A CASEBOOK ON IRISH LAND LAW

by
J.C.W. WYLIE
LL.M. (Harvard), LL.D. (Belfast)
Professor of Law,
University College, Cardiff

PROFESSIONAL BOOKS LIMITED
1984

Published in 1984 by
Professional Books Limited,
Milton Trading Estate, Abingdon, Oxon.
Typeset by Oxford Publishing Services, Oxford
and printed in Great Britain by
The Alden Press, Oxford

ISBN: Hardback: 0 86205 064 2
Paperback: 0 86205 074 X

J.C.W. WYLIE
1984

PREFACE

This is the first of two casebooks designed to be companion volumes to *Irish Land Law* (1975; Supp. 1975–80, 1981). The second casebook, which is in the course of preparation, will be entitled *A Casebook on Equity and Trusts in Ireland* and between them the two casebooks will cover substantially the ground covered by the textbook. Why two casebooks rather than one? The answer is simply that the scope and range of topics covered by the textbook is vast and any attempt to provide primary source material for all those topics in one book would result in a volume of quite unmanageable proportions. The obvious solution was to split the subject into the well-recognised, if often somewhat ill-defined, devision between land law on the one hand and equity and trusts on the other, as adopted by many law school curricula.

The present casebook aims to provide in one volume the leading cases and the main statutory provisions relating to the topics covered by it. In this respect it is something more than a pure 'casebook'. On the other hand, problems of space have ruled out the incorporation of secondary source material. I have, however, included several unreported judgments of significance.

Several points should be emphasised about the contents of the casebook. First, it must be reiterated that it is designed to be a companion to the main textbook. This explains why there is no extensive commentary on the cases; this will be found in the textbook and at every stage appropriate cross-references to the textbook have been inserted. On the same reasoning, those seeking guidance for further reading on particular topics (periodical literature and so on) have only to refer to the relevant section of the textbook. I have, however, in the 'notes and questions' appearing after most cases raised various points of interest and queries to provide food for thought!

Secondly, the author of a casebook such as this is immediately faced with the question of how much editing of the material should be done. In the end of the day, it comes down to the object and purpose of the casebook, subject, of course, to the practical limitations of space and other commercial considerations. The view I have taken is that this casebook, like the textbook, is designed for use by both students and practitioners. It seems to me that the needs of the latter militate against excessive editing – I can think of nothing more disconcerting to a practitioner seeking guidance on a difficult point of law to find the case report chopped to pieces, with large chunks of the judgments missing. Indeed, any deletions, however apparently small, may create the suspicion in the practitioner's mind that neverthe-less that small section might have been relevant to his particular point. Practitioners using this book can rest assured that no editing of this kind has been done; rather than cram lots of extracts from numerous cases into the book, I have instead concentrated on what I regard as the leading authorities on the topics in question and have reproduced the judgments (all of them where multiple ones are involved) *verbatim*. I have also avoided the temptation to delete statements of the facts in judgments in each case – they are the clearest indication of the base from which the judge operated and often are crucial to understanding the reasoning. To assist those who want assistance I have often provided a brief preliminary summary of the facts, but this can always be checked against statements in the judgments. No attempt has been made to provide a statement of what was held in each case – practitioners should prefer to work this out for themselves and students certainly should be required to do this.

This brings me to the needs of students and their use of the book. What I have just said about editing seems to me to apply *à fortiori* to them. It should be a fundamental part of their education that they are required to read the judgments in full and learn to understand the whole process of reasoning. I am convinced after many years of teaching and examining land law that it is better that students master the twenty-odd leading cases than skim through and acquire only a superficial knowledge of dozens of cases, with little understanding of the principles involved. It would, of course, be foolish to expect that everyone will agree with the selection of cases I have made, but I feel confident in saying that if a student masters the cases included in this casebook he or she will have had an excellent grounding in the principles of Irish land law.

I hope that the collection in one place of many of the cases frequently referred to in the textbook, and much of the basic legislation on the subject, will encourage students and practitioners to study this primary source material in a way which I suspect is seldom achieved at the moment because so much of it is not easily accessible. If familiarity with and understanding of the rich heritage of caselaw on Irish land law is increased to some degree by the casebook's publication, I shall feel that I have largely achieved my purpose.

Finally, a few points of detail. Unlike the textbook which seeks to deal with both parts of Ireland, the casebook concentrates on the law in the Republic, though some Northern Ireland cases are included where they give the leading statements on areas of law equally applicable to the Republic. And, of course, most of the cases from the Republic are equally relevant to Northern Ireland. In a sense this anticipates a change which I expect to execute in the new edition of the textbook which is being planned. The law in the North is likely to be changed quite radically within a few years as a result of the activities of the Land Law Working Group of which I am a member. These changes will make the sort to dual treatment of the two jurisdictions in the one textbook executed in the original version of *Irish Land Law* well-nigh impossible to achieve. It is expected, then, that the new edition of the textbook will, like the present casebook, concentrate on the law of the Republic. Some readers will also be aware that a new book on *Irish Landlord and Tenant Law* is currently being written by myself, in conjunction with John Farrell S.C., and this too will be confined to the law of the Republic. This will enable me to reduce considerably the treatment of that subject in the new edition of *Irish Land Law*; it is likely that the new edition will confine itself to what may best be described as general principles and the detailed treatment of special legislation like the Landlord and Tenants Acts, Rent Restriction Acts, etc. will be left to the new book. In anticipation of this, and in an effort to keep the thing within reasonable bounds, the present casebook confines itself to general principles of landlord and tenant law.

Lastly, it is with deep regret that I draw attention to the fact that, unlike in the case of my previous publications, I have not had the benefit of Mr. Justice Kenny's wise counsel in preparing this casebook. The tragic illness which forced his all too premature retirement from the Bench and caused such a loss to the Irish judiciary has disrupted the splendid working relationship he and I enjoyed for over ten years. I am consoled by the appearance of so many of his judgments in this book and feel sure that he would wish for no better tribute.

J.C.W. WYLIE
Cardiff, 15th June, 1984

ACKNOWLEDGMENTS

The publishers and the authors gratefully acknowledge permission from the following to reproduce materials from the sources indicated:

The Controller of the Stationery Office, Dublin: excerpts from Irish statutes.

Department of Justice: unreported judgments.

The Incorporated Council of Law Reporting for Ireland: *Irish Reports*.

The Round Hall Press: *Irish Law Times Reports*, *Irish Law Reports Monthly*.

The Incorporated Council of Law Reporting for Northern Ireland: *Northern Ireland Law Reports*.

CONTENTS

TABLE OF STATUTES

[*N.B.* Page references in **bold** type indicate statutory provisions reproduced in full in the text.]

1. STATUTES OF THE PARLIAMENT OF IRELAND

2. STATUTES OF THE PARLIAMENTS OF ENGLAND, GREAT BRITAIN AND THE UNITED KINGDOM

3. STATUTES OF SAORSTÁT ÉIREANN AND OF THE OIREACHTAS

4. STATUTES OF THE PARLIAMENT OF NORTHERN IRELAND

5. STATUTES OF OTHER JURISDICTIONS

TABLE OF ARTICLES OF IRISH CONSTITUTION

1973 CONSTITUTION

TABLE OF CASES

[*N.B.* Page references in **bold** type indicate cases whose judgments are reproduced in full in the text]

Chapter 1

HISTORICAL BACKGROUND

This chapter contains material which highlights some of the major developments in the history of Irish land law as we know it today. It begins with the establishment of the common law system, goes on to deal with the concept of tenure, which was enshrined in that system, and ends with a subject which has achieved considerable significance in the Republic of Ireland, the protection of property rights under the Constitution. Chapter 2 then deals with some fundamental concepts which continue to underpin Irish land law, such as the doctrine of notice.

I. ESTABLISHMENT OF THE COMMON LAW SYSTEM

The displacement of the ancient Irish law by the English common law was achieved finally during the seventeenth century, a century which was heralded by the refusal of the judges of the King's Bench in Dublin to recognise the Irish customary modes of succession known as *tanistry* and *gavelkind*: see *Irish Land Law*, para. 1.27 *et seq.* However, this has not prevented the Irish courts from referring in comparatively recent times to the earlier Brehon Laws which were once in force in Ireland, in cases where these laws still appeared relevant, e.g. in determining claims to ancient fishing rights: see *Irish Land Law*, para. 6.042.

THE CASE OF TANISTRY
(1607) Dav. 28 (King's Bench)

[Note: Rather than subject the lawyers of today to the Norman-French of the original report of this case, it has been decided to reproduce instead the instructive note on the case written many years ago by the late Professor F. H. Newark, see (1952) 9 N.I.L.Q. 215. This is done with the kind permission of his widow and the Editor of the *Northern Ireland Legal Quarterly*. The footnotes are Professor Newark's.]

All Irish lawyers know that the ancient Irish tenure of Tanistry was abolished by the *Case of Tanistry*[1] in 1607. And that is usually the full extent of their knowledge.

The reason for this lack of any further and better particulars of the case is probably due to the fact that Davies reported the case in Norman-French (or rather what passed for Norman-French at the beginning of the seventeen century) with copious quotations from documents in Latin. And though most enquiring lawyers could grapple with phrases such as 'le custom de drier nets sur terre d'un auter en favour de fishing and maintenance de navigation', there are harder passages which require a considerable vocabulary.

The following notes set out briefly how the case arose, what arguments were adduced, what the court decided, and what happened afterwards. Some of the facts

---

[1] Davies' Reports, 28. Davies was successively Solicitor-General and Attorney-General in Ireland during the period 1603–1619. In 1626 he was appointed a Chief Justice but he celebrated the promotion with a dinner of such magnitude that he died from apoplexy. He was also a poet with a penchant for acrostic and patriotic verse. Several of his poems have the initial letter of the lines spelling ELIZABETH REGINA.

in the report of the case are not quite accurate and have been corrected from other sources.

The Facts

The case concerned the castle and lands of Drominyn (Dromaneen) in Publicallaghan[2] in the County of Cork. From 'time out of mind' these lands had been held according to the Irish custom of tanistry. The custom was that when any person died possessed of land it descended to the eldest and worthiest male of the blood and name of the deceased, and in no circumstances could a woman inherit.

When the story opens the lands in question were held by Donogh macTeige O'Callaghan (hereinafter called Donogh macTeige the elder), who had family as follows:

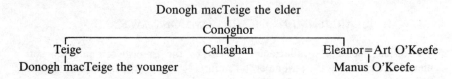

Donogh macTeige the elder
Conoghor

Teige   Callaghan   Eleanor=Art O'Keefe
Donogh macTeige the younger   Manus O'Keefe

Conoghor and Teige died sometime before 1574 while Donogh macTeige the elder was still alive. It was probably this fact of his only son and eldest grandson predeceasing him that led Donogh macTeige the elder to take steps to 'keep the land in the family'[3], and in 1574 he settled the land by conveying it by a common law feoffment to Callaghan for life, remainder to Donogh macTeige the younger for life, remainder to the heirs male of the body of Callaghan, remainder to the heirs male of the body of Donogh macTeige the younger, remainder to the right heirs of Donogh macTeige the elder.

Donogh macTeige the elder died in 1578 and a year later Callaghan, the first life tenant under the settlement, was drowned. He left no legitimate issue, but there was an illegitimate son, Cahir O'Callaghan, of whom we shall hear later.

Donogh macTeige the younger now succeeded as second life tenant under the settlement, but he died in 1584 without issue. As both Callaghan and Donogh macTeige the younger had died without issue neither estate tail took effect and the land then passed under the ultimate remainder to the right heir of the settler. This was Eleanor O'Keefe, but the spectacle of a woman succeeding to the O'Callaghan patrimony was too much for the mere Irish and there appeared on the scene a more distant relative, Conoghor O'Callaghan, known as Conoghor of the Rock, who claimed that he was the eldest and worthiest male of the name and blood of O'Callaghan.[4] He accordingly seized and occupied the land in accordance with the custom of tanistry.

In 1569 a statute of the Irish Parliament – 12 Eliz. c. 4 – empowered the Irish or degenerate English holding land by Irish custom to surrender their holding to the Queen and receive a regrant valid by English Law. In 1593 Conoghor of the Rock, not despising the forms of English law if they could do him any good, made a surrender under this Act and received a regrant in fee simple. He then sold the fee simple to one Fagan, who in turn sold it to Brian MacOwen.[5]

---

[2] The Anglicised version of the Irish, 'Pobul I Callaghan.'

[3] Donogh macTeige the elder was the eldest of seven brothers and he had quietly succeeded his father, apparently under the custom of tanistry.

[4] Conogher of the Rock had an elder brother, so Conoghor must have justified his claim as being 'worthier' than his elder brother.

[5] He was related to the O'Callaghans and was a possible candidate for tanist.

At this point the heirs of Donogh macTeige the elder seem to have awakened to their rights. Art O'Keefe and Eleanor were dead by this time, but Manus O'Keefe entered on the land and conveyed it to Cahir O'Callaghan, the bastard son of the Callaghan who was drowned.

The present case was brought to test the respective titles of Brian MacOwen and Cahir O'Callaghan.[6] Brian MacOwen's title was based on Conoghor of the Rock's claim as tanist, or alternatively, Conoghor of the Rock's title derived from the surrender and regrant. Cahir O'Callaghan's title depended on the validity of the settlement made by Donogh macTeige the elder.

The Argument for the Plaintiff
(1) The custom of tanistry is good at common law. It conforms to the requirements of a custom –
    (a) antiquity – tanistry is 'as old as memory';
    (b) continuance – tanistry has continued 'from time out of mind';
    (c) reasonableness – who can better till the soil and defend the land than the eldest and worthiest?
    (d) certainty – the 'eldest' is easily ascertainable, and the 'worthiest' means no more than the eldest – Littleton frequently equates 'the eldest' and 'the best'.
(2) Even if the positive part of the custom is bad, the negative part which says that a woman cannot inherit is good.
(3) The custom has not been abolished by the introduction of English common law –
    (a) because the custom was reasonable – e.g. when English common law was introduced into Wales some reasonable customs were allowed to continue;
    (b) because even in England local customs survived the Norman conquest;
    (c) because the statute 12 Eliz. c. 4 assumes that tanistry was not abolished.
(4) Donogh macTeige the elder's conveyance in tail with remainder to the right heirs of the grantor did not destroy the custom in this land, because –
    (a) Donogh macTeige the elder held by the custom of tanistry under which he held the land no more than a life estate;
    (b) the custom of tanistry 'runs with the land'.
(5) In any event Conoghor obtained a good title by the surrender and regrant.

The Argument for the Defendant
(1) the custom of tanistry is bad –
    (a) it is unreasonable –
        (i) because it is uncertain who is to succeed, i.e. in the lifetime of the holder there is no heir apparent;
        (ii) because it leaves the inheritance in abeyance on the death of the holder;
        (iii) because to give the land to the 'worthiest' is to encourage men to demonstrate their 'worthiness' by tyrannising over others;
        (iv) the negative part of the custom which excludes women is bad.[7]
    (b) it is void for uncertainty –
        (i) it is uncertain as to the individual – the 'worthiest' depends on public

---

[6] The action was one of ejectment and technically was brought by Brian MacOwen's lessee against Cahir O'Callaghan.
[7] The defendant's argument on this point was weak and amounted to no more than that any principle opposed to a principle of English law was necessarily unreasonable.

opinion, 'which is the most uncertain thing in the world.' – 'worthiest' cannot mean 'eldest' because that would mean a redundancy in the phrase 'eldest and worthiest';

(ii) it is uncertain as to the estate – the tanist has no estate of inheritance of which the law can take notice.

(c) the custom was interrupted by the creation of the estate tail by Donogh macTeige the elder – when a man creates an estate according to the course of common law in what was previously held by customary tenure, the customary tenure is destroyed;

(d) the custom of tanistry is void because it infringes the King's prerogative – the custom deprives the King of warships and marriages.

(2) Even if the custom were good, still the introduction of the common law of England into Ireland abolished it, and now each subject shall inherit his land 'according to the just and honourable law of England'. For tanistry was not a local custom but the former common law of Ireland and therefore it is abolished by the introduction of a new common law.

(3) A good title was not obtained by Conoghor O'Callaghan's surrender and regrant. The regrant was only made in consideration of the surrender, and he had nothing to surrender since he claimed only as a tanist. In any event the formalities of 12 Eliz. c. 4 relating to the surrender of Irish lands do not appear to have been complied with.

Argument for Plaintiff in Reply

Queen Elizabeth was in possession of the lands by virtue of conquest and therefore Donogh macTeige the elder had no title as against the Queen. Therefore the regrant by Queen Elizabeth was good.

Argument for the Defendant in Rejoinder

English sovereigns are royal monarchs and not seignorial monarchs or tyrants. When an English sovereign conquers a land he may obtain a paramount lordship over all land, but he does not obtain possession by confiscation. These foreign writers like Bodin and Chopin are wrong in stating that William the Conqueror confiscated by right of war all land in England.

The Decision

The reports do not give any judgment of the court. The arguments for the defendant are prefaced by the words: 'It was argued for the defendant and was resolved by the court. . . .' We are thus left to assume that the court accepted the defendant's arguments in toto. Since the defendant's counsel was Davies himself as Attorney-General it is not unreasonable to assume that the defendant's arguments, if not devised in concert with the judges, were at least directed along lines known to be acceptable to them.

The Result

The report states that the case was pending in the King's Bench for three or four years and was argued several times on the various points and opinions were given on these points at different times. Finally the litigants came to terms and the case was settled with the approval of the court. It is not clear why the defendant, who seems to have had the court whole-heartedly with him, should have agreed to a settlement. It may have been that though the judges had given their opinions on the various points no definite judgment was in sight and the litigants got tired of waiting. Or it may have been that for some reason of policy the court preferred not to give a definite judgment. Or it may have been that the litigation was in the nature of a test case and the parties were not really at arms length and thus agreed to divide the spoils.

However, in the settlement the defendant got the better bargain, for the portion of the lands which he obtained included the castle.

However, the story has a happy ending. Sometime about 1631, a marriage took place between Elena, the grand-daughter and surviving descendant of Conoghor of the Rock, and Donogh, the son and heir of Cahir O'Callaghan, the defendant in the case. The two rival claims now merged. This last Donogh, son of Cahir came to grips with Cromwell and was transplanted to Clare, where in 1666 he was given a lease of lands at a peppercorn rent for a thousand years or until such time as he should be restored to his estate at Dromaneen. But he never got back there and O'Callaghans still flourish in Clare.

When we regard this case as abolishing the custom of Tanistry we must not imagine that its effect was instantaneous. The doctrine of *stare decisis* was not a highly perfected instrument at the beginning of the seventeenth century as it is to-day. Consequently for some years after we find the English government regarding tanistry as something still to be extirpated. In 1611 among the Acts thought fit to be propounded at the next parliament held in Ireland, was 'An Act to extinguish tanistry,[8] and in 1613 a commission issued to the Lord Deputy and others 'to enquire into the new plantation of Wexford . . . whether they hold by descent or tanistry.[9] But eventually the custom disappeared and the defendant's arguments in the case remain as the justification for the final taking away of what had been law in Ireland 'from time out of mind'.

F.H.N.

Note
See also the *Case of Gavelkind* (1605) Dav. 49.

MOORE V. ATTORNEY GENERAL FOR SOARSTÁT ÉIREANN AND OTHERS
[1934] I.R.44; 68 I.L.T.R. 55 (Supreme Court)

The plaintiffs brought an action claiming a declaration that they were entitled to a several fishery for salmon and all other fish in the entire tidal portion of the River Erne, in the County of Donegal. The defendants were a number of local fishermen (who, in 1925 for the first time, had challenged the plaintiffs' title) and the Attorney-General of the Irish Free State, who was sued as representing the public and the State.

An appeal was lodged from the judgment and order of Johnston J. (reported [1929] I.R. 191) declaring, *inter alia*, the plaintiffs to be entitled to and possessed of a several fishery for salmon and all other kinds of fish in the entire tidal portion of the River Erne in the County of Donegal from the Falls of Assaroe at Ballyshannon to the high sea or bar of Ballyshannon and the bed and soil underlying the said waters. The said order also granted the plaintiffs a perpetual injunction restraining the defendants (other than the Attorney-General) from trespassing upon the said several fishery and from fishing therein or taking fish thereout, and it ordered the defendants to pay the plaintiffs their costs of the action, such costs not to be levied against the Attorney-General in his personal capacity.

The notice of appeal by the defendants other than the Attorney-General applied for an order that the entire of the judgment of Johnston J. be reversed and that in lieu thereof it be ordered that the action be dismissed, on the grounds that the judgment and order were erroneous in law and erroneous in fact, and that the findings and judgment of Johnston J. were bad in law, and that the said findings were against the evidence and the weight of

---

[8] Irish State Papers, 1611, p. 190.
[9] Irish State Papers, 1613, p. 437.

evidence, and that the trial Judge misdirected himself both in law and on the facts in finding that the plaintiffs were entitled to the relief claimed in the action or any part thereof.

The Attorney-General at first served notice of appeal limited only to the incidence of the costs of the action. This notice applied for an order setting aside that portion of the order in the action which directed that the defendants pay to the plaintiffs their costs of the action when taxed and ascertained in so far as it imposed any liability on the defendant, the Attorney-General, to pay such costs, and for an order declaring that the Attorney-General was not liable to pay any part of the plaintiffs' costs of the action.

Upon the hearing of a preliminary objection by the plaintiffs to the competency of the appeal by the defendants other than the Attorney-General, it was held by the Supreme Court that the appeal of the defendants other than the Attorney-General was competent only to the extent of the special relief granted against them, viz. the injunctions, etc., and that an appeal against the declaratory part of the order lay solely within the competence of the Attorney-General. This decision is reported ([1930] I.R. 471). Subsequently to that decision, the Attorney-General applied for and obtained an extension of time for the purpose of serving notice of appeal against so much of the order of Johnston J. as was not the subject of his pending appeal (reported [1930] I.R. 500).

This (second) notice of appeal by the Attorney-General applied for an order that the whole of the order of Johnston J. (not the subject of his (the Attorney-General's) pending appeal) be reversed and that the action be dismissed.

Kennedy C.J.:

What I am about to read, represents the joint opinion of Mr. Justice Murnaghan and myself on all the questions for decision by the Court. I am reading it for both; but I wish to acknowledge that the great labour of putting it together has been his.

The appeal in this action has been brought by the Attorney-General against the judgment of Mr. Justice Johnston, whereby he declared that the plaintiffs were entitled to a several fishery for salmon and all other kinds of fish in the entire tidal portion of the River Erne in the County of Donegal from the falls of Assaroe at Balyshannon to the high seas or bar of Ballyshannon, and whereby the Court ordered that the plaintiffs be quieted in the possession of the said several fishery, and granted a perpetual injunction against the special defendants and all other persons from trespassing upon the said several fishery, or interfering with the plaintiffs in the exclusive use and enjoyment of the said several fishery.

The nature of the case has required that a great mass of documentary evidence should be tendered and oral evidence of considerable volume has been brought forward upon the historical questions involved, while the legal arguments have extended over a wide range. The points involved may, however, be dealt with under three heads. In the first place the plaintiffs claim a parliamentary title to the several fishery under a Landed Estates Court Conveyance. Failing this, they seek to make title to a several fishery according to the rules of common law as laid down in Magna Charta. In addition, they rely upon various statutes of Charles I whereby titles, passed under Commissions of Grace, were validated and given statutory authority.

By a Landed Estates Court Conveyance, dated 11th March, 1869, the predecessors of the plaintiffs in consideration of the sum of £45,520 acquired certain fisheries therein set forth and described. These several fisheries included not only those in the tidal portion of the River Erne but also other several fisheries in the inland waters of the Erne and Abbey rivers and all waters in communication therewith. It appears, however, that the several fisheries in the tidal portion of the River Erne are the most valuable – especially the salmon fishery – of all the fisheries granted by this Landed Estates Court Conveyance. The material portions of this Landed Estates Court Conveyance are set out in paragraph 17 of the Statement of Claim in this action, and they will be found in the report of an application for a mandamus heard in this Court, *R. (Moore)* v. *O'Hanrahan* ([1927] I.R. 406). In his judgment at the trial of this action Mr. Justice Johnston says ([1929] I.R. at p. 210): 'I do not think that the Supreme Court intended in *R. (Moore)* v. *O'Hanrahan* to decide anything as to the operative force and effect of the deed poll of 1869 other than that, in the proceedings before the District Justice, it was not final and conclusive as evidence of the complainants' title.' The learned Judge is under a misapprehension. The Court did, as the report will show, find it necessary to arrive at a construction of the deed poll. Murnaghan J. there stated his opinion as to its proper construction in these words ([1927] I.R. at p. 451):

'The granting of the right, measured by reference to the former title, is quite at variance with the idea of a grant made with the full exercise of the authority of the court and having the full sanction of the statutory title. I am, therefore, of opinion that the Landed Estates Court took the middle course of granting the several fishery rights so far as they had valid legal existence, and that the purchaser was well aware that he had obtained a title not guaranteed under the full force of an incontestable conveyance, but one which could only be founded upon the validity of the title previously enjoyed.' In the view just stated he was in agreement with the judgment of Kennedy C.J., reported at p. 433 of the report. He says: 'In the second place, I am of opinion that the descriptive parcels with which we are concerned did not purport to describe a several fishery, but used equivocal terms for the purpose of covering, without defining, the existing fishery rights of Thomas Connolly. In my opinion' (he continued), 'on the true construction of the deed poll, the Court did only convey by the first description what indeed it purports to convey, namely, the salmon fishery rights of Thomas Connolly in the rivers Erne and Abbey, whatever those rights might be, leaving all questions as to the extent and quality of such rights, if questioned, to be determined elsewhere.'

On the hearing of this appeal it was again argued that the deed poll granted the several fisheries mentioned in it with all the force of a parliamentary conveyance and that the grant was not in any way limited to such property in these several fisheries as was formerly possessed by Thomas Connolly. When the case of *R. (Moore)* v. *O'Hanrahan* ([1927] I.R. 406) was previously before this Court we were not aware that as far back as the year 1883 this very point upon the construction of the deed poll had been decided by the House of Lords. It appears that the diligent investigation made by the solicitor for the special defendants put him on the track of an action, *Mecredy and Others* v. *Alexander and Others* (Unreported) and the full proceedings in that action with the judgments in the various Courts have, by the process of discovery of documents, been obtained from the plaintiffs. The action referred to dealt with a several fishery in the inland waters of the Erne which came within the literal words of the grant – the identical grant with which this case is concerned – if it were not qualified by reference to the previous title of Thomas Connolly. For the jury found that the several fishery in question had never been enjoyed by Thomas Connolly but had, prior to the date of the Landed Estates Court Conveyance, been in the possession of the Marquis of Ely. There was indeed a remarkable divergence of judicial opinion as to the proper construction of the deed poll. The Court of Common Pleas, Morris C.J., Lawson and Harrington JJ., held that the deed poll only purported to grant whatever fishery for salmon Thomas Connolly had. The Court of Appeal, May C.J., FitzGibbon and Deasy LL.J. (Lord Chancellor Nash dissenting), reversed this decision and held that the purchaser under the deed poll obtained a parliamentary grant to the fishery in question quite irrespective of the previous title. The case went, however, to the House of Lords and the Lord Chancellor interpreted the words of the deed poll by holding 'that what is given before is part and parcel of the same thing which is here again described but described in terms showing that everything which Thomas Connolly had and nothing more was meant to pass.' Lords Blackburn, Watson, Bramwell, and FitGerald agreed with the Lord Chancellor and unanimously reversed the decision of the Court of Appeal in Ireland. At the hearing before us it was sought to extract from the additional reasons given by Lord Blackburn a view that he did not adopt the construction that the grant was to be interpreted by reference to the title of Thomas Connolly. We do not think that this inference is correct but certainly there is no ambiguity in the views of Lord FizGerald, who said: 'My Lords, looking at the subject-matter of this conveyance by itself, I entirely agree in all that has fallen from the noble and learned Earl on the Woolsack, and I adopt his conclusion that what was decribed here, and what was intended to be conveyed, is not a general and exclusive fishery from one end of the River Erne to the other from its source to its mouth but that fishery which Thomas Connolly had, and which it appears equally clearly from the conveyance was in the hands of the lessees.' We adhere in this point to the opinion which we have previously expressed, and we are happy in a matter of such moment to find that we are fortified by the views of the eminent authorities we have named, embodied in a decision of the House of Lords fifty years ago. There is one further point upon the construction of the deed which we desire to notice as it was made the basis of an argument put before us. It was suggested that the deed poll granted the several fishery *de facto* enjoyed by Thomas Connolly – that there was no doubt that Thomas Connolly was *de facto* in enjoyment of the fisheries in question and that he had accordingly an indefeasible title to these fisheries. This point is dealt with by the Lord Chancellor, who referred to the great difficulty in establishing the title to fisheries, and he says: 'If the purchaser knows that he takes a title which is not indefeasible, and is content to take it, no injustice is done to him, although he does not get the benefit of an indefeasable title which – if the title had been established in such a way as to justify the Court in granting it – he might have had.' And again he says: 'It may well be that for excellent reasons the Court may qualify the description of that subject in such a way as, on the one hand, to prevent the conveyance from taking away the right of third parties, who have never been put upon proving them, or establishing them, and against whom probably no claim whatever has been made, and to whom therefore no notice was necessarily given, and, on the other hand, taking away from the purchaser any portion of those rights which Mr. Connolly might have been able to give him.'

Accordingly the plaintiffs have acquired under the Landed Estates Court Conveyance any fishery rights to which Thomas Connolly could have made title. This consideration opens up the second branch of the case which, indeed, occupied the greater portion of the hearing before Mr. Justice Johnston. It has been admitted by the Attorney-General and has in fact been proved (because at the hearing proof was insisted upon by the special defendants), that since the beginning of the reign of James I the plaintiffs and their predecessors in title have been in possession of the fishery in question. The Attorney-General has not disputed that the title of the plaintiffs can be traced to numerous Crown leases, grants and patents made at various dates between 1603 and 1639, but he contends that under the law applicable the plaintiffs have not shown any right in law to the several fisheries in question. If the law really were as stated in the *Case of the Royal Fishery of the Banne* (Dav. Rep. 149) heard in Mich. T., 8 Jacobi, and reported in Sir John Davies' Reports, Dublin edition, 1762, p. 149, the plaintiffs' title would be very clear. For the second point stated at p. 152 to have been resolved is: 'Secondly, there are two kinds of rivers, navigable and not navigable. Every navigable river, so high as the sea flows and ebbs in it, is a royal river, and the fishery of it is a royal fishery, and belongs to the King by his prerogative; but in every other river not navigable, and in the fishery of such river, the ter-tenants on each side have an interest of common right. The reason for which the King hath an interest in such navigable river, so high as the sea flows and ebbs in it, is because such river participates of the nature of the sea, and is said to be a branch of the sea so far as it flows. . . . Also the King shall have the grand fishes of the sea, whales and sturgeons, etc., which are royal fishes, and no subject can have them without the King's special grant. . . . And that the King hath the same prerogative and interest in the branches of the sea and navigable rivers, so high as the sea flows and ebbs in them, which he hath *in alto mari*, is manifest by several authorities and records.' And at p. 155: 'And although the King permit his people, for their ease and commodity, to have common passage over such navigable rivers, yet he hath a sole interest in the soil of such rivers, and also in the fishery, although the profit of it is not commonly taken and appropriated by the King, if it be not of extraordinary and certain value, as the fishery of the Banne hath at all times been. . . . Wherefore it was resolved, that the River Banne, so far as the sea flows and ebbs in it, is a royal river; and the fishery of salmon there is a royal fishery, which belongs to the King as a several fishery. . . .'

The *Case of the Royal Banne* (Dav. Rep. 149) as reported by Sir John Davies contains the resolutions of the chief Judges of Ireland, members of the Privy Council, to whom the question was referred by the Lord Deputy. In substance the opinion of the Judges was that the fishing in every tidal navigable river in the kingdom belonged to the King by virtue of his prerogative and that he had the sole right therein. The Judges did not seem to advert to the possibility that the King was, or ever had been, limited in any way by Magna Charta.

This statement of the law as expounded in the reign of James I in Ireland is quite at variance with the law laid down in modern times by cases of the highest authority decided by the House of Lords. Yet such was the temper of the time that, even if we turn to Coke's exposition of Magna Charta contained in his Second Institutes, we find in reference to Chapter XVI – the portion dealing with fisheries – that he limits himself to these words: 'This statute, saith the Mirrour, is out of use,' and he quotes from the Mirrour words to this effect. Coke himself did not venture to say that Chapter XVI of Magna Charta was heeded in the least. This statement of the law was given effect in the Inquisition of Rathmullan, 1 Jacobi (5th September, 1603), by which it is found that 'the regalities and all the fishings of the bays, ports or rivers of Donegal and Callbeg (in the County aforesaid) up to the limit of the flow of the sea of those rivers belong and appertain to the said Lord King in right of his crown (by virtue of the statute in that behalf enacted).' And it is similarly found 'that all the fishings and fishing weirs of the lough pool and river called Loughearne (as well of eels as of other fish) and also all the fishings as well of salmon and herrings as of other fish in the ports or bays of Ballyshannon and Bundroyse (with all other neighbouring places, bays and ports in which fish are wont to be caught) belong and appertain to the said Lord the King in right of his crown and from the said Lord the King for a long time are concealed and unjustly withheld and they are worth yearly besides deductions 20s. sterling'. It will be necessary to return to the consideration of this Inquisition, but we refer to it now because it is obviously based upon the view of the law stated in Davies' Reports.

There is, however, no question as to the law which we must apply, as it has been declared several times in the House of Lords. The Great Charter was transmitted to Ireland in the reign of Henry III in a form somewhat different from that published by King John in England, but the latter has for centuries been held to apply to Ireland. Poynings' Act applied to Ireland the statutes lately made in England, and this description will include the statutory confirmations of the Great Charter made at various times in England. Magna Charta prohibited the recognition of a several fishery in tidal rivers unless the several fishery had prior to the death of Henry II existed as the possession of some private individual, or unless the public had already at that date been excluded by the Crown. In *Malcomson* v. *O'Dea* (10 H.L.C. 593) dealing with a several fishery in Ireland, the provisions of Magna Charta on the subject-matter in hand were fully dealt with, and affirmed as law. The same statement of the law will be found in *Neill* v. *Duke of Devonshire* (8 App. Cas. 135). In this case Lord Blackburn (at p. 180) quoted with approval this passage from *Malcomson* v. *O'Dea* (10 H.L.C. 593): 'It is not law, and this can never be too often repeated, that the Crown cannot grant a several fishery in tidal waters since Magna Charta. Such a statement is illusory and contrary to law. it can grant a several fishery in such waters since Magna Charta, if that fishery existed before Magna Charta. If a tidal river in which there was *prima facie* a right in the public to fish was appropriated by an individual or by the Crown before Magna Charta, that individual or the Crown, if the Crown has got it back, can grant it after Magna Charta.'

Under the law as now authoritatively laid down, in order to sustain their claim to the several fishery the plaintiffs must prove as a matter of fact by reasonable evidence that a several fishery in the tidal waters, the subject-matter of this action, was appropriated by the Crown itself or was in fact possessed by someone else prior to the year 1189. Willes J. in the opinion of the Judges delivered in the House of Lords in *Malcomson* v. *O'Dea* (10 H.L.C. 593, at p. 618) explains the kind of evidence that is reasonable proof of a fact reaching back far into the dim recesses of the past. He says: 'If evidence be given of long enjoyment of a fishery, to the exclusion of others, of such a character as to establish that it has been dealt with as of right as a distinct and separate property, and there is nothing to show that its origin was modern, the result is, not that you say, this is a usurpation, for it is not traced back to the time of Henry II, but that you presume that the fishery being reasonably shown to have been dealt with as property, must have become such in due course of law, and therefore must have been created before legal memory.'

There is, however, an insuperable difficulty in the way of holding that any such separate fishery was appropriated by the Crown as far back as the year 1189, and the plaintiffs do not suggest that any such appropriation was made. It is a matter of historical knowledge that Tirconnaill was not conquered by England for almost four hundred years after the death of Henry II. In the *Case of Tanistry* (Dav. Rep. 78), heard in Hil., 5 Jacobi, Sir John Davies' Reports, Dublin Edn., 1762, at p. 101, it is stated: 'But as to the introduction of the common law of England into this Kingdom of Ireland, it is to be observed that as this island was not fully conquered and reduced to subjection of the crown of England, all at one time, but by parcels, and in several ages; so the common law of England was not communicated to all the inhabitants, *simul et semel*, but from time to time, and to special persons and families of the Irishry, to whom the King was pleased to grant the benefit and protection of his laws.' The submission of Manus O'Donnel, Chief of Tirconnell, in 35 Henry VIII is the earliest date at which it is suggested that in reality and in fact Tirconnaill became subject to the Crown of England. The date at which English law was first extended to Tirconnaill may be gathered from the citations made in the *Case of Tanistry* (Dav. Rep. 78) (Sir John Davies' Reports, Dublin Edn., 1762, p. 106). After citing 40 Ed. 3, he goes on to say:

'And although by the same statute of Kilkenny, the Brehon law, which was the common law of the Irishry, was declared to be no law, but a lewd custom, yet it was not utterly abolished amongst the Irish, but only defended and prohibited to be used amongst those who were of English race, and the Irish were left at large, to be ruled by their barbarous customs as they were before.

'After the making of this statute of Kilkenny, in all other statutes made in the time of the several kings, until the time of Hen. 8., where any mention is made of the troubles and wars in this kingdom, the English are called rebels, and the Irish are called enemies.

'But after the Act of 33 Hen. 8. c. I. by which it is recited, that although the King of England, by the name of Lord of Ireland, had all manner of royal power and jurisdiction in this land, yet inasmuch as he had not assumed the name and stile of King, the Irish inhabitants of this realm had not been so obedient to the King of England and his laws as by right they ought to be: wherefore it is enacted that King Hen. 8, his heirs and successors, should always be Kings of Ireland, and have the name stile and title of king in this land, with all honours prerogatives and dignities appertaining to the state and majesty of king, as united and annexed to the imperial crown of England. After the making of this Act, the said difference of English rebels and Irish enemies is not to be found of record, but all the meer Irish were from thenceforth accepted and reputed subjects and liege-men to the kings and queens of England, and had the benefit and protection of the law of England, when they would use or demand it.'

Sir John Davies interprets this Act, 33 Hen. 8., as extending the law of England to the whole of Ireland – including Donegal. So far as the English King and the Legislature had power to apply the law of England this statute (in our opinion) did apply it. There is no doubt that the statutes dealing with the dissolution of monasteries were held to apply to Tirconnaill – as witness the Inquisition of Assaroe held in 1588. But legal declaration is not the same thing as actual fact, and it is a matter of historical knowledge that large portions of Ireland did not in fact adopt the use of English law. To continue the quotation from the *Case of Tanistry* (Dav. Rep. 78):

'And to the end that the law of England might have a free course in and through all the kingdom of Ireland (as it is expressed in the stat. 11 Eliz. c. 9), it was provided in several parliaments, viz. 3 & 4 Phil. & Mar. c. 3 and 11 Eliz. c. 9, that commission should be awarded, and all the Irish countries which were not shireground before, reduced into shires and hundreds: and accordingly in the several governments of Thomas, Earl of Sussex, Sir Henry Sidney and Sir John Perrot, not only the Irish territories in the confines of Leinster, but also the entire provinces of Connaught and Ulster, being out of all shire-ground before, were divided and distinguished into several counties and hundreds, and several sheriffs, coroners and justices of the peace, and other officers and ministers of the law of England, have been from time to time constituted in these counties, by several patents and commissions under the great seal of Ireland; and by this means the common law hath been communiated to all persons, and executed through all this kingdome for several years passed.'

When the *Case of Tanistry* (Dav. Rep. 78) was heard in Dublin in Hilary Term, 5 Jacobi, Donegal had been shire-ground for many years. This event, as is stated in the evidence, occurred in the year 1584, and a sheriff had been sent to the town of Donegal with troops to protect him. If it was not possible to carry these statutes into complete execution neverthless, according to the law of Ireland, the English law as in vigour in Ireland or parts of it had been proclaimed to extend to the newly-formed county of Donegal before the advent of James I to the throne.

It may be of interest to quote one other paragraph from the *Case of Tanistry* (p. 108) (Dav. Rep. 78):

'Lastly, our lord the King who now is, by a special proclamation, in the third year of his reign, declared and published that he received all the natives of this kingdom into his royal protection, etc., by which it was clearly resolved that the common law of England is now established universally through all this kingdom of Ireland, and that all persons and possessions within this kingdom ought to be governed by the rules of this law, and that every subject shall inherit his land in Ireland by the just and honourable law of England, vz. in such manner and by the same law by which the king inherits the crown of Ireland. And by these degrees, the common law was introduced and established in this kingdom.'

The application of English law, even at a date long after Magna Charta, to new territory includes the provisions of Magna Charta dealing with the fisheries in tidal waters, and consequently an appropriation by the Crown cannot in such a case lawfully be made. This principle is fully recognised in *Attorney-General for British Columbia* v. *Attorney-General for Canada* ([1914] A.C. 153), where it is expressly stated that the application of the law of England to a territory not previously subject to this law involves that the public right of fishing in tidal waters can be ousted only if there has been an appropriation against the public at some time anterior to the death of Henry II. The claim which is, however, put forward by the plaintiffs that the evidence justifies an inference that the fishing in tidal waters of the River Erne was, prior to the year 1189, appropriated into private hands, and that the grant by the Crown in the reign of King James is not a creation, or attempted creation, of a several fishery, but is a transfer of property which had been in private hands prior to the death of King Henry II and which subsequently came into possession of the Crown. If these facts can be substantiated the case falls within the very terms of the principle already quoted from the speech of Lord Blackburn in *Neill* v. *Duke of Devonshire* (8 App. Cas. 135, at p. 180).

The plaintiffs have proved that they and their predecessors in title have been in exclusive possession of the several fishery for almost three hundred and thirty years. This possession must be of enormous weight and no Court could, save for the strongest and most convincing reasons, ascribe an enjoyment so long continued to an illegal origin. In England or that part of Ireland where the English law has prevailed since the coming of Henry II the mere fact of such possession should be ascribed to a legal origin and therefore to an appropriation prior to the death of Henry II and those who might seek to contest the legality of the origin should do so by clear and manifest proofs. In a land such as was Tirconnaill, not subject to English law, the subsequent possession has not the same weight in proving the fact required to make the origin legal in English law, viz., an appropriation into private hands during the period 1180 to 1603 – but nevertheless such long continued possession justifies every assumption which can be made in support of a legal title. We cannot help feeling that the plaintiffs' title, if it rested upon long continued possession alone, would be stronger than possession founded upon a grant from the Crown subsequent to the Inquisition of Rathmullen. For this Inquisition, taken in 1603, is based upon the view then prevalent and expounded in Davies' Reports. At that time the Crown, ignoring the provisions of Magna Charta, claimed the fisheries in tidal waters by virtue of the royal prerogative. The infirmity of this claim is now recognised, but the possession which has endured under a Crown grant based upon it must suffer somewhat from the same infirmity.

Another serious difficulty in the way of the plaintiffs on this point is that Tirconnaill was not subject to English law for about four hundred years after 1180. The appropriation into private hands of fishing in tidal waters is part of the feudal system introduced into England by the Normans. No such right was recognised in Roman law, under which fishing in such waters was considered to be *iuris publici*. This is noted by Sir John Davies, *The Case of the Royal Fishery of the Banne* (Dav. Rep. 149), at p. 150, where he refers to the rule of the civil law 'that *Flumina et portus publica sunt, ideoque jus piscandi amnibus commune est in portu fluminibus-que*, which rule is found in Bracton, lib. 2, cap. 12.' (In Bracton, Totell's edition, 1569, Fol. 8 r.) In Tirconnaill, during the period we are considering the Brehon law was in force – that is from the year 1189 until the introduction of English law. The material point, therefore, is to determine whether under the Brehon law an appropriation of the fishing in tidal waters was possible, because if such an appropriation was not possible, it makes it extremely improbable that an appropriation did in fact take place contrary to the recognised law.

The plaintiffs seek to establish that during the period whilst Tirconnaill was subject to Brehon law the several fishery in the tidal portion of the Erne was appropriated as the private property of the ruling princes of the House of O'Donnell and the princes of the ruling family prior to the accession of the O'Donnell to the rank of prince. In support of this argument they refer to an Exchequer Inquisition, 26th November, 1588, held to ascertain the property of dissolved abbeys. This Inquisition finds:

'There is a certain abbey monastery or house of monks of the Order of Saint Bernard in the town of Asseroe near Bealashennon in this County of Downegall,' and they (the Jurors) 'say that the Abbot and Convent of the Abbey aforesaid had in right of their abbey or house aforesaid liberty for two fishermen to fish for salmon in the place of the stream or river called the Erne which is called Asseroe near Bealashennon every year during times in which salmon are caught. And the second cast or draught (in English the second draught) of all the fishermen of Asseroe when they begin to fish and liberty for one skiff for fishing for salmon or other fish from the island up to the sea below which fishing is of the yearly value of three shillings and four pence sterling money of England aforesaid which premises are temporalities of the Abbey aforesaid in the said County of Downegall.' This Abbey, it should be observed, did not enjoy the several fishery claimed by the plaintiffs, but the suggestion is that, as the owner of a several fishery in English law could create somewhat similar rights by grant out of his several fishery, the proper inference is that the rights of the Abbey were created by the owner of a several fishery. This argument, however, is not of any value unless it can be shown that by the Brehon law as by the law of England a several fishery might exist in tidal waters. The Abbey of Asseroe was founded as early as 1184 by Flaherty O'Muldory – some writers say in 1178 by Rory O'Canacan – and we think it would be justifiable to infer that the Abbey rights of fishing existed from the foundation of the monastery and accordingly prior to the year 1189. Most of the monasteries sought to acquire fishing rights of some description, and these rights are mentioned in various charters and grants which were given in evidence. King John, on 1st April, 1203, confirmed to the monks of Mellifont the fishery in the water of Buni (The Boyne) the grant which he made while he was Count of Moreton. Hervey de Monte Morisco founded the Monastery of St. Mary of Dunbrothy, and by grant, dated 1175, gave lands with fishings in pools to the monastery for the benefit of the monks. In 1177 John de Curci granted to the monastery of Neddrum lands and fisheries – but all these grants were made by Normans in accordance with their own laws. Ferns Abbey was founded about the year 1150 by Dermot, King of the Leinstermen. The grant, which included lands and fisheries, was made by the counsel and assent of his princes and magnates. The Abbey of St. Mary Newry in 1159 obtained a charter from Maurice MacLochlain with the unanimous will and general consent of the nobles of Ultonia and Ergallia. It will be at once seen that all of these grants which were not made by Normans are more like legislative enactments than gifts by the private owner of a several fishery. One Inquisition, taken at

Donegal 13th November, 1603, makes mention of a religious house at Clonleigh, near Lifford, and states that the inhabitants of the college lands were wont from time to time to fish in and upon the river aforesaid by a license of Lord O'Donnell for that purpose obtained with one small skiff (in English a cott) by night only at the ebb of the river (in English the ebb water). The Franciscan Monastery at Donegal was founded in 1474 and it is recorded that Hugh Roe O'Donnell gave the friars a perpetual right to fish for salmon. Both these records are altogether indefinite on the point which it is material to ascertain – viz. whether The O'Donnell had the exclusive right of fishing in the places referred to, while they may be explained as meaning that The O'Donnell was instrumental in securing the privilege for the monks in whatever might have been the form required at the time and place in question. On the other hand, Professor McNeill and Professor Daniel Binchy gave detailed evidence showing that in the Brehon law an exclusive right of fishing in tidal waters was not recognised. Professor McNeill pointed out that in the 'Ancient Laws of Ireland,' Vol. V., at p. 483, among the things which are specified as the full property of every Tuath (kingdom) belonging in equal right to every condition of persons are the salmon of the place. According to the commentary 'one killing of it is lawful.' It is perfectly clear that, as in Roman law, the right of fishing was *publici juris*, so in Brehon law the right of fishing for salmon was vested in the inhabitants of the Tuath and an effort was made to secure equality for all by allowing each person to take one salmon. It has also been explained by Professor McNeill that, as the monks who founded the monasteries usually came from outside the Tuath, they required a kind of legislative sanction to partake of the rights belonging to the inhabitants. In fact the Abbey of Assaroe was derived through Boyle from Mellifont. Mr. Justice Johnston arrived at the conclusion that the texts stating the Brehon law were composed in the eighth century and he was not satisfied that the law remained the same until the twelfth century, at which time he thought the ownership of a several fishery may well have been established; and, further, he regarded the texts of the Brehon law rather as an attempt to lay down regulations of an eleemosynary or charitable character and not as a statement of proprietorial rights, whether of a corporeal or incorporeal character.

Lawyers are so much dominated by the ideas of the system which they administer, that it is difficult to enter into the atmosphere of a code of law alien to that to which they are accustomed. What we call the feudal system was an integral part of the law administered by the Normans in England – and it may have to some extent developed in England prior to the advent of the Norman conquerors. Mr. Justice Willes, in his opinion to the House of Lords in *Malcomson* v. *O'Dea* (10 H.L.C. 593, at p. 620), said: 'There is no improbability in the early appropriation of this always valuable property, or even a more extensive fishery, either in the time of the Irish princes, or in that of the Ostmen, who in this [Limerick] and other ports displaced the ancient inhabitants, and who no doubt gave the name of Lax Wear (Leax Waer, or Lachs Wehr) to the chief accessory of the fishery, or by Henry II in his grant to the companion of Strongbow.' We do not think that this expression of opinion can be transferred to the land of Tirconnaill, where, according to the evidence, the Brehon law continued to be in force until it was extirpated in the sixteenth century by the introduction of English law. The plaintiffs did not attempt to prove that a several fishery or anything equivalent to it was recognised by the Brehon law. It is impossible to recapitulate at length all the evidence given, but we are clearly of opinion that the Brehon law of the twelfth century did not incorporate the feudal notion of the ownership of fishing in tidal waters. Tirconnaill was removed from contiguity with the feudal law of the Norman invaders of Ireland, and it is, we believe, contrary both to historical fact and to legal possibility that in the time of Henry II the fishings in the tidal portion of the river Erne were appropriated into the possession of Flaherty O'Muldory or any native prince who reigned before the advent of the family of O'Donnell in the year 1202. It is pointed out in the evidence that in the sixteenth century, when the chiefs began to accept grants and confirmations of their lands from the English, English legal ideas began to prevail in such grants although English law was not at the time fully introduced into Tirconnaill. In 1565 Calvert O'Donnell surrendered to the Queen 'all regal services and rights in Connalia' (Calendar of the Patent and Close Rolls of Chancery in Ireland, No. 23 of 8 Eliz.). Possibly he accepted a grant from the Queen of the territory, because in the grant made in 1600–01 to Neal Garrowe O'Donnell (Calendar of the Patent and Close Rolls of Chancery in Ireland, No. 34 of 43 Eliz.) the custody of the county is given to him as granted to Calvert O'Donnell except, *inter alia*, 'the fishings of the Earne'. This dealing with the fishery is on the same plane as the Inquisition of Rathmullan, and it appears to have been treated as a royal right rather than private property of The O'Donnell under the Brehon law. Mention is made in an Inquisition taken at Ballyshannon in 1623 of one weir for catching eels called 'O'Donnell's weare' with the appurtenances in the river Erne. This is the only reference in the documents to the O'Donnells in connection with the fisheries and it is limited to one weir for catching eels. The conclusion that no title existed in the O'Donnells to the entire fishings in the river Erne is made clear by the Inquisition at Rathmullan. No one thought of seeking a title in the Crown through the possession of any private individual because this notion was contrary to the law as conceived at the time. If the fishing in all tidal and navigable rivers belonged to the Crown by the royal prerogative, no private title could exist except by grant from the Crown and it was not necessary for the Crown to seek its title through a private title in The O'Donnell. In the grant to Neal Garrowe O'Donnell and in the Inquisition of Rathmullan the fishings in question were dealt with as regalities of the Crown.

In the earliest document dealing with the fishing as a private several fishery – the lease from King James to John Binglie for 21 years from 14th October, 1603 – the King's title is based on the statement that the fishing was 'parcell of the Kings Majesties auntient inheritaunce.' In the Inquisition of Lifford, 21st March, 18 Jac. (1620), the fishing is described as 'a Royal salmon fyshings in the sea . . . where it doth ebbe and flowe' in the precise words used in Davies' Reports. We look in vain for any reference to a several fishery in private hands which had come to the King. If any such several fishery in private hands had come to the King it would have been found, like property belonging to dissolved monasteries, to have come to the King. In the legal view prevalent the royal salmon fishery belonged to the King and it could not belong to a subject except by grant from the King.

In our opinion the plaintiffs are not entitled to an ancient fishery appropriated to private ownership prior to Magna Charta.

Their title, however, under the statutes of Charles I remains to be considered.

By Letters Patent bearing date 30th August, 15 Car. I, Thomas, Lord ffolliott, obtained a grant of very extensive tracts of land and also of the several fisheries, the subject-matter of this action. This grant is recited to have been made 'according to the intention and effect of our Commission under our Great Seal of England bearing date at Canbury in our said Kingdom of England on the first day of September in the fourteenth year of our reign'. Among the numerous properties granted by the Letters Patent we find the rights formerly attached on the Abbey of Assaroe and the several fishery with which we are dealing is granted in the words following: 'And also all the Creek bay or river of Beallashenny otherwise Ballyshannon, viz.: from the high sea to the rock in English "the rocks or waterfall"

commonly called the Salmon Leaps otherwise the fall of Asheroe near the Castle of
Ballyshanny aforesaid And also all the aforesaid rock or salmon leap or fall of
Asheroe with the appurtenances And also all and singular loughs weirs islands
rocks in English "rockes" and waterfall in within or near the aforesaid Bay creek
and river of Ballyshanny otherwise Ballyshannon aforesaid And all the bottom soil
land and water of the aforesaid creek bay or river and all land covered and to be
covered with water there and also the whole fishing and liberty of fishing and to fish
for and catch salmon and all other kinds of fish whatsoever in or within the
aforesaid creek bay and river aforesaid and on the rocks aforesaid And also a weir
for catching eels commonly called O'Donnell's "Weare" with the appurtenances in
the river of Earne And also the liberty of having nets and other Instruments
necessary for fishing on the rocks creeks river and bay aforesaid And also the
liberty of having nets and other Instruments necessary for fishing on the rocks
creeks river and bay aforesaid And also the liberty of carrying off all fish and catch
of fish of every kind from the aforesaid rocks in English "rockes" creeks river or
bays or from any part thereof with all other liberties privileges advantages and
emoluments whatsoever of whatever quality to the premises or any part thereof
belonging or appertaining in the aforesaid counties of Donegal Sligoe and fferma-
nagh or any of them.' This grant undoubtedly in terms includes the several fishery
in question but on account of the provisions of Magna Charta it, standing alone,
would have no legal effect. The plaintiffs, however, strongly urge that by reason of
the several statutes passed in the reign of Charles I the grant so made under the
King's commission by Letters Patent was given statutory confirmation and that it is
valid notwithstanding the provisions of Magna Charta.

This grant by Letters Patent to Thomas, Baron ffolliott, was mentioned in
paragraph 10 of the statement of claim merely as a link in the plaintiffs' title, but by
an amended statement of claim delivered on 12th July, 1928, during the course of
the trial the plaintiffs pleaded that the hereditaments and premises granted as
aforesaid under the Letters Patent were plantation lands in the said Counties of
Donegal and Fermanagh within the meaning of 10 Car. 1, sess. 3, cap. 3, and that
the grant under the Letters Patent was good and valid as well against the King's
most excellent Majesty, his heirs and successors, including the Irish Free State, as
against all and every other person and persons whatsoever.' By a further and
alternative amendment the plaintiffs alleged 'that the said hereditaments and
premises so granted . . . lay within the plantations mentioned in the statute, 15 Car.
I, c. 6, section 1, and that by virtue of section 1 of the said statute the Letters Patent
were good, sufficient, effectual and indefeasible to all intents, constructions and
purposes as well against His Majesty King Charles I, his heirs and successors,
including the Irish Free State, as against all and every other person and persons
whatsoever.' And the plea went on to allege 'that at the date of the said Letters
Patent His Majesty King Charles I was by sect. 1 of the said statute, 10 Car. I, sess.
3, cap. 3, and by sect. 2. of the said statute, 15 Car. I, cap. 6, absolutely and
indefeasibly entitled to the said hereditaments expressed to be granted by the said
Letters Patent in right of his Imperial crown'. The Letters Patent include, as well as
the several fishery the subject-matter of this action, a very great number of
denominations of land in the Counties of Donegal, Fermanagh, Sligo and Leitrim
which are all set out with great particularity, but the substance of the allegation is
that the several fisheries granted were 'plantation lands' under 10 Car. I, sess. 3,
cap. 3, or 'lay within the plantations' under 15 Car. I, cap. 6, s. 1. The Attorney-
General contends that the fisheries in question were not 'plantation lands' and did
not 'lay within the plantations' mentioned, and he further contends that the statutes
referred to did not intend to repeal the provisions of Magna Charta.

A great amount of minute historical investigation was directed to the point whether the several fisheries in question were 'plantation lands,' but before approaching this question it is necessary to deal with an argument based upon the proper construction of the statutes referred to. This argument is that all lands and hereditaments situate in the counties of Donegal and Fermanagh, as well as other counties named in the statutes, were declared to be plantation lands. If this construction were held to be the proper one no question of fact would remain open on this point. In the construction of these statutes we have derived much help from the arguments of counsel, not only at the hearing of the appeal, but also at a subsequent argument limited to this point which we had set down. These statutes do not appear to have been judicially construed in any reported case and we desired on account of the importance of the matter to give them the fullest consideration. The importance of the point raised is apparent as it affects not only the plaintiffs but also every grantee under similar grants in the several counties named.

In approaching the consideration of these statutes it is necessary to keep in mind the causes which led up to their enactment. From the recitals contained in 10 Car. I, cap. 3, we can learn that owners of land had their titles drawn in question on widely different grounds. In some cases no grant from the Crown could be pointed to, and in other cases where Crown grants did exist objection was taken to the validity of the grants; while in the case of plantation lands it might also be contended that the lands had been forfeited to the Crown by reason of failure to observe the conditions of the plantation. By way of remedy for this state of affairs the Crown made fresh grants and in doing so seized the opportunity of increasing its revenues; while the owners desired parliamentary confirmation of the grants so obtained. The first statute, 10 Car. I, cap. 3, styled 'An Act for confirming of Letters Patent hereafter to be past upon His Majesties commission of grace for the remedy of defective titles,' bound the King but expressly saved the rights of others. The matters so intended to be dealt with were more fully provided for in an Act, 10 Car. I, sess. 3, cap. 2, passed as an explanation of the first mentioned statute. Another Act 10 Car. I, sess. 3, cap. 3, was passed at the same time for securing of the estates of the undertakers, servitors, natives and others holding lands in all and every the plantation made in the several counties specified. This is the first of the statutes relied upon in the statement of claim and we will quote the material passage upon which the argument is founded. After an elaborate recital it is enacted: 'That Your Majesty your heirs and successors shall be rightly and by good lawfull and indefeasable title and estate in fee simple deemed and adjudged to be in the actuall and reall possession and seizin in right of your imperiall crown of England and Ireland of all the castles mannors lands tenements and hereditaments lying and being in the said severall counties of Tyrone, Armagh, Donegall, Fermanagh, Cavan, Londonderry, Leytrim and Longford and of and in the severall territories precincts and countries commonly known or called by the name or names of Ely O'Carroll alias O'Carrolls conntrey' [Then follow similar territories] 'and also of and in the several townes or villages lands tenements and hereditaments known esteemed or usually called plantation lands in or neere the territory or country of Clincol-man alias O'Melaghlins countrey' (and several territories are then similarly decribed) 'and also of and in all the castles mannors lands tenements and hereditaments in the severall counties of Waterford, Corke, Limericke, Kerry and Tipperary aforesaid usually called plantation land or heretofore passed or mentioned to be passed by letters patent to any British undertaker or undertakers respectively as plantation lands, at such time or times whensoever any of the forementioned castles mannors lands tenements or hereditaments shall be within the space of five years next ensuing the end of this present session of Parliament new passed granted or confirmed to any person or persons bodies politique or corporate respectively, by letters patents under the greate seale of this Kingdom by warrant of the lord deputy for the time being and commissioners nominated or to be nominated in and by His Majestie's commission of grace for the remedy of defective titles now in being or hereafter to be, being former patentees or proprietors or reputed patentees or reputed proprietors or such as by former distribution assignation or appointment have taken the profits thereof their heirs or assignes respectively.' This language although prolix is not involved and it is clear that the castles, mannors, lands, tenements and hereditaments in the counties first mentioned are indicated by an earlier recital. This recital runs: 'That whereas for the better government and security of this Your Kingdom of Ireland sundry plantations have at severall times been made in the severall counties of Waterford, Corke, Limericke, Kerry, Tipperary, Wexford, Wickeloe, King's County, Queen's County, Westmeath, Leitrim, Longford, Tyrone, Armagh, Donegall, Farmanagh, Cavan and Londonderry, grounded as well upon ancient as recent title of your Crown declared as well by inquisitions as other records and evidences; upon all which divers patents have been passed, and thereby very many undertakers and others of British birth and very many of the natives of best quality and condition have been there planted and settled and severall lands, tenements and hereditaments granted and disposal to corporations forts incumbents of churches schooles and other good uses.' The reading of this statute contended for by the plaintiffs is that all lands, tenements and hereditaments in the counties mentioned are by it declared plantation lands irrespective of whether they were granted in pursuance of the scheme of plantation referred to. But the literal reading of the section is not a notional vesting in the King of the entire counties named, but a notional vesting of the estate passed by the new Letters Patent (in lieu of the previous plantation grant) at the date of the making of the new Letters Patent. Further, it seems to us that the aim and purpose of this Act is shown by the recital immediately preceding the enacting words above quoted: – 'And whereas it hath pleased your most excellent Majestie by your principall officers and ministers here to make known that for the better encouragement of your said subjects to proceede cheerfully in their intended course of planting and civilizing the said severall planted countries and settling a good and happy commonwealth among them Your Majesty would be graciously pleased to grant unto Your said subjects that their estates intended unto them in the said plantations should by all convenient means be secured.'

The estates intended unto them in the said plantations must necessarily be estates given by plantation grants. Grants were made by the Crown of lands and other hereditaments during the years anterior to the plantation in the counties named. The construction which we are asked to place on this statute is that such grants, although not in fact plantation grants, were declared to be plantation grants. In our opinion the title of the Act itself, all the recitals and the enacting words themselves are directly opposed to any such construction. The Act deals with plantation grants and deems the King to be in actual seison of . . . all lands . . . in the county of Donegal . . . at the date whensoever any of the same should be granted to any person or persons, 'being former patentees or proprietors or reputed patentees or reputed proprietors or such as by former distribution assignation or appointment have taken the profits thereof.' In reciting the plantation the statute has already used the words 'upon all which divers patents have been passed . . . some other parcells of the said lands being onely distributed and assigned and not passed by reason of restraints for some years past'. To our minds it is clear that the new grants under the statute are to be made to the persons who obtained lands under the scheme of the plantation, and that persons who did not obtain lands under the plantations were governed by the statute, 10 Car. I, sess. 3, cap. 2, immediately preceding.

Another statute of a comprehensive character was passed in 15 Car. I. This statute, 15 Car. I, cap. 6. 'An Act for strengthening of letters patents past and to be past upon any of His Majesty's commissions of grace for the remedy of defective titles,' became necessary by reason of the fact that the period of five years mentioned in 10 Car. I, sess. 3, cap. 3, was coming to an end. By this statute all Letters Patent past or thereafter to be past upon any of His Majesties commissions of grace for the remedy of defective titles were to be 'deemed and adjudged to be good, sufficient effectuall and indefeazable to all intents constructions and purposes' – in the words of the statute – 'in manner following (that is to say) for and concerning all and every the lands liberties franchises immunities and other hereditaments and premises whatsoever lying or being within every or any of the late plantations within this kingdome made by our late sovereign lady Queen Elizabeth, our late most gracious lord King James and made or to be made by the King's most excellent Majesty that now is or by any of them as well against His Majesty, his heirs and successors as against all and every other person and persons bodies politick and corporate as well spiritual as temporal whatsoever: and for and concerning all the rest of the premises against His Majesty, his heirs and successors only, notwithstanding any defect whatsoever or any statute ordinance law cause matter or thing which might or may any way impeach infeeble avoid or destroy any of the said letters patents in all or any point or points whatsoever.'

This statute in its express terms deals with the two subject-matters dealt with separately in the previous statutes, lands, etc., lying or being within the plantations, and other lands, etc., which cannot be so described. It proceeds to enact that the grantees 'shall and may thenceforth peaceably and quietly have hold possess and enjoy all and singular and every the lands tenements hereditaments and other the premisses lying or being within all and every or any of the plantations aforesaid and specified or mentioned in any of the said letters patents to have been granted or hereafter to be granted or mentioned to be granted as aforesaid as well against His Majesty his heirs and successors as against all and every other person and persons bodies politick and incorporate spiritual and temporal whatsoever and all other the lands tenements hereditaments and premisses mentioned to have been granted or hereafter to be granted or mentioned to be granted in any of the said letters patents as aforesaid onely against His Majesty his heirs and successors. . .'. Sect. 2 of this statute, which was strongly relied upon on behalf of the plaintiffs, is framed substantially in the same way as the corresponding passages already cited from the latter portion of 10 Car. I, sess. 3, cap. 3. This sect. 2 enacts: 'That His said Majesty, his heirs and successors respectively be and shall be deemed adjudged seised and vested in the actual and real seisin and possession of a good lawful indefeazable and absolute estate to him or them his or their heirs and successors in right of his and their imperial crown of and in all and singular and every the castles honours mannors towns villages hamlets lands tenements and hereditaments situate lying or being in the several counties of Tyrone, Ardmagh, Donegal, Fermanagh, Cavan, Leitrim and Longford; and likewise of all the several territories precincts of land and countries commonly known or called by the name or names of Ely O'Carrol alias O'Carrols country' (then follow a number of other territories similarly described) 'and also of all the several towns villages hamlets lands tenements and hereditaments known esteemed reputed or usually called plantation lands in or neere the territories or countries of Cloncolman alias O'Melaghlin's country in the county of Westmeath; and in or near the territory and country of Faran O'Nan in or near the county of Wexford; and of and in the towns and lands of Tourboy in or near the territory of Ranelagh aforesaid; and also of all and singular the castles honours mannors towns villages hamlets lands tenements and hereditaments in the several counties of Waterford, Cork, Limerick, Kerry, and Typerary usually called or reputed as plantation lands or heretofore past or mentioned to have been past by letters patents to any British undertaker or undertakers by birth blood or descent their heirs or assigns respectively as plantation lands, at every such time and times respectively whensoever any of the same beforementioned castles honours man- nors towns villages hamlets lands tenements and hereditaments shall be within the space of five years next ensuing the end of this present session of Parliament new passed granted confirmed released or assured or mentioned to be new passed granted confirmed released or assured to any person or persons bodies politick of incorporate spirituall or temporall respectively, by letters patents under the great seale of this kingdom by vertue or pretence of or reference unto any such commis- sions of grace now being or hereafter to be within this realme being either former patentees or reputed inheritors or proprietors or by former assignation distribution or appointment have taken the profits thereof. . . .' The words here used are practically a repetition of those employed in 10 Car. I, sess. 3, cap. 3, in which statute, as we have said, the recitals make it abundantly clear that the grants intended to be made indefeasable as well against the Crown as against all other persons were grants made in pursuance of the scheme of plantation. The main operative words in sect. I give the indefeasible title against all persons in respect of lands, tenements and hereditaments lying or being within all and every or any of the plantation aforesaid. Sect. 2 is fully satisfied as meaning that all lands etc. in the counties mentioned are to be deemed to be in the actual seisin of the Crown at the date when the new Letters Patent under the commissions of grace may have been or may be issued within the five years following granting to the former grantees of plantation lands in these counties the same lands under a fresh grant. It is, in our opinion, impossible to extract from this section a declaration that all lands etc. in the counties named shall be deemed to be within the plantations whether they were so in fact or not. To support any such view the letters patent granted under the commissions of grace would be good against the Crown and all persons whatsoever if made to a person who had not obtained a plantation grant; but under the statute the grant should be made to a former patentee or reputed inheritor or proprietor or to one who by former assignation distribution or appointment had taken the profits thereof, the very words which in 10 Car. I, sess. 3, cap. 3, are used in reference to persons who took under plantation grants. For these reasons, in our opinion, there is no statutory declaration that all lands granted in the counties named are grants of lands, etc., lying or being within the plantations. No Court, so far as we are aware, has ever construed the statute in this sense and we do not think this construction the correct one. Accordingly, it remains to be determined as a matter of fact whether the several fishery claimed by the plaintiffs can be said to be 'plantation lands' or to lay within the plantations as alleged in the statement of claim.

The documents given in evidence show the dealings with the several fishery subsequent to the Inquisition of Rathmallan which found under the law as then administered the fisheries to be part of the regalities of the Crown. Mr. Justice Johnston remarked that the documents were not easy to reconcile but we think they are consistent and show very clearly the legal dealings. On October 14th, 1603, a lease was made by the Crown to John Binglie for 21 years at a rent of 40s. of which 10s. was in respect of the rivers of Donegall and Caelbeg and 30s. in respect of the fishings in Lougherne and Bondrois. A certified copy of this lease from the patent Rolls 1 Jac. I, part 2,was given in evidence. In the Crown Rental, Ireland, 1613, mention is made of a rent of 40s. due from John Binglie, 'gent' farmer of the whole regalities of the fishings and the fishings of the bays ports havens creeks rivers floudes and streams of Dunegall and Caelbegg And also of the whole fishing and catching of fish of the lakes pools rivers and streams called Lougherne of every kind of fish there being And also of the whole fishing for and catching of salmon and herrings and of all other fish in the porte creeks bayes and streames of Ballishannon and Boundwise with all other places bayes ports havens and creekes next adjacent in which fish were wont to be caught yearly.' This lease is noted to be supposed to be a double chardy and it is also noted that Sir Henry ffolliott was assignee of John Binglie. The date of the assignment from John Binglie to Sir Henry ffolliott is not mentioned but in the Inquisition of Donegal held 21st March, 1621, 18 Jacobi I, it is stated ffolliott had been in possession for over sixteen years. Sir Henry ffolliott obtained a lease for 21 years from 7th June, 1606, of the fishing rights formerly attached to the Abbey of Assaroe, as well as the fishings in the Binglie lease, and again for 20 years from 6th July, 1607. Twenty-one years was the longest term which the Commission was empowered to grant. On 20th July, 1609, Sir Arthur Chichester, Deputy General, in pursuance of the King's letter, dated 29th November, 1608, made a grant to Mary, Baroness Delvin, and Sir Richard Nugent, her son, of lands in many parts of Ireland. One of the subject-matters granted was the fishing and liberty of fishing and the catching of salmon and all other kinds of fish whatsoever in or within the creek bay river stream or pool of Ballishannon. This grant included the rents and profits of all and singular the premises above by the same presents given. In respect of the several fishery so granted an annual payment of £6 13s. 4d. was reserved to the King. Baroness Delvin and Sir Richard Nugent by deed of feoffment, dated 20th January, 1609, granted this several fishery to Sir Henry ffolliott as is found in an Inquisition of Ballyshannon, 2nd January, 1620. On 12th April, 1608, Letters Patent were issued by Sir Arthur Chichester, Deputy General, in pursuance of a letter of King James, dated 27th October – presumably 1607 – granting to Francis Gofton and his heirs the rights of fishing formerly enjoyed by the Abbey of Assaroe at the annual rent of £8 10s. 0d. On 20th may, 1608, as found in the Inquisition of Ballyshannon, 2nd January, 1620, the said Francis Gofton assigned and conveyed these fishings to Sir Henry ffolliott. As noted in the Crown Rental, Sir Henry ffolliott had obtained a lease for 21 years on 7th June, 1606, of portion at least of these fishings. By Letters Patent dated 9th April, 1622, King James made a fresh grant to Sir Henry ffolliott uniting into one grant a great many lands in his possession held under various titles.

The evidence established very clearly that Sir Henry ffolliott was an undertaker and possessed plantation lands, viz., the Manor of Newputon in the County of Fermanagh. It was, however, argued on behalf of the Attorney-General that the fisheries, the subject-matter of this action, were not plantation lands because they did not appear in Pynnar's Survey of the Plantation. This merely negative evidence hardly satisfied in a legal way the point sought to be proved, but evidence was given of the official project for the division of the escheated kingdoms in Ulster done under the commission of King James on 23rd January, 1608, and also of the plan and conditions of the plantation. Prior to this date, viz., on 29th November, 1608 (the year then beginning in March) the King's letter for the grant to Mary, Baroness Delvin, and Sir Richard Nugent had been drawn up. This grant comprised a great number of denominations of land in Cavan but it also granted lands in Westmeath, Roscommon, Cork, Kildare, Dublin, Wicklow, the City of Dublin, Meath, King's County; much of the land granted is stated to have come to the Crown by the dissolution of monasteries, and the grant contains no trace of being a plantation grant. Indeed the date of this grant makes it impossible that it should have been made as part of the scheme of the plantation. Yet it is as assignee of this grant, so far as the fishings are concerned, that Sir Henry ffolliott derived his title, save so far as he already had the lessee's interest as assignee of John Binglie for the residue of the term of 21 years.

To prove that the several fisheries were held under plantation grants an argument of an indirect nature was put forward on behalf of the plaintiffs. It was pointed out that by the Letters Patent of 30th August, 1639, Thomas Lord ffolliott is released from all and singular the conditions covenants articles mandates instructions and agreements of the plantation and it was urged that this clause in the Letters Patent is proof that the several fisheries were granted under a plantation grant. If these several fisheries were the only premises granted the point would deserve consideration but it was truly pointed out that the grant included the manor of Newputon in the County of Fermanagh to which the clause will naturally have reference. It was also urged that by the same grant a general clause, releasing many properties, including fisheries by name from various obligations, contained a release from the obligations under the articles of the plantation. But there is no necessary inference that each named item of property must have been subject to each and every of the obligations mentioned and this clause gives no proof whatever that the fisheries were plantation lands or that they lay within the plantations. It should also be observed that in the Letters Patent of 1639 separate and distinct rents are created in respect of the Donegal lands and the Fermanagh lands. The earlier title of the Donegal lands appears from the documents and most of these lands, if not all, were derived under grants which were not plantation grants. We are accordingly of opinion that neither 10 Car. I, sess. 3, cap. 3, nor 15 Car. I, cap. 6., gave to the Letters Patent of 1639 any statutory authority to override the provisions of Magna Charta in respect of the several fisheries the subject matter of this action and accordingly the grant of these several fisheries under these Letters Patent did not bind the public.

We have to add, with reference to the statutes strongly pressed by Mr. Jellett, 31 Geo. 2, c. 13, 3 Geo. 3, c. 35, that these statutes, which refer to the private several fisheries in the Erne, had no intention of altering Magna Charta and that they cannot be relied upon for this purpose. If in regulating fisheries they referred to fisheries which were enjoyed *de facto* as several fisheries, these statutes cannot be construed as a statutory validation of these fisheries contrary to the provisions of Magna Charta. No more did the statutes regulating fisheries or authorising the use of fixed engines intend that the question involved in this action should be incidentally determined by applications under those Acts.

With Mr. Justice Johnston we feel deeply that ancient landmarks should not lightly be removed. In this case, however, the plaintiffs put forward a title which depends upon the Inquisition of Rathmullan, the lease to John Binglie, the grant to Mary, Baroness Delvin, and Sir Richard Nugent and the Letters Patent to Sir Thomas ffolliott. They ask the Court to declare their title and bind the public for all time. In our opinion the plaintiffs' title depends upon the view stated in Sir John Davies' Reports which was prevalent in Ireland in the times of the Stuart Kings, and was perhaps held even in England under Queen Elizabeth. In 1859 this very fishery came before the Court in *R. (Gilles)* v. *County Donegal Justices* (5 Ir. Jur. N.S. 185) which is not a very satisfactory case but it indicates the ideas which even then prevailed. When, contrary to the law stated in Davies' Reports, the House of Lords in 1863 reasserted the provisions of Magna Charta in *Malcomson* v. *O'Dea* (10 H.L.C. 593) the foundations upon which the plaintiffs' title might be said to rest disappeared and, if we must state our opinion to be that the plaintiffs' claim is invalid, it is the decision of the House of Lords in *Malcolmson* v. *O'Dea* (10 H.L.C. 593) which has produced this result.

FitzGibbon J.:

The claim of the plaintiffs in the present action is to establish their right to a several fishery for salmon and all other kinds of fish in the entire tidal portion of the river Erne in the county of Donegal, from the Falls of Assaroe at Ballyshannon to the high sea or bar of Ballyshannon, and the bed and soil underlying the said waters.

The waters in question are navigable as well as tidal, and accordingly the claim of the plaintiffs is one to an exclusive right of fishing in tidal navigable waters in Ireland. So far as England is concerned, 'since the decision of the House of Lords in *Malcomson* v. *O'Dea* (10 H.L.C. 593), it has been unquestioned law that since Magna Charta no new exclusive fishery could be created by Royal grant in tidal waters, and that no public right of fishing in such waters, then existing, can be taken away without competent legislation': *Attorney-General for British Columbia* v. *Attorney-General for Canada* ([1914] A.C. 153, at p. 170). I rather think that this 'was unquestioned law' in England long before the decision in *Malcomson* v. *O'Dea*, and the case law upon the subject in England, of which there is an enormous volume, turns in the main upon the sufficiency of the evidence in each particular case to establish the existence of an exclusive right of fishing at a date prior to Magna Charta. 'If evidence be given of long enjoyment of a fishery, to the exclusion of others, of such a character as to establish that it has been dealt with as of right as a distinct and separate property, and there is nothing to show that its origin was modern, the result is, not that you say, this is a usurpation, for it is not traced back to the time of Henry II, but that you presume that the fishery, being reasonably shown to have been dealt with as property, must have become such in due course of law, and therefore must have been created before legal memory': *per* Willes J. in *Malcomson* v. *O'Dea* (10 H.L.C. 593, at p. 618).

Now, there seems to be no doubt that, in England, long before Magna Charta, Kings of England had in fact appropriated to themselves by an exercise of the royal prerogative which was made illegal after 1189, and had granted to their feudatories or to religious houses, exclusive rights of fishing in tidal navigable waters, and accordingly there was no intrinsic objection to the presumption of such an appropriation founded upon evidence of the character described by Willes J., and similar principles would apply in any country in which the law of England upon the subject was in force. In *Malcomson* v. *O'Dea* (10 H.L.C. 593) itself, though it does appear in the very brief summary of the evidence on p. 595 of the report, the proved title to the fishery commenced with a charter from King John dated 12th January, 1200, to William de Braosa of 'the honor of Lymerick with all its appurtenances in . . . fishponds and fisheries and ponds . . . as King Henry our father that honor gave to Philip de Braosa uncle of the aforesaid William,' and there is a passing reference to this grant of Henry II in the judgment of Willes J. at p. 621, showing that in one part of Ireland at least a grant had been made by an English King in exercise of his prerogative, before the date fixed by Magna Charta, of a several fishery in tidal navigable waters.

The main ground upon which the plaintiffs' claim is challenged is thus stated in par. 21 of the defence of the special defendants, and par. 1 of the defence of the Attorney-General, respectively: 'The said defendants contend that, on the true construction of the documents of title in the statement of claim set forth, the plaintiffs have not in fact shown title to a several or sole and exclusive fishery in the *locus in quo*, viz., from the falls of Assaroe to the high sea; and, further, that by the provisions of Magna Charta the Crown was prohibited from granting a several or sole and exclusive fishery in the *locus in quo* in case such was not existing therein in or before the year 1189, and any grant by the Crown contrary to the provisions aforesaid is null and void; and, further, that a several or sole and exclusive fishery in the *locus in quo* in or before the year 1189 did not in fact exist and is not historically possible; and the said documents of title and the historical evidence show that the claim to a several or sole and exclusive fishery in the *locus in quo* is modern in origin and dates at earliest from the times of Queen Elizabeth and King James the First.' 'The Attorney-General for Saorstát Eireann . . . denies that the tidal portion of the river Erne in the County of Donegal from the falls of Assaroe at Ballyshannon to the high sea or bar of Ballyshannon or any part thereof or the bed and soil underlying the said waters or any part thereof or the sole and exclusive or several rights of fishing for salmon or any other fish in the said waters or any part thereof had been put in defence from time whereof the memory of man is not to the contrary or at any time prior to the date of Magna Charta.'

Put shortly, these contentions, to establish which a mass of historical evidence was given at the trial, are that by the law which existed in Ireland before the date fixed by Magna Charta as the latest date upon which a several fishery could be created in tidal navigable waters by an exercise of the royal prerogative, no such fishery did or could exist; that the creation of this particular fishery took place, at the earliest, in the reign of Elizabeth, when, it is alleged, such an exercise of the prerogative was prohibited by Magna Charta; and, accordingly, that its origin was modern, and therefore illegal, within the terms of the opinion of Willes J. in *Malcomson* v. *O'Dea* (10 H.L.C. 593), and of the Privy Council in *Attorney-General for British Columbia* v. *Attorney-General for Canada* ([1914] A. C. 153).

I shall not set out here the documentary evidence in detail, but I can say that I have examined it over and over again with all the attention of which I am capable, and I am satisfied that there is no trace of any grant by any English King or Queen before the reign of Queen Elizabeth, and the first actual grant given in evidence was one by King James I. Of course, if a several fishery had in fact existed in the waters in question before 1189, and this fishery had become vested in the Crown for the first time after that date, either by conquest, escheat, forfeiture, or otherwise, there would be no merger, and the Crown could make a new grant of it as an existing fishery, unfettered by the provisions of Magna Charta. I refer, in support of this opinion, to the judgment of Martin B. in the *Duke of Northumberland* v. *Houghton* (L.R. 5 Ex. 127), and especially to the speech of Lord Blackburn in *Neill* v. *Duke of Devonshire* (8 App. Cas. 135, at pp. 179, 180), where he adopts with the full concurrence of his colleagues, Selborne L. C. and Lords O'Hagan and Watson, the judgment of Sir Edward Sullivan M. R. in the Court of Appeal in Ireland.

The defendants have, however, undertaken the burden of proving that no several fishery did, or could under the Irish law which prevailed in Donegal or Tirconnaill until the reign of Queen Elizabeth, exist in the tidal navigable waters of the river Erne. Upon this question I have found myself compelled to come to a conclusion of fact different from that of the learned Judge by whom the case was tried. The plaintiffs tendered no evidence upon the laws of Ireland in respect of fisheries, and the evidence of Professor John Macneill, Dr. de Largy, and Professor Binchy, has satisfied me that there was under the ancient Irish law nothing which corresponded to the several fishery dealt with in Magna Charta and the cases of *Malcomson* v. *O'Dea* (10 H.L.C. 593) and *Neill* v. *Duke of Devonshire* (8 App. Cas. 135).

It has been suggested on behalf of the plaintiffs that the appropriation of a fishery to the people of a Tuath amounted to the creation of a several fishery, but in my opinion the people of a Tuath were 'the public' against whom no appropriation was permitted, and the right of fishing in tidal navigable waters enjoyed by the people of a Tuath to the exclusion of the rest of the inhabitants of Ireland would be analogous to a public right of fishing, and not to the legal conception of a several fishery.

The plaintiffs have also founded an argument upon the right of fishing which is proved to have been enjoyed by several religious houses, and in particular in these very waters of the Erne by the monks of St. Bernard, who occupied the Abbey of Assaroe, which was granted to them in or about 1184 by Flaherty O'Muldory, Lord of Kinel Connel, for the good of his soul. The fishing rights of the Abbey of Assaroe are defined in an Inquisition taken on the spot on the 26th of November, 1588, pursuant to the Acts for dissolution of the Monasteries, and are found to be as follows: 'The Abbot and Convent of the Abbey aforesaid had in right of their Abbey or House aforesaid liberty for two fishermen to fish for salmon in the place of the river or stream called the Erne which is termed Asseroe near Bealashenan [Ballyshannon] every year during times in which salmon are caught And the second cast or draught [in English the second draught] of all the fishermen at Asseroe when they begin to fish And liberty for one skiff for fishing for salmon or other fish from the island up to the sea below, which fishing is of the yearly value of three shillings and fourpence sterling English money aforesaid, which premises are the temporal (possessions) of the aforesaid Abbey'. This is no 'several fishery' but a limited liberty of fishing in the tidal waters of the Erne, granted to the members of a religious community, but the use which the plaintiffs seek to make of it is that they contend that the grantor – who is unnamed – of this liberty must himself have been the owner of an entire and exclusive right of fishing out of which this liberty was carved, and accordingly that the grant of this liberty is evidence of the existence in 1184, when Flaherty O'Muldroy endowed the Abbey, or at some date between that and 1189, of a several fishery owned by him or by some unknown person who made the grant of the liberty to the monks of Assaroe. This argument depends upon a number of pure assumptions, and in my opinion the explanation suggested by Professor MacNeill is less improbable, while it is more consistent with the Brehon law concerning fishing rights. It is quite likely that when the Bernardine monks came into Tirhugh at the invitation of Flaherty O'Muldory from their mother Abbey at Boyle, they came as foreigners to the Tuath, and were permitted a limited liberty of fishing in the waters of the Tuath as an appurtenance to their monastery by the Chief and people of the Tuath. This view is confirmed by one of the pre-Norman grants to a religious house which has been given in evidence, viz. the Charter from Dermot, King of the Leinstermen, to the Abbey at Ferns, which is stated to have been made 'by the counsel and assent of my princes and magnates,' and the Charter of Maurice MacLochlain, King of All Ireland, to the Cistercian Abbey of Newry is made 'with the unanimous will and general consent of the nobles of Ultonia and Ergalla and Oneach.' Grants in such form savour far more of a popular legislative act than of a feoffment or assignment of lands or of an incorporeal hereditament by a proprietor in his own right. When we come to grants such as those by John de Courcy in 1179 to the Monastery of Neddrum, of King John in 1179 to the Abbey of Jerpoint and in 1203 to the Abbey of Mellifont, and of Hervey de Monte Morisco in 1175 to the Abbey of Dunbrody, there is nothing surprising in the conveyance by a conqueror, or by the grantee of a conqueror, of property acquired by conquest, to the Religious whom he found in actual occupation of a monastery upon the conquered territory, nor in the circumstance that his grant is made in the form in use in England at the time. Indeed, it is recited in the memorandum on the grant of John de Courey to the Monastery of Neddrum that he had 'subjugated Ultonia' in the twenty-third year of King Henry, i.e. 1177–8. He had in fact 'gained the maritime coasts thereof from the Boyne to the Banne, and thereupon was made Earl of Ulster.' (Sir J. Davies, 'Discovery', p. 15). I find myself coerced by the evidence to the conclusion that the conjectures of Lord Chancellor Brady (5 Ir. Ch. R. at p. 234) that it was 'highly probable that rights of this kind' (several fisheries in tidal navigable waters) 'may have been enjoyed by the native princes,' and of Willes J. (10 H.L.C. at p. 620) that 'there is no improbability in the early appropriation of this always valuable property, or even a more extensive fishery, . . . in the time of the Irish Princes' cannot be successfully maintained in the light of our greater knowledge of the Brehon law, and that the plaintiffs must assert a right to a several fishery in the tidal navigable waters of the River Erne which had no existence as such until at earliest the later years of the reign of Queen Elizabeth.

Before I come to consider the documentary title of the plaintiffs, which commences with the Inquisition taken at Rathmullan on the 5th of September, 1603, I wish to guard myself against any suggestion that I have decided, or expressed any opinion upon, a question which seems to me to lie at the root of the plaintiffs' title, but upon which no evidence has been offered, and to which no argument has been addressed. It may be that there is nothing in it, and, if so, I have erred *ex abundante cautela*, and I can only plead in extenuation the reference to the same question by the Chief Justice in *R. (Moore)* v. *O'Hanrahan* ([1927] I.R. 406, at pp. 422–7).

There used to be a general belief, which originated I suppose in some loose observations by Lord Coke in the Institutes (I Inst. 141 b.) and in *Calvin's Case* (7 Rep. 1, at p. 17 b.), and which has been fostered by elementary and inaccurate history books, that Ireland was conquered once for all in the reign of King Henry II, and that the laws and usages of England were in force throughout the length and breadth of the land from the time of King John, or, at the latest, from the date of what is called Poynings' Act, 'whereby all the statutes made in England before that time were enacted established and made of force in Ireland. Neither did he only respect the time past, but provided also for the time to come, for he caused another law to be made, that no Act should be propounded in any parliament of Ireland, but such as should be first transmitted into England, and approved by the King and Council there as good and expedient for that land, and so returned back again under the great seal of England' (Sir J. Davies, 'Discovery,' p. 173). 'These laws, and others as important as these, for the making a commonwealth in Ireland were made in the government of Sir Edward Poynings, *But these laws did not spread their virtue beyond the English Pale* though they were made generally for the whole kingdom. For the Province without the pale, which during the war of York and Lancaster had wholly cast off the English Government, were not apt to receive this seed of reformation because they were not first broken and mastered again with the sword. *Besides, the Irish countries, which contained two third parts of the kingdom, were not reduced to shire ground, so that in them the laws of England could not possibly be put in execution.* Therefore these good laws and provisions, made by Sir Edward Poynings, were like good lessons for a lute that is broken and out of tune; of which little use can be made, till the lute be made fit to be played on' (Ibid. at pp. 176–7.)

This passage, from Sir John Davies' 'Discovery of the true causes why Ireland was never entirely subdued and brought under obedience to the Crown of England, until the beginning of his Majesty's happy reign,' is only an abridgement of portion of the judgment of the Court of King's Bench in *The Case of Tanistry* (Davies' Reports 78, at p. 101), where the statutes and the records of the Court are considered at length, which is introduced by the following passage: 'But as to the introduction of the common law of England into this Kingdom of Ireland, it is to be observed that as this island was not fully conquered and reduced to subjection of the Crown of England, all at one time, but by parcels, and in several ages; so the common law of England was not communicated to all the inhabitants, *simul et semel*, but from time to time, and to special persons and families of the Irishry, to whom the King was pleased to grant the benefit and protection of his laws.' And the same judgments goes on to refer to the pleadings and records in the well-known cases in which issues were tried whether the respective plaintiffs were 'mere *Hibernici, et non de quinque sanguinibus qui per concessionem progenitorum Domini Regis liberatatibus Anglicis gaudere debent et utuntur,'* or, in another case, '*non de sanguine aut progenie eorum, qui gaudeant lege Anglicana, quoad brevia portanda*'. Even in the statutes down to the 33rd Henry VIII the English disturbers of the peace are styled 'rebels', but the Irish are called 'enemies'. It was a good plea to an action by an Irishman that the plaintiff was not an Englishman, nor one of the 'five bloods' who enjoyed the privilege of being allowed to maintain suits in the Courts, and it was a good plea to an indictment for murder that the slain man '*fuit Hibernicus et non de libero sanguine.*' There are extant numerous patents of denization, granted to '*Hibernici,*' '*quod ipse de caetero in Hibernia utatur legibus Anglicanis, et prohibemus ne quisquam contra hanc concessionem nostram dictum C— F— D— in aliquo perturbet,*' and even '*omni modo terras, tenementa, redditus, et servitia perquirere possit sibi et haeredibus suis in perpetuum,*' etc. Even the head of one of the five bloods, 'O'Neale himself, in 20 Edward the Fourth, upon his marriage with a daughter of the house of Kildare (to satisfy the friends of the lady), was made a denizen by a special Act of Parliament, 20 Edward the Fourth, c. 8' (Davies, 'Discovery,' p. 79). 'Now we know as a matter of general history,' says the Chief Justice in *R. (Moore)* v. *O'Hanrahan*, ([1927] I.R. 406, at p. 427), 'that Tirconnaill at this time' (i.e., Henry II and John) 'escaped invasion, and that the chiefs of Cinel Connel did not render feudal homage to Henry, and did not accept him as their overlord.' The evidence of the historians in the present case carries our knowledge to a later date. Professor Binchy at Question 1648 and following questions: 'From 1171 down to the year 1541 is there any evidence of any submission by a chieftain of Tirconnaill to the Kings of England?' 'No. None whatever.' 'I take it that from any time down to 1541 there is no evidence of any submissions or claims to sovereignty by the Kings of England over Tirconnaill?' 'Not that I have ever seen.' 'No acknowledgement of a right of sovereignty?' 'No, no acknowledgement.' 'From the time that the O'Donnells succeeded to the Chieftaincy of Tirconnaill did they continue as Irish Chiefs up to 1541?' 'Yes, *and probably later.*' 'Certainly up to 1541 for the moment?' 'Yes.' 'For example was there a general submission of the Irish Chiefs to Richard II in 1392?' 'Yes.' 'And in that submission was the Chief of Tirconnaill a notable absentee?' 'He was the great absentee, the most notable absentee.' 'Were there any settlements of foreigners made in Tirconnaill?' 'No permanent ones of any kind.' 'Was there any evidence of any attempts to introduce into Tirconnaill English rule or English law?' 'Not until the very late sixteenth century.' 'In 1541 Manus O'Donnell made his submission?' 'He did.' '*Was that submission followed by any attempt to set up English administration*?' 'No, it was not.' To this testimony I venture to add that of Sir John Davies, Attorney-General in Ireland from 1603 to 1616, who accompanied the Lord Deputy on his visit to the Counties of Monaghan, Cavan, and Fermanagh in 1607 after the death in rebellion of Hugh M'Guyre, and was one of the Commissioners for disposing of the forefeited or conquered lands in Ulster. It was on this visit that the Lord Deputy went to Ballyshannon itself. Of the submissions in 18 Ric. II to which reference was made in the evidence of Professor Binchy Sir John Davies says ('Discovery,' p. 37): 'Yet did he not increase his revenue thereby one sterling pound, nor enlarge the English borders the breadth of one acre of land; neither did he extend the jurisdiction of his courts of justice one foot further than the English colonies, wherein it was used and exercised before.' After Sir Henry Sidney, Sir John Perrot, who held the last parliament in this kingdom, did advance the reformation in three principal points: First, in establishing the great composition of

Connaught, in which service the wisdom and industry of Sir Richard Bingham did concur with him, next, in reducing the unreformed parts of Ulster into seven shires, namely, Ardmagh, Monahan, Tirone, Coleraine, Donegall, Fermanagh, and Cavan; *though in his time the law was never executed in these new counties by any sheriffs or justices of assize, but the people left to be ruled still by their own barbarous lords and laws'* (Ibid., p. 191). 'Sir George Cary (who was a prudent Governor, and a just, and made a fair entry into the right way of reforming this kingdom) did, in the first year of his Majesty's reign, make the first sheriffs that ever were made in Tyrone and Tirconnel; and, shortly after, sent Sir Edmund Pelham Chief Baron *and myself* thither, the first justices of assize that ever sat in those countries; and in that circuit we visited all the shires of that province' (Ibid., p. 197).

It is abundantly clear from these passages that Sir John Davies, who had first hand knowledge of the subject, did not consider that the English laws had been extended to Donegal in the reign of Henry VIII. From these extracts, and from a mass of other evidence, it seems to be an ascertained historical fact that the land and inhabitants of Tirconnaill never came into subjection to the Crown of England until the last year of Queen Elizabeth or the first year of King James I, and were then acquired by conquest.

But that conquest did not of itself extend to the conquered territory and its inhabitants the laws of England. In *Campbell v. Hall* (20 St. Tr. 239) the manner in which the laws of England are imparted to Dominions, Colonies, and ceded or conquered territory, was the subject of adjudication in the Court of King's Bench, and the case of Ireland came under particular consideration. Lord Mansfield (at p. 324) expressed the clear opinion of the Court that it was the prerogative of the King to promulgate new laws, without the concurrence of parliament, for a *conquered* country. 'This is not a matter of disputed right; it has hitherto been uncontroverted that the King may change part or all of the political form of government over a conquered dominion. To go into the history of conquests made by the Crown of England. The alteration of the laws of Ireland has been much discussed by the lawyers and writers of great fame.' (The 'Discovery' of Sir John Davies, to which I have referred, was largely cited, especially by the celebrated Mr. Francis Hargrave, in the three arguments which took place.) 'No man ever said the change was made by the parliament; no man, unless perhaps Mr. Molyneux, ever said the King could not do it.' In *Fabrigas* v. *Mostyn* (20 St. Tr. 81), de Grey C.J., with whom Gould, Blackstone, and Nares JJ. agreed; declared that it was the right of the King in Council to make regulations for the government of the conquered island of Minorca, and in *Jephson* v. *Riera* (3 Knapp, 130, at p. 152) the Privy Council, on appeal from the Supreme Court of Gibraltar, held, following *Campbell* v. *Hall* (20 St. Tr. 230), that the power of making laws for the conquered territory was 'vested in the Crown, without any limitation as to the advice under which it may be exercised.'

It appears to me to follow from these authorities that the date upon which the provisions of Magna Charta, or of any other English law, became applicable to the newly conquered territory of Tirconnaill depends upon, and must be ascertained from the proclamation or Order in Council, if any, by which the laws of England were extended to the new subjects of the King, and if no such proclamation was made, then from whatever statute, either of the English or the Irish Parliament, made the existing laws of England or Ireland of force in that territory. It further appears to me that in the interval between the conquest and the promulgation of English law, the King for whom the territory had been conquered by his army, could exercise the royal prerogative of making grants of the conquered land, and of creating several fisheries in the tidal navigable waters around its coasts, unfettered by the limitations imposed upon him in respect of his English Dominions, or, of the Irish Pale, by Magna Charta.

If I am right in the opinion that the laws of England had not been extended in Tirconnaill when the first grant of a serveral fishery in the tidal waters of the Erne at Ballyshannon was made to a subject of Queen Elizabeth or of King James, the grantee would have just as good a title to it as William de Braosa had to the fishery which was the subject matter of the decision in *Malcomson* v. *O'Dea* (10 H.L.C. 592). The *Case of Tanistry* (Davies' Reports, 111) also supports the view that English law was not in force in Tirconnaill until about the year 1607 or later. We have not been referred to any proclamation, and I do not know whether any proclamation was made, before the first grant of a several fishery in the tidal navigable waters of the River Erne on October 14th, 1603, but there was a statute passed in the Parliament of Ireland, held in the eleventh, twelfth, and thirteenth years of King James I, cap. 5, entitled 'An Act of Repeale of diverse Statutes concerning the natives of this Kingdom of Ireland,' by which, after a recital 'that all the natives and inhabitants of this kingdome, without difference and distinction, are taken into his Majestie's gratious protection, and doe *now* live under one law as dutiful subjects of our Sovereigne Lord and Monarch,' a number of statutes against the Irish and their customs were repealed. That Act is dated 1612, the year in which the session had commenced. Of the earlier chapters, the first, also 1612, is 'a most joyful and just Recognition of his Majestie's lawfull, undoubted and absolute right and Title to the Crown of Ireland,' and after reciting that until the suppression of the late rebellion, presumably that of the Earls of Tyrone and Tyrconnell in 1607, 'the unreformed parts of this land, which being ruled only by Irish lords and customs, *had never before received the lawes and civill government of England,*' refers to the securing the lands and estates of his Majestie's subjects by the strengthening of defective titles and regranting of estates, and finally to the reduction 'to your Majestie's hands and possession' of 'great scopes of land' in the Province of Ulster by the 'defection and attainder' of 'divers wicked and ungrateful trayators' in those parts, and 'the civill plantation of those escheated lands.' Chapter 4 is the 'Act for the Attainder of Hugh, late Earl of Tyrone; Rory late Earl of Tyrconnell; Sir Cahir O'Dogherty, knight, and others,' and by it all their lands are forfeited to his Majesty, with a proviso saving 'any graunt, gift, lease, or demise,' made by his Majesty 'to any person or persons by letters patents under the great seal of Ireland or under the great seal of England.' The fishery which is in dispute in the present case had been leased nine years before the date of this statute by King James to one, Binglie or Bingley, and had been for several years in the actual possession of Sir Henry ffolliott, from whom the plaintiffs derive their title.

I mention, lest it should be supposed that I have overlooked them amongst the mass of documents in this case, three instruments which record dealings between the Crown and Irish Chieftains of Tirconnaill. The first is a 'Treaty between the Lord Deputy and Calvart O'Donnel by which O'Donnell surrenders to the Queen all regal services and rights in Connalia.' It bears date 8 Elizabeth, that is 1565, and is attested by three of the O'Donnell family, by Donald Magonnell, Bishop of Raphoe, O'Doghertie, Chief of his name, three of the McSwines, of whom one was the Chief of his name, 'and other gentlemen of Connalia.' Calvart O'Donnell agrees, *inter alia*, that, 'Her Majesty shall have the donation of all bishops and other ecclesiastical persons in Connalia.' We know from Sir John Davies that the Queen never succeeded in putting this power into execution in Tirconnaill, and this 'Treaty' is not, as is manifest from its provisions, an unconditional surrender by the King or Chief of a conquered country, and, in any event, it is difficult to see how Calvart O'Donnell, whose title was subject to the Brehon law, could make a valid surrender of the lands of his Tuath. Several of the attesting witnesses were subsequently attainted, and Donald Magonnell, Bishop of Raphaoe, is that Donaldus Magoniall, Hibernus, Epise, Rapotensis, whose name is recorded amongst the Episcopi Pii IV, in the concluding Sessions of the Council of Trent. The next document is a Grant of March 18th, 43rd Elizabeth (? 1601), to Neal Garve, or Garrowe, O'Donnell, Chief of his name, of the custody of the country or territory of Tirreconnell, 'with all lordships, manors, lands, customs, rents and services which had been granted to Calvart O'Donnell, grandfather of Neal; *excepting* the castle and town of Ballishannon, 800 acres of land adjacent, *the fishings of the Earne* and all rights and royalties in Connalia and the donations of the bishoprics, presentation of churches and all lands and possessions as well spiritual as temporal to hold during pleasure'; and the third is a grant on 10th February, 1603, to Rorie O'Donnell, Earl of Tirreconnell, and his heirs male, remainder to his brother Caffrey and his heirs male of all the territories and countries within the circuit of the land called Tireconell, &c., to hold in as full and ample manner as his brother, Hugh Rufus O'Donell, who was attainted and died in Spain, or as his father, Hugh Manus O'Donell, or any other of his ancestors. This reserves, *inter alia*, 'fishings,' 'the castle or fortress town and circuit of Ballishannon' with the precinct thereof with all lands &c belonging to the said castle, 1000 acres, 'and also the entire fishings belonging to the said castle in all the rivers &c within the said town and 1000 acres'.

With respect to the Elizabethan grants to the O'Donnells, there is a significant resolution of the Court in the *Case of Tanistry* (Davies' Reports, 109). 'A tanist surrenders to the Queen, who regrants the land to him, the Queen's grant is void.' 'It was also resolved that nothing passed by the grant of Queen Elizabeth made to Conoghor O'Callaghan, as it is found by the verdict; for the grant is made in consideration of his surrender, and he claimed nothing but as tanist, who hath no estate of which the common law taketh notice . . . by which the grant of the Queen made in consideration of such estate surrendered is void in law, *Barwick's Case* 5 Co. 93, and the case of *Altonwoods*, 1 Co. 43, 18 Eliz. Dyer 252.' 'Lastly where it was objected by one of the counsel for the plaintiff that Queen Elizabeth should be said to be in possession of this land' (which was in 'Publicallaghan, otherwise O'Callaghan's countrie,' in the County of Cork, a long settled part of Ireland) 'by virtue of the first conquest of Ireland . . . it was resolved against this objection that Queen Elizabeth shall not be said to be in actual posession of this land by virtue of the first conquest, if it doth not appear by some record that the first conqueror had seised the land at the time of the conquest, and appropriated it particularly to himself as parcel of his proper demesne.' The Court then proceeds to state the law as to conquered lands substantially as it was stated by Lord Mansfield in *Campbell* v. *Hall* (20 St. Tr. 239) a hundred and sixty-five years later.

That was a Cork case, but when we turn to Tirconaill, Sir John Davies points out that, instead of seising the lands, 'no Governor during Queen Elizabeth's reign did refuse to grant any of those "Captainships"' (the kind that were granted to the O'Donnells as above mentioned) 'to any pretended Irish lord who would desire, and with his thankfulness deserve the same. And again, though the greatest part of Ulster were vested by Act of Parliament in the actual and real possession of the crown; *yet was there never any seisure made thereof, nor any part thereof brought into charge, but the Irish were permitted to take all the profits without rendering any duty or acknowledgement for the same.*'

I have dealt with this matter, which was not discussed during the argument, at, I fear, inordinate length, but I am anxious to protect myself against any suggestion that I have decided, or that it is involved in my decision, that Magna Charta was in force in Tirconaill before 1612, or that King James I or Queen Elizabeth could not have had any power to create a new several fishery in tidal navigable waters in Tirconaill after that territory had been acquired by conquest, and before a proclamation, Order in Council, or statute had been made extending the laws of England, including Magna Charta, to it and its inhabitants, or that the principles declared in *Attorney-General for British Columbia* v. *Attorney-General for Canada* ([1914] A.C. 152), as applicable to newly settled colonies, have any application to dominions newly acquired by conquest, as was the case with Tirconaill at the beginning of the seventeenth century.

Dealing with the case upon the assumption, which has not been disputed by the plaintiffs' counsel, that Magna Charta was in force in Tirconaill before the reign of Queen Elizabeth, and upon the conclusion at which I have arrived upon the evidence, that no several fishery existed in fact before 1189, I must consider the plaintiffs' alternative case, which is founded upon certain statutes passed in the reign of Charles I for the confirmation of Letters Patent and for the remedying of defective titles, and which was introduced by an amendment of the pleadings during the hearing of the case in the Court of first instance.

The plaintiffs' title is as follows: On the 5th of September, 1603, by an Inquisition taken at Rathmullan in the County of Donegal, it was found that this fishery, with others, belonged to the King (James I) in right of his Crown. I am not satisfied that this finding was induced by any misunderstanding of the law relating to fisheries in tidal navigable waters on the part of Sir John Davies or anyone else. I think, though I do not decide, that this Inquisition, and the later one taken at Lifford on September 12th, 1609, may well have been taken to ascertain the properties acquired for the Crown by conquest from the Chieftains of Kinel-Connel and Kinel-Owen, and included in 'the great scopes of land' in the province of Ulster, which the statute of James I declared to have been reduced into his Majesty's hands and possession and 'had never before received the lawes and civill government of England.' On October 14th, 1603, this fishery was demised to one, John Binglie or Bingley, for a term of 21 years at a rent. What became of Bingley and his lease does not appear, but within three years, viz. on June 7th, 1606, a new lease for 21 years of the self-same fisheries was made by the Crown to Sir Henry ffolliott. This lease comprised the fishing rights of the dissolved Monastery of Assaroe, and all the other rights of fishing in the Ballyshannon waters. For some undiscoverable reason, a second lease of the identical fishing rights was made on July 6th, 1607, to Sir Henry ffolliott for the term of 20 years, that is the unexpired residue of the term created by the previous letting. On April 12th, 1608, a grant in fee of the Abbey fishings was made to one, Francis Gofton, at the annual rent of eight pounds ten shillings, and this grant included the reversion expectant upon any demise 'before this time made,' presumably the reversion expectant upon the lease to ffolliott. At an Inquisition taken at Lifford on the 12th of September, 1609, it was found that the Assaroe Abbey fishings were then in the possession of Sir Henry ffolliott, and 'that the whole countrie of Tireconnell, otherwise called O'Donnell's countrie, and all lands, tenementes, fishings, royalties and hereditamentes within the said com. of Donegall, (except the said countrie and lands of Inishowen and excepte all castles, lands, tenements and hereditamentes abovementioned to belonge to any bishoppricke, deanerie, abbie, monasterie, or religious house) are now in the reall and actuall possession of the Crowne *by reason of the attainder of treason of Rorie late Earle of Tireconnell.*' On July 20th, 1609, a grant of enormous tracts of lands in half a dozen counties, including the fishery in the estuary of Erne at Ballyshannon, was made to the Baroness of Delvin and her son Nugent. This was subject to the term of the lease to Sir Henry ffolliott. These Inquisitions and the grants, the interests under which were subsequently acquired by ffolliott, were all prior to the statutes of 11 Jac. I, which extended the English law to all the inhabitants of Ireland, but which contained an express saving of all grants etc. previously made.

On March 21st, 1620, a second Inquisition was taken at Lifford, at which there was a presentment of a royal fishery for salmon in the sea below Ballyshannon, which was found to have been in the possession of ffolliott and his assigns *for sixteen years past*, which takes us back to the conquest of Tirconaill.

ffolliott appears to have been very assiduous in collecting to himself all the outstanding and conflicting interests in the properties comprised in these different grants and leases, for by an Inquisition taken at Ballyshannon on the 2nd of January, 1620, it appears that he had acquired by purchase from Gofton on May 20th, 1608, the premises comprised in the grant to Gofton of April 12th in the same year, that on July 10th, 1604, he had purchased from one, Robert Leycester, lands and fishings in Fermanagh and Sligo which had been granted by the Crown to Leycester on May 17th, 1604, and finally, that he had purchased from the Baroness Delvin and her son the Ballyshannon fisheries comprised in the grant to them of July 20th, 1609, together with other liberties appertaining to the counties of Donegal, Sligo and Fermanagh. He had also obtained from the King in 1612 a grant of the castle and town of Ballyshannon with about 1,000 acres of lands appertaining thereto. Upon the 9th of April, 1622, by Grant pursuant to Letters Patent dated October 22nd, 1618, King James granted to Sir Henry ffolliott, who was then Baron of Ballyshannon, the entire premises comprised in the different grants and leases to which I have referred, including, with many others, the Abbey of Assaroe, its lands, weirs, and liberties of fishing, the castle, bawn and fort of Ballyshannon, the 1,000 acres, the fairs and tolls, 'and also the entire creek bay or river of Bealashanney, otherwise Ballyshannon, viz.: from the high sea as far as the Bank or Fall of water commonly called the salmon leap, otherwise the fall of Asheroe, near the castle of Ballyshannon and also the aforesaid Bank or Saltus Salmoni, in English the Salmon Leap, otherwise the fall of Asheroe, with its appurtenances and also the lakes, weirs, islands and banks in or near the aforesaid creek, bay and river aforesaid and the soil and ground and water of the aforesaid creek, bay, lake or river and all land covered with water there and also the entire fishing and liberty of fishing to take salmon and all other kinds of fish whatever in or within the aforesaid creek, bay and river aforesaid and upon the banks aforesaid . . . and also the whole and entire river and water of Erne aforesaid from the high sea as far as Lough Earne and the ground and soil of the same with the appurtenances, lying and being in the Counties of Donegal and Fermanagh or either of them, which all and singular the premises above by these presents before granted now are in the tenure and occupation of the aforesaid Henry Lord ffolliott, Baron of Ballyshannon, his tenants or assigns.' The *habendum* of the granted hereditaments is in fee simple as regards the Abbey premises, *in capite* by military service as regards the castle of Ballyshannon and the lands appertaining to it, and as to other lands, etc., in fee and common soccage. This grant contains provisions for the maintenance of the castle of Ballyshannon, and for the placing therein of a constable and wardens during the minority of any heir of Lord ffolliott, and especially full warranties and *non obstante* clauses.

Henry Lord ffolliott died shortly after this grant, and an Inquisition *post mortem* was held at Ballyshannon on March 1st, 1623, by which it was found that he died seised in fee of all the premises granted by the patent of April 9th, 1622, subject to some grants which are not material to the title to the fishery, and to provisions for his widow, two sons and a cousin, and that 'Thomas the present Lord ffolliott his son and next heir was then aged 9 years and 8 months and not married.'

The next document, which is treated either as a continuation of the title of Henry Lord ffolliott, or in the alternative as a fresh root of the plaintiffs' title, is a Grant by Letters Patent under the great seal, dated the 30th of August in the fifteenth year of Charles I, and duly enrolled, whereby there were granted to the said Thomas Lord ffolliott, the eldest son of Henry, together with other hereditaments, all the lately dissolved Abbey of the monks of St. Bernard of Asheroe, with the fishings and liberty of fishing in or near the bay or port of Ballyshannon between the castle of Ballyshannon and the high sea, 'which were reputed and are now reputed to belong to the said Abbey or the Abbot and Convent thereof from a time of which there is no human memory to the contrary,' the castle of Ballyshannon with its appurtenant and adjoining lands, its markets and fairs, 'and also all the creek, bay or river of Beallashenny otherwise Ballyshannon viz.: from the high sea to the rock, in English 'the rocks or waterfall' commonly called 'the Salmon Leaps otherwise the fall of Asheroe' near the castle of Ballyshanny aforesaid And also all the aforesaid rock or salmon leap or fall of Asheroe with the appurtenances And also all and singular loughs weirs islands rockes . . . and waterfall in within or near the aforesaid Bay creek and river of Ballyshanny otherwise Ballyshannon aforesaid And all the bottom soil land and water of the aforesaid creek bay or river and all land covered and to be covered with water there and also the whole fishing and liberty of fishing and to fish for and catch salmon and all other kinds of fish whatsoever in or within the aforesaid creek bay and river aforesaid and on the rocks aforesaid . . .'. Then follow eel weirs and 'the liberty of having nets and other instruments necessary for fishing on the rocks, creeks, river and bay aforesaid and also the liberty of carrying off all fish and catch of fish of every kind from the aforesaid rocks . . . creeks river or bays or from any part thereof,' *Habendum*, as regards the fisheries and fishings, to Thomas Lord ffolliott his heirs and assigns for ever. All the premises are created into one entire manor to be for ever reputed styled and named the Manor of Bealashanny in the County of Donegal.

These Letters Patent are stated to be 'according to the intention and effect of our Commission under our Great Seal of England bearing date at Canbury [Canterbury] in our said Kingdom of England on the first day of September in the fourteenth year of our reign, as well for and in consideration of a certain fine or sum of ninety-nine pounds seven shillings and sixpence,' and they contain in further pursuance of the said Commission a release to Thomas Lord ffolliott from 'all and singular the conditions covenants articles mandates instructions and agreements of the plantation, and all and singular other the conditions covenants agreements and mandates whatsoever and howsoever contained mentioned or specified in any prior Letters Patent of the premises before mentioned or any of them or any parcel thereof made or mentioned to be made to the aforesaid Thomas Lord ffolliott or any other person or persons whomsoever before the date of these our Letters Patent,' a release remittance and quit claim of all penalties, rights of re-entry for breach of any condition in any prior Letters Patent, or by reason of any violation or non-performance of any condition article mandate instruction provision or limitation for the plantation, with only a proviso for the maintenace and repair by Thomas Lord ffolliott, his heirs and assigns, of the castle and fortalice of Ballyshannon, and the reservation of a right to install a constable and ten wardens in the Castle during the minority of any heir. The grant is to be free of all rents, penalties, articles of plantation, covenants for performance of the plantation, forfeitures for nonperformance of the plantation, and, after an elaborate *non obstante* clause, specifying many statutes, 'notwithstanding any other statutes Acts ordinances prohibitions restrictions instructions or provisions or any other thing cause or matter in evacuation and weakening or annulment of these our Letters Patent'.

Of themselves, these Letters Patent would have no more, and no less, force or validity than any other royal grant, but they were made in pursuance of, and were invested with the validity conferred by, a statute passed in the fifteenth year of Charles I (15 Car. 1, c. 6), by which it was enacted, after reciting the creation of divers Commissions of Grace for the remedy of defective titles in Ireland, and the granting of lands and hereditaments upon them 'as well . . . as . . . upon the latter commission of grace bearing date at Canterbury in the realme of England the first day of September in the fourteenth year of his said Majestie's reign,' and that some lands had not yet passed but might thereafter be passed, it was enacted that all letters patent 'which are already past . . . under the greate seale . . . of Ireland' 'by virtue or pretence of or reference unto any commission of grace now in being or hereafter to be within this kingdom or any other former commission or commissions granted since the beginning of his now Majestie's reign to any person or persons . . . shall be by authority of this present Parliament enacted and to be and shall be deemed and adjudged to be good sufficient effectuall and indefeazable to all intents constructions and purposes in manner following (that is to say) for and concerning all . . . lands . . . lying or being within every or any of the late plantations within this kingdom made by our late sovereign lady Queen Elizabeth, our late most gracious lord King James, and made or to be made by the King's most excellent Majesty that now is, or by any of them, as well against his Majesty his heirs and successors, as against all and every other person and persons, bodies politick and corporate, as well spiritual as temporal whatsoever . . . notwithstanding . . . any statute ordinance law cause matter or thing which might or may any way impeach enfeeble avoid or destroy any of the said letters patent in all or any point or points whatsoever.' There follows an enactment for quiet enjoyment. The second section enacts that His Majesty shall be deemed seised of an absolute estate in right of his imperial crown in all lands and hereditaments in the counties of Tyrone, Armagh, Donegal, Fermanagh, Cavan, Leitrim and Longford; in several countries, formerly of the Irish families, in other counties; in several reputed plantation lands in or near certain territories in Westmeath and Wexford; in several hereditaments in the counties of Waterford, Cork, Kerry, Limerick and Tipperary, usually called or theretofore passed as plantation lands, 'at every such time and times respectively, whensoever *any* of the same before mentioned . . . hereditaments shall be within the space of five years next ensuing the end of this present session of parliament new passed granted confirmed released or assured . . . to any person or persons . . . by letters patents under the great seale of this kingdom by virtue or pretence of or reference unto any such commissions of grace now being or hereafter to be within this realme, being either former patentees, or reputed inheritors or proprietors, or by former assignation distribution or appointment have taken the profits thereof,' the grantees shall from and after the passing or sealing of any such letters patent be confirmed in their possession and may hold 'as well against his Majesty his heirs and successors as against all and every other person and persons bodies politick and incorporate' freed and discharged from everything except what shall be saved in the letters patent.

This Act, together with three previous Acts for confirming and strengthening defective titles, appears to me to have been passed with the express object of ensuring to the patentees of the Crown, with the authority of Parliament, the estates which had been granted to them, and it appears also that each statute was passed to remedy some oversight or to meet some objection which had been or which might be made to the validity of a title derived under the previous statutes or some grant which they had been intended to confirm. Thus under 10 Car. I, sess. 1, cap. 3, titles had been confirmed only against the King his heirs and successors and all other parties to the same and persons claiming under them. 10 Car. I, sess. 3, cap. 2, was to meet the case of any failure to enrol or record letters patent, to provide for misrecitals and misnomers, and to acquit patentees of reservations in earlier grants of the same lands, while 10 Car. I, sess. 3, cap. 3, which is in almost identical terms with 15 Car. I, cap. 6, only provided for the validation of grants made within 'five years next ensuing the end of this present session of Parliament,' a period which expired on the 20th of March, 1620. The recitals in 10 Car. I, sess. 3, cap. 3, show the classes of grantees for whose benefit it was enacted. It recites that 'sundry plantations have at severall times been made' in eighteen specified counties which include Donegal, 'grounded as well upon ancient as recent title of your crown, declared as well by inquisitions as other records and evidences; upon all which divers patents have been passed, and thereby very many undertakers, *and others of British birth*, and very many of the natives of best quality and condition have been there planted and settled . . . by occasion of all which, very many castles, bawnes, strong houses, forts and townes walled, have since been built and erected . . . to the unexpected enriching and civilizing of the said several *counties* and territories.' With a view to the confirmation of grants, his Majesty is to be deemed and adjudged seised and vested 'in the actuall and reall possession and seizin' 'by good lawfull and indefeasable title and estate in fee simple,' in right of his imperial crown of England and Ireland of 'all castles, mannors, lands, tenements and hereditaments lying and being in the said severall counties of Tyrone, Armagh, Donegall, Fermanagh, Cavan, Londonderry, Leytrim and Longford,' which is a complete enumeration of eight counties, with no reference to any distinction between 'plantation lands' and any others, though in the following categories of lands elsewhere in Ireland, distinction is drawn between territories, precincts and countries of the Irish families, plantation lands, reputed plantation lands, and lands passed as such. The 15 Car. I, cap. 6, is almost identical, except that for some reason it omits Londonderry and the nomenclature of the Irish families is corrected, and the confirmation is made even more elaborate.

The grant to Thomas Lord ffolliott by letters patent dated August 30th in the 15th Car. I recites that they were made in pursuance of the Commission of Canterbury dated September 1st, 14th Car. I, which was the foundation of the Statute of 15th Car. I, cap. 6, and the grant was duly enrolled within the prescribed period, and from that date down to the recent attempt by the special defendants to invade the possession of the plaintiffs, it is not suggested that the grantees under those letters patent have not been in continuous possession and uninterrupted enjoyment of the fishery at Ballyshannon, and it is admitted that the fishery claimed by the plaintiffs is the same fishery which was granted by the letters patent. The Attorney-General has quite properly admitted that, if the grant by the letters patent of 15 Car. I to be valid, no question arises upon the subsequent devolution of title to the present plaintiffs.

I understand that the validity of this grant is disputed upon two grounds: First, that the lands comprised in it are not 'plantation lands,' and, second, that ffolliott was not an 'undertaker' or a person entitled to share in what is called by the Attorney-General 'the plantation.' The answer to the first objection appears to me to be that the whole of the county of Donegal is declared by the Acts 10 Car. I, sess. 3, cap. 3, and 15 Car. I, cap. 6 to be deemed to have been vested absolutely and indefeasibly in his Majesty for the express purpose of validation of any grants made by him. The counties specified in the first category of lands dealt with by those statutes are those which were the last to be conquered and the same which comprised the territories forfeited to King James I by the 11 Jac. I, cap. 4, when the Earls of Tyrone and Tyrconnell, Sir Cahir O'Dogherty, the O'Reillys of Cavan,

Maguire of Fermanagh, O'Hanlons of Armagh, and many more were attainted and outlawed, and their lands absolutely forfeited to His Majesty. These statutes appear to me by their very terms to put the Ulster counties named into the same position as plantation lands, and certainly to validate all grants of lands in those counties, whether strictly plantation lands or not, and the grants to the ffolliotts are in form plantation grants. It was not necessary to constitute a 'plantation' that a whole county or even a considerable tract of land should be settled. The planting of 'castles, bawnes, strong houses, forts and townes walled,' in or on the border of a hostile country was a 'plantation,' and plantations of this description were effected by English Monarchs and their Deputies long before the great Stuart and Cromwellian schemes of settlement were dreamt of. I can imagine no site more suitable for the plantation of a 'castle, bawne, strong house or fort,' than the great passage of the Erne which has been called Seanach's Ford since the earliest times of which we have even a tradition. The castle, which was put in charge of ffolliott, commanded the ford over the Erne which was the gateway into or out of Tirconaill, which was the pass by which the peoples of Kinel-Connell were wont to start on their raids into Sligo and Connacht, and it was across the ford at Ballyshannon that the forces of O'Donnell passed upon that last disastrous journey which ended for so many of them at Kinsale. It was also the bridge-head for operation against Tirconaill, and corresponded to the great fort upon the Blackwater which was constructed and maintained as a curb upon the activities of Tyrone. All the provisions in the grants of the Ballyshannon estates seem to me to be peculiarly appropriate to the plantation of a Warden of the Ford to protect the neighbouring counties against the aggression of the still unconquered Kinel-Connell.

Upon the second point, Sir Henry ffolliott is termed by manifest implication a 'servitor' in the King's letter dated October 22nd, 1618, a document which recites his interest in this very fishery, and the letter was the authority for the grant to him of April 9th, 1622, by which all the property which he had gathered in from Bingley, Gofton, Leycester, and the Nugent family was created one entire manor of Ballyshannon and granted to him. In the grant to Thomas Lord ffolliott, his son, in 1639, there was actually a clause releasing him from the articles and conditions of the plantation, perhaps because there was no longer need to guard the passage of the Erne against the peoples of Tirconaill.

So far as these two points are concerned, I am in complete agreement with Johnston J. and I adopt what he has said on them.

If there were any doubt or ambiguity concerning the true interpretation of the Statutes 10 Car. I and 15 Car. I, in my opinion, the unchallenged enjoyment of the property for three hundred years ought to be attributed, if it can reasonably be referred, to a lawful origin, and that construction which will support such an origin should be placed upon any ambiguous language in the Statutes. 'I cannot go along with his Lordship (Lord Justice Clerk),' said Lord Brougham, in the *Magistrates of Dunbar* v. *The Duchess of Roxburghe* (3 Cl. & F. 335, at p. 353), 'when for this reason he denies that usage, however long and inveterate, could be binding and operative on the parties. It can be binding and operative upon the parties only as it is the interpreter of a doubtful law, as affording a contemporary interpretation; but it is quite plain that, as against a plain statutory law, no usage is of any avail. But this undeniable proposition supposes the statute to speak a language plainly and indubitably differing from the purport of the usage. Where the statute, speaking on some points, is silent as to others, usage may well supply the defect, especially if it is not inconsistent with the statutory directions, where any are given; *or where the statute uses a language of doubtful import, the acting under it for a long course of years may well give an interpretation to that obscure meaning, and reduce that uncertainty to a fixed rule, optimus legis interpres consuetudo*, which is sometimes termed *contemporanea expositio*; and where you can carry back the usage for a century, and have no proof of a contrary usage before that time, you fairly reach the period of *contemporanea expositio.'*

When I find that not for one century, but for three, the lands comprised in the ffolliott grant have been dealt with as if they were plantation lands, and, so far from any contrary usage appearing, that there has been an uninterrupted and unchallenged enjoyment of the whole property upon this basis, and that the statutes of Charles refer to Donegal in terms which at least admit of the interpretation that the whole county was regarded as plantation land or reputed as such, I think that the principle of interpretation stated by Lord Brougham may be applied to these statutes, and that it is not even necessary to call in aid the express enactments, in the statutes themselves, that they are to receive the construction most favourable to the patentees.

That the language of the statutes *is* at least 'of doubtful import,' and that it does not differ 'plainly and indubitably from the purport of the usage,' is not an unfair deduction from the fact that judicial opinion is evenly divided upon its interpretation; and that usage *has* placed this construction upon the statutes seems to me to be established by the following proved or admitted facts: The patentees and their tenants and assignees have been in actual possession and enjoyment, not alone by a documentary title, but by actual use, of the fishery in question without challenge by the Crown or by anyone else, for over three hundred years. During that period the grantees have paid and the Crown has accepted the rents reserved by the grants and payable in respect of the fishing rights and the several fishery granted to Henry Lord ffolliott and found by Inquisition to have been in his possession since 1603. That the Crown rent was redeemed so recently as 1897 by payment to the Crown through the Land Judges Court of a capital sum; that the existence of this several fishery was recognised as such in at least two public statutes, 31 Geo. II, cap. 13, and 3 Geo. III, cap. 35; that the fishery has been constantly dealt with as property, has been let and sold from time to time; that it has been taxed and rated, as a several fishery, to the relief of the poor for nearly a century; and finally, that the Special Commissioners of Fisheries, under the Acts 5 & 6 Vict. c. 106, and 26 & 27 Vict. c. 114, and the Inspectors of Irish Fisheries under the Fisheries (Ireland) Act, 1869, have given certificates from time to time as required by law that the 'fixed engines' for catching salmon in the estuary or tide-way of the River Erne, owned and worked by the plaintiffs, their predecessors and the lessees of their predecessors, were legal – certificates which could not have been granted unless the owners or users of the engines in question had first satisfied the Commissioners that they had been legally erected 'in a several fishery.' It was the duty of the Commissioners, as a specially appointed statutory tribunal, to inquire into all these fixed engines in estuaries of rivers and to abate and destroy all illegal engines. Such fixed engines were illegal unless they had been erected by a person legally possessed of or entitled to a several fishery, and the title to the fishery was one of the matters which the Commissioners were empowered to investigate. If the Commissioners were 'satisfied' of the legality of the engine, they were to give a certificate to that effect. A special appeal was provided by the statute for any person aggrieved, but the adjudication of the Commission was not removable by *certiorari*. It was held in the *Lax Weir Case* (I.R. 2 C.L. 519, n.) that the decision of the Commissioners under 5 & 6 Vict. c. 106, as to the legality of a weir was a judgment *in rem* and by Palles C.B. and Andrews J. in *Devonshire* v. *Drohan* ([1900] 2 I.R. 161) that the determination of the Commissioners under 26 & 27 Vict. c. 114, as to the legality of a weir, was a judgment *in rem* and conclusive against the world.

Each of these circumstances was a recognition of the existence of a several fishery in the tidal navigable waters of the River Erne as a legal entity which could have existed only if the original grant of the fishery had been made by James I in exercise of his royal prerogative as a conqueror before Magna Charta had been promulgated in Donegal; or if the statutes for confirming defective titles had been generally recognised and construed as applicable to the ffolliott grants; and I hold that I am not only empowered, but bound, to adopt that interpretation of the language of the statutes of 10 and 15 Car. I which will uphold the possession and dealings of three hundred years as legal, provided always that the language of the statutes is reasonably capable of such an interpretation.

It may be observed that the fishery was not the only, or even the principal, hereditament comprised in the grants with which we are concerned. It was only severed from the ffolliott estate in 1869, when the great possessions of the Right Hon. Thomas Connolly were sold in the Landed Estates Court. His father the Right Hon. William Conolly had purchased the ffolliott estates in 1719, but, if the ffolliott grants are invalid as being outside the purview of the Caroline statutes for the strengthening of defective titles, it is not the title to the fishery alone that has been undermined by this decree, but that to all the property comprised in the grant to Thomas, Lord ffolliott. The fact that the Right Hon. William Conolly paid the representatives of Lord ffolliott £48,000 for their property in 1719, and that the predecessors of the present plaintiffs purchased this fishery in the Landed Estates Court for the sum of over £45,000 in 1869, and took a conveyance from the Court, cannot affect the rights of the parties, inasmuch as this Court has already decided that the Landed Estates Court conveyance passed only whatever rights the purchasers might be able to prove had been possessed by Thomas Conolly, and that the consideration for their £45,000 was nothing more than a barren rock in the Erne, and a right to whatever they might be able to establish their title to by litigation. That decision binds me, and I accept it *ex animo*, but I do not read the speeches of the Lords in *Mecredy and Others* v. *Alexander and Others* (Unreported) as deciding what was not before their Lordships' House, or in question in that action, viz. the title of the purchasers under the Landed Estates Court conveyance to a several fishery in the tidal waters of the River Erne at Ballyshannon, which at the date of that decision had been actually possessed and worked by their vendor and his predecessors for two and a half centuries: and I feel considerable doubt whether, if it had been proved to their Lordships, as it has been in this case, that Conolly and his predecessors in title, and his successors, the plaintiffs in *Mecredy and Others* v. *Alexander and Others* (Unreported), had been in actual uninterrupted and exclusive enjoyment of the disputed fishery for three hundred years, and the Marquis of Ely had been an intruder of yesterday, they would have come to the conclusion at which they did in fact arrive. On the other hand, it seems to me that each of the Lords, with perhaps the exception of Lord Bramwell, did express an opinion, *obiter* though it was, that the Landed Estates Court conveyance was effective to pass 'an existing subject which was in lease to tenants named Shiel'; 'the existing and known Ballyshannon salmon and eel fisheries which were separated from the riparian rights by means of the enjoyment of the lessees, and had therefore in that way a real existence at the time when the deed was made'; 'a distinct subject of conveyance . . . that Ballyshannon salmon and eel fishery of Thomas Conolly as to which the leases and tenancies are reserved at the end, and which appears by this schedule to have been a known and existing thing, but which did not include in point of fact Lord Ely's waters': *per* Selborne L.C. Lord Blackburn says: 'On the very face of the instrument by the reference, which the Lord Chancellor has pointed out, to the two leases which are given, it shows that there were *de facto* existing fisheries of the sort which I have mentioned, both in the tidal and in the non-tidal part. It is expressly mentioned in the first lease that there is a salmon fishery in Ballyshannon "through the whole extent of the River Erne and the waters thereof and the river commonly called or known by the name of the Abbey River and the waters thereof and all other rivers and watercourses having communications with the said rivers Erne and Abbey where salmon is known to breed and cast spawn." That plainly is a grant enjoyed by Shiel of a salmon fishery in the tidal part and in the non-tidal part; and embraced within it there is what is called for shortness the salmon fishery of Ballyshannon.' He then proceeds with a passage which I will not quote but of which every word is important, and concludes: 'I say, what does that mean when we know as a matter of fact that there was a separate and several fishery *de facto* severed from the right to the river and everything else and *de facto* enjoyed. It seems to me that, when once you have got that fact brought before you, these words mean neither more nor less than if they had been "I grant firstly the salmon fishery called the Ballyshannon salmon fishery enjoyed by Alicia Shiel."' Lord Bramwell's *argumentum a preposteroso* would scarcely have been employed if he had seen, as we have, the earlier Crown grants in which the identical rights the grant of which he says 'is preposterous on what one may call the fact of it' were actually granted, with even more extensive ones, to the parties from whom Conolly had purchased them in 1719. Lord FitzGerald says that 'what was described here and what was intended to be conveyed is not a general and exclusive fishery from one end of the river Erne to the other, from its source to its mouth, but that fishery which Thomas Conolly had, and which it appears equally clearly from the conveyance was in the hands of the lessees. In fact the leases to the Shiels reserved all that he had; and what the party here claims, *and what he got by the conveyance*, was first the rent of £1,200 a year reserved by the lease to the Shiels, and, when the Shiels lease terminated, *the right to the reversion and enjoyment of that which they had,* namely the Conolly fishery.' 'No one can doubt, upon the documents and upon the evidence now before us, that at the time of the execution of this conveyance Thomas Conolly had an extensive and very valuable fishery popularly known as the Ballyshannon fishery, and which was probably derived at some unknown period from a royal grant. I say so because we find that there was a quit rent reserved and we know that in Ireland quit rents were only reserved in grants from the Crown. We know also that, in addition to this fishery at the mouth of the river, a fishery in the upper waters is only valuable as a breeding ground for the fish which will eventually descend the river and come up again and be captured at the wires; but we know from the succession of Caldwell deeds that Thomas Conolly acquired certain riparian rights quite consistent with the rights of other riparian proprietors. Those rights were what the Shiels had under the lease; those rights were what was bargained for, and for which the purchaser gave £45,000; and we give full effect to that transaction.' The Lords held, affirming the Common Pleas Division, that certain eel-fishings in the non-tidal waters of Lough Erne, which neither Thomas Conolly, nor, so far as the evidence went, any of his ffolliott predecessors, had ever enjoyed or possessed, but which had been continuously enjoyed and possessed by the Marquis of Ely as a riparian proprietor, did not pass under the comprehensive words of the Landed Estates conveyance, but the passages which I have cited show that the Lords did not express any doubt that the Ballyshannon fishery which was at the time under lease from Conolly to the Shiels, was effectually conveyed to, and vested in him by the Landed Estates Court conveyance. As I have already said, the opinions expressed by their Lordships were only *obiter* as regards the Ballyshannon fishery, and the decision of this Court has concluded the matter so far as we are concerned.

Upon the whole case, while I agree with the other members of the Court that there is no evidence from which we could presume that a several fishery existed in the tidal navigable waters of the river Erne at any date prior to the year 1189, I consider that, upon the true construction of the statutes 10 Car. I and 15 Car. I and the Letters Patent to Thomas Lord ffolliott, there was a valid grant of the several fishery claimed in this action, and I express no opinion upon the question whether a valid grant was made either by Queen Elizabeth or by King James I or by King Charles I before the restrictions imposed by Magna Charta upon the exercise of the royal prerogative were extended to what is now the County of Donegal.

Notes and Questions
1. *Cf.* the earlier decision of the Supreme Court in *R. (Moore)* v. *O'Hanrahan* [1927] I.R. 406.
2. What precisely is the *ratio decidendi* of the majority of the Supreme Court in the case just reproduced? What is the point of difference between the majority and FitzGibbon J.? The case involved an appeal from a decision of Johnston J.; consider the application of the Supreme Court's decision by Johnson J. in the later case of *Little* v. *Cooper* [1937] I.R. 1.
3. What was the relevance of the Brehon Laws in the *Moore* case? *Cf.* the reference to them in the *Foyle and Bann Fisheries Ltd.* v. *Att.-Gen.* (1949) 83 I.L.T.R. 29.
4. With respect to the references to Magna Carta, see further *Irish Land Law*, paras. 6.042 and 6.116.

II. TENURE

The notion of tenure was one of the fundamental features of the feudal system of landholding introduced to Ireland by the Normans in the twelfth century. Though much simplified, largely as a result of statutory reforms which commenced as early as the thirteenth century, it remains a basic feature of Irish land law in the twentieth century: see *Irish land Law*, ch. 2.

QUIA EMPTORES, 1290

I. Forasmuch as purchasers of lands and tenements of the fees of great men and other lords, have many times heretofore entered into their fees, to the prejudice of the lords, to whom the freeholders of such great men have sold their lands and tenements to be holden in fee of their feoffors, and not of the chief lord of the fees, whereby the same chief lords have many times lost their escheats, marriages, and wardships of lands and tenements belonging to their fees; which thing seemed very hard and extream unto those lords and other great men, and moreover in this case manifest disheritance: Our lord the King, in his Parliament at Westminster after Easter, the eighteenth year of his reign, that is to wit, in the quinzime of Saint John Baptist, at the instance of the great men of the realm, granted, provided, and ordained.

From henceforth it shall be lawful to every freeman to sell at his own pleasure his lands and tenements, or part of them; so that the feoffee shall hold the same lands or tenements of the chief lord of the same fee, by such service and customs as his feoffor held before.

II. And if he sell any part of such lands or tenements to any, the feoffee shall immediately hold it of the chief lord, and shall be forthwith charged with the services, for so much as pertaineth, or ought to pertain to the said chief lord for the same parcel, according to the quantity of the land or tenement sold: And so in this case the same part of the service shall remain to the lord, to be taken by the hands of the feoffee, for the which he ought to be attendant and answerable to the same chief lord, according to the quantity of the land or tenement sold, for the parcel of the service so due.

III. And it is to be understood, that by the said sales or purchases of lands or tenements, or any parcels of them, such lands or tenements shall in no wise come into mortmain, either in part or in whole, neither by policy ne craft, contrary to the form of the statute made thereupon of late. And it is to wit, that this statute extendeth but only to lands holden in fee simple; and that it extendeth to the time coming; and it shall begin to take effect at the feast of Saint Andrew the Apostle next coming. Given the eighteenth year of the reign of King Edward, son of King Henry.

Notes and Questions
1. What principles of law did *Quia Emptores* establish and to what extent are they still relevant? See *Irish Land Law*, para. 2.42 *et seq.*
2. One aspect of the statute, prohibition of subinfeudation, was often ignored in Ireland, see the decision by the House of Lords in *Delacherois* v. *Delacherois* (1864) 11 H.L.C. 62 and other cases cited in *Irish Land Law*, para. 2.45, ff. 2 and 3. See also *Att.-Gen* v. *Cummins*, p. 131, *post* and *Chute* v. *Busteed*, p. 155, *post*.

RE McNAUL'S ESTATE
[1902] 1 I.R. 114; 36 I.L.T.R. 45 (Court of Appeal)

By a lease for lives renewable for ever, made in the year 1763, the lessee covenanted to pay an additional rent if the lessee, his heirs or assigns, assigned or demised the lands, without the lessor's consent, to a person or persons other than the child or grandchild of the person so aliening or demising the lands. In a fee-farm grant made, in lieu of the said renewable lease, in the year 1852, a precisely similar covenant was inserted.

FitzGibbon L.J.:

In this case Elizabeth C. M'Naul is proceeding before the Land Commission under the Land Purchase Acts to sell in fee-simple, discharged from all superior interests (except a liberty to fish), certain lands of Drumcrottagh, held under a fee-farm grant dated the 7th June, 1852, made under the Renewable Leasehold Conversion Act. The grantor's interest is now vested in Dr. Traill; the grantee's interest is vested in the vendor. In ordinary course an order, dated the 2nd April, 1901, was made that the perpetual yearly rent of £6 8s. reserved by the grant should be redeemed. This order contained the following additional declaration:

'The Court, being of opinion that the covenant of the grantee, her heirs and assigns, in the said grant for payment of the additional rent of £5 10s. 9d. in the event of alienation or demise of all or any part of the premises to any person or persons whatsoever other than a child or grandchild of the person so aliening or demising without the consent of the grantor, his heirs and assigns, as therein provided, is void, doth order that no value be placed thereon in fixing the redemption price of the said rent.'

Dr. Traill has appealed against this declaration, contending that the covenant is a good and valid covenant as between the grantor and grantee, and that he is entitled to have the £5 10s. 9d. in addition to the £6 8s. redeemed, and to be paid the redemption value of both the said rents, and his costs.

The fee-farm grant is founded on a lease of the 13th October, 1763, which was last renewed on the 20th February, 1851. Renewal fines were reserved by the lease, and were duly included in the fee-farm rent of £6 8s. But the grant contained the proviso and further covenant that if the grantee, her heirs and assigns, should at any time thereafter alien or demise all or any part of the premises to any person or persons whatsoever other than a child or grandchild of the person or of some one or other of the persons so aliening or demising without the previous consent of the grantor, his heirs or assigns, in writing under hand and seal, then and in such case the grantee, her heirs and assigns, from and after the time of such alienation or demise, should pay over and above the said yearly rent the further yearly rent of £5 10s. 9d. during the continuance of the demise and grant, the sums to be paid half-yearly upon every 1st May and 1st November, the first payment to be made on such of the said days as should first happen after the alienation or demise; and that the grantor, his heirs and assigns, should have the like remedy by distress and otherwise for recovery of the said yearly rent of £5 10s. 9d. as they might have by virtue of the grant for the recovery of the yearly rent first reserved.

The appeal was opened with the statement that the Court would be called upon to consider whether the decision of the Queen's Bench in *Billing* v. *Welch* (I.R. 6 C.L. 88) in 1871 could be reconciled with the provisions of the Renewable Lease-hold Conversion Act.

That decision bound the Land Commission, but it does not bind this Court, and, so far as we can ascertain, it has never hitherto been considered here. My colleagues will refer to the authorities, and to avoid repetition I abstain from doing so. But we are agreed that *Billing* v. *Welch* (I.R. 6 C.L. 88) cannot be distinguished from this case, though probably the other cases cited might be. We find ourselves reduced to the alternative of overruling *Billing* v. *Welch* (I.R. 6 C.L. 88), or of disobeying the statute. Where a statute is concerned, and the opinion of the Court of Appeal is clear as to its construction and effect, it must prevail against any previous practice or decision of a Court below, because there can be no jurisdiction to disregard it. We hold, upon the words of the Renewable Leasehold Conversion Act, that when the fee-farm grant came to be executed, the grantor was entitled to require that the covenant in question should be retained in it, and that, when it was so retained, it became, and it still is, a valid obligation binding the grantee and the lands.

We hold, in general, that the doctrine of repugnancy applicable at common law to an estate in fee is modified, in the case of fee-farm grants founded on renewable leases, by whatever obligations are lawfully inserted in the grants. The object of the Act was to give a perpetual estate, which was not a common law estate in fee, but was an estate created under the statute, which was to remain subject to all covenants and conditions which had bound the previous leasehold estate, save so far as they were got rid of in the manner provided by the Act. When not so got rid of, they were to be retained in the grant, and the decision in *Billing* v. *Welch* (I.R. 6 C.L. 68) cannot be sustained in so far as it avoids such obligations upon the ground of repugnancy to a common law estate in fee.

The preamble mentions as the mischief against which the Act was directed the 'great expense' constantly secured in procuring renewals under covenants for perpetual renewal, and the 'litigation and inconvenience' arising from tenures under leases with such covenants; and it declares it to be expedient that such tenures should be converted, *in manner thereinafter provided*, into tenures in fee.

This preamble has been repealed by the Statute Law Revision Act, 1892, but with the proviso that such repeal 'shall not affect the construction of the statute, whether as respects the past or the future.' This makes the Revised Edition a trap for any adviser or Court which has to determine the effect of the Act, when the repealed preamble has any effect in indicating the scope or purpose of the statute. Here it defines and limits the operation of the Act to the 'manner hereinafter mentioned,' and it thereby distinguishes the tenure to be created under it from tenures in fee at common law.

Sect. 1 provides that the grant shall be 'subject to the like covenants and conditions for the payment of the perpetual yearly fee-farm rent as are contained in the converted lease with respect to the rent thereby reserved, and with and subject to such other covenants, conditions, exceptions, and reservations (save covenants to grant or to accept and take a renewal of such lease, and such covenants, conditions, exceptions, and reservations as may be commuted as hereinafter mentioned) as are contained in such lease and then subsisting'.

It has not been disputed that the limited covenant restraining alienation without the lessor's consent to descendants of the grantee, by providing for the payment of an additional rent of £5 10s. 9d., was a valid and subsisting provision in the lease. It was, in our opinion, not a covenant prohibiting alienation – on the contrary, it permitted alienation on the terms of paying the additional rent. It could not be omitted from the grant, save on commutation or by consent.

Sect. 3 provides for the commutation of any subsisting exception or reservtion contained in the lease, or any right under covenants or otherwise annexed to the reversion which interferes with the proper cultivation of the land. The provision, therefore, did not apply to the covenant in question here. But it is, at best, optional. It empowers the grantee *if he think fit* to require that such exception, reservation, or right should cease wholly or partially; and in such case it enacts that the grant shall be modified accordingly, and that the fee-farm rent shall be increased by an amount equivalent to the value of such exception, reservation, or right, in so far as it it made to cease as aforesaid, such amount to be ascertained in manner mentioned in the Act, in case the parties differ about the same.

If the lessee does not 'think fit' to commute it, even a covenant which interferes with the proper cultivation must, under this section, remain in the fee-farm grant.

Sect. 4 provides for a similar commutation of any right to timber, bogs, minerals, quarries, or royalties; but it does not make it lawful for the owner of the lease to require that such rights shall cease, either wholly or partially, unless the owner of the reversion and the owner of the lease agree, and in such case the grant is to be modified accordingly.

Sect. 5 provides compensation for the owner of the reversion where the estate into which the reversion would be converted upon a grant under the previous provisions would not afford full compensation for the loss of such reversion, or of any power, benefit, or advantage incident thereto, or enjoyed by the owner thereof, under any Act of Parliament, charter, settlement, or otherwise. It enables the owner of the reversion to require such loss to be compensated, either by an addition to the fee-farm rent, or at his option by the payment of such a gross sum of money (the amount in either case to be ascertained as mentioned in the Act, in case the parties differ about the same) as will afford a full compensation for such loss, to be estimated according to the difference in marketable value.

The observation applies alike to sects. 3, 4, and 5, that it is in no case compulsory upon the parties to modify the terms of the lease: if not modified, the same terms must be contained in the grant; and whenever they are modified, the equivalent or compensation must be provided in manner directed by the Act. In no case can an operative condition or covenant in the lease be omitted from the grant, unless by consent, or upon giving the statutory equivalent or compensation.

Sect. 7 provides that, where the grant is made, the reversion shall be converted into an estate of inheritance in fee-simple in the fee-farm rent made payable by the grant, and the conditions, exceptions, and reservations therein contained, and all rights annexed or belonging to such reversion saved by and not commuted under the Act; and such estate of inheritance in fee-simple as aforesaid shall be transmissible and descendible in like manner as if the same were an estate of inheritance in fee-simple in reversion in the lands on which the fee-farm rent is charged by the grant creating the same, having incident thereto the conditions, exceptions, and reservations contained in the same grant, and such rights respectively as aforesaid; and the estate of inheritance created under every such grant as aforesaid in the lands comprised therein, and the estate of inheritance so created as aforesaid in the fee-farm rent made payable by such grant, shall from and after the execution of such grant be respectively vested in the same persons for the same estates and interests, and be respectively subject to the same uses, trusts, provisos, agreements, and declarations as the estate held under the lease, and the reversion or estate by the owner of which the grant is made, were respectively vested in, subject to, and charged with, immediately before their conversion, or as near thereto as the different natures of the estates and the circumstances of each case will admit.

This section, if it stood alone, might lend some colour to the contention that the statutory estate was 'an estate of inheritance in fee-simple'. But sect. 10 provides that all covenants by law implied on the part of landlord or tenant upon any lease, and every covenant for payment of rent, and every other covenant contained in pursuance of the Act in any such grant as aforesaid, in substitution for a like covenant in the lease, where such last-mentioned covenant is of such a nature as that the burden thereof doth by law run with the land, shall run with the estate in fee-simple into which the estate held under such lease is converted under the Act, and the owner or assignee for the time being of such estate in fee-simple shall be chargeable upon such covenants *in the same manner and to the same extent as if he were owner or assignee of the term or interest created by the lease, and such term or interest and the estate out of which such lease was derived were still subsisting*, and the benefit of such covenants shall run with the estate into which such estate is converted under the Act, and the owner or assignee for the time being of the estate created by such conversion shall have the full benefit of such covenants, and be entitled to maintain actions thereon.

This section makes it impossible to apply the doctrine of repugnancy as affecting estates in fee at common law to an estate which is to be deemed to be *a term created by a lease still subsisting*.

The sections which I have quoted appear to enact as plainly as words can provide, (i) that the limited covenant restricting alienation by making additional rent payable thereon was rightly retained in the grant; (ii) that being so retained it must have the same effect as if the lease were still subsisting. It follows that it cannot be void for repugnancy to a common law estate in fee; and that the appeal must be allowed.

But it does not follow that the grantor is now necessarily entitled to the full redemption price of the additional rent of £5 10s. 9d.; because that rent is not yet payable; and it is not proved that there has, as yet, been any alienation upon which the additional rent began to run.

We must discharge the order appealed from in so far as it declares the covenant to be void. The Land Commission has jurisdiction to redeem the whole interest of the grantor under the grant, and the only relief to which the appellant is entitled is a declaration that, in fixing the amount of the redemption price, regard is to be had to the existence in the grant of the covenant referred to. The price will be enhanced by whatever may be justly ascertained to be 'the difference in marketable value' which the existence in the grant of the condition and covenant respecting the additional rent gives to the grantor. In other words, he is entitled to the price of the chance or prospect that, if the redemption did not take place, the £5 10s. 9d. would have become payable on some future alienation to some person other than a descendant of the grantee for the time being.

It is not for us to indicate, and we have no means of estimating, what the amount of such an enhancement may be. The case will be remitted to the Land Commission, with the foregoing declaration, to proceed thereon as to justice may appertain.

The applicant will be entitled to his taxed costs before the Land Commission and upon this appeal, as costs of the redemption, to be added to the redemption price, or to be paid by the grantee if the redemption is not carried out.

Walker L.J.:

This appeal raises a question of very general application as to the rights of lessors and lessees of leases for lives renewable for ever whose leases have been converted into statutory fee-farm grants.

It was quite common to find in such leases before conversion covenants against alienation, sometimes absolute in form, sometimes qualified as to the persons to whom only alienation is permitted, and sometimes again qualified with a statement such as we have here of the consequences to the lessee which would result from the breach. I have never heard it questioned that all such covenants were lawful while the leases remained unconverted. The effect of the conversion generally compulsorily made against the lessor is what we have to consider, which involves two questions – (1) whether they should be inserted in the grant, and if so (2), whether they are lawful, and their effect in the way of consequence to the grantee if they are broken. I shall recur to this last point when I have dealt with the general one as to the effect of the statute on the leases, and the covenants contained in them.

It is admitted that Mr. Justice Meredith could have made no other order than he did, having regard to the decision in *Billing* v. *Welch* (I.R. 6 C.L. 88) which bound him. But we are compelled to consider the whole question, including, no doubt, the fact that *Billing* v. *Welch* (I.R. 6 C.L. 88) was decided thirty years ago, and has not since, apparently, been quarrelled with.

Before I approach the consideration of the Act of Parliament I should like to refer shortly to the cases cited, none of which, I think, amount to a decision on the question except *Billing* v. *Welch* (I.R. 6 C.L. 88).

The first was *Mahony* v. *Tynte* (1 Ir. Ch. R. 577), but it decided nothing favourable to respondent, and in fact the question discussed before us was not raised.

Re Quin (8 I. Ch. R. 578) was the next. This case was decided upon another sufficient ground, but the Lord Chancellor, no doubt, gives an opinion upon the legality of a covenant against alienation, and the propriety of inserting it, assuming, apparently, the estate granted to be an ordinary estate in fee, unqualified in its incidents. Lord Justice Blackburne expresses no opinion on that point.

In *Jackson's Estate* (11 Ir. Ch. R. 145) it was held that the landlord was entitled to compensation under the 5th section of the Act for the non-insertion of a covenant giving a right to pre-emption which the landlord did not press to have inserted, and the compensation was fixed at 1d. per year.

Gore v. *O'Grady* (I.R. 1 Eq. 1) is in favour of the appellant to this extent, that the execution of the fee-farm grant was held not to alter the pre-existing rights of the landlord in respect of turf cut for sale.

In *Lunham's Estate* (I.R. 5 Eq. 170) the grant was made in 1858, and before the Act of 1860, and no question arose on the effect of a conversion under the Renewable Leasehold Conversion Act.

Billing v. *Welch* (I.R. 6 C.L. 88) is an express authority which we have to consider, for the covenant was as here inserted in the grant. I cannot find any substantial difference between the covenant there and here, and it does appear that counsel referred to the material sections, but I do not think they received sufficient consideration. All Mr. Justice O'Brien says on that point is – 'In the argument before us no sufficient reason has been suggested, either from the provisions of the statute or otherwise, why the covenant which would be void in an ordinary grant should not be held to be also void when inserted in the statutable grant.' I cannot think that sufficient consideration was given to the effect of the statute when the question, which is in my view the only material one, was so summarily dealt with.

The case of *Ex parte Raymond* (I.R. 8 Eq. 231) does seem to proceed on the assumption that a covenant against alienation was one which would not be inserted in a fee-farm grant under the practice then prevailing – in other words, that *Billing* v. *Welch* (I.R. 6 C.L. 88) should regulate that practice.

The case, therefore, is reduced to the question whether we should follow the decision in *Billing* v. *Welch* (I.R. 6 C.L. 88), which we are asked to review, or whether, if we thought that decision wrong, we should consider ourselves bound by the course of practice and professional opinion which have prevailed since *Billing* v. *Welch* (I.R. 6 C.L. 88) was decided.

Now, in the first place, this case depends on the construction of an Act of Parliament creating rights and preserving them, and even a continuous course of decisions on it would not allow us to escape from the responsibility of deciding on its true construction. *The Sara* (14 App. Cas. 209) is a conclusive authority upon that point. Here, too, we have the covenant inserted in the grant, and unless we decide that it is illegal, the appellant is entitled to say that regard must be had to it in fixing the value of the landlord's rights, so that we are driven to decide the net point on the Act of Parliament.

It is true that a clause against alienation is inconsistent with the nature of a common law fee-simple estate, and therefore inoperative where such an estate is granted.

But the real question is whether that doctrine applies to the statutory fee-simple substituted for a lease containing such a covenant, and to the reversion to which it had before been legally incident by contract. That depends on the true construction of the statute as applicable to the subject-matter. The Renewable Leasehold Conversion Act was passed on the 1st August, 1849, and every student of Irish law is aware of the fact that the tenure of leases for lives renewable for ever had for a century previous to 1849 been the cause of much litigation, and accordingly the Act recites that 'it is expedient that such tenures should be converted in manner hereinafter provided into tenures in fee.' There is no doubt that leases for lives renewable for ever contained covenants by lessor and lessee of every kind, the benefit and burden of which ran with the land, and covenants by the lessee in the form of that which we have to consider, and even absolute covenants against alienation were usual and quite legal, and *a priori* one would expect that when the owner of the perpetual lease was authorized by the Act, as he is, to require the owner of the reversion to execute to him a grant under the Act, the reversion was not to be deprived of the benefit derived from the lessee's covenant unless compensation was provided, and we find accordingly that the grant is to be made subject to the like covenants and conditions for securing the payment of the fee-farm rent as are contained in the lease with respect to the rent thereby reserved, 'and with and subject to such other covenants, conditions, exceptions, and reservations (save covenants to grant or to accept and take a renewal of such lease, and such covenants, conditions, exceptions, and reservations as may be commuted as hereinafter mentioned) as are contained in such lease and then subsisting.' The Act then provides that any subsisting exception or reservation contained in the lease which interfered with the proper cultivation of the lands should be commuted, saving, however (unless by consent), rights to timber and the like, and mines, minerals, and royalties.

The 5th section provides for the giving of compensation in cases where there was a loss on the conversion of the reversion into a rent, or the loss of any power, benefit, or advantage incident to such reversion.

The 7th section is important, as it directs that the estate held under the lease shall be converted into an estate of inheritance in fee-simple in the fee-farm rent made payable by the grant, and the conditions, exceptions, and reservations therein contained, and all rights annexed or belonging to the estate by the owner of which such grant is made, saved by and not commuted under the Act. The fee-farm estate is transmissible and descends in like manner as if it were an estate in fee-simple, but the greatest care is shown that the rights between grantor and grantee shall not be altered save as expressly provided for.

The 10th section seems to close all controversy. It deals with implied covenants on the part of landlord and tenant which it enacts shall be implied in the grant, and express covenants transferred from the lease to the grant, the benefit or burden of which ran with the land, and it enacts that they shall run with the estate in fee-simple into which the estate held under the lease is converted, and it proceeds: 'And the owner or assignee for the time being of such estate in fee-simple shall be chargeable upon such covenants in the same manner and to the same extent as if he were owner or assignee of the term or interest created by such lease or underlease, and such term or interest, and the estate out of which such lease or underlease was derived, were still subsisting,' and the section concludes by giving the right to maintain actions on such covenants. This seems to transfer the benefit and burden of every covenant in the lease to the substituted grant, and, further, makes careful provision for the preservation of every right of the landlord and every liability of the tenant. The same policy appears in section 20, which gives rights under the ejectment statutes for the recovery of the fee-farm rent.

In my opinion there is in cases of grants under the Renewable Leasehold Conversion Act, a statutory fee-simple created with a statutory reversion to which are legally incident by statute all covenants in the lease not commuted under the statute; and I think there is no legal justification for excluding from the grant covenants against alienation, much less such a covenant as we have to deal with here, and which in fact we find inserted. I express no opinion as to the mode in which an absolute covenant against alienation is to be dealt with or how it is to be enforced. That point does not arise in the present case. I think the covenant in question now is legal, and I am also of opinion, on the authorities, that it was open to the grantee to break this covenant on the terms of paying the fixed price of the additional rent of £5 10s. 9d. It follows that in fixing the redemption price regard must be had to it, but we cannot say more. The additional rent has never been claimed or enforced, and it is not for us to measure the extra value to be attributed to the redemption price by reason of the existence of the covenant.

Holmes L.J.:

It is strange that the question raised in this case, upon which Lord Chancellor Napier expressed a decided opinion in the year 1858, has not since been brought before an appellate Court. I am disposed to agree with counsel for the respondent that Mr. Napier's view, especially since the judgment in *Billing* v. *Welch* (I.R. 6 C.I. 88), has been generally acted upon by the profession; and although some conveyancers may have entertained doubts as to its soundness, the interests at stake were not worth the risk of litigation, involving an appeal to successive Courts.

The determination of the point at issue depends entirely upon the provisions of the Renewable Leasehold Conversion Act, which became law in 1849. In construing that or any other statute great assistance may be derived from authority; and where a possible and reasonable construction has received judicial sanction in a case that has been subsequently followed without appeal in Courts of first instance, I should be prepared to accept it, even although my own mind might lean to a different interpretation. This Court recently acted on this principle in *Re Kane* ([1901] 1 I.R. 520) where, in consequence of a course of decision extending over thirty years, we adopted a doubtful view of the requirements of the Judgement Mortgage Act.

The Renewable Leasehold Conversion Act was carefully drawn for the purpose of converting leases with covenants for perpetual renewal into tenures in fee, without undue interference with the rights and obligations of the several parties interested in the lands. A lease for lives with a covenant for perpetual renewal is a form of tenure peculiar to Ireland, which doubtless owed its origin to a desire to attach to a perpetual freehold interest the terms, conditions, and covenants to which leaseholds can be legally made subject. At least it is certain that many of these instruments contained the same provisions for the protection of the landlord, and the proper treatment and cultivation of the lands, as are found in agricultural lettings for terms of years. When the tenure substituted by the statute put an end to the reversion, and with it destroyed the only means then known to the law for enforcing such obligations as I have referred to, the policy of the Legislature required that the lessor's rights should be preserved in some other way, or that an equivalent therefore should be given him. Accordingly, we find it provided by the first section of the Act that the grant of the estate of inheritance in fee-simple to be made by the owner of the reversion shall be subject to a fee-farm rent of such amount as therein is specified, 'and subject to the like covenants and conditions for securing the payment of such fee-farm rent as are contained in such lease with respect to the rent thereby reserved, and with and subject to such other covenants, conditions, exceptions, and reservations (save covenants to grant or to accept and take a renewal of such lease, and such covenants, conditions, exceptions, and reservations as may be commuted as hereinafter mentioned) as are contained in such lease and then subsisting.'

The third section provided that where any exception, reservation, or right, under a covenant, or otherwise annexed, or belonging to the reversion, interferes with the proper cultivation of the lands, the lessee may, if he thinks fit, require that such exception, reservation, or right should cease wholly or partially, and in such case the grant shall be modified accordingly, and an equivalent given therefor by an increase of the fee-farm rent.

Section 4 enacts that in the case of certain of the rights mentioned in the preceding section its provisions shall only apply where the owner of the reversion consents.

Section 5 provides for further recompense to the landlord in cases in which the substituted estate taken by him under the previous sections would not afford full compensation for the loss of the reversion; and lest the traditions of the common law might thereafter be used to defeat the desire of Parliament to preserve all the essential features of the contract, it is provided in the tenth section that the burden and benefit of covenants, which, while the lease was subsisting, ran with the lessee's interest, and with the reversion respectively, would continue to run with the substituted estates in the same manner and to the same extent as if the owner in fee-simple were still owner or assignee of the term.

I doubt if a somewhat complicated subject could be dealt with in clearer language. All good and lawful covenants contained in the lease were to be introduced into the fee-farm grant, subject to the proviso that the lessee, if he thought fit, might require the commutation of such of them as interfered with the proper cultivation of the land; and when so introduced the owner of the fee-farm rent, or his assignee for the time being, was, in the words of the tenth section, to 'have the full benefit of such covenants, and be entitled to maintain actions thereon' against the owner or assignee for the time being of the estate in fee-simple, into which the lease had been converted.

Restraints on alienation without the consent of the lessor have been always usual in Irish leases; and so far from being regarded as invalid, or contrary to public policy, they have been treated with special favour by the Legislature. Sometimes the restraint took the form of absolute prohibition; in other cases assignment was permitted in favour of a limited class or on the payment of a fine or an increased rent. In leases for lives perpetually renewable covenants of this kind, although not uncommon, were, when they existed at all, generally of the latter class.

The political history of the country, taken in connexion with the peculiar tenure and the comparatively moderate amount of the rent and fines, suggests that in making these leases the lessors were not influenced solely by pecuniary considerations; and it was natural for them to secure, as far as possible, that the holdings should remain in the hands of friendly tenants. This would seem to have been the object of the covenant contained in the original lease of the 13th October, 1763, by which the lessee, his heirs and assignees, in the event of his or their aliening or demising all or any part of the premises to any person other than a child or grandchild without the consent of the lessor, were bound to pay thereafter, in addition to the rent reserved, the further rent therein provided. When the lease was converted pursuant to the provisions of the statute into a fee-farm grant, dated the 7th June, 1852, a similar covenant was inserted in that instrument; and it is admitted that from that time to the present the event has not happened on which the increased rent was made payable.

In the view I take of the case it is needless for me to consider whether it would be possible to make at common law or under the Statute of Uses a grant of lands in fee-simple subject to a perpetual yearly rentcharge, liable to be increased in the circumstances mentioned in the lease. I am satisfied that the additional rent is not a penalty, that the lessee could not have been prevented by injunction from assigning to a stranger, and, therefore, that the restraint on alienation is of a limited and partial character.

The conclusion at which I have arrived, however, does not depend upon these considerations. It is admitted that the covenant was operative and legal in the lease, and it does not lose this character when embodied into the fee-farm grant pursuant to the statute. Nor is it necessary for me to determine whether it interferes with the proper cultivation of the lands. The lessee is given the right, if he thinks fit, to require the omission and commutation of such covenants; but where he allows them to be inserted in the fee-farm grant he is bound by them. The question in this appeal is answered by reading the sections of the Act which, in my opinion, leave no doubt that the provision for payment of an increased rent in the event specified was properly inserted in the grant, and that such rent would be recoverable if and when such event happened.

It may at first sight appear strange that this is the first occasion upon which the matter in controversy has been discussed in the light of the language of the statute. *Mahony* v. *Tynte* (1 Ir. Ch. R. 577) has been relied on by Mr. Ronan as an authority in favour of the appellant; but Smith, M. R., seems to have decided that case upon the principles of the common law as to feoffments in fee. So, too, in the judgment of Napier, C., in *Re Quin* (8 Ir. Ch. R. 578), there is reference to the special provisions of the Act. *Billing* v. *Welch* (I.R. 6 C.L. 88), which in its facts is undistinguishable from the present case, and which the allowance of this appeal will overrule, gives no indication that the words and intention of the statute were considered by the Courts.

Curious as this is, I think it can be easily accounted for. I have often noticed that lawyers of an earlier time, while admitting the theoretical omnipotence of an Act of Parliament, were slow to believe that the Legislature would disregard those principles of the common law which had been invested by time and learning with an almost sacred character.

In *Riordan* v. *McNamara* (30 L.R. Ir. 495) I made some observations on this subject, which further experience has tended to confirm. We of a later generation, who have seen rampart after rampart of legal feudalism disappear before the steady inroad of legislative innovation, can hardly understand the difficulty which our predecessors had in realising a fee-simple estate moulded and modified by statute. There is, however, one passage in the judgment of Barry, J., in *Morris* v. *Morris* (I.R. 6 C.L. 73), which sets forth the true nature of the estate taken by a grantee under the Act of 1849. 'Whatever be the effect,' he says 'of the fee-farm grant, it can only have such operation as is conferred on it by the statute, and that operation is to be ascertained from the language of the Legislature construed according to the well-known rule that every clause and every word must obtain its full and ordinary force and meaning, unless such construction would lead to some absurdity or some repugnance or inconsistency with the other provisions of the enactment.'

Adopting these words and applying them to the present case, I am unable to hold that a covenant inserted in the fee-farm grant, pursuant to the mandate of the statute and for the enforcement of which special statutory provision is made, is void. Being a good covenant, regard must be had to it in fixing the redemption price of the rent; but to what extent such price will be affected thereby can only be determined by the Land Commission.

This may involve some difficulty; for it must be remembered, that although up to the present time the event upon which the increased rent becomes payable has not yet happened, its happening in the future can hardly be described as a mere chance, inasmuch as the right to redemption is dependent upon a transfer of the lands.

Notes and Questions
1. To what extent does this decision violate the so-called rule against inalienability which was supposed to have been enshrined in *Quia Emptores* (see p. 40, *ante*)? See *Irish Land Law*, paras. 2.46 – 2.47.
2. As regards fee-farm grants executed under the Renewable Leasehold Conversion Act, 1849, see *Irish Land Law*, para. 4.081 *et seq.* See also p. 229, *post*.

TENURES (ABOLITION) ACT (IRELAND), 1662

An Act for taking away the court of wards and liveries, and tenures in capite, and by knights service.

Whereas it hath been found by former experience, that the court of wards and liveries, and tenures by knights service, either of the King or otherwise, or by knights service in capite, or soccage in capite of the King, and the consequence of the same been much more burthensome, grevious and prejudicial to this kingdom, than they have been beneficial to the King;

I. The court of wards and liveries, and all wardships, liveries, primer-seizins, and ousterlemains, values and forfeitures of marriage by reason of any tenures of the Kings Majesty, or of any other by knights service, and all mean rates, and all other gifts, grants, charges, incident or arising for or by reason of wardships, liveries, primer-seizins, or ousterlemains, be taken away and discharged, and are hereby enacted to be taken away and discharged from the three and twentieth day of October, one thousand six hundred forty one; any law, statute, custome or usage to the contrary hereof in any wise notwithstanding.

II. And all fines for alienation, seizures and pardons for alienation, tenures by homage, and all charges incident or arising for or by reason of wardship, livery, primer-seizin, or ousterlemain, or tenure by knights service, escuage, and also aide pur fitz marrier, and pur fair fitz chivalier, and all other charges incident thereunto, be likewise taken away and discharged from the said three and twentieth day of October one thousand six hundred forty one; any law, statute, custome or usage to the contrary hereof in any wise notwithstanding.

III. And all tenure by knights service of the King, or of any other person, and by knights service in capite, and by soccage in capite of the King, and the fruits and consequence thereof happened, or which shall or may happen or arise thereupon or thereby, be taken away or discharged; any law, statute, custome or usage to the contrary hereof in any wise notwithstanding.

IV. And all tenures of any honours, manors, lands, tenements, or hereditaments, or any estate of inheritance at the common law, held either of the King, or of any other person or persons, bodies politick or corporate, are hereby enacted to be turned into free and common soccage to all intents and purposes, from the three and twentieth day of October one thousand six hundred forty one and shall be so construed and adjudged, and deemed to be from the said three and twentieth day of October one thousand six hundred forty one, and for every hereafter turned into free and common soccage; any law, statute, custome or usage to the contrary hereof in any wise notwithstanding.

V. And the same shall for ever hereafter stand and be discharged of all tenure by homage, escuage, voyages royal, and charges for the same, wardships incident to tenure by knights service, and values and forfeitures of marriage, and all other charges incident to tenures by knights service, and of and from aide pur fitz marrier, and aide pur fair fitz chivalier; any law statute, usage or custome to the contrary in any wise notwithstanding.

. . .

VII. And such person or persons, to whom the custody of such child or children hath been or shall be so disposed or devised, shall and may take into his or their custody to the use of such child or children, the profits of all lands, tenements and hereditaments of such child or children, and also the custody, tuition and management of the goods, chattles and personal estate of such child or children, till their respective age of twenty one years, or any lesser time, according to such disposition aforesaid, and may bring such action or actions in relation thereunto, as by law a guardian in soccage might do.

VIII. And all tenures hereafter to be created by the Kings majesty, his heirs or successors, upon any gifts or grants of any manors, lands, tenements or hereditaments of any estate of inheritance at the common law, shall be and be adjudged to be in free and common soccage only, and not by knights service or in capite, and shall be discharged of all wardships, value and forfeiture of marriage, livery, primer seizin, ousterlemain, aide pur fiat fitz chivalier, aide pur fitz marrier; any law, statute or reservation to the contrary thereof in any wise notwithstanding.

IX. Provided nevertheless this act, or any thing herein contained, shall not take away, or be construed to take away, any rents, certain heriots, or suits of court belonging or incident to any former tenure now taken away or altered by virtue of this act, or other service incident or belonging to tenure in common soccage, due or to grow to the Kings Majesty, or mean lords, or other private person, or the fealty and distresses incident thereunto, and that such relief shall be paid in respect of such rents as is paid in case of a death of a tenant in common soccage.

X. Provided also, that this act, or any thing herein contained, shall not take away, or be construed to take away, tenures in frankalmoine, or to subject them to any greater or other service than they now are, nor to alter or change any tenure by copy of court-roll, or any services incident thereunto; nor to take away the honorary services of grand serjeanty, other than of wardship, marriage, and value of forfeiture of marriage, escuages, voyages royal, or other charge incident to tenure by knights service, and other than aide pur fair fitz chivalier, and aide pur fitz marrier.

XII. Provided also, that this act, or any thing therein contained, shall not extend to discharge any apprentice of his apprenticeship.

XIII. Provided also, that neither this act, nor any thing therein contained, shall infringe or hurt any title of honour, feodal or other, by which any person hath or may have right to sit in the lords house of Parliament, as to his or their title of honour or sitting in Parliament, and the privileges belonging to them as peers; this act or any thing therein contained to the contrary in any wise notwithstanding.

Notes and Questions
1. What were the effects, immediate and ultimate, of the 1662 Act? See *Irish Land Law*, paras. 2.48–2.50.
2. What was the form of tenure called free and common socage referred to in the Act? See *ibid.*, paras. 2.25–2.27.
3. Note the savings for 'frankalmoine' and copyhold tenure. See *ibid.*, para. 2.28 *et seq.*

SUCCESSION ACT, 1965

11. – (1) Without prejudice to the succeeding provisions of this section, all existing rules, modes and canons of descent and of devolution by special occupancy are hereby abolished except in so far as they may apply to the descent of an estate tail.

(2) Dower and tenancy by the curtesy are hereby abolished.

(3) Escheat to the State and escheat to a mesne lord for want of heirs are hereby abolished.

. . .

73. – (1) In default of any person taking the estate of an intestate, whether under this Part or otherwise, the State shall take the estate as ultimate intestate successor.

(2) The Minister for Finance may, if he thinks proper to do so, waive, in whole or in part and in favour of such person and upon such terms (whether including or not including the payment of money) as he thinks proper having regard to all the circumstances of the case, the right of the State under this section.

(3) Section 32 of the State Property Act, 1954 (which provides for the disclaimer of certain land devolving on the State by way of escheat or as *bona vacantia*) shall extend to the grantee's interest under a fee-farm grant and the lessee's interest under a lease, where the State has a right to such interest as ultimate intestate successor.

IN THE GOODS OF DOHERTY
[1961] I.R. 219 (High Court)

In 1919 Doherty instructed a firm of Dublin stockbrokers, to whom he was then unknown, to invest £30 in Ordinary shares of Bolands Ltd. He further instructed the stockbrokers to retain the share certificates as he intended going to Australia in the near future. The shares were duly bought. None of the members of the firm of stockbrokers heard from him again. In 1959, advertisements were published in Irish and Australian newspapers seeking information about him but none was obtained. An application was made by the Minister for Finance for an order under s. 30 of the State Property Act, 1954, declaring that the shares, bonus shares and accumulated dividends had devolved upon the State as *bona vacantia*.

Kenny J.:

In 1919 James Doherty instructed L.A. Waldron and Company, a firm of stockbrokers in Dublin, to invest £30 in the ordinary shares of Bolands Limited. He paid them this sum and ten £5 ordinary shares in that Company were purchased on his behalf. He instructed the firm to retain the share certificates as he intended to go to Australia in the near future. None of the members of the firm of stockbrokers had known him before this. The dividends on the shares were payable to him 'c/o L.A. Waldron & Company.' Until 1937, the dividend warrants were cashed by the firm and in 1938 the accumulated sum was placed on deposit receipt. Since 1937 the dividend warrants have not been cashed.

The shares purchased and the bonus issues received in respect of them are now worth about £250 and there is a sum of £37 5s. 3d. on deposit receipt.

None of the members of the firm of stockbrokers have heard from Doherty since 1919 and he did not give them any address. In 1959, three advertisements were published in Australian newspapers and three in Irish newspapers asking for information about him, but without result. The Gárda Siochána have been unable to discover anything about him.

The Minister for Finance now applies under ss. 29 and 30 of the State property Act, 1954, for an order declaring that the shares, the monies on deposit receipt and the amount of the uncashed dividends have become the property of the State as *bona vacantia*. Such an order, if made, is conclusive evidence binding on all persons (whether they had or had not notice of the application) that the property belongs to the State.

The expression, '*bona vacantia*,' is not defined in the State Property Act, 1954. In Blackstone's Commentaries (16th ed., 1925), in the chapter dealing with the King's Revenue, the author writes (at p. 298): 'Besides the particular reasons before given why the King should have the several revenues of royal fish, ship-wrecks, treasure troves, waifs, and estrays, there is also one general reason which holds for them all: and that is, because they are *bona vacantia*, or goods in which no one else can claim a property. And therefore by the law of nature they belonged to the first occupant or finder; and so continued under the imperial law. But, in settling the modern constitutions of most of the governments of Europe, it was thought proper (to prevent that strife and contention which the mere title of occupancy is apt to create and continue, and to provide for the support of public authority in a manner the least burthensome to individuals) that these rights should be annexed to the supreme power by the positive laws of the state.'

When anybody died intestate and was not survived by known next-of-kin his personal property (other than leaseholds) passed to the Crown. The origin and history of this right of the Crown is elaborately discussed in the opinion of the Privy Council in *Dyke* v. *Walford* (1846) 5 Moo. P.C. 434. In that case the Privy Council decided that the ordinary and clergy never had any beneficial right or interest in the property of an intestate, but had merely a right of possession for the purpose of administration. I have not been able to find any Irish case in which the matter is discussed. The right of the Crown to *bona vacantia* is now vested in the State under s. 29, sub-s. 2, of the State Property Act, 1954.

Before I can hold that the property to which this application relates is *bona vacantia*, I must be satisfied that James Doherty is dead, that he died intestate and that he has no known next-of-kin.

The circumstances in which the legal presumption of death arises have been stated by the Vice-Chancellor in *McMahon* v. *McElroy* (1869) I.R. 5 Eq. 1, at p. 12. He said: 'The remaining question is whether, upon the evidence, I am to presume the death of Hugh Morgan, the younger, and interfere at present with the actual possession of the defendant. Of his death there is not any positive evidence, and I am called upon to act entirely on the ordinary presumption as to which, and as to its operation there can be no doubt – namely, that, as a general rule, a man's death will be presumed after an interval seven years since he was last heard of. But this is not an invariable rule, and it admits of exceptions; and indeed in any case the Court in following the analogy of the Statutes, on which analogy the rule depends, is bound to consider the circumstances of the particular case, in order to see whether the presumption is rebutted or rather whether it fairly arises. The circumstances of the present case are not such as, in my opinion, to render it safe to make that presumption at present. Hugh Morgan left Ireland for America some time before the year 1859; resided there for some years; married there; came back to Ireland with his wife in 1859 for a temporary purpose only; he sold all his property in Ireland, and, after a very few months, returned to America, whither his wife and son followed him. It is contended, however, that, because he has not since been heard of by his sister, Mrs. McAdarra, the only member of his family who remains in Ireland, I am therefore to presume, without further inquiry, that he is dead. But suppose that an alien comes into this country and stays for a few months, or that a person, who is not an alien, but has his residence abroad, comes here and stays for a little time, and then leaves, having – to put an extreme case – no relatives here, and is not heard of for seven years, is the presumption, therefore, to be made of his death? I do not think the rule would apply to such cases. If, upon further investigation, it shall appear that the circumstances of this case are such as to bring it within the rule; if it be shown that Hugh Morgan has not been heard of by persons who might reasonably expect to have heard of him, and if proper inquiries be made as to the place of his residence in America, and it is found that he has disappeared from it, and cannot be traced, I should not hesitate to presume him dead.'

I think that the firm of stockbrokers who had purchased these shares for James Doherty could reasonably be expected to have heard from him about them during the last 40 years. Even if the name which he gave was false, I cannot think of anybody who would be more likely to hear from him than the firm which he had instructed to purchase the shares and to retain the share certificate and receive the dividends. I think that this is a case in which the legal presumption of death arises, and I am prepared to presume that James Doherty is dead.

The next question is whether I can safely presume that he died intestate, unmarried and without known next-of-kin. A similar question arose *In re Lavelle*; *Cassidy* v. *Attorney-General* ([1940] Ir. Jur. Rep. 8). In that case, Patrick Lavelle went to the United States of America in 1910 and had not been heard of since then. Mr. Justice Gavan Duffy made an order presuming that he died before 1927 but refused to presume that he had had died either intestate or unmarried and childless. In that case advertisements had been published in the United States of America and no reply to them had been received. When Patrick Lavelle went to the United States of America in 1910, his mother and two sisters were alive, and evidence was given that none of them had heard from him since he left and that he was unmarried in 1910. In my opinion, the Court would, in that case, have been justified in presuming that Patrick Lavelle had died intestate and without issue. The decision in

In re Webb's Estate (I.R. 5 Eq. 235) in which the Court of Appeal in Chancery had held that a presumption that a person died without issue arose in somewhat similar circumstances was not cited to Mr. Justice Gavan Duffy. I do not propose to follow the decision in *In re Lavelle*; *Cassidy* v. *Attorney-General* ([1940] Ir. Jur. Rep. 8) in so far as it decides that on the facts of that case, the Court would not have been justified in presuming that Patrick Lavelle died intestate, unmarried and childness.

I think that I would be justified in this case in presuming that James Doherty died intestate, unmarried and without known next-of-kin, and in declaring that the property to which this application relates has become the property of the State as *bona vacantia.*

I have considered whether I should direct an inquiry as to the next-of-kin of James Doherty, but I am satisfied that the advertisements which would be directed for such an inquiry would be the same as those which have already been made and that no further information would be obtained.

Notes and Questions
1. Note that the Succession Act, 1965, which was enacted after the *Doherty* case was decided, does not refer to *bona vacantia* (see p. 52, *ante*). Why not? Doesn't it make any difference of substance? See *Irish Land Law*, para. 2.52.
2. See further on succession, ch. 10, *post*.

III. CONSTITUTIONAL PROTECTION OF PROPERTY RIGHTS

The adoption of a written constitution in the Republic of Ireland has clearly added an entirely new dimension to the common law system of land law imposed on the island. It is clearly outside the scope of this book to consider this matter in any depth and readers should refer to the specialist works, such as Kelly, *The Irish Constitution* (2nd ed. 1984) and O'Reilly and Redmond, *Cases and Materials on the Irish Constitution* (1980). However, a flavour of the considerable social and political significance of constitutional protection of property rights may be gained from the following material.

BLAKE AND OTHERS V. THE ATTORNEY GENERAL;
MADIGAN V. THE ATTORNEY GENERAL
[1981] I.L.R.M. 34 (Supreme Court)

O'Higgins C.J.: (giving the judgment of the Court):
These two appeals relate to separate actions in which declarations were sought as to the invalidity, having regard to the provisions of the Constitution, of certain parts of the Rent Restrictions Act, 1960, as amended by the Rent Restrictions (Amendment) Act, 1967 and the Landlord and Tenant (Amendment) Act, 1971. In the first action declarations were sought as to the invalidity of Parts II and IV of the said Act of 1960, as amended, and in the second action a similar declaration is sought in respect of Part IV only. Both actions were heard together in the High Court and resulted in declarations as to invalidity being made by the trial Judge, Mr Justice McWilliam, in respect of both Parts of the said Act. Against this decision these appeals have been brought by the Attorney General in respect of the relief granted in each of these actions. As in the High Court, these appeals have been heard together by this Court.

The Act
The Rent Restrictions Act, 1960 (hereinafter called the Act of 1960) is declared

by its long title to be: 'An Act to make provision for restricting the increase of rent and the recovery of possession of premises in certain cases and to provide for other matters connected therewith'. As this long title indicates, the Act of 1960 is intended to operate in respect of lettings of premises to which it applies and, so to operate, in respect of the amount of the rent or the recovery of possession of such premises, irrespective of the terms of any letting agreement, or of the wishes of the landlord. The premises to which the Act applies are termed 'controlled dwellings'. These, with the amendments made by the 1967 Act taken into consideration, are such dwellings, erected before 7 May 1941, which, if houses, do not exceed £40 rateable valuation in Dublin or Dun Laoghaire and £30 elsewhere, and, if separate and self-contained flats, do not exceed £30 rateable valuation in Dublin and Dun Laoghaire and £20 elsewhere. Exclusions from the operation of the Act of 1960 are provided for in s. 3(2). This subsection excludes on various grounds dwellings which by reason of date of erection or valuation would otherwise be controlled. The control effected by the Act of 1960, as amended, is said to extend to between 45,000 and 50,000 dwellings.

Rent Restrictions

Part II of the Act of 1960 provides for the 'Restriction of rent controlled dwellings'. The restriction is effected by providing for the determination of a basic rent for each controlled dwelling which, with such lawful additions as are permitted, becomes the rent which is payable. The determination of the basic rent is provided for in s. 7 and s. 9. Each of these sections was amended by the 1967 Act and they are here referred to in their amended form.

S. 7 applies to a controlled dwelling in respect of which evidence is forthcoming of both (a) that it was on 8 June 1966 held by an occupying tenant under a contract of tenancy not being for more than a term of five years or on a statutory tenancy, and (b) the rent at which it was then so held. The basic rent under the section is the net rent on 8 June 1966. This net rent makes provision for the rates, if paid or allowed for by the landlord. If rates were not paid or allowed for by the landlord, then the rent on 8 June 1966 is the net rent and therefore the basic rent. Otherwise the basic rent is the rent payable under the contract.

If the requirements of s. 7 are not satisfied s. 9 applies. Under this section, the basic rent of controlled dwellings, not falling within s. 7, is determined by the court. Such rent must be the amount which the court considers reasonable having regard, as far as possible, to the rents of comparable dwellings. S. 10 provides for the additions which may be made to the basic rents as determined. S. 11 provides that the lawful rent shall, if there are no permitted additions, be the basic rent. If there be such additions, the section provides that the lawful rent shall be the sum of the basic rent and such additions.

Restrictions on Recovery of Possession

Part IV deals with 'Restrictions on Recovery of Possession of Controlled Premises'. The broad effect of these restrictions is that a landlord cannot normally recover possession of a controlled dwelling from a tenant who pays his rent, observes the other conditions of the tenancy and does not commit nuisance or waste. Provision is, however, made for the recovery of possession by the landlord if he can establish certain special grounds. When an order for possession is refused by reason of the provisions of the Act of 1960, the court makes an order declaring that the tenancy of the tenant, otherwise than by virtue of that Act has terminated, and the tenant then becomes a statutory tenant. Up to the making of such an order, the tenant is commonly referred to as a non-statutory tenant. On the death of the tenant, whether statutory or non-statutory, the surviving spouse, if there be such, and, if not, a member of the family who is bona fide residing with the tenant, becomes entitled to the same protection from dispossession as had been enjoyed by the tenant (s. 31). Furthermore, a statutory tenant is empowered, with the consent of the landlord, to make a voluntary assignment of the dwelling. The landlord's consent can be withheld only if greater hardship would, owing to the special circumstances of the case, be caused by granting such consent than by withholding it (s. 32). The landlord of a statutory tenant is also, for the purposes of some sections of the Act of 1960, made responsible for any repairs for which the tenant is not under a liability under his contract or by virtue of section 42 of the Landlord and Tenant (Amendment) Act (Ireland), 1860 (commonly called Deasy's Act). The restrictions contained in this part may have the result that, in the absence of special grounds, possession of the dwellinghouse can never be recovered by the landlord and that possession thereof, with all the features of statutory protection, can eventually pass to different generations of the tenant's family or of the tenant's assignee.

The First Permanent Statute

The Act of 1960 was the first measure dealing with rent restriction which was not expressed to be of temporary duration. As passed, the Act applied to all dwellings erected before, or in the course of erection on, 7 May 1941, which were within the stated valuation limits and which were not otherwise excluded. This meant that control under the Act extended both to the older dwelling previously defined as '1923 Act' premises and to the later dwellings which had been termed 'non-1923 Act' premises. Rent restriction was effected by Part II and restriction of recovery of possession by Part IV. Under s. 7 (already referred to in its amended form) the basic rent of all controlled dwellings was to be determined by reference to the rent at which they were let on the coming into operation of the Act (31 December 1960) and under s. 9 (already similarly referred to) as being such amount as the court considered reasonable, having regard, as far as possible, to the basic rents of comparable premises. By reason of the provisions of earlier legislation, rents determined under either of these sections were related to the rent which was, or might have been, charged for the dwelling on 3 August 1914, or on 7 May 1941, as the case might be, subject to such flexibility as was given under s. 9 by the words 'as the court considers reasonable'. By s. 8, provision was made for the review, on the application of the landlord, of a basic rent determined under s. 7, where such rent fell short by an amount exceeding one-eighth of the rent which would have been determined under s. 9, if that section had applied, and, on proof that the amount of the basic rent had been affected by special circumstances. Unlike the legislation which it replaced, the Act did not apply to business premises. It was, however, provided by s. 54 that tenants who had retained possession of such premises by reason of the previous legislation should be entitled to the benefit of the Landlord and Tenant Act, 1931. This section has now been repealed by the Landlord and Tenant (Amendment) Act, 1980 (see s. 11 and the Schedule to that Act).

The Act of 1967 and the Landlord and Tenant Act, 1971

The Act of 1960 was amended by the Rent Restrictions (Amendment) Act, 1967 and in minor respects by the Landlord and Tenant (Amendment) Act, 1971. It is that Act, so amended, which is impugned in these proceedings. The 1967 Act decontrolled houses with a rateable valuation exceeding £40 in Dublin and Dun Laoghaire and £30 elsewhere. It also decontrolled self-contained flats with a rateable valuation exceeding £30 in the Dublin area and £20 elsewhere. Tenants of dwellings so decontrolled were, however, given a right to a new tenancy under the Landlord and Tenant Act, 1931. Where, however, in such cases, the rent which would be fixed under the Landlord and Tenant Act, 1931 would cause hardship to the tenant, the court was empowered to grant a new lease for a term not exceeding ten years, subject to such rent as the court felt the tenant should be required to pay, having regard to all the circumstances. Decontrol was also to apply to any house or self-contained flat of which the landlord recovered possession. It also applied to houses having a rateable valuation in excess of £10 and, which, after the passing of the Act, became tenanted by a bachelor or a spinster between 21 and 65 years of age. Such tenants were also given the benefit of the Landlord and Tenant Act, 1931, with the benefit of the special provision for hardship already mentioned.

S. 7 of the Act of 1960 was amended to provide a new method of determining the basic rent of controlled premises. The basic rent was to be the net rent at which the controlled premises were let on 8 June 1966 on a contract of tenancy not being for more than five years or on a statutory tenancy. The net rent was arrived at by deducting from the gross rent the amount of the rates payable by the landlord for the year 1965/1966. An amendment to s. 8 of the 1960 Act enabled a landlord to apply to the District Court to review a basic rent where the landlord owned not more than six controlled houses or self-contained flats with a combined rateable valuation not exceeding £60 (in case one at least of them was situated in the Dublin area) or £40 in any other case. The rent, if adjusted by the court, was to be of such amount as the court considered reasonable, having regard to all the cicumstances of the case, but, in particular, to the necessity of avoiding financial hardship to the tenant and the landlord. It was not to exceed the maximum rent which would be fixed on the renewal of a tenancy under Part III of the Landlord and Tenant Act, 1931. The provision applied only where the landlord owned the premises on 8 June 1966 and continuously thereafter. The time for making such an application was, however, limited to two years after the passing of the Act (9 May 1967). To succeed in such an application, the landlord had to satisfy the court that the basic rent (fixed by reference to the net rent as of 8 June 1966) was less than the rent which would be fixed under s. 9 of the Act of 1960 (as amended), if the case was one to which that section applied. S. 9 was also amended to provide that, in fixing basic rents under that section, the court could have regard to rents of comparable dwellings, whether controlled or uncontrolled. Other amendments effected by the 1967 Act do not appear to the court to be material.

The Landlord and Tenant (Amendment) Act, 1971 effected a limited amendment to the provisions of the Act of 1960 (as amended). By s. 10 of that Act, the right given to a limited category of landlords to apply to the court to revise the basic rent of controlled premises under s. 8 of the Act of 1960 was amended. It revived the time for making such applications, originally fixed at a two-year period from the passing of the Act of 1967, for a further period of one year from the passing of the 1971 Act. This period has expired, as has the power to review contained in s. 8, both in its original and amended form.

As already indicated, these proceedings under appeal question the validity of Parts II and IV of the Act of 1960 as amended. In this judgment separate consideration is given to each of the two impugned Parts having regard to the grounds of invalidity alleged.

Effect of Part II

In relation to Part II, the plaintiffs submit that its provisions have the consequences detailed in the ensuing paragraphs.

The basic rent of the majority of controlled premises must be determined under

s. 7. This will be the net rent at which the premises were let on 8 June 1966. This rent, because of earlier legislation, necessarily has as its base either the 1914 rent, if the premises were erected prior to 1919, or the 1941 rent, if they were erected after the year 1919. While this base has to some extent been broadened by statutory increases, it still operates in restriction of the rent which may be charged, to such an extent that the income derived by the landlord from the letting is slight. In relation to the properties owned by the plaintiffs, the evidence is that the market rent would be between 9 and 19 times the controlled rent. This disproportion between market and controlled rents (which is not necessarily the crucial test in this case) is not unusual and is a direct result of the rent restriction effected by the legislation.

Since the special provision for revision of basic rents, which had been permitted in certain cases by s. 8 of the Act of 1960 (as amended) and by s. 10 of the Landlord and Tenant (Amendment) Act, 1971, no longer operates, basic rents, once they are determined under s. 7, can never be reviewed. This means that the income derived by the landlord in all such cases is effectively frozen and tied to the net rent which was derived from the premises on 8 June 1966. While additions are allowed to this basic or net rent, these are referable to the actual expenditure by the landlord, whether for rates, repairs or general maintenance. Apart from yearly increases in rates, such additions as are permitted under s. 10 are limited to the percentages of the actual expenditure set out in the section.

The imposition on the landlord of full responsibility for all repairs (except such as are the tenant's obligation under his agreement or under Deasy's Act), further accentuates the hardship caused to landlords of controlled dwellings, particularly in the case of older houses where maintenance is heavy and the rents small. Reliance was placed on the particular example of one of the plaintiff's houses, No. 32 Haroldsville Avenue, Dublin. In the case of this house, the evidence established that if the landlord carried out appropriate repairs and maintenance, she would sustain an annual loss of £35. The plaintiffs contend that the general result is virtually to deprive them of all financial benefit from their property.

The plaintiffs contend that Articles 40 and 43 of the Constitution, read in the light of its Preamble, have been contravened and that the legislation is to that extent invalid.

As to the Preamble to the Constitution, the plaintiffs rely on the following paragraph: 'And seeking to promote the common good, with due observance of Prudence, Justice and Charity so that the dignity and freedom of the individual may be assured, true social order attained, the unity of our country restored and concord established with other nations': as being the basis upon which the Constitution was adopted.

As to Article 40, the plaintiffs rely on the following provisions:

1 All citizens shall, as human persons, be held equal before the law. This shall not be held to mean that the State shall not in its enactments have due regard to differences of capacity, physical and moral, and of social function.

3.1 The State guarantees in its laws to respect, and, as far as practicable, by its law to defend and vindicate the personal rights of the citizen.

2 The State shall, in particular, by its laws protect as best it may from unjust attack and, in the case of injustice done, vindicate the life, person, good name and property rights of every citizen.

As to Article 43, the plaintiffs rely on the entire Article, which is in the following terms:

1.1 The State acknowledges that man, in virtue of his rational being, has the natural right, antecedent to positive law, to the private ownership of external goods.

2 The State accordingly guarantees to pass no law attempting to abolish the right to private ownership or the general right to transfer, bequeath, and inherit property.

2.1 The State recognises, however, that the exercise of the rights mentioned in the foregoing provisions of this Article ought, in civil society, to be regulated by the principles of social justice.

2 The State, accordingly, may as occasion requires delimit by law the exercise of the said rights with a view to reconciling their exercise with the exigencies of the common good.

On behalf of both the plaintiffs and the Attorney General, the constitutional issues have been dealt with at length, in pleadings, in written submissions and in oral argument. A condensed summary of what has been thus put forward is necessary to show the background of argument against which the court's decision has been reached.

Arguments Summarised

For the plaintiffs, it has been submitted that they have been denied the requirements of justice and have been treated unequally vis-a-vis other citizens who have let uncontrolled property; that the arbitrary and unfair restriction of their letting rights constitute an unjust attack on their property rights; that the State has failed to vindicate those rights; that the restrictions imposed on the property rights are not regulated by any principle of social justice; that the delimitation of those rights is unrelated to the exigencies of the common good; that if an emergency or other temporary basis for the impugned restriction existed at any stage, it has long since passed; that the imposition of those restrictions on houses and flats merely because they happened to be built before 1941 and to have rateable valuations below specified amounts, is arbitrary, unjustifiably discriminatory and not required by the common good; that such control, regardless as it is of the means of the tenant or the hardship it may cause to the landlord, is unjust and unfair, particularly because, since December 1972, the impugned legislation has left no means of reviewing basic rents once they have been determined by the courts; and that the State's failure since 1971 to amend this legislation and to redress the plaintiffs' grievances amounts to a dereliction by the State of its duty under Article 40.3, to protect them from unjust attack and to vindicate their property rights having regard to the injustice that has been done to them.

On behalf of the Attorney General, the case has been made that this legislation falls to be examined for invalidity under Article 43 of the Constitution; that s. 2 of that Article provides for the regulation and delimitation of property rights according to the principles of social justice and the exigencies of the common good; that what this impugned legislation has done is justified by s. 2 of that Article and that, accordingly, no question of non-compliance with Article 40.3 arises; that the power of regulating or delimiting the rights of private property is vested in the Oireachtas by Article 6 and that it is to be presumed that in exercising that power in relation to Article 43, it acted intra vires and with due regard to the directive principles of social justice set out in Article 45, which are not cognisable in any court; that the court's power to condemn this legislation under either Article 40.3, or under Article 43, cannot arise unless it is shown that what was done was not permitted by Article 43.2; that, if what the Oireachtas has done is permitted by Article 43.2, no question of injustice requiring State action under Article 40.3 s. 2 can arise; that Part II of the Act must be tested for constitutional validity as at the time of its enactment and that it cannot be held to have lost that validity by mere passage of time or changes in economic circumstances; that even if the State had any duty to review rent control periodically, it had in fact done so.

Acts Presumed to be Valid

Neither the Act of 1960, nor the Acts which amended it, are expressed to be Acts passed for the purpose of delimiting the exercise of property rights with a view to reconciling such exercise with the exigencies of the common good. Being Acts of the Oireachtas however, which are not unconstitutional on their face, they enjoy a presumption of validity until the contrary is clearly established. Accordingly, if authority for this legislation can be found under the provisions of Article 43, that Article can be relied on when the legislation is challenged.

Article 43 and Article 40

Article 43 is headed by the words 'Private Property'. It defines the attitude of the State to the concept of the private ownership of external goods and contains the State's acknowledgement that a natural right to such exists, antecedent to positive law, and that the State will not attempt to abolish this right or the associated right to transfer, bequeath and inherit property. The Article does, however, recognise that the State 'may as occasion requires delimit by law the exercise of the said rights with a view to reconciling their exercise with the exigencies of the common good'. It is an Article which prohibits the abolition of private property as an institution, but at the same time permits, in particular circumstances, the regulation of the exercise of that right and of the general right to transfer, bequeath and inherit property. In short, it is an Article directed to the State and to its attitude to these rights, which are declared to be antecedent to positive law. It does not deal with a citizen's right to a particular item of property such as a controlled premises. Such rights are dealt with in Article 40 under the heading 'Personal Rights' and are specifically designated among the personal rights of citizens. Under this Article the State is bound, in its laws, to respect and as far as practicable to defend and vindicate the personal rights of citizens.

There exists, therefore, a double protection for the property rights of a citizen. As far as he is concerned, the State cannot abolish or attempt to abolish the right of private ownership as an institution or the general right to transfer, bequeath and inherit property. In addition he has the further protection under Article 40 as to the exercise by him of his own property rights in particular items of property.

This question of the relationship of Article 40.3.2 to Article 43 was discussed in *The Attorney General* v. *Southern Industrial Trust Limited and Simons* (1960) 94 IL TR 161. In that case Lavery J, when delivering the judgment of the court, said at p. 176: 'In any event, in the opinion of the court, the property rights guaranteed are to be found in Article 43 and not elsewhere, and the rights guaranteed by Article 40 are those stated in Article 43'. The court is unable to accept this view. Article 43 does not state what the rights of property are. It recognises private property as an institution and forbids its abolition. The rights in respect of particular items of property are protected by Article 40.3.2, by which the State undertakes by its laws to protect from unjust attack and in the case of injustice done, to vindicate the property rights of every citizen. It is the duty of the courts to protect such property rights from unjust attack and the decision as to what is such an attack is to be made by the courts. This view has acceptable judicial support. Davitt P in his judgment in the High Court in *The Attorney General* v. *Southern Industrial Trust Limited and Simons* (1960) 94 ILTR 161, gave his view as to the relationship between the two Articles in the following terms:

If the matter were *res integra* and untouched by authority, I confess that my reading of these articles (Article 40.3.2 and Article 43) would be as follows: There is a clear distinction to be drawn between (1) the general and natural rights of men to own property, (2) the right of the individual to the property which he does own, and (3) his right to make what use he likes of that property; and I think this distinction is to be observed in these articles. Article 40.3 seems to me to be the only provision in the Constitution which protects the individual's rights to the property which he does own. By it the State guarantees to respect and as best it may to protect it from unjust attack and where injustice has been done to vindicate it. This is no absolute guarantee but is qualified in more than one respect. It impliedly guarantees that the State itself will not by its laws unjustly attack the right; and I think that the justice or otherwise of any legislative interference with the right has to be considered in relation, *inter alia*, to the proclaimed objects with which the Constitution was enacted, including the promotion of the common good.

Article 40.3.2 applies

In this case the plaintiffs claim that their rights to the private property in question have, by the impugned legislation, been subjected to unjust attack and that what has been done is in breach of Article 40.3.2 of the Constitution. In the opinion of the court, this legislation cannot be regarded as regulating or delimiting the property rights comprehended by Article 43. It accordingly requires to be examined for its validity in relation to the provisions of Article 40.3.2. The Question, therefore, to be decided is whether the impugned provision of the Act of 1960 (as amended) constitute an unjust attack on the property rights of the plaintiffs.

The Necessary Limitation of the Constitutional Challenge

Before entering upon this question, it is necessary to clarify certain matters. As already indicated, the Act of 1960 was amended extensively by the Rent Restrictions Act, 1967. The amendments included an extension of the power to review certain rents given to the court by s. 8 and a widening of the permitted basis for comparison on the determination of rents under s. 9. By s. 4(3) of the Act of 1967, however, it was provided that no application for the review of rent under s. 8 could be made after the expiration of two years from the passing of the Act (9 May 1967). This subsection was in turn amended in so far as it related to reviews under s. 8, s.s. (1)A, by s. 10 of the Landlord and Tenant Act, 1971. This section revived and extended the power of the court to review under that subsection 'for one year after the passing of the Landlord and Tenant (Amendment) Act 1971' (7 December 1971). The power to review has accordingly now ceased. In considering the validity of the impugned parts of this legislation, the court cannot have regard to provisions which have been amended or repealed or which no longer operate. The court proposes to consider this legislation as it now operates following the last amendment effected by s. 10 of the Landlord and Tenant Act, 1971.

Examination of the Legislation – Part II

As already indicated the long title of the Act of 1960 describes it as 'An Act to make provision for restricting the increase of rent and the recovery of possession *in certain cases* and to provide for other matters connected therewith.' Part II contains the statutory provision by means of which rents are determined and increases restricted. The legislation which contains these provisions is not limited in its duration. Its terms are mandatory and, generally, do not permit any person affected by its provisions to contract out of their application. The result is that the property rights of the owners of affected houses and dwellings are interfered with, without their consent, and agreements entered into by them for the letting of such premises are, if contrary to the statutory provisions, overriden and rendered ineffective. To the extent, therefore, that these statutory provisions interfere with and render ineffective the exercise, by the owners of the houses and dwellings affected, of their property rights in relation thereto, they constitute, in the opinion of the court, an attack upon such rights. The question which must be decided, however, is whether such attack is *unjust* and therefore in contravention of the provision of Article 40.3.2 of the Constitution.

In this regard it should first be noted, that in accordance with its long title, the Act makes provision for restricting rents only 'in certain cases'. As already indicated, these cases comprise lettings of houses or dwellings within specified valuation limits which were built or constructed prior to 7 May 1941. No reason for this selection is apparent from the impugned legislation, and, apart from the fact that rent control existed only in such cases in the previous temporary legislation, no reason was advanced by counsel for the Attorney general. The result is that lettings of all houses and dwellings outside the specified valuation limits and of all such houses and dwellings, irrespective of valuation, built after 1941 are free of any form of rent control. Further, the legislation expressly excludes all lettings of dwellings made under the labourers Acts, 1883 to 1958 or the Housing of the Working Classes Acts, 1890 to 1958 (to be read in conjunction with s. 120 of the Housing Act, 1966) and thereby excludes the many thousands of lettings made by local authorities to persons in need of housing assistance. It is further to be noted that the statutory provisions contained in Part II operate in respect of the house or dwelling controlled, irrespective of the means of the tenant. Neither the means of the tenant nor the lack of means or possible hardship to the landlord may be considered in determining the permitted rent. It is, therefore, apparent that in this legislation, rent control is applied only to some houses and dwellings and not to others, that the basis for the selection is not related to the needs of the tenants, to the financial or economic resources of the landlords, or to any established social necessity and, since the legislation is now not limited in duration, is not associated with any particular temporary or emergency situation. Such legislation, to escape the description of being unfair and unjust, would require some adequate compensatory factor for those whose rights are so arbitrarily and detrimentally affected. No such compensatory factor is to be found in the impugned provisions of Part II.

The vast majority of the rents in question are determined under the provisions of s. 7. This section declares that the basic rent of premises to which it applies shall be the net rent at which such premises were let on 8 June 1966. The net rent, where the landlord paid or allowed a deduction in respect of rates, is declared to be the rent payable less the rates. Otherwise it is the rent payable on the specified date. The rent payable on 8 June 1966 was, however, in all cases regulated by the rent control legislation previously in force. This had the effect that all rents so payable were related to the rent chargeable in 1914 in respect of the older controlled dwellings, and to the rent charged on 7 May 1941 in respect of the later ones. It was alleged by the plaintiffs, and not seriously disputed by the Attorney General, that the direct effect of this control has been that rents have been pegged or frozen at a level which is usually oppressively uneconomic and which is further eroded by the statutory obligation to repair and maintain the controlled premises. S. 9 applies only to cases not covered by s. 7. It permits determination by the court of such rent as the court considers reasonable having regard to the rents of 'dwellings which are comparable in regard to location, accommodation, amenities, state of repair and rateable valuation'. It is accepted by the plaintiffs that rents determined under s. 9 are comparably higher than rents determined under s. 7 and that, accordingly, such rents yield an element of profit for the owner.

Once basic rents are determined under s. 7 no review thereof is now permitted. The temporary revival of the power to review in certain s. 7 cases, provided by the Landlord and Tenant Act, 1971, has long since expired. This means that all owners whose rents are controlled are restricted in their income to the amount of the basic rent and to such lawful additions as may be related to increases in rates and to a percentage of actual expenditure on maintenance, repair or improvement. This absence of any power to review such rents, irrespective of changes in conditions, is in itself a circumstance of inherent injustice which cannot be ignored. When this is coupled with the absence of any provision for compensating the owners whose rental incomes are thus permanently frozen, regardless of the significant diminution in the value of money, the conclusion that injustice has been done is inevitable.

In the opinion of the court, the provisions of Part II of the Act of 1960 (as amended) restrict the property rights of one group of citizens for the benefit of another group. This is done without compensation and without regard to the financial capacity or the financial needs of either group, in legislation which provides no limitation on the period of restriction, gives no opportunity for review and allows no modification of the operation of the restriction. It is, therefore, both unfair and arbitrary. These provisions constitute an unjust attack on the property rights of landlords of controlled dwellings and are therefore contrary to the provisions of Article 40.3.2 of the Constitution.

Examination of Part IV

Part IV restricts in s. 29 the landlord's right to recover possession of controlled premises. It is also impugned in these proceedings as being invalid having regard to the provisions of Article 40.3.2 of the Constitution. The relevant provisions in Part IV are mandatory and constitute an interference with the normal property rights of the landlords affected. It is an interference which has the effect, in some cases, of causing an almost permanent alienation from the landlord of the right to get possession of the premises, because of the extensive right of the tenant's family to retain possession after the tenant's death.

In the view of the court, a restriction to this extent of a landlord's right to obtain possession of rented premises is not in itself constitutionally invalid, provided the restriction is made on a basis that is not unconstitutionally unfair or oppressive, or has no due regard both to the personal property rights of the landlord and the rights that should be accorded to tenants having regard to the common good. However, the restriction on the right to recover possession contained in Part IV is not distinguishable, or capable of being saved, by such considerations. It is an integral part of the arbitrary and unfair statutory scheme whereby tenants of controlled dwellings are singled out for specially favourable treatment, both as to rent and as to the right to retain possession, regardless of whether they have any social or financial need for such preferential treatment and regardless of whether the landlords have the ability to bear the burden of providing such preferential treatment.

Even if Part IV could be said not to be infected with the constitutional infirmity which invalidates the provisions governing rent control, it could survive the challenge made to its constitutionality only if it could be held to have been enacted by the Oireachtas in a manner and in a context that would leave it with a separate and self-contained existence as a duly enacted measure representing the law-making will of the Oireachtas: see *Maher* v. *Attorney General* [1973] IR 140, 147; *The State (Attorney General)* v. *Shaw* [1979] IR 136; and the varying views expressed in *King* v. *Director of Public Prosecutions* (31 July 1980).

It is clear that it was not so enacted. It acquired a legislative existence as an integral part of a statutory scheme in which controlled dwellings, and only controlled dwellings, had attached to them restrictions as to rent and as to the right to recover possession. For the reasons given earlier in this judgment, these provisions as to rent restriction amount to an unconstitutional interference with the property rights of the relevant landlords. Even if it could be held that the restrictions on the right to recover possessions contained in Part IV did not suffer from the same fatal invalidity, those provisions could not be given a life of their own as representing duly enacted provisions. The whole of the provisions governing both rent control and right to possession were enacted (and re-enacted) as a package and, as such, were intended to have an interconnected statutory operation. It would be impossible to say that if the Houses of the Oireachtas had been presented with the option of enacting the restrictions on getting possession of controlled premises that are contained in Part IV, as a type of control separate and distinct from the control of the rents of such dwellings, they would have enacted Part IV on its own. It is a hypothesis that never became a parliamentary choice, express or implied. It would be impossible, therefore, to say that the Houses of the Oireachtas ever visualised the existence of Part IV as distinct from Part II. Neither of those Parts can be deemed to have been given a viable statutory existence apart from the other.

Accordingly Part IV must also fall as part of an unconstitutionally unjust attack on the property rights of the landlords affected.

Further Observations

This decision has the effect that a statutory protection which many thousands of families relied on for the continuance of the existing tenancies in the dwellings in which they live is no longer available to them. A ruling of this nature on the constitutional validity of a particular statutory provision usually exhausts the functions of this court. In this instance, however, because of the special feature of the case and the consequences involved, the court considers that some further observations are called for.

The removal from the affected tenants of the degree of security of possession and of rent control which they hitherto enjoyed will leave a statutory void. The court assumes that the situation thereby created will receive the immediate attention of the Oireachtas and that new legislation will be speedily enacted. Such legislation may be expected to provide for the determination of fair rents, for a degree of security of tenure and for other relevant social and economic factors. Pending the enactment of such legislation as may be decided upon, it may be possible in many cases for agreement to be reached between landlord and tenants. Where, however, such agreement is not possible, either because of the tenant's inability to pay the rent demanded or because of the landlord's determination to recover possession, considerable hardship would be caused in certain cases, if possession were obtained by the ejectment of the tenant. This court does not wish to pre-empt or prejudge any situation of litigation that may flow from this judgment. It desires to emphasise, however, that it is the duty of the courts to have regard to the basic requirements of justice when exercising their jurisdiction. In this regard, in the reasonable expectation of new legislation, when a decree for possession is sought, the court should, where justice so warrants, in a case where the now condemned provisions of Part IV would be given in defence against the recovery of possession, either adjourn the case or grant a decree for possession with such stay as appears proper in the circumstances.

Notes

1. Note the reaction of the Oireachtas to this decision, see the Rent Restrictions (Temporary

Provisions) Act, 1981, and the Rent Restrictions (Temporary Provisions) (Continuance) Acts, 1981 and 1982. See also *Re Reference under Article 26 of the Constitution of the Housing (Private Rental Dwellings) Bill 1981* [1983] I.L.R.M. 246.

2. See also *Brennan & Others* v. *Att.- Gen.* [1983] I.L.R.M. 449; *Hamilton* v. *Hamilton* [1982] I.R. 466; [1982] I.L.R.M. 290.

Chapter 2

SOME FUNDAMENTAL CONCEPTS

In this chapter we consider some fundamental concepts which lie at the heart of the land law system. As with so much of Irish land law, they are rooted in history and it must be doubted whether some of them have any rightful place in a modern system. It is surely the case that the conveyancers of today should no longer have to concern themselves with the mysteries of the Statute of Uses. It may also be questioned whether the complexities of the doctrine of notice, which continues to surprise conveyancers and trouble the courts, are really necessary.

I. USES AND FORMS OF CONVEYANCE

STATUTES OF USES (IRELAND), 1634

An Act expressing an order for uses, wills, and enrollments.

Where by the common laws of this realme, lands, tenements and hereditaments, be not divisable by testament, nor ought to be transferred from one to another, but by solemne livery and seizin, matter of record or writing, sufficiently made, bona fide, without covin or fraud; yet nevertheless, divers and sundry imaginations, subtill inventions and practices have been used, whereby the hereditaments of this realme have been conveyed from one to another, by fraudulent feoffments, fines, recoveries, and other assurances, craftily made, to secret uses, intents and trusts, and also by wills and testaments sometime made by nude parolx and words, sometime by signs and tokens, and sometime by writing, and by the most part made by such persons as be visited with sickness in their extreame agonies and pains, or at such time as they have had scantly any good memory or remembrance, at which times they being provoked by greedy and covetous persons, lying in wait about them, do many times dispose indiscreetly and unadvisedly, their lands and hereditaments, by reason whereof, and by occasion of which fraudulent feoffments, fines, recoveries, and other like assurances to uses, confidences and trust, divers and many heires have been unjustly at sundry times disinherited, the lords lost their wards, marriages, reliefs, herriots, escheats, aides pur faire fitz chivaler, & pur file marier, and scantly any person can be certainly assured of any lands by them purchased, nor know surely against whom they shall use their actions or execution for their rights, title and duties: also men married have lost their tenancies by the courtesie, women their dowres, and manifest perjuries, by tryale of such secret wills and uses, have been committed; the Kings Highnesse hath lost the profits of wastes for a year and a day of lands of felons attainted, and the lords their escheats thereof and many other inconveniences have happened, and daily do increase among the Kings subjects, to their great trouble and unquietnesse, and to the utter subversion of the ancient common laws of this realme. For the extirping and extinguishment of all such subtill practised feoffment, fines, recoveries, abuses and errours heretofore used and accustomed in this realme, to the subversion of the good and ancient lawes of the same, and to the intent that the Kings Highness, or any others his subjects of this realme, shall not in any wise hereafter, by any means or inventions, be deceived, damaged, or hurted, by reason of such trusts, uses, or confidences.

I. Where any person or persons stand to be seized, or at any time hereafter shall happen to be seized, of and in any honours, castles, mannors, lands, tenements, rents, services, reversions, remainders, or other hereditaments, to the use, confidence, or trust of any other person or persons, or of any body politique, by reason of any bargaine, sale, feoffment, fine, recovery, covenant, contract, agreement, will or otherwise, by any manner means whatsoever it be, that in every such case, all and every such person and persons, and bodies politique, that have, or hereafter shall have any such use, confidence or trust, in fee simple, fee tayle, for terme of life or years, or otherwise; or any use, confidence, or trust, in remainder or reverter, shall from henceforth stand and be seized, deemed, and adjudged in lawfull seizin, estate and possession, of and in the same honors, castles, mannors, lands, tenements, rents, services, reversions, remainders, and hereditaments, with their appurtenances, to all intents, constructions and purposes in the law, of and in such like estates, as they had or shall have, in use, trust or confidence, of or in the same. And that the estate, tithe, right and possession, that was in such person or persons that were, or hereafter shall be seized, of any lands, tenements, or hereditaments, to the use, confidence or trust, of any such person or persons, or of any body politicke, be from henceforth clearly deemed and adjudged to be in him or them that have, or hereafter shall have such use, confidence or trust, after such quality, manner, form and condition, as they had before, in or to the use, confidence, or trust that was in them.

II. And where divers and many persons be, or hereafter shall happen to be joyntly seized of and in any lands, tenements, rents, reversions, remainders, or other hereditaments, to the use, confidence, or trust of any of them that be so joyntly seized, that in every such case that those person or persons, which have, or hereafter shall have any such uses, confidence or trust, in any such lands, tenements, rents, reversions, remainders, or hereditaments shall from henceforth have, and be deemed and adjudged to have, onely to him or them that have, or hereafter shall have such use, confidence or trust, such estate, possession, and seizin, of and in the same lands, tenements, rents, reversions, remainders, or other hereditaments, in like nature, manner, form, condition and course, as he or they had before in the use, confidence or trust of the same lands, tenements or hereditaments. Saving and reserving to all and singular persons, and bodies politique, their heires and successors, other than those person or persons which be seized, or hereafter shall be seized, of any lands, tenements or hereditaments, to any use, confidence or trust, all such right, title, entry, interest, possession, rents and action, as they or any of them had, or might have had before the making of this act.

III. And also saving to all and singular those persons, and to their heires, which be, or hereafter shall be seized to any use, all such former right, title, entry, interest, possession, rents, customes, services and actions, as they or any of them might have had, to his or their own proper use, in or to any mannors, lands, tenements, rents or hereditaments, whereof they be, or hereafter shall be seized to any other use, as if this present act had never been had or made; any thing contained in this act to the contrary notwithstanding.

IV. And where also divers persons stand and be seized of and in any lands, tenements or hereditaments, in fee simple, or otherwise, to the use or intent that some other person or persons shall have and perceive yearly to them and to his or their heirs, one annuall rent of ten pounds, or more, or lesse, out of the same lands and tenements, and some other person, one annuall rent to him and his assigns, for term of life or years, or for some other speciall time, according to such intent and use as hath been heretofore declared, limited, and made thereof. In every such case, the same persons, their heirs and assigns, that have such use and interest, to have and perceive any such annuall rents out of any lands, tenements or hereditaments, that they and every of them, their heirs and assignes, be adjudged and deemed to be in possession and seizin of the same rent, of and in such like estate, as they had in the title, interest, or use of the said rent or profit, and as if a sufficient grant, or other lawfull conveyance had been made and executed to them by such as were or shall be seized to the use or intent of any such rent to be had, made or payed, according to the very trust and intent thereof ; and that all and every such person or persons as have, or hereafter shall have any title, use and interest, in or to any such rent or profit, shall lawfully distraine for non-payment of the said rent, and in their owne names make advouries, or by their bayliffs or servants, make recognizances and justifications, and have all other suits, entries and remedies, for such rents, as if the same rents had been actually and really granted to them, with sufficient clauses of distresse, re-entry, or otherwise, according to such conditions, pains, or other things limited and appointed upon the trust and intent for payment or surety of such rent.

. . .

XVII. And from the first day of May, which shall be in the yeare of our Lord God, one thousand six hundred thirty and five, no mannors, lands, tenements, or other hereditaments, shall passe, alter or change, from one to another, whereby any state of inheritance or freehold shall be made or take effect in any person or persons, or any use thereof to be made, by reason only of any bargain and sale thereof, except the same bargain and sale be made by writing indented, sealed and inrolled, in any of the Kings courts of record at Dublin, or else within the same county or counties, where the same mannors, lands or tenements, so bargained and sold, lye or be, before the custos rotulorum, and two justices of the peace, and the clarke of the peace of the same county or counties, or two of them at the least, whereof the clarke of the peace to be one; and the same inrollment to be had and made within six months next after the date of the same writings indented; the same custos rotulorum or justices of the peace, and clarke takeing for the inrollment of every such writing indented before them, where the lands comprised in the same writings exceede not the yearely value of forty shillings, two shillings, that is to say, twelve pence to the justices and twelve pence to the clarke; and for the inrolment of every such writing indented before them, wherein the lands comprised exceede the summe of forty shillings in yearly value, five shillings, that is to say, two shillings sixpence to the justices; and two shillings sixpence to the said clarke for the inrolling of the same: and that the clarke of the peace for the time being, within every such county, shall sufficiently inroll and ingrosse in parchment, the same deeds or writings indented, as is aforesaid, and the rolls thereof at the end of every yeare, shall deliver unto the said costos rotulorum of the same county for the time being, there to remaine in the custody of the said custos rotulorum for the time being, amongst other records of the same counties, where any such inrollments shall be so made, to the intent that every party that hath to do therewith, may resort and see the effect and tenor of every such writing so inrolled.

XVIII. Provided alwayes, that this act, nor any thing therein contayned, extend to any mannor, lands, tenements or hereditaments, lying, or being within any citty, burrough, or towne corporate within this realm, wherein the mayors, recorders, chamberlaines, bayliffes, or other office or officers, have authority, or have lawfully used to inroll any evidence, deeds, or other writings within their precincts or limits; any thing in this act contained to the contrary notwithstanding.

Note

For detailed discussion of the operation of the Statute of Uses in Ireland, see *Irish Land Law*, para. 3.015 *et seq.*

REAL PROPERTY ACT, 1845

2. After the first day of October one thousand eight hundred and forty-five all corporeal tenements and hereditaments shall, as regards the conveyance of the immediate freehold thereof, be deemed to lie in grant as well as in livery; . . .

3. A feoffment made after the said first day of October one thousand eight hundred and forty-five, other than a feoffment made under a custom by an infant, shall be void at law, unless evidenced by deed; and a partition and no exchange of any tenements or hereditaments, not being copyhold, and a lease, required by law to be in writing, of any tenements or hereditaments, and an assignment of a chattel interest, not being copyhold, in any tenements or hereditaments, and a surrender in writing of an interest in any tenements or hereditaments, not being a copyhold interest, and not being an interest which might by law have been created without writing, made after the said first day of October one thousand eight hundred and forty-five, shall also be void at law, unless made by deed: Provided always, that the said enactment, so far as the same relates to a release or a surrender, shall not extend to Ireland. [This section was repealed as to landlord and tenant in Ireland, save so far as it relates to feoffments, partitions and exchanges by Deasy's Act (Landlord and Tenant Law Amendment, Ireland, Act, 1860), see s. 104 and Sch. B].

4. A feoffment made after the said first day of October one thousand eight hundred and forty-five shall not have any tortious operation; and an exchange or a partition of any tenements or hereditaments, made by deed executed after the said first day of October one thousand eight hundred and forty-five, shall not imply any condition in law; and the word 'give' or the word 'grant' in a deed executed after the same day, shall not imply any covenant in law in respect of any tenements or hereditaments, except so far as the word 'give' or the word 'grant' may by force of any Act of Parliament imply a covenant.

5. Under an indenture executed after the first day of October one thousand eight hundred and forty-five an immediate estate or interest in any tenements or hereditaments, and the benefit of a condition or covenant respecting any tenements or hereditaments, may be taken, although the taker thereof be not named a party to the same indenture; also, a deed executed after the said first day of October one thousand eight hundred and forty-five, purporting to be an indenture, shall have the effect of an indenture, although not actually indented.

Notes
1. See further on the 1845 Act *Irish Land Law*, para. 3.026 and *Irish Conveyancing Law*, paras. 15.02, 16.007–8 and 16.048–9.
2. *Cf.* conveyances of registered land, i.e. land whose title has been registered under the Local Registration of Title (Ireland) Act, 1891 and now the Registration of Title Act, 1964, see *Irish Conveyancing Law*, ch. 16 (*passim*).

RE SERGIE
[1954] N.I. 1 (Court of Appeal)

Premises held under a fee farm grant were mortgaged by way of a demise for 10,000 years to a Bank to secure advances, the mortgagors covenanting to stand seised of the reversion immediately expectant on the term 'in trust for any purchaser or purchasers of the premises or to convey and dispose thereof as the Bank or any such purchaser or purchasers may at any time direct'. The Bank in exercise of its statutory power of sale sold the premises to S. and thereupon assigned to him the unexpired portion of the term. Neither the Bank nor S. gave any directions to the mortgagors regarding the reversion. S. died and by his will he devised and bequeathed the premises to three persons for life and thereafter to named charities, made a number of specific and pecuniary bequests some of which were expressed to be given 'free of legacy duty', and left his residuary estate consisting of realty and personalty to his executors on trust, inter alia, to pay his debts funeral and testementary expenses and death duties. In a dispute over the payment of estate duty the crucial issue was whether S. had died holding a *legal* fee simple or a lease for the residue of the 10,000 year term plus an *equitable* fee simple reversion. At first instance, Lord MacDermott L.C.J. held that the covenant to stand seised amounted to a declaration of trust by the mortgagors which was executed by the Statute of Uses, thereby giving the mortgagees the *legal* reversion. He then held that under the doctrine of merger (see Ch. 15, *post*) they should be regarded as holding a legal fee simple in the premises, which passed to S. before he died. On appeal, the Court of Appeal reversed this decision.

Porter L.J. stated the facts and continued:

The main question for determination is whether the estate duty and the interest thereon in respect of Bennett Buildings falls to be borne by Bennett Buildings or by the residuary estate, and a great part of the argument in this court turned on the question whether the testator was or was not the legal owner of a fee simple estate in the property.

The Lord Chief Justice held that in addition to the term the testator took an equitable estate in the freehold reversion by virtue of the mortgagors' declaration of trust, that notwithstanding the absence of words of limitation in the declaration of trust he took an estate in fee simple in the reversion, and that the Irish Statute of Uses operated on the declaration so as to vest in the testator a legal estate commensurate with the trust declared in his favour, the result being that the doctrine of merger applied and the testator therefore took a legal estate in fee simple in the property.

Estate duty payable in respect of real property is a charge upon the real property, and if the executors have paid it they are entitled to recover it from the devisee of the property upon which it is charged. Notwithstanding this charge, the Lord Chief Justice was inclined to accept the view that the instruction to pay 'my . . . death duties' would exonerate the devise of Bennett Buildings from estate duty, if the testator had not given several of the legacies 'free of legacy duty.' But since the testator, by the use of these exonerating words, had shewn that he was discriminating between the various dispositions, the Lord Chief Justice held that the direction to pay 'my . . . death duties' could not be construed so as to exonerate the real property from the duties which the law placed upon it.

I propose to discuss this matter first of all on the assumption that the testator was the legal owner of a fee simple estate in Bennett Buildings. Where some legacies are expressed to be free of legacy duty, the natural inference is that the other legacies which are bequeathed simpliciter without any such words must bear their own legacy duty, but it does not follow that a devise of real property must therefore bear its own share of *estate* duty. The estate duty is a charge upon it, irrespective of whether some or all of the legacies are expressed to be free of *legacy* duty, and the real question here is whether the direction to pay 'my . . . death duties' relieves the real property of the burden of estate duty which the law imposes upon it.

Testementary expenses include the estate duty payable in respect of the free personal estate, so that death duties, if they are to bear their ordinary meaning in this connection, comprise (*a*) estate duty upon the real estate, (*b*) legacy duty and (*c*) succession duty. It may well be that the prior bequests of several legacies free of legacy duty restrict this wider meaning, and that the testator did not intend to include legacy duty and succession duty under 'my . . . death duties.' But even if this was his intention it does not follow that he intended to exclude real estate duty from the death duties which he directed his trustees to pay.

If he had intended that all the devises and bequests, except such as were given free of legacy duty, were to bear their own respective duties it is impossible to attribute any meaning whatever to the direction to pay 'my . . . death duties.'

The Lord Chief Justice has referred to two cases which, in my opinion, govern the present case. In *In re Pimm* ([1904] 2 Ch. 345) the testator directed that out of the proceeds of the sale and conversion of his real and personal property his trustees should pay his debts, funeral and testamentary expenses and duties. It was contended that duties must be restricted to such duties as were properly payable out of the residue – that is to say – the estate duty payable on the free personal estate. Farwell J. rejected this contention and decided that the settlement estate duty, as well as the estate duty payable on the specifically devised realty, was payable by the trustees. He said (Ibid. 347): 'The expression "my duties" is certainly a wide phrase, and I can see no ground for restricting its generality. I think it is a compendious way of expressing what he had in his mind, and that he meant to say, "all duties to which my estate is liable by reason of any of the dispositions I have made in my will." I can see no other sensible construction of this direction in the residuary clause of the will.'

This decision was followed by Swinfen Eady J. in *In re Cayley* ([1904] 2 Ch. 781). A testatrix, after bequeathing certain pecuniary legacies 'free of all death duties,' bequeathed certain chattels upon trust for certain persons for life with remainders over. She directed the trustees out of a specific fund which she bequeathed to them on trust to pay 'my funeral and testamentary expenses and debts and the legacies bequeathed by this my will and the death duties payable out of my estate.' The question was whether the settlement estate duty was payable out of the settled chattels or out of the specific fund. Settlement estate duty was not a testamentary expense *In re King* ([1904] 1 Ch. 363) *In re Clemow* ([1900] 2 Ch. 182) and was therefore a burden upon the settled property unless the direction to pay the death duties amounted to an express provision to the contrary within section 19 (1) of the Finance Act, 1894. Swinfen Eady J., after referring to the decision of Farwell J. in *In Re Pimm*, said ([1904] 2 Ch. at 784): 'The expression "the death duties payable out of my estate" extends to all death duties, namely settlement estate duty as well as estate duty. It is a convenient and compendious expression, and I can see no reason to restrict its meaning. The duties must, therefore, be borne by the specific fund.'

This decision appears to rule the present case, for the settlement estate duty (which was abolished in 1914) was a charge upon the settled property just as the estate duty payable in respect of realty is a charge upon the realty. Yet the direction to pay the death duties out of the specific fund was sufficient to exonerate the settled property from the settlement estate duty as well as estate duty.

The meaning of death duties was discussed in In *re Massey* [(1920) 122 L.T. 676; 90 L.J. Ch. 40.] A testatrix by a will and codicil both made in the year 1896 gave two of her executors legacies free of legacy duty and she also gave other legacies and annuities, and devised lands to her husband for life with remainder over. She then directed the residue of her personal estate subject to several annuities after payment of 'all and singular my debts funeral and testamentary expenses including death duties and payment of all legacies directed to be paid immediately' to be invested and the income to be paid to her husband for his life, and gave several pecuniary legacies to be payable at her husband's death and the residuary trust fund to the defendants.

Eve J. said 'that at the time when this will was made and for many years afterwards the true construction to be given to the phrase "testamentary expenses" was uncertain. Whether it extended to cover estate duty payable on personalty was a matter of doubt, and that doubt was not resolved until the decisions of Kekewich J. in the case of *Re Lewis: Lewis* v. *Smith* ([1900] 2 Ch. 176, 180): and *Re Clemow* ([1900] 2 Ch. 182). There was therefore at the date of the will a reason why a testator who intended that the estate duty on the personalty should be paid out of the residue should expressly so state and I think the direction given by this testatrix amounts to this and nothing more "I desire my testamentary expenses to be paid by my executors: if the words 'testamentary expenses' include the death duties payable by my executors that is enough, but if they do not I wish to make it clear that I intend those death duties to be paid as though they were included in the expression. . .". All that she meant was that the executors were to pay such duties as were by law payable out of her estate' ([1920] 122 L.T. 676, 678; (1921) 90 L.J., Ch. 40). He therefore held that the executors were liable to pay only such duties as were by law payable out of her estate, irrespective of the question whether or not they would be included in a simple direction to pay 'testamentary expenses.' He also said that if the direction was intended to include the duties on the legacies immediately payable the direction at the commencement of the will that the legacies to the executors were to be paid free of legacy duty would be quite superfluous. It is clear that the judgment was based mainly upon the form of the expression 'testamentary expenses *including* death duties' and that fact that when the will was made it was uncertain what duties were included in testamentary expenses.

I do not think that this decision is in the slightest degree inconsistent with *In re Pimm* ([1904] 2 Ch. 345) and *In re Cayley* ([1904] 2 Ch. 781). It was a question of the construction of a peculiar expression in a will made at a time when the law regarding death duties and testamentary expenses was still uncertain.

In re Borough ([1938] 1 All E.R. 375) was a case in which a testator, having given a large number of legacies, eight being expressed to be free of duty, the others being given simpliciter, gave his residuary estate upon trust for sale and conversion and to pay out of the proceeds 'my funeral and testamentary expenses and all death duties (payable in consequence of my death) and my debts and also to pay or provide for the legacies and annuities &c., &c.' Simonds J. (as he then was) held that the only death duty payable on testator's death was the estate duty on the personal estate and that those legacies and annuities which were not expressed to be free of duty must bear their own legacy duty.

It was contended that 'all death duties' comprised legacy duty as well as estate duty, but this contention was rejected because the testator had shewn a discrimination between the legacies which were free of legacy duty and those not so free.

This decision dealt only with legacy duty and appears to have no bearing on the present case.

In re King ([1942] Ch. 413) was a case in which a testator gave a number of devises and bequests, some of which were expressed to be 'free of duty' or 'duty free' or 'free of all duty' or 'free of duties', and others were given simpliciter, and after the usual trust for sale and conversion he directed his executor out of the trust property to pay his funeral and testamentary expenses and debts and the pecuniary legacies and *'all duties payable in respect of my estate'* and invest the clear residue &c., &c.

The Court of Appeal, affirming the decision of Simonds J. (as he then was), held that the general direction to pay 'all duties payable in respect of my estate' did not relieve those devises and bequests which were not expressly given free of duty from bearing their own respective duties. Luxmoore L.J., delivering the judgment of the court, said (Ibid. 419–20): 'It is difficult to read this' – i.e. the general direction to pay all duties – 'as being intended to free all the specific gifts and legacies from liability to duty, where, as in this case, the testator has expressly freed some of the gifts from duty, and has not done so in other cases. . . . In our opinion, the question in the present case is: Ought the words in cl. 9, "all duties payable in respect of my estate," to be construed without regard to the fact that certain

dispositions in the testator's will are in express terms given free of duty while other
dispositions in the will and the first codicil are not expressed to be so given, or
ought the words referred to to be construed having regard to that fact? If the
former method of construction is correct, then every disposition taking effect at the
testator's death would be freed from liability for duty although the testator has
apparently in cl. 7 and in the first codicil treated some of his testamentary dispositions differently from others in respect of freedom from duty. In our view, the latter
method of construction appears to be the safer, for it gives effect to the express
directions of the testator and avoids treating the expressions with regard to the
freedom of particular benefits from duty as being tautologous.'

The decision in my opinion is open to criticism on several grounds. It attributes
no meaning or force to the direction to pay *all* duties, and even if the direction is
taken to refer only to (*a*) the duty forming part of the testamentary expenses, and
(*b*) the duties on the legacies which were given free of duty, it is quite superfluous
because the testator had already directed payment of these two classes of duties.
Moreover, the construction adopted by the court runs counter to the well settled
rule that where there are two conflicting clauses in a will, the latter must prevail. If
one seeks to discover the intention of the testator in these conflicting clauses, I
think the natural and probable explanation is that when he came to the clause in
which the usual direction is given for the administration of his estate, realizing that
he had given some legacies free of duty and others not free, he directed his
executors to pay not some duties only but *all duties* payable in respect of his estate,
intending this to cover all duties whatsoever or at all events all those duties for the
payment of which he had not expressly provided. Even if this direction is considered to be tautological, it is, I think, safer to carry out the express intention of
the testator that *all* duties should be paid by the executors rather than to adopt a
technical construction which gives no meaning to these words and is based upon an
inference which is drawn from the fact that some of the legacies are expressed to be
free of duty in the earlier parts of the will. This, in my opinion, is a very doubtful
decision and in any event we are not bound to follow it.

In re Palmer ([1946] Ch. 49) was a case regarding the incidence of legacy duty on
shares of the residuary estate. A testator gave several pecuniary legacies free of
duty and one specific legacy not free of duty and gave his real and personal estate
upon trust for conversion and out of the proceeds of sale and his ready money to
pay his funeral and testamentary expenses, death duties and debts and pay or
provide for legacies. The residue was to be divided into three shares, one settled on
his wife for life, and afterwards to his son on attaining the age of 25 years, another
to his son absolutely and the remaining third for his mother and brother in equal
shares. The legacy duty payable on the different shares of the residue varied from 1
per cent in the case of the son to 10 per cent in the case of the wife. It was
contended on behalf of the residuary legatees that the testator intended to give the
shares of the residue free of legacy duty and that the whole of the legacy duty on the
residue should be first paid although the rates of duty might differ, and the clear
residue divided into three parts and dealt with in accordance with the will.

Uthwatt J. (as he then was) said that the provision as to death duties occurred in
a direction to the trustees as to the course which administration should pursue, and
was not in substance directed to creating beneficial interests so that it was wholly a
matter of machinery and direction to the executors and trustees as to what they
were to do. He said he thought he was bound by the decision in *In re King* ([1942]
Ch. 413) and that having regard to the place in the will where the direction to pay
death duties was found, to the generality of the term, and the circumstance that
certain legacies were given free of duty while one was not, the testator did not

intend to free the various interests in the residue from liability to legacy duty to which they were subjected by the ordinary law and which they themselves must bear.

The decision, which is concerned only with the incidence of the legacy and succession duties on the shares of the residue, is of no assistance in enabling us to decide whether the estate duty on Bennett Buildings ought to be borne by the property itself or is payable out of the general residuary estate. Uthwatt J. seems to treat the direction to pay 'death duties' after the words 'funeral and testamentary expenses' as wholly a matter of administrative machinery and direction to the executors and trustees as to what they are to do, but if he meant to convey that such a direction amounts to nothing more than a mere direction to administer the estate, I cannot agree, and in arriving at this conclusion I have followed the same line of reasoning as was adopted by Farwell J. and Swinfen Eady J. in the two cases which I have cited.

So far I have not touched upon a question which formed no inconsiderable part of the discussion in this court, viz. whether the testator was the legal owner of the freehold in Bennett Buildings or merely the owner of the term of 10,000 years with an equitable estate in the freehold reversion. The covenant by the mortgagors to stand seised of the reversion in trust for the purchaser differs in no material respect from the usual form adopted in cases where the premises are held under a fee farm grant. (See Irish Forms and Precedents, p. 421). The purchaser of the term from the Bank became the equitable owner of the freehold reversion with a right to call upon the mortgagors to convey the legal estate to any person he might name. This is not a simple trust, but one which requires the mortgages '*to convey and dispose of*' the freehold reversion as the purchaser might direct. It is therefore what is called a special trust which necessitates the legal estate remaining in the trustees until they convey it according to the direction of the purchaser. As Parke B. said in *Barker v. Greenwood* [(1838) 4 M. & W. 421] where the trustees have anything to do in the execution of the trusts the legal estate must remain vested in them, and in *Doe d. Shelley v. Edlin* [(1836) 4 Ad. & El. 582] it was said (*per curiam*) that the trustees must take that quantity of interest which the purposes of the trust require. In that case the testatrix devised estates to N. in fee in trust to receive and apply the proceeds to the use of S. for her life and immediately after the death of S. 'to convey the same to such uses as S. should be deed or will appoint'. The court held that the legal estate which was vested in N. did not lapse on the death of S. but vested in N. as an absolute legal fee to be conveyed by him according to the directions given by S.

So also *Doe d. Noble v. Bolton* [(1839) Ad. & El. 188]: where a testator devised his manor and mansion house to trustees in trust to permit and suffer his wife, should she wish to do so, to occupy the same and to receive the rents and profits thereof until his son was of age provided she remained unmarried; and on the son attaining 21 then in trust to release, convey and assure the manor and mansion to his son in fee. The court held that the legal estate in the premises vested in the wife till her son attained the age of 21 and Lord Denman C.J. delivering the judgment of the court said: 'It is plain that the trustees must take the legal estate after the death of Mrs. Noble, in order to convey the same to her son.' The Statute of Uses has no application to a trust of this kind where the trustees have a duty to perform. The Chief Justice holding that the Statute of Uses applied to the trust contained in the covenant to stand seised decided that the purchaser on completing the purchase became clothed with the legal estate in the freehold reversion. According to this view the trust to convey and dispose of the freehold reversion is superfluous and meaningless. In my opinion these words clearly show that the real object of the covenant is to give the purchaser the option of calling for the legal estate in the freehold if he desired to have it. The Bank did not want it and it might well be that the purchaser would prefer not to acquire it if he considered that the rent reserved and the covenants contained in the fee farm grant were too onerous. According to the construction adopted by the Chief Justice the purchaser of the term had no such option, but was obliged to assume the legal estate and thus to undertake direct liability for the rent and the covenants in the fee farm grant. In my opinion such a view would nullify what I conceive to be the real object of this covenant which has been in common use by conveyancers for very many years. I hold, therefore, that the legal estate in the freehold is still outstanding in the trustees or their representatives. The leasehold term, being a legal term, did not merge in the equitable estate of the testator in the reversion, and Bennett Buildings must, therefore, be treated as personal property. The estate duty on these premises, as on the other personal estate of the testator, falls to be paid out of the general residuary estate as part of the testamentary expenses.

In the event it seems to me to be immaterial, so far as estate duty is concerned, whether the property is treated as freehold or leasehold.

The appeal must, therefore, be allowed.

Black L.J. stated the facts and continued:

The question at issue in this appeal is whether the estate duty payable in respect of Bennett Buildings falls to be borne by and is payable out of the property itself, or whether on the other hand it is payable out of the testator's residuary estate.

The arguments addressed to the court fell under two separate heads. In the first place the appellants contended that the interest in Bennett Buildings to which Bennett Sergie was entitled at the date of his death was an interest which passed to his executors as such, so that the estate duty in respect of the premises was payable out of his residuary estate, while the respondents contended that his interest was an estate of freehold, so that the estate duty was a charge upon and payable out of the property itself by virtue of the provisions of section 9(1) of the Finance Act, 1894. And in the second place it was contended by the appellants and denied by the respondents that even if the testator's interest in the property was a freehold interest yet the terms of his will were such as to throw the estate duty, leviable in respect of the property, upon his residuary estate in relief of the specific devisees. It will be convenient to consider these two topics separately.

First then, what was the nature of the interest to which the testator was entitled in the property? The arguments in regard to this centred round the covenant in the mortgage that the mortgagors should stand seised of the reversion expectant upon the term of 10,000 years in trust for any purchaser or purchasers of the premises, or to convey or dispose thereof as the bank or any such purchaser or purchasers might at any time direct. This follows the old form of trust of the nominal reversion after the exercise of the mortgagee's power of sale which used formerly to be inserted in a mortgage by subdemise: (see Davidson, Conveyancing Precedents, 2nd. ed (1858), Vol. II, Part 22, p. 822). The modern practice, of course, is that the mortgagor should simply declare that he will stand possessed of the reversion in trust for the mortgagee, and to dispose thereof as he shall direct. As this does not vest the legal but only an equitable estate in the mortgagee it does not render him personally liable to the lessor or grantor for the rent and covenants of the lease or grant: *Walters* v. *Northern Coal Mining Co.* [(1855) 5 De G.M. & G. 629]. The older form, however, as pointed out in the argument, is retained in the precedent in the Irish Forms and Precedents (at p. 421) of a mortgage by demise of lands held in fee farm. The object of the form is obviously to confer a right to the reversion upon a purchaser of the lands from the mortgagee while avoiding any vesting in the mortgagee of the reversion lest it might subject him to personal liability for the rents and covenants of the grant under which the lands are held.

The Lord Chief Justice, from whose decision the present appeal is taken, held that the effect of the covenant in the mortgage was automatically to vest a legal estate in the reversion by virtue of the operation of the Statute of Uses in a purchaser from the Bank under their power fo sale. And as the legal estate in the 10,000 year term was undoubtedly conveyed to Bennett Sergie by the indenture of March 18, 1930, the Lord Chief Justice had no difficulty in holding that this term must be taken to have merged in the inheritance, so that Bennett Sergie was simply entitled at the date of his death to the grantee's interest under the fee farm grant, an interest which would not, of course, pass to his executors as such.

The appellants, who were concerned to contend that the estate duty on the property was payable not out of the property itself but out of the testator's residuary estate, opposed this conclusion with a variety of arguments. In the first place they submitted that the only interest in the property which ever became vested in Bennett Sergie was the leasehold interest actually conveyed to him by his purchase deed, and that he was not entitled to claim any further interest by relying on the covenant in the mortgage. I cannot accept this view. If the provision in the mortgage regarding the reversion is not invalid by reason of any rule of law, I see no reason why a purchaser from the bank should not be entitled to the benefit of it. Quite apart from the provisions of the Real Property Act, 1845, it appears to have always been recognised that a person could take an estate in remainder or an estate by way of use or trust under an indenture inter partes although he was not a party to the deed. It was, however, contended by the appellants that the provision that the mortgagors should stand seised of the reversion in trust for a purchaser was invalid as transgressing the rule against perpetuities. I am unable also to accept this contention. The provision in question in conjunction with the demise to the mortgagee of a long term of years is only a device for creating a satisfactory security over the premises, and for enabling a purchaser from the mortgagee to obtain a right to the whole of the mortgagor's interest in the property which was intended to constitute the security for the loan; in other words the provision is merely ancillary to the mortgagee's power to realise his security by a sale of the mortgaged premises, and is designed to enable that power of sale to be carried out effectively. In *Knightsbridge Estates Trust Ltd.* v. *Byrne* ([1938] Ch. 741; [1939] Ch. 441) it is laid down in broad terms that the rule against perpetuities does not apply to mortgages. Certainly it seems always to have been assumed that the rule does not apply to the mortgagee's power of sale or his other powers for enforcing his security. If this is so it could hardly be held to apply to a power which is merely ancillary to the power of sale, and the only object of which is to enable the mortgagee to realise his security effectively and to confer a satisfactory title upon the purchaser. Until the latter half of the nineteenth century the form of mortgage of leaseholds by subdemise to be found in the standard collections of precedents normally contained a provision regarding the nominal reversion which was to all intents similar to that contained in the mortgage in the present case: (see the observations in Davidson, 4th ed. (1881) Vol. II, Part 2, p. 119). So far as I am aware it was never suggested that such a provision might transgress the rule against perpetuities.

So far then as the provision in the mortgage relating to the nominal reversion is concerned, the main questions to be considered are in regard to the nature and the extent of the interest in the reversion which will be taken by a purchaser from the mortgagee. Is it a legal interest or an equitable interest? Is it a life interest or an absolute interest? This is a pure question of construction. Reading the relevant portion of the mortgage it seems to me quite clear that the parties contemplated that after the exercise by the bank of their power of sale the legal interest in the reversion would still be found to be vested in the mortgagors, and that the purchaser would only have an equitable right to call for a conveyance of this reversion, but that this equitable right would be to call for a conveyance of the whole of the mortgagors' interest in the reversion, and not merely an interest limited to the duration of the purchaser's life. How could the mortgagors, after a sale by the Bank, perform their obligation to convey and dispose of the reversion as the Bank or a purchaser should direct unless they still had some estate or interest in the reversion? And as the obligation to convey and dispose of the reversion as the Bank or a purchaser should direct is executory in its nature, and as the obvious intention is that the Bank or a purchaser should be entitled to call upon the morgagors to convey the whole of their interest in the reversion, this intention can be given effect to without any words of limitation being required, the trust being an executory one. In such circumstances it would be odd to a degree if the alternative trust in favour of a purchaser himself should (as was seriously argued by the appellants) be construed as giving the purchaser only a life interest in the reversion. It is to be remembered that we have not here to construe a settlement but a document executed for a money consideration. In my opinion a court of equity should not be slow to construe it so as to carry out the obvious intention of the parties, and for my part I would be prepared to hold that on the true construction of the document the effect of the clause under discussion was that after a sale by the Bank the mortgagees would still retain the legal estate in the freehold reversion, but that they would hold it in trust for the purchaser so that he would become entitled absolutely to the equitable estate in that reversion.

The Lord Chief Justice, however, took a different view. He held that there was nothing to prevent section 1 of the Irish Statute of Uses, 1634, operating upon the declaration that the mortgagors would stand seised of the reversion in trust for the purchaser, and accordingly he came to the conclusion that by virtue of the Statute of Uses the legal and not merely an equitable estate in the reversion became vested in the purchaser. This view however, if I may respectfully say so, appears to me to be beset with difficulties. In the first place, what becomes of the words 'or to convey or dispose thereof as any such purchaser or purchasers may at any time direct'? Are these words to be treated as in effect adding nothing to the declaration that the mortgagors will stand seised of the reversion in trust for any purchaser or purchasers, and may they accordingly simply be disregarded? Or are they to be disregarded on the principle that if there are two conflicting provisions in a deed the earlier one is to prevail? But even if it is legitimate to accept the view that we must focus our attention solely upon the declaration that the mortgagors shall stand seised of the reversion in trust for any purchaser or purchasers of the premises, and must therefore disregard the following words, grave difficulties still appear to me to remain. No doubt the Statute of Uses executes trusts and confidences as well as uses. But if we are to apply the Statute of Uses in the present instance it is necessary to be clear as to the nature of the transaction and as to the operation of the statute upon it. The mortgagers do not purport to convey the reversion of all; they merely covenant that they will stand seised of it in trust for the purchaser or purchasers. The declaration of the use in favour of the purchaser or purchasers is accordingly one (to use the old phrase) operating without transmutation of possession. In cases of this type where the seisin was unchanged no use could be created without consideration: (Norton on Deeds, 2nd ed. p. 224). The consideration might take the form either of money or money's worth or of blood or marriage. In the latter case the declaration of the use was termed simply a covenant to stand seised, but where the consideration was money or money's worth, it was styled a bargain and sale. In the present case the consideration for the declaration of trust by the mortgagors was obviously money or money's worth, and accordingly this declaration of trust is a bargain and sale and falls to be treated as such. The uses raised by a bargain and sale were not necessarily in favour only of the person himself who paid the consideration; they might be to himself with remainder to other persons, or to other persons alone by his direction: (Sanders on Uses, 5th ed. Vol. II, p. 58: Challis, Real Property, 3rd ed. p. 421 n.).

As is well known, the English Statute of Uses was followed in the same year by the Statute of Inrolments which provided that no lands should pass from one to another whereby an estate of inheritance or freehold should take effect in any person or any use thereof to be made by reason only of any bargain or sale thereof except the said bargain and sale be made by writing indented sealed and inrolled within six months. No separate Statute of Inrolments was enacted in Ireland, but section 17 of the Irish Statute of Uses reproduced in terms these provisions of the English Statute of Inrolments so that after the passing of the Irish statute the legal position in regard to a bargain and sale of freehold lands was the same in Ireland as in England. A mere covenant for valuable consideration that a person should stand seised to the use of another clearly amounted to a bargain and sale within the Statute of Inrolments: (Sanders on Uses, 5th ed. Vol. 11, p. 96; *Bedell's case* [(1608) 7 Co. Rep. 40 (*a*),); *Goodtitle and Pattoe* [(1731) Fitz.-G. 299, 301, 40 (*b*)] (per Raymond L.C.J.). As is said in Bacon's Abridgment (tit. Bargain and Sale (*c*)) 7th ed. Vol. 1, p. 686: 'It is not necessary to use the words bargain and sale, but any words equivalent are sufficient, and whatever words upon valuable consideration would have raised an use of any lands etc. at common law, the same amount to a bargain and sale within this Act (sc. 27 Hen. VIII c. 16); as if a man by deed etc. for a valuable consideration covenants to stand seised to the use of another etc.' It was this necessity of enrolling covenants for valuable consideration to stand seised of freeholds that led to the institution of the system of conveyancing by lease and release which remained for over two hundred years the ordinary method of conveying freehold lands in England. The matter is succintly put in Jenks' Modern Land Law at p. 304.: 'To have allowed a covenant made in consideration of money or valuable consideration to escape the Statute of Inrolments would have been to connive at the grossest evasion of the intention of Parliament. And accordingly covenants to stand seised in consideration of value have always been treated as Bargains and Sales within the Statute.'

If then the covenant in the mortgage is to be regarded as falling within the operation of section 1 of the Irish Statute of Uses it would be subject also to the provisions of section 17 of the Statute and the mortgage deed would require enrolment, unless indeed it were exempted from the necessity of enrolment by section 18 to which I shall advert presently. No evidence was adduced to show that the mortgage was enrolled within six months, as required by section 17. It is, of course, highly improbable that it would ever have occurred to anyone to enrol such a deed, but for the sake of certainty I have caused enquiry to be made in the offices of the court, and I have been informed that in fact the mortgage never was enrolled there.

By a proviso contained in the English Statute of Inrolments it was enacted that lands in cities boroughs or towns corporate that had the privilege of enrolments were not within the Act. Though the intention of the statute doubtless was to have them excepted from enrolments in the courts at Westminster only, yet the proviso was so worded as to exempt them from any enrolment at all: (Bacon's Abridgment (Tit. Bargain and Sales E.2) 7th ed. vol. I, p. 600 ; *Chibborne's* case [(1564) Dyer

220(a)]; *Darby* v. *Boice* [(1607) Yelv. 123)]. Section 18 of the Irish Statute of Uses followed exactly the wording of this proviso in the English Statute of Inrolments, and provided 'that this act nor anything therein contained extend to any lands within any city borough or town corporate wherein the mayors recorders chamberlaines bayliffs or other officers have authority or have lawfully used to inroll any evidences deeds or other writings within their precincts or limits.' The effect of this introduction at the end of the Irish Statute of Uses of the proviso to the English Statute of Inrolments would prima facie appear to have the effect of excluding lands in cities boroughs and towns having the privilege of enrolment from the operation of the Irish Statute of Uses altogether, though presumably the intention of the proviso merely was to exclude them from the operation of section 17 of the Irish Statute requiring bargains and sales of freehold lands to be enrolled within six months. However this may be, the question whether Belfast was, at the time of the passing of the Irish Statute of Uses, a town in which the municipal officers had authority or had lawfully used to enroll any evidences deeds or other writings, is of course a question of fact. But no evidence in regard to this question was placed before the court. As is well known Belfast obtained its first charter of incorporation in 1613, and this was the charter in force at the time of the passing of the Irish Statute of Uses in 1634. In order to discover whether the officers of the borough had been granted authority to enroll deeds one naturally turns to the terms of the charter. I have gone carefully through the charter and I cannot find anything in it which I could construe as conferring such authority. And an examination of the earlier entries in the Town Book of Belfast (Mr. R. M. Young's edition) hardly suggests to me that it could be said in 1634 that these officers had up to then used to enrol evidences deeds or other writings. At any rate there is no evidence before the court to show that Belfast fell in 1634 within the category of cities boroughs and towns exempted from the enrolment provisions of the Irish Statute of Uses, and I assume accordingly that the declaration of trust contained in the mortgage ought to have been enrolled under the provisions of section 17 of the Irish Statute of Uses if the statute were to operate upon it.

What then is the position in regard to a transaction constituting a bargain and sale within the meaning of the statute which is not enrolled within the six months? Though it does not pass the legal estate under the statute it is not a nullity. Equity would treat it as an agreement to convey and would protect the bargainee accordingly: (Cruise's Digest, 4th ed. (1835) vol. IV, p. 251 ; *Mestaer* v. *Gillespie* [(1805) 11 Ves. 622, 625 per Lord Eldon). In other words the bargainee would be in substantially the same position as he was before the passing of the statute. Before the Statute of Uses the Court of Chancery, upon a bargain and sale for valuable consideration, would have decreed an estate in fee simple in the bargainee even though his heirs had not been mentioned: (Sanders on Uses, 5th ed. vol. I, p. 123 ; *Corbet's* case [(1600) 1 Co. Rep. 77(b)] *Shelley's* case [(1581) 1 Co. Rep. 88(b) 100(b)]. I know of no reason why a different view should now be taken by the courts in a case in which the statute fails to operate by reason of the absence of enrolment. On the other hand it appears to be the better view that a bargain and sale operating under the Statute, if made without words of limitation, will only give the bargainee a life estate at law: (Sanders on Uses, loc. cit.; Williams on Real Property, 21st ed. p. 203(n)).

My view accordingly is that even if we are only to have regard to so much of the covenant in the mortgage as provides that the mortgagors shall stand seised of the reversion expectant upon the term of 10,000 years in trust for any purchaser or purchasers of the premises, the effect of this provision is not to vest the legal estate in the reversion in the purchaser, but to confer on him an equitable estate in fee. I appreciate that the conveyance of March 18, 1930, only purported to convey to Bennett Sergie the term of 10,000 years, and that perhaps if he had so desired he might have entered into some arrangement or have taken some step to manifest an intention that he was merely taking an assignment of the term itself and was not taking any estate or interest in the reversion. But in the absence of some evidence of such non-acceptance of the rights in regard to the reversion to which, under the terms of the covenant in the mortgage he was entitled as the purchaser of the premises, I am of opinion that he should not be held to have renounced those rights. There does not appear to me to be any reason why he should not have accepted the interest in the reversion to which a purchaser was entitled under the terms of the covenant. So long as the legal estate in the reversion was not vested in him he would not become personally liable to the grantor for the rent and the grantees' covenants under the grant.

In my view, therefore, upon the execution of the conveyance of March 18, 1930, Bennett Sergie became entitled (a) to a legal estate in the term of 10,000 years and (b) subject to that term of 10,000 years to an equitable estate in the grantees' interest under the fee farm grant. I do not think that this is a case where the doctrine of merger could be invoked, for in no instance can the legal estate merge in the equitable ownership (Mayhew on Merger pp. 7 and 21). In such circumstances, however, since the beneficial interest in the term and the beneficial interest in the reversion had become vested in the same person, the term according to the old authorities would have been regarded as attendant upon the inheritance. If the owner of the term and the reversion had died intestate, his whole interest in the property would have passed to his heir at law and not to his personal representatives. Or if he had made a will devising his realty to one person and bequeathing his personalty to another, it would have passed to the devisee of the realty: (Cruise's Digest. 4th ed. (1835) vol. 1, Tit. XII Trust Ch. 111 ss. 30, 31). 'The general rule is, that where the same person has the inheritance and the term in himself, although he has in one the equitable interest, and in the other the legal interest, there the inheritance by implication draws to itself the term, and makes that attendant upon it.' (Story, Equity Jurisprudence, 10th ed., vol. II, pp. 196–197). It matters not that the person concerned has a legal interest in the term but only an equitable interest in the freehold reversion. 'A term may become attendant upon the inheritance, without any express declaration for that purpose, either where the legal interest in the term is vested in the trustee and the legal freehold in the owner of the inheritance, or where the owner is beneficially or equitably entitled to the inheritance and is legally possessed of the term, or where the legal estate, both of the term and of the inheritance, is vested in trustees.' (Sanders on Uses, 5th ed. vol. I, p. 318). As instances where the legal estate in the term was held to be attendant on an equitable estate in the freehold reversion I would refer to *Dowse* v. *Percival* [(1682) Vern 104]; *Cooke* v. *Cooke* [(1740) 2 Atk. 67]; *Capel* v. *Girdler* [(1804) 9 Ves. 509].

I am accordingly of opinion that whatever in the circumstances may have been the effect of the Satisfied Terms Act, 1845, Bennett Sergie's interest in Bennett Buildings at the time of his death in 1947 was an interest which fell to be treated as real estate. It was therefore an interest which did not pass to his executors as such, and so the estate duty on the property would, by reason of the provisions of section 9 (1) of the Finance Act, 1894, be a charge upon the property itself, unless the burden of the duty is shifted by the terms of Bennett Sergie's will.

I turn now to the second question which was argued before us, namely, whether (on the assumption of course that Bennett Sergie's interest in Bennett Buildings was an interest which did not pass to his executors as such) the terms of his will were such as to throw the burden of the estate duty payable in respect of Bennett Buildings upon his residuary estate in relief of the specific devisees of that property.

The appellants base their argument upon the terms of the residuary clause in Bennett Sergie's will, which directs his trustees to convert his residuary real and personal estate into money, and to pay out of the mixed fund thereby created 'my debts funeral and testamentary expenses and death duties and all legacies under this my will or any codicil hereto in case I shall not have sufficient ready cash to pay same.' The appellants contend that this phrase 'my death duties' is effectual to direct the payment of the estate duty in respect of Bennett Buildings out of the testator's residuary estate. In the judgment appealed from it has been held that on consideration of the whole of the will this phrase 'my death duties' must be construed as referring only to such part of the estate duty as executors are liable to pay in the absence of any specific direction, namely the duty in respect of that portion of the testator's property which in the terms of the Finance Act, 1894, passes to his executors as such.

This is, of course, a question of the construction of the will. We were referred to a considerable number of authorities, but as in all questions of construction, the decision in each case must depend upon the terms of the particular will under consideration, and after reading all the reported decisions bearing on this point which I have been able to trace I do not find that any of them lays down a principle which is clearly decisive of the present case.

One or two principles, however, appear to emerge from the decisions. In *In re Pimm* ([1904] 2 Ch. 345) Farwell J. held that the phrase, 'my duties' in such a connection was prima facie one of wide generality. So far as I am aware this view has never been dissented from, and the same view appears to be taken by Lord Greene M.R. when delivering the judgment of the Court of Appeal in *In re Joel* ([1943] Ch. 311, 323). Accordingly, in the absence of anything in Bennett Sergie's will to show a contrary intention, the phrase 'my death duties' would be wide enough to cover the portion of his estate duty which is attributable to Bennett Buildings. Again while undoubtedly the phrase 'my testamentary expenses' when used by a testator is sufficient to cover the estate duty in respect of such part of his estate as passes to his executors as such, that is to say his free personalty, yet on the other hand it is well established that estate duty payable in respect of realty is not a testamentary expense (*In re Sharman* [1901] 2 Ch. 280). And so a direction to pay 'testamentary expenses including death duties' would not be construed to include duties upon property not passing to the executors as such, as for example the estate duty on real estate (*Re Massey* [1921] 90 L.J. Ch. 40). The appellants accordingly argue that the words 'and death duties' in Bennett Sergie's will following as they do the words 'my debts funeral and testamentary expenses' must be regarded as referring to something more than what would be included in 'testamentary expenses,' otherwise these words 'and death duties' would be otiose. Another point which, perhaps, should not be left out of consideration is the principle for which there is the authority of the English Court of Appeal in *In re Owers* ([1941] Ch. 17) that inasmuch as a general direction to pay legacies out of a mixed fund or residue charges them rateably on the portion attributable to realty and personalty, it follows that so far as the legacies are payable out of the portion attributable to realty they must bear their own estate duty, notwithstanding a direction to pay 'testamentary expenses' out of the mixed fund. In the present case it appears from the Inland Revenue affidavit that the testator was possessed of real estate of very considerable value so that, if the decision under appeal stands, the pecuniary legatees, whose legacies the testator had expressly declared to be free of legacy duty, will presumably have to bear quite an appreciable burden of estate duty.

The respondents in this part of the case relied on such authorities as *In re Massey*[(1921) 90 L.J. Ch. 40] and *In re Borough* ([1938] 1 All E.R. 375) in which it was held that where under a will some legacies had been given expressly free of duty and others were not expressed to be free of duty, a general direction to pay death duties out of residue did not extend to the legacy duty on the legacies not given free of duty.

To hold otherwise would have been inconsistent with the discrimination which the testator had obviously been making between the different legatees. So in *In re King* ([1942] Ch. 413) the Court of Appeal held that in a will where some devises were expressed to be free of duties and others were not, a general direction to pay out of residue 'all duties payable in respect of my estate' did not relieve the latter class of devises from their proportion of estate duty. And this decision was followed by Uthwatt J. in *In re Palmer* ([1946] Ch. 49). I respectfully accept these decisions but I am not satisfied that they apply to the will under consideration in the present case. The argument of the respondents is based entirely on the fact that in Bennett Sergie's will some of the legacies are expressed to be free of legacy duty and others are not. It may well be that it would be inconsistent with this discrimination to hold that the phrase 'my death duties' was wide enough to include legacy duty. But it does not appear to follow that there would be any inconsistency in holding it wide enough to cover the estate duty on real propery, a duty which it would normally include in the absence of any indication in the will to the contrary. Estate duty and legacy duty are two quite different types of duty. Estate duty, which was first introduced by the Finance Act, 1894, becomes payable on a person's death upon the whole of his property, whatever may be the dispositions of it made by his will, or even if he makes no disposition of it at all and dies intestate. Legacy duty, on the other hand, was leviable under much earlier Acts, and the rates at which it was payable varied over a wide range according to the relationship of the beneficiary to the deceased. In one case indeed, that of a legacy for charitable purposes in Ireland, no legacy duty was payable at all by virtue of the provisions of 5 & 6 Vict. c. 82, s. 38. I think that the most natural conclusion on reading Bennett Sergie's will is that the expression 'my death duties' is wide enough to cover all the duties payable merely in consequence of his death, whatever his testamentary dispositions may be, even though by reason of the discrimination shown in other parts of the will it may not be wide enough to cover a duty not payable merely in consequence of his death but leviable because of some particular disposition of his will. This view is, to my mind, reinforced by the consideration urged by the appellants that if the phrase 'and death duties' is construed as meaning only the estate duty payable in respect of personalty it adds nothing to the preceding phrase 'my testamentary expenses'. No canon of construction is more firmly established than that in construing a will we must, if possible, give a meaning to every word used: see the authorities collected in the *English and Empire Digest* vol. 44, pp. 574–575. 'Now I take it to be one rule in the construction of a will, that you are not to impute to a testator, unless the context requires it, that he uses additional words except for some additional purpose; that you are not to suppose he uses additional words for no purpose': *Oddie* v. *Woodford* [(1825) 3 My. & Cr. 584 per Lord Eldon. If we are to give the words 'and death duties' in Bennett Sergie's will any meaning at all additional to that conveyed by the preceding words 'testamentary expenses' the words must be held to be wide enough to cover the duty at issue in this appeal. It is to be noted that the very similar clause which was before the Court in the case of *In re Owers* ([1941] Ch. 17) if the respondents' contention in the present case were held to be correct should be wholly overlooked. The result would be that legacies which the testator had expressly designed to be free of legacy duty would apparently be subject to a substantial burden of estate duty. This would be an odd result. It is, of course, a possible result, as is indeed shown by *In re Owers*. But where one possible construction of a clause in a will leads to an odd result, while another possible construction does not, this I think is some slight indication in favour of the latter construction.

On the whole, therefore, with the natural hesitation which I feel in differing from the view taken by the Lord Chief Justice on a very arguable point of construction, I am of opinion that under the terms of Bennett Sergie's will the estate duty on the property known as Bennett Buildings is payable out of his residuary estate.

Curran J.:

I agree with the conclusion arrived at in each of the judgments just read as to the true construction of the will of Bennett Sergie deceased.

If there is a difficulty in construing the will it appears to me to be limited to the question whether the expression 'death duties' in the will includes 'legacy duty,' having regard to the fact that certain legacies in the will were expressly given free of such duty and others were not.

We are concerned in the present case with 'estate duty' which is undoubtedly covered by the term 'death duties'. I see no difficulty, accordingly, in giving effect to the testator's express provision that the executors are to pay his 'death duties' by finding that the executors must pay the estate duty payable inter alia in respect of Bennett Buildings.

Notes and Questions
1. Why did the demise for 10,000 years in the *Sergie* case contain such a covenant to stand seised? See *Irish Land Law*, paras. 3.027–30.
2. Does there remain any advantage nowadays in using one of the older forms of conveyance instead of the modern deed of grant, in any circumstances? See *Irish Conveyancing Law*, para. 15.02. See also on the older forms of conveyance, *Bayley* v. *Conyngham*, p. 311, *post*.
3. See also on the Statute of Uses, *Att. Gen.* v. *Cummins*, p. 131, *post*, *Bank of Ireland and Others* v. *Domvile*, p. 178, *post*.

II. DOCTRINE OF NOTICE
CONVEYANCING ACT, 1882

3. – (1) A purchaser shall not be prejudicially affected by notice of any instrument, fact, or thing unless –

  (i) It is within his own knowledge, or would have come to his knowledge if such inquiries and inspections had been made as ought reasonably to have been made by him; or

  (ii) In the same transaction with respect to which a question of notice to the purchaser arises, it has come to the knowledge of his counsel, as such, or of his solicitor, or other agent, as such, if such inquiries and inspections had been made as ought reasonably to have been made by the solicitor or other agent.

(2) This section shall not exempt a purchaser from any liability under, or any obligation to perform or observe, any covenant, condition, provision, or restriction contained in any instrument under which his title is derived, mediately or immediately; and such liability or obligation may be enforced in the same manner and to the same extent as if this section had not been enacted.

(3) A purchaser shall not by reason of anything in this section be affected by notice in any case where he would not have been so affected if this section had not been enacted.

(4) This section applies to purchases made either before or after the commencement of this Act. . . . (remainder repealed by the Statute Law Revision Act, 1898).

ALLIED IRISH BANKS LTD. V. GLYNN
[1973] I.R. 188 (High Court)

The first defendant was the registered owner of freehold registered land and he conveyed the land in fee simple to his son, the second defendant, subject to the right of the first defendant to reside in a house on the land. In June, 1963, the second defendant was registered as full owner of the land subject to the right of residence which was entered as a burden on the folio. In December, 1964, the second defendant deposited the land certificate with the plaintiffs as security for money to be advanced to him by the plaintiffs. In March, 1968, the Circuit Court made an order setting aside the conveyance in an action instituted by the first defendant against the second defendant in June, 1967. The first defendant was registered again as full owner of the land in July, 1968, and the burden was cancelled. The plaintiffs did not receive notice of the Circuit Court proceedings. The plaintiffs brought an action against the defendants in the High Court and claimed a declaration that moneys advanced by them to the second defendant were well charged on the interests of the defendants in the registered land.

Kenny J.:

On the 3rd November, 1960, the first defendant was registered as full owner of the lands comprised in Folio 33488 of the register of freeholders for County Roscommon. On the 9th April, 1963, he transferred the lands to his son Michael, the second defendant, subject to his right to reside in the dwellinghouse on the lands to be suitably supported and maintained there; but there was no covenant in connection with this. On the 17th June, 1963, the second defendant was registered as full owner and the right of the first defendant to reside in the dwellinghouse and to be supported and maintained was entered as a burden on the folio.

In October, 1964, the second defendant applied to the plaintiffs for an advance to be secured by a deposit of the land certificate relating to the folio. The land certificate was issued by the Land Registry to the second defendant's solicitor on the 19th November, 1964. On the 5th December, 1964, the second defendant deposited the land certificate with the plaintiffs as security for advances to be made to him; he now owes £893 for principal to the plaintiffs.

In June, 1967, the first defendant issued a civil bill in the Circuit Court against the second defendant claiming to have the deed of transfer of the 9th April, 1963, set aside because when the first defendant signed it he was entirely under the influence of the second defendant and had no independent advice, and because it was obtained by fraud and undue influence. The order made by the Court on the 6th March, 1968, recited that the second defendant's solicitor had entered an appearance and defence in that action but that he had not received any instructions for the hearing; and the order declared that the transfer deed was void, that the second defendant was to hand it up to the first defendant for the purpose of being cancelled (though it is not easy to understand how he could do this when it had been lodged in the Land Registry) and 'that the land registry (*sic*) be rectified by deletion of the registration of the defendant as full owner on the said Folio 33488 of the Register of County Roscommon and the entry of the plaintiff as full owner thereof on the said Register.' No enquiry seems to have been made by the Circuit Court about the custody of the land certificate although the folio showed that it had been issued, and the plaintiffs in this action had no notice of the proceedings in the Circuit Court and did not know anything about them until the Land Registry requested them to lodge the land certificate so that the first defendant could be registered as owner. The plaintiffs refused to do this but, despite this, the first defendant was registered as full owner on the 3rd July, 1968, and the burden in his favour was deleted. I think that a court should not order that a folio in the Land Registry should be rectified by deleting the name of one person as full owner and substituting someone else without requiring the land certificate to be produced when the folio shows that it has been issued. Such an order offends against elementary principle.

The plaintiffs have now sued the defendants for a declaration that they are entitled to a charge on the lands arising out of the deposit of the land certificate with them, and for a sale of the lands. At the time when the deposit was made, the Registration of Title (Ireland) Act, 1891, was in force and s. 81, sub-s. 5, of that Act provided that, subject to any registered rights, the deposit of a land certificate or certificate of charge should, for the purpose of creating a lien on the land or charge to which the certificate related, have the same effect as the deposit of the title deeds of land or of a charge thereon had theretofore: see now s. 105 of the Registration of Title Act, 1964.

The deposit, as security, of documents of title to land which is not registered gives the person with whom it is made an equitable estate in the lands until the money secured by it is repaid: the remedy for securing payment is to apply to the court for a declaration that the deposit has given a charge on the lands. The right created by the deposit is not limited to keeping the deeds until the money has been paid but gives an equitable estate in the lands. The plaintiffs' contention is that they took the deposit without notice of the first defendant's claim and that, although they got an equitable interest only, it ranks before the first defendant's equity. The terms 'equity' and 'equitable state' and 'equitable interest' have been used in different senses in Acts of Parliament, in decided cases and in text books; the difference between them is not capable of complete definition. The main difference is, I think, that 'an equity' does not create or give any estate in the land: it is a right against persons and is enforceable against those who were parties to the transaction which created it.

In *National Provincial Bank Ltd.* v. *Ainsworth* ([1965] A.C. 1175) Lord Upjohn emphasised that 'an equity' does not create an estate or right in land. At pp. 1237–8 of the report he said: 'So in principle, in my opinion, to create a right over the land of another that right must in contemplation of law be such that it creates a legal or equitable estate or interest in that land and notice of something though relating to land which falls short of an estate or interest is insufficient. There are no doubt many cases where judges have said the purchaser "takes subject to all equities" but they meant "equitable interests". . . . An equity to which a subsequent purchaser is subject must create an interest in the land.'

When Parliament provided in s. 29, sub-s. 3, of the Act of 1891 that registration of a person as owner could be made subject to any rights or equities arising from the interest vested in him being deemed to be a graft upon his previous interest in the land, it meant that estates or interests existing at the time of registration were enforceable against the registered owner. The rights saved by the note as to equities in the Act of 1891 were equitable estates or interests and not equities. Parliament, like judges, sometimes uses imprecise language.

But what was the first defendant's interest in the lands when the deposit with the plaintiffs was made? It cannot be challenged accurately as having been 'an equity' only for, if the deed was procured by fraud or undue influence, the first defendant would acquire an estate in the lands when he succeeded in setting it aside. What he had was a *chose in action* which could become an estate if he brought proceedings and if they were successful. Lord Upjohn was dealing with the equity of a deserted wife to retain possession against a mortgagee from her husband who gave the security after he had left her: her claim could never become an estate and so the passage I have quoted does not assist the plaintiffs.

The plaintiffs' main argument is that they took the deposit in good faith without notice of the first defendant's claim and so have a valid security against both defendants; in my view that submission is correct. They had no notice of the facts giving rise to the claim to set the deed aside and there is persuasive authority that a purchaser or mortgagee of an equitable interest who takes in good faith without notice of a claim or the facts giving rise to it is not bound by it. Lord Westbury said in *Phillips* v. *Phillips* [(1861) 4 De G.F. & J. 208] that this was the law and Mr. Justice Fry expressed the same view in *Bainbrigge* v. *Browne* [(1881) 18 Ch. D. 188].

The land certificate deposited with the plaintiffs showed them that the deed of 1963 was a transfer between father and son because of the similarity of the surnames and the addresses, and the burden entered was appropriate for such a transaction. But knowledge that the transfer was between father and son was not notice that it had been procured by fraud or undue influence and there was nothing to suggest that it would be set aside subsequently.

The plaintiffs argued that, if their main contention failed, they were entitled to a charge on the lands against the first defendant, the registered owner, because their interest, though later in time, was superior in equity to his and should be preferred. Mr. Matheson relied on the much-discussed decision of the Irish Court of Appeal (*In re Ffrench's Estate* [(1887) 21 L.R. Ir. 283]) to support this, but, as the plaintiffs succeed on their main contention, it is not necessary to deal with this difficult and controversial problem on which the Irish Court of Appeal have expressed one view and the House of Lords another.

The next issue is whether the plaintiffs' interest is subject to any claim of the first defendant to reside on the lands and to be suported and maintained there. When the plaintiffs took the deposit of the land certificate, they got notice that these rights existed. If the first defendant had not brought the proceedings in the Circuit Court, his rights under the deed of 1963 would rank before those of the plaintiffs. The plaintiffs submitted that the first defendant cannot approbate and reprobate and that, as he brought successful proceedings to have the deed of 1963 set aside, he cannot now invoke the rights which it created. As the deed has been declared void, the rights which it created do not now exist. They have been deleted from the folio and the first defendant cannot revive them as an answer to the plaintiffs' claim. This has the unintended consequence that the plaintiffs' security has been improved in value by what the first defendant did but this is the result of his action, not of theirs.

Therefore, there will be a declaration that the sum secured by the equitable mortgage by deposit of the land certificate relating to the lands comprised in the folio is well charged on the interest of the first and second defendants in the lands.

Note

As regards *Re Ffrench's Estate* and the distinction between equitable interests and mere equities, see *Irish Land Law*, para. 3.077 *et seq*.

NORTHERN BANK LTD. V. HENRY
[1981] I.R. 1 (Supreme Court)

The second and the first defendants were husband and wife. They had separated but the defendant's wife continued to reside in the family home with the children of the marriage. Prior to the separation the defendant husband had purchased a leasehold interest in the house with the wife's money, but the assignment of that interest was made to the husband alone. Negotiations took place between the husband and the wife about the assurance of the leasehold interest to the wife but nothing had been determined when, on the 22nd January, 1974, the wife instituted in the High Court an action against the husband in which she claimed a declaration that she was entitled in equity to the leasehold interest in the house and that the husband held that interest in trust for her. On the same day the husband mortgaged the house to the plaintiff bank by sub-demise to secure the repayment of moneys owed by the husband to the plaintiffs. Prior to the execution of the mortgage by the husband the plaintiffs, apart from making a search in the Registry of Deeds, made no investigation whatever of the husband's title to the house. On the 14th February, 1975, the High Court declared that the husband held the leasehold interest in trust for the wife and ordered the husband to assign that interest to her.

Subsequently, the plaintiff's claimed in the High Court a declaration that their estate in the property under the husband's mortgage was superior to the interests of the husband and the wife and that the mortgage was well charged on that property; the plaintiffs also claimed ancillary relief. The defendant wife contended that her interest in the house prevailed against the claim of the plaintiffs since at the date of the mortgage the plaintiffs had constructive notice of her claim on the house. McWilliam J. dismissed the plaintiffs' claim and they appealed to the Supreme Court.

Henchy J.:

The contest in this case is between the plaintiff bank and the wife of one of its customers. The wife is the first defendant. The husband, who was the customer, is the second defendant; in 1969 he granted a legal mortgage of the family home to the third defendant.

In 1974 the husband's account with the plaintiff bank was heavily overdrawn and his finances were in disarray generally. It was a source of urgent worry to the plaintiffs, who badly needed a collateral security for their debt. The plaintiffs needed that security quickly, for there were other creditors of the husband and cheques drawn by him in favour of some of those creditors had been dishonoured by the plaintiffs. The only substantial item of property that he appeared to have was the family home, and it was mortgaged to the third defendant. However, as a security it was better than nothing in the eyes of the plaintiffs; they required the husband to give a second mortgage on it and he agreed to do so.

The plaintiffs doubtless felt that they had to carry through the transaction swiftly. Advised by their legal department in Belfast, the plaintiffs took up the documents of title and saw the investigation of title that had been carried out when the mortgage to the third defendant was executed in 1969; the plaintiffs made no further investigation of the title, other than to get a Dublin firm of solicitors to have a negative search carried out in the Registry of Deeds. Having thereby established that no dealing with the property had been registered since 1969, the plaintiffs did not investigate the title further, although they knew that the property was the family home and that the husband had ceased to use it as his address in his correspondence with them. A competent solicitor, acting for a normal purchaser of the property, would not have been content to take the title on such a cursory investigation. But all the plaintiffs wanted was a second mortgage, and the advisers probably felt that if they took time to investigate the title fully they might lose priority to another creditor. For that reason I do not wish to criticise them for telescoping the investigation in the interests of business expediency. So, with the title thus looked at summarily, the plaintiffs got the second mortgage executed.

As was later proved, the husband had no title whatsoever to the property. If the plaintiffs had pursued the matter by means of appropriate requisitions on title, they would have discovered not only that it was the wife who was in occupation of the house but that she was in the process of formulating against the husband a claim that she was beneficially entitled to it. The High Court has made a declaration to that effect and that decision stands unchallenged. What the plaintiffs seek primarily to establish in these proceedings is that, as purchasers for value without notice of the wife's title, they should have priority over her.

Section 3, sub-s. 1 of the Conveyancing Act, 1882, deprives the plaintiffs of that priority if the wife's entitlement 'would have come to [*the plaintiffs*' knowledge if such inquiries and inspections had been made as ought reasonably to have been made. . . .' Counsel for the wife argues that the plaintiffs ought reasonably to have inquired as to who was in occupation and as to whether there was any litigation threatened or pending affecting the property and that, if they had done so, they would have learned of the wife's claim. Accordingly, the argument goes, the plaintiffs should not be allowed to dislodge the wife from the property (which she admittedly owned at the time the plaintiffs got the second mortgage of it) because their abstention from making the suggested inquiries fixed them with constructive notice of the wife's claim. The answer depends on the scope or meaning that should be given to the expression 'such inquiries and inspections . . . as ought reasonably to have been made' in s. 3, sub.-s 1, of the Act of 1882.

In my judgment, the test of what inquiries and inspections ought reasonably to have been made by the plaintiffs is an objective test which depends not on what the particular purchaser thought proper to do in the particular circumstances but on what a purchaser of the particular property ought reasonably to have done in order to acquire title to it. The words 'purchaser' and 'purchase' in this context have the meanings ascribed to them by s. 1 of the Act of 1882 and thus include 'mortgagee' and 'mortgage'. In a particular case a purchaser, looking only at his own interest, may justifiably and reasonably consider that in the circumstances some of the normal inquiries and inspections may or should be dispensed with. The special circumstances, thus narrowly viewed, may justify the shortcut taken, or the purchaser may consider that they do so. In either event, such a purchaser is not the purchaser envisaged by s. 3, sub-s. 1, of the Act of 1882. That provision, because it is laying down the circumstances in which a purchaser is not to be prejudicially affected by notice of any instrument, fact or thing, is setting as a standard of conduct that which is to be expected from a reasonable purchaser. Reasonableness in this context must be judged by reference to what should be done to acquire the estate or interest being purchased, rather than by the motive for or the purpose of the particular purchaser.

A purchaser cannot be held to be empowered to set his own standard of reasonableness for the purpose of the sub-section. He must expect to be judged by what an ordinary purchaser, advised by a competent lawyer, would reasonably inquire about or inspect for the purpose of getting a good title. If his personal preference, or the exigencies of the situation, impel him to lower the level of investigation of title below that standard, he is entitled to do so; but, if he does so, he cannot claim the immunity which s. 3, sub-s. 1, reserves for a reasonable purchaser. A reasonable purchaser is one who not only consults his own needs or preferences but also has regard to whether the purchase may affect, prejudicially and unfairly, the rights of third parties in the property. In particular, a reasonable purchaser would be expected to make such inquiries and inspections as would normally disclose whether the purchase will trench, fraudulently or unconsciously, on the rights of such third parties in the property.

In this case, the plaintiffs made no inquiry as to who was in occupation of the property. I consider that a reasonable purchaser would have done so. The minimum requirement for the proper investigation of a title is to see that a purchaser will either get vacant possession on completion or, if the contract or the needs of the purchaser do not so permit or require, get evidence of any estate or interest that will stand between him and vacant possession. Considering the many ways, both at common law and under statute, in which a person in occupation may have an estate or interest adverse to that of the vendor, and which would not appear on an investigation of the vendor's paper title, I consider that the plaintiffs, as purchasers, ought reasonably to have investigated this aspect of the title. Had the plaintiffs done so, the fact of the wife's possession of the proeprty would have come to light, as well as her well-founded claim to the beneficial ownership of it.

Nor did the plaintiffs make any inquiry as to whether any litigation was threatened or pending in respect of the property. I consider that this also was an inquiry which a purchaser ought reasonably to have made. The plaintiffs knew that this was a 'purchase' from the husband of the family home. Even if it had not been a family home, it was foolhardly for a purchaser not to inquire about pending or threatened litigation, particularly litigation stemming from statutory notices served under statutes such as the Housing Acts or the Planning Acts, which might fatally flaw the title. This property was known to the plaintiffs to be the family home. Notwithstanding that the purchase took place before the passing of the Family Home Protection Act 1976 (which makes a transaction of this kind void for want of the prior written consent of the wife), the plaintiffs, as purchasers, ought reasonably to have adverted to the fact that there were decisions showing that a wife who has made payments towards the acquisition of the home, or towards the payment of the mortgage instalments on it, acquired a corresponding share in the beneficial ownership. As a matter of ordinary care, therefore, an inquiry as to threatened or pending claims was called for. In fact there was such an impending claim by the wife. By not inquiring about its existence the plaintiffs became an unwitting party to an unconscionable, if not an actual fraudulent, effort by the husband to mortgage the family home behind his wife's back at a time when he had no beneficial title to it. The plaintiffs, by not making the normal inquiry as to threated or impending litigation affecting the property (indeed, by making no requisitions on title whatsoever), facilitated the husband in nefariously concealing his wife's well-founded claim to the ownership of the property. Because of that, the plaintiffs cannot be said to have shown the care to be expected from a reasonable purchaser. It must be held, therefore, that knowledge of the wife's claim would have been acquired by the plaintiffs if they had made the inquiries that ought reasonably to have been made.

The interpretation given in this judgment to s. 3, sub-s. 1, of the Act of 1882 does not amount to the imposition of any novel or unfair duty of investigation of title on purchasers. Well before the enactment of the Act of 1882, which aimed at setting statutory bounds to the existing doctrine of constructive notice, the Chancery judges had evolved this same test for determining whether a purchaser or mortgagee should have constructive notice attributed to him. Sir Edward Sugden (later Lord St. Leonards), in his Law of Vendors and Purchasers (14th ed. 1862), summed up the pre-1882 approach of the Chancery judges to the question of constructive notice as follows, at p. 755:

> 'The question upon constructive notice is not whether the purchaser had the means of obtaining, and might, by prudent caution, have obtained the knowledge in question, but whether the not obtaining it was an act of gross or culpable negligence.'

Nineteenth century judges were prone to stigmatising actionable negligence as 'gross' or 'culpable.' Indeed, Rolfe B. at pp. 115–6 of the report of *Wilson* v. *Brett* (1843) 11 M. & W. 113, said that he 'could see no difference between *negligence* and *gross* negligence – that it was the same thing, with the addition of a vitupera-tive epithet:' this incisive view was approved by Willes J. in *Grill* v. *General Iron Screw Collier Co.* (1866) L.R.1 C.P. 600. When, therefore, the pre-1882 Chancery judges applied the test of negligence to determine whether a purchaser should be fixed with constructive notice, they were doing no more than asking whether the purchaser's lack of knowledge was consistent with the conduct to be expected from a reasonable man in the circumstances.

Section 3, sub-s. 1, of the Act of 1882, in providing that a purchaser is not to be prejudicially affected by notice of any instrument, fact, or thing unless 'it is within his own knowledge, or would have come to his knowledge if such inquiries and inspections had been made as ought reasonably to have been made by him,' gave statutory stress to the existing judicial insistence that constructive notice could be found only when the lack of knowledge was due to such careless inactivity as would not be expected in the circumstances from a reasonable man. The default of a reasonable man is to be distinguished from the default of a prudent man. The prudence of the worldly wise may justifiably persuade a purchaser that it would be unbusinesslike to stop and look more deeply into certain aspects of the title. But the reasonable man, in the eyes of the law, will be expected to look beyond the impact of his decisions on his own affairs, and to consider whether they may unfairly and prejudicially affect his 'neighbour,' in the sense in which the word has been given juristic currency by Lord Atkin in *Donoghue* v. *Stevenson* [1932] A.C. 562.

In the present case, the plaintiffs may have been justified as a matter of business prudence in taking the second mortgage from the husband, hurriedly and without any proper investigation of the title. But it would be impossible to hold that a purchaser in this situation, given competent legal advice and having due regard to the prejudicial consequences to persons in proximity to him (such as the wife) that could result from a skimped investigation of the title, would have acted reasonably in thus taking a conveyance of the family home. The test for constructive notice is legal reasonableness, not business prudence.

I would reject this appeal by the plaintiffs, thus affirming the decision of Mr. Justice McWilliam which dismissed, on the ground of their constructive notice of the wife's title, the plaintiffs' claim to be given priority over her.

Kenny J.:

The first and second defendants were married in 1952. The wife's father bought a house for them at Montebello, Blackrock, in the county of Dublin and the con-veyance of it was made to her only. The husband contributed nothing to the purchase price. He prospered in the early 1960s and they decided to sell the house at Montebello and to buy one in Sandycove Avenue, West, which was held under two leases. The purchase money of Montebello was not sufficient to pay for the house at Sandycove and so the husband negotiated a mortgage from the third defendant. The two sales and the mortgage to the third defendant were carried out in 1964. The wife gave the husband the amount realised on the sale of Montebello so that he could complete the purchase of the house at Sandycove. The wife's evidence was that she understood that that house was to be put in her name, but her testimony about this was very vague and I think it more probable that the third defendant refused to make an advance to her but was prepared to make one to the husband. I can take judicial notice of the fact that building societies are most reluctant to make advances to persons who have not an income which will make it possible for them to pay the instalments. The house at Sandycove was assigned to the husband and he gave a mortgage on it to the third defendant. The result was that the wife's name was not mentioned in any of the documents of title.

At a later date the husband applied to the third defendant for a bigger advance which it agreed to give; the mortgage of 1964 was paid off and a new one was given by the husband to the third defendant on the 16th July, 1969. Again, the wife's name was not mentioned. The mortgage was made by the husband to the third defendant to secure an advance. It was made by demise for the terms for which the property at Sandycove was held (less the last ten days of each term) and the third defendant was given all the documents of title. Requisitions on title were made by the third defendant when the first mortgage was about to be completed in 1964, but none were made in 1969.

The husband was a director of a firm of insurance brokers, and he also dealt extensively in shares. He had a number of accounts with different banks; one of these was with the plaintiffs. In April, 1972, the husband had permission to overdraw his account with the plaintiffs up to a specified limit and that limit was increased subsequently. He had purchased shares in public companies on a large scale and the rapid fall in prices beginning in 1972 caused him great difficulties. In September, 1972, his overdraft exceeded the limit and he was warned by the plaintiffs that any cheques of his which increased the overdraft would not be paid. In October, 1972, the plaintiffs gave the husband a term loan, which was to be cleared in three years, and they warned him that his current ccount was to remain in credit. All his correspondence with the plaintiffs was from the house in Sandycove in his handwriting. In February, 1973, he had the full amount of the term loan outstanding and his current account was in debit. He continued to draw cheques on it and on the 14th May, 1973, the plaintiffs marked a number of his cheques 'refer to drawer'. In May, 1973, he asked the plaintiffs to send all letters to him not to Sandycove but to No. 71 Upper Leeson Street which was the address of the insurance brokers.

The husband had deposited with the plaintiffs the share certificates relating to securities which he had purchased and in July, 1973, the plaintiffs threatened to sell the shares. The husband wrote to the plaintiffs offering a second mortgage on 'my' house in Sandycove if they did not sell any of the securities for a period of two months. On the 27th July, 1973, the husband gave the plaintiffs a signed authority to the third defendant to forward the deeds of the property at Sandycove to his solicitors and on the same day the plaintiffs wrote to the husband's solicitors asking for their assistance in the completion of the second mortgage. The solicitors received the title deeds from the third defendant but in September, 1973, they told the plaintiffs that the second mortgage 'was not going ahead'. The third defendant had consented to the second mortgage and the plaintiffs did not understand why it had not been completed. On the 18th November, 1973, the husband's solicitors wrote to the plaintiffs and said that 'they were unable to attend to this matter further because of pressure of work' and informed the plaintiffs that they were returning the documents to the third defendant. On the 31st December, 1973, the plaintiffs obtained from the third defendant the deeds and the requisitions which had been made in 1964.

The plaintiffs sent the deeds to their legal department in Belfast with instructions to prepare a second mortgage and a search was made in the Registry of Deeds against the husband and it did not disclose any acts by him. The plaintiffs were not aware that in May, 1973, the husband and the wife had separated, and that the wife had consulted a firm of solicitors who advised her to take proceedings against her husband claiming a declaration that she was the beneficial owner of the house at Sandycove and an order directing the husband to assign it to her. She continued to live in the house at Sandycove.

The plaintiffs' solicitors prepared the second mortgage by sub-demise for the whole of the terms granted by the leases under which the property was held, less the last days. They did not make any inquiries or requisitions of any kind and the husband executed the second mortgage to the plaintiffs on the 22nd January, 1974. On the same day the wife began proceedings against the husband for a declaration that she was the beneficial owner of the house at Sandycove and for an order directing him to transfer it to her. The plaintiffs first became aware of the wife's claim on the 17th July, 1974, when her solicitors wrote to them. The husband did not enter an appearance to the summons by his wife and on the 14th February, 1975, when I was a judge of the High Court, I made an order declaring that he held the property at Sandycove in trust for the wife and ordered him to assign it to her, subject only to the mortgage to the third defendant. The existence of the mortgage to the plaintiffs was not disclosed to me and, if I had a been aware of it, I would not have made that order without hearing the plaintiffs. The plaintiffs had no notice of the wife's application for judgment.

On the 31st July, 1975, the plaintiffs began these proceedings in which they claim a declaration that under their mortgage a substantial sum was owed to them and was well charged on the estate and interest of the husband and the wife in the property, and a declaration that their mortgage ranked before the wife's claim. The wife contended that her interest was superior to that of the plaintiffs because they had constructive notice of her claim when their mortgage was excuted. As all parties admit that the third defendant's mortgage of 1969 ranks before the interests of the plaintiffs and of the husband and the wife, the third defendant did not take any part in the action but submitted its rights to the Court.

It has not been suggested that the plaintiffs had actual notice of the wife's interest and the whole debate has related to constructive notice. Neither the husband nor any solicitor or official from the plaintiffs' legal department in Belfast gave evidence at the hearing. Mr. Justice McWilliam, in the course of his judgment, said:

'Two of the formal inquiries which would be made normally and which, therefore, ought reasonably to have been made are: "Who is in the actual occupation of the property?" and "Is there any litigation pending or threatened in respect of the property?" If these inquiries had been made, the plaintiffs should have had notice of the position or should have been given information which would have led to further inquiries as to it. As these inquiries were not made, I hold that the plaintiffs are deemed to have had notice of the interest of the wife.'

In the middle of the last century there were considerable differences of opinion between judges in Ireland and England in relation to the doctrine of constructive notice. Some wanted to extend it to protect equitable interests: others wanted to restrict it to give certainty to titles. The law is now stated in s. 3 of the Conveyancing Act, 1882, but to understand this it is necessary to deal with the pre-1882 position. The most authoritative statement of the doctrine of constructive notice before the Act of 1882 is that of Lord Cranworth at p. 473 of the report of *Ware* v. *Lord Egmont* (1854) 4 De G.M. & G. 460:

'Where a person has actual notice of any matter of fact there can be no danger of doing injustice if he is held to be bound by all the consequences of that which he knows to exist. But where he has not actual notice, he ought not to be treated as if he had notice, unless the circumstances are such as enable the Court to say, not only that he might have acquired, but also, that he ought to have acquired, the notice with which it is sought to affect him – that he would have acquired it but for his gross negligence in the conduct of the business in question.'

Where it was sought before 1882 to affect a purchaser with constructive notice, the question was not whether he had the means of getting, and might by prudent conduct have got, the knowledge in question, but whether his failure to obtain it was caused by an act of gross or culpable negligence.

For present purposes the relevant parts of s. 3 of the Act of 1882 state:

'(1) A purchaser shall not be prejudicially affected by notice of any instrument, fact, or thing unless –
>   (i) It is within his own knowledge, or would have come to his knowledge if such inquiries and inspections had been made as ought reasonably to have been made by him; or
>   (ii) In the same transaction with respect to which a question of notice to the purchaser arises, it has come to the knowledge of his counsel, as such, or of his solicitor, or other agent, as such, or would have come to the knowledge of his solicitor, or other agent as such, if such inquiries and inspections had been made as ought reasonably to have been made by the solicitor or other agent. . . .

(3) A purchaser shall not by reason of anything in this section be affected by notice in any case where he would not have been so affected if this section had not been enacted.'

I confess that this section has always created considerable difficulties for me. Sub-section 3 seems to have the effect that a purchaser after 1882 is not affected by notice in any case where he would not have been regarded as having constructive notice before the Act of 1882 was passed. This would suggest that the standard to be applied in determining whether a purchaser got constructive notice was the standard stated by Lord Cranworth in *Ware* v. *Lord Egmont* (1854) 4 De G.M. & G. 460, but the standard stated in s. 3 of the Act of 1882 is much wider than that stated by Lord Cranworth. The standard in s. 3 is the prudent purchaser who has obtained competent legal advice while that stated by Lord Cranworth is that of gross negligence. Is then the effect of s. 3, sub-s.3, of the Act of 1882 to nullify the much wider test in sub-s. 1 of that section? Although that is the literal meaning, it would be an absurdity and it has never been suggested by any writer since the section was passed.

None of the decided cases deals with the difficulty created by s. 3, sub-s. 3, of the Act of 1882, and so I turn to the recognised text-books on the subject. None of them refers to this difficulty but they are unanimous that a purchaser or mortgagee who omits to make such inquiries and inspections as a prudent and reasonable purchaser, or mortgagee, acting on skilled advice would have made will be fixed with notice of what he would have discovered if he had made the inquiries and inspections which ought reasonably to have been made by him.

In Wylie's Irish Land Law the question of constructive notice is dealt with at pp. 103–4 and at pp. 643–3. At pp. 103–4 this passage appears:

'The concept of constructive notice is really grounded upon the basic principles of conveyancing. Here the guiding rule of thumb is *caveat emptor*. The onus is upon the purchaser to take proper steps to ensure that the transaction is carried out and its consequencs go according to his plans. The risk is upon him if anything goes wrong. Upon this principle is based the concept of investigation of title which is the purchaser's responsibility. It is to this sort of procedure that section 3(1) of the 1882 Act is referring when it speaks of "inquiries and inspections" which "ought reasonably to have been made". What these are in any particular case depends upon the circumstances, but in essence the general principle is what is regarded as the usual standard conveyancing procedures appropriate for such a case. If the purchaser does not carry these out he will be fixed nevertheless with constructive notice of matters which carrying out such procedures would have brought to his notice. . . . Omissions to carry out the proper steps due to carelessness or negligence are also caught by this rule.'

At pp. 643–4 this appears: 'Further, if the mortgagee fails to follow the usual conveyancing practice in connection with his mortgage, in particular, if he fails to make a proper investigation of title, he will again be fixed with constructive notice of what such investigation would show.'

Section 3 of the Act of 1882 was repealed in England; it was replaced by almost similar provisions in s. 199 of the Law of Property Act, 1925. In Megarry and Wade's Law of Real Property (4th ed. – 1975), the authors wrote at p. 122: 'A purchaser accordingly has constructive notice of a fact if he (i) had actual notice that there was some incumbrance and a proper inquiry would have revealed what it was, or (ii) omitted by carelessness or for any other reason to make an inquiry which a purchaser acting on skilled advice ought to make and which would have revealed the incumbrance.' In Cheshire's Modern Law of Real Property (12th ed. – 1976) under the heading 'Constructive Notice' the author writes (at p. 64) that the test of constructive notice is to ask what ought a prudent careful man to do when he is purchasing an estate.

These passages are in accord with the remarks of Lindley L.J., a great authority on this subject, when giving the judgment of the Court of Appeal in England in *Bailey* v. *Barnes* [1894] 1 Ch. 25; having referred to the passage, *supra*. from the judgment of Lord Cranworth in *Ware* v. *Lord Egmont*, (1854) 4 De G.M. & G. 460, Lindley L.J. said at p. 35 of the report:

'"Gross or culpable negligence" in this passage does not import a breach of a legal duty, for a purchaser of property is under no legal obligation to investigate his vendor's title. But in dealing with real property, as in other matters of business, regard is had to the usual course of business; and a purchaser who wilfully departs from it in order to avoid acquiring a knowledge of his vendor's title is not allowed to derive any advantage from his wilful ignorance of defects which would have come to his knowledge if he had transacted his business in the ordinary way. In the celebrated judgment of Vice-Chancellor Wigram in *Jones* v. *Smith*, [(1841) 1 Hare 43] the cases of constructive notice are reduced to two classes; the first comprises cases in which a purchaser has actual notice of some defect, inquiry into which would disclose others; and the second comprises cases in which a purchaser has purposely abstained from making inquiries for fear he should discover something wrong. The Conveyancing Act, 1882, really does no more than state the law as it was before, but its negative form shews that a restriction rather than an extension of the doctrine of notice was intended by the Legislature.'

Having referred to s. 3 of the Act of 1882, Lindley L.J. went on to say: 'The expression "ought reasonably" must mean ought as a matter of prudence, having regard to what is usually done by men of business under similar circumstances.'

The test then is the prudent purchaser acting on skilled advice. Such a purchaser would certainly not abstain from inquiry in an attempt to avoid having notice. Therefore, I propose to adopt the standard of the prudent purchaser acting on skilled advice, for no such man who was without legal qualifications would undertake the investigation of title to land.

As the husband used moneys which belonged to the wife in her own right to purchase the property at Sandycove, she had an equitable estate and interest in the property to the extent of that money and he was a trustee for her. I do not think that it matters whether one calls her interest 'an estate' or 'an interest'. The effect is the same. That estate arose in 1964 and was prior in point of time to the plaintiffs' interest which was acquired in 1974. So the estate which the plaintiffs acquired under their mortgage was taken by them subject to the wife's equitable interest, if the plaintiffs had constructive notice of that interest. The plaintiffs made no inquiries whatever about the title or other interests in the property when they took their mortgage. They relied on the answers to the requisitions given to the third defendant in 1964. There was no evidence that they carried out any investigation of the title. They were prepared to take whatever interest in the property the husband had 'warts and all' as Mr. McCracken said.

The standard to be applied is an objective one. The question is not whether the plaintiffs acted reasonably in the circumstances of the instant case but whether a reasonable mortgagee would have acted in the way they did. As the wife's proceedings commenced on the 22nd January, 1974, there must have been some correspondence in which the wife's claim would have been asserted before that date and if the standard requisition (is there any litigation pending or threatened affecting the property?) had been made, the plaintiffs would have discovered that the wife was asserting the claim which she now makes. The fact that the solicitors who had acted for the husband in earlier transactions refused to act because of 'pressure of work' created a difficulty for the plaintiffs but they could have insisted on the husband coming to their office and answering the questions himself. In my opinion, they did not act as reasonable mortgagees would normally do.

There was no discussion whatever as to whether the plaintiffs acquired a legal interest. Therefore, I do not express any opinion on the question whether their second mortgage by sub-demise, given after a first mortgage made in the same way, gave them a legal interest.

In addition, the onus of proving that the plaintiffs were purchasers for value without notice rests on them: *Attorney-General* v. *Biphosphated Guano Company* (1879) 11 Ch. D. 327 (at p. 337); *In re Nisbet and Potts' Contract* [1906] 1 Ch. 386 (at p. 402) and *Heneghan* v. *Davitt* [1983] I.R. 375 (at pp. 377, 379).

In my opinion, without taking into account the question of onus of proof, the evidence establishes that the plaintiffs had constructive notice of the wife's estate when they took their mortgage. When the burden of proof is taken into account, the plaintiffs have failed to establish that they took their mortgage without constructive notice of the wife's rights.

Counsel for the plaintiffs placed great reliance on the judgments in *Hunt* v. *Luck* [1902] 1 Ch. 428, which is a decision of the Court of Appeal in England. It is relevant only on the question whether the plaintiffs should have inspected the property and found out whether it was occupied or not. I do not think that a mortgagee is bound to inspect the property on which he is taking a mortgage and the decision is of no assistance on the ground on which I would decide this case.

Accordingly, the plaintiffs' appeal fails and I would dismiss it.

Parke J.:

I also agree that this appeal should be dismissed and I have little to add to the comprehensive judgments which have been delivered, in which the facts and authorities have been so fully reviewed. However, I would like to make some observations upon what I consider to be the duty of a conveyancer who is investigating title on behalf of a purchaser or mortgagee.

This case provides a striking illustration of the necessity of assessing the extent of this duty by applying an objective test, rather than one which is subjective to the needs of a particular purchaser engaged in a particular transaction.

In 1974 the plaintiff bank was in urgent need of some kind of collateral security from the husband, who had only a second mortgage on the house in Sandycove to offer. In the circumstances the plaintiffs were determined to take that security regardless of its quality, and they were anxious to get it as quickly as possible. They did not even wait to get the advice of a lawyer practising in this jurisdiction. They merely instructed the law agent in Belfast to complete the transaction with the least possible delay. In the situation in which they found themselves it could be said that, from their own point of view, the plaintiffs were both 'prudent' and 'reasonable'. That, however, is very far from saying that they were 'reasonable and prudent purchasers' as the phrase is understood in the authorities on the doctrine of constructive notice or that they were protected by the provisions of s. 3 of the Conveyancing Act, 1882. To hold that they were so protected would be to produce the unjust result that, because the plaintiffs deliberately chose not to follow the ordinary and well-established practice of a competent conveyancer, they could unsuccessfully defeat the unquestionable equitable right of the wife to be sole beneficial owner of the house – a right which ought to have become apparent if the title had been investigated in the normal way.

It is right to say that Mr. Barron, on behalf of the plaintiffs does not present his case in quite such an unpalatable way, but it seems to me that this is the inevitable consequence of his argument. Mr. Barron argues that a conveyancer's duty is discharged if he examines the documents of title which have been furnished to him, if he investigates any further documents and facts the existence of which is disclosed by, or may be inferred from, such title documents, and if he directs the proper searches and investigates any acts which may appear. He says that a conveyancer ought not to go outside the material furnished to him or that which is referred to therein, and that he ought not to make further inquiries lest he discovers inadvertently something which might jeopardize his client's right to obtain a good title as a bona fide purchaser without notice. I do not think that his statement fully exhausts the obligations of a competent and qualified conveyancer.

In my view such a conveyancer must also take account of any facts which are within his knowledge, even if they are not actually disclosed by the documents of title. He must then consider such legal principles as appear to apply to such facts. If the application of such principles raises a question in his mind as to the sufficiency of the title, it is his duty to resolve that question by raising the appropriate requisitions. It is, of course, true that investigation of title shares a maxim with the art of cross-examination, i.e. do not ask an unnecessary question lest you receive a disconcerting reply. However, just as no cross-examination can be fully effective unless all the proper questions are asked, no investigation of title can be complete unless all the necessary questions are asked.

In the present case the plaintiffs knew that the house in Sandycove was the husband's and the wife's matrimonial home. The plaintiffs at least had reason to suspect that the husband was no longer residing there. They did not know whether the wife was still living in the house and they did not inquire.

Although the plaintiffs' mortgage was granted prior to the enactment of the Family Home Protection Act, 1976, there was already judicial authority when it was granted (in both this country and in England) that although a matrimonial home might be legally vested in one spouse yet the other spouse could have a claim in equity to at least some share in the ownership of the house. This claim could arise from facts or matters which would not, and frequently could not, be disclosed by a perusal of the documentary title to the property. Although there might not have been complete judicial unanimity as to how the nature of such a claim should be designated, or the exact equitable principle upon which it vested, I have no doubt that by the beginning of the year 1974 any person who was offered a title to a matrimonial home by one spouse should have been alerted to the possibility that the other spouse might have a claim, which would be upheld by the Courts, to at least a share in the beneficial interest in the property. In the present case a proper investigation would have revealed that the wife was not merely entitled to an unquantified share in the house, but to the entire beneficial ownership to the exclusion of the proposed mortgagee.

Having been alerted to the possible existence of such a claim, it is the duty of those investigating the title to dispose of it. It would not be right for me to attempt to suggest how this should have been done, because different conditions may apply to different cases. In the present case the standard requisition as to threatened litigation would have been sufficient because the wife had already threatened proceedings; in other cases it might not. In some cases it might appear to the investigator that it was desirable to obtain evidence of the consent of the other spouse to a sale. A requisition requiring vacant possession (on a sale) or evidence that there was no person in possession of any claim of right (on a mortgage) would have sufficed in the present case because the wife was in possession; but a spouse's claim to an interest in the matrimonial home does not depend upon occupation, so this requisition might be ineffectual. However, these matters are now largely academic, having regard to the provisions of the Family Home Protection Act, 1976.

A conveyancer has not, of course, any duty to third parties – of whose existence he may be unaware. His duty is exclusively to his own client. However, he cannot discharge that duty properly unless he can obtain for his client a title which will not be defeated subsequently by a third party whose right ought to have been discovered on proper investigation.

I would like to say that nothing in this judgment is intended to be, or should be interpreted as being a criticism of the staff of the plaintiff bank's law department. I am sure that they are well qualified, competent and careful. I have no doubt that if this transaction had been presented to them in the normal way with a request to investigate fully the title of a proposed mortgagee they would have made all proper requisitions or, perhaps, would have advised that the matter be referred to solicitors who practised in this jurisdiction. In either event, I would think that the title would not have been accepted.

For these reasons I would dismiss this appeal.

Notes and Questions
1. Is it possible, from the varying descriptions given by the members of the Supreme Court, to describe precisely the test to be applied when considering whether a purchaser or mortgagee has complied with section 3 of the Conveyancing Act, 1882?
2. See further on 'constructive' notice, *Bank of Ireland Finance Ltd.* v. *Rockfield Ltd.* [1979] I.R. 21, espec. at 37–8 (*per* Kenny J.) and *Somers* v. *W.* [1979] I.R. 94 (p. 99, *infra*).

FAMILY HOME PROTECTION ACT, 1976

3. – (1) Where a spouse, without the prior consent in writing of the other spouse, purports to convey any interest in the family home to any person except the other spouse, then, subject to subsections (2) and (3) and section 4, the purported conveyance shall be void.

(2) Subsection (1) does not apply to a conveyance if it is made by a spouse in pursuance of an enforceable agreement made before the marriage of the spouses.

(3) No conveyance shall be void by reason only of subsection (1) –
    (a) if it is made to a purchaser for full value,
    (b) if it is made, by a person other than the spouse making the purported conveyance referred to in subsection (1), to a purchaser for value, or

(c) if its validity depends on the validity of a conveyance in respect of which any of the conditions mentioned in subsection (2) or paragraph (a) or (b) is satisfied.

(4) If any question arises in any proceedings as to whether a conveyance is valid by reason of subsection (2) or (3), the burden of proving that validity shall be on the person alleging it.

(5) In subsection (3), 'full value' means such value as amounts or approximates to the value of that for which it is given.

(6) In this section, 'purchaser' means a grantee, lessee, assignee, mortgagee, chargeant or other person who in good faith acquires an estate or interest in property.

(7) For the purposes of this section, section 3 of the Conveyancing Act, 1882, shall be read as if the words 'as such' wherever they appear in paragraph (ii) of subsection (1) of that section were omitted.

SOMERS V. W.
[1979] I.R. 94; 113 I.L.T.R. 81 (Supreme Court)

Prior to a certain date in 1973 the defendant lived in the county of Dublin with her husband in his house which he held under a lease. On that date the defendant left the house with the children. On the 2nd August, 1976, the husband contracted to sell the house to the plaintiff for its full value. When the plaintiff's solicitor required the defendant's written consent to the sale, he was informed by the husband's solicitor that the defendant had left the house some years ago and was no longer relying on it as her family home, that the husband was abroad and that the defendant's address was unknown. Having returned to Dublin, the husband on the 16th August made a statutory declaration on which he stated that the defendant had not relied on the said house as her family home since he and the defendant had separated and that, by virtue of a separation agreement, she had no interest therein. The separation agreement, which was then produced, did not contain any reference to the house. On the 17th August the plaintiff, relying on the statutory declaration, paid the balance of the purchase money and the husband assigned the house to the plaintiff. When the plaintiff agreed to sell the house in April, 1977, the purchaser insisted on obtaining the defendant's written consent to the sale by her husband. In October 1977, the plaintiff's solicitor asked the defendant, who was living in Dublin, for her consent to that sale and, when the defendant refused to so consent, the plaintiff issued a summons in the High Court seeking an order dispensing with the defendant's consent pursuant to s. 4 of the Act of 1976 on the statutory ground that the defendant was withholding her consent unreasonably. The defendant claimed to have paid some part of the cost of buying the family home. Doyle J. granted the order sought and the defendant appealed to the Supreme Court.

Henchy J.:

This case raises an important conveyancing point under the Family Home Protection Act, 1976. One of the primary objects of this Act is to limit the power of a spouse to alienate the family home without the prior consent in writing of the other spouse. By s. 2 sub-s. 1, the family home is defined as meaning not only a dwelling in which the couple ordinarily reside but also a dwelling in which the spouse whose protection is in issue ordinarily resides or, if that spouse has left the other spouse, ordinarily resided before so leaving.

Section 3 provides that where a spouse, without the prior consent in writing of the other spouse, purports to convey any interest in the family home to any person other than the other spouse then, subject to four specified exceptions, the purported conveyance shall be void. The only one of those exceptions that we are here concerned with is the proviso in s. 3, sub-s. 3, that the prohibition is not to apply if the conveyance is made to 'a purchaser for full value'. That exception gives rise to the issue in this case which is whether the plaintiff, who was the purchaser of the leasehold interest of the defendant's husband in the family home, was a purchaser for full value within the meaning of the Act of 1976.

The dwelling in question was called 'the contract premises' in the judgment of Mr. Justice Doyle, and I shall also employ that description. Before the marriage, the defendant's husband took a lease of the contract premises in his own name in March, 1961. When the husband and the defendant married in July, 1961, those premises became the family home. There were children of the marriage. Unfortunately it turned out an unhappy marriage. The husband is not a party to these proceedings, so we do not know his side of the story. The defendant says that, for stated reasons, she was compelled to leave the contract premises with her children in October, 1973. After she left, she got a tenancy from the Dublin Corporation, first in other premises and then, in June, 1976, at her present address where she has been living since then with her children. She never resumed marital relations with her husband.

On leaving the family home, the defendant went for advice to the centre at Coolock run by F.L.A.C. (i.e. Free Legal Aid Centres), which is the group which supplies free legal aid for those who are in need of legal aid and cannot afford to pay a solicitor. She wished to have custody of the children and to be free of interference by the husband. On the 20th November, 1974, a written separation agreement was executed whereby it was agreed that the defendant and her husband would live separately without interference from each other, that the defendant would have custody of the children subject to stated access by her husband; and that the defendant would keep her husband indemnified against all debts and liabilities which she would contract or incur. The agreement made no provision for any payments by the husband for the maintenance of the defendant and her children; and it was silent as to the family home.

As a result, the defendant's husband retained the family home while incurring no financial commitments to the defendant or his children whereas the defendant, who had to go out to work as a cleaner in a factory, had to struggle to pay the rent of her Corporation house and bring up her children out of her slender wages and the sums she received in the way of social security payments. Whatever the rights or wrongs of the collapse of the marriage, the defendant finished up unfairly and excessively burdened with the problems of life.

On the 2nd August, 1976, the defendant's husband entered into a written agreement to sell his leasehold interest in the contract premises for £6,400 to the plaintiff. The Family Home Protection Act, 1976, had come into operation only a few weeks earlier (12th July, 1976). Both the husband's solicitor and the plaintiff's solicitor were aware that the Act of 1976 had come into force.

[*The judge here referred to letters of the 10th and 11th August, 1976, and continued*] At this time the husband was abroad temporarily so just then his solicitor could not get the defendant's address from him – but he was back in Dublin by the 16th August, 1976. The plaintiff's solicitor did not wait for the husband to return from abroad or for the F.L.A.C. centre to reopen after the summer holidays. Instead, he prepared a statutory declaration, to be made by the husband, stating that the defendant had not relied on the contract premises as her family home since the execution of the separation agreeement and that she 'by virtue of said separation agreement has now no interest therein'. Considering that the plaintiff's solicitor had never seen the separation agreement, which made no reference to the contract premises, this averment was a wild and inaccurate leap in the dark. Without any real inquiry as to the facts and without any inspection of the separation agreement, words which expressed the opposite of the truth were put into the husband's mouth. The defendant's husband executed the statutory declaration thus prepared by the purchaser's solicitor, and the sale was closed on the 17th August, 1976, with the execution of the assignment on that date. The husband had a balance of some £3,400 out of the purchase price after paying off the mortgage and discharging the costs of the sale.

There the matter might have rested, with the husband walking off with the proceeds of the sale, were it not for the fact that the plaintiff, having spent some money on improving the contract premises, agreed to resell those premises in April, 1977, for £10,800. The new purchaser (or, rather, the building society which was financing the new purchaser) required proof that the provisions of s. 3 of the Family Home Protection Act, 1976, had not been breached. The plaintiff's solicitor discovered the defendant's address and wrote to her asking her to give her retrospective consent in writing to the assignment of the 17th August, 1976. The defendant refused, claiming that she was entitled to a proprietary interest in the contract premises. It was in that impasse that the plaintiff instituted the present proceedings in which she seeks an order under s. 4 of the Act of 1976 dispensing with the defendant's consent in writing to the assignment of the 17th August, 1976. In the High Court the judge, holding that the wife's consent was not necessary to that assignment, granted the order sought. It is against that decision that this appeal has been taken.

Section 3, sub-s. 3 (a), of the Act of 1976 allows a conveyance to escape being void under that section if it is made to a purchaser for full value. It is common ground that the plaintiff paid the full value for the contract premises in 1976; but was she 'a purchaser' as defined by s. 3, sub-s. 6, that is to say, was she an assignee 'who in good faith acquires an estate or interest in property?' This is the nub of the case; for the contest is whether she, through her solicitor, acted in good faith in taking the assignment without the prior consent of the defendant. On that issue, the onus of proof rests on the plaintiff: see sub-s. 4 of section 3.

The question whether a purchaser has acted in good faith necessarily depends on the extent of his knowledge of the relevant circumstances. In earlier times the tendency was to judge a purchaser solely by the facts that had actually come to his knowledge. In the course of time it came to be held in the Court of Chancery that it would be unconscionable for the purchaser to take his stand on the facts that had come to his notice to the exclusion of those which ordinary prudent or circumspection or skill should have called to his attention. When the facts at his command beckoned him to look and inquire further, and he refrained from doing so, equity fixed him with constructive notice of what he would have ascertained if he had pursued the further investigation which a person of reasonable care and skill would have felt proper to make in the circumstances. He would not be allowed to say 'I acted in good faith, in ignorance of those facts, of which I learned only after I took the conveyance', if those facts were such as a reasonable man in the circumstances would have brought within his knowledge.

When the Supreme Court of Judicature Act (Ireland), 1877, brought the rules of equity into play in all courts, the equitable doctrine of notice was given supremacy. Further, it was given statutory expression in s. 3 of the Conveyancing Act, 1882. For the purposes of this case the relevant parts of that section are contained in sub-s. 1 which states:

'(1) A purchaser shall not be prejudicially affected by notice of any instrument, fact, or thing unless –

(i) It is within his own knowledge, or would have come to his knowledge if such inquiries and inspections had been made as ought reasonably to have been made by him; or

(ii) In the same transaction with respect to which a question of notice to the purchaser arises, it has come to the knowledge of his counsel, *as such*, or of his solicitor, or other agent, *as such*, if such inquiries and inspections had been made as ought reasonably to have been made by the solicitor or other agent.'

That s. 3 of the Act of 1976 is to be operated within this doctrine of notice is emphasised by the fact that sub-s. 7 of that section amends s. 3 of the Act of 1882 by deleting from it the above italicised words, thus extending the reach of constructive notice.

It is not in contention that the plaintiff did not know, personally or through her solicitor, that the defendant had a prima facie valid properietary interest in the contract premises which the husband was selling. But ought the plaintiff reasonably, through her solicitor, to have ascertained that fact? If she ought, the position is the same as if she actually knew of the claim, in which case she could not be said to have purchased in good faith and the assignment would have to be declared void.

Let us first see what was the extent of the plaintiff's actual knowledge. Through her solicitor (for his knowledge is to be imputed to her) she knew (or was told) that the contract premises were the family home, that the defendant's husband was the vendor, that his marriage had broken up, that there had been a separation agreement, that the vendor's wife was living in a Dublin Corporation house and was no longer claiming that the contract premises were the family home. It was further stated by the vendor's solicitor that the vendor, at the time the title was being investigated, was abroad and that his wife's address was not available. It was against the background of that information that the plaintiff's solicitor decided to close the sale on getting a statutory declaration from the vendor. This statutory declaration, which was drafted by the plaintiff's solicitor, was inaccurate in fact and unfounded in law. It declared that the separation agremeent had been entered into in or about October, 1973 (it was executed in November, 1974) and that by virtue of it the defendant had no interest in the contract premises although the separation agreement did not make any reference whatsoever to those premises.

Furthermore, as we know from the defendant's evidence in the High Court, she has a valid prima facie claim to a proprietary interest in the contract premises on the ground that she made an initial down-payment of £25 for them; that for the first five months of the marriage, when she was still working, she pooled her wages with her husband's; and that at one stage she obtained from her mother and made available to the husband £150 which he used to pay off arrears of rent.

In those circumstances should the plaintiff, as purchaser, be fixed with constructive notice of the contents of the separation agreement and of the existence of the defendant's claim? The answer must be 'Yes'. The contract for sale was executed on the 2nd August and the title had been investigated and the sale completed by the 17th August, 1976. Expedition of that order is to be commended, but not at the expense of due investigation of title. When the plaintiff's solicitor asked to be supplied with the separation agreement and was told that it could not be supplied because the F.L.A.C. centre was closed for the annual holidays, he should not have allowed himself to be fobbed off with that excuse. It is not unusual for sales to be held up for reasons such as this in the month of August at the peak of the holiday season. Considering the dire risk of a void conveyance, it was foolhardy to close the sale without seeing the separation agreement. Had it come to hand it would have shown itself to be worthless as a document of title, and to be no basis for the statutory declaration on which the sale was completed; but it would have given the defendant's then address as a Dublin Corporation tenant so that it would have been possible, through the Corporation, to have traced her to her address at the time of the sale.

In any event, there was never any real difficulty in ascertaining the defendant's address, and discovering whether she was prepared to give her prior consent in writing to the sale. The defendant's husband may have been abroad at some stage, but he was back in Dublin by the 16th August, 1978 (when he executed the statutory declaration) and he well knew the defendant's address. It was folly to close the sale in those circumstances without insisting on the prior consent in writing of the defendant. No sooner was the sale closed than her husband went to the defendant and offered to give her the proceeds of the sale if she would take him back; feeling that she was well rid of him, she refused. But she should have been given the opportunity, before the sale, of withholding her consent unless her claim to an interest in the contract premises was satisfied. If the plaintiff's solicitor had insisted on compliance with his requisition that the defendant's consent should be endorsed on the assignment, the defendant's husband would have had no valid reason for refusing to ask her to do so. The inescapable conclusion is that the true facts, both as to the contents of the separation agreement and as to the existence and nature of the defendant's claim, would have come to the plaintiff's knowledge if (to use the words of the Act of 1882) 'such inquiries and inspections had been made as ought reasonably to have been made'. Therefore, the plaintiff must be held to have purchased with notice of those facts, so that the property she acquired (or purported to acquire) was not acquired in good faith.

The trial judge considered that to hold that the inquiries made by the plaintiff's solicitor were inadequate would add a new dimension to the practice of conveyancing; but that new dimension has been added by s. 3 of the Act of 1976. As a result of that section, a purchaser investigating title must now scrutinise matters that hitherto were not matters of title at all. He must ascertain if the property, because of its present or past use, is a family home within the meaning of the Act of 1976. If it is, he must find out if it is a sale by a spouse and, if so, whether the conveyance should be preceded by the consent in writing of the other spouse so as to prevent its being rendered void under section 3. If that other spouse omits or refuses to consent, the purchaser should require the vendor to apply to the court for an order under s. 4 of the Act of 1976 dispensing with the consent. Where a family home is being purchased from a husband (the converse will be the case if the wife is the vendor), it may, by virtue of the Act, be subject to an inhibition enabling the wife to block a valid sale unless her prior consent in writing is obtained. This inhibition arises for enforcement not only when the wife has acquired (e.g. by payment of rent, rates, mortgage payments or other outgoings) a proprietary interest in the family home but also when the needs of the wife and of the dependent children (as defined) so require in the circumstances.

If the purchaser takes a conveyance without compliance with the requirements as to consent, he carried the onus of proving that the conveyance comes under one of the exemptions in sub-sections 2 and 3. If, as in the present instance, the purchaser's case is that the wife's prior consent did not arise because he was a purchaser for full value without notice, he must show that the consideration amounted or approximated to the full value of the property and also that he, or his agent, made such inquiries or inspections as ought reasonably to have been made. If such inquiries or inspections have not been made but would, if made, have disclosed that the vendor should have obtained either his wife's prior consent in writing or a court order dispensing with that consent, the conveyance will be no less void than if the purchase had actual knowledge that the wife's prior consent in writing required to be sought and he had taken the conveyance in disregard of that requirement.

In this case, the inquiries and inspections which ought reasonably to have been made as a matter of common prudence were not made. Instead, a statement which was unwarranted by any document and which falsely swept aside the defendant's rights was presented to her husband for execution as a statutory declaration and, on the basis of that statutory declaration, the sale by him went through behind his wife's back. It was a transaction of the precise kind that s. 3 of the Act of 1976 was designed to make void. Unfamiliarity with the Act of 1976 seems to have misled both the solicitor for the plaintiff and the solicitor for the defendant's husband.

Finally, a word as to the form of the present proceedings. The plaintiff moved by a special summons in which she asked for an order under s. 4 of the Act of 1976 dispensing with the defendant's prior consent to the sale. This, in my opinion, was not the correct order to seek. If the plaintiff could be said to have been 'a purchaser for full value', the proper order to seek would have been an order declaring the validity of the assignment which had been made without the defendant's prior consent in writing. An order under s. 4 of the Act of 1976 is intended to cover the position *before conveyance* when the spouse omits or refuses to consent. When the conveyance has been executed without the consent, it is either valid without that consent or it is void *ab initio*; in either event an order under s. 4 would be inappropriate.

I would allow this appeal and rule that the assignment to the plaintiff is void.

Griffin J.:

I agree with the judgment delivered by Mr. Justice Henchy. However, I would like to add a few observations of my own.

The long title of the Family Home Protection Act, 1976, is – 'An Act to provide for the protection of the family home and for related matters.' The main purpose of the Act is to ensure that the family home, or any interest in it, cannot be sold or in any way disposed of by the owner over the head of his or her spouse. Although the Act applies to both spouses and, therefore, protects the husband where the wife is the legal owner, for all practical purposes the Act is designed to protect the wife and the dependent children (as defined in s. 1 of the Act) of the family, since in Ireland the legal title to a house is rarely vested in the wife alone.

In respect of any attempted alienation of the family home, the protection afforded by the Act is given by s. 3 and is in the widest terms. Under that section, as applied to this case, the defendant's husband, who has the legal title, cannot convey any interest in the family home to any person except his wife, the defendant, without the prior consent in writing of the defendant and, if he attempts to do so, the purported conveyance is void unless it is within the exceptions in s. 3 of the Act of 1976. 'Conveyance' is defined as including a mortgage, lease, assent, transfer, disclaimer, release and any other disposition of property otherwise than by will or a *donatio mortis causa* and includes an enforceable agreement to make any such conveyance.

Therefore, the prohibition covers every conceivable type of disposition of the family home by the defendant's husband. If, therefore, the husband intends to sell the family home, or to raise a mortgage on the security of it, unless the exceptions in s. 3 apply, he cannot do so without first discussing the matter with the defendant and obtaining her prior consent in writing. Indeed, as the definition of 'conveyance' includes an enforceable agreement to make a conveyance, the section would appear to have been designed to ensure that the defendant's consent in writing should be obtained, where necessary, even before the contract for sale is made. As the defendant's husband not only entered into the contract for sale but executed an assignment of the premises to the plaintiff without obtaining the written consent of the defendant, it is not necessary for the purposes of this case to decide whether the failure to obtain the written consent of the defendant before the contract for sale was made avoided the entire transaction, as the purported assignement was void in any event.

Both solicitors who acted in the purported sale by the husband to the plaintiff either overlooked, or misinterpreted, the provisions in s. 2, sub-s. 1, of the Act of 1976 whereby 'family home' not only means a dwelling in which a married couple ordinarily reside but also comprises a dwelling in which a spouse whose protection is in issue (the defendant), and who has left the other spouse, ordinarily resided before so leaving. There is no doubt that, at all material times, the premises in question were the family home of the defendant and her husband, and that the prior consent in writing of the defendant to the sale was necessary.

Therefore, the transaction is void unless the plaintiff can establish (and the onus is on her) that she was a purchaser for full value who acted in good faith within the meaning of that expression as explained in the judgment of Mr. Justice Henchy. If the appropriate inquiries had been made by the plaintiff's solicitor, he would have ascertained that, prima facie at least, the defendant had a valid claim to a proprietary interest in the premises by reason of investments made by her in the house in paying the deposit and mortgage repayments etc. out of her own monies. As the appropriate inquiries were not made, and as the plaintiff was not an assignee who for full value and in good faith acquired an estate or interest in the premises, the consent of the defendant was necessary and, accordingly, the purported assignment without it was void.

I should like to emphasise that the protection of the Act of 1976 is not confined to a wife who has made financial contribution to the family home. Once the dwelling is a family home within the meaning of the Act, the wife is protected and her consent to the alienation may be required even though she may have left her husband and no longer resides there, provided that, before leaving, she ordinarily resided there. Once the consent of the wife is required, there is no way of dispensing with it except by application to the court under s. 4 of the Act. Any such application must be made *before* a conveyance takes place. The court has no jurisdiction to dispense with the consent where the application is not made until after the conveyance is executed.

Where an application to dispense with the consent is made in proper time, the court may dispense with the consent pursuant to s. 4, sub-s. 1, of the Act. But it is provided by sub-s. 2 of s. 4 that the court *shall not* dispense with the consent unless it considers that it is unreasonable for the wife (or husband) to withhold consent, taking into account all the circumstances, including the respective needs and resources of the husband and wife and of any dependent children of the family, and the suitability of any alternative accommodation offered to the spouse whose consent is required, having regard to the respective degrees of security of tenure in the family home and in the alternative accommodation. The onus of proving that the withholding of the consent is unreasonable in all the particular circumstances is fairly and squarely on the spouse who seeks the order dispensing with the consent.

In the circumstances of this case, if the defendant's husband had brought an application to the court in proper time seeking an order dispensing with the consent of the defendant, in my view the husband could not have discharged the onus of proving that the defendant was unreasonable in withholding her consent. I would allow this appeal.

Parke J.:

I agree with the judgments already delivered. I would allow the appeal.

Notes

1. The Family Home Protection Act, 1976, has been the subject of much litigation, see *Irish Conveyancing Law*, para. 6.31 *et seq*.
2. Note the follow-up to the above decision, *Weir* v. *Somers* [1983] I.L.R.M. 343.

REGISTRATION OF DEEDS ACT (IRELAND), 1707

IV. And further every such deed or conveyance, a memorial whereof shall be duly registered according to the rules and directions in this act prescribed, shall, from and after the said twenty fifth day of March in the year of our Lord one thousand seven hundred and eight, be deemed and taken as good and effectual both in law and equity, according to the priority of time of registering such memorial for and concerning the honors, manors, lands, tenements, and hereditaments in such a deed or conveyance mentioned or contained, according to the right, title, and interest of the person or persons so conveying such honors, manors, lands, tenements, and hereditaments, against all and every other deed, conveyance, or disposition of the honors, manors, lands, tenements or hereditaments, or any part thereof comprised or contained in any such memorial as aforesaid.

V. And further every deed or conveyance not registered, which shall be made and executed from and after the twenty fifth day of March in the year of our Lord one thousand seven hundred and eight, of all or any of the honors, manors, lands, tenements, or hereditaments comprised or contained in such a deed or conveyance, a memorial whereof shall be registered in pursuance of this act, shall be deemed and adjudged as fraudulent and void, not only against such a deed or conveyance registered as aforesaid, but likewise against all and every creditor and creditors by judgment, recognizance, statute-merchant, or of the staple, confessed, acknowledged, or entered into from and after the twenty fifth day of March aforesaid, as for and concerning all or any of the honors, manors, lands, tenements, or hereditaments, contained or expressed in such memorial registered as aforesaid.

O'CONNOR V. McCARTHY
[1982] I.R. 161 (High Court)

On the 18th April, 1977, Fuller & Co. Ltd. contracted in writing to sell to a purchaser a certain shop and yard in Skibbereen in the county of Cork for a sum of money. A memorial of that contract was not registered in the Registry of Deeds pursuant to the Act of 1707. In an action brought by that purchaser against the company in the Circuit Court in 1978, that court ordered the company to perform its contract of the 18th April, 1977, and that order was affirmed by the High Court in 1979. On the 19th April, 1977, the company contracted in writing to sell the same premises to a second purchaser for an increased sum. On the 4th July, 1977, a memorial of the second contract of sale was duly registered in the Registry of Deeds in accordance with the provisions of the Act of 1707. The second purchaser's solicitor had no knowledge of the first contract when he registered the second contract in the Registry of Deeds. Shortly before the registration of the second contract, the second purchaser was informed by someone who was not connected either with the first purchaser or with the company that the first purchaser was claiming to have bought the premises comprised in the second contract; but the second purchaser was satisfied that he had bought the premises and did not give his solicitor that information.

In the winding up of the company, its liquidator applied by motion in the High Court for directions regarding the disposition of the property comprised in the company's two contracts. Notice of the motion was served on the first and the second purchasers who, notwithstanding the orders already made in the first purchaser's action, agreed to be bound by the court's determination of the motion.

Costello J.:

The word 'gazumping' was coined not long ago to describe the practice by which the owner of a property agrees to sell it by means of an agreement which is legally unenforceable and then, on receipt of a higher offer, resiles from his bargain and sells to the new purchaser. The gazumper is concerned with his own commercial advantage and not with any inconvenience distress or loss which his actions may cause to the first purchaser, or with any moral obligations that may have arisen from the first bargain. But he runs certain risks. In particular, if he is not careful, he may find that he has bound himself by two enforceable contracts. This is what has happened to Fuller & Co. Ltd. (the company) which owns certain property in the town of Skibbereen in the county of Cork.

On the 18th April, 1977, the company entered into a written agreement in respect of portion of its properties. Having obtained from a different purchaser a better price for the same property, it entered into a second written agreement 11 days later-in the mistaken belief that the first agreement was unenforceable. The first purchaser instituted proceedings on foot of his contract and the judge of the Cork Circuit Court directed the company to perform the agreement. The company appealed, then changed its mind and consented to a High Court order confirming the order for specific performance. But the purchasers under the second contract had not been idle; they registered their contract in the Registry of Deeds and they claimed that, as they had no notice of the first contract, their contract gets priority over the first one and that they are entitled to the property. It is now accepted that there are two legally enforceable contracts in existence in respect of the company's property; what has to be decided is which purchaser is entitled to a conveyance of the property and which must be content with a claim for damages.

The dispute reaches this Court in the following way. The company was a wholly-owned subsidiary of Kenny & Deey Ltd. Some years ago it went into liquidation and appointed Mr. Austin O'Connor, a chartered accountant practising in Dublin, as its liquidator. The company did not go into liquidation immediately but Mr. O'Connor took charge, with its directors' consent, of its affairs and he was involved in the negotiations for the two sales in 1977 with which we are now concerned. Eventually the company went into voluntary liquidation and Mr. O'Connor was appointed its liquidator. By special summons of the 19th November, 1979, he applied to the Court pursuant to s. 280 of the Companies Act, 1963, for directions in relation to a number of transactions into which the company had entered, including the two sales to which I have just referred. He brought a motion for directions in respect of them and served it on the purchasers under the two contracts. All parties filed affidavits and subsequently agreed that the issues should be heard on oral evidence. In the course of the hearing I pointed out that, if I were to decide that the second contract prevailed over the first, the company could not comply with the order of the Circuit Court and that it would be necessary for the first puchaser to apply to that court to assess damages for breach of contract in lieu of specific performance. So it was agreed by the parties that, in order to avoid multiplicity of proceedings, all the issues between the parties should be determined in this Court. Accordingly, I propose to make such orders on the motion before me as will help to resolve as speedily as possible the several issues that now arise, and to leave over for future determination in this Court those which cannot be resolved now and on which further evidence may be necessary. I will first detail the facts of the two sales, then give my conclusions as to the knowledge (if any) of the first sale possessed by the second purchasers and, finally, consider the relevant legal principles which should be applied in the case.

[*The judge here stated the facts relating to the two contracts and drew certain inferences from those facts. Having done so, he continued his judgment*]

In the light of the facts that I have found, to whom should the premises be conveyed? With the assistance of counsel it has been possible to define within clear limits the legal issues which arise in the proceedings. First, the effect of the provisions of s. 5 of the Registration of Deeds Act, 1707, is that a registered deed or conveyance affecting lands takes priority over an unregistered deed or conveyance. Secondly, whilst undoubtedly it is unusual to register a contract for sale, it has been accepted that such an instrument can be registered: see Wylie's Irish Conveyancing Law at pp. 380, 381. However, it has been argued on Mr. Field's behalf that Messrs. McCarthy and Walsh lost the statutory priority given to them by the Act of 1707 because they had notice of the earlier contract. It is the nature and extent of this equitable doctrine and of the concept of notice, and its application to the facts of this case, that have been the subject of keen debate in these proceedings.

The first submission made by Mr. Blayney on behalf of Mr. Field is that the Courts have drawn a distinction between notice of a prior transaction and knowledge of it, and he referred to two English cases to illustrate the point. In *Cresta Holdings Ltd.* v. *Karlin* [1959] 1 W.L.R. 1055, the plaintiffs sued 12 defendants alleging fraud against the first two, as a result of which the plaintiffs had been defrauded of some £300,000. The eleventh defendants were bankers against whom the plaintiffs alleged that, as a result of the fraud, the bankers received a cheque and the proceeds thereof and 'did not receive the same as purchasers for value without notice'. The bankers sought particulars of this allegation. The judgments of the court drew the distinction between notice and knowledge. At pp. 1057–8 of the report Hodson J. said: 'I do not myself regard the word "notice" as a synonym for the word "knowledge". Notice is a word which involves that knowledge may be imparted by notice, but "notice" and "knowledge" are not the same thing. . .'.

In *Goodyear Tyre & Rubber Co. (Great Britain) Ltd.* v. *Lancashire Batteries Ltd.* [1958] 1 W.L.R. 857, the plaintiffs were tyre manufacturers who applied for an injunction under s. 25 of the Restrictive Trade Practices Act, 1956, to restrain the defendants from selling, at prices lower than those prescribed, goods manufactured by the plaintiffs. Section 25 provided: "Where goods are sold by a supplier subject to a condition as to the price at which those goods may be resold . . . that condition may . . . be enforced by the supplier against any person not party to the sale who subsequently acquires the goods with notice of the condition. . .'. Having referred to the section, Lord Evershed M.R. said at p. 863 of the report:

> 'What is the scope or limit of the words "with notice of the condition"? Prima facie, it would appear to me that if Parliament had meant that the retailer must know the actual terms of the condition, as the judge seems to have thought, Parliament would have said so. The word "notice" to a lawyer, in my judgment, means something less than full knowledge. It means, no doubt, that the thing of which a man must have notice must be brought clearly to his attention. What, in different cases, may be sufficient notice is a matter which will be decided when those cases come before the courts. . .'.

Whilst undoubtedly it may be important, in certain circumstances, for a distinction to be drawn between notice of a prior instrument and knowledge of a prior instrument, I do not think that the distinction is of any great significance in the present case. A person who registers a deed will not gain priority over an earlier unregistered instrument affecting the lands if he had notice of its *existence* and its *nature*; it is not necessary to show that he had any exact knowledge of its terms and conditions. In the present case if it can be established that either Mr. D. McCarthy or Mr. Walsh had actual notice of the Field contract at the relevant time – in the sense that they knew that such a contract existed – then the equitable doctrine which I am considering would apply.

There are, however, well-established distinctions between actual notice, constructive notice and imputed notice. Those distinctions have been explained recently by Mr. Justice Kenny in *Bank of Ireland* v. *Rockfield Ltd.* [1979] I.R. 21, which was a case concerning s. 60 of the Companies Act, 1963. That section provides that it shall not be lawful (apart from certain exceptions) for a company to give, by the provision of security or otherwise, financial assistance in connection with the purchase of its shares, and that any transaction in breach of the section is voidable, at the instance of the company, against any person 'who had notice' of the facts which constituted the breach. Mr. Justice Kenny pointed out that the notice mentioned in the section is actual notice and not constructive notice; at p. 37 of the report he stated:

> 'As there has been considerable confusion as to the meaning of the terms "actual notice" and "imputed notice" and "constructive notice" – a confusion which has been pointed out by many judges and text-book writers – I wish to say that I use the term "actual notice" as meaning in this case that the plaintiff bank, or any of its officials, had been informed, either verbally or in writing, that part of the advance was to be applied in the purchase of shares in the defendant company, or that they knew facts from which they *must* have inferred that part of the advance was to be applied for this purpose. This difficult branch of the law is well summarised at p. 50 of the 27th edition of Snell's Principles of Equity . . . where it is stated:
>
> "From this it is clear that a purchaser is affected by notice of an equity in three cases:
>
> (1) Actual notice: where the equity is within his own knowledge:
>
> (2) Constructive notice: where the equity would have come to his own knowledge if proper inquiries had been made: and
>
> (3) Imputed notice: where his agent as such in the course of the transaction has actual or constructive notice of the equity".'

Now it is well established that it is actual notice of a prior unregistered deed which is necessary in order to give it priority over a later registered deed. The second edition of Madden's Registration of Deeds states at p. 191: 'A party affected with actual knowledge, either personally or through his agent, of a previous unregistered instrument, cannot in equity rely on the statutory priority given by the Registry Act.' At p. 199 of that edition the author states: 'Secondly, a registered deed will not be postponed by constructive notice only – that is to say, it will not be sufficient to bring home directly to the party claiming under it, or to his agent, knowledge of facts from which, in cases unconnected with registration, notice of the unregistered instrument would be inferred.'

Recently the same principle has been restated in Wylie's Irish Land Law. Having referred to the equitable doctrine of notice, the author states at para. 3.089 on p. 111: 'It has been settled, however, that for this principle to operate so as to deprive the purchaser registering of the priority he would otherwise have under the Act, he must have *actual* notice of the prior unregistered deed at the time of the second deed's execution or, at least, at the time of its registration, or notice *imputed* to him because of *actual* notice in his agent. It is not enough to fix him with constructive notice, whether his own or his agent's.'

It was submitted on Mr. Field's behalf that there was circumstantial evidence in the present case which would justify me in holding that the purchasers, and Mr. Walsh in particular, had actual notice of Mr. Field's contract. Certainly they had such notice (it is said) by the 4th July, 1977, when the McCarthy contract was registered. Accordingly, it is claimed that Messrs McCarthy and Walsh have lost their priority. I have already pointed out that I think that, some short time prior to the 4th July, 1977, they had heard rumours that Mr. Field was claiming that he had purchased the property; but did such rumours constitute notice of the prior contract? I do not think so. As has been pointed out in Wylie's Irish Land Law at para. 3.071 on p. 103, where the doctrine of notice is being considered: 'It seems to be the settled view that mere "flying reports" or rumours are not knowledge in this context. The generally accepted principle was stated by Lord Cairns in a leading English case on the subject, *Lloyd* v. *Banks* (1863) 3 Ch. App. 488 – "knowledge which would operate upon the mind of any rational man, or man of business, and make him act with reference to the knowledge he has so acquired".' In *Lloyd* v. *Banks* the question of priority as between an assignee in bankruptcy of a cestui que trust and a subsequent mortgagee (who gave notice in writing of the mortgage to the trustees) was considered. The issue turned on whether the trustee of the fund had notice of the bankruptcy petition. In the course of his judgment Lord Cairns L.C. said at pp. 490–491 of the report:

'. . . I do not think it could be consistent with the principles upon which this Court has always proceeded, or with the authorities which have been referred to, if I were to hold that under no circumstances could a trustee, without express notice from the incumbrancer, be fixed with knowledge of an incumbrance upon the fund of which he is the trustee so as to give the incumbrancer the same benefit which he would have had if he had himself given notice to the trustee. It must depend upon the facts of the case; but I am quite prepared to say that I think the Court would expect to find that those who alleged that the trustee had knowledge of the incumbrance had made it out, not by any evidence of casual conversations, much less by any proof of what would only be constructive notice – but by proof that the mind of the trustee has in some way been brought to an intelligent apprehension of the nature of the incumbrance which has come upon the property, so that a reasonable man, or an ordinary man of business, would act upon the information and would regulate his conduct by it in the execution of the trust.'

I think that the test laid down by Lord Cairns can be applied with advantage to the facts of the present case. Both Mr. D. McCarthy and Mr. Walsh are business-men who would, I am satisfied, have acted reasonably to protect their own interests. Had the information they picked up about Mr. Field's claim to the property been in any way specific – had it, for example, been a clear indication from a reliable source that Mr. Field had concluded a contract at a date prior to their contract – I am satisfied that they would have gone to their solicitor about it. What they obtained was information that someone was claiming ownership of property which they were satisfied they had brought. That did not amount to actual notice of a prior contract. The information was not precise and did not come to them from a source which would have justified them in accepting it as true and which would have caused them to take action on it in the protection of their own interests.

In the light of this conclusion, it is unnecessary for me to decide whether the date of the execution of the McCarthy contract or the date of its registration is the relevant one for the purposes of considering the priorities in this case, since on neither date did the second purchaser have actual notice of the Field contract.

It was then submitted on Mr. Field's behalf that the purchasers under the second contract were disentitled to priority because they had deliberately refrained from making inquiries about the Field contract after they had been told about Mr. Field's claims and that, accordingly, they were mala fide purchasers and were disentitled to priority. The leading case on this subject is *Agra Bank Ltd.* v. *Barry* (1874) L.R. 7 H.L. 135, which was concerned with a question of priority between a legal mortgage and a prior unregistered equitable mortgage, and the effect on such priority of the failure of the solicitor acting for the legal mortgagee to obtain the deeds relating to the title. Lord Cairns, having referred to the doctrine of notice, raised the question as to whether mere negligence could postpone a registered security and then said at p. 149 of the report:

'Of course you may have cases in which there may be such a course of conduct as was indicated in *Kennedy* v. *Green* (1834) 3 My. & K. 699, commented on in the case of *Jones* v. *Smith* (1841) 1 Hare 43, by Vice-Chancellor *Wigram* – conduct so reckless, so intensely negligent, that you are absolutely unable to account for it in any other way than this, that, by reason of a suspicion entertained by the person whose conduct you are examining that there was a registered deed before his, he will abstain from inquiring into the fact, because he is so satisfied that the fact exists, that he feels persuaded that if he did inquire he must find it out. My lords, I do not wish to express any decided opinion at this moment upon a case of that kind . . . there is no such negligence here as, to my mind, carries with it any appearance of fraud.'

As has been pointed out, the court was considering whether absence of inquiry under circumstances leading to an inference of fraud could result in the postponement of a registered deed; it found it unnecessary to decide the question as it was satisfied that the conduct of the solicitor acting for the legal mortgagee was not in any way tainted with mala fides. I am in the same position in this case. Neither Mr. Walsh nor Mr. D McCarthy acted in any way mala fide in abstaining from acting on the rumours they heard. They did not consult their solicitor about them not because they wanted to obtain an advantage over Mr. Field which they thought they might lose if they investigated the rumours but because they genuinely believed that, even if Mr. Field was making the claim reported to them, it was a groundless one. If they did not act in a mala fide manner, then no question of the postponement of their contract could arise from their failure to make further inquiries. I agree with the submission made by Miss Carroll, on behalf of Mr. D. McCarthy and Mr. Walsh, that the whole basis for the equitable doctrine which I am considering is that the Courts of Equity would not allow a mala fide purchaser to take advantage of an Act of Parliament. In the absence of mala fides the statutory priority prevails.

The final submission made by Mr. Blayney was to the following effect. It was pointed out that the Field contract and the McCarthy contract are executory contracts and that the Court is being asked to decide which should be specifically performed. In granting equitable relief the Court should consider the conduct of the parties and, in the exercise of its discretion, it should consider which of the parties is most entitled to relief. Mr. Field should get the property, it is submitted, because the second purchasers had constructive notice of his contract. Had they made proper inquiries after hearing the rumours about his purchase, they would have ascertained the true position and the Court, in the exercise of its discretionary powers, can take this fact into account. To accede to this argument, it seems to me, would be to drive a coach-and-four not just through the statute of Queen Anne but through the long-established doctrine recognised by the Courts of Equity that mere constructive notice of a prior unregistered deed is insufficient to give it priority over a registered one. According to the statute and to the equitable doctrine I have been considering, the second purchasers are entitled to priority because they had not actual notice of the first contract. For the Court to deprive them of the benefit thus conferred on them would amount, in my view, to an improper exercise of its discretionary powers. It follows, then, that Mr. Walsh is entitled to the property.

It is obvious that it is not possible at the present time to determine finally all the matters which have to be settled between the parties; only part of the knot can be unravelled today. The order should recite that the parties have agreed that no further proceedings be taken on foot of the Circuit Court order of the 14th July, 1978, or the High Court order of the 5th October, 1979. It should contain a declaration that the McCarthy contract has obtained priority over the Field contract by virtue of the provisions of the Registration of Deeds Act, 1707, and that it should be specifically enforced if a good title is made out. The order of specific performance should only be conditional at the present time because the purchaser has not yet accepted the title. If any question arises on the title, or on the purchaser's right not to accept it and to claim damages in lieu of specific performance, the motion can be re-entered and, if necessary, a separate issue on such matters tried. The order will also direct Mr. Walsh and Mr. D. McCarthy to give particulars in writing wihin four weeks of today's date of any claim they may wish to make for damages for delay, in addition to specific performance. If such a claim is made and not settled then the motion can be re-entered and an issue tried on the claim. As to the Field contract, I will declare that Mr. Field is entitled to damages in lieu of specific performance on his contract and that he is to furnish to the liquidator within four weeks of today's date particulars of his claim. In default of agreement on it the motion can be re-entered and, if necessary, an issue tried on the point. I will also direct Mr. Field's solicitor to vacate the lis pendens, as the Circuit Court proceedings have now been stayed and the claim for damages does not warrant its retention.

Finally, Mr. Field, Mr. D. McCarthy and Mr. Walsh are each entitled to their costs against the liquidator. The costs should be taxed, in default of agreement, on the basis of the trial of an issue heard on oral evidence; the liquidator is entitled to be recouped out of the assets of the company in respect of such costs. I have been told that the company is solvent and, as the application was a proper one to have been brought, I will direct that the liquidator is entitled to his costs out of the company's assets, taxed on the basis to which I have just referred.

Chapter 3

ESTATES IN LAND

Irish land law has made its own unique contribution to the development and adaptation of the law of estates: see *Irish Land Law*, ch. 4. To the basic concept of the fee simple has been added the fee farm grants of various kinds, some unknown elsewhere in the common law world: *ibid.*, para. 4.057 *et seq*. To the life estate there has been added the lease for lives renewable for ever and the lease for lives combined with a term of years.

I. FEE SIMPLE

1. *Words of limitation*

CONVEYANCING ACT, 1881

51. – (1) In a deed it shall be sufficient, in the limitation of an estate in fee simple, to use the words in fee simple, without the word heirs; and in the limitation of an estate in tail, to use the words in tail without the words heirs of the body: and in the limitation of an estate in tail male or in tail female, to use the words in tail male, or in tail female, as the case requires, without the words heirs male of the body, or heirs female of the body.

(2) This section applies only to deeds executed after the commencement of this Act.

REGISTRATION OF TITLE ACT, 1964

123. – (1) An instrument of transfer of freehold registered land without words of limitation, or any equivalent expression, shall pass the fee simple or other the whole interest which the transferor had power to transfer in the land unless a contrary intention appears in the instrument.

(2) An instrument of transfer of freehold registered land to a corporation sole by his corporate designation without the word 'successors' shall pass to the corporation the fee simple or other the whole interest which the transferor had power to transfer in the land unless a contrary intention appears in the instrument.

(3) In an instrument of transfer of registered land a resulting use or trust for the transferor shall not be implied merely by reason that the property is not expressed to be transferred to the use or benefit of the transferee.

(4) This section applies only to instruments of transfer executed after the commencement of this Act.

SUCCESSION ACT, 1965

94. – Where real estate is devised to a person (including a trustee or executor) without any words of limitation, the devise shall be construed to pass the whole estate or interest which the testator had power to dispose of by will in the real estate, unless a contrary intention appears from the will.

TWADDLE V. MURPHY
(1881) 8 L.R. Ir. 123 (Q.B.D.)

By deed, lands were demised and granted to A and B, to hold to A and B, their heirs and assigns, for the lives of three *cestui que vies*, or for 999 years, or for ever, whichever should last longest, subject to a yearly rent. In an action to recover possession of part of the land the question arose as to whether the deed was a grant in fee (in effect a fee farm grant) or merely a demise of a term of years.

May C.J.: (delivering the judgment of the Court):

The first point to be determined is what estate was created by these instruments (the deeds of 23rd of November, 1814, and 1st November, 1822). It was contended on behalf of the Defendant, that the estate thus created was one for lives with a term of 999 years, concurrent with the term of lives in the first deed, and to take effect in succession after the expiration of the lives of the *cestui que vies* in the second deed, and that the words 'for ever' ought to be rejected as inconsistent with the previous limitations. The limitations of estates in these instruments are unusual and inartificial. Leases for terms of lives, terms of years, either concurrent or in succession, are quite familiar. But no one probably ever met with such a limitation as that which we have to consider in this case. However, we have to construe these deeds according to the usual rules of interpretation. The grammatical meaning of the language used must be adhered to unless some manifest repugnancy be produced by such interpretation, and effect must be given to every term used, if it be possible to do so.

In point of grammatical meaning and construction I see nothing repugnant or inconsistent in limiting lands to a grantee for three periods of time – a term of lives, a term of years, and a further term of perpetual duration. This was apparently the intention of the parties to these deeds. These interests being thus created, the rules of law interpose, and declare that the perpetual interest must be held to absorb these inferior terms: and as it is a maxim that the same person cannot have, in the same right, an absolute and perpetual interest and also a terminable interest, the legal result may be that the intention of the parties is disappointed, and the grantee is held to take an absolute interest in fee. This is a legal result, independent of, but controlling, the intention of the parties. Some stress was laid on the covenants to repair and to yield up in good order at the end of the term, but such covenants are very usual in grants in fee-farm; and I do not think their occurrence in these deeds of much importance on the question of construction. I do not think the term 'for ever,' the import of which is perfectly clear and well understood, can be rejected; and giving these their proper effect, I must hold these deeds to be in effect grants in fee-farm vesting the fee in the grantee. It should be observed that the deed of the 23rd November, 1814, is the more important if the fee was granted by it. The subsequent deed of 1822 could only operate as sanctioning the partition and separating the original single rent.

I come to the conclusion, therefore, that Charles Twaddle was seised in fee of his divided moiety of these lands prior to the deed of 1838.

By that deed, reciting the title of Charles Twaddle under the lease of 1822, and some other interests to be vested in James Twaddle, and that it had been agreed that these respective interests should be conveyed to the trustees of the settlement, upon the trusts after expressed, Charles Twaddle conveyed all his said divided moiety, and all his estate and interest therein, to the trustees, and their heirs, executors, administrators and assigns, for the lives in the lease, and the term of 999 years, fully to be completed, and for ever, subject to the rent, and soforth. James Twaddle conveyed the interests vested in him to the same trustees upon the same trusts. The trusts were declared upon trust for James Twaddle until the intended marriage; and after such marriage, upon trust for James Twaddle for life, with remainder to trustees for a certain term of years, in order to secure a jointure of £30 to Elizabeth Wiggins, the intended wife; and a sum of £300 for the issue, if any, of the marriage. There is also a trust to secure an annuity of £20 to Charles Twaddle, issuing out of the lands conveyed by him, payable to him in case he should cease to reside with James Twaddle. There is no trust declared disposing of the ultimate interests in the several lands conveyed. Charles Twaddle, James Twaddle, and Elizabeth his wife, are dead, and there was no issue of the marriage. The consequence would be, that there was a resulting trust in favour of Charles Twaddle and James Twaddle as to the lands conveyed by them respectively.

James Twaddle died in 1876; Charles Twaddle in 1840.

The Plaintiff is the heir-at-law of Charles Twaddle; and if the tenure by which his lands were held was of a freehold nature, the Plaintiff would be entitled to these lands. If, on the other hand, Charles Twaddle, upon the death of James Twaddle – who would appear to have been the last survivor of the lives named in the deed of November, 1822, and the settlement of 1838 – became entitled to the lands for a term of years, the personal representative of Charles Twaddle would be entitled, not the Plaintiff. In my opinion, the tenure of Charles Twaddle was in fee, and the interest conveyed by him by the deed of 1838 was also in fee.

It was contended that the right of the heir-at-law of Charles Twaddle accrued upon his death, in 1840, and that, therefore, the title of the Plaintiff was barred by the Statute of Limitations. This argument proceeded on the proposition that no estate for life was limited in these lands to James Twaddle. But in my opinion this proposition is wholly without foundation; I cannot find anything in the deed upon which such a construction could be maintained; it is contrary to the recitals, and contrary to the operative portion of the instrument. It is singular that until the marriage both the interests should be limited to James Twaddle; but that after the marriage (which took place), both the interests of Charles and James are limited to James for life is as clear as possibly could be expressed. As James died in 1876, the Statute of Limitations presents no difficulty with respect to the demurrers.

The result will be that the demurrer taken by the Plaintiff to the 2nd paragraph of the Defendant's defence will be allowed. The demurrer of the Defendant to the 2nd paragraph of the Plaintiff's reply will be overruled. The demurrer of the Defendant to the 3rd paragraph of the Plaintiff's reply will be allowed. Elizabeth Twaddle died in her husband's lifetime. The trusts for the securing her jointure never arose, and I think this 3rd paragraph would afford no answer to a defence founded on the Statute of Limitations, if that defence were otherwise maintainable.

Notes and Questions

1. Would the result have been different if the words 'heirs and assigns' had been absent from the deeds? Were the dates of execution of the deeds (i.e. pre-1881) significant? See *Irish Land Law*, para. 4.095.
2. As regards fee farm grants, see further p. 155, *post*.
3. For full discussion of the law relating to words of limitation, see *Irish Land Law*, para. 4.020 *et seq*. See also *Irish Conveyancing Law*, paras 16.049 and 16.088.

RE FORD AND FERGUSON'S CONTRACT
[1906] 1 I.R. 607 (High Court)

By a deed dated 13th October, 1892, freehold land was expressed to be granted 'unto the grantee . . . unto and to the use of the grantee for ever.' The deed also specified that in it the grantee and his 'heirs and assigns' were called 'the grantee', unless a contrary intention appeared. A vendor and purchaser summons was brought for a declaration that the deed was a fee farm grant passing a freehold estate.

Meredith M.R.:

This is one of the cases in which there can be no question as to the intention of the parties to the deed; and if the matter came before the Court in an action for specific performance or rectification, there would be no difficulty in rectifying or reading into the habendum the words of the interpretation clause. But such relief is outside the scope of a vendor and purchaser summons. This is a case where the desire for novelty or economy has brought about bad conveyancing. If there were any authority for holding that, in a case like the present, terms of art could be dispensed with, I would yield to it; but no such case has been cited. In the present deed there is an interpretation clause – [His Lordship read the clause]; but that clause cannot alter the English language. The words are not 'the grantor' or 'the grantee' merely. '*He*, the grantor,' means the grantor only, and 'he, the grantee,' means and can mean the grantee only. It is impossible to incorporate by reference the whole of the interpretation clause, having regard to the use of the words. On the face of the conveyance there is a want of the terms which are essential to the instrument itself. It is far safer to abide by the rule laid down in Key and Elphinstone, and, in the absence of the word 'heirs,' to use the actual words mentioned in the section, 'in fee simple.'

There is no hardship in the present case, as the grantor is living, and there will be no difficulty in rectifying. Under the circumstances, I cannot say that the objections of the purchaser have been sufficiently answered and a good title shown. Costs must follow the result.

Note and Questions
1. As regards a vendor and purchaser summons, see *Irish Conveyancing Law*, para. 12.25 *et seq*.
2. Would the decision have been different if the deed of 1892 had been a will and, if a will, one coming into operation in 1792? See *Irish Land Law*, para. 4.031 *et seq*.
3. What was the significance of the words 'unto and to the use of the grantee' in the 1892 deed? See *ibid*., para. 3.022.

JAMESON V. McGOVERN
[1934] I.R. 758 (Supreme Court)

On a contract for the sale of certain freehold premises, a question arose on the title as to the construction of a marriage settlement.

By this settlement W.H.R. (the intended husband) conveyed to a trustee and his heirs the said premises, and E.A. (the intended wife) assigned to the trustee her reversionary interest in certain moneys, and trusts were declared to pay the income of all and singular the trust premises therein before expressed to be thereby granted assigned and respectively. The first trust was to pay the income under a protected life estate for the husband, followed by a life estate with restraint upon anticipation in favour of the wife during her life, and thereafter a trust for the issue subject to appointment, and in default of appointment in trust for all the children or any the child of the said intended marriage who being sons or a son, should attain the age of twenty-one years, or, being daughters or a daughter, should attain that age or marry, and if more than one in equal shares. The settlement then provided that in default or failure of children (which event happened), 'the said trustees or trustee shall hold the trust premises hereinbefore brought into settlement by the said W.H.R. and the annual income thereof, or so much thereof respectively as shall not have been applied under any of the trusts or powers herein contained in trust for such person or persons and for such estates and interests as the said W.H.R. shall by deed or will appoint, and in default of such appointment and so far as no such appointment shall extend, then for the survivor of them, the said W.H.R. and E.A., absolutely.' No appointment was made by the husband and the wife survived the husband.

The purchasers contended that, as the gift to the survivor (the wife) did not contain any words of limitation, she had only a life estate, the vendors contending that the fee passed to her. The High Court (Sullivan P. and Hanna J.) held that the Irish authorities supported the vendors and refused to follow English cases like *Re Bostock's Settlement* [1921]2 Ch. 469. An appeal was made to the Supreme Court.

Murnaghan J. (delivering the judgment of the Court):

This appeal raises in this Court the question upon which there has been a wide diversity of judicial opinion, viz., whether, in an executed declaration of trust, words and terms known to the common law must be given the same effect in equity, or whether the construction of the trust can be gathered from the intention of the settlor.

In Ireland in the case of *Meyler* v. *Meyler* (11 L.R. Ir. 522) the Vice-Chancellor in interpreting the equitable limitations in a marriage settlement, held that children could not take more than life estates in the absence of words of inheritance. He said (at pp. 529, 530): 'But I have arrived at the conclusion that I am precluded by the authorities upon the subject from going into the question of intention, to be ascertained, as it must be in all cases where the technical rules applicable to deeds do not stand in the way, from a careful perusal of the whole instrument. It is admitted that if this were not the case of a trust estate, as it is, but of a legal estate, with uses executed, there could be no question as to the estates given to the children, who, for want of words of inheritance, could take no greater estates than for their respective lives. It was contended for the defendants that the technical rule on this subject does not apply to declarations of trusts where the whole legal fee is in the trustees, and that in such cases the Court is authorised to act upon the intention ascertained from the whole of the deed. For this contention there is certainly a great weight of opinion of eminent text-writers on the subject. But it appears to me that a series of cases, commencing with *Holliday* v. *Overton* (14 Beav. 467), settles the rule, so far at least as Courts of first instance are concerned, that even in trust estates it is not a question of intention but a technical rule in all cases of deeds executed prior to the Conveyancing and Law or Property Act, 1881, and of all subsequent deeds, save so far as the 51st section of that Act alters that rule.' Chatterton V.C., in thus following the cases of *Holliday* v. *Overton* (14 Beav. 467), *Lucas* v. *Brandreth* (28 Beav. 274) and *Tatham* v. *Vernon* (29 Beav. 604), all decided by Sir John Romilly M.R., supported this position by citations from Lewin on Trusts, and he also directed attention to the 51st section of the Conveyancing Act which applies to future deeds of conveyance, whether of legal or equitable estates, and he observed that this Act 'stopped very far short of enacting that an intention deduced from the context or the actual limitation itself should be sufficient to pass by deed an estate of inheritance without technical words.' It is right to point out that *dicta* of Deasy L.J. in *Lysaght* v. *McGrath* (11 L.R. Ir. 142) in support of the contrary view were cited to the Vice-Chancellor during the argument.

The cases of *Holliday* v. *Overton* (14 Beav. 467) and *Meyler* v. *Meyler* (11 L.R. Ir. 522) appear to have been uniformly followed as, *e.g.*, by Chitty J. in *In re Whiston's Settlement* ([1894] 1 Ch. 661), until in *In re Tringham's Trusts* ([1904] 2 Ch. 487) Joyce J., founding his judgment upon the opinions of earlier conveyancers and some remarks in *Pugh* v. *Drew* (17 W.R. 988), held that, where the intention was clear, an equitable estate could pass in a trust executed without words of inheritance. This decision of Joyce J. ([1904] 2 Ch. 487) has since, I think, been followed consistently in this country in preference to the ruling given by Chatterton V.C. in *Meyler* v. *Meyler* (11 L.R. Ir. 522), as witness *In re Houston, Rogers* v. *Houston* ([1909] 1 I.R. 319) decided by Wylie J.; *In re Stinson's Estate* ([1910] 1 I.R. 47) decided by Ross J.; *In re Cross's Trusts* ([1915] 1 I.R. 304) decided by O'Connor M.R.; and *In re Murphy and Griffin's Contract* ([1919] 1 I.R. 187) decided by Powell J. In England the decision of Joyce J. in *In re Tringham's Trusts* ([1904] 2 Ch. 487), although followed in several cases, was not accepted in many reported decisions, and finally the point came before the Court of Appeal in England in *In re Bostock's Settlement, Norrish* v. *Bostock* ([1921] 2 ch. 469) in which case the decision of Joyce J. was overruled. In the case of *The Land Purchase Trustee, Northern Ireland* v. *Beers* ([1925] N.I. 191) the Court of Appeal in Northern Ireland considered the point subsequently to the decision given in *In re Bostock's Settlement* ([1921] 2 Ch. 469), but the case was determined without the necessity of making a ruling upon the correctness of the Irish decisions given since the case of *In re Tringham's Trusts* ([1904] 2 Ch. 487).

It is desirable at this stage to state briefly the facts upon which the question before the Court has arisen.

Certain premises in the town of Manorhamilton, held under a fee-farm grant made in pursuance of the Renewable Leasehold Conversion Act, were agreed to be sold to the tenant in occupation, and in the making of title a marriage settlement, dated 26th December, 1881, was relied upon as vesting the property in fee in Emily Robinson. By this settlement William Henry Robinson conveyed to a trustee and his heirs the said premises, and the intended wife assigned to the trustee her reversionary interest in certain moneys, and trusts were declared to pay the income 'of all and singular the trust premises hereinbefore expressed to be hereby granted and assigned respectively.' The first trust was to pay the income under a protected life estate for the husband, followed by a life estate with restraint upon anticipation in favour of the wife during her life, and thereafter a trust for the issue subject to appointment and in default of appointment 'in trust for all the children or any the child of the said intended marriage who, being sons or a son, shall attain the age of 21 years, or, being daughters or a daughter, shall attain that age or marry, and if more than one in equal shares.' The settlement went on to provide that in default or failure of children (which event happened) 'the said trustees or trustee shall hold the trust premises hereinbefore brought into settlement by the said William Henry Robinson and the annual income thereof or so much thereof respectively as shall not have been applied under any of the trusts or powers herein contained in trust for such person or persons and for such estates and interests as the said William Henry Robinson shall by deed or will appoint and in default of such appointment and so far as no such appointment shall extend then for the survivor of them, the said William Henry Robinson and Emily Abbey, absolutely.' Emily Abbey, otherwise Emily Robinson, was the survivor, and, as the estate given was an equitable estate, the point to be determined is whether, in the absence of words of inheritance, Emily Robinson became entitled to the equitable fee.

When the system of trusts came to be moulded after the Statute of Uses, the Court of Chancery had to lay down rules for the construction of gifts of these new equitable interests. In 1693 Lord Keeper Sommers in the case of *Sheldon* v. *Dormer* (2 Vern. 309, at p. 310) stated the rule as follows: – 'We are here upon a construction of a trust, where the intent of the party is to govern; and Courts of Equity have always in cases of trusts taken the same rule of expounding trusts, and of pursuing the intention of the parties therein, as in cases of wills; and that even in point of limitations of estates where the letter is to be as strictly pursued, as in any case.' Lord Hardwicke also sought to construe all trusts according to the intention of the parties and even went so far in *Bagshaw* v. *Spencer* (1 Ves. Sen. 142) to deny the distinction between executory trusts and trusts executed. The principles of the Court of Chancery were, however, moulded gradually, and in the time of Lord Northington a definite ruling was made and the distinction between executory trusts and trusts executed became firmly established: *Wright* v. *Pearson* (1 Eden

119). In *Austen* v. *Taylor* (1 Eden p. 369) Lord Northington said: 'But where the trusts and limitations are already expressly declared, the Court has no authority to interfere, and make them different from what they would be at law.' Again, in *White* v. *Carter* (2 Eden at p. 368) Lord Northington said: 'For though the Court has no power, where the limitations are expressly declared, to give the words a different sense from what they would bear at law, yet, where its assistance is required to direct the conveyance, it will give that direction according to the intent of the testator apparent upon the face of the will, if that intent is not contrary to any rule of law.' The distinction taken by Lord Northington became firmly established. I have only to refer to Lord Eldon's decision in *Jervoise* v. *Duke of Northumberland* (1 J. & W. 559). Lord Eldon decided this case in 1820 after a long judicial career in which he systematised the doctrines of equity; and, speaking of executed trusts, he said, at p. 571: 'But these are cases where the testator has clearly decided what the trust is to be; and as equity follows the law, where the testator has left nothing to be done, but has himself expressed it, there the effect must be the same, whether the estate is equitable or legal.'

It is to be remarked that these citations deal with the construction placed by the Court of Chancery upon executed declarations of trust and are independent of other heads in equity, such as, for example, to what extent equity will aid a purchaser for value who has obtained a transfer of an equitable estate without words of limitation. It is remarkable that the opinion which is said to be supported by the eminent conveyancers in the past is dependent upon their text-books and is not supported by any citation of decisions in the Court of Chancery. It is, however, desirable to examine them in detail.

In Cruise's 'Digest of the Law of Real Property,' Title XI, 'Use,' Chap. 2, sect. 32, is found a passage which has been relied upon; 'In the alienation of uses none of those technical words which the law requires in the limitation of particular estates were deemed necessary. Thus, a use might be limited in fee simple without the word heirs: for if a sufficient consideration was given, the Court of Chancery would decree the absolute property of the use to be well vested in the purchaser. And as a use was a thing which consisted merely in confidence and privity, and was not held by any tenure, the rules of the common law were not violated.' This citation deals in terms with uses before the Statute of Uses, and I do not think the author meant it to apply to trusts. Certainly, in the 4th edition of this work published in 1835 the editor did not so understand it. For, in Title XII, 'Trust,' chap. 1, two sections appear to have been added by the editor which sum up in precise language the effect of the decisions which I have dealt with:

'Sect. 87, [Notwithstanding the *dictum* of Lord Hardwicke in the case of *Bagshaw* v. *Spencer* (2 Atk. 246) that all trusts were in notion of law executory (and which has been controverted by Fearne with his usual ability) the distinction is now well established between trusts executed and trusts executory, in marriage articles and wills.

'Sect. 88. Where the devise or trust is directly and wholly declared by the testator or settlor, so as to attach on the lands immediately, under the deed or will itself, it is a trust executed and complete; and must be construed strictly according to its legal import, and in analogy to corresponding limitations of legal estates: but where the devise, trust, or agreement is directory or incomplete, describing the intended limitation of some future conveyance or settlement directed to be made for effectuating it, there the trust is executory; and the Court of Chancery will not construe the devise or articles strictly, but will endeavour to discover the intention, and execute the trust, according to that intention.]'

The next passage relied upon is Butler's note to Coke upon Littleton, 290 *b*

(Note 249), XIV. The passage occurs in what Butler describes as an 'Elementary outline of some leading points in the doctrine of trusts affecting real property.' The passage, as cited, is given in some places as: – 'A mere declaration of trust in favour of another has been held sufficient to transfer to him the equitable fee.' So stated, the passage is cited as laying down a rule for the proper construction of executed trusts. But read in its context, Butler states: – 'An equitable estate is by its nature incapable of livery of seizin, and of every form of conveyance which operates by the Statutes of Uses. In the transfer, therefore, of equitable estates these forms of conveyance have been dispensed with and a mere declaration of trust in favour of another has been held sufficient to transfer to him the equitable fee.' It seems to me that Butler is contrasting the modes of conveyance at common law with a simple declaration of trust, but that he is not at all stating what form a declaration of trust must take.

The next citation relied upon is from Mr. Preston, in Vol. II of his 'Elementary Treatise on Estates,' p. 64. He writes: – 'The general rule is that limitations of trust are to be construed in like manner and by the like rules as limitations of a legal estate; and therefore in deeds the fee cannot pass by grant or transfer *inter vivos* without appropriate words of inheritance. But in contracts to convey, and in trusts declared in a conveyance, the fee may pass, notwithstanding the omission of a limitation to the heirs. Therefore articles to convey to A.B. in fee; or a conveyance to A.B. and his heirs, in trust, to convey to C.D. in fee simple, would confer a right in equity to call for a conveyance of the inheritance. So a conveyance to A. and his heirs in trust, *totidem verbis*, for B. in fee, would pass a fee.' As I understand this passage the first portion states the rule of construction applicable to trusts executed in very distinct terms, while the latter portion mentions certain exceptions which are either contracts executory or conveyances for value where equity will assist in the case of a defective conveyance. Unless by the last example Mr. Preston was stating the rule of equity as to conveyances for value, he states two contradictory propositions.

The last citation is the opinion of Mr. Hayes in his 'Introduction to Conveyancing,' 5th edit., Vol. I, p. 91, published in 1840. He says: 'Trusts like uses before the Statute pursued the course of succession appointed for legal interests of a corresponding description. They were expounded to, by analogy to the rules of legal construction. But these rules did not always govern in equity with absolute sway. The rule, for example, which required the word *heirs* to pass the fee in a conveyance at common law, although it was extended to uses within the Statute, was not rigidly applied to trusts. If land was limited in trust for A. without more, equity, in conformity to the rule of law, gave to A. the beneficial interest for life only; but if it could be collected from the instrument that A. was meant to have the absolute interest, equity, esteeming the intention more than the rule, gave him the beneficial fee without the aid of the word heirs.' Mr. Hayes in this passage was either speaking of a conveyance for value made in the form of conveyance with declaration of trust, which is, I think, more likely, or he was following the opinion of Lord Hardwicke without adverting to the fact that his opinion had been dissented from for over a century.

In his judgment in *In re Tringham's Trusts* ([1904] 2 Ch. 487) Mr. Justice Joyce relied upon these passages above examined, and these and several others were relied upon in *Lysaght* v. *McGrath* (11 L.R. Ir. 142) where the limitations in a voluntary deed were ultimately to named children 'absolutely.' In reference to these citations May C.J. in *Lysaght* v. *McGrath* (11 L.R. Ir 142) says at page 156: 'Practically, however, I apprehend that conveyancers deal with executed trusts just as they would with legal estates.' Deasy L.J. did not decide that the fee passed, although he thought the citations from text-writers might lead to that conclusion. FitzGibbon L.J. appears to have held that the fee did not pass, as he said the plaintiffs were not entitled at law and had no equity upon which to found a claim. Mr. Justice Joyce also relied in his judgment on *Pugh* v. *Drew* (17 W.R. 988). The deed to be construed was one settling freeholds upon such and the same trusts as were declared and contained in a settlement of leaseholds made by another deed. Under the settlement of the leaseholds, they were held in the events which happened for A. and B. in equal shares, share and share alike. The objection was taken that there was no mention of the heirs of A. and B. James V.C. overruled this objection, saying that the absence of words of limitation was not absolutely fatal under all circumstances. I regard the case of *Pugh* v. *Drew* (17 W.R. 988) as a clear case of a referential trust declared by reference to another deed and in its nature executory, where the intention of the settlor can be sought out by the Court.

In the Court of Appeal in England Lord Sterndale M.R. in *In re Bostock's Settlement* ([1921] 2 Ch. 469, at p. 480) did not deal with the authorities in detail, but stated his conclusions in the words used in Lewin on Trusts, 12th ed., p. 125: 'But though technical terms be not absolutely necessary, yet where technical terms are employed they shall be taken in their legal and technical sense. Lord Hardwicke, indeed, once added the qualification: "unless the intention of the testator or author of the trust plainly appeared to the contrary." But his position has since been repeatedly and expressly overruled, and at the present day it must be considered a clear and settled canon that a limitation in a trust, perfected and declared by the settlor, must have the same construction as in the case of a legal estate executed.' Warrington L.J. and Younger L.J. agreed, and it is noticeable that Younger L.J. did not find any such difference of view in the view of older text-writers and conveyancers as has been suggested.

I have dealt at perhaps too great length with the decided cases and the opinions of conveyancers, because I find in so many recent Irish cases a welcome adhesion to the views put forward by Joyce J. in *In re Tringham's Trusts* ([1904] 2 Ch. 487). It may be that Lord Hardwicke was wiser than his successors and that equitable interests would have better flourished if they had not been measured so strictly by analogy to the rules of law. But my reading of the cases and authorities is that the stricter rule has prevailed for almost two centuries, and in my opinion the grounds put forward for departing from the rule were not justified by any authority. I agree with the decision of the Court of Appeal in England in *In re Bostock's Settlement* ([1921] 2 Ch. 469, at p. 480), and am of opinion that so many of the Irish authorities as are based on the authority of *In re Tringham's Trusts* ([1904] 2 Ch. 487) must be overruled.

There is, however, on the facts of the present case a special feature which requires consideration. The settlement was made before marriage and the agreement was to settle the husband's lands on the wife absolutely if she survived him. Every provision with regard to her falls directly within the consideration: *Nairn* v. *Prowse* (6 Ves. 756). In my opinion in this case the wife has an equity independent of the declaration of trust made by the settlor and this equity is sufficient to construe the settlement as giving her the equitable fee which it was contracted that she should have in the events which have happened. *Holliday* v. *Overton* (14 Beav. 467) before Sir John Romilly M.R. was the case of a post-nuptial settlement by a widow, and the Master of the Rolls took the distinction, saying that the children were not purchasers of the fee or of any estate of inheritance under the contract.

But as the case was argued solely upon the point which we have decided in favour of the appellant, and as the respondents do not ask us to make a decree upon the terms as to costs which we would be obliged to order in case of the appellant, in the circumstances the appeal must be allowed.

The same order will be made in the appeal conversant with the promissory note, both appeals being treated as one appeal.

Notes and Questions
1. What precisely is the *ratio decidendi* of this case? Consider the views of Costello J. in *Savage* v. *Nolan, infra*.
2. For further discussion of the point, see *Irish Land Law*, para. 4.033.

SAVAGE V. NOLAN

Unreported (High Court) (1976 No. 2395P) (Judgment delivered 20th July, 1978)
The facts are set out fully in the judgment.

Costello J.:

The plaintiffs and the defendant are sisters and are the only children of the late Mr. and Mrs. Patrick Doran of Glenglass, Killan, County Wexford. At the time Mr. and Mrs. Doran married the plaintiffs allege that a marriage settlement dated the 26th of July 1921 had been executed. They say that Thomas Doran and Margaret Doran (the parties' grandparents) were settlors and that they transferred to Trustees the lands described in Folios 6021, 6022 and 5941 of the Register of Freeholders of the County of Wexford and farming stock, crops, household furniture and other chattels (referred to in the settlement as the 'Trust property') to named Trustees upon trust for Thomas Doran for life (and subject thereto upon trust for Margaret Doran for her life) and subject thereto upon trust for Patrick Doran and Elizabeth White (who subsequently became Mrs. Doran) or the survivors of them for his or her life and subject thereto for the children of the intended marriage as Patrick Doran and Elizabeth White should be Deed jointly appoint and in default of appointment upon trust for the children of the intended marriage in equal shares. The plaintiffs say that no Deed of joint appointment was executed and that accordingly they and the defendant are each entitled absolutely to an undivided third share in the trust property.

The defendant denies that there was any marriage settlement such as the plaintiffs allege. She claims that her father and mother were in exclusive beneficial occupation and possession of 'the trust property' for upwards of thirty years prior to their deaths, that they became beneficially entitled as joint tenants or alternatively as tenants in common to the entire of the property and that under the wills of her father and mother she became absolutely entitled to the land and property, subject only to the payment of a legacy of a thousand pounds to each of the plaintiffs.

Whilst it is true that on the pleadings a formal denial of the *existence* of a marriage settlement was made by the defendant this submission was not seriously stressed at the hearing. The evidence clearly established that a marriage settlement was in fact executed on the 26th of July 1921, that the original deed of settlement was forwarded to the Land Registry in the Four Courts, Dublin and that it was destroyed by the Four Courts fire of the 30th of June, 1922. The Plaintiffs sought to adduce secondary evidence of the contents of the Deed and the first crucial issue which I have to determine is the admissibility of this evidence. Two documents were tendered as secondary evidence; if either is admissible then a further question arises as to whether on the true construction of the admitted document the plaintiffs and the defendant take the trust property in equal shares or whether they merely enjoy life interests only in the property.

The evidence relating to the first issue is this. The Doran family had for many years been clients of a long established firm of solicitors in New Ross now known as Messrs Colfer, Son & Poyntz. Mr. Francis Poyntz joined the firm on the 12th of July, 1908 and was in a position to give very helpful evidence in relation to the matters now in dispute. It appears from his evidence that a Mr. Haughey, and not Mr. Poyntz, was handling the affairs of the Doran Family in 1921 and that Mr. Haughey drew up a marriage settlement relating to the marriage of Elizabeth White and Patrick Doran the parents of the parties herein. Mr. Poyntz has now retired from practice and his evidence was taken on commission on the 22nd of May, 1978, and the present proprietor of the firm of Messrs. Colfer, Son & Poyntz is Miss Kelly. Miss Kelly's evidence establishes that shortly before the 22nd of May she carried out a search of the files in her office and there discovered a document which is typed on purple type (and which for ease of reference I will call the 'purple document'). It is this document which the plaintiffs submit can be accepted as secondary evidence of the lost marriage settlement.

The evidence relating to the purple document is this. As I have stated, Miss Kelly undertook a search amongst the files in the office and found the document in what is termed a 'value file' in a press in her office. The filing system in the firm of Messrs Colfer, Son & Poyntz has, over the years, obviously been a most efficient one. In the 'value file' are kept valuable documents relating to clients affairs. They are kept in envelopes which have an index number relating to the correspondence files of the particular case. The envelope in which the purple document was contained also contained an original assignment of trust of the 24th of July, 1888 and an original assignment of the 5th of May, 1893 also relating to the affairs of the Doran Family. Mr. Poyntz was able to identify the handwriting which appears in and on the typescript of the purple document as the handwriting of Mr. Haughey, and he further established that Mr. Haughey left the firm within a few years of the year 1921. Attached to the purple document were two draft affidavits which would, in the normal course of events, have been sworn for the purpose of authenticating the signatures of the parties to the Deed and sent with the Deed to the Land Registry. The weight of all this evidence satisfies me that the purple document came into existence at about the time of the execution of the original marriage settlement and that it has been in the custody of the Doran family's solicitors ever since.

The reliability of the document as truly representing the contents of the executed Deed must now be considered. It is my opinion that in all probability the document was the final draft from which the original Deed was prepared and is not a copy made after the Deed was executed. If this had been a copy of the executed Deed then the date would have been copied by the copyist and not left blank, as it was, in the typescript. Again, if this was a copy of an executed Deed the names of the attesting witnesses and the signatures of the trustees would have been typed in – but these are absent from it. Again, if it was a copy (and not a draft) then it is reasonable to assume that it would not contain the amendments both in type and in handwriting, which now appear on it. The inference that it is a Draft is strengthened by the fact that two draft affidavits are attached to it and by the fact that a blank space for the date of execution was left when it was originally prepared. That Mr. Colfer's name as the attesting witness to the signatures of Mr. and Mrs. Doran appears as having been typed in the document would not necessarily rebut the conclusion which I have reached – the draftsman could have expected that Mr. Colfer would witness his clients' signatures but might not necessarily witness those of the two trustees or the beneficiaries, and have so provided on the draft.

If, then, it is reasonable to conclude that, on the balance of probabilities, the purple document is a draft of the executed Deed can this draft be relied on as representing the contents of the Deed? I think, again, on the balance of probabilities, that it can. It is true that the evidence on this important aspect of the matter is circumstantial but it is nonetheless persuasive. Mr. Haughey was the solicitor acting for the settlors. His handwriting has been verified by Mr. Poyntz whose evidence satisfies me that Mr. Haughey filled in the date 'the 26th of July' on the draft and who also in all probability made the corrections in handwriting in the typescript where errors had, manifestly, crept in. The practice of the firm, Mr. Poyntz has established, was to keep a copy of all original documents which were lodged with the Land Registry and I think I am entitled to assume that Mr. Haughey must have arranged for this document to be filed in the 'value file' containing original documents relating to the affairs of the Doran family. I am also entitled to assume that he would not have done so unless he was satisfied that it truly represented the contents of the original Deed. Added to these factors is the fact that there is independent evidence that corroborates the contents of part of this document; excerpts from the original Deed were abstracted on the Land Registry Folios and these excerpts correspond with the terms of the document. The abstracted excerpts do not, of course, relate to the clauses relevant to these proceedings but their existence on the Folios helps to support the authenticity and reliability of the document. The weight of the evidence, therefore, has satisfied me that the purple document accurately represents the contents of the lost Deed and I will receive it as secondary evidence unless there is a rule of law which prohibits me from so doing.

As I have already pointed out, the purple document has been only found in the course of these proceedings. Before they were instituted the existence of another document (the 'black document') which the plaintiffs alleged was a copy of the marriage settlement was known to the plaintiffs. A copy of this document was sent to the husband of the first-named plaintiff by Mr. Poyntz in a letter of the 1st of August, 1968 and another copy was sent by Mr. White, the executor of each of the parents of the parties hereto, when he swore affidavits for filing in the estate duty office. The black document differs slightly but in no material way from the purple document. In view of the finding I have made in relation to the purple document it is unnecessary for me to make any finding in relation to the other document. It is also unnecessary for me to consider the submission made on the plaintiffs' behalf that the sworn declaration of the executor of Mr. and Mrs. Doran is an admission that the black document is a true copy of the marriage settlement, and is an admission which binds the defendant.

I have approached the resolution of the first issue in this case by considering as a juror should do whether on the balance of probabilities the purple document truly represents the contents of the lost marriage settlement. I must now consider whether there is any rule in the law of evidence which precludes me from approaching the problem in this way or which, otherwise, would require me to reject the purple document as good secondary evidence.

There is very little Irish authority on the legal principles which I should apply and the English authorities which are cited in the text books are not of recent origin. Mr. Maguire, on behalf of the defendant firstly referred to *Brindley* v. *Woodhouse* (1845) C. & K. 647. This was a case concerning a lost sixty year old Deed. There was tendered in evidence a document purporting to be an attested copy of the lost Deed. The person who attested the copy was dead but his handwriting was proved. The Court, however, refused to receive the copy as secondary evidence of the Deed. That case was referred to in *Halifax Banking Company Limited* v. *Woods* 79 L.T.R. 183 which was, again, a case in which the Court refused to accept secondary evidence of a lost Deed on the ground that the document tendered was a draft which had not been compared with the Deed. It is, however, to be noted that this was a case dealing with a dispute between a vendor and purchaser in which the purchaser refused to accept a copy of a Deed when he had requisitioned the original to compare it with the abstract furnished by the vendor's solicitor. The Court decided that the purchaser was not bound to accept the unauthenticated copy, pointing out;

> 'It seems to me that as between vendor and purchaser a vendor, in the present case, has been by misfortune unable to discharge his duty to the purchaser by verifying the abstracted property' (p. 185).

The Irish case of *Nally* v. *Nally & Others* [1953] I.R. 19 was a case in which an original Deed was lost but the solicitor who prepared it was able to prove its execution and the accuracy of a copy. The copy duly stamped was admitted as evidence of the content of the lost Deed. *Kerins* v. *Davoren* (1861) 12 Irish Chancery Reports 352 was a case in which specific performance was sought of an agreement dated the 1st of November, 1768 to grant a lease for lives renewable for ever. The written agreement on which the action was brought was lost but the plaintiff produced as secondary evidence a document purporting to be a copy of it on which was endorsed in the handwriting of the deceased and his solicitor the fact that he had compared it with the original and that it was a true copy and in which he verified the handwriting of the attesting witnesses. The report quotes the Lord Chancellor as stating 'I cannot receive this evidence' but does not give the reasons for his conclusions.

Mr. Herbert, on behalf of the plaintiffs, referred me to Roscoe's 'Evidence in Civil Actions' (1934 Ed.) Vol. 1. p. 13; Halsbury's 'Laws of England', 4 Ed. 'Evidence' paragraph 130; Wigmore 'Evidence' (1940 Ed.) Vol. 7, paragraph 2143; 'The Laws of Evidence', Baron Gilbert, 1769 Ed. p. 98 and to certain of the cases therein mentioned which, he said, supported the submissions (a) that if the purple document was a copy of the original Deed (as the plaintiffs contended it was) it was admissible as secondary evidence; and (b) that if the purple document was, in fact, a draft it was still admissible in evidence. In support of the proposition that copies produced from proper custody may be treated as good evidence he referred to *Permanent Trustee Company of New South Wales* v. *Fells* [1918] A.C. 879 in which the judicial committee of the privy-council expressed the opinion that 'in certain circumstances copies produced from proper custody may after the lapse of time be treated as good evidence' but which also pointed out that this rule does not apply when an original is in actual existence. *Green* v. *Bailey* (1847) 15 Sim. 542 to which he also referred was a case in which the Court accepted that a lost marriage settlement was in conformity with the draft which was produced at the hearing when there was evidence that the marriage settlement had been recited in an instrument and also in a will: *Waldey* v. *Gray* 20 L.R. Equity, 238 was another case in which the Court admitted secondary evidence of a lost Deed of Mortgage. The secondary evidence consisted of a draft from which the original was engrossed. The Court considered a number of circumstances given in evidence to establish that the draft could safely be acted on and Bacon, V.C. (at p. 250) concluded:

> 'Then it is said, very truly, that there are no degrees of secondary evidence, and that the secondary evidence mainly relied on by the plaintiff consists of drafts of Deeds (with one exception where the draft has been lost) and that, although you may prove the contents of a Deed by a copy, yet you must show that the copy was truly made, that it is not a mere copy of a copy, and further that it is the best evidence which the nature of the case furnishes.

Now it is not suggested that any copy of the Deed was ever made. The drafts are not tendered as copies of the Deeds. The drafts are brought out of the repositories of Waters, who prepared the Deeds; they are there standing as records, to a certain extent, of the contents of the Deeds. The endorsements on them show that the Deeds were engrossed from these identical drafts, and they were duly stamped, and duly executed. In my opinion, that is perfectly good secondary evidence.'

From the authorities which I have examined I cannot conclude that there is a rule of law which would require the rejection as evidence of the purple document in this case. There is no rule which prohibits me from reaching a conclusion that in the circumstances of this case and on the balance of probabilities it represents the contents of the lost Deed or which, having reached this conclusion, prohibits me from admitting the document. I therefore propose to accept it as secondary evidence and turn now to examine the rights of the parties in the light of the marriage settlement as evidenced by this document. The settlors had transferred the 'trust property' to Trustees and after making provision for certain life interests declared that the trust property should be held by the Trustees upon trust 'for the children of the said intended marriage as the said Patrick Doran and Elizabeth White shall by Deed jointly appoint and in default of any such appointment upon trust for the children of the said intended marriage in equal shares'. The defendant points to the absence of words of limitation and say that the children of the marriage only take life interests in the freehold registered land and that after the death of the children there is a resulting trust in favour of the first-named settlor. In support of this construction they rely on *In re Bostock's Settlement* [1921] 2 Ch. 469 and *Jameson* v. *McGovern* [1934] I.R. 758.

It is part of the defendant's contention that the Court cannot consider the intention of the settlor in construing the settlement. For reasons which I will refer to later the plaintiffs contend that the settlor's intention in the present case *is* relevant. Before giving my conclusion on this aspect of the problem I think I should indicate what in my opinion the settlors' intention was. A I have already pointed out, having made provision for what was to happen during the lives of their son and his intended wife they then directed that their trustees would hold the trust property for such of the children of the intended marriage as their son and his wife would by Deed jointly appoint. They then made provision that in default of appointment the children of the intended marriage were to take the trust property in equal shares, and went on to provide that if their son predeceased his intended wife and had no children then she was to be paid a sum of £650 and that the Trustees were to hold the property in trust for the first-named settlor his heirs and assigns in fee simple. It seems to me to be clear from an examination of the settlement that although the settlors did not say that their grandchildren were to get the property 'absolutely' and although they did not use any words of limitation to the effect that they were to take the property 'in fee simple', nonetheless the settlors intended that their grandchildren would take the trust property in equal shares absolutely if no joint appointment was made. This interpretation of their intention is strengthened by the fact that the first-named settlor made specific provision for a reversion of the trust property to himself and his heirs in certain circumstances which he specified, but did not so provide if default was made in a joint appointment by his son and his wife.

The defendant in support of her contention that the Court is not permitted to consider the intention of the settlor in construing the effect of the Deed of Settlement relied, firstly, on *In re Bostock's Settlement* ([1921] 2 Ch. 469). In that case the settlor had mortgaged certain freeholds prior to the settlement. On his second marriage he conveyed the equity of redemption in the freeholds to Trustees in fee simple to the use of his wife and himself for successive life interests and afterwards in trust 'for the child or children of the husband now born or hereafter to be born who shall attain the age of 21 years and if more than one in equal shares as tenants in common and if there shall be no such child then in trust for the right heirs' of the husband. The Court of Appeal held that the trusts in the settlement must have the same construction as in the case of legal estates executed and that in the absence of words of limitation the children took life estates only in the freeholds. The settlement also contained an assignment of leaseholds and chattels to the Trustees upon similar trusts but it was pointed out by the Master of the Rolls (p. 479) that no question arose as to the leaseholds and the chattels. In the present case there is also an assignment of chattels to the Trustees as part of the 'trust property' but the plaintiffs do not contend that this part of the trust property is subject to the same construction as is urged in relation to the freehold registered land. The decision of the Court of Appeal was unanimous. In the course of his judgment Younger L.J. pointed out that the decision was arrived at with considerable reluctance as it was based 'not on any presumed intent in the settlement but in spite of and contrary to what I believe to be its real purpose' (p. 487).

The Supreme Court was required to consider a similar problem in *Jameson* v. *McGovern* [1934] I.R. 758. This, too, was a case relating to the construction of a marriage settlement. The defendant had refused to complete a contract on the grounds that the plaintiffs (who were the vendor's representatives) were unable to make out a good title. It was claimed that the title depended on the gift to a wife in a Deed of Settlement who, in the events that had happened, survived her husband but as no words of limitation were used she obtained only a life interest in the property. As both parties in the present case rely on this authority in support of the construction which they urge should be placed on the marriage settlement in the present case I must examine the judgment in some detail.

Firstly, it is important to observe that what the Court was doing was considering whether in an executed declaration of trust words and terms known to the Common Law must be given the same effect in equity or whether the construction of the trust can be gathered from the intention of the settlor (p. 770). It was urged on behalf of the plaintiffs in that case that, following *Bostock's Settlement*, in the case of an executed declaration of trust the Court is precluded from considering the intention of the settlor and that the Court must construe a limitation in a trust in the same way as in the case of a legal estate executed and that therefore in the absence of words of limitation only a life estate was taken by the wife. After a lengthy review of the authorities Murnaghan, J. concluded that the decision in the Court of Appeal in *Bostock's Settlement* should be followed and that accordingly the Court should not as a general rule consider the intention of the settlor but should in the absence of words of limitation, decide that the wife's interest under the settlement was only a life estate.

In a passage towards the end of the judgment Murnaghan, J. adverted to a special feature of the case as follows:

'The settlement was made before marriage and the agreement was to settle the husband's lands on the wife absolutely if she survived him. Every provision with regard to her falls directly within the consideration: *Nairn* v. *Prowse* (6 Ves 752). In my opinion in this case the wife has an equity independent of the declaration of trust made by the settlor and this equity is sufficient to construe the settlement as giving her the equitable fee which it was contracted that she should have in the events which have happened' (pp. 777–778).

Mr. Gill, on behalf of the plaintiffs, submitted that the passage which I have quoted makes clear that there may be exceptions to the general rule laid down in *Bostock's Settlement*. He suggested that an exception arises when a settlement contains an agreement by virtue of which an equity arises (apart from the declaration of trust) by which a person entitled to the equity can have enforced an agreement to grant an equitable fee. Mr. Gill submits that I can apply this principle in the present case. He submits (1) that the settlor intended that the children of the marriage would take absolute interests and (2) that an enforceable agreement exists to that effect as the children of a marriage are persons within the marriage consideration (see Halsbury's 'Laws of England' 3rd Edition p. 459). In support of this submission he refers to *Holliday* v. *Overton* (15 Beav. 480) in which the Master of the Rolls considered an argument that the children referred to in the instrument he was examining should be regarded as 'purchasers' and that being purchasers a construction of the declaration of the trust was required which would vest the fee in the children without the necessity of employing any words of inheritance for this purpose. In that case the Master of the Rolls observed 'if the children mentioned in this settlement could be considered as purchasers within the meaning of the word, as employed in these passages, some argument might be founded on those authorities'. Mr. Gill says that in the case before me the children of the marriage can be regarded as purchasers.

In my opinion the submissions made on behalf of the plaintiffs are correct. Firstly, the decision of the Supreme Court in *Jameson* v. *McGovern* can only be interpreted as meaning that an exception to the strict rule in *Bostock's Settlement* does exist when the settlement being construed contains an agreement to settle the lands referred to in the Deed on the wife of the intended marriage absolutely. Secondly, I am satisfied that the exception applies to the present case. I have already pointed out that the settlor intended that the children of the intended marriage would, in the events that have happened, take absolute interests – even though such express words were not employed. I accept that it is well established that the children of an intended marriage are within the consideration of the marriage and that accordingly the settlement constitutes an agreement which is enforceable by them by which they are entitled to absolute interests in the events that have happened. Just as the wife in *Jameson* v. *McGovern* had an equity which would have allowed the Court to give effect to the intention of the settlor so, in the present case, the children of the marriage have a similar equity. In my opinion I am, not, therefore, required to follow the strict rule of law laid down in *Bostock's Settlement* but I can decide that the settlement, in the events that have happened, has effectively vested an estate in fee simple in the plaintiffs and the defendant since the death of their mother on the 24th of January, 1973.

I will, in the light of the findings I have just made, consider submissions by the parties as to the form the Court's Order should take.

Notes and Questions
1. Costello J. stated that he was applying an exception to the rule laid down in *Re Bostock's Settlement*. Are there any other exceptions to this rule, or are the so-called exceptions really applications of a general principle of equity? See *Irish Land Law*, para. 4.033.
2. The *Savage* case also concerned the problem of lost deeds, as to which see *Irish Conveyancing Law*, paras 13.52–53.

GILBOURNE V. GILBOURNE
Unreported (High Court) (1974 No. 1635p) (Judgment delivered 9th July, 1975)
The facts are set out fully in the judgment.

Kenny J.:

William Gilburn ('the testator') was the registered owner of part of the lands of Cloonpasteen in the County of Limerick which had been registered on Folio 2798 of the Register of Freeholders for the County of Limerick on the 11th June 1906. He was also registered as owner of part of the lands of Bohard in the same county which had been registered on Folio 10439 of the Register for that county in 1919. Part IV of the Registration of Title Act 1891 applied to the devolution of both these lands.

On the 3rd April 1926 he made his will his signature to which was witnessed by two solicitors. The relevant parts of it read:

'I William Gilburn of Cloonpasteen Kilmeedy in the County of Limerick Farmer made and declare this writing as and for my last will and testament revoking all former wills if any heretofore made by me.

I will devise and bequeath unto my nephews Patrick Gilburn and William Gilburn sons of my brother Robert my lands of Cloonpasteen and Bohard to be held by them as joint tenants so that same shall pass to the heir-at-law of the survivor of them, subject to and charged with the payment of my debts, funeral and testamentary expenses'.

The testator died on the 8th July 1936 and his nephews, who were subsequently registered as limited owners, took possession of the lands. At some time during their joint lives, William transferred his share of the joint tenancy to his son Robert and so severed the joint tenancy for the joint lives or, as the defendants contend, severing the joint tenancy in the fee simple. William Gilburn died on the 14th October 1962 and Patrick on the 14 October 1972. The plaintiff in this action was the heir-at-law of Patrick and claims that he is the owner of the lands under the terms of the testator's will. His case is that the will created a joint tenancy in the two nephews for their lives and when one died, a tenancy for life in the survivor with a contingent remainder in favour of the person who was the heir-at-law of the survivor. The defendants are the next-of-kin of the nephew William and they contend that the effect of the celebrated rule in *Shelley's Case* (1581) 1 Co. Rep. 93 was that the two nephews Patrick and William became owners in fee simple as joint tenants of the lands and that as next-of-kin of William, they are now entitled to one half of them.

The most authoritative statement of this rule is to be found in the speech of Lord Davey in *Van Grutten* v. *Foxwell* [1897] A.C. 658 at pp. 684 and 685. I say 'most authoritative' because it has been cited in all subsequent cases though Lord Macnaghten's speech is more entertaining and in many ways more profound. Lord Davey's statement of the rule is:

'In my opinion the rule in *Shelley's Case* is a rule of law and not a mere rule of construction – i.e. one laid down for the purpose of giving effect to the testator's expressed or presumed intention. The rule is this: that wherever an estate for life is given to the ancestor or propositus, and a subsequent gift is made to take effect after his death, in such terms as to embrace, according to the ordinary principles of construction, the whole series of his heirs or heirs of the body or heirs male of his body or whole inheritable issue taking in a course of succession, the law requires that the heirs, or heirs male of the body, or issue, shall take by descent, and will not permit them to take by purchase, notwithstanding any expression of intention to the contrary. Wherever, therefore, the Court comes to the conclusion that the gift over includes the whole line of heirs, general or special, the rule at once applies, and an estate of inheritance is executed in the ancestor or tenant for life, even though the testator has expressly declared that the ancestor shall take for life and no longer, or has endeavoured to graft upon the words of gift to the heirs, or heirs of the body, additions, conditions or limitations which are repugnant to an estate of inheritance, and such as the law cannot give effect to. The rule, I repeat, is not one of construction, and indeed, usually overrides and defeats the expressed intention of the testator; but the question always remains, whether the language of the gift after the life estate properly construed is such as to embrace the whole line of heirs or heirs of the body or issue, and that question must be determined apart from the rule, according to the ordinary principles of construction, including those which I have already referred to.

The testator may conceivably show by the context that he has used the words 'heirs' or 'heirs of the body' or 'issue' in some limited or restricted sense of his own which is not the legal meaning of the words – e.g. he may have used the words in the sense of children or as designating some individual person who would be heir of the body at the time of the death of the tenant for life or at some other particular time. If the Court is judicially satisfied that the words are so used, I conceive that the premises for the application of the rule in *Shelley's Case* are wanting, and the rule is foreign to the case. But I repeat, that in every case the words are to be interpreted in their legal sense as words of limitation unless it be made plain to the mind of the Court that they are not so used, and in what sense they are used by the testator.'

This decision and the many other reported cases, old and modern, relating to the application of the rule establish these principles which have relevance to the question in this case:

1. While the rule is a rigid rule of law when its application to a deed is being considered, the first question which arises when its application to a will is involved is one of construction, did the testator by the use of the words 'his heirs' or 'heirs of the body' or any corresponding words mean heirs of the ancestor generally or, as it is sometimes put, the whole line of succession or did he mean a specific person who fulfilled the qualification of being 'the heir' or 'the heir of the body' of the ancestor. If he meant one specific person, the rule does not apply.

2. In a deed the word 'heirs' or the words 'heirs of the body' must be used if the rule is to apply (*Mallory's Case* (1601) 5 Co. Rep. 111) but in a will the rule may apply when words having the same meaning as 'heirs' or 'heirs of the body' are used. (Lord Davey's speech in *Van Grutten* v. *Foxwell* [1897] A.C. 658: *Re Keane's Estate* [1903] 1 I.R. 215).

3. When the word 'heir' is used, it is easier for the Court to find an intention that the testator did not mean the whole line of succession but referred only to an individual who fulfilled a qualification. (*Silcocks* v. *Silcocks* [1916] 2 Ch. 161 at p. 166: *In re Hack* [1925] 1 Ch. 633: Megarry and Wade: The law of Real Property 1st edition p. 62).

4. It was not contested that the rule in *Shelley's Case* may apply to the will of an owner of freehold registered land. It seems to me that it does for it is the devolution on intestacy of such land which has been changed.

It seems to me that the construction of the will indicates that the testator was using the word 'heir-at-law' in the sense that he was referring to a designated person, the individual who would be the heir-at-law of the survivor of Patrick and William. My reasons for forming this view are:

1. The testator's signature was witnessed by two solicitors and the language of the will shows that it was drafted by one of them. He would have been aware that the lands would descend to the next-of-kin and not the heir of the survivor of the two joint tenants if the survivor died intestate. It is reasonable therefore to infer that the testator who gave the instructions had the heir-at-law of the survivor in mind and did not intend the words to refer to the whole line of succession but to the designated person, the heir-at-law of the survivor.

2. The limitation is not 'to be held by them as joint tenants and on the death of the survivor to the heir-at-law of such survivor' but 'to be held by them as joint tenants so that the same shall pass to the heir-at-law of the survivor of them'. The use of the words 'so that the same shall pass' indicates that the testator intended the lands to go to a specific person. The case is within Lord Davey's words: 'he may have used the words in the sense of children or as designating some individual person who would be heir of the body at the time of the death of the tenant for life or at some other particular time'.

3. The limitation is not to the *heirs* of the survivor but to the *heir-at-law* of the survivor of them and although the word *heir-at-law* can attract the rule, its use indicates that the testator had in mind a specific individual who fulfilled a qualification, being heir-at-law of the survivor. This taken with the other two points shows that the rule does not apply to this gift. As the rule in *Shelley's Case* does not apply, I reject the contention that the effect of the will was to make the two nephews joint tenants in fee simple. Though the joint tenancy for life was severed, on William's death the lands passed to Patrick for his life and on his death to his heir-at-law.

The questions will be answered accordingly.

Notes and Questions
1. An appeal against this decision was lodged, but was, with consent, dismissed. *Cf. Finch* v. *Foley* [1949] Ir. Jur. Rep. 30; *Re Fallon* [1956] I.R. 286.
2. For further discussion of the rule in *Shelley's Case*, see *Irish Land Law*, para. 4.034 *et seq.* See also *Kennedy and Lawler* v. *Ryan*. p. 372, *post.*
3. On severance of a joint tenancy, see p. 376, *post.*

2. *Classification of Fee Simple Estates*

ATTORNEY-GENERAL V. CUMMINS
[1906] 1 I.R. 406 (Exch. D.)
The facts are set out in the judgment.

Palles C.B. (giving the judgment of the Court):

The first question for decision is the legal effect of the Letters Patent of 5th July, 31 Charles II. By those Letters Patent King Charles II granted to Thomas Lord Audley, Earl of Castlehaven, his heirs and assigns, certain quit rents particularly mentioned in the Patent and therein stated to amount in the whole to the yearly rent or sum of £499 19s. 11¼d., 'to hold the same to the earl, his heirs and assigns, 'till he or they should receive and be paid the sum of £5,000 sterling at one entire payment, and without any manner of account, or any other thing to be rendered or paid unto His Majesty, his heirs and successors, of or for the same or any part thereof.'

By the present information, filed upwards of 200 years after this grant, the Attorney-General asks that Her Majesty shall be at liberty to redeem the quit rents by paying the sum of £5,000; that she may be at liberty to pay that sum into Court; that if necessary a release of the quit rents may be decreed to be executed by all necessary parties; that new trustees of certain instruments may be appointed (such trustees being, as I presume, in the view of the Crown necessary parties to the release); and that the quit rents may be ordered to be put in charge in the Crown rental for collection in future by the proper officer on behalf of Her Majesty.

There has been some argument as to the nature of the estate granted by the Letters Patent. In my opinion, that estate was that which is sometimes called a base or qualified fee (Co. Litt. 1 b; 2 Bl. Com. 109), and sometimes a fee determinable (Plowd. 557). The grant passed the quit rents in fee subject to a condition determining that fee upon the payment by the Crown at any time of the sum of £5,000. Under such a grant the grantee, until the happening of the determining event, has the whole estate in him, and the old Common Law doctrine was undoubtedly that a possibility of reverter, a possibility coupled with an interest, remained in the grantor, and that the fee of the rents would, upon the performance of the condition, revert to the Crown. 'If,' says Plowden (p. 557), 'land is given to a man and to his heirs so long as he shall pay 20s. annually to A, or as long as the Church of St. Paul shall stand, his estate is a fee-simple determinable, in which case he has the whole estate in him, and such perpetuity of an estate which may continue for ever, though, at the same time, there is a contingency *which when it happens will determine the estate*.' The case for the Crown is, that this Common Law doctrine still prevails notwithstanding the modern rule against perpetuities. The defendants, on the other hand, insist that the rule as to perpetuities applies, and defeats the estate in the Crown. Whether it does or not, is the principal question.

It is, however, further contended by the defendants that, as in the case of the Attorney-General, the Crown would on payment of the money have the legal estate, the release sought, or any intervention of this Court as a Court of Equity, would be unnecessary, and that therefore the information should be dismissed. I agree that the Patent is not in the nature of a mortgage; and that as a suit for the redemption of a mortgage, this information cannot be maintained. Nevertheless, as the acts of those claiming through the Patentee have so complicated the title to the quit rents as to render it difficult, if not impossible, for the Crown to ascertain without the aid of this Court the parties entitled to receive the money in question, which, at law, they are entitled to pay, and for which they are entitled to obtain a legal discharge, I cannot entertain any doubt that the Attorney-General is entitled to come into this Court by an information against all the parties having estates in the rents, and have discovery as to the parties entitled to the money, on payment of which the fee will vest in the Crown, to have the rights of those parties determined *inter se*, as in an interpleader suit, and to have the money in question brought in to the credit of the suit, and, pending the ascertainment of the parties entitled to it, to have the sum so lodged treated as having been actually paid to such of the parties in the suit as the Court may ultimately decide to be entitled to it. This relief I conceive the Crown to be entitled to, even upon an information framed as is the present.

Thus, the only real question is whether the estate of the Crown is defeated by the rule against perpetuities.

The grant in question operated at Common Law. It did not take effect under the Statute of Uses, and the modern rule against perpetuities never applied to Common Law conveyances. It is impossible that it could have applied, as it had its origin in the Statute of Uses, as is matter of elementary knowledge; and the subject-matter of that statute did not include conveyances other than those to uses.

There was no doubt a doctrine which was sometimes quaintly and unintelligibly (and indeed, as shown by Lord Northington, erroneously) enunciated as the rule that an estate could not be limited to take effect upon a possibility upon a possibility. This rule related to the ascertainment of the person who was to take, and is shown by Mr. Preston to be confined to cases in which either such person was insufficiently designated, or in which there was no individual who answered the description, if sufficient. This doctrine has no application to the present case.

The only mode by which the Common Law held that a previous estate might be determined before its natural expiration was by means of the annexation of a condition. But if a condition were annexed, then, on the happening of the stipulated event, the estate was defeated, and the donor or his heirs were entitled to enter, and on entry, or in a case like the present, where the subject-matter is incorporeal hereditaments without entry, was in of his former estate. If modern recognition of this Common Law elementary doctrine be required, it will be found, in the opinion of Lord Cairns (then Lord Chancellor), in *The Buckhurst Peerage Case* (2 App. Cas. 1, at p. 26): – 'The Common Law did understand one mode of putting an end to an estate which in the first instance appeared to be granted absolutely, that is to say, it understood the mode of terminating an estate by means of the annexation of a condition. If a condition was annexed to an estate which otherwise would have been absolute, then on the happening of the condition the estate was defeated. But then, my lords, it was not defeated for the benefit of the remainderman; nor could a remainder have been annexed to the condition. It was defeated as defeasible by or *for the donor* who was entitled to enter for condition broken.'

A feoffor making a feoffment in fee, containing such a condition, retained thereafter an interest in the lands which was called a possibility. That possibility was coupled with an interest, and upon the performance of the condition, this interest, by the determination of the estate of the feoffee, expanded into an estate in fee, and the feoffor was in as of his former estate. It was not that the feoffment was construed as containing a limitation of the estate to the feoffor upon the performance of the condition, but that the 'possibility,' which always continued in the feoffor, became in event an estate in fee.

I fear that I have too much laboured these elementary propositions; but it is essential to do so to expose the fallacy which underlies the contention of the defendants.

Now, there is not a trace in the books of any rule which limited the period during which the determination of an estate by condition should take effect, and it is abundantly clear that the modern rule could not have applied, because the donor took not by way of new limitation, but by the determination of the estate given.

An estate to A and his heirs, so long as they were tenants of the manor of Dale, is a form of limitation frequently found in the old books. It was held to vest in A an estate in fee, determinable upon him or his heirs ceasing to be tenants of the manor. There is no instance (as remarked in the *Buckhurst Peerage Case* (2 App. Case. 1)) of such an estate being followed by a remainder to other persons. It was not possible that it could be, because the *whole* fee was vested in the grantee of the determinable fee until the performance of the condition, and a fee could not at Common Law be limited upon a fee; but no doubt was ever entertained that, on the happening of the indicated event and entry by the donor, the estate granted determined. In whom, then, did the fee vest? It was not in the donee, *ex hypothesi* his estate had ceased. It could not have become vested in a stranger, as at Common Law such a limitation would be void. But, necessarily, it should be in someone. The only person in whom it could be – and, therefore, the person in whom it must have been – was the donor, or those claiming through him. Irrespective, therefore, of its non-application to estates, created by Common Law conveyances, the rule against perpetuities could not, from the nature of the estate, apply in a case like the present, without abrogating the elementary principle that, on the happening of the event, the fee in the grantee determined.

These considerations, in my opinion, conclude the case. As, however, it has been so elaborately argued, it may be right that, in deference to the defendants' counsel, I should express my view more fully as to the origin of the rule.

Uses, before the Statute, were not within the cognizance of the Common Law; effect was given to them by Courts of Equity holding that they affected the conscience of the feoffee, and it was of course competent to these Courts to refuse to give effect as against the legal estate to uses which they considered to be injurious to the State. The history of England demonstrates that long prior to this period there was the utmost jealousy against anything that at Common Law would render land inalienable for a lengthened period, such, for instance, as the vesting of it in a corporation. The Lord Chancellors, to whom the origin of this rule is to be traced, did not affect to alter the Common Law, nor was it within their competence to do so; but when, before the statute, the practice became common of conveying to a feoffee or trustee to uses, and where the estate of the *cestui que use* was cognizable in Equity only, they refused the relief of that Court in favour of the *cestui que use* as against the Common Law estate in cases in which, had relief been afforded, the land would have been rendered inalienable for a period which they considered unreasonable. Thus, but for the Statute of Uses, the rule against perpetuity would, until the present, have had no relation to estates created by deed; and, as to other estates, would have remained a purely equitable doctrine. But then came the statute which clothed with the legal estate any use which had been validly created. At this point the Common Law Courts had to intervene, as it was their province to determine where the legal estate was. But to do so they should first determine that the use was a valid one, and in determining this question, which, up to this time, had been purely an equitable one, they adopted the principles which Courts of Equity had theretofore acted upon. Thus the rule as to perpetuities became a Common Law doctrine applicable to springing and shifting uses, and executory and other limitations of property, which could not be created by a Common Law conveyance, and which could take effect only under the Statute of Uses. If I am right in this, the doctrine must be inapplicable to estates created by Common Law conveyances, and especially to estates which reverted to donors on the performance of conditions which determined estates.

In support of what I have said, I shall refer but to two authorities – (1) The Report of the Commissioners appointed to inquire into the law of England respecting real property, including amongst their number such eminent Conveyancers as Mr. Duval, Mr. Hodgson, and Mr. Brodie, who are the very highest authorities upon questions of this nature. In their third report they state as follows: – 'the instances adduced in illustration of the law of perpetuity are all interests springing out of the Statutes of Uses and Wills or deriving effect as executory trusts, and there are interests which, as they have remained interests at the Common Law, and are uninfluenced by the Statute of Uses, or by the doctrine of trusts or devises, have never been considered to be subject to the rules against perpetuity.'

So, too, Lord St. Leonards, in his introduction to his edition of Gilbert on Uses (p. xl), says – '*Remainders* at that time,', *i.e.* before the Statute of Uses, '*might have been limited to take effect at any period*, however remote. Questions of perpetuity did not arise till the simplicity of the Common Law gave way to the complication of modern conveyancing'; and in his work on Powers (p. 1), the same learned personage says: + 'Simplicity was the striking feature of the Common Law, in regard as well to the estates which might be created, as to the modes by which they might be raised. Estates could only be limited in possession, or by way of remainder, that is, on the natural expiration of the preceding estate. A *condition* might, however, have been annexed, as it still may be to an estate on its original creation; but this did not answer for the purpose of a settlement, because, for a breach of the condition, only the grantor or his heir could enter, and his entry would defeat all the remainders dependent on the estate to which the condition was annexed. *Questions of perpetuity did not arise* until the simplicity of the Common Law gave way to the complication of modern conveyancing.'

It is interesting to point out that, even in these modern times, we have cases which depend for their solution upon the validity of Common Law conditions such as the present. I refer to cases of Welsh mortgages, instances of which have occurred even during my own practice at the bar. They are well illustrated by *Howel* v. *Price* (1 P.W. 291; 2 Vern. 701; Pre. Ch. 423, 477). There one Davis mortgaged lands, in Wales, by lease and release, to one Reynolds, and his heirs, for securing £300, with a proviso that if Davis, his heirs or assigns, should, at Michaelmas, 1702, *or at any Michaelmas following*, pay to Reynolds, his heirs or assigns, the sum of £300, and all arrears of rent or interest which should be then due, the conveyance should be void. It was decreed that this was in the nature of a conditional purchase, subject to be defeated on payment by the mortgagor or his heirs of the sum stipulated on Michaelmas Day at the election of the mortgagor or his heirs, and that there was an everlasting subsisting right of redemption, descendible to the heirs of the mortgagor, which could not be forfeited at law like other mortgages, and, therefore, there could be no equity of redemption nor any occasion for the assistance of a Court of Equity, but that the plaintiff might even at law defeat the conveyance by performing the terms and conditions of it, which were not limited to any particular time, but might be performed on *any* Michaelmas Day *to the end of the world*.

For the defendants we have been referred to two cases which ought not to be passed over without notice, viz.: *London and South-Western Railway Company* v. *Gomm* (20 Ch. D. 562), and *Cooper* v. *Stewart* (14 App. Cas. 286).

In the first of these cases the question arose upon a conveyance in fee by the Railway Company which contained a covenant by the grantee that he would, at any time thereafter, whenever the land might be required for the railway or works, and when requested by the Company on a six months' notice, and upon receiving £100, reconvey the lands to the Company. The distinction between that case and the present is that there there was a covenant, here there is a condition; there the jurisdiction was the equitable one of specific performance, here there is the dry legal question as to the estate created by the Common Law conveyance.

In *Cooper* v. *Stewart* (14 App. Cas. 286) the question was the validity of a reservation in a Crown grant of lands in New South Wales of 'such parts of the said lands as are now or shall hereafter be required by the proper officer of His Majesty's Government for a highway or highways, and further any quantity of water and any quantity of land not exceeding ten acres *in any part of* the said grant *as may be required for public purposes*, provided always that such water or lands so required should not interfere with or in any manner injure or prevent the due working of the water mills erected, *or to be erected*, on the lands, and water-courses hereby granted.' There the counsel for the Crown (now Lord Davey) insisted that, although the rule against perpetuities had been applied to conveyances operating under the Statute of Uses, it had not been applied to Common Law conditions or conditional limitations in Common Law grants which would have been valid before that Statute. Lord Watson, having referred to these arguments, says – 'It does not appear to their Lordships to be necessary for the purpose of the present case to decide whether the Crown, in attaching such reservations to grants of land in England, would be affected by the rule against perpetuities.' He then proceeds to decide in favour of the Crown upon the ground that the rule did not, in that colony, apply against the Crown. The case cannot be said to be an authority one way or the other. It does not even show that the question is arguable, as it would have been illogical for the Privy Council to have given an opinion upon a rule which they held to be inapplicable to the case before them.

The only remaining matter which was argued can be disposed of in a few words. It appears that for many years the Patentee has not been in receipt of some of the quit rents which are expressed to be granted, but it does not very clearly appear whether these latter quit rents were vested in the Crown at the date of the Patent. In my view the latter circumstance is immaterial. I am willing to assume that the Crown had not title to this portion of the quit rents. The Attorney-General is content that the declaration of the title of the Crown should be confined to the residue.

But the defendants say that we should compel the Crown, as a condition precedent to our declaring it entitled to this residue of the quit rents, to pay into Court, in addition to the £5,000, the portions of these quit rents which accrued during the last 200 years, and which the defendants allege still remain unpaid. Many answers may be given to this contention; I shall mention but two. Our decree in this suit will do no more than give effect to a legal estate vested in the Crown. Upon lodgment in Court of the £5,000, the rents will, as between the Crown and the defendants, revert to the Crown, and we can no more refuse to direct that those rents shall be put in charge on the Crown rental for collection in future by the proper officer on behalf of Her Majesty than upon an information of intrusion we could refuse the authority of this Court to remove the intruder from the lands of the Crown. It cannot be contended that the defendants have any equitable right to restrain the Crown from insisting upon its legal title. But further (and this goes to the whole merits of this portion of the defence) the grant of Charles II was not one for valuable consideration. It was an act of mere bounty, and it does not contain any warranty of title. Its effect, even had it been the grant of a common person, would have been no more than to pass such estate in the rents as the grantor had, and the grantee would have been without remedy if the title of the grantor turned out to be defective. For this reason it is unnecessary to consider how the case would have stood had the grant been such as had it been that of a common person might have been the foundation of an action against him for damages. Even in that event, I cannot see what jurisdiction we should have had without a petition of right; and even were there such a proceeding, the case would, for other reasons, be full of difficulty.

Upon the whole, then, I am of opinion that both of the defences relied upon by the defendants fail, and that there must be a decree declaring that, upon the true construction of the Patent, the estate thereby granted in the quit rents will, upon payment of the sum of £5,000 late currency to the persons entitled thereto, cease and determine, and (as the defendants are the only persons now in receipt of such quit rent) that upon the lodgment of £5,000 in Court, those quit rents shall be put in charge of the proper officer, and shall thenceforth be collected for the use of Her Majesty. Proper directions will be given for ascertaining the parties entitled to the fund brought into Court.

We have carefully considered the question of costs. Even if the defendants had not relied upon the invalidity of the condition, it would have been necessary, by reason of the complexity of the title to the money, that an information such as the present should be filed; and, having regard to the terms of the grant and the length of time that has elapsed since its execution, I should in that event have thought that the Crown should have paid the defendants' general costs of the suit. Upon the other hand, all the additional costs caused by insisting upon the untenable defences relied on ought to be paid to the Crown by the defendants; and instead of directing a taxation which would be complicated, I think the justice of the case will be met by directing that each party shall bear his own costs down to and including the present hearing.

Notes and Questions
1. What sort of fee simple was the one under consideration in this case? See *Irish Land Law*, para. 4.046 *et seq.*
2. As regards the rule against perpetuities, see further p. 263, *post.*

RE KING'S TRUSTS
(1892) 29 L.R. Ir. 401 (Ch. D.)

A testatrix by her will bequeathed an annuity of £50 a-year to each of the five children of her deceased brother G. (of whom R.K. was one), and directed that the said several annuities should be payable half-yearly from the date of her decease, for their respective lives, or until any of them should marry, and that, on the death or marriage of any of the said children of G. the annuity to any such child should cease and determine. There was no gift over in the event of such death or marriage. R.K. married in the lifetime of the testatrix, but after the date of the will. His wife was still living.

Porter M.R.:

The first question which arises is whether the same principles as to forfeiture apply in the case of a legatee, who marries in the lifetime of the testator, but after the date of the will, as of one who is unmarried at the death, but afterwards marries, and it must be answered in the affirmative.

Andrew v. *Andrew* (1 Coll. 690) is, no doubt, not strictly in point: because the words there were 'remain unmarried'; and a person who was married at the time from which the will speaks could not be said in any sense to 'remain' unmarried, so as to fulfil the condition, and the Vice-Chancellor, in that case, says (p. 691), 'According to my view of the case, therefore, the gift to Eliza Andrew would have been absolute, as she survived the testator, if she had not married in his lifetime. She did marry in his lifetime; and as the gift to her was only so long as she should remain unmarried, it never took effect; and without using the word "lapse" the consequence is the same, so far as she is concerned, as if she had died in the testator's lifetime.'

But *Bullock* v. *Bennett* (7 D.M. & G. 283) is a distinct authority for the proposition. The words of the will are 'Upon trust to pay the income thereof to my daughter, Mary Anne, for her life, or until her marriage, and after her decease or marriage, which shall first happen,' then upon trust over. Mary Anne had been twice married before the date of the testator's will, but was a widow at the time of its execution. Subsequently in the lifetime of the testator she married the defendant.

Turner L.J., says (pp. 285–286): 'Questions of this nature must depend upon the language and context of the instrument, and the point to be ascertained here is, whether the testator is referring to the state of circumstances as they existed at the date of the will, or as they might exist at the time of his death. I state advisedly that, in my judgment, this is the point, notwithstanding the late Wills Act, which by its

24th section enacts, that every will shall be construed with reference to the real and personal estate comprised in it, as if it had been executed immediately before the death of the testator, unless a contrary intention shall appear by the will. It is "with reference to the real and personal estate comprised in it," that the will is to speak, as if executed immediately before the death of the testator. I understand this to mean not with reference to the objects of the testator's bounty, who are to take the real and personal estate, but with reference to the real and personal estate which is to be taken by those objects. Had it been intended otherwise, the words with reference to the real and personal estate would hardly, if at all, have been required to be inserted.

'The statute, therefore, does not in my opinion affect the case, and we must consider the question on the language and context of the will. Now, according to the dispositions of the will, the trustees are to pay the income to the daughter during her life, or until her marriage. It was present, therefore, to the testator's mind, when he made his will, that she was not at that time married, and he has made this more clear by ulterior dispositions by which he has given the fund after her decease or marriage to the children of her first and second husband. Are we then to understand a testator who thus speaks of his legatee as not being married, to refer when he speaks of her future marriage, not to her next marriage, if it should take place in his lifetime, but to any future and subsequent marriage which may take place after his decease? I think not, but that we must apply the words which the testator uses to what his will shows to have been passing in his mind at the time. He demonstrates that he was referring to the circumstances as they then stood, and we must apply his words to those circumstances.'

The curious case of *Rishton* v. *Cobb* (5 Ml. & Cr. 145) is plainly distinguishable from *Andrew* v. *Andrew* (1 Coll. 690); *Bullock* v. *Bennett* (7 D.M. & G. 283), and the present case, because there the legatee was married at the date of the will, though the testator did not know it.

I must therefore deal with the right to the annuity in question as if the marriage of Robert Ebenezer King had taken place after the death of the testatrix.

The law applicable to such cases is, I think, most clearly and succinctly expressed by Sir James Wigram in *Morley* v. *Rennoldson* (2 Ha. 570). There he says:

'The rule of the civil law was referred to in the argument, as it has usually been on questions of this nature, but that law – founded, as Lord Loughborough observes, on social maxims and public policy, so essentially different from our own as to render it difficult to conceive how it could have been adopted by our Courts on this subject – has not been followed with regard to conditions operating in restraint of marriage. The extent to which the civil law has been gradually departed from is to be collected from Lord Thurlow's judgment in *Scott* v. *Tyler* (1 Dick. 712). In the English law a distinction has been taken between the cases in which the restraint operates as a condition precedent, and those in which it is expressed to take effect as a condition subsequent. A distinction has also been made as to whether it is a particular restraint (a partial and reasonable restraint), or whether it is a general restraint; and the decision is generally made to depend upon the question, whether there is a gift over, or no gift over. In *Stackpole* v. *Beaumont* (3 Ves. 88) Lord Loughborough appears to have said, that, such was the state of the authorities, a Judge could not be considered to act too boldly whichever side of the proposition he should adopt. There are some points, however, which seem clearly settled, according to the law as administered in Courts of justice in this country; one is, that, if the restraint is a general restraint, and the condition is subsequent, then the condition is altogether void, and the party retains the interest given to him, discharged of the condition; that is, supposing a gift of a certain duration, and an attempt to abridge it by a condition in restraint of marriage, generally the condition is *prima facie* void, and the original gift remains. But, until I heard the argument in this case, I had certainly understood that, without doubt, where property was limited to a person until she married, and when she married then over, the limitation was good. It is difficult to understand how this could be otherwise; for in such a case there is nothing to give an interest beyond the marriage. If you suppose the case of a gift of a certain interest, and that interest sought to be abridged by a condition, you may strike out the condition, and leave the original gift in operation; but if the gift is until marriage and no longer, there is nothing to carry the gift beyond the marriage. With reference to that point, and also in order that the grounds of my decision might clearly appear to those parties against whom it might be, I wished to look into the authorities; and I am satisfied, from an examination of the authorities, that there is no reason to alter my opinion, that a gift until marriage, and when the party marries then over, is a valid limitation.'

The question in each case where there are words which seem to impose a general restraint upon marriage coupled with a gift over is whether they constitute a limitation or a condition subsequent; and I have to consider the language of the will before me in reference to that question.

The solution of it is to be found in the very words used; and very little help can be derived from decisions in reference to other wills where the language is different.

Here it is to be observed that there is in the first clause a gift which, if it stood alone, would be sufficient to confer a life estate upon each annuitant. The words are, 'I leave and bequeath to my sister Elizabeth Tatam an annuity of £200 a-year; to my brother Robert King an annuity of £300 a-year; to my brother James King an annuity of £200 a-year; to each of the five children of my deceased brother George King, namely, George King, Florence King, Robert Ebenezer King, Helena King, and Isabella King, an annuity of £50 a-year each.'

And when we come to the following clause there are words which might be read as cutting down, in a specified event, that of marriage, the extent of the benefit already given. The testatrix directs that these annuities are to be payable half-yearly from the date of her death, 'for the respective lives of my said brothers and sister, and for the respective lives of my said nephews and nieces, or until any of them shall marry; and on the death or marriage of any of my said nephews or nieces, whichever shall first happen, I direct the annuity to any nephew or niece so dying or marrying shall cease and determine.'

But though this is so, and though for that reason the case is one of much nicety, I am of opinion, on the whole, and endeavouring to construe the words before me in their fair natural meaning and import, that it is a case of limitation and not of condition or defeasance. I think the meaning is that each legatee is to have his or her annuity till death or marriage – whichever first happens; and that, on the authority of such cases as *Evans* v. *Rosser* (2 H. & M. 190) is a limitation merely.

Having given the annuities in general terms the testatrix proceeds to define the mode and time of payment of each – and its duration; and it is to be observed that the words indicating cesser are applied to the event of *death* as well as that of marriage, which would be quite unnecessary if the testatrix had supposed the words first used would, *per se*, confine the benefit, in any event, to a life interest. I think the whole clause must be taken as intimately connected with, and forming a part of the gift itself. Indeed, in the case of the annuities to the brothers and sister of testatrix – as to whom no reference to marriage is made, I suppose, because they were actually married to the knowledge of testatrix – she deemed an express limitation for life necessary or at least proper: a circumstance strongly confirmatory of the view that the clause is to be read as if it were a sort of *habendum*.

As against this view, I drew attention to the terms of the legacies to the Tatams, as to which there is nothing to define the duration of their estate except the general rule of law that an annuity to A B, without more, now means an annuity for his life; and the inference to be derived from this would be that Miss King knew the rule of law, and knew that no *habendum* was needed, and that therefore the subsequent words might more properly be treated as a conditional defeasance than as a limitation in reference to the annuities with which they are connected. It may be, however, that there was some omission of words which the testatrix would have used had her attention been called to it; and having regard to the fact I have pointed out that a distinct and express limitation of an estate to end at death is employed in the case of the brothers and sister – without any such words referring to their or her marriage – I think I am bound, on the whole clause, to hold that the words are words of mere limitation. I confess I should have been better pleased could I have arrived at the opposite conclusion; for it is a hard case that the nephew, who knew nothing of the will, and did not consciously violate the wishes of testatrix, should lose the benefit she meant for him without having any option in the matter. But, on the other hand, there can be no doubt that her intentions are best carried out by the construction I am driven to adopt.

The case is an instance of the very unsatisfactory state of the law on this question. It is little short of disgraceful to our jurisprudence that in reference to a rule professedly founded on considerations of public policy, a gift of an annuity to A B for life, coupled with a proviso that if he married the annuity should cease, whether there be a gift over or not, gives A B a life estate, whether he marries or not; while a gift to C D until he marries or dies, with a gift over, is at an end if C D should marry. The distinction is intelligible to a lawyer; but no testator except a lawyer could be expected to understand it, much less to have regard to it in framing his will. We must, however, take the law as we find it.

On the other point, viz. as to the question of succession duty, I am of opinion that the question must be answered in the negative. The gift of a life interest or any other estate in realty is not a legacy, though such a meaning may be put on the word in cases where it is clear that the testator uses it in that sense. But I do not think that the mere fact of the use of the words 'succession duty,' which, no doubt, are correctly applicable to land or money to be invested in land, is of itself strong enough to lead to the inference that testatrix – who throughout the will elsewhere uses correct language on this point – meant 'legacy' to include the house in Mountjoy-square, especially as the surplus, after paying succession duty may be converted into lands which would be liable to succession duty; but it would be absurd to hold that succession duty would be paid in respect thereof out of a residue supposed to remain after the entire surplus had been so invested.

The following was the curial part of the order:

'The Court doth declare that in the events which have happened the said Robert Ebenezer King has forfeited the annuity of £50 bequeathed to him by the said will. And the Court doth further declare that the duties payable to the Crown in respect of the life interest of the said Ebenezer Rowe in the residuary estate of the testatrix, and in the house and premises in Mountjoy-square, Dublin, in the said will mentioned, are not payable out of the residuary estate, but are payable out of the life estate itself, in the ordinary way.'

Notes and Questions
Do you agree with Porter M.R.'s strictures on the law governing the distinction between a determinable interest and an interest subject to a condition? See *Irish Land Law*, para. 4.049.

RE COGHLAN
[1963] I.R. 246; 98 I.L.T.R. 134 (Supreme Court)

T.C. by his will, dated the 17th August, 1945, bequeathed *inter alia* his farm and dwelling with all stock thereon and all contents to his trustee appointed under the will upon trust for his nephew, *J.C.*, 'provided my said nephew shall marry (if he be not married at my death) and come to reside there within one year from the date of my death, and in the event of my said nephew not marrying and coming to live there as aforesaid, in trust to sell said farm and house and all stock and contents and apply the proceeds of such sale for the celebration of Masses . . .'

The nephew, *J.C.*, contended that the said condition was void for uncertainty and was not severable. Dixon J. held that the conditon was severable and that that part of the condition relating to a residence was void for uncertainty but the part relating to marriage was valid and binding. An appeal was made to the Supreme Court.

Maguire C.J.:

In this case Mr. Justice Dixon has held that the part of the condition in the will of the testator obliging the defendant to marry is not void and that the condition obliges him to marry within one year of the testator's death. He also held that the condition which obliges the defendant to come and reside on the testator's farm within one year from the date of the testator's death is void for uncertainty. This latter finding is accepted. The Court is asked, however, to hold that the condition as regards marriage is void as being contrary to public policy. This submission is unsustainable. The only question which gives rise to any difficulty is whether the two conditions should be regarded as one, with the result that as part of the condition is void the other part must also be held to be void.

As Mr. Justice Dixon says, it is plain that the testator desired that 'within a year of his death his nephew should not only marry but also take up his residence on the farm . . . There are two requirements, therefore, the non-fulfilment of which will work a forfeiture.' He states that the effect of his holding that the condition as to residence is void is that the will would then read as if the residence condition is eliminated from it. The marriage condition remained and if not fulfilled a forfeiture would take place. At the time the judgment was given there still remained a period during which the condition, viz., marriage within twelve months of the testator's death, could have been fulfilled – that time has now elapsed. Accordingly, if the learned Judge's view is right the gift over takes effect.

The appellant's submission is that the two conditions should be treated as one and that the invalidity of a part affects the whole. No authority is cited which is of any help to the appellant. I agree that the desire of the testator was that both of the conditions should be fulfilled in order that the defendant should become entitled under his will. I do not think, however, that one can rely upon this when considering the position which has arisen when it is held that one of the conditions is void. The two conditions are separate and distinct. In my opinion the learned Judge was right in so holding.

The appeal should be dismissed.

Kingsmill Moore J.:

Thomas Coghlan, a farmer of Buttevant in County Cork, died on the 12th November, 1953, a widower, without ascendants or descendants him surviving. His estate consisted of deposit receipts to the amount of £568 7s. 8d. (which are subject to a claim that they were given as a *donatio mortis causa*), a farm of 63 acres, registered land, with a Poor Law Valuation of £41 10s. 0d., stock and machinery on the farm, and household effects in the farm house.

By his will, dated the 17th August, 1945, the testator appointed Cornelius

Motherway to be his sole executor and trustee and, after making a devise and bequest in trust, devised and bequeathed the residue of his estate to his executor to be applied for the celebration of Masses.

The bequest was in the following terms:

'I give devise and bequeath my farm and dwelling with all stock thereon and all contents to my said trustee upon trust for my nephew John Coghlan, son of my brother John, provided my said nephew shall marry (if he be not married at my death) and come to reside there within one year from the date of my death, and in the event of my said nephew not marrying and coming to live there as aforesaid, in trust to sell said farm and house and all stock and contents and apply the proceeds of such sale for the celebration of Masses . . .'

The nephew, who was resident in Cork city and aged about 35, queried the validity of the conditions attached to the gift to him, and the executor accordingly brought a construction summons naming as defendants the nephew and the Attorney General.

Mr. Justice Dixon held that the condition as to residence was framed in too indefinite a manner and was void for uncertainty. Accordingly, being a condition subsequent, it was ineffective to deprive the nephew of the farm, if he chose not to comply with it. Against this portion of his decision there is no appeal.

He held, however, that the condition requiring marriage within the year was a separate and severable condition, to which there could be no legal objection, and that if the nephew did not marry within a year forfeiture would take place.

Against this latter part of the judgment the nephew, John Coghlan, appeals. The only argument adduced on his behalf which it is necessary to consider is the contention that, properly viewed, these are not two independent and severable conditions, but one composite condition, which I may call a condition of 'married residence,' and that as the element of residence is bad for uncertainty the whole composite condition fails.

Certain points seem clear. The residence portion of the condition is bad for uncertainty: *Sifton* v. *Sifton* ([1938] A.C. 656); *Moffat* v. *McCleary* ([1923] 1 I.R. 16). Both conditions – or the composite condition – are conditions subsequent, and conditions subsequent which would operate to defeat a vested estate are to be construed strictly.

'With regard to . . . conditions which are to have the effect of defeating a vested estate, it is a plain rule that such limitations must be construed strictly. That rule is one of very old standing': *Clavering* v. *Ellison* (3 Drew. 451), per Kindersley V.C., at p. 470.

'As conditions subsequent, to defeat vested estates they must be construed strictly, and to work a forfeiture there must be shown a breach of a defined line of conduct which the parties concerned must reasonably have known would work a forfeiture': *Clavering* v. *Ellison* (7 H.L. Cas. 707), per Lord Campbell at p. 721.

'The contingency . . . should be something definite and certain . . . so expressed as not to leave it in any degree doubtful or uncertain what the contingency is which is intended to defeat the prior estate': *Clavering* v. *Ellison* (3 Drew. 451) per Kindersley V.C., at p. 470.

'Where a vested estate is to be defeated by a condition on a contingency that is to happen afterwards, that condition must be such that the Court can see from the beginning, precisely and distinctly, upon the happening of what event it was that the preceding vested estate was to determine': *Clavering* v. *Ellison* (7 H.L. Cas. 707), at p. 725.

I cite these familiar passages for two reasons. First, to show that the condition as to residence was invalid – as to which there is now no dispute – and secondly, to show that if there be doubt as to whether the two conditions are entirely distinct (in which case non-marriage within the year would cause divesting) or are composite (in which case the composite condition would fail for indefiniteness) the doubt should be resolved in such a manner as not to involve divesting.

Grammatically the two conditions are severable, but this is not conclusive. In *Duddy* v. *Gresham* (2 L.R.I. 442) a testator left property to his wife 'on the condition that [she] shall retire immediately after my death into a convent of her own choice,' and, 'she being bound to go into a convent, and not to marry as aforesaid.' His wife survived the testator for seventeen months, never re-married, but did not enter a convent. Morris C.J. considered the main object of the testator was that his wife should not marry again, and the clause as to retirement too uncertain. Christian L.J. thought that the direction to retire into a convent was subsidiary to a condition against re-marriage: that the condition against re-marriage failed as being *in terrorem*, and that it involved the subsidiary condition in its downfall. Deasy L.J. held the condition as to retirement void for uncertainty. Ball C., on the other hand, considered that the two conditions should be read together but in a sense contrary to that which appealed to Christian L.J. and amounted to a condition that the widow should become a nun. I cite the case as showing that it is permissible to construe conditions, in form severable, as being in effect unitary, or conjunct.

What was the object and intention of the testator in the will now before the Court? Undoubtedly he desired a member of the family to take up residence on the family farm, and he desired him to be married when he took up residence. Having regard to what we know of the prevalent desire among Irish countryfolk to preserve a family farm in the hands of the family it is, I think, a reasonable, if not an inevitable, conclusion that the testator inserted the condition as to marriage in order that, when his nephew took up residence on the farm he should beget children who, after his death, should still preserve the connection between the farm and the family. Can we assume that, if owing to the invalidity of the condition as to residence his nephew was not bound to go to reside on the farm but was free to dispose of it at once, the testator would have had any interest in whether he was married or not? Of course it never occurred to the testator that the condition as to residence could be invalid, and the Court is faced with the familiar difficulty of discovering the presumed intentions of a testator in an event which he never contemplated, by his expressed intentions in regard to events which he did contemplate but which have not come to pass. I can only say that it appears to me that the condition as to marriage was in all probability subsidiary to, and dependent on, the condition as to residence, and that if the condition as to residence fails for uncertainty the condition as to marriage fails also. In truth it is not two separate conditions, one good and one bad, but a composite condition which fails by reason of the failure of one of its component parts.

Ó Dálaigh J.:

It is agreed that so much of the condition subsequent as refers to residence is bad for uncertainty; and the major question raised by the appeal is whether the remaining portion of it, referring to marriage, is also bad.

It is the appellant's submission that the condition is a single condition, and being bad in part, that it must accordingly be regarded as bad in its entirety. The respondent disputes this submission and argues that the marriage clause is severable from the residence clause. Counsel have been unable to find any authority on the question at issue and the case therefore stands to be decided as a matter of construction. Did the testator desire to achieve two separate and distinct things (i) the marriage of his nephew and (ii) the nephew's residence on the farm. I can find nothing in the will to indicate that the testator was concerned with either marriage or residence *simpliciter*. It seems to me he wanted a man with a wife to take over his farm. I do not see two conditions, but a single condition, undoubtedly expressed in two clauses but so expressed only because of the exigencies of language. The clauses are so interlocked that one clause cannot be condemned without destroying the entire condition. It would in my opinion be contrary to the testator's wishes to allow the marriage clause to stand alone; it must, I think, fall with the rest of the condition.

Accordingly I also would allow the appeal.

Note

See further on the questions of uncertainty and repugnancy in relation to conditions, *Irish Land Law*, para. 4.053.

CROFTS V. BEAMISH
[1905] 2 I.R. 349 (K.B.D. and Court of Appeal)

B., by his will, left all his property to his wife for life and after her death he devised to each of six of his sons a specific portion of his landed property, and to the other (his third) son he left one shilling. He charged some of these lands so devised with portions for his daughters, and he directed that if any of his sons should die before he attained the age of thirty, the portion of him so dying should go to his 'next eldest brother, and so on, respectively'; and if any of them should die without issue lawfully begotten after attaining the age of thirty years, then his share should go to his 'next eldest brother, and so on, respectively.' Proviso, that no devisee should be at liberty to sell his share to any person save one of his brothers, at a price to be fixed by arbitration.

The testator died in 1867, leaving him surviving his widow and seven sons, all of whom attained thirty. G.B., the eldest son, died in 1900, leaving children surviving. Some of the other sons were unmarried, and some were married, but had no children. The widow died in 1903.

An originating summons was issued to determine the proper construction of the will. The judges of the King's Bench Division dealt with questions of certainty and restrictions on alienation and so their judgments are reproduced. The Court of Appeal dealt only with the narrow point of the meaning of the expression 'next eldest brother.'

Gibson J.:

This was an application for a declaratory order with reference to four points arising on the will of a Mr. Richard Beamish. The questions proposed for our decision are as follows: [His Lordship read the questions].

1. If the executory limitation in this case is not void for uncertainty, it is certainly arbitrary and unreasonable on either of the two constructions submitted to the Court. If the language is clear, the Court must give effect to it, however unreasonable.

Both of these constructions are open to the objections that the brother at one extremity of the series is free from the shifting clause, and the brother at the other end is in a worse position than any of the intervening brothers. Thus if we adopt the descending construction, the eldest brother who dies without issue can never get anything by the gift over, while the second and other brothers dying without issue may have the loss of their estate recouped by getting the estate of an antecedent brother dying without issue. It is apparently admitted that accrued shares are not carried over, and it would be hard on either of the constructions now under consideration to construe 'next eldest brother' as 'next surviving eldest brother.' The result of either of the constructions would be that George Beamish, the eldest son, had the chance of losing his estate without any possibility of benefit from his brothers' death without issue; each of such brothers on losing his own estate had still the chance of succeeding to his next senior's estate, and William, the youngest, not only enjoyed this benefit but whether he lived to thirty or not, and whether he died without issue or not, would have an absolute estate not subject to any shifting clause. The same difficulty, *mutatis mutandis*, applies to the ascending construction, the apparent inequality of treatment being applied to the youngest, instead of the eldest, brother.

This difficulty has induced me to consider whether the words 'next eldest brother' might not receive another interpretation and mean the brother eldest for the time being next at the death, the eldest surviving brother. Such a construction would get rid of the anomalies pointed out as affecting the other construction. In *Bathurst* v. *Errington* (2 A.C. at p. 709), Lord Cairns referred to the possibility of introducing survivorship in the case of brothers. The word 'next' would in this view point to time and survivorship, and not to immediate local proximity in the series to the brother dying. The use of the superlative 'eldest' instead of the comparative might favour this somewhat. It would be intelligible that the eldest for the time being should be benefited; but why the immediate senior or immediate junior should be selected to take under the gift over, I cannot explain. If, however, the testator has so directed, his will must prevail.

The construction I have referred to is not the natural one, and as counsel have declined to support it and have confined themselves to the two already referred to, I have to choose between them if the words 'next eldest brother' are not altogether indeterminate and uncertain.

We have here a series of brothers arranged according to seniority. I think the 'next eldest' points to the brother dying, the purchaser, as being the true eldest for the purpose of reckoning, and the devolution is therefore downwards and not upwards. This would be the ordinary meaning, according to the usage of common speech. I admit, however, the ambiguity of the expression in relation to the divesting of real estate, where the elder would be nearer true heirship than the younger.

If the will had given an estate to the youngest and on his death without issue to the next eldest brother, the next senior brother must have been meant. Apparently the will intended to apply the gift over to all the seven brothers, and it may be argued that when the last brother is reached, that is, the youngest or eldest, according as a descending or ascending construction is adopted, the inquiry then must be who is at that time the next eldest. The word is 'eldest' not 'younger.' If a descending and ascending construction could be applicable to the youngest brother, so that if his elder brother died without issue he would succeed, while if he died without issue the elder would succeed to his estate, this would go far to show that the will was uncertain and unintelligible. William would get Becher's estate, and Becher William's.

With much doubt I think that the descending construction applies.

Mr. Longfield argued that the point did not arise for decision, as the gift over was limited to death within the lifetime of the widow, and he relied on the clause restricting alienation in support of his view. If that clause showed that on the death of his wife the testator intended that the devises should be absolute owners and sell discharged of the shifting clause, I should agree with this contention. But the contention seems inadmissible, inasmuch as the limitation over is irrespective of the duration of the wife's life, and the sale contemplated in the restrictive clause relates to the interests of the devisees, which were in fee-simple though in a certain event defeasible.

2. The next question is, does the limitation fail for uncertainty? With hesitation,

I have come (as already stated) to the conclusion that *prima facie* 'next eldest' contemplates downward computation. This, however, does not dispose of the point. Thomas, one of the brothers, was provided for outside the will, and only gets a levacy of 1s. Is he included or excluded among the brothers in whose favour the gift over operates? If it is impossible to answer this, the executory devise might be uncertain. On the whole, I think that Thomas was named for the purpose (amongst others) of including him in the series to get the same chance of benefit as the others, though he had no stake to lose. My answer therefore here is – No.

3. This question at present hardly requires an answer, and we were requested not to answer it. If 'next eldest' is not equivalent to 'next surviving eldest,' and if accrued shares are not subject to the same shifting limitation, notwithstanding the curious words 'and so on respectively,' a next eldest brother would take the estate of his next senior brother dying without issue, though such next eldest brother had predeceased such senior brother and died without issue: see as to eldest son, *Bathurst* v. *Errington* (2 A.C. at p. 709); *Amyot* v. *Dwarris* ([1904] A.C. 268).

4. I am of opinion that the clause at the end of the will does not restrict the inherent power of alienation attached to the devised estates. It is not expressed to be a condition, and though the testator may have thought that his direction effectually prevented alienation outside the family, I doubt if he intended or desired that, on breach by the devisee, the estate should be defeated and the property revest in himself discharged of the limitations over. Even if the clause was a condition, the class of possible purchasers is not the family, or all blood relations, but the brothers surviving at the time are contemplated, and the condition is plainly inconsistent with freedom of disposition, not merely as to the purchasers, but as to the price, which is to be ascertained by third persons. The restriction is repugnant to the nature of the estate devised, and is void. The purchasing brothers must be alive at time of sale, and if all but one were to die, there would be no effective power of sale.

The difficulty in construing this will fortunately does not arise in reference to the original estates devised, but only affects the gifts over which, if inapplicable or void, disappear, leaving the original devises absolute and unfettered. What the testator's real mind was, or what it would have been if he had known the result of his language, must be a matter of uncertainty. It looks as if his dispositions were made on the ridiculous assumption that a large family, notwithstanding varieties of health, accident, etc., would die necessarily in order of birth. I doubt if he ever contemplated such a devolution as I think the will has carried out. But his intention must be discovered from what he has said, and no matter how improvident and arbitrary it may be, it must, if discoverable, be obeyed.

Boyd J.:

I must confess that I am unable to make up my mind as to whether the testator intended his sons to take in an ascending or descending scale. I do not think he knew himself what he meant. More extraordinary words I have never come across, than those in question, 'That the portion of him so dying shall go to his next eldest brother, and so on, respectively.' I think the whole provision is absolutely uncertain, and is void for uncertainty.

As to the fourth question submitted to us, I agree in what has been said by my brother Gibson.

Wright J.:

The first question is what is the meaning in the will of 'next eldest brother'? and while, generally speaking, the language used in one will is useless as assisting in the interpretation of another, it is said that these very words, or words so nearly alike as to be undistinguishable in meaning from them, have been already construed in two decided cases: the cases referred to are *Fitzgerald* v. *Fitzgerald* (12 Ir. Ch. R. 442), and *Eastwood* v. *Lockwood* (L.R. 3 Eq. 487). In *Fitzgerald* v. *Fitzgerald* (12 Ir. Ch. R. 442) the provision was for younger sons, 'and in case those who die do not leave any wife or children at their death, then the said proportions they were entitled to during their life to go to their eldest brother, and so on to the *youngest*.' It was held that the testator had expressed his intention to give the property in a descending series, inasmuch as he clearly intended to give the shares in such a way that in some events they might ultimately descend to the youngest son, and they could only get to him from the brothers who died by going downwards.

The Lord Chancellor in giving judgment said: + 'It is plain that the testator intended to give the different shares so that, in some event, they might ultimately descend to the youngest son; and from whom were they to go to him? From the brothers who died. It is probable that this testator comtemplated that the order of the death of his children would be that of their birth, so that each elder brother should die before all those junior to him; then, upon the death of each, the next survivor would be, not in reference to the elder brothers who had died, but in regard of the younger brothers who survived, the next eldest brother; and by following this course, it would eventually come down to the youngest son. This construction provides for all cases except the death of the youngest son; but as my impression is that he expected him to die the last, that is no objection to the construction.'

In that case therefore the intention of the testator was found by the Lord Chancellor to be expressed on the face of the will that the shares should go in the descending series. In the other case of *Eastwood* v. *Lockwood* (L.R. 3 Eq. 487), the words of the will are 'the share or shares of him or them so dying to go to my *next surviving son*, according to seniority of age and priority of birth' in like manner as his original share. There is a material difference between the language used there, 'next surviving son,' etc., and 'next eldest brother,' in the will now before the Court; but, apart from that, Vice-Chancellor Page Wood bases his decision that the shares were to go in a descending order of age on the one fact that the testator had in the first gift arranged his children according to the order of their birth, and that 'next' must mean next according to his arrangement, *i.e.* downwards or in the descending line. This I think, with all respect, rather begs the question. I cannot regard either of these cases as deciding, or assisting to decide, the language of the present will; and if I am to decide it, it must be on what is expressed in it.

Testator provides first for his wife; then for his seven sons one after the other in order of birth – a natural order, I would think, for any testator to adopt; then for his five daughters – on the death of any or either of the sons under thirty, the portion of the one so dying 'to go to his next eldest brother, and so on, respectively'; and the same language is used to meet the case of a son dying without issue after attaining the age of thirty. If the descending order is to be adopted, the eldest son fares worst of all, the youngest fares best. I see nothing in the general frame of the will to favour this view, and to so construe the will involves reading 'next eldest' as equivalent to 'next younger.'

With no decision to guide or to help, and with nothing in the will to throw light on the testator's intentions beyond this one clause, I think the words must receive their ordinary meaning, and that 'next eldest' means the next elder brother, at the time of the happening of the event, to a son dying, and that on the death of a son of the testator his share is, by the will, to go to the brother immediately senior to him.

I pass over the second and third questions and come to the fourth, the provision in the will restricting alienation except to a brother, and deal very shortly with the cases cited in argument.

In *Attwater* v. *Attwater* (18 Beav. 330) testator left his estate to his son with an injunction never to sell it out of the family; but if sold at all, it must be sold to one of his brothers. Lord Romilly held this restriction on alienation to be inoperative. In *In re Macleay* (L.R. 20 Eq. 186) Sir George Jessel held that a devise 'to my brother J. on the condition that he never sells out of the family,' followed by gifts to other relatives, was valid, and distinguishes, and certainly does not mention with approval, Lord Romilly's decision in *Attwater* v. *Attwater* (18 Beav. 330). He (Jessel M.R.) held that the condition there was a limited restriction on alienation, and was good; the test being whether the condition takes away *the whole power of alienation substantially*, a question of substance and not of mere form (p. 189). In *Rosher* v. *Rosher* (26 Ch. D. 801) Pearson J., held that a condition in absolute restraint of alienation annexed to a devise in fee is void in law as being repugnant to the nature of an estate in fee, even though its operation is limited to a particular time, and that a condition annexed to a devise in fee of an estate to the testator's son, that his widow should have the option of purchasing the estate for a fifth of its real selling value, was an absolute restraint on alienation during the widow's life, and was void in law, and that the son was entitled to sell the estate as he pleased without first offering it to the widow at the price named in the will.

The recent decision of the Court of Appeal in *McNaul's Estate* ([1902] 1 I.R. 114), overruling *Billing* v. *Welch* (I.R. 6 C.L. 88), turns upon the special provisions of the Renewable Leasehold Conversion Act (12 & 13 Vict. c. 105), and does not deal with the question of a condition in restraint of alienation annexed to the grant of a common law fee-simple estate.

In the present case the testator directs that if any or either of his sons should be disposed to sell his interest in the portion of land willed to him, he or they shall not be at liberty to sell to any other person, save one of his brothers, and that the value of his or their interest, if there should be any difference between them, should be determined by arbitration by three respectable gentlemen, whose decision as to value should be final.

There is thus not merely a restriction as to class (*i.e.* the brothers) to whom a devisee might sell, but on the material question of price or value, the matter is taken out of his hands in case of a difference, and left to a jury of three country gentlemen. In the history of will-making such a power of sale or restriction on alienation was never heard of – practically the power to alienate is completely taken away, and on this question I am glad to find that all the members of the Court agree that this condition is repugnant and void.

The King's Bench made the following order:

'The Court is unable to answer Question No. 1 – Gibson, J., being of opinion that a descending construction, Wright, J., being of opinion that ascending construction, should be adopted, and Boyd, J., being of opinion that the words are uncertain. The Court answers Question No. 2 in the negative. The Court doth not answer Question No. 3, as it is at present unnecessary to do so; and as to Question No. 4, the Court holds that the restriction on alienation is repugnant and void.'

KEARNS AND McCARRON V. MANRESA ESTATES LTD.

Unreported (High Court) (1974 No. 193 Sp) (Judgment delivered 25th July, 1975)

The facts are set out fully in the judgment.

Kenny J.:

This is the third case in our jurisdiction in which the validity and certainty of what is commonly called 'a name and arms' clause has been questioned. In *re Montgomery Deceased, Jellett* v. *Waddington* (1953) 89 I.L.T.R. 62 Mr. Justice Dixon decided that such a clause was void for uncertainty because it was impossible to state when the disuse of the name which the person was bound to assume occurred. In *de Vere Deceased, Jellet* v. *O'Brien* [1961] I.R. 224 Mr. Justice Budd followed Mr. Justice Dixon's decision and held that such a clause was void for uncertainty on grounds corresponding to those given in the first case. Since those two cases have been decided, the Court of Appeal in England, declining to follow a number of earlier English decisions, held in *re Neeld Deceased* [1962] 2 All E.R. 335 that such a clause was valid and was not void for uncertainty. The purchaser in this case is buying a substantial area of land in Clontarf which formerly formed part of the Vernon Estate and as the validity of the vendors' (the plaintiffs) title depends on the acceptance of the correctness of the views taken by the High Court in Ireland, has decided to bring this vendor and purchaser summons. The purchaser maintains, despite the two Irish decisions, that a name and arms clause in a deed made on the 18th December 1933 is valid and effective and that accordingly the vendors have not shown title in accordance with their contract. In order to indicate how the question has arisen it is necessary to deal with the history of the Vernon family to the lands in Clontarf. Unfortunately, this is a most complicated title.

By an Indenture of Settlement made on the 23rd December 1879 made between John Edward Venables Vernon of the first part, Edward Vernon of the second part and numerous other parties, the lands known as the Clontarf Estate were conveyed to the use of John Edward Venables Vernon during his life with remainder to the use of Edward Vernon during his life with remainder to the use of Edward Kingston Vernon during his life with remainder to the first, second, third and every other son of Edward Kingston Vernon successively in remainder one after the other according to priority of birth and the heirs of their respective bodies. John Edward Venables Vernon died on the 29th April 1890, Edward Vernon died on the 20th November 1912 and thereupon Edward Kingston Vernon became entitled to the lands as tenant for life with remainder to his sons in tail male. Edward Kingston Vernon was married in 1911 and had four children. His eldest and only son was Robert Edward Kingston Vernon and he had three younger children, Gwendoline, Elizabeth and Cynthia (subsequently called Mabel Cynthia). These three ladies have married.

By a disentailing deed dated the 18th December 1933 the lands still subject to the settlement of the 23rd December 1879 were conveyed by Edward Kingston Vernon and Robert Edward Kingston Vernon with the consent of Edward Kingston Vernon as protector to John George Oulton and Edward William Davy and their heirs subject to the life estate of Edward Kingston Vernon but discharged from all estates in tail at law or in equity of Robert Edward Kingston Vernon to such uses, for such estates and subject to such powers and provisions as Edward Kingston Vernon and Robert Edward Kingston Vernon should at any time thereafter by any deed, revocable or irrevocable, jointly appoint. Edward Kingston Vernon and Robert Edward Kingston Vernon had agreed to make a settlement of the lands of Clontarf and this was done by a deed made on the same day but executed after the disentailing assurance.

By the deed made on the 18th December 1933 between Edward Kingston Vernon of the first part, Robert Edward Kingston Vernon, the eldest son of the said Edward Kingston Vernon of the second part and John George Oulton and

Edward William Davy of the third part in which the earlier history of the title is elaborately recited, Edward Kingston Vernon and Robert Edward Kingston Vernon, in exercise of the powers vested in them by the disentailing deed appointed Clontarf Estate (which was elaborately described in the First Schedule to the deed) subject to the life estate of Edward Kingston Vernon to the use of the said Robert Edward Kingston Vernon during his life and from and after his decease to the use of the first and every other son of the said Robert Edward Kingston Vernon successively in remainder one after the other according to their respective seniorities and the heirs male of their respective bodies and, in default of issue of the said Robert Edward Kingston Vernon, to the use of Gwendoline Vernon, Elizabeth Vernon, Cynthia Vernon and every other daughter of the said Edward Kingston Vernon successively in remainder one after the other according to their respective seniorities and the heirs of their respective bodies.

The next clause in the settlement is the one which has caused the difficult problem in this case and as the decided authorities turn on niceties of language, it is essential that it should be set out.

It read:

'It is hereby agreed and declared that every person who shall under the limitations hereinbefore contained become entitled as tenant in tail male or in tail by purchase to the possession or receipt of the rents and profits of the said lands and hereditaments hereby settled other than a person who shall then use the surname of Vernon and bear the arms of Vernon shall within one year after he or she shall so become entitled or being an infant within one year after he or she shall attain the age of 21 years and also that the husband of every female so becoming entitled not being a peer or the eldest or only son of a peer shall within one year after such female shall so become entitled or marry which shall last happen assume the surname of Vernon and apply for a proper licence to bear the arms of Vernon either alone or quarterly with his or her own arms and in case such licence is obtained shall forthwith assume such arms unless in either of such cases if such person shall be prevented from so doing by death and if the person so entitled as aforesaid or in the case of a married woman her husband shall refuse or neglect within such year to assume such surname or to apply for such licence as aforesaid or shall at any time afterwards disuse such surname or shall at any time after obtaining such licence disuse such arms then and in every case immediately after the expiration of such year or such disuse if the person so entitled as aforesaid shall be a tenant in tail male or in tail by purchase the estate in tail male or in tail of such person shall absolutely determine and the said lands and hereditaments hereby settled shall immediately devolve on the person next in remainder as if such person were dead without having had issue inheritable under such limitation in tail male or in tail.'

The features of this clause which are relevant for this case are that if any daughter became entitled and married, her husband was to assume the name and arms of Vernon and in addition if either the daughter or her husband 'shall at any time afterwards disuse such surname' the lands were to devolve on the person next in remainder as if the person entitled were dead without having had issue inheritable under such limitation in tail male or in tail.

By a deed dated the 15th July 1937 between the said Edward Kingston Vernon and Robert Edward Kingston Vernon of the one part and the said John George Oulton and Edward William Davy of the other part, which was expressed to be supplemental to the settlement of the 18th December 1933, Edward Kingston Vernon and Robert Edward Kingston Vernon in exercise of the power of appointment given to them by the deed of the 18th December 1933 appointed the lands settled by that settlement of the 18th December 1933 to the same uses as were by that settlement declared in default of any appointment by them save and except the use thereby declared in default of issue of the said Robert Edward Kingston Vernon in favour of Margaret Gwendoline Jane Vernon, Daisy Elizabeth Vernon and Cynthia Mabel Vernon and in lieu of the said use in default of issue of the said Robert Edward Kingston Vernon, the said lands and hereditaments should on his death be held to the use of the said Margaret Gwendoline Jane Vernon, Daisy Elizabeth Vernon and Cynthia Mabel Vernon and every other daughter of the said Edward Kingston Vernon as tenants in common in tail with cross remainders between such daughters as to their original and accruing shares as tenants in common in tail and, subject to this alteration, the said Edward Kingston Vernon and Robert Edward Kingston Vernon confirmed the settlement of the 18th December 1933.

Robert Edward Kingston Vernon died on the 30th June 1945 unmarried and thereupon the three daughters became entitled to the lands as tenants in common in tail. The first daughter married and her husband's name was Kellett. He has not assumed the surname of Vernon and she has not barred the entail so it is said that her estate has been determined. The second daughter Elizabeth married and her husband's name was Shepard and the third daughter called Cynthia in the deed of 1933 and now calling herself Mabel Cynthia married and her name was Mabel Cynthia Rann though there is no evidence what name she now uses.

By a deed made on the 15th January 1962 between Daisy Elizabeth Shepard and Mabel Cynthia Rann of the first part, Edward Kingston Vernon of the second part and Rupert Willoughby Oulton and Leslie Melon of the third part, Daisy Elizabeth Shepard and Mabel Cynthia Rann with the consent of the said Edward Kingston Vernon as protector of the settlement granted two equal undivided third parts of them the said Daisy Elizabeth Shepard and Mabel Cynthia Rann in the lands of Clontarf settled by the deed of the 18th December 1933 to hold the same unto the said Rupert Willoughby Oulton and Leslie Melon and their heirs discharged from the respective estates tail and all estates, powers and interests to take effect after the determination or in defeasance of such respective estates tail, nevertheless as to the share or shares of and in the said hereditaments and premises of which the said Daisy Elizabeth Shepard was previously to the execution of the deed tenant in tail to the use of the said Daisy Elizabeth Shepard her heirs and assigns and, as to the share or shares in the said hereditaments and premises of which the said Mabel Cynthia Rann was previously to such execution tenant in tail, to the use of the said Mabel Cynthia Rann her heirs and assigns. Although the two daughters who executed this deed used their married names they were not then entitled as tenants in tail as Edward Kingston Vernon was alive. He has since died. Gwendoline Kellett's husband has refused to adopt the name of Vernon. There is no evidence in the papers as to whether Gwendoline Kellett has assumed the name of Vernon but I assume from the answers to the requisitions on title that she has. She did not bar her entail by the deed of the 15th January 1962 and is, subject to the name and arms clause if it be valid, a tenant in tail.

The plaintiffs in this summons purchased the lands of Manresa from the three daughters of Edward Kingston Vernon. They had held the lands under two leases for a number of years and then purchased the freehold interest from the three daughters. They have now agreed to sell the lands to the defendants. One of the requisitions on title made by the purchaser was:

'Mrs. Margaret Kellett's husband does not appear to have complied with the provisions of clause 2 of the deed of the 18th December 1933 (name and arms clause) and accordingly the purported conveyance by her of one third of the property for sale contained in the conveyance to the vendors was inoperative and such one third is outstanding in the person next entitled as tenant in tail male of her share. A confirming conveyance from him must be procured.'

To this the answer made was:

'No confirming conveyance necessary. The name and arms clause is void for uncertainty.'

There is no evidence that Mrs. Margaret Kellet's husband has refused to adopt the surname Vernon but the case was argued on the basis that he has and I propose to assume this for the purpose of deciding the questions which have arisen in this case.

A name and arms clause creates a condition subsequent for it divests an existing estate. In the case of such a condition the classic statement of its effect is that of Lord Cranworth in *Clavering* v. *Ellison* [1859] 7 H.L. Cas. 707:

'I consider that from the earliest times one of the cardinal rules on the subject has been this: that where a vested estate is to be defeated by a condition on a contingency that is to happen afterwards, that condition must be such that the Court can see from the beginning, precisely and distinctly, upon the happening of what event it was that the preceeding vested estate was to determine.'

There is however, another statement which has particular application to the problem in this case, that of Mr. Justice Fry in *re Exmouth (Viscount), Exmouth (Viscount)* v. *Praed* (1883) 23 Ch. D 158:

'. . . the condition must be clear and certain. That in my opinion includes not only certainty of expression in the creation of the limitation but also certainty in its operation. It must be such a limitation that at any given moment of time it is ascertainable whether the limitation has or has not taken effect.'

These words were approved by Lord Romer in the advice of the Privy Council in *Sifton* v. *Sifton* [1938] 3 All E.R. 435 and he added:

'If the provision be clearly expressed, it is the fault or the misfortune of the person affected if he should fail to know whether he is committing a breach of it. This is implied however in the language used by Fry J. He said that it must be ascertainable whether the provision has taken effect or not, not that it must be ascertained in fact by the person affected or even that it must be ascertainable by him without difficulty.'

It is therefore essential that the Court must be able to decide whether *at any given moment of time* the person has disused or discontinued to use (and I regard these two expressions as having the same meaning) the surname he is required to use. This is the ground upon which Mr. Justice Dixon held that a name and arms clause if it contained the word 'disuse' is void for uncertainty because the Court cannot say that at any given moment of time the person has ceased to use the particular surname.

Name and arms clauses have appeared in all the standard books of conveyancing precedents for about 150 years and no challenge to their validity was made until 1945. This absence of challenge to their validity has been strongly relied on by the purchasers' counsel as an argument in their favour and he has cited the words of Lord Simonds L.C. in *Bromley* v. *Tryon* [1952] A.C. 205:

'A long course of conveyancing practice cannot, I think, even where titles may be founded on it, be given the same effect as a line of judicial authority. But at the lowest I should hesitate long before I concluded that words which had for nearly a hundred years passed unchallenged by conveyancers, men often profoundly learned in the law of real property and apt to dwell on nice distinctions of language, were after all incapable of sufficiently precise definition.

In a number of English cases (*Lewis Hill Trusts* [1951] W.N. 591), *Bouverie*

Deceased [1952] 1 All E.R. 408, *Wood's Will Trusts* [1952] 1 All E.R. 740 and *in re Kersey* [1952] W.N. 541) Judges of the High Court in England had held that name and arms clauses, insofar as they created a limitation over on the disuse of a surname which a person was required to assume, were void for uncertainty. These cases were considered by Mr. Justice Dixon in *re Montgomery Deceased* (1953) 89 I.L.T.R. 62 and I have had the advantage of consulting the original manuscript of his judgment. In that case a person was required to use and continue to use a particular surname and there was a gift over if the beneficiary discontinued to use and bear the surname. The case had also a similarity to the present case in that the requirement to use and bear the surname applied to the husband of every female who became entitled to the lands and any refusal, neglect or discontinuance by any such husband was to be deemed to be a refusal, neglect or discontinuance by his wife. Mr. Justice Dixon pointed out that the discontinuance of the use of a surname was not so much a definite act as a gradual process but that if the clause were to be held to be valid it was essential that the Court should be able to point to the moment at which the gradual abandonment of the surname was complete. If a person required to assume a particular surname inadvertently uses the original surname or orders goods from a shop using the original surname because the shopkeeper knows who that person is or knows the address or has opened a credit account, is this a disuse of the name which the person is required to use? It is essential if the clause is to be valid that the Court will be able to say with reasonable certainty when the disuse or discontinuance has occurred. It has been conceded in all the cases that the name and arms clause is to be construed as a unit. The whole of the clause must be valid if any of it is to be effective. If a person refuses to adopt a surname, then in relation to that part there is no uncertainty but this does not save the clause. I mention this because although there is no evidence that Mr. Kellett has refused to assume the surname of Vernon, the fact that he has refused to adopt it would not enable the person next entitled to say that in the events which happened the clause was valid, for if the clause is void for uncertainty immediately after the death of the testator or immediately after the execution of the deed in which it is contained, the person bound by it is entitled to rely on this and to say that the whole clause is invalid. If therefore, the part of the clause dealing with disuse is invalid, then the whole of the clause is void for uncertainty. It would be ridiculous that in one set of facts (refusal to adopt the name) the clause was effective to divest, and in another (disuse) it was void for uncertainty.

In *de Vere Deceased Jellett* v. *O'Brien* [1961] I.R. 224 the obligation imposed by will was to continue to use and bear in all deeds and writings which he or she shall sign and upon all occasions the surname of de Vere and there was a subsequent provision that if the person who became entitled should at any time discontinue to use and bear the surname and arms of de Vere, then the estate of that person should absolutely determine and become void. Mr. Justice Budd following the decision of Mr. Justice Dixon held that no one could say when the disuse or discontinuance had occurred and that the whole clause was accordingly void for uncertainty. In this case the person entitled had refused to use the name de Vere at any time.

Both these decisions were given before that of the Court of Appeal in England in *re Neeld, Carpenter* v. *Inigo Jones* [1962] 2 All E.R. 335. In that case in the High Court Mr. Justice Cross had held that a name and arms clause was effective and distinguished the earlier English cases. The three members of the Court of Appeal held that the earlier cases were incorrectly decided and that the introduction of the word 'disuses' or the words 'discontinues to use' did not introduce such uncertainty that the clause was invalid. When the case had been heard in the Court of Appeal, the three Judges gave separate judgments. Lord Evershed, when dealing with the clause about disuse said:

'Equally, as it seems to me, there is no real ambiguity in a divesting provision expressed to take effect if I should at any time "disuse" or "discontinue to use" the surname which I have adopted though I do not say that there might not be circumstances in which a disuse from accident or in some other special circumstances will seriously raise the question of its application.'

But this is precisely the problem. What are the circumstances in which a disuse from accident or some special circumstances will justify the Court in deciding that there has been a disuse. I think that Lord Evershed has stated the problem but not solved it. Upjohn L.J. dealt with the matter at greater length. He said:

'Equally I see no uncertainty if the will directs that the estate is to be forfeited by "discontinuing" or "disusing" the name and arms. Apart from peers and possibly peeresses, and dismissing from consideration those at the other end of the scale, vagrants and criminals, every person must have a surname and, indeed though it is immaterial, a christian name in order that he or she may be identified. A person lives with his name; he cannot do without it; he uses it on all normal occasions for business and social purposes. Many must be familiar with and have experience of persons who, for good reason, have changed their names. There is no difficulty or uncertainty about it. The operation is one which necessarily takes time. Professional and business associates, tradesmen and friends have to be informed of the change of name; that will take some time but in the end, when some time has elapsed, the person who was formerly known as "X" becomes ordinarily known as "Y". He has effectively changed his name. That can be done easily within the year laid down in the clauses in the will. He must then use that name on all occasions. Of course mistakes of forgetfulness will be made to begin with and, with all respect to the opinion of Wilberforce J. in *re Howard's Will Trusts* [1961] 2 All A.E.R. 413 at p. 418, I would think such lapses even after the expiration of the year should be treated as de minimis. No reported case has ever suggested any uncertainty in this operation, as I shall later point out.'

But it is precisely the question as to what lapses are a disuse or a discontinuance that causes the difficulty for the Court. How many deliberate or unintentional lapses bring the 'de minimis' principle into operation? How many lapses are necessary so that it can be said that 'de minimis' does not apply? I have the highest respect for any view expressed by Upjohn L.J. (subsequently Lord Upjohn) but invoking the maxim of de minimis seems to be a way of avoiding the difficulty. None of the judgments in *re Neeld* deal with the question as to how the Court is to decide that at any given moment of time (and that, as Mr. Justice Fry pointed out, is the critical question) a person has disused or discontinued to use the surname which he is obliged to assume. I do not accordingly propose to adopt the reasoning in *re Neeld* [1962] 2 All E.R. 335.

There is another argument to which I attach considerable weight. Since the decisions in *re Montgomery Deceased* (1953) 89 I.L.T.R. 62 and *de Vere Deceased* [1961] I.R. 224 titles to property included in the Vernon estate and in other estates have been accepted on the basis that names and arms clauses are void for uncertainty in Ireland. A decision now that the clauses involved were valid would render these titles bad. Although I am not bound by decisions of other Judges of the High Court, the usual practice is to follow them unless I am satisfied that they were wrongly decided. I am not so satisfied: indeed I think that the reasoning of Mr. Justice Dixon is unanswerable.

To sum up:

1. Since 1953 names and arms clauses have been regarded in Ireland as being void for uncertainty.

2. There were at least five decisions of High Court Judges in England that they were and these included Judges with a high reputation and wide experience of Chancery matters.

3. The fact that a name and arms clause appears in all the standard text books on conveyancing is not of itself conclusive because the validity and certainty of these clauses was never questioned.

4. I think that when there have been two decisions of Judges of the High Court in Ireland, I should follow them and not multiply uncertainty and put titles in doubt.

5. The judgments in *re Neeld Deceased* do not advert to the difficulty that in order to be valid, the Court must be able to say that at any given moment of time the person who has assumed a name has disused it or discontinued to use it. Invocation of the de minimis principle makes the matter even more complicated for how is the Court to say what is the minimum or how many occasions on which the former name was used, be it by inadvertance or deliberately, constitute disuse. If for example it were established that at the end of the year a person who had assumed a surname had on six occasions used his earlier name should I, if I were asked to decide the question (and it is ultimately the Court which decides the question) decide that these exceeded the minimum?

The relief claimed in the summons is a declaration that the requisitions of the defendants in respect of the title to the hereditaments comprised in the contract of the 2nd November 1973 have been sufficiently answered by the plaintiffs who are the vendors. As there were 78 requisitions at least, I cannot make such a declaration. A declaration that a good title has been shown to the said hereditaments in accordance with the particulars and conditions of sale is also claimed but as none of the documents of title were given in evidence and were not discussed during the argument, this declaration cannot be made. I shall accordingly declare that the name and arms clause in the settlement dated the 18th December 1933 and made between Edward Kingston Vernon of the first part, Robert Edward Kingston Vernon of the second part and John George Outon and Edward William Day of the third part is void for uncertainty and that the requisitions of the defendant in respect of that clause have been sufficiently answered by the plaintiffs.

Notes and Questions
1. What precisely was the ground or were the grounds upon which Kenny J. refused to follow the English Court of Appeal decision in *Re Neeld*?
2. Does this decision, and the earlier Irish decisions cited by Kenny J., mean that a 'name and arms' clause is invalid *per se* in Ireland?
3. See further on this general subject, *Irish Land Law*, Supp. (1975 – 80), pp. 16–17.

II. FEE FARM GRANTS

This subject is dealt with in detail in *Irish Land Law*, para. 4.057 *et seq*. See also *Twaddle* v. *Murphy*, p. 113, *ante* and *Re McNaul's Estate*, p. 41, *ante*.

CHUTE v. BUSTEED
(1865) 16 I.C.L.R. 22 (Exch. Cham.)

An action was brought to enforce covenants in a fee farm grant of a mill against a successor to the original grantee. The question arose whether the provisions of the Landlord and Tenant Law Amendment Act, Ireland, 1860 (Deasy's Act) applied to the grant which had been made in 1826. The Court of Exchequer held that they did ((1862) 14 I.C.L.R. 115) and an appeal was made to the Court of Exchequer Chamber.

O'Hagan J.:

This case comes before the Court upon a suggestion of error in the judgment of the Court of Exchequer disallowing the demurrer of the defendant to the summons and plaint, which was shaped under the direction of that Court, to raise clearly or simply the important question with which we have now to deal. Its allegations are that, by an indenture of the 31st of March 1826, one Pierce Chute demised a mill and other premises to one John McCarthy, to hold to him, his heirs and assigns, for ever, the said John McCarthy covenanting for himself, his heirs, executors, administrators, and assigns, that he and they 'should and would, from time to time, and at all times thereafter during the continuance of the said demise, preserve, uphold, support, maintain, and keep the said demised premises, and all improvements made and to be made thereon, in good and sufficient order, repair, and condition, and at the end, surrender, or sooner determination of the demise, to leave and yield up the same to the said Pierce Chute, his heirs, executors, administrators, and assigns.' The summons and plaint goes on to aver that, before the breaches of covenant thereinafter mentioned, or any of them, were committed, and before the passing of the Landlord and Tenant Amendment Act (Ireland), all the estate of the said Pierce Chute in the premises became, and at the time of the committing of the said breaches was, and still continued, duly vested in the plaintiff; and one moiety of the estate and interest of the said John McCarthy had become, and was and continued vested in the defendant. The breach is stated in these terms: - 'The defendant, during the continuance of the said lease, and whilst he was such assignee as aforesaid, broke the covenant, in this, that he did not, during the continuance of the said demise, and whilst he was such assignee as aforesaid of said premises, uphold, support, maintain, and keep the said moiety of the said premises, and the improvements made thereon, in good and sufficient order, repair and condition; but, on the contrary, whilst the plaintiff and defendant were such assignees as aforesaid, and during the said term, and before the passing of the before mentioned Act, the entire of the said dwelling-house and premises became and were, and from thence hitherto have continued to be, and now are, burnt down, dilapidated and destroyed, to the damage of the plaintiff, in respect of his estate in the said moiety, of the sum of £3000.'

This condition of things is apparent upon the allegations of the summons and plaint: – that the grant relied on was a grant in fee reserving rent – in other words, a fee-farm grant; that the covenant relied upon was that of the grantee, to keep the mill and premises in repair; that the rent was assigned, and the interest of the grantee was also assigned before the passing of the Landlord and Tenant Amendment (Ireland) Act 1860; that the covenant was broken before the passing of that statute, though it is a continuing covenant; and the breach is legally assigned as a continuing breach; and that the action is sought, under these circumstances, to be maintained by the assignee of the rent against the assignee of the grantor. The grant having established the tenure between the parties, and the grantor having reserved no reversion to himself, it is clear, and has not I think been disputed, that before the passing of the Landlord and Tenant Act this action could not have been successfully maintained. The question therefore is, whether that Act is to be held to operate retrospectively, as to the subject-matter of the action, and to create rights and impose liabilities which had no existence at the period of its passing, and were not in the contemplation of the grantor and grantee when the grant was executed, or of the persons deriving under them, when the subsequent assignment vested in them, respecting the premises and the rent? It is insisted, on the part of the plaintiff, that the twelfth section of the Act, taken in connection with the third, has this remarkable effect – and the Court of Exchequer has so decided in disallowing the demurrer. The twelfth section provides that 'Every landlord of any lands holden under any lease or contract of tenancy shall have the same action and remedy against the tenant and the assignee of the estate and interest, or their respective heirs, executors, or administrators, in respect of the agreements contained or implied in such lease or contract, as the original landlord might have had against the original tenant, or his heir or personal representative respectively.' For the purpose of maintaining the case of the plaintiff, we must hold that the section is retrospective in its operation, and that it affects fee-farm grants, and fee-farm grants executed before the pasing of the Act; and, in order to come to this conclusion, we must further show that the third section is also retrospective, and operates upon fee-farm grants, so as to establish the relation of landlord and tenant between the grantee and grantor, with all its incidents, though such a relation was never contemplated by them, and formed no part of the basis of their contract with each other. It is manifestly difficult to exaggerate the importance of the question to the proprietors of land in Ireland; so much of it is held under instruments like that which we are considering; and, so greatly must the value of it be affected, in a multitude of instances, if the judgment of the Court of Exchequer be affirmed. I proceed to consider the grounds of that judgment, as presented in the argument for the plaintiff at the Bar. The Landlord and Tenant Amendment Act is a very ponderous piece of legislation, not quite homogeneous in all its parts, or easy of construction in all its provisions; many of the sections are expressly prospective – many of them expressly retrospective – many of them in terms both prospective and retrospective, and many equivocal, from the absence of words distinctly pointing to the past or to the future. I shall not go through those in detail, as was elaborately done in the course of the argument, but numerically, in reference to the distinctions there indicated; they stand apparently thus – six sections are in terms prospective and retrospective; twenty-four are in terms prospective; and seventy-five have no terms making them expressly either retrospective or prospective. The twelfth section properly ranges itself in the last of the classes; its terms are equivocal; it does not contain, like the eleventh section, the words 'after the passing of the Act;' nor has it words pointing clearly to the future, as the sixteenth section, which begins, 'From and after any assignment *hereafter* to be made.' We have had much minute criticism upon it on both sides, with which I do not deem it necesary to coincide or to quarrel; for I think that this section may be held, in a certain sense, and to a certain extent, to be retrospective, and yet the controversy as to its operation on fee-farm grants generally, and especially on fee-farm grants executed before the enactment of it, may remain undetermined. In the case of *Mercer* v. *O'Reilly* (13 Ir. Com. Law Rep. 153), decided by the Court of Common Pleas, and affirmed, on the point which is material here, in the Exchequer Chamber, it was held that the 44th section of the Act, providing that the surrender to, or redemption by a landlord, or eviction of any portion of the premises demised by a lease, shall not in any manner prejudice or affect the rights of the landlord, whether by action, or entry, or ejectment, operates on contracts of tenancy made *prior* to the passing of the Act, as to breaches occurring *after* the passing of it. I think that that decision, and the reasoning on which it was founded, go very far to establish that, as to ordinary contracts between landlord and tenant, though made before the passing of the Act, the twelfth section may have, in a sense, a retrospective operation. In this respect I see no reason for a different rule as to the one section and the other. But, though it be the same as to both, that rule in no way concludes the question here. There seems to be a well-established distinction between Acts which meddle with existing rights, and those which are concerned with the remedies by which such rights may be enforced. Where procedure is dealt with by legislation, it is held that such legislation applies to cases arising either before or after the passing of the statute. The cases of *Freeman* v. *Moyes* (1 A. & E. 338), *Grant* v. *Kemp* (2 C. & M. 636), and others, establish this principle; and they and it were discussed in the case of *Wright* v. *Hale* (6 H. & N. 227), in which it was sustained by the judgment of the Court of Exchequer in England. Upon this principle it will be quite possible to hold very many of the sections of the Landlord and Tenant Act retrospective, in perfect consistency with the decision which should I think be pronounced upon the case before us; and with such consistency we might hold the twelfth section, as the 44th, retrospective, if it was necessary to determine the point at present. For the purposes of the case, however, that determination becomes unimportant, in the view which I take as to the operation of the third section of the statute. The twelfth can have the operation for which the plaintiff contends, only if the third be held to affect fee-farm grants, and fee-farm grants antecedently executed. If it be not so held, the parties to the deed were not 'the original landlord' and the 'original tenant' contemplated by the twelfth section; and it created no contract of tenancy on which 'the landlord' could have his action against 'the tenant' or 'the assignee,' within the meaning of that section. I am of opinion, after the best consideration I have been able to give the matter, that the third section is not retrospective, and does not affect fee-farm grants executed before the framing of the Act. There can be no doubt that the question here is of substantive right, and not of mere procedure; and we are asked to place the parties in a totally new position, and *ex post facto* to create a liability which they never designed to accept or to impose. Now, it is established that, although such a liability *may* be created by the strong exercise of legislative power, its creation must be evidenced by the clearest and most unequivocal language before any Court can assume that the Legislature intended to create it, and this on the plainest grounds. It is consistent with equity and reason, in ordinary cases, that persons who contract with each other should not have their contract enforced, according to their mutual purpose, but should have one wholly different invented for them by a statute passed years after the bargain was complete. The sense of mankind has always revolted against such legislation. It was evidenced by a fundamental maxim of the Roman code, very much in effect the same as that 'rule and law of Parliament' stated by Lord Coke (2 Mot. 292), and relied on in the argument – '*Nova constitutio futuris formam imponere debet, non praeteritis.*' And this principle of construction has been adopted by all our Courts, and is supported by a host of authorities which are familiar to us, and need not be detailed. It is described by Lord Wensleydale – *Moon* v. *Durdin* (2 Exch. 22) – as a principle 'deeply founded on good sense and strict justice.' Lord Cranworth, V.C., says: – 'It is of such obvious convenience and justice, that it must always be adhered to in the construction of statutes, unless in cases where there is something on the face of the enactment putting it beyond doubt that the Legislature meant it to operate retrospectively.' And Chief Justice Erle – *Midland Railway Company appellant, Pye respondent* (10 C.B., N.S. 198) - presents it thus: – 'Those whose duty it is to administer the law very properly guard against giving to an Act of Parliament a retrospective operation, unless the intention of the Legislature that it should be so construed is expressed in plain, clear, and unambiguous language; because it manifestly strikes our sense of justice that an act, legal at the time of doing it, should be made unlawful by some new enactment. Modern legislation has almost entirely removed this blemish from the law; and, wherever it is possible to put upon an Act of Parliament a construction not retrospective, the Court will always adopt that construction.'

Now, looking at the language of the third section of the Landlord and Tenant Act in the light of this principle, I cannot discern anything compelling us to put upon it a construction which must 'shock one's sense of justice' and work manifest wrong in the case before us and very many others. In the first place, I observe that there are in it no expressly retrospective words – 'plain, clear and unambiguous' – such as are used in other sections of the statute, where it was designed that those sections should have an *ex post facto* operation. This being so, is it not fair to assume – the matter in hand being of great importance, and the construction contended for very inconsistent with natural justice – that the Legislature omitted such express words because it did not intend to produce the wrongful result which they would have made unavoidable? But, further, considering carefully the words which *have* been used, do any of them coerce us to the construction contended for? I repeat them: 'The relation of landlord and tenant shall be deemed to be founded on the express or implied contract of the parties, and not on tenure or service; and a reversion shall not be necessary to such relation, which shall be deemed to subsist in all cases in which there shall be an agreement by one party to hold land *from or under another*, in consideration of any rent.' It seems to me that the words of the section naturally point to the future and not to the past. The words 'shall be deemed' are at least capable of being applied in either way, and such words have been expressly held not to be sufficient to compel a retrospective construction: *Hitchcock* v. *Way* (6 Ad. & Ell. 943); *Thompson* v. *Lack* (3 C.B. 540). And it is enough for the argument I am adopting, if the phrase be ambiguous; and afford us therefore the opportunity of construing in accordance with justice and the reason of the thing. Again, the words 'and a reversion *shall not* be necessary to such relation,' taken in connection with those which follow, 'in all cases in which there shall be an agreement,' seem to me more prospective than retrospective in their scope and import; and, at the lowest, are not retrospective so clearly and unambiguously as to coerce us to give them an *ex post facto* operation. I am, therefore, of opinion that whether the section has or has not reference to fee-farm grants generally, it should not be held to affect such grants, if executed before the passing of the Act. And this is enough to carry the consequence that the 12th section cannot aid the plaintiff; and, therefore, that the judgment of the Exchequer was wrong and ought to be reversed; that it has been further and, in my opinion, necessarily argued that the third section should not be held to affect fee-farm grants at all. When in the 25th and 52nd sections the Legislature designs to deal with such interests, it says so, and uses the word 'grant' expressly. Why should it have done otherwise in passing the third section, if the section also was meant to apply to a fee-farm grant? Again, the third section declares that the relation of landlord and tenant shall be deemed to subsist only in cases 'in which there shall be an agreement by one party to hold land *from or under* another in consideration of any rent.' Now, the statute of *Quia Emptores* is not repealed by the Landlord and Tenant Amendment Act; and the grantee in such a case as that before us does *not* hold in fee under the grantor. He holds, not under the grantor, but under the superior lord; and, therefore, his position does not come within the description of the cases affected by the section in which 'there shall be an agreement by one party to hold land *from or under* another.' The grantee never agreed to hold *from or under* the grantor; the assignees of the grantee never agreed to hold from or under the assignee of the grantor; and, therefore, the very terms of the section mean to exclude from its operation such grants as this, in which the condition of that operation – the agreement to hold *from* another – has no existence. I should, on these grounds, hold, if it were necessary, that fee-farm grants generally are not affected by the section; but it is sufficient for the purposes of this judgment to determine that they are not affected by it retrospectively. I do not think it needful further to discuss in detail the arguments which have been presented on either side. The judgment of the Court of

Exchequer appears to have gone very much upon the view that the Landlord and Tenant Act constitutes a code consolidating and amending the laws relating to landlord and tenant, and that it should be presumed, save where otherwise expressly provided, to apply to all contracts connected with their relation, whether before or after the passing of it. On this, I shall only observe – first; that the Act cannot, in my mind, be said to constitute within itself a complete code, so as to dispense with the consideration of the principles of law which were in force at the time of its enactment, and are still in force, notwithstanding its operation. There are very many cases in which it distinctly applies a different rule as to the transactions of the past and of the future, and there are some which it leaves unequivocally to be dealt with by the antecdent law. It is not, therefore, in my judgment, right or reasonable to suppose that it meant so comprehensively to affect *all* the relations of the owners and occupiers of the soil, that all of them, including that created by the fee-farm grant, must be assumed to be affected by it; and I should think it still less right or reasonable, if, proceeding on this groundless assumption, we should further proceed to reverse the established rules of construction in its regard – as ancient as they are wise, as universal as they are equitable, – and presume in favour of its retrospective operation, in the absence of express words to the contrary, instead of making the very opposite presumption, and holding its provisions prospective, save when we are forced by the plainest and most unequivocal language to hold that they are *not*.

For the reasons I have given, I think that the judgment of the Court of Exchequer should be reversed and the demurrer of the defendant allowed.

Fitzgerald J., concurred with **O'Hagan J.**

Hayes, J.:

We are called upon here to say whether the 12th section of the Landlord and Tenant Act is prospective or retrospective. But it would be well, in the first place, to settle clearly whether those words are to apply to the contracts, or to the cases arising upon the contracts, or to the remedies to be applied to those cases. As to the first, it would be extraordinary if an Act, which in its third section declared that the relation of landlord and tenant should thereafter be deemed to be founded on contract, should expressly or impliedly exclude from its operation every contract that had theretofore been made on the subject and was then in course of performance. The case of *Mercer* v. *O'Reilly* (13 Ir. Com. Law Rep. 153), already before this Court on Error from the Common Pleas, and indeed almost every case reported upon the Act, shows that contracts of tenancy entered into before the statute, as well as those made since its enactment are within its operation (*Pentland* v. *Murtagh* (12 Ir. Com. Law Rep., *App*.'ii); *McAreavy* v. *Hannan* (13 Ir. Com. Law Rep. 70); *Bell* v. *Bell* (13 Ir. Com. Law Rep., *App*. xivii). But taking it as clear that contracts made prior to the Act are within its operation, the next question is, whether cases upon such contracts, and which have arisen before the Act, are at all within the Act? This question is more difficult, and requires a more particular notice in reference to the case now before us. The contract dates from the year 1826, and by it Pierce Chute demised to John McCarthy a dwellinghouse, mill and premises, to hold in fee-farm, at a certain rent payable half-yearly; and McCarthy covenanted for himself, his heirs and assigns, to keep and deliver up the premises in good repair. Afterwards, and prior to the Act, the interest of the grantor became vested in the plaintiff, and that of the grantee in the defendant. The breach of covenant complained of in the plaint is, the defendant's not *keeping* the mill in repair whilst he was assignee, it having been previously burned.

A preliminary question has been raised, whether a fee-farm grant, such as existed before the Renewable Leasehold Act, is at all within the 12th section of the Landlord and Tenant Act. In my opinion it is: the Act proposes to consolidate and amend the laws, and not any particular branch of the laws, relating to landlord and tenant in Ireland. The word 'landlord' is interpreted to include the person entitled in possession to the estate of the original landlord *under any lease or other contract of tenancy*; which, by the third section, is 'deemed to subsist in all cases in which there shall be an agreement by one party to hold land from or under another, in consideration of any rent.' 'And a reversion shall not be necessary for such relation.' The expression 'perpetual interest' is also interpreted to comprehend, 'in addition to any greater interest, any lease or *grant* for one or more lives, or for years absolute or determinable on one or more lives, with a covenant for perpetual renewal of such lease or grant.' From the language of these interpretation clauses, I think it plain that the Legislature meant to include the contracts set forth in the old fee-farm grants, such as we have now before us; and that in legislating on such contracts, the word landlord is to include the person entitled to the estate of the original grantor; and the word tenant is to mean the person entitled to any lands under any lease or other contract of tenancy.

The 25th section, under the terms 'perpetual interest under any grant,' is plainly conversant with fee-farm grants; and the proviso which introduces a restriction in respect of those under the "Renewable Leasehold Conversion Act" show that the others were also before the mind of the Legislature. So also the 52nd section gives the remedy by ejectment whenever a year's rent shall be in arrear in respect of lands held under *any fee-farm grant*, lease, or other contract of tenancy. Upon the whole then, I entertain little doubt that the large and general terms used in the 12th section embrace the cases of fee-farm grants other than those referred to in the Renewable Leasehold Conversion Act. It has been urged that as the statute of *Quia Emptores* is still unrepealed, it cannot be said that the grantee in fee-farm holds under any one but the Crown or other chief lord; and therefore fee-farm grants cannot be included in the Act. This might have been a serious objection so long as the law of landlord and tenant was regulated by and founded upon tenure, by which the tenant became liable to fealty or services as an incident; but now that the whole is but a network of contracts, the expression as to lands in fee-farm *being held under any person* is resorted to, for want of a more appropriate phrase, to designate the person with whom the party entitled to the lands has entered into a contract for payment of the rent or other compensation.

To the plaint, setting forth the facts I have already adverted to, the defendant has demurred, and he insists that, as the assignee of John McCarthy the original grantee, he is not liable for any breaches of the covenant entered into by McCarthy with Pierce Chute, for which any other assignee of the grantee before the Act would not have been liable. The 12th section enacts in brief, that 'every landlord shall have the same action and remedy against the tenant and the assignee of his estate, or their respective heirs, in respect of the agreements contained or implied in the contract of tenancy, as the original landlord might have had against the original tenant or his heir respectively.' Until the above section became law, it is quite clear that no person to whom the interest of the grantee in fee-farm was or would thereafter be assigned would thereby incur any liability on the covenant entered into by the grantee for keeping the premises in repair; and this exemption from liability would no doubt greatly influence the proceedings of persons negotiating for such assignment. And it is needless to remark that such a liability which, by the passing of the Act, was *eo instanti* imposed on all persons who had completed their contracts, without any notice of the coming burden, might be reasonably complained of and resisted as an interference with the principles of justice and good faith which should always belong to contracts, and which are so confidently looked for that nothing less than coercive language of the Legislature would justify the Court by its construction to disappoint that expectation. But in truth the clause is conversant only with 'action and remedy' for breaches of the contract, and not with any variation of the rights or liabilities of the parties to antecedent contracts. In the case of *Mercer* v. *O'Reilly* it has been already held by this Court, while administering the remedy thereby provided for non-payment of rent under a contract made before the Act, that such remedy did not apply to the rent which had accrued due before the Act, but only to that which had accrued due subsequently. So, acting in analogy to that case, I think the action and remedy provided by the 12th section ought not to be applied to cases of assignment before the Act, but only to those which occurred after the Act; so that the rights of persons claiming under the contract of assignment might not be unduly or unjustly interfered with. In short, I understand the 12th section merely to say that for the enforcement of any right which the landlord now has or shall hereafter have against the tenant or his assignee, he shall have the same action and remedy as the original landlord might have had against the original tenant; but it gives no new rights in respect of bygone assignments upon which that remedy was to operate. Under the covenant by the grantee in the original fee-farm grant, the grantor had as against the assignee of the tenant no such right as is here claimed. This not being a covenant running with the land, the burden of it did not extend further than the covenantor and his representatives; and the section of the Act ought not to be so construed as to interfere with the rights of parties to contracts of assignment which have been made previous to its passing.

I am, therefore, of opinion that the plaintiff is not justified in the claim which he has made in the plaint, and that the demurrer to it ought to be allowed.

O'Brien J., concurred with **Hayes J.**

Christian J.:

The difference of opinion in the Court below in this case proceeded upon a ground which raises very pointedly, for the consideration of this Court, the most important question which could arise in administering this new statute, namely, what are the proper place and office which, while it is left in force, it has a right to occupy in the law of landlord and tenant in Ireland?

The difference between the learned Barons arose from their having viewed that question from precisely opposite points. It might safely be said that each would be right if you would only place yourself on his particular standing point. It obviously did not occur to the Chief Baron to regard this Act as anything but an ordinary one, subject to all the ordinary rules of construction. He took his stand therefore on the anterior law; he cast on those who asserted that that law was altered in the case before him the burden of showing that it was so consistently with established rules of construction; and finding that one of the best settled of those rules was the one stated by *Lord Coke* in *2nd Inst.* – '*Nova constitutio futuris formam imponere debet, non præteritis*,' – he applied that rule; and doing so he showed, with unanswerable force of reasoning, that there was not, either in the twelfth or the third sections of the statute, any such clear legislation as that rule requires, before a Court could be warranted in holding that, not in procedure or in remedy merely, but in *right and obligation*, the condition of parties to existing contracts was retrospectively metamorphosed.

The other Members of the Court, however, took ground in an entirely opposite direction. This is no common Act, to be dealt with on commonplace principles. As one of the learned Barons observed, 'It is a statement of the law by which ever thereafter that abstract thing, the relation of landlord and tenant, shall be understood.' . . . 'The third section in particular (the same learned Baron says) seems designed as a new basis, not only of this statute, but of the whole law of landlord and tenant.' And the pith of the judgment is to be found in this sentence: 'I am of opinion that, *except when otherwise expressly provided*, the Act, and in particular the third section, *does* apply to agreements made prior to its passing.' That is to say, the old rule of construction relied on by the Chief Baron, and which it must be admitted does still apply to common statutes, is, as to this Act, reversed; the presumption not against but in favour of retrospection; and that presumption can only be rebutted, in any particular case, by showing some *express* provision to the contrary in the Act. Another of the Barons takes still higher ground. He observes: 'The object of the Act apparently was to codify the laws governing this important relation – to place within the limits of one Act all the provisions affecting it which were scattered throughout the Irish and Imperial Statute Books, and to place them in a small compass, within the reach of every member of the community, under such improvements as, in their opinion, experience had suggested. Are we to suppose that the Legislature intended that the existing generation of landlords and tenants were to be excluded from the enjoyment of the benefits thus intended to be conferred; and that as to them the Act was never to have any operation; but as to them the repealed enactments were to be still in force; and that they were to grope through the statute books for the provisions regulating their rights and liabilities? I think such a construction would defeat the object which the Legislature had declared having had in view, viz., consolidating and amending the laws relating to landlord and tenant; and instead of that would create two distinct states of the law – one affecting contracts previous, and the other affecting contracts subsequent to the passing of the Act.' And both the learned Barons dwell at length upon the inconvenience, as if it were something altogether novel and unusual, of having two separate and distinct codes (as they call them) in operation at one and the same time, for an indefinite period – one for past transactions, the other for future.

This is not the first case in which pretensions so exalted have been advanced, and successfully advanced, on behalf of this statute. Some few years ago there was a case in the Court of Common Pleas, of *Bayley* v. *The Marquis of Conyngham* [see p. 311, *post*]. It was not referred to in the argument; and it is not I believe reported; but it bears very closely upon the case before us. It was an action by the plaintiff for disturbance of a right of shooting and fishing on the land of the defendant. The issue was, whether the defendant demised to the plaintiff the shooting and fishing. The evidence was, that the defendant's agent agreed by word of mouth, without writing, to let the shooting and fishing to the plaintiff for one year. The sole question was, as to the validity in law of that letting. The difficulties in the plaintiff's way were these: – considered as an actual demise, the letting was void at Common Law for want of a deed, the subject being an incorporeal hereditament. Considered as an agreement to demise, it was void for want of a writing, under the second section of the Irish Statute of Frauds. The fourth section of the present Landlord and Tenant Act, which requires leases to be by deed or in writing, does not apply to lettings from year to year, or any lesser period; but the second section of the Statute of Frauds did apply to them, and is expressly left unrepealed by the present statute. The 104th section of this Act provides that the several Acts and parts of Acts set forth in the schedule shall, to the extent to which such Acts or parts of Acts are by such schedule expressed to be repealed, *and not further or otherwise*, be and are hereby repealed. The schedule includes the Statute of Frauds (7 *W*. 3, c. 12, sec. 1). Therefore the statute expressly repealed section 1, and equally expressly declared that all the rest, including section 2, should remain unrepealed. Well, this put the Counsel for the plaintiff in *Bayley* v. *The Marquis of Conyngham* rather in a difficulty; but he was equal to the occasion. He took up this Landlord and Tenant Act 1860, and boldly insisted that it swept all other law, common or statute, from the ground. It was a great code, which must be taken as embracing all landlord and tenant law within its own four corners, supplanting and putting to silence all that lay outside it; and under its third section (the fourth not applying to a lease for a year) this demise by words of an incorporeal hereditament was valid, though the Common Law required a deed; and the second section of the Statute of Frauds required at least a writing. Well, three Judges of the Court decided in favour of the Counsel who made that argument. They did not, I need hardly say, adopt the trenchant and uncompromising language of Counsel; but they did *hold* that, by the operation of the third section of this statute, both the Common Law and the second section of the Statute of Frauds were displaced, and that the demise, by words, of an incorporeal hereditament was a good demise. The way in which the second section of the Statute of Frauds, which stood right in the path of the decision, was disposed of was this – it was said that it was *impliedly repealed*. Impliedly repealed! Now, considering that the 104th section and the schedule, taken together, had expressly declared, in the strongest negative language, that *nothing* but the first section *should* be repealed, it is plain that this implied repeal of the second section must have been meant in some other sense than the one in which it would be used in the case of an ordinary statute; for of course you cannot say that, in the common sense, one statute can *impliedly* repeal another, when the former says *expressly* that the latter shall *not* be repealed. The only way in which I was able then, or I confess have ever been able since, to comprehend that decision is, by supposing that the Court adopted the argument of Counsel, and considered that such was the codifying potency of this statute that it superseded, supplanted, silenced all other existing law, even that contained in statutes which it itself expressly preserved in force.

I have felt it necessary to call attention to that decision, because it was not cited at the Bar, and because, complying with the views of the majority in the Exchequer, in the present case it becomes at once apparent how imperatively desirable it is that some clear understanding should, once for all, be arrived at on this subject.

We are now in the Court of Exchequer Chamber; and I hope the case will not be parted with without some expression of opinion from those who can speak with authority, upon this, the very point on which the Judges differed in the Court below. I can do no more than submit the opinion of one very humble individual. I must say then that I am unable to view this Act in the light in which it was viewed by the majority of the Exchequer, as, in *Bayley* v. *The Marquis of Conyngham*, I was unable to view it as it was viewed by the majority of the Court. I can see in it nothing but a statute passed for two not very novel or unusual purposes – one to consolidate (*i.e.*, to gather into one Act) several existing statutes; the other, amendment – *i.e.*, to make some partial improvements or changes, here or there, in the existing Common or Statute Law. As to the notion of its being *a code*, which means a constitution embracing within itself the whole of the department of law with which it deals, and supplanting or silencing all other law on that subject, that I believe to be wholly without foundation; and if not in the plan, so neither, I confess, in the execution do I find anything to entitle this statute to exemption from the ordinary rules of construction. It is not I think remarkable for skill in composition, for acquaintance with its subject, or for circumspection or foresight in anticipating and providing against questions – I will not say possible, but probable – and, like the present, even certain to arise.

In no light therefore, whether as regards its plan, its composition, or its history, can I regard this statute as having any claim to the high pretensions which have been advanced on its behalf.

Neither I confess can I appreciate the force of what was so much dwelt on in the Court below, the having two distinct states of the law – one affecting contracts previous, and the other affecting contracts subsequent to the passing of the Act. Surely that is but the orindary consequence of the introduction of new measures. The same thing occurs in the great Criminal Consolidation Statutes of 1861, which really do possess some resemblance to a code. There, not 39 statutes, on which stress was laid in this case, but 106, were repealed, and a new body of law prescribed for all offences committed after the 1st of November 1861; but the old statutes were kept in force, and are still in force, as to all offences committed before that day.

The clause in the 104th section of this Act, which provides for the keeping in force the old statutes to support existing contracts, and to support proceedings theretofore commenced, was much criticised, as if the latter were inconsistent with the idea of the statute not being generally retrospective. Those expressions, however, have ample subject-matter in the clauses of the Act which are expressly made retrospective.

The rule of construction by which this Act should be interpreted is, in my opinion, the reverse of that laid down in the Court of Exchequer. I am of opinion that, except when otherwise provided, either expressly or by implication, the Act, and in particular the third section, does *not* apply to agreements made prior to its passing.

Having once got the point of view from which the Act is to be regarded, I have said almost all that is necessary for me to say. The case having been treated from that point of view, in one of those exhaustive and masterly judgments of the Lord Chief Baron, which constitute the value of the *Irish Reports* of the present day, I am absolved from the necessity of going into the details of the argument. If he be right in holding that, upon this, as upon other Acts, the presumption is against retrospection, his conclusion is inevitable; as, on the other hand, if Baron Fitzgerald were right in holding that upon this, differently from other Acts, the presumption is in favour of retrospection, *his* conclusion would be equally inevitable.

There is one short view, however, which was not adverted to by the Chief Baron, but which appears to me to be itself sufficient to decide this case against the plaintiff. Assume that, speaking generally, the third and twelfth sections of the statute are retrospective, and do apply to grants in fee-farm, do they apply to the particular fee-farm grant before us? That depends on whether it comes within their language. The twelfth section gives no help to the plaintiff without the aid of the third. That is obvious, and will be found clearly put by Baron Fitzgerald, at pp. 125 and 126 of his judgment. The third section provides that the relation of landlord and tenant 'shall be deemed to subsist in all cases in which there shall be an agreement by one party *to hold* land *from or under* another, in consideration of any rent.' Is there, in this fee-farm grant of the 31st of March 1836, an agreement by John McCarthy *to hold these lands from or under* Pierce Chute? If there is not, then, *ex vi termini*, the Act does not apply. Well, if there be such an agreement, it must be either express or implied. Express agreement to that effect there is none. I remember having some years ago, when at the Bar, seen a lease, which was really an assignment, executed about the time of the decision in *Pluck* v. *Digges* (5 Bligh N.S. 31), which contained a covenant by the lessee to the effect that, notwithstanding the want of a reversion, the relation of landlord and tenant should for all purposes of remedy be deemed to subsist between the parties, and that the grantee would not, in case of ejectment or distress, set up as a defence the want of a reversion. Now I apprehend that, before the late statute, that clause would not prevent the tenant from defeating an ejectment for non-payment under the statute, or a general avowry in an action of replevin; but that its effect would be, either that the grantor would have his action for breach of the covenant, or that a Court of Equity would restrain the grantee from setting up that defence. But, as soon as the late Act was passed, I apprehend that, if the third section *be* retrospective, that case would fall under it by reason of the express agreement, the relation of landlord and tenant would be thenceforth deemed to exist, and the grantor could, without assistance from a Court of Equity, maintain his ejectment on his general avowry. But there is no such express agreement in this fee-farm grant. Is there then any implied agreement to that effect? Well, in construing a legal instrument you must construe it with reference to the law as it was at the time it was executed. Did this fee-farm grant contain an implied agreement on the 31st of March 1826, and thenceforth to 1860, when the new Act was passed, by McCarthy to *hold from or under* Chute? Now you cannot raise by implication an agreement contrary to what is the legal effect of the language of the instrument. But the legal effect of the language was to make McCarthy hold, not from or under Chute, but from or under whoever Chute held under. So said the statute of *Quia Emptores*. Implication contrary to the legal effect of the language would be wholly inadmissible. The consequence is that, when the new Act was passed, there was not in this fee-farm grant any agreement, either express or implied, that the one party should hold from or under the other; and therefore this case is excluded by the very terms of the Act itself. It was said in argument that this would prevent the third section of the Act applying even to fee-farm grants made after it passed, inasmuch as the statute of *Quia Emptores* is not repealed. Well, I confess, if that consequence did follow, I should not be much appalled by it. But it *does* not I think necessarily follow. For I think it might fairly be argued that an instrument executed after this statute had been passed, ought to be construed with reference to the new law founded by the statute; and that if worded as this deed is, like an ordinary lease, it should be held to embody an agreement that the new statutable relation of landlord and tenant should exist, – a relation discharged of the element of tenure and reversion, and resting exclusively in contract.

On this ground, in addition to those which will be found in the Chief Baron's judgments in this case, and in *McAreavy* v. *Hannan*, I concur in thinking that the judgment of the Court of Exchequer should be reversed.

Keogh J. and **Monahan C.J.** concurred with **Christian J.**
Lefroy C.J.:

I concur in the views entertained by my Brethren. It appears to me that the weight of argument is against our giving a retrospective operation to the Landlord and Tenant Law Amendment Act; also, against the supposition that the Legislature intended to make it so – more particularly as we find that in some instances where the Legislature did intend to make the Act retrospective, it has done so in express terms, as in the 10th and 18th sections. Some of the views taken of the statute, and pressed upon us in the course of the argument, would upset the foundations of the laws of real property, and no new foundation was suggested. This Court should be slow *quieta movere*.

Notes and Questions
1. Note the several reference to *Quia Emptores* (see p. 40, *ante*), as to which see *Irish Land Law*, paras. 2.45 and 4.092.

2. What difference would it have made if Deasy's Act had been held to be retrospective?
3. As regards Deasy's Act, see ch. 12, *post* and generally *Irish Land Law*, ch. 17.

III. FEE TAIL

DE DONIS CONDITIONALIBUS, 1285

First, concerning lands that many times are given upon condition, that is to wit, where any giveth his land to any man and his wife, and to the heirs begotten of the bodies of the same man and his wife, with such condition expressed that if the same man and his wife die without heirs of their bodies between them begotten, the land so given shall revert to the giver or his heir: In case also where one giveth lands in free marriage, which gift hath a condition annexed, though it be not expressed in the deed of gift, which is this, that if the husband and wife die without heir of their bodies begotten, the land so given shall revert to the giver or his heir: In case also where one giveth land to another, and the heirs of his body issuing; it seemed very hard, and yet seemeth to the givers and their heirs, that their will being expressed in the gift, was not heretofore, nor yet is observed: In all the cases aforesaid, after issue begotten and born between them, to whom the lands were given under such condition, heretofore such feoffees had power to aliene the land so given, and to disherit their issue of the land, contrary to the minds of the givers, and contrary to the form expressed in the gift: And further, when the issue of such feoffee is failing, the land so given ought to return to the giver, or his heir, by form of the gift expressed in the deed, though the issue, if any were, had died: Yet by the deed and feoffment of them, to whom land was so given upon condition, the donors have heretofore been barred of their reversion, which was directly repugnant to the form of the gift: Wherefore our lord the King, perceiving how necessary and expedient it should be to provide remedy in the aforesaid cases, hath ordained, that the will of the giver, according to the form in the deed of gift manifestly expressed, shall be from henceforth observed; so that they to whom the land was given under such condition, shall have no power to aliene the land so given, but that it shall remain unto the issue of them to whom it was given after their death, or shall revert unto the giver or his heirs, if issue fail whereas there is no issue at all, or if any issue be, and fail by death, or heir of the body of such issue failing. Neither shall the second husband of any such woman, from henceforth, have anything in the land so given upon condition, after the death of his wife, by the law of England, nor the issue of the second husband and wife shall succeed in the inheritance, but immediately after the death of the husband and wife, to whom the land was so given, it shall come to their issue, or return unto the giver, or his heir as before is said . . . [Rep. S.L.R. 1887] And it is to wit that this statute shall hold place touching alienation of land contrary to the form of the gift hereafter to be made, and shall not extend to gifts made before. And if a fine be levied hereafter upon such lands, it shall be void in the law; neither shall the heirs, or such as the reversion belongeth unto, though they be of full age, within England, and out of prison, need to make their claim.

FINES AND RECOVERIES (IRELAND) ACT, 1834

II. . . . after the Thirty-first Day of *October* One thousand eight hundred and thirty-four no Fine shall be levied or Common Recovery suffered of Lands of any Tenure in *Ireland*, except where Parties intending to levy a Fine or suffer a Common Recovery shall before the Thirty-first Day of *October* One thousand eight hundred and thirty-four have sued out a Writ of Dedimus or any other Writ in the regular Proceedings of such Fine or Recovery; and any Fine or Common Recovery which shall be levied or suffered contrary to this Provision shall be absolutely void.

. . .

XII. . . . after the Thirty-first Day of *October* One thousand eight hundred and thirty-four every actual Tenant in Tail, whether in Possession, Remainder, Contingency, or otherwise shall have full Power to dispose of, for an Estate in Fee Simple absolute, or for any less Estate, the Lands entailed, as against all Persons claiming the Lands entailed by force of any Estate Tail which shall be vested in or might be claimed by, or which but for some previous Act would have been vested in or might have been claimed by, the Person making the Disposition, at the Time of his making the same, and also as against all Persons whose Estates are to take effect after the Determination or in Defeasance of any such Estate Tail, including the King's most Excellent Majesty, His Heirs and Successors, as regards the Title to His Majesty to any Reversion or Remainder created or reserved by any Settlement or Will, and which Reversion or Remainder shall have come or shall hereafter come to the Crown in consequence of the Attainder of any Person to whom the forfeited Reversion or Remainder was previously to such Forfeiture limited by any Settlement or Will, but not in any other Case, or where the Title to the Crown shall have accrued by any other Means; saving always the Rights of all Persons in respect of Estates prior to the Estate Tail in respect of which such Disposition shall be made, and the Rights of all other Persons, except those against whom such Disposition is by this Act authorized to be made.

. . .

XV. Provided always . . . the Power of Disposition herein-before contained shall not extend to Tenants in Tail after Possibility of Issue extinct.

XVI. . . . after the Thirty-first Day of *October* One thousand eight hundred and thirty-four, in every Case in which an Estate Tail in any Lands shall have been barred and converted into a Base Fee, either before or on or after that Day, the Person who if such Estate Tail had not been barred would have been actual Tenant in Tail of the same Lands shall have full Power to dispose of such Lands as against all Persons whose Estates are to take effect after the Determination or in Defeasance of the Base Fee into which the Estate Tail shall have been converted, so as to enlarge the Base Fee into a Fee Simpe absolute, including the King's most Excellent Majesty, His Heirs and Successors, as regards the Title to His Majesty to any Reversion or Remainder created or reserved by any Settlement or Will, and which Reversion or Remainder shall have come or shall hereafter come to the Crown in consequence of the Attainder of any Person to whom the forfeited Reversion or Remainder was previously to such Forfeiture limited by any Settlement or Will, but not in any other Case, or where the Title to the Crown shall have accrued by any other Means; saving always the Rights of all Persons in respect of Estates prior to the Estate Tail which shall have been converted into a Base Fee, and the Rights of all other Persons, except those against whom such Disposition is by this Act authorized to be made: Provided always, that nothing in this Act contained shall authorize any Tenant in Tail or other Person to defeat or bar any Estate or Interest which may at the Time of passing this Act have been granted to any Person or Persons by His Majesty or any of His Predecessors, in any Reversion or Remainder which may have come to the Crown by Attainder or otherwise.

. . .

XIX. . . . if at the Time when there shall be a Tenant in Tail of Lands under a Settlement there shall be subsisting in the same Lands or any of them under the same Settlement any Estate for Years determinable on the dropping of a Life or

Lives, or any greater Estate, (not being an Estate for Years,) prior to the Estate Tail, then the Person who shall be the Owner of the prior Estate, or the first of such prior Estates if more than One, then subsisting under the same Settlement, or who would have been so if no absolute Disposition thereof had been made, (the first of such prior Estates, if more than One, being for all the Purposes of this Act deemed the prior Estate,) shall be the Protector of the Settlement so far as regards the Lands in which such prior Estate shall be subsisting, and shall for all the Purposes of this Act be deemed the Owner of such prior Estate, although the same may have been charged or incumbered, either by the Owner thereof or by the Settler, or otherwise howsoever, and although the whole of the Rents and Profits be exhausted, or required for the Payment of the Charges and Incumbrances on such prior Estate, and although such prior Estate may have ben absolutely disposed of by the Owner thereof, or by or in consequence of the Bankruptcy or Insolvency of such Owner, or by any other Act or Default of such Owner; and that an Estate by the Curtesy, in respect of the Estate Tail, or of any prior Estate created by the same Settlement, shall be deemed a prior Estate under the same Settlement within the Meaning of this Clause; and that an Estate by way of resulting Use or Trust to or for the Settlor shall be deemed an Estate under the same Settlement within the Meaning of this Clause.

. . .

XXXII. Provided always . . . if at the Time when any Person, actual Tenant in Tail of Lands under a Settlement, but not entitled to the Remainder or Reversion in Fee immediately expectant on the Determination of his Estate Tail, shall be desirous of making under this Act a Disposition of the Lands entailed, there shall be a Protector of such Settlement, then and in every such Case the Consent of such Protector shall be requisite to enable such actual Tenant in Tail to dispose of the Lands entailed to the full Extent to which he is herein-before authorized to dispose of the same; but such actual Tenant in Tail may without such Consent make a Disposition under this Act of the Lands entailed, which shall be good against all Persons who by force of any Estate Tail which shall be vested in or might be claimed by, or which but for some previous Act or Default would have been vested in or might have been claimed by, the Person making the Disposition at the Time of his making the same, shall claim the Lands entailed.

XXXIII. Provided always . . . where an Estate Tail shall have been converted into a Base Fee, in such Case, so long as there shall be a Protector of the Settlement by which the Estate Tail was created, the Consent of such Protector shall be requisite to enable the Person who would have been Tenant of the Estate Tail if the same had not been barred to exercise, as to the Lands in respect of which there shall be such Protector, the Power of Disposition hereinbefore contained.

XXXIV. . . . any Device, Shift, or Contrivance by which it shall be attempted to control the Protector of a Settlement in giving his Consent, or to prevent him in any way from using his absolute Discretion in regard to his Consent, and also any Agreement entered into by the Protector of a Settlement to withhold his Consent, shall be void; and that the Protector of a Settlement shall not be deemed to be a Trustee in respect of his Power of Consent; and a Court of Equity shall not control or interfere to restrain the Exercise of his Power or Consent, nor treat his giving Consent as a Breach of Trust.

. . .

XXXVII. . . . if a Base Fee in any Lands, and the Remainder or Reversion in Fee in the same Lands, shall at the Time of the passing of this Act, or at any Time afterwards, be united in the same Person, and at any Time after the passing of this Act there shall be no intermediate Estate between the Base Fee and the Remainder or Reversion, then and in such Case the Base Fee shall not merge, but shall be *ipso facto* enlarged into as large an Estate as the Tenant in Tail, with the Consent of the Protector, if any, might have created by any Disposition under this Act if such Reminder or Reversion had been vested in any other person.

. . .

XXXIX. Provided always . . . no Assurance by which any Disposition of Lands shall be effected under this Act by a Tenant in Tail thereof (except a Lease for any Term not exceeding Twenty-one Years, to commence from the Date of such Lease, or from any Time not exceeding Twelve Calendar Months from the Date of such Lease, where a Rent shall be thereby reserved which at the Time of granting such Lease shall be a Rack Rent, or not less than Five Sixth Parts of a Rack Rent,) shall have any Operation under this Act unless it be inrolled in His Majesty's High Court of Chancery in *Ireland* within Six Calendar Months after the Execution thereof; and if the Assurance by which any Disposition of Lands shall be effected under this Act shall be a Bargain and Sale, such Assurance, although not inrolled within the Time prescribed by the Act passed in the Tenth Year of the Reign of His Majesty King *Charles* the First, intitled *An Act expressing an Order for Uses, Wills, and Testaments,* shall, if inrolled in the said Court of Chancery within the Time prescribed by this Clause, be as good and valid as the same would have been if the same had been inrolled in the said Court within the Time prescribed by the said Act of the Tenth Year of the Reign of King *Charles* the First.

SUCCESSION ACT, 1965

95. – (1) An estate tail (whether general, in tail male, in tail female or in tail special) in real estate may be created by will only by the use of the same words of limitation as those by which a similar estate tail may be created by deed.

(2) Words of limitation contained in a will in respect of real estate which have not the effect of creating an estate in fee simple or an estate tail shall have the same effect, as near as may be, as similar words used in a deed in respect of personal property.

Notes and Questions
1. On the subject of fees tail generally, see *Irish Land Law*, para. 4.112 *et seq.*
2. What precisely is the purpose of section 95 of the Succession Act, 1965, and does it achieve its purpose: see *ibid.*, para. 4.132.

WITHAM V. NOTLEY
[1913] 2 I.R. 281 (Court of Appeal)

M.N. by his will devised certain lands to D. and her minor children for their lives with remainder to F.N. in tail, with remainders over. Shortly after M.N.'s death in 1823, F.N. conveyed the lands to E. for the purpose of making him a tenant to the præcipe, and then suffered a common recovery with double vouchers with E. as tenant to the præcipe. A bill in Chancery was subsequently filed by D. and her children against F.N., alleging that he was in possession of the said lands for them, and had not sufficiently accounted for the rents and profits, and in the alternative alleging that he had wrongfully disseised them, and praying for an account, which bill was afterwards dismissed by consent, the plaintiffs' costs being paid by the defendant. An action for rent was brought against the occupying tenants of the lands by the plaintiffs, who, under the will of F.N. and subsequent conveyances, claimed the fee-simple in remainder after the death in 1905 of the survivor of D. and her children. On a case stated by Kenny J. the King's Bench Division held that the defendants were entitled to question the validity of the recovery and, in the absence of proof of disseisin of D. and her children, the plaintiffs were not entitled to recover the rent. The plaintiffs appealed to the Court of Appeal.

O'Brien L.C.:

This is an appeal by the plaintiffs against the judgment of the King's Bench Division, declaring that the plaintiffs' title to the lands in question had not been substantiated, and that the civil bill brought for rent against the defendants should accordingly be dismissed. The lands held by the defendants are parcels of the lands of Cloonboniagh, situate in the county Leitrim. In his lifetime they were the property of Matthew Nesbitt, of Derrycarne in that county, and by his will, dated October 14th, 1912, they, with several other denominations of lands, were devised by the testator to his only son, Francis Nesbitt, in tail male, subject to certain charges, bequests, annuities, and debts. By a codicil to his will, dated October 30th 1821, Matthew Nesbitt changed his will, to the extent of devising the lands of Cloonboniagh to a woman named Anne Doyle and to her five children, who were, no doubt, his progeny too, share and share alike during their lives or the life of the survivor. Long years afterwards a question arose regarding the true nature of the devise. It was raised in the course of proceedings for sale taken by Thomas Croker, the holder of a mortgage from the Doyles. In the first instance the Landed Estates Court had made an order for the sale of the fee-simple of the lands. That order was challenged by Captain Francis William Henry Nesbitt, the heir-at-law of Francis Nesbitt aforesaid, and on his application to have the order for sale amended, the Landed Estates Court, by order dated March 15th 1866, corrected the previous order for sale, and declared that the Doyles' estate in the lands of Cloonboniagh was a life tenancy only, with cross-remainders amongst the mother and the five children named. That decision was confirmed by the Court of Appeal by their judgment of June 7th 1866. It is a significant fact, desirable to have made clear at an early stage. By the codicil a charge of £64 a year was imposed on the lands in favour of the testator's brother, John Nesbitt, subject to which, as I have stated, the lands were devised to Anne Doyle and to her five children, for the estates described.

We were informed by Mr. Conner, K.C., that the Court should be at liberty to draw inferences of fact. Matthew Nesbitt died in 1823, and letters of administration to him, with his will and codicil annexed, were, on June 1st 1823, granted to his son Francis. The conclusion, in my view, to be drawn from the case is, that Francis Nesbitt was living with his father at Derrycarne, and after the father's death he continued to live there during the rest of his life. Anne Doyle lived some distance away; the exact distance has not been indicated. The whole family appear to have lived together. Francis Nesbitt must have been busily engaged for years after the father's death in getting the affairs of the estates settled. The Doyle family did not for many years go to take physical possession of the lands of Cloonboniagh. I have come to the conclusion, however, that they were aware of the interest in the lands which had been devised to them, and I am satisfied that since the father's will became known Francis Nesbitt knew the rights of the Doyles in Cloonboniagh, and that he never in any way whatever questioned them. It would be impossible for the Court to form a confident opinion as to what the precise arrangements were, made between the Doyles and Francis Nesbitt, for a considerable period. I am satisfied that since his father's death he uniformly recognized the rights of the Doyles. From the admission made by the Doyles in their bill in Chancery in 1838, it is clear that he had been accustomed to pay them £24 a year, which, he said, was the surplus of proceeds of Cloonboniagh, after he had paid the annuity charged upon the lands by the codicil in favour of his uncle, John Nesbitt. That bill is a notable fact in this case. Then there are the admission and statement of fact I have just mentioned, and the circumstances that on June 27th 1838, by consent of the parties, it was agreed that the bill should be dismissed, but that Francis Nesbitt and the other defendant named William Pennefather, who had been named as an appointed trustee of Matthew's will, should pay the plaintiffs' (that is the Doyle family's) costs of the proceedings. It is plainly to be concluded that some satisfactory further arrangement was come to. Probably, there was an improvement for the Doyles. A definite change had taken place, at any rate, in the year 1855. From that year it is certain that the Doyles were in possession of Cloonboniagh, and so far as it was tenanted, they and their successors in the property received the rents from it, down to 1905, when the last of the Doyles mentioned in the codicil died. Prior, however, to that date the Doyles had by mortgages divested themselves of their interest in the lands, and it was on the petition of Thomas Croker, a mortgagee, in 1866, that the character of the devise was, both by the Landed Estates Court, and by the Court of Appeal, declared and defined to be that which I have already described. All this time, accordingly, Francis Nesbitt and his descendants, or the grantees from his descendants, never obtained so far as it is stated, any part of the rents and profits out of the lands of Cloonboniagh. If the Doyles in the bill of 1838 are to be credited, Francis Nesbitt professed to have fully accounted for the rents and profits of those lands in the previous years by the payment of the annuity of £60 and the surplus sums paid to them. In 1869, as I understand, Francis William Henry Nesbitt, heir-at-law of Francis, the devisee of Matthew, mortgaged his interest in Cloonboniagh, on a loan of £2000. I gather that the present plaintiffs now represent the interests of the mortgagee – the mortgage having, apparently, been a professed conveyance of the fee-simple, subject to the outstanding life tenancies of the Doyles. On the death, accordingly, of the last Doyle, life tenant, in 1905, the plaintiffs put forward claims against the defendants and other tenants on the lands, but heretofore, the defendants have withheld payment of rent – awaiting the vindication of the plaintiffs' title. That is the problem involved. For the better understanding of it, and shortening, I hope, of what I have to say on the case, I consider it was desirable to give the statement I have made of the general facts regarding the use and possession of the lands. The plaintiffs' title now, according to the definite statement of their learned counsel, is expressly rested on a recovery with a double voucher, suffered in the Easter Term of 1831, by Francis Nesbitt, the devisee of Matthew Nesbitt's lands, by which recovery it is contended Francis Nesbitt there and then barred the entail, and a fee-simple estate became established and vested in him. I do not, by that language, intend to convey that the learned counsel for the plaintiffs maintained that the Doyle estate was interfered with or got rid of – though I am unable to recall what definite position they were prepared to concede the Doyles would and did hold throughout in the case. Both the learned counsel fought the question of title on the recovery of 1831; and, according to my notes, Mr. Conner, K.C., said plainly that the plaintiffs' title, as now presented at any rate, was admitted to be subject to the validity of that recovery.

On the will and codicil taken together it is not possible to suggest – and indeed it never was suggested – that on his father's death Francis Nesbitt was anything else but a tenant in tail of the lands of Cloonboniagh, in remainder upon the life tenancies created in favour of the various members of the Doyle family. His estate was postponed to the precedent freehold granted to the Doyles, which lasted, indeed, from Matthew Nesbitt's death, for the full period up to 1905. The question is whether or not in the facts of the case, as, to my mind, they existed, it was possible for Francis Nesbitt, by the recovery suffered by him, to convert his actual estate in the lands in 1831 into a fee-simple. Admittedly, as it is well known, it was a necessary, preliminary, and essential step towards a valid recovery, to constitute a tenant to the præcipe, as a good and perfect tenant of the áctual freehold of the lands. A man named Thomas Egan was, by the deed of May 9th 1831, to which Francis Nesbitt was a party, professedly constituted such a tenant in the cast of the lands of Cloonboniagh, and he was thereby assumed to be a regular and efficient tenant to the præcipe. By that deed the whole scheme and purpose of the intended course was plainly set out, providing that Thomas Blake was to be the demandant, and that in due course Francis Nesbitt himself was to be the first voucher, and the common vouchee of the Court, the second. It is right to mention that the other lands devised to Francis Nesbitt were included in the recovery, and it may be, inasmuch as Cloonboniagh was included in the full list of lands demised to Francis Nesbitt, in the original will, that inadvertently, rather than by any design, these special lands were introduced into the deed and into the remaining proceedings. And then there was the judgment eventually given in favour of Blake, but who, under the arrangement, had to hold the fee-simple adjudged to him in favour of Francis Nesbitt, his heirs, and assigns for ever. The validity of the course taken essentially depends on Thomas Egan having been, at the time, a good and perfect tenant of the actual freehold of the lands – and unless he was, the whole proceeding, so far as we are now concerned, was invalid and abortive. Francis Nesbitt had no estate depending on any title which would warrant him in making Egan a tenant of the actual freehold. The case relied on is placed wholly on the basis that Francis Nesbitt was, in 1831, a disseisor of the lands, and in full possession of them, and, therefore, qualified to make a valid tenant to the præcipe for the purpose of the recovery. The mere continuance of Francis Nesbitt at Derrycarne and on the lands, after the death of his father, was not a disseisin to justify the view presented here. Having considered the authorities, so far as they were produced, or I could trace them, it would not, in my judgment, be possible to hold that there had been any disseisin of Cloonboniagh, within the meaning of the law pressed on us by the learned counsel for the appellants. A mere naked possession on the part of Francis Nesbitt, who never challenged the estate of the Doyles in the lands, and from the death of Matthew paid the net proceeds from them to the Doyles, up to the time when the latter, in fact, took the entire control, could not, in any sense of the term, be regarded as a disseisin. Francis Nesbitt never made any claim or attempt to oust the Doyles, and, so far as the evidence goes, there is not a trace of his desire to do so in the formal inclusion of Cloonboniagh in the deed, making Egan the tenant of the freehold in the lands. He had no power or title to do so; he had no possession or estate to validate the attempt, if his action were conscious, so far as Cloonboniagh was concerned, to invest Egan with the tenancy in freehold, for the purpose of the proceedings for recovery. The Doyles never had any knowledge of the proceedings, and were in no way concurring parties in it. Lord Coke describes disseisin in simple and striking words at 153 (*b*) of his Commentary upon Littleton. He says that 'Disseisin is a putting out of a man out of seisin, and ever implieth a wrong.' In the same paragraph he, later on, said – 'And of ancient time a disseisin was defined thus: 'Disseisin est un personel trespasse de tortious ouster del seisin''.' In 153 (*b*) Lord Coke referred to opinions of others, but, I think, the two short sentences I have quoted clearly represent his own opinion, and it is in all places taken to do so. A reference also to 257 (*b*) in the Commentary will show that he there also said – 'It is to be understood that there is a force implied in law, as every trespasse and rescous and disseisin implieth a force and is *vi et armis*.' Lord Coke was there speaking of the writ of entry, and the damages recoverable. To the same effect was Bracton's view in the matter, and it is further said that Lord Coke adopted his definition. He has enumerated various modes of disseisin, wherein the main distinction taken, between disseisin and trespass, appears to be founded on the criteria and character of the acts of the disseisor, as whether the putting out was *violenter, injuste et sine judicio*, and so as to a keeping out, if the possession had been vacant, whether it were *animo clamandi*, or *contra voluntatem possidentis*. I have quoted from the note on p. 600 of *Jerritt* v. *Weare* (3 Price, 575).

The judgment of Baron Graham in *Jerritt* v. *Weare* (3 Price, 575) has a close bearing on the present controversy. The head-note is as follows: 'A lease by a stranger, and entry by the lessee, is not a disseisin in fact, without any entry by force, or an avowed intention to disseise.' In his judgment in the case the learned Baron, referring to the judgment of Mr. Justice Aston in *Doe* v. *Horde* (1 Cowper 689) summarized the decision in the latter case by the following statement: 'Mr. Justice Aston, reasoning on the doctrine of recoveries, held that none could be suffered, without the concurrence of the party having the estate for life; and that the deed could only authorize a recovery with the consent of the tenant for life and tenant in tail. Sir Robert Atkyns, however, having contrived to get possession, his levying a fine to make a tenant to the præcipe was held a fraud for want of the concurrence of the jointress, and the estate went to the person entitled under the limitation. The cases would be stretched to an unsustainable latitude if a tenant by sufferance, or tenant at will, making a lease the mere act, should be construed to amount to a disseisin. A manifest intention to oust must be clearly shown.' The case will be recognized as that appearing in Smith's Leading Cases under the title *Taylor* d. *Atkyns* v. *Horde* (Smith's L. Cas., 10th ed., vol. ii, p. 559). But the occasion was another hearing, and not that at which Lord Mansfield gave his judgment. The relevance and force of Baron Graham's summary are manifest, but a few sentences from Judge Aston's judgment itself in 1 Cowper, at p. 698, appear to be exactly applicable to the present case, and decisive of it. He says: 'The great question upon the record is, whether a common recovery suffered in the year 1710 by Sir Robert Atkyns, the younger, is a good recovery. If it is, it has barred the lessor of the plaintiff's right. But that depends on these circumstances: First, whether Sir Robert Atkyns, the younger, was, at the time of the recovery suffered, tenant in tail in possession or tenant in tail in remainder; and secondly, if he was tenant in tail in remainder only, whether there was a good tenant to the præcipe.' At p. 702, he stated, 'The ground of our opinion, therefore, is founded on this: that here there was no actual nor constructive disseisin; Sir Robert Atkyns gained no freehold by it, he had only a naked possession: there was no ouster of the true owner; but the freehold remained not displaced, with Dame Anne, remainder in tail to Sir Robert Atkyns.' I cannot but say that if the names were changed that decision would be an apt and striking judgment in the present case. Sir Robert was relying on the possession by the fine, but he had not obtained the surrender of the precedent estate of Dame Anne as jointress, and she had in no way concurred in the attempt to constitute a real tenant to the præcipe. That is exactly what happened in principle in the case now before the Court. The authorities demonstrate that the real state of affairs disclosed in this case vitiates the recovery of 1831, in relation to the lands of Cloonboniagh. There was no intention of an ouster of seisin on the part of Francis Nesbitt. He was in no sense a disseisor of the outstanding freehold of the Doyles, and we know that it actually existed continuously up to the year 1905. He was not in the position to make Egan a tenant to the præcipe, in the case of Cloonboniagh. To adjudge Francis Nesbitt, in the circumstances, as a disseisor would be to misunderstand the history of the doctrine and its not unnatural growth in the conditions of life prevailing in periods long removed. The notion would be against the whole foundation and spirit of the law. Not therefore being qualified to do so, it was in the actual situation a perfunctory and fruitless attempt on Francis Nesbitt's part, if conscious as regards Cloonboniagh, to make Egan a tenant of it to the præcipe. I need not occupy further time by references to the report of *Taylor* d. *Atkyns* v. *Horde* (1 Burr. 60) and the judgment of Lord Mansfield. I have said already that the case has, in principle, a rare analogy to the present one before us, and the result ought to be the same. The judgment of the learned Lord will attract the attention of everyone interested in the question involved; and as it is so well known and so accessible, it would be superfluous to do more than rely on its manifest application and power.

The special considerations arising from the facts that several of the children, life tenants among the Doyle family in 1831, were minors need not, I think, be dwelt on, in the general view the Court takes. But no impression must be taken that I disagree with the opinion of the learned Judges in the King's Bench in that respect. Agreeing with the judgment of the Divisional Court, the appeal must be refused with costs. This Court, however, thinks that, as the facts relating to the present condition of the Nesbitt family are probably not fully known, and considering the possible effect of further knowledge on the plaintiffs' ability to have their title perfected, the most prudent order to make is that the civil bills be dismissed, but without prejudice.

Holmes L.J.:
The two civil bills which led to the statement of this case by Kenny, J., were brought to recover rents payable by two yearly tenants of portions of the lands of Cloonboniagh in County Leitrim. There is no doubt that the rents sued for are payable to some person. The tenants paid rent down to the year 1905 to Colonel Clements, whose interest in the lands was an estate for the life of Matthew Doyle, who died in March of that year. The plaintiffs' predecessors in title had more than thirty years previously purchased what they believed was the fee-simple of the lands, subject to certain life estates, of which the last was that of Matthew Doyle; and assuming that, on his death, their estate had vested in possession, they issued civil bills in 1909 for the rent then due. It was, of course, necessary for them to show their title, which was of a very complicated character, and in which the crucial point was the effect of a common recovery, with double vouchers, suffered by Francis Nesbitt in the year 1831. If this had the effect of barring an estate in tail male in remainder then vested in Francis Nesbitt, and certain estates subsequent thereto, the plaintiffs are entitled to succeed; but if the recovery only converted Francis Nesbitt's estate in tail male into a base fee leaving the subsequent estates unbarred, then it would be impossible to give the plaintiffs a decree for the rent on the facts before the Court. It would be very difficult to ascertain who is entitled to it, as it would depend on births and deaths that must have occurred long since.

The only question of title raised in the case depends on a narrow point; and I hope to state the grounds of my decision with comparative brevity. In the year 1812, Matthew Nesbitt executed his will, by which he devised all his real estate, which was very extensive, including the lands of Cloonboniagh, to his son, Francis Nesbitt, in tail male, with remainder to his daughter, Elizabeth, in either tail general or tail male (of this there is some doubt), with remainder to several other daughters to be equally divided between them.

In the year 1821, Matthew Nesbitt, by a codicil to his will, gave the lands of Cloonboniagh to Anne Doyle, and her five children, share and share alike, during their lives or the life of the survivor or longest liver of them, with certain further directions as to their respective shares, which it is unnecessary for me to quote, inasmuch as it was long afterwards decided by the Landed Estates Court and the

Court of Chancery Appeal that the true construction was to give a succession of life estates, of which the last to come to an end was that of Matthew Doyle, who, as already mentioned, died in 1905. There is no question that, subject thereto, the limittions of the will of 1812 apply to the lands of Cloonboniagh.

Matthew Nesbitt died in 1823, and his son, Francis, obtained letters of administration, with the will and codicil annexed. It is obvious that Mrs. Doyle was the testator's mistress, and that he was the father of the children. They were supported in some way, and the natural inference is that their support was derived, as the testator intended, from the lands of Cloonboniagh, of which they were made tenants for life. The next step in the title is the common recovery in 1831. There was included in it all the lands devised to Francis in tail male by the will of 1812; and by a deed of the 9th May, 1831, purported to convey all these lands, including Cloonboniagh, to Thomas Egan, as tenant to the præcipe; and the fictitious judgment and record included Cloonboniagh as well as the other lands. The proposition on which counsel for the plaintiffs and appellants rely is, that when a tenant in tail in remainder had previous to his suffering a common recovery disseised a prior life tenant, he was, for the purpose of creating a tenant to the præcipe, in the same position as a tenant in tail in possession – in other words, if the latter has actual seisin of the freehold, it is immaterial whether such be by right or wrong.

In 1831, most, if not all, of the Doyle children were minors, and there has been some discussion as to whether the remainderman could disseise an infant tenant for life; but, as I hold that there is no evidence of disseisin on which the Court can act, it is unnecessary for me to consider this difficult question.

By consent of the parties, we are at liberty to draw inferences of fact, and I am unable to draw from the evidence the inference which would entitle the plaintiffs to succeed, much as I would desire to do so. I start with the proposition that, *prima facie* and until the contrary is proved, seisin and possession must be assumed to go with title, and there is no doubt that from the year 1823 the life estates were as of right vested in the Doyles; and it is equally certain that they have been in receipt of the rents from the year 1855. There is actual evidence of this, and it is unlikely that living witnesses could go farther back. Therefore, this fact is rightly found in the case stated.

There is not any evidence of seisin or possession from 1823 to 1831, except the fact that the Doyles were entitled thereto; and I cannot assume the contrary. The deed executed in that year preliminary to the common recovery includes the lands of Cloonboniagh, but this is no evidence against the Doyles; nor is the fictitious judgment that followed, which being in all respects regular on its face, could not be questioned by writ of error.

Thus matters stood, down to the year 1838, when Mrs. Doyle, her husband, and five children, the devisees under the codicil of 1821, filed a bill in the Court of Chancery, seeking for a declaration of their title to the lands.

It alleges that Francis Nesbitt, the defendant, had dispossessed them, and contains, in the mode of pleading then in use, the allegation of pretences put forward by him. Plaintiffs' counsel argue that we can only have regard to the bringing of such an action, and that the allegations of the suppliants are not evidence against their clients. As, however, the plaintiffs rely on the bill to prove disseisin, they cannot, I think, object to its averments; nor can they say that we are not at liberty to consider the result which was given in evidence by themselves. The bill was dismissed by consent soon after it was filed, the defendant paying the suppliants' costs. The natural inference from this is that the plaintiffs were advised that they could not succeed. This could not have arisen from their not being entitled to the lands, as of this there have never been any doubt. The reason is probably to be found in one of the pretences alleged to have been put forward by the defendant Francis Nesbitt. This was, that he claimed to have collected the rents for the persons entitled, and that, after paying an annuity of £60 charged on the lands, there only remained £25 a year, which he paid to the suppliants. The inference I draw is that he acted, or purported to act, as the suppliants' agent; and that the object of the bill was to obtain from him an account, to avoid which he paid the costs, leaving the tenants for life to manage the lands for the future. This, so far from proving disseisin, would be inconsistent with it; and I am obliged to draw an inference that defeats the plaintiffs. I regret it because they paid a high price for what they were doubtless advised was a good title, and there may not be any other claimants. No one up to the present has sought to enforce his right by litigation; and it is possible, if not probable, that when F.W.H. Nesbitt in 1869 and 1870 conveyed the lands subject to the lift estate to the plaintiffs' predecessors in title, he was the owner in remainder of either the whole or a large undivided share of the fee-simple estate. It is very unlikely that the children of Matthew Nesbitt, other than his son Francis, who took under the will of 1812 estates in remainder to his estate in tail male, ever thought that they would have any real interest in the lands of Cloonboniagh; and if they had all died without issue and intestate as to these lands before 1870, F.W.H. Nesbitt would have been then entitled thereto as their heir-at-law. I find in the first edition of Sir Bernard Burke's Landed Property that Francis was his only son, and that but one of his daughters married, becoming the wife of a clergyman called Nugent, and mother of one child – a daughter, born more than sixty years ago.

It think that, as hitherto there has been no other claimant, it would be more satisfactory to dismiss the civil bills without prejudice; but of course the plaintiffs must pay all the costs of the present litigation.

Cherry L.J.:

Three questions have been stated for the determination of the Court in this case by Kenny, J., namely:

(1) Whether the recovery suffered by Francis Nesbitt in 1831 was effectual to bar the entail?

(2) Whether the defendants in the present proceedings are entitled to question the validity of the recovery? and

(3) Whether the right to question the validity of the recovery is not statute-barred?

The answer to the first question depends upon whether Francis Nesbitt was seised in possession of a freehold estate in the lands at the time that the recovery was suffered. He could not have been rightfully so seised, as there is no doubt that under a codicil to the will of Matthew Nesbitt, which conferred the estate in tail male upon him, the Doyle family were entitled to an estate for their joint lives in the lands of Cloonboniagh. The Doyles' life estate only terminated in 1905, and there is no doubt that for fifty years prior to that date they were in possession by virtue of the devise to them by Matthew Nesbitt.

The contention of the plaintiffs here is that, although Francis Nesbitt was only entitled to an estate in remainder in the lands, he had, prior to 1831, disseised the Doyles; and they argue that under the old law a tenant in tail in remainder, who had wrongfully entered prior to the determination of the life estate, had by disseisin a sufficient estate to appoint a tenant to the præcipe, and so could effectually bar the entail. The case was argued in the Court below on the assumption that this proposition of law was correct, though Gibson, J., appears to think that, under such circumstances, only a base fee could have been created, which would confer no estate upon the plaintiffs in the present case. In this Court it was certainly not admitted by the defendants' counsel, who argued most strenuously that the law before the Act for the abolition of fines and recoveries was the same as it is at present, and that to effect a valid recovery, the consent of the owners of the first estate of freehold in possession was then, as now, necessary, whether there had or had not been a disseisin. In support of this contention they relied on the 3rd section of the 21 Geo. 2, c.11 (Ir.), now repealed, which corresponded in its terms with the 11th section of 3 & 4 Wm, c.74, at present in force.

It is not necessary for us to determine this abstruse question of law, as we are all of opinion that there is no evidence of the disseisin of the Doyles by Francis Nesbitt. The fact that the recovery itself was sufficient cannot be evidence of disseisin, as there is nothing to show that the Doyles had any notice of the proceedings. Nor can the bill in Chancery, presented in 1838, be such evidence, for it actually avers on its face that Francis Nesbitt had accounted to the Doyles for the rents and profits of Cloonboniagh, which would be, if true, inconsistent with a disseisin. It is true that it also avers adverse possession by Francis Nesbitt, but it is impossible to say which of the two inconsistent averments was true. The plaintiffs have, therefore, in my opinion, failed to establish that the recovery suffered in 1831 was effectual to bar the entail, and that they have now any estate in the lands.

On the second question, I also entertain no doubt that the decision in the Court below was correct. The plaintiffs have never been in possession or receipt of the rents and profits of these lands. The tenants who are in actual occupation are, in our view of the facts, liable to be sued either for rent or for mesne rates by the person or persons entitled in remainder under the will, after the determination of the estate in tail male of Francis Nesbitt, which occurred on the death of his only son, Francis W.H. Nesbitt, in 1879. The tenants cannot be called upon to pay their rents twice over, and they are clearly entitled to put any claimants of rent from them on proof of their title.

On the third question I also agree with the judgment of Gibson, J., that proceedings by writ of error only relate to patent defects appearing on the record, and that when there was no valid tenant to the præcipe the whole proceedings were void *ab initio*. It is proceedings by writ of error only which are barred after twenty years.

The dismisses granted by the County Court Judge in these cases should therefore be affirmed, but as the plaintiffs only fail by defect of proof, and as they may be able to establish title in some other way, I think the dismisses should be 'without prejudice,' and not 'on the merits.'

Notes and Questions
1. On fines and recoveries, see *Irish Land Law*, para. 4.117 *et seq*. See also *Cole* v. *Sewell*, p. 246, *post*.
2. What is the answer to the 'abstruse question of law' mentioned by Cherry L.J.?

BANK OF IRELAND AND OTHERS v. DOMVILE
[1956] I.R. 37 (High Court)

Under and by virtue of three deeds of settlement three different estates, the S, M and K estates, were limited upon trust as to the K and S estates for *C.M.D.* for life in tail male in possession and as to the M estate as tenant in tail general in possession with remainder as to the three estates to *M.D.* in tail general. In 1885 *C.M.D.* was found to be a person of unsound mind. In 1886 *M.D.* married *W.P.* There was issue of the marriage one son, *H.P.*, and one daughter, *I.P.* Prior to the marriage *M.D.* executed two disentailing deeds in respect of the estates in tail in remainder limited by the three deeds of settlement and thereby reserved to herself powers of appointment by deed or will in respect of the settled property.

At the date of the execution of the said deeds of disentailment *C.M.D.* was the protector of the M and the S estates and it was not possible for *M.D.* to obtain his consent as he was a person of unsound mind. The effect these three disentailing deeds was decided by the Court in 1933 to be that as to the K. estate *M.D.* became entitled to the fee simple but as to the S and the M estates she became entitled only to a fee simple defeasible on the failure of her own male issue or issue respectively.

C.M.D. died in 1935 without having married and without his estates in tail having been enlarged. *M.D.* died in 1929 and by her will bequeathed all her property to her trustees upon trust for conversion and to stand possessed of the proceeds, in the events which happened, for her son and daughter, *H.P.* and *I.P.*, in equal shares upon certain trusts under which each took at least a life estate. From 1935 to 1952 the income from the settled estates had been paid to *C.F.*, the receiver and committee of the estate of *H.P.* (who was a person of unsound mind) and he had applied the income equally between *H.P.* and *I.P.*

By the year 1935 the lands comprised in the M estate and the S estate had been almost all sold under the provisions of the Land Acts and were represented by invested capital monies, the proceeds of the sale of the land.

A summons was taken out by the plaintiffs as trustees for the determination by the High Court of questions arising upon the administration of the trusts of the said indentures of settlement. One question was whether the disentailing deeds executed by *M.D.* in respect of the M and S estates (which in default of the consent of the protector of the settlement had created base fees) had after the expiration of twelve years from the date of the death of *C.M.D.* by virtue of s.6 of the Real Property Limitation Act, 1874, become effectual to bar all estates limited by the settlements to take effect after or in defeasance of the estates in tail.

Another question concerned the fact that during his lifetime *H.P.* had through his committee and with the approval of the Court executed deeds of disentailment and resettlement for the purpose of the sale of certain parts of the S estate. Two of these disentailing deeds were to two grantees, neither of whom executed the deeds. One of the grantees, *R.N.W.*, who was serving in the British Navy, was at the date of the execution of the deeds missing and subsequently believed to have been lost at sea on the 22nd May, 1941, when his ship was sunk in action. No order presuming his death had been obtained from the Court. It was contended that the circumstances of his death or uncertainty as to the true position invalidated the disentailing deeds of which he was one of the grantees.

Dixon J.:

The questions to be determined in this case relate to three estates which have been in the Domvile family for many years, and which, for convenience, may be shortly referred to as the Santry estate, the Mayo estate and the Kilternan estate, respectively. The first and third of these, as the names suggest, are situated in the County of Dublin. The greater part of these estates has been sold under the provisions of the Irish Land Acts and in other ways and is now represented by invested capital monies; but some portions of the Santry and Kilternan estates still remain unsold. As to all the estates, questions arise as to the exercise by will of a power of appointment in respect of them. As to the Santry estate, questions arise as to whether the base fee which subsisted therein has been enlarged, either in respect of both the unsold lands and the investments representing the lands sold or in respect of any part of either. As to the Mayo estate, the same question arises as to the possible enlargement of a base fee, but only in respect of investments representing lands sold, since all the lands comprised in this estate had been sold by the relevant date. The Kilternan estate was not at any time held on a base fee.

The question of enlargement may conveniently be dealt with first. For this purpose, the history of the estates goes back to the year 1854, when Sir Compton Domvile was owner in fee of the Mayo and Kilternan estates and was tenant for life of the Santry estate with remainder therein to his eldest then surviving son, Charles

Compton William Domvile, in tail. In that year, his second surviving son, William Compton Domvile, married Miss Caroline Meade; and two settlements were entered into. In the same year, Sir Compton made what proved to be his last will. As a result of these three documents, all three estates became settled or resettled in ways that require to be stated in a little detail.

The Kilternan estate was first dealt with, in a settlement dated the 22nd August, 1854, entered into pursuant to marriage articles of the 8th July, 1854, whereby Sir Compton Domvile had agreed to settle both the Kilternan estate and the Mayo estate. The net effect of this settlement was that the Kilternan estate was limited to Sir Compton Domvile for life, with remainder to the second son, William Compton Domvile, for life and, after his death, to his first and other sons successively in tail male, with the reversion to Sir Compton Domvile in fee. This document may conveniently be called the Kilternan settlement.

The Santry estate was settled by a deed of the 24th August, 1854, the way having been paved for this by a disentailing deed executed the previous day by Sir Compton and the eldest son, Charles Compton William. This deed may be called the Santry settlement, although it also dealt with the Kilternan estate in a way that will appear shortly. The net effect of it was to limit the Santry estate to uses which, so far as now material, were successively as follows: Sir Compton Domvile for life; the eldest son, Charles Compton William Domvile, for life; the second son, William Compton Domvile, for life; his first and other sons successively in tail male; the first and other daughters of William Compton Domvile successively in tail male; Anne Helena, wife of Sir Thomas Edward Winnington and eldest daughter of Sir Compton Domvile, for life; Francis Salway Winnington, second son of the said Anne Helena Winnington, for life; his first and other sons successively in tail male; the third and other subsequently born sons of the said Anne Helena Winnington in tail male; Helena Caroline Winnington, eldest daughter of the said Anne Helena Winnington, for life; her first and other sons successively in tail male; Edith Joanna Winnington, second daughter of the said Anne Helena Winnington, for life; her first and other sons successively in tail male; the third and other subsequently born daughters of the said Anne Helena Winnington in tail male; the first and other daughters of William Compton Domvile in tail general; the first and other daughters of Anne Helena Winnington in tail general; and finally, Sir Compton Domvile his heirs and assigns for ever.

In this statement, some uses, which failed to take effect or can no longer take effect, have been omitted.

This deed also settled, on the same uses as the Santry estate, the reversion in fee of the Kilternan estate under the Kilternan settlement. In the event, Sir Compton Meade Domvile, the only son of William Compton Domvile's marriage with Miss Caroline Meade, became tenant in tail male of the Kilternan estate. As he died without having been married and without having barred the entail, this estate reverted in fee to the settlor (Sir Compton Domvile) under the Kilternan settlement. Consequently, as from the death of Sir Compton Meade Domvile, which occurred in 1935, the Kilternan estate became subject to the uses of the Santry settlement so far as then capable of taking effect. By that time, as will be seen later, the uses of the Santry settlement in favour of the first and other daughters of William Compton Domvile had become operative.

One other provision in the settlement under consideration – the Santry settlement – requires to be noted. It is a 'shifting clause' which provided that, if the said Francis Salway Winnington or any male issue of the said Anne Helena Winnington, being a tenant in tail male by purchase under any of the limitations therein contained, should succeed to the baronetcy then enjoyed by the said Sir Thomas Edward Winnington, then the estate should go and remain to the uses and upon the trusts to which the same would have stood limited and settled thereunder if the person so succeeding to such baronetcy were dead without issue male.

The third estate – the Mayo estate – was dealt with by Sir Compton Domvile in his last will, dated the 28th August, 1854. He thereby devised the Mayo estate to trustees upon trust to convey it to the uses and upon the trusts provided for in the marriage articles of the 8th July, 1854 subject thereto, to the uses and upon the trusts of the Santry settlement. He died in 1857, and a formal settlement of the Mayo estate was executed by the trustees on the 3rd August, 1877. The uses declared by this document were successively as follows: William Compton Domvile for life; his first and every other son successively in tail general; his first and every other daughter successively in tail general; the uses of the Santry settlement relating to the reversion in the Kilternan estate.

As in the case of the Kilternan estate, on the death of Sir Compton Meade Domvile, already referred to, the use in favour of the first and other daughters of William Compton Domvile in tail became operative as to the Mayo estate.

As will appear shortly, the entail of the Kilternan estate and the estates in remainder thereto have been barred and the interest enlarged into a fee simple absolute. As to the Santry and Mayo estates, however, there is still a question as to how far the trusts of the respective settlements are still operative and a possibility that one or other of the subsequent limitations therein may take effect or be capable of taking effect in certain events. It is material, therefore, that these interests should be adequately represented on any consideration of matters likely to affect them. For this purpose, the defendants, Eric Thomas Henry Hanbury-Tracy and Thomas Foley Churchill Winnington, have been made defendants. From the pedigrees which have been exhibited, and which are not disputed, it appears that one or other of these defendants is the person now entitled, in remainder expectant on the failure of issue of the first and other daughters of William Compton Domvile, as tenant in tail male in respect of the Santry estate and as tenant in tail in respect of the Mayo estate. Which of them it is depends on whether the 'shifting clause' already quoted from the Santry settlement has operated. All the interests in remainder expectant after such failure of issue have this much in common, that they are contingent on that failure and are therefore equally concerned with the questions involved in the present case, since those questions do not touch on the nature of those interests or any possible conflicts between them but on whether, in the events that have happened, any of such interests are capable of taking effect even in the event of such failure of issue.

Accordingly, I think it would be proper to make a representative order in the present case. As the interests in question may also have been restored or re-created by two documents which have to be considered later, the representation should extend to the interests under those documents. The full representation order would then be to appoint these two defendants to represent the class of remaindermen entitled under the limitations of the Santry and Mayo settlements respectively after the failure or determination of the respective estates thereby limited to the first and other daughters of William Compton Domvile in tail male and in tail respectively and also the class of remaindermen entitled under the limitations and trusts contained in the deed of enlargement, dated the 10th December, 1941, and the deed of resettlement, dated the 20th January, 1947, to take effect after the death and failure of male issue of Sir Hugo Compton Domvile Poë-Domvile, for the purpose of the determination of the questions herein.

Some support can, I think, be found for making such an order in the present case in the decisions of Kay J. in *In re Foster* (45 Ch. D. 629, at p. 631), and of Stirling J. in *In re Nash* ([1893] W.N. 99).

While the various settlements, which have been summarised above, appear somewhat complex in their provisions, the actual history of the devolution of the three estates is comparatively short and simple, because Charles Compton William Domvile died in July, 1884, without issue, and William Compton Domvile died a few months later. His surviving issue were one son, Sir Compton Meade Domvile, who succeeded to the baronetcy, and one daughter, Mary Adelaide Domvile. The effect of the settlements and documents already referred to was that this son became tenant in tail male in possession of the Kilternan and Santry estates and tenant in tail general in possession of the Mayo estate, with remainder to his sister, Mary Adelaide Domvile, in tail male and in tail general respectively.

The next important date is the year 1886, when a marriage took place between Mary Adelaide Domvile and Colonel Sir William Hutcheson Poë. Prior to her marriage she executed two disentailing deeds, both dated the 12th January, 1886. One of these dealt with her estate in remainder in the Kilternan and Santry estates, the other with her estate in remainder in the Mayo estate. The validity and effect of these documents, as disentailing assurances, came before, and was decided by, Mr. Justice Johnston in 1939. The documents themselves were not before him, having been lost and only since found, but he had, and decided that he had, sufficient evidence of execution and enrolment and of their contents to determine the questions involved. The effect of his decision was that the entail of the interest of Mary Adelaide Domvile and all estates in remainder thereto had been effectually barred as to the Kilternan estate, while only the entail had been barred as to the Santry and Mayo estates. Thus, her interest in remainder expectant on the death of her brother, Sir Compton Meade Domvile, without male issue or without issue, as the case might be, had become, as to the Kilternan estate, a fee simple, but, as to the other two estates, had become only a fee simple defeasible on the failure of her own male issue or issue, respectively, that is, a base fee.

The reason for the distinction between the Kilternan estate and the other estates is that the interests of Sir Compton and his sister arose, as to the Kilternan estate, under different instruments while, in the case of the other two estates, the instrument was the same in each case. Accordingly, as to these two estates, Sir Compton, as tenant in tail in possession, was the protector of the relevant settlement. It was not, however, possible to obtain his consent or concurrence, for the reason that he was, and had on the 15th April, 1885, been so found, a person of unsound mind. The assistance of the Court, which could have authorised the exercise of his powers, was not sought, but, as was pointed out by Mr. Justice Johnston, it is very doubtful if the Court would have intervened in view of the principle laid down by the Court of Appeal in England in *In re E.D.S.* ([1914] 1 Ch. 618) and to which reference may have to be made later.

It is material, for the purpose of some of the questions to be answered, to set out the uses expressed in the disentailing deeds. In the case of the Kilternan and Santry estates, the grant was to Richard Walter Tweedie (the grantee) and his heirs to have and to hold the premises, subject to the estate in tail male in possession of Sir Compton Meade Domvile and to a term of years not now material, unto the said Richard Walter Tweedie and his heirs freed and discharged from all estates in tail male or in tail of the said Mary Adelaide Domvile to such uses upon such trusts and with under and subject to such powers provisions and limitations as the said Mary Adelaide Domvile by any deed or deeds with or without power of revocation and new appointment or by her last will or any codicil thereto should appoint; and, in default of and until such appointment and so far as any such appointment should not extend, the uses were to be those of the settlement of the 24th August, 1854, that is, the Santry settlement.

In the case of the Mayo estates, the uses were expressed in a similar manner, except that, in default of appointment, the uses were to be those of the settlement of the 3rd August, 1877, that is, the Mayo settlement.

In fact, Mary Adelaide Domvile – or, as it will now be convenient to call her, Lady Poë – did not survive Sir Compton Meade Domvile. She died on the 28th March, 1929, while he died six years later, on the 22nd April, 1935. The latter is an important date in connection with the question of enlargement, since, as already stated, Sir Compton Meade Domvile died without ever having married and without his estates tail having been enlarged. In consequence, the fee simple in the Kilternan estate and the base fees in the other estates devolved in accordance with the uses expressed in the respective disentailing deeds of the 12th January, 1886. Lady Poë purported to exercise by will the powers of appointment reserved by those deeds and the devolution accordingly depended, and depends, on whether, and how far, the exercise of those powers was effective. These are matters that have to be decided in this suit, although, to some extent, they have already been dealt with by Mr. Justice Johnston in the proceedings already referred to, since part of his decision was to the effect that her will was effectual to pass to the trustees thereof an estate in fee simple in the Kilternan estate and a base fee in the Santry and Mayo estates.

Lady Poë's will consisted of two testamentary documents both duly executed on the same day, 28th January, 1926, and which were admitted together to probate here as one will by Mr. Justice Hanna. A difficulty of construction, as to which part of this composite will dealt with the estates now in question, was decided by Mr. Justice Johnston in the former proceedings and does not now have to be considered. At the date of her will and at her death, Lady Poë had two children surviving. They were Sir Hugo Compton Domvile Poë and Isabel Mary Poë. The latter is a party to these proceedings as is Sir Hugo by his committee, he having been declared a person of unsound mind by order of the 10th May, 1929, and having been a ward of Court since then. In order to comply with a 'name and arms' clause in the Santry settlement of the 24th August, 1854, steps were taken on his behalf in 1936, both in England and here, to authorise him to assume the name of Domvile and to bear the arms of Domvile quartered with those of Poë. His full title is, therefore, Sir Hugo Compton Domvile Poë-Domvile, but it will be convenient to refer to him as Sir Hugo.

For the moment, the effect of Lady Poë's will, as interpreted by Mr. Justice Johnston need only be shortly stated; it will have to be considered in more detail later. It devised and bequeathed all her real and personal property including property over which she should have a general power of appointment or disposition by will upon trust for conversion into money. After providing for certain payments out of the fund so formed, it directed the trustees to invest the residue of the said monies (called 'the Trust Fund') and the income of the Trust Fund was to be paid to her husband for his life, and, on his death, the trustees were to stand possessed of the capital and future income of the Trust Fund for her son and her daughter in equal shares but subject as next thereinafter provided. There then followed a series of complicated provisions as to the 'son's share' and the 'daughter's share' of the Trust Fund, as to which it is sufficient to say, for the moment, that each took at least a life interest in the appropriate share.

Sir William Hutcheson Poë survived Lady Poë by a few years, dying on the 30th November, 1934, but, as he thus died before the tenant in tail in possession, Sir Compton Meade Domvile, he did not enter into receipt of the income of any of the estates now in question. From and after the death of Sir Compton, on the 22nd April, 1935, that income seems to have been received by Cecil Henry FitzHerbert, the present committee of Sir Hugo. He had been in possession as receiver appointed during the wardship of Sir Compton and was also committee (with Elizabeth Patton) of Sir Hugo as from March, 1935, and sole committee of Sir Hugo as from May, 1935, after the death of Elizabeth Patton in that month. He was also receiver in the matter of Sir Hugo as from the 9th October, 1941. As from the latter date, he applied the income equally as between Sir Hugo and Isabel Mary Poë, while a moiety of the income received between the death of Sir Compton in 1935 and the 9th October, 1941, was accounted for and subsequently paid to Miss Poë. The beneficiaries under the will of Lady Poë have, thus, been in receipt of the income in the proportions provided for in the will and, as between them and Cecil Henry FitzHerbert, he must, in my view, so far as he was in possession, be regarded as merely their agent. The trustees of the will had, of course, and continue to have, legal seisin of the estates.

If the disentailing deeds of 1886 had been executed after the death of Sir Compton Meade Domvile, they would have been effectual not only to bar the entail but also to bar all estates to take effect after or in defeasance of the estate tail; and the question therefore arises whether they have become so effectual, under s. 6 of the Real Property Limitation Act, 1874, after the expiration of 12 years from such death, that is, as from the 22nd April, 1947. As of this latter date, the Mayo estate had all been sold; but the Santry estate consisted partly of invested proceeds of sale and partly of unsold lands; and the effect of the section must be considered in relation to both the investments and the unsold lands.

Sect. 6 – which replaced s. 23 of the Real Property Limitation Act, 1833, and reduced the period from twenty to twelve years – reads as follows:

'When a tenant in tail of any land or rent shall have made an assurance thereof which shall not operate to bar the estate or estates to take effect after or in defeasance of his estate tail, and any person shall by virtue of such assurance at the time of the execution thereof, or at any time afterwards, be in possession or receipt of the profits of such land, or in receipt of such rent, and the same person or any other person whosoever (other than some person entitled to such possession or receipt in respect of an estate which shall have taken effect after or in defeasance of the estate tail) shall continue or be in such possession or receipt for the period of twelve years next after the commencement of the time at which such assurance, if it had then been executed by such tenant in tail, or the person who would have been entitled to his estate tail if such assurance had not been executed, would, without the consent of any other person, have operated to bar such estate or estates as aforesaid, then, at the expiration of such period of twelve years, such assurance shall be and be deemed to have been effectual as against any person claiming any estate, interest, or right to take effect after or in defeasance of such estate tail.'

This section does not expressly say that the assurance referred to in it must have been one that was effective to bar the entail, e.g., by being duly enrolled under the Fines and Recoveries Act, 1834; but this was decided to have been the meaning of the corresponding s. 21 of the Act of 1833, which was in substantially the same wording. This was decided by Lord Cranworth in *Penny* v. *Allen* (7 De G.M. and G. 409) and by Lord Romilly M.R. in *Morgan* v. *Morgan* (10 L.R. Eq. 99). These cases were also cited in support of the proposition that the section under consideration should, as an enactment of limitation, receive a strict construction; but this proposition was assented to by all the parties.

Lord Cranworth put the matter succinctly thus (at p. 426): 'The object of the 23rd section was to give effect to acts of a tenant in tail against remaindermen and reversioners, and to give effect to assurances, which, although they were effectual to bar the issue, were ineffectual to bar those entitled in remainder.'

There is no doubt now that the disentailing deeds of 1886 were effectual to bar

Lady Poë's own issue; and the questions to be decided, then, are whether they constitute in every other respect assurances of the type contemplated by the section and whether there has been possession of the type contemplated for the requisite period by virtue of such assurances. This paraphrase of the section may be said to involve the assumption that the possession must be, and continue during the twelve years to be, a possession by virtue of the assurance. This may not be strictly accurate, as the reference to 'any other person whosoever' would appear to contemplate a successor in title whose possession might not be correctly described as being by virtue of the original assurance; but such successor must, in my view, derive his title from or under some person who entered into possession by virtue of the assurance. Even on the most liberal reading of the section, possession must at some time have been held by virtue of the assurance.

The uses of the disentailing deeds have been already quoted, and, subject to the power of appointment reserved to Lady Poë, were merely the uses of the existing settlements. This power of appointment added nothing to their effect, being merely a recognition of the power of disposition of a limited interest which Lady Poë obtained by the disentailing process itself. They amount, therefore, to no more than disentailing deeds. The nature of such a deed was considered in *In re Gaskell and Walters' Contract* ([1906] 2 Ch. 1), by the Court of Appeal in England, and it was there held that a disentailing deed was not an 'alienation' within the meaning of s. 8 of the Forfeiture Act, 1870; and, accordingly, it could be executed by a convict. Cozens-Hardy L.J. said (at p. 10): 'Alienation implies a transaction by which property is given to another person, but here there is no other person, unless a grantee to uses can be so regarded.' Similarly, in *Lord Lilford* v. *Attorney-General* (L.R. 2 H.L. 63), it was held that a disentailing deed executed by a tenant in tail does not destroy the interest he possesses in the estate, but enables him, by the exercise of the power which that interest gives him, to render it perpetual. This, of course, refers to a case where there is no protector or the consent of the protector, if there is one, is obtained; but the principle is the same where the result of the deed is a base fee rather than a fee simple. In reference to the power of disposition thus acquired, Lord Cranworth said (L.R. 2 H.L. 63): 'And, therefore, when he executed the disentailing deed . . . and so became the owner in fee simple, he may be treated as having . . . been competent to dispose by will of a continuing interest in the property . . . He was competent to dispose by will of an interest in the property coming from the predecessor to him and continuing to his devisees.' In the same way, Lady Poë became competent to dispose by will, apart from any power of appointment, of an interest which might come to her under the settlements and might enure for the benefit of her devisees.

It is in line with this view of the purpose and effect of a disentailing deed that the Irish Court of Appeal, affirming Porter M.R., held in *Lynch* v. *Clarkin* ([1900] 1 I.R. 178), that, where the uses declared did not exhaust the fee, the deed was still effective to bar the entail and there was a resulting trust of the fee in favour of the former tenant in tail.

Reference should also be made to *Cannon* v. *Rimington* (12 C.B. 1), which was a decision on s. 21 of the Limitation Act of 1833. This section purported to bar the right of the remaindermen where the right of the tenant in tail to make an entry or distress had become barred by lapse of time; and it was held, in that case, that the section did not apply where the tenant in tail had made a feoffment and thus put it out of his power to bring an action or make an entry, time only running against the remaindermen from his death. There is considerable force in the argument that s. 6 of the Act of 1874, regarded as a re-enactment of s. 23 of the Act of 1833, is complementary to s.21 of the Act of 1833, and, thus, makes provision, in favour of the feoffee and his successors, for such a feoffment. This possibility was suggested in the argument of counsel for the demandant in *Cannon* v. *Rimington* (12 C.B. 1, at p. 12) in these words: 'The 21st and 22nd sections are pure clauses of limitation: they do not apply to validate invalid conveyances; that is done, in a very guarded manner, by section 23'. Although the general effect of the argument was adopted by the Court, this point was not expressly dealt with.

On the foregoing cases and on a consideration of the section as a whole, I have formed the view that a mere disentailing deed was not the type of assurance contemplated by it. If it were so, the section would necessarily apply where a tenant in tail had executed a disentailing deed, without the consent of the protector, and subsequently came into possession and remained in possession for twelve years after the death of the protector, although at any time during the twelve years he could have enlarged the base fee by taking the appropriate steps. It is difficult to conceive of the Legislature intending to provide for such a case, while it is easy to see some force in the claim of a purchaser or grantee from the tenant in tail, who might not be able to obtain or compel an enlargement, to protection. If it be said that, while the section contemplated and provided for the latter case, its terms are wide enough to include the former, this would be to give the section a wide rather than a narrow construction, contrary to the agreed method of approach.

It is difficult to divorce this question from a consideration of the requirement that there should be possession by virtue of the assurance, because this requirement itself suggests that the assurance must be of a kind that confers or is capable of conferring a right to possession, and this does not hold good of a mere disentailing deed. Such a deed does not confer any fresh right to possession on the disentailor or a right to possession on any other person; and, if the disentailor is already in possession, he continues in possession by virtue of the original settlement and not by virtue of the disentailing deed. This is the effect of the decision of Joyce J. in *In re Trevanion, Trevanion* v. *Lennox* ([1910] 2 Ch. 538), applied by Peterson J. in *In re Fowler, Fowler* v. *Fowler* ([1917] 2 Ch. 307), and I respectfully adopt the views of these learned judges.

There is, therefore, I think, no doubt that, if Lady Poë had survived Sir Compton Meade Domvile, she would have entered into possession by virtue of the settlements and so continued in possession although she had, by her own act, altered the character of her interest. When she did not survive him, is it possible to say that the trustees of her will or the beneficiaries thereunder entered into possession by virtue of the disentailing deeds of 1886? Those deeds enabled Lady Poë to make an effective disposition of the lands by will, but I find it impossible to take the view that the right to possession of the trustees or of the beneficiaries did not depend, at least primarily if not exclusively, on her will. Even if I were disposed to take the view – which I am not – that such possession could be said to be by virtue of the combined effect of those deeds and the will, I do not think this would satisfy the requirement of the section that possession should be 'by virtue of such assurance.' This view is not modified by the circumstance that the provisions in the will were clearly intended to be an exercise of the powers of appointment contained in the deeds. In the first place, as already pointed out, the power of testamentary disposition existed independently of its expression or reservation in the deeds. Secondly, I do not think the principle applied in cases like *Attorney-General* v. *Earl of Selborne* ([1902] 1 K.B. 388), that the estates created by the execution of a power take effect in the same manner as if created by the deed that raised the power, can be applied to the interpretation of the words used in s. 6 of the Act of 1874. In any event, such estates, as recognised in the statement of the principle, are *created* by the exercise of the power and, normally, take effect from the time of execution.

Similarly, here, the right to possession was created by the will and took effect from the date of operation of the will, the death of Lady Poë.

This view as to the proper construction of s. 6 disposes of the question of enlargement under that section as to both the unsold lands and the invested proceeds of lands sold. If, however, I am wrong as to the application of the section to the unsold lands, I take the view that the section does not apply to the invested proceeds of any lands sold prior to the expiration of the period of twelve years. In other words, the section applies only to land as a corporeal hereditament. This is what the definition section says. Sect. 1 of the Act of 1833 – which, by virtue of s. 9 of the Act of 1874, is also the definition section for the Act of 1874 – defines 'land' as extending 'to manors, messuages, and all other corporeal hereditaments whatsoever, and also to tithes (other than tithes belonging to a spiritual or eleemosynary corporation sole), and also to any share, estate, or interest in them or any of them, whether the same shall be a freehold or chattel interest, and whether freehold or copyhold, or held according to any other tenure.' There follows a definition of 'rent' and there is a reference to 'rent' in s. 6, but it is conceded that this means something in the nature of a rentcharge and has no application in the present case. Several sections of these Acts can be pointed to which could only apply to land as a corporeal entity – sections referring to making an entry or distress – while no section was referred to which required 'land' to be read in the sense of the proceeds of sale of land or of money directed to be laid out on land. It was, however, contended that the provisions of s. 22, sub-s. 5, of the Settled Land Act, 1882, attracted the provisions of s. 6 of the Act of 1874 so as to make them applicable to capital monies arising under the Settled Land Acts. The sub-section in question provides: 'Capital money arising under this Act while remaining uninvested or unapplied, and securities on which an investment of any such capital money is made, shall, for all purposes of disposition, transmission, and devolution, be considered as land, and the same shall be held for and go to the same persons successively, in the same manner and for and on the same estates, interests, and trusts, as the land wherefrom the money arises would, if not disposed of, have been held and have gone under the settlement.'

There might have been considerable cogency in this argument if the sub-section had merely provided that the capital monies should be considered as land for all purposes and the last portion of the sub-section had been omitted. They are, however, only made land for the specified purposes of disposition, transmission, and devolution; and the last portion of the sub-section strongly indicates that the object was to secure that they should continue to be subject to the limitations and trusts of the settlement. The meaning of this sub-section was considered in *In re Midleton's Settlement* ([1947] 1 Ch. 583), where Lord Greene M.R. said (at p. 591): 'In my view, it is quite a mistake to regard this sub-section as equivalent to or as expressing the same results as would arise on a conversion under the ordinary equitable doctrine of conversion . . . It does not say anything of the kind. It is only for certain limited and stated purposes that the proceeds are to "be considered as land" and they are to be 'held for and go to the same persons successively, in the same manner and for and on the same estates, interests, and trusts, as the land wherefrom the money arises would, if not disposed of, have been held and have gone under the settlement.' The object clearly is to preserve the beneficial interests and cause them to attach to the capital money in the same way as they attached to the land from which it was derived. The decision of the Court of Appeal in this case was affirmed in the House of Lords ([1949] A.C. 418). So far as that decision was concerned with assessment to estate duty not being a purpose of devolution within the sub-section, it may not be consistent with that of our own Divisional Court in *In re Stoughton* ([1941] I.R. 166); but nothing in the latter case conflicts with the view of the sub-section which I have quoted and which I adopt.

It was, however, contended that the effect of s. 6, like other limitation enactments dealing with real property, was not merely to bar a right but to confer a title to the land, and that this amounted to a 'disposition' within s. 33, sub-s. 5. It is true that expressions can be found in reported cases suggesting a transfer of ownership: such as by Parke B. in *Doe d. Jukes* v. *Sumner* (14 M. and W. 39, at p. 42): – 'The effect of the Act is to make a parliamentary conveyance of the land to the person in possession after that period of twenty years has elapsed'; and by Jessel M.R. in *Dawkins* v. *Lord Penrhyn* (6 Ch.D. 318, at p. 323): ' . . . it is a divesting of title or a transfer of title to somebody else.' These expressions were however *obiter* as to whether there was an actual transfer of title from the dispossessed owner; and the more correct view seems to be that of Holmes L.J. in *O'Connor* v. *Foley* ([1906] 1 I.R. 20, at p. 38). He there said: 'I prefer to hold that, although there is not a direct transfer to the wrongdoer who has been in possession, yet the title gained by such possession is limited by rights yet remaining unextinguished, and is commensurate with the interest which the rightful owners lost by the operation of the statute, and has the same legal character.' Apart from the doubt I feel whether s. 22, sub-s. 5, applies at all to an involuntary transaction, so far as a 'disposition' is concerned, I do not think the type of operation effected by the statutes of limitation is within the contemplated purposes.

Neither of these base fees having then, in my view, been enlarged by the operation of s. 6 of the Real Property Limitation Act of 1874, the question arises whether there was an enlargement by the operation of s. 16 of the Fines and Recoveries (Ireland) Act, 1834. This section may have operated in respect of three deeds executed by Sir Hugo through his committee, two of them being executed in 1941 and one in 1946. These deeds were followed by a deed of resettlement of the 20th January, 1947, as to the validity and effect of which questions also arise. All these deeds dealt only with the Santry estate so that, if there has been an enlargement, it is only as to the Santry estate; and the Mayo estate continues to be held on a base fee.

Sir Compton Meade Domvile having died on the 22nd April, 1935, and Lady Poë being then dead, Sir Hugo would have become, under the Santry settlement, as from that date, tenant in tail male in possession of the Santry estate, and, as such, entitled to enlarge the base fee and bar all interests in remainder or reversion after the estate tail. This is the effect of s. 16 of the Act of 1834, substituting a deed for the old process of suffering a recovery. This section reads: ' . . . after the thirty-first day of October one thousand eight hundred and thirty-four, in every case in which an estate tail in any lands shall have been barred and converted into a base fee, either before or on or after that day, the person who if such estate tail had not been barred would have been actual tenant in tail of the same lands shall have full power to dispose of such lands as against all persons whose estates are to take effect after the determination or in defeasance of the base fee into which the estate tail shall have been converted, so as to enlarge the base fee into a fee simple absolute . . .' There follows then a saving clause as to the rights of the Crown in certain events and as to the rights of all persons in respect of estates prior to the estate tail and of all other persons except those against whom such disposition is by the Act authorised to be made. This clause is not material for present purposes.

It will be observed that the person authorised to make the enlarging disposition is the person who would have been 'actual tenant in tail' if the estate tail had not been barred; and, according to s. 1 of the Act, this expression 'shall mean exclusively the tenant of an estate tail which shall not have been barred, and such tenant shall be deemed an actual tenant in tail, although the estate tail may have been divested or turned to a right.' It has been held, accordingly, that the corresponding section of the English Act is not confined to cases where the tenant in tail is owner of the base fee into which his estate tail has been converted: *Bankes* v. *Small* (36 Ch.D. 716). Sir Hugo, in fact, acquired an interest in the base fee under the will of his mother, Lady Poë; but this circumstance is irrelevant to his having the power conferred by s. 16. His incapacity, however, would have prevented him exercising the power during the relevant period, although it could be exercised on his behalf by the Court of which he was a ward, if that Court thought fit.

The matter did in fact arise and was considered by that Court, in the year 1940, in connection with a proposed acquisition of part of the Santry estate by the Dublin Corporation; and an order was made on the 30th July, 1940, by the President of the High Court in the matter of Sir Hugo Compton Domvile Poë-Domvile, a ward of Court. The curial part of that order read as follows: 'It is ordered that the petitioner as committee of the ward be at liberty in the name and on behalf of the ward to execute a deed enlarging the base fee in that part of the Santry estate comprising Santry Court and Demesne and the premises 25, 26 and 27 Chancery Street and numbers 1 to 4 inclusive Greek Street being the premises acquired by the Corporation of Dublin into an estate in fee simple such deed to be conditional on the payment of the net proceeds of the sale of the property comprised in the said deed of enlargement to the trustees for the time being of the settlement of 24th August, 1854, for the purposes of the Settled Land Acts, 1882–1890, and on the execution by the trustees of the will of Dame Mary Adelaide Poë by Miss Isabel Mary Poë and by the petitioner Cecil Henry FitzHerbert on behalf of the ward of an indenture resettling the said net proceeds to the satisfaction of the Registrar in such manner that after the death and failure of male issue of the ward the said net proceeds and the investments representing the same shall be applied in the purchase of freeholds of inheritance in Eire, England or Wales to be assured to such uses upon such trusts and subject to such powers and provisions as would have been operative in respect of the said lands and premises after the death and failure of male issue of the ward had such sales not been made and such enlarging deed not been executed.'

Pausing here for a moment, it seems perfectly clear what this order contemplated and was designed to effect. In the first place, for the purpose of carrying out a sale, which was presumably for the ward's benefit and was apparently, in any event, in the nature of a compulsory acqusition, the committee was authorised to exercise the ward's power of enlargement on his behalf. This enlargement was, however, only intended to be effective so far as was necessary to carry out the sale. In other words, while an indefeasible title would be conferred on the purchaser, the transaction was neither to affect adversely nor to enlarge the rights or interests which would have subsisted if no sale had taken place. This would involve attaching those rights and interests to the proceeds of sale and, in particular, restoring, so far as it could be done, the base fee. A difficulty was, however, created by the Act itself, which does not contemplate anything in the nature of a provisional or limited enlargement but, rather, that an enlargement should be effective for all purposes. Sect. 18 of the Act does provide for limited dispositions but only in the sense that certain dispositions of a limited character shall not operate as enlargements at all. This difficulty was met by the portion of the order which made the exercise of the power of enlargement conditional on the execution of a deed of resettlement of the nature indicated. The base fee would only have subsisted so long as the ward lived and so long as there might be male issue of the ward; but, so long as it subsisted, it could have been dealt with, and interests could have existed in it, as if it were a fee simple, as, for example, under the provisions of Lady Poë's will. This is, then, the meaning of the portion of the order that provides that, after the death and failure of male issue of the ward, the limitations of the resettlement are to be those that would have been operative if there had been no sale or enlargement. These would be the estates, interests, or rights, taking effect after or in defeasance of the estate tail which had been converted into a base fee. Pending such death and failure of male issue, the proceeds would presumably be held on the same trusts as the base fee, that is, in the present cae, the trusts of Lady Poë's will. The direction to lay out the net proceeds and the investments representing the same, at the appropriate time, in the purchase of freeholds of inheritance would effect a conversion into reality if this were necessary to enable those estates, interests, or rights to take effect. The parties who were to join in the resettlement were all represented on the hearing of the petition and were bound by the order made thereon.

This view of the order of the 30th July, 1940, accords with the practice of a Court exercising the jurisdiction in lunacy, as laid down in the case of *In re E.D.S.* ([1914] 1 Ch. 618), already referred to. It was there decided by the Court of Appeal in England that a lunatic's power to bar the entail is a power vested in him for his own benefit and that the Court has jurisdiction in lunacy to authorise the committee to sell the property so as to bar the entail. It was, however, added by the Court that, under ordinary circumstances, the proceeds of sale should be resettled by the Court under its general jurisdiction so as not to prejudice the remaindermen; and an approved form of order is set out (at p. 630 of the report) which does not differ materially in substance from the order under consideration. The judgments contain the following observations: – 'It is settled that the Judge in Lunacy ought not, in ordering a sale, to defeat the interests of the remaindermen': per Cozens-Hardy M.R., at p. 624; '. . . according to the practice of the Court in Lunacy the consent of the Court to the sale is given only upon the terms that the proceeds are resettled to the same uses as before': per Buckley L.J., at p. 627; and '. . . it is the settled rule in lunacy to avoid anything that will prejudice the next of kin, heirs, or successors in title of a lunatic': per Phillimore L.J., at p. 629. The same approach to this question is noted in Vaizey on Settlements at p. 1596, where authority is quoted for the principle that the entail of a lunatic's property ought not to be barred further than is necessary for the purpose of the particular transaction and that, as between the lunatic and the remaindermen, it is the duty of the Court not to alter the nature of the property or the devolution of the estate after the death of the lunatic.

I can now return to the order of the 30th July, 1940, of which I have cited the portion giving rise to the observations just made. The remaining portion of that order conferred a similar power of enlargement on the committee as to any other portion of the Santry estate for the purpose of enabling dispositions to be made, but subject to an application for approval being made to the Court and subject to a similar condition as to the trusts of the net capital monies received or arising on any such disposition. This last condition was, in fact, even more specific as to these trusts than the earlier portion of the order had been. This second portion of the order reads as follows:

'And it is further ordered that the petitioner as such committee be at liberty in the name and on behalf of the ward to execute a further deed or further deeds of enlargement to the extent and for the purpose of enabling grants to be made of other portions of the Santry estate to purchasers or lessees for such terms of years as such purchasers or lessees should require provided that notice of every intended sale or lease shall be given to the said trustees of the said settlement and that an application for approval of each such sale or lease shall be made in the matter of Sir

Hugo Compton Domvile Poë-Domvile a ward of Court and that the net capital monies received or arising on every sale or lease be paid to the trustees or trustee for the time being of the said settlement and invested and during the life of the ward and the lives and life of his male issue (if any) the income arising from all sales and leases of parts of the Santry estate be paid to the trustees or trustee of the said will of Dame Mary Adelaide Poë to be applied in accordance with the trusts and powers therein declared and contained and that after the death and faiure of male issue of the ward the monies and investments arising from sales or leases of portions of the Santry estate the subject of other deeds of enlargement shall be applied in the like manner as hereinbefore provided in respect of the net proceeds of the sale of Santry Court and Demesne.'

I think there can be no doubt, from the whole terms of this order which I have quoted, that the President of the High Court was concerned to ensure that any enlargement effected as a result of the order would not prejudice the rights of any persons entitled after the determination or in defeasance of the base fee created by Lady Poë.

A supplemental order was made in the same matter the following year, on the 22nd June, 1941. It was made on the application of the committee and the curial part reads as follows: 'It is ordered by the President of the High Court that the committee be at liberty in the name and on behalf of the ward to execute a deed enlarging the base fee in the Santry estate (excepting the portions specifically dealt with in the said order of the 30th July, 1940) for the purpose and to the extent of enabling leases for terms of years of any length in possession or reversion to be granted of portions of the Santry estate all such leases to be approved by the Registrar of Wards of Court and all monies received by way of fine on the granting of any lease to be paid and applied as by the said order directed in respect of net capital monies.'

Pursuant to these orders, three deeds were executed, two of them on the 10th December, 1941, and the third on the 28th October, 1946. Of those executed in 1941, one was expressed to be supplemental to the other and to have been executed after it. The parties to both these deeds were the ward by his committee and the committee of the first part, Isabel Mary Poë of the second part, George Ambrose Congreve Webb and Cecil Henry FitzHerbert (the committee) of the third part and Charles Spottiswoode Weir and Richard Nesham Weir (thereinafter together called 'the grantees') of the fourth part. The first deed of the 10th December 1941, recited the prior history of the title to and dealings with the Santry estate, and from these recitals it appears that the parties of the third part, George Ambrose Congreve Webb and Cecil Henry FitzHerbert, had become the trustees for the purposes of the Settled Land Acts of the Santry settlement, and that the grantees, the parties of the fourth part, had become the trustees of the will of Lady Poë. There was also a recital of the order of the 30th July, 1940, already quoted, and of the fact that the Corporation of Dublin had called for a conveyance of the property. The indenture then witnessed that in pursuance of the said order and for effectuating the purposes thereinbefore mentioned the ward acting by the committee as such committee and the committee as such committee with the approbation of Isabel Mary Poë and of the trustees of the Santry settlement as such trustees thereby respectively granted and confirmed unto the grantees the hereditaments specified in the schedule.

The schedule comprised the plots of ground with the buildings thereon known as nos. 25, 26, 27 Chancery Street and number 1 and 4 Greek Street, in the City of Dublin, and also part of the lands of Santry demesne containing 222 acres and 1 perch together with the mansion house known as Santry Court and other buildings erected thereon, in the County of Dublin. For some unexplained reason, this schedule did not include numbers 2 and 3 Greek Street, although the order of the 30th July, 1940, as already seen, specifically dealt with nos. 1 to 4, inclusive, Greek Street.

The habendum in this deed was to hold the hereditaments unto the grantees and their heirs discharged from all estates, rights, interests and powers to take effect after the determination of the base fee created by the recited indenture of the 12th January, 1886, to the intent that such base fee might be enlarged into a fee simple absolute to the use of the grantees and their heirs upon trust to sell and convey the said hereditaments to such person, persons or bodies of persons corporate or unincorporate and at such prices and on and subject to such terms and conditions as had been or might be approved by the President of the High Court, including the conditions as to payment and resettlement of the several purchase monies contained in the said order of the 30th July, 1940. There followed a proviso that if the contemplated sale should not be completed within twelve months the deed should become and be wholly void and the grantees should stand seised of and entitled to the hereditaments for the like estate and interest as the same were then vested for under the will of Lady Poë in the grantees as trustees of the said will. This proviso again illustrates the limited intention of the enlargement. In the event, the sale took place within the twelve months and the proviso did not become operative.

The supplemental deed of the same date, having referred to the first deed, recited that other portions of the Santry estate of which Lady Poë had at her death been seised for an estate in base fee were devised under her will to trustees in trust for sale and that it was desirable that the will trustees should be able to grant leases for terms of years without thereby prejudicing the right of succession of the parties entitled under the Santry settlement on the determination of the said base fee. It then referred to the orders of the 30th July, 1940, and the 22nd June, 1941, and went on to witness that in pursuance of the said orders and for effectuating the said purposes the ward acting by the committee and the committee as such with the approbation of Isabel Mary Poë and of the settlement trustees granted and confirmed unto the will trustees (Charles Spottiswoode Weir and Richard Nesham Weir) all messuages lands and premises situate in the City or County of Dublin being part of the Santry estate except the portions thereof specifically dealt within the order of the 30th July, 1940. As the latter order specifically dealt with nos. 2 and 3 Greek Street, these premises were not captured by this general description and, as will be seen, were dealt with separately in the third deed of enlargement, that of the 28th October, 1946.

The habendum of this second deed of the 10th December, 1941, was expressed to be to hold the premises unto the will trustees and their heirs to the use of the will trustees for the term of 10,000 years from the date of the indenture to the end and intent that the will trustees should and might grant leases and tenancies of any portions of the same for any term or terms of years consistent with the term thereby vested in them in possession or reversion or from year to year or any shorter period at such rent or rents and subject to such covenants agreements and conditions as should be reasonable and proper, such leases and tenancies to be binding upon all persons interested under the settlement, and from and after the determination of the said term and in the meantime subject thereto and to the trusts thereof to the uses upon the trusts and subject to the powers and provisions which in the events which had happened were or would but for the execution of the disentailing assurance of the 12th January, 1886, be subsisting in respect of the hereditaments under or by virtue of the Santry settlement. These uses and trusts were then set out as being to the use of the ward and the heirs male of his body with remainders expressed in the same terms as those in the Santry settlement after the death and failure of male issue of any daughter of William Compton Domvile so far as then capable of taking effect; that is, the remainders were those capable of operating after the determination of the base fee created by Lady Poë.

· This deed contained a proviso which is of importance as showing the intention of preserving the subsisting trusts of the base fee and the rights which might arise on its determination. It was to the effect that during the life of the ward or until his discharge from wardship, whichever should be the shorter period, all leases and tenancies should receive the approval of the Registrar and all monies paid in consideration thereof should be paid to the settlement trustees to be invested by them in the purchase of freeholds of inheritance to be conveyed to the uses on the trusts and subject to the powers and provisions which under the settlement were subsisting with respect to the unsold portions of the Santry estate or as near thereto as circumstances would permit and that the income arising from such investment should during the life of the ward be paid to the will trustees, and, in case the ward should leave an heir male or heirs male of the body and pending the execution and enrolment of a further deed enlarging the base fee into a fee simple absolute, continue to be paid to the will trustees and be applied by them in accordance with the trusts of the said will.

Both of these deeds were duly enrolled but, before passing to the third deed of enlargement, a circumstance must be noted and considered in relation to them, which does not apply to the third deed, and which it is contended invalidates them. This is that, while they were executed by all the other parties, they were not executed by Richard Nesham Weir, one of the will trustees. It appears from subsequent documents that Richard Nesham Weir was serving in the British Navy in 1941 and it was certified on the 7th May, 1945, by the Lords Commissioners of the Admiralty that he was presumed by the Admiralty for official purposes to have died on the 22nd May, 1941. This certificate is recited in an appointment of new trustees, dated the 22nd July, 1946, and it is therein also recited that he was, on the 22nd May, 1941, an officer serving in the Royal Navy and was lost at sea on that date when his ship was sunk in action off the island of Crete. No order has been made presuming his death, but this appointment of new trustees and the subsequent documents have been executed on the basis of his death on the 22nd May, 1941, being an established fact. I think it would be legitimate to approach the question of the validity of the two documents of the 10th December, 1941, on the same basis.

In support of the contention that this circumstance, or, alternatively, the uncertainty as to the true position, invalidated these documents, reference was made to the decision in *Peacock* v. *Eastland* (L.R. 10 Eq. 17) of Lord Romilly M.R. In that case a disentailing deed granted the estate to 'A.' and 'B.' and their heirs to the use of them and their heirs in trust for the grantor. The deed was enrolled but not executed by the grantees and they subsequently executed a deed of disclaimer. It was held that the disentailing deed operated as a grant and not by the Statute of Uses and that it was rendered inoperative by the subsequent disclaimer by the trustess. Lord Romilly, in the course of his judgment, said (at p. 20): – 'The real question seems to me to be this: whether, by grant at common law, any man can confer upon another, against his will and without his consent, any estate whatever in any property? Consequently, in my opinion, all the cases which refer to the releasee to uses being a mere conduit-pipe have no application to this case.' This decision, however, was not wholly inconsistent with the deed being voidable rather than void *ab initio*, because, as Lord Romilly pointed out, the difficulty in the case of *Thompson* v. *Leech* (2 Vent. 198), of the absence of evidence of the attitude of the grantees, did not arise in the case before him: and he went on to quote an important passage from Lord Tenterden in *Townson* v. *Tickell* (3 B. and Ald. 31). Portion of this was to the following effect: – '*Prima facie*, every estate, whether given by will or otherwise, is supposed to be beneficial to the party to whom it is so given. Of that, however, he is the best judge; and if it turn out that the party to whom the gift is made does not consider it beneficial, the law will certainly, by some mode or other, allow him to renounce or refuse the gift.'

There is no doubt that, in form, the deeds of the 10th December, 1941, correspond to that in *Peacock* v. *Eastland* (L.R. 10 Eq. 17) rather than to that in *Nelson* v. *Agnew* (I.R. 6 Eq. 232), where the deed operated by virtue of the Statute of Uses and it was held that assent or execution by the grantees to uses was unnecessary. It would seem, therefore, that the authority of *Peacock* v. *Eastland* (L.R. 10 Eq. 17) would extend to the proposition that, if the grantees or one of them had disclaimed the deeds, they would have been void as to the grantees or as to the one disclaiming. It has been said that, in such a case, the avoidance is *ab initio*, but the position has been more clearly and accurately stated by Byrne J. in *Mallott* v. *Wilson* ([1903] 2 Ch. 494). The following passage from his judgment (at p. 501) shows the more limited meaning that should be given to this statement: '. . . I am satisfied now that the true meaning is that, not in regard to all persons and for all purposes is the case to be treated as though the legal estate had never passed, but that as regards the trustee and the person to whom the grant was made, he is, in respect of his liabilities, his burdens, and his rights, in exactly the same position as though no conveyance had ever been made to him.' The learned judge cited *Thompson* v. *Leach* (2 Vent. 198) already mentioned, and other cases, in support of his view.

In the present case, therefore, if it is to be considered as uncertain whether Richard Nesham Weir was alive on the 10th Decmeber, 1941, the deeds are not less valid than they would have been in the case of a grantee who did not execute or expressly assent, but who, at the same time, had not disclaimed; that is, they would have been good until disclaimer. In the case of a disclaimer by one of two joint grantees, I am inclined to think that this does not invalidate the document as to the other grantee or as to its general effect. If, on the other hand, it is to be presumed that Richard Nesham Weir was already dead on the 10th December, 1941, I do not see why the document should not still be valid as to the other grantee and in its general effect. The principle here involved seems to me to be the same as in the proposition laid down in Norton on Deeds (2nd ed., at p. 437) in these words: 'If the limitation be to two, and one cannot take, the other shall take the whole.' On either view of the matter, there was an appointment of new trustees, already referred to, on the 22nd July, 1946, which is not alleged to have been invalid or ineffective. Finally, it is doubtful whether this point is one that can be allowed to be taken by anyone who was a party to the deeds of the 10th December, 1941.

For these reasons, I am of opinion that the deeds in question are not invalid in the way alleged. Accordingly, attention may now be directed to the third deed of enlargement, that of the 28th October, 1946.

This deed dealt only with the property apparently overlooked in the earlier deeds, namely, nos. 2 and 3 Greek Street, Dublin; and, accordingly, it was supplemental to the first deed of the 10th December, 1941. The parties to it were the ward by his committee and the committee of the first part, Isabel Mary Poë of the second part, the Governor and Company of the Bank of Ireland and the Bank of Ireland Nominees Limited and the committee of the third part and Charles Spottiswoode Weir and Forbes Spottiswoode Weir of the fourth part. It appears from the recitals that the parties of the third part had become the trustees of the settlement of the 24th August, 1854 (the Santry settlement), and the parties of the fourth part had become the trustees of Lady Poë's will. It also similarly appears that the Corporation of Dublin had acquired the premises and called for a conveyance thereof, and that, accordingly, it was necessary that the deed should be executed and enrolled for the purpose of enlarging the base fee in the premises into a fee simple absolute. The indenture then witnessed that, in pursuance of the order of the 30th July, 1940, and for effectuating such enlargement the ward acting by the committee and the committee as such with the approbation of Isabel Mary Poë and of the trustees of the settlement granted and confirmed unto the trustees of the will the premises. These were to be held unto the trustees of the will and their heirs discharged from all estates, rights, interests and powers to take effect after the determination of the base fee created by the indenture of the 12th January, 1886, to the intent that such base fee might be enlarged into a fee simple absolute, to the use of the trustees of the will and their heirs upon trust to convey and dispose of the same to the Corporation at the price at which the same had been acquired and on and subject to such terms and conditions as had been or might be approved by the President of the High Court including the conditions as to payment and resettlement of the purchase money contained in the said order of the 30th July, 1940. This deed was duly enrolled.

There is no ambiguity in this deed, any more than in the principal indenture of the 10th December, 1941 (as to Santry Court and Demesne and the other property therein), as to the intention of enlargement; nor apart from the point already dealt with as to the earlier indenture, was any good reason suggested for doubting their validity and effectiveness as enlarging assurances. The second deed of the 10th December, 1941, was also expressly intended to effect an enlargement but, as already seen, it adopted a somewhat different form. The reason for the differences, in particular the creation of the term of 10,000 years, probably lies in the purpose of the document, namely, to enable leases to be made from time to time. This probably also explains why this deed included a resettlement, subject to that term of years, of the property and of the proceeds of such leases. This was obviously a more convenient course than having a resettlement, complying with the orders made in lunacy, executed on the occasion of each separate lease. It will be noted that the limitations of the resettlement are such as to carry out what I have suggested was the intention of those orders, that is, not to prejudice, any more than was necessary for the immediate transactions, the rights of persons entitled after the determination or in defeasance of the base fee.

This deed, although made to enable leasing and for that purpose creating the long term of years, was, in the first instance, a grant to the will trustees and their heirs, that is, a grant in fee simple, and it was made by the person who would have been the actual tenant in tail but for the creation of the base fee. It appears to me, therefore, that it also operated as an enlargement by virtue of s.16 of the Act of 1834. If authority were needed for this conclusion, apart from the case of *Bankes* v. *Small* (36 Ch.D. 716), already cited, it can be found in the decision of Sullivan M.R., in somewhat analogous circumstances, in *Nelson* v. *Agnew* (I.R. 6 Eq. 232), referred to above. He there held that a disentailing deed need not pursue any particular form of conveyance; any deed which by its legal operation would have conveyed the fee simple, if the grantor had been seised in fee, will, if executed by a tenant in tail in possession, and if duly enrolled, bar the entail.

I am of opinion, accordingly, that these three deeds were effective to, and did, enlarge the base fee into a fee simple absolute in respect of the portions of the Santry estate dealt with in them respectively. This, however, as may have been already gathered, does not mean that it is my view that the parties entitled in

remainder after the base fee have necessarily lost thereby any advantage they
previously had or that the beneficiaries under the will of Lady Poë have gained in
estate thereby. The resettlements effected, in part by the second enlarging deed of
the 10th December, 1941, and in part by the deed of resettlement of the 20th
January, 1947 (still to be considered), cannot be disregarded, if those resettlements
were validly made. The beneficiaries and the trustees of the will of Lady Poë were
parties to those resettlements, as were also the trustees of the Santry settlement. It
was, of course, of interest and concern to the latter that the trusts of the settlement
should be preserved so far as possible. On the other hand, the beneficiaries and
trustees of the will had no equity, right, or duty to require more than that their
interests should not be prejudiced or diminished. The sales and leases must be
presumed to have been for the benefit of the estate of Lady Poë or, at least, since
the trustees were a party to the orders authorising them, of no disadvantage to that
estate. That estate had no claim to any greater benefit merely because these sales
and leases could not be effected without a preliminary enlargement. As regards the
ward, Sir Hugo, the orders would not have been made unless they were considered
to be for his benefit. His power of enlargement, which he could exercise if he were
discharged from wardship, should not of course be prejudiced by any resettlement;
and this power, to override the resettlements thus, was preserved. As will have
been noted, this power is preserved by the form and terms of the second deed (as to
leasing) of the 10th December, 1941; while it will be seen that it is also preserved by
the deed of resettlement of the 20th January, 1947, which now requires to be
considered. It should first, however, be pointed out that, once an enlargementtt was
effected – as I have held it was – by the three deeds which have been considered,
the ward, acting through his committee and under the supervisory jurisdiction of
the Court, and the will trustees, became, between them, competent to dispose of
the whole interest in fee simple in the property involved and, therefore, competent
to resettle it. They became, in effect, the settlors in the (leasing) deed of the 10th
December, 1941, so far as it was a resettlement, and also in the deed of
resettlement of the 20th January, 1947. The beneficiaries under the will of Lady
Poë, so far as their interests might not be represented by the will trustees, were also
parties to these documents. In addition, if it were necessary, Miss Poë, as will
appear later, was competent to represent any possible interest on the basis of a
resulting trust, in favour of Lady Poë's estate, arising on the terms or effect of the
appointment of the property contained in her will.

The uses of this second deed of the 10th December, 1941, have already been set
out; and the proviso in it, as to the application of income during the life of the ward
and of any male heir of the ward, has been referred to. The effect of these
provisions is clearly to restore or recreate the base fee subsisting before the
execution of the deed of enlargement.

The deed of resettlement of the 20th January, 1947, dealt with the net proceeds
of the sale of Santry Court and Demesne and of the premises in Chancery Street
and Greek Street, that is all the property dealt with in the first deed of enlargement
of 10th December, 1941, and in the deed of enlargement of 28th October, 1946.
Amongst other matters, it was recited that the settlement trustees held investments
representing £18,345 15s. 2d., portion of such net proceeds, and £890 2s. 0d., cash,
representing the balance of the net proceeds. It was also recited that the parties to
the deed, the ward acting by his committee, had agreed to execute it in obedience
to the order of the 30th July, 19440, and that the Registrar of Wards of Court had
approved of it.

The parties to the deed were the trustees of the will of Lady Poë, the ward by his
committee and the committee, Isabel Mary Poë, and the trustees of the Santry

settlement; and it was witnessed that the parties agreed and declared as set out in the deed. After provisions giving the trustees power to alter investments and directing the investment of the sum held in cash, the deed continued as follows: –

'3. The settlement trustees shall during the life of the ward and so long as any male heir of the body of the ward shall be living pay the income arising from the said investments to the said Charles Spottiswoode Weir and Forbes Spottiswoode Weir or other the trustees or trustee for the time being of the first will of Dame Mary Adelaide Poë to be applied as by the said first will directed.'

This provision clearly limits the period during which the trustees of the will and the estate of Lady Poë are entitled to the income to that which would have been the period of enjoyment if there had been no enlargement, namely, the continuance of the base fee. It, and the following provision dealing with the period after the determination of the base fee, together carry out the intention of the order of the 30th July, 1940. This following provision reads thus:

'4. From and after the death and failure of male issue of the ward the settlement trustees shall stand possessed of and entitled to the investments to be held by them as aforesaid upon trust to convert the same into money and to lay out the proceeds of conversion in the purchase of freeholds of inheritance situate or arising in Eire, England or Wales and shall cause the hereditaments so purchased to be assured to such uses upon such trusts and subject to such powers and provisions as would have been subsisting in relation to the hereditaments the subject of the said sales had the same not been sold or in relation to the proceeds thereof had the same been sold under the settlement and no such disentailing deed and deed of enlargement had been executed.'

As these provisions in effect restored or recreated the base fee, it was clearly necessary to preserve the ward's power of enlargement in respect thereof, since the Court did not purport to make a final decision in the matter on his behalf either way. Accordingly, the last-quoted provision was followed by this proviso:

'Provided always that nothing herein contained shall affect or prejudice the right of the ward if discharged from wardship or any male heir of the body of the ward by a further deed of enlargement duly enrolled to bar all estates rights interests and powers by the settlement limited to take effect after the determination or in defeasance of the estate in tail male thereby limited to Dame Mary Adelaide Poë.'

The deed concluded with a release by Miss Poë of her power of appointment, given to her by the will of Lady Poë, as to the investments and the income arising therefrom after the death and failure of male issue of the ward. This, of course, does not prevent her dealing with her interest therein so long as, and for as long as, the period of the base fee continues.

I think sufficient has been said to indicate my view that this deed not only carries out the intention of the Court but is also a valid and effective resettlement; and it is unnecessary to pursue this topic further.

The last set of questions are concerned with the effect of the provisions in Lady Poë's will by which she purported to exercise the powers of appointment reserved in the disentailing deeds of 1886. It has already been noted that she included any property over which she had a general power of appointment in the devise and bequest to the trustees of her will upon trust for conversion. The will then provided that, out of the moneys so arising, and out of her ready money, the trustees were to pay her funeral and testamentary expenses and debts and the legacies given by her will or any codicil and all death duties which under or by virtue of any direction or bequest free of duty (*sic*) was payable out of her general personal estate and to make provision for the payment of any annuities bequeathed by her. Then, after directions as to the investment of the residue of such monies (thereinafter called 'the Trust Fund'), the trustees were directed to pay the income of the Trust Fund to her husband during his life. The will then proceeded: 'After the death of my said husband my trustees shall stand possessed of the capital and future income of the Trust Fund in trust for my said son and my said daughter in equal shares but subject as next hereinafter provided.' The provisions which follow deal with the respective shares of the son and the daughter but need not be set out for the moment, beyond saying that they do not exhaust all the possible contingencies and leave in each case at least one contingency in which each share is not expressly disposed of. There arises, therefore, the question whether there is an absolute gift to the son or daughter, as the case may be, in such contingency, or a resulting trust.

The preliminary question thus arises whether, if there were a resulting trust, it would be to the uses limited by the disentailing deeds in default of appointment or so far as an appointment should not extend. I think it is quite clear, and the contrary was not really contended for, that the provisions of Lady Poë's will were intended to, and did, withdraw the property from the instruments reserving the powers of appointment, whether or not the powers were fully exercised as regards her own estate. It is sufficient to quote the following passage from Farwell on Powers (3rd ed., at p. 274): 'It follows that an appointment by will to the appointor's executors and administrators, followed by directions which either fail or do not exhaust the fund, makes the appointed fund part of the appointor's assets. If, therefore, the appointment be to executors as executors and if the appointed fund be treated as blended with the appointor's own property, that will afford ground for presuming that the testator intended to make the fund his own for all purposes.' The case of *Brickenden* v. *Williams* (7 Eq. 310) is then cited as an instance of a case in which a testatrix had treated everything over which she had any power of testamentary appointment (and which would have included any savings of her separate estate) as one mass, giving it as one mass to her executors as executors, and constituting it one property, to be dealt with as her will directed. The position seems to me to be exactly the same in the case of Lady Poë's will.

The question then arises whether she fully exercised the powers, or should be held to have intended to do so, as regards her own beneficiaries. This turns on a consideration of the whole of the relevant provisions in the will. The next provision, after those already just quoted, reads: 'Provided nevertheless and I hereby declare that the shares of the trust fund hereinbefore given to my said son and daughter and hereinafter respectively called "the son's share" and "the daughter's share" shall not vest absolutely in them respectively but shall be retained by my trustees and held by them upon the following trusts respectively.' The trusts which follow deal separately with the son's share and the daughter's share. It is not necessary, for present purposes, to do more than summarise them.

As to the son's share, the trustees were given a discretion as to paying or applying the income for the personal support or benefit of the son, with power to withhold all or any part and to accumulate, with a like discretion as to the accumulations. They were also given power in any year to make up the income of that year, to the figure of £7,000, out of the capital of the son's share. It was then provided that, if her son should survive her for more than 21 years, any accumulations should then be applied in the same manner as if the son had died a bachelor. If the son were married at her death or should marry thereafter the trustees were directed to make a settlement of the share. If the son should die in her lifetime leaving issue living at her death the trustees were to hold the share for all such issue as being male attained 21 years or being female attained that age or married under that age. If the son should die in her lifetime leaving no issue living at her death his share was to go and accrue by way of addition to the daughter's share.

It will be seen, from this summary, that the share was not fully dealt with. In particular, no provision was made for the event of Sir Hugo surviving her but dying without ever having been married. The effect of what I have already decided as to the continued existence of a base fee or of limitations of an equivalent nature is, of course, that any gift over or resulting trust could not take effect, in respect of the property in question, in the event of Sir Hugo dying without issue or without male issue, as the case might be. There is, however, other property as to which the matter is of importance.

In the case of the daughter's share, the provisions were similar but not identical. It was first directed that the trustees should pay the income of her share to the daughter during her life or spinsterhood. If the daughter should die a spinster, the trustees were to stand possessed of the capital and future income for such person or persons and in such manner as the daughter might by will or codicil appoint. If she were married at the death of Lady Poë or should marry thereafter, the trustees were to make a settlement of the share. If the daughter should die in the lifetime of Lady Poë leaving issue living at the death of Lady Poë the trustees were to hold the daughter's share in trust for all such issue as being male should attain 21 years or being female should attain that age or marry under that age. If the daughter should die in her lifetime leaving no issue living at her death, the daughter's share was to go and accrue as an addition to the son's share.

As in the case of the son's share, it will be seen that this share was not fully dealt with. In particular, no provision was made for the event of Miss Poë dying unmarried and without having exercised her power of appointment. Again, so far as the property is held on a base fee or equivalent limitations, the interest of Miss Poë can only continue so long as there is issue or male issue, as the case may be, of Sir Hugo.

If the matter were one of first impression, it might seem more in accord with the intentions of the testatrix that effect should be given to these detailed provisions only to far as they extend, and that the donees were not intended to benefit except to the extent and in the manner provided. If that were so, there would be a resulting trust, in favour of the estate of Lady Poë, in the event of any of the contingencies unprovided for occurring. It was contended, however, and not seriously challenged, that the will in question is one to which what is called 'the rule in *Lassence* v. *Tierney*' (1 Mac. and G. 551) applies. That case, which was a decision of Lord Cottenham, laid down several propositions as to the construction of wills containing provisions on similar lines to those under consideration here; but the portion that is usually quoted as 'the rule' is that given first in the headnote. It is to the effect that, if a testator leaves a legacy absolutely as regards his estate, but restricts the mode of the legatee's enjoyment of it, to secure certain objects for the benefit of the legatee, upon failure of such objects, the absolute gift prevails. The converse of this is stated in the proposition that, if there be no such absolute gift as between the legatee and the estate, and particular modes of enjoyment are prescribed, which fail, the legacy forms part of the testator's estate. Lord Cottenham added the necessary qualification that, in the case of a will containing such a disposition, the intention of the testator is to be collected from the whole will, and not from words which, standing alone, would constitute an absolute gift. It may also be noted that, in the particular case, the Lord Chancellor held that there was not an absolute gift.

The fundamental question, therefore, is whether, on the construction of the whole of the relevant provisions, an absolute gift was intended. It may be that, in considering this question, some of the reported decisions could be suggested to have paid insufficient attention to the qualification that the inclusion of words which, standing alone, would constitute an absolute gift, is not sufficient to attract the rule; but the cases have gone a considerable distance towards a rather liberal interpretation in this respect. Thus, it has been held that a provision, such as occurs in the present case, that the gift is not to vest absolutely in the donee, does not necessarily exclude the application of the rule: *Re Gatti* ([1936] 2 All E.R. 1489); *In re Marshall* ([1928] 1 Ch. 661). In the latter case, Eve J. distinguished the decision of Astbury J. in *In re Payne* ([1927] 2 Ch. 1), where there was a similar expression, on the ground of the language of the wills being a little different. In the case before him there was a gift over, which proved to be invalid, while in the case before Astbury J. there was no gift over. Again, it has been held that it is immaterial to the application of the rule whether the restrictions on the mode of enjoyment are for the benefit of the donee or not: *Fyfe* v. *Irwin* ([1939] 2 All E.R. 271, at p. 281 (H.L.)). Other cases referred to, and holding that there was an absolute gift, were *Kellett* v. *Kellett* (L.R. 3 H.L. 160) and *Handcock* v. *Watson* ([1902] A.C. 14). Apart from *Lassence* v. *Tierney* (1 Mac. and G. 551) itself and *In re Payne* ([1927] 1 Ch. 661), already cited, the contrary view was taken, again by Lord Cottenham, in *Gompertz* v. *Gompertz* (2 Phil. 107).

I confess to some doubt in the present case. The direction to the trustees to stand possessed of the capital and future income of the trust fund for the son and daughter in equal shares would, of course, if it stopped there and stood alone, be an absolute gift; but this direction is immediately qualified by the addition of the words, 'but subject as next hereinafter provided.' This qualification renders the direction at least ambiguous as to the nature of the gift. It is, however, of some significance that the subsequent provisions, while quite elaborate as has been seen, did not exhaust all the foreseeable contingencies but left some unprovided for by way of gift over or otherwise. This is a circumstance that was adverted to by Lord Cottenham in *Lassence* v. *Tierney* (1 Mac. and G. 551) in the view expressed by him that a disposition of the subject-matter of the gift, in every possible event that could arise, would be totally inconsistent with an intention to make an absolute gift (p. 567). The absence of such complete provision might, then, be some indication that all that was intended was to limit the enjoyment of a gift, otherwise absolute, in certain ways in the specified events, and that, in other events, the absolute gift would take effect. Again, in the case of Sir Hugo, although he was not made a ward of Court until three years after the date of Lady Poe's will, she may have felt there was some special need to restrict the mode of enjoyment in his case. For these reasons, and in view of the trend of the authorities and the absence of serious challenge, I think I should decide that the present is a case in which the will severed the property from the estate of Lady Poë so as to exclude an intestacy and that, in any of the events unprovided for, the property involved goes to the particular donee or his or her estate.

It should be added that the interests concerned with the decision of this question appear to be sufficiently represented in the present proceedings. Sir William Hutcheson Poë survived Lady Poë by a few years but his estate has been fully administered and Miss Poë, who is represented here, is his universal devisee and legatee; while Sir Hugo, the only son of Sir William and Lady Poë, is also, of course, represented.

This view of the effect of Lady Poë's will may prove to be somewhat academic so far as the Mayo and Santry estates are concerned. This follows from my decision that a base fee still subsists so far as the Mayo estate is concerned and that portions of the Santry estate have been resettled to uses equivalent to preserving the base fee in respect of them. The remainder of the Santry estate – the capital monies representing prior sales of portions of the estate – are also, of course, held on a base fee. Accordingly, if Sir Hugo dies without having been married, and without any enlargement of these base fees having been made by him or on his behalf, the uses operating after the determination of the base fees must take effect; and his estate will take no interest, under Lady Poë's will, in either the Mayo or the Santry estate. Similarly, in the case of Miss Poë, the interest of her estate would be dependent on whether the base fees were still subsisting at the date of her death; and that interest would, in any case only be co-extensive with and not greater than a base fee in a moiety of the Mayo and Santry estates.

The questions raised in this matter can be answered in the light of and in accordance with the foregoing observations.

Notes
1. As to disentailing deeds, see also *Re Blake's Settled Estates*, p. 406, *post*.
2. As to base fees, see *Irish Land Law*, para. 4.136 *et seq*.
3. As to operation of the doctrine of adverse possession, see ch. 14, *post*.
4. As to the rule in *Lassence* v. *Tierney*, see *Irish Land Law*, para. 14.40.

IV. LIFE ESTATE

DOHERTY V. ALLMAN
(1878) 3 App. Cas. 709 (House of Lords)

Two leases were granted of pieces of land with some buildings on them, one granted in 1798 for 999 years, the other granted in 1824 for 988 years. There was no reservation of a power of re-entry for breach of covenant, nor was there any negative covenant obliging the lessee not to change the use of the premises. There was a power of re-entry, for rent in arrear and no sufficient distress on the premises. In each lease there was a covenant by the lessee that he, his executors, etc., will 'during the term hereby granted preserve, uphold, support, maintain, and keep the said demised premises, and all improvements made and to be made thereon, in good and sufficient order, repair, and condition; and at the end or sooner determination of this demise, shall and will so leave and deliver up the same unto,' the lessor, his heirs, etc. The premises had been used as corn stores for some years; and afterwards as artillery barracks, and dwellings for married soldiers. They had fallen into disrepair: it became necessary to repair them; the lessee thought it would be beneficial to convert the store buildings into dwelling-houses, which would much increase their value, and was proceeding to convert them accordingly, when the lessor filed a bill to restrain him, alleging waste. Chatterton V.-C. held that it was waste and granted a perpetual injunction to restrain it. On appeal, the Court of Appeal in Ireland directed that the injunction be dissolved, but without prejudice to the right of the plaintiff to proceed at law, see I.R. 10 Eq. 362. An appeal was then made to the House of Lords.

Lord Cairns L.C.:

The question in this case arises upon two leases which are now vested in the Respondent. One of them is dated in the year 1798, and is for the long term of 999 years; the other was granted in 1824, and is for the term of 988 years; the first being at the rent of £10, and the second at a rent of £32 19s. The reversion to both these leases is vested in the present Appellant.

The property demised is thus described: [His Lordship read the description of the premises contained in each lease, and also the words of the covenant in each.]

There is not in either of these leases any power of entry for breach of covenant, but there is a power that if rent was not duly paid and no sufficient distress found on the premises to satisfy the arrears, it should be lawful to the lessor to re-enter and re-possess himself of his former estate.

That is the substance of the two leases. The property demised, so far as it consisted of buildings, was in the form of stores – and, as we understand, stores for storing corn. It is stated in evidence, and does not appear to be a matter of controversy between the parties, that since the date of these leases a considerable change has occurred with reference to the demand for buildings of this description in the neighbourhood of *Bandon*; and it is stated, and does not appear to be seriously controverted, that in the town of *Bandon*, which seems to lie at a lower level than where these stores are built, there is now a considerable – perhaps an exuberant – supply of store buildings, access to which, or facility of carriage, is greater than to this higher ground, and that, therefore, there is serious difficulty in obtaining a tenant for this property used as stores. Under these circumstances the Respondent has had specifications prepared, which appear to be prepared in a careful proper, and business-like way, and he has had a contract made in accordance with those specifications, by which the external walls of this building are to be retained, and those external walls, where one part of the building is of a lower height than the rest, are to be raised, so that the building may be of a uniform height; internal changes are to be made, internal party walls are to be introduced, the flooring is to be altered in its level, and six dwelling-houses are to be made out of this which now is one long store. Your Lordships have before you a photograph of the building as it now appears, and an elevation of the building as it is proposed to be, has also been put in evidence; and certainly it does appear a strange thing to any spectator that it should ever come to be a matter of grave dispute between two rational men as to whether that which was proposed to be done is not almost as great an improvement as could be effected. However, so it is, and with that state of things your Lordships have to deal.

The Appellant objects to this being done. The owner of the reversion subject to this long term of years objects to that which the holder of the lease proposes to do. He objects upon two grounds. He says, first, that what is proposed to be done is waste; and, secondly, that it is a breach of contract. I will invert the two grounds, because undoubtedly, if there is a breach of the contract, that is a higher and a stronger ground upon which to appeal to a Court of Equity. If there should be no ground for interposing by reason of a breach of contract, there may still, however, be ground for interposing on the ground of waste, which I will consider afterwards.

My Lords, we will, therefore, first consider the question as to the breach of contract. Your Lordships will observe that the contract is an affirmative one. There are no negative terms in it. There are no terms obliging the lessee negatively, by way of contract, not to use these premises for any purpose but stores, and not to make any alteration which would render them suitable for any purpose but that of storing corn or for goods of the same kind. Your Lordships will also see that the covenant in the first of the two leases is to 'preserve, uphold, support, and maintain,' not merely the demised premises, but 'all improvements made and to be made thereon,' and to yield them up; while the covenant in the second lease is to 'preserve, uphold, support, and maintain,' not only the demised premises, but 'all houses, offices, and improvements made and to be made thereon, in good and sufficient order, repair, and condition,' and to yield them up. The mention of stores occurs in the parcels in the demising part of the lease. In the one case the building is called 'stores,' and in the other 'store-house,' and undoubtedly they were stores and store-houses at the time, and probably they could not be called anything but that which they are called in the lease.

I should not wish to decide or to express an opinion absolutely upon the construction of this covenant. I am going to give to the Appellant the benefit of any doubt there may be in my mind upon the subject, but I am bound to say there is in my mind very considerable doubt as to the construction of the covenant. I should be sorry to lay down any general rule as to what the word 'improvements' meant in a covenant of this kind, but I must take leave to observe that, dealing with property of this description – demised on the tenure which we have here of 999 years or 988 years, bearing in mind that the stores were at the time of the demise to the Respondent, coarse, open, and unfinished buildings, I should be sorry to say that if it came afterwards to be the case that in a place where the stores were absolutely useless buildings, buildings for which a tenant could not be obtained, whereas on the other hand if these stores were, but internal arrangements and fittings converted into dwelling-houses, the property could be made productive and useful – I should be sorry to say that, in a lease for such a term as this the construction to be given to a covenant of this kind might not be held to be such as that the conversion of the store-house under the circumstances into dwelling-houses would be, or might be an 'improvement' within the meaning of that term. The consequences of a different view are to my mind extremely formidable. Without minutely examining the evidence in this particular case, I may say that there might be a case in which a building of this description, in the lapse of a portion of a very long lease of this sort, would become absolutely useless as a store; and I should be sorry to say that it had been so perpetually impressed with the character of a store, that, under a covenant of this kind, it could not be improved so as to be useful for some other purpose. But, my Lords, I repeat I will give the Appellant the benefit of any doubt there may be upon that point; and I will assume in his favour that the construction is that which he contends for, and that this covenant ought to be read literally as a covenant to maintain the stores as stores, and to deliver them up at the end of the term as stores.

Now, my Lords, let us look at it in that point of view. I said that there is here no negative covenant – not to turn these buildings to any other use. My Lords, if there had been a negative covenant, I apprehend, according to well-settled practice, a Court of Equity would have had no discretion to exercise. If parties, for valuable consideration, with their eyes open, contract that a particular thing shall not be done, all that a Court of Equity has to do is to say, by way of injunction, that which the parties have already said by way of covenant, that the thing shall not be done; and in such case the injunction does nothing more than give the sanction of the process of the Court to that which already is the contract between the parties. It is not then a question of the balance of convenience or inconvenience, or of the amount of damage or of injury – it is the specific performance, by the Court, of that negative bargain which the parties have made, with their eyes open, between themselves. But, my Lords, if there be not a negative covenant but only an affirmative covenant, it appears to me that the case admits of a very different construction. I entirely admit that an affirmative covenant may be of such a character that a Court of Equity, although it cannot enforce affirmatively the performance of the covenant, may, in special cases, interpose to prevent that being done which would be a departure from, and a violation of, the covenant. That is a well-settled and well-known jurisdiction of the Court of Equity. But in that case, my Lords, there appear to me to come in considerations which do not occur in the case of a negative covenant. It may be that a Court of Equity will see that, by interposing in a case of that kind, in place of leaving the parties to their remedy in damages, it would be doing more harm than it could possibly do good, and there are, as we well know, different matters which the Court of Equity will, under those circumstances, take into its view, It will consider for example whether the injury which it is asked to restrain is an injury which if done cannot be remedied. It will consider whether, if done, it can or cannot be sufficiently atoned for by the payment of a sum of money in damages. It will ask also this question, – Suppose the act to be done, would the right to damages for it be decided exhaustively, once and for all, by one action, or would there necessarily be a repetition of actions for the purpose of recovering damages from time to time? Those are matters which a Court of Equity would well look to, and on the other hand a Court of Equity would look to this: If we interfere and say, in aid of this affirmative covenant, that something shall not be done which would be a departure from it, no doubt we shall succour and help the Plaintiff who comes for our assistance. But shall we do that? Will the effect of our doing that be to cause possible damage to the Defendant, very much greater than any possible advantage we can give to the Plaintiff? Now, in a case of that kind, where there is an amount of discretion which the Court must exercise, those are all considerations which the Court will carefully entertain before it decides how it will exercise its discretion.

My Lords, let us then apply those considerations to the present case. Suppose the change which is contemplated by the Respondent here is made in the internal arrangements of this which is now a store, will the injury be irremediable? Clearly not. Beyond all doubt as regards the immediate effect it would be beneficial and not injurious to the reversioner; he will have a much better security for his rent, and the property undoubtedly will be increased in value, and if, when the lease comes to an end, he should have that predilection which he appears now to have for a building of the character which we see represented in this photograph, it would be merely a question of money, and that not a very large sum of money, in order that the building might be brought back to the state in which it now is. Therefore there would be no injury which would be irremediable. Then will damages be a sufficient compensation? The same answer applies there – an expenditure of a sum of money, of a very moderate amount, as we see from the estimate of even that which is proposed to be done by the Respondents, will bring back the building to the state in which the Appellant wishes it to be. Then, again, will there be a necessity for repeated actions for damages? Certainly not; it will be one payment, and one only, and by that means the lessor will get the whole of his right.

But then, my Lords, let us look at the other side – what would be the effect upon the Respondents of the interposition of the Court? Here is a lease for 999 years, of which 900 years and more are unexpired, and there is a rental on that lease, and on the second lease, amounting together to £42 19s. a year. If the evidence is to be believed it is either the case now, or it may become the case, that the premises are absolutely untenantable – that no tenant can be obtained for them, or obtained for them at a rent which will produce the rent which the Respondents have to pay. Repair, then, they must, for they are bound to do so by the covenant, and they have been called upon to do so. They must therefore lay out money in repairing something for which they cannot get, when it is done, an equivalent in the shape of a remunerative rent, and the Court therefore for 900 years will be sentencing them, or those who succeed them, to keep the premises in a shape which will not enable them to get a remunerative rent; while, on the other hand, they would be bound to pay the substantial rent of £42 19s. a year to the landlord. It will bear hardly upon the person who stands in the position of the lessee, but it will give no present benefit whatever to the Appellant, and even supposing he should ever become entitled to the lease, anything he would be entitled to would be represented by the payment of an extremely moderate sum of money.

Now, my Lords, that being the case, I do not think it is denied at the Bar that on a covenant of this kind the Court of Chancery before it interferes to prevent what was said to be a departure from the terms of the covenant must exercise its discretion with regard to the whole of the circumstances of the case – it appears to me that what I have said will probably convince your Lordships that there is every reason against the exercise, by the Court of Chancery, of its power of giving an injunction, and everything in favour of its leaving this matter to be the subject of damages, for any person who thinks it worth while to bring an action for damages. My Lords, I therefore think that the case, so far as it is founded on the covenant, is one which, looking upon it as an application for an injunction, entirely fails.

Then with regard to the question of waste: there is no doubt that the Court of Chancery exercises a jurisdiction in restraining waste, and where waste is committed in requiring an account of the waste for the purpose of recompensing the person who has suffered; but I apprehend it is perfectly clear that the Court of Chancery, acting in that case in advance of the common law right, will, in the first place, consider whether there is, or is not, any substantial damage which would accrue, and which is sought to be prevented, and will make that inquiry. In the present case it appears to me to be extremely doubtful whether any jury could be found, who, after this work shall be executed in the way that is proposed, would say that any damage had been done by the work to the inheritance. And I doubt, farther, whether it must not be taken as clear from the evidence here that any jury, or any tribunal judging upon the question of fact, would not say that, if there be technically what in the eye of the common law is called waste, still it is that amelioratinnng waste which has been spoken of in several of the cases cited at the Bar. That which is done if it be technically waste – and here again I will assume in favour of the Appellant that it is technically according to the common law, waste – yet it seems to me to be that ameliorating waste which so far from doing injury to the inheritance, improves the inheritance. Now, there again the course which the Court of Chancery ought undoubtedly to adopt would be to leave those who think they can obtain damages at common law to try what damages they can so obtain. Certainly, I think here again, the Court of Chancery would be doing very great injury to the one side for the purpose of securing to the other, that slightest possible sum which would at common law be considered the full equivalent to which he was entitled. My Lords, this was the view, in substance, taken by the Lord Chancellor of *Ireland* and the Lord Justice of the Court of Appeal, who in this respect differed from the Vice-Chancellor. I must say that I entirely concur with the decision at which they arrived, and therefore I would advise your Lordships, and move your Lordships, to dismiss this appeal with costs.

Lord O'Hagan:

My Lords, I am of the same opinion. I have given much attention to the case in the course of the argument, which was certainly very ably conducted from beginning to end, and I have no reason to doubt that your Lordships ought to concur with the view of my noble and learned friend on the woolsack. The first consideration in the case is I think this – and it is one which has not been and could not be disputed at the Bar – that the jurisdiction as to injunctions in cases like the present is a jurisdiction to be exercised according to the discretion of the Court of Equity. Lord *St. Leonards*, in the case to which reference has been made, speaks of the true mode of exercising that discretion, manifestly assuming that the discretion exists, and ought to be exercised; and that being so, the question is not whether it should be exercised wildly, indiscreetly, and capriciously, as has been suggested in the course of the argument – at all events against such an exercise a very proper protest has been made – it must be exercised according to settled principles and according to the order and practice of Courts of Equity.

Now we have, I think, established for the purposes of this decision the principles in this case by which we ought to abide. In the case of *Mollineux* v. *Powell* (3 P. Wms. 268, n. (F)), which contains perhaps the clearest dictum we have upon the matter, two conditions as to the exercise of jurisdiction in cases of waste have been very clearly pointed out, and one at least of those conditions is expressly recognised afterwards in the Irish case of *Coppinger* v. *Gubbins* (3 J. & Lat. 411). Those conditions are that the waste with which a Court of Equity, or your Lordships acting as a Court of Equity, ought to interfere, should be not ameliorating waste, nor trivial waste. It must be waste of an injurious character – it must be waste of not only an injurious character, but of a substantially injurious character, and if either the waste be really ameliorating waste – that is a proceeding which results in benefit and not in injury – the Court of Equity, and your Lordships acting as a Court of Equity, ought not to interfere to prevent it. I think that is perfectly well established. On the other hand, if the waste be so small as to be indifferent to the one party or the other – if it be, as has been said by a great authority in our law, such a thing as twelvepence worth of waste, a Court of Equity, and your Lordships acting as a Court of Equity, ought not to interfere on account of the triviality of the matter. Now, in my view of the case, those principles decide the question so far as this portion of it is concerned; for it appears to me that we have here established to the full satisfaction of your Lordships, by a series of authorities to which I shall not refer, that the waste, to be of any sort of effect with a view to an injunction, must be a waste resulting in substantial damage. Your Lordships are the Judges not only of the propriety of exercising your discretion, but of the facts by which the exercise of that discretion ought to be regulated. Now, with reference in the first place to the materiality of the waste, we have in the analogy of proceedings in the Courts of Law a very important guide for the exercise of our equitable jurisdiction. It is established not only in the case of *The Governors of the Harrow School* v. *Alderton* (2 B. & P. 86), before Lord *Eldon*, but in every case, that if there be a trial at law, and if the result of such trial is that the jury is compelled to give nominal damages, such as three farthings in that case, the verdict will be entered, not for the man who obtained the nominal damages, but for the Defendant in the case. It is rather an extraordinary jurisdiction, no doubt – it is an equitable jurisdiction exercised by a Court of Law – but it seems to be quite established and quite recognised, and being so I think it is impossible to say that when we come to exercise our jurisdiction, which is a discretionary jurisdiction, we should act upon any other principle, or to say that if we see that the damage has not really been substantial and important, we should do that in a Court of Equity according to our discretion, which even in the strictness of a Court of Common Law is not done because of the reason given.

I think that the judgment in the Court below in the first instance went very much upon the view that the waste here had the effect of destroying the evidence of title. A great deal was said also at the Bar upon that subject, and a great deal certainly was said by the learned Judge who pronounced the original judgment in this case. Now I cannot myself see that there is anything at all in that. I do not think that in the particular circumstances of this case there is any interference with the evidence of title. You may do what you please with this particular building (according to the plans and views of the parties connected with it), and yet not destroy any evidence of title at all. The building is to be modified – is to be improved – but it is to remain where it was, it is to be of the same proportions, it is to have the same position, it is to have the same surroundings; and I cannot see how what is proposed to be done would injure or affect the Appellant's evidence of title. Independently of that, I think we must take this into account, that owing to the circumstances in which property is now situated in this country, in *Scotland*, and in *Ireland*, evidence of title of this kind is not at all of the same importance as it was in other times and other circumstances. When you have an Ordnance Survey, when you have a Registry of Deeds, when you have a system of conveyancing, the value as evidence of title, of a place of this sort retaining its particular position, is very sensibly diminished. At all events, I see no reason upon that ground to hold that there has been any diminution of the evidence of title of which the lessor of these premises can properly complain.

We have heard much comment, on the one side and the other, with reference to the length of the term in this case. I do not rely upon that as the only circumstance in the case on which the judgment of the Court of Appeal should be sustained; but when, in a case of this sort, we are asked to exercise our discretionary jurisdiction, it surely is material to see that the interest of the individual who is only to come into possession of the premises at the end of 900 years is infinitesimally small compared with the interest of the man who is the tenant, and who, with his successors, is to hold the premises all that time, upon whom the effect of our exercise of this jurisdiction would be to tie up his hands, to destroy their property, and to inflict great damage upon them during the course of these many centuries that are yet to come. I think, that being so, we have only to say this in addition, that it is scarcely a matter of possible controversy here whether or no this change is a beneficial change. We have most conclusive evidence that the change will be beneficial. We have the most clear evidence that, as the matter stands, this old dilapidated store has become useless, I presume, to any human being. Circumstances have changed; the necessity for a store of that kind has ceased, and the result has been that the store, if it be allowed to continue in its present condition – because the parties are compelled to leave it in its present condition – till the end of this term of 999 years, the whole premises will be utterly valueless; whereas, upon the other side, if you substitute for this store the houses which are contemplated you double, you treble the security of the landlord, and give him, or whoever may live at the end of the term of 999 years, certainly not an injured property but an improved one. Therefore, inasmuch as the waste, if waste there be, is ameliorating waste, and the injury to the property produced by the waste is not merely trivial but absolutely non-existent, it appears to me that upon that ground the judgment of the Court below may very fairly be maintained.

Now there was one case, I think it is the only case, referred to by the very able and learned Judge who had this matter first before him, the case before Lord *Romilly* to which reference has been made from time to time, *Smyth* v. *Carter* (18 Beav. 78), which would be very strong authority if we are to take it as expressing, in the words that are used, the full opinion of that learned Lord, and an opinion reached with reference to facts which have analogy to the facts before your Lordships. But in the first place, that was a mere *obiter dictum* of Lord *Romilly*. It was in an interlocutory proceeding. It was without any sort of argument; and the case has, I think, no application to the case before your Lordships, and for this important reason, that in that case the observations may have been applied to the limited interest of a tenant from year to year, whereas we have to deal here with the interest of a tenant for 900 years. The circumstances are wholly different, the conditions are wholly unlike, and, therefore, the authority does not, in my opinion apply at all to the case before us.

But beyond all that, if the latter words of the dictum, that the landlord has a right to exercise his own judgment and caprice as to whether there shall be any change, were to be taken in their literal sense, and as applicable to this case, the effect would be to make the landlord absolute arbiter of the fortune, good or ill, of his tenant with reference to these premises for a period of 900 years. Now, my Lords, I for one should be prepared to exercise the jurisdiction of this House, and say that this is not and cannot be the law. Upon this ground I think that the judgment may now well be sustained.

As to the matter of the covenant, my noble and learned friend on the woolsack has dealt with that so largely and so well that I shall not make any observation upon it, except to say that, though it appears to me that it is not necessary to give an opinion upon the construction of that covenant, yet, looking at it in its plain and simple sense, the word 'improvements' inserted in that covenant appears to me large enough to let in a change of this description, and indeed indicates that there existed in the minds of those who entered into that contract at the time, a very reasonable view that, the term being so enormously long, and the changes of the world and of society being such as they necessarily must be during that period, there ought to be a precaution taken so that in the course of these many centuries there might be made, according to circumstances, changes which in themselves would be improvements, according to the exigencies of society and the position of the individuals concerned. Therefore I think that, if it were necessary to decide that question, it would be very difficult to hold that there was a breach of this covenant in that particular regard, and that the word 'improvements' might not possibly – I only say that – might not possibly be held to reach a case of this description, where it is proposed to substitute for a tumble-down old store a substantial house or set of houses, from which the tenant would derive a very fair income, and from which the landlord would derive a very much enlarged security. Therefore with reference to the covenant, there being no negative words in it, it appears to me impossible, having regard to the authorities, to say that if the case of the Appellant fails with reference to the waste, it ought to succeed on the matter of the covenant.

On the whole, I fully concur with my noble and learned friend, that, if there be damage in the case, a Court of Law can deal with that question, and I am quite clear that, our jurisdiction being discretionary, our discretion ought to be exercised in refusing the injunction.

Lord Blackburn:
My Lords, I am of the same opinion. The jurisdiction of the Court of Equity to enforce the specific performance, or to grant an injunction to prevent the breach of a covenant, is no doubt a discretionary jurisdiction, but I perfectly agree with the view expressed by your Lordships that the discretion is not one to be exercised according to the fancy of whoever is to exercise the jurisdiction of Equity, but is a discretion to be exercised according to the rules which have been established by a long series of decisions, and which are now settled to be the proper guide to Judges in Courts of Equity. Without professing to speak definitely as to the every day practice of such Courts, with which I have not always been familiar, I may observe, though with diffidence, that very early in the consideration of this case I came to the conclusion that, in this particular instance, the Judges of Appeal in *Ireland* were quite right in exercising their discretion and refusing to grant the injunction.

I will take the question of the covenant in the contract first. Wherever a consideration of a covenant, and examination into its words and meaning, reveal that the plain intention of the parties was that the lessee might have possession of the land, whatever it may be, on the express bargain that a particular structure was to be kept up, or a particular thing was not to be done, and that the lessor stipulated for that, and the lessee came in and took possession of the premises on the terms that he was to keep that bargain, there, as a general rule, the Court of Equity would not do its duty if it did not enforce the contract, because mere damages would not then afford a sufficient or adequate remedy. A very good instance of it was in the case (*Kemp* v. *Sober*, 1 Sim. (N.S) 517; 20 L.J. (Eq.) 602) where it appeared clearly that the landlord of a house for some reason, no matter what, thought it desirable for him that the house should not be used as a ladies school, and accordingly he in express terms in the contract under which he let the house, bargained that it should not be used as a ladies school, and a tenant, or an assignee of the tenant, came in, and occupied the premises under the contract, and yet proceeded to use them as a ladies school. In such a case I say it would have been monstrous if a Court of Equity had for a moment hesitated, and had said that the using of the premises as a ladies school would do the landlord no harm. The answer would be plain, whether the damages were great or little, the very bargain, on which the premises were taken, was that the tenant or his assignees should not use them as a ladies school, and therefore he should of course be prevented from doing so.

I think, however, it would be but seldom that you could have it appear distinctly upon a lease that it was intended that a thing should not be done unless there were negative words used. But I am not inclined for my own part to base my opinion upon the mere technical difference between negative words and affirmative words in a covenant. Whether they are negative words or affirmative words are very excellent reasons in considering whether it is meant that the thing should be done, or whether it is not meant, but I do not think it is advisable upon that ground to say that while negative words would shew *primâ facie* you are not to do the thing, affirmative words may mean, but do not necessarily mean that, unless the whole context shews that such is the intention of the parties. Even where there have been negative words, circumstances may change, so that though the covenant still remains it would not be reasonable that it should be enforced. I think the case of *The Duke of Bedford* v. *The Trustees of the British Museum* (2 My. & K. 552) illustrates very well what I mean. There a covenant not to raise a garden wall above a certain height was made between the Duke of *Bedford* and Lord *Montagu* when they were occupying two large houses with gardens adjoining each other, and the covenant remained after *Montagu House* had been turned into the *British Museum*, and after the Duke of *Bedford's* garden had been turned into *Bedford Square*, and it was then sought to enforce it in Equity against the *British Museum*; the Duke of *Bedford* acting no doubt for the benefit of the tenants of his houses in the square. What Lord *Eldon* said was, If he has a right to enforce the contract he may enforce it, but circumstances have been so changed by time that it is unjust and unreasonable to enforce in Equity this contract against the *British Museum* in favour of *Bedford Square*, though he would enforce it without much hesitation in favour of the Duke of *Bedford* against Lord *Montagu*, if they had been both occupying their gardens at the time. That strikes me at once as the common sense view of the matter. As long as it fair and right and proper that the Court should enforce the bargain which is made, the Court does enforce it, even although it might think the bargain a foolish one; it is a bargain, and being one must be enforced.

I am inclined to think that construing the covenant in the present lease as one would construe a covenant at law, it means that the lessee should keep up the store-house or stores such as they were, that they were to be kept repaired and maintained. And although there are other words to say that they are also to maintain any improvements there, and, in the second lease, that they are also to keep up and repair any houses that may be built (showing clearly enough that the parties contemplated that improvements of the buildings might be made), still I am inclined to think that the meaning of the covenant was that the stores should be kept and maintained and repaired; and to pull them down and make a serious alteration of them, however it might appear to improve the property, would be a breach of that contract. I do not think it is necessary to decide that, but I think, putting it in the most favourable way that it can be put for the Appellant, the contract may be said to bear that meaning, and I will assume it bears that meaning;

but I am equally clear that no one after reading that contract, and having no regard to the technical point as to there being affirmative or negative words, could say there is anything in that contract that amounted to a stipulation such as the one which I have mentioned of not using the house as a ladies school. There is nothing in the covenant which would be of the essence of the contract, or a stipulation of that sort which would lead a Court of Equity in its discretion to say that the parties have bargained that this should be a store, and never should be changed from a store, and that therefore the bargain so made shall be kept in force for the 999 years.

When a bargain of that sort is made, the question as to whether the Court of Equity would or would not interfere to enforce it must depend upon circumstances. A case might very well arise where affirmative words involve a negative. I think myself the true construction of saying I will maintain a storehouse involves the negative – I will not pull it down. But when a Court of Equity has to consider whether it shall interfere, it would take into its view these grounds – I will not repeat them – which the Lord Chancellor has mentioned to be considered. Is it a contract which must be enforced because damages will be inadequate? No. In the case of the school it was so. Is it a case in which irreparable mischief and damage would be done by pulling down the storehouse? I do not say there could not be such a case, and a very important element to consider is whether the term of the lease be long or short. In such a case as that of *Smyth* v. *Carter* (18 Beav. 78), if it could be really established that there was a tenancy from year to year, and that the notice to quit would expire at the end of eighteen months, I am not at present required to say, and I do not decide, that a Court of Equity might not say, that when a man was pulling down the house for the purpose of making improvements, such an act would be irreparable. The Court might say to the tenant: You are going to build a brewhouse which you say would be much better, but you will not finish that brewhouse before your notice to quit expires. You cannot get any good out of it, your alteration is one which can do you no good, and which the landlord says he objects to strongly, and upon such a matter as that I think he would be entitled to exercise his own will, though that might not be an advantage to him.

I am not by any means prepared to say a Court of Equity would not interfere there and grant an injunction, and very properly. But when we come to such a case as this, where there was originally a long term of 999 years of which upwards of 900 still remained to run, and the premises as they are proposed to be altered will evidently be more than ample security for the rent the risk of damage to the Plaintiff is extremely small, and, as was pointed out by the noble and learned Lord on the woolsack – I will not repeat it – the certainty of inconvenience and injury to the tenant is very great; therefore it seems to me upon these grounds, so far as the covenant is concerned, the Judges of Appeal were quite right, in the exercise of their discretionary power, to refuse to grant an injunction to prohibit the alterations on the ground of the covenant. My Lords, I have already said that, whilst I feel no doubt about that, I am very glad that the Lord Chancellor, who has had so much more experience in Equity matters, has taken the opportunity of stating the course of practice in the Courts of Equity in dealing with these matters, which practice agrees exactly with what seems to me to be the common sense of the thing, as derived from the considerations as to what would be the effect of covenants of this sort.

Now, as the question of waste, I think that is even still clearer.

The old writ of waste is gone, and we have nothing to do with it now, but an action in the nature of waste still exists in the Courts of Common Law. It is perfectly clear that in an action of waste you cannot recover nominal damages only, you must get real damages. The jurors must not find for you unless they think there is substantial and real damage. Now, as to what constitutes real damage, it is clear that in a case where jurymen found three farthings they found no damages at all; and in the case of *Doe* d. *Grubb* v. *Lord Burlington* (5 B. & Ad. 517), where it was a question whether it was waste so as to forfeit a copyhold, the probabilities are that the pulling down of a barn there was not waste, because it was a taking down of an old structure which had become practically useless, and the act was not an injury to the inheritance at all. But even supposing there was an injury, and that there was something for which there might be damages recovered, is it obligatory upon a Court of Chancery to grant an injunction to prevent it under all circumstances? I think not. I think it goes on much the same principles as have been mentioned before. I find in that case of *Greene* v. *Cole* (2 Wms. Saund. 252) it is laid down that the Court of Equity would not interfere and grant an injunction to restrain waste where the damages are trivial. Lord *Eldon*, in *The Governors of Harrow School* v. *Alderton* (2 B. & P. 86), mentioned the practice which the Courts of Law have established, that they would not enter judgment for the Defendant where the damages were very small. *Blackstone* says (3 Com. 228) twelve pence, but what the value of that twelve pence was you must go back to the days of King *Richard* to ascertain. I suppose it would be a larger sum than now, but still a small sum. I do not know whether stronger words could be used than those of Lord *Eldon* as to what was or was not trivial. That was his view of the matter. In the case Mr. *Kay* was referring to (*Greene* v. *Cole*, 2 Wms. Saund. 252, sec. 259, n; *Cole* v. *Green*, 1 Lev. 109, see p. 111), the jury found it was improving waste, but it was held to be waste 'notwithstanding the melioration, by reason of the alteration of the nature of the thing, and the evidence thereof,' and the jury gave a verdict accordingly with 100 marks damages, and the Lord Chancellor seems to have entertained the suggestion that he might relieve the Defendant from that verdict. What the Lord Chancellor did was at the Defendant's instance, who had these damages awarded against him. The report is rather unintelligible, but it is evident that the Lord Chancellor, so far from thinking that the Court of Equity would be bound to grant its aid to enforce proceedings for waste where the property was actually improved, though its nature was altered, entertained serious doubt whether he would give relief in such a case. But when you come to the later cases, I think they are all uniform, that if the waste be something that would improve or would only trivially affect the inheritance, the Court will not interfere. Lord Chancellor *Sugden*, in the case in *Ireland* (*Coppinger* v. *Gubbins*, 3 J. & Lat. 397) which has been cited, explains that point, I think, very clearly. In the particular case where the waste was, he did grant the injunction – and that is intelligible enough – where from inadvertence in granting a long lease, a lease renewable for ever, mines or something of that sort which were not known or thought of were not included in the lease, and where the landlord could not enter upon the mines because he did not reserve the power, the only thing to be done under the circumstances was for the lessor and lessee to make an agreement as to how they should divide the profits of the mines. That was obviously the right course to take. Now, in such a case as that, where the tenant chooses to take upon himself to carry away the minerals bodily, it seems but right he should not be allowed to do that, and that there should be an injunction to prevent it. That was exactly the case before Lord Chancellor *Sugden*. It was not, however, a case of a mine of copper ore, but was a turbary from which the lessee was cutting the peats and selling them at the rate of £300 or £400 a year, and deriving a large revenue from their sale, it was quite plain that the lessor was entitled to say, 'You have no right whatever to cut and carry away this turf of mine without my consent, and my consent you must pay for – you must make a bargain,' and that, I take it, was the ground upon which Lord Chancellor *Sugden's* decision rested. I have no occasion to say whether that was right or wrong, but it was intelligible, and very different from the present case. Here the whole story shews that if there be waste, and I think it very doubtful that a jury would say there had been a real substantial damage even to the value of a shilling, the mischief that would accrue to the tenant from forbidding him to make this alteration would be so very great, and the mischief which could possibly, upon any reasonable contemplation of the matter, accrue to the Plaintiff, the lessor, would be so very small and remote, that I think that upon that ground the Court was quite right in saying that their discretionary power to restrain should not be exercised.

I will only say one word about the alteration of evidence of title. I can perfectly understand that five or six hundred years ago that was an extremely serious matter, that where the evidence of title depended entirely upon the memory of witnesses, to change a meadow into a wood or a wood into a meadow would have been a serious matter as far as regards the evidence of title. After a few years it might be very difficult to trace which had been which. But now-a-days, when there are Ordnance surveys, and where, as in *Ireland*, there is a Court especially dealing with the titles to estates, giving titles, and where the property is marked out on a map, which map can be identified with the Ordnance map – and these maps it may well be supposed will continue to exist and may be referred to to the end of the term – any damage in regard to evidence of title is quite wild and chimerical, or is at least merely nominal. I think, if it is put in that way, it would scarcely be gravely said that a Court of Equity should grant an injunction or that the Court should act upon the rules of a former time and grant an injunction, because of a theoretical absurdity such as a supposed injury to title. I think, therefore, upon the whole, that the decision of the Court of Appeal was perfectly right, and should be affirmed with costs.

Lord Gordon entirely concurred.

Notes and Questions
1. Note that this case did not, in fact, involve a life estate, but rather leasehold estates. Does that make any difference as regards the principles of law or equity applicable? See *Irish Land Law*, para. 4.149 *et seq.* and 17.057–8. See also *Craig* v. *Greer*, p. 616, *post*.
2. To what extent does this case portray the differing attitudes of the common law and equity to waste? Will an injunction to restrain ameliorating waste ever be granted? Will substantial as opposed to nominal damages ever be granted in respect of such waste?

GILMORE V. THE O'CONOR DON AND ANOTHER
[1947] I.R. 462; 82 I.L.T.R. 141 (Supreme Court)

A., a tenant for life of settled lands, unimpeachable for waste, entered into three contracts with G. for the sale to him of certain growing timber, to be cut and removed by G. G. paid the full contract price on the first and second contracts to A. and on the third he paid him part on account. A. did not disclose to G. that he was only a tenant for life, and G., in fact, made no inquiries as to A.'s title. A. described himself, in one of the contracts, as 'landed proprietor.' G. pleaded that he had always regarded A. as absolute owner of the lands.

G. did not cut the trees for some time and before he had started to cut them A. died and B. became tenant for life in succession. B. immediately repudiated the contracts made by his predecessor and forbade G. to cut or remove the trees. B., in fact, sold the trees to another firm of timber merchants, who cut and carried away a very large number of the trees already sold to G. G. sued B. to enforce his rights under the three contracts, joining C. as defendant as personal representative of A. At an early stage of the case the action was discontinued against C. on her undertaking to return to G. all money paid by him for which he had not received trees.

Gavan Duffy J. held that the three agreements must be referred to the vendor's powers under the Settled Land Act, 1882, because a vendor's contracts must, in equity, be attributed to that power which will make them effective. A Court of Equity must take the vendor to have engaged with his purchaser to make his contracts as effective as he has power to make them. The plaintiff was therefore entitled to damages against the first-named defendant for breach of contract.

An appeal was made to the Supreme Court.

Maguire C.J.:

I have read the judgment which Mr. Justice Murnaghan is about to read. I agree with it and have nothing to add.

Murnaghan J.:

This appeal has been brought by Rev. Charles Denis O'Conor, O'Conor Don, against an order of the High Court dated 4th February, 1946, made by Mr Justice Gavan Duffy, now President of the High Court. This order was made in an action brought by John Gilmore against the present appellant and against Gertrude Gwendoline O'Conor, who was sued as personal representative of Owen Phelim O'Conor, deceased. This action arose out of an agreement for the sale of growing timber made by Owen Phelim O'Connor, O'Conor Don, in his lifetime, and the substantial question involved is whether the estate of Clonalis which was, at the date of the contract and still is, under settlement, was bound by this contract after the death of Owen Phelim O'Conor.

Owen Phelim O'Conor, O'Conor Don, became, under the will made by Denis Charles O'Conor, O'Conor Don, dated 5th September, 1916, and two codicils dated respectively 30th November, 1916, and 21st December, 1916, tenant for life without impeachment for waste of all the testator's freehold lands and hereditaments. Since he came into possession on 23rd February, 1917, he frequently exercised his common law right of licensing purchasers to cut and carry away growing timber on the estate, and he retained, as he was fully entitled to do, the purchase money paid in respect of such timber. It is well established that the common law right of the tenant for life without impeachment for waste extends only to trees actually severed from the soil during the lifetime of such tenant for life, and any license given by him to cut timber ceases at his death.

In the year 1941 there was a considerable demand for timber, and about the end of January Owen Phelim O'Conor notified the plaintiff that he had a considerable number of trees at Clonalis, in the County of Roscommon, marked for sale. The plaintiff resides at Moylough, County Galway, and is a timber merchant and, at the time, was actively engaged in purchasing growing timber and cutting it for sale. Negotiations followed, during which the purchaser to be made no inquiry as to the title of Owen Phelim O'Conor, whom he says he always regarded as absolute owner; nor did the O'Conor Don disclose his title beyond the description contained in the agreement in writing where he is called 'landed proprietor.' It was necessary to comply with certain provisions of the Forestry Act and after these had been satisfied an agreement in writing, signed in duplicate, one by the purchaser and one by the vendor, was entered into. By this agreement the plaintiff agreed to buy from O'Conor Don a specified number of trees, already marked and agreed to, for the sum of £1,383, payable on signing the agreement. The agreement made provision as to the use of a sawbench and incidental matters and the purchaser bound himself to repair fences, walls, gates and gate piers damaged by his men. He also undertook to leave Clonalis within two years after signing the agreement, viz., two years from 10th April, 1941. A deposit of £200 had been paid to Owen Phelim O'Conor on the

19th February, 1941, and the balance remaining was similarly paid on the 15th April, 1941, and a receipt given by Owen Phelim O'Conor.

In the years following, two other contracts were made by correspondence for the sale of two other lots, one on the 3rd August, 1942, for £440, and the second on the 6th February, 1943, for £718 10s. 0d. The plaintiff, who was busy in other parts of the country, did not cut any of the trees, and by letter dated the 29th December, 1942, Owen Phelim O'Conor wrote to him saying: 'You are dreadfully slow in starting to cut the Clonalis trees.' He urged the pressing necessity of cutting before the war should be over, and in respect to one of the lots at that time under negotiation he said: 'I am not a seller when war is over.' On the 11th February, 1943, Owen Phelim O'Conor wrote to the plaintiff saying that he had written to the authorities for an extension of time for the cutting of the trees in the first purchase. The conditions of the permit, obtained under the Forestry Act, required that these trees should be cut in a specified time and that re-planting should be done by the licensee, Owen Phelim O'Conor. Owen Phelim O'Conor, O'Conor Don, died on the 1st March, 1943.

On the death of Owen Phelim O'Conor the present appellant became tenant for life without impeachment for waste under the settlement already referred to. Immediately after the death of Owen Phelim O'Conor the plaintiff wrote to the appellant that he was desirous of starting to cut the trees which had been agreed to be sold to him by the previous tenant for life. As early as 1940 the appellant had written to the Forestry Department asking them not to sanction the cutting of such a number of trees as the then tenant for life was seeking to have a licence for. The appellant was not willing to allow the plaintiff to cut the trees specified in the contracts made by Owen Phelim O'Conor, and warned the plaintiff to desist from cutting under this contract. No agreement was reached between the plaintiff and the appellant and the appellant subsequently made an agreement with other parties for the cutting of a limited number of the trees claimed by the plaintiff, and these trees have since been cut and removed.

At the hearing of the action the defendant Gertrude Gwendoline O'Conor undertook to return to the plaintiff the purchase money received by her deceased husband, and the action proceeded against the appellant alone, Gertrude Gwendoline O'Conor being struck out as a defendant. By the order of the High Court inquiries were directed as follows:

1. An inquiry as to which trees comprised in the contracts in the pleadings mentioned have been felled by or by the permission of the defendant, Charles Denis O'Conor.

2. An inquiry as to what damage the plaintiff has sustained by reason of the refusal of the defendant, Charles Denis O'Conor, to permit the plaintiff to fell and take the said trees.

In so far as the actual intention of Owen Phelim O'Conor may be material it is perfectly clear that he intended that the purchase moneys of the trees should be his own private property. This intention was not directly stated to the plaintiff but is proved from correspondence between Owen Phelim O'Conor and the Forestry Department, and that such was the intention of Owen Phelim O'Conor is expressly found by the learned President. Whatever the legal position may be it was certainly a source of loss to the personal estate of Owen Phelim O'Conor that the trees were not cut in his lifetime. If they had been so cut the purchase moneys would have been, beyond all dispute, his private property.

The learned President interpreted the legal effect of the agreements for the sale of the trees in accordance with the view expressed by Littledale J. in *Smith* v. *Surman* (9 B. & C. 561, at p. 573), and in accordance with the decision in *Jones* v. *Tankerville* ([1909] 2 Ch. 440).

He construed these agreements as licences from the tenant for life to cut the trees specified, and as sales of these trees as chattels when cut. During the argument before this Court, counsel for the appellant did not dispute that an agreement to give a licence to cut growing timber and a sale of the trees when cut might be within the powers of a tenant for life under the Settled Land Act, 1882, and the whole argument has proceeded on this basis.

Originally in the pleadings the plaintiff's claim seems to have been one against the estate of Owen Phelim O'Conor on the ground that he had warranted that he had good right and title to sell the timber and that the said contracts would be valid and enforceable after his death. When the action was at hearing on the 5th and 6th December, 1945, no evidence was forthcoming to support any such alleged warranty. After reserving his decision, the learned President, by a memorandum in writing read in Court on the 21st December, 1945, intimated that the plaintiff might be entitled to succeed on the ground, *inter alia*, that the contracts ought, in equity, to be attributed to the only effective power – that is, the power of a tenant for life under ss.3 and 31 of the Settled Land Act, 1882. See *Mogridge* v. *Clapp* ([1892] 3 Ch. 382). Subsequently, by an order dated the 15th January, 1946, leave was given to the plaintiff to amend his statement of claim in several ways, but it is only necessary to quote the amendment contained in par. 7 (*c*) which is as follows:

'7 (*c*). In the alternative the plaintiff says that the said Owen Phelim O'Conor should, in equity, be deemed to have entered into the said three contracts for the purpose of carrying into effect his powers as tenant for life under the Settled Land Act, 1882, and that, accordingly, such contracts are binding on and enure for the benefit of the settled estate and are enforceable against the defendant Charles Denis O'Conor as a successor in title for the time being.'

In his judgment the learned President expressed his opinion that if the trees were sold in the manner described under the exercise of a power given by the Settled Land Acts, a tenant for life unimpeachable for waste would nevertheless be entitled to the purchase money of all trees cut in his lifetime. He also held that to make the contract effective for the purchaser the tenant for life although unimpeachable for waste must, in equity, be deemed to have made the contract under the power given by the Settled Land Act. In reference to this matter, he says:

'The agreements have, apparently, become nugatory on the rigid common law view as exercises of the vendor's common law power, because the selling life-tenant died before the trees were felled; but, if the agreements, properly made by the deceased vendor, are attributable to an exercise of his statutory powers, they bind all persons interested under the settlement and in particular continue to bind the defendant, his successor in title, the present tenant for life without impeachment of waste. I hold that the three agreements must be referred to the vendor's powers under the Act of 1882, for the reason that a vendor's contract must, in equity, be attributed to that power which will make them effective, because a Court of Equity must take him to have engaged with his purchaser to make the contracts as effectual as he has power to make them: *Blake* v. *Marnell* (2 Ball & B. 35).'

The elaborate arguments of counsel centred principally around these two matters although quite a number of subsidiary points were dealt with in argument. If the first view expressed be correct, viz., that the purchase money of trees arising from a sale made under the statutory power, will belong to the tenant for life unimpeachable for waste at the time when the trees are severed, no great injustice can occur if the trees are cut in his lifetime. I can, however, find no authority for the view that purchase money of timber arising from a sale under the statutory power is other than capital money or that it can be paid out to a tenant for life unimpeachable for waste if the trees are severed in his time. The only case referred to in support of the view, *Lowndes* v. *Norton* (6 Ch. D. 139), dealt with quite different facts. In that case a life-tenant wrongfully cut down timber and was succeeded by a tenant for life unimpeachable for waste. It was held that the second tenant for life was entitled to the value of the timber which he was entitled to cut by virtue of his common law power, and which he had been prevented from cutting by the wrongful act of his predecessor. So far as authority touching the matter appears to exist, the decision in *In re Llewellin, Llewellin* v. *Williams* (37 Ch. D. 317), leads quite to the contrary conclusion. In my opinion if Owen Phelim O'Conor had sold under the power given by the Settled Land Act, 1882, and all or any of the trees had been severed in his lifetime, he would not have been entitled to the purchase money of the trees so severed.

If the intention of Owen Phelim O'Conor was that he should receive the purchase money for his own benefit and if this result could only be achieved by a cutting in his lifetime under the common law power, I fail to see the ground for compelling a sale under the statutory power which would produce a result quite different. It is, I think, clear that the purchaser thought that he would get the trees in return for his money, but a contract is the concordant agreement of two minds not the opinion of one party alone. In my opinion the plaintiff who failed to make any inquiry as to the vendor's title had constructive notice that the vendor was tenant for life unimpeachable for waste and he should have taken proper steps to protect his own interest.

Mogridge v. *Clapp* ([1892] 3 Ch. 382), was much relied upon in argument on behalf of the respondent. In that case a lease was made for the term of 99 years and it is clear that both parties intended a lease for that period. The lessor, a widower, instead of being owner in fee, as he thought, was only tenant by the courtesy in right of his deceased wife. It is not explicitly stated in the report but it seems too clear to be insisted upon that a widower could not, out of his life interest, grant a lease for 99 years. This case would be analogous if, in the present case, both parties intended that the trees should belong to the plaintiff after the death of Owen Phelim O'Conor; but such an intention would be contrary to the vendor receiving the purchase money as his own proper moneys.

Blake v. *Marnell* (2 Ball & B. 35), dealt with a case in which a debtor charged lands with a lump sum payable in annual instalments. He had a life interest in the lands and also a power to charge under the settlement, and he died before the amount charged was paid off. It was plainly the intention to charge the lands to the amount specified, and as the charge created in terms by the deed was ineffective if limited to the life estate, the Court presumed that the charge was made under the power. It was also held that it was not possible to construe the terms of a deed by parol evidence as to intention. Lord Redesdale stated the principle as follows, at p. 39, *note*: – '. . . where a person acts for valuable consideration, he is understood in equity, to engage with the person whom he deals with, to make the instrument as effectual as he has power to make it . . .'

Lord Redesdale speaks of making the instrument as effectual as he has power to make it. He was dealing with a deed which did, in terms, charge the lands to the full amount of the charge specified. This rule does not, in my opinion, mean that when it is clear what the parties or one of the parties mean, some other contract must be imputed to them in order to make the contract more beneficial to one of the parties. In the present case the intention of Owen Phelim O'Conor to have, as his own, the purchase money of the trees cannot be made effective by a sale under the Settled Land Act, and in my opinion there is no rule of equity which entitles the plaintiff to impute to him a different intention.

I have not thought it necessary to deal with the very elaborate arguments as to failure on the part of the tenant for life to give notice to the trustees of the settlement, or on the failure to pay the purchase money to the trustees for the purposes of the Settled Land Act, 1882.

In my opinion this appeal should be allowed and judgment should be entered for the appellant.

O'Byrne J.:

I concur with the judgment just read by Mr. Justice Murnaghan.

Black J.:

I could state my conclusion in this case and the deciding reason for it in a paragraph. But, with doubt, I have decided that I ought to deal with the problem fully. I think that the learned President's reasoning and the elaborate and logical arguments of Mr. Monks, whether right or wrong, together with the authorities which he marshalled, call for specific examination. I have other reasons also.

First, I think that the equitable principle on which the learned President decided the case ought to be formally affirmed here as settled law; for, without such definite affirmation, the refusal of this Court to apply this principle in the facts of the present case might be taken as casting doubt on the principle itself. Next, I am unable to agree that the case can be decided upon any inference that the late O'Conor Don intended not to exercise his power under the Settled Land Act in making the agreements with which we are concerned. Lastly, as s. 54 of the Settled Land Act, 1882, expressly protects a purchaser dealing in good faith with a tenant for life, and as nobody has suggested that the respondent did not deal in perfect good faith with the last O'Conor Don, the important s. 54, in my view, demands examination, and if it is to be held not to protect the respondent's transactions, I think some adequate reason should be given for arriving at that result.

The learned President construed the relevant agreements as licencees from the then tenant for life to cut the trees in question, and sales of the trees when cut. I accept that construction. Since the then life tenant's interest ended at his death, it follows that, at common law, the licence must terminate at his death and no property could pass to the licensee and purchaser under these agreements in respect of any trees not severed in the lifetime of the then tenant for life. But, if the agreements had been made, or can be treated as having been made, in the exercise of the powers conferred on a tenant for life under the Settled Land Act, 1882, then I think they would be valid and binding on the present tenant for life and all persons entitled in remainder. The agreements did not purport to have been made in the exercise of Settled Land Act powers, nor is there any evidence that the then tenant for life had any intention of exercising such powers or that the respondent here supposed that such powers were being exercised.

Notwithstanding the foregoing, the learned President said: 'I hold that the three agreements must be referred to the vendor's powers under the Act of 1882, for the reason that a vendor's contracts must, in equity, be attributed to that power which will make them effective, because a court of equity must take him to have engaged with his purchaser to make contracts as effectual as he has power to make them.'

The equitable principle thus stated by the President in the very words of Lord Redesdale, as quoted by Christian L.J. in *Pennefather's Case* (I.R. 7 Eq. 300, at p. 318), may, I think, be treated as axiomatic. Its applicability to the agreements in the present case is no doubt arguable, but surely not the principle itself.

It goes back 235 years to *Thomlinson* v. *Dighton* (10 Mod. Rep. 31), and, as the report shows, was no novelty even then. It is restated in *Blake* v. *Marnell* (2 Ball & B. 35), and by Lord St. Leonards in Sugden on Powers, 8th edn., p. 344. It is clearly expounded by the judges in *Pennefather's Case* (I.R. 7 Eq. 300, at p. 318); by Porter M.R., in *L'Estrange* v. *L'Estrange* (25 L.R.I. 399), and, more shortly, by Kekewich J. in *Mogridge* v. *Clapp* ([1892] 3 Ch. 382 at p. 388). We meet a very germane expression of it in Farwell on Powers, 3rd edn., p. 300, in these words: 'where a man has both a power and an interest, and he creates an estate which will not have an effectual continuance in point of time if it be fed out of his interest, it shall take effect by force of power.' In the present case the late O'Conor Don had an interest out of which to dispose of the trees as he did, if cut in his lifetime, and I think he had also a power under the Settled Land Act, 1882, to grant the licences and make the agreements for the sale of the trees when cut, even though not cut in his lifetime. But, since none of trees were cut in his lifetime, the disposition he purported to make would not 'have an effectual continuance in point of time if it be fed out of his interest.' Hence, the respondent submits that it must 'take effect by force of the power.'

It was strongly urged against all this that the late O'Conor Don had no actual intention of exercising any power under the Settled Land Act, and Lord St. Leonards was quoted as saying that 'it is the intention that in these cases governs.' So, too, Sir W.M. James V.C. in *Garth* v. *Townsend* (L.R. 7 Eq. 220, at pp. 223), asked 'Is there a distinct intention to execute the power?' These unquestionable *dicta* require explanation, and they have often been explained; but never more clearly than by Lord O'Hagan L.C. in *Pennefather's Case* (I.R. 7 Eq. 300, at p. 309). Having quoted these *dicta*, Lord O'Hagan said: 'We have next to consider how such an intention can be so demonstrated? . . . It is not necessary . . . that there should be a recital of the power or that the donee of it should consciously design to execute it, or even that he should be aware of the possession of it at the moment. If he intends to convey property or arrange it in such a mode as makes the exercise of the power an essential condition of its validity and effect, the presumption will be, that he did intend to execute it.' Applying the foregoing words to the present case, and assuming, as I think I should assume, in the absence of evidence to the contrary, that the late O'Conor Don was a reasonably honest man, I must infer that he intended to convey or pass the property – that is the licence to cut the trees and to take and keep them when cut – to the respondent; for he took most of the purchase money and contracted to be paid the rest of it, and, as the President has found, he meant to put all this money in his pocket. Such being his intention it made the exercise of the power, in Lord O'Hagan's words, 'an essential condition of its validity and effect' and hence 'the presumption will be, that he did intend to execute it.' Nor, again in the words of Lord O'Hagan, does it affect the presumption that there was no recital of the power in the agreements, nor that the late O'Conor Don might not have consciously designed to execute it, nor even that he should have been aware of the possession of it at the moment.

The same doctrine was also stated by Sir John Romilly in *Carver* v. *Richards* (27 Beav. 488, at p. 495). He said: 'It is, I consider, the rule of this Court, that if the intention to pass the property subject to the power be clearly established, even though the intention to dispose of it under or by virtue of the power is not shown, still that equity will give effect to the disposition, and hold that the property passes under the power.' No less lucid was the exposition of the same principle by Kekewich J. in *Mogridge* v. *Clapp* ([1892] 3 Ch. 382, at p. 388). His words were: 'There is an old rule . . . that where you find an intention to effect a particular object, and there is nothing to exclude the intention to effect it by a power which is available, and there are no means of effecting it except by that power, then you conclude that the intention was to effect it by means of that power, because otherwise it would not be effected at all. That rule has been applied in a large number of reported cases . . . I think, therefore, that, notwithstanding the existence of the statutory power of leasing was not present to the minds of the parties . . . and really was absent from their minds, I must hold that there was in law an intention that this lease should operate under this Act – that is to say, there was an intention that it should operate . . . in the only way in which it could operate – that is, under the Act.'

In the present case I have felt bound to infer that the late O'Conor Don intended to pass the property in question to the respondent. The late O'Conor Don knew that he was only tenant for life and that he might die before the necessarily lengthy operation of cutting the trees was completed or even before it was begun. I think he must also have known well that the respondent would never have paid the large sum of money he did pay if it had ever dawned upon his mind that, if the vendor of the trees died before the cutting was completed or begun, he would not get all, or perhaps any, of the trees for which he had paid. Would the late O'Conor Don have allowed the respondent to make such a bargain without disclosing his limited ownership and the serious possibility mentioned, if he, the O'Conor Don, had thought there was such a possibility, and can he have had any other intention than that the respondent should get the trees for which the O'Conor Don took his money, whether they were cut in the O'Conor Don's lifetime or not? My answer is 'no,' unless I am to attribute to the late O'Conor Don a code of ethics to which normally honest men would not subscribe. The man is dead and cannot vindicate himself. I therefore think it right to give him credit for having honourably intended that the respondent should get the trees for which he had paid or bound himself to pay whether the O'Conor Don lived or died, in the absence of any evidence suggesting the slightest probability that he had not that honourable intention. Once that intention is inferred, then we are brought face to face with the rule rightly stated by the learned President, and enunciated by the above-quoted authorities and many others, whereby it is presumed that where the property intended to pass can only pass by virtue of a given power, it must be presumed to have been intended to pass by virtue of that power.

The aforesaid rule, however, like many other rules, is subject to exceptions, and the question then arises whether the facts of the present case bring it within any of these exceptions, or in other words, whether the learned President, being incontestably right in accepting the rule as to the equitable presumption, was right or wrong in treating that rule as applicable to the present case. As I understand the argument for the appellant, two exceptions to the rule, or reasons for not applying it and for not presuming that the agreements were made in execution of the Settled Land Act power, were relied upon. These were, first, that the late O'Conor Don intended not to exercise the power, and, second, that even if he intended to exercise the power and had said so expressly, the agreements in question could not have been validly made or enforced under that power. If either of these contentions is correct, the rule that the agreements must be presumed to have been made under the power does not apply; for equity does not make the presumption in question if the person who makes an agreement intended not to make it under the disputed power or if that power would not enable the agreement to be made or enforced even if the parties intended that it should be.

Now, the authorities I have quoted draw a clear distinction between the absence of an intention to exercise the power and an actual intention not to exercise it, and they emphasise that it is only an actual intention not to exercise the power that prevents the presumption being made that it was intended to be exercised, the mere absence of an intention to exercise the power having no effect upon the making of the presumption. In *Pennefather's Case* (I.R. 7 Eq. 300, at p. 311), Lord O'Hagan said: 'It is often, as was said in *Carver* v. *Richards* (27 Beav. 496), 'extremely difficult to distinguish or define the limits between an intention not to execute a power, and the case of no knowledge of the existence of the power; in which case, strictly speaking, there is no intention to execute it; while, in the former, there is an intention not to execute it.' '

In the present case it is contended that because the President found that the late tenant for life meant to put the money in his own pocket, this shows that he intended not to exercise the Settled Land Act power. In my opinion it is impossible to conclude that this finding shows any such intention. I do not think it even shows the absence of an intention to exercise the power, immaterial as such mere absence of intention would be, even if it did. Of course, it is not at all unlikely that when the late O'Conor Don made these agreements, neither the possibility of his own death nor the exercise of the Settled Land Act power was present to his mind at all. But, it is also possible that both these matters were present to his mind, together with the knowledge that the agreements would cease to be effective after his death, and that in order to keep the respondent safe in that eventuality, he meant the agreements to operate under the statutory power, believing, as the learned President of the High Court has held, that they could legally so operate. He may well have thought, as the President has also held, that he could take the purchase money in the first instance under the power subject to his estate being liable to the interested parties in the event of all or any part of that money becoming payable to them on his death before any or all of the trees were cut. To say that this hypothesis seems improbable could only be a guess; but if it is reasonably possible it cannot be ruled out be guesswork or without evidence, and I see none, to justify its rejection. Hence, whatever my suspicion might be, I see no justification for actually holding that the late O'Conor Don did not intend to exercise the statutory power when he made these agreements.

But if, contrary to what I have said, I could feel satisfied that he did not intend to exercise the statutory power in making these agreements, I should feel it utterly impossible to draw the further, quite distinct, and all important conclusion that he actually intended not to exercise the statutory power. My reason is this. I think it not only possible, but extremely probable, that when the O'Conor Don made these agreements he had not present to his mind at all the possibility of his death before all the trees were cut and taken away by the respondent. We must use our own knowledge of human nature in these problems. I think it is well known that people sometimes die intestate though in life they had a horror of such an eventuality. They have done so because, though well aware that anybody may die unexpectedly, being in good health and preoccupied with business or pleasure, the possibility was not present to their minds or operative in their calculations. And as it is with the making of wills so it is with the making of contracts and financial commitments. Quite provident people often put the possibility of death within a few years out of of their minds and calculations, even though they are well aware of it. So in this case the late O'Conor Don when making these agreements may never have thought of death and, therefore, may never have thought of his power under the Settled Land Act. Indeed, if I give him credit for being conscientious in his dealings with the respondent, which I think I should do, I should have to conclude that it was not only possible, but actually probable, that in making these agreements he never thought either of death or of the Settled Land Act. If at that time his power under the Settled Land Act was not present to his mind at all then he could not have had an intention to exercise it, but equally he could not have had an intention not to exercise it. One cannot have an intention at any given time either to do a thing or not to do it, unless that thing is present to one's mind at that particular time.

If I were to determine that the late O'Conor Don, at the material times, had his own death and his statutory power in mind at all, so as to make possible an actual intention not to exercise the power, I could only so determine by an arbitrary guess, which I think is not permissible; and, indeed, if it were, I should probably guess the other way. But, of legal evidence as to whether he intended to exercise the power or intended not to exercise, or had no intention either way in regard to it, in my opinion there is none. That being my view, the first of the two objections to the equitable presumption that he did intend to exercise the power, in my judgement, falls to the ground.

The second objection to the equitable presumption in question is that, as it was argued, the agreements could not have been made or enforced under the power even if it had been proved to have been the actual intention of the late O'Conor Don that they should be. This is said to be the case because there were, at the time, no trustees for the purposes of the Settled Land Act and because the purchase money would have been capital money arising under the Act, and the agreements required it to be paid, most of it in fact being paid, to the late tenant for life contrary to s. 22 of the Settled Land Act, 1882, which requires that it be paid to the trustees or else at the option of the tenant for life paid into Court. As to the first of these two reasons -- the absence of trustees, *Hughes* v. *Fanagan* (30 L.R.I. 111), was strongly relied on; but as a decision it does not help. All that it decided, or that it was necessary to decide, was that an agreement for a lease by a tenant for life under the Act did not bind the remaindermen when there were no trustees *and the intending lessee knew that he was dealing with a tenant for life and knew that there were no trustees.* As a decision, that case would only be in point by way of analogy if the present respondent had known that the late O'Conor Don was only tenant for life and that there were no trustees. There is no evidence that he knew either of these facts. But all the judgments in *Hughes* v. *Fanagan* (30 L.R.I. 111), contained *dicta* quite irreconcilable with the judgments, and I think even with the decision in *Mogridge* v. *Clapp* ([1892] 3 Ch. 382), so strongly relied on by counsel for the respondent. Thus, Barry L.J. thought that the appointment of trustees, and even the service of notices upon them, as prescribed by s. 45 of the Act of 1882, are 'part of the means whereby the inheritance is to be bound' and conditions precedent without the fulfilment of which the contract would not bind the remainderman. Porter M.R. and FitzGibbon L.J., while emphasising the intending lessee's knowledge that there were no trustees, nevertheless used words of similar import to those of Barry L.J., without any express limitation to cases where there was actual knowledge of the omission to appoint trustees.

On the other hand, in *Mogridge* v. *Clapp* ([1892] 3 Ch. 382), the English Court of Appeal, unanimously affirming Kekewich J., held that a lease under the power in the Settled Land Act, 1882, was valid and bound all parties though there were no trustees, at least when the lessee did not know that there were no trustees. Further, Lindley L.J., at p. 395, and Kay L.J., at p. 401, both said that the lease would still bind the remainderman even if the lessee had taken it knowing that there were no trustees. Bowen L.J. concurred. It was also held, in the words of Kay L.J., that 'a lessee has only constructive notice of the lessor's title, and the non-existence of trustees is not . . . a defect of the title of the tenant for life or of his power to grant the lease.'

In Hood and Challis' Conveyancing Acts, 7th edn., p. 224, it is noted that *Mogridge* v. *Clapp* ([1892) 3 Ch. 382), was a case of a lease; but the authors suggest that in a case of a sale 'the principle would be the same.' This view is supported by Lindley L.J. in *Mogridge* v. *Clapp* ([1892] 3 ch. 382). He said that the *Marquis of Ailesbury's Case* ([1892] 1 Ch. 506), went far to show 'that the title would be good even if there were no trustees and the purchaser or lessee knew, in fact, that such was the case.' His use of the word 'purchaser' shows that his opinion applied to a sale as well as to a lease. In *Hatten* v. *Russell* (38 Ch. D. 334, at p. 344), Kay J. applied a like opinion to a case of a sale – at least where the purchaser was unaware that there were no trustees. Again, in *In re Fisher and Grazebrook's Contract* ([1898] 2 Ch. 660, at p. 662), Romer J. said: 'I quite agree that if the purchaser in this case, supposing there had been trustees and in ignorance of the fact that there were no trustees, had paid his money into Court, he would have got a good title.'

However, I think it is unnecessary to express any opinion on this point in the present case; because the failure to appoint trustees appears to be overshadowed by the mistake of the respondent in agreeing to pay the money to the tenant for life. This mistake, if the money were capital money arising under the Act, was a non-compliance with s. 22 or the Settled Land Act, 1882, which prescribes that such money shall be paid either to the trustees or into Court at the election of the tenant for life. If that mistake does not invalidate the agreements, I cannot imagine that the non-appointment of trustees alone would do so. Conversely, if the mistake about the payment of the money does invalidate the agreements it is unnecessary to trouble about the non-existence of trustees.

The appellant's contention that the agreements could not be presumed to have been made under the Settled Land Act power because the purchase money was agreed to be paid and most of it was paid to the tenant for life in contravention of s. 22 of the Act was rejected by the learned President on the ground, I think, that no part of this money was capital money arising under the Act, and that s. 22 was, therefore, inapplicable. He held that in the events that have happened the whole of the money would be payable to the appellant as the present tenant for life. On this point there is one case worthy of notice – *Lowndes* v. *Norton* (6 Ch. D. 139). In that case there were two successive tenants for life, the first impeachable for waste and the second not. The first of these tenants cut down a great number of trees. In so doing she was a wrongdoer. In an injunction proceeding, the proceeds of the trees thus wrongfully cut were ordered to be paid into Court. On the wrongdoer's death, the next tenant for life, being unimpeachable for waste, claimed the money in Court, on the ground that the trees, if they had not been wrongfully cut, would have come to him to do what he liked with them, and that, therefore, he was entitled to the money realised by their wrongful sale. Hall V.C. upheld his contention.

In that case the second tenant for life, being unimpeachable for waste, would have been entitled to cut and sell the trees if they had not been wrongfully cut by his predecessor. His right to the trees was never divested, since the wrongful act of this predecessor could not divest him of it, though its exercise had been rendered impossible. Hence, as his right had never been taken away, he was held entitled to the money, since it represented the proceeds of the sale of his own property.

In the present case the respondent contends that notwithstanding the death of the tenant for life he is entitled to cut and sell the trees specified in the agreements. If the agreements gave him that right, then it seems to me they must have thereby divested the succeeding and present tenant for life of the right to cut and dispose of the trees, which, being unimpeachable for waste, he would otherwise have had during his lifetime; and if the agreements divested the present tenant for life of all future right to cut and sell the trees he cannot have any equitable right to the price of the trees such as, on the authority of *Lowndes* v. *Norton* (6 Ch. D. 139), he would have had if the trees had been wrongfully cut by someone having no legal right to cut them. In other words, if the agreements put an end to the appellant's right to the trees he cannot have any right to the price of the trees, having lost his right to the trees themselves. The learned President, however, said: 'If in the events that have happened I attribute the agreements to the vendor's statutory powers, the defendant (that is the appellant) will be absolutely entitled to the moneys representing the purchase price of the timber from any trees, the subject of the agreements, felled since the vendor's death.' Mr. Justice Murnaghan has rejected this view, saying that he can find no authority for it. In this regard I find myself in agreement with Mr. Justice Murnaghan, not because there is no authority for the view he rejects, for neither is there any direct authority for the opposite view; but because the clear and precise ground on which *Lowndes* v. *Norton* (6 Ch. D. 139) was decided appears to me the only possible ground on which it could have been decided, and its complete inapplicability to the facts of the present case seems to me to render *Lowndes* v. *Norton* (6 Ch. D. 139) an indirect authority against the view that the appellant has any possible claim to the price paid, or agreed to be paid, by the respondent to the late tenant for life.

I, therefore, cannot agree that if the agreements in this case are treated as made under the Settled Land Act power, the money in question can be anything else but capital money arising under the Act. Its payment, and the agreements to pay it, to the late tenant for life were, therefore, in direct contravention of s. 22 of the Act of 1882. Is the effect of that to render the whole transaction void unless there is some special dispensation in the statute which prevents that result? On this point one may consider another requirement of the Act by way of analogy. Thus, in *Mogridge* v. *Clapp* ([1892] 3 Ch. 382) – the very case most relied on by the respondent – Kay L.J. referred to the requirement in s. 7, sub-s. 2, that every lease shall reserve the best rent, and said that there was no provision in the Act that the lease should be void if the best rent was not reserved, but that 'following the analogy of leases under powers in a settlement, that would probably be the case.' Now, it seems to me that the requirement in s. 22, sub-s. 1, is quite as important as the requirement in s. 7, sub-s. 2, and that if a contravention of the latter would make the transaction void, so would a contravention of the former. I think also that a tenant for life selling under the power and contracting to have the purchase money paid to himself in contravention of s. 22, sub-s. 1, would be guilty of a breach of trust, since he is made a trustee for all parties interested by s. 53, and I do not feel able to dissent from the view that if the purchaser made himself a party to such a contract, it could not be enforced against the parties entitled in remainder, unless the purchaser could invoke some dispensing provision in the Act. There is, however, such a dispensing provision in s. 54. It provides that '. . . a purchaser . . . dealing in good faith with a tenant for life shall, as against all parties entitled under the settlement, be conclusively taken to have given the best price . . . and to have complied with all the requisitions of this Act.' In *Mogridge* v. *Clapp* ([1892] 3 Ch. 382), Kay L.J. stressed these last words and had them placed in inverted commas in the report. The words are 'and to have complied with all the requisitions of this Act.' Clearly the requirements in s. 22, sub-s. 1, as to payment of capital money is one of these requisitions.

Hence, by s. 54 a purchaser dealing in good faith with a tenant for life must be conclusively taken to have complied with s. 22, even though he has not done so in fact. Good faith, then, is the test.

I imagine there is no more serious requisition in the Act than that in s. 4, sub-s.1, that every sale shall be made at the best price that can reasonably be obtained. Yet, in *Hurrell* v. *Littlejohn* ([1904] 1 Ch. 689), there was a sale of property by a tenant for life for £2,000 and the very next day the purchaser resold it for £3,000. But the Court refused to set aside the sale on the ground that there was no evidence that the purchaser had acted otherwise than in good faith within the meaning of s. 54. So, in

In re Handman and Wilcox's Contract ([1902] 1 Ch. 599), Buckley J. held a lease bad, not because it did not comply with the statutory requirement as regards rent, which alone would not have been sufficient, but because of that fact, together with the further fact that the lessee did not act in good faith within s. 54.

Sect. 54 would have no meaning or effect at all if it did not protect transactions which otherwise would be invalid or unenforceable where the purchaser or other person in question had dealt in good faith with the tenant for life. It is implicit in the section that a person may fail to comply with any of the requirements of the Act and yet do so in good faith. Otherwise s. 54 could never give any protection at all when a purchaser, lessee, or mortgagee had failed to comply with the requirements of the Act. Failure to comply with a requisition of the Act is a mistake and a serious mistake, and the section plainly contemplates that such a mistake may be made in good faith. A mistake must be either of fact or of law. The protection of s. 54 must extend to either or to both. It can hardly be doubted that it extends at least to a *bona fide* mistake of fact, such as a mistake honestly made as to the best price. Possibly such a mistake was made in *Hurrell* v. *Littlejohn* ([1904] 1 Ch. 689), and Joyce J. held that s. 54 protected the purchaser.

But, s. 54 gives no indication that its protection only extends to mistakes of fact, and it would seem as possible to make a mistake of law in good faith as to make a *bona fide* mistake of fact. In *Chandler* v. *Bradley* ([1897] 1 Ch. 315, at p. 323), Stirling J. – a very experienced Chancery Judge – suggested as a possible instance of mistake which s. 54 might protect, the case of a *bona fide* mistake 'as to the proper mode of paying' a fine agreed on for a lease by a tenant for life. In that case, Stirling J. held that the payment was not really a fine but a bribe to be kept by the tenant for life for himself, with the result that the rent reserved was not the best rent, which rendered it void as being in contravention of s. 7, sub-s. 2. The reason that s. 54 gave no protection was that the lessee who knew his payment was a bribe did not deal with the tenant for life in good faith. But, if Stirling J. was right in suggesting that s. 54 might protect the lessee if he paid a genuine fine, but made some *bona fide* mistake 'as to the proper mode of paying it,' this could protect against a *bona fide* mistake of law; for a mistake in the mode of paying a fine suggests a mistake of law rather than a mistake of fact. If the present respondent had given evidence, for instance, that he knew or even suspected that the late O'Conor Don was only tenant for life, and that he knew the requirements of s. 22, sub-s. 1, but that by a *bona fide* mistake he misconstrued it, and thought that payment by him to the tenant for life, who is made a trustee for all parties by s. 53, was equivalent to payment to the trustees for the purposes of the Act, it may be that he could have invoked the protection of s. 54. Similarly, if he gave evidence that, like the President of the High Court himself, he acted in the belief that s. 22, sub-s. 1 did not apply to the money in question, it may be that s. 54 would protect the transaction from being invalidated. In the circumstances I do not think it is necessary to express any opinion on this point; for the respondent tendered no legal evidence at all as to why he made the mistake of paying or agreeing to pay the money to the tenant for life.

It seems to me that if a purchaser seeks to uphold an agreement which contravenes a serious requirement of the Act, which may gravely damnify innocent persons entitled in remainder, and for that purpose invokes the great favour given by s. 54 on condition that he dealt in good faith, the onus must be cast upon him to show by clear evidence that he did deal in good faith. In the present case no legal evidence was given on the point at all. But the respondent, through his counsel, made the case that he dealt with the late O'Conor Don, believing him to be the absolute owner, and not a mere tenant for life. That was the mistake, and the only mistake, on which he sought to rely; and although this was not proved in sworn evidence, I see no reason to doubt that he was absolutely truthful in instructing his counsel to make that case for him. If it were a mistake which would enable him to invoke the protection of s. 54, I think that it should have been stated in sworn evidence. But I take the view that it is not a mistake in respect of which he can claim protection under s. 54. I do not forget, and have very much in mind, all that was said about constructive notice in *Bailey* v. *Barnes* ([1894] 1 Ch. 25) in *Kettlewell* v. *Watson* (21 Ch. D. 685) by Lord Cranworth in his classic pronouncement in *Ware* v. *Lord Egmont* (4 De G.M. & G. 460), and particularly by Lindley L.J. in *Mogridge* v. *Clapp* [(1892) 3 Ch. 382). But all this does not get rid of the fact that the respondent must be deemed to have had notice of the late O'Conor Don's title. In the very case of *Mogridge* v. *Clapp* ([1892] 3 Ch. 382) itself, Kay L.J. said that the lessee had notice – that is constructive notice – of the lessor's title, and Kekewich J. said that he must be taken to have known that the lessor there 'could only make the lease as tenant by the curtesy – that is by virtue of the Settled Land Act.' So, here, I think the respondent must be deemed to have had notice, though I do not suggest that he had it in fact, that the late O'Conor Don could only make the agreements in question as tenant for life – that is by virtue of the Settled Land Act. Now, if he must be deemed to have had that notice in law, he must be treated as if he had it in actual fact, and cannot be heard to say that he had not that notice. If he purported to make that case, in evidence, it would have to be ignored, and it must, therefore, be ignored *a fortiori* when he makes it merely through the argument of his counsel. Yet, it is only by seeking to make that case that he could show that he dealt in good faith with the late tenant for life. Nobody has even suggested that he did not, in fact, deal in perfect good faith with the late O'Conor Don. It is, therefore, unfortunate for him tha the legal doctrine which imputes to him the knowledge that the late O'Conor Don was only tenant for life, even though he did not in fact possess that knowledge, deprives him of the only means by which, on his own case, he could prove that he dealt in good faith so as to obtain the protection of s. 54.

As I must, therefore, conclude that the respondent cannot invoke the protection of s. 54, and as I have already concluded, though for the reasons I have stated only, that the other grounds on which his case was based must fail, I am unable to dissent from the net decision of the Court that the appellant must succeed in this appeal.

Notes and Questions
1. What precisely were the grounds upon which the Supreme Court reversed Gavan Duffy P.?
2. As regards timber rights, see *Irish Land Law*, para. 4.152. See also *Kirkpatrick and Maunsell* v. *Naper, infra*.
3. As regards sales under the Settled Land Acts, see ch. 7, *post*.

KIRKPATRICK AND MAUNSELL V. NAPER
[1945] 79 I.L.T.R. 40 (High Court)

K. and M. were executors and trustees of the will and codicil of W.L.N. and agreed to sell such trees as were 'ripe and fit for cutting' to T. & C.M. for £13,800. A permit for cutting was issued subject to the usual provisions for clearing and re-planting. The action was brought to determine the title (having regard to the provisions of the will and codicil) to the moneys realised, whereof only a small portion represented the price of timber properly so called, as both timber and non-timber trees were sold. W.L.N. by the codicil to his will bequeathed to his wife, A.M.N., absolutely so much of his residuary estate as consisted of goods and chattels, personal effects, farming implements and stock. The trustees were given the fullest powers of postponement of the sale of the property and decided in their discretion to postpone the sale of the land and premises wherein W.L.N. and A.M.N. had resided, and in fact A.M.N. continued to reside there at the time of the suit. W.L.N. deemed A.M.N. in his will and codicil 'the tenant for life' of the 'rents, profits and income' of his estate whereon he and A.M.N., his wife, had lived. A.M.N. did not seek or get any Order from the Court to put her into posession as the person deemed by statute to be tenant for life, and the trustees, therefore, retained the management of the property. But there was no doubt that A.M.N. would receive the whole income of the property during her life under the express terms of the will.

The sale was made at an exceptionally high price owing to the then prevailing war conditions. A question arose as to A.M.N.'s right to receive any share of the net proceeds of sale of the timber for her own use and benefit.

Gavan Duffy, J.:

Acting on the advice of Colonel Magan, a timber expert, the trustees of the will and codicil of Captain William Lenox Naper agreed with a purchaser on September 15th, 1943, to sell such of the trees on his estate at Lougherow, Oldcastle, Co. Meath, as were ripe and fit for cutting; the trees, numbering nearly 3,000, are described in the agreement as mature. On October 1st, 1943, a permit was issued to Mrs. Naper, the testator's widow, as vendor, in the name of the Department for Industry and Commerce, authorising the sale under the Emergency Powers (Control of Timber) Order, S.R. & O. No. 294 of 1941, which entrusted the control of the country's timber to the Minister for Supplies; the permit specifies the trees to be sold as follows:

Species	Approximate Quantity in Cubic feet
606 Scots Pine Trees	44,062
1,697 Larch Trees	164,362
40 Oak Trees	2,580
1 Elm Tree	54
175 Spruce Trees	20,591
152 Silver Fir Trees	40,595
41 Sycamore Trees	1,566
215 Ash Trees	7,536

The sale price was £13,800. According to the supplementary evidence for which I deferred judgment, the cost of clearing and replanting is estimated at £964 10s. 0d. and there will probably be a Government grant of £380 to set off against that sum, reducing it to a sum of £584 10s. 0d. The net produce of the sale would on those figures be £13,315 10s. 0d., minus the fees due to the trustees' expert. There is also evidence that the sale price at pre-war prices, on the cubic content of the wood sold, would have been £5,930, so that the trustees, selling last autumn in order to get the benefit of the abnormal demand in a time of war, claim to have realised a gross sum of £7,870 more than the price prevailing four years earlier for the same quantity of the same materials.

This action is brought to determine the title to the moneys realised, whereof only a small portion represents the price of timber properly so called. I hold that 'timber' for my present purpose denotes oak, ash, and elm; I reject the suggestion that the meaning of the word at common law disappeared in Ireland under the influence of certain Georgian statutes, the whole policy of which strongly favoured, not the remainderman, but the actual occupant, who was encouraged to plant trees. An Act of the Irish Parliament of 1776, 15 and 16 Geo. 11, c. 26, entitled 'An Act for encouraging the cultivation, and for the better preservation of trees, shrubs, plants and roots,' recited earlier Acts which had failed to attain the same and punished the spoilers and destroyers of trees and plants; for the purposes of that Act and of every other Act then in force relative to timber trees, the Act gave the name of timber to many trees, including, I think, every species of tree mentioned in the Government permit; but I find nothing in the Act to suggest any intention of touching the well-established meaning of timber at common law, and in my opinion the statutory definition must, on its text and on the manifest policy of the Georgian Acts, be limited to its declared ambit.

Captain Naper died on October 25, 1942. By his will, dated April 10th, 1942, he had given all his residuary estate to his widow absolutely, but he revoked that gift by a codicil, dated June 19th, 1942, and he thereby bequeathed to his widow absolutely so much of his residuary estate as consisted of goods and chattels, personal effects, farming implements and stock. The gift of the farm implements and stock suggests that the testator expected his wife to continue to occupy the land near Oldcastle, on which he and she resided; but he did not secure the place as a home for her, though he did insist in her favour that his debts should not be paid out of 'the rents or profits or income,' whereof he designated her 'the tenant for life,' if she survived him. The codicil gave the remainder of the residuary estate, real and personal, unto and to the use of the trustees upon trust for conversion, with the fullest power of postponement, and went on to direct them to 'pay the income from the net rents and profits, interest, dividends and annual produce of the said real and personal residuary estate (after payment of all outgoings and expenses which may be payable thereout . . .)' to his wife during her life. This gift was followed by curious gifts in remainder, but I am not now directly concerned with the construction of the ultimate limitations of the property, either real or personal.

The trustees depose that since her husband's death Mrs. Naper has continued in possession of his residence and demesne with their consent and that she now resides there. They decided in their discretion to postpone the sale of the property and I have no doubt that this decision is in the spirit of the testator's own wishes and that this is the arrangement most congenial to his widow who is still living in her own home; but she has not sought from the Court any order to put her into possession as the person deemed by statute to be tenant for life and the trustees retain the burden of managing the property.

Though Mrs. Naper is not in the strict sense tenant for life, she is solely entitled, after payment of the outgoings, to the whole of the profits and annual produce of the property under the express terms of the will; the net income is produced during her life for her alone, and I have to see how far her rights, on the issue now before me, differ, if they differ at all, from those of a tenant for life in possession.

I shall consider first the rights arising from the felling of the trees which are not timber. If Mrs. Naper were the tenant for life in possession, I apprehend that the most doughty champion of the interests in remainder would not have the forehead to contest her title to the proceeds of the sale of those trees; she would clearly be entitled on the principle illustrated by the decision of Mr. Justice Simonds in *Re Harker* [1938] 1 All E.R. 145. The sale it is insisted was undoubtedly made at a quite exceptional price, but the relevance of that consideration eludes me. The sale was in every respect a proper sale in the course of careful management of the woods under expert advice; the trees to be cut down were 'mature,' 'ripe,' 'fit for cutting.' The value of the usufructuary interest now realised happens to have been more than doubled as a result of a world war, the interest thus benefited by the sale remains precisely the same usufructuary interest, and no statute has yet declared that a war outside our territory is to be deemed to have converted income into capital. Had a tenant for life in possession sold at a moment when there happened to be a glut of similar wood in the market, no portion of the comparative loss would have fallen upon capital. So, in plain justice, the entire increment must here have belonged to the evidence that gain to the usufructuary would in no way whatever impair in the smallest degree the lawful interests of the remaindermen. There is here, upon the evidence, no premature sale and no premature profit from a windfall; therefore the principle which governed the decision in *Re Harison*, 28 Ch. D. 220, and *Re Terry* 87 L.J. (Ch.) 557, the principle that it is the duty of the Court to prevent an accident from enriching a tenant for life at the expense of the remainderman, has nothing whatever here upon which to operate. I can find in the incidental and accidental influence of an external war no justification, either in law or in logic, for depriving a tenant for life in possession of any part of the fruits of the soil, which, were there no war, would belong to the beneficiary and to nobody else. But does the same argument apply to a lady who receives the income, but is not tenant for life in possession? Clearly it does. It is agreed that Mrs. Naper under the will takes all the income, whether the residuary property producing it be converted or unconverted. Her position differs from that of a tenant for life in possession mainly in her immunity from the duties of management and her inability *mero motu* to exercise the statutory powers of a tenant for life; the main difference for the trustees lies in the much heavier onus upon them. I see in the distinction between the two positions no ground for taking the pernancy of these sylvan winnings away from the sole owner of all the profits and annual produce, after payment of the outgoings; the proceeds of sale are all hers, except that, since the trustees as good foresters must clear and replant, they are bound to require Mrs. Naper to defray the consequent expenses, attributable to the non-timber trees, including in their claim a proportion of the fees incurred by them to the expert by whom they were advised. (*Cf. Re Trevor-Batye's Settlement*, [1912] 2 Ch. 339.)

I turn to the timber proper. Timber is by long tradition a part of the inheritance; here again the evidence shows the oak and ash and elm trees to have been properly felled; so the money will be invested and Mrs. Naper will enjoy the resultant income. I should ordinarily, of course, take some guidance, in favour of an equitable claimant with a life interest, from section 35 of the Settled Land Act, 1882, and allow him a bonus out of the proceeds of timber sold, though the analogy is imperfect and a Court will not, as a matter of course, take a person deemed under section 63 of the Act to be tenant for life as having precisely the same claim on the capital money, when timber is sold, as a tenant for life in possession has obtained by statute; I think that the equitable claim and its extent must depend on the circumstances as a whole. In the present instance there is no suggestion that Mrs. Naper will directly or indirectly suffer any loss or injury of any kind as a result of the felling of timber, a very small proportion of the total clearance. Her 'equity' to share in this particular conversion of residue would on the actual facts be as hard to formulate in a convincing theorem as the illusory equity set up for the inheritance to dip into the accretion of income from the sale of pine and larch; for I cannot at this point shut out the fact, a very pertinent fact at this point, that, if my view is right, the fortunes of war have proved marvellously kind to her in the matter of the bulk of the same transaction. Mrs. Naper must be content to let the trust capital keep the whole of its own little benefit. Her own rich harvest from the enhanced income that is hers seems to me to supply a conclusive answer here to the claim that she might in other circumstances have made, as a matter of fair play, to a grant from the timber fund. Accordingly, I hold that the trustees, when the necessary apportionment is made, must appropriate the entire proceeds of the timber trees as capital, after allocating against the sale price of those trees their fair proportion of the clearing and planting expenses and the expert's fees.

As this is a friendly suit, I presume that the precise figures will be ascertained without an inquiry in Chambers. But the parties will have liberty to apply. I wish to add that this case has been a pleasure to try, because counsel have combined to give me the benefit of their erudition and research in admirably documented arguments of conspicuous clarity.

One further matter: with respect to the land comprised in the settlement read by statute into Captain Naper's codicil, Mrs. Naper applies for leave to exercise, under sections 6, 7 and 13 of the Settled Land Act, 1882, the powers of a tenant for life in relation to leases and surrenders: the trustees consent; and I shall make that order.

Notes and Questions
1. What is the justification for Gavan Duffy J.'s interpretation of the Irish Timber Acts? Do you agree with this view?
2. See further on the position of a tenant for life, p. 412, *post.*

V. LEASE FOR LIVES RENEWABLE FOR EVER

RENEWABLE LEASEHOLD CONVERSION ACT, 1849
An Act for converting the renewable Leasehold Tenure of Lands in Ireland into a Tenure in Fee.
[*Preamble rep. by S.L.R.* 1891.]

1. Where lands in Ireland are held under any lease in perpetuity, the owner of such lease in perpetuity, and whether the time for renewal has or has not arrived, may require the owner of the reversion to execute a grant, according to the provisions of the Act, of the lands comprised in such lease; and the owner of the reversion, upon being so required as aforesaid, shall execute a grant to the owner of such lease of an estate of inheritance in fee simple in such lands, subject to a perpetual yearly fee-farm rent, of such amount as herein-after mentioned, to be charged upon such lands, and to be payable on the same days and times as the yearly rent made payable by such lease, and subject to the like covenants and conditions for securing the payment of such fee-farm rent as are contained in such lease with respect to the rent thereby reserved, and with and subject to such other covenants, conditions, exceptions, and reservations, (save covenants to grant or to accept and take a renewal of such lease, and such covenants, conditions, exceptions, and reservations as may be commuted as herein-after mentioned) as are contained in such lease, and then subsisting; and where lands in Ireland are held under any under-lease in perpetuity of any degree of tenure, the owner of such under-lease, and whether the time for renewal has or has not arrived, may require the owner of the lease or under-lease in perpetuity out of which such first-mentioned under-lease is derived, or the owner of the estate of inheritance which may have been granted in respect of the lease or under-lease out of which such first-mentioned under-lease is derived, to execute a grant, according to the provisions of this Act, of the lands comprised in such first-mentioned under-lease; and the owner so required shall thereupon execute a grant to the owner of such under-lease of an estate of inheritance in fee simple in such lands, subject to a perpetual yearly fee-farm rent, of such amount as herein-after mentioned, to be charged upon such lands, and to be payable by such under-lease, and subject to the like covenants and conditions for securing such fee-farm rent as are contained in such under-lease with respect to the rent thereby reserved, and subject to such other covenants, conditions, exceptions, and reservations, (save covenants to grant or to accept and take a renewal of such lease, and such covenants, conditions, exceptions and

reservations as may be commuted as herein-after mentioned) as are contained in such under-lease, and then subsisting; and upon the delivery of every such grant as aforesaid to the owner requiring the same, he shall execute and deliver to the owner executing such grant a counterpart thereof; and the expense of the preparation and execution of such grant and counterpart shall be paid by the owner to whom the grant is made: Provided always, that the owner required to make any such grant as aforesaid shall not be obliged to execute such grant until, where the time for renewal of the lease or under-lease by the owner of which the grant is required has not arrived, all such arrears or sums, if any, of or in respect of rent as, if the time had arrived for renewal of such lease or under-lease, and a bill had been filed for the renewal thereof, would have been required by a court of equity to be paid on such renewal, and where the time for renewal of such lease or under-lease has arrived, or where there has not been a renewal of such lease or under-lease at or after the time at which the same might have been last renewed according to the covenant for renewal, all such arrears or sums, if any, of or in respect of rent, and also all such fines and fees, if any, and interest, as would have been required by a court of equity to be paid on renewal of such lease or under-lease, are paid: Provided also, that no owner required to execute any such grant as aforesaid shall be obliged to execute such grant where the right of renewal is lost both at law and in equity; and where any owner required to execute any such grant as aforesaid disputes the right of the party requiring such grant to require the execution of such grant, such owner shall, within one calendar month after he is so required as aforesaid, serve on the person by whom such grant has been required a notice in writing stating that the right to require such grant is disputed, and the grounds on which such right is so disputed.

2. The fee-farm rent to be made payable by every such grant as aforesaid shall, where the lease or under-lease (as the case may be) to the owner of which the grant is made is renewable without fine, or upon payment of a peppercorn or other merely nominal fine of like nature, be of the like amount as the yearly rent made payable by such lease or under-lease, and shall, where such lease or under-lease is renewable upon payment of a fine or fines not merely nominal, be of an amount equal to the aggregate amount of the yearly rent made payable by such lease or under-lease, and the value of the renewal fine or fines and fees (if any), such value to be estimated or computed with regard to the probable duration of the subsisting term, the average duration of life, and the respective periods for renewal, but without regard to and exclusively of any penal rents or sums made payable upon neglect, delay, or refusal to apply for or take renewal, and to be ascertained as herein-after mentioned, if the parties differ about the same.

3. Where any subsisting exception or reservation contained in the lease or under-lease in perpetuity by the owner of which a grant is required as aforesaid, or any right under covenant or otherwise annexed or belonging to the reversion or estate from the owner of which a grant is required, interferes with the proper cultivation of the lands comprised in such lease or under-lease, the owner of such lease or under-lease requiring such grant as aforesaid may (if he think fit) require that such exception, reservation, or right should cease, wholly or partially, and in such case the grant shall be modified accordingly, and the fee-farm rent to be made payable by such grant shall be increased by such an amount as is equivalent to the value of such exception, reservation, or right, in so far as it is made to cease as aforesaid, such amount to be ascertained in manner herein-after mentioned, in case the parties differ about the same.

4. Provided always, that where any right to timber, timber trees or other trees, woods, underwood, or underground woods, bogs, mosses, turbaries, mines,

minerals, quarries, or royalties, whether under express exception or reservation contained in the lease or under-lease in perpetuity or otherwise, is annexed to or belongs to the reversion or estate from the owner of which a grant is required, it shall not be lawful for the owner of the lease or under-lease in perpetuity requiring the grant to require that such right should cease, either wholly or partially, but in every such case the owner of the reversion or estate from the owner of which the grant is required, and the owner of the lease or under-lease requiring the grant, may agree that such right should cease or pass under the grant, either wholly or partially, and in such case the grant shall be modified accordingly, and the yearly fee-farm rent to be made payable by such grant shall be increased by such an amount as is equivalent to the value of such right, so far as it is made to cease or pass as aforesaid.

5. Provided also, that where the estate into which the reversion from the owner of which a grant is required as aforesaid would be converted upon such grant under the provisions herein-before contained would not afford full compensation for the loss of such reversion, or of any power, benefit, or advantage incident thereto, or exercised or enjoyed by or on behalf of the owner thereof under any local or personal Act of Parliament, charter, settlement, or otherwise, the owner of such reversion may require such loss to be compensated by such an addition in respect thereof to the fee-farm rent to be made payable under such grant, or, at the option of the owner of such reversion, by the payment of such a gross sum of money, (the amount in either case to be ascertained as herein-after mentioned, in case the parties differ about the same,) as will afford a full compensation for such loss, to be estimated according to the difference in marketable value; and where upon a grant made or to be made under this Act to the owner of a lease in perpetuity such addition or payment as aforesaid has been made or may be required to be made, the owner of such lease, or of the estate into which the same has been converted under this Act, upon being required to make a grant under this Act to the owner of an under-lease in perpetuity derived out of such lease, may require an addition to be made to the fee-farm rent to be made payable under such last-mentioned grant, or the payment of a gross sum of money, of the like or a proportionate amount (as the case may require); and in like manner, where upon a grant made or to be made under this Act to the owner of any under-lease in perpetuity an addition to the fee-farm rent payable under such grant, or the payment of a gross sum of money, has been made or may be required to be made under this provision, the owner of such under-lease, or of the estate into which the same has been converted, may require an addition to be made to the fee-farm rent to be made payable on any grant which he may be required to execute to the owner of any inferior under-lease, or the payment of a gross sum of money, of the like or a proportionate amount (as the case may require).

6. Where the owner required to execute such grant as aforesaid and the owner requiring the same shall so agree, a part of the lands comprised in the lease or under-lease by the owner of which such grant is required, and not comprised in any inferior under-lease in perpetuity, may be allocated in fee simple in lieu of the fee-farm rent which would have been made payable by such grant, or of any portion thereof, or such fee-farm rent, or any portion thereof, in lieu of which land is not allocated as aforesaid, may be made payable out of any sufficient part only, to be specified in the grant, of the lands comprised in such lease or under-lease, and the residue of the lands shall be discharged therefrom; and where land is allocated as aforesaid the same shall by the same grant be conveyed or surrendered by the owner of the lease or under-lease to the owner to whom the fee-farm rent in lieu of which or of a portion of which the same is allocated would have been payable.

7. From and after the execution of such grant to the owner of a lease in perpetuity, or to the owner of an under-lease in perpetuity, as aforesaid, such grant shall, where such grant is made to the owner of the lease in perpetuity, bind all persons interested in the reversion and in such lease, and all persons bound by such lease, and such reversion shall be converted into an estate of inheritance in fee simple in the fee-farm rent made payable by such grant, and the conditions, exceptions, and reservations therein contained, and all rights annexed or belonging to such reversion saved by and not commuted under this Act; and such grant shall, where such grant is made to the owner of an under-lease in perpetuity, bind all persons interested in the lease or superior under-lease, or the estate of inheritance granted in respect thereof by the owner of which the grant is made, and in the under-lease to the owner of which the grant is made, and all persons bound by such under-lease; and the estate held under such lease or superior under-lease, or such estate of inheritance as aforesaid, shall be converted into an estate of inheritance in fee simple in the fee-farm rent made payable by such grant, and the conditions, exceptions, and reservations therein contained, and all rights annexed or belonging to the estate by the owner of which such grant is made saved by and not commuted under this Act; and each such estate of inheritance in fee simple as aforesaid shall be transmissible and descendible in like manner as if the same were an estate of inheritance in fee simple in reversion in the lands on which the fee-farm rent is charged by the grant creating the same, having incident thereto the conditions, exceptions, and reservations contained in the same grant, and such rights respectively as aforesaid; and the estate of inheritance created under every such grant as aforesaid in the lands comprised therein, save any part thereof allocated in lieu of a fee-farm rent or any portion thereof, under the provision herein contained, and the estate of inheritance so created as aforesaid in the fee-farm rent made payable by such grant, and in any land so allocated as aforesaid, shall from and after the execution of such grant be respectively vested in the same persons, for the same estates and interests, and be respectively subject to the same uses, trusts, provisoes, agreements, and declarations, and be respectively charged with and subject to the same charges, liens, judgments, incumbrances, and equities, as the estate held under the lease or under-lease in perpetuiuty to the owner of which the grant is made, and the reversion or estate by the owner of which the grant is made, were respectively vested in, subject to, and charged with immediately before their conversion into such respective estates of inheritance as aforesaid was affected, or as near thereto as the different natures of the estates and the circumstances of each case will admit; but all land allocated as aforesaid shall remain subject to all demises and tenancies inferior in tenure to the lease or under-lease by the owner of which such land may have been so allocated.

8. The conversion of any estate under this Act shall not prevent or prejudice the operation of any devise, bequest, or testamentary appointment, made before such conversion, of such estate, or any interest therein, but such device, bequest, or testamentary appointment shall operate upon the estate or interest created or acquired under this Act, as fully and effectually to all intents and purposes whatever, as the same would have operated upon the respective estate or interest previously subsisting if no conversion had taken place.

9. No conversion under this Act of any estate shall operate to give dower or curtesy to the widow or husband of any person becoming entitled under this Act to an estate of inheritance, in any case where the estate converted would not have been liable to dower or curtesy, and such widow or husband was married to such person before such conversion, or to defeat or affect any rights of lords of manors or reputed manors, or of owners of reversions in fee simple, to courts leet or courts

baron, and services at the same, escheats, fairs, markets, franchises, rights, liberties, privileges of chase or free warren, hunting, hawking, fowling, piscaries, fisheries and rights of fishing, or any rights in any mines or minerals, quarries, or royalties, within or under the lands included in any estate converted under this Act, save in so far as the same may be commuted under this Act.

10. All covenants by law implied on the part of landlord or tenant upon any lease or under-lease in perpetuity to the owner of which a grant is made under this Act shall be implied upon such grant, and every covenant for payment of rent, and every other covenant contained in pursuance of this Act in any such grant as aforesaid, in substitution for a like covenant in the lease or under-lease to the owner of which such grant is made, where such last-mentioned covenant is of such a nature as that the burden thereof doth by law run with the land, and bind the assignee of such lease or under-lease, and every covenant implied under this Act upon any such grant, where the burden of the implied covenant for which the same is in substitution was upon the owner of such lease or under-lease, shall run with the estate in fee simple into which the estate held under such lease or under-lease is converted under this Act, and the owner or assignee for the time being of such estate in fee simple shall be chargeable upon such covenants in the same manner and to the same extent as if he were owner or assignee of the term or interest created by such lease or under-lease, and such term or interest, and the estate out of which such lease or under-lease was derived, were still subsisting, and the benefit of such covenants shall run with the estate into which such estate is converted under this Act, and the owner or assignee for the time being of the estate created by such conversion shall have the full benefit of such covenants, and be entitled to maintain actions thereon; and every covenant contained in pursuance of this Act in any such grant as aforesaid, in substitution for a like covenant in such lease or under-lease as aforesaid, where such last-mentioned covenant is of such a nature as that the burden thereof doth by law run with the estate out of which such lease or under-lease was derived, or bind the assignee of such estate, and every covenant implied under this Act upon any such grant, where the burden of the implied covenant for which the same is in substitution was upon the owner of the estate out of which such lease or under-lease was derived, shall run with the estate into which such estate is converted under this Act; and the owner or assignee for the time being of the estate created by such conversion shall be chargeable upon such covenants in the same manner and to the same extent as if he were owner or assignee of such estate so converted, and such estate and lease or under-lease were still subsisting, and the benefit of such covenants shall run with the estate in fee simple into which the estate held under such lease or under-lease is converted under this Act, and the owner or assignee for the time being of such estate in fee simple shall have the full benefit of such covenants, and be entitled to maintain actions thereon.

. . .

20. The fee-farm rent made payable by any grant under this Act, or by any grant made after the passing of this Act, shall be recoverable by distress, ejectment for nonpayment of rent, action of debt, covenant, and all other ways, means, remedies, actions, suits, or otherwise, by which rent-service reserved on any common lease or demise for a life or lives is or may be by law recoverable; and all the enactments relating to ejectment for nonpayment of rent, distress, or other remedies for recovery thereof, shall apply to every such fee-farm rent as aforesaid, as fully and effectually as if the same were rent-service reserved on a lease for a life or lives; and in proceedings by ejectment for nonpayment of such fee-farm rent, under the statutes for the time being in force in Ireland in relation to ejectment for nonpayment of rent made applicable under this Act to such fee-farm rent as

aforesaid, the receipt of such fee-farm rent for three years by the lessor of the plaintiff, or any person or persons through whom he claims, shall have the same force and effect as a similar receipt of rent-service reserved on any lease for life or lives would have in proceedings by ejectment for nonpayment of such rent under such statutes; . . . [Rep., S.L.R. 1892] and in actions of replevin, debt, or covenant, or other proceeding founded on such grant as aforesaid, proof that the said plaintiff or other person, or any person or persons through whom he claims, has or have been in possession or in receipt of such fee-farm rent for three years shall be sufficient evidence of the title of the plaintiff or other person thereto, as in cases of ejectment for nonpayment of rent under the statutes in force in relation thereto; and if in any such action of ejectment as aforesaid judgment be given for the plaintiff, and execution executed, or if any entry be made in respect of such fee-farm rent as aforesaid, or by virtue of any condition for re-entry contained in any such grant as aforesaid, then the estate in the lands acquired under such judgment and execution or by such entry shall be of the like nature, and shall be subject to the same or the like uses, trusts, charges, liens, equities, rights, and incumbrances, as if such judgment and execution or such entry had been in respect of an estate in reversion, and of a rent or of a condition, as the case may be, incident thereto, and such estate in reversion had stood limited to the same uses and trusts, and subject to the same charges, liens, equities, rights, and incumbrances, to which such fee-farm rent stood limited or subject.

21. If in any action of ejectment brought on account of the nonpayment of any fee-farm rent made payable by any such grant as aforesaid, pursuant to the statutes for the time being in force in Ireland as to actions of ejectment for nonpayment of rent, judgment be given for the plaintiff, and execution executed, and the person who has made default in payment of the rent, or the person who but for such ejectment would for the time being have been the party to make the payment from time to time thereafter becoming due, do not, within six calendar months from the time of such execution executed, do such acts or take such proceedings as are or may be by law necessary for the redemption of the lands from the said judgment and execution, (all which acts and proceedings he is hereby authorized to do and take, in the same manner and with the same effect, to all intents and purposes, as if he were the tenant or lessee of the person causing such ejectment to be brought,) then and in every such case it shall be lawful for the owner of or any person having an estate or interest in any fee-farm rent made payable by any such grant as aforesaid out of the whole or any part of such lands, or for the owner of or any person having an estate or interest in the lands out of which such fee-farm rent is payable, or any part thereof, within nine calendar months after such execution executed, to do such acts and take such proceedings for the redemption of the said lands from the said judgment and execution, and for obtaining relief in respect of the same, as under the statutes last aforesaid any mortgagee of a lease might do or take for the redemption of such lease, or his estate or interest therein, from any judgment and execution in any action of ejectment for nonpayment of rent pursuant to such statutes, and for obtaining relief in respect of the same; and any redemption made pursuant to such statutes shall operate so as to restore all estates and interests in rents or in lands which shall have been defeated by the entry or ejectment; and when such redemption as last aforesaid had been made, or when any such redemption has been made under the statutes aforesaid by any mortgagee or any other person, which redemption he is hereby authorized to make, all sums of money paid or advanced on account thereof, and the costs thereof, shall be and be deemed a lien and charge in favour of the person paying the same, his executors or administrators, not only upon the estate or interest of the person making such

default as aforesaid, but upon all the inheritance in which such estate or interest is subsisting, in priority to all other interests or charges whatsoever upon such inheritance, save and except any charges created under the Acts relating to the drainage of lands or to the improvement of lands in Ireland; and such sums of money and costs shall also be recoverable by the person paying the same from the person who has made such default, or his representatives, in and by an action of debt; and all sums of money paid and costs incurred in respect of such lien or charge by any person damnified thereby shall also be recoverable by such person from the person who has made default, or his representatives, in manner aforesaid; and it shall be lawful for any person having the benefit of such lien or charge, or damnified thereby as aforesaid, to apply by petition in a summary way to the Court of Chancery . . . [Rep, S.L.R. 1892] for the appointment of a receiver over such estate, interest, or inheritance, and which receiver it shall be lawful for the said courts respectively to appoint, and to continue until all such sums of money and costs, with interest, and the costs of such petition and of the proceedings thereunder, are fully paid and discharged, and to make such order in reference to such petition as to such courts respectively may seem fit.

. . .

37. Every lease of lands in Ireland for one or more life or lives, with or without a term of years, or for years determinable upon one or more life or lives, or for years absolute, with a covenant or agreement for perpetual renewal, made after the passing of this Act by any person competent to convey an estate of inheritance in fee simple, (and not so made in pursuance of a covenant or agreement entered into before the passing of this Act,) shall, notwithstanding anything therein contained to the contrary, be deemed to be and shall operate as a conveyance of the lands specified therein to the intended lessee, his heirs and assigns for ever, at a fee-farm rent equal to the rent expressed to be reserved in such lease; and all reservation of fine or fines upon or fees for or in respect of such renewal, and all and every covenant, contract, or agreement for the payment of such fine or fees, shall be altogether void; and every contract for such a lease entered into after the passing of this Act by any such person as aforesaid (not being a renewal of a contract in pursuance of an agreement in that behalf made before the passing of this Act) shall, notwithstanding anything therein contained to the contrary, be deemed to be a contract for a conveyance of the lands specified therein to the intended lessee, his heirs and assigns, at a fee-farm rent equal to the rent in such contract proposed to be reserved; and any such fee-farm rent shall be recoverable by all the means and remedies provided for the recovery of fee-farm rents made payable by a grant under this Act, and the provisions of this Act, so far as the same may be applicable, shall be applied to such cases.

. . .

39. In citing this Act in other Acts of Parliament, or in legal instruments or pleadings, it shall be sufficient to use the expression 'The Renewable Leasehold Conversion Act'; and in like manner, in like cases, in describing any fee-farm rent payable under the provisions of this Act, it shall be sufficient to use the expression 'fee-farm rent under the Renewable Leasehold Conversion Act.'

40. This Act shall extend only to lands situated within Ireland.

Note

For detailed discussion of the 1849 Act, see *Irish Land Law*, para. 4.081 *et seq.*

LANDLORD AND TENANT (AMENDMENT) ACT, 1980

74. – A person entitled to an interest in land the title to which interest originated under a lease for lives renewable forever which was created prior to the 1st day of August, 1849, and was not converted into a fee farm grant under the Renewable Leasehold Conversion Act, 1849, shall from the commencement of this Act hold the land for an estate in fee simple. The said estate shall be deemed to be a graft upon the previous interest and shall be subject to any rights or equities arising from its being such graft.

Notes and Questions
1. See *Irish Land Law*, Supp. (1975–80), pp. 18–19.
2. What is the purpose of this section? Does it operate in respect of pre-1849 leases like section 37 of the 1849 Act operated in respect of post-1849 leases?
3. As regards the doctrine of graft, see *Irish Land Law*, paras 9.063–7.

TENANTRY ACT (IRELAND), 1779
An Act for the relief of tenants holding under leases for lives containing covenants for perpetual renewals.

Whereas great parts of the lands in this kingdom are held under leases for lives with covenants for perpetual renewals upon payment of certain fines at the times therein respectively mentioned for each renewal: and whereas from various accidents and causes such tenants, and those deriving under them, have frequently neglected to pay or tender such fines within the times prescribed by such covenants after the fall of such lives respectively: and whereas many such leases are settled to make provision for families and creditors, most of whom must be utterly ruined, if advantage shall be taken of such neglects, which will occasion much confusion and distress in the kingdom: and whereas it has been for a long time a received opinion in this kingdom, to which some decisions in courts of equity and declarations of judges have given countenance, that courts of equity would in such cases relieve against the lapse of time upon giving an adequate compensation to the persons, to whom such fines were payable, or their representatives: and to the end that such interests may not be defeated by a mere neglect, where no fraud appears to have been intended, upon making full satisfaction to the lessors, or those deriving under them;

I. Courts of equity upon an adequate compensation being made shall relieve such tenants and their assigns against such lapse of time, if no circumstance of fraud be proved against such tenants or their assigns; unless it shall be proved to the satisfaction of such courts, that the landlords or lessors, or persons entitled to receive such fines, had demanded such fines from such tenants or their assigns, and that the same had been refused or neglected to be paid within a reasonable time after such demand.

II. Provided always, that in case the landlord shall find any difficulty in discovering his tenant or the assignee of such tenant, so as to make a demand on such tenant or assignee, that then and in every such case a demand made of the said fine on the lands from the principal occupier of the same together with a notice of such demand, to be inserted for the space of two months in the London and Dublin Gazettes [*Iris Oifigiúil*], shall be considered to all intents and purposes a demand within this act.

RE McDERMOTT'S ESTATE
[1921] 1 I.R. 114 (Court of Appeal)
The last renewal of a life under a lease for lives renewable forever (dated July 1707) was made in 1872 and the *cestuis que vie* named therein died or were presumed to have died 69, 43 and 32 years before respectively. It was admitted that £105 was owing for fines accrued due.

No renewal was made nor were any fines paid or demanded up to 1917. The current lessee claimed that the lessor was not entitled to interest on the fines for the full period. Ross J. allowed 6 years' arrears of interest only in respect of each renewal fine, see [1920] 1 I.R. 257. The lessor appealed to the Court of Appeal.

Sir James Campbell C.:

We are all agreed that the words of this statute are too strong to enable the limited construction adopted by Ross J. to be placed upon the words 'adequate compensation.' Had the clause merely provided that the lessee should be entitled to relief on payment of adequate compensation, it might well have been held that it was left to the discretion of the Judge in each case, having regard to the circumstances and facts, to arrive at the true measure of such compensation. It is impossible, however, to leave out of consideration the previous words of the preamble, on which Mr. Brown has properly laid stress, – 'and to the end that such interests' – that is, the interests of the tenants – 'may not be defeated by a mere neglect, where no fraud appears to have been intended, *upon making full satisfaction* to the lessors.' In view of these words, we are driven to the conclusion that the words 'adequate compensation' in the enacting portion of the clause are equivalent to the foregoing words, 'full satisfaction,' and that the limited construction put upon these words by Ross J. cannot be upheld. This construction is in accordance with what appears to have been the unbroken course of procedure and authority during a lengthy period of years; and, in the absence of any authority to the contrary, we are bound to give full effect to what we consider to be the true meaning of the words 'adequate compensation.' The appeal will accordingly be allowed.

Ronan and **O'Connor L.JJ.** concurred.

Note

See also the litigation involved in *Hussey* v. *Domvile* [1900] I.R. 417; *Hussey* v. *Domvile (No. 2)* [1903] 1 I.R. 265. And see *Irish Land Law*, para. 4.171 *et seq.*

VI. LEASE FOR LIVES COMBINED WITH A TERM OF YEARS

DUCKETT V. KEENE
[1903] 1 I.R. 409; 2 N.I.J.R. 226; 36 I.L.T.R. 111 (Court of Appeal)

A lease made the 23rd day of August, 1821, demised certain lands from the 25th day of March last for and during the life and lives of A B and C and the survivors and survivor of them, 'and for and during the full end and term of ninety-nine years from thence next ensuing'. In an action for, *inter alia*, a declaration that on the true construction of the lease the terms were concurrent the Master of the Rolls held that the term of years was reversionary, i.e., it did not commence until after expiration of the lease for lives. An appeal was made to the Court of Appeal.

Fitz Gibbon L.J.:

We have to deal with a lease – an executed instrument – and not with an agreement; it must be construed according to its words; and no help to ascertain its legal effect can be obtained from the conduct of the parties, though it affords us the consolation of knowing that what we regard as the legal meaning of the deed was put upon it by those who held under it.

This assurance was executed in 1821, when conveyancing was more technical than it is now; it refers to the statute for transferring uses into possession, and it operated by way of lease and re-lease in so far as it created an estate of freehold, and as a demise in so far as it created a term.

The *habendum* is unto Thomas Palmer, his heirs, executors, administrators and assigns, words applicable to both freehold and chattel. The demise runs 'from the 25th day of March last.' These words have no effect upon the duration of the freehold, because it came into existence on the execution of the lease, and its termination must coincide with the fall of the last life. The rent was to be computed 'from the 25th day of March last.' For how long was it to run? 'For and during the natural life and lives of George Palmer, Thomas Palmer, and Isaac Palmer, and the survivors and survivor of them, *and* for and during the full end and term of ninety-nine years.' The respondents rely on this word '*and*' as the advantage of fixing the time when the tenure would end. The law and authorities are practically Irish: Davidson's Precedents do not contain a lease in either form, though they include a lease for ninety-nine years determinable on the fall of three lives – a tenure almost unknown here. The inconveniences of a demise for three lives with a long reversionary term are very great, and there is no corresponding advantage; special provisions have been made by statute to meet the difficulty of proving the deaths of *cestuis que vie*; but this difficulty would be immensely increased if the proof did not become necessary, or ever producible, until ninety-nine years after the dropping of the last life.

The earliest case (1770) is *Lord Netterville* v. *Marshall* (Wallis, by Lyne, p. 80). It is not a decision on the point before us, and it is cited for an observation of Lord Lifford. The question was, whether an agreement for a lease for three lives or thirty-one years, *whichever should longest last*, could be executed under a power to make leases for three lives *or* thirty-one years in possession. The Lord Chancellor, who differed from Lord Annaly, thought that, as it was an agreement for a lease (not as here an executed lease) the intention of the parties should prevail, and that they intended to give and accept a term for three lives at all events. He adds:

> 'If the word 'or' in the *habendum* be changed for the word 'and,' there will be a perfect term of years concurrent with the freehold term, and such constructions were frequently made.'

With all respect, the proposed change would be wrong, because 'three lives *and* thirty-one years, whichever should longest last,' would be bad English, and the observation is material only to show that terms of lives and years concurrent are frequent.

Jones v. *Duggan* (4 Ir. L.R. 86) also arose upon articles of agreement for a lease for lives and years to commence *in futuro*, which was void as to the freehold. Its importance lies in the explanation by Burton, J. of the legal operation of such a demise. He incidentally shows that the concurrent interpretation is the primary one, and he also shows that '*and*' is appropriate, because the term of years, though concurrent, is additional:

> 'With respect to the intention of the parties, it is perfectly clear that the intention was to give the tenant a lease for three lives and for the lives and life of the survivors and survivor, and a *concurrent* term for thirty-one years; the operation of which expressed properly would be a freehold lease for three lives, with a contingent remainder of thirty-one years, to commence upon the 25th March next following the date of the instrument, but the years not to be in legal existence until the determination of the lives. Now it is quite true that this intention fails, by the grant for lives being to commence at a future time, and this makes the contract, so far as respects the lives executory, but that does not

make it executory as respects the term of thirty-one years. The entire intention of the parties would be substantially effected by this construction; namely, that the lessee should have a freehold lease for the lives named, and a chattel interest from the 25th March then next after the execution of the instrument, and the term is not thereby merged, but merely suspended while the freehold interests subsists.'

Blackhall v. *Nugent* (5 Ir. Ch. Rep. 323), decided by Brady C. in 1855, was a suit for specific performance of an agreement by Sir Peter Nugent to give 'a lease for three lives *and* sixty-one years,' the lessee to commence his tenancy at the expiration of an existing lease, and paying a large fine at the date of the agreement. No lease was executed, and the existing lease did not expire in the lifetime of Sir Peter Nugent. After his death his devisees for life carried out his agreement by making a lease for three lives with a reversionary term of sixty-one years. After their deaths the remainderman sought to impeach the lease, as not being within the terms of the agreement. Brady C. decided the case on the intention of the parties; he acted on evidence, such as the fine, not admissible for the interpretation of an executed deed, and he said that, even upon an agreement, specific performance might have been difficult if Sir P. Nugent was before the Court, and insisted that he had been misled by the form of expression used. He treated the acts of the tenants for life in granting a lease and acting on the petitioner's construction, as evidence that they considered themselves bound by the words to grant the larger estate, and he held that there was nothing to deprive the words of what he held to be 'their natural meaning.'

We have much stronger evidence here, if it were admissible, that every one acting or holding under this lease treated the term as concurrent; the sub-leases were all kept within the period which a concurrent term would allow. Brady C. did not lay down that the words *necessarily* imported a reversionary term in *Nugent's Case* (5 Ir. Ch. Rep. 323), for he says:

'It is true that the case of *Vignolles* v. *Bowen* (12 Ir. Eq. Rep. 194) shows that a concurrent term of years may be taken as satisfying the construction of words like these. A lease for lives with a concurrent term, however, is not, properly speaking, in contemplation of law a lease for lives and years, as it does not confer on the same person the freehold and chattel interest.'

This is not so, if Burton J. is right; nor unless we add the qualification '*at the same time.*'

Vignolles v. *Bowen* (12 Ir. Eq. Rep. 194) was decided in 1847 by Smith M.R., who held that the description of a lease as being for three lives and thirty-one years, when in fact it was a lease for three lives and only so much of the thirty-one years as might be in existence after the death of the survivor, was not such a misdescription as entitled a purchaser to be discharged. He did not dispose of the case on the evidence of misleading, but on the construction of the rental. He said:

'Leases for three lives and thirty-one years concurrent are common in this country, and the legal operation of such leases is that the lessee holds for the three lives and for so many of the years, if any, as shall be unexpired at the death of the surviving life. Lord Tenterden adverts to such leases in *Long* v. *Rankin*, reported in the Appendix to Sugden on Powers (2 Sug. on Powers App., p., 513); and I do not think that I am to construe the rental as describing the thirty-one years to be a term to take effect for that period at the death of the surviving life, so as to raise a question of misdescription.'

The importance of that case here is the decision that there was nothing to warrant a purchaser in assuming that a lease for lives *and* years is for consecutive and not concurrent terms.

Lastly, we have *O'Connor and Small's Contract* (33 I.L.T.R. 43), decided in 1898 by the Master of the Rolls on a vendor and purchaser summons in respect of a sale of part of the lands comprised in this very lease, and held under a sub-lease containing the same terms. The Master of the Rolls said:

> '*If you put aside the word 'thence,'* everything points to a reversionary term, and the word itself, though *strictly referable* to the date mentioned at the beginning of the *habendum*, may very well be referred to the death of the last of the three lives, the idea of which you can easily see was present to the mind of the draftsman, though *the language used does not give actual expression to it.*'

It is to be regretted that the question first arose in a summary way, and that the Master of the Rolls, when it was more fully discussed, was practically bound by his previous decision. But I cannot think that we are at liberty to 'put aside the word "thence," ' nor to apply it to any date except that to which it is 'strictly referable,' nor can I see that any idea was present to the mind of the draftsman to which the language used did not give actual expression, and, for the reasons which I have given, the language of this deed is, in my opinion, best satisfied by holding that the term of years ran from the 25th March, 1821, and was therefore concurrent with the lives.

Walker L.J.: I concur.

Holmes L.J.:

There is a manifest fallacy in the argument addressed to us on behalf of the defendant. It is assumed that if the term of lives and the term of years are concurrent no force is given to the word 'and.' Now whether the terms are concurrent or the term of years begins when the last surviving life falls the proper connecting word is 'and'; and 'or' would be ungrammatical and inaccurate. In neither case would the terms be alternative. In both cases the terms would be cumulative. The sole question is at what date does the term of years begin to run. I am unable to refer the words 'thence ensuing' to any period except the only date specifically named – the 25th day of the previous March.

Note

See further, *Irish Land Law*, paras 4.117–8.

ADAMS V. McGOLDRICK
[1927] N.I. 127 (High Court)

A sub-lease made on the 27th April, 1869, demised certain lands from its date for the life of the surviving *cestui qui vie* named in the head lease of the 1st April, 1812, 'and for and during the term of 61 years.' On a sale of the land a requisition on title was raised to the effect that the term of years was concurrent and not reversionary. A vendor and purchaser summons was brought to determine the point.

Wilson J.:

This is an application by the purchaser Adams for a declaration that his objections to the title of the vendor under the above contract have not been sufficiently answered, and that a good title to the vendor's interest in the premises under the said contract has not been shown and for a return of the deposit and other relief.

The vendor's interest was as lessee under a sub-lease dated the 27th day of August, 1869, from Henry Joy McCracken to Arthur Lester for the life of William

McCormick (since deceased) and for and during the term of sixty-one years. The head lease under which Henry Joy McCracken held was dated the 1st day of April, 1812, and was for three lives and the life of the survivor of them (William McCormick) and for and during the term, time and space of sixty-one years. The Harrison estate is the head landlord. It is apparent that the above words are capable of meaning for three lives and the life of the survivor and sixty-one years concurrent, or sixty-one years in addition to the three lives. Many cases have been decided on similar words in other cases, and reasons given for coming to directly opposite conclusions. I am not convinced that the reasons given by the learned judges for their decisions are sound or conclusive. Having read these conflicting cases the reasoning seems to me like trying to find some good foundation for a conclusion already held. In this case the last of the lives in the head lease, viz., William McCormick, died on the 27th February, 1895. The head landlord then brought an ejectment to recover possession of these premises against Henry Joy McCracken, the lessee, and his sub-tenants, on the ground that the term had expired as all the lives were dead and the term of sixty-one years, if counted from the 1st day of April, 1812, the date of the head lease, had expired on the 31st day of March, 1873. The case was heard by Palles C.B. on appeal from the County Court Judge of Down on the 13th day of July, 1896, at the Summer Assizes. He affirmed the dismiss with costs and it is sworn before me that he held that the term of sixty-one years clearly ran from the death of the last life on the 27th day of February, 1895. The head lessee has ever since held the premises under the terms of the lease of the 1st day of April, 1812, and the head landlord has ever since adopted that position and received the rent reserved by the head lease. It is now certain that the head lessee whose interest the vendor has, is entitled to hold these premises till the 27th day of February, 1956, against the head landlord on paying the rent and performing the covenants in the head lease and he has the interest under the words of the *habendum* in the head lease. Henry Joy McCracken, having that interest in the premises, made the sub-lease to Lester the vendor's predecessor on the 27th day of August, 1869, to hold from the 27th day of August, 1869, for the life of William McCormick and for and during the term of sixty-one years. Mr. Adams now says that the meaning of these words is for the life of William McCormick and sixty-one years from the 1st day of April, 1812. It would have to mean on his contention, for the life of William McCormick and sixty-one years from the 27th day of August, 1869. There is only one mention of the head lease in the *habendum* of the sub-lease, viz., when it described William McCormick as 'the surviving *cestui qui vie* in the original lease of the 1st day of April 1812.' It seems to me that in this sub-lease the sixty-one years must commence on the death of William McCormick, or the 27th day of August, 1869. I have no difficulty in holding that, as it has been judicially determined in relation to this very property the original term of sixty-one years ran from the death of the surviving *cestui qui vie*, and not from the date of the head lease, so it would be a refusal of justice to do otherwise than determine between the head lessee and his sub-lessee and between that sub-lessee, the vendor, and his purchaser Adams, that the sixty-one years mentioned in the sub-lease of the 27th day of August, 1869, run from the death of the surviving *cestui qui vie*, William McCormick.

In my opinion in considering the construction of this lease, it should be borne in mind that the landlord prepared these leases and they should be construed as strongly as possible against him, and in case of doubt the construction most favourable to the tenant should be adopted. For these reasons, without considering critically the previous cases, I am of opinion that a good title to the vendor's interest in this leasehold has been established. I accordingly refuse the plaintiff's application and order him to pay the vendor's taxed costs.

Chapter 4
FUTURE INTERESTS

This is, perhaps, the most difficult of all areas of land law to master and the task is made no easier in the Republic of Ireland where so many of the old and complicated rules survive unchecked by modern legislation: see *Irish Land Law*, ch. 5.

I. CLASSIFICATION

It is crucial when considering the validity of a future interest to determine first the nature of the interest: e.g., is it a contingent remainder subject to common law rules, or a springing or shifting use subject to equitable principles, or a legal executory interest operating under the Statute of Uses or caught by the rule in *Purefoy* v. *Rogers*. Then there is the possible application of the various rules against remoteness to be considered.

REAL PROPERTY ACT, 1845

6. After the first day of October one thousand eight hundred and forty-five a contingent, an executory, and a future interest and a possibility coupled with an interest, in any tenements or hereditaments of any tenure whether the object of the gift or limitation of such interest or possibility be or be not ascertained . . . may be disposed of by deed; but no such disposition shall by force only of this Act defeat or enlarge an estate tail; and every such disposition by a married woman shall be made conformably to the provisions relative to dispositions by married women . . . in Ireland of the Fines and Recoveries (Ireland) Act, 1834.

8. A contingent remainder existing at any time after the thirty-first day of December one thousand eight hundred and forty-four shall be, and, if created before the passing of this Act, shall be deemed to have been, capable of taking effect, notwithstanding the determination, by forfeiture, surrender, or merger, of any preceding estate of freehold, in the same manner in all respects as if such determination had not happened.

Note
As regards disposition by will, see now section 76 of the Succession Act, 1965: 'A person may by his will, executed in accordance with this Act, dispose of all property which he is beneficially entitled to at the time of his death and which on his death devolves on his personal representatives.'

CONTINGENT REMAINDERS ACT, 1877

1. Every contingent remainder . . . which would have been valid as a springing or shifting use or executory devise or other limitation had it not had a sufficient estate to support it as a contingent remainder, shall, in the event of the particular estate determining before the contingent remainder vests, be capable of taking effect in all respects as if the contingent remainder had originally been created as a springing or shifting use or executory devise or other executory limitation.

RE MURPHY'S ESTATE
[1964] I.R. 308 (High Court)

M.M. made his will in 1935. He devised his freehold farm in trust for his wife for her life and after her death in trust 'for my son' S. 'absolutely provided he has attained the age of twenty-five and in the event of my said son' S. 'predeceasing my said wife or dying before reaching the said age of twenty-five years then in trust for my son' M. 'provided he attains the said age of twenty-five years.' The will contained a residuary clause. M.M. died on the 10th April, 1935; his widow died on the 1st November, 1937. S. attained twenty-five years on the 13th May, 1956. Questions arose on the construction of the said will 1, as to whether S. took a vested estate on the death of the testator's widow on the 1st November, 1937, or on his attaining twenty-five on the 13th May, 1956, and 2, as to the destination of the income arising from the farm between the said dates.

Kenny J.:

Michael Murphy, of Geoghanstown, County Kildare, a farmer, made his will on the 10th April, 1935. He appointed the defendants, Patrick Murphy and James J. Byrne, to be his executors and trustees and then provided:

'I leave my holding at Geoghanstown aforesaid to my said trustees in trust for my wife for life or until such time as she may remarry and after her death or on her remarriage in trust for my son Sean absolutely provided he has attained the age of twenty-five and in the event of my said son Sean predeceasing my said wife or dying before reaching the said age of twenty-five years then in trust for my son Michael provided he attains the said age of twenty-five years. I charge the said lands with the payment to each of my sons Michael and Brendan of the sum of £300 said sums to be paid to them at such times as my said executors may in their absolute discretion deem fit. In the event of the said lands passing to my said son Michael then I charge same with the payment of the sum of £600 to my said son Brendan to be paid by my executors in manner aforesaid and in which event the said charge of £300 in favour of my said son Michael is to be determined. I also charge the said lands with the payment of the debt due by me to the Munster and Leinster Bank. All the rest residue and remainder of my property of every nature and description I leave to my said trustees to apply the income or proceeds thereof in paying the outgoings of said lands and the support and maintenance of my wife and children and the education as befits their station in life of my said children and for the purposes aforesaid it is my will that my said trustees consult my wife's wishes especially in respect to my children over whom I appoint her sole guardian.'

When this will was made, the testator had three sons, Sean, who was almost four, Michael, who was two and a half, and Brendan, who was one. The testator, who died on the 10th April, 1935, owned a farm which was registered under the Registration of Title Acts on Folio 5798R of the Register of Freeholders, County Kildare: it was valued for estate duty purposes at £1,850. The only other property which he had was livestock valued at £400.

The testator's widow, Frances Murphy, died on the 1st November, 1937, without having remarried and Sean Murphy, his eldest son, attained the age of 25 years on the 13th May, 1956. The two sums of £300 mentioned in the will have been paid to Michael and Brendan Murphy. On the 30th October, 1961, an order for the administration of the estate of Michael Murphy was made and accounts and inquiries for this purpose were ordered. Before these can be taken, it is necessary to decide whether Sean Murphy had a vested or contingent estate in the lands at Geoghanstown between the 1st November, 1937, and the 13th May, 1956, and whether he was entitled to all the income of the lands between those two dates.

If I were not handicapped by three decisions of the House of Lords given before 1921 (and therefore binding on me) and by the rule of construction which they establish, I would unhesitatingly decide that Sean Murphy had no interest in the lands at Geoghanstown until he attained twenty-five and that the income of the lands until then passed under the residuary clause in the will. It has, however, been argued that the rule of construction, usually referred to as the rule in *Edwards* v.

Hammond [(1683) 3 Lev. 122] and sometimes referred to as the rule in *Phipps* v. *Ackers* (9 Cl. & F. 583), compels me to hold that under the will Sean Murphy got a vested interest in the lands and, that on the death of his mother in 1937, this interest vested in possession but was liable to be divested if he died before he reached the age of twenty-five. The result of the application of this rule would be that the words 'in trust for my son Sean absolutely provided he has attained the age of twenty-five,' created a condition subsequent and not a condition precedent. In Hawkins on Wills (3rd ed., 1925), at p. 286 the rule is stated in these terms: – 'If real estate be devised to A. 'if' or 'when', he shall attain a given age, the attainment of the given age is held to be a condition subsequent and not precedent, and A. takes an immediate vested estate, subject to be divested upon his death under the specified age.' The rule has been held to apply when the condition attached to the devise or gift began with the word 'provided': see *Simmonds* v. *Cock* (29 Beav. 455).

The reason given to support this remarkable rule is that when property is given to a person when he attains a specified age and is then given over if he dies under that age, he takes all that the testator had to give except what is comprised in the gift over as any other construction would cause an intestacy. To give effect to the view that the testator must have intended to dispose of all his interest, the words of condition were treated as creating a condition subsequent so that the estate became vested before the specified age had been reached and was liable to be divested by death before the age was reached. The reasoning on which the rule was based is plainly fallacious when there is a residuary clause as it is then probable that the testator intended that the income of the property devised on condition should form part of the residuary estate until the attainment of the specified age. The rule did not have its origin in the reasoning which was subsequently developed in its defence but in the common law doctrine that the seisin and legal estate in freehold lands had to have an owner so that the subsequent estate which was contingent would not be destroyed by not having a particular estate to support it. The rule made its first appearance in *Edwards* v. *Hammond* [(1683) 3 Lev. 132], in which a copyholder surrendered lands to the use of himself for life and then to the use of his eldest son and his heirs if he lived to the age of 21 years provided, and upon condition, that if he dies before 21 it should remain to the person making the surrender and his heirs. The lands were held under the tenure known as Borough English in which lands descended to the youngest son on an intestacy and when the surrenderer died the youngest son entered: the eldest son who was seventeen then brought an eject-ment. The Court held that though the first words seemed to create a condition precedent, yet, taking all the words together, they were a present devise to the eldest son subject to and defeasible on the condition subsequent that he did not attain the age of 21. Another report of the case appears in a note, at p. 324, of 1 Bos. and P.N.R.

The rule was approved by all the judges of the Court of Common Pleas in *Bromfield* v. *Crowder* [(1805) 1 Bos. and P.N.R. 313] in which the Master of the Rolls referred the construction of the will to the Court of Common Pleas for the advice of the judges of that Court, presumably because the devise was of freehold and copyhold lands. The existence of the rule was recognised by the House of Lords in *Randall* v. *Doe d. Roake* [(1817) 5 Dow 202] and in *Phipps* v. *Ackers* (9 Cl. & F. 583) it was held to apply to equitable interests. In the latter case the opinions in the House of Lords were given after the advice of eleven Common Law judges had been heard. In *Phipps* v. *Ackers* (9 Cl. & F. 582) the testator left his lands (other than the lands of Wheelock) to his trustees upon certain trusts: in relation to the lands of Wheelock the will provided: '. . . my trustees shall stand seised and be possessed thereof in trust and to the intent and purpose to assign, convey and assure the same unto my godson, George H. Ackers . . . when and so soon as he, my said godson, shall attain his age of 21 years . . . But in case my said godson, G. H. Ackers, shall depart this life before he attains the said age of 21 years without leaving issue of his body, lawfully to be begotten, then and in such case the said messuages, lands and premises in Wheelock aforesaid, hereinbefore given and devised to him . . . shall sink into and become part of the residue of my real and personal estate, and go according to the disposition thereof hereinafter expressed and contained,' and the residue of the real and personal estate was then given to James Coops. At the date of the death of the testator, George H. Ackers was 12 years old: he subsequently attained the age of 21. The opinion of the Judges was sought on the question as to what estate George H. Ackers took in the lands at Wheelock. The Judges advised that the earlier cases went on the principle 'that the subsequent gift over in the event of the devisee dying under 21, sufficiently shows the meaning of the testator to have been that the first devisee should take whatever interest the party claiming under the devise over is not entitled to, which of course gives him the immediate interest, subject only to the chance of its being divested on a future contingency.' They stated that the question whether the doctrine on which the cases rested was originally altogether satisfactory was a point which they had not to discuss as the rule of construction had been established and recognised as settled in all the Courts. The Lord Chancellor (Lord Lyndhurst) said that he agreed with the advice of the Judges and that the only question that remained to be considered was whether a different construction should be put on the will as it was dealing with an equitable estate: he said that he was of opinion that the same construction should be put upon the words when used in connection with an equitable estate as those which the rule requires to be put upon them when they were used in connection with a legal estate. Lord Brougham, who did not like the rule, did not wish to extend it to equitable interests but said that the authorities required him to hold that it applied to them.

The existence of the rule was again recognised and affirmed by the House of Lords in *Pearks* v. *Moseley* (5 App. Cas. 714).

The rule has been recognised and applied in many modern cases: it has been extended to personal estate (see *In re Heath. Public Trustee* v. *Heath* ([1936] 1 Ch. 259)) and was discussed by Black L.J. in the High Court in Northern Ireland in *McGredy* v. *Inland Revenue Commissioners* ([1951] N.I. 155). The judgment of the Lord Justice contains the following passages (at p. 161): 'The rule,' [the rule in *Edwards* v. *Hammond*] 'though so firmly settled and repeated in almost identical terms in all the text books, can hardly fail to strike one as a somewhat artificial and technical rule, involving, to use Lord Selborne's words, a rather violent and unnatural construction of words of contingency. The justification of the rule put forward in the authorities is the doctrine . . . that from the existence of the devise over the courts discover an intention that the first devisee shall take all that the testator has to give except what he has given to the devisee over, an intestacy in the meantime not being intended, and that in order to give effect to that intention they hold, by force of the language of the will, that the first devise is not contingent but vested, subject to be divested upon the happening of the event upon which the property is given over. To some minds this reasoning may not appear entirely convincing . . . . But whatever doubts one may have about the soundness of the reasoning on which the rule has been sought to be justified, there can be no doubt that the rule itself, as now enunciated in all the text books, must, for good or for evil, be accepted as a settled rule of construction binding on our coursts'

I think it undesirable that I should be forced by any rule of construction to give a meaning to a will which I am convinced the testator and his legal advisers did not intend. While rules of construction are of assistance when the words used are ambiguous, I cannot see why a rule of construction should be recognised by our Courts when it fixes on the language used by Mr. Murphy a meaning which it may have had in 1683 in England but which it certainly had not in Ireland in 1935. The history of the rule shows that it was imposed on the Chancery Courts by the Common Law judges. However, despite my objection to it, I feel that the three decisions of the House of Lords compel me to recognise its existence as a rule of construction.

In my opinion, however, the rule does not apply to the will of Michael Murphy. The basis of the rule is that the first devisee is to take all that the testator had to give except what has been given to the person entitled under the gift over; if, however, there is a condition or words of contingency attached to the gift over, the whole basis of the rule disappears for there is not then any intention of the testator to dispose of all his interest in the property by the first contingent gift and the absolute gift over. This conclusion is stronger when there is a residuary clause, for then the testator has disposed of all his interest in the property by the combined effect of the first gift, the conditional gift over and the residuary clause. In this case the gift over which was expressed to take effect in the event of Sean Murphy predeceasing the testator's wife or dying before reaching the age of 25 years was 'in trust for my son Michael provided he attains the said age of twenty-five years.' The gift is conditional and there is therefore no basis for applying the rule of construction and I can give the words their natural meaning.

The questions which have arisen on the taking of the accounts are referred to in the affidavit of the plaintiff, sworn on the 3rd May, 1962. The answers to the questions will be:

1. The farm of Geoghanstown passed to Sean Murphy absolutely on the 13th May, 1956, when he attained the age of twenty-five.

2. The income from the said farm between the 1st November, 1937, when Frances Murphy died, and the 13th May, 1956, was held by the trustees on the trusts declared by the residuary clause in the said will.

I express no opinion on the question whether the plaintiff is entitled to any share of the income captured by the residuary clause as this matter has not been argued.

Notes and Questions
1. Do you agree with Kenny J.'s criticism of the rule in *Phipps* v. *Ackers*? Do you think he should have felt bound to apply it?
2. See further *Irish Land Law*, para. 5.010.

COLE V. SEWELL
(1848) 2 H.L.C. 186 (House of Lords)

Lands, held in fee simple, were, by settlement made in 1752, conveyed to trustees, to the use of the settler for life; remainder to the use of his three daughters for their lives, as tenants in common; remainder to the use of trustees to preserve; remainder, as to the share of each daughter, to the use of her first and other sons successively in tail male; remainder, in case of the death of any one or more of the daughters without issue male, to the use of the survivors or survivor, during their or her respective lives or life, as tenants in common in case of two survivors, with remainder, in like manner as to the original share, to the use of the first and other sons of such surviving daughters or daughter in tail male; remainder, in case all the daughters should die without issue male, as to the share of each, to the use of their daughters as tenants in common in tail; and in case one or two of the settlor's daughters should die *without issue*, the share or shares of such daughter or daughters, to go to the use of the daughters of the survivors or survivor, as tenants in common in tail general; and in case all three should die without issue, then remainder over, with ultimate remainder to the use of the settlor in fee. He died soon after without disposing of the reversion.

One only of the settlor's daughters had issue, four daughters and no son; L.E.S., one of the four, in 1779, while her sisters, mother, and aunts were living, executed a post-nuptial settlement, which recited the said deed of 1752 – and another of 1749, under which she was entitled to a vested estate tail in lands called the B. estate, on the death of her father – and that she was entitled in remainder or reversion, expectant and to take effect in possession on the determination of certain prior estates, to several parts of lands in the deed of 1752 mentioned. It also recited a post-nuptial settlement of 1776, in which were recited L.E.S.'s title to certain shares in remainder or reversion expectant, etc., and her desire to limit and assure the same, and that it was thereby witnessed, that in order to bar the estates in remainder or reversion expectant and to take effect in possession as aforesaid, *then vested in her*, but without prejudice to the prior estates, she and her husband covenanted to levy fines of her said undivided shares in remainder, to enure to these uses, namely, that the trustee should, out of the hereditaments comprised in the deeds of 1749 and 1752, *first falling into possession*, take an annuity of £300, and out of those *next falling into possession*, a similar annuity, both being for L.E.S.'s separate use, and, subject thereto, to the use of her husband for life, remainder to herself in fee. It further recited that no fines were levied under the deed of 1776, and that L.E.S. was desirous of securing payment of certain debts, and, subject thereto, of settling the said remainders and reversions expectant and to take effect as aforesaid, for the benefit of her two children, and had agreed to settle the same, and all her right and interest in the premises, to the uses thereinafter mentioned; and it was, by the deed of 1779, witnessed that, in order to bar the estate tail in remainder or reversion expectant upon and to take effect as aforesaid, *then vested* in L.E.S. in the hereditaments comprised in the deeds of 1749 and 1752, without prejudice to the prior estates, the said L.E.S. and her husband covenanted to levy fines of all her undivided shares in remainder or reversion expectant, and to take effect as aforesaid in the said hereditaments, to enure to trustees for 1000 years, to raise the amount of the aforesaid debts; remainder to other trustees for 2000 years to raise an annuity of £100 out of the lands *first falling* into possession, and a similar annuity out of those *next falling* into possession for maintenance of her only son; remainder to trustees for 3000 years, to raise £3000 for her only daughter; remainder to the use of the son and his issue, in strict settlement; remainder to the use of the daughter and her daughters in tail.

The settlor's three daughters died – one in 1784, *s.p.*, another, the mother of L.E.S., in 1793, the third, in 1799, *s.p.* – all intestate and without having disposed of the reversion vested in them by descent. One of L.E.S.'s sisters died in 1788, intestate and without issue. In 1809, one-third of the lands comprised in the deed of 1752 was, on partition, allotted to L.E.S., and by a decree for sale made in 1820, in a suit instituted against her by the trustees of the term of 1000 years comprised in the deed of 1779, it was declared that the whole of the one-third so allotted was subject to the trusts of the term, and bound by that deed, and the fines levied in pursuance thereof. By a deed executed in 1825, it was witnessed that for barring all estates tail therein mentioned, and settling the lands therein comprised, L.E.S. and her husband and a trustee of the deed of 1779, conveyed all the said one-third part, so allotted in severally to L.E.S. as aforesaid, and also her undivided third part of the B. estate (which had then by the death of her father come into possesion) to a trustee, that recoveries might be suffered of the said lands, and it was covenanted that they should enure, as to such of the said undivided parts as were comprised in the deed of 1779, to the uses therein mentioned, and in confirmation thereof and of the terms of 1000 years; and – after reciting that three specified denominations of lands of which L.E.S. was stated to be seised in tail in remainder, at the date of the deed of 1779, were not comprised therein or in the fines levied in pursuance thereof, and reciting the said suit and decree for sale therein made, and that L.E.S. had agreed to make the said denominations subject to the said term – it was further agreed and declared that the said recoveries should enure to confirm the sale of the said three denominations for the said term, and to give validity to the said decree, and, subject to the said term, to such uses as L.E.S. should appoint, and, as to the lands comprised in the deed of 1779, to such further uses as had not been thereby declared concerning the same, as L.E.S. should by deed or will appoint.

By her will L.E.S. devised all her real estate in fee to her grandson F.S.C. who filed a bill in Chancery in Ireland claiming under the devise part of L.E.S.'s share allotted to her on partition of the land. Sugden L.C., after sending a case for and receiving the opinion of the judges of the Court of Common Pleas [see (1842) 5 Ir. L.R. 190], dismissed the bill, see (1843) 4 Dr. & War. 1; 2 Con. & L. 344 ; 6 Ir. Eq. R. 66. F.S.C. appealed to the House of Lords.

Lord Cottenham L.C.:

In this case the first question is, whether the gift over upon failure of issue of the daughters is too remote.

On the 5th of February, 1752, Peter Daly settled estates upon his three daughters for life, as tenants in common, with remainder to their first and other sons in tail male, respectively; if there were no such heir male to any, then life estates in those shares were given to the survivors, with remainder to their first and other sons in tail male; if all died without issue male, the estates were given to the daughters respectively, as tenants in common in tail general; if any died without issue, they were given to the daughters of the survivors, as tenants in common in tail general; if all died without issue, remainder over.

It is said that this last limitation is too remote, because, there being no previous limitation to issue generally, there might be a failure of all the prior limitations, and yet issue, as in the case of a son of a daughter, might exist, so that this last limitation would not take effect. But if this be a remainder, it would be barrable, and the objection, therefore, would not arise.

The rule is to construe the limitation as a remainder, if possible; *Carwardine* v. *Carwardine* (1 Eden, 27). What then prevents this being a remainder? Assuming the words to receive their strict construction, the limitation would be this: to each daughter for life, with remainder to the sons of each daughter, if any, in tail male; then, if no sons, to other daughters for life; remainder, if no sons of any, to daughters of the daughters in tail general; remainder to daughters of surviving daughters in tail general. But to this last is added a condition that it is to take place only if there be no issue of the daughters, and not only a failure of sons and daughters. But does the interposing of this condition convert this remainder into a shifting use? In the case of *Jack* v. *Fetherstone* (2 Hud. and B. 320), decided by the Courts of Common Pleas and Exchequer Chamber in Ireland, it was held that it was a remainder, and rightly so held. The whole is a series of gifts to take effect upon the death of each daughter, or upon the failure of the prior limitations, all of which are estates tail; but the last has a particular contingency attached to it. So had the cases referred to by Sir Edward Sugden in Fearne (page 5) and in Leonard (vol. 4, page 237). It is therefore a contingent remainder, and barrable; *Nicolls* v. *Sheffield* (2 Bro. C.C. 215) is in point.

The next question is, whether the daughters of Margaretta, who died in 1793, became entitled under the deed to the share of Anastatia, who died in 1799 without issue; the gift over, in the event of any daughter dying without issue, being to the use or behoof of the daughter or daughters of such survivors of the daughters. This is not question of cross-remainders being implied, for cross-remainders are distinctly given, but the question is, whether upon the construction of such gift, the word 'survivor' is not to be construed 'other,' and I think it is such a case, the intention being clear, that all daughters of any daughter should take the share of any other daughter dying without issue. *Doe* v. *Wainewright* (5 T. Rep. 427) is directly in point.

Upon the second point I think it clear, that all the estates and interests to which Lady Elizabeth Sewell was entitled under the limitations of the settlement of 1752, passed under and were bound by the settlement of the 23rd of February, 1779, and the fines levied in pursuance thereof. The case of *Doe* v. *Oliver* (10 Barn. and Cr. 181) is decisive.

The last question, as to the effect of the deed and recoveries of 1825, upon the interest in the property, which at the date of the deed of 1779 belonged to Matilda, who did not die till 1788, is certainly one of some difficulty, arising from the fact that in 1825 the true state of Lady Elizabeth Sewell's (then Russell) title does not appear to have been distinctly understood.

In 1809 there was a partition of the Daly Estate, and one-third was decreed to belong to Lady Elizabeth, which was correct, and in 1812 the trustees of a term created by the deed of 1779, filed a bill for raising the money charged upon such term; and upon a reference to the Master to inquire what lands were comprised in that term, the Master reported, in 1820, that the term applied to the whole of the one-third, and a decree accordingly was made for the sale of a sufficient part of such one-third.

With this decision, as to the state of her title to the one-third of the Daly Estate, namely, that it was all comprised in the deed of 1779, Lady Elizabeth, in 1825, suffered recoveries of the property, described in terms comprehending the interest in question, but with the additional description of being comprised in the deed of 1779; and the question now is, whether the share which was vested in Lady Matilda, at the date of the deed of 1779, and was therefore not included in that deed, was affected by the deed of 1825. Upon this subject, I concur in the judgment of Sir Edward Sugden, and with less doubt than he expressed.

The description of the property in the deed is large enough to include every interest therein, and is expressed to be 'as to Lady Elizabeth's estate and interest therein,' and at that time the estate and interest now in question was in her, and she had been told, by the decree in the partition suit, that the whole of such estate and interest was comprised in the deed of 1779; and this deed of 1825, therefore, so describes it, in addition to the more general description, but that inaccurate description cannot take out of the operation of the deed an estate and interest comprehended in the general description, and which, it is clear, she intended to include in it.

Upon all the points, therefore, I think that the Judges of the Court of Common Pleas in Ireland and Sir Edward Sugden, came to a just conclusion, and that the appeal must be dismissed with costs.

Lord Brougham.:

I entirely agree with my noble and learned friend in the view which he has taken of this case, and I agree also in the certificate of the Court of Common Pleas upon the case sent to them, and in the judgment that was afterwards come to by the learned Lord Chancellor of Ireland upon that certificate being returned, in which the learned Judges expressed their opinion upon the three points referred to them by the Lord Chancellor.

On looking at the learned and able arguments in the Court below, as reported (4 Dru. and War. 1), which I have read carefully, I was a good deal surprised to find that there was a question raised about the remoteness of the limitation. Now, whatever doubt may have arisen in the earlier periods of the learning of the law of contingent uses, whatever confusion of expression, perhaps, rather than of substance, may be found in the reports, giving rise to an impression that there is in such a case a rule similar to the rule with respect to perpetuities in the case of springing uses and executory devises, which, on account of the law respecting perpetuities, may be too remote; whatever difficulty, confusion, or doubt may have arisen in earlier cases as to this, I am quite confident that for upwards of a hundred years the rule has been settled, as will be clearly seen if you search through the authorities. I have been led to do so from the curiosity of the case, and from seeing that the learned gentlemen, particularly Mr. Serjeant Warren, who argued this case below, raised the point, and, therefore, we would suppose that there must be some foundation for it; I wished, therefore, to trace what that foundation was, because it opened to my mind a new and a strange view of the law, applying that to contingent remainders which I had always understood must be, from the very nature of the thing, confined to springing uses, and executory devises : and why? In the case of a contingent remainder, if the limitation is to operate by way of remainder, it must be supported by a preceding particular estate of freehold, an estate for life or an estate tail, and it is absolutely useless unless it is to take effect *eo instanti* that the preceding estate determines; that is the very nature of it, the bond of the existence, if I may so speak, of a contingent remainder.

But then, if I have an estate limited upon a fee, that is to say, an estate to A. and his heirs, and upon the determination of that estate in fee, that is, when the heirs shall cease, then over; that cannot operate by way of remainder; it is quite clear that that is void as a remainder, and it is quite clear that if that is to take effect by way of executory devise or springing use (the only way in which it can take effect) there is no end of it. It may be a perpetuity to all intents and purposes, because if the fee is first limited to A. and his heirs, then, as long as there are heirs, the contingent use, the springing use, or, in the case of a will, the executory devisee, cannot come into possession, cannot exist, and cannot be available; consequently, there might be a perpetuity created from the condition of a former use not coming into *esse*, that condition being the general failure of heirs. What is the consequence then? That the law has said, 'to prevent the possibility of this perpetuity, we will fix certain bounds, beyond which the limitation shall not take effect.' Therefore, there may be an estate given to A. and his heirs ; that is a fee; but you cannot limit a remainder upon that. If you give an estate to A. and his heirs, and for want of such issue, or if A. shall die without heirs during the life of B., then over, that will do, that will operate by way of springing use or executory devise, because the life of B. limits the period during which that shall be held in *suspenso*, and that is the origin of the rule. In the same way, I will take the ordinary case of a fee limited upon a fee, that is, a fee to come into use, to come into possession upon the determination of the estate of A. and his heirs, living B.; that prevents the perpetuity, because it limits the period to dying during the life of B.

But suppose another instance of an executory devise or springing use; suppose I give an estate to commence *in futuro*(and a case of that kind is to be found in the books); if there is an estate for life given to A., and one year after to B.; the Courts say, 'No; you cannot do that;' and this was the origin of the application of the rule, because it maybe one year after the life estate of A. terminates, it may be a thousand years, and so it might end in a perpetuity. But, however the law has settled that, it must be only for a life or lives in being, and twenty-one years after, and no more. That has been found to be the law first, I think, properly and justly recognised in the Duke of Norfolk's Case (3 Chan. Cas. 1), in the end of the century before the last, but subsequently more effectually recognised in a case which I heard here, when I held the Great Seal. The famous case of *Cadell* v. *Palmer* (1 Clark and F. 372), in which we had the benefit of the attendance of the learned Judges, and in which, for the first time, it was authoritatively laid down, that without regard to the origin of the rule against perpetuities, you may tie up a bequest by way of executory devise, – and consequently a limitation in a settlement by way of springing use, – for a life or lives in being, and for twenty-one years longer. And as I had often heard ventilated the notion that there could be no such thing as a term in gross, at all, of twenty-one years, I put the question expressly to the learned Judges (and in the judgment I gave in the case, I argued it upon that ground), namely, can there, without the least regard being had to the fact out of which the rule arose (for that is the origin of the rule), without the least regard being had to the fact of the heir of A., the life or last of the lives in being, not being able to cut off or to bar the remainder, by suffering a recovery or levying a fine, till he is twenty-one, – without any regard to that, but supposing there to be no question of the heir at all; supposing there to be no question of levying a fine or suffering a recovery, or barring the remainder over at all, can by law the life or lives in being have the addition of a term in gross of twenty-one years? The Judges held that that is now the law, whatever may have been its origin. It most clearly arises from a mistake. The law never meant to give a further term of twenty-one years, much less any period of gestation. The law never meant to say that there shall be twenty-one years added to the life or lives in being, and that within those limits you may entail the estate, but what the law meant to say was this: until the heir of the last of the lives in being attains twenty-one, by law a recovery cannot be suffered, and consequently the discontinuance of the estate cannot be effected, and for that reason, says the law, you shall have the twenty-one years added, because that is the fact and not the law, namely, that till a person reached the age of twenty-one he could not cut off the entail. For that reason and in that way it has crept in by degrees; *Communis error facit jus*; and that rule never was applied more accurately than in *Cadell* v. *Palmer*.

I have said this much upon the ground, and the only ground, upon which this case has been argued. But, my Lords, this is not the case of an executory devise in which any argument against perpetuity on the ground of remoteness can be raised, and the doctrine of remoteness has been therefore, I think, most erroneously imported into this case, with which it can have nothing whatever to do, because it cannot be an executory devise, if it can operate by way of contingent remainder; and there cannot be remoteness created here, because the preceding estates tail are all barable; at all events, you have the most perfect security against a perpetuity ever creeping into it, because if it is a contingent remainder, it must take effect on being barable, and it is gone for ever *eo instanti* that the particular estate arises. The law upon that subject is not confined to the case of *Carwardine* v. *Carwardine* (1 Eden, 27), which was only decided in 1757 by the very able judgment of Lord Northington, but long before that, it had been understood, and a great deal of learning upon the subject is to be found in former cases; if I recollect rightly, they are mentioned in Saunders, but certainly in Mr. Serjeant Williams' notes to Saunders; and in various cases it has been held, and that is now a great landmark of the law, that whatever use can operate by way of remainder shall never be held to operate by way of executory devise.

My noble and learned friend also called your Lordships' attention to the other point in the case, that is, with respect to the expression 'survive or survivors.' Now, certainly I am of opinion that there is no ground for saying, for I have watched it very narrowly, that Lord Eldon threw any discredit upon the doctrine which has been laid down in other cases, viz. that 'survivor or survivors' may, regard being had to the circumstances, operate as the word 'other' or 'others.' I find that Lord Eldon, in *Davidson* v. *Dallas* (14 Ves. 576), is supposed by the learned reporter (but I think most erroneously supposed) to have thrown discredit upon that principle. Sir E. Sugden very justly observes that, though Lord Eldon may have had doubts upon it, he always decided according to it, – he always adopted it, – a thing which I have not unfrequently known to happen to that most able and learned Judge, that though he might carp at a principle which had been recognized, he was very slow in overruling if it had been once adopted. But on looking into that case I find that what Lord Eldon says, is this, 'The Judges of the Court have, under the necessity of construction, had recourse to the reading of 'survivors' as 'other' instead of 'survivors,' where the parties have not survived at the time in question, under the pressure of construction, to effectuate the plain meaning of the parties, and that there might not be a complete failure of the accomplishment of that purpose.' That is what his Lordship says; but he does not anywhere say that he disapproves of the principle. Now, my Lords, I never saw a case in which that was more completely carried into effect than in the present case, and I entirely agree with my noble and learned friend, who is more clear upon this subject than the learned Lord Chancellor of Ireland. I do not see any reason for the doubts and hesitation with which he seems to have arrived at that conclusion. The only point which I had any doubt about was upon the one-fourth of the one-third, Lady Matilda's portion, but when I come to look at that, it is evident that it would clearly defeat the very design and object and frame of the instrument if you were to open it.

Then it is said in the Court below that this is a settlement and not a will, and what signifies the intention in a settlement? My Lords, there never was a greater fallacy, and I think I must take this opportunity of reprehending the fallacy, of saying that we are not to construe a settlement or any other instrument *inter vivos* in the same way as we should construe a will, but that we are to adopt a totally different rule of construction in the two cases; in other words, that we are to attend to the intention in the case of a will, and not to care for the intention in the case of a settlement. If there are not certain words used which have acquired a technical meaning, it is a different thing; for example, if there are no words of limitation used, you are not to say, there is an estate tail created, but only an estate for life. But it cannot be said that if I give an estate in Blackacre to A., in a settlement, that will not do to carry a fee, that will only be an estate for life, because there are no words of inheritance; but if I give all my estate in Blackacre to A. in a will, that will do to carry the fee. If any one had gone so far as to contend for that proposition, we should have found no great difficulty in disposing of it. But when a man says in his will, 'I give all the estate I have to A., now being in the occupation of John Noakes' (which is clearly demonstrative of the nature of the limitation, and is a clear description of the particular property that he meant to give), it is too late to deny or to doubt, and the Courts have so held; and that is now the law, that in a will that carries the fee, without the assistance of words of inheritance, that a fee would pass 'by all my estate in Blackacre, farmed by J. Noakes.' That would, no doubt, be the case, because there are certain words which have, by technical construction (for it is merely technical), in the case of a will, a certain meaning given to them, which meaning is not given to them in the case of a settlement. I recollect when I was arguing a case before Lord Ellenborough, happening to use the argument of the difference between a deed and a will, and Lord Ellenborough's observation was this, 'What? Are we not to look at the meaning of the parties? Are we to make nonsense of the words that they use? Are not we rather to take a construction which effectuates their purpose and accomplishes their object, than a construction which defeats it? Most certainly you are to do so, admitting at the same time the technical difference of the rules in the one case and in the other.' You are clearly, said his Lordship, to get at the intention of parties in a deed as well as in a will, though rules have been adopted for getting at their intention differently in a will.

Upon the whole, I entirely agree with my noble and learned friend, that there is no reason for doubt in this case; that the Judges of the Court of Common Pleas, in their certificate, took a sound view of the question, and that your Lordships ought to affirm the judgment of the Court below, which judgment appears to have been given with some hesitation, and with more reluctance, I might say, than my noble and learned friend seemed to entertain, and that hesitation on the part of the Lord Chancellor of Ireland I could not quite understand, and I wanted to look into his edition of Saunders to see whether he had ever committed himself by any opinion he had there expressed; for when persons come upon the Bench, they sometimes feel a little remains of the author about them, as we have seen in more Judges than one, in one case in particular of a late most learned Judge upon Bills of Exchange, who has frequently shown instances of remembering his former statements, perhaps more than we should have wished to have seen, and that, I thought, might have been the case here, but I have not found anything to warrant that impression.

The decree was affirmed, with costs.

Notes
1. This case involved various important features of traditional land law. As regards suffering a recovery, see *Irish Land Law*, para. 4.117 *et seq.*, and as regards partition, see *ibid.*, paras. 7.35–6: also p. 383; *post.*
2. Note also the discussion of the development of the rule against perpetuities, as to which see p. 263, *post.*
3. The House of Lords affirmed Sugden L.C.'s decision and apparently approved the latter's analysis of the rules against remoteness, including the rule in *Whitby* v. *Mitchell*, see *Irish Land Law*, paras. 5.043–4.

II. RULES AGAINST REMOTENESS

1. *Rule against Inalienability*
The application of this rule to dispositions of land was dealt with earlier, see ch. 1, p. 40, *ante* and ch. 3, p. 144, *ante*. Other aspects of the rule, e.g., its application to trusts such as trusts for non-charitable purposes, are outside the scope of this casebook, but see *Irish Land Law*, para. 5.034 *et seq.*

2. *Rule in Whitby* v. *Mitchell*

PEYTON V. LAMBERT
(1858) 8 I.C.L.R. 485 (Queen's Bench)

A testator, in 1783, devised fee-simple lands to A, for life, with remainder to the first son of A. for life, with remainder in tail male to the first and every other son of such first son, and their issue male successively, with a devise over in case A should die without leaving issue male of his body, lawfully begotten. The testator then limited similar devises of the same lands to B. and M., moietively, and to their respective eldest sons and their issue male; and, to prevent any misunderstanding of the said limitations to A, and his eldest son, for their respective lives, the testator declared his meaning to be, that in case such eldest son of A should die without issue male, then his real estates should go to the second, third, fourth and every other son of A successively, and to the first and every other son of such second, third, fourth and every other son of A; such second son of A and his issue male to be preferred to such third, fourth and other sons and their issue; and the like rules to be observed with respect to the second, third and other sons of B. and M. respectively; and in case either B. or M. should die without leaving issue male, the share of either so dying should go to the survivor, or, if she were dead, to her first and every other son, if she leave issue male, under the same limitations as the testator had already annexed to the shares of B. and M. respectively, with devise over to the daughters of A, in case both B. and M. should die without issue male.

Crampton, J.:
This case was heard in the last Term, before my Brother O'Brien and myself. The case is one of great importance; and we felt that it was likely that the parties would carry it to the Court of Error. Under these circumstances, on the last day of

the Term, we gave a formal judgment in the case, in order that the parties might not be delayed in their proceedings; intimating, however, our intention upon a future day to state the grounds of our decision; and this being a convenient time for the purpose, I now proceed to state the reasons upon which we arrived at the conclusion that the plaintiff was entitled to judgment.

This was an ejectment upon the title, brought for recovery of an *undivided moiety* of certain lands, called the Loughscur estate, in the county of Leitrim. The Loughscur estate comprised a great many denominations of land, ninety (it was said) in number, and, of these ninety denominations, sixteen were somewhat differently circumstanced, as to the devolution of title, from the other denominations. The pedigree of the parties, so far as it is necessary for the understanding of the case, is as follows: In the year 1765, George Reynolds was seised and possessed of the entire of the Loughscur estate; he has been in the argument called George the first ; he died in the year 1769, leaving an only son, George Nugent Reynolds the younger, who has been called in the argument George the second. This George the second died in the year 1787, leaving three children, viz., his only son, George Nugent Reynolds, the grandson, who has been called in the argument George the third, and two daughters, Mary Anne and Bridget. George the third died in the year 1802, without issue, leaving his two sisters his co-heiresses-at-law. Mary Anne was twice married, first to Colonel Peyton, by whom she had two children, namely, John Reynolds Peyton, the father of the plaintiff Richard Reynolds Peyton, and Jane, who married John Lambert, and who, with her husband, are the defendants in this record. Colonel Peyton died in the year 1805; and, in the year 1817, Mary Anne, his widow, intermarried with Major Richard Macnamara, her second husband ; and of this marriage there was no issue. Major Macnamara died in the year 1848, leaving Mary Anne, his widow, him surviving. Bridget Reynolds intermarried with Richard Young, who took the name of Reynolds; and of this marriage there was no issue. Bridget Reynolds died in the year 1842; and her husband, Richard Young Reynolds, died in 1848. On the 23rd of November 1836, John Reynolds Peyton intermarried with Alicia Ennis, and died in the year 1850, leaving the plaintiff, Richard Reynolds Peyton, his son and heir. In the year 1855, Mrs. Macnamara died.

This case turns altogether upon the construction of the deeds and wills which were given in evidence at the trial. A verdict was directed for the plaintiffs; but, by consent of the parties, and with the sanction of the learned Judge who tried the case (Mr. Justice Christian), the verdict was ultimately to be entered for the party who should, in the opinion of this Court, be entitled thereto.

Having heard the case very ably and elaborately argued, my opinion is, that the plaintiffs are entitled to a verdict for the whole of the premises comprised in the ejectment; and I shall now state the grounds upon which I entertain that opinion. I shall not, for the present, notice the peculiar circumstances of the sixteen demoninations which I have referred to, but shall consider the case with reference to the bulk of the property which is the subject of this action, and as if all the ninety denominations rested upon the same derivative title. There are three documents, upon the construction of which the decision of this case must turn; these are the will of 1783 , the will of 1795 and the deed of 1836. Upon the will of 1783 the main question in the cause arises; and that is, what estate did George the third take under the will of 1783? The defendants contend that, under this will, George the third took an estate tail; the plaintiffs contend that he took an estate for life only. I think that the plaintiffs' is the true construction. – [His Lordship here read the will of George N. Reynolds (George the second), 1783.] – Now I think, upon the reading of this will, it is manifest that the testator's principal object and intention was, to keep the Loughscur estate in the name and blood of Reynolds as long as possible. It is equally clear that it was with that view and for that purpose that he gave, after the life estates devised to his son and daughters, successive life estates to the unborn sons of his own children, with estates in tail to the children of those unborn children. This kind of limitation, as tending to perpetuity, the law will not permit. Accordingly, if we were to construe this will strictly according to its terms, all the limitations after the life estates would be void for remoteness, and the necessary result (giving effect to the law upon this subject) would be to defeat the main object and intent of the testator, which was to continue the estate in his family and name as long as the law would permit. In order to prevent this result, the defendants' Counsel would construe this will as giving an estate tail to George the third; but it appears to me that this construction is plainly inadmissible. By giving an estate tail to George third, the testator's primary object would be altogether frustrated, since, by a recovery or disentailing deed, the first taker, George third, could have at once made himself owner of the fee-simple, and thus destroyed all the laboriously framed limitations of the will. The only mode, as it appears to me, by which the main, the ruling intention of the testator can be accomplished, is, to apply the *cy pres* doctrine to this will. That doctrine is founded upon the rule that the primary, the paramount intention of the testator shall be carried out, although at the sacrifice of subordinate views expressed by the terms of the will. The Court, in its interpretation of the instrument, does for the testator that which he probably would have done for himself, had he been aware of the impracticability of reconciling the main object of his will with the subordinate limitations which he had in view. Numerous cases there are upon this subject, from *Humberston* v. *Humberston* (1 P. Wms. 332) and *Pitt* v. *Jackson* (2 Bro. C.C. 51), down to *Vanderplank* v. *King* (3 Hare, 1), which is quite in point with the present case. In *Vanderplank* v. *King*, there was a devise to the daughter of the testator, for her life, with remainder to her unborn child, for life, with remainder to the children of the unborn child, in tail. Vice-Chancellor Wigram thought it right to apply the *cy pres* doctrine to that case, and says (p. 10): 'I have considered the question during the argument, with reference to the *cy pres* doctrine, and, upon that part of the case, I do not think that I am at liberty to exercise any discretion. That point is now sufficiently simple and is well established, though sometimes of difficult application.' He then examines the cases referred to, and, again taking up the case before him, after consideration, he reiterates the doctrine which I have just stated, as the ground upon which he decided that particular case. That case is a leading one upon the subject – one which has not been questioned, and upon which I might very well found the opinion I entertain upon this part of the testator's will. Now, in this will we have the general and paramount intention of the testator, that the estate shall not go over as long as there shall be male descendants of his son and daughters. This intention may be carried out, and can be carried out only, not by giving life estates to the unborn children of the tenants for life then *in esse*, but by giving them estates tail; and thus, without violating the rule against perpetuities, we are enabled to carry out the main object and intention of the testator. I think, therefore, that, under the will of 1783, George third took only an estate for life, with remainder to his first and other sons, in tail male, and that, on his death without issue, his sisters took an estate for life each, as tenants in common, with remainder, as to a moiety, to their first and other sons, in tail, with cross remainders over.

This being so, the will of 1795 could not affect the main body of the Loughscur estate; it could only affect those denominations of which the then testator, George the third, was seised in fee. – [His Lordship here read the will of George N. Reynolds (George the third), of 1795.] – By this will of 1795, it appears to me that the sisters Bridget and Mary Anne took each an estate tail in common, with cross remainders over, the reversion in fee being limited to one Hugh Connell.

We have nothing to do here with Mary Ann's moiety; that moiety, we are given to understand, was disposed of by a suit in Chancery. Our concern now is with Bridget's moiety. Taking then Bridget to have been tenant in tail of her moiety in the year 1836, we find that in that year two deeds were executed, the effect of which we have now to consider. Upon the marriage of John Reynolds Peyton in that year, a marriage settlement, dated the 23rd of November 1836, was executed by the parties thereto, and, amongst others, by Richard Young Reynolds and Bridget his wife. Contemporaneously with this settlement, a second deed, of the same date, was executed by Mrs. Reynolds and her husband; this has been called the disentailing deed; but the effect of both deeds plainly was, reserving her life estate to Mrs. Reynolds, to vest the fee of her moiety in trustees, to the uses of the marriage settlement. The plaintiff R.R. Peyton is the eldest son of that marriage, and tenant in tail under the settlement. It was vainly contended by the defendants' Counsel that, inasmuch as the settlement of 1836 was not acknowledged by Bridget Y. Reynolds, before a Judge or a Commissioner, that it was inoperative as to her, and those deriving under her; but the answer to that argument is, that the disentailing deed of the same date with the settlement was acknowledged regularly before a Judge, and with the manifest view of assuring to the uses of the settlement the moiety in question: so that the conclusion upon the whole is, that the plaintiffs are now entitled to the whole of the premises for which the ejectment was brought. Our decision, therefore, is that the plaintiffs shall have judgment for the whole.

O'Brien, J.:

I concur in the clear and satisfactory judgment which has been pronounced by my Brother Crampton.

The first question raised upon the will of George Reynolds the second (1783) was, as to the application of the *cy pres* doctrine to the limitations in favour of testator's son, George Reynolds the third, and his sons. The cases to which my Brother Crampton has referred show clearly that the doctrine is applicable to those limitations; but defendants' Counsel contend that the result of such application would be to give an estate in tail male to George the third, instead of giving to his first and other sons successively, as purchasers, estates in tail male, in remainder expectant upon his life estate. In my opinion, such a proposition cannot be maintained, consistently with the nature and principles of the *cy pres* doctrine. That doctrine has been applied by the Courts to limitations such as those in question, for the purpose of effectuating as far as possible, a testator's general intention to preserve his property in a family, and for the purpose of preventing the total disappointment of that intention by the rule against perpetuities. If, for example, lands be devised to an unborn person, for life, with remainder to his sons, in tail, then (as such limitations in remainder are void and incapable of taking effect in the manner intended), the doctrine of *cy pres* gives to the unborn devisee for life the estate in tail, which was designed for, but could not be legally given to his sons, and which estate tail, so given to the devisee for life, would (if not barred) comprise in its devolutions by descent all the persons intended to have been made tenants in tail by purchase.

In the first part of the will of 1783, the limitations are 'to *George Reynolds the third* (who was then unmarried), *for his life, with remainder to his first son, for his life, with remainder to the sons of such first son successively, in tail male.*' In that part of the will there are no limitations to the second and other sons of George

Reynolds the third; but I am of opinion (and it has indeed been conceded in the argument), that the limitations in favour of the second and other unborn sons of George the third and their sons, which are contained in the subsequent clause of the will, that commences with the words, '*and to prevent any misunderstanding*,' should (though differing in some respect from the limitations in favour of the first unborn son and his issue) have the same effect as if the first part of the will had contained express limitations in their favour, similar to those contained in favour of the first unborn son and his sons.

Now, as estates in tail in remainder expectant upon the life estate of the unborn sons of George Reynolds the third could not be legally given to their sons respectively, I think it clearly follows, from the principle above stated, that the *cy pres* doctrine should be applied by giving to the unborn sons of George Reynolds the third the estate tail which were designed for, but which could not be legally given to, their first and other sons. What authority or reason is there for applying the *cy pres* doctrine (as contended for by defendant), so as to give an estate tail to George Reynolds the third? He took an estate for life under the will; the limitation of an estate for life, to his first and unborn son was valid in itself; but the limitation of estates tail in remainder to the sons of such unborn son was invalid, though an estate tail might have been legally given, by express words, to such unborn son himself. It is necessary, for the purpose of effectuating the testator's general intention, and of observing the rule against prepetuities, that we should (as contended for by plaintiff's Counsel) substitute an estate tail in such unborn son for the life estate and the invalid estates tail in remainder, which were intended to be devised to him and to his issue; but it is *not* necessary, for the foregoing purpose, that we should (as urged by defendants' Counsel) adopt such a construction of the will as would substitute an estate tail in George Reynolds the third, for the life estate expressly given to him, and the remainders over to his sons and grandsons. This latter construction would not only depart, more than is necessary, from the express limitations of the will, but would tend to the further disappointment of the testator's general intention, by unnecessarily accelerating the period at which such intention could be defeated; as (if George Reynolds the third took an estate tail under the will) he could, by suffering a recovery, destroy the limitations over, and alienate the property from the family, at a much earlier period than could be done by his sons. I am, therefore, of opinion that the construction contended for by defendant, as to the *cy pres* doctrine, cannot be maintained, and that, under the part of the will to which I have referred, George Reynolds the third took an immediate estate for life, with remainder to his first and other sons successively, in tail male.

The defendants' Counsel, however, next contended that even if George the third took under the will an immediate estate for life only, with remainder (by the application of the *cy pres* doctrine) to his sons, in tail male, yet that the effect of the words in the will, '*and in case my said son George shall die without leaving issue male of his body lawfully begotten*' (which precede the limitations to testator's daughters), is to give George the third an estate in tail male, in remainder expectant upon the estate in tail male given to his sons. Now, although in many cases, where a devise to a party is followed by a limitation contingent upon '*the failure of his issue*,'' or upon '*his dying without issue*', and the effect of these words, or of expressions of a similar import, has been to give an estate tail, by implication, to that party; yet it has been settled that, where those expressions (even without the word '*such*' being used) are preceded by a devise to the issue of that party, which embraces, in its terms, *all* the issue whose failure is contemplated, then the words importing a failure of issue should be construed as if the word '*such*' had been used, as referring to the objects of the prior devise, and not to issue at large, as intended to provide for the failure or determination of the estate previously given to the issue, and not to give an estate tail, by implication to that party. This principle is established by the case of *Baker* v. *Tucker* (11 Ir. Eq. Rep. 102 ; S.C., H.L. Cas 106), and several other cases cited in the argument. In the will now before us, the words importing a failure of the issue male of George the third are preceded by a devise which, under the *cy pres* doctrine is (as I have already stated) to be construed as a devise to his first and other sons successively, in tail male. This devise embraces, in its terms, all his issue male; and it follows, therefore, that the words in question have not the effect of giving George Reynolds the third an estate tail by implication, but only denote the event upon which there would be a failure or determination of the estate in tail male, previously given to the sons of George Reynolds the third.

The limitations next contained in the will are those to the testator's daughters Bridget and Mary (who were also then unmarried), for their respective lives, as tenants in common, with remainder, as to each daughter's share, to her first son (then unborn), for his life, with remainder to the sons of such first unborn son successively, in tail male; and in the subsequent part of the will to which I have already referred, he directs that the like rules should be observed with respect to the second and other sons of his daughters, as he had directed with respect to the second and other son of George Reynolds the third. I think (for the reasons I have already stated) that, by the application of the *cy pres* doctrine, Bridget and Mary took, under these limitations, life estates only in their respective moities, with remainder to their respective first and other sons successively, in tail male. I think also, that, by the subsequent limitation, in the nature of cross remainders, each sister would (upon the determination of the life estate and estates tail given to the other sister and her sons as aforesaid) take an estate for her life, with remainder to her sons successively, in tail male, in that other sister's moiety.

The will then contains a limitation to the daughters of George Reynolds the third. It is necessary to consider its construction, because, though the limitations to the sons of Bridget and Mary (under which the plaintiff claims) are contained in a prior part of the will, yet the testator, by his codicil, declares that the limitations to the issue female of George Reynolds the third should operate in priority to the limitations to the issue male of Bridget and Mary. The limitation to the daughters of George Reynolds the third is in the following terms: 'I devise all my said real estates *to the daughters of my said son George, as tenants in common, and not as joint tenants, under the same limitations and restrictions as I have hereinbefore devised the same to my said daughters Bridget and Mary, and their issue*'. This limitation is inaccurately drawn, and could not be carried out in the particular manner expressed. If the testator had repeated in it the precise terms of the preceding limitation to Bridget and Mary and their issue, the result would be an attempt to give to the unborn daughters of George the third estates for life, in their respective shares, as tenants in common, with remainder, as to said respective shares, to the first and other sons successively of each unborn daughter, for life, with remainder to the first and other sons of such sons successively, in tail male. Such a devise could not, of course, be carried out according to its terms. It would be a further violation of the rule against perpetuities, by attempting to interpose life estates in the sons of the unborn daughters between the life estates of those daughters and the estates tail purported to be given to the sons of those sons. It has not, however, been suggested by the defendant's Counsel that the peculiar form of this limitation creates any greater difficulty, in the application to it of the *cy pres* doctrine, than exists in the application of that doctrine to the limitations in favour of Bridget and Mary and their issue male; and I am of opinion that, by the application of that doctrine to the limitations in favour of the daughters of George Reynolds the third, and having regard to the testator's general intention, as collected from other parts of the will, the results would be to give to the daughters of George Reynolds the third estates in tail male, in their respective shares, as tenants in common, with cross remainders between them. In this view of the case, the limitations of estates in tail male, which (as I have already stated) were given to the sons of Bridget and Mary, by the preceding parts of the will (but which were, by the codicil, postponed to the limitations in favour of the daughters of George Reynolds the third), would not, as contended for by the defendant's Counsel, be void for remoteness.

The parts of the will to which I have referred were those principally relied on in the argument; and I do not think that, for the purposes of this case, their construction is affected by the devise in the codicil to the testator's wife for her life, with remainders over in the event of all the testator's children dying without issue.

Part of the plaintiff's claim in this ejectment is for Bridget's moiety of the fee-simple lands of George Reynolds the second, which passed by the said will and codicil of 1783. It appears that George Reynolds the third died without ever having had any issue; and, therefore, according to the foregoing construction of the said will and codicil, the plaintiff's father (who was the only son of Mary) became entitled to an estate in tail male, in Bridget's moiety, in remainder expectant upon the death of Bridget and of Mary, and upon the failure or determination of the estates in tail male given to the sons of Bridget, in that moiety. By the disentailing deed and settlement of November 1836, executed on the marriage of the plaintiff's father (who has since died), his said estate was barred, and Bridget's moiety was settled to the uses mentioned in said settlement. Bridget died in 1842, without ever having had any issue; Mary died in 1855, and the plaintiff, under the uses of that settlement, is now entitled to Bridget's moiety of said fee-simple lands of George Reynolds the second.

The residue of the lands mentioned in the ejectment were the fee-simple estates of George Reynolds the third; and the plaintiff claims also to be entitled to Bridget's moiety of those lands, under the will of George Reynolds the third (died in 1795), and under the disentailing deed and settlement of November 1836; contending that Bridget took, under said will of 1795, an estate tail in her said moiety. The defendants, on the other hand, contend that, under said will, Bridget took in her moiety an estate in fee-simple, with an executory devise over to Mary, in tail, in the event of Bridget dying *without issue living at her death*; that, as such event happened, Bridget's estate determined, and that the executory devise to Mary was not affected by the disentailing deed or settlement of 1836. In my opinion, the construction of this will contended for by the plaintiff's Counsel is correct. The testator in the first part of his will gives '*all his real and personal estate*' to his sisters Bridget and Mary, share and share alike. This would have given Bridget an estate in fee in her moiety of the real estate; but there is a subsequent clause whereby testator, '*in case Bridget should happen to die without issue*,' bequeaths her moiety of his real and personal estate to her husband, Richard Young, for his life, '*and to descend immediately upon his death to Mary and her issue*'. Now as a general rule, respecting wills made before 1837, if a devise of lands to a party in fee be followed by a limitation over, in the event of that part '*dying without issue*', those words are construed as importing an indefinite failure of issue, and as giving to that party, an estate tail by implication, instead of the estate in fee, which he would have taken under the preceding devise. I admit, however, there are several cases where the words importing a failure of issue in the party taking an estate in fee under the preceding devise were (by force of other expressions in the will) restricted to a failure of issue at the death of that party, or at some other period, and were accordingly held to have the effect, not of creating an estate tail in that party, but of subjecting his previous estate in fee-simple to an executory devise over, in the event of the failure of his issue occurring at his death, or at such other period. In the case now before the Court, the devise of a life estate to Richard Young, in the event of Bridget dying without issue, and the direction that her moiety should descend immediately upon his death to Mary and her issue, are relied on by the defendant's Counsel as grounds for adopting the restricted construction of the words '*dying without issue*,' instead of giving them their legal and natural construction. Now the circumstances of a subsequent devise of lands for life is not of itself sufficient to confine the failure of issue to a failure at the death of the first taker. Estates for life are frequently limited in remainder after estates tail. In the case of *Roe* v. *Jeffrey* (7 T.R. 589) which was relied on by the defendant's Counsel, all the subsequent devises were of life estates; and in the subsequent case of *Barlow* v. *Salter* (17 Ves. 483) and *Doe* v. *Owen* (1 B. & Ad. 321), the authority of the decision in *Roe* v. *Jeffrey* has been confined to cases where that state of fact occurs. That case does not, therefore, govern the case now before the Court, as in the will of 1795, there are devises in tail and in fee, subsequent to the devise of a life estate to R. Young. With respect to the direction that, in the event of Bridget dying without issue, '*her moiety should descend immediately on the death of Richard Young to Mary and her issue*', cases have been cited in which expressions, referring to the death of the party whose issue was to fail, have been held as restricting the import of the words '*dying without issue*', to a failure of issue at the death of that party; but in the case now before the Court, the words '*descend immediately*' refer to the death of Richard Young and not to the death of Bridget; and it has not been contended by the defendant's counsel that the words '*dying without issue*' could be restricted to a failure of her issue at the death of Richard Young.

The defendant's Counsel have also relied on the circumstance that the testator's real and personal estate are included in the same devises and clauses of his will. But this is no ground for giving to the words '*dying without issue*' the restricted construction as regards the real estate, though we should give them that construction with respect to the personal estate. It has been decided in *Forth* v. *Chapman* (1 P. Wms. 663) and other cases, that where real and personal estates are devised in the same clauses and by the same terms, a different construction may be given to the words '*dying without issue*' (or to similar expressions), as regards the real estate, from what is given to them as regards the personal estate.

There are other limitations in the will of 1795, which, in my opinion, furnish grounds for our adopting the natural instead of the restricted construction of the words in question, and for our holding that Bridget took an estate tail in her moiety of the real estate. Supposing it should be held (as contended for by the defendant) that Bridget and Mary took in their respective moities estates in fee-simple, with executory devises over in the event of their dying without issue living at their respective deaths, it is admitted (even on such a construction), that, if either of them died without issue living at her death, the other sister would, under the devise '*to her and her issue*', take an estate tail in the moiety of that sister so dying. There is then in the will a limitation of the entire real estate to H. Connell, in fee, in the event of both sisters '*dying without issue*'. Now what construction is to be given to those words, as applied to this devise to Connell? They are immediately preceded by limitations of a estate tail to each sister in the moiety originally devised to the other sister; and, having regard to those limitations alone, the natural and obvious construction would be, that the testator intended that the failure of issue, upon which the property was to go over to Connell, was to be identical with that on which the immediately preceding estates were made determinable, namely, an indefinite failure of issue. But, in order to avoid the objection of putting different constructions upon the same words in different parts of the will, the defendant's Counsel contend, that the words '*dying without issue*', as applied to the limitation of the entire real estate to Connell, should receive the same restricted construction as in the limitation of Bridget's and Mary's moieties, and should be construed as meaning 'dying without issue at their respective deaths'. The result then of the entire will, according to the defendant's construction, would be, as to one moiety, a devise to Bridget, in fee, with an executory devise over (in the event of her dying without issue living at her death) to Richard Young, for life, and then to Mary, in tail, and with a further executory devise over to H. Connell, in fee, in the event of Mary also dying without issue living at her death; and as to the other moiety, a devise to Mary, in fee, with an executory devise over (in the event of her dying without issue living at her death) to Bridget, in tail, with a further executory devise over (in the event of Bridget also dying without issue living at her death), to Richard Young, for life, and then to H. Connell, in *fee*. Such devises could, no doubt, have been legally made by the testator; but it will be found that, by adopting this construction, results would follow which could hardly be considered as consistent with the testator's intention, or as having been contemplated by him. In the event (which has actually happened) of Bridget dying in Mary's lifetime, without leaving issue living at her death, then, according to the defendant's construction, Mary would (subject to Richard Young's life estate) take an estate tail in Bridget's moiety, with an executory devise over to H. Connell, in fee, in the event of her dying without issue living at her death; and by suffering a recovery she might defeat that executory devise, and acquire the absolute interest and fee-simple in Bridget's moiety; whereas, in her own original moiety, she would have only an estate in fee determinable upon the same event of her dying without issue at her death, and with an executory devise over, on that event, to H. Connell, in fee, which she could not defeat. It is not likely that the testator contemplated such a result. It was more probably his intention that, if either sister became entitled to the moiety of the other sisters, she was to have the same estate in and dominion over that other moiety as she had got in her own original moiety. Suppose again, that after the death of Bridget, without leaving issue at her death, Mary died leaving issue at her death (but without having suffered a recovery), then, according to the defendant's construction, the executory devise to H. Connell as to both moieties would be defeated and incapable of taking effect. Mary's estate in fee in her own original moiety and her estate tail in Bridget's moiety would become absolute; but the reversion expectant in that event upon her estate tail in Bridget's moiety would have been undisposed of by the will, and, if Mary's issue afterwards determined, without a recovery being suffered, Bridget's moiety would revert to the testator's heir-at-law, namely, to the heir of Bridget and Mary themselves. Such a result could not be considered as in accordance with the testator's intention, which appears to have been to provide for every contingency, and to dispose of the entire interest in his real estate. Other results might also follow, from the defendant's construction of the will, which would be equally at variance with the testator's apparent intention.

The defendant's Counsel have also referred to the terms of the limitation of Mary's moiety, 'that in case she should die without issue, *then* her moiety was to descend *upon her death* to Bridget and her issue', and have relied upon the expressions '*then*,' and '*upon her death*,' as giving the restricted construction to the words 'dying without issue' in that part of the will, and as affording an explanation of their import in the previous part relating to Bridget's moiety. Considering, however, the other limitations of the will, to which I have referred, I think that, although the expressions relied on by the defendant's Counsel have in some cases had the effect for which they contend, yet that, in the present case we should regard those expressions as having been used by the testator to denote that the limitation to Bridget was to take effect immediately after or upon the failure of the estate which Mary took under the preceding limitation, and under the words, '*in case she shall die without issue*', and not as intended to fix the death of Mary as the period for ascertaining whether her estate would determine or become absolute: *Water v. Drew* (Comyns, 372).

It appears to me, upon the whole of the will, more in accordance with the testator's intention, and the purposes he had in view, to hold that he intended to give to each sister similar estates in her original moiety, and also in the moiety of her sister, when the same should accrue to her, and that he did not intend to use the words '*dying without issue*' in a sense different from their ordinary and legal construction of an indefinite failure of issue. I am accordingly of opinion, that each sister took an estate tail in her original moiety, with remainders, as to Bridget's moiety, to R. Young for life, then to Mary in tail, and then to H. Connell in fee, and with remainder, as to Mary's moiety, to Bridget in tail, then to R. Young for life, and then to H. Connell in fee. I do not think that the bequest of a life annuity to P. Brennan, in the event of the devise to Connell taking effect (which has been also relied on by the defendant's Counsel), furnishes any sufficient argument against this construction, as such an annuity might well be limited after the determination of previous estates tail.

The defendant's Counsel have further contended that, even supposing Bridget took, under the will of 1795, an estate tail in the fee-simple lands of George Reynolds the third, yet that the plaintiffs are not entitled to that moiety, under the disentailing deed and settlement of November 1836, inasmuch as the settlement, though executed by her, was not also acknowledged by her, pursuant to the Fines and Recoveries Abolition Act (she being then a married woman). It appears, however, that the disentailing deed was duly acknowledged by her under the statute. That deed, though hearing the same date, appears to have been executed subsequent to the settlement. It recites the settlement, and that the lands were thereby conveyed '*to the uses, trusts, &c. in said settlement expressed*'. It also recites that Bridget and her husband had thereby covenanted to execute such further assurance, whether in the nature of a fine or recovery, or otherwise, as should be requisite for more effectually assuring the lands to the uses and trusts of the settlement. The disentailing deed then conveys the lands to the uses, &c., already declared by the settlement. I think it clear, therefore, that it was not necessary that the settlement should be also acknowledged by Bridget under the statute. The uses and trusts, &c., declared by it were as effectually incorporated in the disentailing deed, by reference and recital, as if they had been repeated in terms in the operative part of that deed. With respect to the reservation clauses in the disentailing deed and settlement, which were relied on by the defendant's Counsel, I think they only referred (as regards Bridget's and Mary's estate) to the life estates to which under the will of 1783 they were entitled in Bridget's moiety of the fee-simple lands of George Reynolds the second, in priority to the estate tail of the plaintiff's father, but did not affect his rights to any of the lands on the death of Bridget and Mary.

The plaintiffs are, therefore, now entitled to Bridget's moiety of all the lands mentioned in the ejectment.

Notes

1. See further on the rule in *Whitby* v. *Mitchell* and the *cy-près* doctrine, *Irish Land Law*, para. 5.042 *et seq*.
2. As to the meaning of 'die without issue', see *ibid* paras. 14.44–6.

3. *Rule against Perpetuities*

EXHAM V. BEAMISH

[1939] I.R. 336 (High Court)

Freehold land was settled by a husband and wife by a voluntary deed unto and to the use of them (the settlors) and their assigns during their joint lives and after the decease of either of them to the use of the survivor during his or her life, and after the decease of the survivor upon trust by demised sale or on mortgage of the settled hereditaments to raise and levy the sum of £7,000 for their younger children, and, subject thereto, to the use of their eldest son for life with remainder to his son or sons as he should appoint, with remainder to the use of their second son for life with remainder to his son or sons in like manner, with remainder to the use of their two daughters, equally, as tenants in common and of their assigns during their lives, and after the decease of either of them to the use of the child, if but one, or of the children equally share and share alike, and of his, her or their heirs as tenants in common if more than one of such of them the said two daughters as should first happen to die, until the day of the decease of the survivor of the said two duaghters, but if there should be no such children, or there being such, they should all happen to die under the age of 21 years in the lifetime of such survivor of the said two daughters and without leaving issue, then, as to the share of such of the said two daughters as should so die without a child or remoter issue in the lifetime of the survivor, to the use of the survivor of the said two daughters during her life, and after the decease of the survivor of the said two daughters upon trust that the trustees or trustee for the time being should, and they were expressly so directed and empowered, make sale and absolutely dispose of all the said lands and hereditaments and stand and be possessed of the moneys to arise from such sale upon trust to pay and hand over the proceeds thereof equally share and share alike unto, between and amongst all and every the grandchildren of the settlors upon their respectively attaining the age of 21 years as to sons and the like age or day of marriage as to daughters, but if any such grandchild should have previously died leaving issue, such issue to take the share to which their parent would have been entitled if living. The trustees of the settlement sought determination of various questions, including whether the gift in favour of the grandchildren was void for remoteness.

Gavan Duffy J.:

This case concerns a voluntary settlement of freehold land in Ireland, made in 1865, which, in the events that have happened, directed the trustees from and immediately after the decease of the survivor of two named tenants for life, daughters of the settlor, to sell the settled land and stand possessed of the moneys to arise from the sale in trust to pay and hand over the proceeds equally, share and share alike, unto and amongst all and every the grandchildren of the settlor and his wife upon their respectively attaining 21 (or marriage as to granddaughters), but, if any such grandchild should have previously died leaving issue, such issue were to take the share to which their parent would have been entitled if living: there was a hotchpot clause and a gift over in default of all such issue.

The settlor, as I shall call him for convenience, the Rev. William Hamilton Thompson, died in 1895 and his wife in 1892; they had four children, all born before 1865; they survived two of these children, who died unmarried; the other two, who became tenants for life, were Mrs. Edith Annie Beamish, who died in 1932, and Mrs. Frances de Courcy Fenwick, who died on the 20th of August, 1937. The only grandchildren were (a) Mrs. Beamish's children: the defendant, Ludlow Hamilton, born in 1871; Ethel Hilda Frances, born in 1873, who died a spinster in 1894, after attaining her majority; and Harold Délacour, born in 1874, who died without issue in 1934; and (b) Mrs. Fenwick's only child, Gerard de Borrowden, born in 1875, who died two days before his mother without issue. I omit for the time being, since the evidence omits, a child of Mrs. Beamish, dying in infancy, who appears as the eldest child on a family tree, which has been handed in, but not proved.

The provision in the settlement for grandchildren is wide enough to include the children of any fifth or younger child who might (theoretically at least) have been born to Mr. and Mrs. Thompson after the date of the settlement. For this reason, though all the grandchildren were in fact born during the lifetime of Mr. and Mrs. Thompson and they had no fifth child, it is now contended that the whole of the limitations for grandchildren are void for remoteness, on the principle of *Jee* v. *Audley* (1 Cox, Eq. Cas, 324) and *Ward* v. *Van der Loeff* ([1924] A.C. 653); and the first question in the summons asks if they are so. In the view that I take of this case the time at which the interests of the grandchildren vested will not affect the question of remoteness and I need not decide it. The question of remoteness will turn upon the ascertainability within the permitted limits of the class of grandchildren who are to take under the settlement; the contingent provisions for their issue are merely substitutional.

If I were construing a will, it is contended that, despite the provision for 'all and every' the grandchildren, I should have to restrict the class and close it at Mrs. Fenwick's death, since Ludlow Hamilton Beamish was then entitled to call for payment of his share; the same rule applies whether the interests of the grandchildren vest at 21 or earlier; see Hawkins, 2nd ed., pp. 100–101. There is no doubt that the rule applies in Ireland. Then it is urged that, if that be so, I must do the same thing in construing a deed, making the time limit start at the date of the deed instead of the date of testator's death. I am satisfied from the reasoning of North J. in *In re Knapp's Settlement* ([1895] 1 Ch. 91) that the same rule for the artificial ascertainment of a class applies to a voluntary settlement.

Mr. Price contends that I am not at liberty to ascertain and close the class of grandchildren at the death of Mrs. Fenwick, because of the rule against perpetuities; for, if I were so to determine the class, I should be ignoring the rule against perpetuities and, still worse, I should thus contrive to defeat it. Now, the rule of the Court, which I must allow the rule against perpetuities to override, is (I quote from Roper, 4th end. at pp. 45–6, 50 and 53) a settled rule for the ascertainment of a class, a rule which all the cases agree in establishing, a rule based on convenience and necessity, and a rule which only clear evidence of a different intention will be allowed to disturb. The rule, says Sir George Jessel, is not founded on any view of the donor's intention: *In re Emmet's Estate* (13 C.D. 484, at p. 490); it is the law that makes the donees certain, says Lord Eldon, who disliked the rule: *Barrington* v. *Tristram* (6 Ves. 345, at p. 349); hence, whether or not the donor would have wished it and whether the Court likes it or not, the donor must be taken to have closed the class of donees at a moment fixed by the rule of the Court. That is the rule that, when reading Mr. Thompson's settlement, I am called upon to put aside in deference to the rule against perpetuities.

It is urged that, where the rule against perpetuities is concerned, I must look at possible, not at actual events and that, if in 1865 the class might, if left to nature, eventually have proved too remote, the Court cannot step in to determine it according to events. It is misleading to say that the Court cannot look at the actual events, for the actual age of a donee is often decisive of remoteness. Mr. Price has to admit that, but at least, he says, you cannot consider actual events occurring after the date of the deed or after the date of a testator's death. Mr. Price, in asking me to disregard the state of affairs at Mrs. Fenwick's death, may seem to lay himself open to the charge of inverting the ordinary method of approaching the construction of a document. I find this clear statement in Marsden on Perpetuities, p. 105: 'Limitations to classes are frequently ambiguous as regards the definition of the class, the persons intended to be included, and the time of vesting. Where this is the case, the true construction of the instrument must be ascertained before the question of remoteness can be answered. The time for ascertaining the class is determined by the ordinary rules of construction without regard to the question of remoteness'. If in the normal way I go through the settlement in the first instance to ascertain the effect of what the donor has written, without reference to the rule against perpetuities, I shall in so doing, upon the argument of Mr. Chadwick, find the class of grandchildren closed by a recognised rule of the Court at Mrs. Fenwick's death, that is, if I read the document with a knowledge of the material external facts, and in particular the date of the death of Mrs. Fenwick and the date of the birth of the surviving and eldest grandchild; then, going back over the document, into which I shall have been bound to read a closing of the class at the time for distribution, I shall find no remoteness. Mr. Chadwick relies upon *Kevern* v. *Williams* (5 Sim. 171) to entitle and compel me to ascertain the class as at the death of the surviving tenant for life; that case, if good law, gives solid support to his argument; the decision, though not of the highest authority and sometimes subjected to unfriendly criticism, has not been overruled and it is strongly defended by Professor Gray (para. 638–639aa), whose only objection is that it did not go far enough. *Cf.* Lewis, p. 173 (par. 9): *id certum est quod certum reddi potest*; see also the reference to Baron Parke's opinion below (12 Cl. & F. 546; see the rejected opinion of Parke B. at pp. 599–600).

On the other hand, I find Lord Kenyon in *Jee* v. *Audley* (1 Cox. Eq. Cas. 324, at p. 326) saying 'the single question before me is, not whether the limitation is good in the events which have happened, but whether it was good in its creation; and if it were not I cannot make it so'. The same rule is laid down in *Dungannon* v. *Smith* (12 Cl. & F. 546; see the rejected opinion of Parke B. at pp. 599–600); see, for instance, Lord Lyndhurst's speech at pp. 622–3. It is re-stated by Lord Hatherley in *Cattlin* v. *Brown* (11 Ha. 372, at pp. 375, 377) and in *Hale* v. *Hale* (3 C.D. 643, at pp. 645–6) by Sir George Jessel, rejecting the submission of counsel that the question of remoteness could not be decided until the period of distribution, when it could be seen what shares of the residue there bequeathed had vested at that time. And in *Pearks* v. *Moseley* (5 A.C. 714, at p. 722) Lord Selborne says that the 'question has always been investigated by looking to the state of things as it was at the testator's death, and, if at that time the whole might be too remote, then you could not rectify it by looking to the way in which events actually turned out at any later time'.

I am citing no mere dicta, but opinions vital or material to the cases in which they were given. The cases themselves are distinguishable, but their common characteristic is the one firm principle running through them, the narrow, rigid principle whereby the rule against perpetuities prevails against all later events, if once its application be found at the testator's death (or here the date of the settlement) to defeat the limitations; in such a case the Court never gets an opportunity to apply its rule for the determination of a class at the death of a tenant for life, because in the face of the rule against perpetuities it cannot make use of the facts essential to that determination, as to births, deaths and ages as at that critical moment; the Court can consider only the actual facts at the creation of the interests. The admissibility of after-events to determine remoteness under powers of appointment (see, for instance, Gray, par. 523 e) stands in sharp contrast to its inadmissibility to determine remoteness in other cases.

There seems to be no doubt that the law, as enunciated in the leading English cases, is the same in Ireland; it was clearly so considered by Sir Michael O'Loghlen M.R. nearly a century ago in *Smith* v. *Dungannon* (Flan. & K. 638), to the report of which in the House of Lords I have already referred.

It occurs to me that the case of *Kevern* v. *Williams* (5 Sim. 171) may really be less anomalous than it looks; in that case the tenant for life, after whose death the grandchildren of testator's brother were to take residuary estate (payment to be made at 25), died within one month or so of testator's death and the class of grandchildren alive at the two deaths seems to have been identical; therefore a decision in favour of the grandchildren living at the death of the tenant for life was a decision for those alive when testator died and, except as a matter of accurate expression, the closing of the class at either of the two dates must have comprised exactly the same grandchildren.

However that may be, I could not in the present case let the state of affairs at the death of the tenant for life influence my decision without disregarding the law long settled by an array of authority too weighty for this Court to ignore. To the first question in the originating summons I must answer 'Yes', subject, however, to one reservation; that is, that, if Mr. Chadwick asks me to receive evidence directed to proving that, as has been suggested in the course of the hearing, it was in 1865 physically impossible for Mr. and Mrs. Thompson, by reason of the lady's age, to have further children, I shall be willing to do so and to postpone my final decision until I have seen that evidence and any evidence that may be filed to reply to it, because I see no principle upon which I can exclude such evidence of a material fact as at the date when the settlement was created. At present I do not know the ages of Mr. and Mrs. Thompson nor whether any cogent evidence of that kind can be adduced; when I speak of the physically impossible, I am not thinking of anything like mathematical proof, which cannot be expected, but I mean evidence that in the ordinary course of nature, now well ascertained by long observation and experience, the thing cannot happen. I am assured that the law precludes me from receiving any such testimony, but that is not my view of our law. The theory which I am asked to accept means that, if the settlement had been made by two octogenarians, I should by our law be compelled to defeat its limitations to the grandchildren by assuming that the octogenarians might have had another child and rejecting any evidence to the contrary, because, so it is said, that was the view of a great jurist at a remote period in another country and because, it is implied, that view has been accepted as part of the law of Ireland.

As a matter of practice, we constantly refer to judgments in the English Courts and such judgments, as every lawyer will recognise, have often proved to be of great service to us; but let us be clear. In my opinion, when Saorstát Éireann, and afterwards Éire, continued the laws in force, they did not make binding on their Courts anything short of law. In my opinion, judicial decisions in Ireland before the treaty, and English decisions which were followed here, are binding upon this court only when they represent a law so well settled or pronounced by so weighty a juristic authority that they may fairly be regarded, in a system built up upon the principle of *stare decisis*, as having become established as part of the law of the land before the Treaty; and to bind, they must, of course, not be inconsistent with the Constitution. The traditionalism of lawyers, practising under a law of precedent, tends to obscure the fact that the High Court of Justice established in 1924, was in simple truth, and not merely on paper, a new Court under a new constitution. The High Court today is a new Court under a new Constitution. In my opinion, this Court cannot be fettered in the exercise of the judicial power by opinions of very different Courts under the old régime, unless those opinions must reasonably be considered to have had the force of law in Ireland, so that they formed part of the code expressly retained. For the rest, we must give to Irish judicial views and to judgments in England and elsewhere interpreting a similar jurisprudence, that respect which their intrinsic worth may entitle them to claim, though here, too, in many a case of doubt one may reasonably incline to follow precedent in order to avoid unsettling a law in the course of becoming established.

But I must go further. If, before the Treaty, a particular law was administered in a way so repugnant to the common sense of our citizens as to make the law look ridiculous, it is not in the public interest that we should repeat the mistake. Our new High Court must mould its own *cursus curiae*; in so doing I hold that it is free, indeed bound, to decline to treat any such absurdity in the machinery of administration as having been imposed on it as part of the law of the land; nothing is law here which is inconsistent with derivation from the People. The severe exclusion of evidence about after-events under the rule against perpetuities is not congenial to me, but it is not an absurdity and I am bound to give effect to it; moreover, it goes deeper than the points of practice with which I am now dealing, the domain in which a wide difference of outlook from the views of the past is most likely to be found. Now, the admissibility of evidence as to the age of child-bearing stands on a different footing from evidence of after-events; I am now invited to treat as law here certain opinions on this subject, given in another context, which, if they did represent the practice, would seem to me absurd.

Lord Coke appears to have declared (for purposes of dower) that the law could not adjudge it impossible for a boy four years old to have a child, or a woman albeit 100 years old. (Co. Litt., vol. 1, c. 5, s. 53). In *Jee* v. *Audley* (1 Cox, Eq. Cas. 324, at pp. 325–6) Lord Kenyon, whom I have already quoted on a different issue, refused to hold it impossible for a woman of 70 (not the testatrix) to have a child; it would be 'a very dangerous experiment', he said, 'to give latitude to such a sort of conjecture'; he did not reject medical evidence, for none was tendered. This decision was highly commended in *Dungannon* v. *Smith* (12 Cl. & F. 546). Malins V.C. gave conflicting decisions (*In re Sayer's Trusts*, 6 Eq. 319; *Cooper* v. *Laroche*, 17 C.D. 368), but in *In re Dawson* (39 C.D. 155) Chitty J., purporting to follow Lord Kenyon and then invoking Lord Coke, refused to receive evidence designed to exclude remoteness by showing that an old woman could not have had a child; she was not the testatrix. I have been referred to no similar decision by any Irish Court. The Courts, both here and in England, where there had been no question of remoteness, have readily recognised that a woman of advanced age is past child-bearing; see *Browne* v. *Warnock* (7 L.R. Ir. 3), *Persse* v. *Mitchell* (34 Ir. L.T.R. 135) and *In re Toppin's Estate* ([1915] 1 I.R. 198, 330) and the cases therein cited. Reliance is placed on some dicta in *Ward* v. *Van der Loeff* ([1924] A.C. 653), but the report clearly shows that Viscount Cave and Lord Blanesburgh spoke under the impression that Lord Kenyon had rejected evidence, whereas he says himself that he refuses to conjecture. Moreover, I propose to receive, if adduced, evidence as to the settlor's own wife, a party to the settlement, and, indeed, as I read the trust deed, the person who should most accurately be called the settlor; I am not concerned with a third party's age, the conclusion therefrom, nor with a testator's knowledge of the age of a third party, as Lord Kenyon was, as Malins V.C. and Chitty J. were, as the House of Lords was in 1924; so that my problem is different from theirs.

Again, whether the view I have expressed be right or wrong, I disclaim any intention of making such an attempt as was made by counsel in *Ward* v. *Van der Loeff* ([1924] A.C. 653) to construe the plain words of a document by extrinsic evidence. This is emphatically not a question of construction, where the reception of the evidence in question is concerned, for the rule against perpetuities is not a rule of construction. I should admit the evidence solely as proof of an existing fact, material at the date of the settlement, to the determination of the question of remoteness, and I should admit it in precisely the same way and for precisely the same purpose as I should admit evidence that the settlor's wife was in fact dead at the date of the deed, if that were the fact.

Accordingly, where mere improbability of further issue will not do, if it should be satisfactorily proved that modern medical science would regard as an absurdity the supposition that another child might in the ordinary course of nature have been born to Mr. and Mrs. Thompson after the date of the settlement, I should not hold myself bound, as a matter of legal practice in dealing with the rule against perpetuities, to treat the absurdity as being in the eyes of the law a possible event, which must determine my decision, by reason of Lord Coke's commentaries (in a very different connection) in the early seventeenth century or the refusal of Lord Kenyon to conjecture (under different circumstances) in the late eighteenth.

Notes and Questions
1. Do you accept (a) Gavan Duffy J's strictures on the rule governing evidence as to capacity for child-bearing and (b) his views on the jurisdication of the High Court to repudiate the rule. Cf. Kenny J's views on the pre-1921 English decisions in *Re Murphy's Estate*, p. 246 *ante*. See also the views of McCarthy J. (*cf.* O'Higgins C.J. and Griffin J.) in *Irish Shell Ltd.* v. *Elm Motors Ltd.* Unreported (Supreme Court; 128–82) (Judgments delivered 17th June, 1983).
2. See further on this aspect of the rule against perpetuities, *Irish Land Law*, para. 5.060.

RE POE
[1942] I.R. 535 (High Court)

Testator by his will devised and bequeathed certain property 'to be divided in equal portions between the children of my brother. . . . I order that my trustees shall have power to dispose of my [property] as they think best, and to use the money and other property for the best advantage of the children of my [said] brother until each of them shall reach the age of twenty-five years when each of them is to receive his or her share on reaching the age of twenty-five years. The children of [my said brother] to include any children he may have at a future date'. Various questions were raised concerning the construction of the will.

Black J.:

The terms of the will of the late Major Poe raise in an acute form what is very often one of the most difficult of all technical legal problems, *viz.*, the effect of the rule against perpetuities upon the validity of a particular testamentary disposition.

The material part of the will in question is as follows: [Read portions of the will]

The opening disposition of all the testator's 'land, money, investments, live stock, furniture, and all other property', etc., in favour of the children of his brother, Captain Arthur Percy Poe, is virtually a bequest of the residue of his property after a number of specified legacies have been paid. Captain Poe is still living. He has three children, all of whom are also living, and all of whom had attained the age of 25 years at the date of the testator's death. If the property in question was vested, and not merely contingent, at the testator's death, the whole class in whose favour the disposition was made being ascertained and closed, there could be no question of remoteness or invalidity in the purported disposition. On the other hand, if the attempted disposition was contingent, and if the class was not closed, but possible future-born children of Captain Poe would legally form members of the class, assuming that the disposition were not invalidated by the rule against perpetuities, then, admittedly and obviously, the disposition in question in favour of such future children would be void for remoteness.

Now, while the problem before me raises some points that are controversial to the last degree, there are at any rate two initial propositions which are not open to question.

The first is that where there is an immediate disposition by will in favour of children as a class, and there are such children alive at the death of the testator, then these children then so living and no others compose the class and are objects of the disposition, unless a contrary intention is to be found in the will. It was not always so. According to older cases, the objects were to be ascertained at the date of the will. But, the rule in question, which has been called 'a rule of convenience' in both Jarman and Theobald, is now axiomatic. If there be nothing in the present will to displace it, the late Major Poe's provision for the children of Captain Poe was a valid disposition in favour of the three children living at the testator's death and still living, and future-born children, if there should be any, can have no interest in it.

The second indisputable rule is that where such a disposition in favour of children as a class is accompanied by a provision postponing payment or distribution of the share of each of the children until the attainment of a certain age, then when the first child attains that age, the class is automatically closed, and children born after that are excluded. This might be referred to as the rule in *Andrews* v. *Partington* (3 Bro. C.C. 401), although it has been re-stated in other decisions too numerous to mention. It also, and more generally, perhaps, than the first rule I have mentioned, has been called a rule of convenience, although, as Chitty J. said in *In re Wenmoth's Estate*, *Wenmoth* v. *Wenmoth* (37 Ch. D. 266, at p. 270) it is a rule that must be very inconvenient to those children who may be born after the period of distribution. Its convenience consists in obviating the inconvenience of making the child who has attained the age of distribution wait an indefinite, and possibly very lengthy, period for his share. Of course if there be other children then living, the eldest child's ultimate and maximum share cannot then be ascertained, for some of the other children may die before reaching the prescribed age, and the child who has reached the required age will then be entitled to his proportion of any share or shares so falling in. But his minimum share can be ascertained when the class is closed by reason of his having attained the prescribed age. Now, if the first rule I mentioned be displaced here by the terms of the will, then the rule in *Andrews* v. *Partington* (3 Bro. C.C. 401), if it also be not excepted by the will, would equally save the disposition with which I am dealing, inasmuch as the three existing children had attained 25 years of age at the testator's death, and the class would then have been closed.

This rule as to the closing of the class can sometimes operate so as to save a devise or bequest from being invalidated by remoteness. An illustration is the case of *Picken* v. *Matthews* (10 Ch. D. 264) where property was left on trust for such children of the testator's daughters as should attain 25. One daughter had a child who had attained 25 at the testator's death. As this closed the class and confined it to children living and ascertained at the testator's death, subject to their attaining a certain age, the gift was valid. In the same way, it may be invoked if that be necessary in the present case. That depends upon whether a contrary or inconsistent intention is to be gathered from the rest of the will.

Before considering that, yet a third rule may be mentioned. It is that when some of the objects that form a class are too remote and others were born within the period permitted by law, the disposition cannot be split into portions, treating it as invalid only as affecting the objects that would be too remote, but valid as regards the objects, being persons, born within the permitted limits of time. In other words, if the vice of remoteness may affect any unascertained member of the class, it affects the class as a whole. For this purpose, the disposition cannot be treated like the curate's egg – good in parts. This principle might perhaps be looked upon as the rule in *Leakey* v. *Robinson* (2 Mer. 363). It was supported by the Court of Appeal in *Smith* v. *Smith* (I.R. 5 Ch. 342) and in *Hale* v. *Hale* (3 Ch. D. 643). On the other hand, in *In re Moseley's Trusts* (L.R. 11 Eq. 499), Malins V.C. held that in such a case the whole gift was not void as infringing the rule against perpetuities, but that it might be severed, and the limitation held good as to some shares, and bad as to others. The same clause of the same will was considered by Jessell M.R. (11 Ch. D. 555), who held the exact contrary of what had been decided by the Vice-Chancellor. On appeal, the Court of Appeal felt bound by the decision of a former Court of Appeal to affirm the Master of the Rolls; the second Court of Appeal at the same time indicating that it favoured the view of the Vice-Chancellor, and only affirmed the Master of the Rolls in deference to the decision of the former Court of Appeal in *Smith* v. *Smith* (L.R. 5 Ch. 342).

As there were three Judges in the second Court of Appeal and only two in the first, this furnishes a curious instance of a principle being settled for the time being by a minority decision of the appellate tribunal. However, the matter was finally concluded by the House of Lords, reported *sub. nom. Pearks* v. *Moseley and Others* (5 App. Cas. 714) when it was settled once for all that in such a case as indicated, there could be no severance, and that if any unascertained member of a class may be too remote, the whole disposition in favour of the class is invalidated. The result is that, if under Major Poe's will the class of children comprises children of Captain Poe who may yet be born, the entire disposition fails, and it cannot be upheld even *quoad* the three children who were living at the testator's death and are still living.

I have now to consider two other provisions in the will, and in my opinion they involve most perplexing difficulties which I have found intensified by many of the cases and judgments – often conflicting – which I have felt it necessary to study in seeking to unravel the problem.

First, there is a provision empowering the trustee to dispose of the property in question, 'and to use the money and property for the best advantage of the children of my brother A. Percy Poe until each of them shall reach the age of twenty-five years, when each is to receive his or her share on reaching the age of twenty-five years'. Now, this clause purports to postpone the distribution of the property left to the children until they attain the age of twenty-five. That clause, if it is not to be disregarded, would bring the rule in *Andrews* v. *Partington* (3 Bro. C.C. 401) into operation, unless there is something else in the will to prevent that result. If the rule in *Andrews* v. *Partington* operates, it would seem to me to lead to the same result as it did in *Picken* v. *Matthews* (10 Ch. D. 264), namely to close the class when the eldest child attained 25 years of age, thus excluding future born children, and getting rid of all question of the rule against perpetuities.

I defer for the moment considering the final words of the will saying that the children are to include any children Captain Poe may have at a future date.

Now, there are a number of reported cases in which the Courts have had to consider the effect upon the period of distribution of a provision making a gift to a class payable only on the attaining of a certain age. Most of these cases did not involve any question of the rule against perpetuities; but some of them did involve that question, and even those that did not are germane to the present problem. First, there is the case of *Fox* v. *Fox* (L.R. 19 Eq. 286). It has been distinguished, criticised, and dissented from; but never, so far as I am aware, actually overruled. In that case a testator directed his trustees, after the determination of some prior life interests, to divide and transfer a portion of £15,000 to and amongst the children of a named party equally as and when they should respectively attain the age of 25 years. He also directed the trustees to apply from time to time the income of the presumptive share of each child, or so much thereof as they should think fit, for his, her, or their maintenance and education until such share should become payable as aforesaid. If there should be no children surviving the testator, or if they should die before attaining 21, there was a gift over. Jessel M.R. said at p. 290: 'Being opposed to the frittering away of general rules, and thinking that such rules, so long as they remain rules, ought to be followed, I hold that a gift contained in a direction to pay and divide amongst a class at a specific age, followed by a direction to apply the whole income for maintenance in the meantime, is vested, and not the less so because there is a discretion conferred on the trustees to apply less than the whole income for that purpose'. He added at p. 291, 'I also think that the gift over, if not conclusive on the question, certainly aids the construction adopted by me'. This was a strongly expressed decision by a great Judge. It will be seen from the words I have quoted, that his opinion was formed quite independently of the gift over, his reference to which was only a confirmatory addendum. I note this because in the 7th edition of Jarman on Wills, p. 1388, it is submitted that the approval of *Fox* v. *Fox* (L.R. 19 Eq. 286) given by the Court of Appeal in *In re Turney* ([1899] 2 Ch. 739) 'had reference to the effect of a gift over in conferring vested interests subject to be divested'. On the other hand, in *Vawdry* v. *Geddes* (R. & My. 202) Leach M.R. took the view that a gift over, so far from aiding the presumption of an immediate vesting, caused that presumption to fail entirely. But certainly in *In re Turney* ([1899] 2 Ch. 739), the gift over seems to have been the decisive point in favour of immediate vesting. See the judgment of Romer L.J. particularly ([1899] 2 Ch. at p. 748). The Court of Appeal said that *Fox* v. *Fox* (L.R. 19 Eq. 286) was very good sense and very good law. Nevertheless, in *In re Wintle, Tucker* v. *Wintle* ([1896] 2 Ch. 711) North J. expressly dissented from it. There was a great similarity between the respective dispositions in *Fox* v. *Fox* (L.R. 19 Eq. 286) and those in the later case of *In re Mervin, Mervin* v. *Crossman* ([1891] 3 Ch. 197) which was decided in the opposite sense, it being held that the children, in spite of the discretionary power to pay all or part of the income for their maintenance, did not take vested interests, and the gift over was void for remoteness. In *In re Williams, Williams* v. *Williams* ([1907] 1 Ch. 180), *Fox* v. *Fox* (L.R. 19 Eq. 286) was distinguished on the words of the will there, Neville J. doubting whether *Fox* v. *Fox* (L.R. 19 Eq. 286) and in *In re Wintle* ([1896] 2 Ch. 711) could stand together. It may seem equally difficult for Fox v. *Fox* (L.R. 19 Eq. 286) and in *In re Mervin* ([1891] 3 Ch. 197) to stand together. In *In re Grimshaw's Trusts* (11 CH. D. 406, at p. 411). Hall V.C. seems to explain *Fox* v. *Fox* (L.R. 19 Eq. 286) on the ground that 'the first trust there was of the capital fund, and after the gift of that in the first instance to the children there followed, as a sort of annex to that trust, these words' – the words referred to being those empowering the trustees to pay the income for maintenance. But in *In re Mervin* ([1891] 3 Ch. 197), the first trust was also of the capital fund, followed by an 'annex' providing for maintenance.

I am inclined to think the most plausible distinction between the cases is that suggested by Stirling J. in *In re Mervin* ([1891] 3 Ch. 197, at p. 201). He said of *Fox* v. *Fox* (L.R. 19 Eq. 286): 'There, however, the fund was divided into as many shares as the son had children, and the income of each share was directed to be applied for the maintenance of the particular child for whom the share was destined. Here the income of the whole fund is made applicable for the maintenance of all the children'. Again, in *In re Parker, Barker* v. *Barker* (16 Ch. D. 44), the trustees were to hold certain investments upon trust to pay the income thereof, or such part of the same as they should deem expedient, for the maintenance and education of the children of the testatrix until they attained 21, and then upon trust to pay them the capital, following which provision the trustees were empowered 'to dispose of any competent part, not exceeding one half of the presumptive share of any of my children' for their advancement in life. The same Judge who decided *Fox* v. *Fox* – Jessel M.R. – held that an infant who had died did not take a vested interest in his share. He said at p. 45: 'When a legacy is payable at a certain age, but is, in terms, contingent, the legacy becomes vested when there is a direction to pay the interest in the meantime to the person to whom the legacy is given; and not the less or when there is superadded a direction that the trustees "shall pay the whole or such part of the interest as they shall think fit".' If this be right, and I should be ready to follow it, the fact that the trustees' power is discretionary to pay all or only part of the income, does not matter. But Jessel M.R. continued at p. 46: 'But I am not aware of any case where, the gift being of an entire fund payable to a class of persons equally on their attaining a certain age, a direction to apply the income of the whole fund in the meantime for their maintenance has been held to create a vested interest in a member of the class who does not attain that age'. He added that there was nothing in the will before him 'giving an aliquot share of income to any individual child'. Similarly, in *In re Gossling, Gossling* v. *Elcock* ([1903] 1 Ch. 448] where each child was held to take an immediate vested interest in his or her share, the very feature was present which Jessel M.R. held to be absent in *In re Parker* (16 Ch. D. 44), as by the terms of the will in *Gossling's Case* ([1903] 1 Ch. 448) the testator 'intended that the income of the aliquot share coming to the particular child should be payable for the maintenance of that child until he or she attained the age of 21'.

In view of these quotations, I think that *Fox* v. *Fox* (L.R. 19 Eq. 286) and *In re Mervin* ([1891] 3 Ch. 197) can be distinguished and may stand together; but the presence or absence of anything giving an aliquot share of income to any individual child does not seem to me to enable *Fox* v. *Fox* (L.R. 19 Eq. 286) and *In re Wintle* ([1896] 2 Ch. 711) to be reconciled, in view of the wording of the maintenance provision in *In re Wintle* ([1896] 2 Ch. 711), which I find hard to distinguish from the like clause in the will in *Fox* v. *Fox* (L.R. 19 Eq. 286). The maintenance clause in the will of Major Poe stands out by itself; but I do not think it makes clear that each child is to get an aliquot share of the income. Taking the cases I have quoted together, I think it is very doubtful whether *Fox* v. *Fox* (L.R. 19 Eq. 286) could be applied in the interpretation of the present will.

Whether it is necessary for those representing the existing children's interest to invoke *Fox* v. *Fox* (L.R. 19 Eq. 286) at all is another matter. Before coming to that, I must consider the last words of the will, which clearly define the term 'children' by saying that they are to include any children of the said A.P. Poe which he may have at a future date. If the gift in this case were not immediate, those words would not affect in any way the old rule that such words of futurity do not let in children born after the first share has become payable. In Hawkins on Wills, 2nd ed., p. 93, the view is taken that in the case of an immediate gift also, such words will generally be considered as intended only to provide for the case of children coming into existence between the date of the will and the testator's death. A number of cases are cited in support of this rule. One of them – *Sprackling* v. *Ranier* (1 Dick, 344) turned upon the use of the word 'then', and is perhaps in no way an authority for the proposition that such words do not enlarge the class. See note (t) at page 1695 of the 6th edition of Jarman. But there is ample authority left. There are the decisions in *Storrs* v. *Benbow* (2 My. & K. 46); *Butler* v. *Lower* (10 Sim, 317) and the dicta in *Mann* v. *Thompson* (Kay, 638). As against this, *Mogg* v. *Mogg* (1 Mer. 654) is undoubtedly a decision in the contrary sense. In accordance with the practice at the time, and the circumstances, no reasons were given for it. Besides this, its authority is not increased by the way it was dealt with in the Privy Council in *Dias* v. *De Livera* (5 App. Cas. 123). In the latter case the authorities in support of the old rule that such words as 'born and to be born' in a bequest which is immediate to children as a class do not enlarge the class to let in those born after the testator's death, are reinforced by a citation of the weighty opinion of Mr. Justice Williams. See p. 134. The case of *Defflis* v. *Goldschmidt* (1 Mer. 417) which may be said to support *Mogg* v. *Mogg* (1 Mer. 654) turned upon very special wording not present in Major Poe's will. I should not be satisfied that these two cases suffice to supplant the old rule as to the effect of such words of futurity as 'to be born' or 'to be begotten'.

In *Bateman* v. *Gray* (L.R. 6 Eq. 215) the words were 'to the children of A. now or hereafter to be born who shall attain the age of 21 years'. These were followed by a power of advancement out of the vested or presumptive share of any object of the gift. Lord Romilly M.R. thought the word 'vested' was very strong, and held that the class of children to take was not ascertained when the eldest attained 21. The word 'vested' does not appear in the clause of the present will authorising the use of the money until the children reach 25. A like decision was given in *Iredell* v. *Iredell* (25 Beav. 485). But there the clause authorising the maintenance contained the words 'whether the child should or should not attain 21'. In *In re Deloitte, Griffiths* v. *Allbeury* ([1919] 2 Ch. 209), Eve J. said that *Bateman* v. *Gray* (L.R. 6 Eq. 215) was not satisfactorily reported, and that the matter before the Court of Appeal could not be concluded in any way by that case. In *Gimblett* v. *Purton* (L.R. 12 Eq. 427) Malins V.C. said at p. 431, that even if he was dealing with a clause for advancement similar to that in *Bateman* v. *Gray* (L.R. 6 Eq. 215) he would have declined to follow that decision 'as it tends to throw a doubt upon a rule which is as well settled as any rule of interpretation in the Courts'. He held in that case that a power to apply the interest of the presumptive shares of grandchildren towards their maintenance did not prevent those born after the eldest attained the age of distribution from being excluded. It is true that in this case there were no words of futurity such as 'to be born'; but the case is none the less relevant, and also of interest for the view the Vice-Chancellor took of *Bateman* v. *Gray* (L.R. 6 Eq. 215).

Upon all the authorities, I should not be prepared to hold that in the present case children born after the eldest child attained 25 years of age form members of the class of children in whose favour the testator made his disposition. On the other hand, I do not think the matter is free from doubt, and I can quite understand that it might present itself differently to another mind. The view to which I incline tends to avoid intestacy and to evade the rule against perpetuities. Both Judges and text-writers have complained that various questionable decisions have been given under the influence of a desire to evade that rule. I can only hope that I am not adding to the number of these errors so influenced. The words of Lord Selborne L.C. in *Pearks* v. *Moseley and Others* (5 App. Cas. 714) were impressed on me. He said at p. 719: 'You do not import the law of remoteness into the construction of the instrument, by which you investigate the expressed intention of the testator. You take his words, and endeavour to arrive at their meaning exactly as if there had been no such law, and as if the whole intention expressed by the words could lawfully take effect'. But I think that pronouncement cannot be taken to mean that I must leave the law of remoteness entirely out of account in all circumstances. I think there are circumstances in which I may take it into account. Indeed, the very next words of Lord Selborne make that clear. He proceeds to say: 'I do not mean, that, in dealing with words that are obscure or ambiguous, weight, even in a question of remoteness, may not sometimes be given to the consideration that it is better to effectuate than to destroy the intention'. I consider the words of the will before me to be ambiguous and indeterminate, and such that in construing them, I should be justified in giving some weight, if necessary, to the consequences that would ensue from adopting a construction that would admit afterborn children to the class in whose favour the disposition was made – a construction which I do not think would give effect to the testator's intention. But, even without any such consideration of consequences, I should take the same view, albeit with the doubt which so many conflicting authorities appear to me to render inevitable.

But, apart from all the foregoing considerations, I am of opinion that the words of Major Poe's will are more like the words used in the will in *Kevern* v. *Williams* (5 Sim. 171) than those in any of the cases I have referred to. In that case the property was given in trust for the grandchildren in the first instance, and then followed the words 'to be by them received in equal proportions when they shall severally attain the age of 25 years'. It was held that the class was limited to those born in the lifetime of the person who took the anterior life interest. Here there is likewise in the first instance an unqualified disposition in favour of the children. In a much later part of the will there is a distinct provision – 'a sort of annex' as it was called in *In re Grimshaw's Trusts* (11 Ch. D. 406, at p. 411) – to the effect that each child is to receive his share on reaching the age of 25 years. Paraphrasing the words of Mr. Jarman at p. 1399 of the 6th edition, it would seem to me that futurity is not annexed to the substance of the gift, but appears rather to relate to the time of payment. *Kevern* v. *Williams* (5 Sim. 171) has not escaped criticism, including that of the learned author of 'Gray on Perpetuities'. Yet it is said in Gray that 'assuming that the postponement of payment was too remote, it is submitted that the decision was correct'. It was suggested that on the facts in that case, the time of payment was not too remote. (See Gray on Perpetuities, 2nd edn. p. 480, s. 638.) If that be so, the postponement of payment in this present case would surely be too remote. I am not aware that *Kevern* v. *Williams* (5 Sim. 171) has ever been overruled. In most of the cases quoted, the postponement of payment was part and parcel of the gift itself. If the two can be divorced here, the postponement of the period of distribution not being annexed to the substance of the prior unqualified gift, then the vesting would have been *instanter*, and Mr. McCann would have been right in his contention that what he was pleased to call 'the tags' – at any rate, the postponement clause – could be disregarded.

If the gift here and the quite separate clause regarding postponement of distribution can be treated as disconnected – and there are a series of legacies sandwiched between then – then I think the cases cited in argument of *Cooke* v. *Cooke* (38 Ch. D. 202) and *In the matter of the estate of Herbert Clarke* (39 I.L.T.R. 78) would be illustrations of a principle that might be applied to the construction of this will. I incline to the view that they may be regarded as distinct.

Therefore, on the several alternative grounds I have indicated, I take the view upon the whole that the disposition in favour of the children of Captain Poe was valid, and that children born after the eldest child attained 25 years of age, if there had been any, would have been excluded. For the same reason, future children, if there should ever be any, would have no claim upon the property left to the children of Captain Poe.

Notes

See further on the application of the rule against perpetuities to class gifts and the operation of the rule in *Andrews* v. *Partington*, *Irish Land Law*, para. 5.080 *et seq.*

RE HAY
[1932] N.I. 215 (High Court)

The testator by his will devised a portion of his estate upon trust, after the death of his wife (which happened), to pay the rents and profits thereof in certain shares to five of his children, Francis, Joseph, Grace, Jane and Margaret during their respective lives, with powers of appointment and gifts over in default of appointment as therein mentioned. The testator directed that from and after the death of the survivor of his said five children, his trustees should hold the shares of any of them, which might remain unappointed by will, for his sons, James and William Thomas jointly for life, and after the death of the survivor, for the first son of Francis for life, and after his death, for such of his children, grand-children, brothers, sisters, nephews and neices as he should by his last will appoint, and in default of appointment, for the second and every other son of the said Francis, severally, according to their respective seniorities with limitations and powers of appointment similar to those given to the first son of Francis. Then followed the words: 'and in default of the same then for the first and every other son of the said Joseph successively according to their respective seniorities in like manner and with like limitations and power of appointment as is hereby given to the first and other sons of Francis'. Similar provisions were made in favour of the first and every other son of the testator's sons and daughters, James, William, Thomas, Grace, Jane and Margaret, all of which provisions were introduced by the words: 'and in default', while the ultimate limitation was expressed in the words – 'in default for my own right heirs for ever.'

The testator's last surviving son was William Thomas, who prior to his death, was entitled to a life interest in the shares of Francis and Margaret, both of whom died without issue and without having exercised the powers of appointment given to them by the will.

The question for determination was as to who was entitled, on the death of William Thomas, to the shares of Francis and Margaret.

The claimants were Edward Norman, the only son of the testator's son Joseph, and appointee under his will of all his (Joseph's) interest under the will of the testator, and Edward James, the only son of the testator's eldest son, James, who claimed to be entitled under an alleged intestacy. Both claimants were born during the lifetime of the testator.

It was admitted that the gift over which immediately followed the life estate to the first son of the testator's son, Francis (or, as there was no such son, the gift which in the events which happened, immediately followed the life estate of William Thomas) offended against the rule against perpetuities and was void.

It was argued on behalf of Edward Norman that he was entitled to a life estate under the immediately succeeding gift in favour of 'the first and every other son of Joseph'.

On behalf of Edward James it was contended that, as the limitation in favour of the children of the first son was void, all ulterior limitations were also void. It was thus submitted that an intestacy arose upon the death of William Thomas, the last tenant for life, and that the interest in question thereupon passed to the heir-at-law of the testator, namely, his eldest son, James, who had by his will appointed all his estate and interest in the lands to his only son, the said Edward James.

Andrew L.J. (sitting as Chancery Judge):

The case has given me a considerable amount of anxiety, as the relevant authorities do not appear to be wholly free from conflict, and the decisions depend in so many cases upon the particular phraseology employed by the testator. The view which I have formed, however, renders it unnecessary for me to refer to the greater part of the authority cited by Counsel or perused by me.

Upon the question of the construction of the words 'and in default of the same', which introduce the limitations in favour of the first and every other son of Joseph, I am of opinion that Mr. Chambers' submission is the correct one, and that their true meaning is 'in default of the exercise of the power of appointment' which was conferred in the immediately preceding line of the will. Not only does it seem unnatural in finding a subject matter for the words 'of the same' to refer back, as Mr. McGonigal contends we should do, to certain selected objects named in practically the opening words of the preceding clause, namely, the sons of Francis, but also any construction which did not make the words 'in default of the same' relate to the immediately preceding power of appointment, would leave unprovided for, if the limitations had been, as the testator assumed they were, valid, the contingency of there being objects of the power but no appointment. The Court is always slow, especially in the case of such series of limitations as are before us in this will, to put such a construction upon ambiguous words as would create an intestacy.

To this extent, therefore, I agree with Mr. Chambers' argument, but I differ from him in the conclusions which he asks me to draw. *Proctor* v. *Bishop of Bath and Wells* (2 H.Bl. 358), and many other cases which could be cited, amply support the proposition to be found in Jarman on Wills, 7th Ed. 324, that, where a gift is void for remoteness, all limitations ulterior to and dependent on such remote gift are also void; but on page 326 the learned editors also rightly lay it down that a limitation following one which is too remote may be good, if it can take effect independently of the void limitation. Now in my opinion a gift over in default of appointment does take effect independently of the preceding power, and it may, accordingly, be good though the power itself be bad for remoteness. Other text books express the same clear view in unhesitating manner. Thus in Theobald on Wills, 7th Ed. 605, the learned editors, after pointing out that limitations following as remainders upon limitations void for perpetuity are themselves void, whether within the line of perpetuity or not, proceed immediately to add: 'But where a power of appointment is given to arise upon an event beyond the limits of perpetuity a gift in default of appointment is valid'. The reason assigned for the difference in the law applicable to the two cases is both clear and authoritative, namely, that in the former class of cases the remaindermen are only intended to take if there is no one to take under the prior limitations; in the latter, the gift in default of appointment is intended to take effect unless displaced by a valid exercise of the power. Finally, the same view is shortly expressed in Halsbury, vol. 22, 360, where it is stated that 'the fact that a power may be exercised in a manner contrary to the rule does not affect a gift in default of appointment which takes effect unless it is itself obnoxious to the rule against perpetuities. This is so because until the power is exercised the property remains vested in those who take in default of appointment.'

Such unanimity of opinion would not, of course, exist without ample authority to support it. Two cases are especially in point, *Webb* v. *Sadler* (L.R. 1 Ch. 419), and *In re Abbott, Peacock* v. *Frigout* ([1893] 1 Ch. 54). The former is a decision of Lord Selborne, L.C. and James and Mellish, L.JJ.; the latter is a considered judgment of Stirling, J. I do not propose to examine them in detail, as the grounds and effect of the decisions are embodied in the passages from the text books which I have cited. Both cases in my opinion support the view that the principle that a limitation, depending or expectant upon a prior limitation which is void for remoteness, is invalid, does not necessarily apply to limitations in default of appointment, as in most cases of such limitations the intention is that they should take effect independently of and unless displaced by a valid exercise of the preceding power of appointment.

This is, in my opinion, the true view in the present case. The testator intended that after the death of the survivor of his sons James and William Thomas the unappointed shares of his children Grace Taylor, Jane, Margaret Anne, Francis and Joseph should pass to the first, second and other sons of Francis, and afterwards to the first and every other son of Joseph unless displaced by the exercise of the powers of appointment which were invalid for remoteness. I therefore hold that on the true construction of the will of the testator and in the events which have happened, Edward Norman Hay is entitled to a life interest in the twelve one hundredths shares of Margaret Anne Wray and of Francis Hay respectively, and I answer questions 2 and 3 of the summons accordingly. All parties are entitled to their costs out of the estate.

Note

See further on subsequent independent and dependent gifts, *Irish Land Law*, para. 5.091 *et seq. Cf. Re Ramadge's Settlement* [1919] 1 I.R. 205.

RE HALLINAN'S TRUSTS

[1904] 1 I.R. 452; 4 N.I.J.R. 237; 38 I.L.T.R. 165 (Court of Appeal)

A testator being entitled, under settlement executed on his marriage in 1877, to a life interest in lands, with power of appointment to child or children after his death, by his will dated 20th May, 1896, appointed all the lands comprised in the settlement to one daughter on her attaining twenty-five. The testator died in 1901, when the appointee was fifteen years old.

Porter M.R.:

The facts of the case are shortly these. By marriage settlement of 26th April, 1877, executed on the marriage of John Hallinan, junior, with Mary Frances O'Farrell, a life estate in lands was limited to John Hallinan, junior, and after his death the property the subject of the settlement was to go 'in trust for all or such one or more exclusively of the other or others of the children and remoter issue of the said intended marriage, at such ages or times, or age or time, and in such shares, if more than one, and upon such conditions, and in such manner, as the said Mary Frances O'Farrell and John Hallinan, junior, or the survivor of them, should by any deed or by his or her will appoint', and in default for the children of the marriage equally. John Hallinan, junior, died 9th June, 1901, having survived his wife, and leaving a number of children, of whom Maude Beatrice attained eighteen in March, 1904, and there are other children younger. John Hallinan, junior, previous to his death, by his will dated 26th May, 1896, appointed to his daughter, Maude Beatrice, all the lands, comprised in the settlement on her attaining the age of twenty-five years; but he did not dispose of the income of the property which should accrue between the date of his death and her attainment of the age of twenty-five.

The question now arises as to whether the appointment in favour of Maude Beatrice Hallinan is a valid execution of the power created by the settlement of 1877, or is void on account of remoteness. The settlement would not have authorised an express appointment to unborn children on attainment of twenty-five, because that would be practically twenty-five years longer than a life in being. But the question is not quite so simple, and will have to be considered in reference to the facts. Maude Beatrice was born in 1886, and the appointment in her favour would necessarily take effect in much less than twenty-five years from the date of her father's death.

The question is whether she takes any interest under the appointment, or whether it is void for remoteness. The general rule is stated by Lord St. Leonards in his book on Powers. He says (p. 396): 'It is well established, therefore, that under a particular power, as a power to appoint to children, no estate can be created which would not have been valid if limited in the deed creating the power.' He then refers to *Massey* v. *Barton* (7 Ir. Eq. R. 95), and says: 'The test of the validity of the estates raised is to place them in the deed creating the power, in lieu of the power itself. Thus, if by a settlement an estate be limited to A for life, remainder to his children as he shall appoint, and he afterwards appoint to a son born subsequently to the settlement for life, remainder to the children of that son as purchasers; read the limitations as if inserted in the settlement in the place of the power, and they will stand thus: to A for life, remainder to his unborn son for life, remainder to the sons of that son as purchasers. Now, the limitation to the grandchildren would have been void if contained in the settlement; and therefore it cannot be sustained as a due execution of the power. But it is important in these cases to consider whether the power was *created* by will or deed: this speaks from the execution of it; that from the death of the testator: so that in the case of a power *created* by will, children born in the testator's lifetime, though *after his will*, stand in the same situaiton as children born at the execution of the deed where the power is created by deed.' 'We must be careful,' he says, 'not to destroy this distinction by extending it to an instrument *executing* a power; for whether the power be executed by deed or will, the limitation, in regard to the question of perpetuity, must receive the same construction. The point of inquiry is the instrument *creating*, and not the instrument *executing* the power.'

The only case he refers to in support of the general proposition is *Massey* v. *Barton* (7 Ir. Eq. R. 95), and *Massey* v. *Barton* was a decision of Mr. Blackburne when Master of the Rolls. That case goes the whole length of the statement in Lord St. Leonards' book: but, curiously enough, Lord St. Leonards relies on *Massey* v. *Barton* (7 Ir. Eq. R. 95) in support of his statement of the law, and *Massey* v. *Barton* (7 Ir. Eq. R. 95) seems to have been decided on the authority of the *dictum* in Lord St. Leonards' book. The suit of *Massey* v . *Barton* (7 Ir. Eq. R. 95) was brought for the purpose of taking the opinion of the Court on a question which arose upon the marriage settlement and will of Mr. George William Massey, who was the father of the plaintiffs in the action. In his judgment the Master of the Rolls says: 'In this case a pecuniary fund was vested in trustees on the marriage of George William Massey, the father of the minors, with Miss Narcissa S. Barry, in trust for him and his lady for their lives, which trusts have ceased by their deaths; and subject to their life estates, as to the principal money, on trust for the issue of the marriage in such shares and proportions, and at such times and with such benefit of survivorship, as George W. Massey should by his last will and testament, attested by two witnesses, appoint; and in default of appointment, to be equally divided between them; the shares of such of them as should be sons to become vested interests on their attaining the ages of twenty-one years. There were three sons, the only issue of the marriage, who are plaintiffs in the cause; and two of them having attained the age of twenty-one years, apply to be paid their shares of the fund. It appears that Mr. Massey made a will attested as the power required, and bequeathed the fund amongst his children, but not to be paid until they attained their respective ages of twenty-five years, and not before; this postponement is contended to be void by the two sons who make the present application. This is the case of a particular power restricted as to its objects to the children of the marriage.' Then he quotes Sir Edward Sugden, and says: 'Adopting this test, the result would be, that by this settlement the fund would be limited to the issue of the marriage then unborn, on the death of the father; but would not become vested for a period that *might* exceed twenty-one years from the time of his death; such a limitation would be clearly void for remoteness: *Lade* v. *Holford* (Amb. 479), and *Proctor* v. *Bishop of Bath and Wells* (2 H. Bl. 358); in which latter case a devise to the eldest unborn son of the testatrix's grandson, who should be bred a clergyman and be in holy orders, was held to be void, as he could not be in orders until twenty-four years of age; until which time there was, therefore, a possible suspense of property.'

In that case, which was heard in November, 1844, George William Massey had died nine years before, but the dates are not given in reference to the objects of the power at all, and I only take the decision as being a general statement of a general proposition. Oddly enough (and I mention it merely as matter of curiosity), I find a note of mine, made years ago, in my own copy of the report: '*Query* as to this case', and setting out reasons – 'In 1835 two, and most probably all, of the sons were upwards of twelve years old, and to give them the fund upon their attaining twenty-five was merely, in other words, to give it to them provided they should be living respectively in thirteen years to be computed from that time. . . . The mistake appears to be in confounding a limitation in the settlement to *any* son who should attain twenty-five – which might or might not be within the rule against perpetuities, and the limitation to ascertained sons who must attain the vesting age within that period.' In this case the gift is 'unto my daughter, Maude Beatrice Hallinan, on her attaining the age of twenty-five years'.

The matter is not very clear; and, in his extremely able argument, Mr. Clery relied very largely on *Wilkinson* v. *Duncan* (30 Beav. 111), which might at first sight appear to be quite undistinguishable from the case before me. It was a question about a will, but I find that it was not decided on any such ground. *Massey* v. *Barton* (7 Ir. Eq. R. 95) was not referred to. The view the Master of the Rolls took was this. He says (p. 117): 'The view I take of the case generally is that which I have stated, viz. where the shares of each person is ascertained, the gifts to those who happen to be within the limits of the rule against perpetuity may be good as to them, though the gifts be invalid as to the others who are beyond that limit, because the number and amount of the shares are ascertained at the proper period, and within the proper limit of time'. He looked into the matter further, and in a supplemental judgment he says: 'I think this will affords instances of both the rules stated by Vice-Chancellor Wood. In the gift to the daughters a sum is specifically given to each, which is not dependent on the gift to the others, and consequently those will take it who can take it within the time allowed by the law against perpetuities. With respect to the gift to the sons, it illustrates the other rule. I am of opinion that it is a gift to a class which cannot be ascertained until all the members of it shall have attained twenty-four, and, therefore, with respect to them, the appointment of the residue is wholly void for remoteness. With respect to the daughters, as the number of sums of £2000 were ascertained at the death of the nephew, I think that those who attain their age of twenty-four within the period of twenty-one years from the death of the nephew are entitled to their shares, and the residue will go as unappointed.' That case was one no doubt in which the question arose upon a power created by will; but the simple question which arose for decision was whether what were good gifts in exercise of the power in reference to the actual attainment of twenty-four within the limit of twenty-one years were bad, because the appointment was not restricted to the age of twenty-one, after lives in being at the creation of the power.

Von Brockdorff v. *Malcolm* (30 Ch. D. 172) was also a case of the exercise of a special power of appointment, and it was held that an appointment 'upon trust for all and every my daughters and daughter who shall survive me, and shall, either in my lifetime or after my decease, attain the age of twenty-four years, and if more than one, in equal shares as tenants in common,' was not void for remoteness. The discussion of the case and judgment were largely cognizant with a different question, viz., as to whether there was an exercise of the power at all; but the question as to remoteness was argued as a subsidiary matter, and Cozens-Hardy, J., puts it this way: 'All the limitations to children are void, as in the case of daughters they might possibly be too remote. A daughter might not attain twenty-four till more than twenty-one years after the death of the testator. The gift is to a class, and, if part of it is void, the whole is void: *Pearks* v. *Moseley* (5 A.C. 714).' Then Mr.

Wright, who appeared for the trustees, says: 'The youngest child was three years old at the time of the testator's death. The class of children must, therefore, be ascertained within twenty-one years from his death: *Wilkinson* v. *Duncan* (30 Beav. 111). The gift is therefore good, and the point which was decided in *Pearks* v. *Moseley* (5 A.C. 714) did not arise. It is immaterial whether the gift is to a class or individuals. The state of things at the time of the testator's death must be looked at. The daughters take absolutely; the direction to settle their shares is of course void;' and Pearson, J., says: 'I think that *Wilkinson* v. *Duncan* (30 Beav. 111) applies, and that the appointment is not void for remoteness.' The result follows that whether the power is created by will or deed, if it is exercised in favour of a person named or described, and if it be directed to vest at a period exceeding twenty-one years after a life in being, but must in the nature of things actually vest before the expiration of twenty years after the determination of the life in being at the creation of the power, in that case there is a good exercise of the power, and I so hold in this case.

(Frances Hallinan appealed to the Court of Appeal **FitzGibbon**, **Walker** and **Holmes**, **L.JJ**.

The Court affirmed the decision of the Master of the Rolls, and dismissed the appeal.)

Note
See further on the application of the rule against perpetuities to powers of appointment, *Irish Land Law*, para. 5.118 *et seq*.

JAMESON V. SQUIRE
[1948] I.R. 153; 82 I.L.T.R. 46 (Supreme Court)

A letting agreement for three years of a dwelling house provided that 'the tenant shall have the option at any time after the expiration of two years of the term hereby granted . . . of purchasing the premises' for a specified sum and on terms therein provided. These terms were that the sale should be carried out by a sub-lease for the entire of the landlord's reversionary term less one day at a specified rent. The tenant remained in possession after the expiry of the original term of three years, becoming a tenant from year to year of the premises, and subsequently sought to exercise the option.

An action was brought by the tenant to compel the landlord to grant a sub-lease in accordance with the option. Gavan Duffy P. held that the option was exercisable only during the third year of the original term and the tenant's attempt to exercise it was too late. The tenant appealed to the Supreme Court.

Maguire C.J.:
This is an appeal from a judgment in favour of the defendants, pronounced by the President of the High Court on the trial of the action.

The action was brought for a declaration that an option contained in an agreement, dated the 15th of October, 1941, was a valid and subsisting option, and for an order that, on payment of the sum of £1,720 by the plaintiff to the defendants, the defendants do execute to the plaintiff a proper sub-lease of the premises the subject of the option. There was also a claim for damages, but this part of the claim is not persisted in.

[He referred to the terms of the agreement and continued:]

After the expiration of the term of three years the plaintiff remained on in possession as a tenant, and on payment of rent, which was accepted by the defendants, he became a yearly tenant. On the 18th November, 1945, he gave notice to the defendants that he intended to exercise the option contained in the agreement. The defendants, through their solicitor, replied that the option was 'not exercisable in the events which have happened.' Thereupon the plaintiff commenced these proceedings.

The President of the High Court held that, on the fair reading of the agreement, the option was a right given to the tenant conditionally on its exercise within the term of three years created by the agreement. Holding that the tenant's attempt to exercise the option came too late, he dismissed the action.

I find myself unable to agree with the learned President in his interpretation of the agreement. The provision that the option might be exercised 'at any time' after the expiration of two years, and the omission of words limiting the period during which it might be exercised, make it plain to my mind that the option was to continue as long as the relationship of landlord and tenant under the agreement lasted. Consequently I hold that, being a term of the original agreement which was not inconsistent with the yearly tenancy which arose after the expiration of the original lease it was carried into the yearly tenancy.

It is contended however that the option is rendered invalid by the rule against perpetuities. If the agreement is to be read as giving only an option to the plaintiff personally, or to his assignee, and is exercisable only during the life of the plaintiff, no question would arise as to the rule against perpetuities. This Court has not been asked to read the agreement in that way. The case has been argued on the basis that, provided it be held that the option to purchase is incorporated in the yearly tenancy, it is capable of being exercised beyond the period permitted by the rule. The appellant contends that, although the option is styled an option to purchase, the rule against perpetuities does not apply because the agreement is to grant a new lease on payment of a premium or fine. If the option was to purchase the fee, it is clear that it would be void for remoteness. Whether the exception of covenants to renew a lease from the rule against perpetuities can be justified on principle, (Romer J. in *Woodall* v. *Clifton* ([1905] 2 Ch. 257) expressed the view that it cannot) it is settled by a long series of decisions that they are outside the rule.

Can the option given here be regarded as a covenant for renewal of a lease? The lease to be granted is a new lease on completely different terms to the original lease. It is to commence at a date which overlaps the original lease. It is to be a sub-lease at a rent which appears to be but a portion of the head-rent reserved by the lease under which the defendants hold the premises. A very substantial purchase money is to be paid. The covenants which it is to contain are such covenants in the superior lease as are applicable to the premises. *McGowan* v. *Harrison* ([1941] I.R. 331) was relied on by the respondents as showing that the transaction to be carried through on the exercise of the option is a sale and not a lease. It was argued that if it is to be regarded as an option to purchase the land it is against the rule against perpetuities. *Rider* v. *Ford* ([1923] 1 Ch. 541) was cited by counsel for the appellant. The facts there were that an agreement for a lease provided that a prospective tenant should 'take the house for three, five, or seven years, and have the option of purchasing either the freehold . . . or a lease of ninety-seven years'. Russell J. held that the option to purchase the freehold was inoperative and invalid because of the rule against perpetuities. At p. 546 he says: 'As to the right to call for a lease of the premises the position is different; it is not disputed that under the authorities a covenant for what is called a renewal of the lease is outside the rule against perpetuities. It was argued that this was not a covenant for the renewal of a lease because the agreement in terms describes it as a right to purchase. That is merely a question of language, and it is quite inaccurate to describe as a right to purchase a lease that which is really a right to call for a lease. It was further argued that although a right to renew a lease was outside the rule this was not such a right because it was a right to call for a lease on different terms from the original. But the right to renew is a right to call for a fresh lease. The new lease is the result of a fresh demise. Even if all the provisions in the fresh lease were the same as in the old lease it would none the less be a fresh demise, and a fresh term with fresh covenants. I am unable to see any reason why the position as regards the rule against perpetuities should be any different in the case of a right to call for a lease, even though the terms may not be in all respects the same as the terms of the original lease, and in the case of a right to call for a lease in which every provision may be word for word the same as in the old lease. In my opinion the right to call for the lease of ninety-seven years, to run from the expiration of the existing tenancy, is not invalidated by the rule against perpetuities and may be exercised by the defendant.'

It is said, however, that this decision, which is not binding on this Court, is in conflict with the decision of this court in *McGowan* v. *Harrison* ([1941] I.R. 331). I do not consider that there is a conflict. In *McGowan* v. *Harrison* ([1941] I.R. 331) the *ratio decidendi* was that the fact that a sale of a house was carried out by means of an under-lease did not suffice to establish that the purchaser was a tenant, holding under 'a contract for letting for habitation of a dwelling-house,' within the meaning of s. 31, sub-s. 1, of the Housing (Miscellaneous Provisions) Act, 1931. The case is, in my view, clearly distinguishable from *Rider* v. *Ford* ([1923] 1 Ch. 541).

The important point is that although the option given here may be described as a sale by means of sub-lease, the question as to whether it is outside the rule against perpetuities depends upon the nature of the interest in the land which is to be granted, not on whether it is described as a sale. The new lease will, in its terms, differ greatly from those in the original lease. I accept the reasoning of Russell J. in *Rider* v. *Ford* ([1923] 1 Ch. 541) as sound. Applying it to this case I am of opinion that the plaintiff is entitled to the declaration which he seeks.

Since the case was argued my attention has been drawn by Mr. Justice Murnaghan to the case of the *South Eastern Railway* v. *Associated Portland Cement Manufacturers* (1900) *Ltd.* ([1910] 1 Ch. 12), where it was held by the Court of Appeal, consisting of Cozens-Hardy M.R., Fletcher Moulton L.J. and Farwell L.J., affirming Swinfen Eady J., that as against the original covenantors the provision in an agreement was a personal contract and was not obnoxious to the rule against perpetuities. Swinfen Eady J. (at p. 25) says: 'In the present case the plaintiffs themselves entered into the contract to grant and granted the easement of tunnelling and they are the very parties who now wish to restrain the defendants from exercising that easement. There is no question here as to the validity of the grant of an easement *in futuro* . . . . Again I wholly fail to appreciate why the plaintiffs are not bound by their own personal contract, which has nothing whatever to do with the rule against perpetuities.' Cozens-Hardy M.R. (at p. 28) said: 'I have listened with some amazement to the contention that the rule of perpetuities applies where the action is brought, not against an assign of the covenantor, but against the covenantor himself, . . .' Fletcher Moulton, L.J. agreed with this view stating (at p. 32) that personal covenants do not fall within any rule against perpetuities. Farwell L.J. (at p. 33) took it to be 'settled beyond argument that an agreement merely personal not creating any interest in land is not within the rule against perpetuities.'

If this is good law, as I am inclined to think it is, it rules the present case. The case was not cited in argument and accordingly I am content to rest my opinion on the grounds already stated in this judgment.

I have had an opportunity of reading the judgment of Mr. Justice Murnaghan. I have not considered the grounds upon which he rests his judgment. If he is right in his view as to the effect of Deasy's Act upon the relationship of landlord and tenant, the reasoning upon which he bases his conclusion in this case seems unassailable. As, again, this line of reasoning was not developed so as to become the subject of critical discussion in argument, I prefer not to express an opinion upon it.

Accordingly, in my opinion, this appeal should be allowed. The plaintiff should have a declaration that the option contained in the agreement of the 15th October, 1941, is a valid and subsisting option and an order that, on payment of the sum of £1,720, the defendant do execute a sub-lease of the premises in accordance with the terms of clause IV of the agreement.

Murnaghan J.: [After referring to the facts as set out *ante*].

It appears to be common ground that on the 15th October, 1943, and until the 14th October, 1944, the tenant could have exercised the option. If he did so exercise it on the 15th October, 1943, it seems to me that the residue of the three years' terms would have ceased by merger in the sublease which he would acquire under the option.

At the end of the three years' term Thomas H. Jameson remained on in possession and he subsequently paid rent which was accepted by the landlord. A tenancy from year to year arose by implication of law. On the 18th November, 1945, the tenant purported to exercise his option. The learned President of the High Court has ruled that he is not entitled to do so. He said: 'I have reached the conclusion that on the fair reading of the tenancy agreement the option was a right given to the tenant conditionally upon its exercise within the third year of the term of three years created by the agreement, provided the tenancy still subsisted when the option was exercised. In my opinion, the tenant's attempt to exercise the option came too late and this action fails.'

The argument for the appellant was mainly, if not altogether, based on the view that the option clause contained in the written agreement was a separate and distinct agreement and was not merely part of the terms of the three year tenancy. If this can be established, it seems to me impossible to limit the words 'at any time after the expiration of two years of the term hereby granted and provided that the tenancy shall not have been determined in pursuance of the provisions of paragraph 3 hereof' to the period of the third year of the term. Clauses of this kind have been considered by Courts in England: see *Moss* v. *Barton* (L.R. 1 Eq. 474) and *Buckland* v. *Papillon* ((L.R. 1 Eq. 477; L.R. 2 Ch. App. 67). In the latter case, where a term of three years had come to an end and a tenancy from year to year had been raised by implication of law, Lord Chelmsford held that the option clause was not part of the terms of the yearly tenancy so created, but he seems to have regarded the clause in the original agreement as subsisting as long as the relation of landlord and tenant remained. In England, the relation of landlord and tenant is based upon tenure, and it may be that Lord Chelmsford did not consider an option to purchase as in any way regulating the relation of landlord and tenant, and that it must be an independent agreement. In *Lewis* v. *Stephenson* (67 L.J.Q.B. 296, at p. 300) Bruce J. said: 'As to the period within which the option is to be exercised when nothing is specified, I think I am doing no violence to the ordinary canon of construction when I say I think that must be taken to mean within a reasonable time before the expiration of the original lease.' This opinion was disapproved of by the Court of Appeal in Ireland in *Allen* v. *Murphy* ([1917] 1 I.R. 484), but in the present case the time is specified and it is merely a question of construction as to what this time may be. If the principle stated by Lord Chelmsford applied in Ireland I should feel it impossible to limit the period of exercise of the option to the third year of the original tenancy.

In Ireland, however, under Deasy's Act (23 & 24 Vict., c.154), s. 3, it is expressly enacted that the relation of landlord and tenant shall be deemed to be founded on the express or implied contract of the parties and not upon tenure or service. This distinction is emphasised by FitzGibbon L.J. In his judgment in *O'Connor* v. *Foley* ([1906] 1 I.R. 20 at p. 27) in the Court of Appeal in Ireland where he says: 'Deasy's Act, section 3, founds the relation of landlord and tenant in Ireland upon the express or implied contract of the parties, and, as at present advised, I think that possession of a tenancy, when acquired under the State of Limitations, carries with it terms of *tenancy* – as distinguished from terms of *personal contract* – the same as those on which the barred tenant held, and that, in Ireland, those terms are founded on *contract*.'

Apart, however, from the particular question dealt with by FitzGibbon L.J., the general principle stated in s. 3 of Deasy's Act seems to me clearly to involve that the clause in the agreement of the 15th October, 1941, giving the option to purchase, is part of the contract of tenancy, and as much part of that contract as any other term of the agreement. The entire terms of the agreement were to govern the relations of the parties during the term and did not, in my opinion, extend to govern these relations after the end of the term. The plaintiff can, in my opinion, therefore, derive no help from the option contained in the agreement of the 15th October, 1941.

The case does not, however, end here. When the term of three years expired, the parties, by their conduct, created a new tenancy – a tenancy from year to year. In *Meath* v. *Megan* ([1897] 2 I.R. 477) in the Court of Appeal in Ireland, Fitzgibbon L.J. says (at p. 479): 'Where a tenant holds under a lease or agreement in writing, for a term which comes to an end, and he continues in possession without making any fresh agreement, there is a presumption that all the terms of the old agreement continue to apply, except so far as they are rendered inapplicable by the change in the duration of the tenancy.' In the third year of the old term one of the contractual terms of the tenancy was that the tenant had an option to purchase during the tenancy, and, in my opinion, this contractual term was applied and made applicable as a contractual term of the tenancy from year to year. I see no difficulty in the textual wording of the clause 'at any time after the expiration of two years of the term'. In substance and in fact, the tenant had an option in the third year of the term, and this option was, I think, a term of the old agreement which continues to apply and there is nothing in the terms of the tenancy from year to year which renders this option inapplicable.

I am therefore of opinion that subject to the question of application of the rule against perpetuities the plaintiff is entitled, under the terms of his tenancy from year to year, to exercise the option.

It is not denied that the plaintiff, at the date of the notice of his intention to exercise the option – the 28th November, 1945 – was in possession and in occupation of the premises as tenant from year to year.

There was considerable discussion whether the rule against perpetuities did or did not apply. This discussion can reasonably arise if the right depends upon a contract contained in the original agreement, but I can see no application for the rule if, as I hold, the option arises upon the terms of the tenancy from year to year. The option in such case lasts for one year only, and is renewed each time the tenancy is continued by the conduct of the parties for a further year. Either party can end the tenancy by giving due notice and thus put an end to the option applicable during the year. Of course the parties may not determine the tenancy from year to year and it may last for many years. But during no year can it be said that the option is entitled to be exercised at a time beyond that allowed by the rule against perpetuities. For this reason, in my opinion, the rule against perpetuities does not apply.

There is another aspect of the case which I think it right to mention, although it was not discussed in argument. In *South Eastern Railway* v. *Associated Portland Cement Manufacturers* (1900) *Ltd.* ([1910] 1 Ch. 12), the Court of Appeal in England emphatically laid down the proposition that no question of perpetuity arises where the original contractor is sued on his personal contract. Cozens-Hardy M.R. referred to *London and South Western Railway Co.* v. *Gomm* (20 Ch. D. 562), which affirmed that the rule against perpetuities had the widest scope, but quoted Jessel M.R. in that case as stating that the rule against perpetuities had no application where the original contracting party was sued. Fletcher Moulton L.J. said (at p. 32): 'They are bound by that agreement because, as the Master of the Rolls said, personal covenants do not fall within any rule of perpetuities and they are the actual covenantors'. Farwell L.J. stated his opinion that the rule against perpetuities has no application to a personal covenant. The learned authors of Gray on Perpetuities do not approve of the law as stated in *South Eastern Railway* v. *Associated Portland Cement Manufacturers* (1900) *Ltd* ([1910] 1 Ch. 12) and consider this ruling as a newly created exception. It seems to me, however, that any action against the original contracting party – especially a living person – must be brought within a life in being. It is interesting to observe that as far back as the year 1852, Romilly M.R. in *Stocker* v. *Dean* (16 Beav. 161) intimated his opinion that a right of pre-emption 'at all times thereafter' could be enforced during the life of the owner.

O'Byrne J.:

I have read the judgment of Mr. Justice Murnaghan: I agree with it and have nothing to add.

Black J.:

Our problem in this case can, I think, be reduced to two net questions: 1, was the plaintiff's option ever a valid right unaffected by the rule gainst perpetuities? and 2, if it was, had it ceased to be a live right at the date when the plaintiff sought to exercise it? These questions are capable of raising several points as abstruse as they are important.

The preceding judgments agree that the rule against perpetuities had no application, but differ as regards the reasons for that conclusion. When the judge appealed from, or a member of this Court, makes a certain reason part of his *ratio decidendi*, it is my principle not to ignore it, but if I cannot presently accept it, to explain why, both in deference to the learned judge and to prevent silence from being deemed to imply consent. I shall, therefore, state my position in regard to certain reasons which have been referred to.

The first is that the tenancy from year to year 'lasts for one year only, and is renewed each time the tenancy is continued by the conduct of the parties for a further year'. As I understand this reason, it is that the option, like the tenancy into which it is supposed to be incorporated, ends each year, and therefore can never be exercised, at a date later than one year from its creation or re-creation, and thus can never infringe the rule against perpetuities. This conception of a tenancy from year to year seems to be founded on *Wright* v. *Tracy* (I.R. 7 C.L., 134; I.R. 8 C.L. 478), where the Exchequer Chamber, by a bare majority of four to three, held that a tenancy from year to year is not greater in duration than a tenancy for a year certain, within the meaning of s. 69 of the Landlord and Tenant Act, 1870. Since the Exchequer Chamber was constituted by judges of the King's Bench, Common Pleas, and Exchequer, it was possible for a minority of those judges to override the opinion of a majority of their number, if that minority happened to be sitting for the occasion, and to constitute a majority, in the Exchequer Chamber. That is what happened in *Wright* v. *Tracy* (I.R. 7 C.L., 134; I.R. 8 C.L. 478). Four judges in the Exchequer Chamber overbore the opinion, not only of their three colleagues sitting with them, but also of three judges of the Common Pleas. It was thus really a minority decision, taking the judges of equal status as a whole. It had other enfeebling factors also. First, in *Lord Arran* v. *Wills* (14 L.R.I. 200 at pp. 212, 213) Lawson J. declared that he was not bound by *Wright* v. *Tracy* (I.R. 7 C.L. 134; I.R. 8 C.L. 478), suggesting that Palles C.B., one of the bare majority in that case, had since changed his view. I do not know whether this was so or not, but if it was, the decision should have been different. Next, another member of the majority, Whiteside C.J., in so far as he expressed any reasons of his own, relied on the decision of the Queen's Bench in *Gandy* v. *Jubber* (5 B. & S. 78), ignoring, doubtless *per incuriam*, that the decision he thus relied on had been reversed unanimously by seven judges in the Exchequer Chamber (5 B. & S. 485; 9 B. & S. 15).

Nevertheless, I do not say that the foregoing strange factors are reasons for rejecting *Wright* v. *Tracy* (I.R. 7 C.L. 134; I.R. 8 C.L. 478), but I do suggest that they are reasons for confining it to the irreducible minimum of what it actually decided. It was concerned with the nature of a tenancy from year to year within the meaning of s. 69 of the Landlord and Tenant Act, 1870 (33 & 34 Vict. c. 46) which made notice to quit necessary in all tenancies less than from year to year. It was held that 'less' meant 'less in duration,' and the majority thought that the Legislature meant to include only tenancies of which the duration was *necessarily* less than the *definite* duration of a tenancy from year to year. Thus, Palles C.B. said (at p. 499) that s. 69 'constitutes a tenancy from year to year a standard of duration, . . . and the use of such a tenancy as a standard of time would appear to me, *per se*, to show that the Legislature regarded its duration as fixed and certain'. He added, 'We are thus driven to ascertain what is the necessary duration incident to such a tenancy. . . . We find that such duration is a term fixed and certain – the term of one year.' It will be noted that he spoke of such a tenancy's *necessary* duration.

Fitzgerald B., another member of the majority, with whom Whiteside C.J. agreed, expressed the same idea. He said (at p. 496) that the words 'lesser period' must mean 'lesser definite period', and that he knew of no 'definite' period created by a tenancy from year to year greater than one year certain. Assuming the majority was right about the aim of the section, the language, just quoted, means no more than that, for the purposes of the particular section, their intention was to treat a tenancy from year to year as a standard of duration and, therefore, to regard only its *definite* and *necessary* duration. It does not seem to follow that, apart from that section and its purposes, a tenancy from year to year should not also, by its very nature, have an unnecessary and indefinite duration. To read the decision as meaning that every tenancy from year to year lasts for one year only, so that where there is neither surrender nor notice to quit, and the tenant remains on and pays rent, there is an implied recommencement or re-letting for another year and so on indeterminately would be to suppose that the majority in *Wright* v. *Tracy* (I.R. 7 C.L. 134; I.R. 8 C.L. 478) intended to reject the unanimous decision of the Exchequer Chamber in *Gandy* v. *Jubber* (9 B. & S. 15) which has been accepted uniformly as settled law for the last eighty years. If the majority intended to do that, I am sure they would have said so; yet although Dowse and Deasy BB. who were in the minority, both quoted and relied on *Gandy* v. *Jubber*(9 B. & S. 15), no member of the majority even mentioned it, except Whiteside C.J., who, as I have said, mistook the overruled decision for the final one. Indeed, this leading decision was anticipated in Ireland in *Hayes* v. *Fitzgibbon* (I.R. 4 C.L. 500) by Fitzgerald and Deasy BB., the former being one of the majority in *Wright* v. *Tracy* (I.R. 7 C.L. 134; I.R. 8 C.L. 478), though he also seems to have mistaken the overruled decision for the final one, and he therefore questioned it. Hence he would have approved of the final decision. With Deasy B. he quoted and approved of *Mackay* v. *Mackreth* (4 Doug. 213) as holding that a tenancy from year to year does not end each year and then get re-created as a new letting, but is a continuing tenancy which leaves the tenant a reversion after a demise by deed for twenty-one years on which an action of covenant could be maintained. *Gandy* v. *Jubber* (9 B. & S. 15) has been quoted and applied to weekly and monthly tenancies in various cases such as *Bowen* v. *Anderson* ([1894] 1 Q.B. 164), *Queen's Club Gardens Estates, Ltd.* v. *Bignell* ([1924] 1 K.B. 117) and *Precious* v. *Reedie* ([1924] 2 K.B. 149). In *Jones* v. *Mills* ([1924] 2 K.B. 149), Williams J. said (at p. 798): 'It cannot be said that there was a new contract each week. . . . If it had been a tenancy from year to year, it would have undoubtedly subsisted until it was terminated by a proper notice'. As Furlong on Landlord and Tenant (2nd ed., vol. 1, at p. 224) expresses it: 'a tenancy from year to year is a tenancy for a term; and the holding is considered a lease for so many years as the party shall occupy, unless in the meantime it shall be determined by notice to quit upon one side, or notice of surrender on the other; so that if the lessee occupy for ten years or more, such period by computation from the time past makes a lease for so many years; and either the landlord or the tenant may declare on the demise as having been made for such number of years.'

Nobody will deny that a tenancy from year to year is a continuing tenancy and may continue for many years. If, according to the proposition I am considering, 'it lasts for one year only and is renewed each time the tenancy is continued,' it must surely follow that it comes to an end each year and recommences at once for another year. That is precisely what the Exchequer Chamber in *Gandy* v. *Jubber* (9 B. & S. 15) said that it did not do. Here are the relevant words of the judgment (at p. 18 of the report); 'There is not in contemplation of law recommencing or re-letting at the beginning of each year'. I have sought to show that the decision in *Wright* v. *Tracy* (I.R. 7 C.L. 134; I.R. 8 C.L. 478) is consistent with that pronouncement. In my opinion, the theory that the tenancy 'lasts for one year only and is renewed each time the tenancy is continued' is not consistent with the said pronouncement. I cannot, therefore, agree that the present plaintiff's tenancy from year to year, which supervened on the expiration of his three-year term and has lasted since for a number of years as one continuing tenancy, was ever a tenancy lasting for one year only, so as to make the option it is said to have incorporated an option for one year only, and on that account outside the rule against perpetuities.

A second reason for getting rid of the rule against perpetuities has been extracted from the decision of the English Court of Appeal in *South Eastern Railway* v. *Associated Portland Cement Manufacturers* (1900) *Ltd.* ([1910] 1 Ch. 12) to the effect that that rule does not apply where the action is brought against the covenantor himself. I do not think any previous authority was produced really supporting this proposition. It has evoked very outspoken criticism from the most reputed expert writers upon this subject. Thus in Gray on Perpetuities (4th ed., at pp. 366, 367, n) it is suggested that 'the learned judges seem to have decided the case *quasi in furore*'. The learned author points out what he considers a vital oversight in the decision, and cites American cases in which the Courts refused to follow it. His view seems to have been fully shared by another outstanding specialist in the law of real property. In an elaborately reasoned article in the Solicitors' Journal (Vol. 54, pp. 471 and 501), Mr. T. Cyprian Williams subjects this decision to a criticism which appears to me, on the first reading, to be of the most devastating character. An earlier article in 42 Solicitors' Journal, p. 650, is of equal interest. I shall confine myself to one summarising extract from the second article in 54 Solicitors' Journal. The learned author writes:

'The Court' (in *South Eastern Railway* v. *Associated Portland Cement Manufacturers* (1900) *Ltd*. ([1910] 1 Ch. 12)) 'declared that the rule laid down in *London & South Western Railway Co*. v. *Gomm* (20 Ch. D. 562) has no application where the action is brought against the original contractor, but relates solely to actions against the original contractor's assigns. The reader will remember that in *Gomm's Case* the Court of Appeal declined to enforce specifically . . . a contract giving an option to re-purchase a piece of land at any future time on the ground that if such a contract were specifically enforceable, it would in effect create an equitable interest in the land, which might arise at a time remoter than the end of the period allowed by the rule against perpetuities. . . . If the rule in *Gomm's Case* (20 Ch. D. 562) should indeed have no application where an action is brought against the original contractor, the result would be that a corporation (which enjoys immortal existence) could make a valid contract specifically enforceable against itself to make some executory limitation of land to take effect at any future time (however remote), notwithstanding that such limitation, if actually attempted to be made by deed at the time of the contract, would at once be void for remoteness. This appears to be an absurd conclusion. And yet (with the greatest respect be it spoken) this was the conclusion at which the Court of Appeal actually arrived in the *South Eastern Railway's Co's Case* ([1910] 1 Ch. 12); for if Lord Justice Farwell's *dictum* be correct, an actual grant by that company . . . by deed (without any prior contract) of the right of future entry and future easement in question would have been void. . . . The true doctrine of *Gomm's Case* (20 Ch. D. 562) is that a contract to make some executory limitation of land, which may take effect at a future time more remote than the end of the period allowed by the rule against perpetuities, shall not operate to confer an equitable interest in that land, *in whosesoever hand it may be*.' The italics are in the original article. Mr. Williams respectfully suggests that this doctrine is properly applicable where the land remains in the original contractor's hands as well as where it has been assigned over.

I do not express any final opinion on this controversy (See *Hutton* v. *Watling* [1948] 1 Ch. 26 – Ed). The doctrine in *South Eastern Railway* v. *Associated Portland Cement Manufacturers* ([1910] 1 Ch. 12) may be right. But, I make it a rule never blindly to accept any pronouncmeent other than that of a Court that binds me, if I happen to know that leading specialists in the branch of law involved have analysed and rejected it, unless I feel able to formulate a satisfactory answer to their criticism and to explain that answer in my judgment. That, I am at present unable to do in relation to the reasoned criticism of Mr. Cyprian Williams in the elaborate articles to which I have referred. If I should ever have to decide the matter *ad hoc*, I should hope to have the aid of an intensive argument by counsel and more time than I have thought necessary to employ on the present occasion to weigh and re-weigh that argument. Hence, I am not prepared to base any conclusion, in this appeal, on the doctrine enunciated in *South Eastern Railway* v. *Associated Portland Cemement Manufacturers* ([1910] 1 Ch. 12).

There is, however, another reason quite different from those I have been considering which, in my view, does justify me in holding that the rule against perpetuities does not affect the plaintiff's option in this case, assuming that that option is otherwise valid. It is a rule so well settled as not to require the citation of the authorities, namely, that the rule against perpetuities has no application to covenants for the renewal of a lease. I need not go into the several suggestions that judges and text writers have made to explain the existence of this somewhat anomalous exception. No lawyer, I think, questions its existence to-day. In my view, the plaintiff's option here is, in reality and in substance, an option to call for the renewal of his lease. Two objections to this have been suggested: first, that the agreement, in terms, describes the option as an option for purchasing, and secondly, that the lease for which it entitled the appellant to call was a lease quite different, in its terms, from the original lease. However, both these factors were present in *Rider* v. *Ford* ([1923] 1 Ch. 541), and they did not prevent Russell J. from holding that the option in that case was for the renewal of a lease and unaffected by the rule against perpetuities. I think the reasons assigned by Russell J. were sound and that *Rider* v. *Ford* is a good decision.

Then, a distinction is suggested between that case and the present one, because here the lessor reserved only a nominal reversion. In *Rider* v. *Ford* ([1923] 1 Ch. 541) the option was alternative, namely to purchase for the fee or for a renewal. It would thus seem that the lessors were owners in fee, and if so, they would have had a valuable reversion after the expiration of the lease for which the lessee had an option to call. The suggestion is that the option in the present case is only colourably an option to call for a lease, and is substantially an option to purchase the fee. *McGowan* v. *Harrison* ([1941] I.R. 331) was said to conclude the case on this point. I think it does not. There, as Sullivan C.J. pointed out, the lease was of the lessor's entire interest. Here there was at least a nominal reversion. But, putting aside that point, *McGowan* v. *Harrison* ([1941] I.R. 331) was decided on the presumed intention of the Legislature in the Housing Act, 1931, which, according to Meredith J., was that the relevant section, s. 31, sub-s. 1, 'is to be restricted to lettings which are not sales' – meaning which are not sales in substance. This Court did not say that a transaction might not be a sale and a lease at one and the same time, and thus in a sense dimorphous. The making of such a lease was held to be a valid exercise of a power of sale in *In re Judd and Poland and Skelcher's Contract* ([1906] 1 Ch. 684), being, as was said, 'a conveyancer's expedient' and 'a mere piece of machinery for carrying out a sale where the property was held with other property under one lease, the object being to avoid any difficulty about rent apportionment'. Again, in *In re Webb, Still* v. *Webb* ([1897] 1 Ch. 144) an under-lease was held a sale for a particular purpose, namely, preventing the solicitor from charging double costs for one and the same transaction. In neither case was it held that the lease was not a lease for any purpose or in any sense, though for a particular purpose it was treated as a sale. In the Housing Act, 1931, which imposed a serious burden on those making lettings, the Legislature may well have intended to confine that new burden to lettings which could not possibly be treated as sales in substance. There is no ground for supposing that the judges who evolved the principle which places renewals of leases outside the rule against perpetuities, had any analogous or other special reason for confining that principle to leases where the lessor retained a substantial reversion.

Having thus got rid of the rule gainst perpetuities, there remains the question whether the option had not ceased to exist before the appellant sought to exercise it. In the preceding judgments it is agreed that this option passed into the tenancy from year to year which supervened when the appellant continued to occupy and pay rent after his original three-year term expired, and he certainly did so continue up to and after the date on which he sought to exercise his option. I am afraid I am unable to feel so sure about this point. No doubt, both in England and in this country, when a tenancy from year to year supervenes in the way indicated upon the expiration of a lease, all the terms of the lease are carried into the tenancy from year to year so far as they are consistent with the character of such a tenancy. In the present case, after the first two years of his term the appellant had an option to get a new lease for 150 years save one day from the 1st May, 1939. His original three-year term commenced from 15th October, 1941. If, then, he exercised the option and got the promised lease during the currency of any year of the tenancy from year to year, the lessor would, thereupon, be deprived of his right to terminate the tenancy from year to year, at the end of the year in question, by notice to quit. The right to determine a tenancy from year to year by notice to quit is a necessary incident in such a tenancy. So it is expressed in Woodfall's Landlord and Tenant (1934 ed., p. 429) and I think never disputed. The exercise of the option would thus take away from the tenancy from year to year 'a necessary incident'. Would such an option be consistent with the nature of a tenancy from year to year? There are many express decisions which seem to make this, at least, doubtful. In *Gray* v. *Spyer* ([1921] 2 Ch. 549) there was an agreement which Younger L.J. held to create a tenancy from year to year. There was a stipulation in this which purported to give the tenant a right to get a perpetual renewal. Younger L.J. held that such a right would be repugnant to a tenancy from year to year; 'for', he said, 'it cannot be a characteristic of such a tenancy that one of the parties to it shall have no right to determine it'. His decision that the tenancy in question was from year to year was reversed ([1922] 2 Ch. 22), but it was not doubted by the judges in the Court of Appeal that if the tenancy had been a tenancy from year to year, the stipulation for perpetual renewal would, as Younger L.J. had held, be repugnant to it. Lord Sterndale said (at p. 28): 'I agree with the learned judge that the two things are inconsistent, and that there cannot be a tenancy from year to year, qualified by a right to perpetual renewal which deprives the tenancy of a necessary incident, that is to say, the right of the landlord to terminate it by a six months' notice to quit'. Of course the parties might agree upon a shorter notice. But, then Lord Sterndale's *dictum* would only be modified accordingly. An option, the exercise of which during the currency of a tenancy from year to year would deprive the landlord of a necessary incident of such a tenancy, namely his right to terminate it by notice to quit, would seem to be repugnant to that kind of tenancy. The principle asserted in *Gray* v. *Spyer* ([1921] 2 Ch. 549; [1922] 2 Ch. 22) found clear expression in *Doe* v. *Browne* (8 East 165); *Browne* v. *Warner* (14 Ves. 156, 409); *Wood* v. *Beard* (2 Ex. D. 30, 38); *Cheshire Lines* v. *Lewis* (50 L.J.Q.B. 121) and in this country in *Holmes* v. *Day* (I.R. 8 C.L. 235); for, in this last case, although the Court was equally divided, no member of it disputed that, if the tenancy there was a tenancy from year to year, a clause which would prevent it from being determined by notice to quit would be repugnant to the nature of such a tenancy. If the agreement in the present case gave the tenant an option which might be exercised during the currency of the tenancy from year to year, then, if it was so exercised, the landlord could not determine that tenancy at the end of the current year or the following year by notice to quit.

Of course, if notwithstanding the foregoing considerations, the appellant's option was carried into the tenancy from year to year, the rule against perpetuities would not affect it. But, in view of my doubt on that point, I must consider the position on the assumption that the exercise of the option now must depend on the original three-year agreement alone. What then? In England there can, I think, be no doubt that the option would continue exercisable as long as the supervening tenancy from year to year continues. So it was held in *Moss* v. *Barton* (L.R. 1 Eq. 474); *Buckland* v. *Papillon* (L.R. 1 Eq. 477; L.R. 2 Ch. App. 67) and *Rider* v. *Ford* ([1923] 1 Ch. 541). The present appellant's option could not be exercised until the end of the second year of his three-year term, but after that, no time whatever was specified within which it must be exercised. No doubt, in Ireland the relationship of landlord and tenant is based upon contract and not upon tenure, but I do not well see why this should prevent the option in the original agreement from being exercised now, seeing that this agreement provided that, after the first two years, the option should be exercisable 'at any time'. The words 'at any time' are, I think, plainly incompatible with a specification of a time limit. This view seems to be borne out by the decision of the former Irish Court of Appeal in *Allen* v. *Murphy* ([1917] 1 I.R. 484). In that case, a lease, originally for twenty-nine years, contained a covenant for renewal every thirty years during a period of 999 years, no time being fixed within which renewal might be demanded. Several renewals, each for thirty years, had been obtained. The last of these expired in 1904. After that, the then tenant remained on, paying rent to the original lessor's successor in title, but sought no fresh renewal for a period of nineteen years. The tenant then sought and obtained a renewal for sixty years instead of thirty years. He then sold his interest and the purchaser objected to the title, alleging that the sixty-year renewal was inoperative, because it was granted nineteen years after the term granted by the last previous renewal had expired. The Court of Appeal held that this was not correct and expressly disapproved of the view of Bruce J. in *Lewis* v. *Stephenson* (67 L.J. Q.B. 296) that application for renewal must be made before the expiration of the lease. Sir Ignatius O'Brien C. adopted the statement in Fry on Specific perform-ance (5th ed., p. 541) that 'where no time has been originally limited within which a tenant's option to have a lease must be exercised, and the landlord has never called upon the tenant to declare his option, mere lapse of time will not preclude the tenant or his assign or legal personal representative from exercising it'. The Lord Chancellor said (at p. 488): 'The landlord continues to receive the rents. If a renewal is made ten, twenty, thirty or forty years after the expiration of the lease, is it to be presumed that it is not effective?' His answer was in the negative. He also said (at p. 487) in commenting on the case of *Lewis* v. *Stephenson* (67 L.J. Q.B. 296): 'If the case is an authority for the proportion that where no time is specified, the application for renewal must be made before the expiration of the lease, I dissent from that as a general proposition'.

Now, it seems to me that that proposition from which he dissented is the very proposition put forward in this case in support of the view that, unless the option was carried into the yearly tenancy, it must have been exercised during the term of the three-year lease and could not be exercised afterwards. In this three-year agreement, assuredly, no time was specified, to use the Lord Chancellor's words. The words used were 'at any time after the expiration of two years of the term'. We are asked to say that though 'no time is specified within which the option must be exercised' nevertheless it must be exercised 'before the expiration of the lease'. I am equally unable to reconcile that contention with the following words of Lord Justice Ronan (at p. 491):

'Where there is the exercise of a power of renewal. . . .; where no time is fixed by the lease for applying for the renewal; where no notice has been served by the landlord calling upon the tenant to elect whether he will ask for a renewal or not; and where everything has gone on as if a renewal had been taken out, the reasonable presumption is that the parties had agreed to let the technicality of renewal lie over, and that neither party had any intention of raising any question as to the forfeiture of the tenant's rights'. All the conditions postulated by Ronan L.J. exist here. There was a lease or letting for three years. It contained an option or right to get a renewal. No time was fixed for applying for the renewal. Everything went on as if a renewal had been taken out, the tenant continuing as tenant. Why then Lord Justice Ronan's conclusion that the tenant's right or option still remains does not clearly follow, I am unable to imagine. Moloney L.J. expressed his view to the same effect as the other judges.

The above pronouncements would seem to indicate that just as, on the facts of the present case, the English Courts following the principle of *Moss* v. *Barton* (L.R. 1 Eq. 474) and *Buckland* v. *Papillon* (L.R. 1 Eq. 477), would hold that the option did not expire with the original term, so our late Court of Appeal would have drawn the same conclusion in this country.

Accordingly, even if my doubts as to the option having been carried into the tenancy from year to year are not unjustified, I am of opinion that the appellant's option, given him by the original agreement, is still exercisable and that his appeal should be allowed.

Notes

1. See also the discussion in *Re Tyrrell's Estate* [1907] I.R. 292; *cf. Re Garde Browne* [1911] 1 I.R. 205. And see *Irish Land Law*, para. 5.136–7.
2. As regards section 3 of Deasy's Act, see p. 543, *post*.
3. As regards Black J.'s discussion of matters inconsistent with the nature of a tenancy from year to year, *cf. Centaploy Ltd* v. *Matlodge Ltd*. [1974] Ch. 1.

Chapter 5
INCORPOREAL HEREDITAMENTS

Only two types of incorporeal hereditainment remain of any practical significance in Ireland. The first is the category of easements and profits, a subject which has produced much litigation before the Irish courts, and the second is rentcharges: see *Irish Land Law*, ch. 6.

I. EASEMENTS AND PROFITS

1. *Nature*
LATIMER V. THE OFFICIAL CO-OPERATIVE SOCIETY
(1885) 16 L.R.Ir. 305 (Common Pleas Division)

A, B, and C were the owners of three consecutively adjoining houses in a street. B's house intervened between those of A and C. A's premises were destroyed by fire and rebuilt. After rebuilding, B's side wall separated from C's premises, the adjacent wall in which became cracked.

In an action by C against A for damages, evidence of architects was given to show that the crack was caused by the settling down of A's new building on soft clay, and drawing over with it B's premises; and, on the other hand, architects were produced on behalf of A, who proved that the rebuilding was properly executed, and attributed the separation to an old settlement increasing gradually.

The jury, upon the question being submitted to them, found that A was guilty of negligence; but the learned Judge at the trial directed a verdict for A, being of opinion that there was no evidence of negligence. The plaintiff moved to have the verdict reversed.

Morris C.J.:

In this case the action has been brought by the occupier of the house No. 3, Harcourt-place, against the Co-operative Society, who are the occupiers and owners of No. 1, for injuries sustained by the house No. 3 by reason of the operations performed by the Defendants in the erection of a new building on the site of No. 1. There is an intervening house, No. 2, occupied by a person named Graham. The injuries as proved at the trial were, that the house No. 3, which previously to the operations of the Defendants in the house No. 1, had joined No. 2, though not built into No. 2, was, by reason of these operations, separated from No. 2. The stack of chimneys of No. 3 were actually in the side walls of No. 2.

In consequence of the operations of the Defendants on the side of No. 1, a crack took place between No. 3 and No. 2; and for the injuries sustained, and for the loss in remedying that, the jury awarded the Plaintiff £60. Mr. Justice Murphy directed a verdict for the Defendants, but took the opinion of the jury as to the proper amount of damages, in the event of a verdict being entered in favour of the Plaintiff.

A number of cases were cited, to which it is unnecessary to refer. The principle of law is well settled in the highest quarter, viz. in the case of *Dalton* v. *Angus* (6 App. Cas. 740), which establishes that where there is an ancient building, which is supported by adjacent soil, it has acquired a right to such support of that soil as it immemorially enjoyed, and that a right of action exists against the owner of the adjacent soil if he disturbs his own land so as to take away the lateral support previously afforded. Applying that to the present case, the Plaintiff is entitled to judgment. The house No. 3 immemorially existed. The evidence shows that the injuries sustained by No. 3 arose from the operations on the site of No. 1, namely, that of building on the soft soil of No. 1 a heavier building than previously existed; the result was the Mr. Graham's house, though uninjured itself, tilted slightly over towards No. 1, and detached itself from No. 3, leaving the crack which is the subject-matter of the injuries complained of. If it was No. 2 that suffered the injury, the case would be that of *Dalton* v. *Angus* (6 App. Cas. 740). The only question is, does the fact of No. 2 not having suffered any injury take it out of that principle. It does not, in my opinion. The principle is that the house, having for a length of time derived a right to the support of the adjacent soil, that right shall not be interfered with. No. 3, upon the facts here, had a right to the support of the soil on which No. 1 stands.

The case of *Solomon* v. *Vintners' Company* (4 H. & N. 585), relied on by the Defendants, does not appear to me to affect this case. It merely decided that the plaintiff's house, which did not adjoin the defendant's, had no right to the support of the defendant's house.

A question was submitted to the jury by the learned Judge, as to whether there was a negligence in performing the operations on No. 1. It does not appear to me that the operations on No. 1 were performed negligently; but, even if skilfully performed, it necessarily resulted in doing injury to No. 3. The verdict should be turned into a verdict for the plaintiff.

Harrison and **Murphy JJ.**, concurred.

Notes and Questions
   Was the right recognised by the Court in this case an easement of support or a natural right of support? What difference does it make? The *Irish Land Law*, para. 6.039.

ABERCROMBY V. TOWN COMMISSIONERS OF FERMOY
[1900] 1 I.R. 302 (Court of Appeal)

   An action was brought by an owner in fee for a declaration of title to a strip of land on the bank of the River Blackwater, adjoining the town of Fermoy, called 'The Barnane Walk,' subject to a right of way on foot possessed by the public over the premises. The evidence adduced regarding the character and user of the premises showed that so long as memory went back it had been devoted to the recreation of the inhabitants of the town, by whom it was used as a promenade. Chatterton V.-C. granted such a declaration and an injunction against the defendants compelling them to remove posts and chains erected on the land and restraining them from such erection. The Commissioners appealed.

Lord Ashbourne C.:
Lord Justice Holmes will deliver the judgment of the Court.

Holmes L.J.:
   Fermoy is a good provincial town, pleasantly situated on the Blackwater, which is said to be the most picturesque of Irish rivers. The Barnane Walk, with which this action is conversant, seems to be an attractive feature of the place. It begins in the town at a street called West-quay, and runs for about half-a-mile along the right bank of the river. It is somewhat curious that the oral evidence, while very abundant in reference to two or three matters of minor importance, gives hardly any description of the walk itself, or of the mode in which it has been used by the townspeople. It is said by counsel that its breadth varies from 8 to 12 yards; it keeps for its whole length close by the bank of the river; and the photographs produced show that it is shaded at least in some placed by handsome trees. It has existed substantially in its present condition as long as living memory goes back; and a map dated 1795 shows a walk bearing a different name in the same situation, and

apparently of the same width and length. It passes when it leaves West-quay for some distance through lands owned by the plaintiff, and for the remainder of its course through what is called in the evidence the Cliffe estate, which has not been connected in title with the plaintiff's property at least during the present century, and probably for long before. In the year 1837 the earliest date spoken to by any witness West-quay and Barnane Walk were separated from each other by a dividing wall extending across the entrance to the latter, having in the centre a stile about 6 or 8 feet broad, and consisting of four steps on each side with a flat stone on the top. It does not appear when or by whom this barrier was erected; but there is evidence that it was rebuilt or repaired on one or two occasions by the predecesors in title of the plaintiff. At one time there was an opening in the wall at the south side of the stile through which a small cart could pass. An old witness, who I think is both truthful and accurate, says that this aperture first appeared and was probably caused by the action of a high flood in the year 1852; and I am not satisfied that it was ever subsequently closed; but the remainder of the wall continued to exist until it was removed in 1882, under circumstances to which I shall presently refer.

By a lease dated the 2nd February, 1835, the then owners of the property now vested in the plaintiff demised to Robert Briscoe for a term of lives renewable for ever a plot of ground extending from Barnane Walk southward to the King-street. This plot does not include the walk itself, which is separated from it by a high wall, and is in fact the northern boundary of the demised premises; nor was any right of way over it granted to the lessee in express terms. One or more houses were built on the land facing King-street; and there is a wicket gate or door in the boundary wall by which a garden or orchard at the rere of one of these houses can be entered from the walk. There was formerly another wicket leading to a cottage; but both the cottage and the entrance to it are now gone. The evidence regarding the end of the walk farthest from the town is wanting in precision. The maps show it as continuing at a fairly uniform width up to a certain point, and then terminating without any trace of way or path beyond. We have been told by counsel that there is a wooden barrier at this point; but the only evidence of this fact is an item of expenditure in the defendants' accounts, and one witness spoke of a beaten track leading from the end of the walk through the fields. It is not alleged, however, that the public has any right of way in this direction; and if people occasionally wander alongside the river, they probably do so by permission of the owner of the land, if they are not trespassers pure and simple. There seems to have been so little controversy at the trial as to the manner in which Barnane Walk was used by the inhabitants of Fermoy that only casual references to the mode of user can be found in the evidence. One witness states that it was a walk for the populace of the town, children, and all, and that there was a band on the river. Another says that it was maintained as a public walk; a third swears that for the forty-five years he has known the place it was used by the people of Fermoy. An old man tells that 'oft when the work was done, we went down there, and there were plenty there besides me.' It also appears that there were seats upon the walk, some moveable and some fastened to the ground. There was no objection to perambulators passing over it; but when cyclists became aggressive, the defendants endeavoured to prevent them riding on it.

It is easy to understand from the foregoing evidence and facts, what have been the character and user of the walk as long as memory goes back. Indeed no better description of it can be given than what is contained in an agreement dated the 29th April, 1882, between Sir Robert John Abercromby, the then owner in fee-simple of the lands now belonging to the plaintiff, and the Fermoy Boat Club, by which the latter were given permission to erect a shed for the use of their boats on the

Barnane Walk, subject to certain conditions, one of which was to preserve the entire walk from injury, 'and to permit nothing to be done that should unfit it for the use and recreation of the inhabitants of the town by whom it is used as a promenade.'

It seems to me that the only questions admitting of doubt that arise in this action are 1, whether the townspeople of Fermoy have any legal rights over the walk; and, 2, if so, what are the nature and extent of such rights?

An attempt was made on behalf of the plaintiff to show that it is and has been a public highway for carriages and other vehicles; and many witnesses were examined on this issue. It is difficult to see how it is relevant to the plaintiff's case and even if it were he has failed to prove it. The existence of the wall across the entrance at the earliest date deposed to, and the fact that it was afterwards rebuilt or repaired by the owners of the soil in 1841 and 1850, its continuance until 1882, and its removal then not by such owner but by the Town Commissioners for a special purpose, are circumstances absolutely inconsistent either with a public highway for carriages by dedication or a private right of way for carriages acquired by lost grant or prescription.

Equally futile were the efforts of the Town Commissioners of Fermoy to show that they had such a property in or authority over the walk as justified them in erecting the posts and chains complained of by the plaintiff.

A local and personal Act of Parliament, passed in the year 1808, created in Fermoy a body of Commissioners who were authorised to fill up vacancies in their number by co-option, and who were invested with wide powers of control over the streets and ways in the town; but there is no proof that these Commissioners interfered at any time with Barnane Walk. Their records, if they kept records, are not forthcoming; and there is no other evidence on the subject. At a date not specified, but sometime between the years 1854 and 1861, the provisions of the Towns Improvement (Ireland) Act, 1854, were adopted with the consent of the old body of Commissioners, the effect of which, according to the fifth section thereof, was to put an end to the operation of the local Act.

The Commissioners that have been since elected, pursuant to the provisions of the statute of 1854, seem from the first to have taken the walk under their management. They alone have kept it in repair, expending for this purpose considerable sums of money from time to time. The wall with the stile across the entrance, or what remained of it, was taken down by their direction in 1882, to allow the military to draw water out of the river higher up. Their permission was asked by the boat club before erecting the boathouse under the agreement already referred to. They placed seats on the walk for the use of the public. They took steps to keep it free from nuisance and from practices calculated to cause discomfort or annoyance: such as cycling, playing objectionable games, and bathing at unseasonable hours.

It is unnecessary to consider whether the control thus exercised was with or without authority. It was for the benefit of the town, and no one complained of it. The first time the action of the Commissioners in regard to Barnane Walk was objected to was the occasion that has led to the present litigation.

In August, 1896, it was resolved by the Commissioners to place a barrier at the entrance to Barnane Walk from West Quay. This subject came before the body on several occasions afterwards; but the resolution does not seem to have been acted on until the following year, when metal columns connected by horizontal chains, with openings on each side for foot-passengers, were erected near the site of the wall which had been removed in 1882. The only reasons given in the minute-book for the step thus taken were to prevent the deposit of broken glass bottles and other rubbish near the boathouse, and to put a stop to bicycle-riding on the walk. It is possible that there was a third reason, which, although not expressed, influenced the Commissioners at least as strongly as the other two.

The interest under the lease of 1835 has been for some time vested in a lady called Hodder, and about the date of the barrier resolutions she was contemplating building three or four houses on the demised premises, fronting towards the river, and to be approached from West Quay by the walk. The first of those houses was to have been begun in October, 1897; but the project was probably spoken of for some time before, and the townspeople not unnaturally were opposed to their promenade being used as a carriage-way to the new houses. Whether this had anything to do with the action of the Commissioners I am unable to say with certainty; but there is no doubt that Mr. Hodder in October, 1897, applied to them to have the barrier removed, as it was a great inconvenience and a serious injury to his wife's property. This application was refused, and as far as I can see Mr. Hodder was not in a position to compel the Commissioners to yield to it. The walk was not included in his lease, nor was a right to use it, with horses and carriages, given to the lessee either by express grant or as appurtenant to the demised lands. Mr. Hodder's request was followed a few weeks later by a peremptory demand on behalf of the plaintiff to take away the barrier; and as the Commissioners insisted on their right to retain it, the present action was instituted to establish the plaintiff's title to that part of the town of Fermoy called Barnane Walk, subject to a right of way for the public over the same, and to compel the defendants to remove the posts and chains.

I do not think that it was ever alleged by the defendants that the plaintiff is not the owner of the land which forms the walk up to the point where it enters the Cliffe Estate, and his title thereto has not been seriously disputed in the argument in this Court. I am also of opinion that the defendants have failed to show any right on their part to erect the posts and chains. Their only claim to do so is by the authority conferred upon them as Commissioners of Fermoy by the Towns Improvement (Ireland) Act, 1854, and by a Provisional Order transferring to them the powers and duties of the Grand Jury in respect of the roads within the town; and there is no provision in either the Towns Improvement or the Grand Jury code by which the acts complained of can be justified. Counsel referred to the 52nd section of the Commissioners' Clauses Act, 1847, incorporated with the statute of 1854; but that section is confined to placing fences and posts on the side of the footways of streets or in the carriage ways thereof, so as to make the crossing thereof less dangerous for foot-passengers; and it cannot be said that the posts and chains at the entrance of Barnane Walk come under this enactment.

The remaining matter in controversy – the question to which the discussion here was almost exclusively directed – is the extent to which the dominion of the plaintiff over the walk is limited by rights acquired either by the public generally or by the inhabitants of Fermoy. A public right of way over it, that is to say, a right of way on foot is admitted in the pleadings and declared by the judgment of the Vice-Chancellor. This implies, according to the contention of the plaintiff, that while members of the public are entitled to walk from one end of it to the other and back, the plaintiff, provided he leaves sufficient space for two persons to pass each other, can use the remainder of the walk for any purpose he thinks fit. He may fence off a path four or five feet in width for the use of the public, and beyond its limits he may erect buildings, dig pits or raise crops. I am disposed to think that this would be in the plaintiff's power if the land is only subject to a public right of way; but I must add that if it were a matter for decision, I should have some difficulty in finding that such a right exists at all. There are three reasons for holding that it does not:

1. It is well settled that although there may be a dedication of a way to the public for a limited purpose, there cannot be a dedication to a *limited part* of the public: *Poole* v. *Huskinson* (11 M. & W. 827). In the present case, all the evidence points to a dedication for the benefit of the people of Fermoy.

2. A public right of way, originating in dedication, generally means a right to the public to pass from one public place to another public place: *Campbell* v. *Land* (1 Macqueen, H. of L. 451); and although the terminus of a public highway may be sufficient without having in the ordinary sense an exit, a mere private place not admitting of a passage through or beyond it, cannot be such a terminus: *Young* v. *Cuthbertson* (1 Macqueen, H. of L. 455). It is unnecessary for my present purpose to consider under what circumstances a *cul de sac* can be a public highway; but I may mention that before giving judgment in *The Giants Causeway Case* (Not reported. 14th Jan., 1898. There is a summary of this case in Vol. 32 of the Irish Law Times at p. 211) I sought in vain for an instance of the public being held entitled to a way terminating in private lands where such way was used for no other purpose than to enjoy a pleasant walk.

3. I am satisfied that the Barnane Walk was not used even by the inhabitants of Fermoy for the sake of reaching any definite point or place. The townspeople assembled on it as a place of recreation to walk, to saunter, to lounge, to chat, to meet their friends.

Dedication of a public right of way cannot I think be inferred from user of this kind; but our law has always recognised that the people of a district – a town, a parish, or a hamlet – are capable of acquiring by dedication or custom, certain rights over land which cannot be gained by the general public. Lord St. Leonards in the case of *Dyce* v *Lady James Hay* (1 Macqueen, H. of L. 305), pointed out the distinction, and illustrated it by village greens, and village playgrounds. Probably the young men and maidens of Fermoy have never at any period of their history danced round the maypole. Their sense of humour, if there was no other reason, has kept them from indulging in such 'awful mirth.' But legal principle does not require that rights of this nature should be limited to certain ancient pastimes. Popular amusement takes many shapes; and there is no outdoor recreation so general and perennial as the promenade. It may be asked how does this differ from a right of way. I think that it differs as much in legal conception as it certainly differs from it in point of fact. It implies that those who use the walk may wander over every portion of its surface, either in groups or in solitary meditation. It implies that the owner of the soil cannot encroach upon it in the manner contended for by the plaintiff's counsel. It implies, I should also think, that he could not convert it into a public road to be traversed by all kinds of vehicles; and that if he is at liberty to grant to individuals the right to pass over it with carriages, such grant must be subject to the condition that the use of it by the inhabitants of the town is not to be interfered with thereby. I believe that this was not the view of the Vice-Chancellor, as I gather from his judgment that he was of opinion that the lands were only subject to an ordinary public right of way on foot.

I think, therefore, that his judgment should be amended by declaring that the plaintiff is entitled as owner in fee to that part of the town of Fermoy called Barnane Walk, as far as the boundary of the Cliffe estate, subject to the right of the inhabitants of the town to use it for their recreation as a promenade. I am of opinion that this alteration has an important bearing upon the principal issue in controversy between the parties. I have already indicated my opinion as to what its effect will be; and as the result is to place the inhabitants of the town, whose battle has been fought by the defendants in a much better position than that contended for by the plaintiff or given them by the judgment, I think that the plaintiff is not entitled to the costs of either the action or the appeal. At the same time, as the injunction stands, and as the appeal was taken from the judgment as a whole, he ought not to be obliged to pay the defendants' costs in either court. This determination renders it unnecessary to hear Mr. Ronan on the point which he asked to be left open.

Notes and Questions
1. What was the precise nature of the right over the plaintiff's land held by the inhabitants of Fermoy? Was it a public right or a local customary right? Whatever it was, how was it acquired? *Irish Land Law*, para. 6.041 *et seq.*
2. See further on public rights, *Moore* v. *Att.-Gen.*, p. 5, *ante.*

SCOTT V. GOULDING PROPERTIES LTD
[1973] I.R. 200 (Supreme Court)

The plaintiff, assignee of a lease for 150 years of premises in Dublin, claimed damages from the defendants for the obstruction of the light reaching her premises by the building being erected by the defendants on their adjacent land. Teevan J. awarded £1700 damages for diminution of light and the defendants appealed to the Supreme Court.

Walsh J.:

This is an appeal brought by the defendants against the judgment and order of Mr. Justice Teevan dated the 31st July, 1968, awarding a sum of £1,700 damages to the plaintiff against the defendants for diminution of access of light to the plaintiff's dwellinghouse, No. 11 Lad Lane, Dublin, which had been caused by the erection of a building on the south-east side of the plaintiff's dwellinghouse by the defendants.

The plaintiff's premises are a mews premises which were converted into a residence by the plaintiff. The defendants' premises, which are the cause of the complaint, comprise a very substantial building erected in three sections. The centre section is a twelve-storey structure which is 124 feet high and is flanked on either side by three-storied sections which are 40 feet high. The defendants' premises are directly opposite the plaintiff's residence, being about 20 feet from the entrance gate to her premises and about 40 feet from the main wall of her residence. The total cost of the erection of the defendants' premises was in the region of £600,000. Before the defendants commenced the building operations, they received a letter on the 9th May, 1967, from the plaintiff's solicitors advising them that their proposed structure would almost certainly diminish the light being received by the plaintiff's residence. The letter advised the defendants that the plaintiff was about to have light measurements taken and it offered the defendants the facility of taking similar measurements at that time. An assurance was sought that no building would be put up which would interfere in any way with the light to the plaintiff's premises or the amenities thereof. The letter contained a warning that, if the defendants proceeded with their building in spite of the letter from the plaintiff's solicitors, the plaintiff would take such steps as might be necessary to protect her interests. The letter also enquired if the defendants would permit the plaintiff's solicitors to have a set of the working drawings for the benefit of the plaintiff's light experts. No reply was received to that letter and a further letter was sent on the 19th May asking for a reply to that of the 9th May. On the 26th May a letter was written by the defendants' solicitors acknowledging the receipt of the letter from the plaintiff's solicitors and declaring that the defendants were quite satisfied that their proposed building would not cause any material interference with the light enjoyed by the plaintiff's premises. From the evidence given in the High Court it was abundantly clear that the defendants did not carry out any inspection of the plaintiff's premises before they settled upon their building plans and did not avail of her offer to have the light measurements made before the building commenced.

The learned High Court judge found that the light to the plaintiff's premises had been interfered with by the defendants' structure and that it was a serious interference with the plaintiff's right to light and that it was of a character which of necessity must continue. The interference in the main resulted from one of the lower sections of the defendants' structure, but to some degree it was caused by the twelve-storey structure also. In the course of the evidence it was stated that it would cost about £10,000 to remove the third floor of the offending low structure and that, if the high block was to come down, it would cost between £60,000 and £70,000. The learned trial judge refused an injunction and awarded £1,700 damages. Against this verdict the defendants have appealed, first, on the ground that the learned trial judge erred in law in awarding damages to the plaintiff for the obstruction of access of light to windows which did not enjoy ancient lights. The defendants also complained that the damages assessed were repetitive and covered the same items under alternative headings and, furthermore, that the plaintiff was not entitled to damages which the judge awarded and included in the sum already mentioned for loss of amenity in addition to damages based on the diminution of the value of the property as a result of the obstruction of the light. It was also claimed that the damages awarded were excessive.

The first ground of appeal raises the most important point in this case. It was found as a fact, and was not disputed, that some of the windows and apertures whose light had been diminished by the defendants' buildings had been only made in the residence when the plaintiff converted them subsequent to the year 1959. Other apertures and windows clearly enjoyed the right of ancient lights. It was also clearly established that the defendants' buildings had diminished the light to the apertures which enjoyed the ancient lights as well as the light to the more recent apertures. The plaintiff has undoubtedly suffered damage both to her ancient lights and to what I would call, for the sake of brevity, her modern lights. It is abundantly clear that no cause of action would arise without the damage to the ancient lights. Once the cause of action has arisen, the net question is whether the plaintiff is also entitled to receive damages in respect of her modern lights as the diminution of light in that quarter is the direct result of the unlawful act of the defendants in infringing the plaintiff's ancient lights. The learned trial judge found that she was so entitled.

Successive editions of Salmond on Torts support the learned trial judge's view of the law. The most recent edition of that work (15th) was produced under the distinguished editorship of Professor R.F.V. Heuston; it states the law as follows at p. 717: 'it sometimes happens that damage which is in itself *damnum sine injuria* is caused by an act which, by reason of some other kind of damage also caused by it to the same person, is wrongful and actionable at the suit of that person. For example, a building which wrongfully obstructs the ancient lights of an adjoining building may at the same time obstruct other windows in that building which have not yet acquired legal protection. In such cases the damages recoverable for the wrongful act include compensation for the whole loss so caused, even though part of that loss is in itself *damnum sine injuria*: *Griffith* v. *Richard Clay & Sons Ltd*([1912] 2 Ch. 291). Again the protection of privacy, or redress for purely economic loss carelessly caused, is often dependent on some other cause of action: *Jackson* v. *Watson & Sons* ([1909] 2 K.B. 193); *Campbell* v. *Paddington Corporation* ([1911] 1 K.B. 869). This has been aptly called the "parasitic" element in damage.' The law is stated in somewhat similar terms in Mayne and McGregor on Damages (12th ed.) at para. 110 *et seq*. The principle of law involved is the ability to recover damages for what is termed a secondary interest where a separate liability in respect of a primary interest has been established. These paragraphs give examples of the various types of cases where damages for interference with the secondary interest were held to be recoverable and the types where they were not. Cases of infringement of rights to light fall within the former.

Dealing with the question of whether or not he should grant an injunction, the learned trial judge used the following words: 'This is not a case for an injunction for a number of reasons; the principal one being that, having regard to the amount expended by the defendants, the plaintiff does not press for an injunction. The other reasons are that it would be excessively costly and oppressive to compel the defendants to reduce the height of the offending part of parts of their building; and that it cannot be said that the defendants arrogantly proceeded in disregard of the plaintiff's rights for they acted on professional advice in a case where there is, as we now, know, a wide divergence of expert opinion. Nevertheless, there has been a serious interference with the plaintiff's right to light and the defendants have created a nuisance which of necessity must continue.' If an injunction had been granted in the case, the order would have restrained the defendants from erecting their building so as to darken, injure or obstruct any of the ancient lights of the plaintiff and also from permitting to remain any building already erected which would cause any such obstruction. On the facts of this case the juxtaposition of the ancient and the modern lights was such that an injunction in those terms to remove the infringement of the ancient lights would also remove the cause of the diminution of light to the modern openings. Is the plaintiff then to be in a worse position because she is awarded damages instead of an injunction? It was urged on behalf of the defendants that the answer should be in the affirmitive, even though the reason why the injunction was not granted in this case was to save the defendants the appalling cost which would fall upon them if an injunction had been given.

There can be no question that the defendants were fully aware of the effect which their building would have upon the light which the plaintiff was receiving in all the openings, both old and new, and it is clear beyond doubt that the defendants could not plead, nor have they endeavoured to plead, that the damage was such as they could not have foreseen.

The point of law at present under review was expressly dealt with in *Griffith* v. *Richard Clay & Sons Ltd* ([1912] 2 Ch. 291). In that case the defendants had erected a building on the side of a street opposite to the plaintiff's two houses which fronted on the other side of the street. The plaintiff's windows facing the street were ancient lights. He was also the owner of a piece of land immediately to the rear of and adjoining his houses. The whole site occupied by the plaintiff's buildings was in such a dilapidated condition that they would soon have had to be demolished and, as the neighbourhood was no longer residential, the property would have been suitable as a site for a warehouse or a factory; it was submitted that the value of the building site as a whole was diminished by the obstruction to the light in front. It was held in that case that the damages recoverable by the plaintiff were not limited to the depreciation in the value of the house but extended to the diminution in value of the whole of the plaintiff's premises, considered as one building site. This affirmed the decision of the trial judge in the Chancery Division. In the course of his judgment in the Court of Appeal, Cozens-Hardy M.R. at p. 296 of the report that if the plaintiff had obtained an injunction 'it is clear that that injunction, by virtue of these ancient lights, would have prevented the defendants from building any part of that which is opposite to the plaintiff's houses above what is called the line shown on the model. That would have enured for the benefit of the whole site, and it would have been competent without doubt for the plaintiff to have utilized this site in the only way in which a sensible man of business would use it, namely, by treating it as a whole . . . Well, it is said that that may be so as to an injunction; it may be that in that indirect way the plaintiff could have got protection for the whole of this building site; but further it is said that has nothing whatever to do with a case in which no injunction is asked for. It was asked for in the writ and statement of claim, but no injunction was asked for at the hearing, and it is said that the considerations to which I have alluded have no application to a case where merely damages are asked for. Well, I ask myself, why not? A wrongful act has been committed by the defendants: what damage has the plaintiff suffered?' Having considered the judgment of Lord Esher in *London, Tilbury and Southend Railway Co. and the Trustees of Gower's Walk School* ([1889] 24 Q.B.D. 326), he went on to say at p. 299: 'I therefore think that this is a case in which we are at liberty to consider not merely what damage has been done in respect to these ancient lights in these ancient buildings, but also to consider what is the damage which the plaintiff has suffered by reason of the wrongful act of the defendants in creating a nuisance by interfering with the ancient lights.'

The question is also answered in the same way by Buckley L.J. in giving his judgment in that appeal. At p. 301 of the report he said: 'Suppose a man had a warehouse bounded by a large and high blank wall on the road having in it only one window, say for the purpose of lighting a counting-house on the ground floor. The owner of that building might open any number of windows – modern windows – in his blank wall, but in respect of these he would not be entitled to sue. Suppose a man on the opposite side of the road raised his building, and it was found that there was a legal nuisance to the one small ancient window. The owner would be entitled, under proper circumstances, to an injunction. If he obtained an injunction his injunction would operate to protect not only the one ancient window in the counting-house, but also in fact although not as of right any modern windows which might have been opened in the wall. Suppose he failed to get an injunction, but got damages, what damages would he be entitled to? He would be entitled to damages measured by the depreciation of the building, not with the one little window on the ground floor only, but with all the other windows. That would be the extent to which he had been injured, and it seems to me as matter of principle that that would be the proper measure of damages.' He goes on to point out that the fallacy of the argument to the contrary stems from the assumption that the action is brought for the pecuniary value of the access of light to each particular room through each particular window. He points out that that is not so and that the action is not in respect of that but in respect of the injury to the house as a whole. The thing to be ascertained is the injury to the house as a whole by reason of the infringement of the right to light to certain of its windows. At p. 302 of the report he said: 'What is the house as a whole? The house as a whole does not mean merely those rooms which look to the front. It includes rooms which look to the back . . . the whole property is to be taken into consideration in determining what is the amount of the damage sustained.' He also approves of what Lord Esher said in the *Tilbury Case* ((1889) 24 Q.B.D. 326.

In the third judgment of the Court of Appeal in *Griffith's Case* ([1912] 2 Ch. 291) Kennedy L.J. was also of the same opinion. He said also that he could not accept the argument that, in assessing damages, only the diminution of light to the ancient lights is to be taken into account; he said that the value of the premises as a whole is to be regarded and that the damages should represent the injury to the premises as a whole resulting from the unlawful act or nuisance of the defendant. He said that it is correct to say that the wrongful act is actionable in so far only as it has affected the ancient lights. At pp. 304–5 of the report he said: 'But directly the wrong has been inflicted it produces, as a natural and necessary consequence, the deprivation of the advantage which the protection of the ancient lights gave to the owner of the property to which those lights belong.' In the present case it is clear that so long as the ancient lights were protected the modern lights were also protected.

The *Tilbury Case* ((1889) 24 Q.B.D. 326) was one where a railway company in exercise of powers erected a warehouse which obstructed the lights of the windows of the plaintiffs' building. The plaintiffs' building was a new one which they had erected on the site of a former building which had ancient lights. The position of certain portions of the windows in the new building coincided with that of the old windows while others occupied wholly different positions. The matter was approached on the basis of whether, at common law, the damages could extend to the modern windows as well as the old, and also on the basis of the provisions of s. 16 of the Railway Clauses Act, 1845, which would have extended to both. Lord Esher M.R. founded his judgment on the common-law point and at pp. 329–30 of the report he stated: 'On this point the rule seems to me to be that where a plaintiff has a cause of action for a wrongful act of the defendant the plaintiff is entitled to recover for all the damage caused which was the direct consequence of the wrongful act and so probable a consequence that, if the defendant had considered the matter, he must have foreseen that the whole damage would result from that act. If that be so, and a person puts up buildings, the inevitable consequence of their erection being to obstruct ancient and modern lights, should he not be taken to have foreseen that in obstructing the one he would obstruct the other? If that were proved in a common law action the plaintiff would be entitled to damages for the whole of the consequences of the wrongful act of obstructing ancient lights, which would include damage to the new as much as to the old lights. If so, it seems to me obvious that compensation must be given under the statute to the same extent.' Lord Esher took the view that s. 16 of the Act of 1845 would give the plaintiff everything he was entitled to by way of legal damages; he went on to say that, even if there was some damage which would not be included in the legal damages, the additional damage would be included in the statutory provision. It is clear, however, that he expressed the view and decided the case on the equation of the two in that particular instance. The other two judges in that case based their decisions on the provisions of s. 16 of the Act of 1845 rather than on the common law.

Lord Esher's view of the damages recoverable at common law was approved and adopted by Cozens-Hardy M.R. and the other two judges in the Court of Appeal in *Griffith's Case* ([1912] 2 Ch. 291). Those two judges, Buckley and Kennedy L.JJ., were also two of the three members of the Court of Appeal in *Horton* v. *Colwyn Bay and Colwyn Urban Council* ([1908] 1 K.B. 327). In that case Buckley L.J. at p. 341 of the report interpreted the *Tilbury Case* ((1889) 24 Q.B.D. 326.) as having decided that a plaintiff who is entitled to sue by reason of a wrong 'may in that action recover all the damage he has sustained, including damage which he could not have recovered if this latter had been the only damage done him.' Kennedy L.J. agreed. *Horton's Case* ([1908] 1 K.B. 327) dealt with a claim for damages by reason of works carried out under the Public Health Act, 1875, and rejected the claim of a person on whose lands sewers were in part constructed who claimed damages on the ground that the value of his lands would be depreciated by the contemplated user of the sewerage station which was not on his lands but on adjoining land. The plaintiff in that case lost because no actionable wrong had been done to him in the first instance and, therefore, the question of a secondary wrong did not arise. What is notable, however, is the interpretation which Buckley L.J. gave to the decision in the *Tilbury Case* ((1889) 24 Q.B.D. 326). Cozens-Hardy M.R. referred expressly to the fact that Buckley L.J. had so interpreted the matter of the common-law case for damages in the *Tilbury Case* ((1889) 24 Q.B.D. 326), and in their concurring judgments Buckley and Kennedy L.J.J. not only did not disagree with that interpretation but reinforced it. Even if it might be said, as was urged on behalf of the defendants in this case, that the original dictum of Lord Esher in the *Tilbury Case* ((1889) 24 Q.B.D. 326) was obiter (which it was not) or because of the provisions of s. 16 of the Act of 1845 was unnecessary (which it probably was), the principle was adopted as the *ratio decidendi* in *Griffith's Case* ([1912] 2 Ch. 291).

In my view *Levet* v. *Gas Light & Coal Co* ([1919 1 Ch. 24) is of no relevance to the question under immediate discussion. All that case purported to decide was that where a right to light is claimed under the Prescription Act, 1832, the enjoyment must have been had to and for a building in which there was an aperture which cannot be an ordinary doorway. My view that the case was concerned with nothing else is reinforced by the fact that no mention whatsoever is made of it in the *Tilbury Case* ((1889) 24 Q.B.D. 326), *Horton's Case* ([1908] 1 K.B. 327) and *Griffith's Case* ([1912] 2 Ch. 291).

The principle of law being discussed appeared in a somewhat different context a year before the decision in *Griffith's Case* ([1912] 2 Ch. 291). In *Campbell* v. *Paddington Corporation* ([1911] 1 K.B. 869) the plaintiff recovered damages for loss of profit which she would have made but for the defendants' act in erecting a stand which constituted a public nuisance and which obstructed the view of the main thoroughfare from the windows of the plaintiff's home. The occasion was the funeral procession of King Edward VII. The plaintiff was in the habit of letting seats in her rooms, having windows facing the road, to persons wishing to view public processions passing down that road. It was quite clear that she had no enforceable right to a view from her premises but the defendants were guilty of a public nuisance by the unlawful obstruction of the highway in erecting the stand and, as a result, she was entitled to maintain an action to recover the damages in respect of the loss sustained by her which flowed directly from the unlawful act of the defendants. On appeal from the country court, Avory J. said at pp. 875–6 of the report: 'I agree that the law does not recognize a view or prospect from a house as a right in the nature of an easement which can belong to anybody as of right, and that no period of enjoyment will give a person a right of action against another who on his own land erects a structure or plants trees which obstruct the view or prospect. But that is not this case. This is the case of a person, a corporation in point of fact, not in the exercise of any right, but unlawfully and without any authority, erecting a structure in the public street which seriously interfered with the enjoyment by the plaintiff of her house. That is enough to give the plaintiff a right of action on the case for disturbing her in the enjoyment, use, and occupation of her house; and, moreover, as the wrongful act of the defendants constituted a public nuisance, the plaintiff, having in my opinion established the fact that she has sustained special damage over and above the general public inconvenience, has established a cause of action on this ground also.' At pp. 878–9 of the report Lush J. said: 'In the same way, where a person without having acquired a right of light enjoys in fact the uninterrupted access of light to his windows, he has no legal right to complain of the conduct of another who by an innocent act obstructs that light. In short, in the one case as in the other the person affected has no right in the sense that he has no easement. But in the present case the act of the defendants, apart from depriving the plaintiff of the view or prospect from her windows, was a wrongful act on independent grounds, and not merely in that it deprived the plaintiff of the view or prospect from her house. The defendants begin with an act wrongful in itself; if such an act is the source and origin of loss to the plaintiff, then, provided the loss is sufficiently closely connected with the wrongful act, it is a loss for which the plaintiff is entitled to redress.' He goes on then to discuss other cases in which wrongful acts causing loss of enjoyment of benefits which could not themselves be enforced but which nevertheless furnished grounds for the award of damages when those particular benefits were injured.

In *Sheffield Masonic Hall Co. Ltd.* v. *Sheffield Corporation* ((1932) 48 T.L.R. 336) at p. 337 of the report Maugham J. approved the opinion voiced in *Griffith's Case* ([1912] 2 Ch. 291). The passages in Mayne and McGregor to which I have referred contain ample illustrations of the several different types of actions in which damages are awarded for the secondary loss in addition to the primary loss; they even include cases where the further damage is of a type totally different from the primary loss. These include actions founded on negligence, inducing a breach of contract, conspiracy, cattle trespass, seduction and others. For the purpose of this case it is unnecessary to explore these decisions; it is sufficient to say that there is more than ample authority for supporting the proposition in cases where the secondary loss is of the same type or character as the primary loss, that is to say, the same type or character as the damage to the right which is protected by the law.

Apart from the ample authority on the subject, in my view, it is demonstrably correct in principle that this arises in cases of infringements of easements of light because the damages are damages for the injury to the hereditament which enjoys the easement which is the direct result of the unlawful act, not just damages for the particular quantity of light interfered with coming through windows which were protected by a right enforceable at law. Once the defendant by his wrongful act has directly caused the damage complained of, he cannot seek to segregate one part of it from another where the whole of the damage resulting from his act was known and foreseeable by him. In such a case it would be completely contrary to legal principle that he should be permitted by an unlawful act to cause damage with impunity to another. The authorities which I have mentioned remain undisturbed in their support of the application of this principle to the case of ancient lights; I have already cited the most up-to-date text-books on the subject as being a correct statement of the law. I have no hesitation in expressing the view that the learned trial judge was correct in taking the view which he did on this aspect of the case, and that he was correct in principle in awarding damages for the injury suffered by the plaintiff so as to include the damage caused to her residence by the diminution of light not merely through those apertures which were entitled to ancient lights but also in respect of the diminution of the light coming through the modern lights.

I turn now to consider the defendants' submissions that the damages assessed were repetitive and that the learned trial judge was wrong in allowing damages for loss of amenity in addition to damages based in the diminution of the value of the plaintiff's residence as a result of the obstruction of the lights. During the course of the evidence at the trial it was submitted on behalf of the plaintiff by her expert that there had been a serious diminution of light. The defendants' expert was emphatic that the interference, if any, was only marginal and insignificant. There was a clear conflict of opinion on this matter which had to be resolved by the learned trial judge. In addition there was the plaintiff's own evidence, which the judge fully accepted, to the effect that much of the light to the premises had been diminished. After a careful weighing of the evidence on both sides the learned trial judge was satisfied that the defendants' building had caused a serious diminution of light. Having considered the evidence and the judge's assessment and analysis of it, I do not see any reason to disturb his finding on this point.

It was agreed that the conversion of the premises which had been carried out by the plaintiff had been carried out with great taste and discrimination and that the premises had been turned into a residence of considerable charm. It is clearly impossible to abate the nuisance which has been caused by the defendants' building without removing the offending portions of the defendants' building which would be an extremely costly matter. The result is, therefore, that the plaintiff's residence will now suffer a permanent diminution of light and that is bound to affect the value. The total sum awarded by the learned trial judge was £1,700, which is made up of damages for depreciation in the value of the property and for loss of amenity. While the judgment and the order do not reveal the ingredients of the amount, from queries raised during the course of the hearing of this appeal it was ascertained that when the sum had been awarded counsel for the defendants asked the judge how the sum was made up and he was told that £1,500 was for depreciation of value and £200 for loss of amenity. The land valuer called on behalf of the plaintiff estimated that the effect of the diminution of light to the premises would reduce the market value of it by £1,500. The valuer for the defendants offered the view that the diminution of light would have no adverse effect on the market value. The plaintiff's valuer placed a valuation of £6,000 on the premises if the light had not been diminished, whereas the defendants' valuer gave evidence to the effect that the premises were worth at least £7,000 even in their existing condition. The defendants' witness did concede that there had perhaps been some diminution of light caused by the defendants' building. In the ordinary course of events one would naturally assume that this would reduce the value of a property but the case being made on behalf of the defendants' here was that this type of property was subject to a special type of demand which was not really very much affected by the diminution of light of the order contended for by the defendants who did not, of course, agree that the diminution of light had been to the extent contended for by the plaintiff. However, one must not lose sight of the fact that the learned trial judge found as a fact that there had been a serious diminution of light and it was not denied by the experts on either side that a prospective purchaser would be affected by such things as the lighting of the premises. I do not see any reason to disagree with the learned trial judge's acceptance of the evidence of the plaintiff's valuer on this point. Indeed, bearing in mind the fact that the defendants' valuer was inclined to put a higher value on the premises in any event, the diminution of light found by the judge to have been caused by the defendants would, if anything, probably cause even greater depreciation in the value of the property. However, there was no cross-appeal by the plaintiff on this point.

In the circumstances I do not consider that the judge's assessment of £200, in respect of the damages to be awarded for loss of amenity, was in any way unreasonable. The damages awarded for this sum must bear a ratio to the diminution in the value of the property itself. It is true to say that if the plaintiff were to put the property up for sale immediately after the damage had been caused she would have taken the full shock of the depreciation in the value of the property but on the other hand would have suffered comparatively little loss under the heading of amenity loss. However, the longer she stayed in the premises and continued to live in them there would be a certain discount of the figure for the depreciation in the value of the premises but on the other hand, of course, the loss of amenity would appreciate in value so that one might say the longer one stays in the premises the less the depreciation in value may be felt because it is spread over so many years but the greater is the immediate effect of the diminution of light, namely, the loss of amenity. In the result, therefore, whether one takes the figure of £1,700 as being the full figure of £1,500 for loss of value and £200 for loss of amenity or the sum of two figures which bear different ratio to each other depending on how long the plaintiff will stay in the house, I think the total sum of £1,700 is quite reasonable.

If the evidence had been that the plaintiff would never sell but would remain for the rest of her days in the house the judge might very well have awarded virtually the whole of this sum for loss of amenity and the balance for depreciation in value. In a case such as this what the judge has to try to do is to arrive at a global figure which will cover the various contingencies either of immediate sale and little suffering in the sphere of amenities or long tenure with consequent higher amenity loss. If the judge gave full value of the depreciation of the property and also damages for loss of amenity based on a lifetime occupancy there would undoubtedly be a double element in the damages. In the present case there may be some slight overlapping but, in my view, it is of no significance because as the one element decreases the other one increases. As was pointed out by Dixon J. in *McGrath* v. *Munster and Leinster Bank Ltd* ([1959] I.R. 313, 328), the assessment in a case such as this involves taking into consideration not merely the depreciation in the value of the property but such intangible injuries as loss of amenity. One takes a global view of the whole matter and, bearing in mind the possibility of duplication if the relative positions of depreciation in value and loss of amenity are not kept in proper perspective, one fixes a figure to cover the situation which will include both of these to the extent to which they exist or may exist.

There can be little doubt that in this case these premises which were so well and tastefully converted from an old mews to a residence depended a great deal upon the amount of light which was available and on the evidence the judge was quite justified in being satisfied that any appreciable diminution of light, let alone the serious diminution which he found, must adversely affect the value of the premises if offered for sale or the enjoyment of the person who lives in them if he does not offer them for sale. There was ample evidence in this case from the plaintiff, as the occupant, of the effect of the diminution of light on which the judge could find that there was an appreciable disturbance in the enjoyment of the premises and that this would of necessity continue.

Having regard to the fact that this case was mainly concerned with the principles applicable to the law on this subject, I have not found it necessary to go into any detail on the actual changes made in the premises by describing which window was a new window and which was an old one, or the fact that what had hitherto been a doorway with a fan-light has now been converted into a window. As the case was concerned with the overall effect on the premises of the loss of lighting, in my view this was unnecessary. For the reasons I have given I would uphold the order of the High Court and dismiss this appeal.

FitzGerald J.:

Prior to her marriage the plaintiff was, and still is, the owner and occupier of the two-storey premises known as No. 11 Lad Lane, Dublin 2, which is a mews at the rear of the house known as No. 11 Fitzwilliam Place. She acquired the mews in 1959. It had been used previously as a coach-house with accommodation for horses on the ground floor and accommodation for the coachman on the upper storey. In addition to the building the plaintiff acquired both the courtyard between the building and Lad Lane and a portion of the garden, some 30 feet in length, at the rear of No. 11 Fitzwilliam Place. On acquiring this property, the plaintiff proceeded to have it converted into a dwellinghouse. Prior to its conversion, the premises had unobstructed light to two windows on the upper floor and to a fan-light over the door on the ground floor and to a glass panel beside this door. These apertures had been in existence for many years – in fact since the original mews were erected – and it is clear that in law they were ancient lights, and the judge so found. That finding has not been challenged on this appeal.

In the course of converting the mews into a dwellinghouse, the coach-house doors on the ground floor were removed and replaced by glass which was divided up into a number of frames, including two main windows which occupy the whole aperture previously filled by the doors of the coach-house. In addition, a new window was built to provide light for a kitchen erected on the ground floor. From the time of the renovation in 1959 up to 1967 these two new windows, and smaller panes of glass occupying the coach-house aperture, had the benefit of light save in so far as it may have been obstructed by the 14 foot wall between the courtyard and the laneway. This wall was 21 feet 2 inches from the windows. The light reaching the new windows was unobstructed for some eight years and did not in that time acquire the status of ancient lights.

In 1967 the defendants proceeded to erect a large office building on the opposite side of Lad Lane from the plaintiff's premises. The defendants' building had a centre section which was 124 feet high and two wing sections which were 40 feet high. The nearest point of the defendants' premises is some 20 feet from the plaintiff's gateway on Lad Lane and some 43 feet from the plaintiff's new ground-floor windows. The defendants' building, and particularly one of the 40 foot wing sections, obstructs the light to all the plaintiff's windows which face the courtyard. In addition to the windows facing the courtyard the plaintiff's premises enjoy light from windows facing the garden at the back of No. 11 Fitzwilliam Place.

Prior to the erection by the defendants of their building, they were notified in correspondence that the plaintiff apprehended that their proposed building would obstruct light to the plaintiff's premises and were amply warned that the plaintiff would assert her right to unrestricted light. The defendants proceeded with the building notwithstanding this warning.

The plaintiff resides with her husband in the said mews; she has resided there since the conversion in 1959. On the 12 October, 1967, the plaintiff instituted proceedings by prenary summons claiming an injunction to restrain the defendants from continuing to erect a building which would obstruct and diminish the light coming to her dwellinghouse so as to amount to a nuisance. She also claimed damages and, alternatively, further damages if the building was completed. In her statement of claim she claimed that there were four windows which were ancient lights, *viz.* (a) the lounge windows on the ground floor, (b) the kitchen window on the ground floor, (c) a bedroom window on the first floor, and (d) another bedroom window on the first floor. She repeated her claim for an injunction to restrain further building; she added a claim for a mandatory injunction to have the building pulled down; and she repeated her claim for damages. The defendants in their defence denied (a) that any of the windows were ancient lights, (b) that their building diminished the light to the plaintiff's windows, and (c) that any nuisance would be caused to the plaintiff or that she would be deprived of enjoyment of her dwellinghouse or that her premises would be unfit for use by her in her profession as an author. They further denied that the plaintiff had suffered or would suffer the alleged or any damage and denied that she was entitled to the relief claimed. There does not appear to have been any application made by the plaintiff for either an interim or an interlocutory injunction and the action came for trial before Teevan J. on the 17th and 18th May, 1968. Reserved judgment was delivered on the 31 July, 1968.

The learned judge declined to grant an injunction but awarded a sum of £1,700 to the plaintiff as compensation for damage sustained by her through the diminution of light to her dwellinghouse. The order of the High Court does not indicate that the learned judge, in assessing the compensation, differentiated between the ancient lights and the modern lights. However, the matter is clarified in his written judgment. He appears to have accepted a contention of the plaintiff's counsel, based on the decision of Peterson J. in *Levet* v. *Gas Light & Coal Co* ([1919] 1 Ch. 24.), that the windows now occupying the space which was formerly filled by the coach-house doors had acquired a right to light as if they were ancient lights. The defendants have appealed against the verdict of £1,700 on the ground that the trial judge misdirected himself in awarding damages in respect of obstruction of light to the new windows which were not ancient lights. They further complain that the damages awarded by the trial judge were repetitive in that the plaintiff was not entitled to damages for loss of amenity in addition to damages based on the diminution in the value of her preperty, and they submitted that the damages were excessive.

It is not disputed that the defendants, by the erection of their new building, have obstructed the light to the windows in the upper floor of the premises which had acquired the status of ancient lights. A wrong having been done to the plaintiff in respect of her ancient lights, the net question on this issue is whether she is also entitled to damages in respect of the obstruction of light to the new windows on the ground floor. It is undoubtedly true that a plaintiff who is the owner of premises which enjoy light through ancient windows is entitled to have the damages measured not merely on the basis of the loss of light to those particular windows but also general damages to be assessed on the basis of loss of amenity and enjoyment of the property and loss of the value of the property. However, the modern text-books appear to take the view that general damages may include compensation for obstruction to the light of modern windows, as if they were ancient windows; this is apparently on the basis that, once the wrongful act of obstruction of the light to the ancient windows is proved, compensation for the obstruction of modern lights (which, of itself, would be *damnum sine injuria*) can then be granted as what has been called 'parasitic damages.' This view appears to be based on *Griffith* v. *Richard Clay & Sons Ltd* ([1912] 2 Ch. 291). The Court of Appeal in that case decided that the damages recoverable by the plaintiff in an action in respect of alleged obstruction of light were not limited to the depreciation in the value of the houses, but extended to the diminution in value of the whole of the plaintiff's premises when considered as one entity. The decision does not appear to me to establish that obstruction of modern lights can attract damages in the same way as if they were ancient lights. If that were to be the law, a new building of 10 or 15 stories with hundreds of windows would be entitled to have damages assessed in respect of the obstruction to those hundreds of windows if the building it had replaced, perhaps one storey in height, had possessed one window which was an ancient light and the neighbouring owner, in the course of erecting a building on his property, were to obstruct the light to that one window and the hundreds of windows in the new building. In my view, a modern window cannot acquire a right to light which should be protected on the same basis as if it were a window enjoying ancient light.

However, it is quite clear that in assessing damages the judge is entitled to take into account the loss of amenity to the plaintiff in the future use of the premises and is entitled to have regard to the reduction in the selling value of the property if the plaintiff should be disposed to sell it. The learned trial judge does not indicate in his judgment how he obtained the figure of £1,700 which he awarded as damages. It appears, however, that on enquiry being made by the defendants' counsel the judge indicated that he was allowing £1,500 for depreciation in value and £200 for loss of amenity. Damages for loss of amenity are properly awarded in respect of the injury sustained up to the date of the trial and for such further period, if it can be estimated, as the plaintiff may continue to occupy the premises. In my view, damages for depreciation should relate to loss in selling value in the future if and when the plaintiff decides to dispose of the property. Where there is no definite evidence as to whether or when the plaintiff is likely to dispose of the property, a global figure for general damages has to be awarded without necessarily segregating the figure in compartments for loss of amenity and depreciation on future sale. It appears to me, however, that the amount of £1,700 which the trial judge awarded bears no reasonable relation to the extent of the injury suffered by the plaintiff as a result of the obstruction of light to the ancient windows themselves and the loss of amenity or depreciation in value. Consequently, in my opinion, the appeal should be allowed and the judgment for £1,700 set aside.

McLoughlin J.:
I agree with the judgment of Mr. Justice FitzGerald.

[The parties agreed to have the damages re-assessed by the Supreme Court, and on the 11th May, 1972, that court assessed the damages at £1,200]

Notes
1. Do you agree with Walsh J. or FitzGerald J. on the issue of the extent to which modern windows can attract damages for obstruction? To what extent did the plaintiff's claim in this case depend upon the existence of an easement (right of light)? What would have been the result of granting an injunction instead of awarding damages?
2. See further on rights of light, *Irish Land Law*, paras. 6. 108–9.

2. Acquisition

CONVEYANCING ACT, 1881

6. – (1) A conveyance of land shall be deemed to include and shall by virtue of this Act operate to convey, with the land, all buildings, erections, fixtures, commons, hedges, ditches, fences, ways, waters, watercourses, liberties, privileges, easements, rights, and advantages whatsoever, appertaining or reputed to appertain to the land, or any part thereof, or at the time of conveyance demised, occupied, or enjoyed with, or reputed or known as part or parcel of or appurtenant to the land or any part thereof.

(2) A conveyance of land, having houses or other buildings thereon, shall be deemed to include and shall by virtue of this Act operate to convey, with the land, houses, or other buildings, all outhouses, erections, fixtures, cellars, areas, courts, courtyards, cisterns, sewers, gutters, drains, ways, passages, lights, watercourses, liberties, privileges, easements, rights, and advantages, whatsoever, appertaining or reputed to appertain to the land, houses, or other buildings conveyed, or any of them, or any part thereof, or at the time of conveyance demised, occupied, or enjoyed with, or reputed or known as part or parcel of or appurtenant to, the land, houses, or other buildings, conveyed, or any of them, or any part thereof.

(3) A conveyance of a manor shall be deemed to include and shall by virtue of this Act operate to convey, with the manor, all pastures, feedings, wastes, warrens, commons, mines, minerals, quarries, furzes, trees, woods, underwoods, coppices, and the ground and soil thereof, fishings, fisheries, fowlings, courts leet, courts baron, and other courts, view of frankpledge and all that to view of frankpledge doth belong, mills, mulctures, customs, tolls, duties, reliefs, heriots, fines, sums of money, amerciaments, waifs, estrays, chief-rents, quit-rents, rentscharge, rents seck, rents of assize, fee farm rents, services, royalties, jurisdictions, franchises, liberties, privileges, easements, profits, advantages, rights, emoluments, and here-

ditaments whatsoever, to the manor appertaining or reputed to appertain, or at the time of conveyance demised, occupied, or enjoyed with the same, or reputed or known as part, parcel, or member thereof.

(4) This section applies only if and as far as a contrary intention is not expressed in the conveyance, and shall have effect subject to the terms of the conveyance and to the provisions therein contained.

(5) This section shall not be construed as giving to any person a better title to any property, right, or thing in this section mentioned than the title which the conveyance gives to him to the land or manor expressed to be conveyed, or as conveying to him any property, right, or thing in this section mentioned, further or otherwise than as the same could have been conveyed to him by the conveying parties.

(6) This section applies only to conveyances made after the commencement of this Act.

62. – (1) A conveyance of freehold land to the use that any person may have, for an estate or interest not exceeding in duration the estate conveyed in the land, any easement, right, liberty, or privilege in, or over, or with respect to that land, or any part thereof, shall operate to vest in possession in that person that easement, right, liberty, or privilege, for the estate or interest expressed to be limited to him; and he, and the persons deriving title under him, shall have, use, and enjoy the same accordingly.

(2) This section applies only to conveyances made after the commencement of this Act.

BAYLEY V. MARQUIS CONYNGHAM
(1863) 15 I.C.L.R. 406 (Common Pleas)

An action was brought for the interruption and hindrance of the plaintiff in his fishery, &c., which had been let to him by the defendant by parol for a year. The defendant traversed the fact of the letting of the fishery to the plaintiff.

Monahan C.J.

This case arises upon the construction of the recent Landlord and Tenant Act; and I regret very much that the Court have not been able to come to an unanimous decision. I must say, however, for myself, that I have had great difficulty and much consideration in arriving at the conclusion to which the majority of the Court have come. The action was brought by Mr. Bayley against the Marquis Conyngham, for having disturbed him in the enjoyment of certain shootings and fishings, which it was alleged by the summons and plaint the agent of the Marquis Conyngham had let to him for one year. The summons and plaint contained six counts. – [His Lordship then stated the substance of the pleadings.] – Some negotiation having taken place as to certain fishings and shootings on the property of the Marquis Conyngham in the county of Donegal, the plaintiff agreed to take them for a period of four or five years, at a rent of £150 per annum. After some time, Mr. Bayley, finding that the shooting and fishing were not as good as he had expected, made a further agreement with the agent of the Marquis Conyngham, that what was originally a letting for five years should be only for one year from the month of August, for which he should pay a sum of £150. Mr. Bayley paid the sum of £75, leaving the balance unpaid. It appears that before the close of the year the Marquis Conyngham refused to allow Mr. Bayley or his friends to fish on the property in question; and in consquence of that Mr. Bayley brought his action to recover damages against the Marquis Conyngham. The real dispute between the parties, was, whether the letting was for a year, or only the unexpired portion of the fishing and shooting season. The jury found that the letting was for a year. The defendant's Counsel submitted that, this being an incorporeal hereditament, the letting relied upon could not have been made without a deed; and, as there was no deed, they called upon me to nonsuit the plaintiff, or direct a verdict for the defendant. I declined to do so, but reserved leave for the defendant to move to have the verdict entered up for him. The question is, whether a right to fish or shoot on the river and lands of a party can be conferred in consideration of a certain rent for one year, unless by deed – whether in fact such an interest can be created by parol? The question is what is really the effect of the 3rd and 4th sections of the recent Landlord and Tenant Act? In order to come to a satisfactory conclusion on this point, it will be advisable to consider what the Common Law was, and what alteration was made in it by the Statute of Frauds. At Common Law no legal estate could be created in an incorporeal hereditament, save by grant under seal; but it is equally certain that at Common Law no freehold estate in land could be created, save by livery of seisin or by deed; that is, no freehold estate in land could be created by mere writing unaccompanied by livery of seisin, unless it were by bargain and sale, or by lease and release, which always implies a deed. But a valid agreement at Common Law could be made either by parol or by writing without seal, for the sale or for making a lease of any lands, or any estate or interest therein; and no doubt a binding contract for the sale or letting a right of fishing or shooting over a party's lands could be made by parol at Common Law. That being so, the Statute of Frauds was passed. The 1st section of that statute provides that no estate in lands and tenements should be created by parol, except leases which did not exceed three years; and it was further enacted by the 2nd section that no agreement respecting any contract or sale of lands should be binding unless it was in writing, and signed by the parties to be charged therewith. The effect of that was this, that a mere agreement by parol, either to lease or sell lands or incorporeal hereditaments, was not binding, but that an actual lease of lands would be valid, provided that it did not exceed three years; but this did not extend to incorporeal hereditaments, an interest in which could not be granted save by deed; and, in the same way, a freehold estate in lands could not be created, prior to the late statute, unless by deed or by livery of seisin. This Act of Parliament is then passed, entitled 'An Act to Consolidate and Amend the Law of Landlord and Tenant in Ireland.' Now, the first observation which arises is, that the object of this Act of Parliament was to reduce into one Act the various Acts regulating the relations subsisting between landlord and tenant. The Acts contained in schedule B to the Act are repealed, except so far as may be necessary to support any lease or contract entered into prior to the passing of the Act. The 1st section of the Statute of Frauds is included in it, and is therefore expressly repealed. The 1st section enacts. – [His Lordship read it.] – The question then arises, is there anything in this Act of Parliament which enables such an estate, or for a period not exceeding a year, to be created without a deed; because at Common Law, before the passing of this Act, no estate in an incorporeal hereditament, nor a freehold estate in lands, could be created without a deed. What then is the effect of this Act of Parliament? Formerly, nothing short of an actual demise created the relation of landlord and tenant. This Act of Parliament makes this revolution in the law, that the relation of landlord and tenant is now created, wherever it is agreed by one party to hold land from another in consideration of rent, or of anything in the nature of rent. If the matter stood there, is there anything to show that the relation of landlord and tenant can be created only by an agreement in writing? By the 3rd section of that Act of Parliament it is enacted that the relation of landlord and tenant shall be deemed to be founded on the express or implied contract of the parties. There was in this case an express contract between the parties; and I see nothing in the 3rd section which requires that it should be in writing. Now I ask could it be contended, if there was a note in writing with respect to incorporeal hereditaments, creating the relation of landlord and tenant for a period exceeding a year, or creating a freehold estate in lands, that would not be sufficient under the 4th section of this Act? – [His Lordship read the section.] – It is clear that the meaning of the 3rd and 4th sections, taken together, is that, wherever the relation of landlord and tenant is intended to be created in corporeal or incorporeal hereditaments, it may be done by an agreement in writing. If therefore, according to the true construction of this agreement, the letting was for less than a year, it might have been done by parol, which could not have been the case under the Statute of Frauds, as the 2nd section of that statute relates to all agreements respecting land. It occurs to me, and to the majority of the Court, that if we are at liberty to give any effect to the glossary of the Act, the word 'lands' embraces incorporeal hereditaments, and that it was the intention of the Legislature to place lands and incorporeal hereditaments on the same footing, so far as relates to landlord and tenant; and that therefore whatever is sufficient to create the relation of landlord and tenant in corporeal, is sufficient also with respect to incorporeal hereditaments. Very much weight has been attached to the argument that an incorporeal hereditament could only pass by deed. Now under the 4th section of the Landlord and Tenant Act, a freehold estate in lands can be created by an agreement in writing; and why should not an interest respecting incorporeal hereditaments be created in the same way? I am aware that the 1st section of the Statute of Frauds is expressly repealed by the 3rd section of the Landlord and Tenant Act; but it does not therefore follow that the 2nd section of the Statute of Frauds may not be partially implied repealed by the same Act. There has been no decision to the effect that the express repeal of one section of an Act of Parliament prevents the implied repeal of another section, if the Act should be inconsistent with it.

Upon the whole of this case, which is one of considerable difficulty, we are of opinion that the verdict should stand, with the damages for the plaintiff at one shilling.

Ball and **Keogh, JJ.**, concurred.

Christian, J (*dissentiente*)

I am of opinion that the verdict should be entered for the defendant, pursuant to the leave reserved. The action was for disturbance of the plaintiff in the enjoyment of a right of shooting and fishing, alleged to have been demised to him by the defendant for one year. To the maintaining of such an action, of course a valid demise was essential. The defence consisted substantially of a traverse of the demise, and the issues were all, in substance, did the defendant demise? The plaintiff proved a verbal agreement by the defendant's agent, to let to him this shooting and fishing, which, upon the finding of the jury, must now be taken to have been an agreement for a year, and not for the shooting and fishing season only, as the defendant contended. The Counsel for the defendant called for a nonsuit, upon the ground that a verbal letting or agreement for a letting of an incorporeal hereditament was invalid to create an estate therein, and that consequently, there was no evidence in support of the issue. The Lord Chief Justice refused to nonsuit, but reserved liberty to apply; and upon motion founded on that liberty (the verdict having been for the plaintiff), the case is now before us.

We are all agreed that if the plaintiff can sustain his verdict at all, it must be upon a clause or clauses in the late Act for Amendment of the Law of Landlord and Tenant (23 & 24 *Vic, c.,* 154). Mr. *Macdonagh*, who, as leading Counsel for the plaintiff, opened the motion to show cause against the rule *nisi*, evinced, I thought, considerable misgiving upon that part of his case, for he began by labouring the case much upon Common Law considerations, founded on the acts of the parties, and the difference between contracts executory and executed, referring to cases in which corporations had been held liable on executed considerations, though there was no contract under seal. The learned Judge, however, was not asked to leave any question to the jury, as to the effect of those acts and dealings, as founding a presumption that a grant under seal was in fact executed. We are all, I believe I may venture to say, of opinion, that if the matter rested on the Common Law, this verbal demise of an incorporeal hereditament, though only for a year, would be void. Finding the Court strongly against him upon that, Mr. *Macdonogh* then fell back upon the statute. He relied upon one section only, *the 4th*, as interpreted by the glossary in the 1st. The Counsel for the defendant were then heard, and applied themselves exclusively to the 4th section, and it was not until the plaintiff's second Counsel came to address the Court in reply that the 3rd section was even mentioned. I shall now proceed to consider the questions in the case, in the order in which they were argued, viz., first upon the 4th section alone, secondly upon the 3rd section, whether alone or conjointly with the 4th.

The argument upon the 4th section, as I understood it was this – that because that section required that 'Every lease or contract whereby the relation of landlord and tenant is intended to be created *for any freehold estate or interest, or for any definite period of time, not being from year to year, or any lesser period*, shall be by deed or note in writing,' that therefore it is to be inferred or implied that estates or interests from year to year, or any lesser period, may be without either deed or writing, and simply by words. Well, I really do not know how better to answer that argument, than by simply reading the section. These smaller estates and interests are simply out of that section. Whatever be the efficacy of the 4th section, whatever be its legislation, these small estates and interests are simply excluded from it. It is precisely as if the section had concluded with a proviso, 'that nothing herein contained, shall in any way apply to or affect estates from year to year, or for any lesser period.' It is really, therefore, too clear for rational argument, that in order to find the law applicable to those smaller interests, we must look somewhere or other outside this 4th section of the 23 & 24 *Vic.*, c. 154. Well, if we have only the Common Law to look to, the answer is immediate. No estate or interest whatever, however small, can be created in such a heriditament as this, except by deed under seal. But then, Mr. *Ball*, the plaintiff's second Counsel, contends that the 3rd section of the statute has altered all; and that is what I have now to consider.

By the 3rd section it is enacted – [reads it]. The argument is founded on the concluding sentence of the section. It is said, that by it, all differences between one sort of hereditament and another, as regards the relation of landlord and tenant is abolished; and furthermore, that but for the 4th section, all differences between agreements verbal and in writing would be abolished, and that all that would be necessary in any case to constitute the relations of landlord and tenant would be an agreement, either verbal or written, by one party to hold under another in consideration of a rent. And then, it is said, as the 4th section, which requires a deed or writing, does not apply (as I have myself shown it does not) to estates from year to year, or any lesser period, those estates or interests remain under the 3rd section alone, and may consequently be created in any species of property whatever, by word of mouth only. Well now, the first answer to that is a very simple one. It is true that the 4th section of the late Act does not apply to such a case as this, but the 2nd section of the Statute of Frauds does, and is not repealed by this statute. The first section is repealed, but the second is not, and one of the provisions of that second section, as we all know, is, that no action shall be brought 'upon any contract, or sale of lands, tenements, or hereditaments, or any interest in or concerning them, unless the agreement, or some memorandum or note therof, shall be in writing, and signed,' &c. Well, that is still in full force, and under that the agreement proved in evidence here is void, for want of at least a writing, even if a deed under seal were not necessary. Therefore, there is here no valid agreement to hold in consideration of a rent, and therefore the 3rd section is *ex vi terminorum* simply inapplicable. Well, that is a very plain and simple ground by which that section is put wholly out of the argument. The able and skilful Counsel who raised the point perfectly well knew this, that, if even the Court could look outside the new Act, his point on the 3rd section must vanish. How then did he endeavour to anticipate it? Of course he did not venture to assert that the 2nd section of the Statute of Frauds was repealed: that was out of the question, because the late statute, so far from repealing that section, declares in express terms that it shall *not* be repealed. By the 104th section of the late statute, it is provided that the acts and parts of acts set forth in the schedule, so far as they relate to the relation of landlord and tenant, and 'to the extent to which such Acts or parts of Acts are by such schedule expressed to be repealed, *and not further or otherwise*, shall be and are hereby repealed.' Well, the schedule mentions only section 1 of the Statute of Frauds; and of course, in the face of those express negative words, no one could contend for anything so merely irrational as it would be to say that expressly or impliedly the 2nd or any other section of the Statute of Frauds than the 1st was repealed by the 23 & 24 *Vic.*, c. 154. Counsel did not argue anything so absurd as that; he kept the Statute of Frauds entirely out of view; and the way in which he endeavoured to attain his object was by presenting a view, which I must take the liberty of calling one of the boldest I ever heard advanced in a Court of Justice. His proposition was this: you must confine yourselves within the Act of 23 & 24 of *The Queen*, you must not look outside it, either at the Common Law or at any other statute, because that Act constitutes in itself a complete *code* of the Law of Landlord and Tenant in Ireland; which, if it means anything, means this (and to give any value to the argument must be so understood), that it has superseded the whole body of the Law of Landlord and Tenant, whether written or unwritten; and that it is within the four corners of this statute that for the future we must look for all law upon that great subject. I totally deny that such is the nature of the statute. It is not an Act of codification, but, which is a totally different thing, an Act of consolidation and amendment. Its functions are two-fold. First, it collects into one Act provisions from various former Acts, which Acts it wholly or partially, repeals; secondly, it amends certain experienced evils in the Law, both Statute and Common. But, subject to those partial operations, it leaves the Common and Statute Law in full force. It is in the first of those functions that it deals with the Statute of Frauds, and it does so by repealing, so far as regards the relation of landlord and tenant, the 1st section only (re-enacting it in its own 4th section), whilst it expressly declares that the 2nd section shall remain in full force in its bearing on the relation of landlord and tenant, as well as in all other respects; and, as I have already pointed out, that section entirely annuls the point upon the 3rd section of the new statute. But, independently of the 2nd section of the Statute of Frauds, suppose that section did not, as it plainly does, remove the 3rd section of the new statute out of the present field of discussion altogether, I should have no hesitation in stating my opinion to be that the function and object of that section have been entirely misapprehended. That section is plainly an example of the second of the two functions which I have ascribed to the statute. Two well-known evils existed in the law – the first, that however clearly parties might have shown their intention to create between them the relations of landlord and tenant, yet if the whole interest of the intending lessor passed, the relation could not exist, for want of a reversion, and the remedies incident to that relation were lost: the second, that if the instrument were worded as an executory agreement for a lease, and not as at present actual demise (a fertile source of litigation and conflicting decision), then the relation of landlord and tenant would not be presently constituted. The 3rd section was passed to remove both those evils, but there its operation ends. It is so part of its province to alter the law of conveyancing, but which, with respect to any particular species of property, a particular species of instrument is required to constitute a demise. Its effect, as I read it, is simply this, that whenever there is a transaction between parties, so carried out and evidenced as that the relation of landlord and tenant would be constituted, but for one or both of two reasons, namely, that there was no reversion, or that the language used was executory, then the relation *shall* be constituted, notwithstanding those objections. But as to the conveyancing formalities with which the transaction must be clothed, whether as to this or that species of property, it may be by parol, or must be in writing, or must be by deed, this section in my opinion leaves that to be dealt with by the rules of law which lie outside itself. And when we look outside it for the rules which apply to such a case as that before us, a letting for one year of an incorporeal hereditament, finding that the 4th section expressly excludes all letting for such a term from its operation, we have nothing left to look to but the Common Law, and the 2nd section of the Statute of Frauds. The letting here was by parol – it is therefore void.

I shall now avert briefly to an argument *ab inconvenienti*, which was much pressed upon the Court. It was said that, unless the plaintiff's construction of the 4th section be adopted, the consequences will follow that, while a lease for 1000 years of an incorporeal hereditament will be good by writing without deed, a lease for one year or one day can only be by deed. Well, the first answer I give to that is, that if such an incongruity does arise upon the section, we cannot help it. The Legislature must be had recourse to. We have no right to resort to fanciful inferences or implications upon the statute, in order to avoid an inconvenience flowing (if it does flow) from its obvious construction. Plainly the Legislature has left these smaller interests to the governance of the law which lies outside this statute, and whatever be the consequences of that, we can only accept them. Beyond that reason it is not necessary to go; but I must confess I am not at all as yet convinced that this supposed inconvenience or incongruity does exist. It is better to avoid expressing opinions upon this new Act of Parliament, when the case does not necessarily call for them; and therefore I shall say no more at present than that, whenever the question arises whether the 4th section enables a lease of an incorporeal hereditament to be made for any term whatever, by writing without deed, it may be very strongly argued in the negative. It may well be contended that all the statute requires is, that there must in all cases be either a deed or a writing to constitute the relation with which it deals – a writing at least, but that it by no means allows that in all cases whatever a writing shall be sufficient; so that if there be any cases in which the Common Law gives the preference to a deed over a mere writing, the statute leaves full scope to the Common Law in that respect. That is precisely the way in which the Statute of Frauds has been construed. By the first section of that statute, leases of any hereditament, corporeal or incorporeal, created by livery of seisin only, *or by parol and not put in writing, and signed, &c.*, shall have the force and effect of leases at will only. It never occurred to anyone to argue that, because that statute thus required that all leases must be in writing, it followed that a writing should be in all cases sufficient, and that therefore, a deed was no longer necessary to the grant of an incorporeal hereditament. And so, although the Statute of Frauds excepts all leases not exceeding three years, made at a certain rent, no one ever thought of arguing that the effect of that was to exempt from the necessity of either deed or writing such leases in cases in which the Common Law required them to be by deed. Really, if the plaintiff's argument upon the new statute be well founded, it is incomprehensible how it happened that all the lawyers who flourished in the two kingdoms since the Statute of Frauds was passed in the reign of William the Third should have continued blind to a point which plainly arose on that statute, precisely as it does on this. Well, this 4th section was a re-enactment of the 1st section of the Statute of Frauds, which is repealed by this Act; and it may well be contended, whenever the question arises, that the same construction must be put upon it, which for nearly two centuries before it was put upon the Statute of Frauds. And if the section were thought incapable of this distributive construction then, there would, to my mind, be considerable ground for contending that for that reason this 4th section does not apply to incorporeal hereditaments at all: it certainly does not without the aid of the glossary. But the introductory terms of the 1st section prevent the glossary from extending the proper meaning of the terms, in any section where there is anything in the subject or context of the section repugnant thereto. Now, the subject of this section being to supply the place of the 1st section of the Statute of Frauds. *i.e.* to superadd the solemnity of a writing to that which at Common Law might be done by parol, it might well be argued that it would be repugnant to the subject of that section to apply it to a species of property for which the Common Law itself required not merely a writing, but a deed, and thus give to the section in that respect the operation of diminishing instead of adding to the solemnities of conveyancing.

For these reasons, my opinion is that the case is untouched by either the 3rd or 4th sections of the new Act, and that the plaintiff ought to have been nonsuited, or a verdict directed for the defendant.

Notes and Questions
1. What is the significance of the majority decision in relation to the oft cited maxim 'all easements lie in grant'? See *Irish Land Law*, para. 6.054.
2. See further on section 3 of Deasy's Act, p. 543, *post*.

RE FLANIGAN AND McGARVEY AND THOMPSON'S CONTRACT
[1945] N.I. 32 (High Court)

The owner of two adjoining houses one of which he held for the residue of a term of 989 years, sub-let that house on a quarterly tenancy; a path led from the country road over portion of the lands attached to the other house to the back door of the house so sub-let, and to no other place; the path was convenient but not essential for the enjoyment of the house; it was clearly visible to anyone viewing the premises. On a sale of the other house by the executors of the owner, under an agreement which did not mention the path, the vendors claimed that they were entitled to except and reserve from the conveyance to the purchaser of the house so sold, a right of way for the residue of the said term of 989 years over the path for the benefit of the house so sub-let.

Black J.:

Under a Lease dated the 24th day of July, 1920, a Mr. Patrick Flanigan became the lessee for a term of 989 years of a plot of ground at Portadown, situated on the north-west side of the Armagh Road, and having a frontage to the Armagh Road of 100 feet. This plot of ground is the portion coloured green on the map referred to in Mr. H. W. Thompson's affidavit and for convenience I shall refer to it as the green plot. On this plot of ground Mr. Flanigan erected in 1920 and 1921 a pair of semi-detached villas fronting to the Armagh Road. Of these two villas the one on the south-western side was from time to time occupied by tenants of Mr. Flanigan. It is at present occupied by a Mr. Henry Luther Bell and it will be convenient to refer to it as Bell's house. The two villas had a total frontage to the Armagh Road of about 68 feet. They are built on the north-east part of the green portion, and accordingly after their erection there was left – unbuilt upon – on the south-western side of Bell's house a part of the green plot having a frontage of about 32 feet to the road. Bell's house was provided with a back door for the usual purpose of taking in coal, etc., and taking out refuse and ashes. The natural means of access to this door from the road would be over the green plot along the side of Bell's house and it appears that immediately after the villas were erected a path about three feet wide was made to the back door of the house. The position of this path is shown and coloured blue on the map. I gather that at first this path was not fenced off in any way from the remainder of the portion of the green plot which had not been built upon.

The next stage in the history is that on the 18th May, 1923, Mr. Flanigan obtained a lease for a term of 990 years of a plot of ground coloured pink on the map, and having a frontage of 118 feet to the Armagh Road. This ground immediately adjoined the south-western boundary of the green plot and I shall refer to it as the pink plot. And on the 21st July, 1924, Mr. Flanigan obtained a lease for a term of 995 years of a plot of ground extending along the rear of the green plot and the pink plot and having a depth from front to rear of about 40 feet. This plot is coloured yellow in the map and I shall refer to it as the yellow plot. After obtaining these two leases Mr. Flanigan was in possession of a site comprising the pink portion, the yellow portion and the unbuilt-upon part of the green portion, and on this site he proceeded to build for himself a residence to which he gave the name of Aughavanagh. This house was erected in 1924 and 1925 and Mr. Flanigan went into occupation of it in July, 1925. Shortly after going into occupation of Aughavanagh Mr. Flanigan planted a laurel hedge along the edge of the path and erected gates and gate pillars at the road. The gates consist of a double gate opposite what appears to be the garage of Aughavanagh and alongside this double gate a small gate opposite the end of the path. Mr. Bell, who came into possession of his present house in July, 1931, says that the laurel hedge originally continued down to the gate pillars but that about 10 years ago an opening was made in it at the end next the road to allow an entrance to Aughavanagh without opening the large gate at the main entrance. At any rate for a considerable number of years the small gate has served both as an entrance to Aughavanagh and also to the path leading up to the backdoor of Bell's house. So far as Bell's house is concerned it was first occupied by a Mr. Geraghty. Then a Mr. Galbraith became tenant in November, 1924, and remained in occupation till May, 1930. Apparently the house lay vacant from May, 1930 to July, 1931, when Mr. Bell went into occupation as a tenant of Mr. Flanigan. Mr. Bell now holds from Mr. Flanigan's representatives who still retain the ownership of the house as a quarterly tenant and is entitled to the protection afforded by the Rent and Mortgage Interest (Restrictions) Acts.

Mr. Flanigan died on the 29th April, 1942, and by an agreement in writing, dated 19th April, 1943, his executors, Mrs. May Flanigan and Mr. Patrick Joseph McGarvey, agreed to sell Aughavanagh to Mr. Herbert William Thompson for £2,500. At the time when this Agreement was prepared the title deeds seem to have been in the possession of a Building Society which had a mortgage on the property and in the Agreement the premises sold are described as 'Firstly All that Dwelling house and premises known as Aughavanagh . . . held under Lease, dated 18th day of May, 1923 . . . and Secondly All that Garden and premises situate at the rear of the premises hereinbefore Firstly described being portion of the premises held under

Lease dated the 21st July, 1924.' This description was inaccurate. As appears from the map part of the grounds of Aughavanagh was comprised in the Lease of 24th July, 1920, which is not mentioned at all in the Agreement; and as regards the actual site of the house itself part of it is on ground comprised in the 1923 Lease part of it on ground comprised in the 1924 Lease and a small part is on ground comprised in the 1920 Lease. No point, however, is taken by the Purchaser in regard to these matters. The parties, however, are at difference in regard to the path on the south-western side of Bell's house. Whatever may be the rights in regard to this path as between the Vendors and the Purchaser there would appear to be little doubt but that Mr. Bell is entitled as an incident of his quarterly tenancy to use this path as a means of access to the back door of his house. In the absence of any arrangement under which Mr. Bell might agree to abandon this right he will continue to be entitled to use the path so long as his quarterly tenancy continues. And even if his tenancy is determined he will still continue to be entitled to use the path if and so long as he retains possession of the house as a statutory tenant under the provisions of s. 18 (1) of the Rent and Mortgage Interest (Restrictions) Act (N.I.), 1940. By letter of 27th July, 1943, the Vendor's solicitors sent to the Purchaser's solicitors the map which has been put in evidence and called attention to the path which they described as 'a right of way coloured blue over the premises to the rear of the adjoining premises belonging to the deceased (Mr. Flanigan).' They suggested that the whole of the premises edged red on the map should be conveyed to the Purchaser reserving to the Vendors a right of way on foot and with barrow over and along the path. By their reply, dated 12th August, 1943, the Purchaser's solicitors refused to agree that the vendors were entitled to have such a right of way reserved and they submitted for approval a draft Assignment making no mention of such a right. The Vendors' solicitors amended the draft Assignment by inserting a provision 'Excepting and reserving to the Vendors their and each of their executors administrators and assigns and their tenants and servants full right and liberty at all times hereafter during the continuance of the said term created by said Indenture of Lease of 24th July, 1920, on foot and with hand barrows only to go pass and repass along and over and upon the passage three feet wide, coloured blue on the map endorsed hereon and situate on the north-east side of the premises hereby firstly assigned.' The Purchaser's solicitors refused to accept this amendment and a correspondence ensued in which each side adhered to their own point of view. I could not help echoing the observation in the Vendors' solicitors' letter of 20th September, 1943, that it seems a pity that there should be any litigation over so small a matter and I deferred giving judgment in order to afford the parties an opportunity of arriving at an amicable arrangement which I understood might possibly be negotiated. I have been informed, however, that it has not been found possible to reach agreement and accordingly I have now to pronounce as best I can on what are the parties' legal rights in regard to the matter.

Mr. Porter's first contention on behalf of the Vendors was that not merely were they entitled to reserve a right of way over the path in dispute but that the path itself did not form part of the premises comprised in the contract of sale and that the Vendors were accordingly entitled to exclude it altogether from the conveyance to the Purchaser. His contention was that the path actually formed part of the premises which I have called Bell's house, and did not form part of the premises Aughavanagh which the Vendors had agreed to sell. It is somewhat remarkable that this contention was never put forward in the correspondence which passed between the solicitors nor is such a contention even hinted at in the affidavit filed on behalf of the Vendors in these proceedings. The Vendors' solicitors who prepared the Agreement for sale never suggested that the path itself was not intended to be comprised in the premises agreed to be sold. In their letter of 10th August, 1943, written after the contest had arisen they speak of the path as separated by the laurel hedge from the *remainder* of the premises sold. The highest that they ever put the Vendors' claim is that the Vendors are entitled to reserve a right of way over the path. And the map prepared on behalf of the Vendors by their architect clearly shows the site of the path as included in the premises purchased by Mr. Thompson. I think that the conclusion to which this evidence clearly points is that the parties had no other idea but that the premises purchased by Mr. Thompson and described in the Agreement as the dwellinghouse and premises known as 'Aughavanagh' extended up to the gable wall of Bell's house and included the site of the path; and if it could by any possibility be maintained that the description of the premises in the actual written Agreement is not in accordance with this intention I think it would be difficult in the circumstances for the Vendors to resist a claim by the Purchaser for the rectification of the Agreement. Accordingly I proceed on the basis that the premises agreed to be sold to the Purchaser included the site of the path.

What then is the legal position on this basis? As I have observed Mr. Bell appears to be entitled to a right of way over the path as an incident of his quarterly tenancy. That right being a right vested in a third party cannot be destroyed by an contract between the present Vendors and the present Purchaser. Accordingly if the Purchaser was coming before the Court seeking specific performance of his contract he could only obtain such specific performance subject to Mr. Bell's rights. On the other hand could the Vendors enforce specific performance against the Purchaser and compel him to accept a conveyance subject to Mr. Bell's rights over the path? The Vendors claim that they could in view of the provision in Clause 10 of the Agreement that the premises are sold subject to rights of way. But I do not think that in the circumstances the Vendors are entitled to rely on the provisions of Clause 10. The Vendors must have been fully aware of Mr. Bell's rights over the path and it is well settled that such a Clause as Clause 10 does not absolve Vendors from their duty to disclose to the Purchaser all matters affecting the property which are within their knowledge. It is to be construed as applying only to matters of which the Vendors are not aware when they enter into the contract (*Heywood* v. *Mallalieu* (25 Ch. D. 357), *Nottingham Patent Brick and Tile Co.* v. *Butler* (15 Q.B.D. 261. 271; 16 Q.B.D. 778, 786–787) per Wills, J., per Lord Esher, M. R., *Simpson* v. *Gilley* (92 L.J. Ch. 194, 201–202), per Astbury, J.).

On the other hand the Purchaser inspected the premises with some care before he entered into the contract. He must have seen the 3 foot wide path bounded by the gable wall of Bell's house on one side and by the laurel hedge on the other side and it must have been quite apparent to him that the purpose of the path, and its only purpose, was to afford a means of access to the back door of Bell's house. It is well settled that a purchaser of property must take it subject to any defects which are patent on inspection and are not inconsistent with the description contained in the contract for sale. The authorities for this proposition cited in the books are mostly old cases such as *Bowles* v. *Round* (5 Ves. 508), which was approved in Ireland by Sugden, L. C., in *Martin* v. *Cotter* (3 Jo. and Lat, 496), at p. 506. But the existence of the principle that in the case of a patent defect the rule *caveat emptor* applies has been recognised in quite a number of modern cases, *Ashburner* v. *Sewell* ([1891] 3 Ch. 405); *Yandle* v. *Sutton* (([1922] 2 Ch. 199); *Simpson* v. *Gilley* (92 L.J. Ch. 194). In order that a defect may be a patent defect within the meaning of this rule it is not enough that there exists on the land an object of sense that might put a careful purchaser on inquiry. To be a patent defect the defect must either be visible to the eye, or arise by necessary implication from something visible to the eye. In each of the three modern cases to which I have just referred, while the existence of the rule was recognised, the defect was held not to be a patent defect, but a latent defect. In the present case, however, I think the defect is a patent defect. I think that the existence and the nature of the path, leading nowhere but to the back door of Bell's house, showed that it served no purpose other than as a way from the road to this back door to which there was no other means of access, and necessarily indicated as a practical certainty to anyone who saw it that the occupier of Bell's house would have a right of way over it to the back door of his house. Being therefore of opinion that Mr. Bell's right of way over the path during the currency of his tenancy is a patent defect, as that term is used in the authorities, I hold that the Purchaser is compellable to take the property subject to Mr. Bell's right and it would follow that the Vendors are entitled to have the conveyance of Aughavanagh expressed to be subject to this right.

On behalf of the Vendors it is contended, however, that not only must the Purchaser take the property subject to the right vested in Mr. Bell under his tenancy but that the Vendors are entitled to except and reserve from the conveyance of Aughavanagh a right of way over the path for the benefit of Bell's house not merely for the duration of Bell's tenancy but also for the whole of the residue of the 989 years Lease under which the green plot is held. The way that this contention is put is this. No doubt it is well settled by *Wheeldon* v. *Burrows* (12 Ch. D. 31) that where the same person owns two adjoining tenements A and B, and has used a path over A for the more convenient occupation and enjoyment of B then if he sells and conveys tenement A to a purchaser he will *prima facie* not be entitled to contend that any reservation of a right of way over the path is to be implied for the benefit of tenement B which he retains. I need not refer to the subsequent cases in which this principle has been recognized and applied. A good illustrative case is *Taws* v. *Knowles* ([1891] 2 Q.B. 564) – a decision of the English Court of Appeal. But it is said that there are certain recognized exceptions to this rule and it is alleged that this case falls under one or other of these exceptions. The exceptions particularly relied upon are (*a*) where the right sought to be reserved is a right of way of necessity, and (*b*) the exception supposed to be established by the case of *Thomas* v. *Owen* (20 Q.B.D. 225).

Now in the first place it may be a question whether these cases are really applicable to the circumstances of the present case at all. The point for consideration in all these cases was as to whether an exception or reservation was to be implied in completed conveyances. In the present case the point is not as to what implication should be drawn from a conveyance already completed but rather as to what precise form the conveyance when completed is to take. The matter here is still in contract. Our task is not to draw implications from a conveyance, but to find what wording of a conveyance will carry the parties' contract into effect. That there is a distinction between the two points – the construction of a completed conveyance and the form which a conveyance is to take in order to give effect to a contract – is brought out by Chitty, J., in *In re Peck and London School Board* ([1893] 2 Ch. 315) and by Astbury, J., in the recent case of *Simpson* v. *Gilley* (92 L.J. Ch. 194), to which I have already referred. The distinction is not always emphasised in the text books. In discussing what reservations a Vendor of land is entitled in pursuance of his contract to have inserted in the conveyance the text book writers constantly refer to the cases decided on the reservations to be implied from completed conveyances. This may indeed be the legal position. It appears to be borne out by the judgment of Chitty, J., in the case of *Beddington* v. *Atlee* (35 Ch. D. 317). But in *Simpson* v. *Gilley* (92 L.J. Ch. 194) Astbury, J. (at p. 200) after making reference to *Thomas* v. *Owen* (20 Q.B.D. 225), proceeded to dismiss such cases as irrelevant to the questions which he had to try, *videlicet* as to whether under the contract the Vendor was entitled to have a right of way reserved by the conveyance. He obviously considered that where there is a clear and unqualified contract for the absolute sale of a parcel of land without reference to any reservation for the Vendor's benefit it would require a good deal to persuade him that the Vendor could claim to have inserted in the conveyance a reservation of a right of way over the land sold. This appears to be in accordance with the view adopted in *Webster on Conditions of Sale*, 2nd Ed. at p. 8, where the learned author, not dealing at this point with completed conveyances but discussing Contracts for Sale under the heading of Particulars of Sale, sets out the legal position quite simply in these words: 'If the Vendor intends to reserve any easements over the land, or rights inconsistent with the full enjoyment of the land, he must express his intention in clear and explicit language.' It may possibly be that this broad statement should be subject to a qualification in cases where the right which the Vendor claims to have reserved is clearly essential to the enjoyment of the property retained (see *Dart on Vendors and Purchasers*, 7th Ed., Vol, I, p. 563). But if the statement even with this qualification is to be regarded as good law then it is clear that in the present case the Vendors would not be entitled to have inserted in the conveyance the reservation which they claim.

If, however, on the other hand the same rules in regard to the reservations to be implied from completed conveyances apply also to contracts we are driven to consider the exceptions upon which the Vendors here rely from the principle in regard to implied reservations laid down in *Wheeldon* v. *Burrows* (12 Ch. D. 31). An undoubted exception – fully recognized in the judgment in *Wheeldon* v. *Burrows* (12 Ch. D. 31) itself – is what are called easements of necessity; and it is said on behalf of the Vendors that the enjoyment of a right of access along the path by the occupier for the time being of Bell's house is an easement of necessity within the meaning of the exception. But it is well settled that an easement of necessity, as referred to in this exception, means an easement without which the property retained cannot be used at all, and not one merely necessary to the reasonable enjoyment of that property. (*Union Lighterage Co.* v. *London Graving Dock Co.* ([1902] 2 Ch. 557), per Stirling, L.J., at p. 573; *Greg v. Planque* ([1936] 1 K.B. 669), per Slesser, L.J., at p. 676). A right of access to the back door of Bell's house along the path may be very convenient and even almost necessary for the comfortable enjoyment of that house. But it cannot be pretended that it is essential and that without it the house could not be used at all. Accordingly I am clearly of opinion that in the circumstances of the present case the Vendors are not entitled to rely on this exception. Then in the alternative the Vendors claim that they are entitled to rely on the exception said to be established by the case of *Thomas* v. *Owen* (20 Q.B.D. 225). They say that inasmuch as Bell's house is in the occupation of a tenant who is entitled to a right of way over the path as against the Vendors during his tenancy the effect of *Thomas v. Owen* (20 Q.B.D. 225) is to entitle the Vendors by reason of the existence of this tenancy to secure a reservation of such right of way not merely for the duration of Bell's tenancy but for the duration of the whole of the long lease for which the Vendors hold the green plot. This would seem *prima facie* a very startling result to follow from the fact of Bell's house being in the occupation of a quarterly tenant. If Bell's house were vacant – as it apparently was from May, 1930, to July 1931, – or if it were in the personal occupation of the Vendors themselves then in view of the principle as regards implied reservations laid down in *Wheeldon* v. *Burrows* (12 Ch. D. 31) no claim could be sustained upon the sale to the present Purchaser of a reservation to the Vendors of a right of way over the path. Can it possibly be that the mere fact of the house being in the occupation of a tenant under a short tenancy so completely reverses the legal position as to subject the Purchaser to the burden of such an easement during the whole residue of the 989 years Lease? I have read and re-read *Thomas* v. *Owen* (20 Q.B.D. 225), and I think all the subsequent reported cases in which *Thomas* v. *Owen* (20 Q.B.D. 225) has been referred to in an earnest endeavour to see if I could formulate the precise principle upon which *Thomas v. Owen* (20 Q.B.D. 225) was decided and set the case on its proper place in a logical framework of exceptions to the principle which I have quoted from *Wheeldon* v. *Burrows* (12 Ch. D. 31). I cannot profess to have succeeded. *Thomas* v. *Owen* (20 Q.B.D. 225) was undoubtedly a decision of a strong court. But subsequent Courts and text book writers have found obvious difficulty in enunciating a rule derived from *Thomas v. Owen* (12 Ch. D. 31) which can stand logically with the undoubted authority of *Wheeldon* v. *Burrows* (12 Ch. D. 31). Some tribunals no doubt have been able to accept *Thomas* v. *Owen* (20 Q.B.D. 225) without question. Thus in *Westwood* v. *Heywood* ([1921] 2 Ch. 130), Astbury J., at p. 139, finds himself able to speak of 'the rule in *Thomas v. Owen*' (20 Q.B.D. 225). On the other hand a few years later in *Aldridge* v. *Wright* ([1929] 1 K.B. 381), Shearman, J., stated that *Thomas* v. *Owen* (20 Q.B.D. 225) and *Wheeldon* v. *Burrows* (12 Ch. D. 31) obviously conflicted, and went on to say that in his opinion *Wheeldon v. Burrows* (12 Ch. D. 31) and the cases which approve of it express the rule which ought to be applied in both the King's Bench and the Chancery Divisions, and in the same case Finlay, J., apparently takes the same view though he does not express it quite so bluntly. It is perhaps worth while to note as Shearman, J., points out in *Aldridge* v. *Wright* ([1929] 1 K.B. 381) that so far as appears from the reports *Wheeldon* v. *Burrows* (12 Ch. D. 31) was not mentioned either in *Thomas* v. *Owen* (20 Q.B.D. 225) or in *Westwood* v. *Heywood* ([1921] 2 Ch. 130), though I can hardly think that the Court which decided *Thomas* v. *Owen* (20 Q.B.D. 225) had forgotten *Wheeldon* v. *Burrows* (12 Ch. D. 31). Shearman, J.'s, criticism is so far as I know the most outspoken criticism of *Thomas* v. *Owen* (20 Q.B.D. 225) in subsequent cases, but it is impossible to read the judgments in other cases in which *Thomas* v. *Owen* has been discussed without feeling that there is considerable difficulty in extracting a clear principle from it which can be fitted in satisfactorily with the principle in regard to implied reservations established by the authoritative decision in *Suffield* v. *Brown* (4 De. G. J. & S. 185) and *Wheeldon* v. *Burrows* (12 Ch. D. 31). As regards the text books I cannot find either in the original edition of Halsbury's *Laws of England* or in the new Hailsham Edition any statement at all corresponding to what is said to be this rule established by *Thomas* v. *Owen* (20 Q.B.D. 225) and in Gale on *Easements*, 11th Ed., p. 199, the learned editors appear disposed to treat *Thomas* v. *Owen* (20 Q.B.D. 225) as resting on very special circumstances which are scarcely likely to occur again, which I suppose means that in their view it cannot be taken as laying down any principle. In two recent cases *Aldridge* v. *Wright* ([1929] 2 K.B. 117) and *Liddiard* v. *Waldron* ([1934] 1 K.B. 435), it appeared that the precise relationship between *Wheeldon* v. *Burrows* (12 Ch. D. 31) and *Thomas* v. *Owen* (20 Q.B.D. 225) would arise for actual decision by the English Court of Appeal but unfortunately each case went off on the fact that it had not been satisfactorily established that the tenant was entitled as of right to the easement or quasi-easement which was alleged to be the subject matter of the reservation sought to be implied. In *Liddiard* v. *Waldron* ([1934] 1 K.B. 435), however, Lawrence, L.J.; after referring at length to *Thomas* v. *Owen* (20 Q.B.D. 225), obviously feels pressed by the difficulty which I have mentioned of holding that the mere fact of the quasidominant tenement being let on a short tenancy so radically alters the normal position between Vendor and Purchaser as to endow the Vendor with a right in perpetuity or at any rate for the whole duration of his interest in the premises retained and says (at p. 445) that in his opinion the principle as applied in *Thomas* v. *Owen* (20 Q.B.D. 225) could not be held to govern a case where there is only a weekly tenancy of the quasi-dominant tenement. And I think that the same point may have been in Scrutton, L.J., mind when he says (at p. 439): 'I confess that the idea of a weekly tenant wandering about with a series of easements when he can be got rid of by a week's notice is a thing of which the law will not take much notice.' If this alleged principle in *Thomas* v. *Owen* (20 Q.B.D. 225) cannot be held to apply where there is only a weekly tenancy I think that for exactly the same reason it cannot apply where there is only a quarterly tenancy so as impliedly to create an easement for the entire duration of a term of 989 years which on the basis of the principle in *Wheeldon* v. *Burrows* (12 Ch. D. 31) would not have been implied at all if the landlord had been personally in occupation of the quasi-dominant tenement instead of having it let to a quarterly tenant. Accordingly even if the same principle as to implying reservations which applies to completed conveyances applies also to contracts I do not think that the legal position is such as to entitle the Vendors in the present case to sustain their claim to reserve an easement over the property sold for the whole residue of the 989 years term.

I will therefore declare that under the contract the Vendors are not entitled to except or reserve from the conveyance to the Purchaser of the Property sold any right of way over or upon the passage three feet wide coloured blue on the map referred to in the Originating Summons; but that they are entitled if they so wish to have the Assignment to the Purchaser so worded as to convey the property subject during the existing quarterly tenancy of Bell's house and any statutory tenancy which may arise upon the determination of the said quarterly tenancy by virtue of the Rent and Mortgage Interest (Restrictions) Acts, to such a right of way over and along the said passage as the present tenant of Bell's house his executors administrators or assigns may be entitled to as an incident of the said quarterly tenancy. I say 'if they so wish' for the Vendors are conveying as personal representatives and accordingly no covenant for title will be implied on their part except a covenant that they have not personally done anything to affect or incumber the property. If the parties were not at arm's length I take it they might be wishful to arrange that a reference to the right of a quarterly tenant of adjoining property might not be put on permanent record on the face of the Purchaser's muniments of title.

Note
See further on the rule in *Wheeldon* v. *Burrows* and easements of necessity, *Irish Land Law*, paras. 6.060–65 and 6.070–1.

HENRY LTD V. McGLADE
[1926] N.I. 144 (Court of Appeal)

The defendants, the proprietors of a licensed house and cafe in Belfast, claimed the right to advertise their premises by keeping a man with an advertisement board at the entrance to the Q. Arcade, which led up to and past defendant's premises. The plaintiffs were the owners of the Q. Arcade and the shops in it, and also of the shops in D. Place adjoining the entrance to the arcade. The plaintiffs had acquired this property in 1919, subject to the tenancies then existing. The defendant's premises were let on 20th July, 1899 to P. &. F. M'G. for 21 years from 1st May, 1899, at an annual rent of £250. On 29th April, 1920, the plaintiffs made a quarterly letting of the premises to P. M.'G. at an annual rent of £600. and by a lease dated 15th February, 1921, the plaintiffs let the premises to P. M'G. in consideration of a fine of £12,000. at a peppercorn rent for one hundred years. The defendants' premises, while held under the lease of 20th July. 1899, were advertised amongst other means by a man standing with an advertisement board at the entrance to the arcade. In 1912, when structural alterations were made in the arcade, it was arranged that thenceforth the defendants could always advertise their premises by means of a man standing with a board at the entrance to the arcade.

An action was brought for a declaration that the defendant was not entitled to advertise his premises by means of a man standing with an advertisement board at the entrance to the arcade. Wilson J. held that the right or privelage passed to the defendant on the assignment of the premises to him and the acts complained of were done in enerise of that right or privilege. The plaintiff appealed to the Court of Appeal.

Andrews L.J.:

The facts of this case are so fully set out by Mr. Justice Wilson that I shall content myself with adopting his statement of them as my own, making only a brief reference to the principle points which they establish.

No attempt has been made by the plaintiffs to controvert the evidence that the defendant's premises, when held under the lease from Sir Otto Jaffe of 20th July, 1899, were advertised amongst other means by a man standing with an advertisement board at the entrance to the Arcade though until 1905 his position was admittedly close to the kerbstone of the footpath. So, also, it has not been denied that the defendant and Sir Otto Jaffe's agent entered into an arrangement in 1912, when structural alternations were being made in the Arcade, that henceforth the defendants could always advertise their premises by means of a man standing with a board at the entrance to the Arcade; and it is admitted that a man has since stood there daily with his advertisement board. The right or privilege was, accordingly, being exercised to the knowledge of all parties interested in the year 1919 when the plaintiffs acquired the Jaffe interest, and also in 1920 and 1921, when the quarterly letting and lease were respectively made by the plaintiff to the defendant. This lease included in express terms a demise of all rights, liberties, privileges and appurtenances to the said premises belonging or in anywise appertaining or therewith used or enjoyed.

In these circumstances the case has been argued before us on one narrow legal issue: Is the right or privilege claimed, namely, to maintain and keep a man with the advertisement board at the entrance of the Arcade, between certain specified hours daily, a right or privilege known to the law? If it is, the judgment of Mr. Justice Wilson must be affirmed.

The only difficulty, in my opinion, in the case is that no authority can be cited in which such a claim, involving the existence of a mobile human element, has been considered by the Courts.

It was expressly admitted by plaintiff's counsel during the argument that the defendant would not have any difficulty in upholding his claim, if, instead of the post to which the advertisement board is affixed being supported by a man, it had been inserted in a hole or socket in the ground. The plaintiffs' contention is that the precise point at which the man may stand is not defined and may vary from day to day, provided he does not transgress the limits fixed by Mr. Justice Wilson's Order, namely, 'at the Donegall Place entrance to the said Queen's Arcade'; and, accordingly, that the right claimed is in its essence a jus spatiandi which is not known to the law.

There can, in my opinion, be no doubt that the demise in the lease of 'rights . . . privileges and appurtenances to the said premises belonging . . . or therewith used or enjoyed' only includes a demise of such rights and privileges as are known to the law. This was clearly laid down by Farwell, J., when dealing with the corresponding and almost identical words of section 6 of the Conveyancing Act, 1881, *Burrows* v. *Lang* ([1901] 2 Ch., 502). The same learned judge further expounded this branch of the law in *International Tea Stores Co.* v. *Hobbs* ([1903] 2 Ch., 165), where he pointed out that such words are sufficiently wide to embrace privileges permissively enjoyed, something essentially different from such strictly legal rights as easements. In that sense such privileges or rights may be precarious: still they must be rights of a character known to the law, and a mere jus spatiandi is not such a right (see page 172). If further authority were required for the latter part of this proposition it is to be found in yet another judgment of Farwell, J., in *Attorney-General v. Antrobus*, ([1905] 2 Ch. 188) – better known as 'the Stonehenge case' – where the learned judge said (at p. 198): 'The public as such cannot prescribe, nor is jus spatiandi known to our law as a possible subject matter of grant or prescription'; and, quoting the words of Sir Francis North's argument in *Potter* v. *North* ([1669] 1 Vent. 387) he adds – 'For such things as can have no lawful beginning nor be created at this day by any manner of grant, or reservation, or deed that can be supposed, no prescription is good.'

I find it unnecessary, however, to refer to further authority on this subject for Mr. Campbell, who appeared for the defendant, freely and most properly admitted the proposition that the jus spatiandi is not known to our law. His answer to the plaintiffs' argument is simply that what his client claims is not a jus spatiandi. In this, in my opinion, he is quite right. The jus spatiandi means or implies a right of walking about, spreading out, or expanding; the right which is claimed and which has been upheld by the learned judge is, in my opinion, rather a jus morandi or a jus manendi. The plaintiffs' counsel contended that if the judgment were upheld it would be competent for the defendant, should he so desire, to change the position of the man with the board from the Donegall Place to the Fountain Lane end of the Arcade, or to keep him walking up and down the Arcade, but clearly this is not so. The judgment merely gives the right to maintain and keep the man at the Donegall Place entrance to the Arcade. Further, he is not empowered by the terms of the order to wander about with his advertisement board at the entrance, thereby causing inconvenience to persons frequenting or lawfully using the Arcade. On the contrary, the judgment expressly declares that the right to maintain and keep the man is subject to the limitation that he does not thereby cause any greater obstruction than is necessary; and it is right to add that the notes of the learned judge do not contain a scintilla of evidence in support of a claim to or assertion of any such right. No doubt the judgment does not define to the inch the precise spot upon which the man must take his stand; but common sense tells us that if his advertisement is to be seen by people passing up and down Donegall Place his position will be central at the mouth of the Arcade, not so far out as to cause an obstruction or to interfere with the rights of the public in Donegall Place, yet not so far back into the Arcade as to have the clear view of the advertisement board interfered with by the corner shops. The Arcade is only 10 feet in width, and it seems that if the effective character of the advertisement is to be maintained a distance of two, or at most, three feet in width and the same in depth represents fairly the practical limits of deviation in the position of this partly human and partly inanimate advertisement. If ever the principle of de minimis non curat lex is held to apply, surely it should be to such a case. I decline to hold that the right exercised within this restricted area can be properly designated as a jus spatiandi.

I am clearly of opinion that the plaintiffs' case fails, and that the appeal should be dismissed with costs.

Best L.J., [having stated the facts as above set out] proceeded as follows:

In the argument before us it was contended by Mr. M'Gonigal, that the right to have a man, with an advertisement board, at the entrance to the Arcade was a right unknown to the law; and that therefore it could not pass by the words in the lease of 15th February, 1921, which are relied upon by defendant. In that lease the premises are demised to Patrick M'Glade, together with 'all rights, liberties, privileges and appurtenances to the said premises belonging or in any wise appertaining or therewith used or enjoyed.'

The contention put forward on behalf of the defendant is that from 20th July, 1899, onwards, or, at any rate, from the year 1912 onwards the tenants of the Queen's Cafe had used and enjoyed as such tenants the right or privilege of keeping between the hours of 8 a.m. and 5 p.m. on weekdays a man with an advertisement board advertising the Queen's Cafe premises, at the Donegall Place entrance to the arcade, and that that right was being actually used and enjoyed by M'Glade as such tenant in possession both when the quarterly letting of 29th April, 1920, was made and also when the lease of 15th February, 1921, was given to Patrick M'Glade, and that this right passed to him as lessee under the said lease by virtue of the words already cited.

Mr. M'Gonigal opened the case to us by urging that what was claimed here was virtually a jus spatiandi but as the argument developed it appeared that practically the sole question between the parties was whether or not the right to have a man with an advertisement board standing at a defined point at the entrance to the Arcade is a right known to the law, and, as such, whether it could be passed by the general words of the lease dealing with rights, liberties, privileges, etc.

We were referred to numerous cases on the question as to what rights of the nature in question in this suit are, or are not, known to the law. *Burrows* v. *Lang* ([1901] 2 Ch., 502), *International Tea Stores Company* v. *Hobbs* ([1903] 2 Ch., 165), and several other cases were cited.

Mr. Campbell, made it clear that the defendant was not claiming a jus spatiandi, but, as he put it himself, that he was claiming a locus standi at or about the very centre of the entrance to the Arcade.

If a socket had been made at the entrance to the Arcade in which a pole containing a board and advertisement similar to the one in this action had been placed, and if it had been proved that that board and advertisement had been placed in that way from 1912 onwards could it have been contended that the right to continue that method of advertising would not have been given to the defendant under the words of the lease which have already been cited?

I can see no difference in principle between the right to have an advertisement on a board which is fastened to a pole stuck into the ground and the right to have such an advertisement held up by a man who is stationed at the precise point where the pole goes into the ground.

The matter that has troubled me in the case is the difficulty of controlling the human element in the advertisement. My colleague does not, however, take such a narrow view on this aspect of the case as I do, and I feel that I should not be justified in coming to a conclusion different from that at which he has arrived.

I agree that the appeal should be dismissed with costs.

Notes and Questions
1. Was the right recognised in this case an easement? *Cf. Re Ellenborough Park* [1956] Ch. 131. What would the position have been if the lease had not contained the clause 'all rights, liberties. . . .'?
2. As regards section 6 of the Conveyancy Act, 1881, see *Irish Land Law*, para. 6.066 *et seq*.

PRESCRIPTION ACT, 1832

[*Note*: This Act was extended to Ireland as from 1st January, 1859, by the Prescription (Ireland) Act, 1858. See *Irish Land Law*, para. 6.085 *et seq*.]

1. . . . No claim which may be lawfully made at the common law, by custom, prescription, or grant, to any right of common or other profit or benefit to be taken and enjoyed from or upon any land of our sovereign lord the King . . . or of any ecclesiastical or lay person, or body corporate, except such matters and things as are herein specially provided for, and except tithes, rent, and services, shall, where such right, profit, or benefit shall have been actually taken and enjoyed by any person claiming right thereto without interruption for the full period of thirty years, be defeated or destroyed by showing only that such right, profit, or benefit was first taken or enjoyed at any time prior to such period of thirty years, but nevertheless such claim may be defeated in any other way by which the same is now liable to be defeated; and when such right, profit, or benefit shall have been so taken and enjoyed as aforesaid for the full period of sixty years, the right thereto shall be deemed absolute and indefeasible, unless it shall appear that the same was taken and enjoyed by some consent or agreement expressly made or given for that purpose by deed or writing.

2. . . . No claim which may be lawfully made at the common law, by custom, prescription, or grant, to any way or other easement, or to any watercourse, or the use of any water, to be enjoyed or derived upon, over, or from any land or water of our said lord the King . . . or being the property of any ecclesiastical or lay person, or body corporate, when such way or other matter as herein last before mentioned shall have actually enjoyed by any person claiming right thereto without interruption for the full period of twenty years, shall be defeated or destroyed by showing only that such way or other matter was first enjoyed at any time prior to such period of twenty years, but nevertheless such claim may be defeated in any other way by which the same is now liable to be defeated; and where such way or other matter as herein last before mentioned shall have been so enjoyed as aforesaid for the full period of forty years, the right thereto shall be deemed absolute and indefeasible, unless it shall appear that the same was enjoyed by some consent or agreement expressly given or made for that purpose by deed or writing.

3. . . . When the access and use of light to and for any dwelling house, workshop, or other building shall have been actually enjoyed therewith for the full period of twenty years without interruption, the right thereto shall be deemed absolute and indefeasible, any local usage or custom to the contrary notwithstanding, unless it shall appear that the same was enjoyed by some consent or agreement expressly made or given for that purpose by deed or writing.

4. . . . Each of the respective periods of years herein-before mentioned shall be deemed and taken to be the period next before some suit or action wherein the claim or matter to which such period may relate shall have been or shall be brought into question; and . . . no act or other matter shall be deemed to be an interruption, within the meaning of this statute, unless the same shall have been or shall be submitted to or acquiesced in for one year after the party interrupted shall have had or shall have notice thereof, and of then person making or authorizing the same to be made.

5. . . . In all actions upon the case and other pleadings, wherein the party claiming may now by law allege his right generally, without averring the existence of such right from time immemorial, such general allegation shall still be deemed sufficient, and if the same shall be denied, all and every the matters in this Act mentioned and provided, which shall be applicable to the case, shall be admissible in evidence to sustain or rebut such allegation; and . . . in all pleadings to actions of trespass, and in all other pleadings wherein before the passing of this Act it would have been necessary to allege the right to have existed from time immemorial, it shall be sufficient to allege the enjoyment thereof as of right by the occupiers of the tenement in respect whereof the same is claimed for and during such of the periods mentioned in this Act as may be applicable to the case, and without claiming in the name or right of the owner of the fee, as is now usually done; and if the other party shall intend to rely on any proviso, exception, incapacity, disability,

contract, agreement, or other matter herein-before mentioned, or on any clause or matter of fact or of law not inconsistent with the simple fact of enjoyment, the same shall be specially alleged and set forth in answer to the allegation of the party claiming, and shall not be received in evidence on any general traverse or denial of such allegation.

6. . . . In the several cases mentioned in and provided for by this Act, no presumption shall be allowed or made in favour or support of any claim, upon proof of the exercise or enjoyment of the right or matter claimed for any less period of time or number of years than for such period or number mentioned in this Act as may be applicable to the case and to the nature of the claim.

7. Provided also, that the time during which any person otherwise capable of resisting any claim to any of the matters before mentioned shall have been or shall be an infant, idiot, non compos mentis, feme covert, or tenant for life, or during which any action or suit shall have been pending, and which shall have been diligently prosecuted, until abated by the death of any party or parties thereto, shall be excluded in the computation of the periods herein-before mentioned, except only in cases where the right or claim is hereby declared to be absolute and indefeasible.

8. Provided always, . . . that when any land or water upon, over or from which any such way or other convenient watercourse or use of water shall have been or shall be enjoyed or derived hath been or shall be held under or by virtue of any term of life, or any term of years exceeding three years from the granting thereof, the time of the enjoyment of any such way or other matter as herein last before mentioned, during the continuance of such term, shall be excluded in the computation of the said period of forty years, in case the claim shall within three years next after the end or sooner determination of such term be resisted by any person entitled to any reversion expectant on the determination thereof.

Note

For detailed discussion of the operation of the Act, see *Irish Land Law*, para. 6.085 *et seq*.

HANNA V. POLLOCK
[1900] 2 I.R. 664 (Court of Appeal)

Prior to 1894 (when they purchased their holdings through the Irish Land Commission) H. and P. were tenants of adjoining farms on the same estate. In 1861 the predecessor of H., for the better drainage of his holding constructed a drain through his lands to a neighbouring river, and at the same time a weir was constructed on the course of this drain, and a 'carry' or conduit, by which some of the water was led in a different direction along H.'s side of the boundary between the two farms to the public road, and thence along that road (which ran through P.'s holding supplying a tank on P's holding with water, and ultimately finding its way to the river at a point lower down its course. In 1896 H. altered the drainage of his lands and removed the 'carry,' so that it no longer supplied P.'s tank. P. entered on H.'s land and restored it. H sued for damages for trespass, obstruction of the watercourse, and for flooding the lands. P. justified under an alleged lost grant, and by prescription. At the trial the jury found a lost grant, but found there was no flow of water as of right prior to the drainage operations in 1861, and the Judge directed a verdict for the defendant. On appeal to the Queen's Bench, the majority found for the plaintiff, see [1898] 2 I.R. 532, and the defendants appealed to the Court of Appeal.

FitzGibbon L.J.:

This case being reported ([1898] 2 I.R. 532), I shall refer to that report with its map, and avoid, as far as I can, repeating what appears therein.

We propose to consider two questions – (1), the question of fact, – Whether there was sufficient evidence to sustain the first and second findings of the jury, of a lost grant by M'Curdy Hamilton to James Pollock of liberty to erect a 'carry' or 'weir,' to the defendant's farm? (2), the question of law, – Whether, the period of user being less than forty years, and the parties to the alleged grant being termors only, and there being no evidence except of user to sustain the plea, the Judge was at liberty to leave the question of lost grant to the jury? In other words, is the judgment in *Bright* v. *Walker* (1 C.M. &. R. 211), as hitherto understood, and as applied to the provisions of the Prescription Act, relating to twenty years' user, law or not?

If the question of fact be decided in favour of the plaintiff, who is the owner of the alleged servient tenement, the discussion of the question of law becomes, as it did in *Timmons* v. *Hewitt* (22 L.R. Ir. 627), unnecessary to the decision of the case; and though my colleagues think it right for us to express our opinions upon it, those opinions cannot bind this Court, or even ourselves, in any future case.

I am clearly of opinion that there is no sufficient evidence in fact to found the presumption of a lost grant. The presumption must always be founded upon intention inferred from circumstances, from user, and from conduct. Upon the undisputed facts of this case, I find it impossible to put into black and white any form of instrument sufficient to confer the right claimed by the defendants, which any person with the lowest measure of regard for self-interest could consent to execute, and in the evidence for the defendants, which includes that of the sup-posed grantee, James Pollock, I find sufficient proof both of what the transaction upon which it is now sought to found the fiction of a grant really was, and also that neither party has at any time dealt with the water in question in the way which would be essential to constitute such a user as of right as would be necessary to sustain the finding of the jury.

In discussing the case I shall fully accept the position which *Angus* v. *Dalton* (6 App. Cas. 740) has, perhaps, advanced farther than any other case, that not only is belief in the existence of the presumed grant unnecessary, but that even where its existence is negatived, the jury not only may, but ought to, give to user as of right for the prescribed period the full effect of an actual grant, wherever the presump-tion can be lawfully made. In dealing with the facts, I shall rely only on the defendants' evidence, or on what is admitted.

In short, I shall discuss the case upon the most favourable assumption for the defendants, as indeed I am bound to do when the jury have found in their favour.

Speaking generally, I concur upon the question of fact, with Andrews, J., but it is my duty to give a detailed judgment of my own.

I take the evidence, as far as I can, in order of date, and I refer to the map printed in the Report. The oldest witness was the defendant, James Pollock, aged 89, who knows the place all his life. John Taylor, John Kerr, and Thomas M'Ken-non also knew it before 1861. These witnesses prove that the water in dispute rises north of the Ballycastle road in lands now belonging to the plaintiff, called White-gate or Chequer Hall. The land, both above and below the road, has a slight fall towards the Killaggan water, a natural stream, and the natural outlet for the water from the land above the road.

At the commencement of the evidence, what is now the county road to Clogh Mills was an 'old avenue' running at an angle from the Ballycastle road past the defendants' farm. At that time, as now, water accumulated above the Ballycastle road, on the plaintiff's lands. Until 1861, this water made its way to the Killaggan water by two courses, neither of which was a natural stream. A pipe from C on the map, carried most of the water which flowed in any defined course down to the Killaggan water. James Pollock, Taylor, Kerr, and M'Kennon all agree that before M'Curdy Hamilton, the presumed grantor, altered the flow of the water, a portion of it came straight down from Whitegate past Pollock's by a shough at the left-hand side of the Clough Mills road to N, where it was taken under the road or 'avenue' to Pollock's house through a hole which he made, and for which the county afterwards substituted a culvert. All the water running through the pipe from C, reached the Killaggan water above a scutch mill now belonging to John Mullen, but the water which ran down the Clough Mills road past Pollock's house fell into the Killaggan water below the mill. The land both above and below the Ballycastle road, east of the Clough Mills road, belonged to the plaintiff's predecessor, and from its low-lying and boggy character it needed drainage and improvement of the outlet for the water.

In this state of facts M'Curdy Hamilton, in or about 1861, made the water-course, which is now the subject of dispute, from B, about half-way between C and the intersection of the roads, past the point where the carry in dispute was put up, and thence on to the Killaggan water at S, above the scutch mill.

This water-course was wide and shallow; its purpose was the drainage of Hamilton's lands; and it discharges more water from the lands above the road than had previously found its way either through the pipe from C, or down the shough along the road.

The main case which the defendants tried to make in evidence at the trial was that, before M'Curdy Hamilton's operations, water ran down to the site of the carry, and from that site to the Clough Mills road, and thence to Pollock's house. In short, the defendants tried to prove that the carry was put up originally in order to leave them water to which they were entitled, and of which they had a user as of right. This case was met, not only by evidence, part of which was given by witnesses produced for the defendants, that no water ever came to the site of the carry until the new cut made by M'Curdy Hamilton brought it there, but by the fact, admitted by James Pollock himself, that 'the water had to be taken a wee bit up hill' from the new course to the Clough Mills road by making the 'carry' in question.

The jury found, upon ample evidence, against the defendants, that 'before the drainage operations of 1861, *no water* flowed as of right from the site of the carry to the Clough Mills road and thence to the defendant's farm.' Upon the question whether there is any evidence to sustain the presumption of a grant, this finding appears to me to be of vital importance.

I take the transaction of 1861 from the evidence of the defendant James Pollock, who was a party to it. After proving that he fetched water to the hole which he made under the Clough Mills road before the carry was made, but discounting that evidence by the finding that this water was not brought as of right from the site of the carry - which implies that it came down the side of the road - he says, 'M'Curdy Hamilton was draining, and he and I made an agreement to send the whole water this road,' meaning down from B.

The map and the levels show that the effect of opening the drain from B was to carry the water that previously went down the pipes from C eastwards to the upper end of the new drain at B and also possibly to carry some of the water which previously ran down the Clogh Mills road westwards to the same point. Kerr worked for Hamilton in making the new course. I accept his evidence, that Hamilton told him 'that James Pollock was to be left his water,' but he describes the operation in these words: 'M'Curdy Hamilton drained the property. I worked at the drains. When we commenced the drainage works we deepened the course from B. That course was not previously carrying any water. When we deepened it, it could carry water away, and then we put up the carry that Pollock might have the water he had been in the habit of getting. We sunk and cleaned out the drain: we did that to drain the land. I put up the carry to bring to Pollock the portion of water that he was in the habit of getting. The carry was there twenty-five years ago in the same place in which it is now.'

Bearing in mind that the jury have found that until these operations no water flowed as of right to the carry and thence to the defendant's farm, and the evidence that the water which previously reached Pollock's farm ran down beside the Clough Mills road, and that such water, and such water only, fell into the Killaggan water below the scutch mill, neither Hamilton nor Pollock can have had any right in 1861 to divert any additional water from the scutch mill; Pollock could not get, and Hamilton could not grant, any right to water diverted from the pipe at C to the new course from B.

I shall presently refer to the evidence of Mullen and of the defendant Nathaniel Pollock as to the diversion of water from the mill. Pollock's operations were, in the words of the jury, 'drainage operations.' Their object was to facilitate the discharge of surface water from Hamilton's lands above the road through Hamilton's lands below the road. Hamilton, in the words of the plaintiff, 'did not want the water himself.' Hamilton and Pollock were friends'; nothing could be more natural than that Pollock should be allowed to take water from the carry to the pipe under the road; but it would be most unnatural and inconsistent with the object of the whole business, if Hamilton were to grant to Pollock a right which would involve the inability ever to deepen his drain, or even to alter or improve the escape of the drainage water from his own lands. Besides, neither he nor Pollock could divert to Pollock's farm any water which previously fell into the Killaggan water above the scutch mill. The carry in question has been dignified with the name of a weir. James Pollock graphically says 'at first it wasn't very high; it was a row of sods, and a wee row of stones high' across a shallow shough which had a fall of only 'about one inch' in its entire length of 500 feet. It appears to me to be absolutely unreasonable to impute to Hamilton any intention to grant, or to Pollock any intention to acquire, any right to water lying in this new course which would not be subject to Hamilton's retention of his right to do everything from time to time that might be reasonable for the drainage of his lands – always remembering that the jury have found that Pollock had no user as of right of any water at the *locus in quo* before the 'drainage operations' of 1861. A fair way to test the reasonableness of presuming a grant is to take the facts as they stood in 1861 as instructions for the preparation of a deed to confer the right now presumed.

Is it conceivable that Hamilton would impose upon himself and his successors an obligation to maintain the bottom of his shough and the top of the 'wee row' of sods and stones always at their then level, and never to improve or deepen his own drains? The only inference which I can draw from the facts is that he might give to Pollock liberty to carry to his farm any drainage water which Hamilton 'did not want,' and which could be taken without the knowledge or with the permission of the owner of the scutch mill, reserving Hamilton's power to drain his own land in a reasonable manner from time to time. The acts now complained of consist only of scouring the water-course for the purpose of drainage, and of removing the 'carry' in the course of so doing. It is proved that Pollock's supply of water could have been restored by similarly scouring the drain from the carry to his house: in short, by merely lowering the level of both drains alike. As the plaintiff puts it: 'When I cleaned out the shough, the water would all go to the Killaggan river, unless the defendants cleaned out their own fence.'

The defendants' engineer, Mr Pinkerton, swears that the defendants' drains 'could be altered for £2, so as to give them all the water and not flood the plaintiff's land.'

The way in which the defendants met this state of facts appears to me to show

conclusively that the right claimed has no legal existence. Nathaniel Pollock says:–
'When the plaintiff sank the stream from the carry to the river, and took the carry
away, I challenged him for it. He told me to sink the shough three inches. I was
threatened by Mullen with law if I did.' And *he didn't*. Mullen swore that when he
heard, seventeen years ago, of the Pollocks taking the water, he went up and spoke
to them and drew their attention to it, and said he would not let them take it unless
they would turn it to his mill again; they promised to return it, but never did, and
recently he served written notice on the defendants, which is in evidence, to send in
the water that they had deprived him of for the last seventeen years, and threaten-
ing proceedings if they failed to do so. With the finding of the jury that there was no
flow of water as of right from the carry before 1861, and the defendant's practical
admission that he did not deepen his own alleged watercourse even by three inches,
because the mill-owner objected, I find it impossible to conceive a grant which
could confer an absolute right to the flow of water through the course in question, it
being indisputably clear that to sustain the findings, that grant must have imposed
an obligation on the grantor not to carry his drainage operations any further, and
for ever thereafter during his term to maintain the bottom of the shough which he
made in 1861 at the same level at which it was originally constructed, and all this for
the sole purpose of voluntarily giving to his neighbour a right, which the jury have
found that he did not previously possess, of supplying his farm with water from a
new cut which the grantor made for the more effective drainage of his own land,
and therefore primarily for his own benefit. The whole doctrine of presumed grant
rests upon the desire of the law to create a legal foundation for the long-continued
enjoyment, *as of right*, of advantages which are *prima facie* inexplicable in the
absence of legal title. In cases such as this, where the grant is admittedly a fiction, it
is all the more incumbent on the Judge to see, before the question is left to the jury,
that the circumstances and character of the user import that it has been '*as of right*.'
It appears to me, in the present case, that the evidence is inconsistent with right,
and that the user is consistent only with permission to enjoy what the supposed
grantor did not want, if and so long as that user might be consistent with the rights
of third parties, and also with the grantor's right to use his own property from time
to time in a reasonable manner. Such a user never could have been as of right in its
inception; it could never acquire during its continuance any higher than a permissive character, and it therefore never could be, or become, a foundation for the
presumption of a grant.

I shall refer very shortly to the cases which establish the distinction, which
common sense indicates, between the cases of artificial and of natural watercourses. *Arkwright* v. *Gell* (5 M. & W. 203) shows that user can confer no right of
action against the owners of an artificial water-course made for a particular purpose, when that purpose was known to the person who used the water, and when
the circumstances showed that its flow was attributable to the exigencies of those
who constructed it. It was there held that from such circumstances no presumption
of a grant could arise. In *Wood* v. *Wand* (3 Exch. 748) more than sixty years
enjoyment was held to give no right of action for diversion of the water of an
artificial course, where the flow, from the nature of the case, appeared to depend
upon temporary circumstances, and where the interruption was by a person standing in the position of a grantor. *Greatrex* v. *Hayward* (8 Exch. 291) is almost
identical with the present case, and it decided that the enjoyment for twenty years
of a flow of water from a drain made for the purpose of agricultural improvement
did not give a right to the neighbour to preclude the proprietor from altering the
level of his drain for the improvement of his land, although, in that case as in this,
the jury had found in favour of the right. This principle was sanctioned, and *Wood*

v. *Wand* (3 Exch. 748) was expressly affirmed, by the Privy Council in *Rameshur Pershad Narain Singh* v. *Koonj Bahari Pattuk* (4 App. Cas. 121), although in that case it was found, upon the facts, that the circumstances fairly supported the presumption of a legal right to surplus water, subject to the right of the defendant to irrigate his own lands, and to take by proper channels and other proper means, so much of the water as might be proper and requisite for such purpose.

Consistently with this last case, the only right which the defendants in the present case could have, would be a right to such water, not exceeding the flow since 1861, as they could take by adapting their carry and drain to the plaintiff's drainage works as altered from time to time. But such a right would not sustain the defence, first because there is no evidence that the plaintiff's scouring of his drains has been in any way unreasonable or improper as a drainage operation, and secondly because the defendants did not make the changes in their carry and drain which would have continued the flow of water as it was before the plaintiff scoured his drain, because they would not face the opposition of the owner of the scutch mill. They cannot make the plaintiff answerable for that.

In my opinion, therefore, upon the third finding of the jury, there was no sufficient evidence to sustain the first and second findings, the plaintiff is entitled to judgment, and the Appeal ought to be dismissed with costs.

Upon the question of law, namely, whether since the Prescription Act, a fictitious grant can be presumed as the foundation of a right upon less than forty years user by a termor against a termor, the Queen's Bench was under the impression that there were Irish decisions that such a right could be so established when the fee was not bound. I read all the Irish cases with care, and it is my impression that, in the High Court, the question has never been *decided* in the affirmative, although opinions to that effect have been expressed by some Judges. It certainly has not been decided by this Court, and in *Timmons* v. *Hewitt* (22 L.R. Ir. 627), when the question was raised before a larger Court than the present, consisting of the Lord Chancellor, Barry and Naish, L.JJ., and myself, the expression of any opinion upon it was declined, because, in that case, as in this, the decision went against the claimant upon the question of fact, and the question of law therefore became immaterial to the judgment. I believe that we ought to take the same course now, but my colleagues think that we ought to express our opinions, and I do so in deference to them, though such expression is unnecessary to our decision, and consequently is not binding either on the Court or on ourselves.

I take the Irish cases in order of date. *Deeble* v. *Linehan* (12 I.C.L.R. 1) was decided on the 9th June, 1860. The acts were done and the action was commenced before the 1st January, 1859, the day upon which 21 & 22 Vict. c. 42 extended the Prescription Act to Ireland. It is remarkable that whenever *Deeble* v. *Linehan* (12 I.C.L.R. 1) has been relied on in the High Court as an authority for the proposition that one termor can prescribe against another, it has not been observed that the dates prevent its application to *Bright* v. *Walker* (1 C.M. & R. 211) or to the Prescription Act, and therefore that it can be no authority upon the point now at issue, viz. the effect of that Act upon the presumption of a lost grant from twenty years user. The case is open to other important observations. Although the servient tenement was held under a bishop's lease, the evidence going to establish the right against the middle estate was extremely strong as circumstantial evidence of a grant in fact. The original watercourse was granted by deed for the purposes of a mill, which had been worked by means of it for 144 years. The watercourse in question was only a substitution for a small part of the granted stream, necessitated by an alteration of a public road for which the owner of the servient tenement had received compensation. Evidence was given, and was held sufficient, of acquiescence by the servient termor; the Court held, under the circumstances, that a grant might be presumed, though not found to have been actually executed. But for the existence of the fee in the bishop, the case could go no farther than *Angus* v. *Dalton* (6 App. Cas. 740) upon the law, and upon the facts it was an incomparably stronger case for maintaining the right. If it were generally applicable to all cases of twenty years' user by termor against termor, I could not reconcile it with *Hanks* v. *Cribbin* (7 I.C.L.R. 489) decided by the Common Pleas in 1857. To treat it as an authority for prescribing for an easement from user over land not held in fee, makes it inconsistent with principle, and with several of the English judgments to which my colleagues will refer. The case becomes completely reconcileable with principle and authority, if it be assumed that the remote reversion of the bishop was treated as unaffected, or as bound by whatever bound the substantial interest, practically the fee, of the middleman.

In *Deeble* v. *Linehan* (12 I.C.L.R. 1) *Bright* v. *Walker* (1 C.M. & R. 211) was cited only to show that the presumption of a lost grant did not involve belief in its actual execution, but the dates prevented it from deciding anything upon the effect of the Prescription Act as laid down in *Bright* v. *Walker* (1 C.M. & R. 211).

Wilson v. *Stanley* (12 I.C.L.R. 345), decided by the Exchequer in 1861 and reported in the same volume, *was* a decision on the Prescription Act, and if Pigot, C.B. rightly interpreted *Bright* v. *Walker* (1 C.M. R. 211), it rules this case. Wilson sued for obstructing a mill-stream which ran across the defendant's lands. Under a lease of 1775 which expired in 1840, under which the plaintiff's and defendant's lands were held, the mill-stream was made and enjoyed for more than forty years. The holding being divided, in 1841 the defendants' lands, with the mill-stream then running across them, were leased for twenty-one years to the defendant's predecessor. In 1843, the mill, with the right to the water, was demised for two lives or thirty-one years to the plaintiff's predecessor, and the stream was enjoyed without interruption until 1860. At the expiration of the lease of 1775, and at the dates of the leases of 1841 and 1843, the reversion was held by a tenant for life. There had been actual user for more than forty years before the action. The plaintiff contended that this forty years' enjoyment gave an absolute right under the Prescription Act, sect. 2; or at all events that there had been twenty years' enjoyment, which but for the Prescription Act would have raised the presumption of a grant; that the Prescription Act could not be held to have superseded the Common Law; and that *Bright* v. *Walker* (1 C.M. & R. 211) was inconsistent with *Wright* v. *Williams* (1 M. & W. 77), and would lead to great injustice, especially in Ireland. Pigot, C.B. said as to the Prescription Act:

'Two results follow from its enactments, according to *Bright* v. *Walker* (1 C.M. &. R. 211), viz. 1. Presumptive title founded on a presumed grant, cannot now be established at all by proof of long uninterrupted enjoyment alone. 2. The prescriptive title which the statute has given the means of establishing, can only be applied where enjoyment has been *such as to bind all estates*, comprising the whole fee-simple, in the servient tenement.'

He says it might have been consistent with the Act to hold prescription should be applied where the enjoyment was had for the periods defined in the earlier sections, and where the prescription was not negatived by other means than by showing commencement of enjoyment within legal memory, but that where prescription was not applicable (as where all estates in the land were not bound), a presumption of a legal origin of the enjoyment in a grant for some competent party might still be made against the party against whom, before the Act, such presumption would have had the sanction of constant practice and established user. But he says:

'It was however *otherwise held* in the exposition of the statute given in the judgment in *Bright* v. *Walker* (1 C.M. & R. 211).'

He refers to that decision, as never having been expressly over-ruled or even mentioned with disapprobation for more than a quarter of a century, and he held himself, in a Court of co-ordinate jurisdiction, bound by it, notwithstanding its special importance in Ireland, where

'It was most important that rights to water, as well as other incorporeal privileges, should be capable of being proved by evidence of long enjoyment, not only against the owners of the fee in possession, but against owners of derivative interests, which, in some instances, are of little less value than the fee.'

He said, equally distinctly, that the decision in *Bright* v. *Walker* (1 C.M. & R. 211) would have precluded the Judge at the trial from leaving it to the jury to presume a grant,

'For, besides the long enjoyment, there were *no other circumstance* presented by the evidence, from which an inference could be drawn that a grant had been made.'

That is the state of the evidence here, and I follow Pigot, C. B., as to its effect. As to reconciling *Wright* v. *Williams* (1 M. & W. 77) with *Bright* v. *Walker* (1 C.M. & R. 211), he says that the only distinction which he could see between these cases was that in *Bright* v. *Walker* (1 C. M. & R. 211) the enjoyment had been for less than forty years, though for more than twenty, and that in *Wright* v. *Williams* (1 M. & W. 77) it had continued for more than forty years; that the latter case therefore was decided upon the forty years' enjoyment and the language of the Act, especially in sect. 8, relating to an enjoyment for that period.

In this he anticipated the decision in *Beggan* v. *McDonald* (2 L.R. Ir. 560), and he limited the effect of *Bright* v. *Walker* (1 C.M. & R. 211) to the twenty years enjoyment only; and as to enjoyment for the shorter period, he accepted the judgment of Parke, B., as law.

Beggan v. *McDonald* (2 L.R. Ir. 560) was decided by the Exchequer in 1877. In that case there were two counts for trespass *quare clausum fregit*. The defendant justified by user as of right for twenty years, and he also justified, in a distinct plea, by like user for forty years. The plaintiff's land had been held under a lease for more than forty years before the action, for a term still subsisting. There was no evidence of acquiescence on the part of the landlord, and the defendant and his predecessors were termors under another landlord. The jury found for the defendants on both pleas. Dowse, B., held that both the landlord and tenant had the burthen imposed on them by the forty years user, the tenant during his lease, and the landlord, unless he put it off under sect 8, within three years after the expiration of the lease. He says (I.R. 11 C.I. 362):

'*Bright* v. *Walker* (1 C.M. & R. 211) has been often questioned, but never overruled. This Court has no authority to overrule it, and, even if I were sitting in a Court of Error, I would find great difficulty in overruling a judgment that, unsatisfactory as it may be in part, has so much to be said in its favour. That case *dealt only with a twenty years user*, and so far as it laid down the law applicable to that period of enjoyment, I consider myself bound by its decision. . . . to a case of twenty years' enjoyment, the reasoning of *Bright* v. *Walker* (1 C.M. & R.

211) distinctly applies. The 8th section has nothing to do with this part of the case. If we were to hold here that the landlord is bound, he is bound without any possible way of freeing himself from the obligation, and this anomalous state of the law would be established, that the landlord could free himself when he was bound for forty years, and he could not free himself when he was bound for twenty years. It is clear the landlord is not bound at all. From whence, to quote *Bright* v. *Walker* (1 C. M. & R. 211), we are led to conclude that an enjoyment of twenty years, if it give not a good title against all, *gives no good title at all.*'

Every Judge, both in the Exchequer and in the Court of Appeal, treated *Bright* v. *Walker* (1 C. M. & R. 211) as concluding the defendant upon the plea of twenty years' user – the only user which exists here; but Dowse, B., Palles, C. B. and the whole Court of Appeal upheld the defence upon the forty years' user, upon the difference of the provisions of the Prescription Act as to the two periods. Deasy, B., and Fitzgerald, B., decided in favour of the plaintiff upon both pleas. Deasy, B., applied the doctrine of *Bright* v. *Walker* (1 C.M. & R. 211) alike to both periods, and therefore dissented from *Wright* v. *Williams* (1 M. & W. 77). Fitzgerald, B. distinguished the effect of the enjoyment for the two periods; and as to the twenty years, Palles, C.B., adopted his judgment, though he dissented from the ground of 'inconclusiveness,' on which Fitzgerald, B., decided against the right on the forty years' enjoyment. Fitzgerald B. says:

'In cases under the 2nd section, if the evidence of twenty years' enjoyment be such as, under the circumstances of the case, could not before the statute have been left to the jury *as evidence of title affecting the fee*, neither can it be since the statute. . . . The jury was rightly told that the evidence of enjoyment could not, under the circumstances of the case (*i.e.*, in the absence of acquiescence), be left to them as evidence of title affecting the fee, and that being so, the plea of twenty years' enjoyment under the statute was not maintained.'

In this Palles, C.B., Dowse, B., and this Court all agreed. Palles, C.B., says:

'We all agree that the object of the statute was to shorten the time of prescription, and that the periods mentioned in it are to be deemed new times of prescription. We also agree that an enjoyment, to create a title against a particular estate in the servient tenement should be, first, such as to be *capable* of giving a good title against the whole fee-simple estate, and secondly, such as will in fact give that title without any further act done by the owner of the dominant tenement, provided the reversioner in the servient tenement shall not resist within three years from the determination of the lease. The sole difference between us is this, my brothers Deasy and Fitzgerald are of opinion that the easement cannot exist at all, unless it binds the fee *absolutely and in every event*. My brother Dowse and myself are of opinion that an enjoyment, although insufficient to bind the fee in the event of the reversioner resisting within three years, is effectual to bind, and does bind, the fee defeasibly, that is, unless and until the reversioner shall within the three years resist.'. . .

He quotes *Bright* v. *Walker* (1 C.M. & R. 211), italicising the words, 'an enjoyment for twenty years,' and says:

'The conclusion at which I have arrived from the consideration of this judgment is, that although expressions are used in it which undoubtedly, taken literally, indicate an opinion that an easement defeasible or subject to determination on the happening of a condition, could not be created by enjoyment under the statute, yet the Court, in using these expressions, had in its contemplation an enjoyment for twenty years only, and that the limited application of sect. 8 rendered it unnecessary to consider the question now before us. . . .'

He reconciled *Wright* v. *Williams* (1 M. & W. 77), with *Bright* v. *Walker* (1 C.M. & R. 211) by holding that the opinion conveyed by the observations of Parke, B., in their more general sense, was subsequently modified so as to exclude their application to forty years' enjoyment, and said that:

'In that sense *Wright* v. *Williams* (1 M. & W. 77) did not interfere with the decision in *Bright* v. *Walker* (1 C.M. & R. 211): it but modified *dicta* unnecessary to the judgment.'

He adds an observation on *Wilson* v. *Stanley* (12 I.C.L.R. 345), which if, correct, rules this case:

'I take the effect of that decision to be no more than this, that *Bright* v. *Walker* (1 C.M. & R. 211) *has established, now beyond controversy in this Court*, that a user for twenty years will not create an easement binding any estate in the servient tenement, unless it bind the fee. . . . If the evidence of the thirty or twenty years' enjoyment be such as, under the circumstances of the case, could not before the Act have been left to the jury *as evidence of a grant* affecting the fee, it will, since the Act, be insufficient to establish the right. But whatever the circumstances may be under which the enjoyment for sixty or forty years took place, it will (if it were as of right and without interruption), as matter of law, *create* the right, unless in the case of the forty years it will come within the qualification in the 8th section. . . . The 6th section enacts that no presumption shall be allowed or made in favour or support of any claim upon proof of the exercise or enjoyment of the matter claimed, for any less period of time than such period mentioned in the Act as applicable to the case and nature of the claim. The operation of this section is in no sense restricted to the cases where, but for the Act, the claim would have been to a prescription at Common Law, *i.e.* from time immemorial. Cases so familiar before the statute in which juries were advised to *presume a grant* from the owner of some estate in the servient tenement less than fee-simple, are *plainly within the enactment. In such a case, since the statute, the presumption of a grant cannot be made* from the mere user for a period less than that specified in the Act, unaccompanied by other circumstances aiding the presumption. . . . The object of the Act was to abolish the unpleasant course of juries presuming grants, which they were convinced had never been executed in fact. The possibility of drawing this presumption *is abolished*, but the rights of the parties are left without the presumption, as if, in every case, in which forty years' enjoyment under the statute has existed, the presumption, which before the statute *might* have been drawn, had been, in fact, drawn.'

The Court affirmed Dowse, B., and Palles, C. B., in *Beggan* v. *McDonald* (2 L.R. Ir. 560). From the headnote it appears to have been understood as a decision that the doctrine of *Bright* v. *Walker* (1 C.M. & R. 211) does not apply where the enjoyment on which the right depends has been for a period of forty years, implying that the doctrine does apply to an enjoyment for twenty years. Ball, C. says:

'In the case of the user for twenty years, it has been decided by the judgment of the English Court of Exchequer in *Bright* v. *Walker* (1 C.M. & R. 211), that no user will avail unless adequate to bind the fee; it will not suffice that it was asserted against a lessee under the fee, and further, if it does not bind the fee, it is held not to bind anyone. This judgment has not escaped criticism, of which a summary, distinguished by the learning and acuteness that characterised the late Pigot, C. B., may be found in *Wilson* v. *Stanley* (12 I.C.L.R. 345). But however the judgment may be criticised, it seems to me that is it now too late to question the authority of the case itself, and that *whenever we are concerned with only a twenty years' user, it must be followed.'*

May, C.J. gives reason and authority for sustaining the doctrine of *Bright* v, *Walker* (1 C.M. & R. 211) as applied to twenty years' user. He says:

'The object of the Legislature' (in the Prescription Act) 'seems to have been definitely to fix and ascertain the periods, and the circumstances, during and under which the user of the incorporeal rights therein dealt with should be deemed to confer a title to such rights The language of Lord Westbury in *Tapling* v. *Jones* (11 H.L.C. 304) in reference to the right to the access of light is, I think, applicable to all the easements with which the Act is conversant. "It is material", said the Chancellor, 'to observe that the right to what is called an ancient light now depends upon positive enactment. It is matter *positivi juris*, and does not require, and therefore, ought not to be rested *upon any assumption of grant*, or fiction of a license having to been obtained from the adjoining proprietor. . . ." The statutory enactments confer the right, and the mode in which it is conferred can properly be ascertained only by a reference to the Act itself.'

Morris, C.J. concurred with the other members of the Court in the judgment pronounced in favour of the defendant, upon the enjoyment for forty years, and on that alone.

Fahey v. *Dwyer* (4 L.R. Ir. 271) was decided by the Common Pleas to the same effect in 1879. There were pleas of prescription for twenty and for forty years. The jury found for the defendants on both. Lawson, J., says:

'If there was any difficulty about the case, *Beggan* v. *M'Donald* (4 L.R. Ir. 271) appears to remove it, for it decided that a period of *forty years'* enjoyment is absolute and indefeasible, and that *Bright* v. *Walker* (1 C.M. & R. 211) *applies only to a twenty years' enjoyment.'*

It is immaterial to the present purpose to consider whether tenure under a common landlord ought to have made a difference.

Timmons v. *Hewitt* (22 L.R. Ir. 627) was tried before Holmes, J., in 1887 upon pleas of twenty and of forty years' user. The plaintiff's counsel asked for a direction, on the ground that one tenant from year to year could not prescribe for a right of way over the land of another yearly tenant under a common landlord. The learned Judge 'acceded' to this proposition as far as twenty years' prescription was concerned, but he left the question of forty years' enjoyment to the jury, with a second question whether the landlord, at the creation of the defendant's tenancy, reserved the way in question in favour of the plaintiff's holding. He reported that he told the jury,

'That they must be satisfied before they could find the first question for the plaintiff, that the user had existed *for the full period of forty years* and that, however clear the evidence might be of user for a shorter period, *no inference ought to be drawn from this without actual evidence.'*

As every prescription, by its nature, rests on the presumption of a lost grant before legal memory, this direction must, in the mind of any one who remembers the rudimentary principle of the law, apply to the presumption of a grant, and it must rest on an adoption of the doctrine of *Bright* v. *Walker* (1 C.M. & R. 211), as applied to user for less than forty years. In the Exchequer, Palles, C. B. referred to *Fahey* v. *Dwyer* (4 L.R. Ir. 271), *Beggan* v. *M'Donald* (2 L.R. Ir. 560), and *Clancy* v. *Byrne* (I.R. 11 C.L. 355), and laid down that user and enjoyment by one tenant against another 'is not as of right within the meaning of the Prescription Act, sect. 2 . . .' He says:

'It is a user by a termor who, if he aquire the right, must acquire it as incident to the land of which he is termor, and thus for the benefit of his reversioner. Such user cannot be as of right, unless a reversioner can in law by user acquire a right against himself.'

He starts the question whether, and he expresses his own opinion that,

'It is competent for the jury to infer from twenty years' enjoyment, as of right and without interruption of an easement claimed by the owner of one of the tenements over the land of the other tenement, held under a common landlord, *either* a grant by deed from one tenant to the other tenant of such easement, *or* where the user is proved' (as it was there) 'to have existed as far back as the memory of the witnesses can go a jury may infer that the alleged dominant tenement was such dominant tenement, when originally demised by the land-lord, that is, that it consisted not of the land merely but of the land with a right of way as appurtenant.'

Upon the first of these propositions, he says that:

'The decision of the Exchequer Chamber in *Deeble* v. *Linehan* (12 I.C.L.R. 1) appears to be a conclusive authority.'

With all respect for his almost unvarying accuracy, I feel that the omission to observe that *Deeble* v. *Linehan* (12 I.C.L.R. 1) was decided upon the law as it stood before the Prescription Act was extended to Ireland, deprives the opinion which he formed upon that question of any possibility of support from the only authority upon which he founded it. *Deeble* v. *Linehan* (12 I.C.L.R. 1) can have had no application either to the doctrine of *Bright* v. *Walker* (1 C.M. & R. 211), or to the effect of the Prescription Act, which are the only matters with which we have now to deal.

In this Court these questions were argued in *Timmons* v. *Hewitt* (22 L.R. Ir. 627); but the Court expressly declined to express any opinion upon them, holding that there was, upon the report of the learned Judge, sufficient evidence to sustain both the findings of the jury, and therefore that the verdict should stand as well under *Beggan* v. *M'Donald* (2 L.R. Ir. 560) on the ground of forty years user, which bound the fee, as also upon the principle of *Clancy* v. *Byrne* (I.R. 11 C.L. 355), that the way in question was appurtenant to the plaintiff's holding at the time of its creation.

Therefore *Timmons* v. *Hewitt* (22 L.R. Ir. 627), applies to the point now before us only in the direction which Holmes, J., gave the jury, that no right could be acquired by user for twenty years, and in the opinion of the Chief Baron, founded on *Deeble* v. *Linehan* (12 I.C.L.R. 1) in the belief that it applied to the Prescription Act.

O'Kane v. *O'Kane* (30 L.R. Ir. 489) was tried by Palles, C B., who repeated his opinion that twenty years user was sufficient to authorize the jury to presume a grant from one tenant to another. The jury found twenty years user, and negatived forty years user, and therefore apparently the Queen's Bench was brought face to face with the question which we are now discussing; but because the defendant's counsel had not objected to the question which the Chief Baron had left to the jury, the course of the trial was made the sole ground of the decision. O'Brien, C.J., said:

'The course of the trial precludes the defendant from all right to insist on the objection. It is plain that the trial proceeded on the basis that the right claimed could have been created by grant. . . . Had counsel desired that the question of lost grant should be put expressly to the jury he should have said so at the trial; and if he meant to contend that such a right could not have been, under the circumstances of the particular case, created by grant, he should have made the objection. . . . We decide this case upon the course of the trial; we do not formally decide whether one tenant can or cannot confer upon another such a right of way by grant.'

No doubt he goes on to say that he does not see why a tenant from year to year should not be able to grant such a right so long as his tenancy lasted; but as the foundation for this opinion, he adopt the view of Pigot, C.B., in *Deeble* v. *Linehan* (12 I.C.L.R. 1), and he says that the course indicated by that learned Judge should as a general rule be adopted. He also omits to notice the anachronism in relying upon that case as an authority upon the Prescription Act or upon *Bright* v. *Walker* (1 C.M. & R. 211).

This is the last Irish case upon the subject.

Before expressing my own conclusion, I must point out the extraordinary position in which the supposed right has been left in the present case as the result of the trial. The Chief Baron reports that the title of neither plaintiff nor defendant was proved by legal evidence. The plaintiff put in an assignment of January 25th, 1867, from M'Curdy Hamilton to Ann Hanna of lands demised by two leases, one dated April 10th, 1807, for eighty-seven years, which expired before action on November 1st, 1893; the second lease, dated November 4th, 1836, was of other lands, and was for thirty-one years and certain lives. The leases themselves were not put in evidence; it did not appear what part of plaintiff's lands had been held under the last lease, nor who were the lives in the lease of 1836, nor whether they were alive or dead. The plaintiff also gave in evidence a vesting order of the Land Commission dated April 25th, 1894, whereby the fee-simple of the lands, subject to the two leases, was vested in the plaintiff.

Though he directed a verdict and gave judgment for the defendants on the findings of the jury, the Chief Baron reports that he abstained from giving judgment in reference to the injunction which the defendants sought by their counterclaim, *i.e.* he refused to quiet the defendants in the possession of the right, because it appeared to him that the evidence was 'in the last degree unsatisfactory' on what, in his view, was an essential part of the case, viz., the continuance of the lives in the leases under which the plaintiffs and defendants respectively held before they acquired the fee from the Land Commission.

In the view which he took and continued to take of the case, the right acquired under the lost grant found by the jury was limited to the continuance both of the defendant's lease, which does not appear to have been given in evidence at all, and of the lease of the 4th November, 1836. No evidence was given of any of the lives being in existence at the date of the writ, nor were even their names disclosed. The report concludes:

'The verdict for the defendants rested upon the direction which I gave the jury that the lives must be presumed to be in existence until the contrary was proved.'

No more striking instance could well be given of the inexpediency of weakening the effect of the doctrine in *Bright* v. *Walker* (1 C.M. & R. 211), which gives to the Prescription Act the effect of substituting definite absolute and statutory rights, for limited conditional or temporary rights founded on the fiction of grants. As the result of the trial, the defendants cannot enforce the rights to which the jury have found them entitled, unless they can prove the continuance of the lease of 1836, and then only until the last life drops, unless, contrary to the opinion and direction of the Judge at the trial, a question upon the effect of the Land Purchase Acts is decided in their favour. I believe that we are all agreed that this question is not to be discussed until it arises, and it cannot arise until the lease of 1836 is proved to have expired.

My own conclusion upon the whole matter may be shortly stated; repeating that I state it only in deference to my colleagues, who think it their duty to discuss it, and that I hold myself and the Court free to reconsider it if it becomes essential to a judgment in any future case.

The doctrine of *Bright* v. *Walker* (1 C.M. & R. 211), when restricted to the enactment as to twenty years' user, appears to me to be reasonable and logical. Prescription before the Act necessarily involved the presumption of a grant before legal memory. Therefore an enactment to 'shorten the times of prescription in certain cases' dealt expressly with cases of enjoyment only; but it impliedly dealt with every case where the right rested on mere enjoyment. Whenever this was supplemented before the Act, the case was outside the Act, and the presumption may still be made independently of the Act, and for that purpose the plea of 'lost grant' remains still legitimately in use. By the words of section 2, twenty years' enjoyment only removed the liability to defeat by proof that the enjoyment of what was claimed as of right had commenced within legal memory, and left the claim in all other respects as defeasible as before. Forty years user on the other hand, under the combined operation of sections 2 and 8, conferred the right, subject only to defeasance by a particular person, namely, the reversioner, within the prescribed time, namely, within three years after the reversion fell into possession. Section 6 prohibits any presumption, including the presumption of a lost grant, from enjoyment for any period shorter than those fixed by the Act. Therefore, in every case in which the evidence of the right consists *only*, as it does here, of *mere user*, the presumption cannot be made unless the user covers the statutory period required to confer the right, namely, forty years, and the claim remains liable, as it was before the Act, to defeat by proof that the fee is not bound, if the user is shorter than forty years.

This is quite consistent with retaining the right to make the presumption of the lost grant from evidence, or from circumstances other than the mere user with which alone the Act is conversant.

The Irish decisions since the Act appear to me to have repeatedly recognised the application of the doctrine in *Bright* v. *Walker* (1 C.M. & R. 211.) to twenty years' enjoyment, and no English decision appears to me to be inconsistent with it. It is still recognised as an authority in every text-book.

In Ireland the only reported *opinions* to the contrary rest upon *Deeble* v. *Linehan* (12 I.C.L.R. 1), without observing that the case did not apply to the Prescription Act. A *decision* to the contrary would appear to me to be inconsistent with the view of the object of the Act which I have quoted from Pigot, C. B., Palles, C. B., Ball, C., and May, C. J. It would be equally inconsistent with all the recognisitions of the authority of *Bright* v. *Walker* (1 C.M. & R. 211), as restricted to twenty years enjoyment, which I have quoted from the Irish cases.

I am not prepared now to assume that, in every one of those cases, the result would have been the opposite of what it was, if the plea of twenty years user had been supplemented by a plea of a lost grant. I cannot assume that the right was defeated in all those cases by the mere omission of a plea. There are expressions in English cases, to which my colleagues will refer, which indicate the opinion of some individual judges that the Prescription Act left it open to the jury to find a lost grant in every case in which it might have been presumed before the statute; but if these opinions are right, or if they extend to the case of mere user by one termor against another for less than forty years, *Bright* v. *Walker* (1 C.M. & R. 211)must be wrong, and the object of the Act, as hitherto stated, must be defeated.

I have quoted Lord Westbury (*Tapling* v. *Jones*, 11 H.L.C. 304), and I might quote Lindley, L. J., and other judges to the contrary effect; but finding the state of Irish authority to be what it is, I hold myself bound to uphold *Bright* v. *Walker* (1 C.M. & R. 211) as applicable to the case before us, and to leave it to the House of Lords to throw it open again to juries, in every case of mere enjoyment, to make the false presumption of a grant against the fact, a power which the Prescription Act was, in my opinion, intended, in the words of Palles, C.B., to '*abolish*' in the cases to which the Act applied.

If I am told that the practice on circuit upon Civil Bill Appeals makes this an important question, I answer, first, that that practice, if it exists, cannot guide this Court; but I also say that the practice of ignoring *Bright* v. *Walker* (1 C.M. & R. 211) is not proved. In my experience, in every case in which it is possible to do so, evidence of acquiescence is given, in order to bind the superior estate through the acts, or even through the inaction, of landlords, of agents, or of bailiffs; or to carry back the evidence to a period of forty years, or to give circumstantial evidence of a grant in fact. In every case in which evidence of mere user has been thus supplemented, the additional evidence would have been unnecessary, if user alone would have sufficed. In most cases, proof of user for twenty years raises some presumptive evidence of user for forty, unless the commencement of the user between the two limits is proved. Speaking from an experience of eighteen years at the Bar, and of twenty years on the Bench, I can distinctly say that *Bright* v. *Walker* (1 C.M. & R. 211) has always been a stumbling-block in the way of relying on mere user for twenty years as sufficient to create a right against a term, and I cannot call to mind a single instance in which mere user for twenty years (forty years' user being disproved) has been made the basis for presuming a grant by a tenant, which would not bind the fee. If we discount the cases in which forty years enjoyment, or acquiescence of the owner in fee, or circumstantial evidence of a grant in fact, was called in aid, I believe that it will be found that the cases in which *Bright* v. *Walker* (1 C.M. & R. 211) has been disregarded, if any such exist, are very limited indeed in number, and are at least as questionable in law and justice as the present case appears to me to be.

I am obliged to close my lengthened contribution to this discussion, by repeating that it is at best, in my opinion, only an exercitation, because the defendants have failed upon the question of fact.

Walker L.J.:

This case involves two questions, one depending on the inference to be drawn from the facts, and only of interest to the parties concerned, and the other of great general importance in Ireland, viz, whether there can arise from user as of right for twenty years, a presumption of a grant of a right of water from one termor to another termor?

As to the first question, the defendant claims a right to have a flow of water through an artificial cut, or channel, formed in 1861, continued by the maintenance of a carry from the point 'Weir' on the map to N, along the mearing fence, and thence to the defendant's tank; and it must be taken that this flow has continued since 1861 to the removal of the carry before action by the plaintiff for the purpose of drainage works.

The fact that the watercourse is entirely artificial does not determine the question, because it is well settled that a right may be acquired as such, under some legal origin, whether grant or arrangement. As is said by Wood, V.-C., in *N. E. Railway Company* v. *Elliot* (1 J. & H. 145):

> 'The true distinction does not depend, as was said in *Magor* v. *Chadwick* (11 Ad. & E. 571), upon whether the channel is artificial or natural, but upon the purpose and origin of the work, and the circumstances of the enjoyment consequent upon it.'

The facts are hardly in dispute. The plaintiff's farm is flooded by springs called the Checker Hall Springs, and before 1861, his predecessor in title had attempted to drain the farm by a pipe running from the point C to the Killaggan river, considerably above the present cut.

In 1861, the plaintiff's predecessor altered his mode of drainage, and constructed the present cut through his own lands down to the point market 'Weir,' and thence along the mearing drain to S, at the Killaggan river.

The jury have found that before the drainage operations of 1861, no water flowed as of right from the point 'Weir' to N, and there could scarcely have been any other finding, for N is at a higher level than 'Weir,' and the mearing ditch was choked up to 1861.

There had always been, I think, some water flowing from Whitegate above to N, and through a hole there along the road to the defendant's tank, but not from the 'Weir,' and when the plaintiff's predecessor made the cut, and the mearing fences were cleared from 'Weir' to N, and 'Weir' to S, probably as a joint work, a carry was erected which turned some of the water coming down the cut to N. The plaintiff swears that the drain from 'Weir' to S is his own drain, which is all the evidence we have on that subject. What I think we have to ascertain is, what was the origin and purpose of the work constructed in 1861? I think upon the whole, it was – like the pipe for which it was substituted – a mere drainage operation for the plaintiff's own purposes, and on his own lands, which from the nature of the thing he could alter, or improve, or put in another place, and any grant of water which the defendant got must be of the same character as the work out of which it issued, and therefore, *ex natura rai*, temporary, and if temporary, the use must have been permissive, and could not form the foundation for a lost grant. It seems difficult to contend that the plaintiff should always be compelled to drain his farm in that place, and by a drain of the same depth, incapable of improvement or alteration. I think the origin and purpose of the cut rebut the idea of permanency, or creation of right. This is the view taken by Mr. Justice Andrews, with whose judgment, after consideration, I concur.

If I could think that any benefit could result from a new trial, I should be disposed to say that the case ought to be tried again, as the objection with which I am dealing was not made at the trial; but the facts are really not in dispute, and must always bring up the question as to what was the origin and purpose of the work done in 1861.

The view I have taken would be sufficient to dispose of the case in favour of the respondents, and under ordinary circumstances it would be unnecessary to express any opinion upon the question, as to whether there can be any presumption of a lost grant arising from a twenty years' enjoyment, as distinguished from a forty years' enjoyment, of an easement such as claimed in this case, where the grant must be presumed to have been made by one tenant to another, either where the tenants hold under different landlords, or, as here, under the same landlord.

In this country, where long leases are so common, and even tenancies from year to year have become almost perpetuities, the importance of a decision adverse to the possible existence of such a right cannot be exaggerated.

I think it right to say, that having given the fullest consideration to the question, I am not prepared to concur with the view of Lord Justice FitzGibbon. In my opinion, the decision in *Timmons* v. *Hewitt* (22 L.R. Ir. 627, 641) was right.

It is interesting to trace in this country the course of decision, which is a progressive one, ultimately terminating in the decision in the Courts of first instance of the very question which we have to decide.

In *Beggan* v. *M'Donald* (2 I.R. Ir. 560) it was held by the Court of Appeal that a period of forty years' uninterrupted enjoyment of a way by one tenant against another created, under the Prescription Act, sections 2 and 8 together, a right absolute and indefeasible, though liable to be defeated by the reversioner within three years after the determination of the term, which in that case had not expired. The questions there arose between tenants holding under different landlords. It must be distinctly observed that it was not considered necessary that the fee should be absolutely bound. In fact the point of the case is that it was only so conditionally. In *Beggan* v. *M'Donald* (2 I.R. Ir. 560), Fitzgerald, B., and Deasy, B., in the Court of Exchequer, held that no title was given to the easement by the forty years' enjoyment, having regard to the 8th section of the Act, and *Bright* v. *Walker* (1 C.M. & R. 211) was treated as an authority for that. Both Dowse, B., and the Chief Baron expressed the opinion that *Bright* v. *Walker* (1 C.M. & R. 211) decided that the plea of twenty years' user could not be sustained under the Prescription Act, inasmuch as the servient tenement was under lease. No question of lost grant between the termors arose, or was discussed in that case. The case was dealt with solely on the Prescription Act.

In *Fahey* v. *Dwyer* (4 L.R. Ir. 271) the same question arose on a forty years' user between two tenants claiming under the same landlord, and the Court of Common Pleas decided that the defendant was entitled to succeed. In both these cases the action was one of trespass, and the defendant justified under a plea of a prescriptive right of way, and in *Fahey* v. *Dwyer* (4 L.R. Ir. 271) the case of *Gayford* v. *Moffat* (L.R. 4 Ch. 133) was relied on for the plaintiff.

The question next arose in *Timmons* v. *Hewitt* (22 L.R. Ir. 627), tried before Lord Justice Holmes. That case also was one between tenants from year to year, holding under the same landlord, and the action was for obstructing a right of way. The learned Judge left to the jury two questions – 1, Did the plaintiff and his predecessors in title enjoy, as of right, and without interruption, the way on foot, and with horses and carts, for forty years before action? and 2, Did the landlord at the creation of the defendant's tenancy reserve the way in favour of the plaintiff's? The jury found both issues for the plaintiff, and a verdict and judgment were entered for him accordingly. The case was argued before the Court of Exchequer. The Chief Baron who delivered the judgment upholding the plaintiff's verdict declined to rest it upon the doctrine of prescription, but supported it on the ground that from the enjoyment it was competent for the jury to presume a grant of the easement from one tenant to the other. The Chief Baron says (p. 647): 'It is competent for the jury to infer from twenty years' enjoyment as of right and without interruption of an easement claimed by the owner of one of the tenements over the land of the other tenement, a grant by deed from one tenant to the other tenant of such easement.' The defendant appealed, and the Court dismissed the appeal, holding that there was evidence to sustain both findings of the jury, *i.e.* the finding of forty years' user, and also the reservation by the landlord of the way at the creation of the defendant's tenancy.

The case, therefore, is no authority as an appeal decision beyond this, that the Judges must have condsidered that the fact that the tenants held under the same landlord did not prevent the existence of the right. In *O'Kane* v. *O'Kane* (30 L.R. Ir. 489) the question also arose between two tenants from year to year, holding under the same landlord; the case was tried before the Chief Baron, and he left to the jury the question whether the plaintiff for the twenty years next before the suit enjoyed as of right and without interruption the way claimed, and the jury so found. On the Chief Baron's report the Court of Queen's Bench came to the conclusion that the question had been left with the view of raising the presumption of a lost grant, and that no sufficient objection had been made by defendant's counsel, and that the course of the trial precluded him from contending that the right could not have been created by grant.

The Chief Justice, however, says: 'We do not see why a tenant from year to year should not be able to grant such a right as long as the tenancy lasted. He could, in my opinion, confer by express grant such a right as long as his tenancy subsisted, and as to the doctrine of lost grant, I consider it a very useful one, and I think this case is an example of the salutary effect of this fiction of a lost grant.'

I think it cannot be disputed that those views of the Judges of first instance are in some respects at variance with the decision in *Bright* v. *Walker* (1 C.M. & R. 221). I read that case as deciding that at all events since the Prescription Act the qualified right from termor to termor cannot arise out of a presumption of lost grant founded on an enjoyment for twenty years, and the observations in *Wheaton* v. *Maple* ([1893] 3 Ch 48) are to the same effect, and are also as it appears to me inconsistent with *Beggan* v. *M'Donald* (1 I.R. Ir. 560). Being, therefore, forced to choose between the decisions in this country, and that in *Bright* v. *Walker* (1 C.M. & R. 221), I shall proceed to state the reasons which induce me to prefer to follow the Irish decisions.

It will be material to see – 1, what the law was as to the presumption of a lost grant when the Prescription Act was passed, and 2, whether that Act altered the law applicable to this doctrine.

Prescription at common law involved that the user began before the time of legal memory; and, it followed from that, none could prescribe except those whose interests were sufficiently permanent – a tenancy in fee was the only continuing estate, which could have an origin coeval with legal memory, and therefore neither tenant for life or for years could prescribe, and a prescription in a *que* estate should always be laid in the person who was seized of the fee-simple. The instability of other estates necessarily imported that they began within the memory of man. Hence prescription at common law was always defeated by proof of the commencement or origin of it. Still even in prescription at common law it was allowed only to supply the loss of a grant, and upon immemorial usage the law presumed an ancient grant and lawful beginning.

But in order to create a legal title which would be in harmony with long enjoyment it was in very early times established that proof of long enjoyment, though beginning within legal memory, would support a title under a fiction of lost grant, presumed from enjoyment, provided it were not by force, or secret, or by permission, and this period of enjoyment was ultimately adapted in time to the analogous period fixed by the statute 21 Jac. 1, as to lands, viz. twenty years. The principle was to quiet a possession had against another, and attribute to it for that purpose a lawful origin, the analogy of which would apply to a grant from termor to termor. No doubt the precedents of pleas of lost grant are all from owner in fee to owner in fee, which may be accounted for by their origin being at a time when the practice as to instructing a jury to presume a grant from twenty years' enjoyment, though the origin was fixed, had not become settled on this subject. However, the observations of Parke, B., in *Bright* v. *Walker* (1 C.M. & R. 211) leave the matter free from doubt. He says at p. 221: 'Before the statute this possession,' *i.e.* for twenty years, 'would indeed have been evidence to support a plea or claim by a non-existing grant from the termor in the *locus in quo* to the termor under whom the plaintiff claims, though such a claim was by no means of ordinary occurrence, and in practice the usual course was to state a grant by an owner in fee to an owner in fee, but' (he adds) 'since the statute such a qualified right we think is not given by an enjoyment for twenty years.'

The case of *Deeble* v. *Linehan* (12 I.C.L.R. 1) in this country decided before the Prescription Act in the Court of Error, and therefore binding on us, is an express authority to the same effect. There there had been an enjoyment of a watercourse from 1826, against occupiers of land, of which one Lyne was the reversioner. Lyne was himself sub-lessee in the second degree under the see of Cork, to which the fee belonged, and Lyne having evicted the lands and got into possession and obstructed the watercourse, it was held that there was evidence to go to the jury of a presumption, as distinguished from the actual execution of a grant, of the right, with the acquiescence of Lyne the reversioner; as he was the person who obstructed the watercourse it was necessary to establish the right against him. So in the case of *Wilson* v. *Stanley* (12 I.C.L.R. at p. 357), Pigot, C. B. in describing the objections to the reasoning in *Bright* v. *Walker* (1 C.M. & R. 211), says – 'It would apparently be consistent with the purpose disclosed in the preamble' (*i.e.* of the Act) 'that where prescription was not applicable (as where all the estates in the land were not bound) a presumption of a legal origin of the enjoyment in a grant from some competent party might still be made against the party against whom, before the Act, such presumption would have had the sanction of constant practice and established user.' It would seem to me, therefore, that before the Prescription Act a presumption of a lost grant might have been made between two termors.

In *Bright* v. *Walker* (1 C.M. & R. 211), every defence, including the defence of a way under a lost grant was open under the plea of not guilty, and there is no doubt that the Court decided that since the Act such a grant could not be available against anyone, unless it bound the fee – in other words, that the doctrine of lost grant was materially interfered with by the statute. Parke B., says – 'We have had considerable difficulty in coming to a conclusion on the point, but upon the fullest consideration we think that no title at all is gained by an user which does not give a valid title against all and permanently affect the see' – in that case the fee.

Lord St. Leonards, in his work on Real Property Statutes, referring to the question decided, says – 'It must be admitted that it is a question of great nicety.' It may well be, and I assume, that as regards prescriptive titles the shortening of the title under that head left applicable to the new period all the doctrines which applied to prescription at common law, so that such prescriptive title would still be defeated by showing that the alleged servient tenement was held under a lease for years, but I cannot see any reason for attributing to it an intention to interfere with the doctrine of presumption of a lost grant, so far as that existed before the Act. On the contrary there are opinions of several Judges distinctly opposed to any such idea. In *Angus* v. *Dalton* (3 Q.B.D. at pp. 118, 119), Cockburn, C.J., says – 'Does the statute apply to the presumption of a lost grant at all?' He observed that the Act professes to deal with the matter of prescription alone, and in proof of that refers to the preamble. He says further on – 'As regards the presumption of a lost deed as rights arising from supposed grant, although the statute may have introduced easements created by grant for the purpose of making such rights indefeasible by prescription at the end of forty years, it is difficult to see how the presumption arising from an enjoyment for twenty years can be in any way affected by the Act'; and he concludes, 'The only conclusion therefore at which I can arrive is that, as regards the effect of twenty years' user or enjoyment in the matter of easements by presumed grant, the law stands exactly as it did before the passing of the Act.'

The same view appears in the judgment of Mellish, L. J. in *Aynsley* v. *Glover* (I.R. 10 Ch. 255). He says 'The statute 2 & 3 Wm.4,c.71, has not, as I apprehend, taken away any of the modes of claiming easements which existed before the statute. Indeed, as the statute requires the twenty years or forty years (as the case may be), the enjoyment during which confers a right, to be the twenty years or forty years next immediately before some suit or action is brought with respect to the easement, there would be a variety of valuable easements which would be altogether destroyed if a plaintiff was not entitled to resort to the proof which he could have resorted to before the Act passed.' In some practice a plea of a right under a non-existing grant is still usual, and will be applicable, as already pointed out, where a plea of user under the statute would be defeated, *e.g.* if the evidence of user does not go down to the action, or where there has been an interruption of enjoyment within the prescribed statutory period: see *Lowe* v. *Carpenter* (6 Ex. 825), where the defendant was given liberty to amend by putting on the record a plea of non-existing grant.

In *Bright* v. *Walker* (1 C.M. & R. 211) the jury found that they would not presume any grant of a right of way by the bishop, the owner in fee, and the Court held, first, that enjoyment gave no right against the bishop, bringing in aid in support of that view section 8 – a view which, so far as resting on section 8 has been criticised, and even dissented from.

Now, as before the Prescription Act, possession for over twenty years would have been evidence to support a claim or plea of lost grant from termor to termor, nothing was wanted in the way of legislation to extend this if facilities were intended to be given for supporting title founded on enjoyment. But prescription stood on a different footing. It should have been from time immemorial, and titles by immemorial prescription were such as absolutely bound the fee. On principle it would seem that the shortening by the statute of the term of prescription would still leave its character the same, and, therefore it should be a user against the fee if you rest your claim on prescription.

But it seems strange that the making the prescriptive title easier by shortening the duration of the necessary user to twenty years should be held to take away the qualified right which existed before it, the presumed grant from termor to termor which I assume to have existed before. Parke, B., says, 'The statute nowhere contains any intimation that there may be different classes of rights – qualified and absolute – valid as to some and invalid as to others'(*Bright* v. *Walker*, 1 C.M. & R. 211). True, but it contains no contrary intimation, and I can conceive no reason for saying that a statute which was intended to facilitate title by enjoyment should be held to take away a class of title by enjoyment which existed before it and which from its qualified character does not interfere with, and is not inconsistent with, title by prescription in its old character from user from time immemorial against the fee, or its statutory character of twenty years against the fee.

It is admitted in the judgment that nothing in the statute prevents the operation of an actual grant from lessee to lessee though lost, if the proof of the loss be given, and secondary evidence of its contents adduced.

In the case of a presumed lost grant the jury always found its existence by presumption, being directed that they might so find, and I think I may add, even though they did not believe it was ever made, and it is difficult to see why presumed grant and actual grant should stand on a different footing for the confirming of the right. I assume that no circumstance is attached to the enjoyment which would have defeated the presumption before the statute, such as that it was secret or permissive, &c. Section 2 of the Prescription Act creates an additional mode of claiming easements, but that has not abolished the former modes, and if the mode of claiming an easement under a presumed though really non-existing grant survives the statute at all, why should it not survive with all its incidents, one of which was that a termor might be presumed to have granted to another, when he might have done so before?

To say that the statute has not created a new class of easements is one thing, but to say it has destroyed a previously existing kind is another. It is true that there are *dicta* that an easement for a limited time, or available only against a particular owner or occupier of the alleged servient tenement, could not have been created before the statute, or since it, save by a grant to be proved as a fact and not inferred by legal presumption.

But the case of *Deeble* v. *Linehan* (12 I.C.L.R. 1) is an express authority binding on us that before the statute a right to the enjoyment of a watercourse may be established under the doctrine of presumed lost grant against a tenant, when the fee is not bound. It cannot be disputed that there are observations made by the present Master of the Rolls in England in the case of *Wheaton* v. *Maple* ([1893] 3 Ch. 48) which are inconsistent with the views I have stated. The plaintiff claimed an easement of light. The defendants were lessees of the Crown under a lease expiring in 1914, which they surrendered on the 5th September, 1892, and the Crown agreed to grant them a new lease, and the defendants agreed to erect a new building which they proceeded to do. The plaintiff's house had been built in 1852, and he had enjoyed his lights against the Crown lessees for more than forty years before the action, which was brought in March, 1893, within three years after the surrender. The Court dealt with the case independently of the Prescription Act, and, secondly, under it. It was argued that a grant should be presumed from the lessee of the Crown, and the Master of the Rolls says that he is not aware of an authority for presuming as a matter of law a lost grant by a lessee for years in the case of ordinary easements, and he states that he was not prepared to introduce another fiction to support a claim to a novel prescriptive right, and further on he refers with approval to *Bright* v. *Walker* (1 C.M. & R. 211), as establishing that the Act had not created an easement for a limited time only, or available only against particular owners or occupiers of the servient tenement, and the observations of A.L. Smith, L.J. are to the same effect.

Apparently, the Master of the Rolls would, if *Beggan* v. *McDonald* (2 L.R. Ir. 560) were before him, have taken the same view as in that case Fitzgerald, B. did in the Court of Exchequer; but it seems to me obvious that these observations are inconsistent with two decisions which I consider binding on me, viz. *Deeble* v. *Linehan* (12 I.C.L.R. 1), and, in its result, *Beggan* v. *McDonald* (2 L.R. Ir. 560).

I have already stated the reasons which induce me to think that it makes no difference in the case that the right is claimed between two tenants holding under the same landlord. Such a right could not be established under the doctrine of prescription proper, as this would lead to a reversioner getting a right against himself; but if the qualified right can exist when it is claimed by one tenant against another, in the case of tenants holding under different landlords, the doctrine of *Gayford* v. *Moffat* (L.R. 4 Ch. 133) is not invaded by the qualified right being established in favour of one tenant against his co-tenant, both holding under the same landlord. It can exist admittedly in the case of an express grant in such a case.

We have to decide whether we will over-rule the view of the Court of Exchequer in *Timmons* v. *Hewitt* (22 L.R. Ir. 627). If we are bound in point of law to do so we must follow *Bright* v. *Walker* (1 C.M. & R. 211) in this respect; but such a result would be in this country extremely inconvenient, and I am glad to be able to come to a conclusion in accordance with the decision of the Court of Exchequer in *Timmons* v. *Hewitt* (22 L.R. Ir. 627) and the result of *O'Kane* v. *O'Kane* (30 L.R. Ir. 489) in the Court of Queen's Bench that a lost grant of a right to water or a right of way may still be presumed from enjoyment of twenty years between two tenants, whether holding under the same landlord or not.

Holmes L.J.:

We are confronted at the threshold of this case with the question whether it is legally possible to presume a lost grant of an easement by a lessee, where the only evidence is user as of right during twenty years of his term, and where it is practically certain that no such grant was actually made.

If this question had been raised before the Judge of Assize or the Queen's Bench Division, those Courts would doubtless have held that they were bound to follow the decision in *Timmons* v. *Hewitt* (22 L.R. Ir. 627); and during the discussion before us, I was under the impression that we were also in the fortunate position of having the point ruled for us by a coercive authority. I did not notice until after the argument had closed that the case of *Deeble* v. *Linehan* (12 I.C.L.R. 1), although it was heard in both the Common Pleas and the Exchequer Chamber after the Prescription Act had been applied to Ireland, had been tried some months before that event, and consequently was determined under the old law. I am not aware that the question has been since decided either in this Court, or in any Irish Court of co-ordinate jurisdiction. It was probably argued on the appeal in *Timmons* v. *Hewitt* (22 L.R. Ir. 627), but there is no full report of the judgment, and I understand it was decided on other grounds. This therefore is, as far as I know, the first occasion on which an appellate tribunal in this country is called on to form an opinion on a question the importance of which in relation to the enjoyment of landed property in Ireland it would be impossible to exaggerate.

There is I think, no room for doubt as to the state of the law before the Prescription Act. To establish a prescriptive right to an easement, it was necessary to show user extending over the full period of legal memory. Such user was inferred where it had continued as long as living memory went back; but once the beginning of the user was shown, prescription as the foundation of the alleged right failed. It was to meet the manifest inconvenience of this doctrine that the legal fiction of a lost grant was invented. The Courts laid down that the same kind of user, which, if it had existed during legal memory, would have established a right by prescription would, if it had continued for twenty years, afford grounds for presuming that it originated in a grant subsequently lost. It was never necessary to have evidence of a grant in fact. In most cases, it was recognized that the grant was purely imaginary. Formerly Judges were in the habit of advising juries that they were at liberty to presume it without actually directing them to do so; but in later times it has been laid down that it is the duty of juries to make the presumption, if they are satisfied that there has been what is called 'user as of right' for twenty years.

It was part of the common law doctrine of prescription that the fee must be bound. This indeed was almost a necessary consequence from the immemorial user, which was its foundation. User going beyond legal memory would have begun previous to all existing interests; and if it bound the lands at all, it must bind every estate therein.

The same consequence does not logically follow from the doctrine of lost grant. If an owner in fee from evidence of user be presumed to have made an imaginary deed binding the inheritance, which, if it were a real instrument, could not have existed thirty years ago, there seems to be no good reason for not presuming under similar circumstances that a lessee had made an imaginary deed binding his lease-hold interest. Accordingly we find it, as I believe, settled law that before the Prescription Act a non-existing grant by a termor might be presumed. *Deeble* v. *Linehan* (12 I.C.L.R. 1), a case in the Irish Exchequer Chamber, which, in my opinion, this Court is bound to follow, depends entirely upon this proposition; and the point actually decided therein was that the Judge who tried the case was wrong in telling the jury that they must find in order to give a verdict for the defendant that a deed had been actually executed by the termor as a matter of fact. In *Bright* v. *Walker* (1 C.M. & R. 211), Baron Parke said that, 'Before the statute this possession' *i.e.* possession of a right of way for twenty years during a lease, 'would have been evidence to support a plea or claim by a non-existing grant from the termor in the *locus in quo* to the termor under whom the plaintiff claims.'

As far as I am able to form an opinion this was accepted law in England as well as in Ireland. At all events, since *Deeble* v. *Linehan* (12 I.C.L.R. 1) no Irish Court can reject it, and we have only to consider whether it has been affected by the Prescription Act.

In answering this question, it is necessary to refer to the language of the Legislature and to subsequent judicial authority; but before doing so, I desire to point out again that the two methods of establishing a right to an easement to which I have referred, differ in their origin, character, and incidents. The first, to which the name of prescription was especially attached seems to have been coeval with our Common Law. Although the right that springs from it presupposes a grant, or something equivalent to a grant, the element of grant does not enter into its legal conception or definition. Its foundation is enjoyment from the time of King Richard the First, and when once established it is absolute and indefeasible. The second has been often referred to, and denounced as a modern instance of judge-made law; and it seems to have been first heard of during the eighteenth century. Its admitted object was to supply a legal basis for rights other than the common law doctrine of prescription; and those rights might have been conditional on the continuance, or limited to the duration, of particular estates in the lands over which they were to be exercised.

There was one feature common to both methods. Each depended on a fiction. It has been said by some Judges that it is scandalous to require a jury to find the loss of a deed that has never existed. To my mind, it is not more scandalous than to ask a jury to affirm a claim or defence founded on prescription at common law. In the majority of cases it is impossible that an easement could have been enjoyed for the full period of legal memory. Legal anomalies of this kind might, perhaps, be corrected, but there is no scandal involved in them. A fiction, recognised by and incorporated with the law, ceases to be a fiction. It then becomes the formal mode of expressing a reality; and it is this reality – such as user, as long as living memory goes back, or user for twenty years before action – that is affirmed by the jury. Still, in 1832 there was ample room for improvement in this branch of our jurisprudence. If the legislative reformer of that year had succeeded in defining, with precision, the extent and nature both of the user capable of conferring a right, and of the right capable of being thus conferred, he would have been a public benefactor. Perhaps his aim was less ambitious; but whatever was his object, the result has been of little practical value. It is, however, no part of my duty to criticise the Prescription Act as a whole. I am concerned with only one of the perplexities that followed it, namely whether it altered or modified the doctrine of lost grant, and I have only referred to its general character for the purpose of showing that it does not purport to be a code, and only deals with a comparatively small portion of the law of easements.

The title of the Act describes its object as 'shortening the time of prescription in certain cases.' Assuming that the word 'prescription' is used here generally and in its widest sense, the cases referred to do not include those of lost grant, for the period of user for twenty years, upon which this presumption was founded is the shortest period mentioned in the statute. The preamble refers exclusively to the inconvenience arising from the legal meaning attached to the expression, 'time immemorial,' whereby title to what has been long enjoyed is sometimes defeated by showing the commencement of such enjoyment. The first and second sections which, with the third, embody the substance of the new legislation, seem to be framed with the special object of leaving a litigant all the means which he therefore possessed of establishing title by user, while giving him, in certain cases additional facilities. Each of these sections relates to a 'claim which may be lawfully made at the common law by custom, prescription, or grant.' These words are not technically appropriate to a claim founded on the modern doctrine of lost grant, which Lord Blackburn says must have originated after 1623, and which he is unable to trace to an earlier date than 1761 (*Angus* v. *Dalton*, 6 App. Cas. 812). Moreover the enactments thus introduced – namely, that no such claim, as aforesaid, after there has been actual enjoyment of the matter claimed for thirty years under the first section, or twenty years under the second, shall be defeated or destroyed by showing only that it was first enjoyed prior to these respective periods – would not be relevant to a claim, one of the essential features of which was that it could not be defeated by merely showing that the user relied on began within legal memory, provided that it had continued for twenty years.

The inference from these provisions, as well as from the other sections, is that the statute is confined to amending the common law of prescription, and that this is done by giving a statutory mode of prescription *in addition* to the methods than existing for establishing rights by evidence of enjoyment. In *Aynsley* v. *Glover* (L.R. 10 Ch. App. 283), Mellish, L.J., having referred during the argument to the every day practise of pleading – 1, enjoyment for twenty years before action; 2, enjoyment for forty years before action; 3, enjoyment from time immemorial; and 4, lost grant – says in his judgment: 'The statute 2 & 3 Wm. 4, c. 71 has not, I apprehend, taken away any of the modes of claiming easements which existed before the statute.' If this be law (and it forms the *ratio decidendi* in the case), it is decisive of the question now under consideration in a Court bound by the decision in *Deeble* v. *Linehan* (12 I.C.L.R. 1).

There is, however, the earlier case of *Bright* v. *Walker* (1 C.M. & R. 211), an authority always referred to in this connexion, and one which cannot be ignored in any discussion of the subject. There the question of a right of way arose between two leaseholders under a bishop. I gather from Baron Parke's judgment that, prior to the Act, the owner of the tenement would, or might, in the same state of facts have been held entitled to the right claimed over the servient tenement during the residue of the lessee's interest therein; but the Court decided that as the law stood after the statute, such a claim could not be sustained. Now, in so far as the plaintiff's alleged right, based, be it observed, on an enjoyment for *twenty* years, depended on the recently passed Prescription Act, I am not to be understood as casting any doubt on this decision. To this extent it has been approved of by subsequent judicial critics, and can be supported by the very persuasive reasoning. But the judgment goes much further than this, for it lays down that the qualified right, which before the statute might have arisen from the presumption of a lost grant by one termor to the other, could no longer be inferred from enjoyment for twenty years. 'Since the statute,' says Baron Parke, 'such a qualified right is not given by an enjoyment for twenty years, for in the first place the statute is for shortening the time of prescription, and if the periods mentioned in it are to be deemed new times of prescription, it must have been intended that the enjoyment for these periods should give a good title against all, for titles by immemorial prescription are absolute and valid against all. They are such as absolutely bind the fee in the land, and in the next place the statute nowhere contains any intimation that there may be different classes of rights, qualified and absolute, valid as to some persons, and invalid as to others.'

Although the second of these propositions is inconsistent with the judgment of this Court in *Beggan* v. *McDonald* (2 L.R. Ir. 560), I am of opinion that if the passage quoted had been confined to a claim under the Prescription Act, based on twenty years' user, it is an accurate statement of the law; but there appears to me to be a manifest fallacy in assuming that the new terms of prescription were to supersede all the former methods by which rights could be acquired by user. I have already endeavoured to show that this is not the true construction of the statute, and I have pointed out that the contrary view was afterwards taken by Mellish, L.J., and James, L.J., in *Aynsley* v. *Glover* (L.R. 10 Ch. App. 283).

I now proceed to consider to what extent *Bright* v. *Walker* (1 C.M. & R. 211), in so far as it relates to the doctrine of lost grant, has been followed in subsequent practice and by later authority. The logical consequence of Baron Parke's judgment was to banish from our law the fiction of lost grant. But pleadings with which we have been long familiar show that this result has not followed; and it is – at least in Ireland – as often acted on at the present day as at any period of the century and a-half of its legal history.

There has been, I think, no subject in modern times that has received fuller judicial consideration than this question of lost grant in the case of *Angus* v. *Dalton* (3 Q.B.D. 85) – first in 1877 by three Judges in the Queen's Bench Division, again in 1878 by the Court of Appeal (4 Q.B.D. 162), consisting also of three members, and finally in 1881 by the House of Lords, assisted by seven Judges. The case gave rise to great difference of opinion, to which it is unnecessary for me to refer; but I have not been able to find in it the trace of suggestion that the doctrine of lost grant had been affected by the Prescription Act. It is referred to by every Judge. Its introduction into our jurisprudence by judicial authority at a comparatively recent time, is condemned by some of the Judges and defended by others; but all agree that it had taken a place in English law, from which it could only be removed by legislation. The very matter with which I am now dealing, although not strictly relevant to the points in controversy, is not passed over. Cockburn, C.J. (3 Q.B.D. p. 119), after using some of the arguments I have ventured to offer, says, 'The only conclusion, therefore, at which I can arrive, is that as regards the effect of twenty years' user in enjoyment in the matter of easements by presumed grant, the law stands exactly as it did before the passing of the Act.' Cotton, L. J. (4 Q.B.D. p. 185), referring to the means by which an easement is capable of being acquired independently of the Prescription Act says, 'They are either an enjoyment beyond living memory, from which in the absence of evidence to the contrary, enjoyment before the time of legal memory would be presumed, or by enjoyment for such a time as would be sufficient in the absence of evidence to the contrary to justify a presumption of a modern grant that has been lost.' Lord Blackburn is as distinct as Cockburn, C.J. (6 App. Cas. 814). He says, 'Lord Tenterden's Act, so far as it went, made that a direct bar, which was before only a bar by the intervention of a

Jury and the use of an artificial fiction of law. But it did not abolish the old doctrine; if it had, old rights even from time immemorial would have been put an end to by unity of occupation for the space of a year. But this is not done: see *Aynsley* v. *Glover* (L.R. 10 Ch. App. 283). I think the law, as far as regards this subject, is the same as it was before the Act was passed.'

The only authority subsequent to *Bright* v. *Walker* (1 C.M. & R 211) that adopts in its entirety the reasoning in that case, is *Wheaton* v. *Maple and Co.* ([1863] 3 Ch. 48, p. 63). Speaking of a lost grant from a lessee, Lindley, L.J. says, 'Although such a grant commensurate with his lease might be inferred as a fact, if there was evidence to justify the inference, there is no legal presumption as distinguished from an inference in fact, in favour of such grant.' The action was one for obstructing ancient lights, and in an earlier part of his judgment, the Lord Justice says in reply to the argument, that a grant of the easement ought to be presumed, 'no such grant is required to account for the state of things which exists, nor is any fiction or presumption necessary to render legal conduct of the plaintiff which would have been illegal without it. The plaintiff has simply been enjoying his own property as he was perfectly entitled to do.' This proposition got rid of the very foundation for the presumption; and when the Lord Justice afterwards referred to this branch of the law, he naturally deals with it somewhat perfunctorily. For example, he says, 'I am not aware of any authority for presuming as a matter of law, a lost grant by a lessee for years in the case of ordinary easements, and I am not prepared to introduce another fiction to support a claim to a novel prescriptive right.' He here seems to have forgotten that according to *Bright* v. *Walker* (1 C.M. & R. 211) itself, this was the law before the Prescription Act; and he had probably never heard of *Deeble* v. *Linehan* (12 I.C.L.R. 1), or *Timmons* v. *Hewitt* (22 L.R. Ir. 627). Indeed, much that is said both by him and the other Judges cannot, as far as I can see, be reconciled with *Beggan* v. *M'Donald* (2 L.R. Ir. 560) in this country, and this naturally weakens its authority as far as we are concerned.

I now turn from England to Ireland, where either from the mode in which land is held, or from the character of the people, there is probably more litigation about easements than in any other part of the empire. The current of decision in this country has not been favourable to the view taken in *Bright* v. *Walker* (1 C.M. & R. 211) of the effect of the Prescription Act upon the doctrine of lost grant. That statute became law in Ireland on the 1st January, 1859, and in 1861 the subject was exhaustively treated by Pigot, C. B., in *Wilson* v. *Stanley* (12 I.C.L.R. 346). He was evidently unable to follow the reasoning in *Bright* v. *Walker* (1 C.M. & R. 211), but sitting in a Court of co-ordinate jurisdiction, he felt bound by it as an authority. At the same time he criticised it very freely. He pointed out that while even in England the Prescription Act as therein expounded had materially abridged the rights previously resulting from long enjoyment, the change in the law would have a far more serious effect in Ireland in consequence of the different circumstances of the two countries. If this were so in 1861, how much more reason is there for repeating it now when through intervening legislation the ordinary Irish agricultural tenant, although presumably holding for a term of years, enjoys practically fixity of tenure?

The inconvenience and confusion that must have arisen in Ireland, if Baron Parke's propositions had been accepted, led to their being often disregarded in practice. Actions relating to easements were especially common on the circuit of which I was a member. They were generally small cases, which would not be disposed of in the Civil Bill Court under its extended jurisdiction; and although counsel asked for a direction on the authority of *Bright* v. *Walker* (1 C.M. & R. 211) where it applied, as it often did, I never remember it given. The verdict of the jury settled them, and the litigants had not the means or inclination to bring them further. *Love* v. *Taylor* (Unreported) was in its time a well-known case, famous for the sturdy spirit of both plaintiff and defendant. I held a brief in it at six Assizes, at three of which it was tried out; but the jury always disagreed. It was tried again on either one or two occasions after I had left the circuit, with the same result. It was known to counsel on both sides that unless the passages I have quoted from *Bright* v. *Walker* (1 C.M. & R. 211) were disregarded, there must be judgment for the plaintiff; but successive Judges, although strongly pressed for a direction at the plaintiff's risk, declined to give it. At length the late Lord Justice Barry announced his intention to direct, whereupon the parties, finding that the battle would be transferred to another field, agreed to refer the whole subject in dispute to arbitration, which resulted, I believe, in a bad award. I have often thought that if judges and counsel had felt any real confidence in the soundness of the law laid down in *Bright* v. *Walker* (1 C.M. & R. 211), this long and expensive litigation would have been avoided, or curtailed. At length the very point now before us arose in the Exchequer Division in *Timmons* v. *Hewitt* (22 L.R. Ir. 627), under somewhat peculiar circumstances. The action was tried by me; and the question of lost grant was not discussed at the trial. The experience of *Love* v. *Taylor* (Unreported) had led me, when hearing civil bill appeals, or sitting at *Nisi Prius*, to follow rigidly *Bright* v. *Walker* (1 C.M. & R. 211), except in such points as are plainly inconsistent with later authorities. The counsel were aware that I should have declined to frame a question for the jury based on the doctrine of lost grant, and this was probably involved in my refusal to have a finding as to user for twenty years. My first question was put in pursuance of the judgment in *Fahey* v. *Dwyer* (4 L.R. Ir. 271). My second, which is not connected with anything dealt with in *Bright* v. *Walker* (1 C.M. & R. 211), would have disposed of the case if an answer to it in the affirmative could have been supported. But for reasons to which I need not refer, it was very difficult to support an affirmative answer; and I have no doubt that it was this which led counsel to press so strongly, and the Court to consider so fully, the first question. It is clear that the Exchequer Division had the gravest doubt as to *Fahey* v. *Dwyer* (4 L.R. Ir. 271) doubts which I fully share; and hence it made use of the first finding to support a proposition which it laid down in the following terms: 'Where two parcels of land are held under a common landlord by tenancies, each of which has existed for upwards of twenty years, it is competent for the jury to infer, from twenty years' enjoyment as of right and without interruption of an easement claimed by the owner of one of the tenements over the land of the other tenement, a grant by deed from one tenant to the other tenant of such easement.' The Divisional Court made this principle a distinct ground for upholding the verdict, although it was also of opinion that the answer to the second question would have supported it. This Court, on appeal, upheld the judgment; but I believe, in doing so, it neither affirmed nor dissented from the proposition I have quoted.

In *Timmons* v. *Hewitt* (22 I.R. Ir. 627) there was no finding of a lost grant by the jury; and as I have already explained, there was no intention to put such a question. In the circumstances of that case, this point was merely formal. Having found the user, the jury ought to have presumed a lost grant, and would undoubtedly have done so, if the law had been explained to them. I have no doubt, however, that the proper course is to submit to the jury a definite question on the subject, as was done in the present case by the Chief Baron. The presumption is not 'juris et de jure'; and it may be rebutted. It ought probably to be made in all cases where the only relevant circumstance proved is uninterrupted user for twenty years before action; and it cannot be rebutted by merely showing that in point of fact no grant was executed. In most, if not in all, cases the fact that would rebut the presumption would also show that the 'user' had not been of right; but it is always desirable to have the question submitted to the jury in precise form, accompanied with such an explanation of the law as is appropriate to the circumstances of the case.

Precisely the same question as was decided in *Timmons* v. *Hewitt* (22 I.R. Ir. 627) arose in *O'Kane* v. *O'Kane* (20 L.R. Ir. 489). There the judgment of the Court was based on the course of the trial; but the Lord Chief Justice speaking apparently for his colleagues as well as himself, expresses a very definite opinion. He says: 'We do not formally decide whether one tenant can or cannot confer upon another such a right of way by grant; but we do not see why a tenant from year to year should not be able to grant such a right as long as his tenancy lasted. He could, in my opinion, confer by express grant such a right as long as his tenancy subsisted; and as to the doctrine of lost grant, I consider it a very useful one, and I think this case is an example of the salutary effects of this fiction of a lost grant by which a state of things which has existed uninterruptedly for a long series of years can be validated.' He then quotes with approbation a passage from the judgment of Lawson, J., in *Tennent* v. *Neill* (I.R. 5 C.L. p. 439), in which the Judge expresses his opinion that the doctrine is not to be limited, but on the contrary is to be extended by the Courts, and points out that it is not necessary that the jury should believe, as a matter of fact, that such grant was executed.

For the last ten years the law as thus expounded has been acted on without challenge in every Assize Court in Ireland, and even on the present occasion Serjeant Dodd told us that he argued against it with the greatest reluctance. Now that the point is to be decided for the first time by the Court of Appeal, we are obliged to make it the subject of independent consideration. While weighing with respectful deference the reasoning and opinions of the distinguished Judges who have proceeded us, and while recognizing the inconvenience and confusion that must follow from altering the rule that has been acted on by the Courts of first instance, I have sought to apply the touchstone of legal principle. Taking the law before the Prescription Act from Baron Parke's exposition of it in *Bright* v. *Walker* (1 C.M. 9 R. 211), and from the judgment of the Exchequer Chamber in *Deeble* v. *Linehan* (12 I.C.L.R. 1), I hold that in so far as that law relates to the presumption of a lost grant, it remains unchanged. I am compelled to reject Baron Parke's reasoning as founded on an assumption that cannot be supported, and as repugnant to the canons of construction applicable to statutes dealing with private rights. Such rights are not to be abridged by legislation relating to a different subject-matter, unless the intention to do so appears either expressly or by clear intendment, and I can find in the Prescription Act neither the one nor other. As before that statute, it was legally possible to presume from twenty years' user as of right the grant of an easement by a termor without further evidence, I hold that it is so still, and that therefore there was no objection in legal principle to the questions on this subject left to the jury.

Having arrived at this conclusion on the matter of law, I have little to say about the rest of the case. The Chief Baron, I have no doubt, framed the two questions relating to the grant to Pollock in the form in which they appear, in deference to the suggestion of the Lord Chief Justice in *O'Kane* v. *O'Kane* (30 L.R. Ir. 489), in which I concur; but he could not have forgotten to instruct the jury that the answer to them depended upon whether there had been user as of right for twenty years. In the case of an artificial watercourse, there could not be such user if the watercourse was in its nature temporary, or if it was not intended to be permanent. If this was not told the jury, it must have been because it was assumed on both sides that the channel made in 1861 was to be permanent. In the absence of any requisition on this subject or objection to the charge, the Court must assume that the findings on questions 1 and 2 negative the temporary theory. This being so, the verdict for the defendant must stand unless there was conclusive evidence that the present channel is temporary only. I have read the careful judgment of Mr. Justice Andrews; and it seems to me to proceed on an assumption which the jury was not bound to make. He says that although the new channel 'was an improvement to the old drain, it was clearly of as temporary a character as the old drain, and as open to alteration or abandonment at any time.' I could understand this if the old and new channels were field drains and nothing more; but it was open to the jury to take a different view of them. The change of channel originated doubtless in drainage improvement, but it is often part of a drainage scheme to change permanently the course of a natural stream. The water discharged by the channels was the outflow from springs which must reach the river in some way. The old course was probably permanent till it was altered; and I see no reason for the jury not concluding that the substituted one was also intended to be permanent. For some reason it was conceived that the change could not be made without the co-operation of Pollock, and it was carried out by both tenants acting in combination. The result was to send by means of a weir a portion of the water into Pollock's land, and to discharge the remainder into the river through Hanna's land. It is impossible now to ascertain the cause of this. Each party seemed to obtain a benefit and to incur the burden; and there is no reason for thinking that the arrangement was not regarded as final by both. The jury was the proper tribunal to decide; and this Court is not at liberty to disregard their verdict. As to the question of merger, I adopt the view of Kenny, J., and, like him, I do not think it necessary to consider the 8th and 9th sections of the Purchase of Land (Ireland) Act, 1885. These are provisions of great importance; but as they do not form the ground of my judgment, I have formed no final opinion as to their effect.

Having taken the foregoing view of the findings of the jury – a view which, until this morning, I believed was held by the majority of the Court – I could not have avoided considering the legal questions to which the greater part of my observations has been directed. I may, however, add that I should not have felt myself relieved from this duty, even if I had agreed with my brethren in their conclusion as to the evidence and verdict. It would, I think, have been a matter for regret if this Court had for the second time refrained from expressing its opinion upon such an important legal problem as that raised in *Timmons* v. *Hewitt* (22 L.R. Ir. 627), and in the present case.

Notes and Questions

1. After this survey of the Irish authorities by the Court of Appeal, how would you summarise the position regarding application of the law of prescription to leasehold property in Ireland? How does it compare with the position in England? *Cf.* the views of later judges, see, *e.g.*, *Flynn* v. *Harte* [1913] 2 I.R. 322; *Fallon* v. *Ennis* [1937] I.R. 549; *Tisdall* v. *McArthur & Co (Steel and Metal) Ltd., infra.*

2. See further on this complicated subject, *Irish Land Law*, para. 6.078 *et seq. Cf.* Delany, 'Lessees and Doctrine of Lost Grant' (1958) 74 L.Q.R. 82; Chua, 'Termors in Prescription in Ireland' (1964) 15 N.I.L.Q. 489.

TISDALL V. McARTHUR & CO. (STEEL AND METAL) LTD.
[1951] I.R 228; 84 I.L.T.R. 173 (Supreme Court)

The plaintiff was the occupier under a monthly tenancy of certain premises in the city of Dublin the ground floor portion of which was used by him for carrying on his business as merchant. The defendant company was the occupier of the adjoining premises, which were held by it for the unexpired residue of a term of years and were used by it for the purposes of its business. On one side the premises of the plaintiff were lighted through windows which looked on to a covered yard the property of the company. The roof of this yard was partly of glass and light after passing through this glass into the yard found its way through the windows into the premises of the plaintiff.

The company, in spite of a refusal of permission by both the plaintiff and the latter's landlord, proceeded through the second-named defendant, who was a builder, to block up the windows, thereby depriving the plaintiff of the light from the glass roof hitherto enjoyed by him. The plaintiff instituted proceedings claiming an injunction to restrain the company and the builder from so obstructing his light.

Upon the evidence the Court found that the two premises had been erected early in the nineteenth century, that until about the year 1900 the yard had been unroofed. Subsequent to the erection of the roof and for more than twenty years prior to the institution of the action the plaintiff's windows had been receiving a substantial quantity of light from the sky through that portion of the roof which was constructed of glass.

The company contended, firstly, that by reason of the light having to pass through a glass roof on the servient tenement before reaching the plaintiff's premises it did not constitute natural light and could not be the subject of prescription under s. 3 of the Prescription Act, 1832, and, secondly, that since the passing of that Act the doctrine of the presumption of a lost modern grant no longer applies to an easement of light. In view of the interesting discussion of the law by Kingsmill Moore J. at first instance, his judgment is reproduced as well as those of the Supreme Court discussing the appeal from him.

Kingsmill Moore J., after referring to the facts, continued as follows:

It is admitted that for over twenty years before the institution of these proceedings light from the sky had been passing through the glass portion of the roof of the company's yard and then entering the plaintiff's windows. If the glass portion of the roof were removed a person looking out from these windows would have an uninterrupted view of the sky through the aperture so caused. It is also admitted that the light was not enjoyed by virtue of any written consent or agreement. It would appear at first sight that the light so enjoyed by the plaintiff's was completely secured to him by s. 3 of the Prescription Act, which enacts 'that when the access and use of light to and for any dwelling house, workshop, or other building shall have been actually enjoyed therewith for the full period of twenty years without interruption, the right thereto shall be deemed absolute and indefeasible . . . unless it shall appear that the same was enjoyed by some consent or agreement expressly made or given for that purpose by deed or writing.' But it is argued for the defendants that the Prescription Act did not create any new kind of easement but only altered the methods of acquiring easements already recognized by law – a proposition which is not contested – and that English law has never recognised the possibilty of an easement of light other than light coming directly from the sky, and not transmitted through, or reflected by, any man-made medium. There is no direct authority either for or against the proposition that an easement cannot be acquired to light transmitted through glass. The plaintiff says that the reason for the absence of authority is that the right to such an easement has never been contested. The defendants explain the absence of authority by saying that such a right has never been asserted. I should have thought that the question must have arisen on many occasions. With the increasing congestion of cities it is often necessary to provide for the access of light through light wells or small courts and I believe that I have on more than one occasion seen such wells or courts covered with a glass roof. It is clear that the matter may become of importance but apparently it is left to me to decide it as a problem of first instance.

Various reasons were suggested why such a right could not exist. It was suggested that in some way the whole nature of light was altered by its passage through glass, a proposition which would seem to involve some novel theories in physics. Light may be reflected, refracted or blocked, but the light which emerges from one side of a pane of glass is essentially the light – or part of the light – which impinged on the other side. I dismiss all the arguments based on physics.

Next it was sought to draw an analogy between transmitted and reflected light and to show by authority that no easement could be acquired in reflected light. I am not convinced of the perfection of the analogy, nor do I think that the authorities establish the proposition for which they were quoted. In *Dent* v. *Auction Mart Co.* (L.R. 2 Eq. 238) the defendants were proposing to build in such a way as to obscure the ancient lights of the plaintiff, but they argued that by the use of white tiles the direct light, which had been obscured, could be adequately replaced by reflected light, The Vice-Chancellor held that this was no answer. 'A person who wishes to preserve his light has no power to compel his neighbour to preserve the tiles, or a mirror which might be better, or to keep them clean, nor has he covenants for these purposes that will run with the land, or affect persons who take without notice; and, therefore, it is quite preposterous to say, "Let us damage you, provided we apply such and such a remedy".' In *Staight* v. *Burn* (5 Ch. App. 163), a similar case, Giffard L.J. said: 'It has been suggested that if the wall is allowed to stand, although there will not be the same direct light, there will be a great amount of reflected light. The answer to that is, that the plaintiffs are entitled to have a light of the same nature as they have had.' In both these cases it was held that a servient owner could not at his own volition take away direct light from the dominant tenement and substitute reflected light. Giffard L.J. puts his decision on this ground that reflected light is a different light, from direct light. The Vice-Chancellor seems to prefer the ground that there would be no means, apart from covenant, to secure the continuance of the substituted light. The dominant owner by acquiescing in the obstruction of his original lighting would lose the right to it: and if the servient owner then proceeded to do away with the substituted light before a prescriptive right to its continuance had been acquired, the dominant owner would have no remedy except perhaps a covenant which might be worthless. Christian L.J. in *Mackey* v. *Scottish Widows Society* (I.R. 11 Eq. 541, at pp. 562 and 563) adopts, explains, and amplifies the judgment of the Vice-Chancellor and shows that the same reasoning applies to a case where a servient owner proposes to substitute for direct light, not reflected light, but another source of direct light.

The matter came very indirectly under notice in *Smith* v. *Evangelization Society (Incorporated) Trust* ([1933] 1 Ch. 515). The servient owner obstructed an ancient light in such a way as to amount to a nuisance in the physical state of facts which existed at the date of the obstruction: but the deprivation of light would not have been sufficient to amount to a nuisance if the dominant owner had not removed two skylights, which would have given sufficient light to the darkened room and which he was in a position to replace. Counsel for the dominant owner was forced to argue that light from a skylight was less beneficial and of a different nature from light coming through a side window and he cited Giffard L.J. to support his contention that the dominant owner could not be forced by the servient owner to put up with light of a different nature from the light which was being obstructed. To this argument the simple answer which was accepted by both Maugham J. and the Court of Appeal is that there is no essential difference between light coming through a skylight and light coming through a side window. But in the course of his judgment Maugham J., at p. 523, refers to the view of Giffard L.J., that direct light is of a different nature from reflected light, and says: 'I agree with the contention of counsel for the plaintiff that reflected light is altogether different from the light pointed to in s. 3 of the Prescription Act, 1832.' This remark appears to be purely *obiter*.

In the Court of Appeal Lawrence L.J. remarked, at p. 536, that 'there is no analogy between reflected light and the direct light coming through a skylight into the room.' He seems to accept that the Courts have drawn a clear distinction between reflected light and direct light, to the extent that a servient owner cannot say, as a justification for his obstruction of direct light, that there is sufficient reflected light left. He does not attempt to analyse the reasons for this conclusion.

These authorities clearly establish the proposition that a servient owner cannot justify an interference with light coming directly to the dominant tenement by showing that he has provided an equivalent amount of reflected light. They do not, in my opinion, establish the proposition that reflected light is of a radically different nature from direct light, or the proposition that an easement can never be acquired by prescription to reflected light; and they certainly do not establish the proposition that an easement cannot be acquired to direct light passing through a glass roof on a servient tenement to the windows of the dominant tenement.

Some assistance may, I think, be derived from *Duke of Norfolk* v. *Arbuthnot* (4 C.P.D. 290; on appeal, 5 C.P.D. 390). A chapel belonging to the Dukes of Norfolk, latterly used only as a burying-place for members of the family, was connected by an interior arch with Arundel Church. Originally, and for many centuries after the construction of the building, light came through the arch from the chapel to benefit the church, and from the church through the archway to benefit the chapel. Of latter years this mutually profitable access of light had been obstructed, first by an ornamental grill, and then by an altar and reredos, which almost completely occluded the light. Certain disharmony having arisen between the vicar and the Duke, the Duke finally built up the arch, and the vicar, after four years, took an action to compel the Duke to remove the obstruction. It was tried first before Lord Coleridge L.C.J., and on appeal before Bramwell L.J., Baggallay L.J. and Brett L.J. A number of reasons were given why the action could not succeed. It was said that the church was not a building within the Prescription Act; that it was doubtful whether, when an arch was built for the common benefit of the two buildings, there could be an enjoyment of light through it sufficient to found a legal right to its continuance; that there had been submission to the interruption for more than a year, and that the prior actions of the vicar and the parishioners had made the right negligible and worthless. Not one of the four judges however suggested that no right could be acquired to the light passing through the arch from the chapel because that light must first have entered the chapel through its own windows. It seems unlikely that so simple and obvious an answer to the plaintiff's claim would, if sound, have escaped the attention of four such eminent judges. The report does not expressly say that the windows in the chapel were glazed, but the chapel was apparently built at the same time as, and as part of, the church in the fourteenth or fifteenth centuries, and it is reasonable to assume that the windows were provided with glass.

To decide that in no case could a prescriptive right be acquired to light coming through a glass roof would, I think, be adverse to the interests of the community. A man having ancient lights looking into his neighbour's yard might be quite satisfied with the amount of light, reaching them through a glass roof erected over that yard by his neighbour, yet, if the defendant is right, he would, by acquiescing in its existence for a year, lose all rights under the Prescription Act and have to submit to a subsequent building up of his windows. To avoid such a result he would be forced to take proceedings to prevent his neighbour from building a roof to which he did not object and which would be of great value to his neighbour. In the absence of any authority or any convincing argument I refuse to be the first to lay down a proposition which seems to me not required by principle and calculated to work great inconvenience in practise.

When this case was opened I suggested that it might be possible to avoid deciding the question already considered. The physical facts point to the conclusion that for about a century after it was built the rere of Number 14 enjoyed the right of light coming to its windows over the yard of Number 15. From such user it seemed to me that I should assume a lost grant confirming the right to such light, a right which had already become absolute at the time when a roof was first placed over the yard. The light could not be lost by such acquiescence as would imply abandonment, or could be modified by agreement. But it seemed to me that consent to a partial obstruction of the light could not be construed as an abandonment of the right to receive such light as was left, or as an agreement to surrender all right to such light; and that the proper inference was that there had been an agreement to allow a roof to be put over the yard of Number 15 on condition that the central portion was of glass. Mr. Moloney, however, has tried to block this way of escape by arguing, first, that since the passing of the Prescription Act no right to any easement (or alternatively no right to an easement of light) can be claimed under the doctrine of lost grant; and, secondly, that, even if it is possible to support a claim on the basis of a lost grant, the presumption of lost grant should not prevail in the circumstances of this case. The view that a right to light cannot be claimed under the doctrine of a lost grant is not, as far as my researches have gone, accepted by any text-book, but Mr. Moloney has cited several authorities for his contention which must be examined.

He relied chiefly on *Tapling* v. *Jones* (11 H.L. Cas. 290), a decision of Lord Westbury, Lord Cranworth and Lord Chelmsford and so of the highest possible authority. The judgments certainly contain passages which, if read as being of universal application, and if necessary for the decision, seem at first to be entirely in favour of Mr. Moloney's contention. The Lord Chancellor, at p. 304, after reading s. 3 of the Prescription Act, says: 'Upon this section it is material to observe, with reference to the present appeal, that the right to what is called an ancient light now depends upon positive enactment. It is matter *juris positivi*, and does not require, and therefore ought not to be rested on, any presumption of grant or fiction of a license having been obtained from the adjoining proprietor. . . . This observation is natural, because I think it will be found that error in some decided cases has arisen from the fact of the Courts treating the right as originating in a presumed grant or license.' Lord Cranworth, at p. 310, says: 'The right to enjoy light through a window looking on a neighbour's land, on whatever foundation it may have rested previous to the passing of the 2 & 3 Will. 4, c. 71, depends now on the provisions of that statute.'

To understand this passage it is necessary to look at the pleadings and arguments in the case. The pleadings are set out succinctly at p. 291 and more fully in the report of the hearing before the Court of Common Pleas (11 C.B. (N.S.) 283). In the plaintiff's declaration there is not one word about a lost grant or common law prescription. He pleads only ancient lights, the right to access of light through such ancient lights, and obstruction by the defendant. In his arguments he appears to base his case on the Prescription Act, and it was to meet an argument based on the Prescription Act that counsel for the *defendant* (who was plaintiff in error) introduced considerations based on the law applicable to a claim preferred on the basis of a lost grant. The Attorney General begins his argument for the defendant (at p. 293) by saying: 'The theory of the law as to an easement or a servitude before the Prescription Act, was that some grant might be presumed as its origin. Evidence of uninterrupted user was taken to establish this presumption.' He goes on to argue: 'As the statute proceeds on the principle of a grant, the rules which would relate to a grant must be applied to the statutory confirmation of the easement.' This then was the only way in which the matter of a lost grant came before the Court – in an argument that the Prescription Act was a statutory mode of claiming an easement, incorporating the principles applicable to a claim on a lost grant, and that the law applicable to acquisition by lost grant should be considered applicable to a claim under the Prescription Act. This argument the Court decisively rejected. Lord Chelmsford was careful to use words which make this clear. At p. 318 he says: 'It was argued on behalf of the appellant that under this Act the right to the enjoyment of lights was still made to rest on the footing of a grant. I do not see what benefit his case would derive from the establishment of this position; but it appears to me to be contrary to the express words of the statute.' I think the passages which I have quoted from Lord Westbury and Lord Cranworth should be read as dealing only with the considerations which arise when a case is pleaded and argued on the Prescription Act. Lord Westbury prefaces his remarks by reading s. 3 and saying: '*Upon this section* it is material to observe. . . .' Lord Cranworth expresses himself more widely but his remarks may also have been intended to refer only to cases where the claim was rested on the Act, and to exclude from the consideration of such claims matters which would be relevant when considering claims based on the doctrine of lost grant. If, however, the learned Lords were purporting to lay down in general terms the proposition that, since the Prescription Act, no claim to light could be based on the doctrine of lost grant, their remarks were clearly *obiter*. In as far as the pleadings or arguments show no question of a claim based on lost grant arose. It is of interest to note that other opinions expressed by the learned Lords in this case, and not necessary for the decision, are now accepted as incorrect. All the judges assume that a period of twenty years' enjoyment of the access and use of light creates an absolute and indefeasible right immediately on the expiration of the period of twenty years. It is now accepted law that the effect of s. 4 is to make the period of twenty years not a period in gross but a period next before some action in which the claim or matter to which such period relates is brought in question: *Colls* v. *Home and Colonial Stores, Ltd.* ([1904] A.C. 179) per Lord MacNaghten at pp. 189, 190; *Hyman* v. *Van den Bergh* ([1908] 1 Ch. 167.) The mistaken view of the Judges on this latter point may well have affected their opinions on the question as to whether a claim may still be based on a lost grant. Such a claim need not be based on enjoyment for a period immediately before an action. One argument for holding that the Prescription Act was not meant to take away the right to plead a lost grant is that the Prescription Act, which was passed to facilitate the proof of claims by long user, should not be interpreted as abolishing a mode of proof which was in some ways more convenient, inasmuch as the user under a lost grant need not extend to the point of time immediately before an action.

In *Jordeson* v. *Sutton, Southcoates and Drypool Gas Co.* ([1898] 2 Ch. 614) an argument was advanced for the defendant company similar to that which had been advanced for the defendant in *Tapling* v. *Jones* (11 H.L. Cas. 290). It was contended that no right to light could be acquired against the company because it would have been incapable of granting any rights which might be inconsistent with its statutory duty. North J. met this contention by the same reply as was used by Lord Westbury – that the right to light *under the statute* did not require and should not be rested on any presumption of grant, but was a matter of positive enactment. This proposition is undoubted and the case does not advance in any way Mr. Moloney's argument. But Mr. Moloney does derive support from the words of Farwell L.J., at p. 176 of *Van den Bergh's Case* ([1908] 1 Ch. 167). That case was decided by all the Lords Justices on the ground that where it is sought to place reliance on a lost grant this ground of claim must be specially pleaded. But Farwell L.J. – carefully prefacing his remarks by the statement that he was speaking for himself alone – gave it as his opinion that, since the passing of the Prescription Act, no claim to light could be based on the doctrine of a lost grant, unless the period of user on which the claim to the lost grant was made was antecedent to the passing of the Act. The remarks of Farwell L.J. were individual and not necessary for the decision and, with great respect, I cannot take the same view as he does of *Tapling* v. *Jones* (11 H.L. Cas. 290), for the reasons I have already given. Nor can I accept his view as to the limited nature of the dictum of Mellish J. in *Aynsley* v. *Glover* (10 Ch. App. 283).

There seems to me abundant authority for the view that a claim to an easement by long user may be rested on the presumption of lost grant, and that this is so even in the case of an easement of light. *Aynsley* v. *Glover* (10 Ch. App. 283) was a case where a right to light was claimed in respect of two cottages which had been standing for seventy-five years at least. For twenty-six years before action brought there had been unity of possession of the dominant and servient tenements. This stood in the way of a claim under the Prescription Act. The Court held that the plaintiff was entitled to succeed on a claim of prescription from time immemorial, there being evidence that the cottages were standing for as long as living memory went back, and no positive evidence as to when they were built. Mellish L.J. says, at p. 284: 'It is everyday practice to plead, 1, enjoyment for twenty years before action; 2, enjoyment for forty years before action; 3, enjoyment from time immemorial; 4, a lost grant; and it has always been understood that a right may be supported on the third ground, although it may be incapable of being supported under the first or second. There are no negative words in the statute to take away rights existing independently of it.' And at p. 285 he says: 'The statute 2 & 3 Will. 4, c. 71, has not, as I apprehend, taken away any of the modes of claiming easements which existed before that statute. Indeed, as the statute requires the twenty years or forty years (as the case may be), the enjoyment during which confers a right, to be the twenty years or forty years next immediately before some suit or action is brought with respect to the easement, there would be a variety of valuable easements which would be altogether destroyed if a plaintiff were not entitled to resort to the proof which he could have resorted to before the Act passed.' He then proceeded to give judgment on the basis of immemorial prescription. James L.J. agreed with his decision. It seems to me that nothing could be plainer or more categorical than the words of Mellish L.J., and that he meant to indicate a considered opinion that a claim to light could still be grounded both on immemorial prescription and on the basis of a lost modern grant.

Wheaton v. *Maple & Co.* ([1893] 3 Ch. 48) was a case in which a claim to light was preferred both against a termor and the reversioner on the term, who was the Crown, and this claim was based both on the Prescription Act and on the basis of a lost grant. Kekewich J. held that as the Crown was not mentioned in s. 3 it was not bound by the provisions of the section, but that it was still possible to base a claim against the Crown on the basis of a lost modern grant. In the circumstances he refused to find a lost grant but allowed the claim against the termor under the Prescription Act. The Court of Appeal accepted that a right might be claimed against the Crown on the basis of a lost grant, but, with Mr. Justice Kekewich, refused to find the existence of such grant. The claim against the termor was also refused on the ground that, as the Crown who owned the fee was not bound, there could be no easement for a limited period prescribing against the termor only. This portion of the decision can no longer be regarded as good law in Ireland since the decision in *Hanna* v. *Pollock* ([1909] 2 I.R. 664).

In *Harris* v. *de Pinna* (33 Ch. D. 238) Chitty J., at pp. 245, 246, was clearly of opinion that a claim to light could be based upon a modern lost grant in a suitable case. This was also the view of Stirling J. in *Smith* v. *Baxter* ([1900] 2 Ch. 138, at p. 146), and of the judges in *Ecclesiastical Commissioners* v. *Kino* (14 Ch. D. 213).

I have already referred to *Duke of Norfolk* v. *Arbuthnot* (5 C.P.D. 390). There again all four judges who considered the case gave judgment on the basis that a claim to light might be based on the theory of lost modern grant, but refused to find such a grant in fact.

Few cases have been more elaborately considered or considered by more judges than *Dalton* v. *Angus* (3 Q.B.D. 85: 4 Q.B.D. 162; 6 App. Cas. 740). Lord Blackburn, at p. 814 of the House of Lords report, says, in reference to the plea of a lost modern grant: 'Lord Tenterden's Act (2 & 3 Will. 4, c. 71), so far as it went, made that a direct bar which was before only a bar by the intervention of a jury and the use of an artificial fiction of law. But it did not abolish the old doctrine; if it had, old rights even from time immemorial would have been put an end to by unity of occupation for the space of a year. But this was not done: see *Aynsley* v. *Glover* (10 Ch. App. 283). I think the law, as far as regards this subject, is the same as it was before that Act was passed.' The same opinion seems to have been held by Cockburn C. J. (3 Q.B.D., at p. 119), and by Cotton L.J. (4 Q.B.D. at p. 185). It is true that none of those eminent lawyers were referring specifically to an easement of light, but their language is wide enough to include, and was, I think, meant to include, all easements.

I turn next to Irish authority and here it is not necessary to go further than *Hanna* v. *Pollock* ([1900] 2 I.R. 664), where all the earlier cases were microscopically examined. It is true, as was pointed out by FitzGibbon L.J., that the views on law therein expressed are but legal exercitations for the decision in fact arrived at by the majority of the Court (Walker L.J. and FitzGibbon L.J.) concluded the matter of any view of the law. Nevertheless the members of the Court, realising the vital importance to the Irish community of the legal questions discussed, considered them with such care and expressed their views at such length and in such detail that those views, even if technically no more than dicta, have greater weight than many formal decisions. The immediate question in debate was whether one termor could acquire an easement of water against another termor by means of the presumption of a lost modern grant. Walker L.J. and Holmes L.J. held that he could, on proof of twenty years user. FitzGibbon dissented from this view though he admitted that such a right could be acquired between termors on proof of forty years' user, or in cases where there was additional evidence to show that the fee as well as the term was bound. Neither Holmes L.J. nor Walker L.J. deals specifically with the case of an easement to light and the last paragraph in the judgment of Walker L.J. if read by itself could lead to the conclusion that he meant to confine his remarks to easements of way and water. It is, however, clear, if the judgments are read carefully, that those judges were of opinion that the right to an easement of light could be founded on a presumption of a modern lost grant. The Lord Justice expressly disagrees with the views of the Master of the Rolls in *Wheaton* v. *Maple & Co.* ([1893] 3 Ch. 48), where he holds that a right to light as between two termors cannot be acquired on the assumption of lost modern grant, and considers these views to be inconsistent with *Deeble* v. *Linehan* (12 I.C.L.R. 1) and *Beggan* v. *Mcdonald* (2 L.R.I 560). He evidently considered that in *Wheaton* v. *Maple & Co.* ([1893] 3 Ch. 48) the Court should have held that an easement of light as between two termors could be upheld on the presumption of a lost modern grant, and if it can be upheld as between termors then *a fortiori* it can be upheld on the same presumption between owners in fee. Holmes L.J. is more specific. At p. 704 he says: – 'The inference from those provisions' (he is dealing with ss. 1 and 2 of the Prescription Act), '*as well as from the other sections*' (the italics are mine), 'is that the statute is confined to amending the common law of prescription, and that this is done by giving a statutory mode of prescription *in addition* to the methods then existing for establishing rights by evidence of enjoyment.' He goes on to quote with approval the words of Mellish L.J. in *Aynsley* v. *Glover* (10 Ch. App. 283), a case of light to which I have already referred.

So far as I know, since *Hanna* v. *Pollock* ([1900] 2 I.R. 664) it has always been considered to be settled law in Ireland that any easement can be properly claimed on the basis of a lost modern grant. The balance of English authority seems to me to point to the same conclusion and this also seems to be the view of all the text-book writers whom I have been able to consult. Mr. Combe in his 'Law of Light' tentatively supported a contrary view in regard to an easement of light, but he seems to have recanted, for he is the author of the article on easements in the second edition of Halsbury's Laws of England where it is stated that an easement of light can be sustained on the presumption of lost modern grant.

Accordingly I reject Mr. Moloney's contention that I am not legally entitled to find that a right to light for the windows of Number 14 had been acquired on the assumption of a lost grant from a competent grantor. The question remains whether I ought so to find. Apart from conclusions to be drawn from the physical nature of the premises I have no direct evidence of enjoyment, and though I know that Number 14 and Number 15 are now held in fee by different owners I have no evidence of the state of the titles at earlier periods.

Number 14 and Number 15 are structurally separate with no connecting door or way and present the appearance of having been two self-contained entities since the day they were built. As far as appearance goes there is nothing to suggest there was ever unity of possession. They are about 150 years old – Number 14 probably older than Number 15 – and the windows in question appear of the same age as the building. All the probabilities point to the conclusion that for something like a century the windows of Number 14 enjoyed light coming over the yard of Number 15. It is a fundamental principle of law that a legal origin should be presumed for privileges which have been long enjoyed if a legal origin is possible. The words of Lord Herschell in *Phillips* v. *Halliday* ([1891] AC. 228) have been quoted with approval by judge after judge. He says (at p. 231): '. . . When there has been long-continued possession in asserting a right, it is a well-settled principle of English law that the right should be presumed to have had a legal origin if such a legal origin was possible, and that the Courts will presume that those acts were done and those circumstances existed which were necessary to the creation of a valid title'; and in *Attorney General* v. *Simpson* ([1901] 2 Ch. 671, at p. 698), Farwell J. says: '. . . when the Court finds an open and uninterrupted enjoyment of property for a long period unexplained, *omnia praesumuntur rite esse acta*, and the Court will, if reasonably possible, find a lawful origin for the right in question.' The principle has been applied against the Crown, not merely a lost grant but a lost charter being assumed. A somewhat extreme example is to be found in *Warrick* v. *Queen's College, Oxford* (6 Ch. App, 728). If there were documentary evidence before me that at any time during the nineteenth century, and prior to the roofing of the yard of Number 15, Numbers 14 and 15 were held in fee by different owners for a period of twenty years I think I should be not only entitled but bound to find that the right to light for the windows of Number 14 over the yard of Number 15 had been acquired by a lost grant and was an absolute right when the yard was first covered, a date which would appear on the physical evidence to have been not before the conclusion of that century. 'But,' urges Mr. Moloney, 'such documentary evidence is not forthcoming. Numbers 14 and 15 may have been in one possession. Number 15 may have been held by a termor who would only make a grant binding his term. There may have been express permission given to the owner of Number 14 by the owner of Number 15. The owner of Number 14 may have built Number 15 and sold it without reserving any right to light.' Certain of those assumptions, even if correct, would not necessarily defeat the claim of the plaintiff: *Angus* v. *Dalton* (4 Q.B.D. 162), per Thesiger L. J., at pp. 172–175; per Cotton L. J. at p. 186. But I do not consider it is necessary to examine those hypothetical assumptions in detail. Mr. Moloney has made no attempt to give any evidence of them. He has not produced his title deeds which might be expected to show the nature of the possession of his client's predecessors in title of the two tenements. If I am in a position to find that for a period greatly in excess of twenty years light coming over one tenement was enjoyed by the windows of the other tenement and that those tenements were apparently in different possessions, the onus shifts to Mr. Moloney to show that these were facts which would prevent an easement of light from being acquired.

In English law possession is *prima facie* evidence of ownership. (See Pollock & Wright on Possession in the Common Law, at p. 25, r. 8.) All the physical facts are in favour of separate possession and so, in default of any evidence to the contrary, are evidence of separate ownership. I do not think it is my duty to speculate on unlikely possibilities. Accordingly I find that, at the time when the yard of Number 15 was first roofed, there was a complete and established right, founded on a lost grant, to the access of light to the plaintiff's windows in Number 14 over the yard of Number 15.

What assumption, then, is to be drawn from the apparent acquiescence of the owner of Number 14 in the roofing of the yard of Number 15? That there must have been a partial interference with his light is clear, but acquiescence in a partial interference does not warrant an assumption of complete abandonment. The most probable explanation is that the owner of Number 14 acquiesced in the roofing on the condition that a roof was constructed of such a nature as to give him as much light as he required. I cannot hold that by partially obscuring the light to the windows of Number 14 the owner of Number 15 acquired a right subsequently to obscure that light completely. I hold that there was no total abandonment of that light and (if it is necessary to go further) that there was an agreement to the erection of the roof on condition that it transmitted sufficient light for the purposes of Number 14 through a glazed portion thereof.

Accordingly I grant the injunctions claimed, both on the ground of trespass and of nuisance. I award to the plaintiff the costs of the motion to be treated as the trial of an action. As no damages have been claimed in addition to the injunction I cannot award damages in spite of the unduly assertive actions of the defendants.

[From this judgment the defendants appealed to the Supreme Court.]

Maguire C.J.:

This is an appeal from a judgment and order of Mr. Justice Kingsmill Moore granting to the plaintiff an order that the defendants, their contractors, servants and agents be restrained from building or continuing to build so as to be a nuisance to the plaintiff or so as to obstruct or diminish the access of light and air to the windows or any of them on the plaintiff's premises at Number 14 Merchant's Quay in the City of Dublin or so as to trespass on the window sills or any of them on the said premises.

The facts are somewhat unusual. The plaintiff is the tenant of the premises at Number 14 Merchant's Quay which consist of what was formerly a dwelling-house but which is now being used by the plaintiff for the purpose of his business. The premises in question were found by the trial Judge in his judgment to have been built in the period of Georgian building in the City of Dublin at an approximate date estimated by him to be about 150 years ago.

On one wall of the premises are certain windows which overlook portion of the first-named defendants' premises which was found by the learned trial Judge to have been at one time an open yard across which light flowed from the open sky to the side wall of the plaintiff's premises. At some time subsequently a roof was thrown across the open yard. Whether this roof when first erected completely cut off all the light from the sky is not clear, but it has been established in the case that for well over twenty years there has been a roof erected over the yard which consisted to a substantial degree of glass and it is unchallenged that during that period light has flowed from the sky through the glass portion of the roof on to the yard beneath and so to the plaintiff's windows.

The plaintiff does not deny that the amount of light now reaching his premises is less than that which must have reached them prior to the erection of the roof, and certain measurements taken on behalf of the defendant's suggest that only about one-tenth of the light from the sky has been able to reach the plaintiff's premises since the erection of the roof.

It seems to be clear that if the light which has been reaching the plaintiff's windows had come through an opening in the roof upon which there had been no glass the plaintiff's case would be established, but the defendants' claim that the interposition of glass between the sun and plaintiff's windows has altered the nature of the light flowing to the windows so as to deprive the plaintiff of any right in law to the enjoyment of a continuance of the flow of such light.

The defendants' suggestion is that the light is altered in its nature and legal attributes by refraction as a result of its passage through the glass portion of the roof and that a flow of refracted light cannot give rise, however long it may be enjoyed, to any legal right under the Prescription Act, 1832. I am not convinced, however, that light, through refracted, does not remain 'light' within the meaning of that Act.

We are told that the matter is free from authority and that may be so. Many reasons may be imagined for the lack of authority. Rarely would a dominant owner tolerate such a substantial interference with his light as was submitted to here. I have little doubt that, when the roof was first put up, an application for an injunction to remove it would have succeeded. The question here however is whether a right to the diminished light can be established.

There is one case, referred to by Mr. Justice Murnaghan in the course of the argument, namely, *Radcliffe* v. *The Duke of Portland* (3 Giff. 702), in which the effect of the interposition of glass on a stream of light was considered and the decision appears to be material in this case. In that case a glass screen was put up consisting of glass which distorted the light and prevented persons from seeing through it. An injunction was sought to compel its removal but the Court held that the screen did not materially interfere with the flow of light, though it appears that had the erection been made of a substance other than glass an injunction would have been granted.

In the present case the light which reached the plaintiff's windows in my opinion was 'light' within the meaning of s. 3 of the Prescription Act, and the plaintiff is accordingly entitled to a right to continue to enjoy so much of it as he has enjoyed for the past twenty years. Accordingly it is not necessary for me to consider the question which was argued at considerable length on this appeal, namely, whether a right to light can, since the passing of that Act, be properly claimed on the basis of the doctrine of modern lost grant.

The terms of the injunction in the order of the trial Judge are based both on a right to light and a right to air having been enjoyed by the plaintiff. No argument has been addressed to us on the right to air and we have not considered the matter.

In my opinion the appeal should be dismissed and the order of the Court below affirmed.

Murnaghan J.:

I agree.

This action was tried without pleadings but the plaintiff, who was a monthly tenant, claimed on the basis that his right to light had been enjoyed for some twenty-five years.

The three windows on the plaintiff's premises with which this action is concerned looked into a building which, formerly an open yard belonging to the defendant Company, has for a considerable period of time been roofed over with a roof composed largely of glass. The plaintiff has proved every requirement necessary to establish his right under the Prescription Act, subject to this, that the light which he enjoyed was light coming through this glass roof. The defendants contend that this fact takes the case outside the Prescription Act.

The argument put forward on behalf of the defendants is that the light has been 'interrupted' within the meaning of s. 3 of that Act. I do not think, however, that light passing through a clear pane of glass can be said to be 'interrupted,' and accordingly, even though it passed over the servient tenement in this manner, the light which in fact did reach the dominant tenement was not, in my opinion, interrupted. There is no proof in fact that a sensible amount of light was not enjoyed by the plaintiff throughout the statutory period.

The Duke of Portland's Case (3 Giff. 702) may, as we have been told, be the only reported decision in point, but it does appear to support the plaintiff's case. I see no reason why light passing through clear glass cannot be the subject of an easement.

The trial Judge gave judgment for the plaintiff on the alternative ground of having found a lost modern grant and his decision has been contested on this matter. If I am correct in holding that the light which the plaintiff in fact enjoyed can be the subject of an easement within the Prescription Act it becomes unnecessary to consider the application in this case of the doctrine of lost modern grant.

O'Byrne J.:

I have come to the same conclusion but I desire to base my decision entirely upon s. 3 of the Prescription Act, 1832, which provides that 'when the access and use of light to and for any dwelling-house, workshop, or other building, shall have been actually enjoyed therewith for the full period of twenty years without interruption, the right thereto shall be deemed absolute and indefeasible, any local usage or custom to the contrary notwithstanding, unless it shall appear that the same was enjoyed by some consent or agreement expressly made or given for that purpose by deed or writing'.

So far as this section is concerned only one question arises. The light in which the easement is claimed came to the plaintiff's building and has been actually enjoyed therewith for upwards of twenty years without interruption. The only question which arises is as to whether this constitutes 'the access and use of light' within the meaning of the section.

I agree with the contention of the appellants' counsel that the word 'light' is not used in the section in its widest sense and that it does not include artificial light. It must be natural light and therefore the question is whether the light which was enjoyed in this case was such natural light as comes within the section.

Counsel for the appellants say that the type of light enjoyed, being refracted light, was not the type of light contemplated by the section. I know very little about the refraction of light and no evidence was tendered upon the matter, but it is a matter of common knowledge that light does in fact pass through glass and I would have thought that such light, where it was natural light in its origin, continued to be natural light after it had passed through the glass.

In this case the glass, I assume, was put in the roof deliberately for the purpose of letting light through. After the roof with the glass was erected the plaintiff no longer enjoyed the same quantum of light as before, but he did enjoy some light. He claims only that reduced quantum of light.

In my opinion the light so enjoyed by him was 'light' within the meaning of the section, and the plaintiff has established his right to the continued use of same without interference. For this reason I am of opinion that the appeal should be dismissed.

Black J.:

So much time and learning have already expended on this case that I do not wish to add unnecessarily thereto.

I agree with the result arrived at by my colleagues and substantially for the same reasons.

I refrain from expressing any view upon the application of the doctrine of lost modern grant and I offer no opinion as to whether the plaintiff could complain if the defendants were to decline to clear away from the glass roof any dirt which might collect there and act as an obstruction to the passage of light to the windows, though I incline to the view that he could not, and that the plaintiff's right with regard to the maintenance of the flow of light through the roof would extend only to require the defendants not to commit any misfeasance in that regard and that mere non-feasance by the defendants would give no cause of action.

I fully agree with the view of Mr. Justice Murnaghan that the light which the plaintiff enjoyed, notwithstanding that it was light passing through glass, might give rise to the creation of an easement, but I do not agree that such light was enjoyed without interruption. I am of opinion that the light must have been at least slightly refracted and, therefore, interrupted, but I do not consider that that disposes of the matter in the defendants' favour, because in my view the word, 'light', as used in the section is capable of including light whether enjoyed without interruption or, as in this case, subject to a measure of interruption, by reason of its passing through glass. Accordingly, it seems to me that it is clear that the plaintiff has enjoyed light, albeit interrupted to the extent to which it passed through glass, for upwards of twenty years.

Notes and Questions
1. Do you agree with Kingsmill Moore J.'s view on the applicability of the doctrine of lost modern grant to a right of light? Why was the Supreme Court reluctant to deal with the point? See *Irish Land Law*, para. 6.099.
2. On the meaning of 'without interruption' see further, *Irish Land Law*, paras. 6.093–4.

II. RENTCHARGES

LAW OF PROPERTY (AMENDMENT) ACT, 1859
10. The Release from a Rentcharge of Part of the Hereditaments charged therewith shall not extinguish the whole Rentcharge, but shall operate only to bar the Right to recover any Part of the Rentcharge out of the Hereditaments released, without Prejudice nevertheless to the Rights of all Persons interested in the Hereditaments remaining unreleased, and not concurring in or confirming the Release.

CONVEYANCING ACT, 1881

5. – (1) Where land subject to any incumbrance, whether immediately payable or not, is sold by the Court, or out of Court, the Court may, if it thinks fit, on the application of any party to the sale, direct or allow payment into Court, in case of an annual sum charged on the land, or of a capital sum charged on a determinable interest in the land, of such amount as, when invested in Government securities, the Court considers will be sufficient, by means for that charge, and in any other case of capital money charged on the land, of the amount sufficient to meet the incumbrance and any interest due thereon; but in either case there shall also be paid into Court such additional amount as the Court considers will be sufficient to meet the contingency of further costs, expenses, and interest, and any other contingency, except depreciation of investments, not exceeding one-tenth part of the original amount to be paid in, unless the Court for special reason thinks fit to require a larger additional amount.

(2) Thereupon, the Court may, if it thinks fit, and either after or without any notice to the incumbrancer, as the Court thinks fit, declare the land to be freed from the incumbrance, and make any order for conveyance, or vesting order, proper for giving effect to the sale, and give directions for the retention and investment of the money in Court.

(3) After notice served on the persons interested in or entitled to the money or fund in Court, the Court may direct payment or transfer thereof to the persons entitled to receive or give a discharge for the same, and generally may give directions respecting the application or distribution of the capital or income thereof.

(4) This section applies to sales not completed at the commencement of this Act, and to sales thereafter made.

. . .

44. – (1) Where a person is entitled to receive out of any land, or out of the income of any land, any annual sum, payable half-yearly or otherwise, whether charged on the land or on the income of the land, and whether by way of rentcharge or otherwise, not being rent incident to a reverion, then, subject and without prejudice to all estates, interests, and rights having priority to the annual sum, the person entitled to receive the same shall have such remedies for recovering and compelling payment of the same as are described in this section, as far as those remedies might have been conferred by the instrument under which the annual sum arises, but not further.

(2) If at any time the annual sum or any part thereof is unpaid for twenty-one days next after the time appointed for any payment in respect thereof, the person entitled to receive the annual sum may enter into and distrain on the land charged or any part thereof, and dispose according to law of any distress found, to the intent that thereby or otherwise the annual sum and all arrears thereof, and all costs and expenses occasioned by non-payment thereof, may be fully paid.

(3) If at any time the annual sum or any part thereof is unpaid for forty days next after the time appointed for any payment in respect thereof, then, although no legal demand has been made for payment thereof, the person entitled to receive the annual sum may enter into possesion of and hold the land charged or any part thereof, and take the income thereof, until thereby or otherwise the annual sum and all arrears thereof due at the time of his entry, or afterwards becoming due during his continuance in possession, and all costs and expenses occasioned by nonpayment of the annual sum, are fully paid; and such possession when taken shall be without impeachment of waste.

(4) In the like case the person entitled to the annual charge, whether taking possession or not, may also by deed demise the land charged, or any part thereof,

to a trustee for a term of years, with or without impeachment of waste, on trust, by mortgage, or sale, or demise, for all or any part of the term, of the land charged, or of any part thereof, or by receipt of the income thereof, or by all or any of those means, or by any other reasonable means, to raise and pay the annual sum and all arrears thereof due or to become due, and all costs and expenses occasioned by non-payment of the annual sum, or incurred in compelling or obtaining payment thereof, or otherwise relating thereto, including the costs of the preparation and execution of the deed of demise, and the costs of the execution of the trusts of that deed; and the surplus, if any, of the money raised, or of the income received, under the trusts of that deed shall be paid to the person for the time being entitled to the land therein comprised in reversion immediately expectant on the term thereby created.

(5) This section applies only if and as far as a contrary intention is not expressed in the instrument under which the annual sum arises, and shall have effect subject to the terms of that instrument and to the provisions therein contained.

(6) This section applies only where that instrument comes into operation after the commencement of this Act.

CONVEYANCING ACT, 1911

1. On any application under section five of the Act of 1881 the court may, if it thinks fit, as respects any purchaser or vendor, dispense with the service of any notice which is, by section sixty-nine of that Act, required to be served on the purchaser or vendor.

RE McSWINEY AND HARNETT'S CONTRACT
[1921] 1 I.R. 178; 55 I.T.L.R. 127 (High Court)

The owner of land obtained in 1919 a court order permitting him to lodge in court a sum to meet an incumbrance on the title (a mortgage dated 1880), plus interest, together with an additional sum to meet the contingency of further costs and expenses. The owner later put the land up for sale and the investigation of the title showed up the mortgage. No demand for any money due under the mortgage nor any acknowledgment of the right to interest had been made or given since 1900. The owner of the land brought a summons asking that the money lodged in court be paid out to him.

Powell J.:

The money of which payment out is now asked was lodged under sect. 5 of the Conveyancing Act, 1881. The affidavit in support of the application for liberty to lodge it left open questions which might at another time be raised – questions as to whether the incumbrance was statute-barred or had been kept alive by payments or by acknowledgment of the debt. Mr. Walker argues that the order allowing payment into Court was a judgment in rem. But the words in sect. 5 do not refer to a particular incumbrance, but refer generally to 'any incumbrance.' 'With regard to these judgments in rem, they are conclusive as to nothing which might not have been in question or was not material'; 2 Smith's Leading Cases, p. 780. The question whether this was a charge which could be enforced, or which was barred, was not material to the order allowing payment into Court. These were matters not raised and not in question when I made the order under sect. 5. Therefore I have come to the conclusion that this order was not a judgment in rem, and that, while it is true that there was a charge in existence, the vendor is at liberty now to assert that the incumbrance was at the date of his application and still is statute-barred, and is entitled to have the money in Court paid out to him.

Note
See further on section 5 of the 1881 Act, *Irish Land Law*, para. 6.145.

Chapter 6
CO-OWNERSHIP

Various forms of co-ownershop have been recognised in Irish land law, but some like co-parcenary and tenancies by the entireties have ceased to have practical significance: see *Irish Land Law,* ch. 7. Joint tenancies and tenancies in common remain an every day occurrence, to which new twists are constantly being added by the courts and the legislature.

FAMILY HOME PROTECTION ACT, 1976
14. No stamp duty, land registration fee, Registry of Deeds fee or court fee shall be payable on any transaction creating a joint tenancy between spouses in respect of a family home where the home was immediately prior to such transaction owned by either spouse or by both spouses otherwise than as joint tenants.

Notes and Questions
1. What is the point of this provision and how effective is it in achieving its purpose? See *Irish Land Law,* Supp. (1975–80), p. 23.
2. On the 1976 Act generally, see *Irish Conveyancing Law,* para. 6.31 *et seq.*

KENNEDY AND LAWLER V. RYAN
[1938] I.R. 620 (High Court)

Certain freehold premises were conveyed to G.R. and S.R., his wife, 'to hold the said premises unto and to the use of the said G.R. and S.R. their and each of their heirs and assigns,' the entire purchase money being paid by G.R. A summons was brought to determine the proper construction of the conveyance.

Gavan Duffy J.:

I have to determine the construction of a deed, dated the 24th of August, 1934, whereby one, Thomas Gavigan, in consideration of a substantial sum of money, granted and conveyed the freehold house, No. 1 Fownes's Street in the City of Dublin, unto George Ryan and Sheila Ryan 'to hold the said premises unto and to the use of the said George Ryan and Sheila Ryan their and each of their heirs and assigns' and purported to assign unto the said George Ryan and Sheila Ryan the seven day licence (for liquor) attached to the premises 'to hold the same unto the said George Ryan and Sheila Ryan absolutely.'

The difficulty arises upon the words 'their and each of their heirs'; it would be unsafe to base any conclusion upon the presence of the word 'assigns': *Brookman* v. *Smith* ; since 1883, where real estate in conveyed to husband and wife jointly, they take as joint tenants and I am pressed by Mr. Vaughan Wilson to hold that Mr. and Mrs. Ryan, who were husband and wife, took the property as joint tenants in fee simple.

Mr. Ryan died on the 19th February, 1938, leaving the defendant, Sheila Ryan, his widow, and a son and daughter, infants, surviving; his will was proved by two plaintiffs and the defendant, who are his executors and trustees. If there was a joint tenancy in fee simple, Mrs. Ryan has the benefit of survivorship; the argument for her is that a grant to husband and wife, their and each of their heirs is a grant to the husband and wife and their heirs, so that the words 'and each of' are superfluous, and, as such, to be rejected in the construction of the deed. The plaintiffs, who are devisees in trust, reply that this contention ignores the clear implication of distinctness or plurality of interest in the expression 'their and each of their heirs,' by the force of which the property, or at least, the inheritance, can only have been held by the grantees as tenants in common.

Mr. Burke for the plaintiffs relies upon a series of cases recognising the partitive force of the word 'respective' to make a tenancy in common, cases in which a devise to A. and B. (being persons who could not marry) and their heirs respectively has been held to give a joint life estate to A. and B., with remainder to each of them as tenants in common after the death of the survivor. This principle has been applied to a devise to two nieces as joint tenants and their several and respective heirs and assigns for ever: *Doe* v. *Green* (4 M. & W. 229); and to a devise to trustees in trust for A., B. and C. and for their respective heirs, executors, administrators and assigns: *In re Atkinson* ([1982] 3 Ch. 52). A devise to two daughters and their issue or to two nieces to hold to them, their heirs and assigns for ever (without the word 'respective') produces the like result, since there are necessarily several inheritances: *Cook* v. *Cook* (2 Vern. 545); *Forrest* v. *Whiteway* (3 Ex. 367). The authority for this construction is to be found in s. 283 of Littleton's Tenures, in a passage to which I shall return; Littleton was dealing with an estate tail, but the principle is equally applicable to an estate in fee simple: *Doe* d., *Littlewood* v. *Green* (4 M. & W. 229, at p. 244). The cases have generally been decided upon wills, but Littleton was speaking of a deed at common law, and the principle was applied in England to a deed, of which we have scanty particulars, in *Wilkinson* v. *Spearman* (cited in 2 P. Wms. at p. 530 (see the correction in 1 De G. & Sm. at p. 79*n*), where the House of Lords appears reluctantly to have followed the same rule upon a grant to two daughters and the heirs of their bodies. The common law position is carefully examined by Brady L.C. in *Fleming* v. *Fleming* (5 Ir. Ch. R. 129), as to the indications necessary to create a tenancy in common; much less definite words have proved sufficient in a will or conveyence to uses. (See Bacon's Abridgement, tit. 'Joint Tenants' (F), and 2 Preston's Abstract, 471). But there is no doubt as to the applicability of Littleton's principle to cases as wide apart as grants at common law and wills, and so to what I may collect under one head as the various intermediate types of assurance.

Romilly M.R., applying Littleton's principle, in *Ex parte Tanner* (20 Beav. 374, at p. 377), says: 'If land were given to a man and woman, and the heirs of the bodies, this would be an estate in special tail, and the word 'respective,' if introduced before the word 'heirs', would have the effect of making the man and woman joint-tenants for life: it would be the same as if the gift were to a man and woman who could not marry and the heirs of their bodies.' This *obiter dictum* if it be correct, may apply to sever the inheritance in fee simple in the present case, provided that the limitation here be equivalent to a limitation to the respective heirs of the husband and the wife, a question which I shall have to examine. The reasoned statement in Littleton deserves to be quoted; that statement, as reproduced in Coke upon Littleton, par. 182*a*, reads:

'Also there may be some joyntenants, which may have a joynt estate, and be joyntenants for terme of their lives, and yet have severall inheritances. As if lands be given to two men and to the heires of their two bodies begotten, in this case the donees have a joynt estate for terme of their two lives, and yet they have severall inheritances . . . And the reason why they shall have severall inheritances is this, inasmuch as they cannot by any possibility have an heir between them ingendered, as a man and woman may have, &c. the law will that their estate and inheritance be such as is reasonable, according to the forme and effect of the words of the gift, and this is to the heires which the one shall beget of his body by any of his wives and to the heires which the other shall beget of his body by any of his wives, &c. so as it behoveth by necessitie of reason, that they have severall inheritances.'

Upon this passage my Lord Coke waxes eloquent on reason as the life of the law and earnestly recommends all students of law to apply their principal endeavour to attain thereunto. The doctrine of a joint tenancy for life is such a case, with a tenancy in common of the inheritance, is here expressly based on necessity, on the physical impossibility of the two men procreating a single heir. (*Cp* Fearne, 9th edn., p. 35; ch. I (V; 4,5).) That doctrine and the specific reason for it are, therefore, singularly inept where the first takers are husband and wife. Happily, however, I am relieved of the necessity for considering whether or not to be guided by Romilly M.R. by the fact that the words which I have to construe are different from those which he puts in his suppositious case.

The expression 'their and each of their heirs' is not unfamiliar in ill-drawn instruments. It may be (I know not) that in loose draftsmanship of this kind the writer uses the words elliptically and inaccurately to mean 'their heirs and the heirs of each of them'; if so, that is not what he has said. The grammatical meaning of the words, as Mr. Vaughan Wilson points out, is plainly 'the heirs of A. and B. and each of those heirs,' and so I see no reason whatever in this particular deed for rejecting the grammatical, in favour of a conjectural meaning. The draftsman may have had in mind, in designating each of the heirs, the immediate heir-at-law, without realising that, if land descends to co-parceners, they 'be but one heir to their ancestor,' but I cannot attribute any such notion to him if the word 'heirs' designates, not individual persons, but a class; on the latter view, on the assumption that he had any clear notion in his mind, when he wrote down 'each', he may have been contemplating each unit in the line of legal successors, but every such unit is already necessarily implied in the word 'heirs'. Now, it is, I think, beyond question that the word 'heirs' in the limitation in this deed is a word of limitation, not a word of puchase; if so, one word describes the whole class of legal successors, the whole line which is to succeed, so that the Rule in Shelley's Case must apply; the word does not designate the individual or particular person answering the description of heir at the death of the ancestor. (See Thomas's note to *Shelley's Case,* (Rep. 106*b*).) In my opinion, since the words 'their and each of their heirs' are directed to a class of successors in law, the mention of 'each' member of the class adds nothing (except a quite otiose emphasis) to the already complete category of 'their heirs' and therefore it involves a redundancy. If that conclusion be correct, the construction of the deed will not be altered by the insertion of this pleonasm, and it makes a joint tenancy in fee simple.

The apparent ambiguity in such expressions as 'to the right heirs of both' (husband and wife) and 'to the right heirs of Walter Read and Mary his wife forever' was resolved in the eighteenth century in such cases as *Row* v. *Quartley* (1 T.R. 630), and *Green* v. *King* (2 Wm. Bl. 1211), by reference to the principle that in law husband and wife are one person. That unity of husband and wife strengthens the argument (if any corroboration be needed) for a joint tenancy in fee simple in the present case, for the Married Women's Property Acts, while enabling a wife to take in joint tenancy with her husband: *Thornely* v. *Thornley* ([1893] 2 Ch. 229), have not abrogated existing principles of law in cases where their provisions do not apply, nor changed the wife's legal position in respect of property, except by altering the wife's right to property as between herself and her husband: *Butler* v. *Butler* (14 Q.B.D. 831, at p. 835); *In re Jupp; Jupp* v. *Buckwell* (39 C.D. 148, at pp. 152, 154), so that the Court should, I think, lean towards a construction which respects that unity. The purchase of the property, with the monies of the husband, if (as I gather) they were his, in the joint names of husband and wife and a resultant joint tenancy in fee simple are, of course, entirely consistent with the presumption of advancement in favour of the wife. And, if we have inherited the traditional tendency of Courts of Equity towards tenancies in common, that consideration can have no weight as against the intrinsic force of the words that I have to construe; as Page Wood V.C. put it in *Kenworthy* v. *Ward* (11 Hare 196, at p. 204), where the Court finds slight words of intention of severance, the course is to act upon them, but, where the words are such as to create a joint tenancy, that must be taken to be the real intent of the conveyance, unless there is some distinct ground to prevent its operation. I see no such ground here. Accordingly, I hold that, upon the true construction of the conveyance of the 24th August, 1934, the late George Ryan and his wife, the defendant Mrs. Sheila Ryan, acquired an estate in fee simple in joint tenancy. I may add that I have not required the infant heir of the late George Ryan to be made a party to this suit, because in my opinion such a proposition as that the heir takes by purchase under this deed would be quite unarguable.

Note
See further on words of severance, *Irish Land Law,* para. 7.15 *et seq.*

L'ESTRANGE V. L'ESTRANGE
[1902] 1 I.R. 467 (Court of Appeal)

A testator devised the residue of his property to trustees for the benefit of six of his children, with power to his said trustees to advance such sum or sums as they might think fit, for the education and advancement in life of his said children. Two of the children claimed the residuary legatees took as joint tenants, so that the survivors took the whole of the residue. Chatterton V.-C. held that they took as tenants in common, see [1902] 1 I.R. 372. An appeal was lodged.

Lord Ashbourne C.:

Notwithstanding the very clear and able arguments of Mr. Molony and Mr. Wilson, we are all of opinion that the decision appealed from is correct. It is a case turning on the construction of a will, and, like all cases of that class, its decision depends upon the intention of the testator, to be gathered from all the language he has used.

There is no doubt that at the commencement of this residuary bequest the testator used words which would, standing alone, make the children joint tenants, but then they are followed by this clause – 'With power to my said trustees to advance such sum or sums of money as they may think fit for the education and advancement in life of my said daughters and my son Patrick.' The question is – Does the use of these words indicate an intention on the part of the testator to cut down the joint tenancy to a tenancy in common? It is one of those clauses of which, when read for the first time, one may not see the full effect, or ascertain how far the words will go; but when read more closely it is clear that the words confer a power, not of maintenance, but of advancement. If a sum, perhaps of a considerable amount, were advanced for one child, it would be right to debit that sum against his or her share, and that debit could not be worked out if these children were joint tenants, and could not be done unless they were tenants in common.

We find abundant authority to support this view. In *Taggart* v. *Taggart* (1 Sch. & Lef. 88) Lord Redesdale said: 'Joint tenancy as a provision for the children of a marriage is an inconvenient mode of settlement, because during their minorities no use can be made of their portions for their advancement, as the joint tenancy cannot be severed.' These words express this view of the question in a clear and pointed manner, and that decision was referred to in *Mayn* v. *Mayn* (L.R. 5 Eq. 150). In the course of the argument counsel said: 'Amongst powers usually inserted in marriage settlements is certainly a power of advancement which, according to

Lord Redesdale's judgment in *Taggart* v. *Taggart* (1 Sch. & Lef. 88), is in itself a presumption against a joint tenancy having been intended.' In giving judgment Lord Hatherley approved of the decision in *Taggart* v. *Taggart* (1 Sch. & Lef. 88). He read the passage from Lord Redesdale's judgment to which I have referred, and he adopted the principle of that decision.

In the present case the testator has used words which show that the governing idea in his mind could only be satisfied by holding that these legatees took the property as tenants in common.

In my opinion the decision of the Vice-Chancellor is right, and should be affirmed, and the appeal dismissed, with costs.

FitzGibbon L.J.:

The incompatibility of a discretionary power of advancement with a joint tenancy is absolute, because the exercise of such a power implies the reduction of several parts of the property into possession. Mr. Molony tried to get out of it by contending that if an advancement was made, it was to be made out of cash, and cash might be produced by savings of income. But the words of the will, which describe the subject of the power, are not confined to cash. There was no obligation to save income, and advancement is usually made out of capital. The words of the testator are – 'the rest, residue, and remainder of my property, real, freehold, and chattel.' He did not confine the power to his cash, though cash must be provided before an advancement could be made. Before any advancement could be made the share of each child would have to be segregated, so that each advancement might be made, not out of the property as a whole, but only out of the share of the child who was to receive the advance. This negatives joint tenancy.

In my opinion the appeal is wholly unsustainable.

Holmes L.J.:

The only ground upon which it would be possible to support this appeal would be by showing that the advancement to the children, which, by the terms of the will, the trustees are given power to make, is an advancement out of the whole of the property, and not out of the share of it devised and bequeathed to the child to whom the advancement is made. But this is opposed to the idea of advancement, which is a term of legal art. It implies that it is to be made out of the property to which the person advanced is actually or contingently entitled. It is now well settled that where a devise or bequest is made to children, followed by a power of advancement, such a power is inconsistent with a joint tenancy in the children, and upon this principle we hold that they took as tenants in common.

Notes and Questions

Were there words of severance in this case? If not, upon what principle did the Court find a tenancy in common? See *Irish Land Law*, para. 7.15.

BYRNE V. BYRNE
Unreported (High Court) (1978 No. 402 Sp.)
(Judgment delivered 18th January, 1980)

The facts are as set out in the judgment.

McWilliam J.:

This summons has been brought for the administration of the estate of William Byrne, (hereinafter called the deceased) who died on 24th Novemeber 1976, but the only issue before me at the moment is as to the effect on a joint tenancy of an agreement by two joint tenants to sell property held by them as such.

The father of the deceased, also William Byrne (hereinafter called the testator), died on 2nd March 1971 having by his last will devised and bequeathed certain lands to the deceased and the defendant as joint tenants. Prior to the death of the testator, the deceased and the defendant had assisted the testator in the working of the lands and, as the testator was aged 78 when he died, they had probably done most of the work for some years previously. After the death of the testator they continued to work the lands although there is some conflict of evidence as to which of the two contributed the most effort, the defendant being also engaged in the business of erecting haysheds in the neighbourhood. I do not consider this slight conflict to be relevant as it appears that everything was considered as a joint venture and all earnings from whatever source were paid into joint accounts, both current and deposit, and no discussions took place about dividing either the land or the money. In 1976 the deceased and the defendant decided to sell the lands, probably due to the failing health of the deceased. A sale was negotiated to some relatives. Again, the evidence with regard to the negotiations does not appear to me to be relevant except that contracts dated 24th February 1976 for the sale of two portions of the lands to two different relatives were prepared and, as the lands had remained in the name of the testator, the contracts were entered into by the executors of the testator as vendors. The sales were not closed until 5th August 1977 nearly a year after the death of the deceased. The plaintiff is one of the next-of-kin of the deceased and claims that the joint tenancy on which the lands were held by the deceased and the defendant was severed by the sale of the lands before the death of the deceased. The defendant, who is occupying a difficult dual capacity, claims that the purchase money representing the lands passed to him in his personal capacity as surviving joint tenant.

A joint tenancy will be severed if any one of the joint tenants alienates his interest in the property, or a part of his interest, by an inter vivos transaction. See page 366 of Wylie's Irish Land Law where it is also stated that no severance occurs if all the joint tenants join together in the alienation. The case of *Hayes' Estate* [1920] 1 I.R. 207 is cited in support of this proposition.

The case is very strongly relied upon on behalf of the defendant. In it there had been a sale by joint tenants to the Congested Districts Board but the purchase price was represented by stock and not money. Two of the joint tenants having died the question arose as to whether the sale had effected a severance. Sir James Campbell said, at p. 209:

'There is no reason in the nature of things why joint tenants might not be equally well satisfied to hold the stock as joint property just in the same way as if, instead of selling the estate for money, they had exchanged it for other lands, or had received some other consideration instead of money for the purchase-price.'

O'Connor, L.J., said at p. 211:

'A mere agreement by persons entitled as joint tenants to convert their property from one species to another does not operate to work a severance.'

Each of the three judges refers to the lack of evidence of an intention to sever and it is clear that they considered that, in order to effect a severance, there must be evidence of an intention to do so.

I have also been referred to the case of *In re Denny; Stokes* v. *Denny* 177 L.T. 291. This was a case in which a third of the residue of an estate had been given to three sisters as joint tenants and, after the deaths of all three, a sum of £1,800 fell in and became subject to the gift. A question arose as to whether the joint tenancy had been severed or whether the whole of the £1,800 formed part of the estate of the survivor. With regard to severance Jenkins, J., said at p. 293:

'A joint tenancy may be served in three ways: in the first place, an act of any one of the persons interested operating upon his own share may create a severance as to that share. . . . Each one is at liberty to dispose of his own interest in such manner as to sever it from the joint fund – losing, of course, at the same time, his own right of survivorship. Secondly, a joint tenancy may be severed by mutual agreement. And, in the third place, there may be a severance by any course of dealing sufficient to intimate that the interests of all were mutually treated as constituting a tenancy in common.'

It seems to be clear from the judgments in these two cases that, on a sale by joint tenants, there must, in order to effect a severance, be evidence of an intention to do so, although, in the case of a sale for money, this would be clear if there was a division of the money between the joint tenants.

I accept also that the burden of proof lies on the person contending that there has been a severance.

There is not, in the present case, any evidence of any sort before me of an intention to sever the joint tenancy and the previous business arrangements between the joint tenants and the fact that they continued to live together after the sale until the deceased became ill and went to live with a sister in Carlingford suggest that no intention had been formed at all. Accordingly, I will declare that, at the date of the death of the deceased, the interest of the deceased and the defendant in the purchase money was as joint tenants.

Note
See further on severance of a joint tenancy, *Irish Land Law,* para. 7.22 *et seq.*

O'CONNELL V. HARRISON
[1927] I.R. 330 (High Court)

A number of shares in the N. bank were, on two separate occasions, purchased for the account of two sisters, M.W. and E.W., and were transferred into their joint names. No evidence was forthcoming as to the source of the money paid or the proportions in which it was contributed for either of the two purchases of these shares. M.W. and E.W. had, previous to the first purchase of shares, acquired their deceased father's business and his investments under his will, including *inter alia* a number of shares in the N. Bank. M.W. and E.W. subsequently entered into a deed whereby they agreed to carry on their father's business for their mutual benefit as tenants in common and not as joint tenants. E.W. married, and subsequently was declared (by her then name of E.H.) to be of unsound mind, and was taken under the care of the Court. Her sister, M.W., having been appointed to be Committee of her person and property, brought in a statement of facts, duly verified by affadavit, wherein she stated that one half of the entire holding of the shares in the N. bank was the property of her sister, E.H., and asked for an order to have these shares transferred into Court to the credit of the matter. The Lord Chancellor made an order declaring that these shares were the property of E.H., and ordering M.W. to sell them and lodge the proceeds to the credit of the matter, which M.W. did. M.W. retained the other half of the entire holding of the shares as her own. Both M.W. and E.H. died, and a question arose as to the nature of the ownership of the shares that they had purchased.

Kennedy C.J.:

The plaintiff, Sir John Robert O'Connell, has taken out this originating summons as executor of Margaret Wooloughan, deceased, claiming to have it determined that he is entitled, as such executor, to a sum of £651 18s., which was lodged by him to the credit of the matter of Elizabeth Harrison, a person of unsound mind, and separate credit of the residuary bequest contained in the will of Margaret

Wooloughan, pursuant to order in that matter, dated 2nd March, 1923. The summons is directed to Henry Harrison, personal representative of the said Elizabeth Harrison, who has died. The case was, by leave, listed before me, the question having arisen for determination upon the winding up of the matter of Elizabeth Harrison.

Margaret Wooloughan and Elizabeth Harrison (formerly Wooloughan) were sisters. Their father, James Wooloughan, prior to his death purchased fifteen shares in the National Bank, Ltd., which he caused to be transferred into the joint names of himself, the said Margaret Wooloughan, and the said Elizabeth Harrison (then Wooloughan).

James Wooloughan died on the 18th December, 1875, having made his will, dated the 3rd August, 1868, and a codicil, dated the 27th June, 1871, which was duly proved on the 12th May, 1876, by Margaret Wooloughan, the executrix therein named. The joint effect of the will and codicil was to give all the residue of the testator's property to his daughters, Margaret and Elizabeth, 'jointly in equal shares.'

On the 19th January, 1880, Messrs. M'Cann & Co., stockbrokers, purchased three shares in the National Bank, Ltd., for the account of Margaret Wooloughan and Elizabeth Wooloughan, and the shares were transferred to the joint names of the two sisters.

On the 15th November, 1880, a deed was made between Elizabeth Wooloughan of the one part, and executed by both sisters. The deed recited the will and codicil of James Wooloughan, and the probate, and that his residuary estate consisted of the shares and other property therein specified, including, amongst other things, fifteen shares in the National Bank. It was then recited that the sisters had agreed to carry on the testator's business of barm brewers for their equal mutual benefit as tenants in common, and not as joint tenants, and that they should also be possessed of, and interested in, the testator's shares and debentures equally as tenants in common, and not as joint tenants, and that Elizabeth should indemnify Margaret as executrix. The deed then contained on the part of Elizabeth Wooloughan a release and indemnity of Margaret Wooloughan as executrix in relation to the estate of James Wooloughan, deceased, followed by a declaration by both parties that they, Margaret Wooloughan and Elizabeth Wooloughan, should thenceforth 'be equally seised and possessed of the said brewery concerns, and carry on the business thereof for their mutual benefit, and hold and be possessed of the said shares equally as tenants in common, and not as joint tenants.' It was assumed in argument that the fifteen shares in the National Bank mentioned in this deed were the same fifteen shares which, as already stated, were purchased by the testator in the joint names of himself and his two daughters. The deed contains no mention of the three shares in the National Bank purchased in January, 1880.

In September, 1881, shares in the National Bank were subdivided into three shares each, so that the eighteen shares standing in the joint names of Margaret Wooloughan and Elizabeth Wooloughan became now fifty-four shares, standing in the same names.

On the 22nd February, 1882, Messrs. M'Cann & Co. purchased an additional ten shares in the National Bank for the account of the two sisters, and again the tranfer was taken into the two names of Margaret Wooloughan and Elizabeth Wooloughan, bringing the total holding in their names up to sixty-four shares, and they so remained until the year 1921. A slip of paper has been exhibited, upon which is a note or memorandum, alleged to be in the handwriting of Margaret Wooloughan, in these words and figures – '64 *National Bank, half Liz.*' No evidence has been given – I am told that none can be given – as to the source of the moneys paid, or the proportions in which contributed, for either of the purchases made through Messrs. M'Cann & Co., so that the matter must rest on inference from the other facts.

In the year 1920, Elizabeth Wooloughan, who had in the meantime married, and become a widow, was (by her then name of Elizabeth Harrison) declared to be of unsound mind, and incapable of managing her property, and was taken under the care of the Court. Margaret was appointed to be Committee of her person and property. Margaret Wooloughan brought in a statement of facts, duly verified by her affidavit, wherein she stated that the property of Elizabeth Harrison comprised (amongst other things) '32 *shares of* £10 *each in the National Bank, Limited,*' and asked to have an order made transferring them into Court to the credit of the matter.

On the 11th January, 1921, an order was made by the then Lord Chacellor confirming the report of the Registrar in Lunacy, which found that the property of the said Elizabeth Harrison consisted of (amongst other things) '32 *shares of* £10 *each in the National Bank, Ltd.*' and, the income of the patient being insufficient to pay the charges for her maintenance and treatment, amounting to £120 a year, the balance over and above £85 a year was charged on the corpus of her property; and it was thereby ordered that Margaret Hooloughan 'sell thirty-two shares of Ten Pounds each in the National Bank, Limited, the property of the said Elizabeth Harrison, now standing in the name of the said Margaret Wooloughan and lodge the proceeds of such sale . . . to the credit of this matter.' Pursuant to this order, the thirty-two shares – that is to say, one half of the joint holding of sixty-four shares – in the National Bank, Ltd., were sold by Margaret Wooloughan, and the proceeds of the sale lodged in Court to the general credit of the matter. The sale was effected by Margaret Wooloughan in a two-fold capacity – personally, as one of the persons in whose names the shares stood, and as Committee of the other of such persons.

Margaret Wooloughan died on the 20th August, 1922, having made a will, dated the 11th October, 1918, and two codicils, dated respectively the 29th October, 1918, and 22nd September, 1919, which will and codicils were duly proved on the 21st October, 1922, by the plaintifff, Sir John Robert O'Connell, one of the executors therein named. The effect of the dispositions made by the testatrix was that, after a number of legacies, her residuary estate was to be realised, and the income to be applied for the benefit of her sister, Elizabeth Harrison, during her life, and after her death the residue was to pass for certain charitable purposes.

On the 2nd March, 1923, an order was made by Molony C.J. in the lunacy matter, on the application of Mr. O'Shaughnessy, who had been appointed Committee in place of Margaret Wooloughan, deceased, and on hearing Sir John R. O'Connell, that Sir John R. O'Connell, as executor of Margaret Wooloughan, 'be at liberty to sell thirty-two shares in the National Bank, Ltd., now standing in the joint names of the said Margaret Wooloughan and Elizabeth Harrison' – that is to say, the residue of the original holding of sixty-four shares; and it was also ordered that he be at liberty to deduct from the proceeds of such sale the amount of his miscellaneous costs, as executor of Margaret Wooloughan, when taxed, and to lodge the balance of the proceeds of the sale in Court to the credit of the lunacy matter, 'and separate credit of the trusts of the residuary bequest contained in the will of Margaret Wooloughan.' The shares were accordingly sold, and the net proceeds, amounting to the sum of £651 18s., lodged to the credit mentioned in the order. This is the sum in question upon the present originating summons.

Elizabeth Harrison died on the 3rd December, 1924, having made her will, dated the 1st April, 1913, which was duly proved on the 24th July, 1925, by the defendant, Henry Harrison, as one of the next-of-kin, to whom letters of administration with the said will annexed were granted. By her will, Elizabeth Harrison bequeathed all her property to her sister, Margaret Wooloughan, who however, pre-deceased her.

The defendant, as personal representative of Elizabeth Harrison, the survivor of the two sisters, put forward a claim that the three shares in the National Bank purchased in January, 1880, and the ten shares purchased in February, 1882, were held by the sisters as joint tenants, with benefit of survivorship, on the ground that, as he suggested, they were purchased out of moneys contributed by them in equal shares. Thereupon, the plaintiff, as personal representative of Margaret Wooloughan, took out the present summons to have the question determined. The sum mentioned in the summons represents the proceeds of sale of thirty-two shares, after deducting costs, and the claim made would only affect so much of that sum as represents nine-and-a-half shares; the whole sixty-four shares having been equally divided, the thirty-two shares sold by Sir John O'Connell would include four-and-a-half of the nine shares, into which the three shares bought in January, 1880, were sub-divided, and five of the ten shares bought in February, 1882.

The first question which I have to determine is whether the shares bought by the two sisters in January, 1880, and February, 1882, were bought by them to be held jointly, with right of survivorship, or were to be held in equity upon a beneficial ownership in common, without right of survivorship. Mr. Walker, for the defendant, urged that it was to be assumed that the moneys invested in the purchase of the shares were contributed by the two sisters in equal shares, and that it was to be inferred from such equal contribution that the shares were acquired to be held in joint tenancy. He relied on the rules stated in White and Tudor's Leading Cases, 8th edition, vol. II, at p. 978 in the notes under the cases of *Lake* v. *Gibson* (1 Eq. Cas. Abr. 291), and *Lake* v. *Craddock* (3 P. Wms. 158).

I am ready to assume, with Mr. Walker, that the purchase money was contributed by these ladies in equal shares, but that assumption does not lead to a conclusive inference of joint tenancy if there is evidence which I may properly consider showing a contrary intention. In the case of *In re Jackson; Smith* v. *Sibthorpe* (34 Ch. D. 732), North J. went behind an express joint account clause in a mortgage upon which three sisters lent money derived by them as tenants in common under a brother's will, and he drew from the circumstances of the case as proved the inference that the three mortgagees were entitled to the moneys in equity as tenants in common. That was, however, a case of money lent on a mortgage, and a curious distinction has crept into the cases between the investment of moneys equally contributed upon a joint purchase of property and the investment of such moneys upon a joint loan. I may refer in passing to the editor's note to *Jackson* v. *Jackson* (9 Ves. 591), to the notes in White and Tudor's Leading Cases in Equity, vol. II, under *Lake* v. *Gibson* (1 Eq. Cas. Abr. 291), and *Lake* v. *Craddock* (3 P. Wms. 158), and to the case of *Steeds* v. *Steeds* (22 Q.B.D. 537).

Among the cases of joint purchase, there is a group of cases quite directly in point upon the question I have to determine. My only hesitation in mentioning them arises from the fact that they were not cited by counsel on either side in the course of the argument. I refer particularly to *Edwards* v. *Fashion* (Prec. Ch. 332); *Robinson* v. *Preston* (4 K. & J. 505); and *Bone* v. *Pollard* (24 Beav. 283), all of which have much in common with the present case on their facts, but especially *Robinson* v. *Preston* (4 K. & J. 505) – always bearing in mind that, as Romilly M.R. said, in *Bone* v. *Pollard* (25 Beav. 283), 'cases of this description must be determined by their own facts' – and these three cases are very helpful as to the facts which may be admitted into consideration in arriving at such a determination. For while, if the only fact be a joint purchase made out of moneys equally contributed, no equity intervenes to take the property out of joint tenancy, and reduce it to a tenancy in common; yet evidence is admissible as to the surrounding circumstances – as to the conduct of the parties whether before or after the purchase, and as to statements against interest (but not as to statements of intention) – and such evidence may establish the true intention of the joint purchasers to have been a purchase for a beneficial tenancy in common, and displace or rebut the inference of equal contribution of the purchase money standing alone: *Robinson* v. *Preston* (4 K. & J. 505); *Edwards* v. *Fashion* (Prec. Ch. 332); *Aveling* v. *Knipe* (19 Ves. 441). See also Phipson on Evidence, 4th edition, at p. 536.

Now let us see what evidence of the character I have mentioned is presented in the present case. In the first place, we find the two ladies acquiring a business concern and certain investments under their father's will, and, a few years later, entering into the deed of 15th November, 1880, for the purpose of affirming that the business, which they continued to carry on, and the investments were held by them beneficially as tenants in common, and not as joint tenants. This deed, at any rate, evinced a strong leaning against joint tenancy on the part of the sisters, then both unmarried, and apparently united in management of their business affairs. (See the observations of Page-Wood V.-C. upon the deed in *Robinson* v. *Preston* (4 K. & J. 505). It is highly probable, but not directly established in evidence, that the two investments now in question were acquired with monies arising from the properties with which the deed was concerned. Then, it is surely not without significance that the ladies purchased two further lots of shares in a company in which they already had a holding standing in their joint names, which they declared by deed to be a held in common, and not in joint tenancy, and that they took the transfers of the new parcels into the same names – as it were, enlarging their existing holding. It is to be remembered that one does not look to find a declaration of a tenancy in common in the transfer instrument of shares or stock in a company.

Nothing relevant then arises after the purchase in 1882 until the year 1920, when Margaret Wooloughan brought in her statement of facts as petitioner in the lunacy matter. There we find her declaration verified on oath, that one-half of the entire holding of shares in the National Bank was the property of her sister, Elizabeth, with her request to have them transferred into Court to the credit of the matter. This is evidence bearing on the question, admissible as evidence of conduct, and also as a declaration against interest affecting property standing in her own name. (See *Robinson* v. *Preston* (4 K. & J. 505), as to a statement made in a will by one of the joint owners.)

In the next place, we have the order of the Lord Chancellor, made at the instance of Margaret Wooloughan, declaring the thirty-two shares to be the property of Elizabeth Harrison, and ordering Margaret Wooloughan to sell them, and lodge the proceeds to the credit of the matter, which she did, as I have already mentioned, in her twofold capacity, while retaining the other thirty-two shares as her own – a fact not without special significance, having regard to the liability attaching to these bank shares.

There is also the slip of paper with the note by Margaret Wooloughan; but I leave it out of consideration. I will only say that it does not conflict with the conclusion at which I arrive otherwise.

From all the circumstances – from the business relations and attitude of mind disclosed by the deed of 15th November, 1880; from the conduct of Margaret Wooloughan in the lunacy matter, manifesting how she understood the transactions, and from her sworn statement of facts – I draw the inference, and I find as a fact established to my satisfaction, that the two parcels of shares in the National

Bank, even if purchased out of moneys contributed in equal amounts, and though transferred into their joint names, were held by Margaret Wooloughan and Elizabeth Harrison in equity as tenants in common.

The decision at which I have arrived as to the fact of tenancy in common disposes of the case, but I wish to add some observations on the other branch of the argument – namely, the contention that, assuming the shares were held in joint tenancy with right of survivorship, the joint tenancy was not severed by the action of the Court in the lunacy matter.

It is the long-settled policy and practice of the Court in the administration of lunatics' estates to preserve the character of their property as far as possible, and to avoid disturbing the succession to such property: *Attorney-General* v. *Ailesbury* (12 App. Cas. 672); Lunacy Regulation (Ireland) Act, 1871, sect. 67 (which deals only with lands). But that policy and practice is always subject to the paramount obligation and duty upon the Court to provide for the maintenance and care of the patient out of his means, and to manage and administer his property in his interest, and for his benefit. There can be no question, in my opinion, of the power of the Court under its statutory jurisdiction to sever such a joint tenancy in funds as the joint tenancy alleged in the present case, and to realise the patient's share, if the patient's interest and benefit so require. Did the patient's interest in the present case require that she should cease to be joint tenant with her sister of these bank shares (if such was the case)? In my opinion, imperatively so, and for two main reasons.

In the first place, Elizabeth Harrison had limited means. Her income was not sufficient to pay the annual charges of the institution in which she was being cared and maintained. An arrangement had to be made with the institution for payment of an annual sum on account, the balance to accumulate, and be charged on the corpus of her property; and, as a basis for such arrangement, it was necessary to make available as large a corpus as circumstances allowed. The paramount claim of the patient's care and maintenance required that her interest in the National Bank shares be realised, even if the result was to sever the joint tenancy, and defeat the right of succession.

In the second place, the shares were liable to heavy calls, from which liability it was essential that the patient's estate should be freed.

Add to these considerations of the patient's interest the fact that her sister, who was petitioner in the matter and Committee, was an actively concurring party in the division of the shares and the sale, and the contention put forward by the defendant here seems to me hopelessly untenable.

I am of opinion, therefore, that the sum of £651 18s., mentioned in the originating summons, is, all of it, the proper moneys of Margaret Wooloughan, deceased, and that the plaintiff is entitled to the declaration for which he prays.

Both parties will have their costs out of the fund; the plaintiff's costs as executor's costs.

Notes and Questions
1. Do you agree with Kennedy C.J.'s criticism of the distinction between the case of money advanced on joint purchase and money advanced on joint loan? See *Irish Land Law*, paras. 7.19 and 7.20.
2. See further on disabilities, ch. 16, *post*.

PARTITION ACT, 1868
1. This Act may be cited as The Partition Act, 1868.

2. In this Act the Term 'the Court' means the Court of Chancery in *England*, the Court of Chancery in *Ireland*, the Landed Estates Court in *Ireland*, and the Court of Chancery of the County Palatine of *Lancaster,* within their respective Jurisdictions.

3. In a Suit for Partition, where, if this Act had not been passed, a Decree for Partition might have been made, then if it appears to the Court that, by reason of the Nature of the Property to which the Suit relates, or of the Number of the Parties interested or presumptively interested therein, or of the Absence or Disability of some of those Parties, or of any other Circumstance, a Sale of the Property and a Distribution of the Proceeds would be more beneficial for the Parties interested than a Division of the Property between or among them, the Court may, if it thinks fit, on the Request of any of the Parties interested, and notwithstanding the Dissent or Disability of any others of them, direct a Sale of the Property accordingly, and may give all necessary or proper consequential Directions.

4. In a Suit for Partition, where, if this Act had not been passed, a Decree for Partition might have been made, then if the Party of Parties interested, individually or collectively, to the Extent of One Moiety or upwards in the Property to which the Suit relates, request the Court to direct a Sale of the Property and a Distribution of the Proceeds instead of a Division of the Property between or among the Parties interested, the Court shall, unless it sees good Reason to the contrary, direct a Sale of the Property accordingly, and give all necessary or proper consequential Directions.

5. In a Suit for Partition, where, if this Act had not been passed, a Decree for Partition might have been made, then if any Party interested in the Property to which the Suit relates requests the Court to direct a Sale of the Property and a Distribution of the Proceeds instead of a Division of the Property between or among the Parties interested, the Court may, if it thinks fit, unless the other Parties interested in the Property, or some of them, undertake to purchase the Share of the Party requesting a Sale, direct a Sale of the Property, and give all necessary or proper consequential Directions, and in case of such Undertaking being given by the Court may order a Valuation of the Share of the Party requesting a Sale in such Manner as the Court thinks fit, and may give all necessary or proper consequential Directions.

6. On any Sale under this Act the Court may, if it thinks fit, allow any of the Parties interested in the Property to bid at the Sale, on such Terms as Nonpayment of Deposit, or as to setting off or accounting for the Purchase Money or any Part thereof instead of paying the same, or as to any other Matters, as to the Court seem reasonable.

. . .

9. Any Person who, if this Act had not been passed, might have maintained a Suit for Partition may maintain such Suit against any One or more of the Parties interested, without serving the other or others (if any) of those Parties; and it shall not be competent to any Defendant in the Suit to object for Want of Parties; and at the hearing of the Cause the Court may direct such Inquiries as to the Nature of the Property, and the Persons interested therein, and other Matters, as it thinks necessary or proper with a view to an Order for Partition or Sale being made on further Consideration; but all Persons who, if this Act had not been passed, would have been necessary Parties to the Suit, shall be served with Notice of the Decree or Order on the Hearing, and after such Notice shall be bound.

PARTITION ACT, 1876

1. This Act may be cited as the Partition Act, 1876, and shall be read as one with the Partition Act, 1868.

2. This Act shall apply to actions pending at the time of the passing of this Act as well as to actions commenced after the passing thereof, and the term 'action' includes a suit, and term 'judgment' includes decree or order.

3. Where in an action for partition it appears to the court that notice of the judgment on the hearing of the cause cannot be served on all the persons on whom that notice is by the Partition Act, 1868, required to be served, or cannot be so served without expense disproportionate to the value of the property to which the action relates, the court may, if it thinks fit, on the request of any of the parties interested in the property, and notwithstanding the dissent or disability of any others of them, by order, dispense with that service on any person or class of persons specified in the order, and, instead thereof, may direct advertisements to be published at such times and in such manner as the court shall think fit, calling upon all persons claiming to be interested in such property who have not been so served to come in and establish their respective claims in respect thereof before the Judge in Chambers within a time to be thereby limited. After the expiration of the time so limited all persons who shall not have so come in and established such claims, whether they are within or without the jurisdiction of the court (including persons under any disability), shall be bound by the proceedings in the action as if on the day of the date of the order dispensing with service they had been served with notice of the judgment, service whereof is dispensed with; and thereupon the powers of the court under the Trustee Act, 1850, shall extend to their interests in the property to which the action relates as if they had been parties to the action; and the court may thereupon, if it shall think fit, direct a sale of the property and give all necessary or proper consequential directions.

4. Where an order is made under this Act dispensing with service of notice on any person or class of persons, and property is sold by order of the court, the following provisions shall have effect:

(1) The proceeds of sale shall be paid into court to abide the further order of the court:

(2) The court shall, by order, fix a time, at the expiration of which the proceeds will be distributed, and may from time to time, by further order, extend that time:

(3) The court shall direct such notices to be given by advertisements or otherwise as it thinks best adapted for notifying to any persons on whom service is dispensed with, who may not have previously come in and established their claims, the fact of the sale, the time of the intended distribution, and the time within which a claim to participate in the proceeds must be made:

(4) If at the expiration of the time so fixed or extended the interests of all the persons interested have not been ascertained, and it appears to the court that they cannot be ascertained, or cannot be ascertained without expense disproportionate to the value of the property or of the unascertained interests, the court shall distribute the proceeds in such manner as appears to the court to be most in accordance with the rights of the persons whose claims to participate in the proceeds have been established, whether all those persons are or are not before the court, and with such reservations (if any) as to the court may seem fit in favour of any other persons (whether ascertained or not) who may appear from the evidence before the court to have any primâ facie rights which ought to be so provided for, although such rights may not have been fully established, but to the exclusion of all other persons, and thereupon all such other persons shall by virtue of this Act be excluded from participation in those proceeds on the distribution thereof, but notwithstanding the distribution any excluded person may recover from any participating person any portion received by him of the share of the excluded person.

5. Where in an action for partition two or more sales are made, if any person who has by virtue of this Act been excluded fom participation in the proceeds of any of those sales establishes his claim to participate in the proceeds of a subsequent sale, the shares of the other persons interested in the proceeds of the subsequent sale shall abate to the extent (if any) to which they were increased by the non-participation of the excluded person in the proceeds of the previous sale, and shall to that extent be applied in or towards payment to that person of the share to which he would have been entitled in the proceeds of the previous sale if his claim thereto had been established in due time.

6. In an action for partition a request for sale may be made or an undertaking to purchase given on the part of a married woman, infant, person of unsound mind, or person under any other disability, by the next friend, guardian, committee in lunacy (if so authorised by order in lunacy), or other person authorised to act on behalf of the person under such disability, but the court shall not be bound to comply with any such request or undertaking on the part of an infant unless it appear that the sale or purchase will be for his benefit.

7. For the purposes of the Partition Act, 1868, and of this Act, an action for partition shall include an action for sale and distribution of the proceeds, and in an action for partition it shall be sufficient to claim a sale and distribution of the proceeds, and it shall not be necessary to claim a partition.

O'D V. O'D
Unreported (High Court) (1983 No.20 CA) (Judgment delivered
18th November, 1983)

The facts are set out in the judgment.

Murphy J:

This is an Appeal from the decision of the Learned President of the Circuit Court given on the 18th July, 1983.

The plaintiff and the defendant were married on the 16th March, 1978, and there was one child of the marriage, namely Robert, who was born on the 14th October, 1980.

The matrimonial home was situated at — and it is common case that the plaintiff and the defendant are each beneficially entitled to a moiety of the said premises.

Since July 1982 – following an application by the defendant for a Barring Order which was unsuccessful – the plaintiff has left the matrimonial home and not returned thereto.

The plaintiff is in some financial difficulty as he lost the executive position which he previously held due to the liquidation of his employer. He has recently started a new enterprise in conjunction with two other persons and whilst it is not yet established how successful or otherwise this business will be he has been drawing a sum of £137 per week by way of emoluments. In fact this figure may be misleading as, due to the fact that the plaintiff has been out of work for some time, he is subject to little or no tax on that income at the present time. Currently he is paying to his wife maintenance at the rate of £55 per week; £40 per week to his father in repayment of a loan to finance the new enterprise and there is due to the Building Society who advanced money in connection with the purchase of the premises in Portmarnock a weekly payment of £52. The payments to the Building Society are not currently being met. Obviously some adjustments can be made in the present arrangement. It would seem that the plaintiff's father might be prepared to postpone the repayment of the loan made by him and perhaps the Building Society loan could be spread over a longer period with a consequent reduction in the amount of the weekly payments. However whatever arrangements may be made it is clear that the present income of the plaintiff is inadequate to meet a reasonable claim for maintenance: the repayment of the mortgage and the repayment of the family loan as well as keeping the defendant and himself in the basic necessities of life. Perhaps surprisingly the defendant is confident that the plaintiff will in fact succeed in his present venture and that further monies will become available as a result. Obviously it would be impossible to rely on such a forecast as a basis on which to make a present decision. Indeed one would have to bear in mind the possibility that a more pessimistic view would be justified.

However the foregoing matters are not really in question at the present time except as a background to the plaintiff's claim that the matrimonial home should be sold and its true value – there was evidence to the effect that it is worth some £43,000 – obtained and out of that sum the Building Society Mortgage repaid and the balance invested in a more modest home for the benefit of the wife during her life and the child at least during its dependency. As the defendant is not agreeable to that course the plaintiff instituted these proceedings claiming a sale of the family home in lieu of partition pursuant to the Partition Acts 1868 to 1876. The learned President did not order a sale of the premises nor did he dispense with the consent of the defendant in the event of a sale taking place. Instead he made an order of partition and adjourned the balance of the proceedings with liberty to re-enter.

In the Appeal it was argued on behalf of the plaintiff that as a joint tenant he was entitled as of right to a decree for partition or that in any event it was a suit where, in the words of section 4 of the Partition Act 1868 'a decree for partition might have been made'. That being so, the argument ran, as the plaintiff was himself entitled to an interest in the property to the extent of one moiety that again he was entitled as of right to the sale of the property unless the Court saw good reason to the contrary. In support of those propositions the cases cited in Carson's Real Property Statutes second edition at page 745 were relied upon. These included *Pitt* v. *Jones* 5 Ch.App. 661; *Drinkwater* v. *Ratcliffe* L.R. 20 Eq. 530; *Pemberton* v. *Barnes* 6 Ch. App. 693; *Re Whitwell* 19 L.R.Ir. 45 and *Re Langdale* I.R. 5 Eq. 572.

This line of argument raises at once the nature and origins of the right to partition itself. There is no doubt that joint tenants and tenants in common did not have the right at common law to compel a partition. The position appears to have been otherwise in relation to co-parceners 'as their co-ownership was cast on them by the act of the law, and not by their own agreement, it was thought right that the perverseness of one should not prevent the other from obtaining a more beneficial method of enjoying the property' (see Williams' Real Property 23rd Edition page 243). The right of joint tenant to compel partition was conferred by a statute in 1542 entitled 'an Act for joint tenants' (33 Henry VIII c. 10). It may be significant to note that the final section to that Act contains a proviso which, translated into contemporary English reads as follows:-

'No such partition, nor severance hereafter to be made by a force of this Act, be nor shall be prejudicial or hurtful to any person or persons their heirs or successors, other than such which be parties or privy unto the said partition, their executors or assigns'.

With only minor amendments the Act of Henry VIII governed the law relating to partition until the passing of the 1868 Act. Prior to that Act there was not jurisdiction vested in the Courts to direct a sale of the property held in common and the only remedy was one of partition.

Authority can be found for the proposition that – during that period at any rate – a decree for partition in a suit instituted and entertained under the Court's equitable jurisdiction was regarded as a matter of right upon proof of title (see 2 Comyns Digest (fifth edition) page 762). In this context it is pertinent to note that in the case of *Turner* v. *Morgan* 8 Ves. 143 that Lord Eldon did partition a single house notwithstanding the very considerable inconvenience that this caused to the parties. In that case the Court enforced the award of the Commission of Perambulation notwithstanding the fact that exception was taken by the defendant on the ground that the Commission had allotted to the plaintiff the whole stack of chimneys, all the fireplaces, the only staircase in the house and all the conveniences in the yard. Certainly this is precedent and authority for the proposition that a single dwelling can be and has been partitioned. In addition the argument made in that case by Counsel on behalf of the plaintiff included a reference to a case of *Benson* in which another house was partitioned 'by actually building up a wall in the middle'.

However the existence of these precedents does not establish conclusively that the order is of right or that the Court is without discretion in the matter. In the Irish case of *North* v. *Guinan* Beatty's Chancery Cases 342 the partition of a house in College Green, Dublin, held under a lease was refused as the landlord might have obtained an injunction to restrain the parties from executing the partition by any act amounting to waste. It seems to me that decision represents both good law and good sense. In general principle the Court would not ordinarily make an order which would be futile. Clearly it is inappropriate to make an order directed to parties to proceedings when its execution depends upon the co-operation of parties not bound by the order.

Reference may also be found to a somewhat esoteric exception to the rule that a house may be partitioned in *Coke on Littleton* 31 B/321 (cited in *Turner* v. *Morgan*) where it is pointed out that a castle can not be partitioned as it may be necessary for the defence of the realm. That particular exception involves a recognition of the principle that partition could not be granted where this conflicted with the public good. Translated into contemporary and more mundane circumstances it would seem to follow that partition of the dwellinghouse should not be directed if, for example, this were to prejudice the proper planning of the area in which the building was located. That the granting of a decree of partition is not an absolute right of the parties or a mere formality of the Courts is made clear by the practice of the Courts as indicated in relation to the High Court in Seton on Decrees but more particularly of the Circuit Court in Babington's County Courts Practice and Carlton's book on the same topic. In the form provided in Babington for the primary order in a partition suit (see page 655) enquiries are directed as to the estate and shares of the parties; the existence of any agreement prohibiting sub-division; the availability of any necessary consent of the landlord; the existence of any charge in favour of the Commissioners of Public Works or the Land Commission and confirmation that all parties interested are before the Court before appointing a surveyor to prepare a map of the proposed division. This procedure seems to me to confirm that the making of the actual order of partition does and always did require the Court to be satisfied by evidence made available to it or to an officer of the Court that it was a proper case in which to make the particular order sought.

As no evidence was produced before the Court – and no inquiries sought or directed – I believe it would be inappropriate to make an absolute order for partition and on that ground alone I would set aside the order of the learned Citcuit Court Judge.

However the matter is even more complex than that. The plaintiff had relied on the 1542 Act as conferring on the Court the jurisdiction to decree partition. In fact that Act was repealed by the Statute Law Revision (Pre-Union Irish Statutes) Act 1962. That this change was not adverted to is not surprising as the error appears to have arisen some considerable time ago and has been perpetuated since. Claims for the partition of the matrimonial home are common indeed and in many if not most of such claims in the High Court the matter is entitled in various Acts including expressly the 1542 Statute.

Why precisely the 1542 Act was repealed in Ireland is not clear. How and why the Partition Action disappeared in England is explained by Overend J. in *Hill* v. *Maunsell-Eyre* [1944] I.R. 499 at 505 and elsewhere. Counsel in the present case were unable to offer any explanation for the repeal in this jurisdiction of the enabling statute. In the circumstances Counsel for the plaintiff/appellant was driven to argue that the jurisdiction to decree partition – as opposed to a sale in lieu of partition – is now exercisable in accordance with the principles which the authorities show as having been established by the decided cases in respect of the practice of the Courts of Chancery. Whilst it is clear that a separate equitable jurisdiction arose (see *Mundy* v. *Mundy* 2 Ves. Jnr. 122) I confess to having some hesitation in accepting that principles which evolved as to the manner in which a statutory jurisdiction might be exercised could survive the repeal of that statute. However, assuming rather than accepting that the jurisdiction of the Courts exists, it is of necessity part of the inherent *equitable* jurisdiction and as such it would seem to me necessarily subject in its exercise to the proper discretion of the Court. In my view the granting of an order of partition on the basis of the evidence available would be wholly inappropriate.

In fact the partition of the family home is not what the plaintiff/appellant seeks. That was the order granted by the learned President of the Circuit Court and it was from that order that the plaintiff/appellant now appeals. What he seeks is an order for sale in lieu of partition. Such an order will not be made where the Court sees good reason to the contrary. What constitutes good reason for the purposes of that section has been considered in a number of decided cases of some antiquity. A number of these cases are reviewed by Monroe J. in *Whitwell's Estate* 19 L.R.Ir. 45. Monroe J. himself appears to have been satisfied that it would be inappropriate to order a sale if it was likely to prove abortive or if it would have involved the parties in accepting a significant sacrifice.

In my view what constitutes good reason at the present time would properly have regard to the rights of the parties under the Family Home Protection Act 1976. Needless to say the old authorites had never considered this problem or anything remotely akin to it. Apart from the fact that the rights conferred by the Family Home Protection Act 1976 in this respect were novel it must be remembered that the Partition Acts preceded the Married Women's Property Act 1882 so that over the centuries and in particular in pursuance of the 1542 Act a partition would have been effected by a husband on behalf and in the right of his wife.

It was argued that the 1976 Act did not repeal the Partition Acts or any of them. It was contended, therefore, that if a proper case for a partition was made out and an appropriate order granted that this dispensed with the necessity for procuring the consent of a spouse under that Act. In my view that argument is not well founded. There is no reason to suppose that an order for partition or sale in lieu thereof was intended to overreach the provisions of the Family Home Protection Act. Even if an order were made under the 1868 Act it must be recognised that this would not consititute a parliamentary conveyance and would not of itself correct imperfections in title. It would only be the fact that the spouses themselves joined in the conveyance that would overcome the need to procure their consent and it seems to me unthinkable that the Court would direct a conveyance to be made under the 1868 Act without having regard to the right of a spouse to withold his or her consent and indeed the express duty imposed on the Court not to dispense with consent without taking into account all the relevant circumstances including in particular those specified in sub-section 2 of Section 4 of the 1976 Act.

Counsel on behalf of the plaintiff/appellant recognised that this argument entailed acceptance of the proposition that a spouse who had no beneficial interest in the Family Home enjoyed the statutory veto on the sale thereof where another spouse who had a beneficial interest, however miniscule, could have his or her statutory veto overborne by a sale directed under the Partition Acts. In my view a Court would be justified in concluding in the circumstances of present times, under our Constitution and of the rights conferred by the Family Home Protection Act that the loss of the statutory veto represented good reasons within the meaning of Section 4 of the Partition Act 1868. This interpretation of the relevant legislation is greatly facilitated by the fact that a contrary conclusion would lead to a result which is unjust to the point of absurdity.

In these circumstances I refuse the Appellant/plaintiff's claim to an order for sale in lieu of partition and I am satisfied that in the circumstances of the case – even if jurisdiction to order partition subsists – that an order would not properly be made in the present case. Accordingly I would set aside so much of the order of the learned President as decreed partition.

Notes and Questions

1. Do you share Murphy J.'s puzzlement about the repeal of the 1542 Act? Note that the English equivalent legislation has also been repealed, but then all the Partition Acts were replaced in England by provisions in the 1925 legistation which have no equivalent in Ireland, see Megarry and Wade, *The Law of Real Property* (4th ed. 1975), p. 428. On the other hand, the 1542 Act has also been repealed in Northern Ireland, see *Irish Land Law,* para. 7.35. Note, however, the wording of the 1868 Act, in particular, the first five words of ss.2–4 – 'In a suit for Partition' – which assume the existence of jurisdiction. That Act remains in force: does this mean that the repeal of the earlier Act should not be taken to affect that jurisdiction?

2. See also *C.H. v. D.G.O'P.* (1978) 109 I.L.T.R. 9.

JONES V. READ
(1876) I.R. 10 C.L. 315 (Exchequer)

In an action for trespass to a wall of the plaintiff, the Defendant pleaded a traverse of the property and of the doing of the acts; evidence was given of a number of facts, some of which, *per se,* afforded evidence of the possession of the entire wall being in the plaintiff, and others of the possession of the entire wall being in the defendant; the act of trespass was the taking down of a portion of the wall and the building on it, so lowered, of the roof of the defendant's store; damages were assessed by the jury rather for the taking down of the wall than for the building of the new roof on it when taken down. The defendant appealed.

Palles, C.B.:

The principal question reserved at the trial was whether there was evidence to go to the jury that the plaintiff and the defendant were tenants in common of the back wall. We are of opinion that there was. There was evidence that the wall was the wall of the plaintiff. That has been admitted in the course of the argument. Again, there was evidence – and undoubtedly very strong evidence, taken by itself – that the wall was the wall of the defendant. The facts relied upon by the contending parties, as establishing their respective cases, are not inconsistent. Every material fact relied upon by the plaintiff is consistent with every material fact relied upon by the defendant. The title, at the time the wall was built, to the land upon which it stands was not shown. There was no evidence whether, at that time, the land was the property of one owner or whether the titles to the plots, now respectively the plaintiff's and the defendant's, had previously become separate. The question is, what inference could, under the circumstances, be drawn by a jury. In the consideration of this question cases such as *Matts* v. *Hawkins* (5 Taunt. 20) have no application. In all cases of that class the title to the land upon which the wall was built was found, and, as a matter of law, the property in the wall followed the property in the land upon which it stood. The next class of case relied upon was that of which *Richards* v. *Rose* (9 Ex. 218) is the type. These cases, we are told, coerce us to hold that one person, and one only, has the property in the entire wall; and that the right, if any, of the other must be in the nature of an easement. Such an argument assumes the question it is intended to establish. In *Richards* v. *Rose* (9 Ex. 218) the deeds, under which the plaintiff and the defendant held, were produced; and, upon the construction of that under which the first purchaser claimed, the Court held that the property in the entire wall passed to him. The determination of the right of the second purchaser was therefore necessarily based upon the hypothesis that the sole property in the wall was in his neighbour. These cases being inapplicable, the question is simple, and one which could well be disposed of irrespective of authority. Evidence of a number of consistent facts some of which, *per se,* afford evidence of the possession of the entire wall being in the plaintiff, and others of which taken by themselves lead to the inference of possession of the same entire wall in the defendant, amount to evidence of a possession in common, and, therefore, of a tenancy in common. If, however, authority were required, we have it in *Wiltshire* v. *Sidford* (1 Man. & Ryl. 404), the judgment of Mr. Justice Bayley in which is decisive on the question.

For the purpose of the next objection we must assume that the parties were tenants in common. I apprehend that there can be no doubt that if a wall, of which two persons are tenants in common, be in a ruinous and dangerous state, either of the co-tenants has a right to take it down for the purpose and with intention of rebuilding it. But the present is not the case of a taking down 'with an intention to rebuild.' Mr. Exham's attention was called during the trial to the omission of these words in the questions he desired to be submitted to the jury, and he declined to insert them. Indeed the facts proved left him no alternative, as I should have been obliged to direct the jury that if the defendant's intention when he took down the wall was to build in the way in which the wall has since in fact been erected, it would not amount to an intention to rebuild. There was clear evidence of ouster by the defendant. There was the taking down, which was in itself a destruction of the common property without the intention necessary to excuse it, and in addition there was a total appropriation of the wall, by the wall-plate being so placed on it as to exclude the plaintiff from her previous use of the wall. Two questions remain, was the verdict against the weight of the evidence, or was it unsatisfactory, having regard to the mode in which the question of damages was left to the jury? As to the first question, having regard to the facts proved and to the absence of evidence of the state of the title, I cannot say that I am dissatisfied with the verdict. I also think that the mode in which the question of damages was submitted to the jury was correct. If the taking down of the wall was justifiable, and the sole acts of trespass were the placing of the wall upon the new structure, the principle upon which the damages were assessed would be erroneous. But when (as we now determine) the taking down the wall was without legal justification it was an act of trespass, and the injury caused to the plaintiff's house by that act was an element for the consideration of the jury in determining the amount of damages. All the grounds upon which the conditional order was obtained therefore fail, and the verdict must stand.

At the same time we should take care that the defendant shall be protected against the plaintiff recovering in any other form of action, as, for instance, in an action for negligently taking down the wall. We shall therefore discharge the conditional order with costs, the plaintiff undertaking not to bring any further action in respect of anything done to the wall by the defendant prior to the commencement of this action, but without prejudice to her compelling the defendant to remove the wall-plate.

Fitzgerald, Deasy and **Dowse, BB.,** concurred.

Note
See further on party walls, *Irish Land Law*, para. 7.53 *et seq.*

Chapter 7
SETTLEMENTS

This is a difficult subject which mercifully is being reduced in significance by modern taxation systems which tend to penalise severely family settlement purporting to tie up land within successive generations of the same family. It continues to be governed in Ireland by the Settled Land Acts, 1882–90, so that the notorious subsuming of trusts for sale within the same statutory regime survives: see generally *Irish Land Law*, ch. 8.

SETTLED LAND ACT, 1882

An Act for facilitating Sales, Leases, and other dispositions of Settled Land, and for promoting the execution of improvements thereon. [10th August 1882.]

I. – PRELIMINARY

1. – (1) This Act may be cited as the Settled Land Act, 1882.

(2) This Act, except where it is otherwise expressed, shall commence and take effect from and immediately after the thirty-first day of December one thousand eight hundred and eighty-two, which time is in this Act referred to as the commencement of this Act.

II. – DEFINITIONS

2. – (1) Any deed, will, agreement for a settlement, or other agreement, covenant to surrender, copy of court roll, Act of Parliament, or other instrument, or any number of instruments, whether made or passed before or after, or partly before and partly after, the commencement of this Act, under or by virtue of which instrument or instruments any land, or any estate or interest in land, stands for the time being limited to or in trust for any persons by way of succession, creates or is for purposes of this Act a settlement, and is in this Act referred to as a settlement, or as the settlement, as the case requires.

(2) An estate or interest in remainder or reversion not disposed of by a settlement, and reverting to the settlor or descending to the testator's heir, is for purposes of this Act an estate or interest coming to the settlor or heir under or by virtue of the settlement, and comprised in the subject of the settlement.

(3) Land, and any estate or interest therein, which is the subject of a settlement, is for purposes of this Act settled land, and is, in relation to the settlement, referred to in this Act as the settled land.

(4) The determination of the question whether land is settled land, for purposes of this Act, or not, is governed by the state of facts, and the limitations of the settlement, at the time of the settlement taking effect.

(5) The person who is for the time being, under a settlement, beneficially entitled to possession of settled land, for his life, is for purposes of this Act the tenant for life of that land, and the tenant for life under that settlement.

(6) If, in any case, there are two or more persons so entitled as tenants in common, or as joint tenants, or for other concurrent estates or interests, they together constitute the tenant for life for purposes of this Act.

(7) A person being tenant for life within the foregoing definitions shall be deemed to be such notwithstanding that, under the settlement or otherwise, the settled land, or his estate or interest therein, is incumbered or charged in any manner or to any extent.

(8) The persons, if any, who are for the time being, under a settlement, trustees with power of sale of settled land, or with power of consent to or approval of the exercise of such a power of sale, or if under a settlement there are no such trustees, then the persons, if any, for the time being, who are by the settlement declared to be trustees thereof for purposes of this Act, are for purposes of this Act trustees of the settlement.

(9) Capital money arising under this Act, and receivable for the trusts and purposes of the settlement, is in this Act referred to as capital money arising under this Act.

(10) In this Act –

   (i) Land includes incorporated hereditaments, also an undivided share in land; income includes rents and profits; and possession includes receipt of income;

   (ii) Rent includes yearly or other rent, and toll, duty, royalty, or other reservation, by the acre, or the ton, or otherwise; and, in relation to rent, payment includes delivery; and fine includes premium or fore-gift, and any payment, consideration, or benefit in the nature of a fine, premium, or fore-gift;

   (iii) Building purposes include the erecting and the improving of, and the adding to, and the repairing of buildings; and a building lease is a lease for any building purposes or purposes connected therewith;

   (iv) Mines and minerals mean mines and minerals whether already opened or in work, or not, and include all minerals and substances in, on, or under the land, obtainable by underground or by surface working; and mining purposes include the sinking and searching for, winning, working, getting, making merchantable, smelting or otherwise converting or working for the purposes of any manufacture, carrying away, and disposing of mines and minerals, in or under the settled land, or any other land, and the erection of buildings, and the execution of engineering and other works, suitable for those purposes; and a mining lease is a lease for any mining purposes or purposes connected therewith, and includes a grant or licence for any mining purposes;

   (v) Manor includes lordship, and reputed manor or lordship;

   (vi) Steward includes deputy steward, or other proper officer, of a manor;

   (vii) Will includes codicil, and other testamentary instrument, and a writing in the nature of a will;

   (viii) Securities include stocks, funds, and shares;

   (xi) Person includes corporation.

III. – SALE: ENFRANCHISEMENT; EXCHANGE; PARTITION
General Powers and Regulations

3. A tenant for life –

   (i) May sell the settled land, or any part thereof, or any easement, right, or privilege of any kind, over or in relation to the same; and

   (ii) Where the settlement comprises a manor – may sell the seignory of any freehold land within the manor, or the freehold and inheritance of any copyhold or customary land, parcel of the manor, with or without any exception or reservation of all or any mines or minerals, or of any rights or powers relative to mining purposes, so as in every such case to effect an enfranchisement; and

   (iii) May make an exchange of the settled land, or any part thereof, for other land, including an exchange in consideration of money paid for equality of exchange; and

(iv) Where the settlement comprises an undivided share in land, or, under the settlement, the settled land has come to be held in undivided shares – may concur in making partition of the entirety, including a partition in consideration of money paid for equality of partition.

4. – (1) Every sale shall be made at the best price that can reasonably be obtained.

(2) Every exchange and every partition shall be made for the best consideration in land or in land and money that can reasonably be obtained.

(3) A sale may be made in one lot or in several lots, and either by auction or by private contract.

(4) On a sale the tenant for life may fix reserve biddings and buy in at an auction.

(5) A sale, exchange, or partition may be made subject to any stipulations respecting title, or evidence of title, or other things.

(6) On a sale, exchange, or partition, any restriction or reservation with respect to buildings on or other user of land, or with respect to mines and minerals, or with respect to or for the purpose of the more beneficial working thereof, or with respect to any other thing, may be imposed or reserved and made binding as far as the law permits, by covenant, condition, or otherwise, on the tenant for life and the settled land, or any part thereof, or on the other party and any land sold or given in exchange or on partition to him.

(7) An enfranchisement may be made with or without a re-grant of any right of common or other right, easement, or privilege theretofore appendant or appurtenant to or held or enjoyed with the land enfranchised, or reputed so to be.

Special Powers

5. Where on a sale, exchange, or partition there is an incumbrance affecting land sold or given in exchange or on partition, the tenant for life, with the consent of the incumbrancer, may charge that incumbrance on any other part of the settled land, whether already charged therewith or not, in exoneration of the part sold or so given, and, by conveyance of the fee simple, or other estate or interest the subject of the settlement, or by creation of a term of years in the settled land, or otherwise, make provision accordingly.

IV. – LEASES
General Powers and Regulations

6. A tenant for life may lease the settled land, or any part thereof, or any easement, right, or privilege of any kind, over or in relation to the same, for any purpose whatever, whether involving waste or not, for any term not exceeding –

(i) In case of a building lease, ninety-nine years [*N.B.* raised to 150 years for land situate in an urban area by s. 62 of the Landlord and Tenant Act, 1931. Now the power to grant building leases has been abolished altogether in respect of 'dwellings' by the Landlord and Tenant (Ground Rents) Act, 1978, see s. 2. See *Irish Land Law*, Supp. (1975–80), p. 2];

(ii) In case of a mining lease, sixty years;

(iii) In case of any other lease, twenty-one years.

7. – (1) Every lease shall be by deed, and be made to take effect in possession not later than twelve months after its date.

(2) Every lease shall reserve the best rent that can reasonably be obtained, regard being had to any fine taken, and to any money laid out or to be laid out for the benefit of the settled land and generally to the circumstances of the case.

(3) Every lease shall contain a covenant by the lessee for payment of the rent, and a condition of re-entry on the rent not being paid within a time therein specified not exceeding thirty days.

(4) A counterpart of every lease shall be executed by the lessee and delivered to the tenant for life; of which execution and delivery the execution of the lease by the tenant for life shall be sufficient evidence.

(5) A statement, contained in a lease or in an indorsement thereon, signed by the tenant for life, respecting any matter of fact or of calculation under this Act in relation to the lease, shall, in favour of the lessee and of those claiming under him, be sufficient evidence of the matter stated.

Building and Mining Leases

8. – (1) Every building lease shall be made partly in consideration of the lessee, or some person by whose direction the lease is granted, or some other person, having erected, or agreeing to erect, buildings, new or additional, or having improved or repaired, or agreeing to improve or repair, buildings, or having executed, or agreeing to execute, on the land leased, an improvement authorised by this Act, for or in connection with building purposes.

(2) A peppercorn rent or a nominal or other rent less than the rent ultimately payable may be made payable for the first five years or any less part of the term.

(3) Where the land is contracted to be leased in lots, the entire amount of rent to be ultimately payable may be apportioned among the lots in any manner; save that –

> (i) The annual rent reserved by any lease shall not be less than ten shillings; and
>
> (ii) The total amount of the rents reserved on all leases for the time being granted shall not be less than the total amount of the rents which, in order that the leases may be in conformity with this Act, ought to be reserved in respect of the whole land for the time being leased; and
>
> (iii) The rent reserved by any lease shall not exceed one-fifth part of the full annual value of the land comprised in that lease with the buildings thereon when completed.

9. – (1) In a mining lease –

> (i) The rent may be made to be ascertainable by or to vary according to the acreage worked, or by or according to the quantities of any mineral or substance gotten, made merchantable, converted, carried away, or disposed of, in or from the settled land, or any other land, or by or according to any facilities given in that behalf; and
>
> (ii) A fixed or minimum rent may be made payable, with or without power for the lessee, in case the rent, according to acreage or quantity, in any specified period does not produce an amount equal to the fixed or minimum rent, to make up the deficiency in any subsequent specified period, free of rent other than the fixed or minimum rent.

(2) A lease may be made partly in consideration of the lessee having executed, or his agreeing to execute, on the land leased, an improvement authorized by this Act, for or in connexion with mining purposes.

10. – (1) Where it is shown to the Court with respect to the district in which any settled land is situate, either –

> (i) That it is the custom for land therein to be leased or granted for building or mining purposes for a longer term or on other conditions than the term or conditions specified in that behalf in this Act, or in perpetuity; or

(ii) That it is difficult to make leases or grants for building or mining purposes of land therein, except for a longer term or on other conditions than the term and conditions specified in that behalf in this Act, or except in perpetuity;

the Court may, if it thinks fit, authorize generally the tenant for life to make from time to time leases or grants of or affecting the settled land in that district, or parts thereof, for any term or in perpetuity, at fee-farm or other rents, secured by condition of re-entry, or otherwise, as in the order of the Court expressed, or may, if it thinks fit, authorize the tenant for life to make any such lease or grant in any particular case.

(2) Thereupon the tenant for life, and, subject to any direction in the order of the Court to the contrary, each of his successors in title being a tenant for life, or having the powers of a tenant for life under this Act, may make in any case, or in the particular case, a lease or grant of or affecting the settled land, or part thereof, in conformity with the order.

11. Under a mining lease, whether the mines or minerals leased are already opened or in work or not, unless a contrary intention is expressed in the settlement, there shall be from time to time set aside, as capital money arising under this Act, part of the rent as follows, namely, – where the tenant for life is impeachable for waste in respect of minerals, three fourth parts of the rent, and otherwise one fourth part thereof, and in every such case the residue of the rent shall go as rents and profits.

. . .

VI. – INVESTMENT OR OTHER APPLICATION OF CAPITAL TRUST MONEY

21. Capital money arising under this Act, subject to payment of claims properly payable thereout, and to application thereof for any special authorized object for which the same was raised, shall, when received, be invested or otherwise applied wholly in one, or partly in one and partly in another or others, of the following modes (namely);

(i) In investment on Government securities, or on other securities on which the trustees of the settlement are by the settlement or by law authorized to invest trust money of the settlement, or on the security of the bonds, mortgages, or debentures, or in the purchase of the debenture stock, of any railway company in Great Britain or Ireland, incorporated by special Act of Parliament, and having for ten years next before the date of investment paid a dividend on its ordinary stock or shares, with power to vary the investment into or for any other such securities;

(ii) In discharge, purchase, or redemption of incumbrances affecting the inheritance of the settled land, or other the whole estate the subject of the settlement, or of land-tax, rent charge in lieu of tithe, Crown rent, chief rent, or quit rent, charged on or payable out of the settled land;

(iii) In payment for any improvement authorized by this Act;

(iv) In payment for equality of exchange or partitition of settled land;

(v) In purchase of the seignory of any part of the settled land, being freehold land, . . .;

(vi) In purchase of the reversion or freehold in fee of any part of the settled land, being leasehold land held for years, or life, or years determinable on life;

(vii) In purchase of land in fee simple, . . . or of leasehold land held for sixty years or more unexpired at the time of purchase, subject or not to any exception or reservation of or in respect of mines or minerals therein, or of or in respect of rights or powers relative to the working of mines or minerals therein, or in other land;

(viii) In purchase, either in fee simple, or for a term of sixty years or more, of mines and minerals convenient to be held or worked with the settled land, or of any easement, right, or privilege convenient to be held with the settled land for mining or other purposes;

(ix) In payment to any person becoming absolutely entitled or empowered to give an absolute discharge;

(x) In payment of costs, charges, and expenses of or incidental to the exercise of any of the powers, or the execution of any of the provisions, of this Act:

(xi) In any other mode in which money produced by the exercise of a power of sale in the settlement is applicable thereunder.

22. – (1) Capital money arising under this Act shall, in order to its being invested or applied as aforesiad, be paid either to the trustees of the settlement or into Court, at the option of the tenant for life, and shall be invested or applied by the trustees, or under the direction of the Court, as the case may be, accordingly.

(2) The investment or other application by the trustees shall be made according to the direction of the tenant for life, and in default thereof, according to the discretion of the trustees, but in the last-mentioned case subject to any consent required or directions given by the settlement with respect to the investment or other application by the trustees of trust money of the settlement; and any investment shall be in the names or under the control of the trustees.

(3) The investment or other application under the direction of the Court shall be made on the application of the tenant for life, or of the trustees.

(4) Any investment or other application shall not during the life of the tenant for life be altered without his consent.

(5) Capital money arising under this Act while remaining uninvested or unapplied, and securities on which an investment of any such capital money is made, shall, for all purposes of disposition, transmission, and devolution, be considered as land, and the same shall be held for and go to the same persons successively, in the same manner and for and on the same estates, interests, and trusts, as the land wherefrom the money arises would, if not disposed of, have been held and have gone under the settlement.

(6) The income of those securities shall be paid or applied as the income of that land, if not disposed of, would have been payable or applicable under the settlement.

(7) Those securities may be converted into money, which shall be capital money arising under this Act.

. . .

IX. – MISCELLANEOUS PROVISIONS

35. – (1) Where a tenant for life is impeachable for waste in respect of timber, and there is on the settled land timber ripe and fit for cutting, the tenant for life, on obtaining the consent of the trustees of the settlement or an order of the Court, may cut and sell that timber, or any part thereof.

(2) Three fourth parts of the net proceeds of the sale shall be set aside as and be capital money arising under this Act, and the other fourth part shall go as rents and profits.

. . .

37. – (1) Where personal chattels are settled on trust so as to devolve with land until a tenant in tail by purchase is born or attains the age of twenty-one years, or so as otherwise to vest in some person becoming entitled to an estate of freehold of inheritance in the land, a tenant for life of the land may sell the chattels or any of them.

(2) The money arising by the sale shall be capital money arising under this Act, and shall be paid, invested, or applied and otherwise dealt with in like manner in all respects as by this Act directed with respect to other capital money arising under this Act, or may be invested in the purchase of other chattels, of the same or any other nature, which, when purchased, shall be settled and held on the same trusts, and shall devolve in the same manner as the chattels sold.

(3) A sale or purchase of chattels under this section shall not be made without an order of the Court.

X. – TRUSTEES

38. – (1) If at any time there are no trustees of a settlement within the definition of this Act, or where in any other case it is expedient, for purposes of this Act, that new trustees of a settlement be appointed, the Court may, if it thinks fit, on the application of the tenant for life or any other person having, under the settlement, an estate or interest in the settled land, in possession, remainder, or otherwise, or, in the case of an infant, of his testamentary or other guardian, or next friend, appoint fit persons to be trustees under the settlement for purposes of this Act.

(2) The person so appointed, and the survivors and survivor of them, while continuing to be trustees or trustee, and, until the appointment of new trustees, the personal representatives or representative for the time being of the last surviving or continuing trustee, shall for purposes of this Act become and be the trustees or trustee of the settlement.

39. – (1) Notwithstanding anything in this Act, capital money arising under this Act shall not be paid to fewer than two persons as trustees of a settlement, unless the settlement authorises the receipt of capital trust money of the settlement by one trustee.

(2) Subject thereto, the provisions of this Act referring to the trustees of a settlement apply to the surviving or continuing trustees or trustee of the settlement for the time being.

40. The receipt in writing of the trustees of a settlement, or where one trustee is empowered to act, of one trustee, or of the personal representatives or representative of the last surviving or continuing trustee, for any money or securities, paid or transferred to the trustees, trustee, representatives, or representative, as the case may be, effectually discharges the payer or transferor therefrom, and from being bound to see to the application or being answerable for any loss or misapplication thereof, and, in case of a mortgagee or other person advancing money, from being concerned to see that any money advanced by him is wanted for any purpose of this Act, or that no more than is wanted is raised.

41. Each person who is for the time being trustee of a setlement is answerable for what he actually receives only, notwithstanding his signing any receipt for conformity, and in respect of his own acts, receipts, and defaults only, and is not answerable in respect of those of any other trustee, or of any banker, broker, or other person, or for the insufficiency or deficiency of any securities, or for any loss not happening through his own wilful default.

42. The trustees of a settlement, or any of them, are not liable for giving any consent, or for not making, bringing, taking, or doing any such application, action, proceeding, or thing, as they might make, bring, take, or do; and in case of purchase of land with capital money arising under this Act, or of an exchange, partition, or lease, are not liable for adopting any contract made by the tenant for life, or bound to inquire as to the propriety of the purchase, exchange, partitition, or lease, or answerable as regards any price, consideration, or fine, and are not liable to see to or answerable for the investigation of the title, or answerable for a conveyance of land, if the conveyance purports to convey the land in the proper mode, or liable in respect of purchase-money paid by them by direction of the tenant for life to any person joining in the conveyance as a conveying party, or as giving a receipt for the purchase-money, or in any other character, or in respect of any other money paid by them by direction of the tenant for life on the purchase, exchange, partition, or lease.

43. The trustees of a settlement may reimburse themselves or pay and discharge out of the trust property all expenses properly incurred by them.

44. If at any time a difference arises between a tenant for life and the trustees of the settlement respecting the exercise of any of the powers of this Act, or respecting any matter relating thereto, the Court may, on the application of either party, give such directions respecting the matter in difference, and respecting the costs of the application, as the Court thinks fit.

45. – (1) A tenant for life, when intending to make a sale, exchange, partition, lease, mortgage, or charge, shall give notice of his intention in that behalf to each of the trustees of the settlement, by posting registered letters containing the notice, addressed to the trustees, severally, each at his usual or last known place of abode in the [Republic of Ireland], and shall give like notice to the solicitor for the trustees, if any such solicitor is known to the tenant for life, by posting a registered letter, containing the notice, addressed to the solicitor at his place of business in the [Republic of Ireland], every letter under this section being posted not less than one month before the making by the tenant for life of the sale, exchange, partition, lease, mortgage, or charge, or of a contract for the same.

(2) Provided that at the date of notice given the number of trustees shall not be less than two, unless a contrary intention is expressed in the settlement.

(3) A person dealing in good faith with the tenant for life is not concerned to inquire respecting the giving of any such notice as is required by this section.

. . .

XII. – RESTRICTION, SAVINGS, AND GENERAL PROVISIONS

50. – (1) The powers under this Act of a tenant for life are not capable of assignment or release, and do not pass to a person as being, by operation of law or otherwise, an assignee of a tenant for life, and remain exerciseable by the tenant for life after and notwithstanding any assignment, by operation of law or otherwise, of his estate or interest under the settlement.

(2) A contract by a tenant for life not to exercise any of his powers under this Act is void.

(3) But this section shall operate without prejudice to the rights of any person being an assignee for value of the estate or interest of the tenant for life; and in that case, the assignee's rights shall not be affected without his consent, except that, unless the assignee is actually in possession of the settled land or part thereof, his consent shall not be requisite for the making of leases thereof, by the tenant for life, provided the leases are made at the best rent that can reasonably be obtained, without fine, and in other respects are in confirmity with this Act.

(4) This section extends to assignments made or coming into operation before or after and to acts done before or after the commencement of this Act; and in this section assignment includes assignment by way of mortgage, and any partial or

qualified assignment, and any charge or incumbrance; and assignee has a meaning corresponding with that of assignment.

51. – (1) If in a settlement, will, assurance, or other instrument executed or made before or after, or partly before and partly after, the commencement of this Act a provision is inserted purporting or attempting, by way of direction, declaration, or otherwise, to forbid a tenant for life to exercise any power under the Act, or attempting, or tending, or intended, by a limitation, gift, or disposition over of settled land, or by a liamitation, gift, or disposition of other real or any personal property, or by the imposition of any condition, or by forfeiture, or in any other manner whatever, to prohibit or prevent him from exercising, or to induce him to abstain from exercising, or to put him into a position inconsistent with his exercising, any power under this Act, that provision, as far as it purports, or attempts, or tends, or is intended to have, or would or might have, the operation aforesaid, shall be deemed to be void.

(2) For the purposes of this section an estate or interest limited to continue so long only as a person abstains from exercising any power shall be and take effect as an estate or interest to continue for the period for which it would continue if that person were to abstain from exercising the power, discharged from liability to determination or cesser by or on his exercising the same.

52. Notwithstanding anything in a settlement, the exercise by the tenant for life of any power under this Act shall not occasion a forfeiture.

53. A tenant for life shall, in exercising any power under this Act, have regard to the interests of all parties entitled under the settlement, and shall, in relation to the exercise thereof by him, be deemed to be in the position and to have the duties and liabilities of a trustee for those parties.

54. On a sale, exchange, partition, lease, mortage, or charge, a purchaser, lessee, mortgagee, or other person dealing in good faith with a tenant for life shall, as against all parties entitled under the settlement, be conclusively taken to have given the best price, consideration, or rent, as the case may require, that could reasonably be obtained by the tenant for life, and to have complied with all the requisitions of this Act.

55. – (1) Powers and authorities conferred by this Act on a tenant for life or trustees or the Court or [the Commissioners of Public Works in Ireland] are exerciseable from time to time.

(2) Where a power of sale, enfranchisement, exchange, partition, leasing, mortgaging, charging, or other power is exercised by a tenant for life, or by the trustees of a settlement, he and they may respectively execute, make, and do all deeds, instruments, and things necessary or proper in that behalf.

(3) Where any provision in this Act refers to sale, purchase, exchange, partition, leasing, or other dealing, or to any power, consent, payment, receipt, deed, assurance, contract, expenses, act, or transaction, the same shall be construed to extend only (unless it is otherwise expressed) to sales, purchases, exchanges, partitions, leasings, dealings, powers, consents, payments, receipts, deeds, assurances, contracts, expenses, acts, and transactions under this Act.

56. – (1) Nothing in this Act shall take away, abridge, or prejudicially affect any power for the time being subsisting under a settlement, or by statute or otherwise, exerciseable by a tenant for life, or by trustees with his consent, or on his request, or by his direction, or otherwise; and the powers given by this Act are cumulative.

(2) But, in case of conflict between the provisions of a settlement and the provisions of this Act, relative to any matter in respect whereof the tenant for life exercises or contracts or intends to exercise any power under this Act, the provisions of this Act shall prevail; and, accordingly, notwithstanding anything in the

settlement, the consent of the tenant for life shall, by virtue of this Act, be necessary to the exercise by the trustees of the settlement or other person of any power conferred by the settlement exerciseable for any purpose provided for in this Act.

(3) If a question arises, or a doubt is entertained, respecting any matter within this section, the Court may, on the application of the trustees of the settlement, or of the tenant for life, or of any other person interested, give its decision, opinion, advice, or direction thereon.

57. – (1) Nothing in this Act shall preclude a settlor from conferring on the tenant for life, or the trustees of the settlement, any powers additional to or larger than those conferred by this Act.

(2) Any additional or larger powers so conferred shall, as far as may be, notwithstanding anything in this Act, operate and be exerciseable in the like manner, and with all the like incidents, effects, and consequences, as if they were conferred by this Act, unless a contrary intention is expressed in the settlement.

XIII. – LIMITED OWNERS GENERALLY

58. – (1) Each person as follows shall, when the estate or interest of each of them is in possession, have the powers of a tenant for life under this Act, as if each of them were a tenant for life as defined in this Act (namely):

   (i) A tenant in tail, including a tenant in tail who is by Act of Parliament restrained from barring or defeating his estate tail, and although the reversion is in the [State], and so that the exercise by him of his powers under this Act shall bind the [State], but not including such a tenant in tail where the land in respect whereof he is so restrained was purchased with money provided by Parliament in consideration of public services:

  (ii) A tenant in fee simple, with an executory limitation, gift, or disposition over, on failure of his issue, or in any other event;

 (iii) A person entitled to a base fee, although the reversion is in the [State], and so that the exercise by him of his powers under this Act shall bind the [State];

  (iv) A tenant for years determinable on life, not holding merely under a lease at a rent;

   (v) A tenant for the life of another, not holding merely under a lease at a rent;

  (vi) A tenant for his own or any other life, or for years determinable on life, whose estate is liable to cease in any event during that life, whether by expiration of the estate, or by conditional limitation, or otherwise, or to be defeated by an executory limitation, gift, or disposition over, or is subject to a trust for accumulation of income for payment of debts or other purpose;

 (vii) A tenant in tail after possibility of issue extinct;

(viii) A tenant by the curtesy [Repealed as regards the estate of a person dying after 1st Jan. 1967 by the Successive Act, 1965, see ss. 8 and 9 and Sch. 2, Pt. III];

  (ix) A person entitled to the income of land under a trust or direction for payment thereof to him during his own or any other life, whether subject to expenses of management or not, or until sale of the land, or until forfeiture of his interest therein on bankruptcy or other event.

(2) In every such case, the provisions of this Act referring to a tenant for life, either as conferring powers on him or otherwise, and to a settlement, and to settled

land, shall extend to each of the persons aforesaid and to the instrument under which his estate or interest arises, and to the land therein comprised.

(3) In any such case any reference in this Act to death as regards a tenant for life shall, where necessary, be deemed to refer to the determination by death or otherwise of such estate or interest as last aforesaid.

XIV. – INFANTS; MARRIED WOMEN; LUNATICS

59. Where a person, who is in his own right seised of or entitled in possession to land, is an infant, then for purposes of this Act the land is settled land, and the infant shall be deemed tenant for life thereof.

60. Where a tenant for life, or a person having the powers of a tenant for life under this Act, is an infant, or an infant would, if he were of full age, be a tenant for life, or have the powers of a tenant for life under this Act, the powers of a tenant for life under this Act may be exercised on his behalf by the trustees of the settlement, and if there are none, then by such person and in such manner as the Court, on the application of a testamentary or other guardian or next friend of the infant, either generally or in a particular instance, orders.

. . .

XV. – SETTLEMENT BY WAY OF TRUSTS FOR SALE

63. – (1) Any land, or any estate or interest in land, which under or by virtue of any deed, will, or agreement, covenant to surrender, copy of court roll, Act of Parliament, or other instrument or any number of instruments, whether made or passed before or after, or partly before and partly after, the commencement of this Act, is subject to a trust or direction for sale of that land, estate, or interest, and for the application or disposal of the money to arise from the sale, or the income of that money, or the income of the land until sale, or any part of that money or income, for the benefit of any person for his life, or any other limited period, or for the benefit of two or more persons concurrently for any limited period, and whether absolutely, or subject to a trust for accumulation of income for payment of debts or other purposes, or to any other restriction, shall be deemed to be settled land, and the instrument or instruments under which the trust arises shall be deemed to be a settlement; and the person for the time being beneficially entitled to the income of the land, estate, or interest aforesaid until sale, whether absolutely or subject as aforesaid, shall be deemed to be tenant for life thereof; or if two or more persons are so entitled concurrently, then those persons shall be deemed to constitute together the tenant for life thereof; and the persons, if any, who are for the time being under the settlement trustees for sale of the settled land, or having power of consent to, or approval of, or control over the sale, or if under the settlement there are no such trustees, then the persons, if any, for the time being, who are by the settlement declared to be trustees thereof for purposes of this Act, are for purposes of this Act trustees of the settlement.

(2) In every such case the provisions of this Act referring to a tenant for life, and to a settlement, and to settled land, shall extend to the person or persons aforesaid, and to the instrument or instruments under which his or their estate or interest arises, and to the land therein comprised, subject and except as in this section provided (that is to say):

(i) Any reference in this Act to the predecessors or successors in title of the tenant for life, or to the remaindermen, or reversioners or other persons interested in the settled land, shall be deemed to refer to the persons interested in succession or otherwise in the money to arise from sale of the land, or the income of that money, or the income of the land, until sale (as the case may require).

(ii) Capital money arising under this Act from the settled land shall not be applied in the purchase of land unless such application is authorized by the settlement in the case of capital money arising thereunder from sales or other dispositions of the settled land, but may, in addition to any other mode of application authorized by this Act, be applied in any mode in which capital money arising under the settlement from any such sale or other disposition is applicable thereunder, subject to any consent required or direction given by the settlement with respect to the application of trust money of the settlement.

(iii) Capital money arising under this Act from the settled land and the securities in which the same is invested, shall not for any purpose of disposition, transmission, or devolution, be considered as land unless the same would, if arising under the settlement from a sale or disposition of the settled land, have been so considered, and the same shall be held in trust for and shall go to the same persons successively in the same manner, and for and on the same estates, interests, and trusts as the same would have gone and been held if arising under the settlement from a sale or disposition of the settled land, and the income of such capital money and securities shall be paid or applied accordingly.

(iv) Land of whatever tenure acquired under this Act by purchase, or in exchange, or on partition, shall be conveyed to and vested in the trustees of the settlement, on the trusts, and subject to the powers and provisions which, under the settlement or by reason of the exercise of any power of appointment or charging therein contained, are subsisting with respect to the settled land, or would be so subsisting if the same had not been sold, or as near thereto as circumstances permit, but so as not to increase or multiply charges or powers of charging.

SETTLED LAND ACT, 1884

An Act to amend the Settled Land Act, 1882. [3rd July 1884].

6. -- (1) In the case of a settlement within the meaning of section sixty-three of the Act of 1882, any consent not required by the terms of the settlement is not by force of anything contained in that Act to be deemed necessary to enable the trustees of the settlement, or any other person, to execute any of the trusts or powers created by the settlement.

(2) In the case of every other settlement, not within the meaning of section sixty-three of the Act of 1882, where two or more persons together constitute the tenant for life for the purposes of that Act, then, notwithstanding anything contained in subsection (2) of section fifty-six of that Act, requiring the consent of all those persons, the consent of one only of those persons is by force of that section to be deemed necessary to the exercise by the trustees of the settlement, or by any other person, of any power conferred by the settlement exerciseable for any purpose provided for in that Act.

(3) This section applies to dealings before, as well as after, the passing of this Act.

7. With respect to the powers conferred by section sixty-three of the Act of 1882, the following provisions are to have effect:

(i) Those powers are not to be exercised without the leave of the Court.

(ii) The Court may by order, in any case in which it thinks fit, give leave to exercise all or any of those powers, and the order is to name the person or persons to whom leave is given.

(iii) The Court may from time to time rescind, or vary, any order made under this section, or may make any new or further order.

(iv) So long as an order under this section is in force, neither the trustees of the settlement, nor any person other than a person having the leave, shall execute any trust or power created by the settlement, for any purpose for which leave is by the order given, to exercise a power conferred by the Act of 1882.

(v) An order under this section may be registered and re-registered, as a lis pendens, against the trustees of the settlement named in the order, describing them on the register as 'Trustees for the purposes of the Settled Land Act, 1882'.

(vi) Any person dealing with the trustees from time to time, or with any other person acting under the trusts or powers of the settlement, is not to be affected by an order under this section, unless and until the order is duly registered, and when necessary re-registered as a lis pendens.

(vii) An application to the Court under this section may be made by the tenant for life, or by the persons who together constitute the tenant for life, within the meaning of section sixty-three of the Act of 1882.

(viii) An application to rescind or vary an order, or to make any new or further order under this section, may be made also by the trustees of the settlement, or by any person beneficially interested under the settlement.

(ix) The person or persons to whom leave is given by an order under this section, shall be deemed to be the proper person or persons to exercise the powers conferred by section sixty-three of the Act of 1882, and shall have, and may exercise those powers accordingly.

(x) This section is not to affect any dealing which has taken place before the passing of this Act, under any trust or power to which this section applies.

. . .

SETTLED LAND ACT, 1890
An Act to amend the Settled Land Acts, 1882 to 1889. [18th August 1890.]

Trustees

16. Where there are for the time being no trustees of the settlement within the meaning and for the purposes of the Act of 1882, then the following persons shall, for the purposes of the Settled Land Acts, 1882 to 1890, be trustees of the settlement; namely,

(i) The persons (if any) who are for the time being under the settlement trustees, with power of or upon trust for sale of any other land comprised in the settlement and subject to the same limitations as the land to be sold, or with power of consent to or approval of the exercise of such a power of sale, or, if there be no such persons, then

(ii) The persons (if any) who are for the time being under the settlement trustes, with future power of sale, or under a future trust for sale of the land to be sold, or with power of consent to or approval of the exercise of such a future power of sale, and whether the power or trust takes effect in all events or not.

. . .

19. The registration of a writ or order affecting land may be vacated pursuant to an order of the High Court or any judge thereof.

SUCCESSION ACT, 1965

50. – . . .

(3) Where land is settled by will and there are no trustees of the settlement, the personal representatives proving the will shall for all purposes be deemed to be trustees of the settlement until trustees of the settlement are appointed, but a sole personal representative shall not be deemed to be a trustee for the purposes of the Settled Land Acts, 1882 to 1890, until at least one other trustee is appointed.

58. – . . .

(2) Where an infant becomes entitled to any estate or interest in land on intestacy and consequently there is no instrument under which the estate or interest of the infant arises or is acquired, that estate or interest shall be deemed to be the subject of a settlement for the purposes of the Settled Land Acts, 1882 to 1890, and the persons who are trustees under section 57 [of the Succession Act] shall be deemed to be the trustees of that settlement.

RE BLAKE'S SETTLED ESTATES
[1932] I.R. 637 (Supreme Court)

An application was made for the appointment of trustees of an alleged 'compound settlement' consisting of a marriage settlement made in 1832, a disentailing deed made in 1864 (between A.W.B. of the first part, J.A.D. of the second part, and R.B. of the third part), and the will of the said J.A.D. made in 1909, and a codicil thereto. Under the marriage settlement lands were settled subject to certain then existing charges and on usual trusts, and the said J.A.D., becoming tenant in tail in possession, subsequently executed the disentailing deed, and became owner in fee subject to these charges. Meredith J. held that after execution of the disentailing deed there was no settlement within the meaning of the Settled Land Acts and the only settlement still existing was under the will of J.A.D. Thus he refused the application and an appeal was lodged to the Supreme Court.

Murnaghan J. (delivering the judgment of the Court):

By an indenture of marriage settlement, dated 30th April, 1864, certain lands in County Galway were subject to certain incumbrances enumerated in a Schedule thereto, settled upon uses and trusts. One of these incumbrances was a mortgage, dated 28th March, 1822, for £5,000 (Irish), and puisne to it was a charge of £3,000 created by a marriage settlement, dated 25th September, 1882, in favour of the younger children of the marriage of Andrew William Blake with Maria Blake, otherwise Daly. By the said settlement, dated 25th September, 1832, a term of 500 years was limited to trustees after the decease of Andrew William Blake, or in his lifetime with his consent, 'by sale or mortgage or any other disposition of the lands for all or any part of the same term or out of the rents, issues and profits to raise the said charge of £3,000.'

John Archer Daly, who was tenant for life under the settlement of 30th April, 1864, became, on the death of his son, Denis Daly in 1901, entitled to the reversion in fee simple, and he, by his will, dated 13th February, 1909, resettled the lands under which will Denise Anne Marie Cole is now tenant for life.

Portions of the lands have been sold in the Court of the Land Commission and the purchase money has been allocated in part payment of the mortgage, dated 25th September, 1822, leaving a considerable sum still due. The portions charge created by the settlement of 1832 was appointed in various sums, and, although no interest has been paid on the greater portion of the charge for many years, it would seem that part at least of the portions charge has had interest paid in recent times so as to keep portion of the charge alive.

With the object of making title to certain lands of Furbough not comprised in the Land Commission sale, application has been made to Mr. Justice Meredith to appoint trustees of the settlement consisting of the portions term of 500 years and the settlement made by the will of John Archer Daly. Mr. Poole, in making the application, drew the attention of Mr. Justice Meredith 'to the remarks of Russell J. in the case of *Lord Alington and the London County Council's Contract* ([1927] 2 Ch. 253), and the learned Judge refused the application. On this appeal we are asked to say that in the circumstances and on the construction of the Settled Land Acts it would be proper to appoint trustees of the settlements above referred to.

Such trustees, if appointed, are frequently referred to as trustees of a 'compound settlement', a refinement of phraseology which throws an air of mystery over such applications. No such term is found in the Settled Land Acts, but the definition of the word 'settlement' as used in the Act of 1882 is 'any deed, will . . . or other instrument, *or any number of instruments*, whether made . . . before or after, or partly before and partly after, the commencement of this Act, under or by virtue of which instrument or instruments any land, or any estate or interest in land, stands for the time being limited to or in trust for any persons by way of succession, creates or is for the purposes of this Act a settlement, and is in this Act referred to as a settlement, or as the settlement, as the case requires'.

Under sect. 20 the tenant for life, exercising the power of sale, can convey or create the estate intended to be dealt with for the estate or interest the subject of the settlement, discharged from all the limitations, powers and provisions of the settlement, and from all estates, interests, and charges subsisting or to arise thereunder, but subject to and with the exception of as there mentioned, viz.:

(i) all estates, interests, and charges having priority to the settlement; and

(ii) all such other, if any, estates, interests, and charges as have been conveyed or created for securing money actually raised at the date of the deed; and

(iii) leases and certain other interests specified.

If the statutory settlement within the meaning of the definition clause in the Act applies, it is highly convenient to appoint trustees of this statutory settlement, and a tenant for life under this statutory settlement can convey the estate without requiring the concurrence of parties having interests under the settlement save those specified in sect. 20, with the result that the claim of such persons attaches to the capital moneys. In *In re Marquis of Ailesbury and Lord Iveagh* ([1893] 2 Ch. 345), Stirling J. held that the tenant for life under a settlement made in 1885 was able to convey the estate free from jointure rent-charges supported by terms of years created by earlier settlements – all the settlements forming a statutory settlement under the Act. In *In re Mundy and Roper's Contract* ([1899] 1 Ch. 275, at p. 290), Lindley and Chitty L.JJ. in a joint judgment interpreted the words 'stands for the time being limited to or in trust for any persons by way of succession' as including the case of a jointure and portions for younger children limited to arise on or after the death of a tenant for life, and the terms of years limited to trustees to secure them. They said in their judgement: 'The jointress and the portioners take an interest in the land, and they succeed to their interests in the land on or after the death of the tenant for life'. Vaughan Williams L.J. stated his view that such terms were mere charges overriding the successive limitations, and coming into operation contemporaneously with those limitations. But he thought a broad view should be taken of the Act so as to enable the tenant for life to sell.

Since the decision of the Court of Appeal in *In re Mundy and Roper's Contract* ([1899] 1 Ch. 275) applications have been successfully made to the Court to appoint trustees of a 'settlement' where jointures and portions, whether secured or not by terms of years, subsist under a settlement prior to another settlement under which there is a person having the powers of a tenant for life. *In re Phillimore's Estate* ([1904] 2 Ch. 460) dealt with lands under which the settlor declared trusts under which he made himself tenant for life with trusts in remainder to pay five annuities for life and subject thereto for himself absolutely, and by his will he resettled the property. It was held, following the decision in *Mundy and Roper's Contract* ([1899] 1 Ch. 275), that the various instruments made one settlement under the Act. In *In re Marshall's Settlement* ([1905] 2 Ch. 325) the settlor took an estate for life and also the remainder in fee subject to a jointure and to a term to raise portions for children. Here there was only one settlement, but it was held that the lands stood for the time being limited 'to or in trust for persons by way of succession'. In *In re Monckton's Settlement* ([1917] 1 Ch. 224) under a settlement lands stood settled to A for life subject to a certain term of years to secure portions and after A's life to a jointure and further portions and thereafter to B in fee. It was likewise held that the lands stood limited for persons by way of succession.

It appears to us that the cases which have already been decided do not involve a principle that the mere existence of a portions charge under a settlement which is otherwise spent is enough to create a limitation of lands to or in trust for persons in succession. We do not think the instrument creating the portions charge so subsisting comes within the definition of a 'settlement' in the Settled Land Act, 1882, and accordingly we are of opinion that Meredith J. was correct in refusing to appoint trustees of a number of instruments of which the instrument including the portions charge was one.

We were pressed with the convenience which would arise if the order were made, but we are bound in the circumstances to say whether the view of the law taken by Meredith J. was correct, and in our opinion it was correct.

Notes

1. See further on the point at issue, *Irish Land Law*, para. 8.025.
2. As to compound settlements, see *ibid.*, para 8.051 *et seq*. See also *Re Domvile and Callwell's Contract*, [1908] 1 I.R. 475 and *Re Earl of Pembroke and Thompson's Contract*, [1932] I.R. 493.

BURKE V. GORE
(1884) 13 L.R. Ir. 367

Residuary personal estate was subject to a trust for investment in the purchase of lands in the counties of Cork and Tyrone, to be settled to the same uses as the testator's real estate, which was devised in strict settlement. No opportunity having occurred to enable such an investment to be made, and the fund representing the residue being in Court to the credit of a suit to carry out the trusts of the will, the trustees applied to the Court, under section 38 of the Settled Land Act, 1882, for leave to enter into an agreement for a transfer of a mortgage for a large amount secured upon fee-simple lands in the counties of Cork and Kerry.

Chatteron V.-C.:.

The fund in Court is personal estate of Colonel Edwards, which, by his will, was vested in trustees upon trust to invest in the purchase of real and freehold estate in the counties of Cork or Tyrone, to be settled to the same uses as those declared as to his other estates, which were devised in strict settlement.

It was necessarily admitted by Mr. Campion that the proposed investment is not within the express trusts of the will, and is one that could not be sanctioned by the Court, acting within its ordinary powers in this administration suit. He sought, therefore, to maintain it under the provisions of the Settled Land Act, 1882. I have had occasion more than once to express my opinion here, that the administration of that Act, so far as it concerns this Court, requires great care and vigilance to guard against its extraordinary powers being used to injure or defraud persons entitled in remainder. It confers powers upon tenants for life to deal with settled lands nearly as if they were absolute owners, imposing checks and conditions upon the exercise of those powers, which, I fear, will, in many cases, be found insufficient to prevent disastrous consequences. With its policy I have nothing to do; but in administering it I do not think that its provisions are to be enlarged beyond what its terms clearly require.

Mr. Campion relied on the 33rd section, which provides that 'where, under a settlement, money is in the hands of trustees, and is liable to be laid out in the purchase of land, to be made subject to the settlement, then, in addition to such powers of dealing therewith as the trustees have, independently of this Act, they may, at the option of the tenant for life, invest or apply the same as capital money arising under this Act.' But this section does not appear to me to apply, as the money sought to be invested is not in the hands of trustees, nor can it be invested, applied, or otherwise dealt with by them. This is the only section that treats money as capital money under the Act, which has not been produced by some dealing with settled land under its provisions. I cannot find any clause which treats the Court as a trustee for its purposes.

The summons asks in the alternative that the Court shall appoint trustees under the 38th section for the purposes of the Act. I do not think that the trustees of the will here are trustees of it as a settlement within the meaning of the Act, as they have no power of sale of settled land, or any power of consent to or approval of the exercise of such a power of sale, and are therefore not within the definition in the 8th sub-division of the 2nd section. The case therefore would be within the 38th section. The exercise of the power under that section is however optional with the Court, and it is with reference to it that I consider that the greatest caution is necessary. When once trustees are thus appointed they and the tenant for life, at whose instance application for their appointment will generally take place, become, in fact, complete masters of the fund. The only protection to those in remainder against the tenant for life in such cases are trustees who, in general, are proposed for approval by him, and as to whom in many cases it will be difficult for the Court to obtain satisfactory information. In my opinion the Court, on application to appoint trustees under this section, should not only require to be satisfied of the fitness of the proposed trustees, but also that the purpose for which their appointment is applied for is such as to render their appointment safe and beneficial to all parties interested.

In this case I am asked to appoint trustees for the purpose of an investment not authorised by the will, and one which may materially interfere with the purpose to which the trust appropriates the fund. To be of any avail it must be followed by an order to transfer this large sum of Stock to the trustees, when so appointed. I am asked to constitute trustees, and to hand over to them this money in order to bring the fund within the terms of the 33rd section. I am not prepared to take this course.

In addition to the reasons I have mentioned, I must bear in mind in exercising my discretion that the purpose to which, by the will, this money is to be devoted, namely, the purchase of land to be settled, requires it to be so invested as to be readily available should an eligible purchase present itself. I regret to say that in the present state of landed property in this country, a mortgage, even on what appears to be abundant security under ordinary circumstances, is not one which would afford reasonable certainty of the money being readily available for the testator's purpose.

Note

See further on the courts' jurisdiction under section 38 of the 1882 Act, *Irish Land Law*, para. 8.036.

RE TUTHILL
[1907] 1 I.R. 305 (Chancery Division)

Under a marriage settlement land was vested in trustees subject to a trust for sale and J.F.T. was tenant for life of one undivided thirteenth share of the land. On sale of the land under the Land Purchase Acts the question arose as to whether J.F.T. was 'deemed' to be tenant for life under section 63 of the Settled Land Act, 1882, and whether the leave of the court should be granted under section 7 of the 1884 Act.

Meredith M.R.:

I hope that the discussion which has taken place will serve a useful purpose. It is, I think, important that all parties concerned in the sale and transfer of estates in this country should understand clearly that a person who, by virtue of sect. 63 of the Settled Land Act, 1882, is 'deemed to be' tenant for life of settled land in Ireland is not entitled, as a mere matter of course, to an order under sect. 7 (ii) of the Settled Land Act, 1884. The law has not been altered by the Irish Land Acts of 1903 and 1904. The most casual reader of the judgment delivered by Barton, J., in the case of *In re Iever's Settlements* ([1904] 1 I.R. 492), cannot fail to observe that the learned Judge acted on the principle established by numerous authorities – of which the cases cited by Mr. Mecredy (*In re Bagot's Settlement* [1894] 1 Ch. 177); *In re Daniell's Settled Estates* [1894] 3 Ch. 503) are typical examples – that applications under sect. 7 (ii) of the Act of 1884 must be dealt with by the Court in the exercise of judicial discretion applied to the circumstances of each particular case. The mere fact that the discretion is invoked in aid of a sale under the Irish Land Acts of 1903 and 1904 is not enough to justify the Court in giving an applicant leave to sell or proceed with a sale of the settled land.

The Court must be satisfied that the sale, if carried out, will be for the benefit of all parties interested under the settlement.

In the case already referred to, Barton, J., was satisfied on the facts before him that the sale was 'an advantageous one for all parties concerned, or entitled under the settlement.' Being so satisfied, he gave his sanction to the sale, notwithstanding the provisions of sect. 48 of the Act of 1903 and sect. 3(1) of the Act of 1904. In the present cases I am satisfied, on the facts before me, that the proposed sales will result in benefit to all parties interested under the respective settlements. The terms arranged are satisfactory.

No doubt the terms arranged would be still more satisfactory to the parties interested – other than the proposed vendors – if the percentage payable under section 48 was in each case to be added to the purchase-money; but I follow the decision of Barton, J., in reference to this somewhat delicate matter, and I respectfully adopt his language (pages 495, 496): 'It is, in my opinion, no objection to an application of this kind that the applicant, if he is otherwise acting honestly and for the advantage of all persons interested, may be influenced by an inducement which the Legislature has, for reasons of public policy, held out to him, or that he will gain a benefit which the Legislature has expressed an intention of conferring upon him. In the absence of any other objection to the application, I see no sufficient ground for withholding the leave of the Court.'

With regard to the question of costs, I confess I have felt considerable difficulty in dealing with the costs of the applicants. The arguments of Mr. Conner and Mr. Wilson, however, have convinced me that in the present cases, at all events, the applicants are entitled to an order directing their costs to be paid out of the proceeds of the respective sales. The trustees are entitled to a like order.

Note
See further *Irish Land Law*, para. 8.046

RE FITZGERALD

[1902] 1 I.R. 162; 36 I.L.T.R. 30 (Chancery Division)

A testatrix gave to A B the use of her house in Dublin during her life as a residence, with a proviso that in the event of A B ceasing to reside in it it should form part of her residuary estate. She also gave A B the income of a sum of £10,000 for life, or so long as she made the house her principal residence, with a like gift over in the event of her ceasing to make the house her principal residence. A B, owing to ill health, wished to cease residing in the house and to exercise her power of sale under the Settled Land Acts. She was willing to forego the income from the proceeds of sale, but without prejudice to her right to continue to receive the income from the £10,000. A summons was issued to determine the matter.

Porter M.R.:

The question raised by the summons is this: The testatrix left the house, 29 Merrion-square, to Miss O'Grady, who is one the plaintiffs in the action, for her life, with a direction that she should make it her principal place of residence, and with a gift over if she did not do so. The gift of the house in this way is clearly within section 51 of the Settled Land Act, 1882, and, therefore, void for the purposes of that Act. If the gift of the house stood alone Miss O'Grady might have found it desirable not to take advantage of it, but there were two legacies of £5000 each, the interest of which was given to her, one by the will, the other by a codicil, for life, or as long as she made the house, 29 Merrion-square, her principal residence, with a direction that upon her death or ceasing to make the house her principal residence these legacies were to fall into the residue. Thus not only is the condition of residence imposed on Miss O'Grady, but there is a gift over if she fails to perform the condition.

The policy of the Settled Land Act, 1882, was to render lands however settled, absolutely disposable by sale, so that there should not be any land not capable of changing hands. Section 51 of that Act is as follows: 'If in a will a provision is inserted purporting or attempting, by way of direction, declaration, or otherwise, to forbid a tenant for life to exercise any power under this Act, or attempting, or tending, or intended by a limitation, gift, or disposition over of settled land, or by a limitation, gift, or disposition of other real or personal property, or by the imposition of any condition, or by forfeiture, or in any other manner whatever, to prohibit or prevent him from exercising, or to induce him to abstain from exercising, or to put him into a position inconsistent with his exercising any power, or tends, or is intended to have, or would or might have the operation aforesaid, shall be deemed to be void.' This applies to the house itself in this case as it is 'settled land'; but the important part of the section for the present purpose is contained in the subsequent words which I have read, which extend the prohibition of an attempt to prevent the tenant for life exercising any power under the Act (*e.g.* the power of sale) to an attempt to do so by a limitation, gift, or disposition of other real or personal property. The only question I have to consider is, does this prohibition apply to a disposition of other, *i.e.* collateral property? It is perfectly clear from the words of the section that it does, even if there was no decision to that effect. The gift to Miss O'Grady of the interest on the two sums of £5000 as long as she makes the house her principal residence is a provision which not only tends to prevent, but has the effect of preventing, her selling the house, and, therefore, it is to be deemed void for the purposes of the Act, with the result that she will not lose the interest on the legacies if she sells the house.

The case of *In re Thompson* (21 L.R. Ir. 107) is a direct authority on the point, and so is the case of *In re Smith, Grose-Smith* v. *Bridge* ([1899] 1 Ch. 331) which goes further than the present case, as there the provision which tended to prevent a sale of the settled land was contained in an instrument different from that under which the tenancy for life of the settled land was created. The policy of the Act is that the tenant for life is to have full power to sell the settled land, and any condition imposed to prevent his exercising this power is not only inapplicable to the settled land, but is to be deemed void, that is to say is inapplicable to any other property to which the condition is attached.

I must, therefore, answer the question asked by the summons by saying that, in the event of the sale of the house, 29 Merrion-square, the gift over of the legacies of £5000 each is void under the Act and does not take effect.

HUGHES V. FANAGAN
(1891) 30 L.R. Ir. 111 (Court of Appeal)

A tenant for life under a settlement, of which there were no trustees for the purposes of the Settled Land Acts, made an agreement to give a lease for thirty-five years to an intending lessee who had knowledge that there were no such trustees, and that he was dealing with a tenant for life. The tenant for life died before the lease was executed. The persons entitled to the lands in remainder were held not entitled to recover possession of the lands from the intending lessee who had gone into possession under the agreement by the Exchequer Division. An appeal was lodged.

Porter M.R.:

If we entertained any serious doubt we should let this case stand for consideration. But inasmuch as the Exchequer Division have reluctantly decided in favour of the defendant, and only because they thought themselves constrained so to decide in deference to certain English authorities, we have the less hesitation in giving our decision at once, seeing it is in accordance with the opinion of the Exchequer Division.

It appears that in July, 1889, the defendant Fanagan agreed with Harvey, the tenant for life under the settlement, to take a lease of the lands for thirty-five years. That agreement does not purport to be one made by virtue of the Settled Land Act, 1882. But I am quite certain that it bound Harvey, and, though not under the Settled Land Act, was in itself perfectly unobjectionable. Harvey died within five months from the making of this agreement. The contract does not in terms purport to bind the persons entitled in remainder with whom Harvey was not in privity; but it is said by the defendant that owing to the provisions of the Settled Land Act, 1882, this contract is binding on the settled land.

It is unfortunate that Fanagan did not see to having the lease completed. However, he omitted to do so while he could, and now as the tenant for life is dead he has lost the opportunity of ever having it executed as a lease.

The contention that the contract is binding on the settled land has been based mainly on the 31st section of the Settled Land Act, 1882, 45 & 46 Vict. c. 38. Sub-section 1, clause iii. of this section provides that the tenant for life may contract to make any lease, and in making the lease may vary the terms, but so that the lease be in conformity with the Act. Next follow three clauses relating to other contracts authorized to be made, and then comes this clause: – 'Every contract shall be binding on, and shall enure for the benefit of the settled land, and shall be enforceable against and by every successor in title for the time being of the tenant for life, and may be carried into effect by any such successor.' Of course the words 'every contract' occurring at the beginning of this clause must receive some rational construction, and manifestly must be restricted so as to include only contracts within or authorized by the Act.

The concluding sub-section of this section calls for some observation. It provides 'that any preliminary contract under this Act for or relating to a lease shall not form part of the title or evidence of the title of any person to the lease.' I agree with what was said by Lord Justice FitzGibbon during the argument, that the only effect of this sub-section is that where a lease has subsequently been duly executed in accordance with such a contract, the lease itself and not the contract is the commencement of the lessee's title.

In all that I have read and in all that precedes in the Act, there is not a word to show any fetter or limitation on the power of the tenant for life to bind the inheritance by his contract; and if the Act had stopped there, there being nothing as yet about the appointment of trustees, I do not think there would have been any difficulty in the way of the defendant's contention. But then come sections 32 to 37, all of which deal with the duties and powers of the trustees of the settlement, and section 38, which provides that if there should be no trustees within the definition of the Act, or where in any other case it is expedient for the purposes of the Act, the Court may, if it thinks fit, appoint them. What are the trustees to do? It is plain they are not to sell or make leases, for the power to do such things has been already conferred on the tenant for life. But by the six preceding sections the trustees are charged with the duty of safeguarding the property comprised in the settlement, and making some sort of provision for the protection of the rights of the persons to take in remainder. Their appointment is not a mere matter of form, but is a matter for the exercise of care. Consequently it was held in *In re Kemp's Settled Estates* (24 Ch. Div. 485) (a case which I have frequently followed in the Rolls), where the Court refused to appoint as trustee under the Act the solicitor for the tenant for life, though he was in other respects a most proper person, being of opinion that his being solicitor to the tenant for life made him unsuitable for an office the duties of which might require him to check the proceedings of the tenant for life. The persons to be appointed trustees, therefore, ought to be independent, and when asked to appoint, the Court must exercise a judicial discretion in the matter. I quite agree that the duties of the trustees are now somewhat shadowy, having been gradually diminished by decisions and legislation till they have become very slender indeed.

The next few sections of the Act deal with payments to and the protection of the trustees, and then comes section 45. [His Lordship read the section.] This section plainly applies to every case of a lease, both where the settlement has appointed its own trustees, and where it has not; and, moreover, in the event of there being none or only one in existence (unless the settlement expresses a contrary intention) it plainly contemplates an appointment being made, so that there may be at least two trustees on whom notice is to be served. In all cases, then, there must be service of the notice on the trustees: every case is covered, and it is not possible to evade the section. Now, what is the meaning of the words 'or of a contract for the same'? The reference is to a contract for some of the things mentioned in the same section. No doubt, the case of a tenant for life making a contract for a lease is not specifically mentioned. Why? Because the section commences 'a tenant for life when intending to make a lease,' and as these words are large enough to include the case of a tenant for life making a contract for a lease (since if he does that, he *intends* to make a lease), there was no need to mention it specifically. I think the construction put upon these words by Mr. Houston and Mr. White is right. I think the sub-section means that one month before the lease or the contract, *i.e.* one month before one or other, the notice is to be served; but I also think that when there are no trustees, if the tenant for life die before the notice is served, the opportunity for serving it is lost, and the notice never can be served so as to comply with the section.

The third sub-section has been relied on as exempting an intending lessee from making inquiries; but it is admitted that it will not cover the case of a lessee who knows that there are no trustees. And the Act of 1884, which provides that the notice may be given in general terms, and that it may be waived by the trustees and still leave them free from responsibility, even that Act does not get rid of, and it is not contended that it does get rid of, any of the provisions in this section or of the need of serving the trustees with notice.

We have been referred to two cases which are said to be authorities in favour of the respondent and which the Exchequer Division thought to be binding on them and to coerce them into deciding as they have done. Those are *The Duke of Marlborough* v. *Sartoris* (32 Ch. Div. 616) and *Hatten* v. *Russell* (38 Ch. Div. 334). But in neither of those cases did the point here debated really arise. They were both cases between a tenant for life and a man who had purchased from him, and they decide nothing as to what is the vital point in this case – the need of the service of the notice in a case where there are no trustees of the settlement and the party dealing with the tenant for life knows there are no trustees. We have been referred to a passage in Clerke's Settled Land Acts, p. 130, 2nd edition, where it is stated that 'the giving of the notice is a matter between the tenant for life and the trustees, and one with which the purchaser is not concerned'; and it is contended here that a similar doctrine applies to the case of a lessee. The passage cited, no doubt, appears to be justified by the decision of Mr. Justice Chitty in *The Duke of Marlborough* v. *Sartoris* (32 Ch. Div. 616), referred to in support of it. What the learned Judge there (at page 623) says is this: 'It seems to me, therefore, that the giving of the notice is a matter between the tenant for life and the trustees, and one with which the purchaser is not concerned. He could not expect to have the notice set out in his abstract. If he inquired whether the notice was given, I can see no reason why the vendor should not say: "That is a matter with which you are not concerned, for the Act says so in so many words." But he goes on: 'Of course the case is different where there are no trustees of the settlement, who are trustees within the Act for the purposes of the Act, in which case an order has to be made apponting trustees for the purposes of the Act.' Therefore, so far as Mr. Justice Chitty's opinion is concerned, it is rather in favour of the appellant. The case of *Hatten* v. *Russell* (38 Ch. Div. 331) is a decision by Mr. Justice Kay, who in his judgment expressly guarded himself from being supposed to decide the point now before us. He says (at p. 344): 'As to the notice there is an express provision in section 45, which is the section that empowers the tenant for life to give notice – that "a person dealing in good faith with the tenant for life is not concerned to inquire respecting the giving any such notice as is required by this section".It is said that that does not absolve a purchaser who knows that no notice has been given, and that in that case he might be liable if he were to complete his purchase. With that point at present I have nothing to do, and I will not pause to give any opinion on it.' Therefore, upon the question, whether it is necessary to give notice where there are no trustees, and that fact is within the knowledge of the lessee or purchaser, Mr. Justice Kay gave no opinion, and the opinion of Mr. Justice Chitty is favourable to the appellant.

There being nothing in these authorities to show that the section should not be construed strictly, it is plain in this case that if the lease had been executed it would have been wholly inoperative, unless the trustees had been appointed and the notice served; and the point which we have to decide is this – Is a person who has not got a lease, but only an agreement for one, to be in a better position by reason of that circumstance? I think the whole scope and object of the Act shows that it was intended that a contract for a lease was to have the same operation and effect as a lease binding the inheritance. But the Act leaves wholly untouched the case where no lease could have been made owing to common misfortune or common default. Without something in the statute to support it, the notion seems a novel one, that, in the absence of what admittedly would give validity to both, a title under an agreement for a lease should be stronger than a title under a lease itself. Besides, I am of opinion that to hold this would be equivalent to striking out of the 48th section the words 'or of a contract for the same,' and to declaring that the tenant for life, by a simple letter of agreement, could bind the inheritance without pursuing the course pointed out by the statute. It was, no doubt, the intention of the Legislature to enable a tenant for life to make a lease so as to bind those entitled in remainder, but the power which the Act gives him is only to be exercised under certain prescribed conditions, and we have no right to extend the provisions of the Act to a case where the prescribed conditions have not been fulfilled.

Mr. Houston has referred to the provisions of the 7th section of the Settled Land Act, 1890 (53 & 54 Vict. c. 69). It provides not in the case of all leases for twenty-one years made by a tenant for life, but in the case of such leases where the lessee is punishable for waste, that the notice prescribed by the 45th section of the Act of 1882 need not be served, and that the lease may be made notwithstanding that there are no trustees of the settlement for the purposes of the Settled Land Acts. The section says: 'A lease for a term not exceeding twenty-one years at the best rent that can be reasonably obtained without fine, and *whereby the lessee is not exempted from punishment for waste*, may be made by a tenant for life – (a), without any notice of an intention to make the same having been given under section 45 of the Act of 1882; and (b), notwithstanding that there are no trustees of the settlement for the purposes of the Settled Land Acts, 1882 to 1890.' 'Whereby the lessee is not exempted from punishment for waste.' What is involved in these words? *Expressio unius est exclusio alterius*. If in a particular case it is expressly provided that neither notice nor trustees are necessary for the making of a valid lease, the obvious inference is that in other cases not included in the section there must be trustees of the settlement for the purposes of the Acts, and that the prescribed notice must be served on them.

I am therefore of opinion that the defendant in this case did not obtain a contract for a lease sufficient under the Acts of Parliament to bind the remaindermen, and that he is not entitled to remain in possession as against them.

FitzGibbon L.J.:

The Settled Land Act, 1882, sect. 45, sub-sect. 2, provides that at the date of the notice directed by sub-sect. 1, there shall be two trustees at least. Sub-sect. 3 enacts that a person dealing in good faith with the tenant for life is not to be concerned to inquire respecting the giving of the notice, but this must mean dealing in the manner prescribed by the Act, and a person who knows that there are no trustees knows that he cannot deal under the Act. Here it is admitted that the defendant knew that he was dealing with a tenant for life, and knew that there were no trustees. It appears, when we look at the agreement, that the defendant was also fully aware of the limited character of the powers possessed by his lessor; for the lease originally agreed on was to have been made in consideration of a fine, and, on its being discovered that the intended letting would have been thereby invalidated, the fine was paid back, the lessor consented to pay costs, and he would have been more than human if, on entering into the new agreement, he had not been tempted to diminish his own personal liability rather than to increase the annual rent to the highest figure. It is plain, therefore, that it was with full knowledge of the difficulties in the way of obtaining a valid lease that the defendant entered into this agreement.

Where there are trustees, a person dealing in good faith with the tenant for life may fairly be exempted from any obligation to look after the interests of the persons entitled in remainder; for the settlement is in that case represented both by the tenant for life and by the trustees, and although these trustees may reduce their action to something perfunctory, if not altogether shadowy, without incurring any personal liability, their powers are not necessarily ineffective, for where they think it necessary, they can bring any matter before the Court and obtain its directions; and I fancy that any Court would have instituted rigorous inquiries before it sanctioned an agreement made under the circumstances disclosed upon the face of the consent here.

According to the defendant's argument, the Act would give to an imperfect inchoate transaction more force and protection than to a completed lease. But I think the words of sect. 45, sub-sect. 1, explicitly require that either before the making of the lease, or before making the contract for it, one month's notice shall be given to trustees of the settlement then existing. If the notice has been given before the contract, it need not be repeated before executing the lease, but if it has not been given before the contract, then it must be given before the completion of the lease, and until it has been given by a tenant for life still 'intending to make' the lease, those claiming under the settlement cannot be bound. I regard the argument as absurd which results in a construction by which a tenant for life needs only to bind himself by an agreement, and then to leave the lease uncompleted until his death, in order to bind the inheritance, without complying with the statutory conditions, though it would not be bound if he had executed the lease agreed upon before he died.

Taking sections 31 and 45 together, and construing them in the light of a transaction like that between Harvey and Fanagan, their effect, in my opinion, is that from the time the contract is entered into it may be enforced against the tenant for life, but that in order to bind the inheritance it must be carried out in the prescribed manner and after the prescribed notice. Where the prescribed notice has not been given, and, through the want of trustees, or the death of the contractor, or for any other reason, cannot be given, the inheritance is not bound, and the purchaser or lessee is – as many other intending purchasers and lessees have been before – relegated to his personal remedies against the party with whom he contracted, or his representatives.

Barry L.J.:

I concur. The only doubt on my mind is caused by the fact of the Lord Chief Baron having come to a different conclusion. At the same time, it is satisfactory to me to know that the learned Judge arrived at his decision only by attributing to two cases a binding significance which I cannot see that they bear. In one of those cases, *The Duke of Marlborough* v. *Sartoris* (32 Ch. Div. at p. 623), where he touches on the question before us, Mr. Justice Chitty has laid it down that if there are no trustees for the purposes of the Act, such trustees must be appointed before a sale under the Act can be effected. So that I cannot see that that case is an authority coercing us to decide in favour of the defendant. The other case also, in my opinion, leaves the question equally open for us to determine. For *Hatten* v. *Russell* (38 Ch. Div. 334) merely decided that the purchaser was bound to complete in a case where, though there were no trustees at the inception of the transaction, they had been subsequently appointed, and the notice served on them – the question under the circumstances being one of conveyancing and not of title. I do not think we are in any way trenching on those cases. If I thought we were I should have liked to have had an opportunity to consider our decision. But I believe we are not deciding anything inconsistent with those two cases.

It seems to me that section 45 of the Settled Land Act requires notice of a sale or lease being made by the tenant for life to be given to the trustees, in order that the latter may have an opportunity of safeguarding the interests of other persons under the settlement. It is quite true, as the Master of the Rolls has felicitously observed, that the functions of the trustees are very shadowy; but it is equally clear that the Legislature intended them to act as a check when the occasion should so require. *Kemp's Settled Estates* (24 Ch. Div. 485) shows that the Court may question the fitness of a person of the most respectable character to act as such trustee by reason of his possibly not being quite independent of the tenant for life. That being so, we cannot regard the appointment of trustees for the purposes of the Act, or the service of the prescribed notice, as a merely formal matter, but as part of the machinery of the Act and part of the means whereby the inheritance is to be bound by the act of the tenant for life. I think the Act of Parliament gives the option to the tenant for life to serve the notice either before the making of the contract or the making of the lease. If after entering into the contract he allows the service of the notice to lie over, as was done here, and an act of God prevents the notice being given before the execution of the lease, the party dealing with the tenant for life must only take the consequences.

Mr. Houston suggests that the policy of the Legislature in passing this Act was a wide policy, and he says that we ought not to thwart it by requiring too strict an observance of the conditions imposed. All I can say is this: I can see no power enabling the tenant for life to do what it is contended that Harvey has done. The conditions he had to fulfil were all conditions precedent: he has failed to fulfil them, and having failed to fulfil them, his contract cannot bind the remainderman. As to the merits I know nothing and I can say nothing. If the defendant has a meritorious case it is a pity that we have to decide against him; but we are here to administer not to amend the law.

Notes and Questions

Does the principle applied by the Court of Appeal apply to any act of non-compliance, however trivial, with the requirements of the Settled Land Acts? Would the position have been different if the defendant had not known he was dealing with a tenant for life? See *Irish Land Law*, para. 8.076. See also *Gilmore* v. *The O'Conor Don*, p. 212, *ante*.

Chapter 8
POWERS OF ATTORNEY

Of the two types of power commonly created in respect of land in Ireland, one, the power of appointment, which has such close affinity with trusts is considered to be outside the scope of this book: see *Irish Land Law,* ch. 11. This chapter relates to the other type of power often created, a power of attorney. The statutory provisions governing this sort of power are far from satisfactory (see *ibid.,* para. 11.29 *et seq.*) and have been completely revised in Northern Ireland, but not yet in the Republic.

CONVEYANCING ACT, 1881
XI – POWERS OF ATTORNEY

46. – (1) The donee of a power of attorney may, if he thinks fit, execute or do any assurance, instrument, or thing in and with his own name and signature and his own seal, where sealing is required, by the authority of the donor of the power; and every assurance, instrument, and thing so executed and done shall be as effectual in law, to all intents, as if it had been executed or done by the donee of the power in the name and with the signature and seal of the donor thereof.

(2) This section applies to powers of attorney created by instruments executed either before or after the commencement of this Act.

47. – (1) Any person making or doing any payment or act, in good faith, in pursuance of a power of attorney, shall not be liable in respect of the payment or act by reason that before the payment or act the donor of the power had died or become lunatic, of unsound mind, or bankrupt, or had revoked the power, if the fact of death, lunacy, unsoundness of mind, bankruptcy, or revocation was not at the time of the payment or act known to the person making or doing the same.

(2) But this section shall not affect any right against the payee of any person interested in any money so paid; and that person shall have the like remedy against the payee as he would have had against the payer if the payment had not been made by him.

(3) This section applies only to payments and acts made and done after the commencement of this Act.

48. – (1) An instrument creating a power of attorney, its execution being verified by affidavit, statutory declaration, or other sufficient evidence, may, with the affidavit or declaration, if any, be deposited in the Central Office of the Supreme Court.

(2) A separate file of instruments so deposited shall be kept, and any person may search that file, and inspect every instrument so deposited, and an office copy thereof shall be delivered out to him on request.

(3) A copy of an instrument so deposited may be presented at the office, and may be stamped or marked as an office copy, and when so stamped or marked shall become and be an office copy.

(4) An office copy of an instrument so deposited shall without further proof be sufficient evidence of the contents of the instrument and of the deposit thereof in the Central Office.

(5) General Rules may be made for purposes of this section, regulating the practice of the Central Office, and prescribing, with the concurrence of the [Department of Finance], the fees to be taken therein.

(6) This section applies to instruments creating powers of attorney executed either before or after the commencement of this Act.

CONVEYANCING ACT, 1882
POWERS OF ATTORNEY

8. – (1) If a power of attorney, given for valuable consideration, is in the instrument creating the power expressed to be irrevocable, then, in favour of a purchaser –

   (i)   The power shall not be revoked at any time, either by anything done by the donor of the power without the concurrence of the donee of the power, or by the death, marriage, lunacy, unsoundness of mind, or bankruptcy of the donor of the power; and

   (ii) Any act done at any time by the donee of the power, in pursuance of the power, shall be as valid as if anything done by the donor of the power without the concurrence of the donee of the power, or the death, marriage, lunacy, unsoundness of mind, or bankruptcy of the donor of the power, had not been done or happened; and

   (iii) Neither the donee of the power nor the purchaser shall at any time be prejudicially affected by notice of anything done by the donor of the power, without the concurrence of the donee of the power, or of the death, marriage, lunacy, unsoundness of mind, or bankruptcy of the donor of the power.

(2) This section applies only to powers of attorney created by instruments executed after the commencement of this Act.

9. – (1) If a power of attorney, whether given for valuable consideration or not, is in the instrument creating the power expressed to be irrevocable for a fixed time therein specified, not exceeding one year from the date of the instrument, then, in favour of a purchaser –

   (i)   The power shall not be revoked, for and during that fixed time, either by anything done by the donor of the power without the concurrence of the donee of the power, or by the death, marriage, lunacy, unsoundness of mind, or bankruptcy of the donor of the power; and

   (ii) Any act done within that fixed time, by the donee of the power, in pursuance of the power, shall be as valid as if anything done by the donor of the power without the concurrence of the donee of the power, or the death, marriage, lunacy, unsoundness of mind, or bankruptcy of the donor of the power, had not been done or happened; and

   (iii) Neither the donee of the power, nor the purchaser, shall at any time be prejudicially affected by notice either during or after that fixed time of anything done by the donor of the power during that fixed time, without the concurrence of the donee of the power, or of the death, marriage, lunacy, unsoundness of mind, or bankruptcy of the donor of the power within that fixed time.

(2) This section applies only to powers of attorney created by instruments executed after the commencement of this Act.

INDUSTRIAL DEVELOPMENT AUTHORITY V. MORAN
[1978] I.R. 159 (Supreme Court)

In 1965 a company issued a debenture to a bank to secure the repayment of moneys which had been advanced by the bank to the company. The debenture created a floating charge over the property of the company in favour of the bank. The conditions of the debenture empowered the bank, upon the principal moneys so secured becoming payable, to appoint a receiver of the company's assets. The conditions provided that such receiver would have power to sell the company's assets and to effect such sale 'by deed in the name and on behalf' of the company, and that such receiver was to be the attorney of the company 'to execute, seal and deliver' any deed required for the purpose of such sale. However, the company's articles of association required that its seal be used only by the authority of the directors of the company. The bank duly appointed a receiver of the company's assets and he agreed to sell certain freehold registered land which the company owned. In the conveyance to the purchaser the company and the receiver, as two distinct grantors, purported to convey the lands to the purchaser in fee simple. The execution of the conveyance by the company was effected by the company's seal being affixed to the conveyance by the receiver opposite the attestation but without the authority of the directors, and the receiver executed the conveyance by signing his name on it. When the purchaser applied to be registered on the relevant folio as full owner of the lands assured, the Registrar of Titles questioned the validity of the conveyance and referred the application to the High Court for its determination. Having considered the reference, the High Court held that the conveyance was ineffective because (a) the receiver had no power to affix the company's seal to the conveyance and (b) the company had no power to authorise an attorney to execute deeds on his behalf within the State. The purchaser appealed to the Supreme Court.

O'Higgins C.J.:

I have read the judgment which Mr. Justice Kenny is about to deliver and I agree with it.

Kenny J.:

Cork Shoe Company Ltd. was incorporated in the State in May, 1947. The regulations in Table A in the first schedule to the Companies (Consolidation) Act, 1908, including Article 71 (with some exceptions which are not relevant to this case) applied to the company. The company subsequently acquired the lands in folio 43689 of the register of freeholders for the county of Cork, on which there were a number of factories.

On the 23rd October, 1965, the company gave a debenture under its seal to the Bank of Ireland to secure all moneys advanced to the company were to be repayable on demand. The company charged its undertaking and all its property with repayment of the sum due and also, as a specific charge, the lands in folio 43689. The debenture was registered as a burden on the folio.

This debenture was issued subject to and with the benefit of the conditions which were endorsed on it and which were to be deemed part of it. Conditions 10 and 14 are so important that I have to set them out:

> 10. 'At any time after the principal moneys hereby secured become payable, the registered holder of this debenture may appoint by writing any person to be a receiver and manager of the property charged by this debenture . . . and any receiver and manager so appointed shall have power . . . (3) To sell or concur in selling, let or concur in letting any of the property charged by this debenture, and to carry any such sale into effect by deed in the name and on behalf of the company, or otherwise, to convey the same to the purchaser . . .
>
> 14. The company hereby irrevocably appoints any receiver or receivers appointed as aforesaid the attorney or attorneys of the company for the company and in its name and on its behalf and as its act and deed to execute, seal and deliver and otherwise perfect any deed assurance agreement instrument or act which may be required or may be deemed proper for any of the purposes aforesaid.'

On the 24th July, 1973, the company adopted new articles of association which provided that the regulations in Table A in the first schedule to the Act of 1908 and in Table A in the first schedule to the Companies Act, 1963, should not apply to the company. The only relevant regulation is article 128 which reads:

'The seal shall be used only by the authority of the directors or of a committee of directors authorised by the directors in that behalf, and every instrument to which the seal shall be affixed shall be signed by a director and shall be countersigned by the secretary or by a second director or by some other person appointed by the directors for the purpose.'

In 1975 there was a substantial sum of money due by the company to the bank, and on the 12th May, 1975, the bank appointed Mr. Michael Gribben as receiver and manager of the company. He agreed to sell part of the lands in the folio to the Industrial Development Authority, who became the purchasers.

On the 8th October, 1976, a deed of transfer was executed; it was expressed to be made between the company of the first part, Michael Gribben of the second part and the purchasers of the third part. It recited that under the powers given by the conditions endorsed on the debenture of the 23rd October, 1965, Mr. Gribben had agreed with the purchasers to sell the lands to which the transfer related. The deed then witnessed that the company, the registered owner, acting by the receiver did thereby convey, and that Mr. Gribben as receiver in exercise of the powers given to him by the conditions endorsed on the debenture transferred, the lands described in the deed to the purchaser in fee simple. The testimonium to this deed reads: 'The common seal of Cork Shoe Company Limited was affixed hereto by the direction of Michael Gribben' and the seal of the company appeared opposite this. Immediately underneath this there appeared the words: 'Signed, sealed and delivered by the said Michael Gribben in the presence of . . .' The deed was then executed by Michael Gribben in his own name, and the witness to the execution by Mr. Gribben signed his name.

When the deed was presented to the Registrar of Titles, he had some doubt about its validity and he referred the matter to the High Court under s.19, sub-s. 2, of the Registration of Title Act, 1964. Mr. Justice Butler held that the seal of the company had been irregularly affixed and that the company had no power to appoint an attorney; the judge declared that the deed of the 8th October, 1976, was ineffectual to transfer to the purchasers the property described in that deed. The purchasers have appealed to this Court.

I think that the judge was correct on the first point concerning the use of the seal but that he was incorrect on the second point. In my view, the deed of the 8th October, 1976, was effective to transfer to the purchasers all the estate and interest of the company in the part of the lands in the folio to which the deed related.

When a receiver is appointed over the assets of a company, the articles of association continue in force and bind him. A receiver, as receiver, has no authority to use the seal of the company. Article 128 required that the seal should be used only by the authority of the directors, and that every instrument to which the seal was affixed should be signed by a director and should be countersigned by the secretary or by a second director. In this case the directors did not authorise the use of the seal and none of them signed the deed of the 8th October, 1976. Accordingly, the first part of the testimonium was without any effect.

The judge reached the conclusion that 'a company has no power to act by attorney to execute deeds within the State' as an inference from s. 40 of the Companies Act, 1963, which reads:

'(1) A company may, by writing under its common seal, empower any person, either generally or in respect of any specified matters, as its attorney, to execute deeds on its behalf in any place outside the State.

(2) A deed signed by such attorney on behalf of the company and under his seal shall bind the company and have the same effect as if it were under its common seal.'

A somewhat similar provision appeared in s. 78 of the Act of 1908 and in s. 55 of the Companies Act, 1862. The inference which the judge drew from s. 40 of the Act of 1963 was incorrect. A company has power to act by attorney to execute deeds within the State and s. 40 of the Act of 1963 is intended to give a company the power to act by attorney outside the State. Some doubt existed whether a company had power to do this and so s. 55 of the Act of 1862 was enacted and was carried forward in the consolidating Acts of 1908 and 1963.

In volume 1 of Palmer's Company Precedents, 17th edition (1956) the author at p. 950 deals with powers of attorney: 'Powers of attorney are frequently required in connection with companies. Prima facie any company can appoint an attorney to act on its behalf, for the attorney is an agent, and as a company can only act by agents, it has an implied power to appoint such agents.' The authority cited for this proposition is *Ferguson* v. *Wilson* [(1866) 2 Ch. App. 77, 89]. The author continues: 'Members of the public dealing with an agent having apparent authority to act on its behalf are in general entitled to assume that he had such authority unless it appears from the company's registered documents that he had not the authority in question . . . Whether, however, in any particular case the directors of a company have power to execute a power of attorney on the company's behalf depends on the article. The general rule is *delegatus non potest delegare*. But directors are generally invested with wide general powers, and in virtue of such powers they are ususally in a position to grant a power of attorney; otherwise the sanction of a general meeting must be obtained.'

The debenture was given in 1965 and so the validity of the appointment must be judged, not by the provisions of the new articles of association adopted in July, 1973, but by the articles in force in 1965. This point was not adverted to in the argument in this Court or before Mr. Justice Butler.

Article 71 of Table A in the Act of 1908, so far as relevant, reads:

'The business of the company shall be managed by the directors, who may pay all expenses incurred in getting up and registering the company, and may exercise all such powers of the company as are not, by the Companies (Consolidation) Act, 1908, or any statutory modification thereof for the time being in force, or by these articles, required to be exercised by the company in general meeting, subject nevertheless to any regulation of these articles, to the provisions of the said Act, and to such regulations, being not inconsistent with the aforesaid regulations or provisions, as may be prescribed by the company in general meeting.'

The articles of this company in force in 1965 did not require that a power of attorney could be given only by the company in general meeting and there was nothing in the Act of 1908 which required this. It is also relevant that a form of debenture with a clause exactly similar to clause 10 of the conditions in this case appears at p. 277 in the third volume of Palmer's Company Precedents, which relates to debentures: 12th ed. – 1920. I take that edition because it was the last one before the English property legislation of 1925 and was edited by Mr. Alfred Topham, a well-known expert on company law. It is inconceivable to me that Mr. Topham would have included such a clause if a company had no power to appoint an attorney to execute deeds on its behalf.

As Mr. Gribben executed the deed of transfer in his own name, the provisions of s. 46, sub-s. 1, of the Conveyancing Act, 1881, make the deed of transfer fully effective. The sub-section reads:

'The donee of a power of attorney may, if he thinks fit, execute or do any assurance, instrument, or thing in and with his own name and signature and his own seal, where sealing is required, by the authority of the donor of the power; and every assurance, instrument, and thing so executed and done shall be as effectual in law, to all intents, as if it had been executed or done by the donee of the power in the name and with the signature and seal of the donor thereof.'

Accordingly, the deed of transfer of the 8th October, 1976, was effectual to transfer the lands described in it to the purchasers, and the order of the 1st may, 1978, should be set aside. This Court should declare that the deed dated the 8th October, 1976, was effective to tranfer to the purchasers the property therein described as being transferred; and the Registrar of Titles should be directed to register its effect on the folio.

While the deed of transfer in this case is effective because of s. 46 of the Conveyancing Act, 1881, I wish to point out that the power given to the receiver by clause 10 is 'to carry any such sale into effect by deed in the name and on behalf of the company.' When a receiver is selling under such a clause, the more usual and better practice is for him to execute the deed of transfer by writing the name of the company and underneath this to write words that indicate that the name of the company has been written by the receiver as attorney of the company under the power of attorney given by the debenture. In addition, he should execute the deed in his own name. In that way he has the best of both worlds. The writing of the name of the company by the authority of the company given when it executed the debenture brings the case within the words of the debenture itself, and execution by the attorney personally gives the advantage of s. 46 of the Conveyancing Act, 1881.

Parke J.:
I have read the judgment delivered by Mr. Justice Kenny and I agree with it.

Chapter 9
MORTGAGES

The material in this chapter covers both the nature and creation of mortgages and the position of the mortgagor and mortgagee once a mortgage has been created: see *Irish Land Law*, chs. 12 and 13. It also deals with judgment mortgages, a subject which has caused much litigation in the Republic of Ireland recently.

I. NATURE AND CREATION OF MORTGAGES

REGISTRATION OF THE ACT, 1964

Charges

62. – (1) A registered owner of land may, subject to the provisions of this Act, charge the land with the payment of money either with or without interest, and either by way of annuity or otherwise, and the owner of the charge shall be registered as such.

(2) There shall be executed on the creation of a charge, otherwise than by will, an instrument of charge in the prescribed form (or an instrument in such other form as may appear to the Registrar to be sufficient to charge the land, provided that such instrument shall expressly charge or reserve out of the land the payment of the money secured) but, until the owner of the charge is registered as such, the instrument shall not confer on the owner of the charge any interest in the land.

(3) A mortgage by way of conveyance with a proviso for redemption or by way of demise or sub-demise shall not of itself operate to charge registered land or be registrable as a charge on registered land.

(4) Any power, howsoever conferred, to borrow or lend money on the security of a mortgage shall be construed as including power to do so on the security of a registered charge.

(5) On registration of the owner of the charge the Registrar shall deliver to him a certificate of charge in the prescribed form.

(6) On registration of the owner of a charge on land for the repayment of any principal sum of money with or without interest, the instrument of charge shall operate as a mortgage by deed within the meaning of the Conveyancing Acts, and the registered owner of the charge shall, for the purpose of enforcing his charge, have all the rights and powers of a mortgagee under a mortgage by deed, including the power to sell the estate or interest which is subject to the charge.

(7) When repayment of the principal money secured by the instrument of charge has become due, the registered owner of the charge or his personal representative may apply to the court in a summary manner for possession of the land or any part of the land, and on the application the court may, if it so thinks proper, order possession of the land or the said part thereof to be delivered to the applicant, and the applicant, upon obtaining possesion of the land or the said part thereof, shall be deemed to be a mortgagee in possession.

(8) On registration of the owner of a charge by way of annuity, the owner of the charge shall have such remedies for recovering and compelling payment of the annuity as are described in section 44 of the Conveyancing Act, 1881, as affected by section 6 of the Conveyancing Act, 1911.

(9) If the registered owner of a charge on land sells the land in pursuance of the

powers referred to in subsection (6), his transferee shall be registered as owner of the land, and thereupon the registration shall have the same effect as registration on a transfer for valuable consideration by a registered owner.

(10) When a transferee from the registered owner of the charge is registered, under subsection (9), as owner of the land, the charge and all estates, interests, burdens and entries puisne to the charge shall be discharged.

(11) When it is expressed in the instrument of charge that any person covenants for repayment of the principal sum charged, there shall be implied a covenant by that person with the registered owner for the time being of the charge to pay the sum charged and interest (if any) thereon at the time and rate specified in the instrument of charge, and also a covenant, if the sum or any part thereof is unpaid at the time so specified, to pay interest half-yearly at the specified rate on so much of the principal sum as for the time being remains unpaid.

63. – (1) A charge registered prior to the commencement of this Act shall not be void or be deemed ever to have been void –

(a) by reason only that it was expressed to have been created by way of mortgage, or

(b) by reason only that the consent of the Land Commission or the Commissioners of Public Works or such other consent as may be provided for by any enactment was not obtained to any demise or sub-demise expressed to have been created by any such mortgage;

and the registration of the charge as a burden on registered land shall not be invalid or be deemed ever to have been invalid for either of these reasons.

(2) In this section 'mortgage' includes both a mortgage by demise or sub-demise and a mortgage by conveyance or assignment with a proviso for redemption.

64. – (1) The registered owner of a charge may transfer the charge to another person as owner thereof, and the transferee shall be registered as owner of the charge.

(2) There shall be executed on the transfer of a charge an instrument of transfer in the prescribed form, or in such other form as may appear to the Registrar to be sufficient to transfer the charge, but until the transferee is registered as owner of the charge, that instrument shall not cooonfer on the transferee any interest in the charge.

(3) The Registrar shall deliver to the registered transferee a certificate of charge in the prescribed form.

(4) On registration of the transferee of a charge, the instrument of transfer shall operate as a conveyance by deed within the meaning of the Conveyancing Acts, and the transferee shall –

(a) have the same title to the charge as a registered transferee of land under this Act has to the land, under a transfer for valuable consideration or without valuable consideration, as the case may be; and

(b) have for enforcing his charge the same rights and powers in respect of the land as if the charge had been originally created in his favour.

65. – (1) The Registrar shall note on the register the satisfaction of a registered charge or of any part of such a charge on registered land, or of the release of any part of registered land from a registered charge, either at the request of the registered owner of the charge, or on proof in such manner as is hereinafter mentioned, or in such other manner as may be prescribed, and thereupon the charge shall to the extent so noted cease to operate.

(2) For the purposes of this section, the receipt of the registered owner for the time being of a charge shall be sufficient proof of the satisfaction of the charge, or of any part of the charge, and a release signed by the registered owner for the time

being of a charge shall be sufficient proof of the release of any part of registered land subject to that charge.

66. – The provisions of this Act with respect to the transmission of registered land and the defeasance of the estate or interest of the registered owner shall apply, with the prescribed modifications, to transmissions and defeasances in the case of registered charges on land.

67. – (1) The registered owner of a charge shall not, merely by reason of his being such owner, be entitled to the possession of the land certificate in respect of the registered land which is subject to the charge.

(2) Every stipulation in relation to a registered charge on land (whether made before or after the creation of the charge) whereby the custody of the land certificate in respect of such land is to be given to the registered owner of such charge shall be void.

105. – . . .

(5) Subject to any registered rights, the deposit of a land certificate or certificate of charge shall, for the purpose of creating a lien on the land or charge to which the certificate relates, have the same effect as a deposit of the title deeds of unregistered land or of a charge thereon.

ANTRIM COUNTY LAND, BUILDING AND INVESTMENT CO. LTD. V. STEWART

[1904] 2 I.R. 357; 3 N.I.J.R. 236; 37 I.L.T.R. 101 (Court of Appeal)

The defendants bought their farm from the landlord, through the Land Commission, under the Land Purchase Acts, in 1886, and by deed dated the 12th August, 1886, the lands were conveyed to them in fee. By the same deed the defendants mortgaged the land to the Irish Land Commission as security for the repayment of the purchase annuity. By a mortgage, dated the 4th May, 1901, the defendants mortgaged the land to the Antrim Building Company to secure the repayment of £1000. The mortgage contained a power of sale and an express statement of the mortgage to the Land Commission. The Antrim Building Company sold the land under the power of sale to Houston.

An action of ejectment on the title was brought by the Company and Houston as co-plaintiffs. Kenny J. found for the plaintiffs, but this decision was reversed by the King's Bench Division. The plaintiff appealed to the Court of Appeal.

Palles C.B.:

I am of opinion that this appeal ought to be allowed. It is brought from an order of the King's Bench Division which changed a verdict for the plaintiffs, directed by Kenny, J., at the trial, into one for the defendants. The question as to the effect of the Judicature Act, on which our judgment must depend, although discussed before the King's Bench, is not referred to in the judgments below, and therefore, we have not the advantage of knowing the view taken of it by the Judges there. As to the question upon which the decision there was based, viz. the proposition that, as the law stood before the Judicature Act, a mortgagor, defendant in an ejectment by a second mortgagee under a mortgage which recited the prior one, was not estopped from relying as a defence upon the legal estate being outstanding, I agree with the view of the King's Bench; and the only reason why I refrain from discussing it at length is that, having regard to the opinion I have formed upon the other question, it does not arise.

The question then upon which the decision of the appeal must rest is one which, having regard to the expected legislation as to land purchase, is of vital moment to purchasing tenants in Ireland, because if the view put forward by Mr. Bartley is right, the sale out of Court by mortgagees of estates purchased through the Land Commission would, so long as any sum remained due on the Government advance, be attended with extreme difficulty, if indeed it would not be practically impossible. Consequently a farm so purchased would for this long period hardly be available as a source of credit. In my opinion this view is not correct. I hold that on the plain construction of the Judicature Act the plaintiff here is, by virtue of his equitable title, entitled to judgment in this action of ejectment, and is so entitled although the Land Commission, in whom the legal estate is, is not before the Court.

It is a mistake to say that the King's Bench Division is a Common Law Court. 'The Court', to use the words of Lord Cairns in *Pugh* v. *Heath* (7 A.C. 237), 'is now not a Court of law, or a Court of Equity, it is a *Court of Complete Jurisdiction*, and if there were a variance between what, before the Judicature Act, a Court of law and a Court of Equity would have done, the rule of the Court of Equity must now prevail'. Where the plaintiff claims to be entitled to any right – such as here, the right of possession of land – by virtue of an equitable estate, the High Court, whatever may be the Division of it in which the suit may happen to be, *must*, so long as the suit remains in the Division, give the same relief as ought to have been given by the Court of Chancery in a suit properly instituted for the like purpose before the Act. This is one of the broadest of the principles which are the bases of the Judicature Act, and we cannot allow it to be frittered away by small technicalities, which it was one of the objects of the Act to extinguish.

From this principle results that which Sir George Jessel (whose loss is greatly to be deplored by all who desire that a wide and liberal interpretation shall be given to the Act), in *The General Finance Co.* v. *Liberator Benefit Building Society* (10 Ch. D. 15, 24), treats as settled law that no action of ejectment can be defeated for the want of the legal estate where the plaintiff has a title to the possession. To my mind that proposition is absolutely incontestable. We have been referred to *Allen* v. *Woods* (68 L.T. 143), in which Lindley, L.J., held that in the peculiar circumstances of the case before him the person who had the legal estate should have been a party to the suit, and in which he refused relief in his absence. The observations of that very learned Judge, which of course must be taken *secundum subjectam materiam*, seem to have been erroneously incorporated in some of the later textbooks, and there treated as laying down the *general* proposition that no one who claims an equitable estate can have any relief unless the legal estate is before the Court. The learned Lord Justice could not have meant to enunciate, and, as I read his judgment, did not in fact enunciate, any such general proposition. The case was one in which the plaintiff could not have succeeded unless direct relief had been given against the absent person. It was essential to that success that such person should have been a trustee for the plaintiff, and as he was not an express trustee, or a person who could be deemed a trustee otherwise than through the judgment of the Court, it was a condition precedent to giving any relief to the plaintiff that the judgment should declare him a trustee – a judgment which it was impossible to give when he was not a party. I therefore pass by that case, and come to the facts of the present one.

It is impossible to contend that the Land Commission are entitled, under the conveyance to them, to go into possession, unless and until default has been made in payment of an instalment. Mr. Bartley referred to case in which mortgagees were held entitled at law to go into possession before default. But the question discussed in those cases was whether the words of the particular mortgage there under consideration had the precision necessary to amount to a demise of the mortgaged premises by the mortgagee to the mortgagor until default. Words operating by way of covenant only were not *at law* sufficient for that purpose, no matter how clear might have been the intention: *Doe* v. *Lightfoot* (8 M. & W. 564); although I think it clear that if the intention that the mortgagor should retain possession till default were manifest on the face of the mortgage, the mortgagee, if he tried to enter before default, would have been restrained by a Court of Equity from so doing. If that be so in the case of an ordinary mortgage, *a fortiori* is it in a case like the present, where the mortgage is to a body like the Land Commission, created by statute for the purpose of carrying out the purchase provisions of a series of Acts, the whole object of which would be defeated if the tenant-purchaser's possession could be interfered with so long as he performed his contract with the State.

These Acts were passed for the benefit of occupying tenants, with the object of continuing them in their occupation, not as tenants but as fee-simple proprietors, and as ancillary to this object of inducing them to purchase the fee-simple of their holdings by making them advances of money repayable by instalments. The deed to the Land Commission is prepared not inaptly to carry out the intention of the Acts, but even had it not been, I should not have had any hesitation in holding that, before the Judicature Act, a Court of Equity would at once have restrained the Land Commission in the almost impossible event of their attempting to use their legal estate to dispossess a purchaser before default – a use which would have been in defiance of the plain terms of the Acts.

If that is so, what is the condition of the parties here? The legal estate is vested in the Land Commission, whose right to punctual payment of the instalments is superior to that of all the parties here. Then, subject to that right, the two parties here are, first, Houston (who is represented by the plaintiffs), a purchaser under a power of sale in the mortgage, who claims the possession under his contract of sale (a contract admittedly binding on the defendant, the mortgagor); and, secondly, the mortgagor himself, who resists the right to possession of the plaintiff, a person plainly entitled to that possession not only against him, but against everyone, including the Land Commission. Is it possible to contend that it is not inequitable that the mortgagor should rely on that legal estate to prejudice the title conferred on the purchaser through his own grant? I hold that, even had there not been a purchaser, the second mortgagees, the Antrim Land Company, could recover in this ejectment. But here there is a purchaser, and *his* right is not to an account of the sum due on the mortgage, or to a receiver, or to a sale. His contract is one of purchase. It is one which is capable of being, and which he is entitled to have, specifically performed, and of that specific performance possession is part and parcel. It follows that the plaintiffs are entitled to the possession; and, in the words of Sir George Jessel, 'the action cannot be defeated for the want of the legal estate'.

This being so, it would serve no useful purpose were I to discuss the exact form of procedure which, before the Judicature Act, ought to have been adopted by a Court of Equity as ancillary to determining the plaintiff's right of possession. It is immaterial whether it would have restrained the defendant from relying on the outstanding legal estate, treating it as a temporary bar (as was done in *Blennerhasset* v. *Day* (2 B. & B. 104)), and let the question be tried in an ejectment; or whether an issue would have been directed; or whether the Court of Chancery itself would have determined the right of possession; or, lastly, whether the outstanding estate was such a temporary bar as might have been dealt with under the Common Law Procedure Act of 1856. Whatever might have been the course adopted, one thing is certain, that through the judgments of two separate Courts the plaintiff would have been put into possession, and what then could have been effected through two Courts can and ought now to be effected by the one Court.

Mr. Bartley's argument ultimately assumed the form of an objection for want of parties. He contended that nothing could be done in the absence of the Land

Commission. I deem it essential to the ends of justice that the Court should lend no colour to an objection for want of parties, unless there be solid, indeed coercive, reason for so doing. So far back as 1843, Sir E. Sugden began the struggle against the enormous costs incurred by the number of parties rendered necessary by the former Rules of Courts of Equity. These Rules were, from time to time, abrogated and further abrogated, until the culmination was reached in our practice under the Judicature Act by Order XVI., Rule 11, of the Rules of 1891.

Under this Rule we are, in the circumstances of this case, enabled, and in my opinion bound, to determine the rights of the parties before us – parties indeed who represent the only rights and interests in dispute. The Land Commission are not interested in the action, or in any question raised in it. They have their paramount claim, no matter which party shall succeed here. It would be a mere waste of time and money to direct that the case should stand over till the Land Commission were made parties.

I have already indicated that were it necessary to consider how the case would have stood had there not been a purchaser, and if the second mortgagees had been the sole plaintiffs, I should still have been of opinion that they were entitled to be put into possession. The old rule that partial relief should not be given has been abrogated, and I hold that in such a case as that supposed the mortgagee, although he had a power to sell, would be entitled to decline to exercise it, without actual possession; so that he might be in a position when selling to guarantee to the purchaser possession on a fixed day. It is no answer to this to say that he could get an order for sale in the Chancery Division. His contract is that he is to have a power of sale, and the Court ought not to deprive him of that power. Nor is it an answer that the purchaser after completion might himself bring an ejectment. Many a person may be willing to purchase a farm under a contract that he will obtain possession on a fixed day without litigation, and quite unwilling to purchase if his right to possession must be established by an action. The necessity of the purchaser entering upon litigation would undoubtedly seriously affect the price.

On these grounds I am of opinion that the order of the King's Bench should be reversed.

FitzGibbon L.J.:

I doubt that the King's Bench can have been conscious of the consequences of its decision in this case. If this action be defeated, it is the defeat of the claim of a mortgagee of a holding acquired under the Land Purchase Acts, and the decision, as it stands, is a decision that no mortgagee of property of that description – a large and increasing class in this country – can enforce payment of his demand by recovering possession of the mortgaged land.

The deed executed under the Purchase Acts first vests the fee-simple in the purchasing tenant, and then transfers it to the Land Commission as security for the payment by instalments of the principal and interest of the purchase-money. It is immaterial that the Land Commission is a public body; the effect of the deed must be the same as if the parties to it were private individuals.

It will throw light on the question to consider the case in three different aspects.

First, what would the rights of the parties have been at Common Law, before the Judicature Act? In an ejectment at law brought by a second mortgagee, being the owner of an equitable estate in the land, the mortgagor could not set up the existence of a prior legal mortgage as a defence against the claim of his own equitable grantee to the possession.

It has been contended that this rule could not apply to this case, because the existence of the first mortgage was disclosed on the face of the second. I cannot conceive how that can be so. The disclosure of the first mortgage on the deed could not have any greater effect than if the puisne mortgagee had express notice of it in any other way. Further, no honestly or properly drawn puisne mortgage could omit to disclose on its face that the lands were subject to a prior mortgage, as the omission might facilitate fraud by enabling the equitable mortgagee to represent himself as the legal owner of the fee, or by making the deed appear to convey the legal estate.

In my opinion, the only distinction which is material for the present purpose is where the second security created only a charge, and gave no equitable estate in the land or equitable right to the possession. Under the old law, the test of the right of a mortgagee, whether puisne or not, to obtain possession of the land, was whether he had the right to foreclose. In Ireland, foreclosure fell into disuse, because there was here a special procedure for realizing mortgages by Court Receivers, and by sales in the Landed Estates Court; but puisne mortgagees had the same right of foreclosure as in England.

In Davidson's Conveyancing (vol. ii., p. 69, 4th ed.) the law is stated thus:-

'The question whether the strict right of an equitable mortgagee is foreclosure or sale has been much discussed. Some confusion seems to have been created by not properly distinguishing between, first, a formal mortgage of an equity of redemption; secondly, a mortgage created by deposit of deeds with an express agreement to execute a formal mortgage; thirdly, a mortgage by deposit without such an agreement, as to which, after conflict of authority, it has been determined that the effect of the deposit alone is to give the mortgagee the right to call for a formal mortgage, so that this case is not distinguishable in principle from the last case; and, fourthly, an equitable security which gives a mere charge or lien on the property without any right to call for a formal mortgage. It appears to be settled that the right of the mortgagee in both the first, and the second, and the third cases is foreclosure, and in the fourth case sale only; but that in the case of a mortgage by deposit the mortgagee can waive his right to foreclosure, and obtain an immediate decree for sale.'

If that is the law, under a puisne mortgage, such as we have here, which in equity granted the land and the right to possession, the mortgagor could not set up the prior legal mortgage as a defence to a simple ejectment on the title at law.

But whether I am right or wrong in that, I have still to consider, secondly, what would have been the rtights of the parties before the Judicature Act, if the puisne mortgagee had either aided his ejectment by an order of a Court of Equity, or had proceeded by suit in Equity. In either case it is, in my opinion, clear that possession of the land could have been recovered. If the ejectment had been brought at law, the order which would have been made by a Court of Equity in aid of that action would have been a decree prohibiting temporary bars from being set up so as to prevent the real right to the property – *i.e.,* to the possession claimed in the action – from being tried and determined. If a suit in Equity had been brought before the Judicature Act, by the present plaintiff against the present defendant, and the defendant had pleaded that the legal estate was in the Land Commission, the one and only thing which a Court of Equity would have done would have been to order notice to be given to the Land Commission as owner of the legal estate. If the Land Commission came in, the Court, on ascertaining that it had the legal right, would inquire whether it desired to go into possession. If not, the equitable mortgagee might have obtained the possession, or had a Receiver, in either case keeping down the charge of the Land Commission.

Seeing that the vesting of the legal estate in the Land Commission is simply part of a system created by statute, for fixing occupying tenants of land in Ireland in their holdings, while securing payment of the purchase-money advanced by the State by instalments covering a long period of years, it would seem to me to be illegal for the Land Commission to put the tenant out, or to go itself into possession, until default in payment of some instalment; and even if the tenant was in default, the Land Commission, when brought before the Court of Equity, on notice, in a suit by the equitable mortgagee, might say, 'We do not want to go into possession', or the Court might say, 'The plaintiff must indemnify the Land Commission' – in other words, he must redeem, or pay the instalments due. In neither case could the mortgagor defeat the claim of the equitable mortgagee to the possession, as the King's Bench has defeated it here.

Lastly, if the action could not have been defeated under the old law, whether at Common Law, or in Equity, or by combining both, there can be no answer to the suit since the Judicature Act. If the defence be treated as an objection for want of parties, the rule requires us to dispose of the case as between the parties before us, unless it is necessary to bring in others in order to provide for their rights. If the defence be treated as a plea in bar, or as matter of substance, then we must obey the Act by giving the same relief which a Court of Equity would have given before – that is, an equitable decree to put the plaintiff into possession, on providing for the payment of the instalments to the Land Commission.

For these reasons I concur with the other members of the Court in holding that the judgment of the King's Bench must be reversed, and that the judgment of Kenny, J., for the possession must be restored.

Holmes L.J.:

I start with the proposition that, since the Judicature Act, where a person is entitled in equity to the possession of land, he can recover such possession by action in the High Court, even although the legal estate is not vested in him. This seems to me to follow from the language of the Act, and it has been laid down by high judicial authority. If I am right in this, the only question is whether the plaintiffs or either of them are entitled in equity to the possession of the premises sued for. What are the relations of the several parties to each other? An occupying tenant purchased his holding from his landlord, borrowing the purchase-money from the Land Commission in the manner prescribed by Lord Ashbourne's Act, which provides that the loan is to be repaid by a terminable annuity to be secured by deed. This security was given in a way afterwards abandoned as inconvenient, namely, by a tripartite instrument, by which the landlord first conveyed the lands to the tenant, and the latter then mortgaged them to the Land Commission to secure the payment of the annuity at the times agreed on. It is manifest that although the legal estate was then vested in the Land Commission, that body was not entitled to take possession of the premises as long as the annuity was not in arrear. Even if the terms of the deed expressly authorized such a step, I should hold the provision to be illegal as being repugnant to the Act of Parliament that authorized the loan and the security; but there is no stipulation of this kind, nor any difficulty in ascertaining the true construction of the document. In this state of things the tenant, who had purchased, mortgaged the lands to the Investment Company. The mortgage deed conveys the premises in fee-simple, and contains a reference to the instrument under which the mortgagor had acquired them, and by which he had vested them in the Land Commission. The mortgagee had thus notice of the terms of that deed, and the effect of the mortgage was to convey to him, subject thereto, all the mortgagor's interest in the lands, including the right to retain possession as long as the annuity was duly paid. The Conveyancing Act attached to the mortgage a power of sale; and the Company subsequently sold to the other plaintiff under circumstances and in a manner which have been held in a former action to have constituted a proper exercise of the power.

The vendor and purchaser seek in the present suit to recover possession from the mortgagor. Why are they not to succeed? I do not understand that the objection of the outstanding legal estate is relied on; but if it is, I have already dealt with it. Mr. Bartley, however, argues that as the Land Commission is entitled at any moment to enter into possession of the premises, the plaintiffs have failed to establish the right which is the foundation of the action. I have pointed out that this is a mistake. As long as the annuity is duly paid, the Land Commission cannot interfere with the possession, and I must assume, in the absence of evidence to the contrary, that the annuity is not in arrear. It was for the defendants, who are relying as against the mortgagee on the security given to the Land Commission, to show that, according to the terms of that instrument, the latter are now entitled to possession.

Mr. Bartley, feeling the force of this proposition, had recourse to an objection for want of parties, and I think I am doing him no injustice in saying that he admitted that if the Land Comnmission had been named as defendants, and if they had not claimed possession, the plaintiffs would have been entitled to judgment. But as the law now stands the misjoinder is not necessarily fatal. If this objection had been taken at the trial – and in the defendants' favour, I deal with the case as if it had been – the Judge, as he is authorized to do by the Judicature Rules, ought to, and I doubt not would, have proceeded to adjudicate on the rights of the parties before him, knowing that the Land Commission would not be affected by his judgment.

If that body has now, or will have hereafter, a right of entry, nothing that is done in this suit can interfere with it. It would be most dangerous to give any countenance to the idea that, where controversies arise as to the possession of premises purchased under the provisions of the Land Purchase Acts, the Land Commission are necessary parties by reason of the annuity charged on the holding.

It will be observed that in giving my reasons for allowing the appeal, I have confined myself to the facts of this action. I have not ventured upon the wider considerations which FitzGibbon, L.J., has referred to, and which are, in my opinion, not free from difficulty. Deeds precisely or substantially similar to the present must be of frequent occurrence in Ireland; and I desire to rest my judgment upon grounds which to my mind are unanswerable, and are at the same time quite independent of the right of the ordinary puisne mortgagee to obtain possession of the mortgaged premises from his mortgagor.

Notes and Questions
1. What precisely was the nature of the interests in the land in question held by the various parties mentioned in the case? As to the various forms of mortgage and similar concepts, see *Irish Land Law*, ch. 12.
2. As to actions of ejectment, see *ibid.*, para. 17.092 *et seq.*
3. As to a mortgagee's right to possession, see p. 447, *post.*
4. As to operation of the mortgagee's power of sale, see p. 447, *post.*
5. As to foreclosure in Ireland, see p. 456, *post.*

FULLERTON V. PROVINCIAL BANK OF IRELAND
[1903] A.C. 309; 1 I.R. 483; 3 N.I.J.R. 309; 37 I.L.T.R. 188 (House of Lords)

A customer of a bank in Ireland having overdrawn his account and being pressed by the bank undertook by letter to deposit a title-deed of an Irish estate as security for his overdraft. He deposited the title-deed with the bank, who did not register the charge. The customer afterwards mortgaged the estate to the appellants, who registered their charge without notice

of the prior charge. The question of the priority of the two incumbrances arose and Meredith J. held that the letter to the bank created an equitable charge which should have been
registered under the Registration of Deeds Act (Ireland), 1707. Since the appellants had
registered their mortgage they had priority. The Irish Court of Appeal reversed this decision
(see *sub nom. Re Stevenson's Estate* [1902] 1 I.R. 23; 2 N.I.J.R. 49; 36 I.L.T.R. 49) on the
grounds that the letters did not amount to an undertaking to deposit the title-deed, so that
registration was not necessary and the bank had priority on the principle laid down in *Re
Burke* (1881) 9 L.R. Ir. 24. The appellants appealed to the House of Lords.

Lord Macnaghten:
My Lords, the point raised by this appeal is a short point, and not, I think, one of
any great difficulty.
The appellants and the respondents were both equitable incumbrancers on
certain property in Westmeath known as the Portlemon estate, and there is a
contest for priority between them. The Portlemon estate has now been sold. But at
the commencement of the contest the equity of redemption was vested in a Colonel
Stevenson, who acquired the property from a Mrs. Treacy; she conveyed it to him
in consideration of the sum of 8000*l.*, which was secured on the property by a legal
mortgage of even date with the conveyance.
The charge in favour of the appellants (who are the trustees of Colonel
Stevenson's marriage settlement) was created by a deed of mortgage dated the 29th
and duly registered on the 31st of July, 1896. There is no question as to the validity
or the regularity of this mortgage.
The charge in favour of the respondents was created or completed by the deposit
on July 15, 1895, of the conveyance to Colonel Stevenson of the Portlemon estate.
Their incumbrance is, therefore, prior in date to that of the appellants.
The respondents' case is that they have not and never had any charge upon the
property in question except the charge that was created by the deposit of Colonel
Stevenson's conveyance; that they had, therefore, nothing to register; that the
statute of Anne has no application to their security, and that according to the law
laid down in *In re Burke* (9 L.R. Ir. 24) they are entitled to the priority which
properly belongs to priority of date.
The case of the appellants is that the deposition which the respondents rely was
accompanied or preceded by certain letters leading up to the actual deposit which
were sufficient to create, and which did in fact create, a valid equitable charge on
Colonel Stevenson's interest in the Portlemon estate; that these letters, therefore,
or some or one of them, ought to have been registered, and that for want of such
registration the claim put forward on behalf of the respondents fails, and their
alleged security must be held to be fraudulent and void against holders of a
subsequent registered mortgage.
The whole question, therefore, depends on the meaning and effect of these
letters. They were written by Colonel Stevenson to the local manager of the
Provincial Bank at Londonderry, where Colonel Stevenson's account was kept.
The earliest in date is one of March 26, 1895. The others are dated May 18, May
24, and June 7. When those letters were written the conveyance of the Portlemon
estate to Colonel Stevenson was not in existence – the arrangement for the sale of
the property to him was only in progress. The conveyance was not executed until
July 11, 1895.
I need not trouble your Lordships by reading these letters. They were read at
length in the course of the argument, and they are discussed very fully in the
judgment of the Court below. Throughout these letters, and more particularly in
the letter of May 18, Colonel Stevenson is making out a case for indulgence and
pleading for forbearance. Apparently the local manager had given him to under-

stand that he himself was likely to get into trouble with the head office over the account, and on May 18 Colonel Stevenson writes: 'All you require is a little patience, and my account will be put upon a satisfactory basis.' That was the tone of the letters throughout. In addition, it is enough for me to remind your Lordships that at the outset of the correspondence on March 26, 1895, Colonel Stevenson writes: 'When I receive the title-deeds of the Portlemon property from my solicitors I will have same at once lodged with you.' That was a clear and definite statement on which the manager of the bank was apparently intended to rely. From that statement Colonel Stevenson never receded. He never qualified it. On the contrary, he repeated it more than once, and in one letter he refers to it as a thing which he had 'undertaken'.

My Lords, if these letters were serious letters meant to be taken seriously, I cannot doubt that they created a valid charge in equity attaching to Colonel Stevenson's interest in the Portlemon estate the very moment the property was conveyed to him, and carrying over his interest by way of security to the bank.

That proposition as a proposition of law was not disputed by the learned Solicitor-General. But he rested his case on two grounds. In the first place he adopted the view taken by FitzGibbon and Holmes L.JJ. that these letters had no contractual force, that they were merely friendly letters of a temporising character and intended to put the manager off – that they were of no real importance, and that the transaction which resulted in the deposit must be taken to have commenced on the occasion of the visit of Colonel Stevenson's solicitor to the solicitor of the bank in Dublin on July 11, 1895.

My Lords, I cannot take that view, and I would point out to your Lordships that the first three letters are formal business letters beginning 'Dear Sir' and addressed to 'The Manager, Provincial Bank, Londonderry'. The last letter no doubt begins 'My dear Mr. Stuart' and contains allusions to private matters. But I am unable to understand how such allusions can detract from the force of a definite undertaking, even though the writer should mingle gossip with business.

The other point on which the learned Solicitor-General relied was that there was no proof of consideration. The promise, he said, if it was a definite promise, was 'nudum pactum' – no doubt, he said, Colonel Stevenson had overdrawn his account but there was no stipulation for forbearance for any definite time. The point does not seem to have been argued in the Courts below, though it was suggested and touched upon by FitzGibbon L.J.

My Lords, this point seems to me to be settled by authority. In such a case as this it is not necessary that there should be an arrangement for forbearance for any definite or particular time. It is quite enough if you can infer from the surrounding circumstances that there was an implied request for forbearance for a time, and that forbearance for a reasonable time was in fact extended to the person who asked for it. That proposition seems to me to be established by the case of *Alliance Bank* v. *Broom* ((1864) 2 Dr. & S. 289), to which my noble and learned friend Lord Lindley referred yesterday, and other cases, among which I may mention *Oldershaw* v. *King* ((1857) 2 H. & N. 517), with the observations on that case and the case in Drewry and Smale, by Bowen L.J. in *Miles* v. *New Zealand Alford Estate Co.* ((1886) 32 Ch. D. 289), and I may add that the proposition seems to be good sense.

On the whole, therefore, though I am impressed by the weight which must attach to the deliberate opinion of such eminent judges as FitzGibbon L.J. and Holmes L.J., I ask your Lordships to take a different view.

I therefore move your Lordships that the appeal be allowed, and the judgment of Meredith J. restored with the costs both here and below.

Lord Shand:

My Lords, I am entirely of the same opinion. I think there was an undertaking to deposit the conveyance. The effect of the correspondence is to shew that there was a large debt due to the bank on the account of Colonel Stevenson which had been overdrawn, and as I gather from the letters there was pressure for the repayment of that debt. In answer to that pressure those letters were written which led to the forbearance of the bank, and I am of opinion that that is sufficient to meet the argument on the second point.

Lord Davey:

My Lords, it might appear to some people that the policy of the Irish Registration Act was to postpone an unregistered transfer of property to a registered one, whether the non-registration arose from negligence or inadvertence or from the fact of the transfer having been effected without any document being executed which was capable of being registered. I must express my personal regret that it was not so held, but it is too late now for your Lordships to interfere with what has become the settled law and is expressed in *In re Burke* (9 L.R. Ir. 24).

My Lords, I do not think that the learned judges who formed the majority in the Court of Appeal differed from Meredith J. and Walker L.J. in the law which they thought applicable to the case: their difference was as to the construction of the letters which passed between Colonel Stevenson and Mr. Stuart, the manager of the bank at Londonderry, in the latter part of the month of May and the beginning of June, 1895. The majority of the Court below thought that those letters were only expressed in the language of expectation and hope, and that they did not express any promise or undertaking which might form a contract between Colonel Stevenson and the bank. My Lords, it appears to me to be important to consider what was the situation at that time. It was this: Mr. Stuart, the manager of the bank at Londonderry, had allowed Colonel Stevenson to overdraw his account to an extent which the directors disapproved, and apparently Mr. Stuart had been instructed by the board at Dublin to press Colonel Stevenson to reduce his overdraft. On the other hand, Colonel Stevenson had at that time contracted to purchase an estate called the Portlemon estate, but it was not yet conveyed to him. I think Colonel Stevenson clearly undertook by his first letter to lodge the deed of conveyance of the Portlemon estate when executed with the bank for the purpose of securing his overdrawn account, and I think as a matter of law that that was a promise to create an equitable mortgage of the property in favour of the bank.

There can be no possible doubt that this promise was accepted by Mr. Stuart on the part of the bank, but it is said that there was no consideration for it. Now in the letter of May 18 (that is the second letter) Colonel Stevenson writes to this effect, addressing Mr. Stuart, 'All you require is a little patience and my account will be put on a satisfactory basis'. I think this means, 'Exercise patience and some forbearance and I will give you the required security and thus put my account in order'. The bank did exercise patience, and gave some forbearance by not demanding, as they might have done, immediate payment of the debt, and by giving Colonel Stevenson the required time to effect the security. I think that such forbearance in fact, although there was no agreement by the bank to forbear suing Colonel Stevenson for any definite period, was sufficient consideration to support his promise to give the security, on the principle stated by Kindersley V.-C. in *Alliance Bank* v. *Broom* (2 Dr. & S. 289). The Vice-Chancellor's judgment in that case was quoted with approval by Lord Bowen in *Miles* v. *New Zealand Alford Estate Co.* (32 Ch. D. 266, 290) as laying down a sound principle. In the case before Lord Bowen the question was whether a guarantee which had been given by the promotor of a company at a general meeting of the shareholders to guarantee a dividend of a certain amount for a certain time on the shares was given with or without consideration, and in referring to the case before him Lord Bowen said, after quoting the Vice-Chancellor's judgment: 'So it will be sufficient here that the directors did forbear, if their forbearance was at the request expressed or implied of the guarantor and in consequence of his guarantee being given, and it seems to me there is no sort of necessity to discover language of any particular form, or writing of any particular character, embodying the resolution of the directors. We must treat the thing in a business way and draw an inference of fact as to what the real nature of the transaction was as between business men'. My Lords, that seems to me to be directly applicable to the present question. There can be no doubt that the forbearance was given in this case, and I think it is a just inference of fact that it was given at the request of Colonel Stevenson in consequence of his undertaking to secure the account and place it on what he describes as a satisfactory basis.

I am, therefore, of opinion that the letters, reading them together, constituted a contract to create an equitable mortgage on the Portlemon estate as soon as the conveyance to Colonel Stevenson was completed. On that event taking place, the contract became absolute and bound the property in his hands. The letters, therefore, constituted a transfer to the bank of the equitable interest in the property, and constituted a conveyance within the meaning of the Registration Act. It ought, therefore, to have been registered in order to secure the priority of the bank; and not having been registered, I think the appellants who claim under a subsequent instrument which was registered are entitled to claim priority over the bank in respect of their advance.

Lord Robertson:

My Lords, this case has been decided by the Court of Appeal on the construction of the four letters of Colonel Stevenson which have been referred to. Now I find it impossible to read the letter of March 26, 1895, otherwise than as a distinct undertaking to lodge the title-deeds as soon as they should be completed. The subsequent letters, so far from detracting from or throwing doubt on the intention and effect of this first letter, are addressed mainly to explaining the delay which had occurred in the execution, and therefore in the deposit, of the promised title-deeds: they all recognise what one of them in terms describes as an undertaking; but the importance of those subsequent letters seems to me to lie in the corroboration which they afford of what primâ facie is the natural construction of the letter of March 26, 1895. Accordingly, I do not encounter the difficulty which FitzGibbon L.J. very justly observes to arise where you have to spell out a contract from several documents.

The only remaining question is, Was it in fulfilment of this undertaking that the title-deeds were in the end delivered? That depends on Mr. Tweedy's evidence, for there is no other evidence on the subject. And Mr. Tweedy's evidence as to delay in lodging the deeds clearly points to an antecedent undertaking in fulfilment of which the title-deeds were ultimately delivered and received.

Lord Lindley:

My Lords, I am of the same opinion. First of all comes the legal question whether an equitable charge is within the Irish statute of Anne. English lawyers are quite familiar with the fact that under the English statutes relating to the registration of deeds and conveyances the various sections of those Acts shew that an equitable charge does come within the word 'conveyance'. I was not myself familiar with the authorities in Ireland on the Irish statutes, but there is no dispute on the point, and

Holmes L.J. says, I believe perfectly accurately: 'It had been long since well settled that the statute of Queen Anne extends to any instrument in writing creating a charge on land'. That was more or less doubtful in this country until it was settled by the case of *Credland* v. *Potter* ((1874) L.R. 10 Ch. 8); and looking into the authorities which proceeded that, cases may be found both ways. It was settled in that case by a judgment delivered by Lord Cairns, James L.J., and Mellish L.J., three of the most eminent men who ever sat on the bench in this country; and their decision was arrived at, not by a short-cut that the word 'conveyance' includes equitable charges, but by studying the subsequent sections of the English Act of Anne, which shew that the word 'conveyance' must be used in a much wider sense than conveyance by deed.

My Lords, having got that legal question clear, the only other question is, What do these letters really mean? do they constitute an equitable charge? With the greatest deference to FitzGibbon L.J. and Holmes L.J., I cannot doubt that they do. We know the position of the parties; we know that Colonel Stevenson's account at the Provincial Bank was largely overdrawn, and that, whether there was pressure or not, he was obviously very anxious about it, for that is apparent from the letters – I infer that there was some kind of pressure – and then he writes that letter of March 26 by which he undertakes to deposit the deed, when he gets it, as a security for his overdraft; what more you want to constitute an equitable charge I cannot conceive.

As regards the difficulty suggested by the Solicitor-General, that it was never so understood or so accepted by the bank manager, the inference I should draw is that it clearly was. It would, in my mind, never have been open to the slightest doubt if the deed had been given to him; but unfortunately it was given to Mr. Tweedy, who knew nothing at all about these letters, and so some confusion has arisen about the way in which the deed came to be deposited. But when you look at the letters and consider the circumstances under which the deed was deposited, it seems to me certain that Colonel Stevenson's deposit was a deposit in pursuance of his obligation.

As to the charge not having been assented to by the bank, in the first place I take it that when you offer a person something to his advantage, as, for example, security for a debt, it is to be inferred that he accepts it unless he dissents. I come to the conclusion that these letters having been offered to the manager for business purposes, he kept them for business purposes, and that his assent to the promise to deposit the deeds must be inferred.

The only other difficulty that was suggested is the want of consideration. That is covered entirely by the case of *Alliance Bank* v. *Broom* (2 Dr. & S. 289).

The result is that this appeal must be allowed.

Notes
1. *Cf. Allied Irish Banks* v. *Glynn*, p. 85, *ante*.
2. As regards operation of the Registry of Deeds, see *Irish Land Law* ch. 22.
3. See further on mortgages by deposit of title documents *Myler* v. *Mr. Pussy's Nite Club Ltd.*, p. 445, *post*.

II. POSITION OF PARTIES UNDER MORTGAGE

CONVEYANCING ACT, 1881
IV. – Mortgages
15. – (1) Where a mortgagor is entitled to redeem, he shall, by virtue of this Act, have power to require the mortgagee instead of re-conveying, and on the

terms on which he would be bound to re-convey, to assign the mortgage debt and convey the mortgaged property to any third person, as the mortgagor directs; and the mortgagee shall, by virtue of this Act, be bound to assign and convey accordingly.

(2) This section does not apply in the case of a mortgagee being or having been in possession.

(3) This section applies to mortgages made either before or after the commencement of this Act, and shall have effect notwithstanding any stipulation to the contrary.

16. – (1) A mortgagor, as long as his right to redeem subsists, shall, by virtue of this Act, be entitled from time to time, at reasonable times, on his request, and at his own cost, and on payment of the mortgagee's costs and expenses in this behalf, to inspect and make copies or abstracts of or extracts from the documents of title relating to the mortgaged property in the custody or power of the mortgagee.

(2) This section applies only to mortgages made after the commencement of this Act, and shall have effect notwithstanding any stipulation to the contrary.

17. – (1) A mortgagor seeking to redeem any one mortgage shall, by virtue of this Act, be entitled to do so, without paying any money due under any separate mortgage made by him, or by any person through whom he claims, on property other than that comprised in the mortgage which he seeks to redeem.

(2) This section applies only if and as far as a contrary intention is not expressed in the mortgage deeds or one of them.

(3) This section applies only where the mortgages or one of them are or is made after the commencement of this Act.

Leases

18. – (1) A mortgagor of land while in possession shall, as against every imcumbrancer, have, by virtue of this Act, power to make from time to time any such lease of the mortgaged land, or any part thereof, as is in this section described and authorised.

(2) A mortgagee of land while in possession shall, as against all prior imcumbrancers, if any, and as against the mortgagor, have, by virtue of this Act, power to make from time to time any such lease as aforesaid.

(3) The leases which this section authorises are –

    (i) An agricultural or occupation lease for any term not exceeding twenty-one years; and

    (ii) A building lease for any term not exceeding ninety-nine years. [This power must now be read subject to the abolition of the power to grant building leases relating to 'dwellings' by the Landlord and Tenant (Ground Rents) Act, 1978

(4) Every person making a lease under this section may execute and do all assurances and things necessary or proper in that behalf.

(5) Every such lease shall be made to take effect in possession not later than twelve months after its date.

(6) Every such lease shall reserve the best rent that can reasonably be obtained, regard being had to the circumstances of the case, but without any fine being taken.

(7) Every such lease shall contain a covenant by the lessee for payment of the rent, and a condition of re-entry on the rent not being paid within a time therein specified not exceeding thirty days.

(8) A counterpart of every such lease shall be executed by the lessee and delivered to the lessor, of which execution and delivery the execution of the lease by the lessor shall, in favour of the lessee and all persons deriving title under him, be sufficient evidence.

(9) Every such building lease shall be made in consideration of the lessee, or some person by whose direction the lease is granted, having erected, or agreeing to erect within not more than five years from the date of the lease, buildings, new or additional, or having improved or repaired buildings, or agreeing to improve or repair buildings within that time, or having executed, or agreeing to execute, within that time, on the land leased, an improvement for or in connexion with building purposes.

(10) In any such building lease a peppercorn rent, or a nominal or other rent less than the rent ultimately payable, may be made payable for the first five years, or any less part of the term.

(11) In case of a lease by the mortgagor, he shall, within one month after making the lease, deliver to the mortgagee, or, where there are more than one, to the mortgagee first in priority, a counterpart of the lease duly executed by the lessee; but the lessee shall not be concerned to see that this provision is complied with.

(12) A contract to make or accept a lease under this section may be enforced by or against every person on whom the lease if granted would be binding.

(13) This section applies only if and as far as a contrary intention is not expressed by the mortgagor and mortgagee in the mortgage deed, or otherwise in writing, and shall have effect subject to the terms of the mortgage deed or of any such writing and to the provisions therein contained.

(14) Nothing in this Act shall prevent the mortgage deed from reserving to or conferring on the mortgagor or the mortgagee, or both, any further or other powers of leasing or having reference to leasing; and any further or other powers so reserved or conferred shall be exerciseable, as far as may be, as if they were conferred by this Act, and with all the like incidents, effects and consequences, unless a contrary intention is expressed in the mortgage deed.

(15) Nothing in this Act shall be construed to enable a mortgagor or mortgagee to make a lease for any longer term or on any other conditions than such as could have been granted or imposed by the mortgagor, with the concurrence of all the incumbrances, if this Act had not been passed.

(16) This section applies only in case of a mortgage made after the commencement of this Act; but the provisions thereof or any of them, may, by agreement in writing made after the commencement of this Act, between mortgagor and mortgagee be applied to a mortgage made before the commencement of this Act, so, nevertheless, that any such agreement shall not prejudicially affect any right or interest of any mortgagee not joining in or adopting the agreement.

(17) The provisions of this section referring to a lease shall be construed to extend and apply, as far as circumstances admit, to any letting, and to an agreement, whether in writing or not for leasing or letting.

Sale; Insurance; Receiver; Timber

19. – (1) A mortgagee, where the mortgage is made by deed, shall, by virtue of this Act, have the following powers, to the like extent as if they had been in terms conferred by the mortgage deed, but not further (namely):

(i) A power, when the mortgage money has become due, to sell, or to concur with any other person in selling, the mortgaged property, or any part thereof, either subject to prior charges, or not, and either together or in lots, by public auction or by private consent, subject to such conditions respecting title, or evidence of title, or other matter, as he (the mortgagee) thinks fit, with power to vary any contract for sale, and to buy in at an auction, or to rescind any contract for sale, and to re-sell, without being answerable for any loss occasioned thereby; and

(ii) A power, at any time, after the date of the mortgage deed, to insure and keep insured against loss or damage by fire any building, or any effects or property of an insurable nature, whether affixed to the freehold or not, being or forming part of the mortgaged property, and the premiums paid for any such insurance shall be a charge on the mortgaged property, in addition to the mortgage money, and with the same priority, and with interest at the same rate, as the mortgage money; and

(iii) A power, when the mortgage money has become due, to appoint a receiver of the income of the mortgaged property, or of any part thereof; and

(iv) A power, while the mortgagee is in possession, to cut and sell timber and other trees ripe for cutting, and not planted or left standing for shelter or ornament, or to contract for any such cutting and sale, to be completed within any time not exceeding twelve months from the making of the contract.

(2) The provisions of this Act relating to the foregoing powers, comprised either in this section, or in any subsequent section regulating the exercise of those powers, may be varied or extended by the mortgage deed, and, as so varied or extended, shall, as far as may be, operate in the like manner and with all the like incidents, effects, and consequences, as if such variations or extensions were contained in this Act.

(3) This section applies only if and as far as a contrary intention is not expressed in the mortgage deed, and shall have effect subject to the terms of the mortgage deed and to the provisions therein contained.

(4) This section applies only where the mortgage deed is executed after the commencement of this Act.

20. A mortgagee shall not exercise the power of sale conferred by this Act unless and until –

(i) Notice requiring payment of the mortgage money has been served on the mortgagor or one of several mortgagors, and default has been made in payment of the mortgage money, or of part thereof, for three months after such service; or

(ii) Some interest under the mortgage is in arrear and unpaid for two months after becoming due; or

(iii) There has been a breach of some provision contained in the mortgage deed or in this Act, and on the part of the mortgagor, or of some person concurring in making the mortgage, to be observed or performed, other than and besides a covenant for payment of the mortgage money or interest thereon.

21. – (1) A mortgagee exercising the power of sale conferred by this Act shall have power, by deed, to convey the property sold, for such estate and interest therein as is the subject of the mortgage, freed from all estates, interests, and rights to which the mortgage has priority, but subject to all estates, interests, and rights which have priority to the mortgage;...

(2) Where a conveyance is made in professed exercise of the power of sale conferred by this Act, the title of the purchaser shall not be impeachable on the ground that no case had arisen to authorise the sale, or that due notice was not given, or that the power was otherwise improperly or irregularly exercised; but any person damnified by an unauthorised, or improper, or irregular exercise of the power shall have his remedy in damages against the person exercising the power.

(3) The money which is received by the mortgagee, arising from the sale, after discharge of prior incumbrances to which the sale is not made subject, if any, or after payment into Court under this Act of a sum to meet any prior incumbrance,

shall be held by him in trust to be applied by him, first, in payment of all costs, charges, and expenses, properly incurred by him, as incident to the sale or any attempted sale, or otherwise; and secondly, in discharge of the mortgage money, interest, and costs, and other money, if any, due under the mortgage; and the residue of the money so received shall be paid to the person entitled to the mortgaged property, or authorised to give receipts for the proceeds of the sale thereof.

(4) The power of sale conferred by this Act may be exercised by any person for the time being entitled to receive and give a discharge for the mortgage money.

(5) The power of sale conferred by this Act shall not affect the right of foreclosure.

(6) The mortgagee, his executors, administrators, or assigns, shall not be answerable for any involuntary loss happening in or about the exercise or execution of the power of sale conferred by this Act or of any trust connected therewith [or of any power or provision contained in the mortgage deed — see s. 5 of 1911 Act, *infra*].

(7) At any time after the power of sale conferred by this Act has become exerciseable, the person entitled to exercise the same may demand and recover from any person, other than a person having in the mortgaged property an estate, interest, or right in priority to the mortgage, all the deeds and documents relating to the property, or to the title thereto, which a purchaser under the power of sale would be entitled to demand and recover from him.

22. – (1) The receipt in writing of a mortgagee shall be sufficient discharge for any money arising under the power of sale conferred by this Act, or for any money or securities comprised in his mortgage, or arising thereunder; and a person paying or transferring the same to the mortgagee shall not be concerned to inquire whether any money remains due under the mortgage.

(2) Money received by a mortgagee under his mortgage or from the proceeds of securities comprised in his mortgage shall be applied in like manner as in this Act directed respecting money received by him arising from a sale under the power of sale conferred by this Act; but with this variation, that the costs, charges, and expenses payable shall include the costs, charges, and expenses properly incurred of recovering and receiving the money or securities, and of conversion of securities into money, instead of those incident to sale.

23. – (1) The amount of an insurance effected by a mortgagee against loss or damage by fire under the power in that behalf conferred by this Act shall not exceed the amount specified in the mortgage deed, or, if no amount is therein specified, then shall not exceed two third parts of the amount that would be required, in case of total destruction, to restore the property insured.

(2) An insurance shall not, under the power conferred by this Act, be effected by a mortgagee in any of the following cases (namely):
  (i) Where there is a declaration in the mortgage deed that no insurance is required:
  (ii) Where an insurance is kept up by or on behalf of the mortgagor in accordance with the mortgage deed:
  (iii) Where the mortgage deed contains no stipulation respecting insurance, and an insurance is kept up by or on behalf of the mortgagor, to the amount in which the mortgagee is by this Act authorized to insure.

(3) All money received on an insurance effected under the mortgage deed or under this Act shall, if the mortgagee so requires, be applied by the mortgagor in making good the loss or damage in respect of which the money is received.

(4) Without prejudice to any obligation to the contrary imposed by law, or by

special contract, a mortgagee may require that all money received on an insurance be applied in or towards discharge of the money due under his mortgage.

24. – (1) A mortgagee entitled to appoint a receiver under the power in that behalf conferred by this Act shall not appoint a receiver until he has become entitled to exercise the power of sale conferred by this Act, but may then, by writing under his hand, appoint such person as he thinks fit to be receiver.

(2) The receiver shall be deemed to be the agent of the mortgagor; and the mortgagor shall be solely responsible for the receiver's acts or defaults, unless the mortgage deed otherwise provides.

(3) The receiver shall have power to demand and recover all the income of the property of which he is appointed receiver, by action, distress, or otherwise, in the name either of the mortgagor or of the mortgagee, to the full extent of the estate or interest which the mortgagor could dispose of, and to give effectual receipts, accordingly, for the same.

(4) A person paying money to the receiver shall not be concerned to inquire whether any case has happened to authorize the receiver to act.

(5) The receiver may be removed, and a new receiver may be appointed, from time to time by the mortgagee by writing under his hand.

(6) The receiver shall be entitled to retain out of any money received by him, for his remuneration, and in satisfaction of all costs, charges, and expenses incurred by him as receiver, a commission at such rate, not exceeding five per centum on the gross amount of all money received, as is specified in his appointment, and if no rate is so specified, then at the rate of five per centum on that gross amount, or at such higher rate as the Court thinks fit to allow, on application made by him for that purpose.

(7) The receiver shall, if so directed in writing by the mortgagee, insure and keep insured against loss or damage by fire, out of money received by him, any building effects, or property comprised in the mortgage, whether affixed to the freehold or not, being of an insurable nature.

(8) The receiver shall apply all money received by him as follows (namely):

  (i) In discharge of all rents, taxes, rates and outgoings whatever affecting the mortgaged property; and

  (ii) In keeping down all annual sums or other payments, and the interest on all principal sums, having priority to the mortgage in right whereof he is receiver; and

  (iii) In payment of his commission, and of the premiums on fire, life, or other insurances, if any, properly payable under the mortgage deed or under this Act, and the cost of executing necessary or proper repairs directed in writing by the mortgagee; and

  (iv) In payment of the interest accruing due in respect of any principal money due under the mortgage;

and shall pay the residue of the money received by him to the person who, but for the possession of the receiver, would have been entitled to receive the income of the mortgaged property, or who is otherwise entitled to that property.

CONVEYANCING ACT, 1882
Mortgages

12. The right of the mortgagor, under section fifteen of the Conveyancing Act of 1881, to require a mortgagee, instead of re-conveying, to assign the mortgage debt and convey the mortgaged property to a third person, shall belong to and be capable of being enforced by each incumbrancer, or by the mortgagor, notwithstanding any intermediate incumbrance; but a requisition of an incumbrancer shall prevail over a requisition of the mortgagor, and, as between incumbrancers, a requisition of a prior incumbrancer shall prevail over a requisition of a subsequent incumbrancer.

CONVEYANCING ACT, 1911

3. – (1) For the purpose only of enabling a lease authorised under section eighteen of the Act of 1881, as varied by this section, aforesaid, or by the mortgage deed (in this section referred to as an authorised lease) to be granted, a mortgagor of land while in possession shall, in like manner as if the legal estate were vested in him and as against every incumbrancer, have, by virtue of this Act, power to accept from time to time a surrender of any lease of the mortgaged land or any part thereof comprised in the lease, with or without an exception of all or any of the mines and minerals therein, or in respect of mines and minerals, or any of them, and, on a surrender of part only of the land or mines and minerals leased, the rent may be apportioned.

(2) For the same purpose, a mortgagee of land while in possession shall, in like manner, and as against all prior or other incumbrancers, if any, and as against the mortgagor, have, by virtue of this Act, power to accept from time to time any such surrender as aforesaid.

(3) On a surrender of part only of the land or mines and minerals leased, the original lease may be varied, provided that the lease when varied would have been valid as an authorised lease if granted by the person accepting the surrender; and, on a surrender and the making of a new or other lease, whether for the same or for any extended or other term, and whether subject or not to the same or to any other covenants, provisions, or conditions, the value of the lessee's interest in the lease surrendered may, subject to the provisions of this section, be taken into account in the determination of the amount of the rent to be reserved, and of the nature of the covenants, provisions, and conditions to be inserted in the new or other lease.

(4) Nothing in this section shall, where any consideration (except an agreement to accept an authorised lease) for the surrender is given by or on behalf of the lessee to or on behalf of the person accepting the surrender, authorise a surrender to a mortgagor without the consent of the incumbrancers, or authorise a surrender to a second or subsequent incumbrancer without the consent of any prior incumbrancer.

(5) No surrender shall, by virtue of this section, be rendered valid unless:-

(a) An authorised lease is granted of the whole of the land or mines and minerals comprised in the surrender to take effect in possession immediately or within one month after the date of the surrender; and

(b) The term certain or interest granted by the new lease is not less in duration than the unexpired term or interest which would have been subsisting under the original lease if that lease had not been surrendered; and

(c) Where the whole of the land mines and minerals originally leased has been surrendered, the rent reserved by the new lease is not less than the rent which would have been payable under the original lease if it had not been surrendered; or where part only of the land or mines and minerals has been surrendered, the aggregate rents respectively remaining payable or reserved under the original lease and new lease are not less than the rent which would have been payable under the originl lease if no partial surrender had been accepted.

(6) A contract to make or accept a surrender under this section may be enforced by or against every person on whom the surrender, if completed, would be binding.

(7) Subsections (13), (16) and (17) of section eighteen of the Act of 1881 shall

have effect as if they were re-enacted in this section and references to the commencement of that Act shall, for the purposes of this section, be read as references to the commencement of this Act.

(8) Nothing in this section shall prevent the mortgage deed from reserving to or conferring on the mortgagor or mortgagee, or both, any further or other powers relating to the surrender of leases; and any further or other powers so conferred or reserved shall be exerciseable, as far as may be, as if they were conferred by this Act, and with the like results, unless a contrary intention is expressed in the mortgage deed.

(9) Nothing in this section shall operate to enable a mortgagor or mortgagee to accept a surrender which could not have been accepted by the mortgagor, with the concurrence of all the incumbrancers, if this Act had not been passed.

(1) For the purposes of this section, and of subsection (1) of section eighteen of the Act of 1881, the expression 'mortgagor' does not include an incumbrancer deriving title under the original mortgagor.

(11) The powers of leasing and of accepting surrenders respectively conferred by section eighteen of the Act of 1881, and this section, shall, after a receiver of the income of the mortgaged property or any part thereof has been appointed by a mortgagee, under that Act, and so long as the receiver acts, be exerciseable by such mortgagee instead of by the mortgagor, as respects any land affected by the receivership, in like manner as if such mortgagee were in possession of the land.

4. – (1) The power of sale conferred on a mortgagee by section nineteen of the Act of 1881 shall include the following powers as incident thereto (namely):-

(i) A power to impose or reserve or make binding, as far as the law permits, by covenant, condition, or otherwise, on the unsold parts of the mortgaged property or any part thereof, or on the purchaser and any property sold, any restriction or reservation with respect to building on or other user of land, or with respect to mines and minerals, or for the purpose of the more beneficial working thereof, or with respect to any other thing:

(ii) A power to sell the mortgaged property, or any part thereof, or any mines and minerals apart from the surface:

(a) With or without a grant or reservation of rights of way, rights of water, easements, rights and privileges for or connected with building or other purposes in relation to the property remaining in mortgage or any part thereof, or to any property sold;

(b) With or without an exception or reservation of all or any of the mines and minerals in or under the mortgaged property, and with or without a grant or reservation of powers of working, wayleaves, or rights of way, rights of water and drainage and other powers, easements, rights, and privileges for or connected with mining purposes in relation to the property remaining unsold or any part thereof, or to any property sold;

(c) With or without covenants by the purchaser to expend money on the land sold.

(2) Subsections (2) and (3) of section nineteen of the Act of 1881 shall apply to the foregoing powers conferred by this section.

(3) This section applies only where the mortgage deed is executed after the commencement of this Act.

(4) For the purpose of exercising any power conferred by this section, an application under section forty-four of the Trustee Act, 1893, as amended by section three of the Trustee Act, 1894, shall not be required.

5. – (1) Upon any sale made in professed exercise of the power conferred on mortgagees by the Act of 1881, a purchaser is not, and never has been, either before or on conveyance, concerned to see or inquire whether a case has arisen to authorise the sale, or due notice has been given, or the power is otherwise properly and regularly exercised.

(2) Subsection (6) of section twenty-one of the Act of 1881 shall, as regards mortgages executed after the commencement of this Act, be read as if the words 'or of any power or provision contained in the mortgage deed' were added at the end thereof.

MYLER V. MR. PUSSY'S NITE CLUB LTD.
Unreported (High Court) (1978 No. 1472 P) (Judgment delivered 11th December, 1979)

The facts are set out in the judgment.

McWilliam J.:

This is an application by the Plaintiffs for an Order of garnishee attaching a sum of £5,000 payable by the Sun Alliance & London Insurance Group, hereinafter called the Insurance Company, in respect of damage by fire to premises at 49, Parnell Square, Dublin, owned by the first-named Defendant, hereinafter called Pussy's.

On 27th July, 1979, the Plaintiffs obtained judgment against all the Defendants except Alan Amsby for the sum of £12,000 and £1,900 for costs.

The Defendants, Liam Ledwich and Tony Keogan, hereinafter called the Insured, are directors of Pussy's and, from 19th September, 1978, until 18th September, 1979, insured the said premises in their own names with the Insurance Company, which has confirmed its liability to pay the sum of £5,000 on foot of the said policy.

The premises are held by Pussy's for the residue of a term of 900 years under an Indenture of Lease made on 10th October, 1759, which contained a covenant by the lessee to repair but did not contain any covenant to insure.

By resolution of Pussy's of 30th September, 1977, the Defendant, Alan Amsby, was authorised to deposit the title deeds of the said premises with the Third Party by way of security for the debts of Pussy's due to the Third Party, and the Defendant, Alan Amsby, did deposit the said title deeds with the Third Party on 30th September, 1977.

Notice of this deposit was furnished to the Insurance Company on 31st January, 1979. The fire which damaged the premises occurred in March, 1979.

The Third Party is opposing this application on the ground that it has an interest in the premises, that the Plaintiffs cannot have a greater interest in the money than the insured, and that the Third Party has a right of some sort to have its security maintained, although no authority has been cited to me for this proposition. The argument is, to some extent, based on the fact that the lessee under the lease was bound to maintain and repair the premises. As regards this submission I would refer to paragraph 1032 at page 522 of Halsbury's Laws of England Vol. 17. It is here stated that a contract of fire insurance is a personal contract which does not pass with the property and that, where mortgaged property has been insured by the mortgagor and is destroyed by fire, the mortgagee is not, in the absence of a covenant as to the application of the insurance money, entitled to have it applied in payment of the mortgage debt. This statement of the law has been continued in all editions of Halsbury including the current (4th) edition. In *Brady* v. *Irish Land Commission* [1921] I.R. 56 the propositon was stated by O'Connor, M.R., at p. 66 as follows:- 'No doubt as between mortgagor and mortgagee, if one of them effects a policy on the subject-matter of the mortgage, the other has no interest in it, and cannot claim the benefit of it apart from special contact. The reason of this is that the mortgagor or mortgagee in whose name the policy is effected is the only person who is privy to it, and the other is a stranger.'

A further argument on behalf of the Third Party is based on the provisions of section 23, subsection (4) of the Conveyancing Act, 1881. Subsection (3) of this section provides as follows:- 'All money received on an insurance effected under the mortgage deed or under this Act shall, if the mortgagee so requires, be applied by the mortgagor in making good the loss or damage in respect of which the money is received.'

Subsection (4) provides:- 'Without prejudice to any obligation to the contrary imposed by law, or by special contract, a mortgagee may require that all money received on an insurance be applied in or towards discharge of the money due under his mortgage.'

Subsection (4) is not restricted to insurances effected under the mortgage deed or under the Act as is the position under subsection (3) and this distinction was recognised in the cases of *J. E. Doherty* [1925] 2 I.R. 246 and *Halifax Building Society* v. *Keighley* [1931] 2 K.B. 252. In *Doherty's* case it was held that a mortgagee was entitled to require insurance money payable under a policy effected by the mortgagor to be paid in discharge of the mortgage debt although the insurance was not effected under the mortgage deed or under the Act. In each of the cases the mortgage was by deed and it has hitherto normally been assumed that the Conveyancing Act, 1881, only applies to mortgages by deed, but clause (vi) of section 2 defines 'mortgage' as including any charge on property for securing money or money's worth. An equitable charge by deposit of title deeds is a charge on property for securing money and it seems to me that the principle enunciated in *Doherty's* case and approved in the *Halifax Building Society* case is equally applicable to a mortgage by deposit of title deeds although the principle stated in Halsbury ought to be read so as to include a reference to a statutory provision in addition to the reference to a covenant as to the application of the insurance money.

It is then submitted on behalf of the Plaintiffs that the Third Party did not give any notice requiring the insurance money to be applied towards the discharge of the mortgage debt. This is so, but the notice of the deposit was given to the insurance company on 31st January, 1979, two months before the fire occurred, and there could have been no reason for giving this notice other than to state that the Third Party had an interest in the insurance money should any claim arise.

Apart from giving such notice, it is also submitted that, as between two claimants, the Plaintiffs are first in making their claim and, therefore, should have priority over the Third Party, and also, that the Plaintiffs' claim should have priority because the Plaintiffs have a judgment which entitles them to execute forthwith whereas the Third Party has only got a cause of action. Both these submissions seem to me to be met by the fact that the Third Party has a statutory right to have the insurance money applied towards discharge of the mortgage debt and had, in exercise of this right, given notice to the insurance company long before the date of the fire.

It is, to me, surprising that this subsection of the 1881 Act has not been considered with regard to a mortgage by equitable deposit of title deeds during the past hundred years, but this appears to be the case. Having regard to the definition of 'mortgage' contained in section 2 of the 1881 Act and the decision in *Doherty's* case, I am of opinion that the Third Party is entitled to have the insurance money applied in discharge of the money due under the mortgage in priority to the judgment debt of the Plaintiffs and that I should discharge the conditional order of garnishee.

Note
See further on mortgage insurance, *Irish Land Law*, paras. 13.007–9.

IRISH PERMANENT BUILDING SOCIETY V. RYAN
[1950] I.R. 12 (High Court)

The defendant mortgaged his dwellinghouse to the plaintiffs, a building society, to secure the repayment of moneys advanced by the plaintiffs. The mortgage deed provided for the payment of quarterly instalments in repayment of the advance, together with interest, and that in case of default of payment for three months the plaintiffs might enter into possession of the mortgaged premises and might sell them. The defendant defaulted in his payments for a space of over three months, and it appeared that he would not be in a position to pay the arrears or to continue paying the quarterly instalments. The defendant having refused to deliver up possession, the plaintiffs sought an order pursuant to Order LV, r. 7, of the Rules of the Supreme Court, 1905, for the delivery of possession of the mortgaged premises by the defendant so that they might sell the premises with vacant possession which would enhance the value of the premises.

Gavan Duffy P.:

Mortgagees have seldom sought possession under Order LV, r. 7, and the Court has been slow to make an order. Nevertheless, I am of opinion that applications such as the present should be encouraged, rather than discouraged in suitable cases, in view of the great saving in costs so far as the defendant is concerned. Having regard to the position of the defendant, I think this is a suitable case.

The defendant executed an indenture of mortgage which contained a special clause, carefully drafted, enabling the mortgagees to enter into possession of the mortgaged premises if the mortgagor should be in default for the space of three calendar months in the payment of some instalment of principal and interest due under the mortgage deed. In the present case the defendant has been in default for the space of twelve months in the payment of the instalments and, in fact, has never paid any of the instalments due under the mortgage deed and has no prospect of paying any. There is evidence that no one but the defendant and the members of his family are in possession of the mortgaged premises and that there is no incumbrance, other than the present mortgage, affecting the premises. By letter, dated the 5th May, 1949, the plaintiffs called upon the defendant to deliver up possession of the premises because of his default in the repayment of these instalments, and no satisfactory reply to this demand was received by the plaintiffs. In the affidavit made by the secretary of the plaintiff society, it is deposed that it would be difficult to effect a sale of the premises if the defendant remained in possession and that the value of the premises would be greatly enhanced by a sale with vacant possession. I am satisfied that a sale with the defendant in possession is likely to be far less satisfactory than a sale with vacant possession. I, therefore, propose making an order for the delivery of possession to the plaintiffs of the premises. I will allow a stay of execution for a period of three calendar months from this date...

Notes
1. See now Order 54, rule 3 of the Rule of the Superior Court, 1962. *Cf.* the decision by Lowry J. in *Re O'Neill* [1967] N.I. 129.
2. See generally on court orders for possession granted to mortgagees, *Irish Land Law*, para. 13.016 *et seq*.

HOLOHAN V. FRIENDS PROVIDENT AND CENTURY LIFE OFFICE
[1966] I.R. 1 (Supreme Court)

A life insurance company in the exercise of its powers of sale as legal mortgagee entered into a contrct for the sale of certain property of which the plaintiff was mortgagor. In negotiating the sale and the purchase price to be paid, the company offered the premises for sale on an investment basis without attempting to disturb the occupying tenants and refused to consider an alternative mode of offering the premises for sale, notwithstanding the advice of auctioneers and house agents that a sale with vacant possession should realise an enhanced purchase price. In an action by the mortgagor against the company, seeking an order restraining the company from completing the sale (to which proceeding the purchaser was not a party) Budd J. refused the relief sought. An appeal was made to the Supreme Court.

Ó Dálaigh C.J.:

This appeal is against an order of Mr. Justice Budd, dated the 15th November, 1964, dismissing the plaintiff's claim for an injunction to restrain the defendant insurance company from completing the sale of the premises, Raglan Hall, Clyde Road, in the city of Dublin, the property of the plaintiff, to one, Francis Sweeney, at the price of £5,500.

The defendants are mortgagees of the property and the sale, the completion of which it is sought to restrain, is a sale in purported exercise of the defendants' powers under an indenture of mortgage, dated the 31st December, 1946. The plaintiff's complaint is that the sale price represents a gross undervalue of the property and that, in the circumstances, the sale is an improper and unreasonable exercise of the power of sale of the defendants.

The premises are held under a Pembroke lease, dated the 29th August, 1857, for a term of 150 years from 1857 (subject to a ground rent of £7 16s. 6d.). The plaintiff acquired the residue of that term on the 31st December, 1946, and on the same date he mortgaged the property to the defendants by way of sub-demise. The mortgage was to secure a loan of £20,000. As additional security for repayment of the sum advanced he also mortgaged on the same date an endowment policy for £27,500, with profits, effected with the defendants, payable on the 25th June, 1966, or at previous death.

The plaintiff fell into arrears with payments of interest and the amount advanced was not repaid. In these circumstances the defendants on the 31st October, 1961, in pursuance of their powers of sale, entered into a contract for the sale of the premises to one, Francis Sweeney, for the price of £5,500. The amount of the plaintiff's indebtedness to the defendants on foot of the mortgage was £12,957 16s 0d. Moreover, the plaintiff was indebted to the defendants in respect of very considerable sums paid by them to maintain the endowment policy. The estimated value of this policy on maturity (1966) was £46,206; but this was less than the total of the amount of the plaintiff's indebtedness to the defendants. In other words, the realisation by the defendants of their securities would fall short of wiping out the plaintiff's indebtedness to them.

The premises, Raglan Hall, which is situated on Clyde Road in the Ballsbridge district, consists of a three-storey, detached Georgian house, with residential mews, surrounded by large garden, and occupies a total site area of 2 roods, 10 perches. The lease permits of additional buildings on payment of a further rent of £20 per annum. At the date of the impugned contract of sale the house was let in three flats and the mews were vacant. The net income was estimated to be £481 per annum. The contract price therefore represents just under 11½ years' purchase of the annual income.

The defendants received various offers to purchase the premises between March, 1959, and October, 1961. The offers ranged from £4,000 to £6,750; the lower offers were rejected by the defendants and the higher offers were eventually withdrawn by the intending purchasers. Mr. Sweeney's offer was the highest firm offer made in the period. In all, there were twelve enquirers. When the defendants decided to sell the premises they had them put on the books of their surveyors, the firm of Messrs.

Harry Lisney & Son, and also on the books of two other Dublin auctioneering firms. Messrs. Lisney, on their own initiative, advertised the premises over a period of a week in the Irish Times in the month of March, 1961. The advertisement was in these terms:

'BALLSBRIDGE – Net income approx. £471 p.a. out of substantial house and mews let to 4 tenants. Details from Lisney and Son, M.I.A.A., 23 St. Stephen's Green. 61976.'

The advertisement appeared twice in a column headed 'Houses and Lands to Let' and four times in a column headed 'Houses and Lands for Sale'. They also circulated to some dozen customers particulars of the property in a roneo-ed document. This document was headed 'Substantial Investment – ripe for development' and in the body of it it was stated that 'there is also a substantial garden which lends itself for further development if required'.

The defendants on a number of occasions prior to the sale were advised as to the value of the premises by their surveyors, Messrs. Harry Lisney & Son. The last advice received prior to the date of the contract of sale with Mr. Sweeney is that contained in a letter dated the 1st November, 1960. It is in these terms:-

'As promised, we confirm that we have further considered the question of the sale of this property.

'These premises are presently leased in four unfurnished units. Three are situated on separate levels in the house and the fourth being in the Lodge on the rear service laneway.

'The following would appear to be the relevant factors:-

'1. That the premises are held under a lease for 150 years from 1857, leaving 47 years to run, subject to rent of £7 16s. 6d. per annum. It is presumed that this is a building lease with continued reversionary rights. It is noted also that the lease contains no restriction against the use of the premises as offices and that additional buildings may be erected save that the ground rent be increased by £20 per annum.

'2. That the existing rateable valuations (four figures) total £91.

'3. That the income from the unfurnished lettings presently totals approximately £493 per annum or approximately £500 per annum after the payment of ground rent and rates.

'As a pure investment the present market value of this property is approximately £4,500 (Four Thousand Five Hundred Pounds).

'During the past twelve or eighteen months, however, there has been a growing demand for offices on the south side of the city as far as the shopping centre in Ballsbridge. The present position, therefore, is that the vacant possession value of this propery is now considerably higher than the investment value. If vacant possession were available, the asking price would probably be in excess of £10,000. £8,000 to £9,000 could be expected and higher figures could be realised as it is the type of property which could suit a particular purchaser although it is admitted that there may be a short waiting period.

'We would advise, therefore, that you commence negotiations with the four tenants with the object of seeking vacant possession and if necessary paying compensation. We would expect this to be up to a level of £500 for each tenant, but in some cases, and particularly in respect of the garden flat, it may prove necessary to pay as much as £1,000. In our opinion the payment of this compensation is worth while whether or not there are potential purchasers in mind at the time of the negotiations or not.

'We trust that these are the comments required and that you will let us hear if we can assist further.'

The defendants themselves did not advertise the sale. Their Dublin office on the receipt of Messrs. Lisney's advice of the 1st November, 1960, forwarded it to their head office in London. The instructions they received from London were to proceed with the sale on an investment basis. The head office indicated that they were not prepared to pay any monies out of the monies available in the plaintiff's account for the payment of compensation to the tenants. Nor were they prepared to put money up for advertising. The defendants did not take legal advice as to the position of the tenants. They did not consult with the tenants as to the terms upon which they might be agreeable to give up possession. Nor did they consult with the Pembroke Estate or the Corporation planning authorities as to what the development possibilities might be.

Mr. Justice Budd was of opinion that the legal position of a mortgagee exercising a power of sale was clearly stated in the cases cited to him; and his summary of the position is given in this sentence:- 'I have only to decide whether the facts support the contention that the defendant Society wilfully sold at a gross undervalue and that the sale was an improper and unreasonable exercise of the power of sale.' What His Lordship understood by the latter part of this test is made clear in the passage immediately before this. There, he said he felt compelled to follow the decision of the House of Lords in *Kennedy* v. *De Trafford* ([1897] A.C. 180) and to apply to the case before him the principles there enunciated, adding:- 'If there were no authority on the point I might take a different view of the matter, because I feel that there is a lot to be said in favour of the suggestion that a mortgagee, when selling, should take all reasonable steps in his power to see that the best price is obtained.'

His Lordship appears to me to have rejected as included in the definition of the duty of the mortgagee to mortgagor that, as well as acting in good faith, the mortgagee must take reasonable steps or precautions to obtain a proper price.

Mr. O'Neill for the defendants did not dispute that, as he put it, the duty to act in good faith included the obligation to take reasonable steps to obtain the best price. But in view of the Judge's statement of the law I think I should survey the cases briefly.

The extent of the duty has been variously stated in the English cases. Lord Herschell in *Kennedy* v. *De Trafford* ([1897] A.C. 180) specifically said (at p. 185) that it was not necessary to give an exhaustive definition of the duty; and left it open as to whether the duty was, *inter alia*, to take reasonable precautions.

The test has been differently stated over the years. Lord Eldon in *Downes* v. *Glazebrook* (3 Mer. 200, at p. 223) said that the mortgagee is a trustee for the benefit of the mortgagor under a power of sale.

Sir John Stuart in *Robertson* v. *Norris* (1 Giff. 421), having quoted Lord Eldon, said at p. 424:- 'That expression is to be understood in this sense, that the power being given to enable him to recover the mortgage money, this Court requires that he shall exercise the power of sale in a provident way, with a due regard to the rights and interests of the mortgagor in the surplus money to be produced by the sale'; and two years later, in *Jenkins* v. *Jones* (2 Giff. 99, at p. 108), he said that the mortgagee 'must take all reasonable means to prevent any sacrifice of the property.'

Mr. Justice Kay in *Warner* v. *Jacob* (20 Ch. D. 220) disapproved of Lord Eldon's dictum, at p. 224, and stated that if the mortgagee 'exercises it [the power of sale] *bona fide* for that purpose, without corruption or collusion with the purchaser, the Court will not interfere even though the sale be very disadvantageous, unless indeed the price is so low as in itself to be evidence of fraud.'

In *Farrar* v. *Farrars, Ltd.* (40 Ch. D. 395) Chitty J. stated the duty of the mortgagee in these words (at p. 398):- 'He is bound to sell fairly, and to take reasonable steps to obtain a proper price; but he may proceed to a forced sale for the purpose of paying the mortgage debt.'

On appeal Lindley L.J., delivering the judgment of the Court of Appeal, said (at p. 410):- 'A mortgagee with a power of sale, though often called a trustee, is in a very different position from a trustee for sale. A mortgagee is under obligations to the mortgagor, but he has rights of his own which he is entitled to exercise adversely to the mortgagor . . . every mortgage confers on the mortgagee the right to realise his security and to find a purchaser if he can, and if in exercise of his power he acts *bona fide* and takes reasonable precautions to obtain a proper price, the mortgagor has no redress, even although more might have been obtained for the property if the sale had been postponed.'

Later in *Kennedy* v. *De Trafford* ([1896] 1 Ch. 762) Lindley L.J. adverted to the words, 'reasonable precautions'. In that case the Vice-Chancellor (of the Duchy of Lancaster) said in the Court of first instance that 'reasonable precautions to obtain a proper price were not used'. Lindley L.J. says (at p. 772):- 'The reason why these words were added was this: a mortgagee is not a trustee of a power of sale for the mortgagor at all; his right is to look after himself first. But he is not at liberty to look after his own interests alone, and it is not right, or proper, or legal, for him, either fraudulently, or wilfully, or recklessly, to sacrifice the property of the mortgagor: that is all.'

On appeal to the House of Lords ([1897] A.C. 180) Lord Herschell, at p. 185, first says:- 'My Lords, I am myself disposed to think that if a mortgagee in exercising his power of sale exercises it in good faith, without any intention of dealing unfairly by his mortgagor, it would be very difficult indeed, if not impossible, to establish that he had been guilty of any breach of duty towards the mortgagor. Lindley L.J., in the Court below, says that, "it is not right or proper or legal for him either fraudulently or wilfully or recklessly to sacrifice the property of the mortgagor". Well, I think that is all covered really by his exercising the power committed to him in good faith. It is very difficult to define exhaustively all that would be included in the words 'good faith', but I think it would be unreasonable to require the mortgagee to do more than exercise his power of sale in that fashion. Of course, if he wilfully and recklessly deals with the property in such a manner that the interests of the mortgagor are sacrificed, I should say that he had not been exercising his power of sale in good faith'.

It had been argued that in addition to a *bona fide* exercise of the power there was also a duty to take reasonable precautions to obtain the best price. Lord Herschell did not find it necessary to decide the point. His words, at p. 185, are:- 'My Lords, it is not necessary in this case to give an exhaustive definition of the duties of a mortgagee to a mortgagor, because it appears to me that, if you were to accept the definition of them for which the appellant contends, namely, that the mortgagee is bound to take reasonable precautions in the exercise of his power of sale, as well as to act in good faith, still in this case he did take reasonable precautions. Of course, all the circumstances of the case must be looked at.'

Lord Macnaghten, at p. 192, says that the conduct of a mortgagee who acts in good faith with regard to a sale cannot be impeached without saying more. Lords Morris and Shandy concur apparently with the two preceding speeches, the latter also expressing his approval of the judgment in the Court of Appeal.

Finally, in *McHugh* v. *Union Bank of Canada* ([1913] A.C. 299), a decision of the Privy Council (consisting of Viscount Haldane L.C. and Lords Macnaghten, Atkinson and Moulton) there is the following unequivocal statement of the duty of the mortgagee:- 'It is well settled law that it is the duty of a mortgagee when realising the mortgaged property by sale to behave in conducting such realisation as a reasonable man would behave in the realisation of his own property, so that the mortgagor may receive credit for the fair value of the property sold': per Lord Moulton, at p. 311. In that instance one of the matters at issue was the right of the mortgagee to deduct the reasonable expenses of such realisation. Lord Moulton added that the doctrine he had enunciated recognises as a necessary corollary the right of the mortgagee to effect such a deduction.

One may say, after a survey of the cases, that the English Courts have vacillated in their definition of the duty of a mortgagee exercising a power of sale. Sir John Stuart's exposition of Lord Eldon's definition, though considered too wide by Kay J. and Lindley L.J. and perhaps by Lords Macnaghten and Shandy, finally appears to have in effect commended itself to the Privy Council in 1913. The reasonable man of 1913 may be equated with the provident man of 1858. The reasonable man sets himself a higher standard than to act in good faith. There is no room for doubting the *bona fides* of a reasonable man. He will, while rightly looking to his own interest, also bear in mind the interest of the mortgagor. Whether or not the property to be sold is value for the amount of the mortgagee's debt the mortgagor has a very real interest in the best price being obtained. If there should be a surplus it is for his benefit; equally he benefits by the best price being obtained: his indebtedness is thereby reduced as much as possible. Mortgagor and mortgagee are not in like case in this respect. A mortgagee who is not fully paid off because the best price is not obtained still has a right to sue the mortgagor for the balance, while the mortgagor must abide the disadvantage of a poor price being realised. Moreover, there is the interest of second and other mortgagees to be safeguarded.

Although the mortgagee holds the land as his security there is, behind, the equity of redemption; and as Kekewich J. said in *Colson* v. *Williams* (56 L.J. Ch. 539), at p. 540:- 'In equity we have always been accustomed to deal with that equity of redemption as if it were the legal estate, and to allow the owner of it to deal with it quite as if he were really the owner, subject, of course, to the mortgage.'

The trial Judge, I am satisfied, applied too lenient a test in judging the conduct of the defendants. The question he should have asked himself was: Did the defendants act as a reasonable man would in selling the plaintiff's property? The defendants' own surveyors, in as plain words as surveyors could use, indicated that a sale with vacant possession would, after payment of compensation to the tenants, probably produce a considerably enhanced price, as much perhaps as £15,000 or even more. The Judge adverted to the fact that the defendants were advised by their surveyors. He says:- 'The advice they received was acted upon, save that the defendants decided to act without reference to development potentialities; but in that regard I consider they were entitled to their views and opinions, and the fact is that the final sale was only agreed upon after numerous other prospective sales had fallen through.'

The evidence does not indicate that the defendants gave any reasonable consideration to the alternative mode of sale recommended by their surveyors. On the contrary, it appears that there was no examination of the possibilities of a sale with vacant possession. The attitude of the defendants may best be indicated by quoting a lengthy passage in the course of the cross-examination of Mr. Pike, chief clerk in the defendants' Dublin office:-

'560.   Q.: Mr. McCann:- It was made clear to you in the letter of the 1st November, 1960, what the investment value was and then it was suggested to you if certain steps were taken the premises might be much more valuable?

'A.: That is correct.

'561.   Q.: It was put to you that it might be necessary to pay the tenants something to get out?

'A.: That is correct.

'562. Q.: Having been given that information, can you give any reason why nobody approached even one of the tenants to ask what he would get out for?

'A.: No, because we had no monies available for negotiating the removal of these tenants from the property, we were not prepared to pay compensation, we had no money to pay compensation out of this account.

'563. Q.: You did not know what the compensation would be. Supposing you went to one of the tenants and he said to you, 'Alright, I will get out if you pay me £300,' would you think it worth while to write to Head Office and say:- 'We can sell the premises with vacant possession for £10,000 or £11,000. I can get tenant A out for £300, tenant B out for £300, tenant C out for £300'?

'A.: We were not prepared to pay any compensation at all.

'564. Q.: At all?

'A.: At all, because we had no monies available.

'565. Q.: (Mr. Justice Budd): You are under a misapprehension. If you were going to get £10,000 or £11,000 and if you found that by negotiating you could get the tenants out for £1,000, would it not occur to you to write to Head Office as to whether or not you would make an arrangement with the tenants on the basis of the sale?

'A.: The position was this, we placed the entire matter, following Messrs. Lisney's report, before Head Office and they gave us instructions to proceed with the sale on an investment basis, they did not authorise us to open negotiations with the tenants.

'566. Q.: That may be so, but had they done so up to that, because this was in the form of advice?

'A.: They got the original of Messrs. Lisney's letter of the 1st November, 1960, and we merely proceeded on the instructions received from Head Office.

'567. Q.: There were no negotiations?

'A.: No, we got clear instructions to proceed with the sale on investment value and not to enter into negotiations as we had no money available for such negotiations.

'568. Q.: Were the instructions in such wide terms that they precluded negotiation on the basis of paying the tenants out of the purchase money?

'A.: No, we did not pursue the matter at all.

'569. Q.: You did not investigate it in any way?

'A.: No.

'570. Q.: (Mr. McCann): At the time of this sale were you aware of the fact that many people were looking for this type of house for development purposes?

'A.: I was aware that some people were looking for it.

'571. Q.: And that very often speculators would take this type of property even with one or two tenants in the property?

'A.: Yes, that is so.

'572. Q.: Have you not seen this type of property advertised in the papers under the following heading: 'Investment property, capable of extensive development.' Did you ever see anything like that?

'A.: Yes.

'573. Q.: May I take it from time to time speculators often come along to your concern for the purpose of borrowing money to buy this sort of property?

'A.: They do, but we do not transact that type of business.

'574. Q.: May I take it they frequently go to you?

'A.: Yes, and we . . .

'575. Q.: You turn them away to somebody else?

'A.: Yes.

'576. Q.: Would you agree with me that since 1961 there have been numerous speculators both in this country and over from England with plenty of money to pay for this sort of property?

'A.: Yes, I am aware of that.

'577. Q.: Would you agree with me that the best way of letting them know about property is to advertise it in the papers?

'A.: Not always, I cannot agree with you.

'578. Q.: Surely, the first thing you will do, if you want to sell your property, is to advertise it in the papers. Does not everybody do it?

'A.: Not by us.

'579. Q.: Can you give any possible reason why this is so?

'A.: Because we had decided to sell it at investment value, we had decided to get what we considered a good offer over the investment value, and the investment value was given to us at £4,500.

'580. Q.: (Mr. Justice Budd): Had you closed your mind then to sell on the basis of possible development?

'A.: We did not pursue that.

'581. Q.: Had you closed your mind to selling any other way but as an investment?

'A.: On the basis of Messrs. Lisney's report, yes. We decided we would sell on an investment basis as we considered it was the only way we could dispose of the property under the circumstances.

'582. Q.: Would you develop that, 'On the basis of Messrs. Lisney's report'?

'A.: The report of the 1st November, 1960. We had a choice in that report of selling on an investment basis and selling, on vacant possession from the tenants, selling the vacant house and site.

'583. Q.: Having told you about the investment value and having told you that there was a demand for this sort of premises a growing demand for offices, they go on to state, 'We would advise therefore that you commence negotiations with the four tenants with the object of seeking vacant possession' etc. How do you say there was a choice given? I would interpret this myself, perhaps wrongly, as being advice to go and negotiate with the tenants to see what you could do with them because there were better prospects?

'A.: Yes, that is quite clear, but it is also qualified by the fact that we would have to offer compensation to the tenants in order to obtain possession of the property.

'584. Q.: Admittedly, but I would have read the letter as saying you could sell on an investment basis but as there is a rising market for offices you can go and interview the tenants to see what would happen?

'A.: Yes, my Lord, that is quite correct, I accept that, but it went on to say we must pay compensation and Head Office indicated they were not prepared to pay any monies out of the monies available in this account for the payment of such compensation, that, therefore, we should proceed on the basis of selling by investment.

'585. Q.: (Mr. Justice Budd): Apparently, then, it was not considered by you or Head Office as to whether it would be advisable to negotiate with the tenants on the basis of paying them out of the purchase money?

'A.: No, that was never considered.'

I do not say that it was unreasonable of the defendants not to have laid out money in paying compensation to the tenants in order to be able to sell with vacant possession. In the absence of information as to what the position was with regard to the tenants one cannot say with certainty what would have been reasonably required of them to safeguard the interests of the mortgagor. I would say that if the position turned out to be as the defendants' own advisers anticipated, I would find it difficult to say it would be reasonable for the defendants to reject out of hand the course proposed to them.

What in fact happened, as has been demonstrated, is that the defendants refused to look into the value of the plaintiff's property on a basis which their own surveyors advised would show a considerably higher price than sale at investment value. Their minds (as their witness admitted) were closed to this course. This was not reasonable; in my opinion it was quite unreasonable. A mortgagee with a power of sale has not power to dispose of the mortgagor's property with the same freedom as if it were his own. The defendants' Head Office appear to have taken an authoritatian line of action in this matter which left their Dublin office with no option but to obey. They declined even to examine into the possibilities of a better price, and this, in my judgment, was such unreasonable conduct on their part and such a disregard of the plaintiff's interests that an injunction should issue to restrain the defendants completing the sale to Mr. Sweeney.

I do not think it necessary to say anything of the plaintiff's failure to protest expressly against the sale proposed to Sweeney as I consider that in the course of the general representations which he made to the defendants' Head Office in London he had made it quite clear he objected fundamentally to a sale on 'investment' basis as not representative of the true value of the property.

I would allow this appeal.

I should add an epilogue. After the original argument concluded, the Court, in the course of considering its judgment, found that a question arose which had not been argued on the appeal, viz., whether, in the absence of the purchaser, Francis Sweeney, as a party to these proceedings and in the light of the provisions of s. 21, sub-s. 2, of the Conveyancing Act, 1881, and of s. 5, sub-s. 1, of the Conveyancing Act, 1911, the plaintiff's remedy (if any) must lie in damages only. The plaintiff had not claimed damages. The Court therefore directed that the case be re-listed for argument. As a result of the further argument we have heard – and counsel on both sides found themselves in agreement in their submissions – I am satisfied, firstly, that s. 21, sub-s. 2, cannot have any application until a conveyance has been made. In this case no conveyance has been made. And, secondly, as to s. 5, sub-s. 1, of the Act of 1911, I am also satisfied that a purchaser who in fact has notice, actual or constructive, of an irregularity in the exercise of the power of sale before completion by conveyance could not get a good title. No question of a remedy in damages between the parties before the Court can arise: the contract of sale is either properly made or it is not. If not, then it cannot be permitted to be completed, and the appropriate remedy is an injunction. Whatever Mr. Sweeney's rights against the mortgagees may be, they are not for consideration now.

Lavery J.:

I have read the judgment delivered by the Chief Justice. I agree with it and I have nothing to add.

Walsh J.:

I agree.

Notes and Questions

1. How would you define now the criterion by which a mortgagee enquiring his power of sale in Ireland should be judged? *Cf.* the English case of *Cuckmere Brick Co. Ltd.* v. *Mutual Finance Ltd.* [1971] Ch. 949. See also *Casey* v. *Irish Intercontinental Bank Ltd.* [1979] I.R. 364; *Van Hool McArdle Ltd.* v. *Rohan Industrial Estates Ltd.* [1980] I.R. 237; *Irish Land Law*, Supp. (1975–80), pp. 38–9.

2. So far as sales by building societies are concerned, see now section 82(1)(*a*) of the Building Societies Act, 1976, which provides that, in exercising any power of sale under a mortgage, a building society 'shall ensure as far as is reasonably practicable that the estate is sold at the best price reasonably obtainable'. Does this differ from the criterion laid down by the Supreme Court in the *Holohan* case? See generally *Irish Land Law*, para. 13.034 *et seq.*

BRUCE V. BROPHY
[1906] 1 I.R. 611 (Court of Appeal)

The plaintiffs, in an undefended mortgagees' suit, sought a decree that, in default of payment of the principal and interest secured by the mortgage on a day to be named, the defendant should stand foreclosed of all right or equity of redemption in the mortgaged premises.

The mortgage was made to secure the entire of the purchase-money of the lands, which had been advanced by the mortgagee to the mortgagor. The plaintiffs alleged that the rents were insufficient to keep down the interest on the mortgage debt; that the proceeds of a sale at twenty-five years' purchase would be insufficient to discharge the said debt, even if the plaintiffs became entitled to the bonus on a sale to the tenants (which was the avowed object of seeking foreclosure), and that there was no other mortgage affecting the premises. Barton J. held that the court should not depart from the well-settled practice of ordering a sale in lieu of foreclosure. The plaintiffs appealed to the Court of Appeal.

Sir Samuel Walker C.:

We do not think that there is any reason for interfering with the order of Barton, J.

It is the right of a mortgagee in ordinary cases, and in this case, to go into possession of the mortgaged property under his deed. The plaintiffs have not done that. They have come to a Court of Equity to realize their charge, and they have come to a Court with a settled practice for centuries of decreeing a sale, and not foreclosure in the sense now asked for.

I do not say that, under special circumstances, and where a special case is made for foreclosure, the Court has not power to grant a decree for foreclosure, and not a sale. No such case has been made here; and I think that, in a case where the defendant has not appeared, and where, being in default, she has naturally trusted that, in the ordinary course of practice adopted by the Court, the property will be sold, and possibly bring more – possibly much more – money than the amount of the mortgage, we should not depart from that ordinary course of practice.

In this case no circumstances of convenience have been shown to lead us to depart from the settled practice, and we do not think that, especially where the defendant has not appeared, we ought to do so.

FitzGibbon L.J.:

It must be borne in mind that there are two rights of a mortgagee which are capable of being enforced. One is to take the land instead of his debt by going into possession, remaining liable to account in equity if the land is worth more than the mortgage-money; if it is not worth more, the mortgagee keeps it. Secondly, the mortgagee has the right to turn his security into an effective means of recovering his money, by going to a Court of Equity, and asking the Court to give him whatever remedy it usually gives, and which it is fair to give. In Ireland it has been long considered that the proper remedy is to have the land turned into money. It was considered that an inquiry as to incumbrances was in the interest both of borrower and lender, even where there was only one mortgagee. When there were several, any one of them had equally the right to take some proceeding to recover his money, and then conversion of the land into money was for the convenience of everybody.

We are here asked to omit the judicial step of ascertaining that the land is not worth more than the debt, and to give it over by a foreclosure decree to the mortgagee, in order to enable him to sell it over again to greater advantage. I say nothing as to jurisdiction. There may be many cases where taking the land *in specie* may be a just and proper course; but where only one side is heard, and where the avowed object is ultimately to convert the land into money, I do not think that we ought to depart from the ordinary practice.

Holmes L.J., concurred.

Notes and Questions

1. What is the reason for the 'well-settled practice' in Ireland? See also FitzGibbon L.J.'s remarks in *Antrim County Land, Building and Investment Co. Ltd.* v. *Stewart*, p. 430, *ante*. *Cf. Irish Land Law*, para. 13.060.
2. Would it have made any difference in the *Bruce* case if both sides had been heard?

BROWNE V. RYAN
[1901] 2 I.R. 653; 1 N.I.J.R. 25; 35 I.L.T.R. 6 (Court of Appeal)

The defendant mortgaged his land to the plaintiff to secure a loan of £200 and interest thereon. The money was raised by the mortgagee by depositing the mortgage as security with a bank. As part of the same transaction the defendant agreed by an independent deed to sell his land within twelve months, and to give the sale thereof to the plaintiff, who was an auctioneer, and that if the said lands were sold otherwise than through the plaintiff he would pay the plaintiff five per cent on the purchase money. The defendant subsequently sold the lands through another auctioneer for £1250. Palles C.B. held at first instance that the covenant to pay five per cent was a clog on the equity of redemption and not such a collateral advantage as could be bargained for by a mortgagee. The Queen's Bench Division (Andrews J. *dissentiente*) held that the mortgagee was entitled to the five per cent. The mortgagor appealed to the Court of Appeal.

Lord Ashbourne C.:

In this case the judgment of the Court will be delivered by Lord Justice Walker.

Walker L.J.:

In this case Patrick Ryan, a farmer, had an intention of selling the lands of Curragh Feakle, which he owned. The plaintiff John Browne is an auctioneer. Ryan wanted a sum of £200 which Browne agreed to give, or procure for him on the security of a mortgage of the farm. Accordingly by a deed dated the 16th June, 1898, between Patrick Ryan on the one part and John Browne of the other – a mortgage in the statutory form – Ryan (in consideration of £200 expressed to be paid by Browne to Ryan) conveyed the lands to Browne for securing payment, on the 16th December, 1898, of the principal sum of £200, with interest at £7 per cent, and also an obligation if the principal was not paid, to pay interest at same rate on every 16th June and 16th December, reducible to £6 per cent if punctually paid.

An agreement under seal was also made which was admitted to form part of the mortgage transaction. It bears date the 21st June, 1898. It is in the following terms:-Whereas the said Patrick Ryan is about selling the lands of Curragh Feakle, in the county of Clare, and whereas the said John Browne has advanced the sum of £200 on the security of the said lands to the said Patrick Ryan, he the said Patrick Ryan agrees to give the said lands to the said John Browne, said lands to be put up for sale by public auction within twelve months from the date hereof, and to pay to the said John Browne the usual commission of £5 per cent on the amount of the purchase-money, and in the event of the said lands being sold otherwise than through the agency of the said John Browne, to pay unto the said John Browne £5 per cent on the amount of such purchase-money.

In point of fact the money was procured from the Bank of Ireland on the security of the lodgment of the mortgage. It is admitted that the parties must be treated as occupying the relation towards each other of mortgagor and mortgagee, and that the agreement must be read as if contained in the mortgage-deed. Patrick Ryan paid off the £200 before the day of redemption arrived, and obtained a reconveyance, dated the 19th November, 1898, by which Browne reconveyed the lands 'discharged from all principal money and interest secured by and from all claims and demands under the said indenture of mortgage'.

Patrick Ryan having thus got up the lands, did not sell them within the twelve months, but he did sell them in 1899 for a sum of £1250; and he did not employ Browne as auctioneer. The conveyance, which is to a man named Purcell, is dated the 24th August, 1899.

The plaintiff thereupon claimed the sum of £62 10s. as being payable to him as commission under the terms of the mortgage agreement.

The defendant contends that the obligation created by the agreement was a fetter on the equity of redemption which cannot be enforced, and the Chief Baron, before whom the case was tried without a jury, was of that opinion, and entered a verdict for the defendant. In the Queen's Bench Division, on a motion to set aside the verdict and enter judgment for plaintiff, Mr. Justice Andrews concurred in opinion with the Chief Baron, but the other Judges, the Lord Chief Justice, and Gibson and Kenny, JJ., were of a different opinion, and directed the verdict to be entered for the plaintiff. We have now to decide between these conflicting views. It is not material to consider what our decision would be if there were not in existence long established rules of Courts of Equity governing the relations between mortgagor and mortgagee, and putting limitations on the stipulations which may be contained in a contract of mortgage. Nor is it material to consider whether such rules had their origin in the laws against usury, because in substantial matters they have survived the abolition of the usury laws. The question is, 1, what the rules of Courts of Equity were in relation to contracts between mortgagor and mortgagee made in connection with the mortgage transaction; 2, how far those rules have been invaded by decisions in recent times not easy to reconcile with each other; and, 3, whether the present case falls within a principle lying at the foundation of the rules, and which, when rightly understood, is unaffected by any decision. As I understand the principle, it is that when a transaction appears, or has been declared to be a mortgage, Courts of Equity regard the instrument only as a security for the repayment of the principal, interest, and costs named and secured, and the mortgagor is entitled to get back his property as free as he gave it, on payment of principal, interest, and costs, and provisions inconsistent with that right cannot be enforced. The equitable rules, 'once a mortgage always a mortgage', and that the mortgagee cannot impose any 'clog or fetter on the equity of redemption', are merely concise statements of the same rule.

I think it has long been settled, and is still the law, that, when once the redemption price has been fixed and arrived at, the mortgagee cannot charge against the mortgagor on account as a charge against the estate to be redeemed any extra payments for commission for himself or otherwise. That rule is distinctly stated by Lord Eldon in *Chambers* v. *Goldwin* (9 Ves. 254), and is followed in *Broad* v. *Selfe* (9 Jur. (N.S.) 885; 11 W.R. 1036; 2 N.R. 541), and also in *Comyns* v. *Comyns* (I.R. 5 Eq. 583), and this, though the bargain for the extra payments may have been deliberately made; such a charge by its mere statement clogs the equity of redemption, and involves an assertion that there shall be no redemption till the extra demands are paid.

It is true that there are observations as distinct from decisions which go to the full extent that a mortgagee cannot stipulate for any collateral benefit for himself, even though the stipulation is not oppressive or unconscionable. Such are the observsations of the Master of the Rolls in *Jennings* v. *Ward* (2 Vern. 520), of Judge Hargreave in *Edwards' Estate* (11 Ir. Ch. R. 367), and of the Master of the Rolls in *Broad* v. *Selfe* (11 W.R. 1036), and apparently also the language of Kay, J., in *Field* v. *Hopkins* (44 Ch. D. 524), decided in January, 1890. In this last case the mortgagees were a solicitor and an auctioneer. There was a foreclosure suit which it was conceded had the same incidents as a suit for redemption. The charges in question included a fee for the valuation of the property by the mortgagee-auctioneer, and Kay, J., assuming that the right to make the charge was covered by a recital in the mortgage deed, held that it was not recoverable. He says (at p. 529):-

'Can a mortgagee stipulate for more than his principal, interest, and costs by a recital of this kind, it being clear that this remuneration would not have been payable but for this recital? It is said by Lord Romilly in *Gregg* v. *Slator* (25 L.J. Ch. 440), and by myself in the recent case of *In re Roberts* (43 Ch. D. 52), that where a solicitor-mortgagee tries to charge against his mortgagor professional costs in connection with the preparation of the mortgage, such a charge has been disallowed, because he is not claiming costs paid to another person, but he is claiming them for himself, and, as the mortgagee is only liable to pay outgoings, he is not bound to pay anything charged by the solicitor for his own benefit. Therefore, this sum charged by the auctioneer, as incidental to the preparation of this mortgage is not a proper charge, unless it is covered by the recital I have read. Then comes the question, Can a mortgagee contract for payment to himself of a profit-payment to which, but for such a contract, he would not be entitled? The matter has been considered in many cases. It is only necessary for me to refer to my own judgment in *James* v. *Kerr* (40 Ch. D. 459), where I quoted the language of the Master of the Rolls in *Jennings* v. *Ward* (2 Vern. 520), that "a man shall not have interest for his money, and a collateral advantage besides for the loan of it, or clog the redemption with any by-agreement." That decision has since been followed in a great many cases: and I go on in my judgment to state that "in *Broad* v. *Selfe* (11 W.R. 1036) Lord Romilly decided that this rule was not affected by the repeal of the usury laws, and he disallowed a commission for which the mortgagee had stipulated in addition to his principal and interest". Until these decisions are reversed I shall feel bound to follow them. Accordingly, the five guineas taken by the auctioneer-mortgagee, which he could not possibly have claimed without a special contract, could not be the subject of a valid contract. According to the mortgage law recognised in this country, a mortgagee cannot make such a contract: he cannot contract to get anything from the estate beyond his principal, interest, and costs: therefore profit-charges, which he is not entitled to be paid, stand on the same footing as commission, which he clearly cannot charge.'

In the Court of Appeal the Judges disposed of the point by holding that the right to make the claim was not covered by the deed, and it was not necessary to go further. So stood the law up to the year 1890, and Mr. Bourke, in his argument, admitted that if the case depended on the decisions up to the year 1890, the plaintiff must fail. But he said the covenant is not found to be oppressive or unconscionable: damages recovered under it are not made a charge on the estate: it is merely a personal and collateral benefit to the mortgagee, and therefore within the principle of *Biggs* v. *Hoddinott* ([1898] 2 Ch. 307); *Santley* v. *Wilde* ([1899] 1 Ch. 747; 2 Ch. 474); therefore the commission secured by the covenant is recoverable; and he further contended that the result would be the same if there had been a personal covenant that a sum of £100 should be paid by the mortgagor to the mortgagee if the lands were redeemed by him. It may be that those two cases indicate a new departure, but we must see how far they have travelled. They certainly have not interfered with the maxim 'once a mortgage always a mortgage', or any case which really falls within that rule. In the first place they profess to save it whole, and in the next place the decision of *Salt* v. *Marquis of Northampton* ([1892] A.C. 1), decided in November, 1891, is an express authority, that the rule remains in full force. Lord Bramwell seems to regret the introduction of the rule, as one which interfered with free contract, and he describes it as follows, the 'right of redemption shall not even by bargain between the creditor and debtor be made more burdensome to the debtor than the original debt, except so far as additional interest and expenses consequent on the debt not having been paid at the time appointed may have occurred or arisen: that any agreement making such right of redemption more burdensome is void: for instance, £1000 out at £5 per cent payable in six months on mortgage, with a proviso that if not paid in six months the right of redemption should not be exercised, except on payment of £6 per cent interest, would be void'.

The facts in *Biggs* v. *Hoddinott* ([1898] 2 Ch. 307) must be examined in order to understand the case. Biggs was a brewer, and the defendants were owners of an hotel, and Biggs lent them £7654, which was secured by a mortgage of 18th March, 1896, repayable with interest at 5 per cent on 18th September, 1896, and the defendants covenanted that during the continuance of the security they would deal with the plaintiff for all beer and malt liquors consumed on the premises. There was a proviso that the loan should not be called in or paid off for five years. The deed in no way charged any money payable for beer, &c., on the premises. In the spring of 1898 the defendants ceased to purchase beer, &c., from the plaintiff, and claimed to be entitled to redeem the mortgage at once, and tendered all moneys due, and as the plaintiff declined it, the defendants took out an originating summons to compel redemption, and the plaintiff then brought his action, claiming an injunction restraining the defendants during the continuance of the security from selling any liquors not purchased from plaintiff and for damages. It was first held that the clause precluding redemption for five years was valid, as had already been decided in *Teevan* v. *Smith* (20 Ch. D. 724) and this disposed of the redemption summons.

The case was then argued on the plaintiff's motion for an injunction. Mr. Justice Romer, after pointing out that the covenant was a reasonable and proper one under the circumstances, first recognised the principle that you cannot by contract clog the equity of redemption, so as to prevent the mortgagor redeeming at the time agreed on, on payment of principal, interest, and costs, and he next held that there was nothing in the covenant which clogged the right of redemption. He says:-

'The mortgagor's right to redeem under the mortgage deed stands exactly the same whether the covenant to take the beer from the brewer, the mortgagee, is in the deed or not. The mortgagee, by virtue of that covenant, has no right to stop or check redemption. He could not stop redemption, because there had been any breach of that covenant. There is no charge upon the mortgaged premises in favour of the mortgagee for any sums which might become due to him under or by virtue, or by reason of any breach of that covenant by the mortgagors' –

and he there held that the observations in some of the cases cited which appeared to lay down that a mortgagee could not stipulate for any collateral advantage were too wide and not necessary for the decisions.

The decision of Romer, J., was affirmed in the Court of Appeal on the same ground, viz. (to use the language of Chitty, L.J.):-

'That it in no way affects the equity of redemption, for it is not stipulated that damages for breach of the covenant shall be covered by the security, and redemption takes place quite independently of the covenant, so this is not a case where the right to redeem is affected' –

and when once the collateral covenant was free from that character, it being reasonable and proper, it was valid, though contained in the mortgage deed.

It will be observed that the covenant there was limited to the continuance of the security, and the obligation under it so limited in no way interfered with the rights as owner of the mortgagor. When the stipulated time for redemption arrived and redemption took place, the covenant fell with it and the nature of the obligation was quite collateral, and had nothing in its character which prevented him redeeming. It would be quite a different matter if the obligation to take the beer – in other words, the position of a tied house – survived redemption under the contract. The case is certainly an authority that fair collateral contracts in a mortgage deed for the benefit of the mortgage which do not prevent or burden redemption or interfere with the position of a free owner after redemption are valid. The case of *Santley* v. *Wilde* ([1899] 1 Ch. 747; 2 Ch. 474) is on its facts more difficult to deal with, though I see nothing in the grounds on which the decision is stated to be rested as distinct from the decision itself, which cannot be accepted.

In *Santley* v. *Wilde* ([1899] 1 Ch. 747; 2 Ch. 474), Miss Santley was sub-lessee of a theatre with an *option* of purchasing a reversionary term for £2000. She borrowed the money for the purpose on a mortgage of the term to secure the £2000 and £6 per cent interest. The reversionary term would expire in June, 1905, and the mortgage money was made repayable by instalments, the last of which would be payable four and a half years before the expiration of the term. The mortgage was made redeemable on payment of the £2000 and interest and all other payments covenanted to be paid, and the deed contained a covenant to pay to the mortgagee one-third of the net profit rental of the theatre during the whole of the mortgagor's term, which would outlast the time for redemption. Byrne J., held that the clause securing the one-third of the profits during the whole term operated to prevent redemption and was void, and that such a provision could not enable the mortgagee to maintain any action for specific performance or account or for damages. The Court of Appeal reversed that decision. The Master of the Rolls states the ground of his judgment as follows: after reading the document he says ([1899] 2 Ch. at p. 476):-

'That means that this lease is granted or assigned by the mortgagor to the mortgagee as security, not only for the payment of the £2000 and interest, but also for the payment of the one-third of the net profit rents to the end of the term. If I am right in the principle which I have laid down, that does not clog the right of redemption upon the performance of the obligation for which the security was given. But it is said that is not good law. Those, however, who say so lose sight of the true principle underlying the expression that there must be no clog or fetter on the equity of redemption. The plaintiff says, "I will pay off the balance of the £2000 and interest, and you will give me back the lease, and this is the end of my obligation." But the mortgagee says, "No, that is not the bargain, you cannot redeem on those terms; on the contrary, you may pay me the £2000 and interest, but if you do you must also pay the one-third profit rents." On principle that is right.'

In other words, they held that the equity of redemption only arose upon the performance of the stipulation to pay one-third of the profits during the whole term, as well as the other stipulations. Collins, L.J., in the last case, *Rice* v. *Noakes* ([1900] 1 Ch. 213; 2 Ch. 445), treats *Santley* v. *Wilde* ([1899] 1 Ch. 747; 2 Ch. 474) as deciding that the one-third profits was part of the subject matter of the security. If that was the true interpretation of the redemption clauses, there was no fetter on the equity of redemption.

The last case on this subject, *Rice* v. *Noakes* ([1900] 1 Ch. 213; 2 Ch. 445), puts the true limitations on what was decided in *Biggs* v. *Hoddinott* ([1898] 2 Ch. 307). It was a mortgage of a leasehold public-house to a brewer. The mortgage money and interest were repayable on demand, but the deed contained the following covenant:-

'And for the considerations aforesaid the mortgagor, so as to charge the premises hereby demised into whatsoever possession they may come, whether by act of the party or by operation of law, or by any other ways or means however, and to the further intent that the obligation of this covenant may run with the land, doth hereby covenant with the company that the mortgagor shall not, nor will at any time during the continuance of the term aforesaid, and whether any principal moneys or interest shall or shall not be owing upon the security of these presents, use or sell, or permit to be used or sold, upon, or about the said demised premises any malt liquors except such as shall be *bona fide* purchased by the mortgagor of the company. And further, that if and whenever there shall be a breach of the said covenant, he, the mortgagor, shall and will pay to the company the sum of £1000, as, and for ascertained liquidated damages for each such breach.'

The question argued was, whether the plaintiff was entitled to get a reconveyance on payment of all moneys due under the mortgage free from the obligation of his house remaining a tied house during the currency of the lease. Cozens-Hardy, J., decided in favour of the mortgagor on the ground that the tie, though valid during the continuance of the security, could not be maintained when all moneys due upon the security had been paid off, and that it was involved in the very idea of a mortgage, that a mortgagee when paid off, should have no estate or interest in the mortgaged premises, and no right to interfere with the mortgagee in his enjoyment or use of the premises. He says at p. 219:-

'The negative covenant or "tie" is expressed to be a "charge" on the premises. I doubt whether this phrase is strictly accurate. The precise operation of such a covenant has been described in different ways. Lord Cottenham, in *Tulk* v. *Moxhay* (2 Ph. 774) calls it an "equity attached to the property by the owner". Sir George Jessel in *London and South Western Railway Co.* v. *Gomm* (20 Ch. D. 583) calls it "an equitable burden". This much at least is clear, that in the hands of the plaintiff and of any person taking with notice, this covenant imposes a fetter upon the enjoyment of the property, and materially lessens its value.'

The decision of Cozens-Hardy, J., was affirmed on appeal on the ground that what was mortgaged was the house without any tie, and that the covenant put it out of the power of the mortgagee to give back to the mortgagor on redemption that which he was bound to return to him, viz. the unincumbered term. Lord Alverstone says:-

'Whatever may be the proper expression, in my opinion the covenant impairs or affects the mortgaged property, so that the mortgagor will not get it back on redemption. It impedes his right to redeem and rescue that which was his own at the time he mortgaged it.'

He adds:-

'Speaking for myself, I should have had a difficulty in arriving at the same conclusion as the Court of Appeal did in *Santley* v. *Wilde*, on the facts of that case.'

I own I confess to the same difficulty, but let us now apply the principles involved in the equitable rule which I have first stated, and those which can be collected from the decision in *Rice* v. *Noakes* ([1900] 1 Ch. 213; 2 Ch. 415), to the present.

The covenant is not that if the mortgagor sells he will employ the plaintiff as auctioneer, nor is the covenant limited to the continuance of the security, or even made an incident to an act enforcing by sale the security. The whole covenant must be considered, and it is not material that the parties might have arrived at practically the same end by using other language.

The first obligation is that the mortgagor shall sell within twelve months. That is a period which outlasts the time for redemption, and attaches an obligation by covenant on the owner to sell, whether he liked or not, after (on the assumption) he had got back his property free. The liability under the covenant sued on only arises in the event of his not selling within the twelve months.

I do not think it material that this 'tie' on the rights of the owner arises through a liability to damages under a covenant as distinct from a burden which a Court of Equity can attach on the lands, or on him in respect of the lands, on the principle of *Tulk* v. *Moxhay* (2 Ph. 774). Equally he is under a burden in respect of his own ownership arising from an obligation alleged to be in force after that ownership should be after redemption free.

I am of opinion that, without at all relying on the rule laid down in the earlier authorities that a mortgagee cannot stipulate for any collateral benefit to himself, this case offends against the principle which underlies the case of *Rice* v. *Noakes* ([1900] 1 Ch. 213; 2 Ch. 445), and that the decision of the Queen's Bench Division should be reversed, and the judgment given by the Chief Baron at the trial restored.

It follows that the appeal must be allowed with costs in this Court and in the Queen's Bench Division.

FitzGibbon L.J.:

As this appeal involves the consideration of an important rule of equity, it is my duty to add a few words. We were pressed with the argument that there has been a change in the rule since 1890. In my opinion the rule, stated in the form in which it applies to the present case, has undergone no change. The essential principle of the rule is, I believe, that where land has been mortgaged as a security for money, when the money secured is paid off, the land, and its owner in the use of it, must be as free as if it had never been mortgaged. Any inroad upon the rule stated in that form must destroy it altogether; and I agree with Lord Justice Walker that, if it does not apply to this case, it must be treated as abrogated.

The rule originated in that wider principle of equity under which the Court of Chancery interfered with contracts between parties who were not in a position to deal with each other on equal terms, e.g., 'catching bargains' with expectant heirs, it being deemed inequitable that a leader should, through the necessities of a borrower, obtain any additional or collateral advantage affecting the right of redemption, beyond the payment of principal and interest and costs. Lord Bramwell's criticism only showed how firmly the principle was established, and though he made no attempt to conceal his dislike of it, he was constrained to act upon it in *Salt* v. *Northampton* ([1892] App. Cas 1).

Biggs v. *Hoddinott* ([1898] 2 Ch. 307), *Santley* v. *Wilde* ([1899] 1 Ch. 747; 2 Ch. 474), and *Rice* v. *Noakes* ([1900] 1 Ch. 213; 2 Ch. 445), do not mitigate or change the rule as I have stated it.

In *Biggs* v. *Hoddinott* ([1898] 2 Ch. 307), there was a covenant not to pay off the mortgage for five years, and also a covenant to deal with the mortgagee for all beer and malt liquors to be consumed on the mortgaged premises *during the continuance of the security*. An attempt was first made to show that the covenant not to redeem for five years was not valid; but, that point being closed by authority, it was next contended that the covenant to deal exclusively with the mortgagee during the continuance of the security was inequitable as an attempt by him to confer a collateral advantage upon himself contrary to the rule. But Romer, J. and the Court of Appeal held that this covenant was reasonable, that it left the mortgagor perfectly free to redeem at the stipulated time, and that it did not affect the equity of redemption. This decision did not infringe the rule as I have stated it, because, on payment of the principal, interest, and costs, in accordance with what were held to be the reasonable terms of the mortgage, the mortgaged property and its owner would become as free as if there had never been any mortgage.

In *Santley* v. *Wilde* ([1899] 1 Ch. 747; 2 Ch. 474), a loan of £2000 was secured by the mortgage of a leasehold term of years in a theatre, for a sum repayable by instalments. The mortgage was redeemable on repayment of the loan and all other moneys covenanted to be repaid by the mortgagor, and the mortgagor covenanted to pay to the mortgagee one-third of the profits of the theatre during the residue of the term for which it was held, which would not expire for nearly five years after the date fixed for payment of the last instalment of the loan. The Court of Appeal decided that this one-third of the profits continued to be payable after the repayment of the last instalment of the loan. If that decision is considered upon the ground stated in the judgment of the Court of Appeal, it affirmed the principle that every mortgage security must be redeemable on discharge of the debt, any provision to the contrary notwithstanding; and that any provision inserted to prevent redemption on payment or performance by the mortgagee of the debt or obligation for which the security is given, is void. But the Court held, upon the facts and instrument in the particular case, that the covenant to pay to the mortgagor one-third of the profits of the theatre *during the stipulated term* was reasonable and valid, and, in effect, that this payment was only part of the stipulated mode of repaying the mortgage debt. I do not think that I could have taken that view of the facts, and I cannot distinguish, in equity, the position of the one-third *extra* profits there, after the payment of the last instalment, from that of the £62 10s. commission claimed on the sale of the redemption here. But the case makes no change in the rule; it only raises a difficulty in understanding its non-application to the particular case.

In *Rice* v. *Noakes* ([1900] 1 Ch. 213; 2 Ch. 445) the mortgagor mortgaged a leasehold public-house to a brewer to secure a loan with interest; and he covenanted to constitute the mortgaged premises a 'tied house' for the residue of his term, which extended beyond the period for redemption. The mortgagor paid off the loan and interest, in accordance with the proviso for redemption, and he then claimed to have his public-house declared free from any further obligation under the covenant to deal with the mortgagee. Cozens-Hardy, J., held that when the money due on the mortgage was paid off, the mortgagor was entitled to have the premises reconveyed freed from this obligation; and this decision was affirmed by the Court of Appeal. It is not necessary for us to attempt to distinguish the facts of that case from those of *Santley's Case* ([1899] 1 Ch. 747; 2 Ch. 474). As a decision upon the force and effect of the rule of equity, it is, in my opinion, decisive of the present case. The covenant was held to have gone the moment the mortgage debt was paid off; the property and its owner in the use of it thereupon became as free as if there had never been any mortgage, and the same result must follow in the case of Ryan's covenant to sell his land, and to pay commission to Browne, after having redeemed the mortgage.

It is admitted that the deed which purported to secure the commission was 'part of the mortgage transaction'. We must take this admission in its natural sense, and we must deal with the case as if the provisions of this deed were contained in the mortgage, and were entered into in consideration of the advance. Thus the transaction, though a mortgage, purports to bind the mortgagor to sell the lands, whether redeemed or not, within twelve months; to give the sale to the plaintiff as auctioneer; and to pay him a commission of £5 per cent upon the purchase money, whether the sale is carried out through him or not. This is plainly an additional and collateral advantage to the mortgagee, purporting to secure a further profit to him, over and above the repayment of his principal, interest, and costs: it affects the equity of redemption, because, if valid, it would compel the mortgagor afterwards, notwithstanding redemption, to sell the mortgaged property, and to pay part of the proceeds to the mortgagee. If enforceable, it would not leave the mortgaged property, or the owner in the use of it, free on repayment of the loan; but the property should be sold, and the price should be shared with the mortgagee.

The Lord Chief Justice says:-

'The auctioneer gives his time, trouble, and credit, in getting the money. The owner of the farm gets all he is contractually entitled to. The auctioneer does not get one penny of money in hand, and the somewhat discredited doctrine of "clog" is invoked to prevent his getting anything for his time, trouble, and the use of his credit. He is to be deprived of the very consideration for which he entered into the contract. The owner of the farm is to be permitted to utilize the contract so far as it operates for his benefit, and to have recourse to the doctrine of "clog" to deprive the auctioneer of the sole and only benefit that it was stipulated he was to get as a consideration for what he was to do.'

I answer, with all respect – the lender is estopped by his own deed from saying that the consideration for the contract was not the loan of £200 at interest, and a mortgage to secure it. The necessary result in equity is that, on repayment of the loan with interest and costs, the property may be redeemed on the terms stated in the proviso for redemption; and the property, and the mortgagor in the use of it, must thenceforth be free. This agreement purports to bind the borrower to convert his property into money whether he redeems it or not; and, in addition to repaying the mortgage debt, it binds him to pay a commission to the mortgagee out of the purchase money. The application of the doctrine of 'clog' to such a stipulation has, so far as I know, never been questioned, far less 'discredited'. I concur with Andrews, J., and I am clearly of opinion that the judgment for the defendant given by the Lord Chief Baron must be restored.

Holmes L.J.:

If a farmer were to agree with an auctioneer, that in consideration of the latter procuring for him a loan from a bank, he would sell his farm within twelve months and pay the auctioneer a stipulated percentage of the purchase money, there would be no illegality nor invalidity in such a contract; and if it were broken, damages would be recoverable. The negotiations between the plaintiff and the defendant which preceded the present litigation opened upon the foregoing lines, and if they had terminated in such an agreement as I have indicated, there would probably have been no necessity for the present action. Unfortunately, however, the transaction assumed a different shape. The money which the plaintiff obtained from the bank was lent by him to the defendant on the security of an indenture of mortgage by which the farm was conveyed to the lender, subject to a proviso for redemption on payment at the end of six months of £200, the amount of the loan with interest thereon at £7 per cent per annum, reducible to £6 per cent in the event of punctual payment. As far as this deed is concerned, the transaction appears to be an ordinary mortgage with the incidents belonging to this kind of security. A few days later a further document was executed which has been already read. It is manifest from its contents, and indeed it is admitted by the plaintiff's counsel, that its provisions formed part of the terms of the loan; and their effect is to bind the mortgagor to sell the mortgaged property within twelve months either through the instrumentality of the mortgagee or of another auctioneer, and to pay the mortgage £5 per cent of the purchase money obtained upon such sale.

I do not know why this mode of obtaining a loan for the defendant was adopted; and it is immaterial to inquire whether the plaintiff obtained or expected to obtain any advantage by assuming the position of lender, and having the mortgage made to himself.

It is enough that he became a mortgagee; and the rights and liabilities of the parties must be ascertained by reference to the rules of law applicable to mortgages. I do not understand the suggestion that the defendant was guilty of fraud in selling the farm through another auctioneer. This was contemplated by the terms of the contract, and unless a litigant is to be held guilty of fraud, because he seeks to rely upon a doctrine of equity which was intended for his protection, I can find no grounds for the imputation.

The decision of the matter in controversy in this action depends altogether upon the effect of the agreement for the loan taken in its entirety. In the first place, it was to be secured by mortgage, and this necessarily implies that upon repayment of the money advanced with interest and expenses, the borrower is entitled to have reconveyed to him his property freed and discharged from all liability or burden in respect of or arising from the contract under which the advance was made. But there were also the terms contained in the collateral agreement by which the mortgagor was obliged to sell the mortgaged premises within twelve months. How can such a stipulation co-exist with the right to redeem? It is not merely a clog or fetter in equity of redemption, but it is absolutely destructive of it. As a matter of fact the farm was redeemed by payment of principal and interest within the twelve months; but did the mortgagor then become the unfettered owner of his property? Certainly not. The effect of a contract must be estimated on the assumption that it is observed; and on this assumption the result would be, that the mortgagor after paying in full the principal and interest due would be obliged to sell his farm. So too if he had not redeemed within the year, the fulfilment of the contract on his part would have destroyed the possibility of redemption. I am unable to conceive any case that would come more completely and unequivocally than the present within the principle, that where a loan is secured by mortgage, the character of a mortgage – that is to say, the right to redeem – cannot be burdened or impeded. Unless it can be successfully argued, that absolute destruction of the right is no fetter on it, this case comes within the rule.

The only ground upon which the contrary has been argued is that the collateral agreement does not place any charge on the mortgaged lands; but there is no authority to support this distinction. On the contrary, the majority of the contracts that have been avoided by reason of their being inconsistent with the fundamental conception of a mortgage security were contracts that carried with them only personal obligation; and in the last reported case – *Rice* v. *Noakes* ([1900] 1 Ch. 213; 2 Ch. 445) – the Master of the Rolls declined to decide, as being immaterial, whether the covenant of the publican to deal with the brewery ran with the licensed premises or not.

It is not part of my duty to justify or explain the introduction into our jurisprudence of the rule that prevents the right of redemption being made more burdensome than what is necessarily involved in a contract by way of mortgage. It is now too firmly established to be weakened by judicial criticism; and I think that there is no reason for saying that it has been discredited in recent times, if by this expression it is meant that the rule has been disregarded or substantially modified. The last occasion on which it was considered by the ultimate tribunal of the kingdom was in the case of *Salt* v. *Marquess of Northampton* ([1892] App. Cas. 1), heard by the House of Lords in the year 1891. The peers who then formed the Court included a very able and thorough-going champion of individualism, the late Lord Bramwell. As might be expected, he spoke with considerable severity of the double condition of things arising from legal rights and equitable rights, and of a system of documents which do not mean what they say. Yet he announced the rule broadly and distinctly; and he acted on it, although he expressed regret to be obliged to give the decision to which it led. It would be superfluous for me after Lord Justice Walker's judgment, which I had an opportunity of reading before it was delivered, to examine the long succession of cases dealing with this branch of law; but as far as I can see, the argument for the plaintiff rests altogether on two authorities: *Biggs* v. *Hoddinott*([1898] 2 Ch. 307), and *Santley* v. *Wilde*([1899] 1 Ch. 747; 2 Ch. 474). Of these the former does not touch the point at all. A mortgagor of licensed premises was not entitled to redeem for five years, and it was held that a contract by him to deal exclusively with the mortgagee for malt liquor during that period was good. But he was entitled to redeem on the usual terms at the stipulated time, whereupon the obligation would terminate. *Rice* v. *Noakes* shows by contrast the point of this decision; for in that case it was held that a similar contract could not be enforced after the time for redemption, and so as to fetter the right of redemption given by the mortgage.

As for the case of *Santley* v. *Wilde*, I admit that I am unable to reconcile it with what I understand to be the established rule of law. I follow the proposition laid down in the judgment of the Court; but the facts of the case seem to me not to fall within the proposition. It cannot, I think, stand together with the subsequent case of *Rice* v. *Noakes*; but even if it had the effect of modifying the law as previously understood, still the contract in the present case cannot be enforced if a shred of the old rule remains.

Note

See generally on this area of the law of mortgages, *Irish Land Law*, para. 13.088 *et seq. Cf. Maxwell* v. *Tipping* [1903] 1 I.R. 498.

III. PRIORITIES

WORKINGMEN'S BENEFIT BUILDING SOCIETY V. DIXON
[1908] 1 I.R. 582 (Court of Appeal)

In 1894 the defendant D. made a proposal to the lessors, to take certain lands on a building lease. The proposal having been accepted by the lessors, D. went into possession of the land, but there was no document accepting the proposal, the custom on the estate being to execute the leases only after the buildings were erected. In 1900 a mortgage of the premises was executed by D. to the plaintiffs, to secure a loan, and the mortgage was registered on the 14th September, 1900. On the 14th July, 1902, the lessors executed to D. a lease of the premises for 150 years, from the 1st May, 1894; and, on the 7th May, 1903, D. obtained possession of the lease from the lessor's solicitors. On the 5th May, 1903, the plaintiffs wrote to the lessor's agents, informing them of their equitable mortgage, and asking that the lease, when executed, should be sent to them; but they received no answer to this letter, and were not informed of the lease being executed and handed to D. On the 20th January, 1904, D. deposited the lease with the defendants, the Bank, to secure a loan, producing to the Bank at the same time a receipt for rent as from 1897. The Bank made no inquiry, and searched only from January,

1902. In 1906 the Bank, after they had received express notice of the plaintiff's equitable mortgage, took a legal mortgage of the premises from D.

The premises were sold, and the proceeds were insufficient to pay both the plaintiffs and the Bank in full.

Ross J.:

The only matter left undetermined in this action is a question of priority as between a charge of the plaintiffs and a charge of the Ulster Bank. The premises have been sold, but have not realized enough to satisfy the claims and costs of both chargeants.

On the 28th June, 1894, the defendant George Dixon signed a proposal to take from the Earl of Longford and Lord de Vesci a plot of ground in Spencer Road, Glenageary, for a term of 150 years, from the 1st May, 1894, at a rent of £3 2s. 6d. The proposal contained a term that the defendant George Dixon, who is a builder, would erect within a year one house, at a cost of at least £500. No agreement was signed by the lessors; but the proposal was accepted. It seems to have been the custom on the estate not to give the lease until the building was completed. The lessee entered into possession, and the house, 19, Spencer Road, Glenageary, was erected, but was not completed until early in the year 1902, or thereabouts. No question was raised by the lessors in respect of the failure of the lessee to complete the work within the time originally specified.

In the year 1900 the lessee applied to the plaintiffs for the loan of £400, to enable him to complete the building. The plaintiffs agreed, and the lessee executed a mortgage of the premises, dated the 22nd August, 1900, for the £400, repayable by instalments as provided by the deed. The mortgage was duly registered on the 14th September, 1900. On the 14th July, 1902, the lease was executed; and on the 7th May, 1903, the lessee obtained it from Messrs. Reeves, the lessors' solicitors, on payment of their costs for its preparation and registration. Messrs. Stewart & Sons are the agents of the lessors; and, on the 5th May, 1903, they received a letter from the plaintiffs, requesting Messrs. Stewart to let them have this lease when completed, along with certain other leases, as they were mortgagees of the premises. It appears that their letter was not answered, and the plaintiffs were not informed that the lease had been executed, and was about to be handed to the lessee.

On the 20th January, 1904, the lessee deposited the lease with the Ulster Bank, by way of equitable mortgage, to secure moneys due or thereafter to be advanced. On the 25th January, 1904, the Bank sent the lease to Messrs. Stewart, requesting an indorsement, that the building covenant had been satisfied. The indorsement was made, and the lease returned. At the time of the deposit the lessee did not inform the Bank of the mortgage to the plaintiffs. The plaintiffs were informed on the 25th June, 1906, by a letter from the lessee's wife, that the lease was deposited with the Bank, and requesting them to put the house up for auction. Thereupon, on the same day, the plaintiffs wrote to the Bank, inquiring if this was so, and what was the amount of the Bank's claim. They intimated that they were about to put the property up for public sale. The Bank replied, on the 26th June, that they were unable to give the information sought, unless instructed to do so by the lessee. On the 28th September, 1906, the lessee executed a legal mortgage to the Bank.

There can be no doubt whatever that from the date of the acceptance of his proposal the defendant, Dixon, had an interest in the premises capable of being affected by a mortgage. The plaintiffs did everything that was necessary to secure their charge upon that interest. Their mortgage accurately defines the premises, and the mortgage was duly registered. They were aware of the custom on the estate, and that no lease or agreement for a lease was in existence. If there had been a lease, and if they had not insisted on getting it into their possession, or, having got it, if they had allowed it to get out of their possession, the case would be different. They were aware that the original time specified had been extended, and that the work was going slowly on. They might reasonably believe that Messrs. Stewart & Sons would not have the lease prepared until the house was ready for occupation.

On the 5th May, 1903, they wrote to Messrs. Stewart informing them of their charge, and asking for the lease. At that time the lease was with Messrs. Reeves, but under the control of the lessors. Through a slip of somebody in the office, the letter was not answered. If Messrs. Stewart & Sons had replied to the effect that the lease was ready in the hands of the estate solicitors, and that they would be obliged to hand it to the lessee, then there would have been something to induce the plaintiffs to take action. But, having no answer to their letter, they had no sufficient reason for anticipating any danger of their security. On the 20th January, 1904, the mischief was done: the lease was deposited in the Bank. It would seem to me exceedingly harsh and unjust to hold that the neglect of the plaintiffs during these seven months to get possession of the lease is such gross negligence as to deprive the plaintiffs of a perfectly valid security.

I have nothing to say about the law in addition to what has been said by Mr Justice Barton in his admirable judgment in *Greer* v. *Greer* ([1907] 1 I.R. 57). In so far as the Bank rely on the equitable mortgage it was taken subject to the prior equities. The legal mortgage cannot help them. It was taken after notice of the prior charge, and with the knowledge that the lessee was a trustee for the plaintiffs. This disposes of the whole case. I only wish to add that if the matter came to the weighing of the respective equities, I think the Bank would not come out better than the plaintiffs. The fact that the term ran from the 1st May, 1894, coupled with the fact that receipts for rent were produced covering a period prior to the date of the lease, might have led the legal advisers of the Bank to the discovery of the existence of the earlier mortgage. I accordingly declare that the plaintiffs' charge takes priority over that of the Ulster Bank. The costs of this action must be added to their charge.

The Ulster Bank appealed to the Court of Appeal.

The Court of Appeal (The Lord Chancellor and FitzGibbon and Holmes, L.JJ.) affirmed the decision of Ross, J., and dismissed the appeal.

Notes and Questions
1. Do you agree with Ross J.'s view on the question of 'gross negligence' by the bank? How does the criterion of 'gross negligence' differ from that of 'constructive notice'? See *Northern Bank Ltd.* v. *Henry*, p. 87, *ante*.
2. On the subject of priorities in relation to mortgages generally, see *Irish Land Law*, para. 13.127 *et seq*. See also on the doctrine of notice, p. 84 *et seq*., *ante*.

RE O'BYRNE'S ESTATE
(1885) 15 L.R. Ir. 373 (Court of Appeal)
The facts are set out in Naish C.'s judgment.

Naish, C.:
The Appellants in this matter, who are mortgagees upon the lands ordered to be sold, under two deeds, dated respectively the 14th January, 1879, and 26th May, 1879, claim to have the sums due to them under these deeds paid in priority to the sum due to the National Bank upon foot of an earlier deed of mortgage, executed by the owner to the Bank on the 13th February, 1878, and registered on the 19th

February, following. This deed of the 13th February, 1878, was executed for the purpose of securing the balance then due by Mr. O'Byrne to the Bank, upon his account with them, and also the balance which might from time to time become due from him to the Bank in respect of bills and notes discounted, or in respect of loans, credits or advances, and the money, as to the priority of which the questions in the case arise, represents a balance due by Mr. O'Byrne to the Bank for advances made by them to him, and therefore *prima facie* secured by the deed, but which advances were made after the owner had executed the mortgages under which the Appellants claim, and after these latter mortgages had been registered. Some of these advances, moreover, were made by the Bank after the filing of the petition for sale and its registration of a *lis pendens*, but before the Bank were served with the conditional order for sale.

It is admitted that the advances so made were made *bonâ fide* by the Bank, without any notice of the deeds of the 14th January, 1879, and 26th May, 1879, or of the claims or rights of the incumbrancers under these deeds, or of the filing of the petition for sale; but it was contended in the Court below, and also here, that, notwithstanding, by force of the registration of the latter deeds, all the advances made by the Bank subsequent to such registration must be postponed to the claims of the incumbrancers under these deeds, and that, in any case, the advances made by the Bank after the registration of the petition for sale as a *lis pendens* are so postponed.

The question raised is therefore one of very great importance, and is this, viz. if a person executes to another person or to a Bank a mortgage to secure future advances, and if, after so doing, he executes a subsequent mortgage, which is registered, or proceedings are taken against him for a sale by a subsequent incumbrancer, and same are registered as a *lis pendens*, whether advances made on foot of the earlier deed *bonâ fide*, and without any notice or knowledge of the subsequent dealings or of the proceedings, are postponed to the claim of the subsequent incumbrancer.

In the Court below Judge Flanagan held they were not postponed, and from his decision this appeal has been brought.

Now, in considering the question before us, it is well to bear in mind that the validity of deeds to secure future advances has never been questioned. The law allows such securities to be created, and, when created, gives effect to them. The mortgagor cannot redeem except on payment of the further advance, and the mortgagee can sell to realize the sums so advanced. Being good against the mortgagor, they are equally good against and binding upon a second mortgagee, or other person deriving through the mortgagor, unless some special ground exists for placing him in a more favourable position than the person through whom he claims. Prior to the case of *Hopkinson* v. *Rolt* (9 H.L. Cas. 514) – a case which, in my opinion, has an important bearing on the question before us, and to which, therefore, I refer – it would appear to have been considered that even where the first mortgagee makes an advance with full knowledge of the existence of the second mortgage, he would nevertheless be entitled to priority; but the House of Lords in that case held that it was otherwise, and that the first mortgagee having notice of the second mortgage when he makes his further advance, must be postponed to the second mortgagee. But the case proceeded on the ground of *notice*. It was on the ground of notice, and of notice alone, that the priority of the first mortgage was interfered with; and, as the ground on which Courts of Equity interfere, where notice is proved, with what otherwise would be the rights of the party, is, that it is necessary to do so in order to prevent fraud, it follows that the ground on which the first mortgagee was postponed was that it was considered that his making, voluntarily and without any legal obligation on his part to do so, a further advance when he knew of the second mortgage, and so knowingly and deliberately ousting, or endeavouring to oust, the right acquired by the second mortgagee, would be, if it were allowed to prevail, a fraudulent act, and as such could not be allowed to stand.

Now, if this be so, and if, independent of the effect of the Registry Acts, the security of the first mortgagee in respect of his further advance is good as against the second mortgagee, except in cases where his assertion of it would be a fraudulent act, let us see whether the Registry Acts make any difference.

It was argued on behalf of the Appellants that if, in England, notice be sufficient to prevent the first mortgagee from making further advances, registration in Ireland should be deemed to have the same effect, and to be effectual for the purpose of fixing the priorities of the parties. But is this so? No doubt registration is for many purposes, under the express provisions of the legislature, attended with the same effect as notice; but still it is not the same thing, and the present case is a very good example of the difference between them. Notice, where it exists, by bringing home to the mind of the first mortgagee the existence of the second mortgage, would render his conduct fraudulent in making an advance, and then endeavouring to oust the second mortgagee; but it would be absurd to argue that the fact of the second deed being registered, when the first mortgagee is wholly ignorant both of its existence and registration, as also probably of the very existence of the second mortgagee – could be held to affect his conscience so as to render his conduct fraudulent, by interfering with rights of which he was not aware.

I am very clearly of opinion, therefore, that mere registration cannot, for the purpose of postponing the first mortgagee be held to be equivalent in its effect to notice.

But a very ingenious argument was pressed upon us by Mr. Madden, who argued that, by the express provisions of the Registration Act, priority was given to his client's deed over the subsequent advances made by the Bank. He argued that his deed being registered, the Act, by its 4th section, gave him priority over every subsequent disposition, and that the subsequent advance was a disposition.

I cannot, however, accede to that argument. The disposition of the estate to the Bank was effected by the deed executed on the 13th February, 1878, and there was no other disposition of it to them; and the case of *Credland* v. *Potter* (L.R. 10 Ch. App. 8), which was relied upon by him, does not appear to me to be in point. There the deed relied upon did not purport to secure future advances. It was given merely to cover the present advance. Here the deed was given to secure future advances, and the Bank claims by virtue of the deed itself. There the first mortgagee did not claim in reality on foot of his deed, but by virtue of the equitable doctrine of tacking, which is a very different thing: and it was held that the second mortgagee, whose deed was registered, was entitled to priority, not over money advanced on the security and within the very terms of the first deed, but over a sum of money not advanced in pursuance of the first deed. If the first deed had been to cover future advances, the result would, I apprehend, have been different.

The Registration Acts must be taken as applying to deeds to secure future advances as well as to others. There is nothing in the Acts excluding such deeds from their operation, or preventing such deeds from sharing in and enjoying the advantages and priorities they confer. This being so, what is there which can be registered except the original deed itself? The making of the advance across the Bank counter, or by placing a sum of money to the credit of the mortgagor is not a transaction which can be registered. It was said the Bank might insist on the execution by the mortgagor of a memorandum, and then register it; but in such case the security would be created in reality, not by the original deed, but by the memorandum; whereas, in reality the security which is acquired in case of a deed to secure future advances, for such future advances, is derived from the deed itself, and when registered the Registry Act does not detract from its force or efficacy as against persons claiming through the mortgagor, and who cannot prove notice so as to affect the conscience of the first mortgagee.

In my opinion, therefore, the registration of a subsequent mortgage, the first mortgagee having no notice of it, does not affect or prejudice the validity of the first mortgage, and does not prevent it from operating as a security for such further advances as against the mortgagor and those deriving under him. To hold otherwise would very materially prejudice the value of such securities, and would be contrary to what is I believe the general understanding as to their effect. And it is to be remembered that if there be a loss in this case, the second mortgagees have themselves to thank for it. When taking their security it is to be supposed they took the common precaution which every mortgagee takes before his deed of mortgage is executed, viz. to search the registry. They would have found there, and most probably did find there, the memorial of the Bank mortgage, which, on the face of it, states it is given to secure future advances, and they could then have served notice on the Bank, and so prevented them from making further advances. They could have done this, but they did not, and they cannot now turn round and say that, having neglected so very obvious a precaution, the Bank shall suffer because they (the Bank) did not adopt the unusual, as I consider it, unnecessary precaution of having fresh searches made before each cheque drawn by Mr. O'Byrne was honoured by them.

As regards the other question raised, viz. as to the effect of the registration of the *lis pendens* on the security of the Bank, the conclusion to which I have come is that, as regards the advances made subsequent to such registration and before service of the conditional order, the Bank is entitled to priority as against the Appellants.

It cannot be argued that the filing of the petition and its registration as a *lis pendens*, of which the Bank was wholly and, in my opinion, excusably ignorant, can have the effect of notice, so as, within the principle of *Hopkinson* v. *Rolt* (9 H.L. Cas. 514), to bring home knowledge to the Bank, and fix them with the consequences of such knowledge.

The object of the registration of an action or proceeding as a *lis pendens* is to prevent the parties to the proceedings from creating new rights inconsistent with the rights and equities asserted in the proceeding. In this case the Bank had taken their security long previous to the institution of the petition for sale. They made the advances, whether it was by way of allowing the account of Mr. O'Byrne to be overdrawn or otherwise, in good faith; and I do not think the doctrine of *lis pendens* can be held to go the length of establishing that securities such as these, being recognised by the law as valid, the person holding such a security is bound to search in the office for the registration of *lis pendens* before each occasion on which he acts on it. Where the party holding the security is a Bank, as is the case here, and the security is given to cover the indebtedness resulting from the usual accommodation afforded by bankers to customers, which includes the overdrawing of a current account, it would follow that the Bank would require to have a continual search kept up. I do not, however, think this is so; and as the Bank are claiming on foot of a security executed long previous to the institution of the proceedings before the Land Judges, the validity and effect of that security are not interfered with by the subsequent *lis pendens*.

On these grounds I am of opinion the order appealed from is correct, and the appeal must be dismissed.

FitzGibbon L.J.:

I concur with the Lord Chancellor, and upon the main question have nothing to add to the reasons given by him for holding that a mere further advance upon an existing mortgage providing for it, is not a 'disposition' of the estate within the meaning of the Registry Act.

As to the *lis pendens* point, I at first felt some difficulty, for it did seem as if advances made after the commencement of the suit adversely affected the rights of the litigating party. Upon consideration I am satisfied that this is not so, for the rights of the parties are to be ascertained according to the law of registration, under which the right of the registered mortgagee to make further advances on this security, until actual notice of the subsequent loan, is protected. *Hopkinson* v. *Rolt* (9 H.L. Cas. 514), as it seems to me, rests entirely on the doctrine of equitable fraud, which arises only on *actual* notice, and the same principle appears to require actual notice, as distinguished from mere registration, of the *lis pendens*. As soon as such notice is given, as in this case it was by the service of the conditional order for sale, all parties have actual knowledge of the claims subsisting against the property, and, under *Hopkinson* v. *Rolt*, cannot afterwards displace any such claim by exercising a power of further advance; but until then the *lis pendens* is in the same position as an incumbrance of which the mortgagee for future advances has not notice. Thus, when we decide that the mere advance of money is not a 'disposition', we seem to me to decide both questions in the case, and to ascertain that the order appealed from is in all respects right.

Barry L.J.:

I also concur in the judgment, and for the reasons given in his judgment by the Lord Chancellor.

I think the two questions are identical: once we arrive at the conclusion that the further advances are covered by the registration of the deed of mortgage to the Bank, I think it follows, as a matter of course, for the same reasons, that the registration of the *lis pendens* does not affect the further advances, there not being actual notice of the *lis*.

Notes

1. See further on the doctrine of tacking, *Irish Land Law*, para. 13.159 *et seq*.
2. As regards registration of a *lis pendens*, see p. 483, *post*.

IV. JUDGMENT MORTGAGES

JUDGMENTS (IRELAND) ACT, 1844

10. . . . from and after the First Day of *November* One thousand eight hundred and forty-four no Lis Pendens shall bind or affect a Purchaser or Mortgagee, without express Notice thereof, unless and until a Memorandum or Minute containing the Name and the usual or last known Place of Abode, and the Title, Trade, or Profession of the Person whose Estate shall be intended to be affected thereby, and the Court of Equity, and the Title of the Cause or Information, and the Day when the Bill or Information was filed, shall be left with such Officer so to be appointed as aforesaid, who shall forthwith enter the same Particulars in a Book as aforesaid, in alphabetical Order, by the Name of the Person whose Estate is intended to be affected by such Lis Pendens, and which Book is to be intituled 'The Index to Lis Pendens'; . . .

JUDGMENT MORTGAGE (IRELAND) ACT, 1850

5. . . . no Lis pendens shall bind or affect a Purchaser or Mortgagee, without express Notice thereof, unless and until a like Memorandum or Minute as is required for a Registry thereof under the said Act of the Eighth Year of Her Majesty to be left with the Officer appointed under that Act, within Five Years before the Execution of the Conveyance, Settlement, Mortgage, Lease, or other Deed or Instrument vesting or transferring the legal or equitable Right to the Estate or Interest in or to such Purchaser or Mortgagee for valuable Consideration, save where such Lis pendens has been registered under the said Act of the Eighth Year of Her Majesty before the passing of this Act, and such Conveyance, Settlement, Mortgage, Lease, or other Deed or Instrument is executed within Five Years after the passing of this Act.

6. . . . where any Judgment shall be entered up after the passing of this Act in any of Her Majesty's Superior Courts at *Dublin*, or any Decree or Order in any Court of Equity, Rule in any Court of Common Law, or Order in Bankruptcy or Lunacy, to which the Effect of a Judgment in One of the Superior Courts of Common Law is given by the said Act of the Fourth Year of Her Majesty, shall be made after the passing of this Act, or any Judgment, Rule, or Order shall be obtained or made in or by any Inferior Court of Record after the passing of this Act, and shall, under the Provisions of the said Act of the Fourth Year of Her Majesty, be removed into One of Her Majesty's Superior Courts of Record at *Dublin*, and the Creditor under any such Judgment, Decree, Order, or Rule shall know or believe that the Person against whom such Judgment, Decree, Order, or Rule is entered up, obtained, or made is seised or possessed at Law or in Equity of any Lands, Tenements, or Hereditaments, of any Nature or Tenure, or has any disposing Power over any such Lands, Tenements, or Hereditaments which he may without the Assent of any other Person exercise for his own Benefit, and where any Judgment has been entered up before the passing of this Act in any of Her Majesty's Superior Courts at *Dublin*, or any Decree or Order in any Court of Equity, Rule in any Court of Common Law, or Order in Bankruptcy or Lunacy, to which the Effect of a Judgment in one of the Superior Courts of Common Law is given by the said Act of the Fourth Year of Her Majesty, has been made before the passing of this Act, or any Judgment, Rule, or Order has been obtained or made in or by any Inferior Court of Record before the passing of this Act, and has been or shall be, under the Provisions of the said Act of the Fourth Year of Her Majesty, removed into one of Her Majesty's Superior Courts at *Dublin*, and the Creditor under any such Judgment, Decree, Order, or Rule shall know or believe that the Person against whom such Judgment, Decree, Order, or Rule is entered up, obtained, or made is seised or possessed as aforesaid of, or has such disposing Power as aforesaid over, any Lands, Tenements, or Hereditaments which by virtue of this Act are exempted from being taken in execution under any Writ of Execution to be issued upon such Judgment, Decree, Order, or Rule, it shall be lawful for such Creditor, at any Time and from Time to Time after the entering up or Removal of such Judgment in or into such Superior Court, or the making of such Decree, Order, or Rule, or the passing of this Act, whichever shall last happen, to make and file in the Superior Court in, by, or into which such Judgment, Rule, or Order is entered up, made, or removed, or in the Court of Equity by which such Decree or Order is made, or in the Case of such Order in Bankruptcy or Lunacy as aforesaid, in the Court of Chancery in *Ireland*, an Affidavit stating the Name or Title of the Cause or Matter, and the Court in which such Judgment, Decree, Order, or Rule has been entered up, obtained, or made, and the Date of such Judgment, Decree, Order, or Rule, and the Names, and the usual or last known Place of Abode, and the Title, Trade, or Profession of the Plaintiff (if there be such), and of the Defendant or Person whose Estate is intended to be affected by the Registration, as herein-after mentioned, of such Affidavit, and the Amount of the Debt, Damages, Costs, or Monies recovered or ordered to be paid by such Judgment, Decree, Order, or Rule, and stating that, to the best of the Knowledge and Belief of the Deponent, the Person against whom such Judgment, Decree, Order, or Rule is entered up, obtained, or made is at the Time of the swearing of such Affidavit so seised or possessed, or has such disposing Power as aforesaid, of or over such Lands, Tenements, or Hereditaments, and such Affidavit shall specify the County and Barony, or the Town or Country of a City, and Parish, or the Town and Parish, in which the Lands to which the Affidavit relates are situate, and where such Lands lie in Two or more Counties or Baronies, or Parishes or Streets, or partly in One Barony, Parish, or Street and partly in another, the same shall be distinctly stated in such Affidavit; and it shall be lawful for the Creditor making such Affidavit to register the same in the Office for registering Deeds, Conveyances, and Wills in *Ireland*, by depositing in such Office an Office Copy of such Affidavit; and such Copy shall be numbered and transcribed, and shall be entered in the Books and Indexes kept in the said Office, in like Manner as if the same were a Memorial of a Deed; and for the Purpose of such Entries the Creditor under such Judgment, Decree, Order, or Rule shall be deemed the Grantee, and the Debtor thereunder shall be deemed the Grantor; and the Amount of the Debt, Damages, Costs, or Monies recovered or ordered to be paid thereby shall be deemed the Consideration; and the like Fee shall be paid on such Registration as in the Case of registering a Memorial of a Deed.

7. . . . the Registration as aforesaid of such Affidavit shall operate to transfer to and vest in the Creditor registering such Affidavit all the Lands, Tenements, and Hereditaments mentioned therein, for all the Estate and Interest of which the Debtor mentioned in such Affidavit shall at the Time of such Registration be seised or possessed at Law or in Equity, or might at such Time create by virtue of any disposing Power which he might then without the Assent of any other Person exercise for his own Benefit, but subject to Redemption on Payment of the Money owing on the Judgment, Decree, Order, or Rule mentioned in such Affidavit; and such Creditor, and all Persons claiming through or under him, shall, in respect of such Lands, Tenements, and Hereditaments, or such Estate or Interest therein as aforesaid, have all such Rights, Powers, and Remedies whatsoever as if an effectual Conveyance, Assignment, Appointment, or other Assurance to such Creditor of all such Estate or Interest, but subject to Redemption as aforesaid, had been made, executed, and registered at the Time of registering such Affidavit.

JUDGMENT MORTGAGE (IRELAND) ACT, 1858

5. . . . when and so soon as such Subscription of a Memorandum of Satisfaction of any Judgment shall be so made to the Entry of any Affidavit which shall have been registered in manner authorized by said Ninth Section of said recited Act, such Registration shall thereupon be deemed and taken as null and void and otherwise as if no such Registration had been effected; and the legal or other Estate in the Lands affected by such Registration shall without any further Deed, Conveyance, or Assurance be and thereby become vested in the Person or Persons in whom such legal or other Estate would have been then vested if no such Registration had been theretofore effected.

REGISTRATION OF TITLE ACT, 1964

71. – (1) The registration of the affidavit required by section 6 of the Judgment Mortgage (Ireland) Act, 1850, for the purpose of registering a judgment as a

mortgage shall, in the case of registered land, be made in the prescribed manner and with such entries as may be prescribed.

(2) In an affidavit registered after the commencement of this Act, the land shall be sufficiently described by reference to the number of the folio of the register and the county in which the land is situate.

(3) The affidavit shall be expressed to be made by the creditor specified in section 6 of the said Act of 1850 or by a person authorised to make it by section 3 of the Judgment Mortgage (Ireland) Act, 1858.

(4) Registration of an affidavit which complies with the said sections and this section shall operate to charge the interest of the judgment debtor subject to-

   (a) the burdens, if any, registered as affecting that interest,

   (b) the burdens to which, though not registered, that interest is subject by virtue of section 72, and

   (c) All unregistered rights subject to which the judgment debtor held that interest at the time of registration of the affidavit,

and the creditor shall have such rights and remedies for the enforcement of the charge as may be conferred on him by order of the court.

MURRAY V. DIAMOND
[1982] I.L.R.M. 113 (High Court)

The plaintiff obtained a judgment against the defendant and registered the judgment as a judgment mortgage against the defendant's family home. The issue to be determined was whether the judgment mortgage in favour of Denis Murray constituted a purported conveyance by David Diamond of his interest in his family home such as would be rendered void by s. 3(1) of the Family Home Protection Act, 1976 by reason of the absence of proper written consent thereto by his spouse. In relying upon s. 6 of the Judgment Mortgage Act, 1850 counsel for the wife submitted that the judgment creditor must know or believe that the judgment debtor is seised or possessed or has disposing power at law or in equity of any lands tenements or hereditaments, which he may without the assent of any other person exercise for his own benefit. It was also submitted that as, under the provisions of the Family Home Protection Act, 1976, the husband can no longer dispose of the family home without the consent of the wife, the husband's interest in the family home was not an interest against which such a judgment mortgage can be registered. Further reliance was placed on ss. 52 and 71(4) of the Registration of Title Act, 1964 (as affecting family homes which are registered lands) on the grounds that the judgment mortgagee or transferee takes his charge of his estate from one spouse but subject to the rights of the other spouse if that other spouse is not a party to the transaction.

BARRINGTON J delivered his judgment on 7 December 1981 saying: This judgment deals with a net point of law raised as an issue between the plaintiff Denis Murray and the defendant David Diamond and his wife Jean Diamond by Carroll J in her order herein made on 6 July 1981.

The issue is set out in the schedule to that order and is as follows:

   Whether the judgment mortgage in favour of Denis Murray constitutes a purported conveyance by David Diamond of his interest in his family home such as would be rendered void by s. 3(1) of the Family Home Protection Act, 1976, by reason of the absence of the prior written consent thereto by his spouse.

The point raised is clearly one of great practical importance raising, as it does, the question of the validity of judgment mortgages registered against the husband's interest in the matrimonial home without the consent of the wife.

The answer to the question raised turns, it appears to me, on the nature of a judgment mortgage itself. The Judgment Mortgage Act, 1850 provides a means whereby a judgment creditor, who complies with the appropriate formalities, can convert his judgment into a judgment mortgage. One of the things he must do is swear and register an affidavit giving particulars of his debt and particulars of the lands sought to be affected. It is this affidavit which, when registered, becomes the judgment mortgage (see *Madden on Deeds* (2nd Ed.) p. 117).

'What is a judgment mortgage?'.Lord Chancellor Brady asked in *Re Flood's Estate* 17 IrChR 116, 125 and answered-

'It is, in fact, the affidavit made for the purpose of registering a judgment as a mortgage'.

S. 6 of the Judgment Mortgage Act, 1850 sets out what such affidavit must contain, and goes on to provide that it will be lawful for the creditor making such affidavit to register same in the Registery of Deeds by depositing an office copy of such affidavit there. It then goes on to provide that:

> Such copy shall be numbered and transcribed and shall be entered in the books and indexes kept in the said office, in like manner as if the same were a memorial of a deed; and for the purpose of such entries the creditor under such judgment, decree, order or rule shall be deemed the the grantee, and the debtor thereunder shall be deemed the grantor; and the amount of the debt, damages, costs or monies recovered or ordered to be paid thereby shall be deemed the consideration . . .

It seems clear from this that it is the registration of the office copy of the affidavit which converts the judgment into a judgment mortgage. But while the section says that for the purpose of the entries made in the register the judgment creditor is to be deemed the grantee and the judgment debtor to be deemed the grantor it is clear that the judgment mortgage comes into existence by operation of the statute and not by virtue of any positive act of the judgment debtor.

S. 3(1) of the Family Home Protection Act, 1976 provides that, subject as therein, the purported conveyance is to be void where 'a spouse, without the prior consent in writing of the other spouse, purports to convey any interest in the family home to any person except the other spouse'.

In my opinion when a judgment mortgage is created the spouse against whom it is registered, does not convey any interest in the family home. *A fortiori* he does not 'purport' to convey any interest in the family home. The spouse against whom the judgment mortgage is registered is merely a patient. The judgment creditor is the agent and the mortgage comes into existence by operation of law.

Needless to say I am not here dealing with a case of fraud or with a case of connivance between one spouse and his or her judgment creditor to defeat the rights of the other spouse.

Apart from fraud or connivance I do not think that the mere fact that a man has, irresponsibility, allowed himself to get into debt, or allowed a judgment to be obtained against him and thereby allowed a situation to develop in which his creditor registers a judgment mortgage against his interest in the family home, would justify a court in saying that he has conveyed or purported to convey his interest in the family home to the judgment mortgagee. This appears to me to be the correct interpretation of the statute. The fact that the Family Home Protection Act, 1976 may afford less protection to the innocent or unsuspecting spouse than some people may have considered does not mean that the purposes of that Act are defeated. I do not think that the principle in *Nestor* v. *Murphy* [1979] IR 326, on which the plaintiffs in the issue relied, has any application in the circumstances of the present case.

The above conclusion appears to dispose of the issue in the present case but, as some other points were argued before me, it may be proper to refer to them.

Counsel for the wife relied upon the reference in s. 6 of the Judgment Mortgage Act to the fact that the judgment creditor must know or believe that the judgment debtor 'is seized or possessed at law or in equity of any lands, tenements, or hereditaments, of any nature or tenure, or has any disposing power over any such lands, tenements or hereditaments, which he may without the assent of any other person exercise for his own benefit'.

Counsel submitted that as, under the provisions of the Family Home Protection Act, 1976, the husband can no longer dispose of the family home without the consent of the wife, the husband's interest in the family home is not an interest against which a judgment mortgage can be registered. It seems clear however from a careful reading of the section that the words 'which he may without the assent of any other person exercise for his own benefit' govern the words 'has any disposing power over any such lands, tenements, or hereditaments' and do not govern the words 'seized or possessed at law or in equity of any lands, tenements or hereditaments of any nature or tenure'. In other words the effect of this section is to allow the judgment creditor to register a mortgage not only against the judgment debtor's interests in lands but also to enable the judgment creditor to register a mortgage against certain 'disposing powers' provided only that the judgment creditor can exercise that disposing power for his own benefit without the consent of any other person (on this see *Wylie Irish Land Law* p. 649).

Counsel for the wife, in the present case, also pointed to the provisions of s. 71(4) and s. 52 of the Registration of Title Act 1964 as affecting family homes which are registered lands. S. 71(4) provides that, in the case of registered lands, registration of the affidavit of the judgment mortgagee operates to charge the interest of the judgment debtor in the land, subject to registered burdens, if any, and burdens to which, though not registered, that interest is subject by virtue of s. 72 and 'all unregistered rights subject to which the judgment debtor held that interest at the time of registration of the affidavit'. S. 52(1) of the same Act provides as follows:

1. On the registration of a transferee of freehold land as full owner with an absolute title, the instrument of transfer shall operate as a conveyance by deed within the meaning of the Conveyancing Acts, and there shall be vested in the registered transferee an estate in fee simple in the land transferred, together with all implied or express rights, privileges and appurtenances belonging or appurtenant thereto, subject to-
a. the burdens, if any, registered as affecting the land, and
b. the burdens to which though not so registered, the land is subject by virtue of s. 72, but shall be free from all other rights, including rights of the state.

The submission is that, in the case of the family home, the judgment mortgagee or transferee takes his charge of his estate from one spouse but subject to the rights of the other spouse if that other spouse is not a party to the transaction. It appears to me that this would be so only if the rights of the other spouse were property rights of the kind contemplated by the provisions of the Registration of Title Act, 1964. But I do not think they are. I prefer to follow the reasoning of Gannon J. in *Guckian* v. *Brennan* (H.C.(Gannon J.) 3 March 1980, No. 126 Sp. 1980) where he held that the rights of the spouse who does not own the family home are valuable rights but not an estate or interest in lands. This reasoning was accepted by McWilliam J. in *Lloyd* v. *Sullivan* H.C., 6 March 1981 No. 39Sp. 1981. See also *National Provincial Bank Ltd.* v. *Ainsworth* [1965] A.C. 1175.

Under these circumstances I think that the answer to the question raised in the issue should be that the judgment mortgage in question does not constitute a purported conveyance by David Diamond such as is rendered void by Section 3(1) of the Family Home Protection Act 1976.

Notes
1. See also *Containercare (Ireland) Ltd.* v. *Wycherley* [1982] I.L.R.M. 143.
2. On the subject of judgment mortgages generally, see *Irish Land Law*, para. 13.163 *et seq.*
3. On the Family Home Protection Act, 1976, see *Irish Conveyancing Law*, para. 6.31 *et seq.*

DARDIS AND DUNNS SEEDS LTD. V. HICKEY
Unreported (High Court) (1972 No. 1165 Sp.) (Judgment delivered 11th July, 1974)
The facts are set out fully in the judgment.

Kenny J.:
On 23rd of March 1971 the plaintiffs in this action, Dardis and Dunns Seeds Limited, got judgment in the Circuit Court against James Hodgins for £421.27 and £15.97 costs. On the 29th of April 1971 the plaintiffs lodged a copy of the affidavit which had been lodged in the Circuit Court in the Registry of Deeds to convert the judgment into a judgment mortgage against lands owned by James Hodgins. Paragraph 6 of the affidavit read:

'That the usual or last known place of abode of the said defendant at the time that the said judgment was so obtained was and at present is Robinstown, Navan, County Meath and the title trade or profession of the said defendant is and at the time when the said judgment was obtained was a farmer.'

Paragraph 9 of the affidavit read:

'I further say that to the best of my knowledge and belief the said James Hodgins the said defendant is at the time of swearing this affidavit, seized or possessed at law or in equity, or has disposing power which he may without the assent of any other person, exercise for his own benefit over certain lands, tenements, hereditaments and premises hereinafter mentioned, that is to say a plot of ground at Robinstown in the Barony of Upper Navan and County of Meath.'

James Hodgins subsequently made an agreement with Michael Hickey, the defendant in this action, for the sale of these lands. The title shown commenced with a scheme of the 2nd August 1890 made under the Educational Endowments (Ireland) Act 1885 in relation to the parochial schools of the diocese of Meath and other endowments. In the First Schedule to the scheme the lands subsequently sold by Hodgins were described as being a school-house in the parish of Bective, in the townland of Balbradagh in the Barony of Upper Navan and in the County of Meath. The title then passed to a deed of the 6th of October 1966 made between the Meath Diocesan Board of Education ('the Board') and James B. Hodgins of Balbradagh, Navan, County Meath who is described as a mechanic. By this deed the Board conveyed to James Hodgins 'all that dwelling-house and premises usually known as Bective school-house situate in the townland of Balbradagh Barony of Upper Navan and County of Meath' in fee simple. By a deed made on the same day which was a mortgage to secure payment of £700 and which recited the conveyance to Hodgins, he conveyed 'all that the premises described in the said recited conveyance of even date and therein described as all that the dwelling-house and premises usually known as Bective school-house situate in the townland of Balbradagh Barony of Upper Navan and County of Meath' to the Board. In this deed Hodgins is described as a mechanic. By a deed made on the 4th of October 1971 between the Board and James Hodgins, who was again described as a mechanic, which recited the mortgage of the 6th of October 1966 and repayment of all monies secured by it, the Board granted and released to Hodgins 'all and singular the hereditaments and premises comprised in or assured by the said indenture of mortgage' discharged from all monies secured by it.

The solicitors acting for Michael Hickey had a hand-search made by Ellis and Ellis, the well-known searchers, against James Hodgins from the 6th of October 1966 to the 31st of August 1971 against lands 'in the townland of Balbradagh in the Barony of Upper Navan and in the County of Meath.' The search disclosed the existence of the mortgage to the Board, but not the judgment mortgage. The solicitors for Michael Hickey searched against the property as it was described in the deeds but as Balbradagh was not mentioned in the judgment mortgage affidavit and as Robinstown was not mentioned in the requisition for the search, it did not disclose the judgment mortgage.

The ordinance survey shows a townland of Balbradagh and a number of houses at a cross roads at a place called Robinstown where there is a Roman Catholic Church and two schools, one of which is the property purchased by Michael Hickey. A certificate of valuation issued by the Valuation Office shows James Hodgins as the occupier of lands which are described as being in the townland of Balbradagh, in the electoral division of Bective and in the County of Meath.

On 5th of October 1971 James Hodgins described as 'of Balbradagh, Navan in the County of Meath mechanic' conveyed to Michael Hickey, the defendant in this action 'all that and those the plot of ground being part of the townland of Balbradagh with the dwelling-house and premises situate thereon in the Barony of Upper Navan and County of Meath as more particularly delineated and described on the map thereof hereto annexed and thereon bounded by a red verge'. The map shows the school-house and the name Robinstown as the name of the place where the premises were situate.

The plaintiffs have now brought this action against Michael Hickey, in which they claim a declaration that the judgment mortgage of the 29th of April 1971 is well charged on his interest in the lands. Although the defendant was a purchaser for value without notice, the judgment mortgage binds his interest in the lands and may be enforced against it if the judgment mortgage affidavit complied with the requirements of the Judgment Mortgage (Ireland) Act 1850. I express no opinion on the question whether the solicitors acting for the defendant should have searched against lands in Robinstown: they probably knew that the property was in that place but as its name did not appear in any of the documents of title, they did not think it necessary to specify it in the requisition for the search.

Section 6 of the Act of 1850 prescribes the contents of the affidavit which converts a judgment into a judgment mortgage. It must state, amongst other things, 'the names, and the usual or last known place of abode, and the title, trade or profession of the plaintiff (if there be such), and of the defendant or person whose estate is intended to be affected by the registration, as hereinafter mentioned, of such affidavit.' It must also state 'that to the best of the knowledge and belief of the deponent, the person against whom such judgment, decree, order or rule is entered up, obtained, or made is at the time of the swearing of such affidavit so seized or possessed, or has such disposing power as aforesaid, of or over such lands tenements or hereditaments and such affidavit shall specify the county and barony or the town or county of a city and parish or the town and parish in which the lands to which the affidavit relates are situate'.

Miss Carroll for the defendant has argued that the affidavit did not create a valid judgment mortgage because it did not describe the lands to be charged with sufficient detail and because James Hodgins was not a farmer. An affidavit by Mr. Michael Regan, the solicitor who acted for James Hodgins, has been filed in which Mr. Regan says that he was informed by his client that his occupation was that of a mechanic and that to the best of his knowledge information and belief, his client was never a farmer.

The first question is whether Robinstown is a town for the purpose of the Act of 1850. Its name suggests that it is and if it be, the affidavit would be defective because it does not specify the parish. I do not think that the name is decisive of the question. There is no definition of the word 'town' in the Act of 1850 and so its meaning must be ascertained by reference to the law as it was and the English language as used in 1850. The original meaning of 'town' was a collection of houses which 'hath, or in time past hath had, a church and celebration of divine service, sacraments and burials' but, wrote Coke, 'if a towne be decayed so as no houses remain, yet it is a towne in law'. I agree with the statement of Chief Baron Pallas in *Archer* v. *The Earl of Caledon* [1894] 2 I.R. 476: 'Town according to my view, like every other word in the English language will bear a different signification according to the object with which it finds a place in any particular piece of legislation.' When the premises are situate in a town, the parish must be stated in the judgment mortgage affidavit, a requirement which was inserted for the purpose of identification only. The question as to the meaning of the word 'town' arose under the Railways Clauses Consolidation Act 1845 in *Elliott* v. *The South Devon Railway Company* (1818) 2 Exch. 725. In it Baron Alderson said: 'What the walls of a town were in ancient times, that is, a boundary, continuous buildings are now. By continuous buildings I do not mean buildings which touch each other, but buildings so reasonably near that the inhabitants may be considered as dwelling together. Within the ambit surrounded by such houses is town. . . .'

The meaning of the word was discussed in some of the many cases which were decided on s. 58 of the Land Law (Ireland) Act 1881. In *Killeen* v. *Lambert* (1882) 10 L.R. Ir. 362, a decision of the Court of Appeal, Lord Justice FitzGibbon referred to Dr. Johnson's definition of a town as 'a collection of houses larger than a village' but as that great authority on the English language defined a village as 'an assemblage of houses smaller than a town', the dictionary does not help. In *McCann* v. *The Marquis of Downshire* [1894] 2 I.R. 611 the same Judge pointed out that population taken alone is not the decisive test. He said that it would not in the least surprise him to find that whether in the popular sense or for the purposes of the Land Acts, one place with a comparatively small population was 'a town' while another with a larger population was a village because the population shown in the census depends on how the boundaries are drawn.

In the Towns Improvement (Ireland) Act 1854 'town' is defined as meaning and including 'a city, town corporate, borough, market town or other town in Ireland containing a population of 1,500 inhabitants or upwards' and Robinstown is not in the list of towns at p. 6 of Vanston's book on the law relating to municipal towns which sets out the towns which satisfy this definition.

The only reported case on the meaning of 'town' in the Act of 1850 is the decision of Mr. Justice Lynch in *re Ulster Banking Company* I.R. 3 Eq. 264 in which that Judge held that Omagh was not a town. This decision is severely criticised by Mr. Justice Madden in his book on the Registration of Deeds where he points out that Omagh was an assize town. I may add that it is in the list of towns in Vanston's book and so the decision is clearly wrong.

The Act of 1850 requires that in the case of lands situate in a town or county of a city, the parish must be stated. This is for the purpose of identification only (see the decision of the House of Lords in *Thorn* v. *Brown* L.R. 2 H.L. 220) and in the case of an assemblage of houses all of which are situate in one parish, there would be no purpose in requiring the statement of the parish if the assemblage were a town. It follows that town in the Act of 1850 means an assemblage of buildings which are in two or more parishes. The whole of Robinstown is in the parish of Bective and the Church of Ireland church for that parish is situate some miles from it. As the whole of Robinstown is in the one parish, I think that Robinstown was, despite its name, a village and not a town in 1850 and that this is still the position.

The Act of 1850 does not require the townland in which the premises to be affected are situate to be stated in the affidavit and so I think that the description of the lands in the judgment mortgage affidavit was sufficient.

There is now a definition of 'town' in the Interpretation Act 1937 but as this applies to Acts of the Oireachtas only, it cannot help in the construction of the Act of 1850.

The next issue is whether the misdescription of James Hodgins as a farmer invalidates the affidavit, for the evidence that he was never a farmer is coercive. The Act of 1850 required that the 'title trade or profession' of the plaintiff and of the defendant was to be stated: if there was a misdescription, the affidavit was not effective to create a mortgage even though no one was deceived. In *Crosbie* v. *Murphy* (1858) 8 Ir. C.L.R. 301 the plaintiff sued the defendant, who was a solicitor, for negligence in the preparation of a judgment mortgage affidavit in which a lady who was an hotel and shopkeeper was described as 'Bridget Curran of Killorghan (sic) in the County of Kerry widow'. Three Judges (Chief Justice Lefroy, Mr. Justice Crampton and Mr. Justice O'Brien) held that this was a misdescription which invalidated the affidavit. Mr. Justice Crampton said: 'It is most material that the designation of the party against whom the judgment mortgage is to be obtained should be stated with precision and accuracy.' In *Murphy* v. *Lacey* (1896) 31 I.L.T.R. 42, one of the plaintiffs was described in the judgment mortgage as a farmer. The evidence established that he had sold his farm in Ireland many years before and had afterwards farmed and done other work in the United States of America. He returned to Ireland with his wife and during the fourteen years prior to the filing the affidavit, his wife and he had resided with the defendant and had helped him without payment in the management of the farm. Porter, M.R. held that the plaintiff was an agricultural labourer and not a farmer, that the description at the date of the affidavit is the material matter and that although the description deceived or misled no one, the affidavit was defective and did not create a valid judgment mortgage.

If the description of farmer applied to one who had been a farmer and subsequently became a farm labourer was sufficient to invalidate an affidavit, the description of a person who was a mechanic and who had never been a farmer as a farmer must have the same effect.

The result is that the plaintiffs' judgment mortgage affidavit was not effective to create a mortgage and that this action must be dismissed.

This case shows that when purchasing lands in a village whose name is not the same as that of the townland in which it is situate, it is essential to search in the Registry of Deeds against the name of the village and of the townland.

Note

See further on the requirements for the affidavit, *Irish Land Law*, para. 13.168 *et seq.* See also *Credit Finance Ltd.* v. *Hennessy*. Unreported (High Court) (1979 No. 21 Sp.) (Judgment delivered 25th May 1979)

FLYNN V. BUCKLEY
Unreported (Supreme Court) (264/79) (Judgment delivered 24th April, 1980)
The facts are set out in the judgment.

O'Higgins C.J. (giving the judgment of the Court):-

The Court has already allowed the Plaintiff's appeal but by reason of the importance in practice of the question raised has reserved until to-day a statement of the reasons for its decision.

The appeal was brought against the Judgment and Order of Mr. Justice McWilliam discharging a lis pendens registered by the Plaintiff against the Defendants' interest in certain property. The Plaintiff had by Plenary Summons issued on the 22nd September 1978 commenced proceedings against the Defendants for the specific performance of a contract for the sale to him by them of their supermarket premises in Mullingar. On the same date he had registered the proceedings as a lis pendens against the Defendants' interest in the property. On the 15th October 1979 the Plaintiff pursuant to an Order of the Master of the High Court extending the time for doing so, delivered his Statement of Claim. By Notice of Motion served for the 5th November 1979 the Defendants applied to the High Court for an Order that the Plaintiff's Lis Pendens registered against the property the subject of the contract for sale be vacated, and, also for an Order that the Plaintiff's proceedings be dismissed or stayed. This Notice of Motion was grounded on affidavits deposing to a rescission of the contract for sale by agreement between the parties prior to action brought. No replying affidavit was filed on behalf of the Plaintiff, although an opportunity to do so was afforded to his advisers prior to the decision from which this appeal was brought. Apparently the reason that such was not done was because counsel on behalf of the Plaintiff took the view that the Defendants' application was not entertainable by the Court. They took the view that there was no jurisdiction to vacate a Lis Pendens without the consent of the registering party. They also took the view that in the circumstances of this case no procedure existed whereby the Plaintiff's proceedings could be dismissed in the absence of a plenary hearing.

In making the application to the Court the Defendants relied on the provisions of the statute 30 and 31 Vict. C.47, known as the Lis Pendens Act 1867. This Act by Section 2, reciting that a registered lis pendens cannot be vacated without the consent of the person by whom it was registered, and, that such consent is sometimes withheld although the suit or proceedings is at an end, or 'is not being bona fide prosecuted', authorises the Court before whom the property sought is in litigation, upon the determination of the lis pendens or during the pendency thereof, where the Court is satisfied that the litigation is not prosecuted bona fide, to make an Order if it sees fit, for the vacating of the lis pendens without the consent of the party who registered it. The Section goes on to provide that if such Order is made 'the Senior Master of the Common Pleas at Westminster shall, upon the filing with him of an office copy of such Order, enter a discharge of such lis pendens. . . .' The Act contains no provisions limiting its application to any particular part of the then United Kingdom. In *Giles* v. *Brady* [1974] I.R. 462 Mr. Justice Kenny, then a Judge of the High Court, had occasion to consider whether this Act applied to Ireland. He came to the conclusion that it did not. In arriving at this conclusion he was influenced by the fact that Section 1 (since repealed) referred to a Section of the Companies Act 1862 which did not apply to Ireland and by the reference in Section 2 to 'the Senior Master of the Common Pleas at Westminster', an office which did not exist in Ireland. His decision in this respect had, however, not been followed by Mr. Justice McWilliam in *Culhane* v. *Hewson* (decided 20th October 1978). [See now [1979] I.R. 8 – Ed.] In that case Mr. Justice

McWilliam came to an opposite conclusion. He was influenced in so doing because of an Order made by this Court on the 28th July 1975 in an unreported case, *Glencourt Investments Limited and The Companies Act*, and also by the fact that in the official index to the statutes for 1867 the Act appears with the letters G.B. and I. opposite to it. Mr. Justice McWilliam's view was later followed in the High Court by Mr. Justice Costello in *Dunville Investments Ltd.* v. *Kelly* (decided 27th April 1979).

I have had an opportunity of looking at the Registrar's note of the proceedings in the Supreme Court in *Glencourt Investments Limited and The Companies Act*. I did not sit on the Court which was presided over by Mr. Justice Walsh. From the Registrar's note it does not appear that the Act of 1867 was either cited or considered. The Court did make an Order vacating the Lis Pendens but it appears to have done so solely because it concluded that the Lis Pendens has been wrongly registered in the first instance. It seems to me, therefore, that this case is of not assistance in determining the issue.

When the Defendants' Motion came on for hearing before him, Mr. Justice McWilliam, having granted the adjournment already referred to, adhered to his previously expressed view that the Act of 1867 did apply to Ireland. Further, in view of the fact that the affidavits filed by the Defendants had not been controverted by the Plaintiff, he concluded that the Plaintiff's proceedings were not being bona fide prosecuted because prior to action brought the Plaintiff had agreed to a rescission of the Contract. Accordingly he made an Order vacating the Lis Pendens. He held, however, that he had no power at that stage to dismiss the Plaintiff's claim.

On the hearing of this appeal counsel on behalf of the Plaintiff have argued that the view expressed by Mr. Justice Kenny in *Giles* v. *Brady* is correct and that the Lis Pendens Act 1867 did not apply to Ireland. On this account they submit that there was and is no power to vacate a Lis Pendens in the absence of consent from the registering party. Alternatively, they submit that Mr. Justice McWilliam was wrong in concluding that the proceedings were not being bona fide prosecuted. In this respect they relied on two specific matters disclosed in the Affidavits filed. One of these was the fact that in the Affidavit of Liam Whyte it was stated that on the occasion of the alleged rescission by consent the Plaintiff's partner concluded the transaction by saying that he would 'see Mr. Buckley in Court'. This was a reference to one of the Defendants and was relied on as being inconsistent with an agreed rescission of the Contract. The other matter relied on was a letter written by the Plaintiff on the day of and subsequent to the alleged rescission. This letter was exhibited in the Affidavit of Mr. Liam Whyte and is addressed to him in the following terms:

'Dear Liam,

    I am sorry that your client remains adamant in his refusal to complete on this contract on the basis offered and you have followed instructions to return the deposit.

    The return of the deposit as Mr. Clancy and I advised you on behalf of your client does not mean we are in any way waiving our position under the contract and all legal steps to enforce the proper completion will now be implemented i.e. specific performance and a list pendence to restrain attempted sale elsewhere and use of the building as we do not want the structure to deteriorate further.

    I am sure you would not attempt to delude another purchaser that clear title could be obtained on this building until we have exhausted all legal process and I hope your client and his solicitor follow suit.

I would like you to ascertain whether your clients solicitor will accept proceedings on Mr. Buckley's behalf or whether we must serve direct'.

And it was signed by the Plaintiff.

As to the first matter it seems to me necessary in view of the conflict of judicial decision, for this Court to decide, authoritatively, whether or not the Act of 1867 did apply to Ireland. The general rule with regard to the operation of a British statute was that the operation of such statute extended to the whole of the then United Kingdom and that if the intention was to limit the operation to a part only, an express limitation was necessary. In addition, in the absence of an express limitation, an intention to limit the application could be gathered by necessary implication from the construction of the statute (see *R.* v. *The Guardians of the Poor of the Mallow Union* 12 Ir. C.L.R. 35). Here is a British statute which is not limited in its application by express terms. It appears in the official index for the year in question as applying to both G.B. and I. Nor can it be said because of the form and terms used that, by necessary implication, an intention not to apply to Ireland can be gathered. The fact that it refers to a Section of the Companies Act 1862 which did not apply in Ireland does not of itself, in my view, indicate that it was intended not to apply to Ireland. Equally, the absence of a proper office or of proper machinery for registering a vacate of a lis pendens cannot be said, by necessary implication, to indicate an intention not to apply to this country. Such indicates, undoubtedly, a defect in the statute and a defect which required remedying. But it does not suggest or indicate any more than this. It is to be noted that four years later Section 21 of the Judgment (Ireland) Act 1871, reciting the absence of sufficient provision for registering vacates of lis pendens, made good the deficiency. I have come to the conclusion that the general rule operates and that this Act was intended to apply to Ireland and did operate satisfactorily on the provision of appropriate machinery for registering vacates under the 1871 Act. In my view, therefore, Mr. Justice McWilliam was correct in holding that he had power to make the Order sought in the absence of the Plaintiff's consent.

I have come to the conclusion, however, that Mr. Justice McWilliam was not correct in the view he formed that the proceedings were not being prosecuted bona fide. Counsel on behalf of the Defendants relied on delay in addition to the alleged rescission. I do not think there was such delay on the part of the Plaintiff as to indicate a lack of bona fides. Nor do I think that the facts deposed to in the Affidavits indicated a clear and unambiguous rescission of the Contract by consent. On the contrary the two matters relied on by the Plaintiffs indicate the possibility of a contrary view. It appears to me on the facts deposed to in the Affidavit that it was not possible to conclude that no issue of fact, between the parties, remained. As Mr. Justice McWilliam in fact came to this conclusion I think he was incorrect. In the result I have come to the conclusion that Mr. Justice McWilliam was not entitled on the evidence before him to conclude that the Plaintiff's claim was not being prosecuted bona fide.

For these reasons I was of the view that the Plaintiff's appeal should be allowed and that the Order vacating the lis pendens should be discharged.

TEMPANY V. HYNES
[1976] I.R. 101 (Supreme Court)

A company owned certain lands and its ownership of the lands was registered under the Registration of Title Act 1964 on two folios. The plaintiff was appointed a receiver of the assets of the company by a debenture holder to whom the company had issued the debenture. In the events which happened, the debenture conferred upon the debenture holder, and upon the receiver appointed by him, a power to sell the assets of the company. The debenture was registered as a burden on one folio but it was not so registered on the other folio. In exercise of his power of sale, the plaintiff contracted to sell to the defendant the lands of the company and the defendant paid to the plaintiff a sum of money as a deposit and as part of the purchase price.

Two judgment mortgages were registered as burdens on the lands comprised in the two folios after the date of the contract and before the sale was completed. The defendant did not accept the plaintiff's contention that he was not obliged to discharge the two post-contract judgment mortgages. At the hearing of the plaintiff's action in the High Court in which he claimed specific performance by the defendant of the contract of sale, the trial judge considered that it was doubtful whether the plaintiff and the company could convey the property free from incumbrances without discharging the judgment mortgages, and so he exercised his discretion by refusing to make the order sought by the plaintiff. The plaintiff appealed to the Supreme Court.

O'Higgins C.J.:

I have read the judgment of Mr. Justice Kenny and I agree with it.

Henchy J.:

The issue in this appeal is whether the defendant, as purchaser of the land, was entitled to repudiate the contract in the circumstances in which he purported to do so. If he was so entitled – and the trial judge so held – he has a good answer to the instant claim by the plaintiff, as vendor, for specific performance of the contract; in that event the dismiss of that claim in the High Court should stand, otherwise this appeal by the plaintiff should succeed.

The relevant circumstances are briefly these. The defendant entered into a written contract to purchase from the plaintiff a garage in Longford for £30,500. The property is registered property which is governed by the Registration of Title Act, 1964. The registered owner was Tractasales (Longford) Ltd, and the plaintiff contracted to sell as receiver of that company. In the present proceedings it has not been questioned that the plaintiff, as receiver, was entitled to stand in the shoes of the registered owner for the purpose of making title.

The defendant's solicitor proceeded to investigate the title. Because of difficulties in the title (such as the discovery that the property was registered on three folios and not on two), the date for completion specified in the contract passed without the parties being ready to complete. Eventually, all the legal difficulties that had arisen were smoothed out, except for one; it transpired that subsequent to the date of the contract two judgment mortgages had been entered on the folios as burdens affecting the interest of the registered owner. The plaintiff was advised that, in order to give a good title, it was not necessary for him to discharge those two post-contract judgment mortgages by paying the amounts due under them; but the defendant's solicitor was reluctant to complete the sale on that basis.

After lengthy negotiations, a compromise was reached by the solicitors. It was agreed by them that the sale would be closed subject to the retention on joint deposit of £4,500 out of the purchase money for a period of six weeks and that an application would be made during that period to the registrar of the Land Registry to register the defendant freed from the post-contract judgment mortgages. It was agreed that if that application were not successful within the six weeks, the £4,500 (which would have been adequate to discharge the amounts due to the judgment mortgagees) would be released to the defendant so that he could discharge those burdens by paying off the judgment mortgagees. In agreeing to that compromise the plaintiff was being eminently reasonable. In effect, he was saying to the defendant:- 'In order to give you a good title I am not bound to discharge the amounts due on foot of the post-contract judgment mortgages but, to allay any fears you may have on that score, I shall put to one side out of the purchase money £4,500 for six weeks so that my opinion may be put to the test in the Land Registry; if I am not proved right in that time, I shall surrender the £4,500 to you so that you may discharge the amounts due on the judgment mortgages.' It is no wonder that the defendant's solicitor agreed to completion on that basis.

However, when the defendant and his solicitor arrived for the appointment with the plaintiff's solicitor to close the sale, the defendant flatly repudiated the basis on which his solicitor had agreed to close. The defendant was prepared to close only if the £4,500 was delivered into his custody forthwith. The plaintiff, who was selling as receiver for a debenture holder, could not agree to that proposal. Although his solicitor strongly advised him to complete the sale on the agreed basis, the defendant adamantly refused to do so. With that impasse the sale broke down. Hence the present proceedings for specific performance.

One thing is clear about the defendant's conduct between contracting to buy the property in February, 1974, and repudiating the contract in March, 1975: he came to regret the contract he had signed and decided to get out of it one way or another. He lived in Dublin, and he had bought this propery with a view to developing it as a roadhouse and garage. But, as he frankly admitted in evidence, for family and other reasons he found the move to Longford undesirable; so from about September, 1974, he was resolved to repudiate the contract. The ground on which he eventually repudiated it in March, 1975, was only the particular pretext he fastened on for that purpose. However, his motives are irrelevant if the ground of repudiation was sound in law.

When a binding contract for the sale of land has been made, whether the purchase money has been paid or not, the law (at least in cases where the parties proceed to the stage of conveyance) treats the beneficial ownership as having passed to the purchaser from the time the contract was made: *Gordon Hill Trust Ltd.* v. *Segall* ([1941] 2 All E.R. 379). From then until the time of completion, regardless of whether the purchase money has been paid or not, the vendor, in whom the legal estate is still vested, is treated for certain purposes (such as the preservation of the property from damage by trespassers) as a trustee for the purchaser. But, coupled with this trusteeship, there is vested in the vendor a substantial interest in the property pending completion. Save where the contract provides otherwise, he is entitled to remain in possession until the purchase money is paid and, as such possessor, he has a common-law lien on the property for the purchase money; even if he parts with possession of the property, he has an equitable lien on it for the unpaid purchase money; and he is entitled to take and keep for his own use the rents and profits up to the date fixed for completion. It is clear, therefore, that between contract and completion the vendor has a beneficial interest in the property which is capable of being charged by a judgment mortgage: see Megarry and Wade on Real Property (4th ed., p. 575), Williams on Vendor and Purchaser (4th ed., pp. 545–7), Lewin on Trusts (16th ed., pp. 153–4) and Halsbury's Laws of England (3rd ed., paras. 484–6).

Therefore, when a judgment mortgage is registered as a burden affecting the interest of a registered owner after an enforceable contract has been made to sell the land, what becomes affected is the transient beneficial interest of the registered owner. Section 71, sub-s. 4, of the Registration of Title Act, 1964, stipulates that on registration of the judgment-mortgage affidavit, the charge thereby created on the interest of the judgment debtor shall be subject to the registered burdens, the burdens taking effect under s. 72 without registration, and 'all unregistered rights subject to which the judgment debtor held that interest at the time of registration of the affidavit'. The latter category applies here, for a 'right' is defined in s. 3, sub-s. 1, of the Act of 1964 as including 'estate, interest, equity and power' – thus covering the estate or interest of the purchaser. Since the judgment creditor (by registering his judgment as a judgment mortgage) could not acquire any greater estate or interest in the land than the registered owner had at the time of such registration, all that could pass to the judgment creditor there was the interest in the land which the registered owner had after the making of the contract to sell, namely, an interest which would pass out of existence once the sale had been completed, the purchase money paid and the purchaser registered as full owner. It follows, therefore, that if the defendant completes the purchase and becomes registered as full owner, the post-contract judgment mortgages will no longer affect the lands and he will be entitled to have them cancelled from the folios.

This conclusion is in line with that of Kennedy C.J. in *In re Murphy and McCormack* ([1930] I.R. 322) and that of the majority of the Supreme Court in *In re Strong* ([1940] I.R. 382). Those decisions were given under the Local Registration of Title (Ireland) Act, 1891, which is now repealed by the Act of 1964. In each of those cases the judgment mortgage had been registered after the execution of the deed of transfer and after payment of the full purchase money whereas, in this case, the judgment mortgage was registered before the deed of transfer had been executed or the full purchase money paid. My concurrence in the conclusion reached in those judgments – that the registered judgment mortgage could not affect the estate or interest of the registered transferee – is in no way affected by the latter difference, for the reasoning in those judgments leading to that conclusion applies with no less force to a case such as the present where the judgment mortgage was registered after the contract of sale but before the execution of the deed of transfer or the payment of the balance of the purchase money.

If a registered judgment mortgage could be classified as 'a charge created on the land for valuable consideration' within the terms of s. 68, sub-s. 3, of the Act of 1964, it would be unaffected by the unregistered right of the purchaser for value; but a judgment mortgage is a process of execution and is not a charge created for valuable consideration: *per* Kennedy C.J. in *In re Murphy and McCormack* ([1930] I.R. 322) and *per* O'Byrne J. in *In re Strong* ([1940] I.R. 382).

The conclusion reached in those judgments – that the unregistered right of a purchaser for value from the registered owner is not subject to a judgment mortgage registered against the registered owner subsequent to the contract to sell – would now appear to have been given statutory recognition because s. 71, sub-s. 4(*c*), of the Act of 1964 provides that the registration of the judgment mortgage affidavit shall charge the interest of the judgment debtor subject to 'all unregistered rights subject to which the judgment debtor held that interest at the time of registration of the affidavit'. In other words, in a case such as this, the unregistered 'right' of the defendant as purchaser is superior to the interest of the registered owner which became charged by the post-contract judgment mortgages.

It follows, in my opinion, that (apart from the effect on pre-contract mortgages of the appointment of the plaintiff as receiver on foot of mortgage debentures, an effect which was not dealt with in the High Court and was only touched on in this appeal) the plaintiff was not bound, in order to make good title, to discharge the moneys due on foot of the post-contract judgment mortgages. Those mortgages took effect subject to the defendant's equitable estate or interest in the land; they could affect only such beneficial estate or interest as the registered owner then had and that estate or interest could not survive the completion of the sale and the registration of the defendant as full owner. The defendant could then have the post-contract judgment mortgages cancelled from the folios.

As the defendant's purported repudiation of the contract was ineffective to rescind it, I would allow the appeal and decree specific performance.

Kenny J.:

Tractasales (Longford) Ltd. (the company) carried on a garage business and were the registered owners under the Registration of Title Act of the lands in folios 9792, 12146 and 12386 in the county of Longford. A first mortgage debenture was made on the 11th September, 1969, between the company and United Dominions Trust (Ireland) Ltd. (the debenture holders), and it recited that the company had requested the debenture holders to lend them £25,000 and that the debenture holders had agreed to make this advance with interest provided that the repayment was secured by a debenture.

By that instrument the company charged its property in the following terms:- 'the company hereby charges its undertakings and all its property assets and goodwill whatsoever and wheresoever both real and personal present and future including therein the uncalled capital of the company for the time being with the repayment to the debenture holder of all the principal and interest and other monies payable under this debenture so that the charge hereby created shall be a first charge on the property charged herein and so that it shall be a floating security only not hindering any sale or other dealings by the company in the ordinary course of its business with its property and assets comprised in the charge but that the company shall not be at liberty to create any mortgage or charge on any of its property or assets ranking in priority to or pari passu with this debenture without the previous consent in writing of the debenture holder provided always that the said charge above referred to so far as it relates to the property comprised in the schedule hereto shall be a specific charge thereon and not a floating charge as on the borrower's other property'. The property described in the schedule was folio 9792. The completion of the debenture had been carried out rapidly because the company were in severe financial difficulties and the solicitor who prepared it had not been told that the company were registered as owners of the lands in folios 12146 and 12386.

The sum advanced under the debenture of the 11th September, 1969, was not sufficient to solve the company's difficulties and they sought further help from the debenture holders who agreed to give it. By a second debenture made on the 1st June, 1971, and registered on folio 9792 only, the company charged its assets and undertaking with all further sums advanced so that the charge was to be a floating charge on all its assets but a specific charge on the property in folio 9792.

On the 26th July, 1971, the debenture holders appointed the plaintiff to be receiver of all the property charged by the two debentures. The plaintiff decided to sell all the property in one lot but he and his solicitors thought that the company were registered as owners of the lands in folios 9792 and 12146 and were not aware that part of the property was in folio 12386. Between the date of the appointment of the plaintiff as receiver and the public auction, two judgment mortgages were registered against the lands included in folios 9792 and one of them had also been registered in folios 12146 and 12386. The conditions of sale described the property as being that comprised in folios 9792 and 12146.

The special conditions provided that the plaintiff was selling the property as receiver in exercise of his power of sale conferred by the mortgage debentures of the 11th September, 1969, and the 1st June, 1971; the conditions also provided:- 'The vendor shall discharge all charges registered against the said folio on or before closing and shall pay all Land Registry fees for the cancellation of such charges.'

The closing date was 28th May, 1974, and, in the event of the sale not being closed on that date, interest at the rate of 18% was to be paid by the purchaser on the balance of the purchase money until completion. The defendant attended the auction on the 26th February, 1974, and purchased the property for £30,500; he paid £7,625 which was paid 'as a deposit and in part payment of the purchase money' and he signed the contract attached to the conditions of sale.

On the 23rd November, 1971, Peter F. Doggett registered a judgment mortgage against the lands in folio 9792 and on the 26th March, 1973, Henry Smith registered a judgment mortgage against the lands comprised in the three folios. These two judgment mortgages were registered after the appointment of the receiver but before the contract for sale had been signed. On the 22nd May, 1974, Longford Arms Motor Works Ltd. registered a judgment mortgage on the three folios and on the 1st July, 1974, Foster Finance Ltd. registered a judgment mortgage on folios 12146 and 12386. The last two mortgges were registered after the contract had been signed.

The defendant had purchased the property because he thought that he could get finance to develop it. He was unable to do this and became determined that he would get out of the sale if he could. He raised questions about planning permission and, when these had been dealt with, he made searches in the Land Registry and on the 23rd January, 1975, he found out that part of the lands surrounding the garage was registered on folio 12386. The plaintiff had forgotten that the land certificate in relation to this had been handed over to him when he was appointed receiver and he had left it in his office in Longford. It was not deposited with him as security.

The defendant's solicitor then required the discharge of the judgment mortgages which had been registered after the date of the contract, and negotiations in connection with this took place. The plaintiff's solicitors had obtained releases of the two judgment mortgages registered before the contract and it was ultimately agreed between the solicitors that the sale should be closed on the 18th March 1975, on an undertaking by the plaintiff's solicitors that they would put £4,500 on deposit in the joint names of the solicitors which was to be held for six weeks. If, within that time, the plaintiff's solicitors had not succeeded in having the two post-contract judgment mortgages removed from the folios, the sum was to be paid to the defendant's solicitors. At this time the plaintiff's solicitors believed that the two judgment mortgages registered before the contract had to be discharged out of the purchase money but that those registered after the contract would be removed by the registrar on registration of the transfer to the defendant. When the parties met at the Four Courts on the 18th March, the defendant refused to close the sale on these terms and insisted that the £4,500 should be paid to him immediately; this was a demand which the plaintiff's solicitors could not accept.

The plaintiff decided to go on with his action for specific performance of the contract – an action which he had begun on the 3rd December, 1974. The action was heard by the President of the High Court and he dismissed it because he thought that the title shown by the plaintiff might involve the defendant in litigation with the post-contract judgment mortgagees. The grounds for his decision were that folio 12386 was not included in the written contract for sale, that the debenture holders were not mortgagees of it by equitable deposit and had not registered either of their debentures against it and that the judgment mortgagees might succeed in a claim that their judgment mortgages were effective against it in priority to the claim of the debenture holders.

The first argument for the plaintiff was that when the contract for sale was signed on the 26th February, 1974, the company became a trustee for the defendant who became the owner of the entire beneficial interest in the lands and that the company did not own any estate or interest on which the two judgment mortgages of the 22nd May and the 1st July, 1974, could operate; it was submitted that those judgment mortgages would be removed from the folio on the registration of the transfer to the defendant.

A vendor who signs a contract with a purchaser for the sale of land becomes a trustee in the sense that he is bound to take reasonable care of the property until the sale is completed, but he becomes a trustee of the beneficial interest to the extent only to which the purchase price is paid. He is not a trustee of the beneficial interest merely because he signs a contract. This is made clear by Lord Cranworth in *Rose* v. *Watson* ((1864) 10 H.L. Case. 672) where he said at pp. 683–4 of the report:- 'There can be no doubt, I apprehend, that when a purchaser has paid his purchase-money, though he has got no conveyance, the vendor becomes a trustee for him of the legal estate, and he is, in equity, considered as the owner of the estate. When, instead of paying the whole of his purchase-money, he pays a part of it, it would seem to follow, as a necessary corollary, that, to the extent to which he has paid his purchase-money, to that extent the vendor is a trustee for him; in other words, that he acquires a lien, exactly in the same way as if upon the payment of part of the purchase-money the vendor had executed a mortgage to him of the estate to that extent.' Until the whole of the purchase money is paid, the vendor has in my opinion a beneficial interest in the land which may be charged by a judgment mortgage.

Some judges and writers of the standard text-books (Cheshire, and Megarry and Wade) who have dealt with this matter have stated that from the date of the signature of the contract (whether the whole or any part of the purchase money has been paid or not) the purchaser is the owner of the entire beneficial interest in the land. Thus in *Shaw* v. *Foster* ((1872) L.R. 5 H.L. 321) Lord Cairns said at p. 338 of the report:- '...there cannot be the slightest doubt of the relation subsisting in the eye of the Court of Equity between the vendor and the purchaser. The vendor was a trustee of the property for the purchaser; the purchaser was the real beneficial owner in the eye of a Court of Equity of the property, subject only to this observation, that the vendor, whom I have called the trustee, was not a mere dormant trustee, he was a trustee having a personal and substantial interest in the property, a right to protect that interest, and an active right to assert that interest if anything should be done in derogation of it.' In *Lysaght* v. *Edwards* ((1876) 2 Ch. D. 499) Jessel M.R. said at p. 506 of the report:- 'the moment you have a valid contract for sale... and the beneficial ownership passes to the purchaser...' Both these statements are inconsistent with the clear principle stated by Lord Cranworth and are, I believe, incorrect. When a contract for sale has been signed, the vendor becomes a trustee of the *beneficial interest* to the extent that the purchase money has been paid.

This issue arose in *Kissock and Currie's Contract* ([1916] 1 I.R. 376) which was a decision of the Court of Appeal in Ireland, in which a judgment mortgage had been registered against a vendor between the date of the contract for sale by him and its completion. The sale was closed without any payment being made to the judgment mortgagee. A subsequent purchaser objected to the title because he maintained that the judgment mortgage was valid and this claim was upheld. Sir Ignatius O'Brien L.C. said at p. 388 of the report:- 'I think that, from the point of view of the judgment-creditor... his debtor had an interest in land after the date of contract for sale and until completion, capable of being affected by the judgment.' If this case was correctly decided, as I think it was, the principle underlying it disposes of the puzzling concept in some of the other cases that such a judgment mortgage is valid when registered but ceases to be effective when the sale is completed because then the vendor's interest is deemed to have passed to the purchaser from the date of the contract. I prefer the principle stated by Lord Cranworth.

Counsel for the plaintiff relied on a passage in the judgment of O'Byrne J. in *In re Strong* ([1940] I.R. 382) at pp. 401–402 of the report. It reads:- 'Under the general rules of law and equity, apart from the provisions of the Local Registration of Title (Ir.) Act, 1891, the position, as between a purchaser of lands, who has paid his purchase money but has not obtained a conveyance, and a judgment debtor [*sic*] who has registered his judgment as a mortgage affecting such lands, seems to be quite clear. Where a contract is entered into for the sale and purchase of lands the vendor becomes a trustee for the purchaser and the latter becomes owner in equity of the lands subject to certain rights of the vendor to secure payment of the balance of the purchase money and to regain possession of the lands should the contract not be completed.' The first sentence is dealing with the position of a purchaser who has paid the whole of the purchase money and has not got a conveyance when a judgment mortgage is registered against the vendor; the purchaser then takes the lands free of the judgment mortgage. The second sentence deals with the position after a contract for sale has been signed and no part, or part only, of the purchase price has been paid. The second sentence is, in my view, important. The structure of the two sentences suggests that the second is explanatory of the first: it is not. It is re-stating the view of Lord Cairns and of Jessel M.R. which I do not accept and which is not consistent with what Lord Cranworth said.

At the date when the two post-contract judgment mortgages were registered on the folios, the deposit only had been paid and they therefore affected whatever beneficial interest the company had in the lands. Therefore, I reject the argument that, because a contract for sale had been signed, the vendor company had no beneficial interest in the lands which could be affected by the post-contract mortgages.

The next argument was based on the provisions of s. 71, sub-s. 4, of the Registration of Title Act, 1964; logically it should have been the first because, if correct, it disposes of the four judgment mortgages. This sub-section appears in a section dealing with the registration and effect of judgment mortgages on registered lands: nothing corresponding to sub-s. 4 of s. 71 is to be found in the Act of 1891. The plaintiff's argument was that, when the receiver was appointed, there was an equitable assignment to the debenture holders of all the property which was subject to the floating charge, and that the result of this was that the claim of the debenture holders in relation to the lands in the three folios ranked before that of the judgment mortgagees.

The two mortgage debentures created a specific charge on the lands in folio 9792 and a floating charge over all the other assets, present and future, of the company; and the effect of the appointment of a receiver under a debenture is that there is an equitable assignment to the debenture holder of all the property which is subject to the floating charge: *Robbie and Co. Ltd.* v. *Witney Warehouse Ltd.* ([1963] 1 W.L.R. 1324); *Rother Iron Works Ltd.* v. *Canterbury Precision Engineers Ltd.* ([1974] Q.B. 1) and *Murphy* v. *The Revenue Commissioners* ([1976] I.R. 15). The word 'right' is defined by s. 3 of the Act of 1964 as including 'estate, interest, equity and power'. The equitable assignment effected by the appointment of the receiver was, in my opinion, an unregistered right subject to which the company held the lands on which the debentures were not registered at the time of the registration of the affidavits creating the four judgment mortgages. A judgment mortgage is a process of execution and the judgment mortgagee is not a purchaser for valuable consideration: *Eyre* v. *McDowell* ((1861) 9 H.L. Cas. 619). Counsel for the defendant said that the Court should not decide this issue in the absence of the judgment mortgagees; but when the defence is made that the title is too doubtful to be forced on a purchaser it is the duty of the Court to decide this question: *Alexander* v. *Mills*((1870) 6 Ch. App. 124); *In re Nichols and Von Joel's Contract* ([1910] 1 Ch. 43).

In my opinion the claim of the debenture holders in relation to the lands in the three folios ranks before the rights of the four judgment mortgages and the vendor has shown a good title to all of the lands in the three folios. When the transfer from the plaintiff and the company to the defendant, the mortgage debentures and the appointment of the receiver are produced to him, it will be the duty of the registrar of titles to cancel the entries of the four judgment mortgages which appear on the folios without proof of the payment of any sum in respect of any of them.

Counsel for the defendant argued that specific performance was a discretionary remedy and that the Court should not interfere with the decision of Mr. Justice Finlay. The President refused specific performance only because he thought the title was too doubtful to be forced on a purchaser and, as his view on this matter was incorrect, the exercise of his discretion should in my opinion be set aside (See [1968] I.R. 11). It is right to say, however, that the effect of the appointment of the receiver does not seem to have been argued before him because he does not refer to it in his judgment.

The contract provides for the payment of interest at the rate of 18% from the date fixed for completion which was the 28th May, 1974. In March, 1975, the solicitors had agreed that one month's interest only would be payable but the defendant repudiated the agreement which they had made and the plaintiff is not now bound by it. It would, however, be inequitable that interest should be payable from the date fixed for completion because the existence of the third folio had not been discovered on that date. In my opinion the order that the contract ought to be specifically performed should provide that interest at 18% should be payable from the 23rd January, 1975, when the parties became aware that part of the property of the company was registered on a third folio.

In my opinion, the appeal should be allowed and there should be an order that the contract ought to be specifically performed with the variation which I have suggested. There will be liberty to apply to the High Court.

Note

See the discussion of this case in *Irish Conveyancing Law*, para. 11.04 *et seq*. See also *Coffey and Moylan* v. *Brunel Construction Co. Ltd.*, Unreported (Sup. Ct.) (324/81)(Judgments delivered 13th May, 1983).

Chapter 10
SUCCESSION

This topic covers a wide range of subjects, wills, intestacies, administration of estates and, what has proved to be a frequent source of litigation recently, family provision. The modern law on these subjects is, of course, now largely enshrined in the Succession Act, 1965; see *Irish Land Law*, chaps. 14–16.

I. WILLS

SUCCESSION ACT, 1965
PART VII
Wills

76. – A person may by his will, executed in accordance with this Act, dispose of all property which he is beneficially entitled to at the time of his death and which on his death devolves on his personal representatives.

77. – (1) To be valid a will shall be made by a person who –

(*a*) has attained the age of eighteen years or is or has been married, and

(*b*) is of sound disposing mind.

(2) A person who is entitled to appoint a guardian of an infant may make the appointment by will notwithstanding that he is not a person to whom paragraph (*a*) of subsection (1) applies.

78. – To be valid a will shall be in writing and be executed in accordance with the following rules:

1. It shall be signed at the foot or end thereof by the testator, or by some person in his presence and by his direction.

2. Such signature shall be made or acknowledged by the testator in the presence of each of two or more witnesses, present at the same time, and each witness shall attest by his signature the signature of the testator in the presence of the testator, but no form of attestation shall be necessary nor shall it be necessary for the witnesses to sign in the presence of each other.

3. So far as concerns the position of the signature of the testator or of the person signing for him under rule 1, it is sufficient if the signature is so placed at or after, or following, or under, or beside, or opposite to the end of the will that it is apparent on the face of the will that the testator intended to give effect by the signature to the writing signed as his will.

4. No such will shall be affected by the circumstances –

(*a*) that the signature does not follow or is not immediately after the foot or end of the will; or

(*b*) that a blank space intervenes between the concluding word of the will and the signature; or

(*c*) that the signature is placed among the words of the testimonium clause or of the clause of attestation, or follows or is after or under the clause of attestation, either with or without a blank space intervening, or follows or is after, or under, or besides the names of one of the names of the attesting witnesses; or

(*d*) that the signature is on a side or page or other portion of the paper or papers containing the will on which no clause or paragraph or disposing part of the will is written above the signature; or

(*e*) that there appears to be sufficient space on or at the bottom of the preceding

side or page or other portion of the same paper on which the will is written to
contain the signature;

and the enumeration of the above circumstances shall not restrict the generality of
rule 1.

5. A signature shall not be operative to give effect to any disposition or direction
inserted after the signature is made.

79. – (1) An appointment made by will, in exercise of any power, shall not be valid
unless it is executed in accordance with this Act.

(2) Every will so executed shall, so far as concerns its execution and attestation, be
a valid execution of a power of appointment by will, notwithstanding that it has been
expressly required that a will made in exercise of such power shall be executed with
some additional or other form of execution or solemnity.

80. – Every will executed in accordance with this Act shall be valid without any
other publication thereof.

81. – If a person who attests the execution of a will is, at the time of execution or at
any time afterwards, incompetent to be admitted a witness to prove the execution,
the will shall not on that account be invalid.

82. – (1) If a person attests the execution of a will, and any devise, bequest, estate,
interest, gift, or appointment, of or affecting any property (other than charges and
directions for the payment of any debt or debts) is given or made by the will to that
person or his spouse, that devise, bequest, estate, interest, gift, or appointment shall,
so far only as concerns the person attesting the execution of the will, or the spouse of
that person, or any person claiming under that person or spouse, be utterly null and
void.

(2) The person so attesting shall be admitted as a witness to prove the execution of
the will, or to prove the validity or invalidity thereof, notwithstanding such devise,
bequest, estate, interest, gift, or appointment.

83. – If by will any estate is charged with any debt or debts, and a creditor, or the
spouse of a creditor, whose debt is so charged, attests the execution of the will, the
creditor, notwithstanding such charge, shall be admitted a witness to prove the
execution of the will, or to prove the validity or invalidity thereof.

84. – A person shall not, by reason only of his being an executor of a will, be
incompetent to be admitted a witness to prove the execution of the will, or a witness to
prove the validity or invalidity thereof.

85. – (1) A will shall be revoked by the subsequent marriage of the testator, except
a will made in contemplation of that marriage, whether so expressed in the will or not.

(2) Subject to subsection (1), no will, or any part thereof, shall be revoked except
by another will or codicil duly executed, or by some writing declaring an intention to
revoke it and executed in the manner in which a will is required to be executed, or by
the burning, tearing, or destruction of it by the testator, or by some person in his
presence and by his direction, with the intention of revoking it.

86. – An obliteration, interlineation, or other alteration made in a will after
execution shall not be valid or have any effect, unless such alteration is executed as is
required for the execution of the will; but the will, with such alteration as part thereof,
shall be deemed to be duly executed if the signature of the testator and the signature
of each witness is made in the margin or on some other part of the will opposite or near
to such alteration, or at the foot or end of or opposite to a memorandum referring to
such alteration, and written at the end of some other part of the will.

87. – No will or any part thereof, which is in any manner revoked, shall be revived
otherwise than by the re-execution thereof or by a codicil duly executed and showing
an intention to revive it; and when any will or codicil which is partly revoked, and
afterwards wholly revoked, is revived, such revival shall not extend to so much

thereof as was revoked before the revocation of the whole thereof, unless an intention to the contrary is shown.

88. – Where, subsequently to the execution of a will, a conveyance or other act is made or done relating to any estate comprised in the will, except an act by which the will is revoked, the conveyance or act shall not prevent the operation of the will with respect to any estate or interest in the property which the testator has power to dispose of by will at the time of his death.

89. – Every will shall, with reference to all estate comprised in the will and every devise or bequest contained in it, be construed to speak and take effect as if it had been executed immediately before the death of the testator, unless a contrary intention appears from the will.

90. – Extrinsic evidence shall be admissible to show the intention of the testator and to assist in the construction of, or to explain any contradiction in, a will.

91. – Unless a contrary intention appears from the will, any estate comprised or intended to be comprised in any devise or bequest contained in the will which fails or is void by reason of the fact that the devisee or legatee did not survive the testator, or by reason of the devise or bequest being contrary to law or otherwise incapable of taking effect, shall be included in any residuary devise or bequest, as the case may be, contained in the will.

92. – A general devise of land shall be construed to include leasehold interests as well as freehold estates, unless a contrary intention appears from the will.

93. – A general devise of land shall be construed to include any land which the testator may have power to appoint in any manner he may think proper, and shall operate as an execution of such power, unless a contrary intention appears from the will; and in like manner a general bequest of the personal estate (other than land) of the testator shall be construed to include any such estate which he may have power to appoint in any manner he may think proper, and shall operate as an execution of such power, unless a contrary intention appears from the will.

. . .

99. – If the purport of a devise or bequest admits of more than one interpretation, then, in case of doubt, the interpretation according to which the devise or bequest will be operative shall be preferred.

CLARKE V. EARLY
[1980] I.R. 223 (Supreme Court)

The deceased died in 1962. In 1964 Sabina Geoghegan, in whose house the deceased had died, produced a testamentary paper which she alleged was his will and by which he appeared to have devised his lands to her. The name of the deceased appeared as a signature at the foot of the note and was followed by the signatures of two witnesses. The document did not record the appointment of an executor and did not contain an attestation clause. In 1978 the applicant applied for a grant of letters of administration of the estate of the deceased, with his alleged will annexed. Although both witnesses were then dead, it was proved that they had been known by the deceased and the signature of one of them was verified. There was some evidence that the alleged signature of the deceased was not his true signature. The application was dismissed by the High Court. An appeal to the Supreme Court was lodged.

O'Higgins C.J.:

This appeal is brought by the applicant against the refusal of Mr. Justice Gannon to accede to his application for an order giving him liberty to obtain letters of administration of the estate of the late Hugh Early, deceased, with his last will dated the 16th April, annexed.

Hugh Early lived in Glencastle, Bunahowen in the county of Mayo. He died at the age of 88 on the 11th May, 1962. He was unmarried and his only known next-of-kin were John Early, a brother, who then lived in England and a Miss Anne Early who was believed to be a cousin. Hugh Early died at Barrack Street, Belmullet, in the county of Mayo in the house of a Mrs Sabina Geoghegan, who was a distant relative and who had cared for and nursed him for some time prior to his death. His only assets consisted of a farm of land at Glencastle, his ownership being registered in folio 23536 of the register of freeholders for the county of Mayo.

On the 16th November, 1964 (being some time after the death of the deceased) Mrs. Sabina Geoghegan handed to Mr. Liam McHale, solicitor, of Ballina a document which she said was the last will of Hugh Early and which was dated the 16th April, 1962. This document had apparently been in her possession since the death of Hugh Early and was handed to Mr. McHale for the purpose of having the same proved as a will. Its terms were as follows:

'I am leaving my land at Glencastle, Bunnahowen to Mrs. Sabina Geoghegan, Barrack Street, Belmullet who is looking after me and I am staying with her. She has to bury me and pay my funeral expenses and get a Mass said for me.'
Under this text appeared the following words:
'Signed: *Hugh Early*.
Witness: *James Mullan*, Fohera, Ballinamore, Co. Leitrim.
Witness: *Patrick Callaghan*, Barrack St., Belmullet.'

At the top of the text was the date '16th April, 1962'. As appears, the document contained no attestation clause nor was an executor named. Mrs. Geoghegan's purpose in handing the document to Mr. McHale was to put her title to the lands in Glencastle in order, as she was negotiating a sale of these lands to Martin McIntyre.

It appears that Mr. McHale sought the assistance of Anne Early for the purpose of extracting a grant of letters of administration with the will annexed. This was not successful as Anne Early first demanded payment for her co-operation and later refused it, alleging that the signature on the document was not that of the late Hugh Early. It does not appear that any approach was made to John Early, the deceased's brother. In any event, Mr. McHale's efforts ended in failure and no further steps were taken at that time to extract a grant of administration with the will annexed. In the meantime, Martin McIntyre, the putative paurchaser, went into occupation of the lands at Glencastle. Apparently, Anne Early also did so. There appears to have been a joint occupation by both these people for a period of years and this was followed by a period in which Martin McIntyre was in exclusive occupation. Eventually Mr. McIntyre emigrated to America in 1972, but he made a practice of returning from time to time to continue his occupation of these lands.

On the 2nd May, 1974, Mrs. Sabina Geoghegan died. She had previously made her will dated the 14th August, 1969, under which she appointed Patrick Lavelle as her executor, and left to her grandson, Michael Hopkins, her house at Belmullet and to her granddaughter, Vera Hopkins, her residuary estate. Vera Hopkins is now Vera Gomez. Sabina Geoghegan's will was duly proved.

Mr. Lavelle having declined to apply, on the 22nd December, 1978, the applicant (acting under power of attorney for Vera Gomez) was granted letters of administration of the estate of Hugh Early, limited for the purpose of instituting proceedings for the preservation of the property of the said deceased. On the same day a plenary summons was issued by the applicant claiming possession of the lands of Glencastle from Mr. Martin McIntyre.

Subsequently, the applicant, as such attorney, applied to the High Court for a grant of letters of administration to the estate of the deceased, with his purported last will annexed. This application was refused by Mr. Justice Gannon by an order dated the 14th February, 1980, and against this refusal this appeal has been brought.

The facts already outlined were deposed to in a number of affidavits on the hearing of the application before Mr. Justice Gannon. In addition, it was established that both persons whose names appeared as witnesses to the purported will were dead. However, the handwriting and signature of the witness James Mullan was identified by his widow, who deposed in an affidavit to the fact that the first seven lines of the writing in the document was in his hand and that his signature appeared thereunder. She could not verify the signature 'Patrick Callaghan' but she deposed to the fact that she knew a man called Patrick Callaghan who resided in Barrack Street, Belmullet, and that she knew him to be a friend of the late Hugh Early. There was, however, no evidence verifying or in any way identifying the signature 'Hugh Early' as being that of the deceased.

Mr. Shanley, for the applicant, urged that this Court should apply the maxim *omnia praesumuntur rite esse acta* to the many shortcomings that appear in the evidence relied upon to support the document as being the last will of the deceased. It seems to me that this is far too large a step to ask the Court to take in the circumstances of this case. I am prepared to accept that the document appears to be a testamentary document. It seems essential, however, that there be evidence that it was actually signed by the deceased. The evidence in support of the application undoubtedly shows that the document was truly signed by one of the witnesses. I am prepared to accept that it was so signed by this person as a witness. The application of the presumption might also carry the apparent attestation of the second witness, since a person bearing that name and address existed and was a friend of the deceased. There is, however, a complete absence of any evidence to verify the signature 'Hugh Early' as being that of the deceased. Not only is there such an absence of evidence but there is an allegation, admittedly of doubtful authenticity, by a near relative that this was not the signature of the deceased.

To apply the maxim *omnia praesumuntur rite esse acta* it is necessary, in my view, that two conditions be observed. In the first place an intention to do some formal act must be established. In the second place there must be an absence of credible evidence that due formality was not observed. Here it can be said that the second condition is established. But what of the first? While the document has a testamentary flavour, it is established that it is not a holograph. In the absence of any evidence that it was signed by the deceased, there is no evidence of an intention on his part to enter into the formality of making a will. Mr. Shanley cited a number of cases in which the presumption he relied upon was applied. I can, however, find no decision which goes as far as he would have this Court go in this case. The strongest authority in favour of the applicant is that of *Harris* v. *Knight* (1890) 15 P.D. 170. In that case probate was granted of a lost will without the production of a copy but with satisfactory evidence as to the contents. Both the attesting witnesses were dead but there was evidence to identify the signature of one of them. There was an allegation that the signature of the testator was a forgery. However there was also evidence (which the trial judge accepted) that it was not a forgery but was in fact the genuine signature of the testator. In other words, in that case there was evidence which the court could accept that the document was signed by the testator and that he intended it to be his will.

Accordingly, I have come to the view that there was not sufficient evidence to justify a grant of administration in this case and that this appeal should be refused. However likely it is that the document in question represented what the late Hugh Early would have wished to do in his will, this is not sufficient to justify this Court ignoring the absence of any evidence that it was in fact his will.

Henchy J.:
    I agree.

Kenny J.:
  I agree.

Parke J.:
  I agree.

O'Higgins C.J.:
  Mr. Justice Griffin, who is unable to be present today, has asked me to say that he agrees with my judgment.

Notes
1. See further on formalities for wills, *Irish Land Law*, para. 14.04 *et seq.*
2. *Cf.* the view of the Court of Appeal in *Clery* v. *Barry* (1884) 21 L.R. Ir. 152.

IN THE GOODS OF COSTER
Unreported (Supreme Court) (Judgments delivered 19th January, 1978)
The facts are set out in Kenny J.'s judgment.

Kenny J.:
  On 1st October, 1971, Hannah Coster ('the deceased'), an elderly childless widow, who lived in Dublin, went to the offices of a well-known firm of solicitors in Dublin to make her will. The solicitors took written instructions for it by which she left a number of charitable gifts and left the residue of her estate to her sister, a nun in the Convent of Mercy in Wexford, for distribution among the poor in Wexford. Two members of the firm of solicitors were appointed executors. When the will had been engrossed and executed in accordance with the formalities prescribed by the Succession Act 1965 ('the Act of 1965'), one of the solicitors put it, a plain copy of it and the written instructions into an envelope which he retained in the office.
  On 18th October 1973 the deceased called to the solicitors office and asked for the original will which she took away. She said nothing to indicate why she wanted it. Between 1st February 1973 and 31st January 1974, she purchased a printed form of will from Messrs Eason. This printed form with nothing written on it by the deceased, was found among her papers after she died on 16th October 1976 when she was over 80. Her only next of kin was her sister, the nun. The original will was not among her papers and was not in her house and although advertisements for it have been published in 3 papers and gazettes, it has not been found. The deceased's sister died on 22nd November 1976 and appointed the applicant who is the Superior of the Convent in Wexford to be her executrix and she has got probate of the sister's will. The applicant then applied to the High Court for an order declaring that the deceased had died intestate and seeking a grant of letters of administration to her estate under s. 27(4) of the Act of 1965.
  The High Court judge (Mr. Justice Gannon) refused the application because he thought that the will of 1973 might have been mislaid and that even if it had been destroyed, the revocation effected by this was conditional on the execution by the deceased of another valid will. The applicant has now appealed to this Court against the whole of the order made in the High Court.
  Sub-s. 2 of s. 85 of the Act of 1965 (which repeals the whole of the Wills Act 1837, the relevant part of sub-s. 2 being however exactly similar to s. 20 of the Wills Act 1837) reads:

  '(2) . . . no will or any part thereof shall be revoked except by another will or codicil duly executed or by some writing declaring an intention to revoke it and executed in the manner in which a will is required to be executed, or by the burning, tearing or destruction of it by the testator or by some person in his presence and by his direction, with the intention of revoking it'.

When a testatrix makes a will and retains the original or subsequently comes into possession of it and it cannot be found after her death and there is no evidence to show what has become of it, there is a presumption that she destroyed it with the intention of revoking it. This presumption, which was applied in the ecclesiastical courts before 1857, is of ancient origin. It is however a presumption only and not an absolute rule so that it may be rebutted. Thus the occurrence of a fire at the testatrix's home or the character of the deceased's custody (see the judgment of Chief Justice Cockburn in *Sugden* v. *Lord St. Leonards* (1876) 1 Prob. Div. 154 at p. 217) or the possibility of a disappointed beneficiary having removed the original will) have to be taken into account as matters which may rebut the presumption.

The classic statement of the rule is that of Baron Parke's when giving the advice of the Privy Council in *Welch* v. *Phillips* (1836) 1 Moore's P.C. 299: 'Now the rule of the law of evidence on this subject, as established by a course of decisions in the Ecclesiastical Court is this: that if a will traced to the possession of the deceased and last seen there, is not forthcoming on his death, it is presumed to have been destroyed by himself; and that presumption must have effect unless there is sufficient evidence to repel it. The onus of proof of such circumstances is undoubtedly on the party propounding the will' (see also *Allan* v. *Morrison* [1900] A.C. 604: *Re Faris (No. 2)* [1911] I.R. 469: *Re Southerden* [1925] P. 177).

In the instant case there is nothing to rebut the presumption that the deceased destroyed the will of 1971 with the intention of revoking it. It has been traced to her custody by coercive evidence and has not been found despite exhaustive searches and inquiries.

Was the revocation by destruction conditional on her making another will? I do not think it was. To make a destruction of a will by a testatrix a conditional revocation only, a mere general intention at the time of destruction to make another will is not, in most cases, effective to make the revocation by destruction conditional. The purchase of the printed form of will shows that the deceased had the making of another will in mind but this does not make the revocation conditional. The rule was pithily summed up by Lord Justice Roskill in *Re Jones deceased* [1976] 1 All E.R. 593 at p. 603. That was a case of revocation by mutilation and the same questions arose as in the instant case. '. . . a mere intention to make a new will, however clearly shown, is not enough of itself, as the authorities show, to make the revocation conditional'.

There is also Irish authority to the same effect. *In the goods of Walsh (John Joseph)* [1947] Ir. Jur. Rep. 44 was a decision of Mr. Justice Haugh, who acted as Probate Judge for many years. He said: 'It has often happened that a person destroying a will with the intention of making another, dies without having made it but I could not hold that because an intention was expressed and not carried out, the formula destroyed should therefore be set up'. In the passage the word 'formula' is clearly a misprint and should read 'will'.

In my opinion, the revocation by destruction was absolute and not conditional. In fairness to Mr. Justice Gannon I should say that neither *Re Jones deceased* [1976] 1 All E.R. 593 nor *In the goods of Walsh (John Joseph) deceased* [1947] Ir. Jur. Rep. 44 was cited to us or to him.

The order made in the High Court should be set aside. This Court should declare that the deceased died intestate and that the applicant be given liberty to apply for a Grant of Letters of Administration to her estate. The applicant's costs of the application to the High Court and of this appeal (when taxed) will be part of her costs of the administration of the estate of the deceased.

O'Higgins C.J. and **Parke J.** concurred.

Note
See further on revocation of wills, *Irish Land Law*, para. 14.17 *et seq.*

ROWE V. LAW
[1978] I.R. 55; 114 I.L.T.R. 86 (Supreme Court)

By her will made in 1967 a testatrix devised and bequeathed all her property, which she called her trust fund, to her trustees on trust (1) to discharge thereout her debts, funeral and testamentary expenses and subject thereto (2) to set aside out of the capital moneys of the trust fund a sum of £1000 to be applied in the purchase and furnishing of a cottage for the use of the second and third defendants during their joint lives and the life of the survivor and subject thereto 'as to any balance then remaining' to invest the same and pay the income to the second and third defendants during their joint lives and to the survivor during his or her life and subject thereto to pay the £1000 or the investments representing it to a named legatee and subject thereto (3) to pay a legacy of £100 and subject thereto (4) to stand possessed of 'the trust fund then remaining' and to pay and transfer it to the plaintiffs in equal shares.

The testatrix died in 1972 and probate of her will was granted to the first defendant. The second and third defendants contended that, by her bequest of 'any balance then remaining' in clause 2 of her will, the testatrix had intended to bequeath to them her entire estate less the payments of her debts, funeral and testamentary expenses, and the £1000. Extrinsic evidence was available to support, and to controvert, that contention. Section 90 of the Succession Act, 1965, states that 'extrinsic evidence shall be admissible to show the intention of the testator and to assist in the construction of, or to explain any contradiction in, a will'. At the hearing of a construction summons issued by the plaintiffs as residuary devisees and legatees it was held by Kenny J., in answering the questions posed, (1) that the words used by the testatrix were not ambiguous and did not raise any difficulty of construction or application, and that she had expressed clearly an intention to give the second and third defendants life interests in the balance of the £1000 only as distinct from the balance of the entire estate; (2) that, in such circumstances, the provisions of s. 90 of the Act of 1965 do not authorise the introduction of extrinsic evidence to establish an alleged intention on the part of the testator which conflicts with the intention he has expressed in his will. The second and third defendants appealed to the Supreme Court.

O'Higgins C.J.:

The testatrix died on the 10th June, 1972, having made her last will and one codicil on the 6th June, 1967, of which probate was granted to a solicitor, the first defendant, on the 6th March, 1973. The testatrix was twice married. She was married first to Patrick Rowe who died many years before the date of her will. She then married Walter Doran from whom she was separated at the date of her will; she had been separated from him for some years before that. She had no family. For many years prior to the date of the will the second defendant and the third defendant resided with the testatrix and worked as labourer and domestic help respectively. They so resided as James Morgan and Mary Germaine because they were then unmarried; they have married since the death of the testatrix.

These proceedings have been brought by the testatrix's two brothers-in-law who are named in the will as residuary legatees and devisees. They seek to determine certain questions which arise on the construction of the main portion of the will.

In the construction summons the questions raised are as follows: 'Does the phrase 'any balance then remaining' contained in paragraph 2 of the said will mean (a) any balance remaining out of the sum of one thousand pounds after the purchase and furnishing of a suitable cottage residence for James Morgan and Mary Morgan (in will referred to as Mary Germaine) or (b) any balance remaining out of the capital moneys of the Trust Fund after the purchase and furnishing of such cottage. . .'.

If these questions were to be determined in accordance with the law prior to the Succession Act, 1965, certain principles of construction would have applied. These would have ordained that the meaning of the words used was to be sought in the will itself, that the words used should be applied in accordance with their plain grammatical meaning and that extrinsic evidence would be inadmissible to assist in the construction.

As to the inadmissibility of extrinsic evidence, paragraph 25 of the 13th edition of Theobold on Wills states: 'This is a basic principle of long standing which has a number of exceptions and much depends on whether or not the exceptions can be prayed in aid. Where the meaning of the will, from the words used, is clear, it is not possible to look at extrinsic evidence. However, when the meaning is not clear, it may be permissible to "sit in the testator's armchair" and take account of the circumstances surrounding the testator at the time of making the will in order to assist in its interpretation. It may thus be possible to look at the facts known to the testator at the time he made his will concerning the persons and property mentioned therein as an aid to construction. The range of admissible surrounding circumstances may determine the nature of the result. Extrinsic evidence may also be admissible in one or two other cases, for example, to explain latent ambiguities or to rebut certain presumptions of law'.

Paragraph 427 of the same work states: 'It has been said, that to construe the will of a testator "you may place yourself, so to speak, in his armchair and consider the circumstances by which he was surrounded when he made his will to assist you in arriving at his intention". But this proposition must be accepted with several reservations. What has to be done is first to construe the will. The meaning placed upon the language used as the result of this process cannot be altered by reference to the surrounding circumstances when the will was executed. The procedure is not – first ascertain the surrounding circumstances and with that knowledge approach the construction of the will, but first construe the will; if the meaning is clear, surrounding circumstances cannot be looked at to throw a doubt upon that meaning, or to give the will a different meaning. . ..'

It seems to me that these two passages set out correctly the common law with regard to the construction of a will. Applying these statements of the law to the will of the testatrix, what is the position? One looks for the meaning of the words 'as to any balance then remaining' in the will itself and one applies these words in their ordinary grammatical sense. Extrinsic evidence would not be admissible unless the meaning were obscure or unless ambiguities existed, or in order to rebut certain presumptions of law. In this case no presumption of law requires rebuttal. Is there, then, in the language used any ambiguity or any uncertainty? It seems to me that there is not. In relation to the setting aside of £1,000 out of the trust fund, the testatrix appears to have established three separate trusts providing for its application and eventual disposal. These three trusts are specified under the same numbered paragraph in the will and they provide first for the initial use of £1,000; then 'as to any balance then remaining' provision is made for the investment of it in some trustee security and the payment of the income to the second and third defendants during their lives; then it is provided that, after the death of the survivor, the £1,000 or the investment representing the same is to go to the parish . . all of this the meaning appears to be clear. There exists no such ambiguity . . . he introduction of extrinsic evidence. Looking only at the terms of . . . ld doubt that the words 'as to any balance then remaining' . . . £1,000 then remaining.

Therefore, in accordance with the law as it existed prior to the Succession Act, 1965, extrinsic evidence would be excluded. This will would be construed accordingly to the plain meaning of the words and it would be held to mean that merely the balance of £1,000 went to the second and third defendants for their lives. It would also be construed as giving the residue of the trust fund to the plaintiffs absolutely and immediately. This would be so even if clear and unequivocal evidence were available to show that such was not what the testatrix wished or intended by the words she used. While having the advantage of finality, such a state of the law also had the obvious and grave disadvantage of frustrating at times the known intentions of testators. The law reports abound with cases in which this must have occurred. I will refer to two as examples.

In *Higgins* v. *Dawson* [1902] A.C.1 the testator, when he made his will, was the owner of some real estate, plate, and china and of two mortgage debts amounting to £13,187, and of nothing else except the accruing interest on the mortgage debts. By his will he made gifts of the residue of the mortgage debts after payment of his debts to a charity. The question was whether the residue of the mortgage debts meant what might remain of the mortgage debts after paying thereout first the legacies and secondly the debts, or whether it meant what remained after paying debts only. Upon the latter construction, if the testator had died the next day, all the legacies would have failed, as there was nothing out of which to pay them. As a matter of fact the testator had, between the date of his will and his death, become entitled to other property which was not sufficient to pay the legacies in full. Approaching the will with a knowledge of these facts, the conclusion was almost irresistible that the legacies were meant to be paid out of the mortgage debts and that 'residue' must mean residue of the mortgage debts after paying the legacies as well as the debts. However, it was held that the evidence was inadmissible. It was held, in accordance with the principles applying to the construction of a will, that the prima facie meaning of the word 'residue' as used in the will was residue deducting debts and that meaning could not be altered by reference to evidence.

In re Julian [1950] I.R. 57 was a case where a Protestant lady by her will bequeathed a sum of money to 'The Seamen's Institute, Sir John Rogerson's Quay, Dublin' and the bequest was subsequently claimed by two bodies, namely, the Catholic Seamen's Institute, Sir John Rogerson's Quay, Dublin, and the Dublin Seamen's Institute, Eden Quay, Dublin. On the hearing of the summons, issued by the executors for the determination by the court of questions arising on the construction of the will, it was sought to prove the intention of the testatrix by the introduction of parol evidence of her religion, of her association with one of the said institutes, namely, the Dublin Seamen's Institute, Eden Quay, and of a mistake, on the part of the solicitor who engrossed the will, in regard to the address of the institute as appearing in the will. It appeared that the testatrix, in the course of her instructions to the solicitor, expressed her doubt as to the correct address of the institute whereupon the solicitor consulted a book of reference in which the only seamen's institute mentioned was that situate at Sir John Rogerson's Quay, Dublin. It was held by Kingsmill Moore J. in the High Court that the parol extrinsic evidence could not be admitted to show the intention of the testatrix because, on the language used, no doubt could exist as to the description of the institute to be benefitted. Accordingly, in accordance with the ruling that the extrinsic evidence was inadmissible, the clear intention of the testatrix was frustrated and the benefit of her gift went to the Catholic Seamen's Institute, Sir John Rogerson's Quay, and not to the Seamen's Institute, Eden Quay, with which she had been associated.

At the end of his judgment (p. 66) Kingsmill Moore J. said: 'This is by no means the first – and, equally certainly, will not be the last – case in which a judge has been forced by the rules of law to give a decision on the construction of a will which he believed to be contrary to the intentions of the testator. The law reports are loud with the comments of judges who found themselves in similar plight; but I consider the law to be well established and conclusive that I must reject Mr. O'Brien's evidence and, in the absence of such evidence, I must hold that the Catholic Seamen's Institute is entitled to the bequest.'

With cases such as these in mind it is not surprising that some modification of the apparent inflexibility of the common law should have been attempted by statute. The exclusion of extrinsic evidence of the intentions of testators in accordance with the common-law principles had produced too many cases in which a will was given a construction which was the complete antithesis of what the testator had intended. In my view, such a modification was one of the purposes which the Oireachtas had in mind when it came to enact the provisions of s. 90 of the Succession Act, 1965, which states:

> 'Extrinsic evidence shall be admissible to show the intention of the testator and to assist in the construction of, or to explain any contradiction in, a will.'

This section, with its marginal note describing it as a new section, was obviously intended to effect a change in the law as it existed at the passing of the Act of 1965. In considering the meaning of this section in his judgment in this case, Mr. Justice Kenny said: 'The first question then must always be whether the will is ambiguous or contradictory. If it is, extrinsic evidence (in the sense in which I have defined it) is admissible as a result of s. 90; if it is not, this evidence is not admissible.' I cannot agree with this view. In my opinion the clear purpose of this section is to give primacy to the actual intention of the testator and to construe the will in accordance with that intention.

Obviously, the ideal construction of any will or document is the one which reflects accurately and exactly the intention of the person who made it. In the absence of evidence to the contrary, it must be taken that a document made by a person reflects his intentions. The important statutory change brought about by s. 90 of the Act of 1965 was to ensure that this could be tested. The section made it mandatory to admit evidence *to show* the intention of the testator when it came to a question of construing a will. If the section had only intended to do little more than put in statutory form the common law as it existed prior to the section, it would have been worded very differently. It is to be particularly noted that the section makes special mention of the contradictions in the will itself which, as the punctuation indicates, is something quite different from the portion of the section preceding that provision. It is also to be noted that s. 99, which also imports a new rule of interpretation into the construction of wills, expressly deals with devises or bequests admitting of more than one interpretation. The fact that that particular problem has a special section to itself leads one to conclude with absolute certainty that it was not intended to be covered by section 90.

If s. 90 had existed when *In re Julian* [1950] I.R.57 was decided the result would have been otherwise, and I have no doubt that it was passed for the purpose of dealing with that kind of case. Of course, if the section were to be interpreted in the manner in which the learned trial judge interpreted it, no change would be possible in cases such as *In re Julian* because, as in this case, the words used in the will are unambiguous and clear and no contradiction exists.

It appears to me clear that s. 90 of the Act of 1965, was drafted to provide for two contingencies: the first where there is a contradiction in the will itself and the second where there is a contradiction between the actual intention of the testator and what was said in the will, given its pre-1965 construction. This latter category would, of course, cover and include situations in which an error had been made by a solicitor or other person writing down the will.

When one looks at the legislative history of this particular Act, one must be fortified in the view that this is the correct construction of the section. When the Bill for the Act was first introduced in the Oireachtas, this subject matter was dealt with in s. 89 of the Bill. This provided that 'extrinsic evidence shall be admissible to assist in the construction of a will or to explain any contradiction therein.' As the Bill progressed through the Oireachtas, amendments were made to this particular section. The first amendment referred to 'extrinsic evidence of the intention' and provided that such should be admissible. The final version provided that 'extrinsic evidence shall be admissible *to show* the intention of the testator' and this, of course, is what is incorporated in s. 90 of the Act of 1965. As passed, the section expressly provides for extrinsic evidence to show the intention of the testator where no such words had been contained in the corresponding section of the Bill as introduced. It seems clear that in the section as enacted an indissoluble link has been created between the testator's intention and the construction of the will.

In fact a true construction of the will cannot be other than a true reflection of the intention of the testator. If there is a difference between them, then it is indisputably clear that the actual intention of the testator has not been reflected in the construction of the will. As the law stood before 1965, it was not possible to ensure against such an event and there is ample evidence to show that in many cases construction of particular wills did not reflect the intention of the testator. The problem before the Oireachtas was to change the law to enable that position to be achieved, i.e. to get rid of the general rule which rendered inadmissible any such extrinsic evidence for the purpose of ascertaining the actual intention of the testator as well as for the purpose of explaining contradictions within the will itself. It is to be noted that the explanatory memorandum published with the Succession Bill (as passed by both Houses of the Oireachtas), having quoted in paragraph 56 the terms of s. 90, contains the following statement: 'At present, extrinsic evidence of a testator's intention is, in general, inadmissible, although there are exceptions to this rule.'

In arriving at the view that the effect of s. 90 is to get rid of the common-law rule which rendered inadmissible extrinsic evidence for the purpose of ascertaining the actual intention of the testator as well as for the purpose of explaining contradictions in the will itself, I am satisfied that the ordinary reading of this section leads to that result. I am, however, fortified by the knowledge that the legislative history of the measure, particularly the express introduction of the phrase 'to show the intention of the testator' before the Bill was finally enacted leads inevitably to the same conclusion. To hold otherwise would, in my opinion, be to run directly contrary to the clearly expressed mandatory provisions of section 90. The words used do not, in my view, permit any court to trat the introduction of extrinsic evidence as to the actual intention of the testator as an exception only, the admissibility of which lies within the discretion of the judge.

The Oireachtas has chosen, and understandably so, to sacrifice the certainty of literal interpretation with its frequently attendant capricious results, in favour of the somewhat more difficult but more understandable task of ascertaining the testator's actual intention. For this reason extrinsic evidence *must* be admitted (where it is sought to do so) to 'show the intention of the testator' and 'to show' the meaning of the will, and thereby to 'assist in the construction' of the will. This may mean in particular cases a susbtantial change in what has been the practice up to this, but this is what the legislature has ordained.

In my view, however, what is permitted is evidence of the testator's intentions as such and that is evidence of his intentions when he came to make his will. Previous expressions of intent or evidence of general disposition would not be admissible nor would, I believe, evidence of subsequent statements by the testator of what his intentions had been at the time he made his will. What is permitted by the section as extrinsic evidence of intention is what was said and done at the time of the making of the will as indicating a testamentary intention at that time.

In this case what is in issue is what the testatrix meant by the words 'any balance then remaining' which appear in paragraph 2 of her will. There are available two accounts of what her testamentary intention was when she made this will. One of these accounts is contained in the attendance docket prepared by her solicitor as a record of her instructions to him for the preparation of her will. One assumes that this attendance docket can be supported by the oral evidence of the solicitor. The other account is contained in an affidavit from the testatrix's brother-in-law, Fr. Francis Rowe, referring to the same attendance upon her solicitor and giving a conflicting account of what her instructions to him were. Fr. Rowe's account of what the testatrix said as indicative of her intentions appears to support the actual construction applied by the learned trial judge having regard to the language used. On the other hand the attendance docket, if it contains a correct account of what the testatrix wished and intended, indicates that quite a different meaning should be attached to the words 'any balance then remaining'. In my view, the true meaning of these words in this will ought not to be considered and cannot be determined without ascertaining what was the true intention of the testatrix at the time she proceeded to make her will. This will entail the resolution of the conflict between the solicitor's account of what was said and that of Fr. Rowe. Obviously this conflict must be resolved and, once it has been resolved, the will must be considered in the light of the evidence as to the true intention of the testatrix.

In my view, the learned judge ought to have permitted extrinsic evidence to be adduced in relation to the construction of this will. In my view, accordingly, his decision ought not to stand and I would order a rehearing of this construction summons in the High Court directing that such extrinsic evidence as may be available with regard to the testatrix's intention ought to be admitted. I would allow this appeal.

Henchy J.:

The chief point arising in this appeal may be stated in this form: where there is a clear and unambiguous disposition in a will of portion only of a fund, and there is extrinsic evidence available in a court of construction to show that the testator really intended to make a disposition of the whole of the fund, does s. 90 of the Succession Act, 1965, allow the court of construction to use that extrinsic evidence for the purpose of superseding the clearly expressed intention in the will? I pose the question in that way because I think there is no doubt that (for the reasons given by Mr. Justice Kenny in the High Court) the words 'any balance then remaining' refer not to the whole of the trust fund created by the will but to the balance then remaining of the portion of it (amounting to £1,000) which was dealt with in the preceding paragraph of the will. If the words in the will prevail, the expression 'any balance then remaining' must be held to refer to any balance then remaining of the £1,000 after it has been applied in accordance with the preceding paragraph.

There is available parole evidence of declarations, made by the testatrix at the time of the making of the will, which show that she intended the expression 'any balance then remaining' to refer to nothing more than the balance of the £1,000 – that is to say, showing that the will truly represents her intention. As against that, evidence is available from the solicitor who drew the will to the effect that the testatrix's instructions to him show that what she had in mind was not the balance of the £1,000 but the balance of the trust fund consisting of her total estate, which estate was valued for probate purposes at some £50,000. If the latter evidence were to be accepted as being correct, and if s. 90 of the Succession Act, 1965, were to be held to allow it to be used to determine the true nature of the testamentary disposition, it would enable the court to rectify the will by giving testamentary effect to a disposition which is not to be found in the will and which actually conflicts with the disposition in the will.

Section 90 of the Succession Act, 1965, reads as follows:

'Extrinsic evidence shall be admissible to show the intention of the testator and to assist in the construction of, or to explain any contradiction in, a will.'

Section 9 of the Wills Act, 1837, laid down a common requirement for all wills, whether of real or personal property, i.e. a written instrument signed by the testator and witnessed by two signing witnesses. Between 1837 and the enactment of the Act of 1965, it was an inflexible rule that, where there was a clear and unambiguous testatorial intention expressed in such a will duly admitted to probate, extrinsic evidence of a different intention could not be received in a court of construction for the purpose of overriding the intention expressed in the will.

In Wigram on Extrinsic Evidence In Aid of the Interpretation of Wills (5th ed.) the author, having proposed (p. 2) the question 'Under what restrictions is the admission of extrinsic evidence, in aid of the exposition of a will, consistent with the provisions of a statute, which makes a writing indispensable to the purpose for which the instrument was made?' gives (at p. 8) the following reply:

'It is said, (and correctly), that the statute, by requiring a will to be in writing, precludes a Court of law from ascribing to a testator any intention which his written will does not express, and, in effect, makes the writing the only legitimate evidence of the testator's intention. . . . At the same time, however, Courts of law, though precluded from ascribing to a testator any intention not expressed in his will, admit their obligation to give effect to every intention which the will properly expounded contains. The answer, therefore, to the question above proposed . . . must be, that any evidence is admissible, which, in its nature, and effect, simply explains what the testator has written; but no evidence can be admissible, which, in its nature or effect, is applicable to the purpose of shewing merely what he intended to have written.'

The rule that extrinsic evidence could not be adduced for the purpose of adding to, varying, or contradicting the terms of a will has been applied firmly in the Courts, even in cases where the upheld interpretation of the will appeared to run counter to the true intention of the testator. For example, in *In re Huxtable* [1902] 2 I.R. 793, the testator bequeathed £4,000 to C. 'for the charitable purposes agreed between us'. It was held that, while evidence could be received to prove what the agreed charitable purposes were, it was impermissible to receive evidence to show that the testator intended that only the income was to go to those purposes – on the ground that such evidence would contradict the will. For the same reason in *In re Rees* [1950] Ch. 204), where the testator left part of his estate 'unto my trustees absolutely they well knowing my wishes concerning the same. . .' the court rejected apparently credible evidence that the testator intended the trustees to take the property absolutely, for such evidence would have rebutted the trust which the will was held to have created. The point, then, is whether s. 90 overthrew that rule.

At the time of the enactment of s. 90, extrinsic evidence was admissible in a variety of circumstances – depending on whether the court was sitting as a court of probate or a court of construction – to show the intention of the testator: the one important qualification being that such evidence could not be received by a court of construction for the purpose of adding to, varying, or contradicting the intention expressed in the will.

I read s. 90 allowing extrinsic evidence to be received if it meets the double requirement of (a) showing the intention of a testator and (b) assisting in the construction of, or explaining any contradiction in, a will. The alternative reading would treat the section as making extrinsic evidence admissible if it meets the requirement of either (a) or (b). That, however, would produce unreasonable and illogical consequences which the legislature could not have intended. If the section made extrinsic evidence admissible merely because it satisfies requirement (a), then in any case the court could go outside the will and receive and act on extrinsic evidence as to the intention of the testator. The grant of probate would no longer provide an exclusive and conclusive version of the testamentary intention as embodied in a will. However, it would be unreasonable and contradictory for the legislature, on the one hand to lay down in s. 78 the formal requirements for the disposition of one's property by will, and on the other to allow by s. 90 (without qualification or limitation as to purpose or circumstances or time) extrinsic evidence of the intention of the testator to be admitted. Such a sweeping and disruptive change, fraught with possibilities for fraud, mistake, unfairness and uncertainty, should not be read into the section if another and reasonable interpretation is open.

Section 90 is no less tainted with repugnancy if it is treated as making extrinsic evidence admissible merely because it satisfied requirement (b), that is to say, if it assists in the construction of, or if it explains a contradiction in, a will. Since the function of a court in construing a will or in finding an explanation of a contradiction in it necessarily involves a search for the intention of the testator, it would have been unnecessary for the section to include requirement (b) if requirement (a) on its own were sufficient to allow the admission of extrinsic evidence.

The plain fact is that the grant of an unlimited and undefined jurisdiction to admit extrinsic evidence to show the testator's intention would be so large in its scope and so untoward in its potential consequences that it would exceed the spirit and purpose of the Act. The necessary delimitation of the jurisdiction to admit such evidence is effected by the second limb of the section: 'and to assist in the construction of, or to explain any contradiction in, a will.' The conjunctive and cumulative 'and' is to be contrasted with the disjunctive and alternative 'or'. It connotes a duality of purpose as a condition for the admission under the section of extrinsic evidence. The necessary conditions are: to show the intention of the testator and to assist in the construction of, or to explain a contradiction in, the will. If either condition is not satisfied, the section does not allow the evidence to be admitted.

Let us now relate s. 90, as so interpreted, to the circumstances of this case. The extrinsic evidence which is sought to be adduced would have the purpose of showing the intention of the testator. The first condition for its admissibility under the section would therefore be satisfied. But what of the second condition, that it would assist in the construction of the will, or explain a contradiction in it? There is no suggestion of a contradiction in the will; so that aspect of the second condition does not arise. The matter then reduces itself to a question whether the proposed evidence would assist in the construction of the will. I am satisfied that it would not. The questioned provision in the will is clear and admits of only one construction. Extrinsic evidence could not possibly assist in its construction. It is only when assistance is needed – because on application of the rules of construction the will may be said to be unclear or uncertain in order to achieve the correct construction of the will that recourse may be had under the section to extrinsic evidence of the testator's intention. That is not the case here. If the proposed evidence were received and acted on, the Court would have to change the expression 'any balance then remaining' (i.e., of the £1,000) to 'any balance then remaining of the Trust Fund' (i.e. of the whole estate). To do that, however, would amount to more that a construction of the will; it would amount to a rectification of it. And it is quite clear that a jurisdiction to rectify a will which has been admitted to probate is outside the contemplation of s. 90; and it was not permitted by the pre-existing law.

I conclude that the jurisdiction given by s. 90 to use extrinsic evidence to assist in the construction of a will is confined to cases where the intention, as expressed in the will, calls for elucidation; my conclusion coincides with the opinion reached by Mr. Justice Kenny in the High Court in this case and by Mr. Justice Parke, when sitting in the High Court, in *Bennett* v. *Bennett* (High Court – 24th January, 1977).

To sum up: s. 90 allows extrinsic evidence of the testator's intention to be used by a court of construction only when there is a legitimate dispute as to the meaning or effect of the language used in the will. In such a case (e.g., *In re Julian* [1950] I.R. 57) it allows the extrinsic evidence to be drawn on so as to give the unclear or contradictory words in the will a meaning which accords with the testator's intention as thus ascertained. The section does not empower the Court to rewrite the will in whole or in part. Such a power would be repugnant to the will-making requirements of s. 78 and would need to be clearly and expressly conferred. The Court must take the will as it has been admitted to probate. If it is clear, unambiguous, and without contradiction then s. 90 has no application. If otherwise, then s. 90 may be used for the purpose of giving the language of the will the meaning and effect which extrinsic evidence shows the testator intended it to have. But s. 90 may not be used for the purpose of rejecting and supplanting the language used in the will.

As the clause of the will in question in this case is clear and unambiguous and does not import any contradiction, s. 90 does not allow extrinsic evidence to be used either to explain it or to supersede it. Accordingly, I would dismiss this appeal.

Griffin J.:

The facts and the relevant terms of the will of the testatrix are fully set out in the judgments of the Chief Justice and of Mr. Justice Kenny (from whose decision in the High Court this appeal by the second and third defendants is taken) and it is not necessary for me to repeat them.

By her will the testatrix gave, devised, and bequeathed all her real and personal estate (which she called 'the Trust Fund') to her trustees upon certain trusts which are set out in the will in numbered paragraphs. Paragraph 1 provided for the payment of her debts, funeral and testamentary expenses out of the Trust fund. In paragraph 2, she carved out of the Trust Fund the sum of £1,000 which she directed should in the first instance be utilised or applied in the purchase and furnishing of a suitable cottage residence for the use and occupation of the appellants during their joint lives and the life of the survivor of them and, subject thereto, 'as to any balance then remaining' to invest the same, the income to be paid to the appellants during their joint lives and then to the survivor for life. In my opinion, her use of the words 'in the first instance' in relation to the use to which the £1,000 was to be put, followed by the trust in respect of 'any balance then remaining' could only be interpreted as being the balance of the £1,000 remaining after the purchase and furnishing of the cottage. Her use of the words 'in the first instance' is important and indicates that one would reasonably expect further references to what is to be done with the remainder of the £1,000 after the purchase of the cottage. Further, her use of the word 'any' before 'balance then remaining' is significant as she could not reasonably have thought that the £1,000 would exhaust her considerable estate. Her use of the phrase 'any balance then remaining' is to be contrasted with her reference to 'the Trust Fund then remaining' in paragraph 4 of the will.

The construction for which the appellants contend would require the insertion of the words 'of the Trust Fund' after the word 'balance', so that the relevant portion of paragraph 2 would then read 'as to any balance of the Trust Fund then remaining'. Apart from the provisions of paragraph 2 there are other provisions in the will which indicate that this construction would not be the correct one. In the last sub-clause of paragraph 2, it is provided that on the death of the survivor of the appellants 'the said sum of £1,000 or the investments for the time being representing the same' are to be given to the parish priest for the time being of the parish of Castledermot. Here is found reference not only to the £1,000, but also to 'the investments for the time being representing the same'. The only investments referred to earlier in the will are those in respect of 'any balance then remaining'. Finally, in paragraph 4 the testatrix expressly referred to 'the Trust Fund then remaining'; this is the expression which the appellants seek to write into the relevant portion of paragraph 2 after the word 'balance' for the purpose of the construction for which they contend. These words clearly refer to the balance of the trust fund after payment of the debts, the £1,000 and the legacy of £100 for Masses bequeathed in paragraph 3. The use of these words in paragraph 4 weigh very heavily against the appellants' claim that they should be written into paragraph 2 for the purpose of arriving at the true construction of that paragraph.

In my opinion, therefore, the construction of this will, as written, leaves no room for doubt in relation to the relevant words in paragraph 2, and the construction given to the words by Mr. Justice Kenny is the correct one.

The question then arises as to whether, having regard to the provisions of s. 90 of the Succession Act, 1965, extrinsic evidence is admissible as to the dispositive intention of the testatrix at the time she gave instructions for the will. Prior to the passing of the Act of 1965, the general principle was that in a court of construction, where the *factum* of the instrument has been previously established in the court of probate, the inquiry was pretty closely restricted to the contents of the instrument itself in order to ascertain the intentions of the testator. As the law required wills both of real and personal estate to be in writing, it could not, consistently with this doctrine, permit parol evidence to be adduced to contradict, add to, or explain the contents of the will.

The general rule was subject to certain qualifications. Evidence of the state of the testator's family and property and other circumstances surrounding the testator was admissible, but evidence of the intention of the testator was not. As Lord Langdale M.R. said in *Martin* v. *Drinkwater* (1840) 2 Beav. 215 (p. 218) you are at liberty to prove the circumstances of the testator, so far as to enable the court to place itself in the situation of the testator, at the time of making his will; but you may not prove either his motives or intentions.

It is quite clear that extrinsic evidence of a testator's intention was admissible only where equivocation arose – i.e., to identify the subject matter or the person with the description in the will where the description is equally (though not completely) applicable in all its parts to two or more subject matters or two or more persons claiming to take: see Lord Cairns L.C. in *Charter* v. *Charter* (1874) L.R.7 H.L. 364 (p. 377); *In re Ray; Cant* v. *Johnstone* [1916] 1 Ch. 461 (p. 465) and *In re Julian* [1950] I.R. 57 (p. 62). In all other cases where extrinsic evidence was allowed, the evidence was purely factual in the sense that it was merely evidence of surrounding circumstances or the meaning of words. 'The procedure is not – first ascertain the surrounding circumstances and with that knowledge approach the construction of the will, but first construe the will; if the meaning is clear, surrounding circumstances cannot be looked at to throw a doubt upon that meaning, or to give the will a different meaning. . .' – Theobald on Wills, 13th ed., para. 427. If the words of the will were definite and free from doubt, parol evidence was not admissible to show that they meant something different. In *Hall* v. *Hill* (1841) 1 Dr. & War. 94,, Sugden L. C. said at p. 122 of the report: 'Now, I think that is the true rule, that if by construction you arrive at a conclusion, you cannot let in evidence for the purpose of contradicting it'.

This was the state of the law at the passing of the Succession Act, 1965. Section 90 of that Act is in the following terms:

'Extrinsic evidence shall be admissible to show the intention of the testator and to assist in the construction of, or to explain any contradiction in, a will.'

It is contended on behalf of the appellants that the words 'extrinsic evidence shall be admissible to show the intention of the testator' should be read disjunctively and interpreted widely and that, in consequence, the evidence of the solicitor who took the instructions of the testatrix and drafted the will should be admissible in relation to the intention of the testatrix. Therefore, it is necessary to consider precisely what extrinsic evidence is admissible under section 90.

Where evidence of intention was admissible at common law, declarations made by the testator before, after, and contemporaneously with the will were admissible. In *Doe d. Allen* v. *Allen* (1840) 12 Ad. & El. 451, Lord Denman C. J. giving the judgment of the court, said at p. 455 of the report: 'Cases are referred to in the books to shew that declarations contemporaneous with the will are alone to be received; but, on examination, none of them establish such a distinction. Neither has any argument been adduced which convinces us that those subsequent to the will ought to be excluded, wherever any evidence of declarations can be received'. And in *Langham* v. *Sandford* (1816) 19 Ves. 641. Eldon L.C. said at p. 649 of the report: 'It is unfortunate, but it is certainly settled, that declarations at the time of making the will, subsequent and previous to it, are all to be admitted: yet we know, that what men state as to their intentions may be conformable to the purpose at the time, but not afterwards: and declarations by a testator, after having made his will, are frequently made for the purpose, not of fairly representing, but of misrepresenting, what he has done'. These latter words, although written over 150 years ago, would seem to be very appropriate to conditions in Ireland today, where it is not unusual for testators to placate several relatives by telling them that they have been looked after in the will. If s. 90 is to be given the interpretation contended for by the appellants, I see no reason whatever why the same rule should not apply as applied at common law when extrinsic evidence was admitted, and why declarations by a testator made years before or after the making of the will should not be admissible. To hold otherwise would require reading into the section limitations that are not there.

In my opinion, however, this submission of the appellants is not well founded and s. 90 of the Act of 1965 should not be construed in the manner contended for, or in isolation. Section 90 is included in Part VII of the Act which deals exclusively with wills., Section 78 of the Act of 1965, which replaced s. 9 of the Wills Act, 1837, and s. 1 of the Wills Act Amendment Act, 1852, sets out in detail the formalities necessary for a valid will. If extrinsic evidence of the dispositive intention of a testator is to be admitted without qualification, the effect of this would be that a new will could be written for the testator, this will to be collected from the statements and declarations of the deceased at the time of, before, or after the making of the will, without compliance with the provisions of section 78. The effect of this would be to nullify those provisions and to render ineffective the safeguards provided therein.

In my view, on the correct construction of s. 90, extrinsic evidence is to be admitted only for the stated purpose of assisting in the construction of, or to explain any contradiction in, a will, and not for the purpose of replacing the dispositive intention of the testator as expressed in the will – for that would be outside the range of purpose permitted by the section.

If the construction of the will is clear, evidence cannot be adduced for the purpose of contradicting the terms of the will or writing a new will for the testator. The section was designed to ensure that, in the case of difficulties which arose in such cases as *In re Julian* [1950] I.R. 57, once the construction of the will is not clear then extrinsic evidence is to be admissible to assist in its construction. Similarly, where there is a contradiction in the will, extrinsic evidence is admissible to explain it. If this section had been in force when *In re Julian* was decided, then in my view that decision would have gone the other way.

In my opinion, therefore, Mr. Justice Kenny was correct in ruling that, once the construction of the will was quite clear, extrinsic evidence to show the dispositive intention of the testatrix was not admissible. Accordingly, I would dismiss this appeal.

Notes and Questions
1. Do you agree with the reasoning of the majority? Do you think the result accords with what the Oireachtas had in mind when section 90 was enacted, or, indeed, what the draftsmen of the section intended?
2. See also *Fitzpatrick* v. *Collins* Unreported (High Court) (1978 No. 4122 P).

II. SPOUSE'S LEGAL RIGHT AND PROVISION FOR CHILDREN
SUCCESSION ACT, 1965
PART IX

109. – (1) Where, after the commencement of this Act, a person dies wholly or partly testate leaving a spouse or children or both spouse and children, the provisions of this Part shall have effect.

(2) In this Part, references to the estate of the testator are to all estate to which he was beneficially entitled for an estate or interest not ceasing on his death and remaining after payment of all expenses, debts and liabilities, (other than estate duty), properly payable thereout.

110. – In deducing any relationship for the purposes of this Part, the provisions of the Legitimacy Act, 1931, and of section 26 of the Adoption Act, 1952, shall apply as they apply in relation to succession on intestacy.

111. – (1) If the testator leaves a spouse and no children, the spouse shall have a right to one-half of the estate.

(2) If the testator leaves a spouse and children, the spouse shall have a right to one-third of the estate.

112. – The right of a spouse under section 111 (which shall be known as a legal right) shall have priority over devises, bequests and shares of intestacy.

113. – The legal right of a spouse may be renounced in an ante-nuptial contract made in writing between the parties to an intended marriage or may be renounced in writing by the spouse after marriage and during the lifetime of the testator.

114. – (1) Where property is devised or bequeathed in a will to a spouse and the devise or bequest is expressed in the will to be in addition to the share as a legal right of the spouse, the testator shall be deemed to have made by the will a gift to the spouse consisting of –

(*a*) a sum equal to the value of the share as a legal right of the spouse, and

(*b*) the property so devised or bequeathed.

(2) In any case, a devise or bequest in a will to a spouse shall be deemed to have been intended by the testator to be in satisfaction of the share as a legal right of the spouse.

115. – (1)(*a*) Where, under the will of a deceased person who dies wholly testate, there is a devise or bequest to a spouse, the spouse may elect to take either that devise or bequest or the share to which he is entitled as a legal right.

(2)(*a*) Where a person dies partly testate and partly intestate, a spouse may elect to take either –

(i) his share as a legal right, or

(ii) his share under the intestacy, together with any devise or bequest to him under the will of the deceased,

(*b*) In default of election, the spouse shall be entitled to take his share under the intestacy, together with any devise or bequest to him under the will, and he shall not be entitled to take any share as a legal right.

(3) A spouse, in electing to take his share as a legal right, may further elect to take any devise or bequest to him less in value than the share in partial satisfaction thereon.

(4) It shall be the duty of the personal representatives to notify the spouse in writing of the right of election conferred by this section. The right shall not be exercisable after the expiration of six months from the receipt by the spouse of such notification or one year from the first taking out of representation of the deceased's estate, whichever is the later.

(5) Where the surviving spouse is a person of unsound mind, the right of election conferred by this section may, if there is a committee of the spouse's estate, be exercised on behalf of the spouse by the committee by leave of the court which has appointed the committee or, if there is no committee, be exercised by the High Court or, in a case within the jurisdiction of the Circuit Court, by that Court.

(6) In this section, but only in its application to a case to which subsection (1) of section 114 applies, 'devise or bequest' means a gift deemed under that subsection to have been made by the will of the testator.

116. – (1) Where a testator, during his lifetime, has made permanent provision for his spouse, whether under contract or otherwise, all property which is the subject of such provision (other than periodical payments made for her maintenance during his lifetime) shall be taken as being given in or towards satisfaction of the share as a legal right of the surviving spouse.

(2) The value of the property shall be reckoned as at the date of the making of the provision.

(3) If the value of the property is equal to or greater than the share of the spouse as a legal right, the spouse shall not be entitled to take any share as a legal right.

(4) If the value of the property is less than the share of the spouse as a legal right, the spouse shall be entitled to receive in satisfaction of such share so much only of the estate as, when added to the value of the property, is sufficient, as nearly as can be estimated, to make up the full amount of that share.

(5) This section shall apply only to a provision made before the commencement of this Act.

117. – (1) Where, on application by or on behalf of a child of a testator, the court is of opinion that the testator has failed in his moral duty to make proper provision for the child in accordance with his means, whether by his will or otherwise, the court may order that such provision shall be made for the child out of the estate as the court thinks just.

(2) The court shall consider the application from the point of view of a prudent and just parent, taking into account the position of each of the children of the testator and any other circumstances which the court may consider of assistance in arriving at a decision that will be as fair as possible to the child to whom the application relates and to the other children.

(3) An order under this section shall not affect the legal right of a surviving spouse or, if the surviving spouse is the mother or father of the child, any devise or bequest to the spouse or any share to which the spouse is entitled on intestacy.

(4) Rules of court shall provide for the conduct of proceedings under this section in a summary manner.

(5) The costs in the proceedings shall be at the discretion of the court.

(6) An order under this section shall not be made except on an application made within twelve months from the first taking out of representation of the deceased's estate.

118. – Property representing the share of a person as a legal right and property which is the subject of an order under section 117 shall bear their due proportions of the estate duty payable on the estate of the deceased.

119. – All proceedings in relation to this Part shall be heard in chambers.

. . .

56. – (1) Where the estate of a deceased person includes a dwelling in which, at the time of the deceased's death, the surviving spouse was ordinarily resident, the surviving spouse may, subject to subsection (5), require the personal representatives in writing to appropriate the dwelling under section 55 in or towards satisfaction of any share of the surviving spouse.

(2) The surviving spouse may also require the personal representatives in writing to appropriate any household chattels in or towards satisfaction of any share of the surviving spouse.

(3) If the share of a surviving spouse is insufficient to enable an appropriation to be made under subsection (1) or (2), as the case may be, the right conferred by the relevant subsection may also be exercised in relation to the share of any infant for whom the surviving spouse is a trustee under section 57 or otherwise.

(4) It shall be the duty of the personal representatives to notify the surviving spouse in writing of the rights conferred by this section.

(5) A right conferred by this section shall not be exercisable –

    (*a*) after the expiration of six months from the receipt by the surviving spouse of such notification or one year from the first taking out of representation of the deceased's estate, whichever is the later, or

    (*b*) in relation to a dwelling, in any of the cases mentioned in subsection (6), unless the court, on application made by the personal representatives or the surviving spouse, is satisfied that the exercise of that right is unlikely to diminish the value of the assets of the deceased, other than the dwelling, or to make it more difficult to dispose of them in due course of administration and authorises its exercise.

(6) Paragraph (*b*) of subsection (5) and paragraph (*d*) of subsection (10) apply to the following cases:

    (*a*) where the dwelling forms part of a building, and an estate or interest in the whole building forms part of the estate;

    (*b*) where the dwelling is held with agricultural land an estate or interest in which forms part of the estate;

(*c*) where the whole or a part of the dwelling was, at the time of the death, used as a hotel, guest house or boarding house;

(*d*) where a part of the dwelling was, at the time of the death, used for purposes other than domestic purposes.

(7) Nothing in subsection (12) of section 55 shall prevent the personal representatives from giving effect to the rights conferred by this section.

(8)(*a*) So long as a right conferred by this section continues to be exercisable, the personal representatives shall not, without the written consent of the surviving spouse or the leave of the court given on the refusal of an application under paragraph (*b*) of subsection (5), sell or otherwise dispose of the dwelling or household chattels except in the course of administration owing to want of other assets.

(*b*) This subsection shall not apply where the surviving spouse is a personal representative.

(*c*) Nothing in this subsection shall confer any right on the surviving spouse against a purchaser from the personal representatives.

(9) The rights conferred by this section on a surviving spouse include a right to require apropriation partly in satisfaction of a share in the deceased's estate and partly in return for a payment of money by the surviving spouse on the spouse's own behalf and also on behalf of any infant for whom the spouse is a trustee under section 57 or otherwise.

(10)(*a*) In addition to the rights to require appropriation conferred by this section, the surviving spouse may, so long as a right conferred by this section continues to be exercisable, apply to the court for appropriation on the spouse's own behalf and also on behalf of any infant for whom the spouse is a trustee under section 57 or otherwise.

(*b*) On any such application, the court may, if of opinion that, in the special circumstances of the case, hardship would otherwise be caused to the surviving spouse or to the surviving spouse and any such infant, order that appropriation to the spouse shall be made without the payment of money provided for in subsection (9) or subject to the payment of such amount as the court considers reasonable.

(*c*) The court may make such further order in relation to the administration of the deceased's estate as may appear to the court to be just and equitable having regard to the provisions of this Act and to all the circumstances.

(*d*) The court shall not make an order under this subsection in relation to a dwelling in any of the cases mentioned in subsection (6), unless it is satisfied that the order would be unlikely to diminish the value of the assets of the deceased, other than the dwelling, or to make it more difficult to dispose of them in due course of administration.

(11) All proceedings in relation to this section shall be heard in chambers.

(12) Where the surviving spouse is a person of unsound mind, a requirement or consent under this section may, if there is a committee of the spouse's estate, be made or given on behalf of the spouse by the committee by leave of the court which has appointed the committee or, if there is no committee, be given or made by the High Court or, in a case within the jurisdiction of the Circuit Court, by that Court.

(13) An appropriation to which this section applies shall for the purposes of succession duty be deemed to be a succession derived from the deceased.

(14) In this section –

'dwelling' means an estate or interest in a building occupied as a separate dwelling or a part, so occupied, of any building and includes any garden or portion of ground attached to and usually occupied with the dwelling or otherwise required for the amenity or convenience of the dwelling;

'household chattels' means furniture, linen, china, glass, books and other chattels of ordinary household use or ornament and also consumable stores, garden effects and domestic animals, but does not include any chattels used at the death of the deceased for business or professional purposes or money or security for money.

RE URQUHART
[1974] I.R. 197 (Supreme Court)

A wife having bequeathed by her will a legacy to her husband on condition that he should survive her for a month; she was not survived by any children of her marriage. Her husband survived her by one day and then died without having made an election pursuant to s. 115 of the Act of 1965, so that the husband's estate was not benefited by a legal right or by the legacy. In these circumstances the plaintiffs claimed that a half share in his wife's estate was property of which the husband was competent to dispose at the time of his death for the purpose of the Finance Act, 1894.

Kenny J. upheld this claim and the husband's executors appealed to the Supreme Court.

Fitzgerald C.J.:

This appeal arises from a claim for estate duty made by the plaintiffs against the defendants who are the executors of Douglas D. Urquhart, deceased. The claim arises in the following circumstances. Douglas D. Urquhart died on the 5th May, 1969, and his wife, Kathleen Mary Urquhart, died on the 4th May, 1969. The husband was unconscious at the time of his wife's death and did not subsequently recover consciousness; up to the time of his death, he was unaware that his wife had predeceased him.

The wife made her last will on the 6th April, 1967, whereby she appointed the defendants to be her executors and trustees. By clause 3 of her will she provided that, if the husband survived her for the space of one calendar month, she gave him all her personal belongings and household furnishings and effects, and the sum of £15,000. She made further bequests, including a bequest of the residue of her estate. By clause 4 of her will it was provided that, in the event of her husband not surviving her by the said period of one calendar month, her property (including the residue) should be disposed of as provided for in the said clause. As the husband failed to survive the wife for the calendar month, clause 3 of her will was inoperative, and her property falls to be divided in accordance with clause 45 subject to the husband's right, if any, arising under the provisions of the Succession Act, 1965. The assets of the wife have been valued at £95,000.

The husband made his own will on the same day as his wife (6th April, 1967) in similar terms to that made by his wife, in that it was subject to the proviso that she took a benefit under his will if, and only if, she survived him by a calendar month. His assets were considerbly less than his wife's. There were no children of the marriage.

The plaintiffs' claim is for a declaration that one-half of the estate of the wife was property of which the husband was 'competent to dispose' within the meaning of the Finance Act, 1894, and for the orders which would follow such a declaration. In the events which have happened, the claim is that the estate of the husband is liable for estate duty on his 'right' to half his wife's assets, in addition to the estate duty for which it is liable as his own estate in possession. Prior to the enactment of the Succession Act, 1965, there would have been no duty payable in respect of the property which is the subject of the plaintiffs' claim as, in the events which happened, the husband would have received no benefit under his wife's will. However, it is submitted on behalf of the plaintiffs that under the provisions of the Act of 1965 the husband had a 'right' to half his wife's estate; and they submit that by virtue of s. 2, sub-s. 1 (a), of the Act of 1894 he was 'competent to dispose' of the half share which thus became part of his assets for the purpose of calculating the estate duty.

The relevant sections of the Act of 1965 would appear to be s. 111 and the immediately following sections in Part IX of the Act which deals with the legal rights of a testator's spouse and the legal rights of children. The Act of 1965 made a number of changes in the law in relation to the functions and duties of executors, the devolution of the estates of intestates and the administration of their assets. The material part of the Act in this case is Part IX. That part of the Act commences at s. 109 and has the effect of limiting the right of a testator to disinherit his spouse or his children. Section 111, sub-s. 1, provides that, where a testator leaves a spouse and no children, the spouse shall have the right to one-half of the estate. Sub-section 2 of s. 111 provides that, where a testator leaves a spouse and children, the spouse shall have a right to one-third of the estate. Section 112 provides that the right of a spouse, created by s. 111, shall have priority over devises, bequests and shares on intestacy. [*The Chief Justice referred to sub-ss.* 1, 4 *and* 5 *of s.* 115 *of the Act of* 1965, *and continued*] There can be no doubt but that the husband had a legal right to half his wife's estate if he elected to take it rather than the bequest to him in his wife's will. However, he would have to exercise his election within the period specified in sub-s. 4 of section 115. In fact the husband was never notified by the executors of his right, and he never elected. In the events which happened, he never became entitled to any share of his wife's estate under her will.

It was contended on behalf of the plaintiffs that liability to estate duty arises by virtue of s. 2, sub-s. 1 (a), of the finance Act, 1894, which provides that: 'Property passing on the death of the deceased shall be deemed to include the property following, that is to say: (a) Property of which the deceased was at the time of his death competent to dispose'. This raises the question as to whether the half-share in the wife's estate, which the husband could have elected to claim as his legal right, was property of which the husband was competent to dispose. In my opinion, the husband's right to establish and receive a half-share of his wife's estate depended upon a number of factors under the Act of 1965. First, it depended upon him surviving his wife. Secondly, it depended upon him becoming aware of the fact that he had survived her. Thirdly, it depended upon the husband then deciding to claim the half-share within the time prescribed. In point of fact, he did survive his wife but he never knew it. Consequently, he was never in a position to decide whether he would elect to claim his right to half his wife's estate or not. In those circumstances, it appears to me that he could not be deemed competent to dispose of the half-share. I am fortified in this opinion by the provisions of s. 115, sub-ss. 4 and 5, of the Act of 1965 which specifically provide for a case where the surviving spouse is of unsound mind and, consequently, not in a position to exercise the election himself.

The plaintiffs placed reliance on the decision of Luxmore J. in *Penrose* v. *Penrose* ([1933] Ch. 793) and on *Parsons* v. *The Attorney General* ([1943] Ch. 12) which was a decision of the English Court of Appeal. In *Penrose's Case* ([1933] Ch. 793), a married woman, by her will, bequeathed and devised her real and personal estate to trustees upon trust to pay the income therefrom to her husband for his life, and upon his death to such persons of a certain class as the husband should by deed or will appoint. The husband survived his wife and by deed appointed a portion of the residuary estate to himself, being one of the class of persons to whom he could appoint. This appointment was valid; he could have appointed the whole of the residue to himself, and not merely a part of it. In those circumstances, it was hardly surprising that the learned judge held that he was competent to dispose of the residue. In point of fact, the case appears to have been appealed and then settled.

In *Parsons' Case* ([1943] Ch. 12) a testatrix gave a legacy of £10,000 to her husband absolutely, and she gave the income of her residuary estate on trust for her husband for life, and after his death on trust for her son absolutely. The husband disclaimed the legacy by a formal deed of disclaimer and the legacy fell into the residue. On the husband's death, the revenue authorities claimed estate duty in respect of the legacy on the ground that, although the husband had disclaimed the legacy, he was competent to dispose of it and the liability for duty was not excluded by s. 52 of the Finance Act, 1894. It was held by the Court of Appeal that during the period between the death of the testatrix and the date of the disclaimer the husband was competent to dispose of the legacy within the meaning of s. 5, sub-s. 2, of the Act of 1894, and that estate duty was payable. On its particular facts, the decision was clearly correct. The surviving husband was in a position to accept or reject the legacy. He was aware of the position and, in point of fact, he decided to disclaim. Those circumstances are very different from those existing in the present case, where the husband never knew that he had survived his wife and that he was in a position, or would be in a position, to elect whether to claim his rights under the Act of 1965 or not.

In my opinion, this action by the plaintiffs is misconceived. The action should have been dismissed; the appeal should be allowed and the order of the High Court set aside.

Walsh J.:

The late Mrs. Kathleen Urquhart died on the 4th May, 1969. She was survived by her husband, Douglas Urquhart, who died on the 5th May, 1969. The wife and her husband were domiciled within the jurisdiction.

The wife made her last will and testament on the 6th April, 1967, and appointed the defendants to be executors and trustees of her will. By paragraph 3 of her will she expressly provided as follows:

'3. If my husband Douglas David Urquhart shall survive me for the space of one calendar month then but not otherwise I make the following dispositions of my property.
(a) To Walter Philip Tappin and his wife Daphne Mary Tappin of The Pines, Sandy Lane, Cobham, Surrey, the sum of £2,000 in equal shares. If either of the legatees predecease me then the said legacy is to be paid to the survivor of them, and in the event of both predeceasing me then said legacy is to be paid in equal shares to their children living at the date of my death.
(b) I give to my husband all my personal belongings and household furniture and effects together with the sum of fifteen thousand pounds.'

By paragraph 4 of her will the wife provided as follows: 'If my said husband shall not survive me for the period aforesaid then and in that case I direct and declare that the following dispositions of my property in this clause No. 4 contained shall take effect but that otherwise this clause No. 4 shall be null and void.'

There followed then a disposition of her property to a number of her relatives. On the same date (6th April, 1967) her husband, Douglas Urquhart, made a will in similar terms relating to his wife. The husband died unaware of his wife's death; he had been unconscious for a period including the time of the death of his wife to the time of his own death. The husband and his wife died leaving no children. The value of the estate of the wife for the purpose of estate duty amounted to approximately £95,000.

The present case has arisen out of the claim for estate duty in respect of the estate of the husband. The defendants delivered an estate-duty affidavit dated the 20th

June, 1969, in the estate of the husband; but they did not include in it any share of the husband by way of legal right in the estate of his predeceased wife. When the question was raised by the plaintiffs, the defendants contended that nothing vested in the husband by reason of the death of his wife and that no property passed on his death under that head. The contention of the plaintiffs was that, by virtue of the provisions of s. 111, sub-s. 1, of the Succession Act, 1965, the husband was entitled as of right to a half share in his deceased wife's free estate. The expression 'free estate' apparently was intended to refer to the estate left after the discharge of the costs and expenses of administration. The plaintiffs claimed that by virtue of s. 118 of the Act of 1965 the half share of the wife's estate bore its due proportion of the estate duty paid on the wife's estate. The defendants disputed the claim on the ground that the husband had never elected to take the legal right in his wife's estate under s. 115 of the Act of 1965 and that, therefore, he was not entitled to any share of the estate or to any benefit under the will.

[*The judge referred to the provisions of s. 115, sub-s. 1, of the Act of 1965, and continued*] It is claimed by the defendants that s. 115, sub-s. 1 (b), of the Act of 1965 had the effect of confining the husband to his rights under the will of his wife because he did not make an election under the section. It is further claimed that the gift to him under the will lapsed as he did not survive his wife by a month. The opposing contention of the plaintiffs is that, where a testator dies leaving a spouse and no children, the effect of s. 111 of the Act of 1965 is that the spouse's right to one-half of the estate is a vested right which takes effect immediately and continues to be effective unless divested by an election made under s. 115 within the period set out in sub-s. 4 of that section. It was submitted on behalf of the plaintiffs that, as he had died without making any such election, the husband at the date of his death was competent to dispose of the half-share of his wife's estate for the purposes of s. 2, sub-s. 1 (a), of the Finance Act, 1894, and that on his death estate duty was payable on this as part of his own estate.

The matter came before Mr. Justice Kenny for decision upon a special summons and he made a declaration to the effect that one-half of the estate of the wife was property of which the husband was competent to dispose at the time of his death within the meaning of the Act of 1894. Against this decision the defendants have taken this appeal.

The Act of 1965 brought about a revolutionary change in the law of succession in this State. Prior to the enactment of this statute, the law of succession in respect of property which passed as personal property in the case of intestacy was determined by the provisions of the (Irish) Statute of Distribution, 1695, and the Intestate Estates Act, 1954. A person who died testate since the coming into operation of the Statute of 1695 could deal with his property as he thought fit. The effect of the Act of 1954 was to give the widow of a man dying intestate and without issue a first charge of £4,000 on his realty and personalty. Prior to the enactment of the Statute of 1695 there was not complete freedom of testamentary disposition. The law was governed by what was called the 'custom of Ireland' which was abolished by s. 10 of the Statute of 1695. By the custom of Ireland only one-third of the personal estate of a deceased person, or a moiety of his personal estate was available for disposition by will. The custom of Ireland is set out in s. 10 of the Statute of 1695 in the following words: 'And whereas it has been held, that there is a certain custom within this kingdom of Ireland to the effect following, that is to say, that if any person dye possessed of or entitled to any goods, things in action, or personal estate whatsoever; and having at the time of his death, a wife, or child, or children, that in such case all the said estate is to be divided into three equal parts, whereof one third part belongs to the wife, another to the child or children, and the other third part only to be subject to the disposition of the party deceased by his last will or testament, in case he make any, or to go in a course of administration in case he dye intestate; and if he leave a wife only, and no child or children, then the said estate to be divided into two parts, whereof the one moiety to go to the wife, and the other moiety only to be subject to his disposition by will as aforesaid, otherwise to go in a course of administration in case he dye intestate; and so in like manner if he shall leave a child or children, and no wife. . . .' The section then goes on to enact as follows: '. . . .now it is hereby declared, that the said custom shall from henceforth be absolutely null and void to all intents and purposes whatsoever, and shall not be taken to be in force, or to be binding to any person or persons whatsoever.'

Part II of the Act of 1965 went a considerable distance in abolishing the difference between real and personal estate for practical purposes. Section 10 of the Act of 1965 provides that all property, real and personal, shall devolve on the personal representatives. Section 11 provides for the abolition of primo geniture, dower, tenancy by the curtesy and all then existing rules, modes and canons of descent and of devolution by special occupancy, except in so far as they apply to the descent of an estate tail. Escheat to the State and escheat to a mesne lord for want of heirs was also abolished. Section 12 confers on the personal representatives the same powers over real estate as they had over personal estate. Section 13 provides that where a person dies intestate, or dies testate but leaves no executor surviving him, his real and personal estate until administration is granted in respect of it shall vest in the President of the High Court, who for that purpose shall be a corporation sole. Section 14 provides that in the subsequent provisions of the Act and in any subsequent enactment a reference to the estate of a deceased person shall include, unless the contrary intention appears, a reference to both the real and personal estate of that deceased person. It is clear that s. 111 of the Act of 1965 operates in respect of the real and personal estate. The reference to a testator leaving a spouse and no children, in which case the spouse would have a right to one-half of the estate, is reminiscent of the custom of Ireland which was abolished by s. 10 of the Statute of 1695. It is clear from s. 10 of the Statute of 1695 that in such a case the wife was entitled as of right to one moiety of the estate.

The questions which arise for decision in this case, in so far as s. 111 of the Act of 1965 is concerned, is whether one-half of the estate goes to the surviving spouse as of right or whether by virtue of the provisions of s. 115 of the Act of 1965 the joint effect of the provisions, in a case where there has been a devise or bequest, is to confer on the surviving spouse simply a right to claim one-half of the estate as distinct from a right to take one-half of the estate. In effect, the defendants' argument is based upon the former interpretation. The wording of s. 111, sub-s. 1, of the Act of 1965 says clearly that what the surviving spouse has is 'a right to one-half of the estate'.

Section 46, sub-s. 3, of that Act provides as follows: 'Where the estate of a deceased person is solvent, it shall, subject to rules of court and the provisions hereinafter contained as to charges on property of the deceased, and to the provisions, if any, contained in his will, be applicable towards the discharge of the funeral, testamentary and administration expenses, debts and liabilities and any legal right in the order mentioned in Part II of the First Schedule'. Sub-section 4 of s. 46 provides that nothing in sub-s. 3 'affects the rights of any creditor of the deceased or the legal right of a spouse'. Sub-section 5 makes provision for persons entitled under a will or intestacy to have assets marshalled where a creditor or spouse entitled to a legal right applies an asset in the wrong order. The beneficiary whose property is being taken by the creditor or by the spouse will stand in the place of the creditor or spouse '*pro tanto* as against any property that, in the said order, is liable before his own estate or interest'. Sub-section 6 provides that 'a claim to a share as a legal right or on intestacy in the estate of a deceased person is a claim against the assets of the estate to a sum equal to the value of that share'. The effect of this section is to make the legal right a debt due by the estate.

Section 115, sub-s. 4, of the Act of 1965 casts upon the personal representative the duty to notify the surviving spouse in writing 'of the right of election conferred by this section'. It goes on to say that the right shall not be exercisable after the expiration of six months from the receipt by the spouse of such notification or one year from the first taking out of representation of the deceased's estate, whichever is the later. The 'right of election' mentioned in sub-s. 4 is a reference to the provisions of sub-s. 1 (a) of section 115.

The provisions of s. 115 must be read in the light of s. 114, which provides that, where a testamentary gift to a spouse is expressed to be in addition to the share as a legal right of the spouse, that share shall be deemed to have been devised or bequeathed under the will in addition to the express devise or bequest already contained in the will. In any other case a devise or bequest in a will to a spouse shall be deemed to have been intended by the testator to have been made in satisfaction of the share as a legal right of the spouse. In the latter event, of course, the right of election under s. 115 arises. Section 113 enables the legal right of a spouse to be renounced in an ante-nuptial contract made in writing between the parties to an intended marriage, or to be renounced in writing by the spouse after marriage and during the lifetime of the testator. Section 112 provides that the right of a spouse under s. 111 (to the legal right) shall have priority over devises, bequests and shares on intestacy.

In my opinion, the whole of this structure presupposes and is based on an assumption implicit in the statute, in addition to what is expressly stated in s. 111, that a legal right arises on the moment of the death of the testator. Where there is no legacy or devise or where there is a legacy or a devise expressed to be in addition to the legal share, the legal share vests upon the death. But when a testator in his will makes a devise or bequest to a spouse and it is not expressed to be in addition to the share as a legal right, then the spouse has a statutory right to take the share as a legal right – but that share does not vest until he takes it. If the spouse does not take the share as a legal right, then the legacy or devise under the will which vested in the spouse at the death of the testator will remain vested in the spouse without his taking any step in relation to it. The spouse can never have both. This result flows from the joint effect of s. 114, sub-s. 2, and section 115.

The right to take the legal share requires a 'taking' to vest the share in the spouse. It may be an actual taking, as by an express election to take it instead of the legacy, or it may be a constructive taking by dealing with the legal share in a manner which is inconsistent with any explanation other than that the spouse, in so dealing with it, has elected not to take the legacy. It appears to me, therefore, that the spouse is not competent to dispose of the legal share until either he has made a formal election or has dealt with it in a way such as I have just described. In effect, that means that actual disposition of the share by the spouse may amount not only to such disposition but it may also be the very act which in itself is the first 'taking' of the share and which for the first time puts the spouse in the position where he can be said to be competent to dispose of it. I think that in a case falling within s. 115 of the Act of 1965 the essential differences between the legacy and the legal right is that in respect of the legacy there is nothing the legatee has to do to make it his own, whereas in respect of the share as a legal right there is something the spouse has to do to make it his own: to state it succinctly, if the spouse does not take it he does not get it.

Therefore, the right to take the legal share is not exercisable at all until something is done, within the period specified in sub-s. 4 of s. 115, which amounts to an election not to take the legacy. If the death of the spouse takes place before such election is made, then the legal share does not form part of the spouse's estate because the spouse had done nothing before death to take the share as a legal right. I think this view is borne out by the terms of sub-s. 5 of s. 115 which provide that even in the case of the surviving spouse being a person of unsound mind the right of election must be exercised either by the committee or, where there is no committee, by the High Court or the Circuit Court as the case may be. Failure of any of these bodies to act will result in a position where the legal right, which the surviving spouse had been entitled to take, had not in fact been taken.

In my view, the true construction of s. 115 of the Act of 1965, in the light of the other sections, is that the surviving spouse is entitled to take the share as a legal right referred to in s. 111, but that it must be taken. Where there is no 'taking' of the property there is no competence to dispose of it though, for the reasons I have given, actual disposition may in itself be sufficient evidence of election.

What the husband had immediately before his death was a statutory right to take the property in question. In so far as that right itself could be said to be 'property', it ceased upon his death and therefore could not be subject to a claim for estate duty. Furthermore, it was a right which was exercisable only in his own favour. The claim made for duty in the present case has been not in respect of the value, if any, of the right as such but in respect of the property which the husband could have obtained if he had elected to take the property. The plaintiffs have relied upon the decision of Luxmoore J. in *Penrose* v. *Penrose* ([1933] Ch. 793) and have endeavoured to equate the statutory right in the present case with the general power of appointment which was the subject matter of that particular case. In that case the deceased was himself one of the objects of the power and appointed to himself. It was held that he was a person 'competent to dispose' within the meaning of s. 5, sub-s. 2, of the Finance Act, 1894. It was sought to argue in that case on behalf of the estate that as the testator had appointed the whole of the property to himself he had simply acquired it but had not disposed of it, and that his power to dispose of it did not arise under the power but after he had exercised it in his own favour. It was held there that the donee of a power who could freely appoint the whole of the fund to himself and so acquire the right to dispose of the fund in accordance with his own volition was competent to dispose of that fund as he thought fit, and that it made no difference that it could only be done by two steps instead of one, namely, by an appointment to himself followed by a subsequent gift or disposition instead of by a direct appointment to the object or objects to which it might finally be given. It was held that if under a power the donee could make the whole of the property subject to it his own, he could by exercising the power in his own favour place himself in the position to dispose of it as he thought fit, and that the power to dispose is a necessary incident of the power to acquire the property in question.

[*The judge referred to the provisions of s. 22, sub-s. 2 (a), of the Finance Act, 1894, and continued*:] The deceased in the present case clearly had no interest or estate in the property but simply a statutory right to take it if he chose to do so. The plaintiffs therefore rely upon the reference to 'such general power' as covering the present case.

The *Penrose Case* ([1933] Ch. 793) dealt with a rather complicated settlement and was one to which s. 5, sub-s. 2, of the Act of 1894 applied. The present case falls within s. 2 of the Act of 1894. In the *Penrose Case* ([1933] Ch. 793) the person who had the power of appointment which he could exercise in his own favour had in fact exercised it. I cannot accept the decision as an authority which should be followed for the general proposition that, if at the time of death the deceased possessed the ability to make property his own by exercising an option or an election, the property must be deemed to pass on his death whatever his wishes or actions in the matter. In so far as any part of the judgment in that case appears to support that proposition it is *obiter* only. To adopt that view, for which the *Penrose Case* ([1933] Ch. 793) was stated to be an authority, would be to hold that under the provisions of the Act of 1965 a person who was entitled to a legal right, and who elected expressly not to accept it, could be held to have been competent to dispose of the property; and that he had in fact disposed of it by refusing to take it. It would also appear to lead, inevitably to the conclusion, absurd though it is, that a spouse who died within the period for election without electing might be charged estate duty on both the share to which he or she was entitled as a legal right and on any legacy or devise because the latter vests immediately upon death; and this would be so although the Act of 1965 expressly provides that the surviving spouse cannot have both.

In my view, the provisions of s. 2 and the particular definition of 'competent to dispose' in s. 22, sub-s. 2 (a), of the Act of 1894 never contemplated that estate duty would be payable in respect of property which a person could obtain by exercising an election and foregoing a testamentary disposition where the property did not pass by the will and where no such election was ever made. The position of the husband in the present case cannot be compared with that of a person to whom a gift has been made by a will and who later chooses to disclaim it; in that situation the legatee, until he disclaims, has from the moment of the death of the testator a full right to dispose of the gift. In such a case a legatee who dies before disclaiming will benefit his estate because his executors or personal representatives can claim the legacy he has not disclaimed. In a case such as the present one, if no election is made then no right becomes vested; and if the election is not made within the statutory time during the lifetime of the person entitled thereto nothing is acquired; and if the person should die before making the election the right of election or the benefit of such an election does not pass to the executors or personal representatives.

At best the legal share provided by the Act of 1965 can be described as a statutory offer which is not binding upon the surviving spouse until it is accepted. The mere ability to make a thing one's own is not sufficient to attract estate duty and the use of such a phrase by Lord Greene M.R. in *Parsons* v. *The Attorney General* ([1943] Ch. 12, 15) must be read in the context in which it appears. In that case a surviving spouse who had been left £10,000 in stock subsequently disclaimed by a deed the benefit of the settlement or bequest; it was held that, notwithstanding the disclaimer, he had during the continuance of the settlement been competent to dispose of the property within the meaning of s. 5, sub-s. 2, of the Act of 1894. It is in that context that Lord Greene's remark must be read, particularly as it is followed by a sentence which reads: 'From the moment of the testatrix's death the husband was able to make the legacy his own.'

For these reasons I am of opinion that at the date of his death the husband, Douglas Urquhart, was entitled to take the half share of his wife's estate as a legal right but that, as he did not do so before his death, it was not property which he was competent to dispose of within the meaning of s. 22, sub-s. 2 (a), of the Act of 1894.

Henchy J.:

The husband, as the surviving spouse, not having been disqualified by any provision in Part IX of the Succession Act, 1965, was entitled under the provisions of s. 115, sub-s. 1 (a), of that Act to elect to take either the bequest in his wife's will or the one-half share in her estate to which he was entitled as a legal right. Since the bequest in the will was conditional on his surviving his wife by one calendar month and, in any event, was of much less value than half her estate, he would no doubt have elected for the legal right. However, he was unconscious when his wife died; and he died a day later without recovering consciousness. In those circumstances, s. 115, sub-s. 1 (b), of the Act of 1965 operated to confine him to his rights under the will, because he did not make an election. But under the will, because he did not survive his wife by a month, the bequest to him lapsed. Therefore, the wife's estate devolved to the persons specified in clause 4 of her will. No argument has been put forward to suggest that the devolution of the wife's estate was otherwise.

The question giving rise to this litigation is whether, as the husband did not elect to take the legal right in lieu of the bequest in the will, estate duty is payable on the amount of the legal right. Therefore, the case falls to be decided on the interpretation of the Finance Act, 1894, a well as the Succession Act, 1965.

Under the Finance Act, 1894, property passing on death is made subject to estate duty. Section 2, sub-s. 1, of the Act of 1894 provides that property of which the deceased at the time of his death, was competent to dispose is deemed to pass on his death. Section 22, sub-s. 2 (a), of the Act of 1894 further provides that a person is deemed competent to dispose of property if he has such an estate or interest in it, or such a power or authority, as would, if he were *sui juris*, enable him to dispose of it as he thinks fit. The plaintiffs contend that estate duty is payable on the amount of the legal right because, although the husband had not elected to take it, he was competent (if only his health had allowed) to dispose of it. The contention of counsel for the defendants, who are the husband's executors, is that he had not acquired a power to dispose of the legal right because an election by him to take it was a condition precedent to the acquisition by him of the legal right.

As far as spouses are concerned, the primary purpose of Part IX of the Act of 1965 is to ensure that (save in the excepted cases) the surviving spouse shall have a legal right to one-half of the estate if there are no children and to one-third if there are children, notwithstanding any testamentary disposition to the contrary. This right is established by Section 111. Section 114 of the Act of 1965 gives a statutory construction to the will of the deceased spouse by providing that, where the will of the deceased spouse by providing that, where the will expresses a devise or bequest to be in addition to the legal right, the will is to be construed as giving both the devise or bequest and the legal right; in the absence of such an expressed intention in a will, a devise or bequest is to be deemed to have been intended to be in satisfaction of the legal right.

Section 115, sub-s. 1, of the Act of 1965 gives the surviving spouse the choice of taking *either* what has been given by the will *or* the one-half or one-third to which he is entitled as a legal right. The election as to which he will take must be made within the time specified in sub-s. 4 of section 115. Sub-section 1 (b) of s. 115 enacts that, in default of election, the surviving spouse will be entitled only to what was given by the will and not to the share representing the legal right. Unless and until an election is made by the surviving spouse within the specified period, the choice of taking either the devise or bequest under the will or the one-half or one-third share (as the case may be) remains open to him as a personal option. No particular formality is prescribed for the making of an election, so it will be a question of fact in each case whether, by words, writing, or other conduct, the spouse has made an unambiguous decision to opt for one or other of the two mutually exclusive benefits open to him.

Such being the law, can it be said that the surviving spouse in the present case, having died the day after his wife's death without having elected to take the one-half share of her estate for which he could (health considerations apart) have elected, was competent to dispose of that one-half share for the purposes of the Finance Act, 1894? Section 22, sub-s. 2 (a), of the Act of 1894 gives the words 'competent to dispose' a specialised connotation by providing that they shall include 'every power or authority enabling the donee or other holder thereof to appoint or dispose of property as he thinks fit' exclusive of powers exercisable in a fiduciary capacity of the kind set out in the sub-section. Therefore, for the estate of the husband in the present case to be liable for estate duty on the one-half share of the wife's estate, it is not necessary for the plaintiffs to show that he had acquired any estate or interest in it. It is sufficient if they can show that he had a power or authority to dispose of it as he thought fit.

The argument of counsel for the defendants is that such power or authority never vested in the husband because, before it could vest in him, it was necessary for him to elect to take the one-half share. It is said that such election – which, admittedly, he never made – was a condition precedent to the acquisition by him of a power or authority to dispose of the one-half share. I readily accept than an election by the husband to take the one-half share was necessary to validate a disposition of it by him. But I do not accept that the election was a condition precedent to the existence of a competency to dispose. I see no reason why the election and the disposition could not have coalesced in one legal act. For example, in a single sentence in a will (such as: 'I will to A.B. the one-half share in my wife's estate to which I am entitled under the Succession Act, 1965') he could have elected to take the one-half share and also made a valid disposition of it. But even if it be said that in such an act two steps are necessary to effect a transfer of ownership (i.e., the election and the testamentary disposition), it would not take from the fact that he had a power of disposition. Once he had the power to make the property his own (as he undoubtedly had) he also had the power to dispose of it. All that stood between him and the exercise of that power was his state of health, and it is agreed that that is an irrelevant consideration for the purposes of this case.

That this is the effect of s. 22, sub-s. 2 (a), of the Act of 1894 has, as far as I know, been unquestioned since the decision in *Penrose* v. *Penrose* ([1933] Ch. 793). In that case a husband had a power of appointment over certain property under his wife's will in favour of a class which included himself, and the issue was whether estate duty was payable on his death in respect of that property. It was held that, since he could have exercised the power of appointment so as to vest the property in himself, he had power to dispose of it and estate duty was therefore payable on it. Dealing with the argument (similar to that made in the present case) that what the husband had was a power to acquire the property rather than a power to dispose of it, Luxmoore J. said at pp. 807–8 of the report: 'It is argued that the power in the present case is a limited power and does not authorize the donee to appoint or dispose of the property subject to it as he thinks fit. It is said that if he appoints to himself he only acquires the property but does not dispose of it, and that his power to dispose of it as he thinks fit does not arise under the power but after he has exercised it in his own favour. In my judgment this is too narrow a construction to place on the words of the definition. A donee of a power who can freely appoint the whole of the fund to himself and so acquire the right to dispose of the fund in accordance with his own volition, is, in my judgment, competent to dispose of that fund as he thinks fit, and it can make no difference that this can only be done by two steps instead of by one – namely, by an appointment to himself, followed by a subsequent gift or disposition, instead of by a direct appointment to the object or objects of his bounty. If under a power the donee can make the whole of the property subject to it his own, he can by exercising the power in his own favour place himself in the position to dispose of it as he thinks fit. The power to dispose is a necessary incident of the power to acquire the property in question.

Therefore, the question in the present case is to be solved by deciding what property the husband was competent at the date of his death to dispose of as he thought fit. As to the bequest to him under the wife's will, he was incompetent to dispose of that, for the effectiveness of that bequest was conditional on his surviving his wife by one month. So if he had made a deed or will purporting to dispose of it, no property would have passed. All he had was a contingent right to the property bequeathed to him, and his death wiped out that right. But as to the one-half share in his wife's estate to which he was entitled under the Act as a legal right, if at the date of his death he had made a deed or a will disposing of that one-half share to somebody, that person would have got a perfectly good title. Leaving aside the husband's health (which counsel for the defendants concedes to be irrelevant for the purpose of this case), the husband's legal capacity to make such a disposition could not be successfully impugned. He was therefore 'competent to dispose' of it in the sense in which those words are defined in s. 22, sub-s. 2 (a), of the Act of 1894 as including 'every power or authority enabling the donee or other holder thereof to appoint or dispose of property as he thinks fit.' If the husband had made a deed or will alienating the one-half share to somebody he would be validly exercising a competency to dispose of it no less effectively than if he had exercised a general power of appointment over it that had been vested in him.

The result is that the one-half share of the wife's estate fell within the reach of the Act of 1894 for the purpose of estate duty. This means that the husband's estate is burdened with estate duty on property that was never part of that estate. However, such an artificial basis for the incidence of estate duty has been part of our law since the passing of the Act of 1894. The result would have been exactly the same – and the basis for it no less artificial – if the husband had done no more than announce that he was electing to take the one-half share and had died before either taking it or disposing of it. If a deceased was 'competent to dispose' of property, estate duty falls inexorably on it according to the terms of the Act of 1894. Whether the wider incidence of that duty resulting from the operation of Part IX of the Succession Act, 1965, should be relieved by amending legislation is a matter for the legislature. I would dismiss the appeal.

Notes
See further *Irish Land Law*, para. 14.56 *et seq.*

H.V.H.
[1978] I.R. 138; 114 I.L.T.R. 1 (Supreme Court)

The plaintiff was the widow of a testator who by his will devised and bequeathed all his property (including 114 acres of agricultural land) to the second defendant subject to the right of the plaintiff to reside during her life in part of a dwellinghouse in which she ordinarily resided and which was situate on and held with the agricultural land. The testator did not leave any children and the plaintiff elected pursuant to s. 115 of the Succession Act, 1965, to take her legal right to a moiety of the estate of the testator instead of the rights of residence and maintenance bequeathed to her in the will. The plaintiff then applied to the High Court and claimed an order pursuant to s. 56 of the Act of 1965 directing the personal representative of the estate of the testator to appropriate, in satisfaction of the plaintiff's share, the dwellinghouse which was held with the agricultural land. The second defendant objected to such appropriation of the dwellinghouse on the ground that it would diminish the value of his remaining share of the estate. In these circumstances s. 56, sub-s. 5, of the Act of 1965 provides that such appropriation shall not be made 'unless the court . . . is satisfied that the exercise of that right is unlikely to diminish the value of the assets of the deceased, other than the dwelling, or to make it more difficult to dispose of them in due course of administration and authorises its exercise'. The personal representative did not contend that it was necessary for him to sell the lands, or any part of them, for the purposes of the due administration of the testator's estate. Kenny J. held, in directing an appropriation pursuant to s. 56 of the Act of 1965, that an applicant under sub-s. 5 (b) must discharge the onus of satisfying the court about both of the requirements specified in the sub-section. He also held that the phrase 'the value of the assets of the deceased, other than the dwelling. . .' must be interpreted as referring to the assets taken by the beneficiaries other than the applicant. The second defendant appealed to the Supreme Court.

Henchy J.:
I have read the judgment of Mr. Justice Parke and I agree with it.

Griffin J.:
I have read that judgment and agree with it.

Parke J.:
This is an appeal against so much of the order of Mr. Justice Kenny dated the 10th December, 1974, as directed the first defendant, as the executor, to appropriate the dwellinghouse on the farm which forms part of the estate of the testator towards the satisfaction of the legal right of the widow of the testator in pursuance of an application by her under s. 56, sub-s. 5 (b), of the Succession Act, 1965.

The plaintiff's application for such an order is only one of a number of disputes between the parties relating to the administration of the testator's estate. After the hearing before Mr. Justice Kenny, the plaintiff in these proceedings instituted a partition suit in relation to the lands forming part of the testator's estate. Judgment in that suit was delivered by Mr. Justice McWilliam on the 12th January, 1977, and we have been informed by counsel for the second defendant that it is his intention to appeal to this court from such judgment. It is clear that no final order for the distribution of the assets of the estate can be made until that appeal is determined by this Court. However, this Court has been asked to determine the issues arising on the construction of s. 56, sub-s. 5 (b), of the Act of 1965 so that the rights of the parties in this respect may be ascertained.

[*The judge here referred to the provisions of sub-s. 1 and sub-s. 5 (b) of s. 56 of the Act of 1965*]

It appears to me that this appeal raises three questions on the construction of sub-s. 5 (b) of section 56. The first relates to the onus of proof. The trial judge held that the onus lies upon an applicant under the sub-section to satisfy the court that the exercise of the right of appropriation is unlikely to diminish the value of the assets of the deceased, other than the dwelling, or to make it more difficult to dispose of them in due course of administration. This finding was not challenged in argument and appears to me to be clearly correct.

The second question is to ascertain the meaning of the words 'the value of the assets of the deceased, other than the dwelling'. The trial judge held that in a case such as the present, where the spouse has exercised her legal right to one half of the estate, these words are limited to the value of the assets of the deceased, other than the dwelling, *and other than those passing to the spouse.* I cannot accept this as being correct. Such a construction would not be in conformity with one of the fundamental rules of interpretation *i.e.,* that words may not be interpolated into a statute unless it is absolutely necessary to do so in order to render it intelligible or to prevent it having an absurd or wholly unreasonable meaning or effect. No such necessity arises here. The words of sub-s. 5 (b) of s. 56 are clear and intelligible as they stand. They refer plainly to *all* the assets of the deceased other than the dwelling. The fact that the dwelling is the only exclusion seems to me to remove any doubt which might exist as to the comprehensiveness of the word 'all'.

The trial judge seems to have considered that he was bound to construe the expression in the way in which he did because he considered that any other construction would render it impossible for any application under paragraph (b) to succeed in respect of a residential agricultural holding. This view is based upon the belief which he expressed in his judgment that a residential agricultural holding is invariably more valuable than a non-residential agricultural holding. With the greatest respect to the learned judge, I do not think that is necessarily so. The common experience of the Courts affords many examples to the contrary. A large, old, and dilapidated dwelling will frequently diminish the value of the holding. In cases, common enough nowadays, where there are two dwellings on a holding the exclusion of one of them will probably enhance the value of what is left. These, and other examples, were cited to us in argument and reinforce the conclusion that it is not necessary to interfere with the clear wording of paragraph (b) on the grounds of avoiding an irrational meaning or effect. In my view the words mean what they say, *viz.*, all the assets of the deceased other than the dwelling.

The third question which arises is as to the meaning and effect of the word 'or' which separates the expressions 'diminish the value of the assets of the deceased, other than the dwelling', and 'to make it more difficult to dispose of them in due course of administration'. It as urged upon us very strongly by counsel for the plaintiff that its effect is disjunctive. He contended that an applicant under s. 56 could discharge the onus of proof by establishing one or other of two things, namely, that the exercise of the right would be unlikely (a) to diminish the value of the assets or (b) to make them more difficult to dispose of in the course of administration, but that such an applicant was not obliged to establish the unlikelihood of *both* consequences. He submitted that in a case such as the present, where no sale of the assets is contemplated, the fact that the exercise of the right might diminish the value of the assets was irrelevant and that the exercise of the right would in no way impede the personal representative in distributing the assets in due course of administration. This was the view taken by the trial judge who interpreted the word 'them' as meaning 'the assets of the deceased other than the dwelling-house' and the word 'dispose' as including voluntary distribution amongst the beneficiaries *in specie*. I regret that I cannot accept these conclusions. Reading paragraph (b) in its entirety, it seems to me clear that what sub-s. 5 (b) of s. 56 requires the court to be satisfied of is that *neither* of the specified eventualities is likely to happen. In my opinion the submissions on behalf of the plaintiff on the construction of this portion of paragraph (b) must also fail.

Accordingly, the appeal must succeed. In my view, it must be held, that the plaintiff has failed to establish under s. 56 of the Act of 1965, the right of appropriation sought by her. Whether she is otherwise entitled to the dwellinghouse is a matter that must await the outcome of the pending appeal in the partition suit.

Section 56, sub-s. 11, of the Act of 1965 requires all proceedings in relation to s. 56 to be heard in chambers. This does not mean that the judgment in such proceedings in chambers may not be published: *per* Lord Denning M.R. in *Wallersteiner* v. *Moir* ([1974] 1 W.L.R. 991, 1003). The decision in this appeal is being given in court rather than in chambers so that the opinion of the Court as to the correct interpretation of s. 56, sub-s. 5 (b), of the Act of 1965 may be promulgated. However, in order to preserve the confidentiality inherent in the requirement of a hearing in chambers, all identifying facts and circumstances, including the names of the parties, are omitted from this judgment.

Note
A second action was begun by the plaintiff in this case and this too ended up before the Supreme Court, see *H.* v. *O.*, *infra*.

H. V. O.

[1978] I.R. 194 (Supreme Court)

Since the plaintiff's request for an order under section 56 of the Succession Act, 1965, was refused in the High Court (see *H.* v. *H., supra*)., she then commenced this action in the High Court and claimed the same division and conveyance by the executor in exercise of his general powers of appropriation under s. 55 of the Act of 1965. The second and third defendants, who were entitled to a moiety of the estate, resisted the plaintiff's claim and sought a sale of the lands and the distribution of the proceeds of sale to the persons entitled thereto.

It was held by McWilliam J. that the provisions of s. 55 of the Act of 1965 empowered the personal representative of the testator's estate to divide the lands in the manner suggested by the plaintiff and to convey to her, in satisfaction *pro tanto* of her claims to the estate, the part of the lands desired by her; and that the personal representative would be ordered to convey to the plaintiff such part accordingly. The second and third defendants appealed to the Supreme Court.

Henchy J.:

The testator was the plaintiff's husband. They had no children. His estate consisted chiefly of a residential farm of 113 acres. Subject to the payment of his debts and his funeral and testamentary expenses, the testator by his will left all his estate to his nephew, the second defendant, subject to certain rights in the dwellinghouse in favour of the plaintiff and subject to and charged with the payment of £150 p.a. in favour of his brother, the third defendant (in addition to rights of residence and support in the dwellinghouse which the latter had under an earlier settlement), and subject also to certain legacies. The first defendant is the personal representative.

On the death of the testator the plaintiff elected under s. 115, sub-s. 1 (a), of the Succession Act, 1965, to take the half share of the estate, for which she became under eligible under s. 111, rather than what had been given to her by the will. The combined effect of the terms of the will and that election is that the plaintiff and the second defendant are each entitled to a half share of the estate, subject to the rights of the third defendant.

The plaintiff instituted proceedings in the High Court seeking an order under s. 56 of the Succession Act, 1965, requiring the first defendant, as personal representative, to appropriate the dwelling on the lands in or towards the satisfaction of her half share. Such an order was made in the High Court, but on appeal to this Court it was held that the plaintiff had failed to discharge the onus cast on her by s. 56, sub-s. 5 (b), of proving that the proposed appropriation of the dwelling was unlikely to diminish the value of the assets other than the dwelling, or to make it more difficult to dispose of them in due course of administration. The plaintiff was held to be disentitled to the order sought, and so the appeal in those proceedings was allowed.

On the very day that the High Court gave judgment in favour of the plaintiff in that action, a second action was instituted in the High Court by the plaintiff. This second action, which is the one now before us on appeal, was aimed primarily at getting an order under s. 55 of the Act of 1965 allowing the first defendant, as personal representative, to appropriate the part of the lands on which the dwelling is situate in or towards satisfaction of the plaintiff's half share. Mr. Justice McWilliam made that order in the High Court. The first defendant and the third defendant were joined as defendants, but they have taken a neutral stance in the matter. The contention in both actions is between the plaintiff and the second defendant. It is to be regretted that all disputes between the plaintiff and the second defendant were not disposed of, as they could readily have been, in a single action rather than in two separate actions which have resulted in two appeals to this Court. In consequence, the estate has been unnecessarily burdened with costs; and the administration of the estate has been unduly delayed.

The Act of 1965 provides a legislative code of rules governing succession to the estates, whether testate or intestate, of deceased persons. The Act abolished many of the old rules as to the descent on death of the real and personal property to which a deceased person was entitled. In regard to intestate succession, Part VI of the Act of 1965 laid down a new set of rules as to who is to succeed and in what shares, giving special emphasis to the standing of a surviving spouse, children, parents, and brothers and sisters. In regard to testate succession, for the first time in this State the legislature has asserted by this Act the primacy of familial obligation, so as to trench on and circumscribe freedom of testation. Where the testator has left a child or children surviving him, the court, if it is of opinion that the testator has failed in his moral duty to make provision for a particular child in accordance with his means, may overrule the will to the extent of making such provisions for the child out of the estate as it thinks just: see section 117. Where the testator has left a spouse and there are no children, the spouse shall have a right to one-half of the estate; if there are children, the spouse has a right to one-third of the estate (s. 111); and in either event the spouse may elect to take either such share or what has been devised or bequeathed to him or her by the will. The latter provision was operated in this case. There being no children, the plaintiff as the surviving spouse had a legal right under s. 111 to a half share of the estate, and she exercised her right of election under s. 115, sub-s. 1, by opting for that half share rather than for what was given to her by the will.

The Act of 1965 provides that the real and personal estate of the deceased person shall on his death, notwithstanding any testamentary disposition, devolve on and become vested in his personal representatives: see section 10. The duty is imposed on the personal representatives of distributing the estate as soon after the death as is reasonably practicable having regard to the nature of the estate, the manner in which it is required to be distributed and all other relevant circumstances: see section 62. Various powers, duties and rights are vested in or imposed on the personal representatives in connection with the administration of the estate, and there are specific rules as to payment of debts where the estate is insolvent and as to the order of application of assets where the estate is solvent; see s. 46 and the first schedule. But nowhere in the Act is there any specific statement as to how the personal representatives are to discharge the surviving spouse's legal right to one-third or one-half of the estate, as the case may be. Section 112 gives the legal right priority over devises, bequests and shares on intestacy. In the general context of the Act of 1965, it must be assumed that the legislative intention was that the legal right (where elected for) is to be discharged in the same manner as if the one-half or one-third of the estate had been expressly given in the will in priority over all devises and bequests.

Subject to the restrictions imposed by s. 50, the personal representatives may sell the whole or any part of the estate for the purpose of distributing the estate among the persons entitled. Sections 55 and 56 enable a share in the estate, including the legal right of a surviving spouse, to be dealt with by appropriation of a specific part of the estate. Section 56 is to the general effect that where the estate includes a dwelling in which, at the time of the deceased's death, the surviving spouse was ordinarily resident, the surviving spouse may, subject to specified conditions, require the personal representatives in writing to appropriate the dwelling, under s.

55, in or towards satisfaction of any share of the surviving spouse. This right, which is not confined to cases where the surviving spouse's share is a legal right under s. 111, may be extended to household chattels, and in certain circumstances may be exercised in relation to the share of an infant. I need not elaborate on the conditions requisite for the valid exercise of the right. It is sufficient to say that the plaintiff, being the surviving spouse and having elected for the one-half share which was her legal right, was unsuccessful in the appeal in the first action in her attempt to obtain an order directing the appropriation of the dwelling in or towards the satisfaction of that share. She failed because she had not discharged the onus cast on her by s. 56, sub-s. 5, of showing, as a pre-condition of the exercise of the right, that its exercise was unlikely to diminish the value of the assets other than the dwelling, or to make it more difficult to dispose of them in due course of administration.

Section 55 allows the personal representatives, subject to the provisions of the section, to appropriate any part of the estate in its actual condition at the time of appropriation in or towards satisfaction of a share. While the right conferred by s. 56 is a right conferred on a surviving spouse, the right conferred by s. 55 is exercisable only by the personal representatives and is not confined to the share of a surviving spouse. When the plaintiff, as the surviving spouse who was entitled to a one-half share as her legal right, sought in the present action to get an order directing the first defendant to appropriate the part of the lands on which the dwelling is situate towards the satisfaction of her share, she was seeking to assert a right to which she was not entitled under section 55. The right of appropriation given by s. 55 is an enabling right which may be exercised only by the personal representative. A person entitled to a share is given no right to compel the personal representative to propose an appropriation under section 55. The first defendant, as personal representative, has not chosen to operate the section so, strictly speaking, the plaintiff was misconceived in her efforts to compel him to do so. In the High Court the judge treated the first defendant as having served the notice of intended appropriation which is required by sub-s. 3 of section 55. I do not think that was correct. The first defendant does not seem to have served any document or delivered any pleading which could be said to be a compliance with sub-s. 3 of section 55. However, both in the High Court and in this Court, counsel for the first defendant has raised no objection to his being deemed to have served the necessary notice, and as all the interested parties are before the Court and have not claimed to be prejudiced in any way by want of notice, I deal with the matter on the footing that the first defendant, as personal representative, is willing to operate s. 55 and that the statutory pre-conditions as to notice have been complied with. I do so particularly because no appeal has been taken by any party against the ruling of the judge in this respect, and also because a dismiss of the action on this ground would probably have the effect of burdening this estate with yet another High Court action.

But I wish to stress that a beneficiary is not given any right to compel a personal representative to exercise a power of appropriation under section 55. It is only because of the special circumstances to which I have referred that the personal representative in this case is being treated as having taken the necessary steps for an appropriation under section 55.

Section 55, sub-s. 1, stipulates that the power of appropriation may be exercised 'subject to the provisions of this section'. The limitations of the power are to be found in the section itself rather than in the terms of analogous powers given elsewhere in the Act. Leaving aside an appropriation of a dwelling under s. 56, the requirements laid down by s. 55 for the valid exercise by personal representatives of their power to appropriate are these –

1. The appropriation must not affect prejudicially any specific devise or bequest: sub-s. 2.

2. Notice of the intended appropriation must be served on all parties entitled to a share in the estate, other than persons who may come into existence after the time of the appropriation or who, after reasonable enquiry, cannot be found or ascertained at that time: sub-s. 3.

3. Apart from certain exceptions which are not applicable in this case, the following consents are necessary: (a) when the appropriation is for the benefit of a person absolutely and beneficially entitled in possession, the consent of that person; (b) when it is in respect of any settled share, the consent of either the trustee thereof, if any (not being also the personal representative), or the person who may for the time being be entitled to the income see sub-s. 4.

4. The personal representatives, in making the appropriation, shall have regard to the rights of any person who may thereafter come into existence, or who cannot after reasonable enquiry be found or ascertained at the time of appropriation, and of any other person whose consent is not required by this section.

The court only acquires jurisdiction in the matter when a party, on being served with notice of an intended appropriation, applies within six weeks to the court to prohibit the appropriation. The section is silent as to how the court is to exercise its jurisdiction, which is essentially supervisory and prohibitive. So it must be assumed, having regard to the tenor, the scope and the purpose of the section, that the court should prohibit an intended appropriation only (a) when the conditions in the section have not been complied with; or (b) when, notwithstanding such compliance, it would not be just or equitable to allow the appropriation to take place, having regard to the rights of all persons who are or will become entitled to an interest in the estate; or (c) when, apart from the section, the appropriation would not be legally permissible. Since the personal representatives hold the estate under s. 10, sub-s. 3, as trustees for the persons by law entitled thereto, the exercise of the statutory discretion to appropriate must be viewed as an incident of the trusteeship, so that it is the court's duty to prohibit the appropriation if it is calculated to operate unjustly or inequitably by unduly benefiting one beneficiary at the expense of another. But otherwise, where the conditions of the section have been observed and the personal representatives have made a bona fide decision to appropriate, the exercise of their discretion to appropriate should not be interfered with unless for some reason unrelated to the terms of the section the appropriation would be legally unacceptable, e.g., if it would amount to a sub-division prohibited by law. Such an approach to the scope of the section is also required by the fact that, when the Act of 1965 was passed, it was settled law that, without any statutory enablement, personal representatives could appropriate a specific part of the estate (such as a leasehold) as part of the share of a beneficiary with his consent, on the ground that they could sell it to the beneficiary and set off the purchase money against his share: see *In re Beverly, Watson* v. *Watson*.

I turn now to the circumstances of the case in hand. The holding of land left by the testator was approximately 113 acres, on which he had 68 head of cattle. Of that 113 acres, 12 acres stand some short distance apart from the remainder. The remainder is bisected by the Ennis–Limerick road which runs from north to south. To the west of that road there are 52 acres on which the dwelling stands. The remaining 48 acres are to the east of the road. Therefore, the house and 52 acres form an easily identifiable and severable block. The proposed appropriation would mean that the first defendant, as the personal representative, would convey to the plaintiff the 52 acres (on which the dwelling is situated) in or towards satisfaction of the half share of the estate to which she is entitled. The plaintiff is ready and willing to accept that appropriation. It is opposed, however, by the second defendant, who is entitled to the balance of the estate, which is subject to five legacies amounting in all to £2,200 and to the annuity of £150 and the rights of residence and support in favour of the third defendant.

There is no question but that in any event the legacies will be paid in full, and it has not been suggested that the proposed appropriation would prejudice the annuity of the third defendant or his rights over the lands. He is at present residing in the dwelling with the plaintiff, and is on amicable terms with her. There is good reason to think that the proposed appropriation would best preserve the status quo as far as he is concerned. On the other hand, it is difficult to see how his rights of residence and support would be effectively preserved if the dwelling and all the lands were to be sold. In fact, no argument against the appropriation has been put forward on behalf of the third defendant. The only person who actively opposes the appropriation is the second defendant. Instead of the appropriation, he wants the first defendant to put all the lands and the house up for sale as a single unit, in which case he would hope to become the purchaser. His object is to annex the lands, by means of such purchase, to his own holding which is nearby.

The second defendant puts his case against the appropriation on two grounds. First, he contends that the testator's primary intention that the lands should pass in their entirety to him would be frustrated by the proposed appropriation; whereas his proposition that all the lands be sold in due course of administration would give him a chance of acquiring them by purchase, thus effectuating the testator's intention that the lands should not be broken up but should pass to him. I must reject this argument. If we were construing the will, the paramount consideration would be the testator's intention: but we are not construing the will. We are dealing with the application of s. 55 in circumstances in which the legislature has specifically allowed the testator's intention to be set aside by enabling the plaintiff as his widow to have, as it were, the will amended so as to give her a half share of the estate in place of the benefits given to her by the testator in his will. It is of the essence of the scheme of the Act in such circumstances that the testator's intention as to the devolution of his estate on his death must be cast aside. In fact, s. 112 categorically stipulates that the half share to which the plaintiff became entitled as her legal right shall have priority over devises and bequests. Therefore, while the plaintiff and the second defendant are each entitled to a half share in the estate, the plaintiff's half share, being a legal right, takes priority over the defendant's half share, which derives from the will. In such circumstances it would be repugnant to the Act of 1965 to apply s. 55 for the purpose of reviving and giving effect to the testator's intention – an intention which the Act requires to be overborne. I consider that the intention of the testator can have no part in the operation of s. 55 in the circumstances of this case.

The other ground on which the second defendant seeks to have the appropriation prohibited is that, in his view, it will unfairly benefit the plaintiff at his expense by making the unappropriated part of the lands worth appreciably less than a half share in the proceeds of the lands if they were sold as a single unit. As I have indicated, if this ground is substantial it would justify a prohibition of the proposed appropriation. Therefore, it is necessary to consider the financial consequences of the proposed appropriation as compared with those of a sale of the lands as a single residential unit.

At the hearing in the High Court three valuers gave evidence, two for the plaintiff and one for the second defendant. For the purpose of their valuations, the rights of the third defendant were disregarded. One of the plaintiff's valuers assessed the market value of the house and all the lands as a single residential farm at £112,000 and the other put their value at £110,200; while the defendant's valuer gave a valuation, by reference to the three component parts, which amounted to £109,600. It is common case, therefore, that a half share of the proceeds of a sale of the house and all the lands as one unit free of the interests of the third defendant, who is now 82, would be approximately £55,000. One of the plaintiff's valuers valued the house and 52 acres (which is the proposed appropriation) at £58,000 if sold separately, the plaintiff's other valuer reached the figure of £59,000, and the valuation of the defendant's valuer was £52,000. The corresponding figures of the valuers for a sale of the rest of the lands were £56,000, £51,000 and £57,000 respectively. No evidence was given of the valuations which the personal representative is empowered by s. 55, sub-s. 10, to get.

Therefore, so far as the evidence in the High Court went, it showed that the proposed appropriation of the house and 52 acres would benefit the plaintiff to the extent of about £55,000, and if the rest of the land went to the second defendant it would represent a financial benefit to him of about the same amount. This is about the same as each would get, or be credited with, if the lands were sold as a single lot. So, instead of supporting the second defendant's claim that the appropriation would unduly benefit the plaintiff at his expense, the evidence indicates that the appropriation would amount to a partitition of the lands on a fifty-fifty basis – the plaintiff and the second defendant each getting landed property of approximately equal value. It is true that the personal representative's valuations may be different from those given in evidence in the High Court, but nothing has emerged to suggest that the value of the appropriation would be appreciably more than half the value of the whole holding. In any event, the holding does not represent the whole of the estate, and the personal representaive will be able to make any necessary set-off or adjustment in the accounts so as to ensure that the plaintiff will not get more than she is entitled to.

Therefore, I hold that the second defendant has not substantiated his claim that the proposed appropriation should be prohibited. Not alone does the objection to the appropriation fail but the appropriation would eminently accord with the merits of the case. If the house and all the lands were to be sold, it would mean that the plaintiff would be ousted from the matrimonial home where she has spent all her married life, and the rights of residence and support to which the third defendant is entitled would be put in jeopardy. If the appropriation is permitted by the Land Commission (as it requires to be), it will ensure that the plaintiff, who is widowed and without children, will not be condemned to the harsh fate of having to leave the dwelling and seek a new home. Instead of getting her share in money she will acquire the house and 52 acres, which will be a viable agricultural holding, and there will be assured to the third defendant in the terminal years of his life his rights to support and maintenance in the dwelling at the hands of the plaintiff in the manner in which those covenanted rights have been satisfactorily accorded to him up to now.

Being satisfied that the proposed apportionment will be a valid exercise of the discretion vested in the personal representative by s. 55 (provided the consent of the Land Commission pursuant to s. 12 of the Land Act, 1965, as obtained), I would dismiss this appeal. However, I would amend the order under appeal by deleting so much of it as orders the personal representative to execute the conveyance mentioned therein. In lieu thereof, I would declare that, subject to obtaining the consent of the Land Commission, the execution of the said conveyance would be a valid exercise of the powers vested in the personal representative by s. 55 of the Succession Act, 1965.

Griffin J.
 I agree.

Park J.
 I agree.

Note
See further, *Irish Land Law*, para. 14.60. See also *C.H.* v. *D.G. O'D.* (1978) 109 I.L.T.R.9.

IN THE GOODS OF G.M.
(1972) 106 I.L.T.R. 82 (High Court)

By his will dated 3rd March, 1961, the testator left all his property in the Republic of Ireland and all his shares and securities to executors upon trust for his wife for her life and after her death for two nephews. The testator had married in 1924. There were no children of the marriage and in 1941 the wife informally adopted the plaintiff. The boy grew up in the testator's home and at the time of the testator's death was aged thirty-two and was married with two children. On the 19th March, 1954, the Adoption Board made an adoption order under the Adoption Act, 1952, (No. 25 of 1952) and the plaintiff became the adopted child of the testator and his wife.

Kenny J.:
 G.E.M. ('the testator') was the owner of a large farm in County Meath which he worked and of lands in England. On the 10th December, 1924, he married B.C. one of the defendants. They had no children and in 1941 she decided to adopt a boy called F.B., the plaintiff, who came to live with them. The informal adoption followed a conversation which she had with her sister and she did not consult the testator who knew nothing of it until she brought the boy to the farm. There was no system of legal adoption in the Republic of Ireland at that time.

The plaintiff attended the national school of A. until he was eight and then went to boarding schools until he was 17 years of age when he became a student at the School of Navigation attached to the University of Southampton for one year. He then joined the Merchant Navy in which he reached the position of first mate. He holds a Master's certificate and since May, 1969, has been working for the British and Irish Steamship Company. He is now 32, lives in Dublin, married and has two children. His basic salary is £1,200 but his total earnings will be about £1,700 this year.

On the 19th March, 1954, *An Bord Uchtala* made an adoption order under the Adoption Act, 1952, by which the plaintiff became the adopted child of the testator and his wife. The application for this must have been signed by the testator and validity of the Order has not been challenged. From the time it was made the plaintiff was called F.M. or F.B.M.

Mrs. M. who is a medical doctor, paid all the expenses of the plaintiff's education and provided him with clothes and pocket money. The testator and the plaintiff were on friendly terms, but the bond of affection which the relationship of father and son usually creates never existed between them. The testator told the plaintiff that he would never become the owner of the farm at F. and all the evidence suggests that the testator never wanted the adoption and signed the documents in connection with it to please his wife. The testator has two nephews, J.A.K. and M.K., the sons of his sister who was a medical doctor who now lives in Northern Ireland. Mrs. K. and one of her sons called on a few occasions to see the testator. Mrs. M. did not welcome their visits and there was not any personal affection or attachment between the testator and his nephews.

On the 3rd March, 1961, the testator made his will by which he appointed his brother, T.A.M. and A., the well-known solicitor, to be his executors and trustees. He left all his property in the Republic of Irleand and his shares and securities to them upon trust for his wife for life and after her death for the two nephews I have mentioned, absolutely. He left his farm at P. in England to them upon trust for his brother-in-law G.A.C. who had been managing it for many years, for his life and after his death to his nephew, M.K. absolutely. The remarkable feature about this will is that the plaintiff is not mentioned in it. The effect of section 24 of the Adoption Act, 1952, was that the plaintiff was to be regarded as the child of the testator and of his wife born to them in what the Act calls 'lawful wedlock' and who for the purpose of property rights was to be treated as a child of the testator if the testator had died intestate.

The testator died on the 19th January, 1968, when he was 93 years of age. He was domiciled in the Republic of Ireland. His property consisted of (a) the farm in Co. Meath subsequently acquired by the Land Commission for £50,000 payable in 8% Land Bonds and which, for the purposes of this application, I intend to value at £45,000; (b) shares and securities in the Republic of Ireland, in England and Scotland, which had a market value of about £65,000; (c) livestock and furniture worth about £8,500 and (d) the farm in England which had a value of about £18,500. His debts and funeral expenses were £2,257 so that the gross value of his estate after deduction of debts, but before deduction of testamentary expenses was about £135,250. The testamentary expenses (excluding the costs of these proceedings which I estimate will be about £5,000) will be about £5,000 so that the testator had disposing power over assets worth about £130,000. The estate duty payable in the Republic of Ireland was £38,067 against which there is a credit of £12,061, the duty paid in England. His widow has elected to take the legal share of one-third of his estate instead of the benefits given to her by the will (see section 111 of the Succession Act, 1965).

There was some discussion as to whether the estate for the purposes of Part IX of the Act of 1965 includes the farm in England, but it has now been conceded that it does not. Section 109(2) of the Act has not changed the judge-made rule that the succession to immoveables is governed by the law of the place where they are situate, while that to moveables is regulated by the law of the domicile of the deceased. Section 109(2) bears a striking similarity to section 66 which appears in Part VI which deals with distribution on intestacy. Both define the type of interest in property with which the two parts are dealing, an estate to which the deceased was beneficially entitled for an interest not ceasing on death.

Part IX of the Act made radical changes in the law relating to the privilege to dispose of all property by will in any manner. The widow is now given a right to choose between what is given her by the will and one-third of the estate when children of the marriage have survived the testator. Section 117 provides that when the court is of opinion that a testator has failed in his moral duty to make proper provision for a child of his in accordance with his means, whether by his will or otherwise, the court may order that such provision shall be made for the child out of the estate as the court thinks just and the effect of section 110 is that a child who has been adopted under an order made by *An Bord Uchtala* is in the same position as a child born of the marriage. Section 120 specifies a number of cases in which a person may be excluded from inheriting. It has not been suggested that the plaintiff has done anything which would justify his omission from benefit under the will of the testator.

Counsel have referred to the legislation in England, New Zealand and in New South Wales which limits the unrestricted power of disposition by will. The Family Protection Act, 1908, of New Zealand was the first legislation of this type, in a common law country while a similar law was made in New South Wales by the Testators (Family Maintenance and Guardianship of Infants) Act, 1916. The legislation in England began with the Inheritance (Family Provision) Act, 1938, which has been amended by the Intestates Estates Act, 1952, and the Family Provision Act, 1966. I have considered many of the decisions on these Acts. *Allardice* v. *Allardice* [1911] A.C. 730; *Re Allen* [1922] N.Z.L.R. 218; *Bosch* v. *Perpetual Trustee Co. Ltd.* [1938] 2 All E.R. 14; *In re Pugh decd.* [1943] Ch. 387 and *In re Goodwin* [1968] 3 All E.R. 12.

The concept underlying the legislation in New Zealand, New South Wales and England is that a testator owes a duty to make reasonable provision for the maintenance of his widow and of his dependants. Our Succession Act, however, is based on the idea that a testator owes a duty to leave part of his estate to his widow (the legal right share) and to make proper provision for his children in accordance with his means. It is not based on a duty to provide maintenance for his widow nor is it limited in its application to children who were dependant on him. The cases decided on the New Zealand, New South Wales and English Act of Parliament are, therefore, of little assistance.

An analysis of section 117 shows that the duty which it creates is not absolute because it does not apply if the testator leaves all his property to his spouse (section 117(3)) nor is it an obligation to each child to leave him something. The obligation to make proper provision may be fulfilled by will or otherwise and so gifts or settlements made during the lifetime of the testator in favour of a child or the provision of an expensive education for one child when the others have not received this may discharge the moral duty. It follows, I think, that the relationship of parent and child does not of itself and without regard to other circumstances create a moral duty to leave anything by will to the child. The duty is not one to make adequate provision but to make proper provision in accordance with the testator's means and in deciding whether this has been done, the court may have regard to immoveable property outside the Republic of Ireland owned by the testator. The court, therefore, when deciding whether the moral duty has been fulfilled, must take all the testator's property (including immoveable property outside the Republic of Ireland) into account, but if it decides that the duty has not been discharged, the provision for the child is to be made out of the estate excluding that immoveable property.

It seems to me that the existence of a moral duty to make proper provision by will for a child must be judged by the facts existing at the date of death and must depend upon (a) the amount left to the surviving spouse or the value of the legal right if the survivor selects to take this, (b) the number of the testator's children, their ages and their positions in life at the date of the testator's death, (c) the means of the testator, (d) the age of the child whose case is being considered and his or her financial position and prospects in life, (e) whether the testator has already in his lifetime made proper provision for the child. The existence of the duty must be decided by objective considerations. The court must decide whether the duty exists and the view of the testator that he did not owe any is not decisive.

The testator in this case never made any provision for the plaintiff except that he allowed him to live at F. The plaintiff was the testator's only child and his mother and he were the only persons to whom the testator owed a duty for there was no one else with any moral claim on him. The estate of the testator was worth about £135,250 before payment of testamentary expenses and estate duty. If I take £10,000 as an estimate of the amount of testamentary expenses and costs, the value of the mother's legal right will be about £36,200 (one-third of £108,500) so that the amount available to make proper provision for the plaintiff is about £89,000. The amount of estate duty payable is £38,000 but as Mrs. M's legal right and any provision made for the plaintiff under section 117 will have to bear their proportions of this duty section (118) I exclude it from the calculation. This is another striking change made in the law because except in relation to real estate, estate duty was, before 1967, payable out of the residue.

In my opinion the circumstances which I have described created a moral duty binding on the testator to make proper provision by will for the plaintiff. He made no provision whatever and so he failed in this duty. The court must, therefore, order that proper provision is to be made out of the estate and must decide this difficult question from the point of view of a prudent and a just parent.

I think that the provision which such a parent would have made in this case would have been to have given one half of the estate (excluding the immoveable property in England) to the plaintiff. The amounts of the testamentary expenses and the costs of the two sets of proceedings will be deducted from the gross amount of the estate to arrive at the figure on which the one half is calculated.

Note
See further, *Irish Land Law*, para. 14.61 *et seq.*

III. ADMINISTRATION OF ESTATES

CROWLEY V. FLYNN
[1983] I.L.R.M. 513 (High Court)

The testatrix Maude Robb died on 15 May 1946 having by her last will dated 4 March 1943 bequeathed her leasehold interest in certain property to her executor and trustee George Robb on trust for sale and to hold proceeds of sale as to two-sixteenths for himself and the balance to be divided equally between her two daughters. A grant of probate was obtained on 11 July 1946. George Robb died on 24 August 1978 and letters of administration *de bonis non* were obtained by the deceased's two daughters on 20 March 1981. Following a contract for sale of the leasehold interest dated 7 August 1979 the purchaser refused to accept title form the administratices *de bonis non*. It was submitted on behalf of the purchaser that: (i) no power of sale had been shown to subsist because no reason had been given for the exercise of such power by personal representatives after the lapse of 33 years, and, (ii) that the delay had been such that an assent to the establishment of the will trust should be inferred. The vendor submitted that, (i) an executor is always entitled to sell for the purposes of distribution of the assets among the beneficiaries, and (ii) that a purchaser would in any event be protected by the provisions of s. 51 of The Succession Act 1965.

Barron J. delivered his judgment on 13 May 1983 saying: The contract for sale in this case is dated 7 August 1979. The questions raised in the summons relate to a leasehold interest in the property in sale which was vested in Maud Robb at the date of her death. She died on 15 May 1946 having by her last will dated 4 March 1943 bequeathed this interest to her executor and trustee George Robb upon trust for sale and to hold the proceeds of sale as to 2/16ths for himself and as to 7/16ths for her daughter Adelaide Maud McCourt and as to the remaining 7/16ths for another daughter Rosalind Mabel Edith Webb. George Robb obtained a Grant of Probate on 11 July 1946. He died on 24 August 1978 and Letters of Administration *de bonis non* were obtained by the deceased's two daughters on 20 March 1981.

The purchaser has refused to accept title from the administratices *de bonis non*. He contends that no power of sale has been shown to subsist because no reason has been given for the exercise of such power by personal representatives after the lapse of 33 years. He further contends that the delay has been such that an assent to the establishment of the will trusts should be inferred. The purchaser in support of his first contention relies upon in re *Molyneux and White* 15 LRI 383 which was affirmed at 15 LRI 383. In this case it was held that a delay of more than 20 years creates a presumption that all the testator's debts have been paid and puts a purchaser on enquiry as to the purpose of the sale.

Against this contention, the vendor submits that an executor is always entitled to sell for the purpose fo distribution of the assets amongst the beneficiaries and relies upon in re *Norwood and Blake's Contract* [1917] 1 I.R. 472. He further submits that a purchaser would in any event be protected by the provisions of s. 51 of the Succession Act 1965. S. 51 sub/s. 1 of the Succession Act 1965 is as follows:

> The purchaser from the personal representative of a deceased person of any property, being the whole or any part of the estate of the deceased, shall be entitled to hold that property freed and discharged from any debts or liabilities of the deceased, except such as are charged otherwise than by the will of the deceased, and from all claims of the persons entitled to any share in the estate, and shall not be concerned to see to the application of the purchase money.

Where there has been a lapse of at least 20 years from the date of death, in re *Molyneux and White* is an authority for the proposition that a purchaser is put upon enquiry. In my view, this means that the vendor, selling as personal representative, must satisfy the purchaser that he has power to sell as such. In *Somers* v. *W* [1979] I.R. 94, it was held by the Supreme Court that the definition of the word purchaser as being somebody who acquired in good faith put such person in notice of all matters which would have come to the knowledge of the purchaser's solicitor if such enquiries had been made as ought reasonably to have been made in the particular sale. The word purchaser is defined in the Family Home Protection Act 1976 as follows:

> the word purchaser means a grantee, lessee, assignee, mortgagee, chargeant, or other person who in good faith acquires an estate or interest in property.

The word purchaser is defined in the same terms in the Succession Act 1965 with the addition of the words 'for valuable consideration', which for the purpose of the present case add nothing to the definition. There is nothing in s. 51 of the Succession Act 1965 nor in s. 19 of the Administration of Estates Act 1959 which it replaces which suggests that a purchaser is never to be upon enquiry. It follows that, if more than 20 years has elapsed since the date of death of the testator, there is nothing in the section to negative the rule in re *Molyneux and White* so that a purchaser is still put on notice to enquire the reason for the sale and if he fails to make such enquiry is bound with notice of what he would have discovered.

The only evidence as to the reason for the delay in the present case is contained in a letter dated 11 June 1980. This letter suggests that administration of the estate of Maud Robb was deliberately postponed by the executor with the consent of the beneficiaries. However the latter also shows that rents were divided between the persons entitled under the will trust. I do not consider that this resume of the facts is sufficiently clear to absolve the purchaser from further enquiry. It seems to me that such evidence of events from the death of the testatrix until the present time as there is shows no more than that the beneficiaries under the trust for sale received the rents in accordance with the shares to which they were entitled. This *prima facie* suggests that the trust for sale was being operated. If there is doubt on the facts, then the purchaser should not be forced to take a title dependent upon such doubt.

The present sale is not to provide for the payment of debts of the deceased. In so far as it is for the distribution of the assets among the beneficiaries, this is not something which the executor is required to do. His duty was to transfer the assets to the will trustee, albeit himself, and it was for him in this latter capacity to distribute the assets. On this basis, there is no ground either for the exercise of a power of sale by the personal representative.

The purchaser's second submission is that an assent to the establishment of the trust for sale should be inferred. Whether or not such inference can be drawn is dependent upon the facts. See *George Attenborough & Son* v. *Solomon* [1913] A.C. 76, which enunciates this principal and *Wise* v. *Whitburn* [1924] 1 Ch. 460, a case in which the inference was drawn. Having regard to the lapse of time since the death of the testatrix and the facts which are known, it seems reasonable to infer that an assent was given to the establishment of the will trust. Even if I am wrong in this view as to the proper inference to be drawn from the delay and from the other evidence available, there would in my view be sufficient doubt as to this to make it unreasonable to require the purchaser to accept the title.

In the circumstances, I accept the contentions made on behalf of the purchaser and I will declare that a good title to the hereditaments has not been shown in accordance with the particulars and conditions of sale.

Notes
Cf. *Shiels* v. *Flynn, infra*. See also *Irish Land Law*, para. 16.50.

SHIELS V. FLYNN
[1975] I.R. 296 (High Court)

The owner of freehold land whose title had been registered pursuant to the Local Registration of Title (Ir.) Act, 1891, died intestate on the 30th March, 1931, and letters of administration of the estate of the owner were granted to the plaintiff in 1931. The plaintiff was not registered as owner but the grant of administration was noted on the relevant folio. The plaintiff, in his capacity as administrator, offered the land for sale by public auction on the 29th January, 1973, when the defendant was declared to be the highest bidder and signed a memorandum of the contract of sale. The defendant, as purchaser, objected that after such lapse of time the sale could not be taking place in due course of the administration of the estate of the deceased owner, but the plaintiff insisted that the administration of the estate of the deceased was still incomplete and that his title and his power to sell the land were unaltered. A summons was issued in the High Court to determine the issue.

Kenny J.:

On the 26th April, 1921, Williams Shiels was registered as full owner (subject to equities) of part of the lands of Barnageeragh in the County of Dublin which were the subject matter of folio 2089 of the register of freeholders for the County of Dublin. Part IV of the Registration of Title Act, 1891, applied to them. He died intestate on the 30th March, 1931, and on the 16th September, 1931, letters of administration to his estate were granted to his son who is the plaintiff in these proceedings. There were four next-of-kin entitled to share in the estate. The death of William Shiels and the grant of letters of administration were noted on the folio, but the plaintiff was not registered as owner.

The plaintiff let the lands in conacre for many years and, on the 29th January, 1973, they were sold by public auction. In the conditions of sale it was stated that the plaintiff was selling the lands as personal representative of William Shiels. The purchaser was the defendant and he objected to the title on the ground that, as William Shiels died 43 years ago, a sale by the plaintiff as personal representative could not be in the due course of the administration of the estate; and the defendant required the plaintiff to have himself registered as full owner on the folio.

In correspondence the defendant's solicitor maintained that the lands could not possibly be assets of the deceased and that it would be unsafe for the defendant to take a transfer from the personal representative as some of the next-of-kin could have become beneficially entitled to the lands. The plaintiff's solicitor informed the defendant's solicitor that the estate of William Shiels had not been administered and that the administration bond had had to be renewed each year. The defendant, who had purchased the lands with the intention of developing them, refused to accept this explanation and the plaintiff has now issued this summons under the Vendor and Purchaser Act, 1874, claiming a declaration that he has shown a good title.

Interesting questions as to whether the decision in *Molyneux* v. *White*([1884] 13 L.R. Ir. 382) was a correct statement of the law in Ireland and as to whether the rule in *Re Tanqueray-Willaume and Landau* ([1882] 20 Ch.D. 465) applies to leaseholds and to registered lands have been discussed. Sections 18 and 19 of the Administration of Estates Act, 1959, and ss. 50 and 51 of the Succession Act, 1965, have the effect that these questions do not now arise in relation to any person who died after 1959.

It seems to me, however, that the answer to the problem in this case is to be found in the Registration of Title Act, 1891. Part IV of the Act of 1891 applied to freehold registered land, that is to say, land which has been at any time sold and conveyed to or vested in a purchaser under any of the provisions of the Purchase of Land (Ireland) Acts.

Section 84, sub-s. 1, in Part IV of the Act of 1891 provided:

'(1) Where any such land is vested in any person without right of survivorship to any other person, it shall, on his death, notwithstanding any testamentary disposition, devolve to and become vested in his personal representatives or representative from time to time as if it were a chattel real vesting in them or him'.

Sub-section 3 of s. 84 provided:

'(3) On the death either of a sole registered full owner or of the survivor of several registered full owners of any such land not being registered as tenants in common, the personal representatives of the sole owner or survivor shall alone be recognised by the registering authority as having any right in respect of the land, and shall have the same powers of dealing with the land, and any registered dispositions by them shall have the same effect, as if they were the registered owners of the land.'

Section 5 of the Administration of Estates Act, 1959, provided that 'the enactments mentioned in column (2) of the Second Schedule to this Act are, as respects the estates of persons dying on or after the 1st day of June, 1959, repealed to the extent specified in column (3) of that Schedule.' Sub-section 3 of s. 84 of the Act of 1891 is included in the second schedule to the Act of 1959 but, as William Shiels died before the 1st June, 1959, sub-s. 3 of s. 84 continued to apply to the administration of his estate. The Registration of Title Act, 1964, repealed the Act of 1891 but s. 113, sub-s. 2, of the Act of 1964 provided that the provisions of Part IV of the Act of 1891, in cases of death before the commencement of the Act of 1964, were to continue to apply to all land which was subject to the provisions of that Part immediately before such commencement. The whole of the Act of 1959 was repealed by the Succession Act, 1965, but s. 9, sub-s. 3, of the Act of 1965 provided: 'Except to the extent to which any provision of this Act expressly provides to the contrary, the provisions of this Act shall not apply to the estate of any person dying before the commencement of this Act'. The result is that the Act of 1959 still applies to the estates of persons who died before the 1st January, 1967, except in the cases where express provision is made to the contrary by the Act of 1965.

It follows that s. 84, sub-s. 3, in Part IV of the Act of 1891 applies to this sale with the result that the personal representative in this case has the same power of dealing with the land as if he were the registered owner and any registered disposition by him has the same effect as if he were the registered owner. Therefore, the plaintiff is able to show a good title to the lands if he can give clear possession, and a purchaser from him will be entitled to be registered on the folio.

Although William Shiels died in 1931, the provisions of s. 51 of the Act of 1965 are an additional protection to the purchaser against the type of claim which his counsel relied on in argument. Section 51 provides:

'(1) A purchaser from the personal representatives of a deceased person of any property, being the whole or any part of the estate of the deceased, shall be entitled to hold that property freed and discharged from any debts or liabilities of the deceased, except such as are charged otherwise than by the will of the deceased, and from all claims of the persons entitled to any share in the estate, and shall not be concerned to see to the application of the purchase money . . . (3) This section applies whether the deceased died before or after the commencement of this Act'.

As there has been a discussion about the power of an administrator to give a good title to a purchaser of leaseholds and of land registered under the Act of 1891 when there has been an interval of more than 20 years between the death before 1959 of a testator or an intestate and the date of the sale, I think I should say that in my opinion the decisions in *Re Whistler* ([1887] 35 Ch.D. 561) and in *Venn and Furze's Contract*([1894] 2 Ch. 101) did not represent the law in Ireland. Those cases decided that when an executor is selling leaseholds he can make good title to them without the concurrence of the beneficiaries and without proof that the debts and administration expenses have been paid when the sale is more than 20 years from the date of the death of the deceased. The subsequent decision in *Verrell's Contract* ([1903] 1 Ch. 65) shows that some doubt existed whether they were correctly decided. I think that the law in Ireland was correctly stated in *Molyneux* v. *White* ([1884] 13 L.R. Ir. 382). In that case the Vice Chancellor and the Court of Appeal decided that an executor could not give a good title to a purchaser without proof that there were unpaid debts when a period of 37 years had passed between the date of death and the sale, because at the expiry of 20 years after the death there was a presumption that all the debts of the deceased had been paid.

The correctness of this view is reinforced by the decision of Cusack Smith M.R. in *Bradley* v. *Flood* ([1864] 16 Ir. Ch.R. 236) where, in the course of an exhaustive judgment dealing with the law before the passing of the Statutes of Distribution, the Master of the Rolls decided that an administrator was not bound to sell chattels real of his intestate in order to distribute the purchase money among the next-of-kin when there were no debts to be paid, and that the next-of-kin were entitled to require him to convey to them their shares in the estate in specie. One of the effects of the Act of 1959 and of the Act of 1965 is that in the case of persons who died on or after the 1st June, 1959, this is no longer the law.

Chapter 11
LANDLORD AND TENANT

This is a vast and complex subject. The materials contained in this chapter deal with the general law governing the relationship of landlord and tenant (see *Irish Land Law,* ch. 17) and not with the more specialist areas, such as the rent restriction legislation (though see p. 55, *ante*) and other systems of statutory control (see *Irish Land Law,* ch. 18).

I. NATURE AND CREATION OF THE RELATIONSHIP

LANDLORD AND TENANT LAW AMENDMENT ACT, IRELAND, 1860

3. The relation of landlord and tenant shall be deemed to be founded on the express or implied contract of the parties, and not upon tenure or service, and a reversion shall not be necessary to such relation, which shall be deemed to subsist in all cases in which there shall be an agreement by one party to hold land from or under another in consideration of any rent.

4. Every lease or contract with respect to lands whereby the relation of landlord and tenant is intended to be created for any freehold estate or interest, or for any definite period of time not being from year to year or any lesser period, shall be by deed executed, or note in writing signed by the landlord or his agent thereunto lawfully authorized in writing.

GATIEN MOTOR CO. LTD. V. CONTINENTAL OIL COMPANY OF IRELAND LTD.
[1979] I.R. 406 (Supreme Court)

The respondent landlord let a certain tenement to a third party for three years from the 6th February, 1970, and the third party used the tenement for the purposes of his business during that period. Before the expiration of that term of years, the third party sought a renewal of his tenancy from the respondent, but the latter was unwilling to grant a renewal unless the third party surrendered possession of the tenement for a week. The third party was unwilling to vacate the premises for such week since he believed that such surrender would damage the goodwill of his business. Ultimately, it was agreed that the third party would remain 'in possession' of the tenement from 6th – 12th February, 1973, as a caretaker for the respondent and not as a tenant, without payment of rent, and that the respondent would grant to the applicant company (formed by the third party) a new tenancy for three years from the 12th February, 1973. The third party was aware that such a compromise was designed to prevent the tenant of the tenement from acquiring a statutory right to a new tenancy under the Act of 1931. The appropriate caretaker's agreement and new tenancy agreement were executed by the relevant parties, and the applicant used the tenement for business purposes as tenant.

On the expiration of the new tenancy on the 12th February, 1976, the applicant claimed to be entitled to a new tenancy under the Act of 1931 and contended that the third party had been in possession of the tenement as a tenant from 6th – 12th February, 1973, and that, accordingly, the tenement had been used by the tenant for the time being thereof for the entire of the three years and three months immediately preceding the 12th February, 1976. At the hearing of an appeal from an order of the Circuit Court declaring the applicant to be entitled to a new tenancy in the tenement under the Act of 1931, the High Court stated a case for the opinion of the Supreme Court and asked that court whether the caretaker's agreement had created a tenancy and, if not, whether that agreement was void under s. 42 of the Act of 1931 on the ground that it indirectly deprived the applicant of a right to a new tenancy under that Act.

Griffin J.:

At all material times the respondents were the owners of the garage known as Gatien Service Station, Rathfarnham, in the city of Dublin, where the well-known petrol known as 'Jet' was sold. By a lease dated the 15th October, 1970, the respondents let the said premises to Leo Gerard Coady, together with the equipment listed in the third schedule to the lease, for the term of three years from the 6th February, 1970, subject to the rent of £1,500 p.a. and to the covenants contained in that lease. The term of the lease of 1970 was intentionally and specifically limited to the period of three years so as to ensure that Coady would not acquire a right to a new tenancy under the Landlord and Tenant Act, 1931.

From the 6th February, 1970, to the 5th February, 1973, inclusive, Coady carried on the business of a service station in the premises. He was anxious to obtain a new lease of the premises and, for that purpose, he had discussions with the respondents' representatives towards the end of 1972. His solicitors were in correspondence with the respondents' solicitors and it was made quite clear to him, and to his solicitors, that the respondents would not consider granting a new lease unless he vacated the premises for the period of one week at the termination of the term of three years. As the respondents were not prepared to agree the terms of any new lease until after Coady had vacated the premises, and he was concerned that the goodwill of the business being carried on by him in the premises would be endangered if he had to vacate the premises, it was agreed between the parties, at the request of Coady and his solicitors, that at the expiration of the said term Coady should be permitted to remain in the premises as a caretaker only.

A caretaker's agreement dated the 6th February, 1973 (but signed by Coady on the 5th February, 1973) was duly entered into by Coady in pursuance of the aforesaid arrangement, and by that agreement he acknowledged that on the 6th February, 1973 he had been put into possession of the premises as a caretaker by and for the respondents and that he was in possession of the said premises and equipment solely as such caretaker of and for the respondents and not under any contract of tenancy. He further acknowledged that he had undertaken and agreed and that he thereby undertook and agreed with the respondents (inter alia) to take care of the premises and equipment for the respondents and to deliver up the possession thereof to the respondents when required so to do. Before entering into the caretaker's agreement Coady knew, and had been so advised by his own solicitors, that he would not be granted a new lease of the premises unless he entered into that agreement and that it was being required in order to prevent him from acquiring rights to relief under the provisions of the Act of 1931; he knew that it was not a tenancy and that under it he was merely a caretaker.

The terms of a new lease were agreed on the 10th February, 1973, whereby the premises and equipment were to be let for a period of three years from the 12th February, 1973. Coady was anxious to take the lease in the name of the applicant company which was then in the process of formation and the shares of which, when formed, were to be beneficially owned by him. Due to the delay in the formation of the applicant company, the lease was not formally executed until the 24th July, 1973.

On the 10th July, 1975, the applicants served notice, pursuant to s. 24 of the Act of 1931, of their intention to claim a new tenancy under Part III of that Act. On 29th March, 1976, the applicants applied to the Circuit Court, pursuant to s. 25 of the Act, for an order determining their right to a new tenancy in the premises; the application was successful and the respondents appealed to the High Court.

On the hearing of the appeal, it was submitted on behalf of the applicants that in reality the caretaker's agreement was a contract of tenancy and that, as he was in possession of the premises for the relevant period, Coady was a tenant and not a licensee. The applicants further contended that, if the caretaker's agreement did not create a tenancy, it was an agreement made with the intention of depriving Coady of his right to relief under the Act of 1931. The appeal was heard by Mr. Justice Murnaghan and, at the conclusion of the evidence, he stated a Case for the opinion of this Court upon the following two questions: –

1. Did the said caretaker's agreement create a tenancy?
2. If the caretaker's agreement did not create a tenancy, is the same null and void under the provisions of s. 42 of the Landlord and Tenant Act, 1931, upon the ground that it indirectly deprives the applicant of its right to relief sought in these proceedings?

The central issue on the hearing of this Case Stated is whether the caretaker's agreement created a tenancy. The question of whether or not the applicants would be entitled to a new tenancy under Part III of the Act of 1931 depends on the relevant provisions of sub-ss. 1*(a)* and 2*(b)* of s. 19 of the Act of 1931.

There was clearly no right to a new tenancy on the expiration of the lease of the 15th October, 1970. In the relevant circumstances a right to any new lease would not arise under s. 19 unless the premises were 'during the whole of the three years next preceeding the termination of such tenancy, bona fide used by the tenant for the time being thereof wholly or partly for the purpose of carrying on a business and, immediately before such termination, either was held by the tenant thereof under . . . or under a lease or other contract of tenancy for a term of not less than one year . . .' Sub-section 2*(b)* of s. 19 provides that the reference in s. 19 to the termination of a tenancy as a point in time shall be construed as referring, in the case of a tenancy terminating by the expiration of a term of years (as in this case), to the day which is three months before the expiration of such term. In other words, user by the tenant for the purpose of carrying on a business for at least three years and three months prior to the day upon which the tenancy expires is necessary before there is a right to a new tenancy. As the lease of 1970 was for three years certain, there was no right to a new tenancy when that lease expired. Indeed, as found by Mr. Justice Murnaghan, that lease was expressly limited to the period of three years for that purpose.

In the same way, there would be no right to a new tenancy in respect of the lease dated the 24th July, 1973, unless it could be established that the premises were used for the purpose of carrying on a business 'by the tenant for the time being thereof' for the whole of the period of three years and three months next preceding the 12th February, 1976. The applicants cannot establish this unless Coady was a tenant between the 6th February and the 12th February, 1973.

As to the first question, it was argued on behalf of the applicants that, for the period during which he occupied the premises during the currency of the caretaker's agreement, Coady was a tenant under an implied tenancy on the same terms, conditions and covenants as those created by the expired lease of 1970. It was alleged that Coady was in exclusive possession of the premises for that period, and it was submitted that he could not have been a caretaker because exclusive possession made him a tenant. It is not necessary for the purpose of this case to consider whether the occupation which Coady enjoyed during that period amounted to exclusive possession because, in my view, it is immaterial on the facts of this case. Whilst exclusive possession is one of the factors to be taken into account in determining whether an implied tenancy exists, it is not a decisive factor. To find whether it was intended to create a relationship of landlord and tenant, one must look at the transaction as a whole and at any indications that are to be found in the terms of the contract between the two parties: *per* Lord Denning at p. 615 and

Buckley L.J. at p. 618 of the report of *Shell-Mex* v. *Manchester Garages* ([1971] 1 W.L.R. 612).

Under s. 3 of the Landlord and Tenant Law Amendment Act, Ireland, 1860, the relation of landlord and tenant is deemed to be founded 'on the express or implied contract of the parties' and such relation shall be deemed to subsist in all cases in which there shall be 'an agreement by one party to hold land from or under another in consideration of any rent'. As there could be no question of an express contract in this case, the applicants were driven to alleging an implied contract. In my view, it would be doing violence to language to hold that an implied contract could exist on the facts of this case; the evidence is coercive in establishing that Coady went into occupation under a caretaker's agreement. In relation to implied tenancies, I would adopt the following passage from the judgment of the President of the High Court (Finlay P.) in *Baumann* v. *Elgin Contractors* ([1973] I.R. 169) at p. 177 of the report:

'As I understand the legal principles applicable, the true origin of an implied tenancy is that the law implies from the conduct of the parties what is, in effect, a silent agreement that their relationship shall be arranged in a certain contractual fashion.'

On the facts of this case, there is no room whatever for inferring a contrary silent agreement. The parties negotiated at arms length, both were fully advised legally, and the caretaker's agreement which was signed by Coady expressed the intention of the parties and was entered into at the behest of the solicitors for the tenant. Before signing it Coady, being the former tenant, was fully aware that unless he agreed to these terms he would not under any circumstances get another lease at a future time. He acknowledged that he was being put into possession as caretaker for the respondents *and not under any contract of tenancy*.

As to the second question, it was argued on behalf of the applicants that if the caretaker's agreement was a valid and subsisting agreement, it amounted to contracting out of the Act of 1931 and that, accordingly, it should be declared void. Section 42 of the Act of 1931 provides: 'A contract, whether made before or after the passing of this Act, by virtue of which a tenant would be directly or indirectly deprived of his right to obtain relief under this Act or any particular such relief shall be void.' The phrase 'relief under this Act' is defined in s. 2 and it includes a new tenancy under Part III of the Act.

When the caretaker's agreement was made, the tenant under the lease of 1970 had no right to a new tenancy under the Act of 1931. The caretaker's agreement was entered into with the express purpose of ensuring that the Act of 1931 would have no application. Indeed, the lease of 1970 was agreed to be for a term of three years with the express purpose of ensuring that the Act of 1931 would not apply. Although it is not lawful to contract out of the Act of 1931, a distinction must be drawn between a provision which attempts to exclude the Act from a transaction to which it applies, and a transaction to which the Act has no application. Thus, in *Hardiman* v. *Galway County Council* ([1966] I.R. 124) this Court held that a covenant by a tenant not to claim compensation for disturbance offended against s. 42 of the Act of 1931 and was void. In that case the term of the lease was 20 years and the tenant would clearly have been entitled to a new tenancy on the expiration of the lease.

Although s. 42 of the Act of 1931 avoids contracting out of the Act, it does not prevent the parties from so arranging matters that there is nothing to which the Act can apply. When the lease of 1970 expired, Coady was fully aware of the fact that he was not entitled to a new lease, and also that the respondents were not prepared to give him, or the company which he was in the process of forming, a new lease which would have the effect of giving the tenant rights under the Act of 1931 on its expiration. Both parties were deliberately and intentionally arranging the transaction in such a way as to ensure that the Act of 1931 did not apply. They understood each other perfectly, and they were fully advised. They were entitled to arrange matters in such a manner as not to attract the control of the Act. The agreement was not for the purpose of evading the Act of 1931 but of preventing the provisions of the Act from applying or, in other words, of arranging a lease which would be outside the scope of the Act. In my opinion, that is not in breach of s. 42 of the Act of 1931.

What is forbidden by s. 42 is a contract which deprives a tenant of 'his right to obtain relief under this Act.' What is envisaged by this section is a contract which would affect a tenant who *has* a right to relief under the Act. When the agreement to enter into the caretaker's agreement was made, Coady had no right to any relief under the Act of 1931 and the effect of that agreement was not to deprive him of any right to obtain such relief. When the lease of 1973 expired, the applicants had no right to a new lease under s. 19 as there had not been occupation of the premises by a *tenant* for the time being for the whole of the three years and three months immediately preceding the 12th February, 1976. There was no contract or agreement depriving the applicants of any right which they had to obtain relief under the Act of 1931, as they had never succeeded in acquiring such a right. This factor is to be contrasted with *Hardiman's Case* where the tenant had acquired rights under the Act of 1931 and the covenant was held to be void because it purported to deprive the tenant of his right to obtain relief.

Therefore, in my opinion, both questions submitted in the Case Stated should be answered in the negative.

Kenny J.:

By a lease made on the 15th October, 1970, the respondent company let to Leo Gerard Coady the Gatien Service Station, Rathfarnham, Dublin (together with the equipment in it) for three years from the 6th February, 1970. Coady covenanted that he would keep the premises open each day for the sale of motor fuels during the three-year period, that he would not carry on or permit to be carried on in the premises any business except that of a garage and petrol filling station without the consent in writing of the respondents, and that he would yield up the premises to them at the termination of the lease.

Section 19 in Part III of the Landlord and Tenant Act, 1931, provides: –

(1) On the termination within the meaning of this section of a tenancy in a tenement, this Part of this Act shall apply to such tenement if such tenement complies with any one of the following conditions, that is to say: –

    (*a*) such tenement was, during the whole of the three years next preceding the termination of such tenancy, bona fide used by the tenant for the time being thereof wholly or partly for the purpose of carrying on a business and, immediately before such termination, either was held by the tenant thereof under a tenancy from year to year or under a lease or other contract of tenancy for a term of not less than one year . . .

(2) References in this section to the termination of a tenancy as a point in time shall be construed as referring . . .

    (*b*) in the case of a tenancy terminating by the expiration of a term of years or other certain period or by any other certain event, to the day which is three months before the expiration of such term or period or the happening of such event . . .'

Section 20 of this Act of 1931 provides that a tenant of a tenement to which 'this

Part of this Act applies' shall, on the termination of his tenancy in such tenement, be entitled to a new tenancy in such tenement. Sections 19 and 20 are included in Part III of the Act of 1931.

Therefore, Coady would not have been entitled to a new tenancy under s. 19 of the Act of 1931 when his tenancy expired on the 6th February, 1973. On the 12th December, 1972, his former solicitor wrote to the respondents asking them whether they were prepared to give his client a new tenancy in the premises when his existing one would expire. The respondents replied that they were prepared to give Coady a new tenancy from the 12th February, 1973, for a period of three years but that Coady would have to vacate the premises for a week from the 6th to the 12th February. Coady went to another firm of solicitors who wrote that their client was worried over the suggestion that he would have to vacate the premises for a week and then resume possession. They also stated that the new lease would be taken in the name of the applicant company, which was then being formed. Negotiations took place between the respondents and Coady's solicitors. Efforts were made to find a method by which Coady would not acquire the right to a new tenancy under the Act of 1931 and, at the same time, would not have to vacate the premises, as he feared that this would damage the goodwill of the business which he had built up.

It was ultimately agreed that Coady would be allowed to remain in the premises as a caretaker only for the period of one week and that the new tenancy would commence on the 12th February, 1973, and would be for a period of three years. Before Coady signed the acknowledgment that he was a caretaker, he knew that he would not be given a new tenancy of the premises unless he did so and that the interval of a week and the acknowledgment were being required to prevent him acquiring rights to a new tenancy under the Act of 1931. He was fully advised on the position by his solicitor before he signed the acknowledgment that he was a caretaker. This document is of such importance that I must set it out in full. It reads: –

'I, Leo Gerard Coady do hereby acknowledge that I have been this day put into the possession of all that the premises and equipment attached thereto Gatien Service Station, Whitechurch Road, Rathfarnham, Co. Dublin, as caretaker by and for Continental Oil Company of Ireland (Conoco) and that now I am in possession of said premises and equipment solely as such caretaker of and for Conoco and not under any contract of tenancy. And I hereby further acknowledge that I have undertaken and agree and I do now hereby undertake and agree with Conoco to take care of the said premises and equipment for him *[sic]* and to preserve same from trespass and injury and to deliver up the possession thereof to Conoco its successors, his heirs *[sic]* or assigns, when required so to do.'

This document is dated the 6th February, 1973; it was signed by Coady on the 5th February and his signature was witnessed by Mr. Prior, who certified that he had read the document to Coady and had explained it to him.

The terms of the new lease were agreed on the 10th February, 1973, but its execution did not take place until the 24th July, 1973, because of the delays experienced in the formation of the applicant company. By the lease of the 24th July, 1973, the respondents let the premises to the applicants for three years from the 12th February, 1973, and the applicants covenanted with the respondents in terms substantially similar to those in the lease of 1970. The lease of 1973 expired on the 12th February, 1976.

On the 10th July, 1975, the applicants served notice of their intention to seek relief under the Act of 1931, and on the 29th March, 1976, they served notice of their intention to apply to the Circuit Court for a new tenancy. In that notice they stated that their tenancy in the premises 'terminated' – within the meaning of that term in s. 19 of the Act of 1931 – on the 12th November, 1975. The applicants' application for a new tenancy succeeded in the Circuit Court and the respondents appealed to the High Court. The applicants' principal arguments in both Courts were that Coady had exclusive possession of the premises from the 6th February to the 12th February, 1973, and that, therefore, he had been a tenant of the premises for that week so that he and the applicants had been using the premises for more than three years as tenants. They also submitted that if this first proposition was wrong, the caretaker's agreement of the 6th February, 1973, was made void by s. 42 of the Act of 1931.

When the evidence and arguments had concluded, the High Court judge said that he was prepared to accept the arguments advanced by counsel for the respondents. Counsel for the applicants then asked the judge to state a Case for the opinion of this Court.

[Having referred to the questions posed in the Case Stated, the judge continued] The applicants' counsel argued that the caretaker's agreement created a tenancy because the tenant was in exclusive possession of the premises from the 6th February to the 12th February, 1973. He said that the law in the Republic of Ireland was different to that in England, and that in this State a person who has exclusive possession of land must be regarded as holding it as a tenant. He went on to argue that the reality of the arrangements made between the respondents and Coady was that they created a tenancy from the 6th February to the 12th February, 1973.

When determining whether a person in possession of land is to be regarded as a tenant or as being in some other category, exclusive possession by the person in possession is undoubtedly a most important consideration but it is not decisive. The existence of the relationship of landlord and tenant or some other relationship is determined by the law on a consideration of many factors and not by the label which the parties put on it. Even if the documents disclose an intention to confer exclusive possession on the person in possession, it does not necessarily follow that he is a tenant. All the terms of the document and the circumstances in which it was entered into have to be considered.

In *Shell-Mex* v. *Manchester Garages* ([1971] 1 W.L.R. 612) Lord Justice Denning M.R. said at pp. 615 – 616 of the report: – 'I turn, therefore, to the point: was this transaction a licence or a tenancy? This does not depend on the label which is put on it. It depends on the nature of the transaction itself: see *Addiscombe Garden Estates Ltd.* v. *Crabbe* ([1958] 1 K.B. 513). Broadly speaking, we have to see whether it is a personal privilege given to a person (in which case it is a licence), or whether it grants an interest in land, in which case it is a tenancy. At one time it used to be thought that exclusive possession was a decisive factor. But that is not so. It depends on broader considerations altogether . . . But Mr. Dillon says that Manchester Garages Ltd. have exclusive possession, and that that carries with it a tenancy. That is old law which is now gone. As I have said many times, exclusive possession is no longer decisive. We have to look at the nature of the transaction to see whether it is a personal privilege or nnot.'

I do not agree with the submission by the applicants' counsel that the law in the Republic of Ireland is different to that in England on this matter. No case has been cited by him which supports this proposition, while there is at least one decision of this Court which seems to me to disprove it. In *Davies* v. *Hiliard* ((1965) 101 I.L.T.R. 50) the defendant signed a caretaker's agreement on the 4th March, 1964, and went into occupation of two flats which were the property of the plaintiff. On the 21st March, 1964, a cheque for £160 for rent for six months payable in advance was given to the plaintiff's solicitor, who paid the sum for which the cheque was drawn to the owners. During this period a proposed tenancy agreement was being discussed but complete agreement was never reached and the document was not executed by either party. The plaintiff demanded possession of the premises and, when this was refused, he issued a caretaker's summons in the District Court. The District Justice made an order for possession and the defendant appealed to the Circuit Court. The Circuit Court judge stated a Case for this Court, and this Court held that the Circuit Court judge should affirm the order of the District Justice as, on the evidence, the defendant did not hold the premises as a tenant of the plaintiff. In that case the defendant had paid rent and was undoubtedly in exclusive possession but, despite that, this Court decided that he did not hold the property as a tenant but as a caretaker.

In principle, therefore, supported by the decision to which I have referred, the argument of the applicants' counsel is incorrect. This conclusion is also supported by a passage at p. 732 in Wylie's Irish Land Law for the accuracy of which, in relation to the law in the Republic of Ireland, I have accepted responsibility: see p. vii of the preface. That passage states: 'The rule now may be stated that, if the "grantee" of the land in question does not have possession of it, he is clearly not a tenant. If he does have possession, he may be a tenant but this is not necessarily the case.'

Coady signed the caretaker's agreement acknowledging that he had been put into possession of the premises as caretaker for the respondents and that he was in possession of the premises and equipment solely as such caretaker for the respondents and not under any contract of tenancy. The tenancy created by the lease of 1970 ended on the 6th February, 1973. The tenancy created by the lease of 1973 commenced on the 12th February, 1973, and neither Coady nor the applicants paid anything in respect of the period 6th – 12th February, 1973. The caretaker's agreement, the non-payment of any sum for the period 6th – 12th February, 1973, and all the surrounding circumstances indicate that Coady was not a tenant from the 6th – 12th February, 1973, and that the caretaker's agreement of the 6th February, 1973, did not create a tenancy.

The second question asked by the High Court judge relates to the effect of the provisions of s. 42 of the Act of 1931. That section provides: 'A contract, whether made before or after the passing of this Act, by virtue of which a tenant would be directly or indirectly deprived of his right to obtain relief under this Act or any particular such relief shall be void.' The phrase 'relief under this Act' is defined by s. 2 of the Act of 1931 which states that it shall be construed as equivalent to the expression 'compensation for improvements or a new tenancy under Part III of this Act.'

In my opinion s. 42 operates to make void a contract which would deprive a tenant of a right which he has to obtain relief under the Act of 1931. He must have such a right before he can rely on the section to make void a contract which, directly or indirectly, deprives him of that right. The foundation of the section is that there is an existing right of a tenant to relief under the Act; if he has this, a contract which deprives him of it, whether directly or indirectly, is void. In the instant case the applicants did not use the premises for the purpose of carrying on a business during the whole of the three years preceding the 12th Novemeber, 1975, and they cannot invoke any part of the period of three years during which Coady was in occupation under the lease of 1970 because neither the applicants nor Coady were in occupation as tenants between the 6th and the 12th February, 1973.

The applicants' counsel also argued that the caretaker's agreement of the 6th February, 1973, had the effect that Coady was deprived of his right to a new tenancy by it. Even if the caretaker's agreement was made void by s. 42 of the Act of 1931 (a proposition which I do not accept), once it is held that it did not create the relationship of landlord and tenant, the applicants are not entitled to a new tenancy because they and Coady were not in possession for the necessary period of three years calculated in accordance with the standard specified in s. 19 of the Act.

Section 42 of the Act of 1931 was considered by this Court in *Hardiman* v. *Galway County Council* ([1966] I.R. 124) but the meaning of the terms "indirectly" deprived' in the section did not arise for determination in that case. I confess that I do not understand what the parliamentary draftsman had in mind when he referred to "indirect" deprivation. How can a tenant be indirectly deprived of his right to obtain relief under the Act of 1931? I was happy to find that in 1932 Mr. T.C. Kingsmill Moore (subsequently Mr. Justice Kingsmill Moore, and a member of this Court) and Mr. Odell had a similar difficulty for, at p. 81 of their book published in 1932, they wrote in relation to this section: – 'It is difficult to see what contracts "indirectly" deprive the tenant of his right to relief.' I reserve the problem of the meaning of this delpic phrase for future consideration because, in my view, a decision as to its meaning is not required in this case.

Both questions in the Case Stated should be answered 'No'.

Parke J.:

I have read the judgments already delivered and I would answer both questions in the negative.

Notes

1. Part III of the Landlord and Tenant Act, 1931, has now been replaced by Part II of the Landlord and Tenant (Amendment) Act, 1980: see *Irish Land Law,* Supp. (1975 – 80), pp. 57 – 59.
2. As regards the distinction between a lease and a licence, see *Irish Land Law,* para. 17.008 *et seq.* See also *Irish Shell and B.P. Ltd* v. *Costello Ltd.* [1981] I.L.R.M. 66; *Bellew* v. *Bellew* [1982] I.R. 447, [1983] I.L.R.M. 128.

IRISH LAND COMMISSION V. HOLMES
(1898) 32 I.L.T.R. 85 (Queen's Bench)

This issue before the Court arose from a case stated by Madden, J., at the Assizes held at Nenagh, July, 1897, on appeal from the County Court Judge of Co. Tipperary. Certain premises known as the Hop Garden, in the town of Nenagh, had been granted in March, 1869, by defendant's predecessor in title to a Mr. Harding to hold for ever, subject to the payment of £1 yearly and certain usual covenants. In March, 1897, the Irish Land Commission issued a Civil Bill against Holmes to recover £4, being the aggregate amount of the tithes rent-charge for six years. The County Court Judge dismissed the appeal.

Palles C.B.:

My difficulty throughout has been to see how argument can arise in this case. The question is whether the defendant Holmes is liable to pay the tithe rent-charge when admittedly by this instrument of March, 1869, he has no estate in the lands. I call it an instrument because the parties are not agreed as to what exactly to call it. Whatever it be called it passed the fee-simple in the lands subject ot the payment of a yearly rent, and was an instrument whereby the relation of landlord and tenant was created under s. 3 of what we are told not to call Deasy's Act. I shall treat it as Dr. Falconer desires on this basis. Dealing with it as though the term fee-simple were inserted instead of 'lease for ever,' it is clear that, referring to the Tithe Rent-charge (Ir.) Act, 1838, s. 7, Harding's estate answers the conditions of the section that the tithes shall be payable by the party having the first estate of inheritance, &c., under which there shall be no perpetual estate or interest. That simple consideration concludes the case, but the arguments have been so elaborate that I do not like to leave it there. Prior to 1861 the relation of landlord and tenant depended upon the existence of a reversion, and the object of s. 3 of the Act of 1860 was to get rid of the inconvenience that this necessity caused, yet in the teeth of the section it is argued that there is a kind of sectional reversion left, which does not amount even to a *scintilla juris,* for that has a real existence. The relationship was made to depend upon contract, not upon actual tenure, and all that one has to do is to look, not to an estate, but to an agreement for the payment of rent – *i.e.,* the relationship of landlord and tenant in respect to the payment of rent does not depend upon an estate in the lands, and so when one finds that relationship it does not go one step towards elucidating the question here, and accordingly the line of decisions referred to by Dr. Falconer does not assist us. [His Lordship here explained the decision in *Adams* v. *Alexander* (28 I.L.T.R. 141).] In this case we have no estate; nothing remains but a rent; and is Stanley's Act applicable to a case of this kind? The policy of the Act without going through its sections is evident – namely, that the tithe composition should attach to the fee. S. 12, after exempting tenancies at will as from year to year from the liability for tithes after 1833, provides that as successive interests in lands determine the liability shall fall upon the next higher interests until ultimately it shall rest upon the fee-simple; and to prevent this policy being defeated with regard to future estates s. 13 was enacted, that in any future setting, letting, or demise of lands the tenant or lessee shall hold free from the payment of tithes or composition for tithes. But even if there could have been a lease of the fee there could have been no liability for tithes upon the lessor, for the estate that is to be freed from liability must be one less than the fee. The meaning of the Act is that liability must rest upon the fee. For all these reasons, whether taken together or separately, the tithe rent-charge is not payable by Holmes.

O'Brien and **Johnson, JJ.,** also delivered concurring judgments.

Notes
1. See further on section 3 of Deasy's Act, *Chute* v. *Busteed*, p. 155, *ante*, *Twaddle* v. *Murphy*, p. 113, *ante* and *Bayley* v. *Conyngham*, p. 311, *ante*. And on the Act generally, see *Lyle* v. *Smith*, p. 575, *post*. See also *Irish Land Law*, para. 17.005 *et seq*.
2. As regards tithe rentcharges, see *ibid*. para. 6.120 *et seq*.

McCAUSLAND V. MURPHY
(1881) 9 L.R.Ir. 9 (Chancery Division)

The defendants' agent, with full authority, though not in writing, advertised a house and farm to be let. Several proposals were sent in – one by the plaintiff, in writing, offering £2 per acre for such term as might be agreed on. The proposals were laid before the defendants by the agent, who explained to them their nature and effect. The plaintiff's and another were selected, and the agent was authorised to accept either, if satisfied with security for the rent. The agent prepared a draft lease from the defendants to the plaintiff for thirty-one years, which he read to the plaintiff, and wrote on the draft the names of the proposed sureties, which he afterwards inserted in the draft as co-lessees with the plaintiff. The plaintiff afterwards attended at an auction of the furniture and farming-stock, and purchased some of the furniture and a large quantity of manure for the farm. In a suit for specific performance, the defendants denied the agent's authority to conclude the agreement for a letting, or to put the plaintiff in possession, and they pleaded the Statute of Frauds, and that the agent was not authorised in writing, as required by the Landlord and Tenant Act, 1860, sect. 4.

Sullivan M.R. said that the defendants the Misses Murphy relied on two defences. First, they say that Mr. Warnock was not authorised by them to conclude an agreement for the letting of the lands; that he was authorised to negotiate for a letting, but he was not authorised to conclude any agreement without their sanction being given to the particular terms of it; and they never sanctioned the letting in the draft lease. Secondly, they say that they are not bound by the agreement in point of law, as Mr. Warnock was not authorised in writing to make the agreement; and they rely on the Statute of Frauds (7 Wm. 3 c. 12, s. 1, Ir.) and on the Landlord and Tenant (Ireland) Act, 1860, s. 4. As to the first defence, His Honor went fully through the evidence, and expressed his opinion that Mr. Warnock was authorised by the defendants on every point – to make the letting, to take the plaintiff M'Causland as tenant, and to give him possession on the terms of the tenancy. As to the legal defence, a question of difficulty was raised as to the construction of the 4th section of the Act of 1860. Previously to that Act, there was a well-marked distinction drawn by the Statute of Frauds. By the 1st section of that Act, an agent, to make a lease for his principal when an interest was intended to be actually passed, must have been authorised in writing; whereas under the 2nd section, where a mere agreement was entered into, the agent need not be authorised in writing. The contrast between the two sections was plain and clear. The Act of 1860 made a great alteration in the law, and one would expect to find its provisions plain and clear, if the intention was to put an end to the distinction between an actual lease and an agreement. But no such intention was expressed in the Act. The 1st section of the Statute of Frauds is repealed by the schedule, and the provisions of the 4th section of the Act of 1860 are substituted for it as to actual leases. But the 2nd section of the Statute of Frauds is not repealed, though by the 1st and 3rd sections of the Act of 1860 the relation of landlord and tenant is founded on the express or implied contract of the parties; and a lease means any instrument in writing containing a contract of tenancy. In this case there was authority to make a preliminary agreement for a future tenancy, and a lease was to be executed. In his opinion, therefore, the plaintiff was entitled to specific performance of the pre-liminary agreement by the execution of a lease in the terms of the draft lease.

Notes
See further *Irish Land Law*, para. 17.017 *et seq.*

II. COVENANTS AND AGREEMENTS

LANDLORD AND TENANT LAW (AMENDMENT) ACT, IRELAND, 1860

11. Every assignee of the estate or interest or any part thereof of any tenant, by lawful assignment, or by devise, bequest, or act and operation of law, made after the passing of this Act, shall be subject to the observance of all agreements in respect of assignment or subletting to the same extent as the original tenant might have been.

12. Every landlord of any lands holden under any lease or other contract of tenancy shall have the same action and remedy against the tenant, and the assignee of his estate or interest, or their respective heirs, executors, or administrators, in respect of the agreements contained or implied in such lease or contract, as the original landlord might have had against the original tenant, or his heir or personal representative respectively; and the heir or personal representative of such land-lord on whom his estate or interest under any such lease or contract shall devolve or should have devolved shall have the like action and remedy against the tenant, and the assignee of his estate or interest, and their respective heirs or personal repre-sentatives, for any damage done to the said estate or interest of such landlord by reason of the breach of any agreement contained or implied in the lease or other contract of tenancy in the lifetime of the landlord, as such landlord himself might have had.

13. Every tenant of any lands shall have the same action and remedy against the landlord and the assignee of his estate or interest, or their respective heirs, executors, or administrators, in respect of the agreements contained or implied in the lease or other contract concerning the lands, as the original tenant might have had against the original landlord, or his heir or personal representative respectively; and the heir or personal representative of such tenant, on whom his estate or interest shall devolve or should have devolved, shall have the like action and remedy against the landlord, and the assignee of his estate or interest, and their respective heirs and personal representatives, for any damage done to the said estate or interest of such tenant by reason of the breach of any agreement contained or implied in the lease or other contract of tenancy in the lifetime of the tenant, as such tenant might have had.

14. No landlord or tenant, being such by assignment, devise, bequest, or act and operation of law only, shall have the benefit or be liable in respect of the breach of any covenant or contract contained or implied in the lease or other contract of tenancy, otherwise than in respect of such rent as shall have accrued due, and such breaches as shall have occurred or continued subsequent to such assignment, and whilst he shall have continued to be such assignee: Provided, however, that no assignment made by any assignee of the estate or interest of any tenant shall discharge such assignee from his liability to the landlord, unless and until notice in writing of the particulars of such assignment shall have been given to the landlord.

15. Every tenant, being an assignee as aforesaid, who shall have assigned his estate or interest in the lease or other contract of tenancy in the interval between two gale days, shall, notwithstanding such assignment, be liable as assignee to the payment of the rent and the performance of the agreements contained in the lease or other contract up to and including the gale day next following the service of notice of the said assignment.

16. From and after any assignment hereafter to be made of the estate or interest of any original tenant in any lease, with the consent of the landlord, testified in manner specified in section ten, the landlord so consenting shall be deemed to have released and discharged the said tenant from all actions and remedies at the suit of such landlord, and all persons claiming by, through, or under him, in respect of any future breach of the agreements contained in the lease, but without prejudice to any remedy or right against the assignee of such estate or interest.

CONVEYANCING ACT, 1881

10. – (1) Rent reserved by a lease, and the benefit of every covenant or provision therein contained, having reference to the subject-matter thereof, and on the lessees part to be observed or performed, and every condition of re-entry and other condition therein contained, shall be annexed and incident to and shall go with the reversionary estate in the land, or in any part thereof, immediately expectant on the term granted by the lease, notwithstanding severance of that reversionary estate, and shall be capable of being recovered, received, enforced, and taken advantage of by the person from time to time entitled, subject ot the term, to the income of the whole or any part, as the case may require, of the land leased.

(2) This section applies only to leases made after the commencement of this Act.

11. – (1) The obligation of a covenant entered into by a lessor with reference to the subject-matter of the lease shall, if and as far as the lessor has power to bind the reversionary estate immediately expectant on the term granted by the lease, be annexed and incident to and shall go with that reversionary estate, or the several parts thereof, notwithstanding severance of that reversionary estate, and may be taken advantage of and enforced by the person in whom the term is from time to time vested by conveyance, devolution in law, or otherwise; and, if and as far as the lessor has power to bind the person from time to time entitled to that reversionary estate, the obligation aforesaid may be taken advantage of and enforced against any person so entitled.

(2) This section applies only to leases made after the commencement of this Act.

LANDLORD AND TENANT (AMENDMENT) ACT, 1980
PART V
COVENANTS IN LEASES OF TENEMENTS

64. – In this Part, 'lease' includes a yearly tenancy arising by operation of law or by inference on the expiration of a lease and a statutory tenancy implied by holding over premises on the expiration of a lease.

65. – Where a lease (whether made before of after the commencement of this Act) of a tenement contains a covenant (whether express or implied and whether general or specific) on the part of the lessee to put or keep the tenement in repair during the currency of the lease or to leave or put the tenement in repair at the expiration of the lease and there has been a breach of the covenant, the subsequent provisions of this section shall have effect.

(2) The damages recoverable in any court for the breach shall not in any case exceed the amount (if any) by which the value of the reversion (whether mediate or immediate) in the tenement is diminished owing to the breach.

(3) Save where the want of repair is shown to be due, wholly or substantially, to wilful damage or wilful waste committed by the lessee no damages shall be recoverable in any court for the breach if it is shown –

(*a*) that, having regard to the age and condition of the tenement, its repair in accordance with the covenant is physically impossible, or

(*b*) that, having regard to the age, condition, character and situation of the tenement, its repair in accordance with the covenant would involve expenditure which is excessive in proportion to the value of the tenement, or

(*c*) that, having regard to the character and situation of the tenement, the tenement could not when so repaired be profitably used or could not be profitably used unless it were re-built, re-constructed or structurally altered to a substantial extent.

66. – A covenant in a lease (whether made before or after the commencement of this Act) of a tenement absolutely prohibiting or restricting the alienation of the tenement, either generally or in any particular manner, shall have effect as if it were a covenant prohibiting or restricting such alienation without the licence or consent of the lessor.

(2) In every lease (whether made before or after the commencment of this Act) in which there is contained or in which there is implied by virtue of the British Statute passed on the 5th day of May, 1826, and entitled 'An Act to amend the Law of Ireland respecting the Assignment and Sub-letting of Lands and Tenements' or by virtue of *subsection (1)* a covenant prohibiting or restricting the alienation, either generally or in any particular manner, of the tenement without the licence or consent of the lessor, the covenant shall, notwithstanding any express provision to the contrary, be subject –

(*a*) to a proviso that the licence or consent shall not be unreasonably withheld, but this proviso shall not preclude the lessor from requiring payment of a reasonable sum in respect of legal or other expenses incurred by him in connection with the licence or consent, and

    (*b*) where the lease is made for a term of more than forty years and is made in consideration wholly or partially of the erection or substantial addition to or improvement or alteration of buildings, to a proviso to the effect that, in the case of any alienation of the tenement in contravention of the covenant effected more than seven years before the end of the term, no such licence or consent shall be required if notice in writing of the transaction is given to the lessor within one month after the transaction is effected, and

    (*c*) where such alienation would cause a transfer or increase of any rates, taxes or other burden to or of the lessor, to a proviso that all expenditure incurred by the lessor by reason of the transfer or increase shall be reimbursed by the lessee to the lessor as and when so incurred and shall be recoverable from the lessee as rent under the lease.

67. – (1) A covenant in a lease (whether made before or after the commencement of this Act) of a tenement absolutely prohibiting the alteration of the user of the tenement shall have effect as if it were a covenant prohibiting such alteration without the licence or consent of the lessor.

(2) In every lease (whether made before or after the commencement of this Act) of a tenement in which there is contained a covenant prohibiting either expressly or by virtue of *subsection (1)* the alteration of the user of the tenement without the licence or consent of the lessor, the covenant shall, notwithstanding any express provision to the contrary, be subject –

    (*a*) to a proviso to the effect that the licence or consent shall not be unreasonably witheld, but this proviso shall not preclude the lessor from requiring payment of a reasonable sum in respect of legal or other expenses incurred by him in connection with the licence or consent, and

    (*b*) unless the alteration involves the erection, provision or reconstruction (otherwise than as an improvement within the meaning of *subsection (3)*) of any building or structure, to a proviso that no fine or sum of money in the nature of a fine (other than any sum authorised by this section) nor any increase of rent shall be payable for or in respect of the licence or consent, and

    (*c*) if the alteration would cause a transfer or increase of any rates, taxes oor other burden to or of the lessor, to a proviso that all exprenditure incurred by the lessor by reason of the transfer or increase shall be reimbursed by the lessee to the lessor as and when so incurred and shall be recoverable from the lessee by the lessor as rent under the lease.

(3) In this section and *section 68*, 'improvement' means any addition to or alteration of a building or structure and includes any structure which is ancillary or subsidiary thereto but does not include any alteration or reconstruction of a building or structure so that it loses its original identity.

(4) The references in section 29 of the Act of 1967 to an improvement shall be construed as references to an improvement within the meaning of *subsection (3)*.

68. – (1) A covenant in a lease (whether made before or after the commencement of this Act) of a tenement absolutely prohibiting the making of any improvement within the meaning of *section 67 (3)* on the tenement shall have effect as if it were a covenant prohibiting the making of the improvment without the licence or consent of the lessor.

(2) In every lease (whether made before or after the commencement of this Act) of a tenement in which there is contained a covenant prohibiting either expressly or

by virtue of *subsection (1),* the making of any improvement within the meaning of *section 67 (3)* on the tenement without the licence or consent of the lessor, the covenant shall, notwithstanding any express provision to the contrary, be subject –

(*a*) to a proviso that the licence or consent shall not be unreasonably witheld, and

(*b*) to a proviso that no fine or sum of money in the nature of a fine (other than a reasonable sum in respect of legal or other expenses incurred by him in connection with the licence or consent) nor any increase of rent shall be payable for or in respect of the licence or consent.

69. – Where –

(*a*) a lease (whether made before or after the commencement of this Act) of a tenement contains a covenant prohibiting or restricting the doing by the lessee of any particular thing without the licence or consent of the lessor, and

(*b*) the rent reserved by the lease has not been paid for five or more years, and

(*c*) the lessor is not known to and cannot be found by the lessee,

the Court may, on the application of the lessee and after the publication of such (if any) advertisements as the Court directs, authorise the lessee, subject to such (if any) conditions as the the Court thinks fit to impose, to do the particular thing so prohibited or restricted and thereupon it shall be lawful for the lessee to do such particular thing without the licence or consent of the lessor, in accordance with the conditions (if any) so imposed.

O'REILLY V. EAST COAST CINEMAS LTD.

In the year 1947 the plaintiffs granted a lease of a tenement and the lessee's estate was assigned to the defendants in the year 1948. In the year 1951 the defendants were informed that the tenement was in a state of disrepair. In the year 1955, when the term of years created by the lease of 1947 had 12 years to run, the defendants surrendered that lease and the plaintiffs granted a new lease of the tenement to the defendants for a term of 35 years. Each lease contained a covenant by the lessee to keep the tenement in good and sufficient repair during the relevant term of years and to deliver possession at the end or sooner determination of the relevant term in such repair. The defendants allowed the tenement to fall into disrepair and, in the year 1959, the plaintiffs claimed in the High Court damages from the defendants for breaches of the covenants for repair. At the trial of the action the defendants contended that the plaintiffs, by accepting the surrender and by granting the lease of 1955, had waived any existing claim for damages for breach of the covenant to repair contained in the lease of 1947.

The defendants also relied on the provisions of s. 55 of the Landlord and Tenant Act, 1931, which provide that, unless a state of disrepair is shown to have been due to 'wilful damage or wilful waste committed' by the lessee, no damages shall be recoverable for the breach by a lessee of a covenant to repair contained in a lease of a tenement if it is shown that it would be impossible or uneconomic to repair the tenement (see now s. 65 of the 1980 Act, p. 555. *ante*). It was agreed that the repair of the tenement would not be an economic proposition and the defendants submitted that the plaintiffs had not shown that the state of disrepair of the tenement was due to 'wilful damage or wilful waste committed' by the defendants. In dismissing the plaintiff's claim it was held by Davitt P., 1, that the plaintiffs had not waived their claim for damages for breach of the covenant to repair contained in the lease of 1947. 2. That that the defendants, intentionally and deliberately, had taken no action to repair the tenement while it fell into rack and ruin but that the defendants' inaction did not constitute wilful damage or wilful waste committed by them within the meaning of s. 55 of the Act of 1931, as interpreted by the Supreme Court in *Gilligan* v. *Silke* [1963] I.R. 1. The plaintiffs appealed to the Supreme Court.

Ó Dálaigh C.J.:

This appeal, which is from a judgment of the former President, Davitt P., is concerned with the correct interpretation of s. 55 (b) of the Landlord and Tenant Act, 1931. The meaning of this section was considered by this Court in *Gilligan* v. *Silke* ([1963] I.R. 1). The former President took the view that the case precluded him from finding in favour of the plaintiffs. He therefore dismissed the action with costs.

The judgment of Davitt P. sets out the facts and circumstances of the case at length. For the purpose of this appeal it will suffice to present a brief summary. The action is for damages for breach of covenant to repair. The premises in question are in Bray, Co. Wicklow. It would appear that they were created about the middle of the last century, and at different times they have been used as assembly rooms, Turkish baths, a skating rink and latterly as a cinema. User as a cinema commenced some time prior to the year 1936 and continued until August, 1947, when a fire occurred in the operating box in the gallery. The fire did not do much damage. It was necessary to close the cinema pending the carrying out of certain alterations required by the local authority. The premises have not been re-opened since then. The building consists of a hall or auditorium with an arched roof and two subsidiary structures. The first of these is a flat-roofed vestibule in the front of the building, and the second is a return building at the rear containing toilets and cloakrooms. The roof of this latter building is A-shaped.

In the year 1936, Mr. Maurice Baum acquired the lessee's interest from a Mrs. McDermott; the McDermott lease expired in 1946. On the 1st April, 1947, the plaintiffs as lessors granted a new lease to Mr. Baum for a period of 21 years from the 1st May, 1946, and in May, 1948, he assigned his interest under the lease to the defendant company of which he is a managing director.

The work required to be done by the local authority following the fire included a provision for a projection box which would be exterior to the premises of the lessees and would overhang the adjoining premises of the lessors. The lessors refused their consent to this structure and, in the result, the alterations were never carried out. In the year 1949 the defendants decided to abandon the idea of reconstructing the premises as a cinema and instead to re-plan them as a repertory theatre. Their architects, Messrs. Good & Siberry, prepared plans and specifications for submission to the lessors. The lessors' approval was given in January, 1949, and subsequently in 1951, after certain modifications were agreed upon, the approval of the local authority was obtained.

Up to the year 1952 it was necessary to obtain a licence from the Department of Industry and Commerce to carry out the reconstruction work envisaged. The only licence which could be obtained was to do work for a cost not exceeding £500 in each year, and for a period of about 4 years the defendants carried out a considerable amount of demolition work. This demolition work may be summarised as follows. The balcony and operating box and the box-office in the vestibule were removed; the front wall between the two entrance doors was broken down to make way for a wider new entrance; the inner wall openings were built up and new ones made; and defective plaster was hacked off the walls. It also appears that during this period of 4 years lead was stripped from the flat roof of the vestibule and from the valley gutters of the return building, but no evidence was given as to how this occurred or who was responsible for it.

When, in 1952, a licence was no longer required for building work, the defendants were faced with raising money to carry through their plans. One of the difficulties was the comparatively short term of their lease. After negotiations with the plaintiffs, the lease of 1947 was surrendered and a new lease for a longer term granted. This is the lease of the 12th March, 1955, which granted the premises for a term of 35 years from the 1st January, 1955. Notwithstanding the grant of a longer term, the defendants appear to have been unsuccessful in finding the necessary finance for the work involved and nothing more was done. The defendants eventually went into voluntary liquidation and in April, 1963, the liquidator surrendered possession of the premises to the plaintiffs. The present proceedings were instituted in 1959 but did not come for hearing until May, 1966.

Davitt P. held that the defendants, intentionally and deliberately, stood by and did nothing in the way of necessary repairs while the premises literally went to rack and ruin. The dilapidated state and condition of the premises was, however, in his view not due to the demolition work which the defendants had carried out. He found that the real cause of the failure was the defendants' failure to keep the premises weatherproof. While defects in the main roof (which the lessors covenanted to keep in repair) may have contributed to the appearance of dry rot, this was not the main cause. The principal cause, as found by Davitt P., was the failure to make the roof of the return building at the rear stauch and weatherproof after the lead gutters had been stripped. In addition Davitt P. held that considerable damage must also have resulted from the failure to replaster the walls after the old plaster had been hacked off. He summarised his findings by saying: 'In short, it was not the acts of demolition whcih caused the damage; it was the failure to secure the premises, temporarily at least, from the effects of the weather during and after the work of demolition.'

Although Davitt P. held that the defendants, intentionally and deliberately, stood by and did nothing in the way of necessary repairs while the premises literally went to rack and ruin, he nevertheless was of opinion that this did not amount to wilful waste within the meaning of s. 55 (b) of the Act of 1931 as interpreted by this Court in *Gilligan* v. *Sike* ([1963] I.R. 1). He said that in that case Maguire J. 'took the view that to constitue wilful waste there would have to be some act or acts committed by the lessee deliberately and intentionally directed towards the spoliation of the tenement.' That had not been established in this case, and he therefore dismissed the plaintiffs' action.

The evidence with regard to the stripping of gutters of the vestibule and return building can be disposed of shortly. The plaintiff, Mr. O'Reilly, was unable to say by whom the lead had been removed; he did not see the actual stripping. Mr. Baum, for the defendants, said that all they did was to put rubberoid on the return building and that no one, to his knowledge, had stripped the lead from either of these buildings. He added that he had not heard of lead being removed until the hearing in court that day. One may summarise the effect of this evidence by saying that the plaintiff did not establish that the stripping of lead from the roof of the vestibule and of the return building was part of the demolition work carried out by the defendant company. The position therefore appears to be that the condition of the roofs of these two buildings is not to be ascribed to any positive action upon the part of the defendants, but that it is due rather to wear or tear and to the action of some third party for whom the defendants are not responsible.

On the 19th November, 1951, the Town Engineer, Mr. Healy, wrote to Mr. Siberry, the defendants' architect, calling his attention to the fact that the roofs of the annexes were leaking rather badly and would need considerable repairs. Notwithstanding this, no step whatever was taken by the defendants to make the roofs of these buildings weatherproof and, as Davitt P. has found, the defendants intentionally and deliberately abstained from doing the necessary repairs. It was this action on their part which he said was the principal cause of the dilapidated condition into which the premises later fell.

The defendants' conduct amounted to wilful permissive waste, that is to say, being aware of the leaking state of the roofs of the annexes from, at latest,

November, 1951, they took no steps, intentionally and deliberately, to prevent the premises falling into a dilapidated condition. Davitt P. clearly interpreted *Gilligan* v. *Silke* ([1963] I.R. 1) as holding that wilful permissive waste was not wilful waste within the meaning of s. 55 (b) of the Act of 1931.

Kingsmill Moore J., who delivered the first judgment in the Supreme Court in *Gilligan's Case* ([1963] I.R. 1), was of opinion that there were certain items of damage in that case which would fall under the heading of 'wilful waste' and, as Davitt P. had not decided that question in *Gilligan's Case* ([1963] I.R. 1), he would have sent the case back for retrial on this point. At p. 20 of the report Kingsmill Moore J. defined 'wilful' as meaning 'conscious and deliberate' or, as he put it later, as 'something deliberate and intentional, something which involves a choice of courses, something to which the mind and will is a party.' He was also of the view that 'waste' was a term of legal art and, as such, was divided into 'voluntary waste' and 'permissive waste'. Moreover, he was clearly of the view that the verb 'commit', in the context of the phrase 'wilful waste committed', covered acts of omission as well as acts of commission and he cited old and established authority for this view. Both Maguire J. and Lavery J. were of opinion that Sheila Gilligan's action should be dismissed. At the invitation of Lavery J., who presided, Maguire J. delivered his judgment before that of Lavery J. Lavery J. in his judgment agreed with Maguire J. In the course of his judgment expressing his agreement, Lavery J. stated (at p. 31 of the report) what he understood Maguire J. to have decided. Lavery J. said: 'Mr. Justice Martin Maguire has also fully explained his view as to the meaning of the term [wilful waste] and is of opinion that mere "permissive waste" cannot be considered "wilful waste" and that what was done, or rather omitted to be done, here was permissive waste only.' Later, at p. 32 of the report, he pointed out that 'wilful' qualified both 'damage' and 'waste' and said he thought the word must be given the same meaning in both cases.

I turn now to the judgment of Maguire J. At p. 27 of the report, in dealing with the terms 'wilful damage' and 'wilful waste' he said: 'In their ordinary meaning they contemplate some acts that are deliberate and intentional. I find myself quite unable to accept the argument that they mean nothing more than spontaneous or accidental, or that they can be construed as implying merely permissive waste in the ordinary meaning attributed to that phrase.' He returned to the same idea at p. 28 of the report where he said that: 'One might say that if the Legislature had meant by "wilful waste" merely permissive waste it could readily have said permissive waste or, simply, waste, without introducing this new expression, "wilful waste". If knowledge of the existing law must be imputed to the draftsmen of this Act, then I think they went more than a little out of their way to introduce a provision new to the law to effect a departure from well established precedent. The onus of showing wilful damage or wilful waste committed by the tenant is thrown upon the landlord. "Waste" must be construed as a term of art. But "wilful waste" is a new term, found for the first time in this Act of the Irish Legislature.' Finally, at p. 29 of the report, he concluded with these words 'In this case there is no evidence of wilful waste, no evidence of any act committed by the defendants deliberately and intentionally directed towards the spoliation of the tenement.'

It was in these last words that Davitt P. in the present case saw the gist of the decision of the majority of the Supreme Court in *Gilligan's Case* ([1963] I.R. 1). From the earlier citations from the judgment of Maguire J. it is clear that he is insisting that wilful waste is not permissive waste *merely*, that the term 'wilful' *adds* something to 'waste' and that 'waste' must be construed as a term of legal art. As such, it includes 'permissive' as well as 'voluntary' waste. He never receded from this view. The words, in the judgment of Maguire J. in *Gilligan's Case* ([1963] I.R.

1), which led Davitt P. in this case to think that Maguire J. was excluding from the term 'wilful waste' wilful permissive waste are the words: '. . . *act committed by the defendants deliberately and intentionally directed towards the spoliation of the tenement.'* If by these words Maguire J. meant to convey that there must be a positive *act* on the part of the lessee (i.e. *committed* by the lessee), then what he was saying was wholly inconsistent with the nature of permissive waste as accepted by him earlier in his judgment, not alone this, but he was overlooking, as Kingsmill Moore J. pointed out in his judgment, that, while the verb 'commit' ordinarily applies to something done actively, it is common to talk of committing an error, fault, or sin, and that the error, fault, or sin may be one of omission. Moreover, and more significant, words like *do* or *make* waste (*firmarii vastum non facient* in the Statute of Marlbridge or *que aver fait vastum* in the Statute of Gloucester) have long since been understood to cover passive as well as active waste. I see in the words 'directed towards the spoliation of the tenement' in the judgment of Maguire J. nothing additional to what is contained in the words 'deliberate and intentional,' that is to say, that the lessee is conscious and well aware of the likely result of his omission. It should, moreover, be pointed out that, having reached the view that the acts of waste alleged against the lessee in *Gilligan's Case* ([1963] I.R. 1) were merely permissive waste, the additional words of Maguire J., which misled Davitt P. in this case, were obiter.

I cannot construe the judgment of Lavery J. in *Gilligan's Case* ([1963] I.R. 1) as rejecting the concept of wilful permissive waste. If the judgment of Maguire J. can be construed as doing so, it is at variance with the views of the other two members of the Court in that case and, as I have indicated, it is quite at variance with the long-established meaning of the term 'waste'. Lavery J., as I have pointed out, was at pains to underline that the argument which was being rejected was that 'wilful' added nothing to mere permissive waste; and, further, that the acts alleged against the lessee in *Gilligan's Case* ([1963] I.R. 1) were in the view of Maguire J., and also in his view, permissive waste only.

The result of this analysis is to show that Davitt P. was in error in this case in the view that *Gilligan's Case* ([1963] I.R. 1) has laid down that 'wilful waste' in s. 55 of the Act of 1931 did not extend to wilful permissive waste. On a careful reading of that case it appears that the Court (or at least two of its members) accepted the contrary view; that is to say, that 'waste' as a term of legal art necessarily included permissive as well as voluntary waste. In the result this appeal should be allowed, and judgment should be entered for the plaintiffs and the matter remitted to the High Court to fix damages.

Haugh J.: I agree.

Walsh J.: I agree.

Budd J.: I agree.

FitzGerald J.: I agree.

Notes and Questions
1. Do you think it was sensible to re-enact the phrase 'wilful damage or wilful waste' in the 1980 Act without change? In the light of the case law, could you improve upon it?
2. *Cf.* 'fraudulent or malicious' waste in section 25 of Deasy's Act: see *Irish Land Law,* para. 17.058.

RICE V. DUBLIN CORPORATION
[1947] I.R. 425; 88 I.L.T.R. 103 (Supreme Court)

A plot of ground was compulsorily acquired by the defendants under the Housing of the Working Classes (Ireland) Acts, 1890 to 1921, and leased to the plaintiffs in separate parcels. Each lease contained covenants by the lessee *(a)* to erect a two-storey shop and residence and *(b)* not to permit the premises so erected to be used for the sale of intoxicating liquor. On the application by the lessees for leave to use their respective premises for the sale of intoxicating liquor, the defendants refused their consent without assigning any reason. The plaintiffs thereupon instituted proceedings for declarations that the defendants had unreasonably withheld their consent. It appeared from the evidence that the defendants' refusal was based upon their general policy not to permit the sale of intoxicating liquor in any premises on their new housing estates. Davitt J. stated a case for the Supreme Court.

Maguire C.J.:

These two Cases stated by Davitt J. raise for our consideration and determination the same questions. Each plaintiff is the lessee of a plot of land which has been compulsorily acquired by the defendants under the provisions of the Housing of the Working Classes Acts, 1890 – 1921. The plots were demised by the defendants to the original lessee in each case for a term of 150 years and in each case contained a covenant that the lessee would, within twelve months, on the site so demised, erect a two storey premises consisting of a shop on the ground floor and a residence on the upper floor, of such design and material as should meet with the approval of the housing architect of the defendants. Each lease, furthermore, contained a covenant by the lessee not to permit or suffer the premises or any part thereof to be used for the sale of intoxicating liquor or occupied as a brothel. Buildings which complied with the terms of the covenant first mentioned, were duly erected by each lessee. Each plaintiff now is lessee of the premises occupied by him or her for the residue of the term of 150 years. Notwithstanding the terms of the covenant mentioned, the plaintiffs, relying upon s. 57 of the Landlord and Tenant Act, 1931, requested the defendants to consent to the user of the premises for the sale of intoxicating liquor. The defendants, without assigning any reason, refused so to consent.

Each plaintiff issued a civil bill seeking a declaration that the defendants had unreasonably witheld their consent to the premises being so used. The Circuit Court Judge granted the declaration asked for by the plaintiff in each case. An appeal was taken to the High Court. At the conclusion of the plaintiffs' case in the High Court, counsel for the defendants asked for a direction on certain grounds which, as they are raised in the questions submitted for determination by this Court, need not be stated here. The learned Judge reserved the points raised for consideration. The defendants gave evidence which formed the basis of the findings of the Circuit Court Judge – *(a)* that the lands demised by the leases under which the respective plaintiffs hold, were compulsorily acquired by the defendants under the provisions of the Housing of the Working Classes Acts, 1890 – 1921, and *(b)* that in the year 1938 the City Manager had decided that leases on the defendants' new housing estates should contain covenants prohibiting the use of the demised premises for the sale of intoxicating liquor; *(c)* that the two plaintiffs were the only lessees who had requested the defendants to waive this prohibition; *(d)* that the applications had been referred to the defendants' housing committee; *(e)* that the housing committee as a matter of general policy decided not to consent, in the case of any lease containing such a prohibition, to the user of the premises for the sale of intoxicating liquor, and that in accordance with this policy the housing committee decided to refuse both the applications.

On the application of counsel for both parties in each case the learned Judge has stated these Cases and submits for our determination in each Case the same five questions.

The first question is: Whether the buildings erected upon the lands demised by plaintiff's lease were provided by the defendants under the Housing of the Working Classes Acts, 1890 – 1921, within the meaning of s. 3 of Landlord and Tenant Act, 1931. This section, so far as material, reads:

'**3.** – Where the buildings on any land or premises were or are provided by a local authority under the Housing of the Working Classes (Ireland) Acts, 1890 – 1921, or the Labourers (Ireland) Acts, 1883 to 1930, the following provisions shall have effect, that is to say: –

(*a*) if such land or premises is or are held by such local authority in fee simple, this Act shall not apply in respect of such land or premises;'

It seems to me on first impression that on the facts in these cases and using the word 'provide' in its ordinary sense one would say that the defendants have provided the lands and the original lessees have provided the houses. It is contended, however, that because the sites leased to the plaintiffs were acquired by the defendants by the exercise of compulsory powers given to local authorities to enable them to provide sites for houses and because the defendants have secured the building of the houses in question by requiring from each lessee of a site a covenant to build, that the defendants can be said to have 'provided' the houses which were built in pursuance of such covenants. To say so, however, is, to my mind, unduly to extend the meaning of the word 'provide'. In my opinion the lessees who caused them to be erected and who made available the moneys wherewith they were built, directly and primarily provided the houses. It is only indirectly and in a secondary sense that the defendants can be said to have done so. In my opinion the aim of s. 3 of the Landlord and Teanant Act, 1931, is to take away from the operation of the Act only those houses for the erection of which a local authority is directly responsible.

The first question submitted for our determination should, therefore, be answered in the negative.

The second question submitted by the learned Judge is:

'If the Landlord and Tenant Act, 1931, applies to the lease in question, is the agreement in the lease not to use the demised premises for the sale of intoxicating liquor an agreement *prohibiting the alteration of the user* of the premises within the meaning of s. 57, sub-s. 1, of the said Act?'

It is contended by Mr. FitzGerald that a contravention of the prohibition contained in the covenant would not be an alteration of user. It would be otherwise, he argues, if the terms of the lease tied the premises to a particular user. It seems to me, however, if, as here, the effect of a covenant is to prohibit the user of the premises for a particular purpose, that to use the premises for this purpose is to alter the user of the premises.

Accordingly, the second question should be answered in the affirmative.

The third question submitted is: – 'If the answer to the second question is in the affirmative does the said agreement *absolutely* prohibit such alteration of user within the meaning of the sub-section?'

The purpose of the Landlord and Tenant Act, 1931, as indicated in the long title, is further to improve and ameliorate the position of tenants in urban areas. Part VI of the Act which includes s. 57 is devoted to the easing of the position of tenants in regard to the type of covenant which in many cases bears hardly on tenants. Sect. 55 limits the liability of a tenant who is guilty of a breach of a covenant to repair. Sect. 56 mitigates the harshness of covenants against alienation. In sub-s. 1 it provides that covenants absolutely prohibiting or restricting alienation, either generally or in a particular manner, shall have effect as if such covenant were a covenant against alienation without the consent of the lessor. There, the contrast is between covenants which allow of no escape from their prohibitory terms and covenants which are similar but from which there is an escape if the consent of the lessor be obtained. The Legislature have thus modified the rigidity of such prohibitory covenants by introducing a qualification which reasonable landlords in practice have accepted. In order that the new proviso shall not be rendered nugatory the section also introduces, by sub-s. 2, a proviso that the landlord's consent shall not be unreasonably witheld. Sect. 57, which is the section we are concerned with here, deals with covenants restrictive of user. Sub-s. 1 reads as follows: –

'Every lease (whether made before or after the passing of this Act) of a tenement which contains a covenant, condition, or agreement absolutely prohibiting the alteration of the user of such tenement shall have effect as if such covenant, condition, or agreement were a covenant, condition or agreement prohibiting the alteration of the user of such tenement without the licence or consent of the lessor.'

The wording of this sub-section is almost similar to that of sub-s. 1 of s. 56.

To my mind, construing the section by reference to the ordinary meaning of the language employed, and having in mind the mischief which it is designed to remedy, the Legislature, in using the word 'absolutely,' is contrasting, as in s. 56, covenants prohibiting the alteration of user from which there is no possibility of relief under the terms of the covenant, with those from which the lessor may grant relief, and has modified them in the same way. In my opinion the word 'absolutely' applies to all covenants which prohibit the alteration of user but do not leave it open to the lessee to seek from the lessor permission to alter the user. Applying this test to the covenant under consideration it seems to me clearly to be within the operation of s. 57, sub-s. 1, and must, as a result of the sub-section, have effect as if it were a covenant prohibiting the alteration of user of the premises without the consent of the lessor. I have considered Mr. FitzGerald's ingenious argument to the contrary but in view of what I hold to be the plain meaning of the section, I am unable to accept it.

Accordingly, the third question submitted for our consideration should be answered in the affirmative.

The remaining questions give very little trouble. The fourth question is: 'If it becomes necessary to determine the issue whether defendants' refusal of their consent to the proposed user by the plaintiff of the demised premises was unreasonable, does the fact that they gave no reason for their refusal shift to them the onus of showing that their refusal was reasonable?'

The fifth question is whether, in determining that issue, it is permissible to have regard to the fact that the defendants' refusal of their consent was not based upon the consideration of any special circumstances of the plaintiff's case, but was the result of a determination not to consent to the user, for the sale of intoxicating liquor, of any premises demised by lease containing a prohibition against such user.

Sub-s. 2 of s. 57 is designed, as is sub-s. 2 of the preceding section, to prevent the statutory modification effected by sub-s. 1 being rendered futile by the refusal of consent of a capricious landlord. It adds a proviso that the licence or consent of the landlord to alteration of user of a tenement shall not be unreasonably witheld. The onus is on a tenant who alleges that consent has been unreasonably witheld to establish his case. This onus is not discharged merely by proving that before the hearing no reason was given by the landlord for his refusal. It is still open to the landlord to state the grounds for such refusal to the Court. It is for the Court to say whether the grounds stated are reasonable or not.

The fourth question should, accordingly, be anwered in the negative.

As regards the fifth question, I am of opinion that while it is the duty of the Court to consider each case upon its merits, there is no reason why a landlord may not properly base a refusal of consent upon grounds of general policy in relation to the management of his estate. The question whether the grounds upon which a decision to refuse consent to the alteration of the user of premises is reasonable in reference to a particular case is a matter for the Court. No general rule can be laid down because it is easy to conceive cases in which a refusal to agree to an alteration of user based on a decision of policy in the management of the landlord's estate would be entirely reasonable. On the other hand the Court may hold that such a ground is not a reasonable ground for witholding consent in a particular case. This answers the fifth question.

Murnaghan J.:

The two Cases Stated now before the Court were heard together and were stated by Davitt J. on the hearing by him of two appeals brought by the Dublin Corporation against two declarations made by the Circuit Court of Dublin in favour of the respective plaintiffs. By its orders the Circuit Court declared that the Dublin Corporation had unreasonably withheld their consent to the waiver of covenants in the leases under which the respective plainiffs held their premises under the Corporation and which prohibited the premises being used for the sale of intoxicating liquor.

By s. 57, sub-s. 1, of the Landlord and Tenant Act, 1931, a lease which contains a covenant absolutely prohibiting the alteration of the user of a tenement is to have effect as if such covenant were a covenant prohibiting the alteration of the user of such tenement without the licence or consent of the lessor. By s. 57, sub-s. 2, of the same Act such a covenant shall be deemed to be subject to a provision to the effect that such licence or consent shall not be unreasonably witheld.

Sect. 3 of the Landlord and Tenant Act, 1931, however, enacts:

'Where the buildings on any land or premises were or are provided by a local authority under the Housing of the Working Classes (Ireland) Acts, 1890 to 1921, or the Labourers (Ireland) Acts, 1883 to 1930, the following provisions shall have effect, that is to say: –

(a) if such land or premises is or are held by such local authority in fee simple, this Act shall not apply in respect of such land or premises;

(b) if such land or premises is or are held by such local authority under a lease, such local authority shall be deemed for the purposes of this Act to be the tenant of such land or premises and to be in exclusive occupation thereof.'

Paragraph 4 of the Case Stated finds: 'The lands upon which the said premises are built were acquired by the defendants compulsorily under the provisions of the Housing of the Working Classes Acts, 1890 – 1932, and are now held by the defendants in fee simple. The Corporation did not, however, actually erect the buildings in question, but in each case they made a lease for 150 years, at rents of £28 and £22 respectively, and in each lease was a covenant which bound the lessee, within a specified period, to erect a two-storey premises consisting of a shop on the ground floor and a residence on the upper floor in a manner to be approved of by the architect employed by the Corporation. Such a lease was made within the powers given to local authorities under the Housing (Ireland) Act, 1919. Sect. 11, sub-s. 1 of that Act enacts: –

'Where a local authority have acquired or appropriated any land for the purposes of Part III of the Act of 1890, then, without prejudice to any of their other powers under that Act, the authority may –

(b) with the consent of the Local Government Board, '[now adapted to be the appropriate Minister] 'sell or lease the land or part thereof to any person for the purpose and under the condition that that person will erect and maintain thereon such number of houses suitable for the working classes as may be fixed by the local authority in accordance with plans approved by them and, when necessary, will lay out and construct public streets or roads and open spaces on the land or will use the land for purposes which, in the opinion of the local authority, are necessary or desirable for or incidental to the development of the land as a building estate in accordance with plans approved by the local authority, including the provision, maintenance, and improvement of houses and gardens and other works or buildings for or for the convenience of persons belonging to the working classes and other persons.'

Sect. 11, sub-s. 1, (d), which may be contrasted with s. 11, sub-s. 1, (b), just cited, enabled the local authority with the consent of the Minister, to sell or lease any houses on the land or erected by them on the land, subject to such covenants and conditions as they might think fit to impose either in regard to the maintenance of the houses as houses for the working classes or otherwise in regard to the use of the houses.

Paragraph 3 of each of the Cases finds specifically that pursuant to, and in compliance with, the covenant contained in each lease the lessee erected a shop and residence on the sites respectively demised. On the facts above stated question No. 1 of each Case asks: '1. Were the buildings erected upon the lands demised by the plaintiff's lease provided by the defendants under the Housing of the Working Classes Acts, 1890 to 1921, within the meaning of s. 3 of the Landlord and Tenant Act, 1931?

On behalf of the Corporation it is urged that, as part of the consideration for which they parted with the land was the performance of a covenant to build, the corporation had provided the buildings. I think it is correct to say that in a constructive sense the Corporation had provided the buildings, but it is equally true that in a factual or concrete sense the lessee had provided the buildings. The Legislature must, however, in circumstances like those under consideration, have used the word 'provided' in only one of these two meanings. The real question involved is, therefore, which sense should be applied in the interpretation of s. 3 of the Act.

An analogous question has already come before this Court in *Collis* v. *Earl of Pembroke* ([1934] I.R. 589). In order to come within the definition of 'building lease' s. 46, sub-s. 1, of the Landlord and Tenant Act, 1931, *inter alia* requires that 'such permanent buildings were erected by the person who, at the time of such erection, was entitled to the lessee's interest under such lease.' In the case referred to the owner in fee simple made a lease which contained a covenant on the lessee's part to build. The lessee did not, in fact, build, but made a sub-lease which contained a covenant that the sub-lessee should build. The buildings were erected by the sub-lessee but the lessee contended that, inasmuch as the consideration for the sub-lease was a covenant that the lessee should build, it should be held that the lessee had 'erected' the buildings. This view was rejected by the High Court and by this Court. In the High Court the judgment of Meredith J. which was approved in this Court, pointed out that the sub-lessess had, in fact, erected the buildings, and that if the lessee could be said to have erected the buildings this was in a secondary sense. It was held to be the plain intention of the Act that the person who should be entitled to a reversionary lease was the person who, by his labour and expense, had erected the buildings.

If s. 3 of the Landlord and Tenant Act, 1931, makes the Act not apply in cases like the present, lessees who, by their labour and expense, have erected the buildings will be deprived of the right to a reversionary lease and the general policy of the Act will be rendered nugatory. Further, in my opinion the Legislature recognised that under the Housing (Ireland) Act, 1919, s. 11, sub-s. 1, (*d*), a local authority might lease houses erected by them on the land, and that it was in reference to such cases that s. 3 of the Landlord and Tenant Act, 1931 made use of the words 'where the buildings on any land or premises were or are provided by a local authority'. For these reasons, in my opinion, the answer to question No. 1 should be: 'No'.

Where leases contain covenants that certain things shall not be done without the consent of the landlord, such consent not to be unreasonably witheld, if the landlord refuses his consent the lessee may do the act and contend, when it is material to do so, that the landlord's refusal was unreasonable. This course was not available to the respective lessees in the present cases, because they cannot sell intoxicating liquors without a licence from the licensing authority and the licensing authority will not grant such a licence to do what is forbidden by the covenant. The lessees accordingly sought from the Court declarations that the landlord's consent was unreasonably witheld. In the consideration of this matter the Cases Stated, in question No. 2, asks a question in respect of the specific covenant in each lease, viz., 'is the agreement in the lease not to use the demised premises for the sale of intoxicating liquor an agreement prohibiting the alteration of the user of the premises within the meaning of s. 57, sub-s. 1 of the said Act?'

On behalf of the Corporation it is contended that the section is intended only to apply if a specific user of the premises is prescribed or contemplated by the parties, e.g. to use the premises as a private dwellinghouse, and that it is only in the case of prohibition of alteration of this user that the section applies. This construction is based upon a strict interpretation of the word 'alteration' in connection with the words 'absolutely prohibiting' and is sought to be supported by a comparison with s. 56 in which the word 'restricting' is used after 'prohibiting.' The leases in the present cases contemplate user as a shop and dwellinghouse and the covenant is in these words: 'And that the said Lessee shall not nor will during the continuance of this demise, permit or suffer the said premises hereby demised, or any part thereof, to be used for the sale of intoxicating liquor or to be used or occupied as a brothel.' It seems to me that the words of this covenant do 'absolutely prohibit the alteration of the user of such tenement' within the meaning of s. 57. The permitted user of the premises within the contemplation of the parties does not include those specified in the covenant, and this covenant absolutely prohibits the alteration of the user contemplated by the parties to the user specified in the covenant. I cannot there-fore hold that the section only applies where one or more specific users are provided for and an alteration of these specific users is prohibited. In my opinion, question No. 2 should be answered: 'Yes.'

Question No. 3 of the Cases Stated asks 'does the said agreement absolutely prohibit the alteration of any such user within the meaning of the sub-section?' It is only necessary to read the sub-section to see that a covenant prohibiting the alteration of the user of such tenement without the licence or consent of the lessor is contrasted with a covenant absolutely prohibiting such alteration. The covenants in the two leases before the Court do not mention the licence or consent of the lessor but are in form absolute prohibitions. This question should in my opinion be answered: 'Yes.'

The Cases Stated find that 'in 1938 the City Manager decided that all future leases on the defendants' new housing estates should contain covenants prohibiting the use of the demised premises for the sale of intoxicating liquor.' The plaintiffs are, so far, the only lessees to request the defendants to waive such a prohibition. 'Their applications were referred to the defendants' housing committeee. The housing committee decided as a matter of general policy not to consent in the case of any lease containing such a prohibition to the user of the demised premises for the sale of intoxicating liquor. In accordance with this policy they decided to refuse the plaintiff's applications.' Question No. 4 is, apparently, stated with reference to these findings. It is as follows: – '4. If it becomes necessary to determine the issue whether defendants' refusal of their consent to the proposed user by the plaintiff of the demised premises was unreasonable, does the fact that they gave no reason for their refusal shift to them the onus of showing that their refusal was reasonable?' Counsel for the plaintiffs did not seek to obtain an affirmative answer to this question. It was admitted at the hearing it was necessary that the plaintiff should establish at least a *prima facie* case. A *prima facie* case is not established merely by showing that the defendants gave no reason for their refusal. The answer to question No. 4 should be: 'No.'

Question No. 5 of the Cases Stated is: 'In determining that issue is it permissible to have regard to the fact that defendants' refusal of their consent was not based upon the consideration of any special circumstances of the plaintiff's case but was the result of a determination not to consent to the user for the sale of intoxicating liquor on any premises demised by lease containing a prohibition against such user?'

It is permissible to have regard to the fact that defendants' refusal of their consent was not based upon the consideration of any special circumstances of the plaintiff's case, but not as a determining factor. The unreasonableness of the defendant's refusal may depend upon considerations which do not arise upon special circumstances of the plaintiffs' case. For example, if it is a question of estate management or the well-being of the estate tenants as a whole, the reasonableness or unreasonableness of the refusal depends upon the facts known to the defendants at the date of refusal. In a case like those before the Court the reasonableness or unreasonableness of the refusal should depend on the facts brought to the knowledge of the Court at the date of the hearing. If the defendants gave no reason for their refusal when made, and could give no reasonable grounds at the hearing in Court, regard might well be given to the fact that they gave no reason when making the refusal. If, however, at the hearing a substantive case is made to rebut a *prima facie* case made at the hearing by the plaintiff, only the slightest regard could be given to the fact that the refusal when made was not accompanied by reasons. In my opinion the answer to question No. 5 should be: 'Yes, but not as a determining factor, and as having the very slightest weight if grounds for reasonableness of the refusal are proved to exist in answer to a *prima facie* case made by the plaintiff in Court.'

Geoghegan J.:

Mr. Justice Murnaghan permitted me to read the judgment which he has just read.

I agree with it, and there is nothing I can usefully add.

O'Byrne J.:

I have arrived at a different conclusion as to the answer which should be given to the first question submitted to us, and propose to state shortly the reasons which have induced me to arrive at that conclusion.

Under s. 3 of the Landlord and Tenant Act, 1931, where the buildings on any land are provided by the local authority under the Housing of the Working Classes

(Ir.) Acts, 1890 to 1921, and such land is held by the local authority in fee simple, the said Act of 1931 shall not apply in respect of such land.

The building, with which this case [Kenny's case] deals consists of a shop and residence known as No. 133 Galtymore Road, Crumlin. This building was erected and stands upon land which was acquired by the local authority, viz., the defendants in these proceedings, under the provisions of the Housing of the Working Classes Acts, 1890 to 1932, and this land is held by the local authority in fee simple. The question, then, as to whether the Act of 1931 applies depends entirely upon the question whether the said building was provided by the local authority under the said Acts and this is the first question submitted for our determination.

The land was acquired compulsorily under and for the purposes of the said Acts, and was demised by the defendants to one Wilde, the plaintiffs' predecessor in title, by indenture of lease dated the 23rd November, 1940, for a term of 150 years from the 25th March, 1940, subject to the yearly rent of £28. The land, as so demised, was a vacant site and the lease contained a covenant, on the part of the lessee to erect thereon, within twelve months from the 21st August, 1940, a two-storey building consisting of a shop on the ground-floor and a residence on the upper-floor. In purusance of that covenant the building with which we are concerned was erected by the lessee. Was this building provided by the local authority within the meaning of s. 3 of the Act of 1931?

Nothing turns upon the nature of the building or the purpose for which it is used. It was, admittedly, within the competence of the local authority to erect such a building under the powers conferred upon them by the said Acts and the case may be dealt with as though the building were erected for, and dedicated to the purpose of, housing members of the working classes. The question, thus, narrows itself down to the question whether the building was provided by the local authority. On this question I have arrived at a clear view.

Having acquired a piece of vacant land for the purposes of the said Acts, there were several ways in which the local authority might have proceeded with a view to having appropriate buildings erected thereon. They might have had the buildings erected by direct labour and, in such event, the buildings would clearly have been provided by the local authority. It is equally clear and conceded in the argument at the bar, that a similar result would have followed, if they had had the buildings erected by a building contractor for a money consideration. I can see no logical distinction between the latter case and the case which we are considering. In each case the local authority had secured the erection of the buildings for the purposes of the said Acts and the only distinction between the two cases is in the nature of the consideration given by the local authority. In the case of the building contractor true consideration is a money payment; in the other case it is a demise of the land, with the buildings to be erected thereon, for the term, and at the rent mentioned in the lease. This is valuable consideration, and was obviously considered by the lessee as ample consideration, for the erection of the house. In determining the question whether the building was provided by the local authority, I cannot see any real distinction between two cases, in one of which the consideration consists of money and in the other of money's worth.

Is it to be held that a building is provided within the meaning of the section only when the local authority pays for it in terms of money? This seems to me to be quite unwarranted and calculated to lead to absurd results. Suppose the erection of the building in this case cost £1,000. If the Corporation had paid that amount to Wilde (the original lessee) for erecting the building, then, *in concessis,* the building would have been provided by the corporation within the meaning of s. 3, though it might have been demised to Wilde the following day for the term, and at the rent mentioned in the lease in consideration of a fine of £1,000. The result in both cases would have been identical; but, in one case, it is admitted that the house would have been provided by the Corporation and, in the other case, it is contended that it would not have been so provided. A construction which leads to such an absurd result is not to be recommended.

Take another case. Suppose the house were erected for the Corporation, not for a money consideration or a demise of the land upon which it was erected, but in consideration of the transfer or demise by the Corporation to the builder of another piece of land. Surely the building in such a case would be provided by the Corporation, and yet, what is the distinction between that case and the present?

The argument on behalf of the plaintiff in this case seems to me to have proceeded substantially on the basis that the word 'provided' in s. 3 of the Act of 1931 is synonomous with 'erected,' using the later word in a narrow sense, and unless some such meaning is attributed to it I fail to see how the first question can be answered in the negative. Yet it seems to me that the word has, and was deliberately intended to have, a wider signification. Under s. 8 of the Housing (Ir.) Act, 1919, the local authority may acquire existing houses, which may be made suitable as houses for the working classes. If it acquired such houses under and for the purposes of these Acts, it could scarcely be argued that they were not provided under the said Acts; but the construction contended for would clearly exclude them.

When, as in this case, land is acquired by a local authority under the Housing Acts and buildings, dedicated to the purposes of the said Acts, are erected thereon in pursuance of a contract for valuable consideration entered into with that authority I am of opinion that such buildings are provided by the local authority within the meaning of s. 3. The local authority has secured the erection of the buildings and has made them available for the purposes of the Housing Acts. This, in my view, is all that is necessary to bring the buildings within the excluding provisions of s. 3 of the Act of 1931.

In my opinion the first question should be answered in the affirmative and the other questions do not arise.

Black J:

The first question in these Cases is whether the defendants 'provided' the houses in question, within the meaning of that term in s. 3 of the Landlord and Tenant Act, 1931. It is not disputed that if they had employed a builder to erect the houses at a price, contemporaneously leasing the sites and the future houses as from that date for a term of years, they would have 'provided' the houses as truly as if they had constructed them with their own hands. But, it is said that because they did not themselves employ the builder, but only bound another person by contract to employ him, they have not 'provided' the houses.

In both cases supposed, they would be, all along, owners of the reversion of both sites and houses, never parting with the seisin, and merely giving the lessees for years an *interesse termini: Lewis* v. *Baker* ([1905] 1 Ch. 46). In both cases they would have furnished the sites and bound another party by contract to build the houses or get them built. In both cases they would have given good consideration for the building of the houses, and none the less because, in one case the consideration would be given directly to the actual builder, whether in a lump sum or in instalments over a period, while in the other case the consideration would be given to the building lessee, and would take the form of a lease of sites and houses together at a ground rent with fixity of tenure for an agreed term. *Prima facie* it does not seem to me that these differences in the method of bringing about the same result can make that result anything but the 'provision' of the houses in both cases alike.

When a thing is brought into existence, he who has made complete provision for its being so brought, and whereby it is brought, into existence, has provided it. At least, the lexicographers seem to define the word 'provide' in that sense.

So far, then, as the point depends solely on the ordinary usage of language, as I understand it, I see no justification for denying the claim of the Corporation to have provided these houses, seeing that they provided the sites and bound the respective plaintiffs' predecessors by contract to erect them, giving them what they deemed adequate consideration for doing so.

I could, however, see great force in the contention, if indeed it were put forward, that the language of the section should not be given the full scope of its natural meaning, on the ground that the policy of the Act indicates that it was meant to have a more restricted meaning. This contention became the *ratio decidendi* of *Collis* v. *Earl of Pembroke* ([1934] I.R. 589), though the case turned on s. 46 with which we are not now concerned. The word in question there was 'erect,' which is a much narrower word than 'provide.' Yet, even there, FitzGibbon J. thought it necessary to give a reason for refusing to apply the maxim *qui facit per alium facit per se*. His reason was based on what he held to be the policy of the Act, and he showed that if the term 'erected' in s. 46 was not restricted to the action of the lessee who employed the actual builder 'the whole policy of the Act could be frustrated' by a process so easy that the Legislature must be supposed to have intended the term 'erected' to be so restricted. Just as FitzGibbon J. thought it necessary to give a reason for refusing to apply the maxim *qui facit per alium facit per se* in a case where the disputed word was 'erected', so I should have liked to hear a reason given in the present case for refusing to apply the same maxim where the word in question is the much wider term 'provided.' I have heard none. But, I think I ought to suggest and consider one myself – namely, the very reason given by FitzGibbon J. in *Collis's Case* ([1934] I.R. 589) – the policy of the Act.

As ss. 56, 57 and 58 show, it was part of that policy to prevent lessors from insisting unreasonably on certain restrictive covenants. Plainly also, as shown by s. 3 it was part of that policy to exempt from those sections local authorities which provided houses under the Housing of the Working Classes Acts. Why should they be exempt from these salutary fetters upon unreasonableness? I have little doubt it was partly because it was felt that public bodies making provision for housing from altruistic motives might be trusted not to insist unreasonably on restrictive covenants, and that legislative interference in their case might be dispensed with. I think the further reason for exempting them was that they should not be discouraged in the public work of providing housing by being exposed to lawsuits by their lessees professing to be aggrieved by such covenants. Obviously these reasons of policy would not be applicable save where the public authority continued to be the lessor of the houses affected. If they leased sites for building and their lessees made sub-leases of the houses they built, no public purpose could be served by exempting such lessees from the same restrictions on their conduct towards their sub-lessees as are imposed by the Act on all other private lessors. Can I then infer that the Legislature intended not to exempt from the Act such holders of building leases from local authorities, and that therefore the word 'provided' in s. 3, should have its full natural scope cut down so as not to exempt such persons? The argument based on the policy of the Act, which was decisive in *Collis* v. *Earl of Pembroke* ([1934] I.R. 589), seemed to me, at one stage, almost equally forcible in the present cases. But, on further reflection, I think it is not. In *Collis's Case* ([1934] I.R. 589), the wider meaning of the word 'erected' would have made easy, as FitzGibbon J.

said, and therefore fairly certain, 'the frustration of the whole policy of the Act.' The Legislature could hardly have overlooked or intended that. But, in the present cases, giving the word 'provided' its full natural scope would not involve any such frustration. The worst that could follow from it would be to let people who got building leases from local authorities and build houses and sub-let them, escape from the provisions of the Act, notwithstanding that there appears no good reason why they should escape. The number of such persons may not be considerable, and the Legislature may have overlooked their exemption from the Act, or not thought it worth while making special provision against it, thinking only of its main purpose of exempting local authorities as lessors of houses which they had built or acquired under the Housing of the Working Classes Acts. Therefore, I do not think that any argument based on the policy of the Act would be strong enough in the present cases to justify our attributing to the Legislature an actual intention that the word 'provided' in s. 3 should have a narrower scope and meaning than, in our common usage of speech, I conceive it to possess. This conclusion would lead me to answer the first question submitted to us in the affirmative, thus rendering the other questions unnecessary. As, however, my view on the first question does not prevail, I must deal with the remaining questions also.

The second question in Patrick Rice's case only differs from the second question in Nora Kenny's Case in that it omits the word 'absolutely' before the word 'prohibiting.' This omission makes no difference, because even if the agreement prohibits in some sense the alteration of the user, it does not prohibit it within the meaning of the section unless it absolutely prohibits it. Hence, the second and third questions in both cases all come down to the single query whether the agreement absolutely prohibits the alteration of the user within the meaning of s. 57 of the Landlord and Tenant Act, 1931.

The Act has been in operation for fifteen years. Yet, the meaning of the phrase 'absolutely prohibiting the alteration of the user' seems never before to have been judicially determined. This is strange; first, because of its widespread practical importance, since it may make a great difference to many landlords and tenants throughout the country; and secondly, because of its highly controversial character. Its doubtfulness was shown by the fact of Mr. Justice Davitt having submitted it to this Court, and also, I often heard it recognized as problematical, and debated out of Court, when I was at the bar. It is, therefore, no question for a mere dogmatic pronouncement; but in my view demands a careful examination of the obvious objections which obstruct each of the alternative interpretations to which it is open.

We have two excellent text-books on this Act of 1931. That which bears the name of Mr. Justice Dixon, as he now is, replete as it is with aids to other problems does not happen to touch this one. But, Messrs. Moore and Odell, in their work, have tried to reason it out. Their conclusion is that 'a covenant which merely restrained the lessee from carrying on as shop, or from carrying on noisome trades, would not come within the words of the section.' If that is right, no agreement which does not prohibit all and every alteration of the user is within that section, and the second and third questions must be answered: 'No.' In my judgment, if one takes the words of s. 57 alone, both language and logic justify this conclusion of the learned authors quoted. A covenant expressed absolutely to prohibit 'the alteration of the user' is a quite different covenant from one that is expressed absolutely to prohibit merely 'a particular alteration of the user,' and *vice-versa*. The former includes the latter; but this, so far from making them both the same covenant, renders it impossible for them to be anything but essentially different covenants. Hence, when in s. 57 the Legislature clearly specified one of these two covenants as that with which the section was conversant, I infer, *prima facie,* that it did not mean the other, which would be an essentially different covenant from that which it meticulously describes.

If a tenant agreed with his landlord in express terms that 'the alteration of the user' of the premises should be 'absolutely prohibited,' nobody could doubt that the effect would be to prohibit all and every alteration of the user. On the other hand, if the parties agreed in express terms merely that 'a particular alteration of the user' should be absolutely prohibited, I imagine that no solicitor for the tenant would advise his client that this agreement 'absolutely prohibited the alteration of the user'. If he did so advise, and the client suffered by assuming in consequence that he could not make any change of user at all, and later on discovered the true position, I think his legal adviser might find himself in an awkward predicament.

An absolute prohibition of a particular change of user is, in my view, a qualified and conditional prohibition – or, in other words, a mere restriction – of 'the alteration of the user.' I think the dictionaries are right when they all give the primary meaning of 'absolute' as 'unconditional,' and also when, like the Oxford Dictionary, they describe a 'condition' as 'a thing upon the fulfilment of which depends that of another.' The 'thing' in question – that is, the condition – may be the failure to obtain one's landlord's consent. But it may equally well be the failure to obtain somebody else's consent, or it may equally well be the doing, refraining from doing, or happening of something which has nothing to do with the obtaining of anybody's consent. So if a tenant is prohibited from changing the user of his premises, but is only so prohibited if – or, in other words, on condition that – the change proposed is of a particular kind of change, then surely the prohibition of the change of the user is clearly conditional. The making of the one particular kind of change in question is 'the thing upon the fulfilment of which depends that of another,' that other being the coming into operation of the prohibition. I find quite incomprehensible the idea that a prohibition which permits every one of the countless possible alterations of user save one exceptional kind of alteration can be said to be an absolute prohibition of the alteration of the user. I find equally incomprehensible the idea that the only kind of condition contemplated by the section as making the prohibition conditional is a condition that the landlord's consent shall not have been obtained. Why all other possible and well-recognised conditions should be treated as not being conditions at all for the purposes of the section I cannot even begin to understand. The only explanation I have heard of this is that s. 57, sub-s. 1, contrasts a covenant prohibiting the alteration of user without the landlord's consent with a covenant prohibiting alteration of user. Naturally, the condition about the landlord's consent is the only condition the section mentions, and for the obvious reason that this is the only conditions which it causes to be implied. That is why it has to mention it. It does not mention any other conditions, simply because there would be no point in doing so, since it does not cause any of them to be implied. But this natural omission to mention any other conditions since there is no reason to mention them in no way indicated to me that no other conditions are contemplated as conditions by being dependent on which the prohibition would be rendered conditional, and, therefore, not absolute.

In the result my first view of s. 57 was that there could not be an absolute prohibition of the alteration of the user unless all and every change of user was unconditionally prohibited, for I thought, and still think, that that is the kind of prohibition that the language, used in its natural sense, connotes. Nevertheless on close examination of the analogous s. 56, I think I can find a reason which entirely changes the position. Sect. 56, introduces a certain implied condition into every lease which contains an agreement 'absolutely prohibiting or restricting the alienation, either generally or in any particular manner . . .' Now, were it not for these words 'either generally or in any particular manner' in s. 56, I should agree with the view taken in the text-book of Messrs. Moore and Odell in regard to s. 57. In substance I think this view is that the word 'restricting' in s. 56, used in contradistinction from the phrase 'absolutely prohibiting', shows, all the more clearly, that prohibition of a particular method of doing the thing in question would be a mere restriction and not an absolute prohibition. By analogy the significant absence of the word 'restricting' from s. 57 would emphasize the natural meaning of the phrase 'absolutely prohibiting' as excluding any prohibition of change of user conditional on its being a change of a particular kind. But the addition of the words 'either generally or in any particular manner' in s. 56 reverses the whole of that concusion. I read s. 56, sub-s. 1 as contemplating that a covenant, condition or agreement may: 1, absolutely prohibit alienation generally; 2, absolutely prohibit it in any particular manner; 3, restrict alienation generally; or 4, restrict alienation in any particular manner. It is easy to understand 1 and 4. But 2 shows that for the purposes of the section the Legislature contemplated that a covenant may absolutely prohibit alienation, though it only prohibits it when effected in a particular manner, provided of course that the prohibition does not depend on any other condition. This is an indication that the the phrase 'absolutely prohibiting' is used in a special sense. Now 'it is a sound rule of construction to give the same meaning to the same words occurring in different parts of an Act of Parliament': *per* Cleasby B. in *Courtauld* v. *Legh* (L.R. 4 Ex. 126, at p. 130), unless there is strong reason for doing otherwise: *In re National Savings Bank Association* (L.R. 1 Ch. 547, at p. 550) and *Reg.* v. *The Poor Law Commissioners, in the Matter of the Holborn Union* (6 A. & E. 56. at p. 68). So, by analogy, as "absolutely prohibiting alienation" in s. 56 includes, for the reason stated, an unconditional prohibition of alienation in one particular manner only, likewise it may be inferred that "absolutely prohibiting the alteration of the user' in s. 57 may be intended to include unconditional prohibition of one or more kinds of alteration only. In other words s. 56, when the context is considered, seems to show that the phrase 'absolutely prohibitng,' as applied to alienation, is used, not in its full and natural sense, but in the special sense just indicated. By analogy and the rule of construction mentioned, the same words 'absolutely prohibiting' may be given the same special meaning when applied in s. 57 to alteration of user. This inference drawn from the wording of s. 56, and this alone, enables me to agree that the words 'absolutely prohibiting' in s. 57 may be interpreted in the special sense indicated. Were it not for s. 56, for my part I could not do so.

Having found, as I think, a reason to justify that view, one can easily see another that fortifies it, though it would not be a justification in itself. It is that if one had to hold that an agreement absolutely prohibiting alteration of user is confined to an agreement which prohibits all and every alteration of user, it would open the door to a device which might easily render the whole of s. 57 quite valueless. This device would be to qualify every covenant against alteration of user by some condition which, theoretically, would prevent it from being absolute, but which actually would never be likely to arise. It follows that I should answer the combined second and third questions in both cases in the affirmative.

As to the fourth question, I should answer it: 'No.' The fact that the defendants gave no reason for their refusal, at the time, has no effect on the onus of proof. If the onus of proof is shifted at all it can only be, as in most other cases, by the fact of the plaintiff's making a *prima facie* case, which in this instance would be a *prima facie* case of unreasonableness on the part of the defendants. It is immaterial to the issue whether the defendants at the time of their refusal gave a good reason for it or even whether they gave any reason at all. All that is material is, whether, in the opinion of the learned judge at the hearing, a reason for the defendants' refusal exists and is sufficient to make their refusal reasonable.

The fifth question seems to suggest that the grounds of refusal which the defendants had or put forward at the time is necessarily material; whereas the material grounds are those which in fact exist. In my view the defendants' grounds of refusal at the time can only be material if no better grounds than those in fact exist at the time of the hearing. Consideration of the plaintiff's special circumstances may be material in determining whether the defendants' refusal is reasonable or not; but it may also be quite immaterial to that determination. If, for instance, the plaintiff proposed to use the premises for an illegal purpose, or possibly, if he sought to open a shop in a locality like Fitzwilliam Square, his special circumstances would be irrelevant; but, on the other hand, if his proposed change of user seemed to the Court reasonable in itself, but the defendants' objections also seemed cogent in themselves, then the material question would be whether in the opinion of the Court the reasonable desire of the plaintiff outweighed, or was outweighed by, the reasonable objections of the defendants.

It is for the learned judge to form his own opinion from the character of the locality and such other circumstances as may exist whether the determination not to consent to the user of the premises for the sale of intoxicating liquor is reasonable in itself, even allowing for any special circumstances which may be established by the plaintiff.

The Cases were accordingly remitted to Davitt J. for decision.

Note
See further, *Irish Land Law*, para. 17.039.

LYLE V. SMITH
[1909] 2 I.R. 58; 43 I.L.T.R. 255 (King's Bench Division)

A lease of lands near the sea contained a covenant by the lessee, that if it became necessary to rebuild or repair a certain sea-wall the lessee, his executors, administrators, or assigns would contribute a certain proportion of the expenses incurred. The sea-wall was not parcel of the demised premises, but lay between them and the sea, and was necessary to protect the subject-matter of the demise from encroachment by the sea, and ultimate destruction.

Lord O'Brien L.C.J.:

This case brings up again a controversy which has existed for some centuries in our law, namely when, does a covenant run with the land? *Spencer's Case* (1 Sm. L.C. (11th ed.), p. 55), however reminiscent of an earlier period, most certainly does not renew our youth. The learning connected with it tells us of those subtle distinctions which in other days delighted the sages of the law, but which, perhaps, did not reflect much credit on the law itself. The facts which give rise to the controversy before us are set forth in the case stated for our determination by my brother Wright. The case stated has been so frequently read that it is not requisite to read it again. The lease to which it refers, and the lessee's interest in which is now vested in the defendant as assignee, contains the covenant upon which the controversy depends. It runs as follows: [His Lordship read the covenant.] The sea-wall which is referred to is not on any part of the demised premises, but is essential to the protection and preservation of the demised premises. Mr. Justice Wright, who tried the case, states: – 'It was further proved that a storm occurred on 26th November, 1905, causing the breaches in the sea-wall shown (coloured pink) at A and B on the plan. The breach at A was so large as to endanger the roadway at that point. These breaches were repaired by the plaintiff at a cost of £242. The whole of the wall and the wall as a whole is necessary for the protection of the coast. If a breach remained unrepaired, the sea would scour behind the remainder, and eventually the entire wall would be swept away. Ultimately the sea would undermine and destroy the roadway and villas beyond.' It is further found that the defendant's proportion, if she is bound to contribute, would be £20 6s. 7d.

The question for our determination is, Is the defendant in fact bound to contribute towards the repair and maintenance of the wall? No question has been argued as to amount, if she is bound to contribute at all. I am of opinion that the defendant, who is assignee of the lessee, is bound to contribute on two grounds: 1st, that the obligation to contribute is not a mere collateral agreement, that it is a covenant which runs with the land; 2nd, on the point secondly argued, that if the agreement or obligation is not one that can be held, strictly speaking, to run with the land, it is at least a covenant incident to and relating to the tenancy, to the subject-matter demised, and being so binds the assignee under the provisions of the 12th section of the Landlord and Tenant (Ireland) Act of 1860.

Firstly, then, does the covenant in question run with the land, and bind an assignee? The word 'assigns' is used in the covenant, and what is provided for is for the benefit, protection, and indeed I might say for the preservation of the subject-matter demised during the continuance of the tenancy. Now it is well settled that a covenant to do something on part of the land – the subject-matter demised – runs with the land, though assigns are not specifically named, and a covenant to do something which is intended to become parcel of the land runs with the land if the word 'assigns' is used. But the cases have gone further. It has been held that though the thing to be done is not upon parcel, nor intended to become parcel, of the subject-matter demised, yet if the thing to be done is clearly for the benefit, support, and maintenance of the subject-matter demised, the obligation to do it runs with the land: see the case of *Easterby* v. *Sampson* (6 Bing. 644). There Alexander, C.B., is reported to have said (p. 652): '*Spencer's Case* (1 Sm. L.C. (11th ed.), p. 55) lays down the rule, that if the lessee covenant for him and his assigns to do anything on the land demised, it will bind the assignee, though the covenant should extend to a thing to be newly made. And in *The Mayor of Congleton* v. *Pattison* (10 East, 130) Lord Ellenborough says: "A covenant in which the assignee is specifically named, though it were for a thing not *in esse* at the time, yet being specifically named, it would bind him if it affected the nature, quality, or value of the thing demised, independently of collateral circumstances; or if it affected the mode of enjoying it." That is the rule to be extracted from *Spencer's Case* (1 Sm. L.C. (11th ed.), p. 56) and from all which have followed it.' And the Chief Baron added later in his judgment that the covenant to build a smelting mill, though it was not to be built on the land demised, yet ran with the land because it was plainly connected with the mines which were demised. See also *Vyvyan* v. *Arthur* (1 V. & C. 410), and *Athol* v. *Midland Great Western Railway* (I.R. 3 C.L. 333).

A covenant to repair a sea-wall which so closely affected the quality, value, identity, and even the existence of the subject-matter demised would plainly run with the land; but the question here which was so much pressed by Mr. Harrison in his able argument is more difficult – much more difficult – it is this: Is the obligation created by the deed to contribute a proportionate sum an obligation which runs with the land? It was contemplated that the lessor's was to be the hand that was to do the entire work – the whole work necessary for the repair of the sea-wall throughout its entire length. Does the obligation on the part of the lessee to pay to the lessor a proportionate sum of this entire liability amount to an obligation running wth the land? Certainly there is no case precisely in point; but I think that, having regard to the object contemplated and provided for, the obligation comes within the class of obligations which run with land. It most intimately touches and concerns the land. A sea-wall is obviously necessary for the protection, indeed for the preservation, of the subject-matter demised. It is manifestly for the interest of the lessee or assignee – for the interest of the person for the time being in possession as lessee or assignee – that the sea-wall should be repaired; and though the instrument of demise contemplates that, in the first instance at least, the hand to make the repair is the hand of the lessor, yet he works for the common benefit of himself and the lessee in a matter that touches and concerns the land, and he may be regarded as an agent *pro tanto* for the lessee, that is, an agent to expend in repair, and to do so much repair as may be covered by a contributive amount, ascertainable by the prescribed method and proportion. I think the obligation to pay the prescribed amount was, in its substance and essence, an obligation that ran with the land.

Before I leave this branch of the argument I should, I think, refer to the case of *Dewar* v. *Goodman* ([1908] 1 K.B. 94), which was pressed upon our attention with so much insistence by counsel for the defendant. That case is, in my judgment, plainly distinguishable from the present. There the thing covenanted to be done, namely, to keep in repair certain houses which were not the subject of the sub-demise, had no reference to what was the subject of the sub-demise. It did not touch the subject-matter of the sub-demise, nor did it support or maintain it in any way. It had no connection whatever with the corpus of the subject-matter sub-demised, or with the mode of enjoyment. There lies the distinction between the case of *Dewar* v. *Goodman* ([1907] 1 K.B. 612; [1908] 1 K.B. 94) and *Easterby* v. *Sampson* (6 Bing. 644). No doubt the non-repair of the houses other than those sub-demised might lead to forfeiture of the estate of the lessee in all the houses, but this would not make the covenant in the under-lease run with the land. This is very clearly put in the judgments of Mr. Justice Jelf and Lord Justice Buckley. Mr. Justice Jelf is reported to have said ([1907] 1 K.B. at p. 622) – 'On principle Mr. Copping argued on behalf of the plaintiff that the covenant in question for perform-ance of the covenants of the head lease does *pro tanto* touch or concern the thing demised in that, if performed, it secures the possession of it by preventing eviction on that ground by the superior landlord, and if not performed it forfeits the under-lease. I was at first much struck with this argument, and if the matter were *res integra* I should be inclined to adopt it; but an examination of the cases cited by Mr. Atherley-Jones for the defendant seems to point to a stricter interpretation of the rule, and to require that, in order to run with the land and the reversion, a covenant must directly, and not indirectly or collaterally, touch the land demised: see, for instance, *Thomas* v. *Hayward* (L.R. 4 Ex. 311), *Mayor of Congleton* v. *Pattison* (10 East, 130, at p. 135), where Lord Ellenborough says a covenant is assignable "if it affects the nature, quality, or value of the thing demised, indepen-dently of collateral circumstances, or if it affects the mode of enjoyment."' Lord Justice Buckley is reported to have said – 'The contention for the plaintiff may, I think, be summarized as follows: A covenant to do an act, not in respect of the demised premises, but which will protect from forfeiture the estate of the lessee in the demised premises, is a covenant which runs with the land.' He added – 'If that proposition is true, it is wholly new. It may, nevertheless, be true, but I am not aware of any authority in support of it.' He then examined the cases, and rejected the proposition. It is plain, I think, that the case of *Dewar* v. *Goodman* ([1907] 1 K.B. 91) is not an authority against the plaintiff.

But now I come to the 12th section of the Landlord and Tenant Act of 1860, and here arises a question of very great general importance. It is interesting from a legal point of view, and, as I said, is of great general importance. I desire to preface my consideration of the actual language, the *ipsissima verba* of the section, by some observations made by Lord Hatherley and by Lord Justice Holmes. Lord Hatherley is reported to have said, in giving judgment in *Liddy* v. *Kennedy* (L.R. 5 H.L. 134, at p. 143), a case in which there was a provision to resume possession of premises, but in which a severance of the reversion had taken place – 'Now, as regards a condition of this kind, very many authorities have been cited to satisfy us that, after severance of the reversion, after this change in the interest of James Kennedy, great difficulty would be experienced, as matters stood after former decisions, in holding that this lease could be terminated, under any circumstances, by the effect of the proviso. But what has happened in Ireland has been this, that, although it may be held in Ireland that the statute of Hen. 8 (to which the statute of Car. 1 in Ireland was analogous), dealing with the interest of assignees of reversions, is not applicable to a case like this, where the reversion has been severed, and therefore does not enable persons, where the reversion has been parted with, to avail themselves of the previous construction of this proviso, yet the statute for Ireland of the 23 & 24 Vict. c. 154, entirely remedied that defect. It appears to me that this statute has been framed for the express purpose of removing some of these technical difficulties which stood in the way of justice, and which, though devised originally with logical regard to consequences, have been found in practice to involve far more frequently the failure of justice than to secure any beneficial result to the parties.' To the same effect is the language of Lord Chelmsford. He says (p. 149): – 'But then, supposing that under the Common Law this clause in the lease might be subject to the objection that the reversion, or a portion of the reversion, was parted with, and that the power or condition, or whatever it may be called, would be subject to the objection that the power was entirely gone, we have in this case the Landlord and Tenant Act in Ireland, the 23 & 24 Vict. c. 154, which appears to me, whatever may have been the Common Law on the subject, to put the question upon an entirely different footing. The clauses of that Act to which attention has been directed appear to me to be perfectly clear on the subject. It seems to have been the intention of the Legislature that parties in the position of James and Victor Kennedy should be entitled to use the power which was conferred upon them for the purpose for which it was intended. Now what is the interpretation clause with regard to the word "landlord." It is to include the person for the time being entitled in possession to the estate or interest of the original landlord under any lease or other contract of tenancy, whether the interest of such landlord shall have been acquired by lawful assignment, devise, bequest, or operation of law, and whether he has a reversion or not. It was said by Mr. M'Mahon that this applies only to the case of the assignee of the original landlord, and not to the original landlord himself. It would be a very extraordinary state of things that the landlord by parting with a portion of an interest should give to the assignee a right, and by the same act should deprive himself of the right which he previously possessed in respect of the interest which he retains. But it appears to me, then, that the words, "entitled to the estate or interest of the original landlord," may very well apply to the case of James Kennedy, because James Kennedy is not in possession of the entire estate and interest of the original landlord. Thus the 12th section provides that "every landlord of any lands holden under any lease or other contract of tenancy shall have the same action and remedy against the tenant and the assignee of his estate or interest, or their respective heirs, executors, or administrators, in respect of the agreements contained or implied in such lease or contract as the original landlord might have had against the original tenant or his heir or personal representative respectively."'

In *Re M'Naul's Estate* ([1902] 1 I.R. 114), Holmes, L.J., when dealing with the rule of construction of statutes, is reported to have said (p. 138): 'In *Riordan* v. *M'Namara* (30 L.R. Ir. 495) I made some observations on this subject, which further experience has tended to confirm. We of a later generation, who have seen rampart on rampart of legal feudalism disappear before the steady inroad of legislative innovation, can hardly understand the difficulty which our predecessors had in realizing a fee-simple estate moulded and modified by statute. There is, however, one passage in the judgment of Barry, J., in *Morris* v. *Morris* (I.R. 6 C.L. 73) which sets forth the true nature of the estate taken by a grantee under the Act of 1849. "Whatever be the effect," he says, "of the fee-farm grant, it can only have such operation as is conferred on it by the statute, and that operation is to be ascertained from the language of the Legislature construed according to the well-known rule, that every clause and every word must obtain its full and ordinary force and meaning, unless such construction would lead to some absurdity or some repugnance or inconsistency with the other provisions of the enactment."'

I may also refer to a passage from the judgment of Jessel, M.R., in *Re Willey* (23 Ch. D. at p. 127), cited in the argument in *Re M'Naul's Estate* ([1902] 1 I.R. 114): 'I never allow my construction of a plain enactment to be biassed in the slightest degree by any number of judicial decisions or dicta as to its meaning, when those decisions or dicta are not actually binding upon me. I read the Act for myself. If I think it clear, I express my opinion about its meaning, as I consider I am bound to do. Of course if other Judges have expressed different views as to the construction, and their decisions are binding on this Court, this Court has simply to bow and submit, whatever its own opinion may be. But when there is no such binding decision, in my view a Judge ought not to allow himself to be biassed in the construction of a plain Act of Parliament by any number of dicta or decisions which are not binding on him.'

Now then, applying these cases to the matter in hand, in the first place, there is no case which decides the question which presents itself on the 12th section of Deasy's Act. I omit for the present the valuable observations of Mr. Justice Andrews in the case of *Burrowes* v. *Delany* (24 L.R. Ir. 503). But taking, as I am told to take, the *ipsissima verba* of the section, is there anything to prevent my giving to them their ordinary meaning? Nothing that I can see. Having regard to the definition of the word 'landlord', in the Act of Parliament, the words of the 12th section fit the case. It is plain that the words 'during the continuance of the tenancy,' which occur in the lease, point to a contractual matter – to use Mr. Justice Andrews' language, incident to the subject-matter of the tenancy. The Landlord and Tenant Act of 1860 has reference to 'land,' and contracts in reference to land, and the contract under consideration is calculated to affect the subject-matter of demise. The relation of landlord and tenant does not, as it did, rest upon tenure; it now rests upon privity of contract, and if the relation of landlord and tenant rests upon privity of contract, why should not an assignee be bound by an instrument in which the word 'assigns' is used, when he takes under that instrument, and must be presumed to have known its contents? Is the landlord to do all the work which may be really necessary for the preservation of the subject-matter demised? and is the assignee, though specifically named, and enjoying the benefit that has accrued to the lands he occupies by work done in his time, to bear no part of the burthen? The defendant has entered on the subject-matter of the tenancy under an instrument of contract which uses the word 'assigns', and now endeavours to renounce the contractual obligations which relate to the subject-matter of the contract. This, in my opinion, he cannot do.

Gibson J.:

The sea-wall was for the common benfit of the landlord and various lessees; it was essential to preserve the property demised, to enable the lessee to perform his covenants as to that property, and to secure the road constituting the approach; it could only be maintained by entrusting the work to the landlord, as the entire length of sea-wall was necessary, and the maintenance could not be left to separate action of lessees dealing with fractions of the structure. Part of the consideration of the lease was the covenant to contribute, and the rent was thereby made less than it otherwise would have been. In these circumstances it seems startling to the ordinary intelligence that though the lessee should be bound, the assignee should not be.

Defendant's counsel, relying on *Spencer's Case* (1 Sm. L.C. (11th ed.), p. 55), contend – (1) That even if the covenant obliged the lessee to do the work himself, his assignee would have been under no such responsibility; (2) that even if he would have been, the covenant to contribute is only a collateral covenant to indemnify, not running with the land. For the plaintiff it is replied that – (1) the contribution was in substance part of the rent; (2) that the covenant ran with the land; (3) that even if it did not, Deasy's Act, sects. 12 and 13, transfers the obligation to the defendant.

The service of cleaning a parish church, ringing the church bell, keeping a grindstone for the use of a parish: *Doe* v. *Benham* (7 Q.B. 976), or labour for the landlord, may be rent, and the variable character of service or payment does not affect the character of rent: *Lloyd* v. *Keys* ([1901] 2 I.R. at p. 421). By a trifling change in drafting the present lease contribution could have been made rent proper; it is in substance a payment by which the rent is reduced. This exhibits the extreme technicality of defendant's argument. It was not, however, introduced into the reddendum as rent, and was not I think, rent. The questions for consideration are, therefore, two. Did the covenant run with the land? If technically it did not do so, did Deasy's Act make the assignee liable?

1. In England, where the maintenance of sea-walls is the subject of express legislation, covenants like the present must often occur: see *Newport Union* v. *Stead* ([1907] 2 K.B. 460) (since reversed by the house of Lords), where, at p. 467, the form of the statute is given. There is no analogous Irish legislation. It was suggested for the plaintiff that the facts here throw on the lessor an implied duty to maintain the wall, and that on his failure to do so, the lessees could have entered to execute the necessary repair, as stated by Lord Romilly in *Morland* v. *Cook* (L.R. 6 Eq. at p. 261). I have not felt it necessary to decide this point, which has not been sufficiently argued; and I will deal with the case on the basis that the lessor was not legally obliged to maintain the wall, though of course in his own interest he would necessarily do so, and it was assumed he would. I have not found any case quite like the present. *Vyvyan* v. *Arthur* (1 B. & C. 410) was a case of service like rent. *Jourdain* v. *Wilson* (4 B. & Als. 266) and *Athol* v. *Midland Great Western Railway* (I.R. 3 C.L. 333) were cases of quasi-easements attached to the demised premises. *Morris* v. *Kennedy* ([1896] 2 I.R. 247) is of the same type. And in *Sampson* v. *Easterby* (9 B. & C. 505), where the question was as to the benefit of the covenant running with the reversion, the smelting mill was part of the mining equipment which the lessee was to enjoy in specie. In *Vernon* v. *Smith* (5 B. & Ald. 1) the insurance money was to be spent on the premises. The only assistance derived from the cases is the principle they lay down. A covenant runs with land when it relates to the support and maintenance of the premises: *Bally* v. *Wells* (Wilmot's Notes, p. 344), cited in *Vernon* v. *Smith* (5 B. & Ald. 1); or which affects the nature, quality, or value of the thing demised, independently of collateral circumstances; or which affects the mode of using it: *Mayor of Congleton* v. *Pattison* (10 East, at p. 135); or

which affects the land itself during the term; or which, *per se,* and not merely from collateral circumstances, affects the value of the land at the end of the term; same case at p. 138. The present covenant appears to fall within the principle. The benefit of the covenant would seem clearly to run with reversion, so that the landlord's grantee could sue the lessee on it: *Rogers* v. *Hosegood* ([1900] 2 Ch. 388), the reasoning in which is important. Must not the burthen equally so run? None of the cases cited for the defendant is in point. They all relate to covenants quite unlike the present. *Dewar's Case* ([1908] 1 K.B. 94) is plainly distinguishable, as there was a limited covenant for quiet enjoyment, and the covenant related to premises not demised. If the covenant for quiet enjoyment had protected the sub-lessee from the sub-lessor's default in performing the covenants in his own lease, that covenant would have certainly run with the demise. The covenant held not to pass had very much the same object. It is unnecessary to criticize the decision, as it is not in point here. In the present case, would not a covenant by the lessor to maintain the sea-wall have run with the land, both as to burthen and benefit? And would the result be different if the covenant was made conditional on the lessee's making contribution to the cost?

Mr. Harrison relies on several special grounds which make (he contends) the covenant collateral: the covenant only arises if the lessor expends money on repair, which he is not bound to do; the wall is at some distance from the leasehold premises; and the money payment is only an indemnity. No doubt the obligation only purports to attach if the repair has been necessary, and has been carried out; but the plain object was to secure the maintenance of the wall, which was assumed to be necessary for the common protection. The fact that a small space intervened between the holding and the wall – part of such space consisting of the road approach – cannot affect the real function of the wall as a shield to the premises. It is not necessary that the wall should be at the defendant's actual boundary; all the parts behind the wall in peril of sea erosion were benefited by it.

As to the covenant being for money contribution and not for physical repair, it is manifest that the wall as an entire thing must be maintained by one person, the landlord; and the only useful obligation that could be imposed on the lessees would be to assist financially. The recital in the statute mentioned in the *Newport Union Case* ([1907] 2 K.B. at p. 467) and *Morland* v. *Cook* (L.R. 6 Eq. 252) illustrates this mode of aid. The money represents the value of the share of labour.

A further objection was that the benefit of the covenant could not run with the lessor's estate if the reversion was severed. The same difficulty would have arisen in *Vyvyan's Case* (1 B. & C. at 410) (as pointed out in *Doe* v. *Reid* (10 B. & C. at p. 857), in *Sampson's Case* (9 B. & C. 505), and in *Coker* v. *Guy* (2 B. & P. 565). When there is such division, the problem often is not easy to solve. See, for example, *White's Case* ([1897] 1 Ch. 767), *Clegg* v. *Hands* (44 Ch. D. 503), *The Manchester Brewery Co.* v. *Coombs* ([1901] 2 Ch. 608). As there has been hitherto no such severance, I decline to pronounce any speculative opinion of future contingencies.

2. Assuming (contrary to my opinion) that in strictness the covenant would not have run with the land, does Deasy's Act, section 12, make the assignee liable? The section consists of two parts. The landlord has the same action and remedy against the assignee in respect of the agreements contained or implied in the lease or contract as the original landlord might have had against the original tenant; and the heir or representative of such landlord on whom his estate or interest under any such lease or contract devolves or should have devolved has the like action and remedy against the tenant and assignee for any damage done to the estate by breach of agreement in the landlord's lifetime as such landlord himself might have

had. I agree with Mr. Harrison that the statute of 11 Anne, c. 2 s. 4 (Irish), gives no assistance; its object was in Ireland, by transferring privity of contract, to get rid of the absurd anomaly, discussed in the notes to *Mostyn* v. *Fabrigas* (1 Sm. L.C. (11th ed.), p. 591), that a lessor's action against an assignee, not being within the statute of Charles 1, and resting therefore on privity of estate, was local and not transitory. The Act was an amendment of the Act of Charles 1, and should receive the construction impressed on that enactment.

Putting the statute of Anne aside as irrelevant, I take up Deasy's Act. Though not in strictness a code, it covers for future lettings, the entire relation of landlord and tenant, abolishing old real property principles, which it replaces by the law of contract. The necessity of a reversion disappears, and transmission of burthen and benefit under the contract no longer depends on the existence of a deed under seal. The assignee is put in the original tenant's place, whether assigns are named in the covenant or not. If the contract of tenancy is assigned, the lessee remains liable until discharged under sect. 16, meanwhile enjoying a right of indemnity against the assignee. Section 16 assumes that when the landlord gives the prescribed consent, the assignee is subjected to all the lessee's liabilities. The intention of the legislation is illustrated by such cases as *Bickford* v. *Parsons* (5 C.B. 920); *Buckworth* v. *Simpson* (1 C.M. & R. 834) and *Cornish* v. *Stubbs* (L.R. 5 C.P. at p. 339). In a demise not under seal, the assignee could only be bound by being substituted under a new tenancy on the old terms: *Elliott* v. *Johnson* (L.R. 2 Q.B. at p. 127). By making the tenancy pass with its liabilities the statute obtained the same result. The statute was intended to put the law of landlord and tenant in Ireland on a modern, simple, and intelligible basis, getting rid of feudal technical rules; and it falls within the observations of Holmes, L.J. in *M'Naul's Case* ([1902] 1 I.R. at p. 138). The express language of sections 12 and 13 cannot be restricted or altered by forcing on it *Spencer's Case* (1 Sm. L.C. (11th ed.), p. 55) applicable to the law of covenants at common law, which was so precious in the eyes of legal schoolmen that they could hardly conceive a statute disregarding it. We must construe the enactment as it stands: *Vagliano's Case* ([1891] A.C. at p. 145). It introduced a wholly new and revolutionary principle, substituting contract for ancient real property law. The effect of sections 12 and 13 has attracted only little attention since 1860, and the authorities on the subject are few. In La Touche's Furlong, at p. 558, and in Nolan & Kane (3rd ed.), pp. 21 and 22, the view is taken that collateral covenants are transferred. In *Athol's Case* (I.R. 3 C.L. 333) and in *Morris* v. *Kennedy* ([1896] 2 I.R. 247) the covenants were held to pass; but the application of the statute was not discussed or considered. The only direct reported authority is the judgment of Andrews, J., in *Burrowes* v. *Delaney* (24 L.R.Ir. at p. 517), where he held that covenants 'incident to the tenancy,' though not strictly running with the land, came within the operation of section 13. In a late case (unreported) in this Divison, in an action brought by a lessor under a provision in the lease appropriating it to the last year's rent of the term; the assignee of the lease obtained a fair rent order under the Act of 1887, reducing the rent; he was held by the Court, presided over by Palles, C.B., on new trial motion, to be entitled to use the money so lodged with the landlord in satisfaction of the rent sued for in the action, though, if the lease had not been determined by the Act of 1887, the time of appropriation had not arrived. I am not aware whether Deasy's Act was relied on. At the trial of this case before me no question was raised on the ground of want of contractual privity. The tendency of the speeches in *Liddy* v. *Kennedy* (L.R. 5 H.L. 134) also favours the wide construction of the statute.

The assignee is made subject to the same action and remedy as the original lessee, and so far as regards terms applicable to the contract of demise as a continuing obligation intended to bind the tenant for the time being, the assignee, who takes the benefit, cannot, as against the landlord, disclaim the burthen. If the intention expressed or implied in the contract is to attach to the tenancy, as part of the demise, obligations relating to the land which are to operate during the term against everyone holding under the contract, the assignee is made liable. On the importance of intention *Rogers* v. *Hosegood* ([1900] 2 Ch. 388) contains some interesting reasoning. It relates to benefit of covenants passing on a sale in fee, and does not directly bear on a demise, or contract liability of the kind created by Deasy's Act.

There may be terms depending on personal considerations and not capable of vicarious performance: *Tolhurst's Case* ([1903] A.C. at p. 417), which might not come within sections 12 and 13; and collateral agreements might be conceived so disconnected with the land and demise that they might not pass to the assignee. Such terms would be construed as not intended – *primâ facie,* at least – to apply or attach to the tenancy proper. It would be undesirable to attempt an exhaustive definition as to covenants which are within or outside the statute. Such cases as *Raymond* v. *Fitch* (5 Tyr. 985), *Doughty* v. *Bowman* (11 Q.B. 444), *Dewar's Case* ([1908] 1 K.B. 94) seem plainly within it. I confine myself to the question of principle. If the covenant here would have been collateral before 1860, the statute now makes it bind the assignee; it concerns the very existence of the subject of demise; it is expressly part of the consideration of the letting; and was intended to impose liability on all owners of the tenancy during the entire duration of the term.

On both grounds, the nature of the covenant and the effect of the statute, I concur in the original conclusion of my brother Wright, in favour of the plaintiff.

Madden J.:

This is an action by a lessor against the assignee of a lease for 999 years upon a covenant in the lease. Two questions arise in the case: one of these depends upon the construction and effect of this particular covenant; and the other is of great general importance. The plaintiff contends, first, that the covenant upon which the action is founded is one which runs with the land, within the meaning of the second resolution in *Spencer's Case* (1 Sm. L.C. (11th ed.), p. 55), and the subsequent authorities; and, secondly, that if he should fail to bring the case within these authorities, the words of the 12th section of the Landlord and Tenant Act of 1860 are sufficiently wide to include certain covenants between lessor and lessee which would be regarded as collateral under the decisions upon the Act of Hen. 8, and the corresponding Irish statute of Charles 1. This section of the Act of 1860 now represents for Ireland the Act of 32 Hen. 8, c. 34, upon which *Spencer's Case* (1 Sm. L.C. (11th ed.), p. 55) was decided. It is undoubtedly, in certain respects, wider in its application than the Irish statutes which it superseded and repealed (10 Car. 1, s.2, c. 4, and 11 Anne, c. 2). It extends to contracts of tenancy not under seal, and it is part of an enactment by which privity of contract is substituted for privity of estate, and by which the principles of tenure are no longer applicable to the relation of landlord and tenant. Thus it had the effect of doing away with much of the technicalities which led to a failure of justice under the older Acts. Whether it has the further effect of transferring the burden and benefit of a class of covenants which must be regarded as collateral under the decisions to which I referred, is a question of great importance, which I do not think it necessary to discuss, by reason of the opinion which I have formed upon the former of the questions which arise in the case. Having regard to the nature of the demised premises, and to the character of the covenant in question, I am clearly of opinion that it is one which touches and concerns the premises demised by the lease within the meaning of the resolution in *Spencer's Case* (1 Sm. L.C. (11th ed.), p. 55), as interpreted by subsequent decisions.

The premises so demised consist of a dwelling-house, one of a number of villas facing Ballyholme Bay. Each villa has a strip of garden running down to a road, and on the sea side of the road there is a grass slope or embankment, beyond which there is a sea-wall, constructed in 1884 by the predecessor in title of the plaintiff for the protection of his property, which is from its situation, and from the composition of the soil, liable to erosion and to consequent encroachment by the sea. It is found in the case that the whole of this wall is necessary for the protection of the coast, and that the result of the non-repair of a breach would be the destruction of the wall by the action of the waves admitted by the breach, and the consequent destruction of the roadway and ultimately of the subject-matter of the demise.

That a covenant which is conversant with the preservation and protection from destruction of the subject-matter of a demise may be fairly regarded as one which touches and concerns it, is a proposition which commends itself to general acceptance. But the second resolution in *Spencer's Case* (1 Sm. L.C. (11th ed.), p. 55) has been overlaid with so complicated a mass of technicalities that it behoves us to consider whether any principle has been laid down in decided cases, in obedience to which we are bound to act in applying to any particular covenant the apparently plain and simple language of the resolution.

The defendant contends that this covenant should be regarded as collateral for three reasons. First, because it is conversant with a thing to be done on the land of the reversioner, and not on the demised premises. Secondly, because the subject-matter of the covenant is the payment of money otherwise than by way of reddendum under the demise; and thirdly, she relies on the decision of the English Court of King's Bench in *Dewar* v. *Goodman* ([1908] 1 K.B. 94) as laying down a principle which we ought to apply to the present case.

As regards the first of these contentions, I should be disposed to regard as collateral a covenant by a lessee to build a house, to repair a wall, or to do any other work on land outside the demised premises, even though it were on the land of the reversioner, in the absence of some clearly established relation between the work to be done and the user and enjoyment of the demised premises. When such a relation exists, there is ample authority for treating the covenant as one which runs with the land.

The existence of this relation may be established in different ways. In *Vyvyan* v. *Arthur* (1 B. & C. 417) the covenant was by the lessee of certain land to grind corn at a mill situated on the land of the lessor. 'It is said that as the thing required to be done by the covenant is not to be done upon the land demised, but upon other land which might or might not continue to be the land of the lessor, it does not, therefore, respect the land demised, and, consequently, that the assignee cannot take advantage of the covenant. I am of opinion, however, inasmuch as the thing to be done is to be done at a mill which belonged to the lessor at the time of making the lease, and which has always continued to belong to the owner of the reversion of the land demised, that the covenant to be implied from the reddendum is in the nature of a covenant to render a rent, and, consequently, that it is a covenant that ran with the lands' (*per* Holroyd, J.). Best, J., observes (p. 417): 'The general principle is that if the performance of the covenant be beneficial to the reversioner, in respect of the lessor's demand, and to no other person, his assignee may sue upon it; but if it be beneficial to the lessor without regard to his continuing owner of the estate, it is a mere collateral covenant, upon which the assignee cannot sue.'

The Court in that case was enabled to apply these general observations to the covenant before it by regarding it, by way of implication from the reddendum, as in the nature of a covenant to pay rent; and Mr. Overend, in an ingenious argument, has endeavoured to call in aid the particular reasoning upon which *Vyvyan* v. *Arthur* (1 B. & C. 417) was decided. But, to my mind, the connexion in this case between the covenant and the demise is so direct that it is unnecessary to have recourse to the artificial reasoning upon which that decision was founded, even if it were applicable to the present case. I can conceive no relation more close than that between a house built on the sand, and the sea-wall which protects it from the action of the sea. The encroachment of the sea along a portion of our coasts is a matter of common knowledge; and the right to protection by the natural barrier of sand and shingle, or by artifical walls or embankments, has come before our Courts in various forms. The case of *Morland* v. *Cook* (L.R. 6 Eq. 252) was not a case between landlord and tenant, and is not directly in point as regards the present case. But it is of value, as illustrating the close relation which, in the eye of a Court of Equity, as well as a matter of common understanding, exists between land liable to encroachment from the sea, and the maintenance of the protecting sea-wall.

Inasmuch as the covenant in the present case is conversant with the preservation of the subject-matter of the demise, it touches and concerns the things demised more directly than a class of covenants which have always been regarded as running with the land. I refer to covenants which affect the user of the demised premises; by which I mean the mode of user, and not the profit to be derived from the user, for covenants of the latter class are only collateral: *Thomas* v. *Hayward* (L.R. 4 Ex. 311). The case of *Easterby* v. *Sampson* (9 B. & C. 505; 6 Biag. 644) is an authority for the proposition that a covenant by a lessee affecting the user of the demised premises will run with the land, although the act to which the covenant relates is to be done on land of the lessor, outside the limits of the demised premises. The covenant in *Easterby* v. *Sampson* (9 B. & C. 505; 6 Biag. 644) was to build a new smelting-house on a part of the lessor's waste land which was not included in the demised premises, but adjoined them. It was held by the Court of Exchequer Chamber, affirming the decision of the Court of King's Bench, that, inasmuch as the covenant affected the mode of enjoying and using the thing demised, the principle laid down by Lord Ellenborough in *Mayor of Congleton* v. *Pattison* (10 East, 135) applied. 'It is impossible to doubt that the demise of the mines is immediately connected with the possession of the smelting-mill' (*per* Alexander, C.B., at p. 650). Upon the same principle it has been decided in several cases, of which the decision of the Court of Appeal in England, *Clegg* v. *Hands* (44 Ch. D. 503), may be taken as an example, that a covenant as to the manner in which a particular business is to be carried on upon the demised premises will run with the land.

I now proceed to consider the second point relied on by the defendant's counsel – the circumstance that the covenant is conversant with the payment of moneys. In *Vernon* v. *Smith* (5 B. & Ald. 1) the lessee of certain premises situated within the weekly bills of mortality covenanted with the lessor at his own expense to insure the demised premises in a certain amount in a public office in London or Westminster. Under the provisions of 14 Geo. 3, c. 78, the landlord of premises lying within those limits had a statutory right to have the amount of the insurance laid out in rebuilding the premises. This circumstance, in the opinion of the Court of King's Bench, brought the case within the principle thus stated by Abbott, C.J.: 'A covenant to lay out a given sum of money in rebuilding or repairing the premises, in case of damage by fire, would clearly be a covenant running with the land, that is, such a covenant as would be binding on the assignees of the lessee and which the assignee of the lessor might enforce.' There are some observations in the judgment of Best, J., which are applicable to the present case – 'A covenant in a lease of which the covenantee cannot, after his assignment, take advantage, and which is beneficial to the assignee as such, will go with the estate assigned. If this were not the law, the tenant could hold the estate discharged from the performance of one of the conditions on which it was granted to him. The original covenantee could not avail himself of this covenant; he sustains no loss by the destruction of the buildings, and, therefore, has no interest to have them insured . . . . By the terms *collateral covenants* which do not pass to the assignee, are meant such as are beneficial to the lessor, without regard to his continuing the owner of the estate.'

In *Vernon* v. *Smith* (5 B. & Ald. 1), as in the present case, the covenant was to be performed by the payment of money. The money paid could not, as in *Vyvyan* v. *Arthur* (1 B. & C. 417), be regarded as in the nature of rent. It was money to be paid to a stranger, not, as here, to the lessor. The connection between the money and the demised premises depended on the fact that the expenditure would result in the restoration of the premises if destroyed by fire. In the present case the money is to be paid for protection against destruction by water. Restoration and preservation are no doubt different things, but I can see no distinction between these things relevant to the question how far each of them touches and concerns the subject-matter of the demise.

It remains to consider the question of the application to the present case of the decision of the English Court of Appeal in *Dewar* v. *Goodman* ([1908] 1 K.B. 94) on appeal from Jelf, J. ([1907] 1 K.B. 612). The distinction between that case and the present becomes apparent on reading the following passage in the judgment of Buckley, L.J.: 'The construction for the plaintiff may I think, be summarized as follows: A covenant to do an act, not in respect of the demised premises, but which will protect from forfeiture the estate of the demised premises, is a covenant which runs with the land. If that proposition is true, it is wholly new. It may nevertheless be true, but I am not aware of any authority in support of it.' The distinction here taken between the estate of the lessee in the demised premises, and the demised premises themselves, is the foundation of the judgment of the learned Lord Justice. The same distinction runs through the judgment of Lord Alverstone, C.J.: 'The covenant in the present case is a covenant to do something on land which was not the subject of the demise, but it is contended for the plaintiff that, as the performance of the covenant was for the benefit and protection of the sub-lessee, and concerned his interest or estate in the land, that is sufficient to bind the assigns; and cases were cited for the purpose of showing that the terms "estate" and "land" were in this construction to be treated as equivalent. But the important thing to observe with regard to the cases cited was that in every one of them the covenant did touch and concern the land demised, in the strictest sense of the word' (p.103). And further on, at p. 104, he uses the words 'interest of the lessee in the land demised' as denoting something different from the land itself, or the user of the land. It is evident from the concluding portion of the judgment of Jelf, J., at p. 623, that if he had not been hampered by the technicalities which have been engrafted upon the clear and simple language of the resolution in *Spencer's Case* (1 Sm. L.C. (11th ed.), p. 55), he might have held with counsel for the plaintiff that 'the covenant in question for performance of the covenants of the head lease does *pro tanto* touch or concern the thing demised in that, if performed, it secures the possession of it by preventing eviction on that ground by the superior landlord, and if not performed it forfeits the underlease.' 'It may be,' he added, 'that the Court of Appeal, if the case is carried there, may be able to take a broader view of the matter, and to break through the legal technicalities which a Court of first instance feels constrained to observe.'

The particular gloss on *Spencer's Case* (1 Sm. L.C. (11th ed.) p. 55) by which

Jelf, J., was chiefly influenced was a passage in the judgment of Lord Ellenborough in the case of *Mayor of Congleton* v. *Pattison* (10 East. 135), to which I have already referred, where he says that a covenant is assignable if it affects the nature, quality, or value of the thing demised, independently of collateral circumstances, or if it affects the mode of enjoyment. Here is to be found the true ground of distinction between the past and present case and *Dewar* v. *Goodman* ([1908] 1 K.B. 94). A covenant relating to the preservation from destruction of the thing demised, affects not merely its nature, quality, or value, but its very existence. Without discussing the grounds upon which it was decided that the covenant in *Dewar* v. *Goodman* ([1908] 1 K.B. 94) did not come within the resolution in *Spencer's Case* (1 Sm. L.C. (11th ed.) p. 55), we can have no difficulty in discerning, or acting upon, the essential difference which exists between the relation born by the covenant in that case to the title to the premises, and in the present case to the very subject-matter of the demise.

A question was suggested during the argument, which if answered in the affirmative would be conclusive of the case: whether a covenant is not implied on the part of the lessor to maintain a protection to the demised premises, the repair of which is admitted to be necessary. The existence of such a liability on the part of the lessor, and the mode of enforcing it – whether by action at law, or by proceeding in equity, in which the lessee would be a plaintiff, and the lessor and the other contributory lessees defendants – are questions of some nicety, as to which I should not like to express an opinion without further consideration and argument. It is not necessary for me to do so, for I am clearly of opinion, for the reasons which I have stated, that the covenant on the part of the lessee, regarded as unilateral, is one which nearly touches and intimately concerns the demised premises, and therefore runs with the land.

Kenny J.:

Two matters have to be borne in mind in dealing with this case: the one, that the claim arises out of and in connection with the relation of landlord and tenant, and the other, that the person who is suing is the original lessor in whom is vested the property in both the wall and the reversion expectant on the determination of the defendant's lease. It is the lessor who, as such owner of the reversion and of the wall, has made the outlay in the repair of the latter. The only point in the case is whether the assignee of the lessee's estate is liable under the covenant for a proportionate part of the expenses incurred in the carrying out of a work which, on the facts as stated by Wright, J., is essentially necessary for the preservation of the defendant's house and premises. So far as merits are concerned they would seem to be altogether on the side of the plaintiff.

It is said that this covenant for contribution is not one that runs with the land so as to lay the burthen of its performance on the shoulders of an assignee of the lessee's estate; that it is a mere collateral covenant, not touching or concerning the demised premises; and that while the lessee might be personally liable on foot of it, his assignee is under no such liability to the owner of the reversion. Even if that contention were correct, it might not save the defendant from ultimate liability, for, if the assignment from the lessee to the defendant be properly drawn, it will most likely be found to contain a covenant on the part of the defendant to indemnify the lessee from the effects of any breaches of the covenants contained in the lease. However that may be, we have to deal only with the question of liability between the reversioner and the assignee of the lessee's estate.

The branch of our law conversant with the subject of covenants running with the land is of an extremely technical character, and the authorities that bear upon it are in many instances on the border-line and difficult of application to any set of circumstances other than those on which they rest. All the cases establish that if the covenant be purely personal and collateral to the thing demised it does not run with the land – while, on the other hand, if it touches or concerns the subject-matter of the tenancy, it does run with the land and is binding on assignees of the covenantor's estate. In some of the cases a more exhaustive definition of a covenant running with the land will be found.

In *Sampson* v. *Easterby* (9 B. & C. 505; 6 Bing. 644) it was held to run with the reversion on the ground that the thing covenanted to be done tended to the support and maintenance of the thing demised. In *The Mayor of Congleton* v. *Pattison* (10 East, 130) Lord Ellenborough in his judgment declares that the covenant would bind the assignee 'if it affected the nature, quality, or value of the thing demised, independently of collateral circumstances, or if it affected the *mode of enjoying it*'; and in *Athol* v. *The Midland Great Western Railway Co.* (I.R. 3 C.L. 333), Whiteside, C.J., in delivering the judgment of the Court refers to the covenant in that case as relating 'directly to the nature and occupation and enjoyment of the very thing demised and connected with it.' Cotton, L.J., in his judgment in *Austerberry* v. *The Corporation of Oldham* (29 Ch. D. 750), discusses the two classes of covenants, and at p. 776, says: 'In order that the benefit may run with the land, the covenant must be one which relates to or touches and concerns the land of the covenantee . . . Looking at the terms of the covenant it is . . . not a covenant having a direct reference to the land, or the enjoyment or the benefit of the land of the covenantee.' *Clegg* v. *Hands* (44 Ch. D. 503) was also a case relating to the benefit of a covenant running with the reversion, where the demise was of a public-house, and the lessee had covenanted to buy all his beer from the lessors whose assignees were the plaintiffs. At the close of his judgment, Lopes, L.J. says: 'In my opinion, it touches and concerns the demised premises; it affects the mode of enjoyment of the premises, and, therefore, it runs with the reversion.' On the other hand, *Thomas* v. *Hayward* (L.R. 4 Ex. 311), if it be still good law, is an authority for this – that touching the beneficial occupation of the thing is not equivalent to touching or concerning the thing itself. Lord Alverstone, C.J., in *Dewar* v. *Goodman* ([1908] 1 K.B. 94; affirmed H.L., W.N., 1908, p. 250) remarks that 'it is said that *Thomas* v. *Hayward* (L.R. 4 Ex. 311) cannot now be considered as good law,' but he adds that he cannot accept that view; but Buckley, L.J. considers that the Chief Justice has placed too much reliance on it, and proceeds to distinguish it. In my opinion, the covenant in the present case is directly connected with the demised premises. It was entered into as part of a scheme for the protection of, amongst others, the lessee's villa residence, which might, in the absence of the wall in question, suffer material damage from the encroachments of the sea. If the lease had been taken without any reference to this wall, it might have become necessary for the defendant, in order adequately to protect his own premises, to take steps for the repair of the wall. I rather incline to the opinion that a frontager to the sea in his position could take steps of this nature. If he were obliged to do so, how was he to be repaid his outlay beyond the proportion of it which his own premises ought to bear? I think the covenant affords an answer. Furthermore, the lessor might have assumed sole liability for the maintenance of the wall, and, if he did, it is not unreasonable to conclude that the rent reserved would have been larger. In my opinion, it follows that there was a consideration for the covenant arising from the very nature, value, and condition of the thing demised. Apart from this, the covenant may be regarded as one to co-operate for the purpose of maintaining a work that is a common protection to the demised premises and to the lessor's other property. If, as is found by Wright, J., the wall is so essential to the continued existence of the defendant's house, cannot it be regarded as in a sense partaking of the very essence of the frontagers' houses, and being part and parcel of the very premises themselves? In my opinion, the latter are so dependent on it for not alone stability, but their very existence as habitable structures, that it is as much a part of the premises as their very foundations. The covenant contemplates the doing of an act on premises so situated, and to my mind is equivalent to a covenant providing for the apportionment of outlay on the premises specifically demised by the lease. If the covenant was one to repay the lessor any outlay he might expend on the premises within the ambit of the lease, there could be no doubt that such a covenant would run with the land.

A case, *Morland* v. *Cook* (L.R. 6 Eq. 252), not unlike the present, came before Lord Romilly, M.R., in 1868. In one particular it differed from it, namely, that it was not a case of landlord and tenant, but one in which the covenant was contained in a partition deed. The several parties to the deed mutually covenanted with one another that the expenses of maintaining a sea-wall should be borne by them, their heirs and assigns, out of the partitioned lands in proportion, and by an acre-scot, payable thereout. It was impossible to say in which of the parties the ownership of the wall – which constituted the southern boundary of the land – was vested. The defendants' lands were situated just within the wall, and did not anywhere abut on the sea. The defendants were assignees, and the suit was instituted for a declaration that they were bound to contribute to the repair of the wall. It was argued that the covenant ran with the lands, and also that it was in affirmance of a common law liability, and *Rex* v. *Commissioners of Sewers in Essex* (1 B. & C. 477) was relied on. Lord Romilly, in giving a decree in favour of plaintiffs, said that the thing to be done by force of the covenant was annexed to and appurtenant to the land partitioned – which goes with the land and binds the assignee though not mentioned.

Morland v. *Cook* (L.R. 6 Eq. 252) is open to the observation that the contribution was by the partition deed actually made a charge on the contributory land, and this criticism was directed against its weight in the case to which I have already referred of *Austerberry* v. *The Corporation of Oldham* (29 Ch. D. 750), where the Court held that a covenant in a purchase deed to maintain a road did not run with the land adjoining. Cotton, L.J., in that case, while admitting to some extent the force of this objection, does not express disapproval of the actual decision or of the arguments by which Lord Romilly justified it. He even adds (p. 777), 'but as regards benefit, a covenant for the keeping up of a sea-wall which would prevent the land in question owned by the plaintiff from being flooded was undoubtedly a covenant with reference to the benefit to be enjoyed by the land by the keeping of the sea out.' Lindley, L.J., considered that *Morland* v. *Cook* was intelligible on the ground that the expense was practically created a rent-charge out of the lands. Fry, L.J., expressed a less decided opinion as to the benefit of the covenant not running with the land, and added that he was more inclined to think that the road in question was so far an incident to the use and occupation of the adjoining lands that it might be conceivable that it came within the principles of 'covenants relating to things incident to the land.'

I am therefore of opinion that the covenant in the present case runs with the land, and that the defendant, as assignee, is liable for her proper proportion of the expenses of repair incurred by the plaintiff.

As to the other point that was argued, namely, that, whether the covenant ran with the land or not, it was one that came within the 12th section of Deasy's Act, it is enough for me to say that I am of opinion that the liability to contribute to the repair of the wall was an incident of the tenancy when the defendant purchased the lessee's interest, and that as assignee of that interest she is liable under the section for the contribution.

III. DETERMINATION OF TENANCIES

LANDLORD AND TENANT LAW AMENDMENT ACT, IRELAND, 1860

7. The estate or interest of any tenant under any lease or other contract of tenancy shall not be surrendered otherwise than by a deed executed, or note in writing signed by the tenant or his agent thereto lawfully authorized in writing, or by act and operation of law.

8. The surrender of any lease made before or after the passing of this Act for the purpose of obtaining a renewal thereof, shall be valid without the surrender of the interests of the under-tenants thereunder; and the owners of such renewed lease for the time being and their representatives shall have the same rights and remedies as against such under-tenants as he or they would have had or have been entitled to had such surrender not been executed; and the chief landlord shall have the same remedies against the premises for the rents and duties reserved in such new lease, not exceeding the rents and duties reserved by the lease out of which such under-tenancies were derived, as he would have been entitled to in case no such surrender had been executed.

. . . .

40. If any dwelling house or other building constituting the substantial matter of the demise, and holden by any tenant under any lease or other contract of tenancy not containing an express covenant or agreement binding on the tenant to repair the same, shall be destroyed, become ruinous and uninhabitable, or incapable of beneficial occupation or enjoyment, by accidental fire or other inevitable accident, and without the default or neglect of the said tenant, it shall be lawful for such tenant to surrender the said premises; and on tendering the said surrender and on payment of all rent and arrears due or accruing due, or tendering the same, the said tenant shall be thenceforth discharged from all obligation to pay the rent or perform the covenants and conditions in the lease thenceforward.

. . . .

44. The surrender to or resumption by a landlord, or eviction of any portion of the premises demised by a lease, shall not in any manner prejudice or affect the rights of the landlord, whether by action, by entry, or ejectment, as to the residue of said premises.

CONVEYANCING ACT, 1881

14. – (1) A right of re-entry or forfeiture under any proviso or stipulation in a lease, for a breach of any covenant or condition in the lease, shall not be enforceable, by action or otherwise, unless and until the lessor serves on the lessee a notice specifying the particular breach complained of and, if the breach is capable of remedy, requiring the lessee to remedy the breach, and, in any case, requiring the lessee to make compensation in money for the breach, and the lessee fails, within a reasonable time thereafter, to remedy the breach, if it is capable of remedy, and to make reasonable compensation in money, to the satisfaction of the lessor, for the breach.

(2) Where a lessor is proceeding, by action or otherwise, to enforce such a right of re-entry or forfeiture, the lessee may, in the lessor's action, if any, or in any action brought by himself, apply to the Court for relief; and the Court may grant or refuse relief, as the Court, having regard to the proceedings and conduct of the parties under the foregoing provisions of this section, and to all the other circumst-

ances, thinks fit; and in case of relief may grant it on such terms, if any, as to costs, expenses, damages, compensation, penalty, or otherwise, including the granting of an injunction to restrain any like breach in the future, as the Court, in the circumstances of each case, thinks fit.

(3) For the purposes of this section a lease includes an original or derivative under-lease, also a grant at a fee farm rent, or securing a rent by condition; and a lessee includes an original or derivative under-lessee and the heirs, executors, administrators, and assigns of a lessee, also a grantee under such a grant as aforesaid, his heirs and assigns; and a lessor includes an original or derivative under-lessor, and the heirs, executors, administrators, and assigns of a lessor, also a grantor as aforesaid, and his heirs and assigns.

(4) This section applies although the proviso or stiplulation under which the right of re-entry or forfeiture accrues is inserted in the lease in pursuance of the directions of any Act of Parliament.

(5) For the purposes of this seciton a lease limited to continue as long only as the lessee abstains from committing a breach of covenant shall be and take effect as a lease to continue for any longer term for which it could subsist, but determinable by a proviso for re-entry on such a breach.

(6) This section does not extend –

(i) To a covenant or condition against the assigning, under-letting, parting with the possession, or disposing of the land leased; or to a condition for forfeiture on the bankruptcy of the lessee, or on the taking in execution of the lessee's interest; or

(ii) In case of a mining lease, to a covenant or condition for allowing the lessor to have access to or inspect books, accounts, records, weighing machines or other things, or to enter or inspect the mine or the workings thereof.

[*Sub. s. (7) rep. by S.L.R. 1894.*]

(8) This section shall not affect the law relating to re-entry or forfeiture or relief in case of non-payment of rent.

(9) This section applies to leases made either before or after the commencement of this Act, and shall have effect notwithstanding any stipulation to the contrary.

CONVEYANCING ACT, 1892
Leases, Under-leases, Forfeiture

2. – (1) A lessor shall be entitled to recover as a debt due to him from a lessee, and in addition to damages (if any) all reasonable costs and expenses properly incurred by the lessor in the employment of a solicitor and surveyor or valuer, or otherwise, in reference to any breach giving rise to a right of re-entry or forfeiture which, at the request of the lessee, is waived by the lessor by writing under his hand, or from which the lessee is relieved, under the provisions of the Conveyancing and Law of Property Act, 1881, or of this Act.

(2) Sub-section six of section fourteen of the Conveyancing and Law of Property Act, 1881, is to apply to a condition for forfeiture on bankruptcy of the lessee, or on taking in execution of the lessee's interest only after the expiration of one year from the date of the bankruptcy, or taking in execution, and provided the lessee's interest be not sold within such one year, but in case the lessee's interest be sold within such one year, sub-section six shall cease to be applicable thereto.

(3) Sub-section two of this section is not to apply to any lease of –

(a) Agricultural or pastoral land:

(b) Mines or minerals:

(c) A house used or intended to be used as a public-house or beershop:

(d) A house let as a dwelling-house, with the use of any furniture, books, works of art, or other chattels not being in the nature of fixtures:

(*e*) Any property with respect to which the personal qualifications of the tenant are of importance for the preservation of the value or character of the property, or on the ground of neighbourhood to the lessor, or to any person holding under him.

3. In all leases containing a covenant, condition, or agreement against assigning, underletting, or parting with the possession, or disposing of the land or property leased with the possession, or disposing of the land or property leased without licence or consent, such covenant, condition, or agreement shall, unless the lease contains an expressed provision to the contrary, be deemed to be subject to a proviso to the effect that no fine or sum of money in the nature of a fine shall be payable for or in respect of such licence or consent; but this proviso shall not preclude the right to require the payment of a reasonable sum in respect of any legal or other expense incurred in relation to such licence or consent.

4. Where a lessor is proceeding by action or otherwise to enforce a right of re-entry or forfeiture under any covenant, proviso, or stipulation in a lease, the court may, on application by any person claiming as under-lessee any estate or interest in the property comprised in the lease or any part thereof either in the lessor's action (if any) or in any action brought by such person for that purpose, make an order vesting for the whole term of the lease or any less term the property comprised in the lease or any part thereof in any person entitled as under-lessee to any estate or interest in such property upon such conditions, as to execution of any deed or other document, payment of rent, costs, expenses, damages, compensation, giving security, or otherwise, as the court in the circumstances of each case shall think fit, but in no case shall any such under-lessee be entitled to require a lease to be granted to him for any longer term than he had under his original sub-lease.

5. In section fourteen of the Conveyancing and Law of Property Act, 1881, as amended by this Act, and in this Act, 'lease' shall also include an agreement for a lease where the lessee has become entitled to have his lease granted, and 'under-lease' shall also include an agreement for an under-lease where the under-lessee has become entitled to have his under-lease granted, and in this Act 'under-lessee' shall include any person deriving title under or from an under-lessee.

LYNCH V. LYNCH
(1843) 6 Ir.L.R. 131 (Exchequer)

L., lessee *pur autre vie,* assented to a new letting by the landlord, of a part of the demised premises to M., who entered into possession accordingly, but there was no surrender in writing of L.'s interest.

Brady C.B.:

This case, which was tried before the Lord Chief Justice, comes before the Court on a motion to set aside the verdict. It is an ejectment on the title, and the lessors of the plaintiff claim under a freehold lease for a life still in being. It appeared in the course of the trial, that in the year 1833 an ejectment for non-payment of rent was brought to evict that lease, and that in order to pay off a portion of the arrears, an arrangement was entered into whereby one Patrick Lynch, the husband of the present defendant Judith Lynch, who is since deceased, on paying a part of the arrears, got into possession of a portion of the lands; for which portion the present ejectment has been brought, and the question made at the trial before the Lord Chief Justice was, whether the arrangment entered into at the time of the ejectment for non-payment of rent, between Mr. Willington, the agent on the part of the head-landlord, and Patrick Lynch, the late husband of the defendant, with the assent of the lessees or their representatives (the present lessors of the plaintiff), was only intended as a means of securing the repayment of the portion of the arrears of rent advanced by him, or whether it was the creation of a term altogether new, directly under the landlord, without any holding under or connexion with the original lessees.

The Chief Justice left the question to the Jury, most strongly in favour of the lessors of the plaintiff, – for he told them, that unless they were certain that at the time of the agreement, the lessees knew of the terms of that agreement and concurred in it, and knew also at the time that their concurring in that agreement, it would have the effect of putting an end to the lease of 1821, and concurred in it with such knowledge of the effect, they would not be warranted in finding for the defendant; and that if they were not fully satisfied thereon, or if they conceived the lessees intended only the making a security to Patrick Lynch for the money he advanced, and either did not know, or did not intend, that their interest in the lease of 1821 should be finally surrendered, they should find for the plaintiff.

The jury under that direction found for the defendant: thus finding unequivocally and distinctly that the lessors of the plaintiff were parties to the settlement or agreement between the landlord and the new tenant Patrick Lynch, and that they concurred with the landlord in making to the person under whom the defendant derives, a new letting of the premises of which they had been previously in possession under the lease of 1821. The Chief Justice in effect told the Jury, that if that was their opinion, they should find for the defendant, because, the transaction so completed, amounted in his opinion to a surrender by operation of law, and that the parties claiming under the original lease could not set it up as against the defendant deriving under the person with whom such new arrangement was made.

The lessors of the plaintiff on this motion insist that this view of the case cannot be upheld, and it has been broadly contended that we are to look behind the cases in England, and in particular the case of *Thomas* v. *Cook* (2 B. & Al. 119), in which this doctrine of surrender by operation of law is said to have originated in modern times. That was the case of a tenancy from year to year, and the Court there held that when the tenant assented to his landlord making a new lease and taking a new party as tenant in his place, the transaction amounted to a valid surrender of his lease by operation of law, although there was no note or surrender in writing. It has been contended by Counsel for the lessors of the plaintiff that that case might have been decided on other grounds, but we find no other grounds suggested in the argument or mentioned by the Members of the Court in the delivery of their judgments. And in the *Nisi Prius* report of the same case (2 Stark. N.P.C. 408), they are the only grounds upon which the case is put.

This is not the only decision upon the subject. The doctrine there established has been followed in the subsequent cases of *Walker* v. *Richardson* (2 M. & W. 882); *Reeve* v. *Bird* (C.M. & R. 31); and *Bees* v. *Williams* (2 C.M. & R. 581); so that we must, I think, on this motion, take it that the doctrine stated and acted on in the case of *Thomas* v. *Cook,* has received the general sanction of the Judges of England, and is now the settled law of the land.

But it is contended that this case is distinguishable from the cases cited, on the ground that this is a lease of a freehold estate, and as such cannot be surrendered without a deed or note in writing, according to the Statute of Frauds (7 W. 3, c. 12, s. 1, Ir.), which enacts that, 'No leases, estates, or interests, either of freehold, terms of years, or any other uncertain interest in any messuages, manors, lands, tenements or hereditaments, shall be surrendered, unless by deed or note in writing, or by *act and operation of law.*'

To judge the force of this objection, let us consider what is the meaning of the expressions thus used in the statute. A surrender by 'act and operation of law,' I think may properly be stated to be a surrender effected by the construction put by the Courts on the acts of the parties, in order to give to those acts the effect substantially intended by them; and when the Courts see that the acts of the parties cannot have any operation, except by holding that a surrender has taken place, they hold it to have taken place accordingly. Surrender by implication is quite a different thing: thus, before the Statute of Frauds, the mere cancelling of the deed may have amounted to a surrender by implication. Now, it is unquestionable that before the Statute of Frauds, a lease for life was equally capable of being surrendered by parol or by operation of law, as a lease for years. The doctrine is so expressly laid down in *Shepherd's Touchstone,* p. 301, where it is said, that 'If lessee for life or years take a new lease of him in reversion, of the same thing in particular contained in the former lease for life or years; this is a surrender in law of the first lease: – as if lessee for his own life, or another's life, in possession or reversion, take a new lease for years; or a lessee for forty years takes a new lease for fifty years; the first lease in both these cases is surrendered. And this rule holdeth, albeit the second lease be for a less time that the first, as if lessee for life accept a lease for years, or lessee for twenty years accept a lease for two years.' Again, in the same passage it is said: 'And this rule, as it seems holdeth also, albeit the second lease be to the lessee and a stranger, or to the lessee and his wife; and albeit the second lease be by word only, and the first lease be by deed, if so be the thing granted by the lease be such a thing as may pass by word without writing.' Now, unquestionably the new agreement in the present case was valid without a lease, for in truth it was no more than the creation of a tenancy from year to year in Patrick Lynch.

It was however contended by Mr. *Lynch* in a very ingenious argument for the lessors of the plaintiff, that there was a distinction between a lease for lives and a lease for years, in regard to the mode in which they could respectively be surrendered; and for that purpose he cited amongst others, a case from 1 *Levintz* (*Mason* v. *Tredway,* p.145). But that case stands upon totally different grounds. The Court was there considering what construction was to be put upon the language of a deed; and in the same chapter from which I have already quoted in *Shepherd's Touchstone* (Chap. xvii. p. 300), a surrender by writing is said to be an instrument testifying by 'apt words' that the particular tenant of the lands or tenements for life or years doth consent, &c.; and the Courts have accordingly held that certain words may have an operation in the case of a lease for years which they cannot have in the case of a lease for lives; and that is the substance of the decision in the case from *Levintz.*

A strong illustration of the anxiety of the Courts to construe the acts of the parties so as to effectuate their intention, occurs in the following instance, viz., where tenant for life joined with the remainder-man or reversioner in making a feoffment; and it bears directly on the question now before us. According to the law before the Statute of Fruads, it was settled that in such a case, if the feoffment was without deed, it operated as the surrender of the estate for life, and as the feoffment of the reversioner or remainder-man; but if the feoffment was by deed, it operated as a grant of the life estate by the tenant for life, and as the confirmation of the remainder-man. This will be found expressly laid down in *Treport's case* (6 Coke, 15a.); and the law upon the subject is thus stated in 2 *Bacon's Abr. Estate* p. 572, 'The next thing to be considered is when tenant for life and he in reversion join in the conveyance; and this has a different operation as the feoffment is with or without deed; for if it be without deed, then this is construed to be a surrender of the estate for life, and the feoffment of him in reversion, for no other interpretation can make the feoffment effectual; for if the estate passes from the tenant for life to the feoffee, it will be a forfeiture of his estate, whereof he in reversion may take advantage, notwithstanding his joining; for he having only the reversion had nothing to do with the freehold, and by consequence could make no feoffment or livery; and it cannot be a grant or confirmation of him for want of a deed, therefore to make it effectual it is construed the surrender of the tenant for life, and the feoffment of him in reversion. But if tenant for life and he in reversion join in a feoffment by deed, then each passes only his own estate; the tenant for life the freehold in possession, and he in reversion his reversion; and this cannot be a forfeiture, because he in reversion joined in a proper conveyance to transfer his reversion, and having passed it to another, has no interest left to entitle him to take advantage of the forfeiture if it was one.' There is a case in *Croc. James,* to the same effect. It is plain then on these authorities that not only could a lease for life have been surrendered by parol at common law, but that the doctrine of surrender by operation of law applied to it equally, and to the same extent as to a lease for years; and this being the case, I see no ground for any distinction on which the Court can act in holding it not to be governed by the case of *Thomas* v. *Cook* (2 B. & Al. 119), and the other cases following it to which I have referred.

If in the present case the Jury had found that the intention of the parties was to make a security to Patrick Lynch only, the case would have been different; but they found directly the contrary. They have given the estate to a new tenant through the landlord, and with the assent of the original lessees. Could the landlord after that insist that the old lease was subsisting, for the purpose of defeating his grant to the new tenant? and if he could not, can the former lessee who concurred in that grant be in a different position?

Upon these grounds then, being of opinion that the case of *Thomas* v. *Cook* was well decided, and that there is no sound distinction between a freehold lease and a lease for years, we think the verdict ought not to be set aside, or a new trial granted.

Pennefather B.:

After the very full judgment just pronounced it may not, perhaps, be expected that I should add any thing; but as it is a question of considerable importance, and I believe the first judicial determination of the exact point in question, I will briefly state the grounds of my concurrence in the Chief Baron's judgment.

The point upon which this case turns was decided, for the first time, in the case of *Thomas* v. *Cook* (2 B. & Al. 119). Before that case, it was settled law on the older authorities, that the acceptance of a new lease by a tenant operated as a surrender of his interest, whether such new lease were for a greater or less estate, whether the first lease had been freehold, or whether it was one for a long term of years. There are many authorities to show that the previous lease, whether of freehold, or for a term of years, was surrendered by the acceptance of a demise though by parol. The case of *Thomas* v. *Cook* (2 B. & Al. 119) carried the law a little further. There the demise was made, not to the former tenant, but to the new occupier, with his privity and assent; and the same construction, and the same operation have been given to that dealing by that case, that would have attended a lease or demise made to the tenant himself.

It was argued, that *Thomas* v. *Cook* (2 B. & Al. 119) might have been decided on other grounds, but no other ground was suggested by any of the learned Judges by whom the case was decided. It was put on the operation of the second demise, and held to be a surrender by operation of law; and in truth, it would appear to me, that (although no allusion is made to it by any of the learned Judges) their decision might derive much support from the passage read by the Chief Baron from

Shepherd's Touchstone (p. 301). For, in that passage it is said, that, although the second demise be made not singly to the tenant, but to the tenant and a stranger, it shall equally have the effect of a surrender by operation of law. Now, what does *Thomas* v. *Cook* decide? It is this, that where the second demise was with the assent of the lessee to a stranger, and the stranger got the possession, the effect was the same as if the demise had been made to the original tenant. That is not very different from, nor does it carry the law much further than, that a demise or lease to the tenant and a stranger operates as a surrender by operation of law.

For a while, however, doubts were entertained of the soundness of the decision in that case, and I confess, that I, myself, participated in those doubts. But whatever the propriety of that decison may be, it has been acted on, and recognised in many subsequent cases; and if it establish, as it does, that a demise to a stranger with the assent of the lessee, possession accompanying the act, is a surrender by operation of law of a chattel interest; I think it must be equally so of a freehold, and that no well founded distinction can be taken between the two.

If the decision in *Thomas* v, *Cook* (2 B. & Al. 119), acted on as it has been, is intended to be controverted, it must be done in such a way as to admit of the case being carried further by way of appeal, and the question should be put upon the record; but on a motion for a new trial, it must be considered a binding authority.

I am, however, far from saying that *Thomas* v. *Cook* (2 B. & Al. 119) was rightly decided, whatever may be the difficulty (and there is much) in that decision arising out of the Statute of Frauds. Assuming, therefore, that case to have been rightly decided, I am unable to distinguish the case of a freehold from that of a chattel, and consequently concur in the judgment of the Chief Baron.

Lefroy B.:
The first question in this case is, whether the cast done by the landlord, as between him and a third person, with the concurrence of the former tenant, will amount to a surrender by operation of law of the tenant's interest.

I was at first inclined to think that *Thomas* v. *Cook* (2 B. & Al. 119) carried the law further than the doctrine of implied surrender had previously gone; but I now think, as the Court has already intimated, that that decision does no more than apply the law to a new case, but does not infringe on the principle of the law as antecedently established. Another question is, whether the doctrine laid down in *Thomas* v. *Cook* is applicable to a freehold lease.

With respect to the first question – consider first, what is the law as to a dealing merely between the landlord and his tenant. According to all the authorities, if a tenant in a dealing between himself and his landlord does an act acquiring a new interest, or a new estate inconsistent with his former estate, that amounts to a surrender of his former estate by operation of law. But each of these ingredients must concur in the transaction in order to constitute it a valid surrender by operation of law; namely: – there must be an *act* affecting the possession – that act must create an interest; and lastly, that interest must be inconsistent with the tenant's former interest. Thus, in 2 *Roll. Ab.* 495, *Surrender, F. pl.* 3, 4, 5, it is said if a tenant grant a *license* to his landlord to make a feoffment, or to make livery, or himself give livery as the attorney of his lessor; in none of these cases will there be a surrender.

The act in which the tenant joins must also create an estate; and accordingly, the accepting of a new lease which is void, does not amount to a surrender, because it creates no new estate, and therefore, no estate inconsistent with the tenant's former interest. It appears to me, that the case of *Thomas* v. *Cook* (2 B. & Al. 119) merely extended that doctrine to an act done by the landlord creating a new interest in a third person inconsistent with the tenant's, the tenant concurring in the act. In that case, the possession was given up by the tenant, pursuant to the new agreement made by the landlord with the tenant's concurrence and assent, and it was held to amount to an implied surrender, or as it is called, a surrender by operation of law. The decision did not rest merely on the tenant's having assented to the agreement, but on his *giving up the possession* pursuant to the agreement; by which a new interest was created inconsistent with the former tenant's interest, on somewhat of the same principle upon which Courts of Equity have held that a parol agreement accompanied by possession takes a case out of the Statute of Frauds.

The distinction between an act done by the tenant affecting the possession, and a mere assent or agreement, has been acted upon in a case in *M'Clelland* and *Younge*, – I allude to the case of *Doe* d. *Huddleston* v. *Johnston* (p. 141). In that case a tenant from year to year agreed by parol with his landlord's agent to quit at the ensuing Lady-day, which was within half-a-year; and the premises were re-let by auction, at which the tenant attended and bid, but the new tenant was not let into possession; and that was held not to amount to a surrender, because the tenant did not do an act affecting the possession inconsistent with his former interest – thus following up the principle of the cases in *Roll's Abridgment*.

The mere fact of the tenant's being a party to the agreement, is not *per se* sufficient to constitute a surrender; but if the tenant be a party to the agreement, and follow it up by giving possession in pursuance of it – that amounts to a surrender by operation of law, and that is precisely the state of facts here. The original lessee not only acceded to the new arrangement or agreement made by the landlord with Patrick Lynch, but followed that up by giving up the possession to Lynch in pursuance of that agreement.

But it is said that this being the case of a freehold lease, is distinguishable on that ground from the case of a chattel interest. In the old cases, however, no distinction is taken in a dealing between the landlord and tenant, whether the lease be freehold or chattel. In *Mellow* v. *May* (Moore, 636), which is recognised in *Hamerton* v. *Stead* (3 B. & C. 483), it was decided that in the case of a lease for life, if the lessee accepted from the landlord a tenancy from year to year, or even a tenancy at will, it amounted to a surrender of the lease; and I see no reason why the doctrine acted upon in the case of *Thomas* v. *Cook* (2 B. & Al. 119) should not apply to the case of a freehold lease as well as a chattel.

Note
See further, *Irish Land Law*, para. 17.084 *et seq.*

HAYES V. FITZGIBBON
(1870) I.R. 4 C.L. 500; 5 I.L.T.R. 7 (Exchequer)
The facts are set out in the judgment.

Fitzgerald B.:
In this case, which was an ejectment tried before Mr. Justice O'Brien at the last Assizes for the county of Cork the material facts are these: A lease, for three lives or thirty-one years, was made in the year 1801, by the then Lady Kingston, to Edmund Hayes, of thirty-six acres of land, for three acres of which the present ejectment was brought. In the year 1862 the interest in this demise came, by assignment, to the plaintiff and his then intended wife. I think it must be assumed, from the learned Judge's report, from the finding of the jury, which I shall presently mention, and from what was admitted to have been the course of the trial, that, previously to the month of February, 1867, the interest in the lease had

vested in the plaintiff only. The last liver of the *cestui que vies* named in the lease died on the 14th of September, 1868. Previously to that event, and while the lease of 1801 was still subsisting, and in the month of February, 1867, a new lease of the same thirty-six acres of land was made by Lord Kingston to the plainiff for three lives, which are still in being.

At the trial the jury found that, at the time of the execution of the lease of the 20th February, 1867, the defendant held the three acres of land in question, as tenant from year to year, of the plaintiff. In point of fact, it was proved at the trial, by the plaintiff himself, that the defendant had paid him a rent of 21*s.* yearly, from 1862 up to March, 1868, being more than a year after the execution of the lease of 1867. Possession of the three acres was demanded by the plaintiff on the 15th September, 1868, being the day after the death of the last living *cestui que vie* in the lease of 1801; and such possession having been refused, the present ejectment was brought.

For the defendant, it was insisted that the ejectment could not be maintained without proof of service of the usual notice to quit on the defendant. Each party insisted that a verdict should be directed for him, without leaving any question to the jury. The learned Judge left to the jury the single question on which they found, as already mentioned, and on such finding directed a verdict for the defendant. It appears that the lease of February, 1867, contains a covenant by the plaintiff against subletting; there was, I understand, none such in the lease of 1801.

On the part of the plaintiff it was, in the first place, insisted that the estate of the defendant was, at the time of the execution of the new lease of February, 1867, at best a tenancy from year to year, determinable, at all events, by the determination of the lease of 1801, according to the original limitation of estate in such lease; and that, therefore, though it might not have been put an end to by the surrender of that lease, it could not endure beyond the life of the last living *cestui que vie* therein named. On this head we were, in the argument before us, referred to the cases establishing that when a parol lease has been made for a term exceeding three years, and which, under the Statute of Frauds, can only operate as a lease at will, and then a tenancy from year to year has arisen from payment of rent, the tenancy so arising determines, at all events, and without notice to quit, on the expiration of the term mentioned in the parol demise. It was further insisted, on the authority in the case of *Gandy* v. *Jubber* (5 B. & S. 78, 485) and the cases therein referred to, that a tenancy from year to year is to be considered as an estate recommencing every year as on a new letting, and that, therefore, so far as any tenancy from year to year in the defendant depended on the acts of the plaintiff in receiving rent after the lease of February, 1867, such letting would be a violation of the covenant against subletting in that lease, and, according to the decisions in this country on the Subletting Acts and the Landlord and Tenant Act of 1860, wholly void, even against the plaintiff.

With respect to the first contention of the plaintiff, the eighth section of the Landlord and Tenant Act, which has been substituted for the repealed fourth section of the Irish Act, 5 Geo. 2, c. 4, provides for the continuance of a lessee's rights and remedies against his subtenants, upon a surrender of his lease and the taking of a new lease, as if there had been no surrender, – in other words, makes the new lease a continuance of such lessee's reversion, which it was not at Common Law; and I cannot doubt that the intention of the Legislature was to preserve the subtenants' interests exactly as the repealed section of the Act of Geo. 2 did in terms preserve them, viz.: 'as the original lease out of which the respective under leases are derived had been still kept of foot *and continued.*'

The section of the Landlord and Tenant Act does not in terms contain a provision for the preservation of the subtenants' interests; but surely a provision for such preservation, coextensive with the rights and remedies given to the lessee against such tenants by making his new lease a continuance of his reversion, must be necessarily implied. It is, no doubt, true, that the tenancy from year to year of the defendant was, prior to the new lease of 1867, dependant for its existence on the duration of the lease of 1801, and determinable with it; but this occurs, not from any express contract, – for none such is found by the jury, – but was the necessary legal consequence of the limited interest of the plaintiff. If no new lease had been taken out by the plaintiff, then if, after the expiration of the lease of 1801, the defendant had continued in possession of the lands, the plaintiff could have had no right to evict him and disturb that possession: – he would then have had no estate in the land himself. A tenant is not estopped from showing that his landlord's estate has ceased.

The plaintiff's right to bring an ejectment against the defendant after the death of the last *cestui que vie* in the lease of 1801, arises solely from the new lease of 1867, which the Statute has for his benefit made a continuance of his reversion, so as to preserve the relation of landlord and tenant between him and the tenant. It would, of course, be otherwise if the tenancy from year to year had originally, by the express contract of the parties, been made determinable on the death of the *cestui que vie* in the lease of 1801, and such liability and determination had not solely arisen from the limited nature of the plaintiff's own estate. This distinguished the present case from the cases on the Statute of Frauds. The Statute of Frauds leaves to the parol demise the effect only of an estate at will, but the express terms of that demise in all other respects, are applied, so far as the nature of the estate will admit, to such estate at will. I think, therefore, that the tenancy from year to year of the defendant became, by the lease of 1867, a tenancy from year to year, determinable with the continued estate of the landlord, but not without notice to quit during the continuance of that estate.

With respect to the further contention of the plaintiff I shall not say much. The case of *Gandy* v. *Jubber,* having regard to the result in the Exchequer Chamber, is at best not a very satisfactory one; but even if it be law, all that it establishes is, that, *for the purpose of an action of nuisance* against the landlord of a tenant from year to year, the landlord's unexercised power of determining the tenancy at the end of each year is to be considered as, in favour of the complainant, *equivalent* to a new setting at the commencement of each year. Be that as it may, I am of opinion that the estate of a tenant from year to year is a continuing estate; and the point appears to me to have been expressly decided on demurrer in a case to which I was referred by my Lord Chief Baron, – that is to say, the case of *Mackay* v. *Macreth* (4 Doug. 213). The estate of tenant from year to year was held to be a continuing estate, and to leave in the tenant for years a reversion after a demise by deed for twenty-one years, on which an action of covenant could be maintained. The same point was, I think, an effect decided in *Oxley* v. *James* (13 M & W. 209). What is said by Mr. Justice Patteson in *Tomkins* v. *Lawrence* (8 C. & P. 909), is explained by Vice-Chancellor Wood, in *Cutty* v. *Arnold* (1 J. & H. 651), and whether satisfactorily explained or not, that learned judge also decided that a tenancy from year to year was a continuing estate; and *Pike* v. *Eyre* (9 B. & C. 909) is another authority for the same position.

I think, therefore, that the second contention of the plaintiff also fails.

I say nothing of what was urged in argument with respect to the effect of a conversation between the plaintiff, the defendant, and the agent of the head landlord. The effect of that conversation was wholly for the jury; but in the present case, each party insisted that no question ought to have been left to the jury at all. I see no reason for considering that the judge's decision to admit a lease of 1826, which expired in 1846, made by the plaintiff's father to a party, from whom the defendant alleged the possession was originally derived to him, was wrong, on the ground that it did not come out of the proper custody; and it was really of no value in the case. On the whole, I think the case shown ought to be allowed.

Deasy, B. concurred.

O' REILLY V. GLEESON
[1975] I.R. 258 (Supreme Court)

The defendant made arrangements to sell by tender the premises demised to her by the plaintiff by a lease dated the 29th August, 1946; the property comprised in that lease was bounded on the east by Leeson Lane. The defendant also arranged to sell some property on the west side of Leeson Lane which was held by her under a lease dated the 12th July, 1933, and granted by a third party. The defendant's particulars and conditions of sale were drawn on the mistaken basis that a parcel of land at the eastern end of the premises demised by the lease of 1946 was held by the defendant as part of the property demised to her by the lease of 1933, and one of the conditions of sale compelled a purchaser to assume and admit that the map endorsed on the lease of 1946 was inaccurate. The plaintiff complained to the defendant about her denial of his title to the parcel at the eastern end of the demise of 1946 but the defendant in correspondence on several occasions repeated her denials of the plaintiff's title. The plaintiff claimed in the High Court the possession of the entire premises demised by the lease of 1946, or the said parcel, on the ground that there had been a forfeiture of the lessee's interest under that lease.

Butler J., in giving judgment for the plaintiff, held that the plaintiff was entitled to forfeit the defendant's interest in the portion of the demise of 1946 which was the subject of the defendant's disclaimer of title, and to recover possession of that portion.

The defendant appealed to the Supreme Court and the appeal was heard by FitzGerald C.J., Henchy and Griffin JJ. The Chief Justice died without having delivered a judgment and the parties agreed to be bound by the judgments of the remaining two members of the Supreme Court.

Henchy J.:

In 1971 the Irish sisters of Charity put up for sale the complex of buildings constituting St. Vincent's Hospital, St. Stephen's Green, Dublin. Those buildings had become vacant when the hospital moved to new premises. It was decided that the sale would be by tender. A brochure was printed and circulated and it gave particulars of the property and set out the general conditions of sale. Amongst the people to whom the brochure was sent was the plaintiff. It was sent to him as a matter of courtesy because he owns the fee simple estate in No. 60 St. Stephen's Green, one of the buildings being sold, and it was thought that he might be interested in tendering for the leasehold estate which was being sold.

The defendant's interest in No. 60 arises under a lease of the 29th August, 1946. By that lease the plaintiff demised the property known as No. 60 St. Stehpen's Green (as more particularly delineated on a map endorsed on the lease to six lessees for the term of 30 years from the 15th July, 1945, at the yearly rent of £295. The lessees were apparently trustees of the Irish Sisters of Charity and the defendant, as the sole survivor of them, has become entitled to the lessees' interest.

When the plaintiff got the brochure, he noticed that it was intended that the purchaser would be bound to accept that the map endorsed on the lease of 1946 was wrong. The brochure said, in effect, that a piece of ground, measuring some 30′ by 50′ and situated at the back of No. 60 St. Stephen's Green, was erroneously included in the lease of 1946, and that the vendors held that piece of ground under a lease of the 12th July, 1933, from the Earl of Pembroke for the term of 10,000 years at the yearly rent of one peppercorn. The plaintiff's solicitor took the matter up forthwith; he claimed that his client's title as lessor was being disclaimed and he threatened proceedings unless the vendors dropped their claim to hold the questioned piece of ground under the lease from the Earl of Pembroke. An acrimonious and unyielding correspondence followed, resulting in the present proceedings in which the plaintiff claims, primarily, possession of the whole of the property demised by the lease of 1946 and, alternatively, possession of the piece of ground which the defendant says was erroneously included in the map endorsed on the lease of 1946 and, alternatively, possession of the piece of ground which the defendant says was erroneously included in the map endorsed on the lease of 1946. The basis of the claim is that the defendant has worked a forfeiture by disclaiming her lessor's title. The claim succeeded in the High Court, for Mr. Justice Butler held that there had been such a disclaimer and that it had effected a forfeiture; but he limited the forfeiture to the disputed piece of ground. From that order the defendant now appeals to this Court.

It goes without question that the defendant, through her agents, has clearly and repeatedly asserted in writing, and has sought to bind a purchaser to the same conclusion, that the plaintiff erroneously included the disputed area in the lease of 1946. While that conduct may possibly not damnify the plaintiff during the currency of the lease, it is calculated to put part of the property demised outside the reach of the plaintiff's reversion. It is an unequivocal denial of the plaintiff's title to part of the property demised. Furthermore, although made bona fide, it would seem to be an unjustified denial; but it would be wrong to express a concluded opinion to that effect in the absence of the Earl of Pembroke who may possibly wish to claim, under the lease of 1933, a reversion in the disputed area.

Where a lessee for a term of years asserts in writing that the lessor erroneously included a particular area in the property demised, does such denial of the lessor's title work a forfeiture of the lease? That is the central question in this case.

The legal rules governing forfeiture of a lease by disclaimer of the lessor's title derive from the feudal law of medieval England. It is said that forfeiture of this kind may be occasioned by act *in pais* (i.e. an act done without legal proceedings) or by matter of record. The legal history of forfeiture by matter of record is summarised in the judgment of Lord Denning M.R. in *Warner* v. *Sampson* ([1959] 1 Q.B. 297). Forfeiture by the record does not arise in this case, so there is no need to consider which version of the law on that kind of forfeiture should now be accepted as correct by this Court in the light of the conflicting judgments in both *Warner* v. *Sampson* ([1959] 1 Q.B. 297) and *Wallace* v. *Daly & Co. Ltd.* ([1949] I.R. 352).

The law of forfeiture by act *in pais* does not always appear clear or coherent in either the text-books or the cases. This is largely due to a failure to appreciate that the law has distinguished tenancies for fixed terms from periodic tenancies for the purpose of this kind of disclaimer. In the case of a periodic tenancy, if the tenant impugns the landlord's title he runs the risk that the landlord may proceed to have him ejected without notice to quit, on the ground that the tenant's disclaimer of title is to be treated as a determination of the tenancy, *per* Lord Denman C.J. in *Doe d. Graves* v. *Wells* ((1839) 10 Ad. & E. 427) and *per* Sir Raymond Evershed in *Wisbech St. Mary Parish council* v. *Lilley* ([1956] 1 W.L.R. 121). But as to leases for a term certain, whatever the law of forfeiture by act *in pais* may have been in its feudal origins, the only reported case in modern times of forfeiture of a term of years by act *in pais* is *Doe d. Ellerbrock* v. *Flynn* ((1834) 1 Cr. M. & R. 137) which turned on the fraud of the tenant in delivering up the possession of the premises and of the lease to a person claiming under a hostile title: see *Doe d. Graves* v. *Wells* ((1839) 10 Ad. & E. 427); *per* Black J. at p. 374 of the report of *Wallace* v. *Daly & Co. Ltd.* ([1949] I.R. 352); and De Moleyns' Landowner's and Agent's Practical Guide (8th ed., vol. I, p. 460). Indeed,

Lord Denning M.R. went so far as to say in *Warner* v. *Sampson* ([1959] 1 Q.B. 297) at p. 316 of the report that 'there is no room for any implied condition that (the tenant) is not to dispute the landlord's title, either on the record or off it'. Leaving aside forfeiture by the record (because it does not arise in this case), I agree that there is no room in the modern law of landlord and tenant for forfeiture of a lease by act *in pais*. No example of it is to be found in the reports since at least 1834 when *Doe d. Ellerbrock* v. *Flynn* ((1834) 1 Cr. M. & R. 137) was decided. In that case a forfeiture was held to have been effected, but the case can be justified in its result as one where the lessee, by his fraudulent conduct in passing possession of the property and of the lease to a person who was asserting a title adverse to the lessor, was held to have thereby determined the term.

In *Doe d. Graves* v. *Wells* ((1839) 10 Ad. & E. 427) at p. 435 of the report Lord Denman C.J. said of *Doe d. Ellerbrock* v. *Flynn* ((1834) 1 Cr. M. & R. 137):

'There it was thought that the tenant had betrayed his landlord's interest by an act that might place him in a worse condition: if the case went farther than that, I should not think it maintainable. The other instances are cases either of disclaimer upon record, which admit of no doubt as to the nature of what is done, or of leases from year to year, in speaking of which the nature of the tenancy has been sometimes lost sight of, and words "forfeiture" and "disclaimer" have been improperly applied. It may be fairly said, when a landlord brings an action to recover the possession from a defendant who has been his tenant from year to year, that evidence of a disclaimer of the landlord's title by the tenant is evidence of the determination of the will of both parties, by which the duration of the tenancy, from its particular nature, was limited. But no case, I think, goes so far as the present: and I feel the danger of allowing an interest in law to be put an end to by mere words.'

Furthermore, it was stated in *Doe d. Graves* v. *Wells* ((1839) 10 Ad. & E. 427) by Patteson J. at p. 436 of the report that 'No case has been cited where a lease for a definite term has been forfeited by mere words.' The reason for the absence of such cases would seem to be that even in the heyday of feudal tenures, mere words, whether spoken or written, would not have produced a forfeiture of a lease for a term certain. The only example of forfeiture by act *in pais* given in Bacon's Abridgment (7th ed., vol. 4 p. 884) is where the tenant alienates the fee; and he says that even then forfeiture will not result if the conveyance is for any reason ineffective to convey the fee. This means that even if a repudiation of the lessor's title appeared from the recitals or the habendum of the ineffective conveyance, a forfeiture would not be caused. Elsewhere (7th ed., vol. 3, p. 196) Bacon makes the position clear when he says: 'In our law these acts which plainly amount to a denial must be done in a court of record, to make them a forfeiture . . . and all other denials, that might be used by great lords for trepanning [*i.e. ensnaring*] their tenants, and for a pretence to seize their estates, by our law were rejected, for such convictions might be made by such great lords where there was no just cause.' That is to say, forfeiture by mere words could arise only by matter of record, and the only recognized forfeiture by act *in pais* was by a tortious feoffment, whereby the tenant for years could convey the fee. With the abolition of the tortious feoffments by s. 4 of the Real Property Act, 1845, there has been no place in the modern law of leaseholds for the operation of forfeiture by acts *in pais*.

Whatever may be the result of a disclaimer of the lessor's title in pleadings (as to which I express no opinion), leases are now held by the courts to be terminated at the instance of a lessor on the ground of forfeiture only when the forfeiture arises from a provision expressly incorporated in the lease: *per* Lord Russell of Killowen (with whom Lord Goddard agreed) in *Cricklewood Property & Investment Trust Ltd.* v. *Leighton's Investment Trust Ltd.* ([1945] A.C. 221, 234).

Therefore, I would hold that the defendant's conduct, even if it amounted to a disclaimer of the lessor's title, would not have worked a forfeiture of the lease for there is no provision in the lease which could be relied on to support a forfeiture on that ground.

Even if a lease could be forfeited by mere disclaimer of the lessor's title by the lessee, the question would arise whether what the defendant did in this case amounted to a disclaimer.

It is fundamental to the relationship of landlord and tenant that the tenant is estopped from denying (i.e. disclaiming) his landlord's title. That is to say, he cannot assert the rights of a tenant and at the same time say, in effect, that there is no tenancy because the landlord had no title to grant the tenancy, or because the title is in himself or in someone else. He cannot have it both ways. If what he does is a repudiation of the relationship of landlord and tenant, then in the case of a periodic tenancy terminable by notice to quit, he is debarred from insisting on the necessity for a notice to quit if the landlord chooses to eject him without serving one. The reason is that a notice to quit is necessary only when there is an admitted tenancy, so when the tenant repudiates the existence of a tenancy he thereby admits that there is nothing to terminate and that a notice to quit is unnecessary. However, as I have pointed out, in the case of a lease for a fixed term not terminable by notice to quit, the estate of the lessee in the land is not defeasible by mere disclaimer of title on his part.

But even if a lease for a fixed term could be forfeited by disclaimer – or if a notice to quit, in the case of a periodic tenancy, is rendered unnecessary because of a disclaimer – the disclaimer must not be of some particular aspect of the landlord's title but of the landlord's whole title *as landlord*. If it were otherwise, the tenant could question, only at the peril of forfeiture or ejectment, any error, large or small, in the extent of the land leased or let, or in the terms of the lease or tenancy, or in the extent of the rights or duties (such as the use of furniture, or trading restrictions) incorporated in the lease or tenancy. The landlord could question such mistakes with impunity and have them rectified, whereas the lessee or tenant would imperil his leasehold or tenancy if he raised them. If that were the law, it would be unequal and oppressive.

In my opinion, the law is correctly stated in Woodfall on Landlord and Tenant (27th ed., para. 2058) as follows: 'In order to make either a verbal or written disclaimer sufficient, it must amount to a direct *repudiation of the relation of landlord and tenant,* or to a distinct claim to hold possession of the estate upon a ground wholly inconsistent with that relation, which by necessary implication is a repudiation of it. A disclaimer, as the word imports, must be a renunciation by the party of his character of tenant, either by setting up a title in another or by claiming title in himself.' What the lessee in the present case did was much less than that. What she wrote, through her agents, amounted to this: 'I acknowledge the plaintiff as my lessor under the lease of 1946 but I say that the lease erroneously included a piece of ground in the area intended to be demised; and I shall require the purchaser of my leasehold interest to accept that the lease is erroneous in that respect.' That was far from being a repudiation of the relationship of landlord and tenant. It was in fact an affirmation of that relationship coupled with a proviso as to an error in the area demised.

It does not follow from this conclusion that a lessor is without remedy if the lessee groundlessly questions or repudiates some aspect of the lease. He may have the true position asserted and protected by bringing proceedings for a declaration or for an injunction or, in an appropriate case, for damages. However, in the present case this aspect need not be looked at further since the plaintiff does not claim to have suffered any loss and since the defendant has given an undertaking to this Court not to repeat, during the currency of the lease of 1946, the allegation of error in that lease.

Two further points need to be made.

First, the authorities show that if the defendant's conduct had produced a forfeiture it would have been a forfeiture of the lease *in toto*. The only case cited in which there was a forfeiture of the part of the property held by the lessee was *Doe d. Phipps* v. *Gowen,* but in that case the piece of ground held to have been forfeited was not demised by the lease but was acquired by the lessee by adverse possession. There cannot be a forfeiture of part of the property demised; this follows as a matter of principle as well as of practicalities. The theory behind recovery of possession on the ground of forfeiture is that the lessor has elected to treat as void the lease which became voidable as a result of the lessee's conduct. Once the court treats that election as legally effective, it treats the lease as being void in every respect. A partial avoidance of the lease is not possible. In practice it would involve a re-writing of the lease in terms of the area demised and, therefore, in terms of rent, covenants, conditions, ets. – thus producing a contractual relationship and a leasehold estate different from that envisaged by the parties and expressed in the lease.

Secondly, I think it is right to point out that, unfortunately, some of the authorities on which this judgment is based were not opened by counsel in the High Court; if they had been, the judgment given in that court might well have been different.

I would allow the defendant's appeal against the order for possession made in the High Court.

Griffin J.:
I agree.

Notes
1. Would it have made any difference if the lessee had held under a lease containing a clause rendering the lease subject to determination by giving notice? Or if the lessee had held under a periodic tenancy?
2. Where there is a forfeiture or re-entry clause in the lease, note the effect now of section 27 of the Landlord and Tenant (Ground Rents) (No. 2) Act, 1978:

    27. – (1) Where a person is entitled to acquire the fee simple in a dwellinghouse by virtue of *Part II* a covenant giving the lessor a right to re-enter and take possession of the premises where rent is in arrear shall not be enforceable against him but this shall not affect any other civil remedy of the lessor.

    (2) Section 52 of the Landlord and Tenant Law Amendment Act, Ireland, 1860 (which provides for proceedings for ejectment for non-payment of a year's rent) shall not apply to a dwellinghouse to which *subsection (1)* relates.

MCB (GALWAY) LTD V. INDUSTRIAL DEVELOPMENT AUTHORITY
[1981] I.L.R.M. 58 (Supreme court)

The plaintiff company took a lease of factory premises from the defendant's predecessor An Foras Tionscal which lease contained a provison for forfeiture should the plaintiff company go into liquidation. The plaintiff company went into liquidation and the defendant purported to terminate the lease. The plaintiff contended that by virtue of the Conveyancing Act the defendant was not entitled to rely upon the forfeiture clause. The defendant appealed against the decision of the High Court holding in favour of the plaintiff's contention.

O'Higgins C.J. delivered his judgment on 21 May 1981 saying: . . . The lease to the plaintiff contained a covenant restricting the use of the premises to the manufacture of copper cylinders and calorifiers as this was the type of industry approved for these premises. The lease contained the following provision:

33.1 If the lessee being a company shall go into liquidation (other than a voluntary liquidation for the purpose of amalgamation or reconstruction) or being an individual shall be adjudicated a bankrupt or take the benefit of any Act for the relief of debtors or if an order is made or an effective resolution passed for the winding-up of the lessee's business or if a receiver is appointed over the property of the lessee then and in any of the cases it shall be lawful for An Foras Tionscal to terminate this lease by serving a Notice of Termination on the lessee. On the service of such notice this lease shall absolutely cease and determine without prejudice to any claim of An Foras Tionscal against the lessee arising out of any antecedent breach or of any condition of this lease.

. . . I turn now to a consideration of the relevant statutory provisions. S. 14 of the Conveyancing Act, 1881 which gave relief against re-entry or forfeiture under any proviso or stipulation in a lease, on the observance of the statutory conditions, did not apply to 'a condition for forfeiture on the bankruptcy of the lessee' [subsection 6(1)]. By s. 2 of the Act 'Bankruptcy includes liquidation by arrangement'. By the combined effect of s. 2 (2) and (3)(e) of the Conveyancing Act, 1892 it is provided that the exclusion the relief provided by s. 14 of the 1881 Act in the event of bankruptcy is only to apply 'after the expiration of one year from the date of the bankruptcy' except in the case of the lease of 'any property with respect to which the personal qualifications of the tenant are of importance for the preservation of the property, or on the ground of neighbourhood to the lessor, or to any person holding under him'.

The question, therefore, is whether on the facts and circumstances of this case the lease made by the defendant's predecessor can be regarded as one in which the personal qualifications of the tenant were of importance for any of the reasons mentioned. In the first place it is to be noted that this lease was made to a company. I find it difficult to associate the words 'personal qualifications' with a company. It is, of course, necessary that the company has the power to accept the lease and to engage in the industrial activity envisaged. It seems to me to be straining language, however, to suggest that the possession of such powers relates to personal qualifications. Even if it could properly be done, however, would the possession by the company of the necessary powers be 'of importance for the preservation of the value or character of the property'? I cannot see that it would. Nor can I see how the suitability or power of the company to take the lease and to engage in the selected activity could be regarded as important 'on the ground of neighbourhood to the lessor'.

In the second place it seems to me that this lease and others made by an An Foras Tionscal and the defendant as its successors are made purely for commercial purposes and are concerned solely with the suitability of the selected lessee in the promotion of industrial activity and the provision of employment. The character of the property is that of a factory and the lease provides that it can only be used as such. The neighbourhood is an industrial estate. In relation to neither the value or character of the premises nor the neighbourhood can the personal qualifications of the selected tenant be regarded as of importance. Finally, it would appear to me that if the defendant's contention were correct the relief provided by the 1892 Act could never apply to leases made either by the defendant or An Foras Tionscal. It would, in my view, require very express words in a statute to bring about such a result.

I have, accordingly, come to the conclusion that McWilliam J. was correct in the view which he formed and the decision which he came to. I would, accordingly, dismiss this appeal.

Griffin J. delivered his judgment on 21 May 1981 saying: . . . Subject to the reservation hereinafter referred to, I agree with the judgment of the Chief Justice.

For the purpose of this appeal it is not necssary to decide whether the words 'the presonal qualifications of the tenant' contained in s. 2, s.s. 3 (e) of the Conveyancing Act, 1892, are capable of applying where the tenant is a limited company. As the Chief Justice has stated, whether these words are applicable to a company or not, in this case such qualifications are not 'of importance for the preservation of the value or character of the property, or on the ground of neighbourhood to the lessor' so as to exclude the provisions of s. 2, s.s. 2 of the 1892 Act. I would expressly reserve my opinion on the question as to whether these words do apply where the tenant is a company until it arises for decision in an appropriate case.

Notes
See further on the 1881 and 1892 provisions, *Irish Land Law*, para. 17.087 *et seq*. See also *O'Connor* v. *Mooney & Co. Ltd.*, *infra*.

O'CONNOR V. MOONEY & CO. LTD
[1982] I.L.R.M. 373 (High Court)

The plaintiff demised premises at Cope St., Dublin, to Cardall Ltd by a 21 year lease in August, 1969. In October, 1973, Cardall secured plaintiff's consent to assign lease to first-named defendants. In January, 1975, plaintiff noticed that premises were in occupation of second-named defendants without her consent. In April 1975, forfeiture notice (for breach of covenant) was served on first-named defendants. In November 1975, Circuit Court ordered that plaintiff was entitled to recover possession and costs and gave liberty for plaintiff to apply in respect of arrears and rent and mesne rates. The defendants appealed and the appeal was deal with on plenary hearing. Second-named defendants claimed they were entitled to relief from forfeiture as sub-lessee pursuant to s. 14 of the 1881 Act notwithstanding that the sub-lease was granted without the consent of the head lessor.

Doyle J. delivered his judgment on 5 October, 1981, saying: This is an appeal by both defendants against a judgment of the Circuit Court ordering that the plaintiff should recover possession of the premises the subject matter of these proceedings against both defendants and further relief ordered by the court. The proceedings were commenced by ejectment civil bill on the title and were for the recovery of possession of the office, store and toilet situated on the ground floor of premises known as No. 8 Cope Street in the City of Dublin and all the basement of the said premises except the small portion thereof in the occupation of the plaintiff, together with the right in common with the plaintiff and the other occupiers of the building to the use of the hall and stairs leading to the said premises; the endorsement of claim went on to allege that the said premises were the property of the plaintiff and that possession of them was wrongfully withheld by the defendants. The plaintiff also claimed mesne rates and the cost of the proceedings. To this civil bill an appearance was entered by solicitors acting on behalf of the first-named defendant Messrs. J.G. Mooney and Co Ltd for brevity hereinafter referred to as 'Mooneys' but no defence was delivered on their behalf. The second-named defendants, International Trading Group Ltd, were not represented by a solicitor on the record but an appearance and defence purported to have been entered on their behalf by Mr Hugh Charlton in person, who, it transpired, was a director of that company.

The first document which I have described as purporting to be a defence bears date 7 July 1975 and is apparently signed by Mr. Charlton. It denies the plaintiff's right to recover the premises sought in the civil bill; claims that the defendants are in possession and, further, that the proceedings 'do not properly belong to the jurisdiction of the Circuit Court. The proceedings properly belong to the jurisdiction of the High Court and are accordingly invalid'. At another paragraph these defendants deny that they wrongfully uphold possession and aver that they hold possession of the premises rightfully and in accordance with law. They also refer to a counter-claim by those defendants for an injunction to restrain the plaintiff from interfering with those defendants' lawful rights and they claim £5,000 damages for interference with such rights and for breach of contract. At paragraph 8 of this document it is claimed 'the plaintiff's statement of claim is invalid because (a) of vagueness (b) it is not in accordance with the rules of court'. Later, that is to say, by a document dated 31 October 1975, these defendants, namely the International Trading Group Ltd, delivered a further defence and counterclaim and prefaced it by a preliminary objection claiming that the suit is not maintainable since the plaintiff claims an unliquidated amount of mesne rates in excess of the jurisdiction of the Circuit Court, and then goes on to plead a defence extending to several pages. This latter document appears in form to be in language to which the courts are more accustomed in documents of this sort and one is led to believe that some assistance by a person used to drawing pleadings may have been obtained. However, it is not stated to have been delivered by a solicitor and does not bear counsel's name. In summary it claims that these defendants are entitled to a declaration that they are lawfully in possession and an order directing the plaintiff to consent to a sub-lease of the premises by Mooneys the other defendant, to these defendants, the International Trading Group. They claim in the alternative that they should have a lease directly from the plaintiffs and they would look for an order if necessary staying the proceedings until the matter of the sub-lease should be determined.

The plaintiff, Sheila O'Connor, moved the court for judgment in default of defence against the first named defendant, 'Mooneys' and sought an order for possession against them of the premises the subject of the action. Next she sought summary judgment against the second-named defendant notwithstanding the delivery of the defence and also an order for possession of the premises against those defendants.

The motion for judgment was grounded *inter alia* upon an affidavit of the plaintiff, Sheila O'Connor, in the course of which she stated that she was the owner of the premises No. 8 Cope Street, Dublin including that part of the premises described in the indorsement of claim on the civil bill and of which possession is sought in these proceedings. She exhibited her documents of title and her title to the premises has not been in dispute. Mrs O'Connor, the plaintiff, went on to aver that by an indenture of lease dated 18 August 1969 she demised the office, store and toilet on the ground floor together with the basement of the premises at No. 8 Cope Street described in the lease to Cardall Ltd for a term of 21 years from 1 January 1969 subject to the yearly rent of £950 and she exhibited this lease to Messrs Cardall.

She went on to say that Cardall Ltd went into occupation and possession of the premises under the lease and that they remained in occupation as lessee until the month of October of 1973 when Cardall Ltd requested Mrs O'Connor's consent to an assignment of the leasehold interest in the property to the first-named defendants 'Mooneys'. Mrs O'Connor gave her consent to the proposed assignment and believed that the lessee's interest was subsequently assigned to the defendants Mooneys who thereupon went into occupation of the premises as lessee and commenced to pay rent to the plaintiff.

Mrs O'Connor further deposed that in the month of January 1975 she discovered that the first-named defendant, Mooneys appeared to have vacated all or part of the property demised to them under the lease and to have allowed the second-named defendant company, International Trading Group Ltd into occupation of all or part of the property. Mrs O'Connor stated that no consent had ever been sought from her by Mooneys to any assignment or sub-letting of their interest in the premises to the second-named defendant. She states in this affidavit that the apparent assignment or sub-letting came to her notice only when she observed employees of the second-named defendant coming in and out of the premises and when she saw large quantities of electrical goods and cartons belonging to the second-named defendant being stored in the premises. These she believed to a very serious fire hazard and it appears that the plaintiff's insurers were of the same mind. Furthermore, the large quantities of goods and cartons created an obstruction and an inconvenience and annoyance to the plaintiff and other users of the premises. She believes that such storage of goods and cartons was an alteration of the use of the premises and different from that for which she had let them. Her insurance company has indicated their concern because of the fire hazard caused by this new user of the premises. She also states that the second-named defendant refused to allow an inspector from her insurance company to have access to the property to assess the situation.

She went on to say that having instructed her solicitors and requested them to ask the defendants to rectify the position without success that she was obliged to take steps to forfeit the lease and she served a notice of forfeiture upon 16 April 1975 pursuant to the provisions of s. 14 of the Conveyancing Act, 1881, upon Mooneys, the first-named defendant who held the leasehold interest as herein described from the plaintiff. In that she set out in the customary manner the breaches of covenant upon which she relied and required them to be remedied before 21 May 1975 and required also payment by way of compensation for the breaches. She states that she received in reply a letter dated 22 April 1975 from the second-named defendants in the course of which those defendants stated 'we will clear the premises altogether before 21 May 1975. However, I think we should go to court and ask the court to interpret the lease so that we can know what rights we have. We assume this is agreeable to your client as it will remove any possibility for disagreement or discord if we have a precise ruling from the court.' This was signed on behalf of International Trading Group Ltd by H. Charlton. The plaintiff did not consider that the second-named defendants had any lawful right or title to be upon the premises at all. She claimed in her affidavit that the breaches of covenant continued up to the time of the notice of motion and that instalments of rent had accrued since 9 October 1974. These instalments amounted to a substantial sum, since increases were payable under the terms of the lease. Moreover the plaintiff complained that she had received no sum by way of rent or mesne rates from either defendant since the proceedings were commenced. A replying affidavit was filed on behalf of Mooneys, the first-named defendants, by Mr Noel S. Cooke, Chartered Accountant, who stated that he was a director of the first-named defendants and authorised by them to make his affidavit. At paragraph two he deposed 'I say to my knowledge the first named defendant has at no time since or including the 20 June 1975 had any use or occupation of the premises described in the civil bill issued herein on behalf of plaintiff nor has the first named defendant received any rents or profits from the said premises during the said period.'

The matter came before the learned Circuit Court judge on 3 November 1975 when having recited that evidence had been adduced, and Mr Cooke counsel for the plaintiff, Mr McCann counsel for the first named defendant appearing and Mr Charlton director of the second named defendant company appearing in person and that it appeared to the court that the plaintiff was entitled to possession of the premises the learned Circuit Court judge ordered that the plaintiff should recover possession of the office, store and toilet situate on the ground floor of the premises known as No. 8 Cope Street in the City of Dublin and all the basement of the said premises except the small portion thereof in the occupation of the plaintiff and the learned Circuit Court judge further ordered that the plaintiff should recover from the defendants and each of them the costs of the proceedings and gave liberty to the plaintiff to apply in respect of arrears of rent and mesne rates. From that decision the present appeal has been taken. Notice of appeal was served by solicitors acting for the first named defendants Mooneys on 12 November 1975. The second named defendants International Trading Group Ltd decided, somewhat belatedly, to instruct solicitors on their behalf and a notice of appeal dated 7 November 1975 against the whole of the judgment of the Circuit Court was delivered on behalf of International Trading Group.

In this Court the matter proceeded to plenary hearing. Mr Cooke for the plaintiffs set out the history of the proceedings in the Circuit Court and the circumstances in which the appeal now came before this Court, stressing the breaches of covenant upon which his client Mrs O'Connor relied. He related the circumstances in which it was found necessary to serve the forfeiture notice that I have already referred to and stated that it had become operative on 20 June 1975 when the ejectment civil bill was served. Mr McCann, for Mooneys, opening his clients' case informed me that both defendants were closely associated and that Mr Charlton to whom I have made reference earlier was a member of the boards of both companies. He dwelt upon the subsequent troubled commercial history of Mooneys and the fact that Mr Charlton was no longer on the boards of both companies. He conceded that there had been breaches of covenant. Mr Callan for the second defendant, International Trading Co, stated that they had been carrying on business for a number of years; that they had obtained a controlling interest in Mooneys and that they arranged to take an assignment from Mooneys of their interest in the premises who had agreed to sub-lease the entire interest to the International Trading Group Ltd.

It was further intimated to me that the International Trading Group would now rely upon a defence that they were in possession of the premises under the agreement for the sub-lease from Mooneys. Mr Callan also referred to the fact that negotiations had taken place between both defendants in relation to the lessee's interest and stated that early in 1975 his clients the International Trading Co had re-leased back the portion of the premises to Mooneys and that this double use as I understood him to submit was one of the circumstances which led for some period to an increased and perhaps excessive user of the premises. He stated that such nuisance or obstruction as was caused thereby had ceased at the date of expiration of the forfeiture notice. He also added that the forfeiture notice had not been served on his client but that they had been sent a copy of it.

I mention these matters because I enquired at this stage from Mr Callen whether his clients were relying upon the allegation in the amended or second defence delivered by Mr Charlton that the sub-lease was valid and subsisting and that his clients sought to look for relief as under lessees. Mr Callan informed me that that was the case and upon this basis the matter proceeded. Mr Callan agreed that Mooneys ought to have sought the consent of the plaintiff to the grant of the sub-lease to his clients.

Liberty having been given to proceed to oral evidence Mr Hugh Charlton was called on behalf of the second named defendants International Trading Group. He deposed that he was joint managing director of these defendants and the only other shareholder was a Mr Gerard Sheehy. They carried on the business of Wholesale Radio and Television Dealers and had been in business for upwards of twenty years. His company had been in touch with a Mr Finucane, the managing director of Messrs Cardall, some six months before the assignment was made by Cardall to Mooneys, who, Mr Charlton claimed, were obtaining the assignment in trust for the International Trading Group. Mr Charlton further alleged that this arrangment was known to the plaintiff Mrs O'Connor and that she consented to this assignment upon those terms. He stated that her husband Mr O'Connor, a stockbroker, had discussed the transaction with him (Mr Charlton) as the premises at Cope Street and enquired what use the International Trading Group proposed for the premises. Mr Charlton assured him that the existing business would be continued there.

Mr Charlton next referred to what appears to have been an incomplete transaction or else one which was subsequently revoked by mutual consent and this related to an assignment by Messrs Cardall Ltd to Messrs Sheehy and Charlton, which purported to be assigned to Messrs Sheehy and Charlton. The feature of this document to which my attention was particularly drawn was what purported to be an assent by the plaintiff Mrs Sheila O'Connor to the transaction and the assignment of the lessee's interest to Messrs Charlton and Sheehy but so as that the consent should not be taken or construed as a general waiver of the covenants against alienation contained in the lease; and this apparently had been duly executed not only by the parties to the assignment but also by Mrs O'Connor the plaintiff in these proceedings. The document was produced to me but it had been torn into two pieces and some pencil marks appear on the face of the document which are consistent with an indication that its provisions were not, or no longer, to be effective. I withhold for the present my view as to the effect of this partially destroyed or damaged assurance.

It is stated however that another arrangement was substituted for the provisions contained in this document and that it was decided to assign the property to the first-named defendants Mooneys. Mr Charlton stated that there was a lease back arrangment which he was privy to because he was a memeber of the board of both companies.

He stated furthermore that there was an agreement that the International Trading Group should sell to Mooneys on 9 May 1973. This transaction was approved he states, at a meeting of Mooneys on 22 June 1973 at which the purchase by Mooneys of the properties of the International Trading Group was approved. At that time he states that Messrs Reddy, Charlton and McKnight were solicitors for the International Trading Group and Messrs Fottrills solicitors for Mooneys. The lease back arrangment, he said, was effected by an indenture between Mooneys of the one part and the International Trading Group Ltd of the other part whereby Mooney's interest in the portion of the premises at No. 8 Cope Street was assigned to the International Trading Group. The assignment is undated but bears the common seal of Mooneys and the signatures of two directors and the secretary and is executed on behalf of the International Trading Groups by Mr Charlton, whereupon, it is stated, the key of the premises was handed by Mr Hickey acting on behalf of Mooneys to the representative of International Trading Group Ltd on 20 November 1973. Mr Charlton went on to say that his company had put some furniture into the premises but he stated that the premises were not necessary and indeed not used for the purposed of his company's business.

Mr Charlton next referred to an arrangement which he described as a compromise agreement made on 12 or 13 January 1975 at the time when he left Mooneys. He stated that 'we paid rent for all the premises including 8 Cope Street to Mooneys up to the date of this compromise agreement'. He continued 'we then started transferring our goods into 8 Cope Street, that is to say, wireless sets, televisions and goods of that character. This commenced on Sunday 12 January 1975.' He denied that any obstruction was caused. 'We didn't store our boxes on the stairs' although he conceded that a carrier employed by his firm might have done so. He said that when he received word of any complaint he gave instructions to see that the matter should be put right and consulted Mrs O'Connor to see that this had been done. This interview with Mrs O'Connor was carried out by a Miss or Mrs Francis who was Mr Charlton's secretary. He states that no other occupants of the buildings or of the adjoining premises made complaints about the nature of his firm's user of the premises. Mr O'Connor however had objected to the carrier at the manner in which the goods were being disposed of in the premises.

Mr Charlton denied that the goods were of a highly inflammable character and in fact he stated that they had had them insured at normal rates. The previous occupants Messrs Cardall had been in the business of dealing in paper and photographic materials which were of a more inflammable character. He agreed that Mrs O'Connor had also objected to the use of the two front offices as stores and Mr Charlton stated that he had the goods removed out of these offices to another alternative room suitable for storage. At some later unspecified date, according to Mr Charlton, Mr O'Connor came to the presises and sought to make arrangements for an insurance inspection to be carried out. Mr Charlton stated that he was busy at the time and said he would have to have notice of any such arrangement.

When cross-examined by Mr Cooke, Mr Charlton alleged that his firm held a lease from Mooneys but also he stated that they were relying upon the circumstances and were making the case that they also held a lease from the O'Connors. He was aware however that the O'Connors had never consented to Mooneys giving a sub-lease to his firm. He assumed that Mooneys had paid the rent all through the year 1974 and he could not say that his company had paid any rent direct to Mr or Mrs O'Connor. He stated that at the date of the compromise agreement on 12 January, 1975, to which he had earlier referred, his company paid rent in respect of all the leases and he produced a paid cheque for £45,000 dated 12 January 1975 drawn by the International Trading Group Ltd in favour of Mooneys. Mr Charlton stated that he was aware that the written consent of the lessor was necessary to effectively give a sub-lease to his company but he could not say if any such consent had ever been given. He was likewise unable to say how much rent had been paid by his company or in respect of what particular period it had been paid. He did say however that they did pay rent and further added that they continually requested from Mooneys a statement of account of outstanding balances including rent.

There was extensive examination as to what the cheque for £45,000 payable to Mooneys was intended to cover and no agreement appears to have been established between Mooneys and the International Trading Group Ltd as to what precisely this figure was intended to discharge. Mr Charlton said there was a claim for £60,000 for outstanding rent and that £45,000 represented a compromise which also incorporated the surrender of certain leases. He then said the £45,000 was to cover all rent outstanding on the remaining leases including the lease of 8 Cope Street, incorporating arrears due to Mooneys in respect of the rent of the premises. Mr Charlton further stated that the £45,000 included some payments of rent in advance in respect of the Cope Street premises. Mr Charlton further stated that his firm was in dispute with Mooneys as to how far in advance rent had been paid and was incorporated into the payment of the £45,000 already referred to and it does not appear that this dispute between those parties has yet been resolved.

It became apparent in the course of further testimony under cross-examination of Mr Charlton that he was aware of the danger of fire which the boxes and containers presented, because vandals had apparently set fire to boxes of that character on the street outside his own premises adjoining. He did not make the appointment sought to enable an inspection to be carried out by the insurance company. He agreed that he had told Mr O'Connor who had sought to make arrangement for such an inspection that he, Mr Charlton, was busy at the time and asked for notice before such an arrangement could be made. He said that Mr O'Connor did not come back to seek again to make such an arrangement. Upon re-examination by Mr Callan the witness stated that the original of the compromise agreement to which he had referred was retained by the Northern Bank Finance Co and the calculations which gave rise to the compromise were also, he said, in the custody of the Northern Bank Finance Corporation.

Mr Gerard Sheehy, who was joint managing director with Mr Charlton of the International Trading Group Ltd, next gave evidence. He mentioned some negotiations he had had with Mr O'Connor regarding payment of the rent of Cope Street which was due and this took place in his Mr Sheehy's house in the autumn of 1974. Mr Sheehy disclaimed any concern with the property end of his company's business and advised Mr O'Connor that he should contact Mr Charlton. He apparently was a party to the negotiations which led up to the so called compromise agreement. He stated that the £45,000 related to certain properties including Cope Street and that the agreement had been drawn up by Mooneys. Mr Sheehy stated that his company had arranged insurance through Messrs Armstrong and Taylor, insurance brokers, and that this cover included the interests of Mrs O'Connor as landlord. Apparently he was also aware that the O'Connors' insurance company, namely, the Irish National Co, had indicated that on account of the nature of the stock they would discontinue their liability under their policy and in consequence the International Trading Group arranged the insurance through Messrs Armstrong and Taylor to which I have referred. Mr Sheehy could not be of great assistance of the main transaction in relation to the tenure of the premises since his business was not concerned with property and he was managing public houses for Mooneys at the material times. Other witnesses to give evidence for the International Trading Co were Miss Eileen Francis who was Mr Charlton's secretary and Mr Rory O'Connor who was the manager of the musical department. The latter witness identified certain photographs of the premises which seemed to me, at any rate to indicate that the user of the premises at the time that these photographs were taken would not be such as to recommend itself to any fire insurance company. Another witness, Mr Brian Warren, who is an electronic service technician in the service of the International Trading Group for a number of years, agreed that a number of the goods which were stored in No. 8 were inflammable in character but he claimed that they were packed in polyester board which reduced any risk of fire to the articles contained in them. Other musical instruments and tape recorders and microphones were sometimes contained in cardboard boxes. He agreed on cross-examination that these would be more of a risk of fire than the articles contained in the polyester containers. Mr Richard Budds the secretary of Mooneys was examined by Mr Callan. He produced the undated indenture of assignment between Mooneys and the International Trading Group Ltd and proved his execution of the documents as secretary of Mooneys and identified his company's seal and the signatures of the other signatories for Mooneys. He stated that this indenture was executed on 9 May 1975 and he fixed this date by reference to a record in the seal book of Mooneys. Minutes of 24 July confirm the signing on behalf of Mooneys of a number of documents which included this indenture. In answer to Mr Cooke who cross-examined him this witness stated that Mooneys had executed this lease in May 1975 although they had notice of forfeiture in April 1975. The witness stated that he was not personally aware of the fact that the forfeiture notice had been served. There was no record in his company's books but he assumed that it would have been known about by the company's solicitors. At that stage the witness stated Mooneys were already in arrears in respect of the rent of the premises which they were now puporting to sub-lease. One copy of the undated demise of the premises by Mooneys to the International Trading Group Ltd bears the words in pencil and I quote 'hold until we receive counsel's advice'. The witness stated that these words were not on the indenture when it was received by Mooneys.

The evidence dealt in a number of respects with the actions of the two defendants but much of it seemed to me not to bear directly on the issue as between either defendant and the plaintiff who was seeking possession for forfeiture. Mr Brian O'Connor, a stockbroker, the husband of the plaintiff who himself has offices in Cope Street gave evidence on behalf of the plaintiff.

He dealt with the transfers by way of lease and sub-lease with various transactions involving the property in dispute. It appears that at one stage, Mr O'Connor and his wife were anxious to obtain back the leasehold interest from Mooneys since they were concerned about the payment of the rent and also about the user of the premises. Goods were arriving 'by the lorry load' Mr O'Connor said, and were being stored in the premises and they were mostly contained in large cardboard boxes except guitars and musical instruments which were in paper wrappings. Mr O'Connor expressed objections to the carriers because of the nature of the goods and because also, as he said, they were blocking the hallway and part of the basement. The whole ground floor including the two offices were stacked with goods. There were empty cartons in the hallway and in the street. Goods were there from time to time in the manner objected to by Mr O'Connor and so as to obstruct normal user of and access to the premises up the Friday before the hearing before me commenced. Mr O'Connor considered that the goods dealt with in this way constituted a fire hazard and also an obstruction and an objectionable feature of the use of the premises. Rent was last received on 1 January 1975. It was requested from Mooneys subsequently but no payment was made. Mr O'Connor described the abortive attempt made by him and the officer of the Irish National Insurance Co to inspect the premises on 18 March. He stated that Mr Charlton refused to give him the key and said it was in another premises. It was never found possible to carry out the inspection required by the insurance company. Mr O'Connor summarised the final situation as being that there was a substantial change in the user of the premises, that there was a subletting made without the consent of Mr O'Connor or of his wife, that the insurance on the premises was in jeopardy and that the rent was unpaid. It seems to me that no substantial answer to these complaints has been established in court.

To sum up the situation: no evidence has been adduced before me which would entitle the first-named defendants to relief from forfeiture and in my opinion the plaintiff is entitled to judgment against them. The second defendants if they are to obtain relief must rely upon the provisions in aid of under-lessees contained in s. 4 of the Conveyancing Act, 1892. That enactment provides:

> 4. Where a lessor is proceeding by action or otherwise to enforce a right of re-entry or forfeiture under any covenant, proviso or stipulation in a lease, the court may, on application by any person claiming as under-lessee any estate or interest in the property comprised in the lease or any part thereof, either in the lessor's action (if any) or in any action brought by such person for that purpose, make an order vesting for the whole term of the lease or any less term the property comprised in the lease or any part thereof in any person entitled as under-lessee to any estate or interest in such property upon such conditions as to execution of any deed or other document, payment of rent, costs, expenses,

damages, compensation, giving security, or otherwise as the Court in the circumstances of each case shall think fit, but in no case shall any such under-lessee
be entitled to require a lease to be granted to him for any longer term than he
had under his original sub-lease.

No doubt the grant of relief of the type sought is a matter within the discretion of
the court, but when one examines the present circumstances it appears that the
court would have difficulty in finding grounds such as would induce it to exercise
this discretion. The sub-lease relied upon is no strong support for the second
defendant's claim. *Prima facie* it was granted in breach of the terms of the head
lease, which required that the consent in writing of the lessor should first be
obtained. Of course such consent ought not reasonably to have been witheld.

Furthermore I am satisfied that there was substance in the plaintiff's complaints
relating to the user of the premises. The storing in the offices demised (and from
time to time the depositing upon the street outside) of the cartons and packing
cases used for the purposes of the business carried on by Mr Callan's clients, the
second defendants International Trading Group, was such as to constitute a nuisance and obstruction not only to persons occupying or resorting to the premises,
but properly also to foot passengers upon the street, as demonstrated in the
photographs which were put in evidence. Perhaps a graver aspect of this misuse of
the premises is the fact that it jeopardized the possibility of obtaining fire insurance
cover for the premises No. 8 Cope Street.

Mr Callan sought also to found his client's claim for relief against forfeiture on
the provisions of the Conveyancing Act, 1881. He claimed that his clients the
International Trading Group Ltd were entitled to a new lease on foot of a document which had been executed but not delivered and which he said was an
agreement to grant a lease. He referred I think to the undated indenture made by
Mooneys by way of sub-lease to the International Trading Group Ltd and also I
think relied upon the document purporting to be an assignment from Cardall Ltd to
Messrs Gerard Sheehy and Hugh Charlton executed but not dated and, as previously referred to, apparently intended not to take effect, for which purpose it had
been partially destroyed. Mr Callan referred to one or other of these documents,
and I quote, 'as an escrow of some sort'.

In the course of a comprehensive argument Mr Callan referred to various English
authorities notably *Peebles* v. *Crosthwaite* (13 T.L.R. 198) and in particular to the
judgment of Romer J therein reported. Mr Callan also referred to the decision in
Treloar v. *Bigge* (L.R. 9 Ex. Ch. 151) and the observations of Kelly, Chief Baron to
the effect that an arbitary refusal of consent to a sub-lease should not be regarded
as effectual.

English authorities upon the relationship of landlord and tenant and their mutual
rights to forfeiture or relief from forfeiture must be approached cautiously since the
relationship in Ireland for many years has been founded upon contract. However
the circumstances in the present case are such that it would be inequitable to force
the plaintiff into privity of contract with, and to compel her to grant a lease to, the
second-named defendants having regard to all the circumstances to which I have
referred. The positions of the Conveyancing and Law of Property Act, 1881 require
the court when exercising its discretion to grant or refuse relief to have regard to
the proceedings and the conduct of the parties. As I have stated, when I have
regard to the circumstances here as I have already recited them, I consider that it
would not be reasonable to saddle the plaintiff with a tenancy the circumstances of
which raise such substantial grounds of objection. The lease to Mooneys prohibited
sub-letting of the premises or any part thereof without the consent in writing of the

landlords. In my opinion the landlord in this case would have been within his reasonable rights to refuse such consent.

Accordingly there will be an order that the plaintiff do recover possession of the office, store and toilet situate on the ground floor of the premises known as No. 8 Cope Street in the City of Dublin and all the basement of the said premises except the small portion thereof in the occupation of the plaintiff. The plaintiff is also entitled to an award in respect of arrears and rent and mesne rates, but this I leave to be determined if it cannot be agreed between the parties. There is not at present sufficient evidence before me to ascertain the amount of such arreas of rent and/or mesne rates.

In deference to the exhaustive argument of Mr Callan, I feel that I should point out that in the second of two documents in the nature of the defences delivered in the Circuit Court and dated 31 October, 1975, the second defendants International Trade Group Ltd allege facts and circumstances which, if proved, might entitle them to damage or other relief against their co-defendants Mooneys, but this issue does not arise in the present proceedings.

Note

Cf. *Enock* v. *Lambert Jones Estates Ltd.* [1982] I.L.R.M. 532

Chapter 12
COVENANTS

Until recently in the Republic of Ireland conveyancers were concerned primarily with leasehold covenants which, despite some odd statutory provisions, generally give rise to few problems: see *Irish Land Law*, paras. 17.061 *et seq.* and 19.03 *et seq.* The position has changed radically since the enactment of the Landlord and Tenant (Ground Rents) Act, 1978 which restricts the right to create leases of dwellings and has resulted in an upsurge in freehold conveyancing. This has necessitated conveyancers becoming familiar with the ramifications of the rule in *Tulk* v. *Moxhay*, the 'estate scheme' rules and so on.

I. LEASEHOLD LAND

CRAIG V. GREER
[1899] 1 I.R. 258 (Court of Appeal)

By lease dated the 15th February, 1854, the Earl of R. demised certain lands near Belfast to W.T., for the term of 1000 years at a yearly rent, and subject, among others, to a covenant on the part of the lessee to expend within three years a sum of £500, at least, in erecting a private dwelling-house on portion of the said demised premises, and a further covenant not to use or allow to be used any house then erected or thereafter to be erected on any part of the demised premises, save for a private dwelling-house or tea and refreshment house, without the consent in writing of the Earl of R. A sub-lease dated 25th December, 1863, was made by W.T. of a portion of these premises containing 2R. 23p, on which a villa residence had been erected called Seville Lodge, to Arabella G. (one of the defendants) for a term of 800 years, subject, however, to all the provisoes, clauses, covenants, and agreements contained in the original lease. All the estate and interest of W.T. became vested in R.F., who in 1891 purchased the reversion in fee of the Earl of R. R.F. died in 1896; and the trustees of his will sold his interest in the premises to A. (the plaintiff).

By a sub-lease dated the 9th Dec., 1896, portion of the premises comprised in the sub-lease of the 25th Dec., 1863, including Seville Lodge, passed into the occupation of B. and C. (the two other defendants). This sub-lease which was for a term of 750 years, excepted and reserved all such matters and things as were excepted and reserved in and by the lease of the 15th February, 1854, and was made subject to all the clauses, covenants, restrictions, reservations, and agreements therein contained so far as they affected the premises demised.

Since the date of the original lease the character of the surrounding neighbourhood had completely changed through the extension of the municipal boundaries of Belfast; and on portion of the premises, adjoining those in occupation of B. and C., the plaintiff herself had recently erected a number of small shops and dwelling-houses. The defendants B. and C. commenced to excavate and remove the soil from the portion of the premises in their occupation, and to erect a large spirit grocery thereon.

The plaintiff sued for damages for breach of covenant in a lease and for waste, and for an injunction.

In view of the interesting discussion of the law relating to enforceability of leasehold covenants where there is no 'privity of estate', e.g., where the occupier of the land is a sub-tenant rather than an assignee of the lease, part of the judgment of first instance is reproduced (see *Irish Land Law*, paras 19.12 (fn. 36) and 19.42. The Court of Appeal did not deal with this point and for this reason their judgments are not reproduced.)

Chatterton V.–C.:

. . . But then it was said that these covenants do not run with the land, and that there was no privity of contract between the plaintiff and the defendants Braithwaite and M'Cann. Of course there is direct privity of contract between her and the defendant Greer. But assuming that the covenants and restrictions do not run with the land, there is the equitable rule, that where a person purchases an interest in land with notice of covenants restricting the use of the land in a particular way, the covenant will be enforced against him, whether the covenant runs with the land or not. In the case of *Tulk* v. *Moxhay* (8 Q.B.D. 403); Lord Cottenham, C., laid down, or rather affirmed the important principle, that the Court of Chancery has jurisdiction to enforce a contract between the owner of land and his neighbours purchasing a part of it, that the latter should either use, not use, or abstain from using the land purchased in a particular way, and stated that he never knew it disputed. He held that the question was not whether the covenant ran with the land, but whether a party shall be permitted to use the land in a manner inconsistent with the contract entered into by his vendor, and with notice of which he purchased. He observed that of course the price would be affected by the covenant, and that nothing could be more inequitable than that the original purchaser should be able to sell the property the next day for a greater price, in consideration of the assignee being allowed to escape from the liability which he had himself undertaken. I may say that the present is an *a fortiori* case, for here the purchaser took expressly subject to the covenants and restrictions in the superior lease.

That case was considered by the Court of Appeal, in *Haywood* v. *Brunswick Building Society* (8 Q.B.D. 403), and was treated as the leading case on the subject and as deciding that an assignee, taking land subject to restrictive covenants, is bound by such covenants if he has had notice of them. The case before the Court was distinguished from *Tulk* v. *Moxhay* (2 Phill. 774), by the fact that the covenants there were not restrictive as in *Tulk* v. *Moxhay* (2 Phill. 774), but affirmative covenants binding the purchaser to expend money, which would not be enforced on an assignee of the land, with whom there was not privity of contract. The defendants in that case were mortgagees. Lindley, L.J., says that it was not a case of landlord and tenant, which was a distinction never to be lost sight of.

In *Hall* v. *Ewin* (37 Ch. D. 74) the case of *Tulk* v. *Moxhay* (2 Phill. 774) was again under the consideration of the Court of Appeal. Cotton, L.J., says of that case: 'There is no doubt that under the principle in *Tulk* v. *Moxhay* (2 Phill. 774), if a man had actually done anything in contravention of the covenants of which he had notice, the Court would grant an injunction.' He adds that the principle there laid down was that if a man bought an underlease, although he was not bound at law by the *restrictive* covenants of the original lease, yet if he purchased with notice of these covenants, the Court of Chancery would not allow him to use the land in contravention of the covenants, and that that is a sound principle. The other Lords Justices agreed in this opinion. The case was decided on the authority of *Haywood* v. *The Brunswick Building Society* (8 Q.B.D. 403), and was said to be distinguished from *Tulk* v. *Moxhay* (2 Phill. 774), on the ground that the injunction sought was in effect to compel the defendant to bring an action against his tenant to prevent him from doing the act complained of. In *Austerberry* v. *Corporation of Oldham* (29 Ch. D. 750) the Court of Appeal again considered this subject, and expressed their approval of the principle laid down in *Tulk* v. *Moxhay* (2 Phill. 774). The facts of that case, which was a proceeding to enforce a covenant to make and maintain a road, are so different from those here, that it is valuable only for the expression of the opinions of the Lords Justices as to the enforcing covenants not running with the land at law. The covenant was not restrictive, and Cotton, L.J., says, 'Undoubtedly where there is a restrictive covenant, the burden and benefit of which do not run at law, Courts of Equity will restrain anyone who takes the property with notice of that covenant from using it in a way inconsistent with the covenant.' In the judgments of Lindley and Fry, L.JJ., they, in considering the question of what covenants run with the land, carefully exclude cases of landlord and tenant from question.

The conclusion to be derived from these authorities is that the principle of *Tulk* v. *Moxhay* (2 Phill. 774) is fully established, but that it is to be confined to restrictive covenants, and not applied to cases where the covenant is to do some act, such as repairing or improving the property, involving the expenditure of money. Therefore, even if the case of the plaintiff rested merely on the principle laid down in *Tulk* v. *Moxhay* (2 Phill. 774), I should have no hesitation in holding that the defendants, who had express notice of these restrictive covenants, when they respectively acquired their interestrs in the premises, are in equity bound by them, and that they should be restrained by injunction from using the demised premises contrary to them. But the plaintiff's case does not rest there, for by the express terms of the leases of 1863 and 1896 the defendants took, subject to all the covenants, clauses, and restrictions contained in the lease of 1854. This, too, is a case between landlord and tenant which, as observed in the cases to which I have referred, is not subject to the same considerations as those where that relation does not subsist between the parties.

The defence chiefly relied on was that from the change in the character of the neighbourhood, which has undoubtedly taken place, it would be inequitable in the proprietor of the ground to claim the assistance of the Court to restrain such building as that now in the course of erection by tenants of Seville Lodge. Such relief has been refused in several cases. It is therefore necessary to consider these cases, and extract from them the general principles on which proceeded.

Before referring to them I must see what the facts are in the present case which are material to this part of the case.

It appears upon the evidence that when the lease of 1863 was granted, the district in which these lands are situated was chiefly occupied with villa residences, of which Seville Lodge was one. But the city of Belfast was gradually spreading, and especially within the last few years, since a tramway service was established, and what were once country roads are being turned into streets of dwelling-houses, in many of which shops were set up. This, of course, greatly enhanced the value of all ground available for building, and offered strong temptation to the owners of it to turn it into streets instead of continuing it as sites for villas. At the other side of Belmont-avenue, opposite the premises demised by the lease of 1854, there is a nearly continuous row of small houses and shops, but the ground in question is still chiefly occupied with villas, there being no less than ten villa residences still occupied as such on the premises demised by the lease of 1854. The only street upon it now consists of houses very recently erected by the plaintiff, and that is at the part furthest from Seville Lodge. The plaintiff herself resides in what appears to be a handsome villa immediately adjoining Seville Lodge. Seville Lodge fell into bad repair, and was for some years occupied as a ladies' school, and since that was discontinued, it has been unoccupied. This change in the district was produced by causes altogether independent of any dealing with the premises by the plaintiff, for I cannot reasonably attribute it to the building of the houses at the far end of them by her, which was quite recent, and after the change in the character of the district had taken place. The place is only about half a mile from Belfast, and was until recently outside the municipal boundary, but that boundary was in the year 1894 extended to over a mile from the old limit. It was alleged that small houses have been lately built on a portion of the ground leased as Seville Lodge, but I think the evidence is that these were not new buildings but were the old offices and stables of Seville Lodge, formerly occupied by some of the servants, which are now, by whose act did not appear, occupied for other purposes. Until the commencement of the defendants' building complained of there do not appear to have been any other houses existing on the grounds of Seville Lodge. There was for a great many years a publichouse at Gelston's corner not upon the plaintiff's lands, but at the opposite side of Belmont-avenue, and not in any way owned by the plaintiff.

The case of *The Duke of Bedford* v. *The Trustees of the British Museum* (2 Myl. & K. 552), is always referred to on this subject, where it was held that if the grantor's deed contained a covenant in effect restricting the grantee to a particular use of the subject of the grant, but those deriving under him had so altered the character of his lands adjoining the subject of the grant that the restrictions in the covenant ceased to be applicable to the new character of the land conveyed, according to the true intent and spirit of the contract, a Court of Equity would not interfere to enforce the covenant, but would leave the grantor to his remedy at law. Lord Eldon impliedly, and Sir T. Plumer expressly, based their judgment on the fact that the acts were those of the grantor, thus creating a personal equity against him, and those deriving from him.

This case was relied on by the defendants, and so was also the case of *Roper* v. *Williams* (T. & R. 18), also before Lord Eldon, where the owner of an estate suitable for building desired to sell it in suitable divisions, and had a general plan of it made, laying the ground out according to which purchasers were required to build, and they covenanted with the owner of the estate to build in conformity with the plan, and not otherwise. The owner, however, relaxed this obligation in favour of certain purchasers, and it was held that as the plan was intended for the general benefit of all, the vendor could not obtain an injunction against other purchasers from infringing their covenants, as he had prevented the general plan from continuing. This was not a case of a change in the character of the neighbourhood, but was the direct act of the vendor alone.

In *German* v. *Chapman* (7 Ch. D. 271), which also was a case of a general scheme laid out for the letting of an estate for building purposes, it was held that a covenant to be entered into by all the purchasers not to use their houses otherwise than as private residences, was not waived by the vendor giving permission to carry on a school in one of the houses on the estate. The case of *Roper* v. *Williams* (T. & R. 18), and also that of *Peck* v. *Mathews* (L.R. 3 Eq . 515) was there referred to and distinguished on the ground that the acts relied upon in those cases as amounting to a waiver were of such a nature as to render nugatory the general building schemes which were intended to be for the benefit of all the purchasers. The opening of a boarding school at a distant portion of the ground, and not interfering with the general design, was held not to amount to a waiver. There is no general building plan in the case before me, nor any covenants for the benefit of a class of purchasers, but a covenant entered into with the lessor alone for the benefit of herself, and the protection of her property.

I shall next refer to the case of *Sayers* v. *Collyer* (28 Ch. D. 103) before the Court of Appeal which has an important bearing on the present. It was the case of a general building scheme laying out a building estate for sale in lots, and provided for covenants from each purchaser not to build a shop on his lot, or to use his house as a shop, or to carry on any trade therein. It was relied on that the covenant was waived by the fact that some of the houses so built had been used as shops; but it was held that the change in the character of the neighbourhood was not in itself a ground for refusing an injunction, because the change was not caused by the conduct of the plaintiff. Bowen, L.J., in his judgment says, that the case of *The Duke of Bedford* v. *The Trustees of the British Museum* (2 Myl. & K. 552) must not be misunderstood or misapplied; that it did not decide that contractural obligations disappeared as the circumstances changed; but that a person, who is entitled to the benefit of a restrictive covenant, may by his conduct or omissions put himself in such an altered relation to the person bound by it, as makes it manifestly unjust for him to ask the Court to insist on its enforcement by injunction. He adds that they did not decide that a mere alteration in the character of the neighbourhood would be sufficient, because there was no evidence that such alteration was caused by the plaintiff. Fry, L.J., says, that the rule in *The Duke of Bedford* v. *The Trustees of the British Museum* (2 Myl. & K. 552) was not applicable to that case; that it applies where an alteration takes place through the acts or permission of the plaintiff or those under whom he claims, so that his enforcing his covenant becomes unreasonable, but that he did not think that it applies to cases where the change which has taken place was beyond the control and independent of the action of the plaintiff. The case was decided on the ground of acquiescence by the plaintiff.

The last case which I shall refer to is *Knight* v. *Simmonds* ([1896] 2 Ch. 294), also in the Court of Appeal, which was one where there had been a sale of an estate in building lots with covenants not to allow any trade or business to be carried on upon the respective lots. It was held that the covenants did not run with the land, but the injunction was granted on the ground that the general scheme had not been materially departed from by permission of the vendor. The facts of that case, however, were so different from the present that I do not think it has a material bearing on the question. No consideration arose there like that in *Sayers* v. *Collyer* (28 Ch. D. 103) to which I have referred as to the change in the character of the neighbourhood.

The principle to be deduced from these authorities seems to me to be that in order to defeat the right of a person with whom a covenant has been entered into restricting the mode of user of lands sold or demised, it must be clearly established that there is a personal equity against him arising from his acts or conduct in sanctioning or knowingly permitting such a change in the character of the neighbourhood as to render it unjust in him to seek to enforce his covenant by injunction: a change resulting from causes independent of him will not have such an operation. As I have already stated, I am of opinion that the general change which has occurred in this neighbourhood arose from causes entirely independent of the plaintiff and those from whom she derives, and upon ground in which she has no estate or interest, and over which she had no control. The building by the plaintiff of the small houses at a remote part of her land cannot in my opinion be deemed such conduct on her part as to disentitle her to obtain an injunction against a breach of contract entered into with her by her tenant on the execution of the lease of 1863. I fail to see any injustice to the defendants in her suing to prevent a breach of covenant confined expressly to the holding called Seville Lodge, because on another portion of her property, at some distance from it, she has built houses which her tenant is precluded by her contract from building on the portion leased to her.

It was contended that the defendant Arabella Greer stands in a better position in this case than her co-defendants, as she is not proved to have authorized or sanctioned the breaches of her own covenant by the others. I do not think that her position is better than theirs. That she has been aware of their intention to erect the building objected to I can have no doubt. If she were now coming forward to disown their acts, she could more plausible urge this contention, but so far from that being so, she has joined with them in resisting the plaintiff's claims. The defences are substantially the same, and delivered by the same solicitor, and she appeared at this trial by the same counsel. In the case of *Maunsell* v. *Hort* (1 L.R.I. 88), which has much resemblance to this, the immediate lessee was made a defendant with the sub-tenants, who actually committed the acts complained of, and sought to escape liability to costs, because he did not actively resist the plaintiff's claim, but still the Master of the Rolls held him liable for costs jointly with his co-defendants. In the case of *Lord Pembroke* v. *Warren* ([1896] 1 I.R. 76) before me, Mr. Warren, the representative of the immediate lessee, was made a defendant with his sub-tenants, who alone were responsible for the acts complained of, and though he not only did not resist the decree sought for, but as far as he could, co-operated with the plaintiff in obtaining it, no one thought of raising the question as to his being made a co-defendant; and though in consequence of his disowning the acts of his tenants, I did not hold him liable to pay the plaintiff's costs, I made him abide his own costs.

The case relied on to exempt Miss Greer from liability in the present suit is that of *Hall* v. *Ewin* (1 L.R.I. 88), but there the sole defendant was a person who was not assignee of the lease containing the covenant, but only of an underlease, and therefore there was no privity of contract as here. He had taken no part in, nor authorized, nor sanctioned the acts of the under-tenant, and alleged that he had done all in his power, saving bringing an action, to prevent the under-tenant's acts. I am of opinion that this case does not support Miss Greer's contention, and I further incline to think that if she had not been joined as co-defendant, it might have been a good objection to the frame of the suit. . . .

Note
See further an enforceability of covenants as between successors to the lessor and lessee, *Lyle* v. *Smith*, p. 575, *ante*.

II. FREEHOLD LAND

CONVEYANCING ACT, 1881

58. – (1) A covenant relating to land of inheritance, or devolving on the heir as special occupant, shall be deemed to be made with the covenantee, his heirs and assigns, and shall have effect as if heirs and assigns were expressed.

(2) A covenant relating to land not of inheritance, or not devolving on the heir as special occupant, shall be deemed to be made with the covenantee, his executors, administrators, and assigns, and shall have effect as if executors, administrators, and assigns were expressed.

(3) This section applies only to covenants made after the commencement of this Act.

59. – (1) A covenant, and a contract under seal, and a bond or obligation under seal, though not expressed to bind the heirs, shall operate in law to bind the heirs and real estate, of the person making the same, as if heirs were expressed.

(2) This section extends to a covenant implied by virtue of this Act.

(3) This section applies only if and as far as a contrary intention is not expressed in the covenant, contract, bond, or obligation, and shall have effect subject to the terms of the covenant, contract, bond, or obligation, and to the provisions therein contained.

(4) This section applies only to a covenant, contract, bond, or obligation made or implied after the commencement of this Act.

Note
These provisions should be compared with ss.78 and 79 of the English Law of Property Act, 1925, which have recently given rise to so much controversy, see *Federated Homes Ltd.* v. *Mill Lodge Properties Ltd.* [1980] 1 All E.R. 371; *Irish Land Law*, Supp. (1975–80), pp. 69–70.

GAW V. CÓRAS IOMPAIR EÍREANN
[1953] I.R. 232; 89 I.T.L.R. 124 (High Court)

M.B., a predecessor in title of the plaintiff, was the owner of a house and land which extended from the house down a cliff to the foreshore. A railway company purchased a strip of the land between the house and the foreshore for the purpose of constructing a railway line thereon, and subsequently to a deed of conveyance to the railway company of the said land a further deed was executed containing a grant by the railway company to *M.B.* of a sole right of way from the house across the said strip of land to the foreshore over a specially constructed passage or footpath. The grant also contained a covenant by the railway company for themselves, their successors and assigns, at all times to keep, repair and maintain the footpath and keep clear the strand at the end thereof.

The plaintiff was the successor in title of *M. B.,* and the defendants by virtue of the provisions of certain public and private statutes were the successors of the undertaking and liabilities of the railway company. The footpath had fallen into a state of disrepair and the strand at the shore end of it had become cluttered with stones and rocks cast up by the tide. In an action against the defendants the plaintiff claimed a declaration of her title to the right of way and sought to enforce the covenant to keep, repair and maintain the footpath and keep clear the strand.

Dixon J.:

A little over a hundred years ago, the Waterford, Wexford, Wicklow and Dublin Railway Company, which had been incorporated in 1846, contemplated the construction of a tunnel for the purposes of the portion of its undertaking connecting Dalkey and Killiney in the County of Dublin. As part of the preliminaries to that construction, the Company entered into an agreement, dated the 25th January, 1848, with one, Martin Burke, described as of Stephen's Green in the City of Dublin. It is only necessary to summarise this agreement. It provided for the sale by Martin Burke to the Company of portion of the lands of Dalkey commons for a sum which was 'to cover all claim for damage by reason of severance or other injury to said lands and the house called Kyber Pass adjoining same by reason of the construction of the said railway and works.' After other provisions not material for present purposes, the agreement provided: 'It is also agreed to give to Mr. Burke the right and facility of passage to the sea on the south side of said land.'

This agreement was followed by a conveyance, dated the 28th February 1848, by Martin Burke to the Company of the lands which had been specified in the agreement to hold the same to the Company their successors and assigns for ever. Martin Burke was therein described as of Stephen's Green in the City of Dublin, hotel keeper. This conveyance contained no reference to any passage to the sea.

There appears to have been some neglect or delay on the part of the Company in giving the right and facility of passage to the sea mentioned in the agreement, because the next record in the transaction is a decretal order made by the Lord Chancellor, on the 21st November, 1853, in the matter of Martin Burke, petitioner, and the Dublin and Wicklow Railway Company, respondents. As will be seen later, an Act of 1851 had altered the name of the Company. This order dealt first with a matter included in the agreement of the 25th January, 1848, viz., the conveyance to Martin Burke of such portions of adjoining lands acquired by the Company as might not be required by the Company for the purposes of their undertaking. This matter was referred to Edward Litton, the Master of the Court in rotation, to enquire and report. The order then proceeded: 'And it is further ordered that the said Master of the Court in rotation, to enquire and report. The order then proceeded: 'And it is further ordered that the said Master do also enquire and report whether the respondents have in fact since the date of the said agreement of 25th January, 1848, given to the petitioner the right and facility of passage from the petitioner's house called Kyber Pass to the sea on the south side of his land as provided by the said agreement and if the Master shall find that the said respondents have not given the same then His Lordship doth declare the respondents bound forthwith to make and at all times thereafter to maintain a convenient and sufficient passage for the purpose of giving such right and facility for the petitioner's use and accommodation And it is further ordered that the parties be at liberty to apply to the Master from time to time in respect of the execution of this part of the decree And that the Master be at liberty if necessary to direct the proper mode of performance thereof.'

The Master did in fact report on the 20th May, 1856, but, before this date, there was a deed of grant by the Company to Martin Burke and the works contemplated would appear to have been executed. The deed is dated the 20th March, 1856, and most of it is of importance for the purposes of the present action. The first three recitals are as follows:

'Whereas the said Martin Burke (party hereto) is now and for several years hath been lawfully seized and possessed of certain lands and premises known as Kyber Pass and situate at Dalkey in the County of Dublin and in the immediate vicinity of the said sea and strand at Dalkey aforesaid and which possessed an ancient passage leading from the south side of the said lands and premises unto the said sea and strand and giving direct easy and convenient access thereto for the purposes of bathing boating fishing and otherwise.

'And whereas by the construction of the railway and works authorised by the said Acts and the several Acts incorporated therewith the said passage and the access and approach to the said sea and strand thereby given were interfered with and interrupted by the said railway and works.

'And whereas under and by virtue of an agreement in writing bearing date the 25th day of January, 1848, and made between the said Martin Burke and the said Company by their said original name and title and entered into between the said parties upon the occasion of and in relation to the purchase by the said Company from him the said Martin Burke of the portion of his said lands and premises required by them for the purposes of the said railway he the said Martin Burke was entitled and the said Company were bound as a part of the terms of the said sale to have the right and facility of passage to the said sea (on the south side of his lands) given and made good unto him the said Martin Burke his heirs under-tenants and assigns by and at the expense of the said Company.

The deed then recited the institution of a suit in equity by Martin Burke for specific performance of the agreement and the order of the 21st November, 1853, already referred to, made therein; and it then proceeded:

'And whereas the reference directed by the said decretal order having been proceeded with the Master found and declared that the said Company had not given the right and facility of passage as provided by the said agreement as aforesaid and the said Master accordingly directed a convenient and sufficient passage for the purpose of giving such right and facility as aforesaid to be made and constructed by and at the expense of the said Company according to a certain plan and specification of and for the same prepared by and under the direction and superintendence of Joseph James Byrne Esquire the engineer appointed by the said Master for that purpose.

'And whereas in pursuance of the said decretal order and the said directions of the said Master thereunder and conformably with the said plan and specification the said footpath road or passage and the works thereof respectively have been made constructed and completed by the said Company from the said house lands and premises of Kyber Pass to the said sea and strand over through and upon a portion of the lands duly acquired by the said Company for the purpose of the said railway now in their possession and hereinafter described under the directions of the said Joseph James Byrne who certified to the said Master their completion.

'And whereas in order to give full effect to the said decretal order and the said Master's directions thereunder and according to a consent entered into between the said parties in the said suit dated the 9th day of August, 1855, the said Company agreed to execute unto the said Martin Burke a grant of the right of passage to the sea with plan and specification annexed over their said lands for the full enjoyment of the said passage in the manner hereinafter mentioned and to enter into such covenants for at all times hereafter maintaining the same in conformity with the said decretal order as are hereinafter contained.'

It will have been observed that, judged by modern practice, these recitals are somewhat prolix, and the grant of the right of passage which follows is even more elaborate. By it, the Company were expressed for themselves and their successors to 'grant covenant and agree with and to the said Martin Burke his heirs and assigns that it shall be lawful for the said Martin Burke his heirs and assigns and his and their agents and servants and the tenants and occupiers for the time being of the said house lands and premises of Kyber Pass situate at Dalkey in the Barony of Rathdown in the County of Dublin aforesaid and of all and every other house or houses lands and premises of the said Martin Burke his heirs and assigns and all and every other person and persons for his and their respective sole use accommodation benefit and advantage or by his or their permission or authority from time to time and at all times for ever hereafter at his and their convenience and respective will and pleasure at all hours and for all purposes whatsoever to have and use the sole right and facility of passage and to go return pass and repass in through along over and upon all that footpath footway road and passage and strand at the foot thereof lately made constructed completed and cleared in upon over or through that part of the land belonging to and in the possession of the said Company on both sides of the road now called and known as the Vico Road situate at Dalkey in the Barony of Rathdown and County of Dublin aforesaid and formed fenced and railed off by the said Company from and out of other portions of their said lands and leading from the south side of the said house lands and premises of Kyber Pass aforesaid first unto and towards the said Vico Road on the south side thereof and then after crossing the said road from the north side thereof along towards unto and upon the strand at foot thereof and thence unto the sea opposite or adjacent thereto and which said footpath road or passage and strand at foot thereof the convenient right and liberty of passage over and using which is hereby granted as aforesaid and the course and direction width length declivity and other particulars and works thereof as laid out constructed executed under the directions of the said Joseph James Byrne by the said Company are more particularly described in the map plan and specification thereof the convenient right and liberty of passage over and using which is hereby granted as aforesaid and the course and direction width length declivity and other particulars and works thereof as laid out constructed executed under the directions of the said Joseph James Byrne by the said Company are more particularly described in the map plan and specification thereof respectively hereunder annexed which said footpath footway road or passage and strand at foot thereof and the several works of the same respectively as described and detailed in the said map and specification respectively and so now made constructed executed and cleared by the said Company as aforesaid they the said Company are under the said decretal order bound henceforth for ever to maintain.'

There follows then, in the deed, a covenant for repair which need not be set out for the moment, as the nature of the grant intended and effected by the portion of the deed just quoted in put in question. The action is brought by the plaintiff as the successor in title of Martin Burke and she claims a declaration that she is entitled from time to time and at all times at all hours and for all purposes to have and use the sole right and facility of passage and to go return pass and repass along over and upon the said passage way and strand. She also alleges that the undertaking of the Dublin and Wicklow Railway Company and of the Dublin Wicklow and Wexford Railway Company is now vested in the defendants and she claims a declaration that they are at all times at their own costs and expenses bound to repair renew amend and maintain and keep repaired amended renewed and maintained in a proper sufficient and workmanlike manner the said passage way and strand; and she claims consequential relief in respect of alleged non-repair.

The defendants, in their defence, say that they 'do not and never have questioned the plaintiff's right to a passage way as claimed in this action, but as regards the plaintiff's claim to have the said passage and works connected therewith maintained and repaired and to have a part of the foreshore cleaned and maintained as a bathing place or otherwise the defendants submit that the statement of claim discloses no cause of action against them.'

This plea would appear to admit the existence of a right of way vested in the plaintiff, but the defendants argued that its effect was not so extensive as it appears at first sight and that it left open the question of the nature of the right. Their contention was that the grant in the deed of the 20th March 1856, was merely that of a personal licence and not of a right of way amounting to an easement. In support of their proposition they could point, with considerable plausibility, to the diffuse and somewhat inconsistent wording of the grant itself. In particular, it was pointed out that the limitation to Martin Burke his heirs and assigns was, so far as the assigns at least were concerned, to the assigns of the grant, not to the assigns of what should have been the dominant tenement, viz., the lands of Kyber Pass; that the grant extended to the tenants and occupiers of all and every house or houses lands and premises of the said Martin Burke, which might, of course, not be situated in Dalkey at all; that it also extended to any person permitted or authorised to use the passage by Martin Burke his heirs and assigns irrespective of any connection of such person with anything in the nature of a dominant tenement; and that the clear intention and meaning of the document as a whole was merely to grant, as was expressed, a 'right and facility of passage.' In the latter connection, they point to the first recital in the deed as showing that the draftsman was well aware of a more accurate way of defining an easement and they also pointed out that the right is not limited to a way to and from the sea or strand but is a right to use both portions of the passage 'for all purposes.'

These are serious difficulties in the construction of the grant and it cannot be said that the meaning is expressed very clearly. There is authority, if it were necessary, that there cannot be a right of way, in the sense of an easement as distinct from a licence merely personal, in gross, that is, without both a dominant and a servient tenement: see, e.g., *Rangeley* v. *Midland Railway Company* (3 Ch. App. 306, at p. 310); *Hawkins* v. *Rutter* ([1892] 1 Q.B. 668, at p. 671). If the right in this case is merely personal, the covenant to repair would necessarily be only a personal one and these circumstances would have a material bearing on the right of the plaintiff to take advantage of it and on the liability of the defendants to perform it.

On the other hand, it was argued on behalf of the plaintiff that the grant was one of an easement. The dominant and servient tenements are clearly indicated, it was said, as being, respectively, the lands of Kyber Pass and the lands belonging to the Company; the terminal points are also indicated, viz., those lands of Kyber Pass at one end and the sea or strand at the other; and the grant is recited as being for the purpose of making good to Martin Burke the 'ancient passage' interrupted by the railway and which was clearly an easement. Further, counsel for the plaintiff pointed out that the actual way was physically well defined and set apart and attached or appurtenant to the lands of Kyber Pass; that the reference to other houses of Martin Burke may have been intended to be or should be limited to houses erected on the lands of Kyber Pass; and that, in any event, if this reference or the extension to persons permitted or authorised to use the way were too wide, the grant could be treated as severable. Finally, they suggested that a merely personal right could and would have been expressed in simpler and clearer language and without reference to the lands of Kyber Pass.

While, as is evident, the matter is not free from difficulty, I have formed the view that the grant, on a reading of the document as a whole, intended to, and did, create an easement. It is true that the phraseology might have been more precise and it is possible that the draftsman may have had some idea of combining the two ideas of an easement and a more extensive personal licence. It is clear that he intended the right to extend to the widest possible user and the widest possible class of persons. If, however, the wording is sufficiently apt – as I think it is – to amount to the grant of a right of way, I think it is immaterial, for present purposes, that something has been added or attempted to be added to it. The addition may be treated as surplusage or severable.

This view is not altered by a consideration of the case of *Ackroyd* v. *Smith* (10 C.B. 164), which was strongly relied on by the defendants. This was an action of trespass in which the defendants sought to justify as assignees of an alleged right of way. Their assignor had been the grantee from the plaintiff of a certain close and of a right of passing and repassing 'for all purposes' over a certain road. It was held, on demurrer, that the grant was not restricted to the use of the way for purposes connected with the occupation of the land conveyed; that the right in question was not one which inhered in the land, or which concerned the premises conveyed, or the mode of occupying and enjoying them, and therefore did not pass to the defendants by the assignment. The difficulty in the position of the defendants was put thus by Cresswell J., delivering the judgment of the Court (at p. 187): 'If the right conferred by the deed set out, was only to use the road in question for purposes connected with the occupation and enjoyment of the land conveyed, it does not justify the acts confessed by the plea. But, if the grant was more ample, and extended to using the road for purposes unconnected with the enjoyment of the land, – and this, we think, is the true construction of it, – it becomes necessary to decide whether the assignee of the land and appurtenances would be entitled to it.' After referring to *Keppel* v. *Bailey* (2 Myl. & K. 517), he proceeded: 'Now, the privilege or right in question does not inhere in the land, does not concern the premises conveyed, or the mode of occupying them; it is not appurtenant to them. A covenant, therefore, that such a right should be enjoyed, would not run with the land. . . . If a way be granted in gross, it is personal only, and cannot be assigned.'

This would appear to be a decision that the true construction of the grant was that it was a right in gross, or, putting it another way, that there was no dominant tenement. This view is supported by the circumstance that the statement of the facts set out in the judgment and also the pleadings suggest that the road in question did not run to the plaintiff's close but merely connected a turnpike road with 'a certain lane called Legram's Lane.' This consideration, although not specifically dealt with in the judgment of Cresswell J., may lend point to his observation (at p. 188) that 'it would be a novel incident annexed to land, that the owner and occupier should, for purposes wholly unconnected with that land, and merely because he is owner and occupier, have a right of road over other land.'

This case was explained in a different way in the case of *Thorpe* v. *Brumfitt* (8 Ch. App. 650), by Sir W. M. James L. J. (at p. 655). He there said: 'The case of *Ackroyd* v. *Smith* (10 C.B. 164) has been misapprehended. It was there in substance said to the defendants, "In any view of the case, you are wrong. If this was a right of way appurtenant to a particular property it could only be used for purposes connected with that property, and you have been using it for other purposes. If it was not, then it was a right in gross, and could not be assigned to you." The case involved no decision that the right of way was in gross.'

Sir G. Mellish L.J. did not agree with his colleague on this last point. He said (at p. 657): 'In *Ackroyd* v. *Smith* (10 C.B. 164), though it was not absolutely necessary to the decision to give any opinion whether the right of way was in gross or not, the Court gave an opinion that it was in gross. But in that case the close to which it was sought to make the way appendant was not at the end of the road . . .'; and he then quoted the observation of Cresswell J. last cited above.

Whatever be the true view of *Ackroyd* v. *Smith* (10 C.B. 164), it has not, in my opinion, any application to the present case. Here my view, as indicated, is that, on the true construction of the grant, the right is appurtenant to the lands of Kyber Pass; and there is no allegation or claim in respect of any user otherwise than in connection with the enjoyment and occupation of those lands. Further, I do not think *Ackroyd* v. *Smith* (10 C.B. 164) is any authority for the proposition that if a right of way is expressed to be 'for all purposes,' it is thereby prevented from being an easement; while *Thorpe* v. *Brumfitt* (8 Ch. App. 650) is an authority to the contrary. Sir G. Mellish L.J. then concluded his judgment with the words (at p. 658): 'There is no authority for holding that the generality of this expression, "for all purposes," makes a right of way not appurtenant where it is expressed to be to or from a particular piece of land.'

Accordingly, if the plaintiff is the successor in title of Martin Burke, she is entitled to a right of way as granted by the deed of the 20th March, 1856. The substance of the action, however, is her claim to be entitled to enforce the covenant to repair the right of way against the defendants. It has been established by the evidence that the actual passageway and the works originally constructed in connection therewith have been neglected for many years; in fact, there was no direct evidence of any repairs or maintenance at any time. As a result of this neglect, and of the combined effect of time and the elements, assisted, it may be inferred, to some extent, by deliberate acts of trespassers or others, it is common case that the right of way is seriously out of repair and that it would cost a considerable sum to restore it to its original condition. I am satisfied by the evidence that the actual user of it, and especially the portion between the public road and the strand, has become difficult and, towards the lower end of it, hazardous and dangerous except for a person both agile and careful.

The terms of the covenant relating to repair in the deed of 1856 are as follows: 'And further that they the said Company their successors and assigns shall and will from time to time and at all times for ever hereafter at their own costs and expenses repair renew amend and maintain and keep repaired renewed amended and maintained in a proper sufficient substantial and workmanlike manner the said footpath footway road or passage and strand at foot thereof as shown and delineated on the said map or plan thereof hereto annexed the right of passage over and the right of using which is hereby granted as aforesaid and all and every the said works and conveniences of or belonging to the same as aforesaid.' The important question in this action is whether the defendants are liable to the plaintiff under that covenant.

So far as the position of the defendants is concerned, no question arises as to whether the covenant to repair is one the burden of which runs, as it is phrased, 'with the land,' since the defendants are in a different position to that of the ordinary successor in title by purchase or by operation of law. The covenant entered into, in the grant of the 20th March, 1856, by the Dublin and Wicklow Railway Company, was clearly an obligation incurred by that Company; and there is a clearly-established chain of succession, either by change of name or by transfer, from that Company to the defendants, of the original undertaking and its liabilities. This is not really questioned by the defendants, but it may be of some advantage to set out briefly the steps involved.

The original undertaking was the Waterford, Wexford, Wicklow and Dublin Railway Company, which was incorporated, under the name, by 9 & 10 Vict., c. *cviii*, in 1846. In 1851 the name was changed, by 14 and 15 Vict., c. *cviii*, to the Dublin and Wicklow Railway Company. A further change of name – to that of Dublin, Wicklow, and Wexford Railway Company – was made in 1860 by 23 Vict., c. *xlvii*; and s. 9 of this Act provided that 'notwithstanding the change of name of the company, all deeds . . . and contracts . . . made under the recited Acts . . shall be as effectual to all intents for, against, and with respect to the company as if the name of the company had remained unchanged.' The recited Acts included those of 1846 and 1851. The next change of name occurred in 1906 when the new title of The Dublin and South Eastern Railway Company was given by 6 Edw. 7, c. *lxxi*; and s. 23 provided that the change of name was subject to Part IV of the Companies Clauses Act, 1863. Under s. 39 of this Part, all deeds, instruments, purchases, sales, securities and contracts before the passing of the Special Act effecting the change, made under any other Act, or with reference to the purposes thereof, are to be as effectual to all intents in favour of against, and with respect to the company as if the name of the company had remained unchanged.

The next step was of a different character and was effected by the Railways Act, 1924 (No. 29 of 1924) and the Great Southern Railways Amalgamation Scheme, 1925 (Stat. R & Or., 1925, No. 1), made thereunder. The effect, for present purposes, was that the Dublin and South Eastern Railway Company was one of the companies amalgamated to form the new undertaking to be known as the Great Southern Railway Company, and Part V of the Railway Clauses Act, 1863, was incorporated. This Part, which relates to amalgamation, contains in ss. 44 and 55 savings for conveyances, contracts, etc., and rights and claims of or against a dissolved company, and the subject-matter extends to covenants, agreements and contracts in force at the time of amalgamation, which are to be as valid and of as full force and effect against or in relation to the amalgamated company as if made by or in relation to that company by name.

A further amalgamation, to which Part V of the Act of 1863 was applied, was effected by the Transport Act of 1944 (No. 21 of 1944) and the name became Córas Iompair Éireann. The final change was made by the Transport Act of 1950 (No. 12 of 1950), which effected a further amalgamation and set up a new undertaking but with the same name. By s. 23, sub-s. 2, and s. 68 existing liabilities and contracts are continued as against the new body.

The effect of all this is that, if the original covenant is still otherwise enforceable, it is enforceable against the defendants by reason of a statutory transfer of liability to them. Such a transfer occurred and was recognised in the cases of *Fortescue* v. *Lostwithiel and Fowey Railway Company* ([1894] 3 Ch. 621) and *Earl of Jersey* v. *Great Western Railway Company* ([1894] 3 Ch. 625 (*footnote*). In those cases it was not suggested there could not be an effective statutory transfer of the liability, the question in each case being whether the particular liability was within the terms of the transfer. It may be of importance to note that this statutory transfer of a liability is not necessarily related to, and may be independent of, any transfer of title or property.

It follows that, if there had been no devolution of the grantee's interest, the covenant would still be enforceable against the plaintiff, as the present successor in title of the grantee, is entitled to the benefit of the covenant. The succession in title, so far as the lands of Kyber Pass are concerned, was proved satisfactorily from the Landed Estates Court conveyance of the 10th August, 1869, to James Milo Burke. That conveyance was made in the matter of the estate of John Hogan Burke and it does not appear how the interest of Martin Burke came to be in John Hogan Burke. At the same time, however, the conveyance granted the right of passage 'in as full and ample a manner as the same was granted to the late Martin Burke by the Dublin and Wicklow Railway Company by indenture dated the 20th day of March, 1856.' The later indenture recited that Martin Burke was then (1856) and for several years had been lawfully seized and possessed of certain lands and premises known as Kyber Pass and situate at Dalkey in the County of Dublin; while portion of the premises conveyed by the Landed Estates Court conveyance was 'part of the lands of Dalkey otherwise Dalkey Commons situate in the Barony of Rathdown and Country of Dublin with the house and premises thereon known as Kyber Pass.' Further, the estate maps of Martin Burke and John Hogan Burke (nos. 55 and 56, respectively, in the plaintiff's affidavit of discovery) both include the same portion of land on which the dwelling, 'Kyber Pass,' is shown. I think there is sufficient to establish the chain of title, so far as the lands are concerned, from Martin Burke to the plaintiff. If the matter turned solely on the right of passage, it is probable that the Landed Estates Court conveyance would be a sufficient commencement, in view of the established nature and effect of such a conveyance. It is, however, of importance to ascertain whether the plaintiff is the owner of the lands in conjunction with which the right of passage was granted and intended to be used; and I consider that the documents proved do establish this sufficiently.

All the documents of title, commencing with the Landed Estates Court conveyance, expressly mention and convey the right of passage, but none of them mentions the covenant to repair. The benefit of such a covenant may be separately assignable, either expressly or by operation of law: see *Ives* v. *Brown* ([1919] 2 Ch. 314); *Chambers* v. *Randall* ([1923] 1 Ch. 149), but that has not happened in the present case. The question, then, is whether the benefit of this covenant could come to the plaintiff without express assignment; that is, whether the benefit 'runs with the land.' There is no doubt that the grant of a right of way imports no obligation on the grantor to repair it but the grantor may become so liable by prescription or by express stipulation: *Pomfret* v. *Ricroft* (1 Wms. Saun. 557). I can find no evidence of any prescriptive liability in the present case, nor do I think this covenant could be regarded as part of the grant in the sense used in a rather obscure and unsatisfactory line of reasoning adopted in some of the authorities. Accordingly, the question reduces to that of covenants running with the land.

The leading authority on this branch of the law is, of course, *Spencer's Case*, as set out and annotated in Smith's Leading Cases (13th ed., 1929), vol. 1, at p. 51. The covenant in question is of the class of covenants not between lessor and lessee dealt with at p. 72. The learned editors divide this class into the two sub-heads of 1, covenants made *with* the owner of the land to which they relate, and 2, covenants made *by* the owner of the lands to which they relate.

Regarding the plaintiff, for the moment, as the owner of the land to which the covenant in question here relates, what is stated of such a covenant is this: 'With respect to the former of these classes, viz., covenants made *with* the owner of the land to which they relate, there seems to be no doubt that the benefit, i.e. the right to sue on such covenants, runs with the land to each successive transferee of it, provided that such transferee be in of the same estate as the original covenantee was.' Illustrations are then given from decided cases, including a covenant to make further assurance: *Middlemore* v. *Goodale* (Cro. Car. 503); a covenant for title: *Kingdom* v. *Nottle* (Mau. & Sel. 53); a covenant for quiet enjoyment: *Campbell* v. *Lewis* (3 B. & A. 392); a covenant for distress by way of indemnity against distress on the grantee for more than the reserved services: *Anon* (Moor (K.B.,) 179); a covenant to supply a close with pure water sufficient to supply the cattle therein: *Sharp* v. *Waterhouse* (7 E. & B. 816).

Covenants of the character dealt with in this passage might be said to be in gross or personal, so far as the covenantor is concerned, since, as is pointed out in the text, the covenantor may be a stranger to the lands in question and his liability is independent of the possession or ownership of any lands of his own. Consequently, the question of the burden of the covenant running with any land does not arise and the original covenantor will remain primarily and, usually, solely, responsible. His responsibility may, of course, devolve on another, but, apart from operation of law, this would only be on a contractual basis or by statute. In the present case, whether the original obligation incurred by the Dublin and Wicklow Railway Company in 1856 was merely personal or something more, it has, in my view, been transferred to the defendants by a series of statutes already cited.

The question, however, immediately arises whether the plaintiff *can* be regarded as the owner of the lands to which the covenant relates. She is the owner in fee of the lands of Kyner Pass and of the right of way; but it is to the latter right and not to the lands of Kyber Pass that the covenant relates. I find it quite impossible to read the covenant as touching or concerning the lands of Kyber Pass, except in a very indirect and, for present purposes, inadmissible way. It does touch and concern the right of way and the proper enquiry seems to be whether such a covenant can run with an incorporeal right or, putting it another way, whether a right of way can be regarded as 'land' within the proposition cited from Smith's Leading Cases (13th ed., 1929), vol. 1, at p. 72. There are several decisions which require to be examined in this connection.

First, however, Gale on Easements (9th ed., 1916), may be referred to as to the nature of the right of way iself. It is there (at p. 10) pointed out that it is now properly described as an incorporeal hereditament and that, generally, an easement appears to fall within the words, 'lands or hereditaments,' in s. 4 of the Statute of frauds and within 'land' in the Vendor and Purchaser Act, 1874, and the Settled Land Acts. The notes to *Spencer's Case* deal (Sm. L. C., 13th ed. 1929, at p. 95 *et seq.*) with the question of the subject-matter with which a covenant may run. Having expressed the view that the principle probably does not extend to personalty and having dealt with the rather exceptional case of ships, *Milnes* v. *Branch* (5 Mau. & Sel. 411) is cited for the proposition that a covenant could not run with rent. This case, however, requires to be carefully considered, as it did not decide that a covenant could not run with a rentcharge, which would be a very different proposition. It is of importance because Brett. L.J. in *Haywood* v. *Brunswick Building Society* (8 Q.B.D. 403, at), largely founded his decision on what would appear to be a misreading or misinterpretation of it. Both cases were similar to the extent that a covenant to erect, and keep in repair, buildings on the land, by way of security for rent reserved in respect of the land, was involved. What Brett L.J. said was: 'I am clearly of opinion, both on principle and on the authority of *Milnes* v. *Branch* (5 Mau & Sel. 411) that the action could not be maintained at common law. *Milnes* v. *Branch* (5 Mau & Sel. 411) must be understood, as it always has been understood, and as Lord St. Leonard's understood it, and it will be seen, on a reference to his book, that he considers the effect of it to be that a covenant to build does not run with the rent in the hands of an assignee.' Cotton L.J., in his judgment, did not refer to the case, but a third member of the Court, Lindley L.J., gave a more accurate account of it and indicated one clear ground of distinction. He said (at p. 410): 'Neither *Milnes* v. *Branch* (5 Mau & Sel. 411) nor comment on them (at p. 591): 'These cases depended upon the *form* of the conveyance. The covenants were held not to run with a rent not granted by the covenantor.' The italics for the word, 'form,' are Lord St. Leonard's; and the edition is the one referred to by Brett L.J.

Most of the other cases cited in Smith's Leading Cases are cases which either were, or could have been, decided by recourse to the statute, 32 Hen. 8, c. 34 (or the corresponding Irish statute, 10 Car. I sess. 2, c. 4) relating to the benefit and burden of covenants as between lessors and lessees and their respective assigns. Consequently, they are more appropriate to the portion of the notes dealing with covenants between lessor and lessee rather than the portion under consideration which purports to deal with covenants not between lessor and lessee. Thus, in *Bally* v. *Wells* (3 Wils. K.B. 25), there had been a demise of the tithes for six years and the question was whether the covenant not to let certain farmers have any part of the tithes bound the lessee's assignee. The question was put in the judgment of the Court of Common Pleas (at p. 26) in the form whether there was 'any difference between land and tithe, with regard to the covenant in this case?' The rather pertinent answer was given (at p. 30) that 'if we can strip the mind of the idea of matter, there seems to be no difference between an inheritance in lands and an inheritance in tithes.' The statute was not there referred to, but the case is not necessarily an authority for more than the proposition that a lease of tithes was within the scope of 32 Hen. 8, c. 34.

Similarly, in *Earl of Egremont* v. *Keene* (2 Jones 307) there was a demise of the tolls of the market and the covenant to pay rent was held binding on the assignee of the lessee. The argument referred to 10 Car. I, sess. 2, c. 4, and Pennefather B. commenced his judgment (at p. 310) by saying: 'The question turns upon the construction of the Statute.'

In *Muskett* v. *Hill* (5 Bing. N.C. 694), a licence (for twenty-one years) to search for, raise and carry away minerals was held to pass an assignable interest, but the question whether the burden of the covenant, to keep six miners at work after notice to that effect, ran with it was not decided. *Earl of Portmore* v. *Bunn* (1 B. & C. 694) was equally inconclusive, it being held that the assignee of the grantee could not be bound by the covenants inasmuch as it appeared that the grantors had not any legal or equitable estate in the real hereditament which the deed set out in the declaration purported to grant.

Martyn v. *Williams* (1 H. & N. 817) was expressly decided on the basis that 32 Hen. 8, c. 34 extended to incorporeal hereditaments. Martin B. (at p. 826) observed that the question depended upon 'the true construction of the statute . . . for it seems to be considered the better opinion that covenants do not run with the reversion at common law.' The latter remark, of course, must be considered as relating to leasehold interests.

Two other cases cited in Smith's Leading cases (13th ed., 1929) are distinguishable on the same ground of coming within the statute. In *Norval* v. *Pascoe* (34 L.J. Ch. 82), there was a mining licence for twenty-one years and a covenant to pay compensation for surface damage was held to be one running with the subject-matter of the grant. In *Hastings* v. *North Eastern Railway Company* ([1899] 1 Ch. 656; [1900] A.C. 260) it was held that the rent reserved, in respect of a way-leave for one thousand years, was payable to the owner of the reversion for the time being within 32 Hen. 8, c. 34. One further case mentioned on this topic is *Butler* v. *Archer* (12. Ir. C.L.R. 104), where the Court was equally divided on the question whether a fee farm grantee could avail, against the assignee of the grantor, of a deduction which the grantor had covenanted to allow in respect of part of the cost of erection of a dwelling-house on the lands. Although one judgment was withdrawn *pro forma* to permit of a writ of error, the parties came to an arrangement and the case did not go further. In any event, as it clear, it was not concerned with a transfer of the benefit of the covenant but with the question whether the assignee of the grantor was affected with the burden of the covenant.

There is, thus, so far, no clear authority that the benefit of a covenant may run at law with an incorporeal hereditament. In fact, doubt is thrown on the possibility by the editors of *Spencer's Case* (Sm. L.C. (13th ed., 1929), vol. 1, at p. 81) in these words: 'It would probably be found somewhat difficult to contend that a covenant could run with such an easement as a watercourse.' The authorities however, they cite in this connection are *Milnes* v. *Branch* (5 Mau. & Sel. 411) and *Earl of Portmore* v. *Bunn* (1 B. & C. 694) which, as already shown, may be discounted as not having any real bearing on the question; while, as a commentary on the case of *Holmes* v. *Buckley* (Prec. in Ch. 39), yet to be considered, it will be found not to be very just. The editors, themselves, immediately proceed to observe that 'covenants like that to pay a rent-charge issuing out of the land have reference to an interest possessed *Randall* v. *Rigby* (4 M. & W. 130), however apply very closely. in *Milnes* v. *Branch* (5 Mau. & Sel. 411), the plaintiff was not assignee in fee of the rent, having only a leasehold interest in that rent.' It is true that he added: 'There are dicta in the judgments, however, which favour the contention of the defendants in this case, and it is impossible not to see that the *burden* of the covenant does not run with the land.' I have italicised the word, 'burden,' in this passage as showing the context of the reference to 'dicta in the judgments' and as showing also what I conceive to be the true ground and extend of the decision in *Haywood* v. *Brunswick Building Society* (8 Q.B.D. 403), viz., that the burden of a positive covenant does not run with the land. I do not think the case decided that the benefit of such a covenant might not run with a rent-charge, provided it was sufficiently related to the rent-charge. The only member of the Court who seems to have decided this was Brett L.J. and he based it on *Milnes* v. *Branch* (5 Mau. & Sel. 411). As already pointed out, Lindley L.J. confined his judgment to the question of the burden of the covenant. Cotton L.J. commenced his with the words (at p. 408): 'I am of the same opinion on both points. I think that a mere covenant that land shall be improved, does not run with the land within the rule in *Spencer's Case* (Sm. L.C. (13th ed., 1929), vol. 1, at p. 89) so as to give the plaintiff a right to sue at law. I also think the plaintiff has no remedy in equity.' The two points he was concerned with, and dealt with, were clearly, therefore, the burden of the covenant and the effect of notice of the covenant. Further, as will be seen, the reference by Lord St. Leonard's to *Milnes* v. *Branch* (5 Mau. & Sel. 411) by no means bears out the statement of Brett L.J. Finally, it may be noted that the decision in *Haywood* v. *Brunswick Building Society* (8 Q.B.D. 403) does not appear to have been reserved.

It is evidently important, in view of the foregoing, to enquire what *Milnes* v. *Branch* (5 Mau. & Sel. 411) did decide. It has already been noted that Lindley L.J. pointed out that it was concerned with a plaintiff who had merely a leasehold interest in a rent which had been reserved in perpetuity, and, consequently, he would not have been in of the same estate as the covenantee. The case, however, is distinguishable on another ground clearly appearing from the judgments. The facts were that the owner in fee had conveyed the lands to the defendant and another to the use that he (the owner) his heirs and assigns might have a rent out of the premises, and, subject thereto, to the use of the defendant in fee; and the defendant covenanted with the owner, his heirs and assigns to pay the rent and within one year to build messuages on the premises for securing the rent and to keep them in repair. The ground of the decision was that the conveyance had not created a rent-charge. Thus Lord Ellenborough (at p. 417): 'I do not see how the analogy, as it regards covenants which run with the land, is to be applied, unless it be shewn that this is land; it might as well be applied to any covenant respecting a matter merely personal The statute, Hen. 8, recites that, at common law, such only as are parties or privies to any covenant can take advantage of it; here is neither privity of contract, nor privity of estate; the rent is reserved out of the original estate.' Bayley J. was even more explicit (at p. 417): 'I am entirely of the same opinion. The argument for the plaintiffs loses sight of the conveyance by which this rent is created. It is incorrect to state it as a rent-charge granted by the owner of the fee; it being a conveyance in fee by Barnsley and Robinson to the defendant to certain uses, one of which is, that they shall receive the rent; so that the rent arises out of the estate of the feoffors. It is therefore not a grant by the owner of the fee, and the covenant is a covenant in gross.' Abbot J. concurred and Holroyd J. gave no judgment.

Randall v. *Rigby* (4 M. & W. 130) is also cited for the proposition that a covenant could not run with a rent, but its authority for any such proposition is suspect on two grounds. First, the proposition is only stated *obiter* and is based on the alleged authority of *Milnes* v. *Branch* (5 Mau. & Sel. 411). Thus, Parke B. (at p. 135: 'No doubt this covenant is collateral or in gross in one sense, that it does not run with the land or rent; for that *Milnes* v. *Branch* (5 Mau. & Sel. 411) is an authority.' Secondly, as pointed out by Lindley L.J. in *Haywood* v. *Brunswick Building Society* (8 Q.B.D. 403) (at p. 410), the decision turned on the proper form of action. The action was brought in debt and it was held that covenant not debt was the proper form of remedy. Lord Abinger C.B. put it (at p. 134) that 'the question here is not whether the defendant is liable, but whether he is liable in this form of action.'

These two cases – *Milnes* v. *Branch* (5 Mau. & Sel. 411) and *Randall* v. *Rigby* (4 M. & W. 130) – are summarised in Sugden on Vendor and Purchaser (14th ed.), at p. 590, and he then makes the short by the covenantee independently of the covenant.' As to this statement, it may be observed that the independent interest is in the rent-charge, not in the lands, and that the owner of a watercourse or of a right of way may have, in the same way, an interest independent of a covenant to cleanse the watercourse or to keep the right of way in repair, as the case may be.

Before coming to the case of *Holmes* v. *Buckley* (Prec. in Ch. 39), just mentioned, it might be better to refer to *Brewster* v. *Kitchen* (1 Raym, 317, (reported as *Brewster* v. *Kidgel* in 12 Mod. 166)), as this case is referred to first in the notes to *Spencer's Case* (Sm. L.C. (13th ed., 1929) vol. 1). The two reports of this case mentioned (there are other reports of it) conflict somewhat, but it is clear that the actual decision was that the plaintiff, who was the successor in title of the original grantee of a rent-charge, which had been covenanted or agreed to be paid without deduction, was entitled to recover it in full. The case mainly turned on the position of the defendant, who was not the original grantor nor shown to be his heir or assignee, and it, therefore, was concerned with the running of the burden. On this aspect, the judges were of opinion that the covenant bound the grantor and his heirs. Lord Holt C.J. then raised the difficulty (which, according to Lord Raymond's report, did not appear to be understood by the other judges) that, the covenant being merely personal, while it might bind the heirs, did not bind an assignee or *terretenant*. The other judges got over this difficulty, whether they understood it or not, by holding (contrary to Lord Holt's view) that the covenant might charge the land 'being in the nature of a grant, or at least a declaration going along with the grant, showing in what manner the thing granted should be taken.' However questionable this part of the decision (which appears from the report in 12 Mod.) may be thought to be, there remains the fact that the benefit of the quasi-grant or declaration, or whatever it might be called, was not disputed to have passed to the plaintiff. On this question, the only expression of opinion (and not dissented from by the other judges) was on the part of Lord Holt who said that he made no doubt but that the assignee of the rent should have covenant against the grantor, because it was a covenant annexed to the thing granted: 12 Mod. 166 (at p. 170).

The next case to be cited on this topic has, if it is trustworthy, considerable analogy with the present case. It is *Holmes* v. *Buckley* (Prec. in Ch. 39). Although these reports are anonymous they appear to have had a considerable reputation as authoritative and accurate. In that case, there was a grant of a watercourse through the lands of the grantors and the deed contained a covenant by the grantors, for them their heirs and assigns, to cleanse the same. It was heard in the Chancellor's Court and the decision, put shortly, was the the plaintiff, to whom the watercourse had come by means assignments, was entitled to an order that the defendant, to whom the lands had come, should cleanse the watercourse, and notwithstanding that the plaintiff and those under whom he claimed had cleansed it for forty years at their own charges. Sugden (14th ed., at p. 593), notes the case very briefly and states the decision as that 'this covenant was held to bind the land in the hands of an assignee, for it was a covenant that ran with the land.' This statement takes no note of the circumstance that the benefit of the covenant apparently ran with the watercourse. The notes to *Spencer's Case* (1 Sm. L.C. (13th ed., 1929), vol. 1, at p. 51) take a different view of it, by concentrating on another aspect of the case. This was that, as stated in the report, the defendant had built upon the land and much heightened the ground that lay over the watercourse and made it much more inconvenient and chargeable to repair, and it was alleged (and in part proved) that the building had much obstructed the watercourse. The report states the opinion of the Court to have been that this was a covenant that ran with the land . . . and, though the plaintiff had cleansed the same at his own charge whilst it was easy to be done, and of little charge; yet, since the right was plain upon the deed, and the cleansing made chargeable by the building, it was reasonable the defendants should do it. The word, 'chargeable,' seems clearly to have been used in the sense of expensive.

The notes in Smith's Leading Cases (13th ed., 1929) vol. 1, rather seek to distinguish this case either on the ground that it might be urged, as in *Brewster* v. *Kitchin* (1 Raym, 317: 12 Mod. 166) that the covenant was, in fact, part of the grant – a view which is even more difficult to follow or understand in the case in question – or that, even if there had been no covenant, the defendant was guilty of a wrongful act when he obstructed and injured the plaintiff's watercourse. This latter suggestion seems rather a strained interpretation in view of the statement of the Court that the right was plain upon the deed, that the obstruction was stated to have been only 'in part' proved, that the reference to the cleansing being made chargeable by the building (and, therefore, its expense of more moment) was clearly an answer to the argument that the plaintiff and his predecessors in title had previously done it, and that the relief granted was not that appropriate to the obstruction of an easement. The editors of Smith's Leading Cases (13th ed., 1929, vol. 1, go on at p. 81) to observe that 'as both parties were assignees . . . it would, in order to support such an action of covenant, be necessary to hold, not merely that the burden of the covenant ran with the land, but that the benefit of it ran with the watercourse.' That seems to be exactly what the case did decide. As the covenant to cleanse the watercourse was positive in its nature, it is hardly now good law that the burden of it should run with the land, but this does not necessarily impair the authority of the case for the proposition that the benefit could run with the watercourse. This view seems to me more acceptable than the opinion of the editors already quoted – and shown to be unsupported by the cases cited in connection with it – that it would probably be found somewhat difficult to contend that a covenant could run with such an easement as a watercourse. It also has regard to the sensible injunction of the Court in *Bally* v. *Wells* (3 Wils. 25) to strip the mind of the idea of matter and to reflect that, as to the matter under the consideration, there seems to be no difference between a corporeal hereditament and an incorporeal one.

It may be useful to cite here a contrary opinion to that in Smith's Leading Cases (13th ed., 1929, vol. 2, at p. 81) from another standard authority, viz., Sugden, *op. cit.* In *Milnes* v. *Branch* (5 Mau & Sel. 411), Lord Ellenborough had commented on the dictum already quoted from Lord Holt to the effect that the assignee of the rent might have covenant against the grantor, because it was a covenant annexed to the thing granted. Lord Ellenborough had said that he was inclined to think that the language of Lord Holt was extrajudicial. The comment of Sugden (14th ed., at p. 591, note II) is as follows: 'There appears to be no foundation for shaking Holt's opinion. The rent-charge is an incorporeal hereditament, and issues out of the land, and the land is bound by it; the covenant, therefore, may well run with the rent in the hands of an assignee; the nature of the subject, which savours of the realty, altogether distinguishes the case from a matter merely personal.' A little later in the same note having referred to *Bally* v. *Wells* (3 Wils. 25), he went on to say: 'And although in this case, the question was as to an assignee of tithes being bound by a covenant entered into by the grantee thereof, yet the principle is the same as though the question were, whether the assignee could take advantage of a covenant entered into *with* the grantee: – in each case the point turns upon the subject of the grant being such as a covenant may run with.'

A different explanation of *Holmes* v. *Buckley* (Prec. in Ch. 39) was given by Cotton L.J. in a case which needs to be carefully considered, viz., *Austerberry* v. *Corporation of Oldham* (29 Ch. D. 750). He there said (at p. 777): '. . . it is suggested that that decision really must not be looked upon as an authority that the benefit of the covenant would run with such an easement; but I should think myself that the watercourse must have been used to convey water to adjoining land of the plaintiff, and probably it was in respect of that land that the covenant was said to run with the land.' It will be seen that this explantion ignores the separate legal existence of the incorporeal right. Lindley L.J. dismisses the case (at p. 82) as one in which the plaintiff was entitled to an injunction of some sort to restrain the defendants from interrupting his watercourse and as being too loosely reported.'

This case of *Austerberry* v. *Corporation of Oldham* (29 Ch. D. 750) is relied on by the defendants; but I cannot read it as an authority that the benefit of a covenant may not run with an incorporeal hereditament. The plaintiff was the successor in title of a landowner who had conveyed a piece of land as part of the site of an intended road and the defendants were the assignees of the original trustees who had made the road and covenanted with the landowner (as well as with other landowners) to keep it in repair and allow the use of it by the public subject to tolls. In these circumstances, it was held that the plaintiff could not enforce the covenant against the defendants, even though the latter had taken with notice of the covenant. The ground of the decision as to the effect of notice was that *Tulk* v. *Moxhay* (2 Ph. 774) was not to be extended beyond restrictive covenants. The question of notice, of course, does not arise where the covenant does in fact run with the land.

The limitation of the scope of *Tulk* v. *Moxhay* (2 Ph. 774) was not to be extended beyond restrictive covenants. The question of notice, of course, does not arise where the covenant does in fact run with the land. This limitation of the scope of *Tulk* v. *Moxhay* (2 Ph. 774)combined with the view – in line with the authorities – that the burden of a covenant does not run with the land at law, except as between landlord and tenant, disposed of the plaintiff's claim in *Austerberry* v. *Corporation of Oldham* (29 Ch. D. 750). Not much was said on the question of the benefit running, and, on this aspect, the view was taken, which was sufficient to dispose of it, that the covenant did not touch and concern any land of the plaintiff. Thus, Cotton, L.J. said (at p. 776): In order that the benefit may run with the land, the covenant must be one which relates to or touches and concerns the land of the covenantee. Here, undoubtedly, what was to be done was not to be done on the land of the covenantee at all, but simply on the land of the purchasers from him – these trustees; and when we look at the particular form of covenant entered into with him it is clear that it was not pointedly with reference to his land that this covenant was entered into – it was a covenant that this strip of land should be kept as a road for the use of the public. . . . Looking at the terms of the covenant, it is rather a covenant for the benefit of such of the public as might be willing to use this road, not a covenant having a direct reference to the land, or the enjoyment or the benefit of the land, of the covenantee, the predecessor in title of the plaintiff.' Lord Lindley L.J. (at p. 781) is somewhat to the same effect: '. . . there is no covenant whatever to do anything on the plantiff's land, and there is nothing pointing to the plaintiff's land in particular. . . . I do not overlook the fact that the plaintiff as a frontager has certain rights of getting on to the road: and if this covenant had been so worded as to shew that there had been an intention to grant him some particular benefit in respect of that particular part of his land, possibly we might have said that the benefit of the covenant did run with this land.' Fry L.J. was rather more favourable to the plaintiff on this branch of the case. He said (at p. 784): 'Upon that point my opinion is perhaps not quite as confident as that of my learned brothers. I am rather more inclined to think that the road connecting the land with the public highway was so far an incident to the use and occupation of the remainder of Mr. Elliott's land that it might be conceivable that it came within the principles of covenants relating to things incident to the land; but, at the same time, I do not desire to express any difference of opinion upon that.'

The foregoing review does not purport to be exhaustive, but it is hoped that it has been sufficiently intense to show that, on the one hand, there is no clear authority against the proposition that the benefit of a covenant may run with an incorporeal hereditament in the same manner as it can run with a corporeal one; while, on the other hand, there is some authority which, rightly regarded, appears to support it. Again, on principle, I find it difficult to understand why the proposition should not be a sound one. From the point of view of legal character and incidents, the only substantial difference to-day between a corporeal hereditament and an incorporeal one seems to be that the latter lies only in grant and not also in livery, but livery has become somewhat outmoded. To take the view that there is a difference in the effectiveness of a covenant according to the character of the hereditament to which it relates would seem to me a retrograde step. It is necessary, of course, that the other conditions should be fulfilled, but I think they are here. Thus, the plaintiff is in of the same estate as the original grantee, she possesses an interest in the subject-matter of the covenant independent of the covenant, and the covenant touches and concerns that interest. It is true that the repair has to be carried out, in the physical sense, on the corporeal hereditament, but it is still a repair for the purposes of, and to make more effective, the right of way. It may also touch and concern the lands of Kyber Pass in the sense hinted at by Lord Justice Fry in the passage just quoted. Accordingly, I am of opinion that the covenant to repair is enforceable against the defendants at the instance of the plaintiff.

The same result might possibly have been arrived at in another way. All the conveyances subsequent to the Landed Estates Court conveyance were executed since the passing of the Conveyancing Act, 1881, and by s. 6 of that Act, would be effectual to pass all rights and advantages whatsoever appertaining to the land or any part thereof; and an easement is 'land' within that Act. Accordingly, if the benefit of the covenant passed by the Landed Estates Court conveyance, the subsequent conveyances would have transferred it to each successive purchaser. If the Landed Estates Court conveyance had not that effect – and the point is doubtful – this gap in the chain might be supplied by the application of the principle of estoppel to the order of the Court of Common Pleas of the 13th June, 1873. That only recorded the consent and agreement of James Milo Burke and the Dublin, Wicklow and Wexford Railway Company that the latter were bound under the deeds of the 20th March, 1856, and the 10th August, 1869, to keep the strand cleared. It was, however, made on consent, and its effect as an estoppel is therefore a little doubtful, and it related only to the strand. Accordingly, I prefer to rest my decision on the other ground.

The next question to be determined is the form of relief to which the plaintiff is entitled in respect of non-repair. She claims an order in the nature of a mandatory injunction directing the defendants to carry out the necessary repairs, while the defendants contend that, if she is entitled to any relief, it should only be damages, and that, in the special circumstances of the case, the amount of the damages must be very limited. These circumstances are, mainly, the absence of any evidence of user or intended user of the right of way and the unlikelihood of any appreciable user. This unlikelihood arises from the present condition of the strand. Whatever may have been its condition one hundred years ago – and it may be recalled that a recital in the grant of 1856 referred to an ancient passage giving access to the sea and strand for the purposes of bathing boating fishing and otherwise – the evidence suggests that the strand is now the least attractive or convenient of spots for any such purposes. It is now entirely covered, probably to a depth of two feet, by natural boulders or rocks, and all trace of sand or surface shingle seems to have disappeared. This condition, which seems to have subsisted now for some years, must be due to the action of the tides if the strand was originally sandy or shingly, and, while it is not inconceivable that the sea might some day restore it to something like the original condition, any such restoration would be necessarily impermanent and possibly short-lived. In its present condition, mere progression over the strand must be a matter of difficulty and some danger, bathing would require extreme enthusiasm and disregard of comfort, and boating similar qualities, apart from the risk of damage to the boat and the absence of any reasonable means of beaching or launching one. On the other hand, as the defendants point out, there are reasonable and more attractive facilities for any of these purposes within easy reach of Kyber Pass. For these reasons, they say, the cost of repair would be out of all proportion to the real value of the right of way to the plaintiff and the damages should be limited to whatever comparatively small addition the possession of the right would make to the market value of Kyber Pass.

The difficulty I see about accepting this view is that the effect of it would be really to compel the plaintiff to sell or surrender the right of way for a money payment, since, as I follow the evidence, it is nearly unusable at the moment and will, if not repaired, become completely so in the course of time. While, in practice, it is reasonable to suppose that the plaintiff will have little occasion or desire to use the right of way to any great extent, I cannot proceed on the basis that this is necessarily so. If, as I have found, she is entitled to the right of way, and if – and I must presume from the fact of the action having been brought – she requires the user of it restored or made good, I think I must attribute to her a genuine desire to have the user of it, however difficult it may be to conceive the utility or object of such user. Consequently, I think the net question is whether the defendants should be ordered to do the repairs or the plaintiff should be awarded damages equivalent to the cost of them.

Prima facie, the case belongs to a category in which the Court will not ordinarily decree specific performance, viz., a contract to build or do similar works. One reason is the difficulty of exercising supervision; another is that usually in such cases damages are an adequate remedy. Counsel for the plaintiff cited two cases, having some analogy to the present, in which agreements to execute works or to render acts of personal service were enforced specifically. In each case, the defendants were a railway company. The first case was *Todd & Co.* v. *Midland Great Western Railway Company* (9 L.R. I. 85), where the defendants had removed a siding which they had previously provided for the plaintiffs under an agreement, but which the plaintiffs had not used. It was held that the plaintiffs were entitled to a decree to replace the siding and keep it in working order, the Court considering damages an insufficient remedy. On the question of damages, the Master of the Rolls relied on the difficulty of estimating the value to a trading concern of having their own siding, and the question was as between specific performance and damages, not as to who should build the siding. It was obviously peculiarly appropriate and convenient that, if the siding were to be built, the railway company should do it.

The other case was that of *Fortescue* v. *Lostwithiel and Fowey Railway Company* ([1894] 3 Ch. 621), already cited in another connection. There, covenants to make and maintain certain accommodation works and also to perform certain acts in the nature of personal service were enforced by an order for specific performance. Again, the execution of accommodation works is peculiarly within the competence and province of a railway company; and the personal services were only enforced as part of a larger contract that could be specifically enforced and as being very special.

The latter case is, however, important for the reason that Kekewich J. (at p. 638) based his decision on a passage in Fry on Specific Performance, on which the plaintiff here relies. The passage (which appears unaltered in the 6th ed., at p. 48) was as follows: 'Whether the Court will, or will not, interfere to enforce all such contracts' – that is, contracts for building and other works of that kind – 'when definite, it appears to be settled that it will assume jurisdiction where we have the following three circumstances: first, that the work to be done is defined; secondly, that the plaintiff has a material interest in its execution, which cannot adequately be compensated by damages; and thirdly, that the defendants have by the contract obtained from the plaintiff possession of the land on which the work is to be done.'

There is no difficulty, in the present case, as to the first of these circumstances, in view of the existence of a very precise and detailed specification for the original works. As regards the second, the plaintiff has a material interest in the execution of the works, but can it be said that it cannot adequately be compensated by damages? If the measure of damages is the cost of the repairs, I am satisfied by the evidence that the only satisfactory manner of estimating the cost would be on a time and material basis which means that the damages cannot be assessed in advance or independently of the work being executed. On this view, the question would simply be as to who should do the work; but, if the plaintiff is only entitled to damages, she cannot be compelled or required to do any repairs and must be left free to retain the damages if she chooses. Further, if she did no repairs or incomplete repairs, difficult questions might arise in the future as to the scope and effect of the covenant now in question. If the measure of damages were the value of the lost amenity or advantage, I should find it even more difficult to put a figure on it.

The third circumstance is not, in terms, fulfilled any more than the second, but, again, there is a considerable analogy. Kekewich J. (at p. 639) thought the third circumstance sufficiently fulfilled by the fact that the land had been acquired by the company by convenance from the predecessors in title of the plaintiff. In the present case it is not clear that the land over which the right of way extends was formerly the property of Martin Burke or acquired from him by the Railway Company. On the other hand, the Company did acquire land from him on the Kyber Pass side of the public road and the 'ancient passage' to the sea which he possessed and which was interfered with by the railway works must have included or extended over land on the sea side of that road. An element – and, perhaps, the material one – in this connection is the possession by the defendants of the lands on which the work is to be done. While I have no doubt that the plaintiff would be afforded every facility in carrying out repairs, the balance of convenience is obviously in favour of the persons in possession being required to execute the works. Another material consideration is that the defendants, by their nature, have equipment and facilities not readily available to the plaintiff or anyone employed by her for the work, and this should result in considerable economy.

There is no definite rule of equity that a covenant of the nature in question here will not be enforced specifically. The question is still one of judicial discretion, having regard to all circumstances of the particular case; and the general tendency of modern decisions is rather towards granting the relief sought if possible. The difficulty as to supervision and enforcement, of course, remains. As to the latter, Kekewich J., dealing with the question of personal services, said (at p. 640) in *Fortescue* v. *Lostwithiel and Fowey Railway Company* ([1894] 3 Ch. 621): 'I agree, I do not see how that can possibly be enforced, if the railway company are recalcitrant, otherwise than by a sequestration.' In the present case, the plaintiff might have less drastic remedies available to her. This matter, and that of supervision, are, however, probably, academic, as I cannot conceive that a responsible corporation like the defendants would fail to carry out what has been decided to be their legal duty, or that, in doing so, they would not act conscientiously and efficiently to the best of their ability. In Scotland, unlike England, the Court sometimes appoints some properly qualified person to supervise the work, and the Courts here might be free to adopt a similar practice if necessary; but, in the present case, I see no necessity for such a course in the first instance. Any difficulty or dispute that may arise as to carrying out the work will be sufficiently provided for by reserving liberty to apply to both parties.

Holding the view, therefore, that this covenant should be ordered to be specifically performed, the question remains as to the manner and extent of the performance that should be required. I think the plaintiff is entitled to have the right of way restored, so far as possible, to the condition provided for by the original specification; but this is subject to one general and two particular qualifications.

The general qualification is that it would be unreasonable to expect or require more than a substantial compliance with the specification, that is to say, minor differences, including the use of different or more modern materials or methods to those obtaining one hundred years ago, should not be regarded as non-compliance. This, of course, would be all the more so if the differences had been agreed between the parties or their engineers.

The first particular qualification arises from the fact that an alteration was made in the right of way as originally specified. It does not appear when or by whom the alteration was made, but it must be presumed to have been made since the original construction. It consists of a flight of steps – of a steeper gradient than anything provided for in the specification – between the points 'N' and 'O' on the plan, in which portion the specification did not provide for any steps. The steps do not extend completely from 'N' to 'O' and the rest of this portion was made level. Originally, there was, or should have been, a uniform slope from 'N' to 'O'. It must be presumed, in favour of the defendants, that this alteration was made by a predecessor in title of the plaintiff, and, therefore, the defendants should not be required to restore the original condition of this portion of the right of way or to do any work in relation thereto.

The second particular qualification relates to the strand. The position as to the strand is obscure. While it may not be accessible to the public, generally, it appears that there are other private ways to it, and, *prima facie*, the foreshore would be vested in the State. With the exception of three steps to be built to the strand, and another provision to be noted in a moment, the specification was silent as to the strand and the works specified ended with a platform at high water mark. It is true that the grant of 1856 purports to confer a right of way over the land over which the rest of the right of way lies. There was some evidence of works (not related to the right of way) by the defendants or their precedessor below high water level but, as evidence of ownership of the foreshore, I do not find it sufficiently unequivocal. The grant is, of course, sufficient as against the defendants for the purpose of a declaration of a right of way over the strand, but this does not conclude the question of repair so far as the idea of repair could be applied at all to the strand. The covenant to repair renew amend and maintain extends to the strand, but I would find it very difficult to give a meaning to this were it not for an indication in the specification and other documents of a special and limited meaning. The grant of 1856 uses the word, 'cleared,' in a context and manner that may have particular reference to the strand, and the only work prescribed by the specification in relation to the strand, apart from the three steps descending to the strand, was that, at this point, 'the strand is to be cleared from all large or rough rubble granite for a breadth of 20 feet.' Further light is thrown on this matter by portion of the Rulings of the Master, dated the 26th February, 1855, in the course of making the enquiries directed by the decretal order of the 21st November, 1853. The portion in question reads: 'That the strand should be cleared of the large stones to such an extent as will allow a passage of twenty feet wide into the sea so as to leave the strand as it was for that twenty feet wide either by casting the stones at either side of this passage or by removing them. Bathers can thus descend or boats be pushed up on the strand as before the obstruction was created and I think that twenty feet wide is an abundant space for such purpose.'

This strongly suggests that the stones referred to in the grant were something in the nature of debris that had come to be on the strand by reason of works executed by the railway company. This is supported to some extent by the next document which is a mandatory injunction, dated 26th August, 1856, issued by the then Lord Chancellor in the equity proceedings. It commanded and enjoined the railway company, under the penalty of £1,000 sterling, forthwith 'to renew clear and repair the strand for the space of twenty feet in breadth from the point "P" at the foot of the passage from Kyber Pass House in the map or working plan referred to in the said Master's Report filed the 22nd day of May, 1856, mentioned, unto the sea at low water mark situate at Dalkey in the County of Dublin by clearing the said strand from all rough rubble granite'.

It will be noted that the obligation, whether under the specification or under the injunction, extended only to the stones of a limited quality and character. The injunction cannot have been very effective, because the matter seems to have been still in dispute in 1860. This is suggested by an affidavit, sworn on the 25th October of that year, in the equity suit, by one, James Pugh. This affidavit relates how, on the direction of the railway company, James Pugh and his workman had, between the 11th and 19th October, cleared the strand to low water as far as the tide admitted for twenty feet in width at the point 'P', but that, on the Monday following the 19th, the stones had been thrown in again by the tide. The deponent then expressed his opinion that during the winter months it would be impossible to keep the works in the order shown on the plan, because the tide often dashed with great fury as high as the point 'O' throwing the stones about in all directions and covering the strand.

Whatever the purpose or effect of that affidavit was, the question had evidently not been finally solved in 1873. On the 13th June of that year there was a consent decree in the Court of Common Pleas in an action which had been taken by James Milo Burke against the Dublin Wicklow and Wexford Railway Company. The material portion provided that it was consented and agreed 'that the defendants should under the deeds of 20th March, 1856, and 10th August, 1869, respectively, be bound to keep the strand referred to cleared pursuant to the provisions of the said deed for an average width of 20 feet and for a length of 39 feet measured seaward from the point "P" . . . and that the aforesaid space to be cleared shall be deemed and taken to be the space so to be cleared and for ever kept cleared and maintained according to the true construction of the said deeds respectively.'

If this consent meant more than that the then defendants were to do more than clear and keep cleared the strand of the 'large or rough rubble granite' or the 'obstruction' that may be presumed to have been placed there by them or their predecessors, it was an extension of what I conceive to have been the scope, in this respect, of the covenant in the grant of 1856. In the absence of evidence as to what were the pleadings or issues in the action in which the consent was entered into, I am very doubtful how far I could hold the present defendants to be estopped or bound by the terms of the consent. Even more in their favour is the practical consideration, suggested by the affidavit of James Pugh, referred to above, and by the evidence given before me, that the clearance of the strand would be a futile undertaking. To carry out now what was contemplated by the consent of 1873 – and this is the most that the plaintiff could ask – would mean that, out of a rock-covered piece of foreshore, perhaps three hundred yards wide, a passage or channel of twenty feet width should be cleared or created. I feel it is more than likely that the first storm, or, possibly, even the first high tide, would substantially undo any such work, and I think any order in respect of the strand would place an unreasonable and unpredictable burden on the defendants.

It is true that there are probably some stones and fragments of masonry, from the original works of the right of way, now on the strand. Apart, however, from the difficulty of precise identification and particularisation, I am satisfied by the evidence that their removal would not alleviate very materially the present inhospitable nature of the surface of the strand. While the defendants may well see fit to remove them, I do not think they should be ordered to do so. Consequently, in my view, any order on foot of the covenant should exclude the strand.

The result is that the plaintiff is entitled to the following relief:

1, A declaration that she is entitled from time to time and at all times and for all purposes to have and use the right and facility of passage and to go return pass and repass along over and upon the passage way and strand as set out in the deed of grant dated the 20th March, 1856, and made between the Dublin and Wicklow Railway Company, of the one part, and Martin Burke, of the other part, and as more particularly described in the map plan and specification thereto annexed.

2, A declaration that the defendants are at all times at their own costs and expenses bound to repair renew amend and maintain and keep repaired renewed amended and maintained in a proper sufficient substantial and workmanlike manner the said passage way other than the portion thereof between the points marked 'N' and 'O' on the said plan.

3, An order directing the defendants to repair renew and amend the said passage way in accordance, so far as may be, with the said specification, but not including any work on or to the said strand or on or to the said portion between the points 'N' and 'O.' To enable the defendants to choose their own time, having regard to weather and other conditions, I think they should be given six months from the perfecting of the order herein to comply with this direction.

There will be liberty to either party to apply and the plaintiff will be entitled to her costs against the defendants.

Notes and Questions
1. This case involved a positive covenant (to repair), so why did the question of the running of the burden not arise? The *Irish Land Law*, para. 19.38 *et seq.*
2. As regards the running of the benefit of freehold covenants, see *ibid.*, para, 19.19 *et seq.*
3. As regards rights of way, see p. 294, *ante*; also *ibid.*, para. 6.107.

FITZPATRICK V. CLANCY
Unreported (High Court) (1964 No. 1879P)
The facts are set out in the judgment.

Kenny J.:

By a lease made on the 4th July 1835 the Earl of Howth let lands on the sea front at Sutton to a Mr. Pier for 100 years from the 1st May 1835 and a large house called Warren House was subsequently built on them. The tenant's interest under this lease was acquired by a Mrs. Conner who made sub-leases of parts of the lands and then, in 1934, assigned the remaining parts of the lands containing about 10 acres to Mr. John Hanley. Mr. Hanley then began negotiations with the Howth Estate Company (which I shall call 'the Company') which had become entitled to the freehold interest in the lands for a reversionary lease of the lands assigned to him. Warren House was, at this time, in a bad state of repair and the Company wanted to impose an obligation to repair it on Mr. Hanley who could not decide whether he wanted to rebuild it as a residence for himself or whether he wanted to pull it down and develop the lands as a building estate. The lands had many attractive features: they are on the main road from Dublin to Sutton and there is a fine view from them over the sea to the Hill of Howth. On the 1st August 1934 Mr. Hanley stated to the agents acting for the Company that he wanted to occupy Warren House as it was and that he had no intention of building on the lands. After long negotiations Mr. Hanley on the 6th November 1934 made a written proposal to the Company: he offered to take a lease of the lands for 999 years from the 1st May 1935 at a rent of £40 per year and undertook to expend money on Warren House to put it into reasonable order within two years from the date of the proposed lease unless the house should, before then, have been pulled down 'in furtherance of a building scheme'. The proposal also provided that Mr. Hanley was to be free to build dwellinghouses on the lands on sites and in accordance with plans to be approved by the Company but an additional rent of £3 per year was to become payable for each dwellinghouse.

The draft lease prepared by the solocitors for the Company contained a covenant by Mr. Hanley for himself and his assigns that he or any other person would not convert, use or occupy the premises let or any part thereof or any building or buildings to be erected on the lands for any purpose save as a private dwellinghouse or houses. The Solicitor acting for Mr. Hanley struck this covenant out of the draft lease and, in place of it, put in a covenant that the tenant would not use the premises for any offensive trade or business. The solicitors for the Company refused to accept this amendment and insisted on the original covenant in the draft. A lease of the 3rd May 1935 between the Representative Church Body (which were mortgagees of the Company), the Company and Mr. John Hanley was the result of these negotiations. By it the lands with the house and other buildings were let by the Representative Church Body at the request of the Company to Mr. Hanley for 999 years from the 1st May 1935 at a yearly rent of £40. There was a provision for a penal rent of £30 for each dwellinghouse built on the lands without the consent of the Company. Mr. Hanley for himself and his assigns covenanted amongst other things, that he would 'within two years from the date hereof in the event of the dwelling-house now standing on the said demised premises not having been previously taken down in furtherance of a building scheme as hereinafter mentioned expend such a sum on the repair of the said dwellinghouse as will put the same in reasonable order and condition' and that he 'or any other person or persons will not at any time during the term hereby granted convert, use or occupy the said premises or any part thereof or any building or buildings to be erected thereon for any purpose save as a private dwellinghouse or houses'. It also contained a clause in these terms: 'Provided always that the lessee shall have the option to build and erect on the said premises such dwellinghouses and buildings as may be agreed on by the Company (the Howth Estate Company) the said houses to be erected on a site the site plans and specifications to be first approved by the Company' and Mr. Hanley was then to pay an additional yearly rent of £3 for each such house. There was also a covenant by the Company for quiet enjoyment.

Mr. Hanley, who was a buyer in a drapery firm in Dublin and who was not a builder, did not demolish Warren House within two years from the date of the lease and lived there until his death. The house was not demolished until 1961 when the first four-named defendants who are the trustees for the Irish Christian Brothers had it demolished.

Early in 1938 the plaintiff, Mr. Thomas Fitzpatrick, who wanted to build a house on part of the lands in the lease, began negotiations with Mr. Hanley to acquire part of the lands which fronted on to the main road to Howth. He retained Mr. Patrick Munden, the well-known architect, to examine the proposed site and to prepare a map. The plaintiff, who wished to build a good house, wanted a site on the west side of the lands and was therefore concerned about the type of house which Mr. Hanley might build on the remaining part of the 536 feet frontage. The plaintiff tried to get an assurance from Mr. Hanley about the kind of houses which might be built on the frontage, and on the 6th December 1938 the solicitors acting for Mr. Hanley wrote to the plaintiff in these terms:

> 'Referring to your call here on the 29th ult. (the 29th November 1938) I communicated with my client with reference to the assurance required by you as to the type of house which my client intended to build on the remaining portion of the frontage at Sutton. Mrs. Hanley called here to-day and informed me that Mr. Hanley was prepared to give an undertaking that any house built on

the plot would be value for at least £1,000. She also stated that it was Mr. Hanley's wish to get the best possible house, but it would be useless going to the expense of preparing plans for houses for the frontage which might have to be altered later on. I think you may take it that Mr. Hanley is as anxious as you are to get a good class house built on his land.'

And on the 23rd February 1939 the plaintiff wrote a letter to Mr. Hanley which contained these paragraphs:

'As a result of Mr. Munden's visit to Sutton on Tuesday I have received from him a draft map showing the plot of ground, having a frontage of 120 feet, and being 120 feet wide at back, together with garden at rear of this plot.

It is clearly set out, and I am satisfied it will be suitable. I am agreeable to take it at the figure agreed upon viz. £750 subject to my solicitor's approval.

It is understood and agreed between us, that if when the plans are in preparation or completed, my architect considers that a further extension of 20 or 30 feet desirable that such an extension can be required at an agreed price. Also that only good type houses costing not less than £1,000 shall be erected on adjoining plots. I would require vacant possession of the lodge.

I intend to get plans prepared immediately, as I am anxious to get on with the work, and I would be glad to have your formal acceptance.' On the 26th February Mr. Hanley wrote to the plaintiff:

'Your communication received. Everything nominated is in order and accepted. Ground is now pegged and a personal visit is advisable.'

A development plan showing a possible layout of the lands with Warren House standing and the plaintiff's house with eight other houses on the frontage was prepared by Mr. Munden in March 1938 on Mr. Hanley's instructions. The plaintiff had not seen this plan at any time before the assignment to him on the 6th July 1939 but he knew that Mr. Hanley with whom he was on friendly terms had consulted Mr. Munden about the development of the frontage. I think that Mr. Munden was acting as architect for the plaintiff and for Mr. Hanley in 1938 and in 1939.

While the plaintiff was negotiating with Mr. Hanley for a site, discussions between Mr. Hanley and a Mr. O'Baoighill for the sale of a plot of land fronting on to the main road but on the east side of the lands let by the lease of 1935 were going on. On the 31st March 1939 Mr. Hanley assigned to Mr. O'Baoighill a plot of land on the east side of the lands in the lease of 1935 for the residue of the term of 999 years subject to the payment of the rent of £40 and to the covenants in the lease of 1935 but indemnified against payment of this rent by the remaining lands in that lease. This assignment had a recital that Mr. O'Baoighill intended to build a house on the lands assigned to him, that he had got the consent of the Company to this and had agreed to pay a rent of £3 to them and he covenanted to pay it. The dimensions of the plot of land assigned to Mr. O'Baoighill did not correspond with those shown on Mr. Munden's development plan for the same site.

On the 6th July 1939 Mr. Hanley assigned to the plaintiff a plot on the western side of the lands let to him by the lease of 1935 for the residue of the term of 999 years subject to the rent of £40 but indemnified against it by the remaining lands in the lease and the plaintiff agreed to pay a rent of £3 to the Company. This assignment contained a recital of the assignment to Mr. O'Baoighill and of the intention of the plaintiff to build a house on the lands assigned to him. Mr. Hanley covenanted with the plaintiff 'that he will henceforth during the continuance of the said term of 999 years pay the said yearly rent of £40 reserved by and perform and observe the covenants on the part of the lessee and conditions contained in the said indenture of lease (the lease of 1935) so far as the same relate to such of the premises thereby demised as are retained by the vendor (Mr. Hanley) and will at all times keep the purchaser (the plaintiff) effectually indemnified against all actions and proceedings, costs, damages, expenses, claims and demands whatsoever by reason or on account of the non-payment of the said yearly rent of £40 or any part thereof or the breach non-performance or non-observance of the said covenants and conditions or any of them insofar as they relate to the premises retained by the vendor (Mr. Hanley)'.

Neither of these assignments contained any covenant or stipulation by Mr. Hanley about the user of the lands retained by him except his covenant to observe the covenants in the lease of 1935. This covenant by Mr. Hanley was a covenant of indemnity only and was not an assignment to the plaintiff or to Mr. O'Baoighill of the benefit or burden of the covenant relating to user in the lease of 1935 and did not impose any restriction on his use of the remaining lands in favour of the plaintiff or Mr. O'Baoighill (*Beattie* v. *Quivey* (1876) I.R. 10 C.L. 516 and *Harris* v. *Boots Limited* [1904] 2 Ch. 376). There was thus no covenant between Mr. Hanley and the plaintiff in connexion with the user of the lands retained by Mr. Hanley.

The plaintiff and Mr. O'Baoighill erected houses on the lands assigned to them. I have, with the consent of all the parties, inspected both of these houses from the outside and the foundations which have been dug for the school. The plaintiff's house is a fine residence with long well-kept gardens in the front and back and has a most attractive view from the front towards the Hill of Howth. I unhesitatingly accept the evidence given by Mr. Gill, a most experience valuer, that the proposed school will reduce the market value of the plaintiff's house by £6,000.

In September 1941 the plaintiff wished to buy some more ground at the back of his house and Mr. Hanley assigned to him another part of the lands in the lease of 1935 for £250 indemnified against the rent of £40 which Mr. Hanley charged on the lands retained by him. This assignment contained a similar covenant of indemnity by Mr. Hanley in relation to the payment of the rent of £40 and the performance and observance of the covenants in the lease of 1935.

Mr. Hanley died on the 16th December 1942 and left all his property to his wife, who on the 31st March 1947 assigned all the lands comprised in the lease of 1935 which had been retained by Mr. Hanley (and which then amounted to about 6 acres) to Margaret Willis. On the 5th June 1953 the Company let a small piece of land on the north-eastern side of the lands included in the lease of 1935 to Mrs. Willis for 981 years. Mrs. Willis wanted to have the lands which had been assigned to her developed as a building estate and had plans for houses on all the lands and not on the frontage only passed by the Town Planning Authority. The plaintiff took keen interest in this proposal and wrote to the Town Planning Authority to emphasise the importance to him of good houses being built on the lands near his house so that its value would be maintained.

Mrs. Willis despaired of the lands being developed and on the 24th November 1959 she agreed to sell (by way of assignment) the lands which had been transferred to her in 1947 and with the benefit of the covenants contained in the assignment to the plaintiff and to Mr. O'Baoighill. The Christian Brothers purchased the lands for the building of a large primary school and, at a later date, of a secondary school. As this user would have been a breach of the covenant in the lease of 1935 to use the lands for private dwellinghouses, the solicitors acting for the Irish Christian Brothers wrote to the Company to find out if this covenant could be altered so that a school could be built on the lands and some inconclusive and diplomatically obscure letters were written by the solicitors acting for the Company.

On the 4th January 1960 Mrs. Willis assigned the lands which had been retained by Mr. Hanley to the first four-named defendants for the residue of the term of years granted by the lease of 1935 subjeca to the rent of £40 and to the covenants in the lease of 1935. This assignment contained a covenant by the first four-named defendants to observe and perform the covenants in the lease of 1935 and to indemnify Mrs. Willis against actions and proceedings by reason or on account of the non-payment of the rent of £40 or the breach non-performance or non-observance of the covenant in the lease of 1935. The Christian Brothers then demolished Warren House and carried out other works on the lands although this was a breach of the covenants in the lease of 1935. The Company threatened to bring proceedings against them but the estate agents acting for the Company advised their clients that the Christian Brothers had rights under the Landlord and Tenant Acts and that they might be able to get permission to build the schools. This advice was plainly wrong for the lands were not 'a tenement' within the meaning of that term as defined in the Landlord and Tenant Act 1931 (see *Corr* v. *Ivers* [1949] I.R. 245 and *McEvoy* v. *Gilbeys of Ireland Limited* [1964] I.R. 30). Ultimately the Company agreed to alter the covenant in the lease about the use of the lands for private dwellings so that buildings for use as a school or college (other than a reformatory or industrial school) might be built on the lands and, for this concession, the rent of £40 payable under the lease of 1935 was increased to £164. This agreement took legal shape in a deed dated the 19th May 1961 (expressed to be supplemental to the lease of 1935) by which the Company authorised the first four-named defendants to demolish the dwellinghouses on the lands and to erect additional buildings (provided that the new buildings did not interfere with the amenities of the existing leaseholds) and to use the new buildings for a school or college.

Plans for the new primary school on the lands have been approved by the Company and by the town planning authority. The primary school is designed to take about 500/600 boys and will be 50 feet from the boundary wall of the plaintiff's premises and a new secondary school may be built at a later date. The primary school (the foundations for which have been opened) is sited so that its front line will be 60 feet beyond the front line of the plaintiff's house and it will seriously interfere with the very attractive view from the windows of the plaintiff's house. Preliminary work on the site for the school began in 1964. The plaintiffs began these proceedings on the 23rd October 1964 and then applied for an interlocutory injunction: on the hearing of this application the first four-named defendants gave an undertaking that they would not proceed with the work until this action had been determined in the High Court. The action was heard in January 1965: many documents were discovered and I have been given a book of all the correspondence. All counsel and solicitors in the case are to be commended for having had the case disposed of so rapidly.

The plaintiff claims an injunction to restrain the Christian Brothers from erecting a school on the lands adjoining his house and an injunction to restrain the Company from authorising this. The Representative Church Body made the lease of 1935 as mortgagees of the Company and their mortgage was paid off in 1945. The second-named plaintiff who is the assignee of Mr. O'Baoighill has served notice of discontinuance of the action.

The plaintiff's case against the Christian Brothers is that the lease of 1935 created 'a building scheme' so that he is entitled to enforce the covenant by the tenant in the lease of 1935 against them as assignees of part of the lands in that lease. The plaintiff's case against the Company is that the grant of the supplemental deed of the 19th May 1961 was a derogation from the grant by the Company of the lease of 1935. In the course of a very able closing speech Mr. Parke made the additional case that what Mr. Hanley did, said and wrote in 1938 and 1939 created 'a building scheme' so that the covenants by the tenant in the lease of 1935 could be enforced by one assignee against another although there was no covenant by Mr. Hanley binding him and his assigns to use the lands retained by him in any way. I wish to emphasise that the only covenants involved are those contained in the lease of 1935: there are no other covenants. It has not been argued that the letters between the plaintiff and Mr. Hanley created a contract or collateral bargain which can be enforced against the Christian Brothers. Legal principles and decided cases of high authority establish that such a case based on a contract or collateral bargain could not succeed against them.

Most of the reported cases dealing with the Chancery doctrine of the 'building scheme' are English and relate to cases where the lands were conveyed in fee in lots with restrictive covenants as to user in each conveyance. In this case section 13 of the Landlord and Tenant Act 1860 gives the plaintiff as assignee of the original tenant in the lease of 1935 the same right to enforce the covenants by the landlord in that lease as Mr. Hanley had but the covenants in the lease of 1935 on which reliance is placed in this action was not by the landlord with Mr. Hanley but were by Mr. Hanley with the Company.

The legal doctrine by which a purchaser or lessee of lands who has purchased them subject to restrictive covenants as to user may enforce similar restrictive covenants entered into by adjoining purchasers or lessees with the person from whom they purchased or leased the lands was developed by the Courts of Chancery in the second half of the 19th century and was a means by which relief could be given in cases where the common law could not do so. The difficulty about giving relief under the common law was that the restrictive covenants which the plaintiff sought to enforce had not been made by the adjoining owner with the plaintiff but had been entered into by the person against whom it was sought to enforce them with the grantor or lessor. There was thus no privity of contract between the plaintiff seeking to enforce the covenants and the person against whom their enforcement was sought.

The first statement of this doctrine is to be found in the judgment of Hall, V.C. (a great authority on the law of property and conveyancing) in *Renals* v. *Cowlishaw* (1878) 9 Ch. D. 125, a judgment which was affirmed by the English Court of Appeal (see ll Ch. D. 866). The Vice Chancellor said (p. 128): 'The law as to the burden of and the persons entitled to the benefit of covenants in conveyances in fee was certainly not in a satisfactory state; but it is now well settled that the burden of a covenant entered into by a grantee in fee for himself his heirs and assigns although not running with the land at law so as to give a legal remedy against the owner thereof for the time being, is binding upon the owner of it for the time being, in equity, having notice thereof. Who then (other than the original covenantee), is entitled to the benefit of the covenant? From the cases of *Mann* v. *Stephens* (15 Sim 377), *Weston* v. *Macdermott* (L.R. 2 Ch. 72) and *Coles* v. *Sims* (5 De G.M. and G.1) it may, I think, be considered as determined that anyone who has acquired land, being one of several lots laid out for sale as building plots, where the Court is satisfied that it was the intention that each one of the several purchasers should be bound by and should, as against the others, have the benefit of the covenants entered into by each of the purchasers, is entitled to the benefit of the covenant; and that this right, that is, the benefit of the covenant, enures to the assign of the first purchaser, in other words, runs with the land of such purchaser. This right exists not only where the several parties execute a mutual deed of covenant, but wherever a mutual contract can be sufficiently established. A purchaser may also be entitled to the benefit of a restrictive covenant entered into with his vendor by another or others where his vendor has contracted with him that he shall be the assign of it, that is, have the benefit of the covenant. And such covenant need not be express, but may be collected from the transaction of sale and purchase. In considering this, the expressed or otherwise apparent purpose or object of the covenant, in reference to its being intended to be annexed to other property, or to its being only obtained to enable the covenantee more advantageously to deal with his property, is important to be attended to. Whether the purchaser is the purchaser of all the land retained by his vendor when the covenant was entered into, is also important. If he is not, it may be important to take into consideration whether his vendor has sold off part of the land so retained, and if he has done so, whether or not he has so sold subject to a similar covenant: whether the purchaser claiming the benefit of the covenant has entered into a similar covenant may not be so important.' In the Court of Appeal Lord Justice James (another great authority on Chancery matters) said that he entirely concurred with every word of the judgment of the Vice Chancellor.

The next case (*Spicer* v. *Martin* (1888) 14 App. Cas. 12) is one of great authority for not merely is it a decision of the House of Lords but is a decision of that House sitting with a majority of Irish Lords of Appeal in Ordinary (Lords Fitzgerald and Macnaghten). In that case Spicer purchased from the Commissioners of the exhibition of 1851 the fee simple interest in a house No. 2 Cromwell Gardens subject to a covenant that he would not permit any trade or business to be carried on there. The conveyance to him in 1867 included a block plan of the seven houses in Cromwell Gardens. By six similar conveyances made on the same day the Commissioners conveyed the six other houses in Cromwell Gardens to Spicer: all the seven houses formed one block of buildings and each conveyance contained a similar restrictive covenant. In 1880 Spicer made a lease of No. 2 Cromwell Gardens to Martin subject to a covenant that the premises would be used as a private dwellinghouse only: this lease, which included a block plan of the seven houses, was for 80 years and was granted for a high premium. In 1885 the promotor of a hotel company arranged for the purchase of five of the houses in Cromwell Gardens with the intention of converting them into a hotel and he negotiated with the Commissioners for a release of the restrictive covenants. At this time some of the houses in Cromwell Gardens were owned by Spicer's devisee who gave his consent to the negotiations with the Commissioners. Martin then sued Spicer's devisee and the promoters to restrain the use of the five houses as a hotel. There was no covenant by Spicer with Martin that the houses in Cromwell Gardens (other than No. 2) would be used as private dwellinghouses but, despite this, Martin was granted a perpetual injunction. In the course of his speech Lord Fitzgerald said: 'It seems to me that these two transactions run into each other and are not to be separated, and that each was subject to and brought about by the same statement that the whole of this property of the seven dwellinghouses was on the part of both the landlord and his lessees subject to the same restriction, that the houses were to be used as private dwellinghouses only, and for no other purpose, and that the purchaser, Martin, was to be subject to and to have the benefit and protection of that restriction'.

. . . .'There is every ingredient in this case from which we may reasonably infer an intention that the lessees or purchasers were to be protected by and have the benefit of the restrictive covenant as between Spicer and the Commissioners and to be bound by a similar obligation entered into by each on his own behalf.

It can make no difference that Spicer's obligation to the Commissioners was split up by the adoption of a separate conveyance in fee of each of the seven building lots'.

'I cannot entertain any reasonable doubt that as between the appellant and the respondent the latter was, according to right and justice, entitled to the full benefit and protection of the restrictive covenant which the vendor had entered into with the Commissioners.'

In the course of his speech Lord Macnaghten said: 'If the site of the houses now known as Cromwell Gardens had been put up for sale by auction in building lots, according to a plan corresponding with that on Mr. Martin's lease, and if the conditions of sale had prescribed that houses should be built such as those which have actually been erected, and that every purchaser should bind himself by a covenant now in question, no one, I think, could have doubted that each purchaser would, as against the vendor, and as against every co-purchaser, have the right to the benefit of the covenent, although there might have been no direct stipulation to that effect, and no express provision for mutual covenants by the purchasers inter se. What difference is there in substance between the case I have supposed and the case which has occurred? The site was laid out in accordance with the building scheme, the houses were to be built as private houses, and to be used for no other purpose: a covenant to that effect was imposed on the builder who bought the ground, and intended to parcel it out and sell it or let it again. The houses were actually built as private houses, and offered to the public as such. Their character was unmistakable; and every person who took one of the houses was required to enter into the same restrictive covenant. All this in one way or another was brought to Mr. Martin's knowledge. Every lessee in ordinary course must have had the same information as Mr. Martin had. Every lessee must have known that every other lessee was bound to use his house as a private residence only. This restriction was obviously for the benefit of all the lessees on the estate; they all had a common interest in maintaining the restriction. This community of interest necessarily, I think, requires and imports reciprocity of obligation.'

Graham v. *Craig* [1902] 1 I.R. 263, a decision of the Court of Appeal in Ireland reversing a judgment of Porter M.R. is the only Irish case on the matter. The issue in that case was whether there was a building scheme: the Court of Appeal held that there was no evidence from which it could be inferred that such a scheme was ever in existence.

In *Elliston* v. *Reacher* [1908] 2 Ch. 374, Mr. Justice Parker (as he then was) stated the law about the enforcement of restrictive covenants in a building scheme in a manner which has been approved in many subsequent cases. He said: 'I pass, therefore, to the consideration of the question whether the plaintiff can enforce these restrictive covenants. In my judgment, in order to bring the principles of *Renals* v. *Cowlishaw* and *Spicer* v. *Martin* into operation it must be proved (1) that both the plaintiffs and the defendants derived title under a common vendor; (2) that previously to selling the lands to which the plaintiffs and the defendants are respectively entitled the vendor laid out his estate, or a defined portion thereof (including the lands purchased by the plaintiffs and defendants respectively), for sale in lots subject to restrictions intended to be imposed on all the lots, and which, though varying in details as to particular lots, are consistent and consistent only with some general scheme of development; (3) that these restrictions were intended by the common vendor to be and were for the benefit of all the lots intended to be sold, whether or not they were also intended to be and were for the benefit of other lands retained by the vendor; and (4) that both the plaintiffs and the defendants, or their predecessors in title, purchased their lots from the common vendor upon the footing that the restrictions subject to which the purchases were made were to enure for the benefit of the other lots included in the general scheme whether or not they were also to enure for the benefit of other lands retained by the vendors. If these four points be established, I think that the plaintiffs would in equity be entitled to enforce the restrictive covenants entered into by the defendants or their predecessors with the common vendor irrespective of the dates of the respective purchases. I may observe, with reference to the third point, that the vendor's object in imposing the restriction must in general be gathered from all the circumstances of the case, including in particular the nature of the restrictions. If a general observance of the restrictions is in fact calculated to enhance the values of the several lots offered for sale, it is an easy inference that the vendor intended the restrictions to be for the benefit of all the lots, even though he might retain other land the value of which might be similarly enhanced, for a vendor may naturally be expected to aim at obtaining the highest possible price for his land. Further, if the first three points be established, the fourth point may readily be inferred, provided the purchasers have notice of the facts involved in the first three points: but if the purchaser purchases in ignorance of any material part of those facts, it will be difficult, if not impossible, to establish the fourth point. It is also observable that the equity arising out of the establishment of the four points I have mentioned has been sometimes explained by the implication of mutual contracts between the various purchasers, and sometimes by the implication of a contract between each purchaser and the common vendor, that each purchaser is to have the benefit of all the covenants by the other purchasers, so that each purchase is in equity an assign of the benefit of these covenants. In my opinion the implication of mutual contract is not always a perfectly satisfactory explanation. It may be satisfactory that all the lots are sold by auction at the same time, but when, as in cases such as *Spicer* v. *Martin*, there is no sale by auction, but all the various sales are by private treaty and at various intervals of time, the circumstances may, at the date of one or more of the sales be such as to preclude the possibility of any actual contract. For example, a prior purchaser may be dead or incapable of contracting at the time of a subsequent purchase, and in any event it is unlikely that the prior and subsequent purchasers are ever brought into personal relationship, and yet the equity may exist between them. It is, I think, enough to say, using Lord Macnaghten's words in *Spicer* v. *Martin*, that where the four points I have mentioned are established, the community of interest imports in equity the reciprocity of obligation which is in fact contemplated by each at the time of his own purchase.' The judgment of Mr. Justice Parker was affirmed by the English Court of Appeal (see [1908] 2 Ch. 665).

I have read a number of other cases, *Reid* v. *Bickerstaff* [1909] 2 Ch. 305, a decision of the English Court of Appeal, *Kelly* v *Barrett* [1924] 2 Ch. 279, a decision of the same Court and *Newton Abbot Co-Operative Society* v. *Williamson* [1952] 1 All E.R. 279, a decision of Mr. Justice Upjohn (as he then wa) but these decisions do not add anything to the principles laid down by the earlier cases.

When these principles are applied to this case, the first of the arguments put forward for the plaintiff, that the lease of 1935 created a building scheme because it contained a covenant to use the premises for the purpose of dwellinghouses, is seen to be incorrect. For this argument the Company must be regarded as the vendor but there is no evidence whatever that the Company had ever laid out the lands in the lease of 1935 or any defined portion of them for sale in lots and all the evidence indicates that they did not ever intend to do so. The only restriction on the lands related to their use and there is no evidence that Mr. Hanley ever took the lease with the intention that any restrictions contained in it which he might subsequently impose on the purchaser or sub-lessee from him were to be for the benefit of any other lots which might be included in the scheme. Indeed, the amendment to the draft lease made by Mr. Hanley's solicitor shows that Mr. Hanley wanted to have liberty to use the lands for purposes other than those of private dwellinghouses. This branch of the case also fails because it is impossible to infer the existence of a building scheme from one lease only.

The next argument was that Mr. Hanley was to be treated as the common vendor. There is evidence that he had had a plan of development of the frontage of the lands prepared in March 1938 but the plaintiff had not seen this nor did he rely on it when he made his purchase. There is, moreover, complete uncertainty about the extent of this scheme of development. Was it to relate to the front only or was it to relate to all the lands assigned to Mr. Hanley? The two assignments made to Mr. Fitzpatrick and Mr. O'Baoighill do not contain any restrictions except those arising from the covenants to observe the conditions and covenants in the lease of 1935. There is no evidence that Mr. Hanley intended to incorporate the restrictions on the user contained in the lease of 1935 in sub-leases or assignments to be made by him so that such incorporation would be for the benefit of all the lots intended to be sold. The covenant as to user contained in the lease of 1935 would of course be enforceable by the Company against any assignee or sub-lessee from Mr. Hanley but it does not seem to me that this creates 'a building scheme'.

In my opinion there was never a building scheme in connexion with these lands in existence.

The plaintiff has also made a claim against the Company because, it was said, they had derogated from their grant by releasing the covenant about user in the lease of 1935. The principle relied on is that an owner cannot sell or let lands for a particular purpose and then, subsequently, do or permit an act which frustrates or materially interferes with the known purpose for which the letting was made. The most authoritative statement of the law on this matter is that in the opinion of Lord Loreburn L.C. when giving the advice of the Privy Council in *Lyttelton Times Company Limited* v. *Warners Limited* [1907] A.C. 476. The Lord Chancellor said: 'At the root of the difficulties in the case as presented to their Lordships in argument lies this question. Ought the fact that one of the parties was the grantor and the other the grantee of a lease to dominate the decision of the case? The maxim that a grantor cannot derogate from his grant expresses the duty ordinarily laid on a man who sells or leases land. But it does not touch a similar and equally binding duty that may in certain cases be laid on a man who buys or hires land. If A lets a plot to B, he may not act so as to frustrate the purpose for which in the contemplation of both parties the land was hired. Also if B takes a plot from A, he may not act so as to frustrate the purpose for which in the contemplation of both parties the adjoining plot remaining in A's hands was destined. The fact that one lets and the other hires does not create any presumption in favour of either in construing an expressed contract. Nor ought it to create a presumption in construing the implied obligation arising out of a contract. When it is a question of what shall be implied from the contract, it is proper to ascertain what in fact was the purpose or what were the purposes to which both intended the land to be put, and having found that, both should be held to all that was implied in the common intention.' The Lord Chancellor uses the phrase 'so as to frustrate the purpose for which in the contemplation of both parties the land was hired' but the later cases (*Browne* v. *Flower* [1911] 1 Ch. 226, *O'Cedar Limited* v. *Slough Trading Company Limited* [1927] 2 K.B. 123 and *Kelly* v. *Battershell* [1949] 2 E.R. 830) suggest that the correct test is whether what is done is a substantial interference with the common purpose for which the premises were let or which renders them materially less fit for that purpose. It was strenuously contended by counsel for the plaintiff that the decision in *Kelly* v. *Battershell* was incorrect and that I should not follow it but the validity of the principle on which the English Court of Appeal acted was not disputed.

In my opinion a school beside the plaintiff's house, though it will substantially reduce its market value, will not render it materially less fit for living in. It may interfere with the plaintiff's privacy and quiet but this is not sufficient to make the house less fit as a dwellinghouse.

It has also been suggested that the Company which had granted the lease of 1935 which contained a restriction as to user by the tenant could not subsequently release the covenant which created this restriction. No decided case or text-book of authority was cited to support this wide proposition. As a general statement of the law, it is certainly incorrect.

The Christian Brothers have also relied on an estoppel against the plaintiff. The plaintiff, it was said, consented to a school being built on the lands adjoining his house and the defendants relied on his consent and started to build the school. The evidence shows that the Christian Brothers did not know or rely on what the plaintiff had said when they started to build the school..

The issue whether the user of the adjoining premises as a school will be a breach of the covenant for quiet enjoyment contained in the lease of 1935 was not mentioned in argument because this matter cannot be tried until evidence of the amount of noise caused by the pupils in the school is available and I express no views on it.

Though the plaintiff's claim against all the defendants fails, I do not wish to hide the sympathy which I have for him.

Note

See further on estate/building schemes, *Irish Land Law*, para. 19.34 *et seq*.

POWER SUPERMARKETS LTD, V. CRUMLIN INVESTMENTS LTD.

Unreported (High Court) 1978 No. 4539 P) (judgment delivered 22nd June, 1981)
The facts are set out in the judgment.

Costello J.:

Power Supermarkets Ltd entered into an agreement with Crumlin Investments Ltd on the 19th day of June 1974 by which Crumlin Investments agreed to grant to Power Supermarkets a lease of portion of a shopping centre in Crumlin which Crumlin Investments was then in the course of developing. The lease was eventually granted to Quinnsworth Ltd (a wholly owned subsidiary of Power Supermarkets). The lease contains a clause by which Crumlin Investments covenanted

'Not during the term to grant a Lease for or to sell or permit or suffer the sale by any of its tenants or so far as within the Landlord's control any sub or under tenants of groceries or food products in or over an area exceeding 3,000 square feet in any one Unit forming part of the Shopping Centre unless so ordered or directed by any Court of competent jurisdiction.'

The meaning of this covenant and its operation on the facts of this case are the subject matter of dispute in this action.

I can dispose of one matter of interpretation immediately. The Defendant's Solicitor took the view that this covenant prohibited Crumlin Investments from making a lease or a letting by which a lessee or a tenant could carry on the prohibited activities, but it did not restrict any trading activities which Crumlin Investments itself might wish to carry on in any unit in the shopping centre. According to this view Crumlin Investments could itself sell groceries and food products in an area over 3,000 square feet if it was so minded. And so an assignee of any part of the freehold would not be bound in any way by the covenant. With respect, I cannot agree with this interpretation. The lessor in my opinion not only covenanted not to allow a tenant to sell groceries and food products in any area exceeding 3,000 square feet in a Unit of the shopping centre but it also covenanted that it would itself not do so. I agree that the covenant was somewhat imperfectly drafted, but the sense must be as I have just suggested. What I have to decide then, is whether this covenant was breached by one or other or both the Defendants.

There are two limited liability companies who are Defendants in this action, Crumlin Investments Ltd., the original lessor, and Dunnes Stores (Crumlin) Ltd. to whom Crumlin Investments conveyed the fee simple interest in a Unit of the shopping centre. The Plaintiffs make two submissions. Firstly, they say that I should look at the reality of the relationship between Crumlin Investments and Dunnes Stores (Crumlin) and hold that Crumlin Investments is in fact carrying on a business in the shopping centre in breach of the covenant. Secondly, and alternatively, they claim that Dunnes Stores (Crumlin) is bound by the landlord's covenant and that it threatens to trade in breach of it.

To deal with the first submission I must refer to the history of the Defendant's involvement in the Crumlin shopping centre. The centre, as I have said, was developed by Crumlin Investments and a number of tenants took leases of different units in it. But the development was not a financial success and a financial institution which held a debenture over the property sought a purchaser of it. It approached the well known commercial enterprise to which I will refer as the Dunnes Stores Group. The Group decided to buy and it acquired the property by purchase of the shares in Crumlin Investments. The purchasing company was Cornellscourt Shopping Centre Ltd, and thus Crumlin Investments became its wholly owned subsidiary. But Cornellscourt Shopping Centre Ltd. is a wholly owned subsidiary of Dunnes Stores Ltd. which in turn is a wholly owned subsidiary of Dunnes Holding Co., an unlimited liability company whose shareholders are trustees of a discretionary trust whose beneficiaries are Mr. Ben Dunne and the members of his family. The Dunne Family in fact control all the companies in the Dunnes Stores Group (of which there are something in the region of 150) and actively participate in their running. It was central to the Group's strategy that a Dunnes Stores Supermarket would be opened in a large vacant unit in the shopping centre. This would not only give the group a new and potentially profitable retail outlet but it was considered that this would attract custom to the whole centre, and would result in the fixing of higher rents on the periodic rent reviews to which all the tenants were subject. But it is the policy of the group that each of its outlets should be operated by a separate company. So, Dunnes Stores (Crumlin) Ltd. was incorporated on the 4th Jun, 1978. Only two shares in this company were issued, and it became a wholly owned subsidiary of Dunnes Stores (George's Street) Ltd, a company which in its turn is a wholly owned subsidiary of Dunnes Stores Ltd., to which I have already referred.

The Plaintiffs are supermarket operators and carry on business in competition with the Dunnes Stores Group. They were, as can well be imagined, watching with keen interest the advent of the Group at the Crumlin Shopping Centre. Immediately it became clear that the Group was taking over the empty unit in the centre and that it proposed to trade in groceries and food products an application for an interim injunction was brought and a temporary restraining order was made on the 28th July, 1978. On the same day the Group's Solicitor sent to the Group's Accountants an engrossment of the conveyance of the fee simple interest of Crumlin Investments in a large vacant unit for execution by Dunne's Stores (Crumlin). I am satisfied that this happened coincidentally with the interim order and the conveyance, which is dated the 1st August, 1978, was not executed in an attempt to defeat the injunction but in pursuance of an arrangement which had already been agreed upon in the Group. As I have already pointed out the Group's Solicitor did not consider that Crumlin Investments were prohibited from trading in the manner referred to in the covenant and as they wished to do and as a lease to the new Company could clearly not be made it had been decided instead to convey to the new company the fee simple in the Unit. By this means it was considered that the new company could trade in groceries and food products in an area in excess of 3,000 square feet in the vacant unit and no infringment of the covenant would take place.

I come now to the actual means and method of trading in this unit of the shopping centre. The Dunne family are actively involved in the running of the Dunnes Stores Group of companies, and their wishes prevail, in respect of each company in the Group, including Crumlin Investments and Dunnes Stores (Crumlin). After the initial meeting of the Board of Directors of Dunnes Stores (Crumlin), which is comprised of members of the Dunne family, in 1978 no meeting of the Board has since been held. There has been no meeting of its shareholders. Company Accounts for one year only have been prepared, but have not been presented to any meeting. No meeting of the Directors was held for the purpose of deciding to take a conveyance of the property in the centre and no meetings were ever held to make decisions on trading and commercial matters. Purchases of stock are made on the company's behalf by the purchasing panel of the Dunnes Stores Group who apportion liability for purchases to each trading company in the Group to whom the goods are invoiced. The Company is managed and controlled not by the members of the Dunne family meeting as Directors of the Company, and not by its shareholders, but by members of the Dunne family (or their servants and agents) meeting informally to manage the affairs of the Group as a whole or by individual members taking decisions on the family's behalf.

An exactly similar situation has prevailed since the purchase of the shares in Crumlin Investments. Since then there has been no meeting of the Board of Directors of Crumlin Investments (which also comprise members of the Dunne family and their Accountant) and no shareholders meeting has taken place. It, too, is managed and controlled in the same way as Dunnes Stores (Crumlin) is managed and controlled. The reality of the relationship between the two companies is highlighted by the conveyance of the fee simple interest in the unit in the shopping centre. The consideration for this conveyance was only £100 which I am satisfied, notwithstanding the explanation for this figure which was advanced in the course of the evidence, must be regarded as a gross undervalue. It contained no covenant requiring the purchasers to carry on the business which Crumlin Investments required in order to make the shopping centre commercially viable. It contained none of the usual easements granted with a conveyance of this sort. It was never registered in the Registry of Deeds. These omissions are readily understandable when it is appreciated that the two companies are merely vehicles for carrying out the wishes of the Dunne family; they would do what the Dunne family told them to do.

The Plaintiffs submit that I should pierce the corporate veil and look to the realities in this case and hold, notwithstanding the fact that Crumlin Investments and Dunnes Stores (Crumlin) are two separate corporate entities, that the business in the unit is being carried on by a single entity. I was referred to *Smith Stone and Knight Ltd.* v. *Birmingham Corporation* [1939] 4 All E.R. 116, a case in which a parent company was held entitled to compensation in respect of a business carried on by its subsidiary on the basis that the subsidiary was in reality carrying it on on behalf of the parent company, and to *D.H.N.* v. *Tower Hamlets London Borough Council* [1976] 1 W.L.R. 852 a case also dealing with the payment of compensation for the compulsory acquisition of property. The claimants in that case were a group of three companies associated in a wholesale grocery business. The Court of Appeal held that it should pierce the corporate veil, and that it should not regard the companies as separate legal entities but treat the group as a single economic entity for the purpose of awarding compensation. I need not refer to the facts of the case; however, the reasons which prompted the court's approach are very material for the resolution of the issues in the present case. Lord Denning pointed out (page 860) that the group of companies was virtually the same as a partnership in which all three were partners; that they should not be treated separately so as to defect the claim to compensation on the technical point; that they should not be deprived of the compensation which should be justly payable for disturbance. So, he decided that the three companes should be treated as one. Lord Shaw (at page 867) pointed out that if each member of the group of companies was to be regarded as a company in isolation that nobody at all could claim compensation 'in a case which plainly calls for it', and he said that the true relationship should not be ignored because to do so would amount to a denial of justice. He too considered that the group should be regarded as a single entity.

It seems to me to be well established from these as well as from other authorities (See *Harold Holdsworth & Co. Ltd.* v. *Caddies* [1955] 1 W.L.R. 352; *Scottish Co-operative Wholesale Society Ltd.* v. *Meyer* [1959] A.C. 324) that a Court may, if the justice of the case so requires, treat two or more related companies as a single entity so that the business notionally carried on by one will be regarded as the business of the group, or another member of the group, if this conforms to the economic and commercial realities of the situation. It would, in my view, be very hard to find a clearer case than the present one for the application of this principle. I appreciate that Crumlin Investments is a property-owning not a trading company but it is clear that the creation of the new company and the conveyance to it of the freehold interest in a unit in the shopping centre were means for carrying out the commercial plans of the Dunne family in the centre. The enterprise had a two-fold aspect (a) the creation of a new retail outlet for the Dunnes Stores Group in the shopping centre and (b) the enhancement of the rents in the centre as a whole which the creation of such an outlet would hopefully produce. To treat the two companies as a single economic entity seems to me to accord fully with the realities of the situation. Not do to so could involve considerable injustice to the Plaintiffs as their rights under the covenant might be defeated by the mere technical device of the creation of a company with a £2 issued capital which had no real independent life of its own. If it is established that the covenant is breached there should in my opinion be an injunction against both Defendants.

Even though the finding I have just made determines the parties' rights in this action I think I should also express my views on the Plaintiff's second, alternative, submissions as the parties may wish to have my decision on all aspects of the case. They urged that the lessor's covenant in this case ran with the land and that Dunnes Stores (Crumlin) were bound by it when they took the conveyance of the 1st August, 1978. The Defendants claimed that they were not and in support of their contention relied on *Thomas* v. *Haywood* L.R. 4 Ex. 311. But that case in my view does not help them – it dealt with the right of the assignee of the *lessee's* interest to sue on a covenant in the lease. The present case is one involving the enforcement of a restrictive covenant against the successor in title to the freehold interest of the covenantor, and different principles apply.

The principle of equity which was developed in the last century is that the burden of a restrictive covenant runs with the land to which it relates so as to bind successors in title of the original covenantor, except in the case of a bona fide purchaser without notice. The basis of this rule is that the covenant is concerned with preserving the value of the land retained by the covenantee. For it to apply there must be a clear intention that the burden is to run. (See: Wylie *Irish Land Law* paragraphs 19.25 to 19.43, and *London and S.W. Railway Co.* v. *Gomm* 20 Ch. D. 562, at 583). Here, I think there can be little doubt that the parties to the lease intended that the lessor's covenant would run with the land. It is true that the lessor did not expressly covenant on behalf of its successors and assigns, but it could not have been intended that the day after the execution of this lease the lessor would have been at liberty to convey the fee simple of a unit in the shopping centre so as to permit a grantee of the fee simple to trade in a way forbidden to a lessee of the same unit. It is equally clear that the covenant is a restrictive one and that Dunnes Stores (Crumlin) had notice of it. If, therefore the trading which is proposed for the unit breaches the covenant Dunnes Stores (Crumlin) should be restrained from continuing it.

That brings me to the last issue in the case – one that can be briefly dealt with. It is admitted that the sale of groceries and food products in the Unit conveyed to Dunnes Stores (Crumlin) has taken place, and will take place if an injunction is not granted. But it is said that the covenant has not been breached because in ascertaining the area embraced by the covenant only the area in which a sale actually takes place can be counted, that it to say only the area where the cashier sits and receives payment. As the check-out areas so occupied in this case are well below 3,000 square feet, there has, it is said, been no breach. Although ingenious, this interpretation fails adequately to have regard to what the parties must have intended by the covenant. The lessor and the lessee were well aware of contemporary methods of retailing in the grocery trade and quite obviously they were agreeing that in consideration of the execution by Quinnsworth of a lease of a unit in the shopping centre a business of substance in competition to Quinnsworth's would not be permitted in another unit in the centre. To limit the clause to the areas now suggested would it seems to me do violence to the parties' intentions.

I will therefore make an order in the terms of paragraph (a) of the prayer in the Statement of Claim. If any dispute arises as to the implementation of this Order the case can be re-entered for argument.

Note
See further on the rules governing the running of the burden of restrictive covenants, *Irish Land Law*, para. 19.38 *et seq*.

Chapter 13
LICENCES AND SIMILAR INTERESTS

This has been, perhaps, one of the most fertile areas of land law in recent decades. In Ireland there has been the additional factor that the courts have long recognized interests in land which seem to share many of the characteristics of the modern licence, e.g., rights of residence and conacre and agistment 'lettings': see *Irish Land Law*, ch. 20.

I. LICENCES

CULLEN V. CULLEN
[1962] I.R. 268 (High Court)

The plaintiff had built up a successful business at Enniscorthy and Adamstown, Co. Wexford. He lived with his family in his premises at Adamstown where he carried on the business of a licensed grocer and merchant. There was also a small farm attached to the business. The eldest son, *S.*, left school in 1945 and joined his father in the business, and the second son, *M.*, did likewise in 1946. A younger son, *P.*, worked in the business from 1954. From about 1945 onwards a series of family quarrels commenced between the father on one side and the mother and sons on the other. In 1952 the plaintiff first accused his wife and children of robbing him. In 1954 *S.* left the house and set up in business on his own. In the same year *M.*, who had previously left the house after a quarrel, returned at the request of his father to take over the complete running of the business, save that the plaintiff reserved the right to sign cheques drawn in connection therewith. About 1956 the plaintiff began making difficulties about signing cheques and ultimately it was agreed that *M.* would hand over the management to his father in January, 1958. *M.* then received £3,500 from his father and bought himself a farm; he continued to reside in the family home. The plaintiff became erratic in some of his business affairs and in 1959 his wife caused him to be examined by doctors, including a mental specialist, who diagnosed a paranoid illness. An attempt was made to remove the plaintiff to a mental hospital but he escaped to Dublin. When in Dublin the plaintiff sent word to his wife by messenger that he was transferring the property at Adamstown to her, and that she should carry on the business in her own name. In return for this he required a signed statement from his wife and sons that he was sane and the withdrawal of any order of arrest which might have been made in connection with the attempt to commit him to a mental hospital.

Early in 1959 the plaintiff's wife won a portable house in a competition. She gave this house to her son, *M.* He offered it to his father who refused it. *M.* began to prepare a site for it on his own lands. When the plaintiff went to Dublin his wife thought it would be suitable to have *M.*'s house erected on the lands at Adamstown, and she sought her husband's permission to do so. He replied by messenger that he was making the place over to her and she could erect the house where she liked. As a result *M.* erected the house on the lands at Adamstown rather than on his own lands.

On the 14th September, 1959, the plaintiff sent letters to *M.* and *P.* requiring them to leave the house and give up any connection with the management of the farm or business.

An action was brought by the plaintiff (commenced in June, 1960) against his sons, *M.* and *P.*, claiming 1, an injunction to restrain the defendants from interfering in the business and from trespassing on the property at Adamstown; 2, accounts; 3, damages for trespass; and a counterclaim was made by *M.* that he was entitled to the house he had built and the site thereof at Adamstown.

Kenny J.:

The plaintiff, Mr. John Cullen, began his career in business as a shop assistant in Enniscorthy. He prospered and established his own shopkeeping business in which he sold boots, shoes and groceries: he also bought a farm near Enniscorthy. He was married in November, 1928, when he was forty-seven and his wife was twenty-three. There were five children of the marriage, Seán, who was born on the 2nd

September, 1929, Martin, Liam, Patrick and Joseph. Joseph has never been in good health and has been away from home for a number of years. After the marriage, Mrs. Cullen helped her husband in the business at Enniscorthy by keeping the books and helping in the shop.

The plaintiff's business continued to prosper and in April, 1944, he purchased for £6,800 premises at Adamstown to which an intoxicating liquor licence was attached. The premises purchased consisted of a bar, a grocery shop, a store, living accommodation, and about 60 acres of land. The family moved from Enniscorthy to Adamstown and have lived there since 1944. The plaintiff retained his business in Enniscorthy which was conducted by a manageress.

In 1945, the eldest son, Seán, left school and went to work in the business: in 1946, the second son, Martin, left school and he too went to work in the business. In 1946, Seán won a prize of £6,250 in a sweepstake but did not receive the money until he was 21 years of age.

From the time that the family moved to Adamstown there were quarrels between them: although it was not a happy household there were not any serious disputes until 1949. I am satisfied that relations between the plaintiff on the one side and Mrs. Cullen and the children on the other got progressively worse from 1945, that there had been numbers of quarrels before 1949 and that from the time that Seán and Martin began to work in the business their father was suspicious of them. In 1949, when Seán was nearly twenty, he came home from a dance at three o'clock in the morning and was told by the plaintiff to go away and not to come back. He remained away for two or three weeks and returned when his mother told him that the plaintiff wanted him to come back.

In 1951 the plaintiff went to Dublin for a serious operation and remained there for about six months. He left his wife to run the business (which had an annual turnover of about £10,000) but left £20 in cash only for the financing of the business. The plaintiff was the only person with authority to draw cheques on the bank account used in connection with the business, and when Mrs. Cullen wanted to pay some debts due to suppliers she sent the cheques to the plaintiff in Dublin for signature: the plaintiff sent her a reply that the accounts were to be paid out of the cash takings of the business or by money order. This happened at a time when the customers of the business were likely to be seeking credit. Mrs. Cullen got a loan of £700 from a friend and opened a bank account in her own name and, when her husband returned in the spring of 1952, this loan was repaid.

When the plaintiff returned, the disputes and quarrels began again. In May, 1952, there was a quarrel between the plaintiff and Seán as a result of which Seán left and went to Dublin where he remained for three weeks. He returned at his mother's request. About this time the plaintiff began to accuse his wife and children of robbing him and made this accusation to a number of customers who were in the shop. Martin Cullen asked a Mr. Lawton who was the accountant of the business to see his father and an interview took place between them in June, 1952. Martin was worried about these charges as his father was in charge of the cash in the business and he thought that his father would try to show a loss in the business so that the view that he was being robbed would be confirmed. When the accounts were completed at the end of 1952, they showed a substantial drop in profits. When the accounts had been received by the plaintiff a further discussion between the plaintiff and Mr. Lawton took place and the plaintiff subsequently told Martin that there would have to be a big change in the running of the business as so much money had gone astray. Unfortunately none of the accounts of the business for any period prior to June, 1959, were given in evidence, and although I indicated at the end of the evidence that I thought that they would be of assistance counsel for the defendants objected strenuously to any of them being handed in.

Patrick had left school in the summer of 1953 and wanted to go to a university: his father was strongly opposed to this as he wished him to go into the business. Seán had got his sweepstake prize and he offered to pay Patrick's university fees and to provide him with money to enable him to stay in Dublin. Patrick went to University College, Dublin, in the autumn of 1953 and returned to Adamstown for the Christmas vacation about the 20th December, 1953. On the morning of the 25th December, 1953, the plaintiff told Seán and Patrick that they were to leave because they had disobeyed him; the disobedience was that Patrick had gone to University College, Dublin, and Seán had provided the money for him to do this. Mrs. Cullen made some reference to the day and thereupon the plaintiff ordered all the family to go. Some two weeks afterwards the plaintiff sent a message to them that he would like them to return and all except Seán returned. Seán went to Dublin for some time and subsequently bought a grocery and bar business and a farm some five or six miles from Adamstown. He has continued to deal with the shop at Adamstown. For some time before Seán left, relations between his father and him were extremely bad; they did not have meals together and hardly ever spoke to each other.

In June, 1954, Martin left Adamstown because of some quarrel with the plaintiff and stayed in Dublin until August when he was asked by Mr. Lawton to return and a Father Scallan brought him a message that his father wished him to return. There was a meeting between the plaintiff and Martin at which a new arrangement for the running of the business was worked out. Martin was to be the manager of the business, was to make his own arrangements for the employment of a staff and the ordering of goods and was to have complete control of it except that the plaintiff was to sign the cheques. This arrangement came into force in January, 1955, and worked reasonably well for some time. A new bank account was opened to which the plaintiff lodged £500 and the business seems to have prospered. However, in 1956, the plaintiff began to refuse to sign cheques and, as many of the goods supplied to the shops came from suppliers who insisted on cash on delivery, the running of the business became difficult. Father Kehoe, the local curate, intervened successfully on a number of occasions and persuaded the plaintiff to sign cheques. In 1957 the plaintiff had a number of quarrels with customers in the shop; these were not serious but they showed that the plaintiff wanted to assume the management and to end the arrangement under which Martin was managing the business. Discussions took place between the plaintiff and Martin and it was agreed that Martin's management would end in January, 1958, and that the plaintiff would pay him £3,550 as a reward for the way in which he had managed the business: this sum was, I think, intended to be a share of the profits which had been made by Martin. Martin bought a farm, called 'Coolnagreina', near Adamstown, for £2,050 with the money which the plaintiff had given him but he continued to live in the premises at Adamstown. The plaintiff did not approve of the purchase of the farm and Martin had been singularly tactless in not consulting him about the purchase. Despite this the relations between them from January, 1958, until March, 1959, seem to have been reasonably good.

The plaintiff took over the management of the business in January, 1958: Mrs. Cullen still worked on the books and did a certain amount of ordering. The plaintiff managed the business without any serious incident until the beginning of 1959 when he refused to order flour or meal and left the business without these for some weeks: he also told a firm who were regular suppliers of the business that goods which they brought to the premises for delivery were to be taken away. In March, 1959, he dismissed an assistant and about this time Mrs. Cullen asked a Dr. Gilroy to see her husband. She complained to him that her husband was interfering in the running of the business, that he was insulting customers and that he was preventing the wholesalers from supplying goods. The plaintiff had not been seen by Dr. Gilroy before this and one of the mysteries of this case is why Mrs. Cullen asked Dr. Gilroy to see her husband and did not consult Dr. Murphy, his regular medical attendant. Dr. Gilroy saw the plaintiff on the 26th March, 1959. In the course of the interview the plaintiff said that he was going to run his business himself and that his wife and family were robbing him. Dr. Gilroy's attempts to persuade the plaintiff to see a psychiatrist or to accept treatment failed. Throughout the interview the plaintiff emphasised that he was not interfering with anybody and, as proof of this, told Dr. Gilroy that he prayed for everybody and that he had composed a prayer which he recited to Dr. Gilroy.

In April Dr. Gilroy was again requested by Mrs. Cullen to see her husband. She had told him that Dr. Murphy was the plaintiff's regular medical attendant and Dr. Gilroy spoke to Dr. Murphy. Dr. Gilroy saw the plaintiff on the 9th April and the interview was similar to that of the 26th March; the plaintiff showed considerable hostility to his family and was not prepared to submit himself to treatment. Some time after this the plaintiff was, at Dr. Gilroy's suggestion, seen by a Dr. Condon, who specialises in mental illnesses. Dr. Condon wished to see the plaintiff a second time and saw him with Dr. Gilroy at the end of April. Dr. Condon suggested that a temporary private patient reception order under s. 185 of the Mental Treatment Act, 1945, should be made and, according to Dr. Gilroy, said that the plaintiff should be given a sedative and removed from Adamstown. Dr. Gilroy's view was that the plaintiff was suffering from a paranoid illness. It is necessary to emphasise that the doctors who gave evidence drew a distinction between a paranoid illness and the condition known as paranoia. Their evidence was that a paranoid illness is a social illness in which the patient believes that people are ill-disposed towards him: it involves delusions and false judgments and is frequently characterised by suspicions held by the patient that his family are trying to ruin him. In this illness the reasoning powers are intact but impaired on some subjects. In paranoia, on the other hand, the patient has a number of systematised delusions which are unshakeable: the paranoic is rational on all matters except on those on which he has the inflexible delusions. It is a form of insanity and is incurable.

In the first week in June, Dr. Gilroy asked Dr. Vincent Crotty, the resident medical superintendent of the Mental Hospital in Waterford, to see the plaintiff. Dr. Crotty first interviewed Mrs. Cullen who told him that she believed that her husband was mentally ill, that he believed people were plotting against him and were plotting to take his property from him. Dr. Crotty saw the plaintiff on the 5th and 6th June. On the first occasion Dr. Gilroy was present and, I think, signed the certificate certifying that the plaintiff was suffering from mental illness and required not more than six months' treatment. Dr. Crotty thought that the plaintiff had an emotional disturbance sufficient to be called a mental illness; the plaintiff repeated to him the accusations against his family and Dr. Crotty was struck by the fact that he seemed to have no human feeling for them. The doctor thought it advisable that Mrs. Cullen should have somebody in the house with her when the plaintiff was there as he thought that there was a risk that the plaintiff would become violent. Dr. Crotty was also of opinion that the plaintiff required treatment and telephoned to Waterford to arrange for the attendance at Adamstown on the next day of two Brothers of the Order of St. John of God who were to remove the plaintiff. Dr.

Crotty saw the plaintiff again the next day and the interview followed the same course as that of the 5th June except that Father Kehoe came to the interview at the plaintiff's request. Father Kehoe was strongly opposed to the removal of the plaintiff to a mental hospital and said that the cause of the plaintiff's trouble was not his mental attitude but the attitude of his wife and children to him and that that would still be there when the plaintiff came back after treatment. Father Kehoe gave evidence that Dr. Crotty said that the plaintiff was a paranoic: Dr. Crotty denied most strenuously that he said this and I think that Father Kehoe is confusing this interview with some other meeting. Dr. Crotty then signed either the medical certificate or the order and gave it to the Brothers. Neither the medical certificate nor the order was proved, but I infer that the certificate given by Dr. Gilroy was given under s. 184 of the Act of 1945 and that the order under that section was made by Dr. Crotty. The order cannot have been made under s. 185 as that requires a certificate of two registered medical practitioners and the consideration of it by the person in charge of the institution. The order made authorised the removal of the plaintiff from Adamstown and his detention for six months from the date of the order.

The plaintiff was determined that he would not be removed to a mental institution. He escaped from Adamstown and persuaded a relative to drive him to Dublin. He took some books and ledgers relating to the business with him so that he would be able to send out accounts, a step which shows that his business faculties were not impaired in any way. The plaintiff gave a dramatic account of the attempt by the two Brothers to give him an injection and says that he then went for Father Kehoe and brought him back. I find it difficult to accept this highly coloured version of what happened and I find it more difficult to understand how the plaintiff escaped. Apparently all the arrangements had been made to bring him to Waterford when the certificate or order had been signed by Dr. Crotty and another of the mysteries in this case is how the plaintiff escaped from Adamstown and why he was not taken into custody.

I regret that the certificate and order made were not proved as s. 186 of the Act of 1945 seems to authorise the arrest of the person to whom the order relates within a period of seven days from the time the order was made, but all the confused and tortuous negotiations which followed were carried on because the plaintiff and his adviser, Father Kavanagh, believed that the order which had been made authorised his arrest long after the seven-day period had expired.

Dr. Crotty's final view of the plaintiff was that he was suffering from some kind of mental illness, but he could not come to any definite conclusion what it was. He thought that the plaintiff's mental illness was caused either by some special external stress which was responsible for his behaviour or that he was suffering from a paranoid illness. I accept the whole of the evidence given by Dr. Crotty. I am satisfied that on the 5th and 6th of June the plaintiff behaved in the way which Dr. Crotty described. Having heard all the evidence, I am convinced that the plaintiff's condition in the year 1959 was caused by his reaction to considerable mental stress and that this stress arose from the conflict between his determination to assert and show his authority on all possible occasions and the attitude of Mrs. Cullen and Patrick to this. The plaintiff was convinced that his family should always give way to him and, when they did not do this, he took refuge in suspicions and fantasies.

As the plaintiff did not return to Adamstown again, except for a short visit in January, 1960, and as he did not meet the members of his family again (except for a short meeting with Patrick) I think that I should now state my conclusions on the events up to June, 1959. I am satisfied that the plaintiff had and has very strong

inflexible opinions about his authority as a husband and father and that he has
equally strong views about the obligation of the members of his family to obey this
authority; he has probably had these views since he was married but they became
more vocal and more intense from 1949 and I am satisfied that the plaintiff never
understood the opposition which these views would provoke in the members of his
family who lived and worked with him. These views made it certain that there
would be trouble with his children when they reached the age of eighteen or
nineteen. The plaintiff is entitled to have these views; they were commonly held 80
or 90 years ago if we accept the evidence given by the literature of that period, but
they were not common in 1959; and though it may be said that they are the views
which should prevail, they are not now generally acted on: any attempt to enforce
them is almost certain to lead to distressing domestic conflicts. The best evidence of
the plaintiff's views on these matters is provided by a number of sentences from his
evidence. In the course of it he said: 'Boys should obey their father and Missus
should obey her husband', at a time when he was speaking about young men of
twenty-three and twenty-four; 'Let him (Patrick) recognise his boss'; and in answer
to the question as to whether he had put Seán out in 1952, his reply was, 'Yes, I had
authority to do it. It was well done for.' Moreover, throughout his evidence there
were references to who was to be the boss and the illuminating remark by him that
he 'ruled his family fairly'. While many think that other parents should apply these
maxims to their children, most of us know that any attempt to apply them to our
own is likely to produce conflict. The plaintiff, however, was determined that he
would apply them to his family and, from the time that Seán was seventeen, the
inevitable quarrels started.

From 1952 until June, 1959, Mrs. Cullen and Seán, Martin and Patrick tried to
deal with the problem presented by the plaintiff's views by ignoring the plaintiff's
orders and by doing their best to avoid quarrels. The situation was one calling for
considerable tact and on Mrs. Cullen's part at least, considerable diplomacy, and
she did not possess either of these qualities. She committed a serious error of
judgment in always siding with her children against the plaintiff and all of them
were foolish in presenting a united front to their father whenever any quarrel or
dispute arose. I accept the candid evidence of Seán Cullen on this aspect of the
case. In the course of it he said that in what led up to the disputes the plaintiff was
not always wrong but that in the actual disputes when they came, he was always
wrong because no one could reason with him. This attitude to the plaintiff by the
members of his family aggravated an already difficult situation; it induced the
plaintiff to try to assert his authority and, above all things, to give public demon-
strations of it, and as his remarkable views about his authority were ignored he
believed that his family were against him. From that it was an easy step to the belief
that he was being robbed by them – an idea which he repeated in the witness box.
The questioned authority is always the one most violently asserted. I think that
Martin's success in running the business did not endear him to the plaintiff, and
when Martin left, Mrs. Cullen thought in a vague way that the business was going
down because of the plaintiff's management. Throughout 1957, 1958 and the early
months of 1959, the plaintiff became more and more convinced of the rightness of
his views about his authority and, when they were not accepted, about the necessity
of demonstrating it in public and of securing its acknowledgement by his wife and
children: when it was not acknowledged, the ideas of persecution, maltreatment
and being robbed grew stronger. The plaintiff withdrew more and more into his
own world of fantasy; he attempted to assert his position by quarrelling with the
customers, by ordering them out, by refusing to accept goods brought to the

premises on the ground that he had not ordered them and, in every way he could, showing that he was the owner of the business.

I am satisfied that Seán, Martin and Patrick did not steal anything from the plaintiff. It may be that in early years they took some pocket money from the cash in the shop but they were being paid very little and the cash arrangements in business in country areas are very different from those which prevail in cities or towns. I cannot help thinking that Joseph's illness had far more to do with this domestic tragedy than any of the witnesses were prepared to allow.

The plaintiff gave evidence and, having heard his evidence, I am perfectly satisfied that he is now sane and he still has considerable business capacity. I think that he is now capable of managing the business at Adamstown, though the management will be somewhat erratic and stormy; but as he still has these views about the necessity for the acknowledgement of his authority, there is a risk that his condition of June, 1959, may revive if he returns to Adamstown when his wife is there.

During the case it was hinted on a number of occasions that the certificate of the 6th June, 1959, was the result of a conspiracy between Mrs. Cullen, Martin, Patrick and the doctors and that all of them knew that the plaintiff was sane at all times. I am satisfied that Mrs. Cullen was responsible for the request to the doctors to come to examine her husband and that though her sons may have known that she was going to do this, they did not attempt to influence the doctors in any way. I reject entirely the suggestion that there was any conspiracy between the doctors and Mrs. Cullen and the suggestion that the doctors knew that the plaintiff did not require treatment and that he was sane. I am satisfied that in June, 1959, the question of the plaintiff's authority was preying so much on his mind that he was suffering from a high degree of nervous tension which caused a temporary mental illness and that it disappeared when he had left the source of the stress which was his family. He still has the views, but it was the resistance to the views which produced the behaviour of June, 1959. Considerable support for this view is to be found in the fact that the plaintiff's relations with his sons who did not live at Adamstown became good when they left: thus his relations with Seán in connection with the running of the farm were good and his relations with Martin seem to be good until he got the idea that Martin was responsible in part at least for bringing the doctors to examine him.

In 1959 Mrs. Cullen wanted the business run by Patrick, Martin and herself as she did not consider the plaintiff fit to run it. She had complained to the doctors that her husband was interfering in the business; as the business was his, this shows that she thought he should be out of it. She did not seem to me to be a domineering woman. In the course of her evidence she said on a number of occasions that she wanted the plaintiff treated because she thought the business was going down. At the end of the case I suggested to counsel for the defendants that the production of the accounts of the business up to the 6th June would be helpful on this issue. I understand that the plaintiff has not got these accounts, but, when the matter was mentioned some time after the evidence had concluded, counsel for the defendants refused to produce the accounts or to allow me to inspect them if they were handed in. The grounds given in support of this attitude were not convincing. Mr. Liston made it clear that the plaintiff would welcome the accounts being handed in. I cannot make any finding on the question whether the business at Adamstown was going down in 1958 and in 1959 in the absence of these accounts but the refusal to allow them to be produced suggests to me that the accounts do not show the suggested reduction in business.

It is now necessary to take up the story of the events after the 6th June. The plaintiff came to Dublin where he met Father Kavanagh, a member of the Vincentian Order, who has been a lifelong friend of his. Father Kavanagh had him medically examined and was told that the plaintiff was sane. Father Kavanagh thought quite rightly that the main thing was to ensure the plaintiff's liberty by getting the order for his arrest withdrawn and that everything possible should be done to achieve this. On the 11th June a discussion took place in Dublin between Mr. Lawton (who I infer had been summoned to Dublin by Father Kavanagh), Father Kavanagh and the plaintiff, and, as a result, Mr. Lawton was authorised to tell Mrs. Cullen that the plaintiff was prepared to make over to her the place at Adamstown. Unfortunately Mr. Lawton was not told that he was to make it clear to Mrs. Cullen that the condition attached to this was that Mrs. Cullen, Martin and Patrick were to acknowledge in writing that the plaintiff was sane and were to take all necessary steps to have the order authorising his arrest withdrawn. Mr. Lawton returned to Enniscorthy on the 11th June and shortly afterwards went to see Mrs. Cullen. He told her that he came with a message from Father Kavanagh and that her husband was transferring his property at Adamstown and the money due in connection with the business to her but that she was not to touch the cattle on the land. He also told her that she should try to get the business going and when she said that she had no capital, he advised her to go to the Provincial Bank, to open an account and to lodge £400 from her own monies and to use the account to run the business. Mrs. Cullen subsequently lodged £403 to a bank account in her name and this account was used to run the business. There was also a discussion about a portable house which Mrs. Cullen had won in a competition organised by the 'Sunday Press'. I shall deal with this in a later part of the judgment. On the 17th June Father Kavanagh went to Enniscorthy to see Dr. Murphy, who was the plaintiff's regular doctor, and was apparently told that the plaintiff could still be arrested on the order which had been made. He came back to Dublin and told the plaintiff that he should get legal advice. The legal advice was that the plaintiff would have to insist on a written withdrawal of the allegations of mental instability and to this the plaintiff added the proviso that his authority as owner of Adamstown had to be recognised. As the negotiations were about the tranfer of Adamstown to Mrs. Cullen, it is difficult to understand why the plaintiff introduced the recognition of his authority as a condition of the transfer, but it provides another illustration that what mattered to the plaintiff was the acknowledgement of his authority. Father Kavanagh again saw Mr. Lawton in August and told him what Mr. Cullen required and this was passed on to Mrs. Cullen.

Since the 6th June Mrs. Cullen has been conducting the business at Adamstown and Martin and Patrick have been working for her. Patrick has been living in the premises all the time and Martin lived there until his marriage in August, 1960.

On the 14th September, 1959, the plaintiff's solicitor wrote to Martin Cullen, requiring him to leave the house at Adamstown and to give up any connection with the management of the farm and business. A similar letter was sent to Patrick and a letter was sent to Mrs. Cullen, requiring her to cease interfering with the business and telling her that her grown-up sons would not in any event be allowed to stay in in the house. Father Kavanagh carried on some further unsuccessful negotiations in an attempt to settle the differences. Mr. Lawton died in November, 1959. On the 18th June, 1960, the plaintiff commenced proceedings against Patrick and Martin, claiming an injunction to restrain them from interfering in the business and from trespassing on the property at Adamstown. An application by the plaintiff for an interlocutory injunction was refused by Mr. Justice Haugh on the 4th April, 1960.

Whatever be the position of children under 21 years of age who live in their father's house, those over 21 are licencees of their father when they are on property (including the family home) belonging to him. If the site of the bungalow is left out of consideration for the moment, the defendants were licencees of the plaintiff when they were on the premises at Adamstown and they had not any proprietary interest in them. As the licence which they had to enter and reside there was revoked by the letters of the 14th September, the grounds upon which it was sought to justify their continued presence on the premises have now to be examined. The first ground is that pleaded in para. 6 of the defence, which reads:

'As a further defence to the matters alleged in paragraphs 4 and 5 of the statement of claim the defendants say that in or about the month of August 1954 the plaintiff agreed with the second-named defendant, Martin Cullen, to hand over to him as from the 1st day of January 1955 the management of the said business at Adamstown save that the plaintiff would retain the sole right to sign cheques on the bank account relating to the said business. The second-named defendant accordingly managed the said business and with the approval of the plaintiff employed the first-named defendant therein and the defendants say that it was in pursuance of the said agreement that the defendants resided in the said dwelling-house and managed or worked in the said business. The said agreement was terminated by the plaintiff in or about the month of January 1958 when the plaintiff resumed the management of the said business but the plaintiff continued to employ the first-named defendant in the said business and permitted both the said defendants to reside in the said dwelling-house.'

The letters of the 14th September, 1959, written by the plaintiff's solicitor to both the defendants required them to leave the premises and were a termination of any contract of employment which existed between the plaintiff and the defendant, Patrick Cullen. The matters pleaded in para. 6 of the defence do not afford a justification of the defendants' presence on the premises.

A further justification is that pleaded in para. 7, which is in these terms: 'The defendants further say that in or about the month of June 1959 the plaintiff voluntarily left the said dwelling-house and went to reside in Dublin and subsequently in Enniscorthy and shortly after his departure informed or caused to be informed the said Sarah M. Cullen that he was making over and transferring to her his said property at Adamstown aforesaid absolutely and that she should open a new account in the Provincial Bank of Ireland, Enniscorthy Branch, in her own name for the purpose of the said business. The said Sarah M. Cullen accordingly opened such account and put to the credit thereof the sum of £400 out of her own money and applied the same for the purpose of carrying on the said business and thereafter carried on and still carries on the said business on the footing that she was legally or in equity entitled to the said property and has employed and still employs the defendants as assistants in the said business and authorised and permitted and still authorises and permits them to reside in the said premises in connection with their employment and the plaintiff was not on the 14th day of September 1959 and has not since been and is not now entitled to terminate and has not lawfully terminated the employment of the defendants or of either of them as such assistants or assistant or the right of the defendants or of either of them to reside on the said premises in connection with such employment.'

Mrs. Cullen is not a party to this action. At the end of the argument I suggested that she should be added as a party so that the claim pleaded in para. 7 could be dealt with. The plaintiff and the defendants declined to make any application to add Mrs. Cullen as a party but despite this I think that I must deal with this claim. I wish, however, to place on record that Mrs. Cullen was in Court throughout the hearing of the case and that she gave evidence for the defendants.

The plaintiff authorised Father Kavanagh to tell Mr. Lawton that he was going to transfer to Mrs. Cullen the place at Adamstown and every blade of grass on it and everything except the cattle on the lands and Mr. Lawton told her of this. It seems to me that this was a statement of intention by the plaintiff of what he proposed to do. He offered to do this because he wanted to retain his liberty and to avoid arrest under the order made under the Mental Treatment Act, 1945. Mr. Matheson has relied on the decision in *Dillwyn* v. *Llewelyn* ((1862) 4 De G.F & J. 517) as an authority for the proposition that the Court should now compel the plaintiff to transfer the lands and premises at Adamstown to Mrs. Cullen. The case is an authority for the proposition that a person claiming under a voluntary agreement will not be assisted by a Court of equity but that the subsequent acts of the donor may give the donee a ground of claim which he did not acquire from the original gift. In that case a father had told his son (the plaintiff) that he should live near him and had offered him a farm in order that the plaintiff might build a house: there was a written memo in which the father confirmed that it was his wish that his widow should give the lands to his son so that he would have a house. The plaintiff expended a large sum of money in building a house on the lands. Lord Westbury held that the making of the promise to give the lands coupled with the knowledge that the plaintiff had spent a considerable sum of money in building the house on the lands gave the plaintiff an equity to call on those claiming through the father to complete the gift. In this case, however, the only act relied on by Mrs. Cullen to create the equity is the putting of £403 into the business on Mr. Lawton's suggestion; she has, however, been in receipt of the profits of the business since the 6th June, 1959, and these are considerably more than the sum which she paid in. Moreover, the balance sheet of the business as at the 31st December, 1960, shows a sum of £680 16s. 2d. to the credit of the bank account (I assume that this is the bank account in her name) and she could at any time since January, 1960, have repaid out of her profits of the business the monies advanced by her. The equity referred to by Lord Westbury is a discretionary one and when I consider the circumstances in which the plaintiff made the statement that he was about to transfer the property at Adamstown to his wife and that he made it because he believed that it was the only way by which he could remain free, I have no doubt whatever that it would be grossly inequitable to regard Mrs. Cullen as being entitled to a transfer of the property at Adamstown or as having acquired any proprietary interest, legal or equitable, in the property as a result of what was said. The use by Mrs. Cullen of her own monies for the running of the business, particularly when she could have repaid this advance at any time, does not, in my opinion, create any claim in conscience or in equity which the Court should enforce or give any ground for disregarding the general principle that equity will not aid an imperfect gift. As Mrs. Cullen has no proprietary interest in the property the defendants cannot shelter behind her permission to them or her employment of them in the business. A further ground relied on was that the plaintiff made no provision for Mrs. Cullen when he left, that she had to run the business to provide maintenance for herself and that she was accordingly entitled to employ the defendants and to license them to reside in the premises. In the circumstances I think that she was entitled to conduct the business when the plaintiff left, but she had no authority to employ either of the defendants in the business or to license them to reside in the premises after the letters of the 14th September.

A further justification pleaded in para. 8 is that the plaintiff made an oral contract with Patrick Cullen in 1954 under which Patrick Cullen agreed to reside in the dwelling-house at Adamstown and to work in the business and that the contract has not been terminated by the plaintiff. There was no evidence to support this and I decline to infer such a contract.

There was no evidence that the defendants had ever excluded the plaintiff from the Adamstown premises or that they had refused to allow him to take part in the management of the business. I think that Patrick (who did not give evidence) ignored his father's orders in 1958 and 1959 and that he placed orders with suppliers without consulting him even though he had been told that he was not to do this. The defendants, however, are trespassers on the plaintiff's property at Adamstown and their continued presence on the property is a continuing trespass. The plaintiff asks for an injunction to restrain them from trespassing and the question whether such an injunction should issue has been the subject of my most anxious consideration; the delay in giving judgment has been due to this aspect of the case. A claim for an injunction by a father against his two adult sons to prevent them coming to what was – and what the father wants to be – the family home is certainly novel; there is no reported case in Ireland on the matter and, as far as I have been able to trace, the problem has not been considered by any of the Courts in the United States of America or in Canada. There are two decided cases on the matter in England.

When Mr. Liston was opening the case he said that the plaintiff wanted an injunction because he wished to return to his property at Adamstown without the fear of being certified under the Mental Treatment Act and because the plaintiff felt that this could not happen if his two sons were not excluded from the property. The defendants' presence on, or absence from, the property at Adamstown does not seem to me to have anything to do with the likelihood of the plaintiff being certified for temporary treatment under the Mental Treatment Act, 1945. Sect. 185 of that Act empowers the wife or a relative of the person to make an application for a temporary reception order and if a certificate is signed by two registered medical practitioners, certifying that the person to whom the certificate relates is suffering from mental illness and requires suitable treatment, the order for temporary reception may be made. This argument does not seem to me to justify the grant of an injunction.

The plaintiff's strongest ground for an injunction is that he is the owner of the property at Adamstown, that he wants his two sons excluded from the property because he wants to run the business and because, as he put it in his evidence, 'the children are a trouble to me and I do not want them'. Moreover, it is highly probable that the plaintiff's nervous tension and nervous condition of June, 1959, will revive if his sons are in Adamstown when he returns. He is not prepared to return so long as they are there and the refusal of an injunction will be a denial of his right of property in the premises at Adamstown.

Against the grant of an injunction it has been urged 1, that it would be inequitable to give an injunction because both the defendants have acted on the plaintiff's promise that he would make over the property at Adamstown to his wife; 2, that he who seeks equity must do equity and that the plaintiff, seeking the equitable relief of an injunction, must carry out his own promises; 3, that as the plaintiff is not seeking an injunction against his wife (which he could not get in any event), there should not be an injunction against the defendants; 4, that the plaintiff is quite free to return and run his business without interference by the defendants; 5, that the result of an injunction would be to cut off the defendants from social relations with their mother so that they could not visit her; 6, that Mrs. Cullen says that she is not prepared to live alone with her husband and that she wants somebody to stay in the house; 7, that if the plaintiff became ill the defendants could not take the risk of going to visit him or make any effort at reconciliation; 8, that neither of the defendants has ever claimed to be entitled to take part in the running of the business; and 9, that the grant of an injunction in this case would be contrary to the provisions of the Constitution dealing with the family.

There was no discussion about the general principles on which the Court decides whether an injunction should be granted or not except for a reference to the two cases in which the suitability of an injunction as a method of preventing a son from entering his parents' home was discussed. The Court has to consider the balance of convenience, but this weighing becomes difficult when the refusal of an injunction amounts to a denial of the plaintiff's right to decide who shall be on his property and the grant of an injunction is the intrusion by the Court into family and domestic relations which should be governed by affection, respect and the sense of moral obligation which all of us have and not by Court orders.

The Directors of the Imperial Gas Light and Coke Co. v. *Broadbent* ((1859) 7 H.L. Cas. 600) was a case in which the plaintiff sought an injunction to restrain a nuisance created by the manufacture of gas near his grounds. The Vice Chancellor granted an injunction and his order was affirmed by the Lord Chancellor, Lord Cranworth. The defendants appealed to the House of Lords and the Lord Chancellor, Lord Campbell, in the course of his opinion said (at p. 610): 'It is argued that it is highly inexpedient in this case to grant an injunction. Why, this is the very case for an injunction, because it is a case in which an action cannot sufficiently indemnify the party who is injured. How can he prove to a jury the exact quantity of pecuniary loss that he may have sustained? He may be able to show the value of the flowers and trees that have been destroyed, but how can he show the irreparable injury done to his trade by his customers leaving him, whom he may find it most difficult or impossible to get back.

'Then we are told that an action is to be brought, I know not how often, I suppose an annual action, that actions are to be multiplied indefinitely. I cannot but think that this would be a denial of justice to a person who has proved the injury he has sustained, especially when the party of whom he complains still obstinately persists in doing what produces effects so injurious to him'; and in the same case Lord Kingsdown said (at p. 612): 'The rule I take to be clearly this: if a plaintiff applies for an injunction to restrain a violation of a common law right, if either the existence of the right or the fact of its violation be disputed, he must establish that right at law; but when he has established his right at law, I apprehend that unless there be something special in the case, he is entitled as of course to an injunction to prevent the recurrence of that violation.'

The Chancery Amendment Act, 1858 (21 & 22 Vict., c. 27), better known as 'Lord Cairns's Act', had not been passed at the time when the *Imperial Gas Light and Coke Co. Case* ((1859) 7 H.L. Cas. 600) was commenced and was not referred to in the argument in that case. Sect. 2 of Lord Cairns's Act (which is in force in Ireland: see *Solomon* v. *Red Bank Restaurant, Ltd.* ([1938] I.R. 793) and *Leeds Industrial Co-operative Society, Ltd.* v. *Slack* ([1924] A.C. 851) provided: 'In all cases in which the Court of Chancery has jurisdiction to entertain an application for an injunction against a breach of any covenant, contract, or agreement, or against the commission or continuance of any wrongful act . . . it shall be lawful for the same Court, if it shall think fit, to award damages to the party injured, either in addition to or in substitution for such injunction', and s. 28 of the Supreme Court of Judicature (Ireland) Act, 1877, provided (so far as material): 'And whereas it is expedient to take occasion of the union of the several Courts whose jurisdiction is

hereby transferred to the said High Court of Justice to amend and declare the law
to be hereafter administered in Ireland as to the matters next hereinafter mentioned: Be it enacted as follows:

'(8) ... and if an injunction is asked, either before, or at, or after the hearing of
any cause or matter, to prevent any threatened or apprehended waste or trespass,
such injunction may be granted, if the Court shall think fit, whether the person
against whom such injunction is sought is or is not in possession under any claim of
title or otherwise, or (if out of possession) does or does not claim a right to do the
act sought to be restrained under any colour of title, and whether the estates
claimed by both or by either of the parties are legal or equitable.'

The effect of Lord Cairns's Act was explained by Lindley L.J. in *Shelfer* v. *City of
London Electric Lighting Co.* ([1895] 1 Ch. 287, at p. 315). He said: 'The jurisdiction to give damages instead of an injunction is in words given in all cases . . . but in
exercising the jurisdiction thus given attention ought to be paid to well settled
principles; and ever since Lord Cairns's Act was passed the Court of Chancery has
repudiated the notion that the Legislature intended to turn that Court into a
tribunal for legalising wrongful acts; or in other words, the Court has always
protested against the notion that it ought to allow a wrong to continue simply
because the wrongdoer is able and willing to pay for the injury he may inflict.
Neither has the circumstance that the wrongdoer is in some sense a public benefactor . . . ever been considered a sufficient reason for refusing to protect by injunction an individual whose rights are being persistently infringed . . . Lord Cairns's
Act was not passed in order to supersede legislation for public purposes, but to
enable the Court of Chancery to administer justice between litigants more effectually than it could before the Act ...

'Without denying the jurisdiction to award damages instead of an injunction,
even in cases of continuing actionable nuisances, such jurisdiction ought not to be
exercised in such cases except under very exceptional circumstances. I will not
attempt to specify them, or to lay down rules for the exercise of judicial discretion.
It is sufficient to refer, by way of example, to trivial and occasional nuisances: cases
in which a plaintiff has shown that he only wants money; vexatious and oppressive
cases; and cases where the plaintiff has so conducted himself as to render it unjust
to give him more than pecuniary relief. In all such cases as these, and in all others
where an action for damages is really an adequate remedy – as where the acts
complained of are already finished – an injunction can be properly refused. There
are no circumstances here which, according to recognised principles, justify the
refusal of an injunction . . .'

In *Colls* v. *Home and Colonial Stores, Ltd.* ([1904] A.C. 179) Lord Macnaghten
said, at p. 192: 'Then, with regard to giving damages in addition to or substitution
for an injunction – that, no doubt, is a delicate matter. It is a matter for the
discretion of the Court, and the discretion is a judicial discretion. It has been said
that an injunction ought to be granted when substantial damages would be given at
law. I have some difficulty in following out this rule. . . . But the recovery of
damages, whatever the amount may be, indicates a violation of right, and in former
times, unless there were something special in the case, would have entitled the
plaintiff as of course to an injunction in equity. I rather doubt whether the amount
of the damages which may be supposed to be recoverable at law affords a satisfactory test. In some cases, of course, an injunction is necessary – if, for instance, the
injury cannot fairly be compensated by money – if the defendant has acted in a
high-handed manner – if he has endeavoured to steal a march upon the plaintiff or
to evade the jurisdiction of the Court. In all these cases an injunction is necessary,
in order to do justice to the plaintiff and as a warning to others.' In the same case,

A Casebook on Irish Land Law

Lord Lindley said, at p. 212: 'The general rule that where a legal right is continuously infringed an injunction to protect it ought to be granted is subject to qualification, as was carefully explained by Sir George Jessel in *Aynsley* v. *Glover* (L.R. 18 Eq. 551 *et seq.*); and more recently by the Court of Appeal in *Shelfer* v. *City of London Electric Lighting Co.* ([1895] 1 Ch. 287).'

The decision of Buckley J. in *Behrens* v. *Richards* ([1905] 2 Ch. 614) is authority for the proposition that a successful plaintiff in an action for trespass is not entitled as of course to an injunction. *Waterhouse* v. *Waterhouse* (94 L.T. 133) is a decision of the same Judge. It was an uncontested application for judgment by a father claiming an injunction to restrain his son, aged 35, from entering his father's house. Buckley J. refused to grant an injunction and in the course of his judgment said: 'An injunction to restrain a trespass is not a matter of course. If a man intrudes into another man's house, or if a man having paid for a seat in the pit of a theatre insists on forcing himself into the stalls, the proper remedy is one much more simple than an application to this Court for an injunction. This plaintiff may, for aught I know, be entitled to such a remedy elsewhere if he has a case for it. But an injunction is a formidable weapon, to be used only when justified by such a state of facts as upon precedents and principles well established in this Court justify its application. Under circumstances, an injunction to restrain a defendant – even though the defendant be the plaintiff's son – from entering on premises would be right. But the facts alleged in this case are far from justifying an order that a son shall not enter his father's house. The duty of a father towards his son does not come to an end when, by reason of the latter having attained his majority or having reached a riper age, he may be properly called upon to provide for himself. Even when a child is an infant the parents' duty to provide maintenance and education is of imperfect obligation, and whether in a Court of law or of equity its direct enforcement may be difficult or impossible. But the duty arising from the relation of parent and child, whether directly enforceable or not, is a duty of which the parent can in no circumstances divest himself. The duty is not limited to providing maintenance during infancy or any other time. It is a duty so to conduct himself in all respects towards his child as is right in him, he being his father. For many purposes this Court deals with questions as between parent and child in manner different from that which would be applied between strangers in blood. The Court as between father and son regards not merely obligations which are legally enforceable, but obligations which arise from the relations between the parties – obligations which are not legal, but may be called moral. There may be cases in which a son by misconduct may have rendered it very difficult for his father to determine how properly to discharge his parental duty. But the duty remains. The son also has his duties, and the father is not only entitled, but ought to use every legitimate means to ensure that his son shall perform them. No misconduct of the son, however, can abrogate the duty of the father. There might be a case in which the father might be entitled (say for the proper discharge of his duty to others) to forbid his son even to enter his house. But except in very grave circumstances this Court would never make an order with the intent and result of severing the connection which ought to exist between parent and child. There are no facts alleged here upon which I should consider it right in this case, even if it could be right in any case, to make an order the result of which would be that, if the son came to see his father, the latter might apply to the Court to commit the son to prison for breach of an injunction. To use every legitimate means to induce or even to drive a man to conduct himself as a good son and a good citizen is, of course, right. But this is not a result which can be achieved by injunctions of this Court. The forces to be employed are those of education, example, influence, and guidance from childhood and throughout life.

These are matters in respect of which a father always owes the duty of a father to his sons. Apart from other considerations, it would be strange if a Court of Justice were to intervene with an order cutting the son off from his father.'

In *Stevens* v. *Stevens* (24 T.L.R. 20) Coleridge J. granted an injunction to a mother to restrain her son from breaking and entering her dwelling-house but, in doing so, he emphasised that the circumstances of the case were very grave.

In *Solomon* v. *Red Bank Restaurant, Ltd.* ([1938] I.R. 793) Johnston J. considered all the authorities on Lord Cairns's Act and remarked that the tendency of the more recent cases suggested a note of encouragement in favour of damages rather than an injunction.

After much consideration I have come to the conclusion that this is not a case in which an injunction should be granted against the defendants. I realise that I am denying the plaintiff one of the incidents of his fundamental right of property but I refuse the injunction because 1, it would make a reconciliation between the plaintiff and his sons impossible and would prevent them visiting him in an effort to restore more normal relations; 2, It would make it impossible for the defendants to visit their mother who is obliged to live with the plaintiff and would mean that she would have to leave her home in order to see them. 3, The defendants have never attempted to exclude the plaintiff by active steps from the control and management of his business. 4, The defendants have stated in Court through their counsel that they do not intend to prevent the plaintiff returning to the premises and that they do not intend to interfere with him in the conduct and management of the business. 5, Relations between fathers and their sons should not be governed by the heavy artillery of Court orders, injunctions or the threat of committal to prison, but by respect, affection, honour and the feeling of moral obligation. 6, There is a risk that the plaintiff's hostility to his wife may revive when he returns to Adamstown and somebody should be in the house to protect her. 7, The plaintiff is in control of the business at Enniscorthy and receives the grazing rents out of Adamstown.

Although an injunction is refused, the plaintiff is entitled to damages against the defendants for their continued acts of trespass. There was no evidence that the defendants received any of the profits of the business and I dismiss the claim for an account against them. I will award £50, damages, against the first-named defendant and £50, damages, against the second-named defendant for trespass.

I come now to deal with the ownership of the site on which the house, won by Mrs. Cullen in the competition in the 'Sunday Press', had been erected. However unfortunate the Cullens may have been in their domestic relations, they have been singularly fortunate in competitions; Seán had won a substantial prize in the Hospitals Sweepstake and in March or April, 1959, Mrs. Cullen had won a fully furnished portable house. She gave this house to Martin and the plaintiff knew this in April, 1959. Martin intended to erect the house on his lands at Coolnagreine and, when representatives from the 'Sunday Press' visited Adamstown in April, 1959, a site on his farm at Coolnagreine was selected. Shortly after this, Martin began to prepare the site for the house and did some work on the foundations. He had offered the house to his father before the 6th June, 1959, as he thought that his father did not approve of the position selected for it, but the offer was not accepted. When the plaintiff left Adamstown on the 6th June, Mrs. Cullen decided that she would like to have the house erected on the farm at Adamstown and, when she was speaking to Mr. Lawton, she told him this and sought her husband's permission for it. Mr. Lawton said that he did not see why the permission was necessary as the property at Adamstown would be transferred to her; she persisted and Mr. Lawton undertook that he would write to Father Kavanagh and would telephone to her when he got a reply. A few days afterwards Mr. Lawton wrote to Father Kavanagh who discussed the matter with the plaintiff. The plaintiff told him that it was not necessary to discuss the matter because he was making over the place at Adamstown to Mrs. Cullen and that she could put the house where she liked. This discussion took place on the 13th or 14th June. Father Kavanagh gave this information to Mr. Lawton who then telephoned Mrs. Cullen and told her that she could go ahead with 'the project as mentioned' and put the house up wherever she liked. Mrs. Cullen sent a message to Martin that he was not to go on with the preparation of the site on his farm and was to put up the house on the lands at Adamstown. He then stopped the preparation of the site on his own lands and began to work on a site for the house at Adamstown. He employed a man to work with him and spent about £200 in installing a water supply and building the foundations. The house arrived at the end of July and was assembled and erected in August. Some time after it was erected Martin heard that his father objected to its being placed at Adamstown and in August, 1960, Martin, who was about to get married, wrote to his father asking him to attend the wedding, and added: 'I am hoping that you will give me the site the bungalow is on and your blessing.'

I am satisfied that Martin would have erected the house on his own lands if the plaintiff had not given Mrs. Cullen permission to put up the house at Adamstown and that he erected the house on the lands at Adamstown because he relied on the permission given. I am convinced that the plaintiff knew at all times that Mrs. Cullen had given the house to Martin and that the house was being erected for Martin to live in. It would cost £700 at least to take it down now and lay foundations for it elsewhere; the cost of the decoration of the house which would be made necessary by its removal would be an additional £100. It has been submitted on the authority of *Ramsden* v. *Dyson* ((1866) L.R. 1 H.L. 129) that Martin Cullen has acquired a right to compel the plaintiff to transfer to him the site on which the house now stands. That case decides that if a stranger begins to build on land which he thinks is his and the real owner, seeing the mistake, abstains from correcting it and leaves him to continue, equity will not afterwards allow the real owner to assert his title to the land; but that if a stranger builds on land knowing it to be the property of another, equity will not prevent the real owner from claiming the lands afterwards. In this case, however, Martin knew that the land belonged to the plaintiff and his letter written in August, 1960, supports this view. In my opinion the argument based on *Ramsden* v. *Dyson* ((1866) L.R. 1 H.L. 129) is incorrect.

I am of opinion, however, that the plaintiff is estopped by his conduct in giving consent to the erection of the house at Adamstown when he knew that the house had been given to Martin and that the plaintiff cannot now assert any title to the site on which the house has been erected. There was a representation by him that he consented to this and that representation was acted on by Martin who spent £200 at least in erecting the house and gave a considerable amount of his time to this work. It seems to me that the principle stated by Denning J. in *Central London Property Trust, Ltd.* v. *High Trees House, Ltd.* ([1947] K.B. 130) and affirmed by the same Judge when he was a Lord Justice of Appeal in *Lyle-Meller* v. *Lewis & Co. (Westminster), Ltd.* ([1956] 1 All E.R. 247) applies to this aspect of the case and that the plaintiff cannot withdraw the permission which he gave for the erection of the house on the lands at Adamstown and cannot now assert a title to the site on which the house stands or to the house. While the estoppel created by the plaintiff's conduct prevents him asserting a title to the site, it does not give Martin a right to require the plaintiff to transfer the site to him: if I had jurisdiction to make such an order I would do so, but I do not think I have. However, neither the plaintiff nor any person claiming through him can now successfully assert a title to the lands on which the house is built by any proceedings and, at the end of the twelve-year period from the date when the erection of the bungalow commenced, Martin will be able to bring a successful application under s. 52 of the Registration of Title Act, 1891, for his registration as owner. If this case goes further, I hope that it will be held that I was wrong in deciding that I had no power to order the plaintiff to transfer the site to Martin. There is a claim in the pleadings that Martin has acquired a lien on the lands but this was not argued. I must accordingly dismiss the counterclaim.

There will be judgment on the plaintiff's claim for £50, damages, against Patrick Cullen and for £50, damages, against Martin Cullen, both up to this date.

I have considered the question of costs. The plaintiff claimed an injunction and has failed on that part of his claim. Much of the time which the hearing of the action took was caused by the case made by the defendants that the plaintiff was obliged to transfer the premises and lands at Adamstown to Mrs. Cullen. That case and the counterclaim have failed. I will award the plaintiff one half of the costs of the action and I will award the defendants the costs of the motion for the interlocutory injunction: the two sets of costs will be set off against each other and the balance due will be certified by the Taxing Master. There will be no costs of the counterclaim. I will give a certificate that it was reasonable to commence these proceedings in the High Court owing to the important nature of the action.

Notes and Questions
1. Do you agree with Kenny J.'s suggestion that the son, if he remained in possession, would acquire title under the Statute of Limitations (as to which see Ch.14, *post*)? See *Irish Land Law*, para. 20.10. Cf. *McMahon* v. *Kerry County Council* [1981] I.L.R.M. 419; *Murphy* v. *Murphy*, p. 696, *post*; *Bellew* v. *Bellew* [1982] I.R. 447, [1983] I.L.R.M. 128.
2. On the application of the doctrine of estoppel, see also *Revenue Commissioners* v. *Moroney* [1972] I.R. 372; *Irish Land Law*, para. 20.07 *et seq.*
3. On the subject of licences generally, see *ibid.* para. 20.02 *et seq.* See also *Bellew* v. *Bellew* [1982] I.R. 447, [1983] I.L.R.M. 128.

II. RIGHTS OF RESIDENCE

NATIONAL BANK LTD. V. KEEGAN
[1931] I.R. 344; 66 I.L.T.R. 101 (Supreme Court)

By a memorandum of agreement, made in 1915, between C.K. and his aunt, M.K., C.K. agreed to give M.K. 'during her life the exclusive use of the drawing-room and bedroom over same, with fuel and suitable support and maintenance', in a certain dwelling-house, 'free of charge, the consideration for same being natural love and affection and services rendered' by M.K. to C.K.; and C.K. thereby agreed with M.K. 'to execute a deed whenever called upon to carry out and give effect to the foregoing contract'. No deed was ever executed pursuant to the said agreement. The agreement was not registered in the Registry of Deeds. M.K. went into exclusive occupation of the two rooms, and so continued, and was supplied with fuel and maintenance. The rest of the house was in the occupation of C.K., who held the premises under a fee-farm grant. In 1921 C.K. deposited the title deeds of the premises with a bank by way of equitable mortgage to secure the payment of present and future advances. In 1927 C.K. being indebted to the bank for a large sum, the bank issued a summary summons to enforce the mortgage against C.K. M.K. claimed to be entitled under the agreement to an equitable life interest in the two rooms, and also to a charge on the whole of the premises in her favour for fuel and suitable support and maintenance during her life, and that the bank's equitable mortgage was puisne to her life interest and charge. She stated in an affidavit that on the faith of the agreement, and on the security of the rights thereby conferred on her, she had from time to time made advances to C.K. of sums amounting to £252. The manager of the bank stated in an affidavit that at the date of the deposit the bank had no knowledge of any claim by M.K. against the premises. Johnston J. held that M.K. was entitled to an equitable life interest in the two rooms, which was not subject to the bank's equitable mortgage. He also held that M.K. was entitled to a charge on the premises for fuel and support and maintenance. An appeal was made to the Supreme Court.

Kennedy C.J.:

This is a mortgage suit instituted by summary summons, issued on the 27th January, 1927, to enforce an equitable mortgage by deposit of title deeds made by the defendant on the 3rd August, 1921, with the plaintiff bank to secure all moneys when due, or thereafter to become due, by the defendant to the bank.

The mortgaged property comprised a dwelling-house and plot of ground in Freemarket, in the occupation of the defendant, with a yard and garden at the rear, situate in that part of the town of Moate called Newtown, and County of Westmeath, held under a fee-farm grant, dated 26th March, 1862.

The documents deposited with the bank by way of mortgage consisted of the original fee-farm grant, under which the property is held, and the original of a conveyance of the property in the year 1887 to one, Patrick Keegan, who died intestate in the year 1909, when the property descended to the defendant as his heir-at-law.

The primary decree in the suit was made on the 24th May, 1928, when the defendant did not appear, and was not represented. The decree stated the amount of the debt then due on the security of the equitable mortgage to be £619 4s. 3d. for principal and £104 4s. 8d. for interest. The usual order for sale in default of payment was made, and the usual accounts and inquiries were directed, and referred to the Examiner.

In Chambers the claim was made by one, Mary Keegan, to be entitled to an equitable interest and charge in priority to the plaintiffs' mortgage. At the request of the plaintiff bank the Examiner put the case in the Judge's list on a memorandum, dated 4th February, 1930, for the purpose of obtaining a decision of the Judge disallowing the claim of Mary Keegan to be in priority to the plaintiffs' claim under the equitable mortgage. This appeal is taken by the plaintiff bank against the order of Johnston J., made on the 7th April, 1930, on the hearing of the memorandum, when he ruled against the claim of the bank.

The claim of Mary Keegan, who is an aunt of the defendant, is founded on an instrument made under the hand of the defendant on the 27th September, 1915, and witnessed by a solicitor. It is necessary that I should read the document in full. [Reads document.]

No deed was in fact ever executed pursuant to the agreement, nor was the agreement registered in the Registry of Deeds.

Mary Keegan, however, went into exclusive occupation of the drawing room and bedroom mentioned in the agreement, and has continued in such occupation ever since. She claims to be entitled under the instrument, in the first place, to an equitable life interest in the specified rooms in the premises, and, secondly, to a charge on the whole of the dwelling-house and premises in her favour of fuel, and suitable support and maintenance during her life, and that the plaintiffs' equitable mortgage is 'puisne', or subject to the life interest and charge she claims.

In her affidavit, filed on the 11th January, 1929, Mary Keegan states that, on the faith of the agreement and on the security of the rights conferred on her by the instrument, she has from time to time made advances to the defendant of sums of money, now amounting in all to £252.

There is no evidence, nor has any suggestion been made, that at the time when he executed the instrument in favour of his aunt the defendant was otherwise than solvent, or that he was unable to meet his creditors, or that there was any fraud involved in the transaction, or that the agreement was intended to defeat existing or future creditors.

At the time of the equitable mortgage to the bank (3rd August, 1921), that is to say, nearly six years after the execution of the instrument in favour of Mary Keegan, the defendant owed the bank some £1,211. He then made the deposit, which comprised, with the title deeds I have mentioned, some shares or other property.

By means of payments on account and by sale of the other property, or part of it, at the date of the institution of the suit the principal debt had been reduced to the sum of £619 4s. 3d.

The bank contends that Mary Keegan should have: (1) registered the agreement in the Registry of Deeds; (2) got in the legal estate in her two rooms by a legal conveyance; and (3) got over possession of the title deeds from the defendant. It was contended that, by reason of her omission to do all or any of these things, she has been guilty of negligence and of laches, which have prejudiced the bank, and deprived her of the right to set up her equitable estate and charge. The bank also contends that Miss Keegan has not, by virtue of the instrument, any estate or interest in or charge on the property.

Johnston J., by the order under appeal, declared that Mary Keegan is entitled, under and by virtue of the agreement of the 27th September, 1915, to an equitable estate for life in the drawing room and bedroom over same in the dwelling-house, the subject-matter of the suit, and that such equitable estate for life is not subject to the plaintiffs' equitable mortgage by deposit of title deeds; and the Judge further declared that Mary Keegan is entitled under and by virtue of the agreement to a charge upon the said lands and premises for fuel and suitable support and maintenance in the said dwelling-house in priority to the plaintiffs' equitable mortgage.

Counsel for the bank have challenged not only the Judge's decision on the question of priority, but also his decision on the construction and effect of the agreement. It is unfortunate that we have not had the assistance of an argument on Mary Keegan's behalf. Her solicitor attended at the opening of the appeal to inform the Court that Mary Keegan was unable to be represented owing to want of means.

The construction and effect of the instrument of 27th September, 1915, must be considered first, before we come to the question of postponement. The instrument presents two problems, viz.: first, as to the residential right, and, second, as to the right of support. The residential rights, which are so commonly given in farm holdings in this country, especially by way of testamentary provision for testators' widows, also frequently by the reservations of rights in settlements made on the marriage of sons, are of two types, namely, the type which is a general right of residence charged on the holding usually coupled with a charge of maintenance; and the type which is a particular right of residence created by reserving or giving the right to the exclusive use during life of a specified room or rooms in the dwelling-house on the holding. The general right of residence charged on a holding is a right capable of being valued in moneys numbered at an annual sum, and of being represented by an annuity or money charge. It is clear that such is not the type of benefit given by the instrument before us. Here we have the second type of case, in which the exclusive use during her life of a specified part of the holding comprising two rooms is given to the beneficiary. If this benefit were given her by a deed or a will, I think that it is clear that she would hold an estate for life in the property, legal or equitable, according to the terms of the instrument. The document of the 27th September, 1925, is an executory agreement to grant such a life estate or interest, and to perfect it by a deed if called for, and Mary Keegan went into immediate occupation and enjoyment of the premises, and took, and has held, exclusive possession thereof ever since (a period of twelve and a half years, up to the primary decree in this suit, to which she was not then a party). In my opinion, Johnston J. rightly held that Mary Keegan is entitled to an equitable estate for life in the two rooms mentioned in the agreement.

The second problem under the agreement is the question as to her right to 'fuel and suitable support and maintenace in the dwelling-house free of charge'. Johnston J., by his order, declared that this right amounted to an equitable charge on the lands and premises. He does not, however, refer to this question in his written considered opinion, which is so full on every other branch of the case. I regret this, because I have not been able to find in the agreement anything to support a charge of the fuel, support, and maintenance agreed to be given to Mary Keegan. In my opinion, if she had called for a deed, she would not have been entitled under the terms of the agreement to ask for anything more than a covenant on the part of the defendant in respect of the fuel, support, and maintenance which he agreed to give her, and she could not have required to have the benefits under the covenant charged on the house and premises. I do not agree, therefore, with so much of the order under appeal as declares Mary Keegan entitled to a charge for fuel, support, and maintenance. In my opinion, therefore, the question of priority only arises with reference to the life interest in the two rooms, and I will consider it as limited to that subject-matter.

I come now to consider the three grounds urged for postponing Miss Keegan's life interest in the premises, and making it subject to the equitable mortgage of the plaintiff bank.

One of these grounds is that she should have got possession of the title deeds which would have prevented the creation of a mortgage by deposit. No authority was cited in support of the proposition which the bank is really driven to submit for the purpose of this argument, viz.: that the owner of an equitable interest in a part of property is entitled to get from the legal owner of the whole the title deeds to his legal estate in the whole. Since it is patent that she had no such right, the case of negligence in omitting to get the deeds into her possession falls to the ground.

The bank then falls back on negligence and laches founded upon Miss Keegan's omission to call for a legal conveyance by deed, and her omission to register the agreement in the Registry of Deeds. It seems to me that the bank in making such a case ignores the facts and the true issue between the parties. The bank's mortgage is a mere equitable deposit, a transaction especially devised to avoid the Registry of Deeds, and to create a good equitable charge, with the right to call for a conveyance by way of legal mortgage (which if registered might have prevailed over Miss Keegan's equitable interest). Miss Keegan has an unregistered equitable estate or interest, with a right to call for a legal conveyance by deed; the bank has an unregistered equitable mortgage, with a right to call for a legal mortgage by deed. The issue is, therefore, between two unregistered equitable interests, taking them as they are found to be, and the onus is on the bank to displace the application of the rule of equity – that the first in time shall prevail. If the bank puts it to a competition of equitable merits, it seems to me that the two parties are on a parity in respect of those merits brought in question, registration and legal conveyance, but the prior equity of Miss Keegan is greatly enhanced by being coupled with actual possession and enjoyment of the premises for a substantial period of time, upwards of twelve years; while the second equity suffers on a comparison of merits by the bank's omission to inquire into the rights and claims of those in actual possession of the property in the deposited deeds. Such inquiry would have revealed Miss Keegan's occuption of part of the property under claim of right, if not already known to the bank manager, as one might well have expected him to know in the case of a client for a number of years in a small country town, a client permitted to borrow to a substantial amount before he was required to give security.

I see no reason for displacing Mary Keegan's priority in time. In my opinion, she is entitled to an equitable life estate in the two rooms, which interest is not subject to the plaintiffs' equitable mortgage. In so far as the order of Johnston J. so declares it should be affirmed; but, so far as it declares that there is a charge on the premises for fuel, support, and maintenance, it should, in my opinion, be reversed.

FitzGibbon J.:

I have read the judgment which has just been delivered, and I agree with it.

Murnaghan J.:

Christopher Keegan was entitled to the grantee's interest, under a fee-farm grant arising upon the conversion of a lease for lives renewable for ever, when he executed the memorandum of agreement, dated 27th September, 1915. I do not accept the argument that this document was merely an incomplete promise. *Manning* v. *Saul* (26 L.R. Ir. 640) shows that words like 'hereby agrees to give' may amount to an assignment if the intention of transferring possession be manifest. As to whether or not the agreement was voluntary, I think on the evidence before us it was: because, assuming, as the memorandum recites, that the consideration was natural love and affection, and services rendered by Mary Keegan to Christopher Keegan, these services may have been past voluntary services, and not services for which Mary Keegan was at law entitled to claim payment.

An agreement of an informal kind should be construed so as to carry out the intention of the parties, as ascertained from the document and the surrounding circumstances. What passed according to the language employed as reasonably construed? The words are: 'the exclusive use of the drawing-room and bedroom over same, with fuel and suitable support and maintenance in the dwelling-house . . . free of charge'. Did this mean an assignment of the rooms for the life of the grantee? If it did, she could let these rooms, and introduce strangers into her nephew's dwelling-house. In my opinion, the words meant a personal use, a personal right of residence in the dwelling-house, for which residence the aunt was assigned the exclusive use of the two rooms specified. A grant of the use of premises may pass the estate in the lands, but the meaning of the word 'use' is flexible, and may be controlled by circumstances. It seems to me that the addition of the words 'with fuel and suitable support and maintenance' indicates that the right of residence was a personal one, as it is, I think, admitted that no one was entitled to support and maintenance except Mary Keegan. In my opinion, the memorandum created an equitable charge upon the premises both for residence and support, and did not amount to an assignment.

There remains the point whether such an equitable right is postponed to a subsequent equitable charge by reason of the failure of the donee to register the charge. The ground upon which this contention is based is that the first chargeant should be postponed because the failure to register is such negligence as to make it inequitable for the charge to maintain its priority. To accept such a doctrine between successive equitable chargeants would result in setting up in priority the latest equity, although it, too, was unregistered.

Greer v. *Greer* ([1907] 1 I.R. 57), which was cited, did not deal with the priorities of equitable chargeants, nor was there in *In re Ffrench* (21 L.R. Ir. 283) a question between equitable rights.

In my opinion, no authority can be brought forward in support of the proposition that an equitable right loses its priority because the person entitled has failed to register his equitable charge.

Notes

1. See the discussion in *Irish Land Law*, para. 20.13 *et seq*. See also *Murphy* v. *Murphy*, p. 696, *post*.
2. On the question of priorities, see further p. 84, *ante*.

III. CONACRE AND AGISTMENT

DEASE V. O'REILLY
(1845) 8 Ir. L.R. 52 (Queen's Bench)

Land was tilled and prepared by A., a tenant for life, and allotted by him, at a certain rate per acre, in small portions to his labourers for the purpose of planting potatoes. All the labour was done at his expense; the potatoes were planted by the labourers and above ground. When A. died, the remainderman prevented the labourers carrying off the crop until they had paid him the rate so agreed upon. The question arose whether the money payable under the contract was 'rent' and therefore apportionable under the apportionment statutes. Brady C.B. held that it was and an appeal was made to the Queen's Bench.

Crampton, J.: delivered judgment of the Court:

[His Lordship having stated the facts of the case proceeded to say]: The main question is, whether a con-acre holding as described in the bill of exception, amounts in legal construction to a holding under a demise, or to a tenancy.

Now, it is plain that the tenancy of a con-acre holder (if any) is not a tenancy from year to year, neither can it be a tenancy of any higher species – it is not a tenancy for half a year either, or for any determinate period – can it be a tenancy at will? No; for the contract cannot be legally terminated at the will of one of the parties only. There is not, in fact, any exclusive right to the party in the con-acre holding – from the time of the contract until the potato planting begins, the possession remains with the landlord; and from that time, although a special possession for a particular purpose is with the con-acre holder, the general possession remains with the landlord. If this be a tenancy, it may be asked, when does it begin, and when does it end? It is said, it begins with the planting, and ends with the digging out of the potatoes. But if so, some part of each man's portion is held for one period, and some for another. For the potatoes are planted from time to time, and they are dug out in like manner and carried away according to the wants or convenience of the owner. It would seem to me that such a contract is not a demise of the land, but a sale of a profit to be derived from the land, a temporary easement, and not an estate in the land; and this view coincides with the doctrine laid down in *Co. Litt.* 10 *b*, where we find it is said that a grant of *vesturam terræ* does not pass the land; the grantee has only a particular right in the land; he has not the houses, the timber trees, mines, or other real things: and this is also the view taken of the subject by Baron Pennefather, in the case of *Close* v. *Brady* (Jones & C. 186), who considers the con-acre dealing as not creating a tenancy, but being only a mode of farming the land.

But secondly, suppose the con-acre holder to be a tenant, then his estate is cut short by the death of his landlord, the tenant for life, and he is entitled to his emblements, as his landlord's executors were for the crops planted by their testator, and growing at his decease. Then, whether there be a tenancy, or whether there be no tenancy, in this case we are of opinion there can be no apportionment. It follows, that the exception must be allowed and a *venire de novo* awarded.

Note
1. See also *Booth* v. *McManus* (1861) 12 I.C.L.R. 418 at 435–6 (*per* Pigot C.B.), *Irish Land Law*, para. 20.26. *Cf.* the views of modern judges in the two cases following.
2. See generally on the subject of conacre and agistment, *Irish Land Law*, para. 20.25 *et seq.*

COLLINS V. O'BRIEN
[1981] I.L.R.M. 328 (High Court)

The plaintiff advertised the letting for grazing of 46 Irish acres of land at Ballinamona, Bulgaden, Co. Limerick. The letting, which was by public auction, took place on 23 March 1979 and the defendants bid of £162 per acre was accepted. The sale was conducted on the usual basis of the eleven months system for grazing lettings although no written or oral term was stipulated by the auctioneer as to the date of termination. The plaintiff maintained that the letting came to an end on the 31 December 1979. There was evidence to the effect that such lettings customarily terminated in the area on that date. Early in January 1980, the plaintiff instructed her solicitors to write to the defendant requiring him to vacate the lands. On 7 February 1980 the defendant did vacate the lands under protest although he maintained that the letting continued until 22 February 1980. The plaintiff claimed for the use and occupation of the lands from 1 January 1980 to 7 February 1980 while the defendants counterclaimed for the loss of the use and enjoyment of the lands from the 7 February 1980 to 22 February 1980 at the rate of £21 per day.

At the trial evidence was given by an auctioneer on behalf of the plaintiff that the phrase 'eleven months system' was descriptive of custom and that, in that part of County Limerick, grazing lands were always vacated on 31 December in any year no matter when the letting commenced, in order to allow the lands to recover for the following year. Evidence was given on behalf of the defendant that, when the lands were let for grazing on the eleven month system, the purchaser was entitled to keep his cattle on the lands for the full eleven months no matter when the letting commenced unless there was a specific term in the letting agreement to the contrary. The price of £162 per acre would have been a fair price for a letting for eleven months and if the defendant had to vacate the lands on 31 December 1979 he would be paying at the rate of £222.75 per acre for eleven months grazing, which sum had never been reached in such lettings. The Circuit Court judge decided that the letting came to an end on 31 December 1979 and gave a decree to the plaintiff and dismissed the counterclaim. Defendants appealed.

Doyle J.: delivered his judgment on 14 October 1981 saying: This is a difficult case to decide because there is no memorandum or note in writing relating to the transaction. A few words on a sheet of paper may have avoided litigation. A grazing letting is a licence to use the lands of another and usually the letting is for less than twelve months. It does not amount to a tenancy: *In re Moore's Estates Ltd., Fitzpatrick* v. *Behan* [1944] I.R. 295. Similarly a letting in conacre is a licence to put in a crop, grow it, dig it, and take it away. In both grazing and conacre lettings the terms of the agreement customarily follow the natural seasons and, in the case of grazing lettings, the parties usually adopt the eleven month system. I accept the evidence of Mr. Quish, auctioneer, when he says that in such lettings it is not unusual for the letting to end on the 31 December of any given year.

Mr. Lee has referred me to the case of *Crane* v. *Naughton* [1912] 2 I.R. 318 in which the plaintiff, who was possessed of freehold lands, instructed an auctioneer to put up for sale by public auction the grazing of a certain portion of those lands for a period of six months. In pursuance of such instructions the auctioneer duly offered the grazing for sale and accepted the bid of the defendant. In the course of his judgment Gibson J. said:

> What is the nature of the contract here? When parties to a contract reduce it to writing nothing can be added to, or taken from, the writing; it speaks for itself and is final and conclusive. But the document required by the Statute of Frauds is of a different character. It is a memorandum of what the contract is. Accordingly, if the memorandum is not in accordance with the true contract it is a bad memorandum. . . . The contract here purports to be a contract for a grazing for a definitive period. The reason for the formula of eleven months has come to be used is because if twelve months were put in for a grazing letting there is a special section of the Land Act, 1881, s. 16, which says that that would be a yearly tenancy. That fact shows that the eleven months is a term in such letting that relates to tenancy of land. The contract therefore comes within s. 4 of Deasy's Act [*Landlord and Tenant Act*, 1860] and, being for less than a year, need not be in writing.

Usually the agreement is, however, reduced to writing which embodies dates for the commencement and termination of the period of grazing. In the present case, on the death of her husband, the plaintiff decided on a clearance sale of her cattle and farm implements by public auction and on the letting of the grazing of her 46 Irish acres. The date of the auction, which was 23 March 1979, was an unusual date for the commencement of a grazing letting. In *Crane* v. *Naughton* (supra) the date was also unusual as the advertisement in the local press stated that it was to be from 9 October 1911 to 1 April 1912. In the present case there is nothing in writing as to when the letting was to end. The conclusion to which I have come is that the plaintiff thought the term was from 23 March 1979 until 31 December 1979. The defendant believed that it was from 23 March 1979 until 22 February 1980. The parties were thus never *ad idem* and so there was no contract between them. In those circumstances I have to ask myself: what would a Court of Equity allow? I approach the case as if on a claim for quantum meruit. If the defendant had taken the grazing from a date in or about the middle of January 1979 to end on 31 December of that year the price for the grazing would be £162 per acre. The plaintiff has not discharged the onus of proof which rested on her to show that, in the circumstances, the term ended on 31 December 1979. The defendant enjoyed the grazing only from 23 March to 7 February 1980 when he was forced to vacate the lands. He lost 15 days grazing and I will give him a decree on his counterclaim for £315 being 15 days at the agreed figure of £21 per day.

Note

See further *Irish Conveyancing Law*, para. 9.009 *et seq.*

MAURICE E. TAYLOR (MERCHANTS) LTD. V. COMMISSIONER OF VALUATION
[1981] N.I.J.B. 236 (Court of Appeal)

The Commissioner of Valuation refused to omit from the valuation list as agricultural buildings under article 2(1)(a) of Schedule 1 to the Rates (Northern Ireland) Order 1977 two buildings occupied by the company at Draperstown, County Londonderry. The company carried on business as a shipper of seed and ware potatoes. Some of these potatoes were grown on about 100 hectares of land taken in conacre by the company. As the land around Draperstown was not suitable, land situated between Moneymore and Dungannon, some of it 10 to 20 miles away from the buildings in question, was taken. These buildings consisted of a dressing shed and a store. The dressing shed was used solely for grading, sorting, bagging and labelling potatoes grown by the company. No potatoes from any other grower were stored in the shed except for a day or two while a consignment was awaiting transport to the docks. The only regular storage in the store was of boxed seed potatoes for future planting by the company except that consignments of potatoes for shipment were put under cover overnight when frost was threatened. The company appealed to the Lands Tribunal which held that the buildings should be omitted from the valuation list as agricultural buildings.

A case was stated to the Court of Appeal and the main judgment was given by Gibson L.J., part of which is reproduced here.

Gibson L.J.:

. . . The land which is claimed to be occupied with the buildings comprises in each year about 100 hectares, the situation and area of which varies from year to year. They are used by the company for the growing of seed potatoes for export. The business which the company carried on is, inter alia, that of a shipper of seed and ware potatoes. Of the total tonnage shipped by the company in each year approximately 12 per cent to 15 per cent is grown by the company on the land so taken and the remainder is purchased from other growers. No part of the land on which the company grows potatoes is owned or leased by it. Unfortunately the land around Draperstown is not scab free, and in order to grow a scab free crop of potatoes it is necessary for the company to take land a considerable distance from Draperstown, and as potatoes should only be grown on a rotation basis the company is driven to take different plots of land each year to grow its crop. The land is invariably taken from different landowners in conacre. It is agreed that the company occupies the dressing shed and store within the meaning of the order, that is to say, in a rating sense, but the fact that the company holds these plots of land as a conacre tenant raises the question whether the plots are also so occupied by it.

Conacre letting is a system of agricultural land tenure which is, I believe, peculiar to Ireland. It has long existed side by side with the other traditional means of letting agricultural land, namely, by tenancy from year to year, and the legal consequences have always been recognised as very different. The reason why conacre lettings came into existence is, I think, to be found in the social and economic condition of the agricultural peasants in Ireland till about 100 years ago. They were in many cases landless, living a hand to mouth existence close to the poverty line. The staple diet was potatoes and, having no money to purchase them, they had to be grown by the peasants themselves. What, therefore, was needed, was a means whereby they could cultivate on the lands of others a crop of potatoes sufficient for the consumption of themselves and their families. The system of conacre letting was devised as one which admirably protected the rights of the landowner and yet which was designed to provide the necessary food for the tenant, who was frequently a labourer employed by the landowner. In its original form the landowner would designate to each conacre tenant a strip of land, already ploughed and manured, sufficient to provide the necessary number of drills of potatoes, or occasionally some other green crop. The tenant was given access to the land for the period necessary to plant, cultivate and harvest the crop, usually 11 months, but did not own the crop until, at the end of the letting, he had paid for it, either in money, by a share of the crop or in labour. See *Booth* v. *McManus* (1862) 12 I.C.L.R. 418, *per* Pigot C.B. at page 436. He was then free to remove the crop and his concern with the land ended. The advantage to the landlord was obvious in that he secured the benefits of a normal letting in return for the use of the land and yet had absolute security, because the crop could not be removed until the indebtedness had been discharged. From a legal point of view also, the practice had considerable advantages for the landlord over a normal letting. He remained in legal ownership and possession of the land and so enjoyed the parliamentary franchise which in those days depended on occupation of property. Also, the right which a tenant from year to year had to compensation for disturbance by his landlord and for improvements made by the tenant was excluded in the case of a conacre tenant by section 15 of the Landlord and Tenant (Ireland) Act 1870. Further, the prohibition against subletting by tenants from year to year did not prevent their making conacre lettings (see section 2 of the Land Law (Ireland) Act 1881), and by section 5 of the same Act a conacre tenant had none of the protective rights conferred on a statutory tenant.

From a rating point of view it is clear from the authorities that the landowner or tenant from year to year was invariably regarded as the occupier of the land farmed by others in conacre and was therefore rated under the Poor Law Act. In this connection it is important to remember that in the 19th century rateable occupation was regarded as restricted to occupation whether by the owner or by a lessee of the land. Judges in the last century were in some difficulty in classifying the interests of a conacre tenant. Pennefather B. in *Close* v. *Brady* (1838–39) Jo. & Car. 187 in common with several other judges regarded a letting in conacre as merely a mode of tilling the land, and the rent as but part of the produce of the land. Crampton J. in *Dease* v. *O'Reilly* (1844) 8 I.L.R. 52 considered a conacre letting as constituting only the sale of a profit to be derived from the land, a temporary easement. The view that it was in the nature of an easement was voiced also by some of the members of the court in *McKeowne* v. *Bradford* (1862) 7 Ir. Jur. (N.S.) 175. Another view was that it was a profit a prendre, but, whatever its character, all were agreed that it conferred neither legal possession nor rateable occupation on the conacre tenant.

The whole concept of conacre lettings has during the last 100 years undergone a radical change. No longer do the original considerations have any practical application, and with their disappearance have gone the early features which I have outlined. Nowadays it would be practically unknown for there to be a conacre letting of a small strip or area of ground having no obvious physical boundaries. The areas now correspond with the areas of fields or farms. The landowner no longer ploughs the land or provides the manure and he no longer reserves any right to exercise any control over or protection of the land, except in so far as the tenant may only grow one crop, is often obliged to fertilise the land and is required to vacate the land at the end of the term. The owner now merely has a claim in debt for the rent, and no longer has any lien or charge on the crop or right to prevent its removal. In perhaps most cases, as for example, where the farmer has retired or dies leaving a widow living in the house on the farm, the same land is let in conacre or agistment year after year, often to the same person, and in that case whether he vacates the land for a month is of little importance to the owner. In not a few cases, as, for example, where the owner is in America, the lettings are made for long periods, occasionally by a single contract to the same tenant, and apart from any special covenants in the agreement no rights are reserved or exercised by or on behalf of the owner over the land during the period of the conacre or agistment agreements.

The terms on which the company takes the lands for the growing of potatoes in this case illustrate the modern practice in so far as it is expressly found as a fact that the conacre landlord is, under the agreements, not to enter upon the land nor to permit anyone else to do so during the period of the take, and not to undersow the potato crop, nor make any other use of the land.

Leaving aside for the moment the fact that the company has the right to be on the land for only 11 months, I am satisfied that the decisions of the Irish courts in the last century to the effect that a conacre tenant is not in occupation of the land for rating or other purposes have been overtaken both by the change in the nature of conacre lettings and also by the law.

The facts found by the Lands Tribunal establish that the company has exclusive occupation of the various plots for the purpose of growing and harvesting the potatoes. It also has the right to exclude all other persons, including the owners of the land, from the lands taken during the period of the take. Whereas, in earlier days, the landowner retained paramount occupation of the land, it is now clear that if there is any question of paramount occupation, which would only arise in the case of some rather exceptional contract, it now resides in the tenant.

Secondly, from the legal point of view the theory that a conacre agreement does not create a tenancy is so well established and embedded in our statute law that it cannot now be questioned. Yet the old notion that rateable occupation could only be found in the owner or lessee of the land has now disappeared from our law . . .

Notes and Questions
1. To what extent do you think Gibson L.J.'s analysis reflects changes in practice in the Republic? To the extent that it does, what are the legal consequences? Conacre and agistment may be more common in the North, see *Irish Land Law*, para. 20.27, fn. 98.
2. Do you think that Gibson L.J.'s analysis should be confined to the issue of rating valuation?

Chapter 14
ADVERSE POSSESSION

This has proved to be a most controversial subject on both sides of the Irish Sea in recent times and the Irish judges have not always seen eye-to-eye with English judges on fundamental issues: see *Irish Land Law*, ch. 23.

STATUTE OF LIMITATIONS, 1957
Actions to recover land

13. – (1) (*a*) subject to paragraphs (*b*) and (*c*) of this subsection, no action shall be brought by a State authority to recover any land after the expiration of thirty years from the date on which the right of action accrued to a State authority or, if it first accrued to some person through whom a State authority claims, to that person.

   (*b*) An action to recover foreshore may be brought by a State authority at any time before the expiration of sixty years from the date on which the right of action accrued to a State authority.

   (*c*) Where any right of action to recover land, which has ceased to be foreshore but remains in the ownership of the State, accrued when the land was foreshore, the action may be brought at any time before the expiration of sixty years from the date of the accrual of the right of action, or of forty years from the date on which the land ceased to be foreshore, whichever period first expires.

(2) The following provisions shall apply to an action by a person (other than a State authority) to recover land –

   (*a*) subject to paragraph (*b*) of this subsection, no such action shall be brought after the expiration of twelve years from the date on which the right of action accrued to the person bringing it or, if it first accrued to some person through whom he claims, to that person;

   (*b*) if the right of action first accrued to a State authority, the action may be brought at any time before the expiration of the period during which the action could have been brought by a State authority, or of twelve years from the date on which the right of action accrued to some person other than a State authority, whichever period first expires.

(3) For the purposes of this Act –

   (*a*) where a right of action to recover any land accrued to the Crown before the 6th day of December, 1922, the right of action shall be deemed to have accrued to a State authority on the date on which the right of action first accrued to the Crown;

   (*b*) where a right of action to recover any land accrued to Saorstát Éireann before the 29th day of December, 1937, the right of action shall be deemed to have accrued to a State authority on the date on which the right of action first accrued to Saorstát Éireann:

   (*c*) where a right of action to recover any land accrued to the State before the operative date, the right of action shall be deemed to have accrued to a State authority on the date on which the right of action first accrued to the State.

· · ·

18. – (1) No right of action to recover land shall be deemed to accrue unless the land is in the possession (in this section referred to as adverse possession) of some person in whose favour the period of limitation can run.

(2) Where –

(*a*) under the foregoing provisions of this Act a right of action to recover land is deemed to accrue on a certain date, and

(*b*) no person is in adverse possession of the land on that date,

the right of action shall not be deemed to accrue unless and until adverse possession is taken of the land.

(3) Where a right of action to recover land has accrued and thereafter, before the right of action is barred, the land ceases to be in adverse possession, the right of action shall no longer be deemed to have accrued and no fresh right of action shall be deemed to accrue unless and until the land is again taken into adverse possession.

(4) For the purposes of this section –

(*a*) possession of any land subject to a rentcharge by a person (other than the person entitled to the rentcharge) who does not pay the rentcharge shall be deemed to be adverse possession of the rentcharge, and

(*b*) receipt of the conventional rent under a lease by a person wrongfully claiming to be entitled to the land in reversion immediately expectant on the determination of the lease shall be deemed to be adverse possession of the land.

. . .

24. – Subject to section 25 of this Act and to section [49 of the Registration of Title Act, 1964 – see *infra*], at the expiration of the period fixed by this Act for any person to bring an action to recover land, the title of that person to the land shall be extinguished.

REGISTRATION OF TITLE ACT, 1964
Title under Statute of Limitations

49. – (1) Subject to the provisions of this section, the Statute of Limitations, 1957, shall apply to registered land as it applies to unregistered land.

(2) Where any person claims to have acquired a title by possession to registered land, he may apply to the Registrar to be registered as owner of the land and the Registrar, if satisfied that the applicant has acquired the title, may cause the applicant to be registered as owner of the land with an absolute, good leasehold, possessory or qualified title, as the case may require, but without prejudice to any right not extinguished by such possession.

(3) Upon such registration, the title of the person whose right of action to recover the land has expired shall be extinguished.

(4) Section 24 of the Statute of Limitations, 1957, is hereby amended by the substitution, for 'section 52 of the Act of 1891', of 'section 49 of the Registration of Title Act, 1964'.

PERRY V. WOODFARM HOMES LTD.
[1975] I.R. 104 (Supreme Court)

The northern extremity of the plaintiff's property was bounded by a laneway which ran from east to west; a narrow strip of ground adjoined the northern side of the laneway. In 1955 the plaintiff entered into adverse possession of portion of the strip of ground, and he continued in such possession without acknowledging the title of any person to that portion. In 1955 the strip of ground (with other lands) was held by a lessee under a lease which created a term of 999 years from the 29th September, 1947. In October, 1970, the lessee purported to assign the strip of ground to the defendants for the residue of the said term; and a month later the lessors conveyed to the defendants the fee-simple estate in the strip of ground. The defendants claimed to be entitled to the possession of the strip of ground, including the portion used by the plaintiff, on the basis that the leasehold interest in the said portion of the strip had been determined by merger on the acquisition by the defendants of the fee-simple estate. The plaintiff issued a plenary summons in the High Court and claimed an injunction restraining the defendants from entering upon the portion of the strip used by the plaintiff. At the trial of the action it was held by O'Keeffe P., in granting a perpetual injunction, that, assuming that there could be a merger of part of the lands demised by the lease, no interest in the plaintiff's portion of the strip was vested in the defendants by the assignment of 1970 since the title of the assignor had been extinguished by the effect of the adverse possession and the operation of the statute and, therefore, the lessee's interest in that portion did not merge in the fee-simple estate acquired by the defendants. The defendants appealed to the Supreme Court.

Walsh J.:

The history of the facts which preceded the action instituted in the present case is so fully and adequately set out in the judgment of the learned President of the High Court, against which the present appeal is taken, that I need not refer to them.

The Statute of Limitations, 1957, provides at s. 13, sub-s. 2, that a person, other than a State authority, cannot bring an action to recover land after the expiration of 12 years from the date on which the right of action accrued to the person bringing it or, if it first accrued to some person through whom he claims, to that person. Section 24 of the Act of 1957 provides that, subject to s. 25 of that Act (which applies to equitable estates in land and to land held in trust) and to s. 49 of the Registration of Title Act, 1964, at the expiration of the period fixed by the Statute of 1957 for any person to bring an action to recover land the title of that person to the land shall be extinguished. The Irish Life Assurance Co. Ltd. which had a leasehold interest in the land which is the subject matter of these proceedings failed to bring any action to recover possession of the same over a period of 12 years during which the plaintiff was in possession of that land to which he had then no title. The 12 years had expired by the 1st December, 1967. On the 5th October, 1970, Irish Life purported to assign their interest in the leasehold premises to the defendants. The defendants subsequently acquired the freehold interest and the registration of their title to the freehold interest was not completed until the 17th December, 1970.

The defendants claim that, upon the acquisition by them of the fee simple interest, the leasehold interest which had originally been vested in Irish Life merged in the freehold and was extinguished. The vital question in the present case is whether or not Irish Life had any leasehold interest at the date of their purported assignment to the defendants because, if Irish Life had no leasehold interest at that date, there could be no question of a merger in the freehold simply because the defendants had subsequently acquired the fee simple.

In support of this claim the defendants relied in the High Court, and in this Court, upon the majority decision of the House of Lords in *St. Marylebone Property Co. Ltd.* v. *Fairweather* ([1963] A.C. 510). In that case the owners of the freehold took what purported to be a surrender from a person claiming to be the holder of a leasehold interest in the lands in question. Prior to the purported surrender the lessee had been out of possession for more than 12 years and the land was in the possession of a squatter. In that case the House of Lords, sitting as a court of four members, decided by a majority that the surrender had determined the leasehold interest and that the owner in fee was entitled to recover possession because the effect of the surrender had been to extinguish the squatter's rights. The effect of the majority judgment in that case was that the passage of time in the corresponding provision of the English Limitation Act only destroyed the lessee's title to recover possession from the squatter and did not affect the lessee's title in relation to anybody else, and that the leasehold interest remained vested in him. The dissenting judge in the *Fairweather Case* ([1963] A.C. 510) was Lord Morris of Borth-y-Gest who took the view that the surrender was ineffective because the lessee had nothing to surrender and, therefore, there could not be any question of the leasehold interest being extinguished so as to give the owner of the fee simple an immediate right to possession. This view commended itself to the learned President of the High Court.

In my view, the defendants, in relying upon the majority decision of the House of Lords in support of their submissions, are asking the Court to hold that s. 24 of the Statute of 1957 does not mean what it says. That section says quite clearly that after the expiration of the period fixed 'the title of that person to the land shall be extinguished'. The interpretation sought to be put upon this is that it simply reads that the right of the person to recover possession of the land shall not be enforceable but that his title to the land itself remains unaffected. That is to equate it with the position which existed formerly in respect of actions for the recovery of chattels which actions, after the expiration of six years under the Common Law Procedure Act, could not be enforced although the title to the goods still remained in the original owner. However, the Statute of 1957 has now provided at s. 12 that the title of the person to the chattel shall be extinguished. There can be no ambiguity about that and it is clearly designed to bring chattels into line with the law relating to land.

In the case of land, the effect of the Statute is to destroy the title of the person dispossessed to the estate from which he has been dispossessed, but it does not destroy the estate itself. The creation of a leasehold estate constitutes in effect an encumbrance upon the freehold the effect of which, so long as the leasehold estate survives, is to prevent the freeholder from entering into possession of the land in question save in accordance with the terms of the lease. The fact that the title of the lessee to the lease is destroyed leaves unimpaired the existence of the lease and, therefore, it leaves unimpaired the encumbrance upon the freehold which prevents the freeholder from repossessing the lands during the continuance of the lease. In my view, a person who has lost all his title to a leasehold estate is not in a position to deal effectively with that estate and, therefore, he has nothing to surrender and nothing to assign. A person who takes a purported assignment or a purported surrender of a leasehold estate cannot be in any stronger position or have any better title than the person making the purported assignment or surrender. Therefore, I am satisfied that the effect of the Statute of 1957 is that Irish Life had no estate or interest to assign to the defendants and, therefore, the question of a merger could not arise when the defendants subsequently acquired the freehold estate.

It is correct to say that the position of the freeholder cannot be prejudiced by the dispossession of the leaseholder by the squatter, and that means that the freeholder is entitled to the benefit of any covenants and is entitled to enforce them against the land. The squatter cannot be disturbed from his possession by the landlords for the duration of the term of the lease but, on the other hand, while the lease did not pass to him by assignment, the squatter may be indirectly forced to carry out the covenants to preserve his possession from ejectment by forfeiture for non-observance of the covenants. The contractual relationship between the lessee and the owner in fee simple remains and the lessee remains liable upon such covenants which may be enforced against him personally by the lessor, if the lessor so chooses. However, in so far as re-entry for breach of covenant may be affected, if that takes place the squatter may be dispossessed, but it will be because of the breach of covenant and not because of any right on the part of the dispossessed lessee to deal with the property. The owner of the fee cannot sue the squatter on foot of the covenants or for the payment of the rent reserved by the lease because there is no privity between them. But because of the threat of re-entry hanging over the squatter in the event of failure to pay rent or to observe the covenants, the lessor is effectively in no worse position than he would have been with the original lessee. In fact he may find himself in a stronger position in so far as he can hold the original lessee to the terms while at the same time he is in a position to enforce indirectly all the covenants against the squatter by the threat of re-entry, if the lease provides for re-entry in the event of failure to observe the covenants.

Furthermore, the lessor is not in danger of having his own title extinguished by the possession of the squatter because the time would only begin to run as from the date or event at which the lessor would be entitled to call for possession. In the case of a continuing leasehold estate that position would not arise until the end of the term demised. I do not find any difficulty in appreciating the distinction between a lessee losing his title to the leasehold property on the one hand and the continuous existence of the lease itself as against the owner in fee of the other.

I think it is well established, and the authorities referring to this point are mentioned by Mr. Justice Griffin in the judgment he is about to deliver, that the effect of the Statute of Limitations, in so far as unregistered land is concerned, is that there is not a statutory conveyance or assignment of the estate to the squatter. The position would, however, appear to be different so far as registered land is concerned. Section 49 of the Registration of Title Act, 1964, provides that, subject to the provisions of that section, the Statute of 1957 shall apply to registered land as it applies to unregistered land. The section then goes on to provide at sub-s. 2 that where any person claims to have acquired a title by possession to registered land he may apply to the registrar to be registereed as owner of the land and the registrar, if satisfied that the applicant has acquired the title, may cause the applicant to be registered as owner of the land with an absolute, good leasehold, possesory or qualified title (as the case may require) but without prejudice to any right not extinguished by such possession. It also provides that upon such registration the title of the person whose right of action to recover the land has expired should be extinguished. This would appear to permit a squatter to have himself registered in the Land Registry as the owner of a leasehold, being registered land, where the squatter has dispossessed the registered owner of the leasehold.

For the reasons I have given I am of opinion that the judgment of the learned President of the High Court was correct and that the injunction which he granted should be confirmed and that this appeal should be dismissed.

Henchy J.:

The small plot of ground in question in this case lies at the back of the plaintiff's house. He never got any paper title to it but he has been in exclusive possession of it since about 1955, without paying any rent or giving an acknowledgement of title to anybody. The paper title to it was a lease of the 27th November, 1947, by which the plot (as part of a larger area) was leased for 999 years. By an assignment dated the 5th October, 1970, the defendants acquired that leasehold interest but, as far as the plot was concerned, the assignment was no use to them for it is agreed that the plaintiff had acquired, as against them, a title by adverse possession. However, the defendants took a conveyance of the fee simple on the 5th November, 1970, and the defendants say that, as a result, the leasehold interest has merged in the fee simple, that the title acquired by the plaintiff was valid only against the leasehold interest, and that now that the leasehold has been wiped out by the merger they, as owners of the fee simple, are entitled to possession.

The defendants have signified their intention of taking over the plot for building purposes, so the plaintiff has begun these proceedings to stop them doing so. He applied in the High Court for an interlocutory injunction to restrain them and, the parties agreeing to have that application treated as the hearing of the action. Mr. Justice O'Keefe granted the plaintiff a perpetual injunction restraining the defendants from using the plot. It is from that order that the defendants appeal to this Court.

It is a net question of law: who is entitled to possession? To answer that, it is first necessary to see what right the plaintiff had acquired at the end of the twelve-year period of limitation. Section 24 of the Statute of Limitations, 1957, says that 'at the expiration of the period fixed by this Act for any person to bring an action to recover land, the title of that person to the land shall be extinguished'. Since the lessee was the person entitled to bring an action to recover the plot in question, it was the lessee's title that was extinguished. The Statute of 1957, like its predecessors, is silent as to what was acquired by the plaintiff.

Whatever may be the legal result when the intention of the dispossessor was merely to oust and replace a tenant or lessee, or when it can be said that by estoppel the dispossessor has acquired an interest in the land identical with that formerly owned by the dispossessed person, I think the authorities both in Ireland and England make it clear that in a case such as this, where the adverse possession has been unqualified, there is no question of the Statute of Limitations having the effect of a parliamentary conveyance of the leasehold interest to the plaintiff: see *O'Connor* v. *Foley* ([1906] 1 I.R. 20) and the judgments, in the Court of Appeal and in the House of Lords, in *St. Marylebone Property Co. Ltd.* v. *Fairweather* ([1963] A.C. 510).

I consider that, immediately before the defendants took a conveyance of the fee simple, the position between the plaintiff and the defendants was that the plaintiff had acquired an unqualified right against the defendants as lessees to remain in possession, and that the defendants' title was totally extinguished. As between the defendants and the owners of the fee simple, nothing had changed. The lease, with all its rights and duties, was unaffected except that the lessees were irrevocably barred from recovering the plot from the plaintiff. The paramount title remained in the owners of the fee simple, whose right fo recover possession would not accrue to them until the lease came to an end, either by effluxion of the term demised by the lease or by the exercise of the proviso for re-entry contained in it. Therefore, so long as the lease existed, neither the lessor nor the lessee could oust the plaintiff from possession of the plot.

What change, then, in the plaintiff's right to possession has been effected now that the lease has disappeared on its merger in the fee simple? The only possibilities would appear to be these:-

1. *The plaintiff is now entitled to the leasehold interest or an interest equivalent to the leasehold interest.*

This is the solution for which counsel for the plaintiff contends but, as I have already indicated, it is not legally possible. In the last century, on the authority of cases such as *Rankin* v. *McMurtry* ((1889) 24 L.R. Ir. 290), it was thought that the effect of the Statute of Limitations was to execute, as it were, a parliamentary conveyance to the dispossessor of the dispossessed's interest in the land. However, in England since *Tichborne* v. *Weir* ((1892) 67 L.T. 735) and in Ireland since *O'Connor* v. *Foley* ([1906] 1 I.R. 20), it has been generally accepted that the effect of the Statute of Limitations is merely negative and divestitive. Those cases, where the operation of the statute was held to vest in the dispossessor the leasehold or tenancy interest of the dispossessed person, or its equivalent, are cases where that result arose, not from the operation of the statute, but from the conduct of the parties. For example, of the four judges who decided in *Rankin* v. *McMurtry* ((1889) 24 L.R. Ir. 290) that the dispossessor had acquired the leasehold interest of the dispossessed leaseholder, two held that this arose by estoppel. I know of no case in Ireland or England where it was held that a person had acquired by adverse possession the lease or tenancy or its equivalent, unless he showed, by at least paying the rent, that he wished to stand in the shoes of the ousted tenant or leaseholder. Even if it could be held in this case that the plaintiff had acquired the leasehold estate, that estate has now disappeared on its merger in the fee simple. Therefore, I reject the submission that the plaintiff, who has never paid rent for the plot, is entitled to the leasehold estate or its equivalent.

2. *The plaintiff is now entitled to the fee simple in the plot.*

In effect, that is what Mr. Justice O'Keefe held, because he granted a perpetual injunction restraining the defendants, who have the paper title to the freehold, from entering on the plot. That is tantamount to saying that, although the defendants are the registered owners of the folio which includes the plot, they are forever barred from making any use of it. I am unable to find any basis for concluding that the ouster of the leaseholder by the operation of the Statute of Limitations could also result in the extinction of the title of the owners of the fee simple. By making the lease of the 27th November, 1947, for the term of 999 years, the owners of the fee simple put the plot out of their reach for the duration of the lease. In the events that have happened, the soonest the Statute of Limitations could have started to run against the owners of the fee simple would have been when the lease merged in the fee simple. I am unable, therefore, to see how the title of the owner of the fee simple could be said to be extinguished or that it could be said to be vested in the plaintiff. Even counsel for the plaintiff does not so contend.

3. *The defendants are entitled to the fee simple in the plot subject to the right of the plaintiff to retain possession of it until the expiration of the period of the lease, i.e., 999 years from 1947.*

This possibility rests on the theory that at common law, on the surrender of a lease to the freeholder or on the merger of the lease in the freehold, an underlessee continues to be protected from eviction. This is undoubtedly true of underleases but, as Lord Denning pointed out at pp. 546–7 of the report in *St. Marylebone Property Co. Ltd.* v. *Fairweather* ([1963] A.C. 510), this is because on the merger of the lease in the freehold or on its surrender to the freeholder the lessee is not allowed to derogate from his grant so as to prejudice the underlessee. This principle, however, has no application to a squatter. If it had, it would mean that in the present case the position of the plaintiff as squatter would be vastly improved as a result of the merger; and the position of the freeholder, against whom the plaintiff never prescribed, would be vastly worse. Since the lease was wholly extinguished on the merger, the defendants as freeholders could not recover rent or sue on the covenants or enforce the proviso for re-entry, whereas the plaintiff and his successors could enjoy the plot rent-free for the unbroken residue of the term of the 999 year lease, free from the risk (which they ran before the merger) that they could be ousted if events entitled the freeholders to enforce the proviso for re-entry. It seems to me to be inequitable and contrary to first principles that, as a result of the merger of the leasehold in the fee simple, the rights of the freeholders should be reduced and those of the squatter who had displaced the lessee should be enlarged. I am satisfied that nothing has happened that would vest in the plaintiff as squatter an unqualified right to retain possession of the plot until the expiration of 999 years from the commencement of the lease in 1947.

4. *The defendants have become entitled since the merger of the lease in the freehold to a right to recover possession of the plot.*

This seems to be the only remaining possibility, and I believe it to be the correct one. If, before the merger, the freeholders had become entitled to determine the lease under the proviso for re-entry, I fail to see how in those circumstances the plaintiff could have resisted a claim by the freeholders to recover possession of the plot. Now that the lease has been determined by its merger in the freehold (a result which the President of the High Court doubted but which has been conceded in this Court) it is not, in my judgment, possible to maintain that the legal result is any less than if the lease had been determined under the proviso for re-entry. As to the conclusion that the squatter's right to possession is wiped out by such an eventuality, I would respectfully adopt what Lord Denning said at p. 548 of the report in *St. Marylebone Property Co. Ltd.* v. *Fairweather* ([1963] A.C. 510): '...I must say that I see no difference between a surrender or merger or a forfeiture. On each of those events the lease is determined and the freeholder is entitled to evict the squatter, even though the squatter has been on the land during the lease for more than 12 years: and on the determination of the lease, time then begins to run against the freeholder'.

In my opinion, therefore, it follows that a right to possession of the plot accrued to the defendants when the leasehold merged in the freehold in 1970. Accordingly, I would allow the appeal, discharge the injunction and dismiss the plaintiff's claim.

Griffin J.:

It is conceded by the defendant that, by reason of 12 years adverse possession against the Irish Life Assurance Company, the plaintiff has acquired a statutory title in respect of that part of the land of which he has been in possession. It is also conceded that the interim injunction was properly granted because the defendants were not at that time registered as full owners of the land now comprised in folio 18621 of the register of freeholders for the county of Dublin.

Shortly stated, the point at issue in this appeal is whether the plaintiff can restrain the defendants from entering upon the plot of land in dispute or whether Irish Life, as lessees under a long lease whose own title had been extinguished by 12 years adverse possession by the plaintiff, could validly assign to the defendants; and whether the defendants, as assignees of the lessee's interest in the lease, by acquiring the fee simple in the land, could enable the lease to be determined by merger and the plaintiff, as squatter, to be dispossessed.

Prior to the passing of the Real Property Limitation Act, 1833, the statutes then in force barred only the remedy and not the right. Section 34 of the Act of 1833 effected a radical change by providing that at the determination of the period limited by the Act to any person for making an entry or bringing any action, *the right and title* of such person to the land was *extinguished*: the period was then 20 years. By s. 1 of the Real Property Limitation Act, 1874, the period for a person to make an entry or to bring an action to recover land was limited to 12 years next after the time at which the right to make such entry or bring such action first accrued to him or to some person through whom he claimed. The Act now in force is the Statute of Limitations, 1957. Under s. 13, sub-s. 2(a), of the Statute of 1957 no action to recover land shall be brought after the expiration of 12 years from the date on which the right of action accrued to the person bringing it or, if it first accrued to some person through whom he claims, to that person. Section 15, sub-s. 1, of the Statute of 1957 provides that where the estate or interest claimed was an estate or interest in reversion or remainder or any future estate or interest and no person has taken possession of the land by virtue of the estate or interest claimed, the right of action to recover any land shall be deemed to have accrued on the date on which the estate or interest fell into possession by the determination of the preceding estate or interest. By s. 24 of the Statute of 1957 it is provided that, subject to s. 49 of the Registration of Title Act, 1964, the title of a peron to land shall be extinguished at the expiration of the period fixed by the Statute of 1957 for that person to bring an action to recover the land.

The argument made on behalf of the defendants may be summarised as follows. The freehold interest to which the defendants became entitled on registration was an estate or interest in reversion or remainder or, alternatively, a future estate within the meaning of s. 15, sub-s. 1, of the Statute of 1957 and, therefore, their right of action only accrued on the determination of the preceding estate or interest which was the lease dated the 27th November, 1947. The defendants said that, as they had acquired by assignment the leasehold interest on the 5th October, 1970, it followed that upon the registration of the defendants as full owners of the land a merger took place as the term and the immediate reversion were then vested in them at the same time; they relied on the majority decision of the House of Lords in *St. Marylebone Property Co. Ltd.* v. *Fairweather* ([1963] A.C. 510) as authority for this proposition.

On the other hand the plaintiff contends that the object of all statutes of limitation is to prevent claims which, although originally valid, must be considered as extinguished where ancient possession is to be clothed with the right and 'to quiet the possessors of land in the estates which they had long enjoyed'. The plaintiff also contends that the effect of s. 13, sub-s. 2, and s. 24 of the Statute of 1957 is to destroy the title of the leaseholder and he relies on a series of Irish cases, starting with *Rankin* v. *McMurtry* ((1889) 24 L.R. Ir. 290), which he submits are inconsistent with *Fairweather's Case* ([1963] A.C. 510) and with *Tichborne* v. *Weir* ((1892) 67 L.T. 735) and he says that the Irish cases should accordingly be followed. The plaintiff also submits that, even if these Irish cases are not followed, the dissenting judgment of Lord Morris of Borth-y-Gest in *Fairweather's Case* ([1963] A.C. 510) is correct and that there was nothing to surrender or merge in the fee simple and that, accordingly, no merger took place in the present case.

In the (English) Limitation Act, 1939, there are provisions similar to the relevant portions of our Statute of 1957 to which I have referred.

Prior to 1892, it was fairly widely accepted in both England and Ireland that the effect of s. 34 of the Real Property Limitation Act, 1833, for all practical purposes, was to convey the estate of the ousted person to the squatter. In *Doe d. Jukes* v. *Sumner* ((1845) 14 M. & W. 39) Parke B. at p. 42 of the report said: 'The effect of the Act is to make a parliamentary conveyance of the land to the person in possession after that period of twenty years has elapsed.' Lord St. Leonards in *Incorporated Society* v. *Richards* ((1841) 1 Dr. & War. 258) and again in *Scott* v. *Nixon* ((1843) 3 Dr. & War. 388), referred to the statute as executing a conveyance or operating as a statutory transfer.

These dicta received the approval of the Queen's Bench Division in *Rankin* v. *McMurtry* ((1889) 24 L.R. Ir. 290) where Johnson J., in dealing with s. 34 of the Real Property Limitation Act, 1833, said at p. 297 of the report: 'The title of a former owner of a leasehold is absolutely barred; he cannot thereafter dispossess the wrong-doer, who can set up the statute against him, but not against the landlord, whose rights are not affected; he can dispose of it by will, whether fee-simple, freehold, or chattel; if he dies intestate, if chattel, it forms part of his assets for administration: *Re Williams* ((1886) 34 Ch. D. 558); and, on the principle decided in *Scott* v. *Nixon* ((1843) 3 Dr. & War. 388), he can sell and convey *inter vivos*, and the title will be forced on an unwilling purchaser.' Holmes J., having stated that he was somewhat unhappy about the expression 'a parliamentary conveyance', said at p. 301 of the report: 'But whatever be the mode of transfer, I am of opinion that the estate and interest, the right to which is extinguished, so far as the original owner is concerned, became vested in the person whose possession has caused such extinction. The opposite conclusion would seriously affect lease-hold tenancies in this country.' Counsel for the plaintiff submits that this case was correctly decided but that it is of no real significance in the present case whether there is a transfer or not.

In *Tichborne* v. *Weir* ((1892) 67 L.T. 735), a decision of the Court of Appeal in England upon which the defendants rely, the dispute had not arisen until after the expiration of the term limited by the lease, and the question which arose for decision was whether the person who had been in possession adverse to the lessee for a number of years was liable on the covenants in the lease after the expiration of the term and after he had gone out of possession. It was held that he was not so liable and the court refused to accept the notion of a parliamentary conveyance as being good law. At p. 737 of the report Bowen L.J. said that the effect of the Act of 1833 was not only to bar the remedy but also to extinguish the title of the person out of possession, and that in that sense the person in possession held by virtue of the Act and not by a fiction of a transfer of title. *Tichborne* v. *Weir* ((1892) 67 L.T. 735) has since been accepted as good law in England and as burying there, once for all, the notion of a parliamentary transfer or conveyance.

The question was considered by the Irish Court of Appeal in *O'Connor* v. *Foley* ([1906] 1 I.R. 20) and FitzGibbon L.J. expressed the view that the dicta of Lord St. Leonards and of Lord Wensleydale when applied to the fee were practically correct. At p. 26 of the report FitzGibbon L.J. said: 'But they have since been quoted in several Irish cases, and applied literally to limited estates, and in particular to tenancies, and I am not prepared to uphold *dicta* in which they so appear against the decision of the Court of Appeal in *Tichborne* v. *Weir* ((1892) 67 L.T. 735) that, though a right is extinguished, and a right is given, *there is not a transfer of a right* by possession for the statutory period.' At p. 39 Holmes L.J. said: 'I have said on a former occasion that the reference to a conveyance is not happily conceived. I prefer to hold that, although there is not a direct transfer to the wrong-doer who has been in possession, yet the title gained by such possession is limited by rights yet remaining unextinguished, and is commensurate with the interest which the rightful owners lost by the operation of the statute, and has the same legal character. This opinion has been universally held in Ireland' – and he cited *Rankin* v. *McMurtry* ((1889) 24 L.R. Ir. 290); *Mulcaire* v. *Lane-Joynt* ((1893) 32 L.R. Ir. 683); *MacCormack* v. *Courtney* ([1895] 2 I.R. 97]; and *In re Hayden* ([1904] 1 I.R. 1). This statement of Holmes L.J. was accepted as 'the more correct view' by Dixon J. in *Bank of Ireland* v. *Domvile* ([1956] I.R. 37, 58). Later, in *In re Ryan, Maher* v. *Harte Barry* ([1960] I.R. 174, 179) Dixon J. said: 'It is not so much a question of interests having been acquired as of rights having been lost. I do not wish to answer the question in a way which would suggest that the Limitation Act effected a transfer of property.'

In *Fairweather's Case* ([1963] A.C. 510), where the ousted lessee purported to surrender to the freeholder, the majority decision of the court (Lord Morris of Borth-y-Gest dissenting) was that an owner in fee simple who held land subject to a term of years had an estate or interest in reversion or remainder and that, accordingly, his right of action against a squatter was deemed to have accrued at the date when the preceding estate or interest (represented by the term) determined in such manner that his estate or interest fell into possession; and the court held that the effect of the extinguishment sections of the Limitation Act was that, when a squatter dispossessed a lessee for the statutory period, it was the lessee's title *as against the squatter* that was finally destroyed and not the lessee's right or title *as against the freeholder* and, accordingly, that the lessee was in a position to surrender to the lessor, that the lease was 'determined' by the surrender made in 1959 by the ousted lessee, and that the freeholder thereupon became entitled to possession of the demised property.

I am unable to accept that, in providing that at the expiration of the period fixed by the Statute of Limitations, 1957, for any person to bring an action to recover land the title of that peron to the land shall be extinguished, the legislature intended that such extinguishment should take place only as against the squatter and not as against the freeholder. If the majority decision in *Fairweather's Case* ([1963] A.C. 510) is to be followed here, it would have a very far reaching effect. Until comparatively recent years, raising representation in the case of small farms was quite rare, the occupiers preferring to rely on the Statute of Limitations, and there must be very few agricultural holdings in this country in which at some time in the past 140 years a tenancy was not 'acquired' under the statute. Again, leases for 999 years (such as the lease of 1947) are now quite common and the effect of this decision is that by collusion between the lessee and the freeholder, the successors in title of a squatter on leasehold land can be ejected however long the lessee has been out of possession – be it 12 years, 120 years or 900 years. It seems to me that such a result would entirely defeat the object of the Statute of Limitations.

Having regard to the opinion hereinafter expressed as to the ability of an ousted lessee to surrender or effect a merger, it is not necessary for the purpose of this case to decide what right, if any, has been gained by the squatter by reason of the title of the lessee having been extinguished. Nevertheless, it seems to me that, though there is no statutory transfer or conveyance to the squatter, what the plaintiff (as squatter) has gained is the right to possession of the premises in dispute as against the defendants (as fee-simple owners) for the unexpired portion of the term of the lease, subject to the risk and the possibility of a forfeiture. During the currency of the term limited by a lease, the lessor has no right to possession of the demised property unless the lessee has incurred a forfeiture for breach of one or more of the covenants in the lease. If a squatter goes into possession, his possession, though adverse to the lessee, is not adverse to the lessor. Until the squatter has been in possession for a period of 12 years, the lessee can recover possession of the premises from him; but once the squatter has been in such possession for 12 years the title of the lessee is extinguished and the lessee, who has lost the right to possession, can no longer eject the squatter. In my view, the squatter has the right to possession not only as against the lessee and any stranger but also as against the lessor for the unexpired portion of the term, subject to the risk of a forfeiture; and this is what the squatter has gained. The ousted lessee continues to be contractually liable to the lessor upon the covenants in the lease. In the present case, at the time when the purported assignment by Irish Life was made, there had been no forfeiture and the plaintiff was accordingly entitled to remain in possession as against the lessor.

The real question for decision is whether the lessee and the freeholder, by a merger or a surrender, can give to the freeholder the right to possession so as to defeat the squatter. The defendants rely on the majority decision in *Fairweather's Case* ([1963] A.C. 510) and in particular on the judgment of Lord Denning who came to the clear conclusion that a surrender operated as a determination of the term; at p. 548 of the report he said that he saw no difference between a surrender, a merger or forfeiture, and that on each of these events the lease would be determined and the freeholder entitled to evict the squatter, even though the squatter has been on the land during the currency of the lease for more than 12 years; and that on the determination of the lease time began to run against the freeholder. The defendants contend that the same considerations apply in the present case.

Whilst the opinion of Lord Denning is deserving of the highest respect, I find it extremely difficult to see how an ousted lessee who has no right to possession could give to the lessors, by a purported surrender or assignment, a right to possession; or how such lessee, as a person whose title has been declared by the statute to be extinguished, has anything to surrender or assign which could affect the possession of the squatter. This was the view of Lord Morris of Borth-y-Gest in *Fairweather's Case* ([1963] A.C. 510); in his dissenting judgment he said at p. 550 of the report: 'When a lessor grants a lease to a lessee for a term of years the lessee is given a right to possession during the term. The lessee will have a right to possession for the period of the term which will be effective as against his lessor and as against everyone else. If thereafter the lessee wishes during the term to place the lessor in the position of having a right to possession as against everyone he does not do this by abandoning any such right to possession as against the lessor as might be thought to exist: he must also be in a position to cede to the lessor rights to possession as against everyone else – which was one part of what he had obtained from the lessor. If, however, he has lost all his rights to possession how can he reinvest his lessor with any of them? Unless he is in a position to transfer those rights to his lessor the lessor must wait until he acquires such rights in some other way. If it can be said in a case where a squatter has during a lease remained in possession for the statutory period that the lessee has merely lost his right to possession vis-à-vis the squatter, how can he give the lessor a right to possession against such squatter?'

If a lessee made an *underlease* and subsequently surrendered the lease to the freeholder, the freeholder could not eject the underlessee during the term of the underlease. This proposition was not contested in *Fairweather's Case* ([1963] A.C. 510), nor was it contested in the present case. The defendants sought to draw a distinction between an underlease and a trespasser, and they relied on the following passage in Coke upon Littleton (Vol. II, s. 338b) which reads: '...having regard to the parties to the surrender, the estate is absolutely drowned. . . . But having regard to strangers, who were not parties or privies thereunto, lest by a voluntary surrender they may receive prejudice touching any right or interest they had before the surrender, the estate surrendered hath in consideration of law a continuance.' The defendants rely upon that passage as protecting an underlessee from eviction during the term of his underlease but not as protecting a trespasser – this being the view taken by Lord Denning. I can see no reason why Coke's statement should be confined to an underlease and should not also apply in the case of a person who has been in adverse possession for the necessary period prescribed by statute. As Lord Morris of Borth-y-Gest put it at p. 552 in *Fairweather's Case* ([1963] A.C. 510), if a lessee who has lawfully assigned or sub-let cannot by a surrender affect the rights of assignees or underlessees, it is difficult to see why a surrender should endow a lessor with a right against an adverse possessor which was not possessed by the lessee.

In the High Court, the learned President was not prepared to accept the majority decision of the House of Lords in *Fairweather's Case* ([1963] A.C. 510) and preferred the reasoning of Lord Morris of Borth-y-Gest. In my opinion, the decision of the learned President was correct. In my judgment, Irish Life, who had lost the right to possession, could not assign to the defendants the right to possession; nor could the defendants, by taking a transfer of the freehold, give themselves any better right to possession than they had before the transfer was effected. I fail to see how a lessee or a purported assignee of a lease, by surrendering the lease, or by purchasing the freehold, can confer a right which he himself has not got. In my judgment, therefore, this appeal fails and should be dismissed.

Notes and Questions
1. Do you agree with the majority views in the Supreme Court on the question of a parliamentary conveyance and the effect of a purported merger? See *Irish Land Law*, para. 23.09 *et seq.*
2. Do you agree with Walsh J.'s comments on the operation of section 49 of the Registration of Title Act, 1964? See *ibid.*, para. 23.43 *et seq. Cf. Spectrum Investment Co. Ltd.* v. *Holmes* [1981] 1 All E.R. 6.
3. As regards merger generally, see ch. 15, *post.*

MURPHY V. MURPHY
[1980] I.R. 183 (Supreme Court)

A testator was the owner of a freehold farm through which a road ran from east to west. By his will the testator devised his farm to trustees on trust for his wife and his two sons (the plaintiff and the defendant) for a period of ten years from the date of his death. The testator directed that during the ten-year period the farm should be managed by the defendant and that all profits therefrom should be lodged in a bank in the joint names of the wife and the defendant. The testator directed that at the end of the ten-year period the portion of his farm situate on the south side of the road should be divided in a particular manner and he devised the eastern part thereof (which included a dwelling-house) to the defendant and he devised the western part to the plaintiff. The testator directed that after the division of his farm his wife should have a right during her life to reside on whichever portion of his lands that she might choose and he bequeathed an annuity to her. The testator devised and bequeathed the residue of his property to his wife. Apart from the residuary devise, the testator's will did not contain any disposition of the testator's estate in the portion of his farm which was situate on the northern side of the road. The testator died on the 23rd June, 1936, and was survived by a widow and by the plaintiff and the defendant, all of whom continued to live in the dwelling-house on the defendant's part of the farm.

The defendant managed the farm during the ten-year period, which expired on the 23rd June, 1946, and he lodged the profits in the joint account in accordance with the terms of the testator's will. The plaintiff left the farm in 1949 and in 1954 he conveyed his part of the land to the defendant, and in the same year the defendant closed the joint account, and thereafter treated the entire farm as his own property. The defendant had treated the northern portion of the farm as part of his property since the end of the ten-year period; he grazed cattle on it, he paid the rates and made improvements to it. The testator's widow left the farm in the year 1968, without having acted as owner of the northern portion of the farm, and went to live in a home for old people where she died on the 25th March, 1971, aged 91 years, having by her will devised and bequeathed all her property to the plaintiff whom she appointed to be executor thereof. In the year 1976 the plaintiff commenced an action in the High Court in which he claimed a declaration that, at the date of her death, the testator's widow was entitled in fee simple to the portion of the farm situate on the northern side of the road. The defendant claimed to have been in possession of the northern portion of the farm since 1946 and contended that the plaintiff's claim failed as more than 12 years had elapsed since a right of action had accrued to the testator's widow, through whom the plaintiff claimed. Costello J. dismissed the plaintiff's action and an appeal was made to the Supreme Court.

O'Higgins J.:
The facts relevant to the issues which arise on this appeal are fully set out in the judgment of the trial judge, Mr. Justice Costello, and in the judgment of Mr. Justice Kenny; therefore, it is unnecessary for me to refer to them in any detail. It suffices to say that the effect of the will of the late Laurence Murphy, who died on

the 23rd June, 1936, was to divide his farm of 153 acres into three parts at the end of the ten-year trust period mentioned in his will. This farm lay north and south of the Loughrea-Kilchreest road in the county of Galway. The portion north of the road contained 40 acres and the portion south of the road contained 113 acres. His widow became entitled as residuary legatee to the 40 acres which were north of the road, while the portion south of the road was divided between his two sons, the plaintiff and the defendant. The widow was given in addition a right of residence and support on whichever portion of the sons' divisions she should choose at the end of the trust period. The ten-year trust provided for the working of the farm as a unit by the defendant as manager under the direction of the trustees of the testator's will, and for the lodging (in a bank account in the joint names of the widow and the defendant) of all profits derived from the working of the farm.

The terms of the will were carried out and for the period of the trust the lands were managed and farmed as one unit by the defendant; the joint bank account was duly kept and the profits of the farm were lodged in it. After the expiration of the trust period, the plaintiff assigned his division of the lands to the defendant by a transfer which became effective in 1954. In that year also the joint account came to an end and since then, and up to the commencement of this action, the defendant has farmed all the lands as the apparent owner. From the death of the testator the widow continued to reside in the family home which was on the defendant's portion of the testator's lands. She was provided for and maintained thereon by the defendant until the year 1968 when she went to a Home where she died on the 25th March, 1971, at the advanced age of 91.

By her will the widow appointed the plaintiff to be executor and sole residuary devisee and legatee. As such, the plaintiff claims that the portion of the lands devised by the testator which is on the north of the Loughrea-Kilchreest road is now the plaintiff's property, and he seeks to recover that portion from the defendant. The defendant claims that he has acquired title to these lands and that the plaintiff's claim thereto is barred by the Statute of Limitations, 1957. In the High Court Mr. Justice Costello decided this issue in favour of the defendant, and the plaintiff has brought this appeal against that decision.

Section 13, sub-s. 2(*a*) of the Act of 1957 provides that no action for the recovery of land may be brought by any person (other than a State authority) 'after the expiration of twelve years from the date on which the right of action accrued to the person bringing it or, if it first accrued to some person through whom he claims, to that person'. The plaintiff claims through his mother, the testator's widow, who became entitled to this portion of the lands under the terms of the will at the expiration of the trust period which occurred in 1946. At that time the testator's widow was residing in the old family home with the defendant. The lands continued to be farmed as one unit with the plaintiff also there, until he left in 1949 to go to England. The plaintiff sold and transferred his share to the defendant in 1954. In that year also the joint account, which had been continued after the expiration of the trust period, was closed and from then on the defendant ran the farm himself on his own account.

[Having referred to s. 18, sub-s. 1, of the Act of 1957, the Chief Justice continued] The question which arises is when, on the facts found by the trial judge, did the widow's right of action to recover these lands accrue? Her title commenced in 1946 but at that time, and until 1954, the joint account continued. The trial judge regarded this period from 1946 to 1954 as being equivocal by reason of the continued existence of the joint account. He took 1954 as the starting point and concluded that from then on all equivocation in relation to the defendant's possession ceased and the limitation period commenced to run. Section 18 of the Act of

1957 defines adverse possession as being possession by some person in whose favour the period of limitation can run. The period would not run in favour of a person in possession as a licensee or as an agent or as a trustee; nor would it run if there were disability or fraud. None of these circumstances exist in this case. Here the trial judge found as a fact that from 1954 onwards the defendant's possession was adverse within the meaning of the Act of 1957 because he was a person who was in possession and in whose favour the limitation period could run.

It is possible that the widow never knew of her rights to the 40 acres under the testator's will and assumed that the entire farm had been divided amongst her sons. In my view, this circumstance is immaterial in the absence of any question of fraud. The possession by the defendant was possession by him on his own behalf. In my view, the fact that the widow continued to live on the farm and continued to be supported thereon did not alter the character of the defendant's possession in any way. On the facts found by the trial judge, the defendant farmed the entire lands as the apparent owner from the year 1954 onwards. He looked after his mother in the house and on the lands but this did not alter the character of his possession in any way. In my view, therefore, the defendant has clearly established a right to these lands pursuant to the Act of 1957 and, for these reasons, I would dismiss this appeal.

Kenny J.:

On 29th March, 1920, Laurence Murphy (the testator) bought the freehold interest in the lands of Gortnamacken in the county of Galway containing 153 acres. The Loughrea-Kilchreest road divides these lands into two portions: the road runs on a bridge which is above the level of the lands but access at ground level from one part of them to the other is obtained through two arches of the bridge. The lands to the north of the road are liable to heavy flooding and are suitable only for the grazing of cattle. The dwelling-house on the lands known as Millmount is on the south side of the road. The land to the south of the road contains 113 acres and the land to the north of it contains 40 acres. When the testator made his will on the 30th May, 1936, there was a cottage known as 'Garvin's' with a small garden attached to it on the north side and very near to the road. Opposite Garvin's garden and on the south side of the road there were two pillars. In a field south of the road there was a herd's house and at the most southern portion of the lands there was a field which was owned by an adjoining occupier and known as 'Martin Ford's tillage field.'

When the testator made his will, he resided in Millmount House with his wife Agnes, his daughter Annette and his two sons (the plaintiff and the defendant). By his will the testator left the lands to his trustees to hold them upon trust for his wife, the plaintiff and the defendant for a term of ten years from the date of his death; he directed that the defendant was to act as manager of the lands and that all profits from them should be lodged in the National Bank at Loughrea in the joint names of his wife and the defendant. He directed that at the end of the period of ten years, legacies were to be paid to his wife and his daughter out of the moneys lodged. He directed that at the end of the period of ten years his lands were to be divided by drawing a line from the two pillars opposite Garvin's garden 'to proceed straight towards the herd's house up to the corner of Martin Ford's tillage field' and he left that part of the lands on the eastern side of the dividing line with the dwelling-house and premises thereon to his trustees upon trust for the defendant absolutely. The lands on the western side of the line were left to trustees upon trust for the plaintiff absolutely.

The will continued: 'I direct that from and after the said division and from and after the vesting of the said respective portions of my said farm and lands in my said sons my said wife shall have the right during her life to reside upon whichever portion of the said lands she chooses and to be supported clothed maintained and fed thereon and thereout and that in addition she shall be paid during her life by my said son Laurence Murphy a sum of ten pounds each year and a similar sum by my said son Thomas Murphy . . .'

The testator left all the residue of his property real or personal to his wife. He died on the 23rd June, 1936, and on the 16th April, 1941, letters of administration with the will annexed were granted to the defendant. The title to the lands at Gortnamackan was never registered under the Local Registration of Title (Ireland) Act, 1891, or under the Registration of Title Act, 1964.

All the lands north and south of the road were farmed by the plaintiff and the defendant until 1951 when the plaintiff agreed to sell to the defendant the lands given to the plaintiff by the testator's will; the plaintiff then left and went to England. This agreement was carried out by a conveyance made on the 9th March, 1954, by which the plaintiff conveyed to the defendant all the lands left to the plaintiff by the testator's will. In 1954 the bank account referred to in the will was closed and the legacies left to the testator's widow and to his daughter were paid. The testator's widow and daughter continued to live in Millmount and were supported and maintained by the defendant who paid the widow the sum referred to in the will. In 1968 the widow left the lands and went into a home for old people and the daughter remained in the dwelling-house. The testator's widow died on the 25th March, 1971, and by her will she left everything she had to the plaintiff.

I am convinced that under the testator's will the lands north of the road became the property of the testator's widow under the residuary clause in his will, but I am equally certain that she never knew this and assumed that from the year 1954 the defendant was the owner of the 153 acres, subject to her right to reside in the house and to be maintained out of the lands south of the road. From the year 1954 the defendant farmed the entire holding and spent money on draining the lands north of the road. The defendant assumed that all the lands north and south of the road belonged to him.

In 1976 the plaintiff brought these proceedings for a declaration that he was the owner of the lands north of the road under the bequest to him made in the widow's will. The defendant claimed that he had acquired a title to them under the Statute of Limitations, 1957. The trial judge, Mr. Justice Costello, held that the widow's right to the lands north of the road had become barred under that statute. I agree with his conclusion. Section 13, sub-s. 2(*a*), and s. 18, sub-s. 1, are the relevant provisions of that statute.

The ignorance of the testator's widow and of the defendant that the lands north of the road belonged to her does not prevent the Act of 1957 applying and does not prevent the defendant being in adverse possession of these lands. In Wylie's Irish Land Law at p. 857 it is stated: 'It is also established that the adverse possession may take place without either party being aware of it.' The widow was not maintained out of the land on the north of the road because, although the whole farm was worked as one unit, her right to maintenance and to the annual sum came out of the lands left by the testator to the plaintiff and the defendant; the only claim the widow had to the lands north of the road was as residuary legatee.

The question is whether the defendant had adverse possession of the lands north of the road from 1954 when the joint account was closed. Before the year 1833 the common law had engrafted the doctrine of non-adverse possession on to the earlier Statute of Limitations so that the title of the true owner was not endangered until there was possession clearly inconsistent with recognition of his title, *i.e.*, adverse possession, and so there had to be an ouster. This doctrine of non-adverse possession was abolished by the Real Property Limitation Act, 1833, in which the words 'adverse possession' were not used (Lord Upjohn in *Paradise Beach & Transportation Co. Ltd.* v. *Price-Robinson* ([1968] A.C. 1072). The use of the words 'adverse possession' in the Act of 1957 does not revive the doctrine of non-adverse possession which existed before 1833. In s. 18 of the Act of 1957 adverse possession means possession of land which is inconsistent with the title of the true owner: this inconsistency necessarily involves an intention to exclude the true owner, and all other persons, from enjoyment of the estate or interest which is being acquired. Adverse possession requires that there should be a person in possession in whose favour time can run. Thus, it cannot run in favour of a licensee or a person in possession as servant or caretaker or a beneficiary under a trust: *Hughes* v. *Griffin* ([1969] 1 W.L.R. 23).

In the instant case the defendant's possession from the year 1954 was inconsistent with the widow's title to the lands north of the road. She never made a claim to be the owner of them because she did not know that she had one. The fact that she lived in Millmount until 1968 and that all the lands were farmed as one unit was not an assertion by her of any claim to the lands north of the road. There is no evidence that she ever went on these lands or made any use of them. This view is strongly supported by a recital in the deed of mortgage of the 14th December, 1954, by which the defendant charged all the 153 acres in favour of the National Bank. The widow joined to postpone her rights under the will to the claim of the bank. In that deed the defendant is called the mortgagor and in the deed, which is signed by the widow and the daughter, there is the recital: 'and whereas the mortgagor is now seised and possessed of the lands in the schedule hereto'. The schedule described the entire holding of 153 acres.

I have considered the decisions of the English Court of Appeal in *Wallis's Holiday Camp* v. *Shell-Mex* ([1975] Q.B. 94) and *Treloar* v. *Nute* ([1976] 1 W.L.R. 1295). In each of those cases the question was whether the person in possession of lands had been in adverse possession. This is ultimately a question of fact: in this case I have no doubt that the defendant was in adverse possession since the year 1954. Therefore, the plaintiff's claim to the lands on the north of the road is barred by the Statute of Limitations. Accordingly, his action fails and should be dismissed.

Parke J.:
I agree with the judgment delivered by Mr. Justice Kenny.

Note
Cf. Browne v. *Fahy* Unreported (High Court) (Judgment delivered 25th October, 1975): see *Irish Land Law*, Supp. (1975–80), p. 75.

Chapter 15
MERGER

The doctrine of merger, or extinguishment as it is sometimes called, is a technical one which seems to have arisen before the Irish courts with considerable frequency: see *Irish Land Law*, ch. 24.

HURLEY V. HURLEY
[1910] 1 I.R. 86; 42 I.L.T.R. 253 (Court of Appeal)
This was an appeal from a decision of Barton J. (see [1908] 1 I.R. 393).

Walker L.C.:
In this case we have had a learned discussion upon a conflict of title between the heir-at-law of a deceased husband and the widow of that husband, to two terms of years which had belonged to the wife when she married, the reversion on which was bought by the husband in the Landed Estates Court on 25th February, 1898.

The widow survived, and claims the terms of years as hers by survivorship. The heir-at-law, on the other hand, says that the husband, by his own act, purchased, and thereby merged the terms; though it would have been otherwise if he had acquired the reversion by act of law only.

It is somewhat refreshing to find that the venerable authorities and *dicta* which have been cited from the blackletter reports are irreconcilably in conflict, and as regards text-writers we have on the one side the high authority of Preston, Conv., vol. 3, pp. 273–303, which we find copied into some respected text-writers, and on the other the equally valuable opinion of Lord St. Leonards in his work on Vendors and Purchasers p. 619, for what he vouches as the opinion, though not the decision, of the Court of the Exchequer in *Jones* v. *Davies* (5 H. & N. 766), affirmed in the Exchequer Chamber (7 H. & N. 505). It is not easy to appreciate the distinction in principle between the act of the party and the act of law, such as marriage or descent, where the husband accepts the *status* and benefits. There was only one case cited as a direct authority on the very question before the Court: *Carter* v. *Lowe* (Owen, 56), which appears to me a somewhat complicated case.

We are I think driven, as Mr. Justice Barton considered he was, to decide the question on principle. The law as to the right of a husband to his wife's chattels real is settled from the earliest times. He can alienate or dispose of them during his life by an act *inter vivos;* and if he survives his wife, they become his absolutely. On the other hand, if the wife survives, without the husband having alienated or disposed of them, she takes them absolutely as survivor. This disposition by him would equally take place if he took a new lease, because this involves a surrender of the old, and this is equal to an assignment. This revival of property in the wife on his death, when she survives, is only defeasible by his disposition of the term during his life.

In the view I take of this case, there has not arisen that incompatibility of the subsistence of two estates, which might have arisen if the husband had conveyed to him, in possession, the fee-simple of the lands as comprised in the leases. This would raise acutely the question discussed by Mr. Preston, and would only leave for discussion the question, whether his having the term in *autre droit* would make a difference. I am disposed to think that, applying the equitable rules to the doctrine of merger, which even in a Court of law now we are bound to apply, the estates would not coalesce to the prejudice of the wife, not being vested in the husband in the same right, unless it could be held that the conveyance to him involved a disposition or surrender of the wife's term. This inference would not be necessary; for his deed, and the transaction of itself, would not show an intention to defeat the wife's right. It would be like the case where a husband has mortgaged his wife's chattels real, which has been held not to defeat the right of the wife to redeem: *Clarke* v. *Burgh* (2 Coll. Ch. Cas. 221). But further in the present case the merger is founded on the deed of 1898, which conveys to him the reversion subject to the chattel terms. Unless the wife's term is dealt with, the former rights, including hers by survivorship, continue; and how can we infer an intention to dispose of, or deal with the terms, of which he was possessed in right of his wife, when the deed purports to preserve them? He could after the deed of 1898, as before, assign or dispose of the terms, but, as he died without doing so, I think the wife's right remains.

I am quite satisfied with the judgment of Mr. Justice Barton, and the reasons on which he has founded it.

FitzGibbon L.J., concurred.

Holmes L.J.:

A lady entitled to the lessee's interest in certain premises under two leases for the respective terms of 300 years married in 1873 without any settlement; and her husband during the coverture purchased, in the Land Judge's Court, the fee-simple estate in the premises, which were conveyed to him by the Land Judge, subject to the two leases.

The wife, who survived her husband, claims in this action the interest under the leases; and her right depends upon whether the purchase by her husband of the reversion in fee did, or did not, operate as a merger of the terms of years. There is no evidence of intention, or of any matter from which intention might be inferred; and if there was merger, it can only have arisen, as the case is presented to us, from the conveyance by the Land Judge. Although the question under consideration has been discussed by Judges and writers on the law of real property for two or three centuries, no conclusion has been hitherto arrived at; and the views of great lawyers are so conflicting as to justify the author of Platt on Leases in not attempting to reconcile them, being as he said convinced that nothing short of a judical decision can reduce this confusion to order.

Mr. Sullivan, in his argument, relied on cases in which it was held that where an executor, possessed of a term of years, puchased the reversion in fee, there was a merger of the leasehold interest, and he contended that this is a much stronger decision than what is asked for by the appellant. It would certainly be so if the executor had no beneficial interest in the term. But I think it clear that in these cases there had been no bequest of the term, and that, therefore, by the old law, it was the property of the executor. This is shown by the fact that, even in such a case, the Courts of Equity would not allow merger to prejudice the testator's creditors.

I asked Mr. Sullivan to refer us to any actual decision of the matter now in controversy, and the only one he could mention was *Carter* v. *Lowe* (Owen, 56; Mo. 358), but I find the facts therein were materially different. The wife had a term of years, and the husband after marriage obtained another lease. He had the same right to surrender the premises demised to his wife as to assign them; and the acceptance of a new lease implied such a surrender. Therefore, it was a case where the husband, being himself a lessee, acquired the fee. In these circumstances, I am not disposed to weigh the opinions of Dyer and Manwood as against Hobart and Holt. I know that Mr. Preston, who seems to have been an enthusiastic champion of merger, preferred the former; and that Lord St. Leonards, in his last edition of the Law of Vendors and Purchasers, appears to lean towards the latter.

I shall try to find some legal principle to guide me. I start with the propositiion that, if the owner of a term of years purchases the reversion in fee, and there is no evidence of intention, merger follows. Why? Because the two estates are vested in the same person, at the same time, and in the same right; and, therefore, there is no reason against their coalescing. But had the husband in the present case the two estates in the same right? I think not. He had certain rights in his wife's leasehold, but so had she. His right was to assign or surrender it; but if he did not do so, it was the property of his wife on his death if he predeceased her, not through him but by reason of her original title thereto. I agree with Barton, J., that both husband and wife are possessed in her right; and, according to *Bracebridge* v. *Cook* (Plowd., 417), if a stranger gets possession, both ought to join in an ejectment, and the wife shall have judgment as well as the husband.

It is now settled, contrary to the opinion of Mr. Preston, that if the husband took the fee by devise there would be no merger. It is also admitted that if, having the reversion, he married the leaseholder, merger would not be the result. It is said that in these cases there was no act on the part of the husband. I would have thought that marriage was as much 'an act' as buying a reversion. Speaking for myself, I regard this doctrine of act of the party as distinguished from act of law, propounded by Mr. Preston, as an ingenious fallacy. The only act of the husband was to purchase the reversion; and I am unable to see how this can affect the respective rights of his wife and himself in the lease.

Notes and Questions
1. Would it have made any difference if the marriage had taken place after 1882? See *Irish Land Law*, para. 25.09 *et seq.*
2. See further on merger, *Re Sergie*, p. 70. *ante*; Craig v. *Greer*, p. 616, *ante*; *Perry* v. *Woodfarm Homes Ltd.*, p. 685, *ante*.

RE TOPPIN'S ESTATE
[1915] 1 I.R. 330 (Court of Appeal)

Lands were limited by will to A. for life, with remainder to her issue as she should appoint, with remainder as she should appoint generally, with an ultimate remainder to A. in fee. On the testator's death A. also became absolutely entitled to a charge on the lands. A. died a spinster aged over seventy years, having by her will devised her real estate and bequeathed her personal estate to different persons, without mention of the charge, and without havng indicated any intention during her life either to keep the charge subsisting or to extinguish it. Ross J. held that the charge had been extinguished. The executors appealed against this decision.

O'Brien L.C.:
Although this is a case of some difficulty, it has been so fully and ably argued that we do not consider it necessary to reserve our judgment.

I shall advert very briefly to the facts. Mrs. Elizabeth Magan, being possessed of considerable real and personal estate, made her will on the 30th April, 1850, in the following terms: [His Lordship referred to the will and continued:]

Mrs. Elizabeth Magan died on the 12th September, 1880, when her daughter Augusta Magan became entitled to whatever estate was devised and bequeathed to her by the will of her mother, and also became absolutely entitled under the provisions of a post-nuptial settlement of the 27th August, 1835, which it is unnecessary to consider in detail, to a charge of £3333 late Irish currency on the freehold property devised by the will. The title to this charge accrued and became a vested interest when she attained the age of twenty-one years, but she was not entitled to the beneficial ownership of the charge until the death of her mother, who had a life interest therein – a fact I mention because it was relied upon in the argument of Serjeant Matheson.

Miss Magan never married; at the date of her mother's death there could have been no presumption against her marrying and having children, but she attained the age of over seventy years, and it is not too much to say that the idea of her having children at that age, or at any time during a period of many years before her death, was one not to be seriously entertained. I say that, fully appreciating the views which appealed to the earlier exponents of our law as to the devolution of real property after possibility of issue extinct – views which I do not find to be followed in the application of modern principles of equity to cases where the Court has to deal with mere charges on land, or with personal property, as distinct from the ownership of real property.

Miss Magan made her will on the 15th January, 1881, and died on the 26th October, 1905, aged, as I have said, over seventy years. By her will she devised to the person or persons who should be her heir or heiress-at-law at her death all her real freehold and chattel real estate, except certain premises in Delgany (which were not affected by the charge of £3333), and after leaving certain legacies she bequeathed the residue of her personal estate to the trustees and executors of her will for the purpose of building or of assisting in building hospitals.

On the one hand, those interested in the personal estate, the charities, now claim that this charge of £3333 has, by operation of law, remained during these many long years in full force and effect, that it formed portion of the personal estate of the testatrix at her death, and should be now raised as such; on the other, the co-heiresses-at-law of this lady claim that this charge must be considered in law as having absolutely disappeared and become extinguished in the freehold of the estate on, or prior to, her death; and that accordingly the legatees of her personal estate cannot sustain the claim which they have put forward.

Ross J., in a short judgment, has said that the test in such cases is, 'whether a period existed when it was absolutely indifferent to the owner of the lands charged and the charge whether it was kept subsisting or not'; and, notwithstanding the long and learned discussion which we have had, extending into many bye-ways both of feudal and equitable law, I have come to the conclusion that that test is the one which must be applied, that it is the test which in common sense ought to be applied, and the one which a proper consideration of the authorities coerces me to apply. It would not, however, be right that I should simply affirm, without more, that view of Ross J., as the authorities which have been cited by Serjeant Matheson and Mr. Brunskill require careful and full consideration.

Serjeant Matheson has contended with great erudition that on the true construction of this will, and having regard to the decision of the Lord Chief Baron on the questions as to whether or not this estate was a settled estate at the date of Miss Magan's death, and whether she remained for some purposes a tenant for life, we ought to hold that, although prior to her death any possibility of her having issue might have disappeared, yet still, until the day of her death, the estate for life, given in the first instance never coalesced with the estate in fee following it, owing to the existence of this contingency, which for many years prior to her death was an absolutely shadowy and unreal contingency, namely, the possibility of her having issue; and he says that as the remainder in fee never was in this lady up to the time of her death, there could be no extinguishment of the charge. Now, at the beginning of the argument, this contention struck me as being not only interesting, but as one which might possibly be right; I do not now, however, entertain any doubt but that it is untenable. Serjeant Matheson has relied upon *Donisthorpe* v. *Porter* (2 Eden, 162), but that case, to which I shall refer later on in my judgment, is not, I consider, in favour of his contention.

Now, as regards charges on estates, it is clear that in feudal law these were not regarded with favour; the estate in the lands, and that alone, was the thing beloved of the feudal lawyer; charges upon land were of comparitively modern growth, and the condition of things which exists in our times, when charges upon an estate may be of greater value that the ownership of the estate itself, would not have at all commended itself to the early English lawyer. Accordingly we find that this question of the preservation or non-preservation of charges, so far from being dependent upon any principles of common law, is dependent upon the principles laid down by courts of equity; and equity has approached the problem of the destruction of charges, as distinct from the merger of estates, from its own peculiar point of view, and has framed rules to aid the Court in arriving at the conclusion as to whether or not, under all the circumstances of each particular case, there has or has not been a destruction of any charge in question. One of the earliest cases in which the view of a court of equity in dealing with this question of extinguisment of charges is contrasted with the technical principles underlying the merger of estates based on common law doctrines with regard to real property, is to be found in a clear and concise passage in the judgment of the Master of the Rolls in *Forbes* v. *Moffat* (18 Ves. 390) – a passage which, so far from being in any way differed from, has re-appeared in successive judgments in later cases as containing a clear and binding statement of the law relating to this question of the destruction of charges, as viewed by courts of equity. 'It is,' the Master of the Rolls says, 'very clear that a person becoming entitled to an estate, subject to a charge for his own benefit, may, if he chooses, at once take the estate, and keep up the charge. Upon this subject a Court of Equity is not guided by the rules of law. It will sometimes hold a charge extinguished, where it would subsist at law; and sometimes preserve it, where at law it would be merged. The question turns upon the intention, actual or pre-sumed, of the person in whom the interests are united. In most instances it is, with reference to the party himself, of no sort of use to have a charge on his own estate; and, where that is the case, it will be held to sink, unless something shall have been done by him to keep it on foot.' Later on in the judgment of the Master of the Rolls we find another reference to this principle: 'In *Wyndham* v. *The Earl of Egremont* (Ambler, 753) the limitation was to Lord Thomond for life, with remainder to trustees to preserve contingent remainders to his first and other sons in tail male, and to his right heirs. Yet it was determined that the charge should be raised for the benefit of his personal representatives. What the counsel for the personal repre-sentatives contended was, that the charge should not merge; unless at some period in Lord Thomond's life it was indifferent to him whether the term should be kept on foot or not. Upon looking into all the cases in which charges have been held to merge, I find nothing which shows that it was not perfectly indifferent to the party in whom the interests had united, whether the charge should or should not subsist; and in that case I have already said it sinks.'

That is the view which has been followed from time to time by all the judges who have had to consider cases involving this question. It is necessary to find whether or not it was a matter of indifference to the person entitled to the charge that it should be kept on foot; if it was a matter of indifference, the presumption is that the charge was destroyed. I studiously avoid the words 'merge' and 'merger', because I find that all the judges in the early cases dealing with the extinguishment of charges are careful to point out that the technical question of merger at law is not the question which courts of equity take into consideration in dealing with charges. It is not a question of equity following the law, because this whole matter of keeping charges alive arose from the equitable view of the need to prevent injustice being done, and equity proceeded, not upon highly refined technicalities, but upon a broad basis of common sense. I do not intend to express any opinion as to whether, as regards the devolution of estate, this lady was at the date of her death seised of an estate in fee in which her former life estate had merged owing to the possibility of her having issue being at an end. I consider it unnecessary to decide that question, although we have listened to a learned argument from both sides in reference to it. I am clearly of opinion that equity in this matter looks only to the intention of the owner of the charge, and I shall now advert to some of the rules which have guided courts of equity in disposing of particular cases which have come before them.

In *Donisthorpe* v. *Porter* (2 Eden, 162) the Lord Chancellor says: 'I do not think it a rule, that a charge upon an estate which can only be got at by trustees, and so be prevented from merging at law, shall be distinct in equity, and go to the administrator, while the estate goes to the heir; but, I think, where the owner has an absolute interest in the estate and charge, the charge is annihilated for the benefit of the estate and heir. The Court does not consider the subtilties of mergers, but discharges the estate from the incumbrance; it would otherwise burthen estates to no purpose.'

That judgment, delivered in 1762, is as applicable to the question now being considered in 1915 as if it had been delivered yesterday. To burden the estate with this charge for the benefit of the charitable legatees would be, in my judgment, to no purpose. Consider the position of this lady. At the time of her death the contingent estate devised to her issue had no reality whatsoever. She reached old age, and for many years had enjoyed the property without interest being paid on the charge, or any account being kept of such interest. It is inconceivable that she herself ever considered this charge, if she knew of it, as a property subsisting apart from her estate in the lands. Her will shows that she intended to deal with her property on two broad lines: she wished that her real estate should go to her co-heiresses; and that her personal estate should go to these charitable objects. She never intended that the charge on her real estate should be preserved and subsequently raised for the benefit of those who were to take her personal estate. Her position for many years prior to her death was that she could have sold this real estate and, at least under an order of a court of equity, have put the proceeds of the sale in her own pocket, notwithstanding this shadowy contingency relied upon by the appellants. What is the law with reference to a position such as that?

I shall refer first to the decision of the Court of Appeal in England in *Thornhill* v. *Nixon* ((1904) W.N. 112). There the Court was asked to make an order for payment out of Court to a mother and her children of certain stock representing a trust fund which had been bequeathed by will upon trust for the mother for her life, and upon her death upon trust for her children on attaining age. The mother was a widow upwards of 52 years of age, and had five children, all of whom had attained 21 years of age. The learned judge in the Court below, Buckley J., refused to make the order sought, but on appeal Vaughan Williams L.J. is reported to have said, that while he did not mean to alter any rule which had been laid down, nor did he wish to be understood as saying that the mere fact that the mother had arrived at the age of 52 was in itself a sufficient reason for making the order, yet the Court had always to look at the circumstances of each case; and, having regard to the circumstances, and bearing in mind that it was a case in which the Court was not interfering with the rights of any living person, he though it safe to make the order. That was an order based on the impossibility of the lady having further issue, and on the fact that the rights of no living person were interfered with. Whether or not this question of the interference with rights of living persons was originally a mere technicality or not, it is clearly settled that it is one of the circumstances of the case which must be taken into consideration.

In *In re Hocking* ([1898] 2 Ch. 567) the Court of Appeal in England refused to make the presumption of a woman being past child-bearing for the purpose of depriving a living person of the possibility of becoming entitled to an interest; and Lindley M.R., after referring to *In re Lowman* ([1895] 2 Ch. 348), says: 'There the Court deprived no living person of a possible interest. Nor, so far as I am aware, has it ever done so . . . I have looked in vain for any case in which the Court has deprived one person of the chance of becoming entitled to property if another should die childless or have a child. Nor ought the Court to do so.' Again, in *In re White* ([1901] 1 Ch. 570), where leaseholds were bequeathed upon trust for a woman for her life, and after her death upon trust for all her children who should live to attain the age of 21 years, Buckley J. made the presumption in favour of the one child born of the woman who attained 21, the mother being a widow aged over 56 years, the learned judge in his judgment saying: 'In giving the whole to him, the Court is not depriving any living person of a possible interest.' That is a perfectly clear and well-settled rule, and the decisions in Ireland are to the same effect.

In *Browne* v. *Warnock* (7 L.R. Ir. 3) Chatterton V.-C. held that a title the validity of which depended upon the presumption that a woman was past child-bearing should be forced upon an unwilling purchaser, and that the purchase-money should go to the person who, in all good sense, was entitled thereto.

A still stronger decision, having regard to the age of the woman, was that of Porter M.R. in *Persse* v. *Mitchell* (34 I.L.T.R. 135), where he held that there was a presumption that there would be no issue of the marriage, the wife being almost 55 years of age, and having lived with her husband for over nineteen years without having a child; and he empowered the trustees to convey trust property to the plaintiffs, who on this presumption were entitled thereto, subject, however, to their entering into a recognizance to restore the estate in the event of there being issue, and the issue being entitled under the trusts of the settlement. That form of order, however, requiring a recognizance to be entered into, was really somewhat of a departure from our modern practice, and the case is not a clear authority on the general principle.

We were pressed by Serjeant Matheson as to the point of time when the charge can be said to have ceased to exist, but I find clear authority as to this, if authority be required, in *Swinfen* v. *Swinfen* (29 Beav. 199, at p. 204). Sir J. Romilly M.R. there says: 'The next question is, at what time this presumption of intention must be considered to arise. I am of opinion that the presumption arises on the death of the person who is entitled both to the estate and to the charge, and that this intention is to be collected from all the circumstances which existed at that period. All the acts of the person so entitled prior to his decease must be taken into account for the purpose of ascertaining his expressed intention, if any such exist, and all the facts affecting his posiiton, down to and at the time of his decease, must also be taken into consideration, for the purpose of ascertaining from thence the intention of the testator, to be presumed from the position in which he stood.'

The first leading fact then in considering this lady's position is that, as I have said, she could have converted the whole estate into money for her own benefit; the second is that she by her will devised her real estate, without mention of the charges, in one way, and bequeathed her personal estate in another. I consider it clear that I am entitled to take the first fact into consideration, and that I can do so with regard to the second is shown by a further passage in the judgment in *Swinfen* v. *Swinfen* (29 Beav. 199, at p. 204), to which I have already referred: 'In this case, as far as there is any expression of intention, it is in favour of the merger, for the will devises the estate without any mention of the charge, which seems, by the Lord Justice Turner, in that case (*Grice* v. *Shaw,* 10 Hare, 76) to have been considered, in the absence of any other circumstances taking away the effect of that act, to constitute some, although a slight, intention to merge the charge.'

I am also entitled to take into consideration the fact that this charge became vested in Miss Magan, not through any act of her own, but by reason of the limitations contained in the settlement of 1835.

It is well settled that when a person having a limited interest in lands, such as a tenant in tail in remainder, himself pays off a charge on those lands, the presumption is that he did so, not with the intention of benefiting the estate, but with that of keeping the charge alive. The presumption is otherwise in the case of a tenant in tail in possession, but that is, I take it, because he has the power at any time of barring the entail. That presumption, however, which arises from the fact that the charge was acquired by the man's own act, has no application in the case where both the charge and the estate in the lands coalesce in the same individual, not by force of any act of his own, but owing to the operation of some will or settlement; and in such cases, in the absence of any evidence of intention to the contrary, the charge is held to disappear. If that be the presumption to be drawn in the case of a tenant in tail even in the extreme case of the charge being acquired by an act of his own, merely by reason of the fact that he could at any time bar the entail, why should any different presumption be applied in a case such as this, where, as I have said, this lady could at any time during a period of many years prior to her death, either by means of an application to the Court, or by entering into a contract for sale, have turned the entire estate into money, for her own exclusive benefit?

Taking all these circumstances into consideration, and being of opinion that it was a matter of the most complete indifference to the owner whether this charge was kept alive or not, I must hold that the charge ceased to exist, and, applying *Swinfen* v. *Swinfen* (29 Beav. 199), that the date when it so ceased to exist was that of the death of this lady.

An argument was addressed to us based on the fact that Miss Magan sold portion of the lands comprised in the settlement as tenant for life and not as absolute owner. That she was advised to do so is, however, readily to be understood by anyone who appreciates the convenient method of making title afforded by the powers conferred by the Settled Land Acts. In *re Marshall's Settlement* ([1905] 2 Ch. 325) – a decision which I have never known to have been doubted, the powers of a tenant for life were held to be rightly exercisable, even although, in one point of view, there was no life tenancy in existence. The fact of Miss Magan having exercised the powers of sale of a tenant for life cannot for a moment outweigh the other considerations to which I have referred.

The appeal must be dismissed with costs.

Cherry L.C.J., and **Ronan L.J.,** concurred.

Note
See further *Irish Land Law,* para. 24.13.

Chapter 16
DISABILITIES

Though the disabilities affecting certain persons in the ownership and disposition of land have been reduced over the decades, several still remain, often of necessity for the protection of the persons in question: see *Irish Land Law*, ch. 25. As regards persons suffering from a mental disorder, see *O'Connell* v. *Harrison*, p. 378, *ante* and *Bank of Ireland* v. *Domvile*, p. 178, *ante*.

BLAKE V. CONCANNON
(1870) I.R. 4 C.L. 323

Certain lands were let to an infant in May, 1866. He possessed and enjoyed the lands until the 20th of April, 1867, when he, being still an infant, left the possession, and, on attaining his majority (which occurred shortly after), he repudiated the contract of tenancy and the tenancy under it.

Pigot C.B.:

In this case I decided, in point of fact, at the hearing at the Assizes, that the Defendant, under a letting made to him of the lands in question, in May, 1866, possessed and enjoyed the lands until the 20th of April, 1867; that he was under the age of twenty-one years when the letting was made and that he still continued an infant on the 20th of April, 1867; that he, on that day, left the possession of the lands; and that, in due time after he had attained his majority (which event occurred shortly after he had left the possession), he repudiated the contract of tenancy, and the tenancy under it; but that in the interval, before he had repudiated, and while he continued in possession and enjoyment of the lands, a gale of the rent sued for became due on the 1st of November, 1866.

Upon these facts I reserved the point, whether, by the repudiation, the Defendant not only became exonerated from liability for the rent, which, if he was liable for it at all, became due on the 1st of May, 1867, but also for that which became due on the 1st of November, 1866, while he continued in possession and enjoyment of the lands.

I read and considered the judgments of Baron Parke, in the cases of *The North-Western Railway Company* v. *M'Michael*, and *The Birkenhead, Lancashire, and Cheshire Junction Railway Company* v. *Pilcher* (5 Exch. 114); especially the judgment in the first of those cases. I also looked into the authorities referred to in those judgments. And, upon the consideration which I then gave to those two judgments, and to those authorities, especially to the terms on which the case of *Ketle* v. *Elliott* is abstracted in 1 Rolle's Abridgment, 731, and to the passage in Bacon's Abridgment, *Infancy and Age* (I.) 8 (referring to that case, and to the three books in which, under different names, it is reported), I formed the opinion, that the Defendant, having repudiated the letting in due time after he had attained his majority, and before he was sued for the rent, was entitled on the ground of his infancy, and of that repudiation, to defend the action brought by this Civil Bill.

The amount of the rent being considerable, and another demand for rent of another farm being made by the same landlord against the same Defendant, and being likely to become the subject of an action, I gave to each of the parties a written statement of my opinion and my reasons.

The Appellant, against whom I expressed my opinion, applied to me to have the case re-argued in Dublin. To this I assented; and after a very considerable time, it was argued by Mr. Monahan for the Appellant, and by Mr. Robinson for the Respondent.

The result of that argument, and of further consideration of the case, and of the reasoning addressed to me by Mr. Monahan, was, that my opinion was changed.

I think, on consideration, that I gave a force and effect to the language of Baron Parke in the judgment before referred to, and also to the passages cited from Rolle's Abridgment, 731, and from Bacon's Abridgment, *Infancy and Age* (I.) 8, which do not properly belong to them.

In the passage in Rolle's Abridgment, 731, the case of *Ketle* v. *Elliott*, decided in the 11 Jac. 1, is stated thus– 'If a lease for years be made to an infant rendering rent, the rent is arrear, and after the infant comes of full age, and afterwards continues the occupation of the land, this will make him chargeable with the arrears incurred during his infancy. Pasch. 11 Jac. 1. Between Kettle and Elliott adjudged.'

It appeared to me that Rolle's understanding of the import and effect of that decision was, that the facts, that the infant attained his majority, and afterwards attained his age, and afterwards continued in occupation of the land, constituted the reason which should make him chargeable with the arrears that accrued during his infancy; that is to say, that, but for the continuance of the Defendant in possession after he became of age, he would not have been liable; and that the mere enjoyment of the lands, while the rent was accruing, and until after it had accrued, would not render the infant liable. I am satisfied, on examining the different reports of *Ketle* v. *Elliott*, not only that it was *not* decided there that the occupation and enjoyment of the infant, until after the rent became payable, would *not* render him liable; but that the Judges, in that case, were of opinion, that such an occupation and enjoyment during infancy *would* create such liability.

In each of the reports of that case, the question is stated to be, whether a lease made to an infant is void. According to the reports in Cro. Jac. 320, and in 2 Bulstrode, 69, it was held, that the lease is voidable at the election of the infant, and that he may make it void by refusing and waiving the land before the rent day comes, and that 'then no action of debt will lie against him.' And the same view appears to have been entertained according to the report in Brownlow, 120. There was, according to the reports in Cro. Jac. and in Brownlow, an additional fact – that the infant became of age before the rent became due; so that it may not have been necessary to determine that he would have been liable if he had then remained an infant. But the proposition which I have stated is laid down in clear terms in Cro. Jac. 320, and in Brownlow, 69.

In 4, Bac. Abridgment, 376, *Infancy and Age* (I.) 8, there is the following passage, for which the case reported in the three reports that I have referred to, and also in Rolle's Abridgment, 731, is cited as an authority: 'If an infant takes a lease for years of land, rendering rent, which is in arrear for several years, then the infant comes of age, and still continues the occupation of the land; this makes him chargeable with all the arrears incurred during his minority; for, though at full age he might have departed from his bargain, and thereby have avoided payment of the arrears which the lessor suffered to incur during his minority, yet his continuance in possession after his full age ratifies and affirms the contract *ab initio*, and so gives remedy for the arrears of rent incurred from the time of the contract made.'

In this passage it is distinctly laid down, that the repudiation of the contract of tenancy, after the lessee has attained his majority, will exonerate him from liability for the arrears of rent which accrued during his minority, and while he was in occupation of the land demised; and in the judgment of Baron Parke, in *The North-Western Railway Company* v. *M'Michael* (5 Exch. 125), that very learned Judge, dealing with an action for calls on railway shares vested in an infant, as analogous to an action for rent reserved upon a lease to an infant, appears to have adopted the view of the case so laid down in Bacon's Abridgment, which is referred to by Baron Parke in that judgment. Baron Parke says, p. 125: 'Under this Act, therefore,' the General Railway Act, 8 & 9 Vict. c. 16, s. 79, 'our opinion is, that an infant is not absolutely bound, but is in the same situation as an infant acquiring real estate, or any permanent interest; he is not deprived of the right which the law gives to every infant, of waiving and disagreeing to a purchase which he has made; and if he waives it, the estate acquired by the purchase is at an end, and with it his liability to pay calls, though the avoidance may not have taken place till the call was due (see Bac. Abridgment, *Infancy and Age* (I.) 8).'

It was upon that passage of Bacon's Abridgment, and upon that passage in Baron Parke's judgment, together with the terms in which the case, cited as *Ketle* v. *Elliott*, is abstracted in Rolle's Abridgment, 731, that I was induced to form the opinion which I first expressed, as to the Defendant's exemption from liability to the arrears sued for in this Civil Bill, by reason of his repudiation of the contract and tenancy, before he was sued for those arrears. But, on consideration, I find nothing in any of the reports of the case cited in Bacon's Abridgment and Rolle's Abridgment (for they appear all to relate to one and the same decision), indicating any opinion or suggestion of the Court, that when the liability to the rent has once attached upon the infant by the demise to him, and by his occupation of the land until after the rent had accrued due, he not only can, by repudiating the demise, divest himself of the estate in the lands, and free himself from all future liability to the rent; but he can also divest the landlord of a right of suit which had become vested in him when the infant, without waiving or repudiating the tenancy, had continued in occupation until after the rent became due.

That an infant is liable to an action of debt for rent reserved on a lease for years made to him for land which he has occupied and used until after the rent became due, appears from very ancient authority. A case in the Year Book, 21 Hen. 6, 31 b., is referred to by Baron Parke in his judgments in the case in 5th Exchequer, and is also referred to twice in *Ketle's Case* (Brownlow, 120), in which the following is stated as law by Newton, Justice: 'If one lease for a term of years, rendering rent, *in fait*' (that is, not by matter of record, see Co. Litt., 380) 'to an infant within age, if he manures the land, a writ of debt is maintainable against him; the cause is, he has a *quid pro quo*.'

Four cases were decided in the Court of Exchequer in England, in which actions were brought for calls on railway shares, and in each of which actions the Defendant relied upon his having been an infant when he became the holder of the shares. In each of these cases the Court considered the liability of the Defendant with reference to the law affecting infant lessees, and infant purchasers of land. The first was *The Newry and Enniskillen Railway Company* v. *Coombe* (3 Exch. 565). There the Court treated the Defendant as having become the holder of the shares only by reason of his having contracted with the Company, and subscribed for the shares; and having been an infant when he did so, and having disaffirmed and repudiated the contract and subscription before the action was brought, he was held exonerated from liability. The next case was *The Leeds and Thirsk Railway Company* v. *Fearnly* (4 Exch. 26). There the Defendant pleaded that, at the time of his becoming and being the holder of the shares, and of the contracting of the debt in respect of the calls, the Defendant was an infant. The plea did not state either that he had become the owner of the shares by reason of a contract with the Company, or that he had repudiated the shares. On demurrer, the Court held him liable. The two next cases were those which I before mentioned: *The North-Western Railway Company* v. *M'Michael*, and *The Birkenhead, Lancashire, and Cheshire Railway*

Company v. *Pilcher*; both reported together in 5 Exchequer, 114. In each, the defence was, that the Defendant became the holder of the shares while he was an infant. In neither did it appear that he became the holder only by contract with the Company, in neither was there any repudiation. And, although in one of the cases (*The North-Western Railway Company* v. *M'Michael*), it was alleged in the plea, that the Defendant had derived no profits from shares, it did not appear that the Defendant was still an infant. The Court, on demurrer to the plea in each case, held the Defendant liable, following their former decision in *The Leeds and Thirsk Railway Company* v. *Fearnly*, and a case previously decided in the Court of Queen's Bench – *The Cork and Bandon Railway Company* v. *Cazenove* (11 Jur. 802; 10 Q.B. 935). In 5 Exch., 123, Baron Parke stated the views which the Courts took of persons becoming shareholders when infants. After stating that, if the effect of the infant becoming a shareholder by an original agreement with the Company, ought to be treated as a contract for a future partnership, and to contribute to the capital for carrying on the undertaking, such a contract could not be presumably beneficial to the infant, and would be not binding on the infant at all; he proceeded to explain the grounds on which infants had, in cases already decided, been held liable. He said, they have been treated 'as persons in a different situation from mere contractors,' for they then would have been exempt; but, in truth, they were purchasers, who have acquired an interest, not in a mere chattel, but in a subject of a permanent nature, either by contract with the Company, or purchase, or devolution from those who have contracted, and with obligations attached to it, which they were bound to discharge; and have been thereby placed in a situation analogous to an infant purchaser of real estate, who has taken possession, and thereby become liable to all the obligations attached to the estate; for instance, to pay rent in the case of a lease rendering rent, and to pay a fine due on admission to a copyhold to which an infant has been admitted: *Evelyn* v. *Chichester* (3 Bur. 1717); unless they have elected to waive or disagree with the purchase altogether, either during infancy or after full age, at either of which times it is competent for an infant to do so: Bac. Abridgment, *Infancy and Age* (I.); Co. Litt. 380. This Court accordingly held, in *The Newry and Enniskillen Railway Company* v. *Coombe* (3 Exch. 565), that an infant who did avoid the contract of purchase during minority was not liable for calls. In the subsequent case of *The Leeds and Thirsk Railway Company* v. *Fearnley* (4 Exch. 26), where there had been no waiver or repudiation of the purchase, we held, in conformity with the previous decision of the Queen's Bench, that the Plaintiff continued liable.' Baron Parke then proceeded to state the dissent of the Court from one of the reasons of the Court of Queen's Bench in *The Cork and Bandon Railway Company* v. *Cazenove*; and to state, at length, the reasons of the Court of Exchequer for holding, in each case, that the Defendant, by analogy to the liability of infant lessees, was liable for the calls.

Long before those decisions the Court of Exchequer in Ireland (in the year 1829) made a similar decision in *Billing* v. *Osbrey*, in an action brought for rent upon a lease by the assignee of the reversion against an infant, sued as assignee of the lessee. The Defendant, by his guardian, pleaded, that at the time the rent became due he was, and at the time of the bringing of the action he still continued, an infant. On demurrer to this plea, the Court held that the infant was answerable for the rent during his enjoyment of the premises. The decision is to be found stated in 1 Furl. Landl. and Ten. 912. It is there stated from a manuscript note of the learned author, whose well-known care and accuracy may be fully relied on.

Two cases have been more recently decided in this country: *Mahon* v. *O'Ferrall* (10 Ir. L.R. 527), and *Kelly* v. *Coote* (5 Ir. C.L.R. 469; 2 Ir. Jur. N.S. 195). In each of these cases (as in that cited by Mr. Furlong), the Defendant was sued, as assignee of a lease, for rent reserved in it; and pleaded, as his defence, that he was an infant when the rent accrued. In each, the liability of the infant was affirmed. But there was not in any of them a repudiation of the estate or tenancy in respect of which the Defendant was sued, and which, upon the record, was treated as having vested in him.

Upon a review of all the authorities, and I am not aware of any others materially affecting the question arising on this Civil Bill, I am satisfied that I was wrong in forming the opinion, which I did reluctantly, that, upon the view which I at first took of the passages in Bacon's Abridgment and in Rolle's Abridgment of the case referred to, and of the judgments of Baron Parke, in 5 Exchequer, the Respondent, the Defendant in the Civil Bill, was discharged from liability to the first gale of rent.

It appears to me now, upon a consideration of the grounds on which an infant is held to be liable where, by the authorities to which I have referred, his liability is established, if he does not waive or repudiate the tenancy and the land, that he ought to be held bound by that liability when it has been once attached to the payment of the rent which accrued while he has occupied, and before he has repudiated. He is not, in an action of debt for the rent, held liable upon the contract of tenancy alone. His liability arises from his occupation and enjoyment of the land, under the tenancy so created. If his liability arose from the contract alone, the repudiation of the contract, by annulling it, would annul its obligations, which would then exist only by reason of the contract. But the infant, though he can repudiate the contract of demise, and the tenancy under it, and can so revest the land in the landlord, cannot repudiate an occupation and enjoyment which are past, or restore to the landlord what he has lost by that occupation and enjoyment of the infant. The reason given by Justice Newton, in 21 Hen. 6,31,b., lies at the root of the infant's liability: 'he has had a/ *quid pro quo.*' Though quaintly expressed, it is a reason sanctioned by common sense, and in accordance with plain justice. The infant owes the rent, because he has an equivalent in the occupation and enjoyment of the lands. The authorities to which I have referred appear to me sufficiently to indicate that, if the infant does not avoid the tenancy under which he occupies before the rent becomes due, the mere fact of infancy constitutes no defence. If, therefore, he continues so to occupy without repudiation, the landlord, on the accruing of the rent, has a vested right of suit against the infant for the rent which has so accrued. I cannot, on consideration, hold that such vested right can be divested by the mere repudiation of the infant, without a direct decision, or some unequivocal and acknowledged authority, sustained by general acquiescence or clear analogy of law. I have found none. The dictum of Baron Parke, in 5 Exchequer, 125, must be regarded with all the respect due to everything that fell from that eminent Judge. But it was not necessary for the decision of the case before him; and it was manifestly founded on the passage in Bac. Abr. *Infancy and Age*, (I.) 8, or was influenced by that passage. And I have shown that the proposition in Bacon's Abridgment, which is there contained, and which appears to have been thus adopted by Baron Parke, was not warranted by the authorities cited in support of it.

On the whole, I am of opinion that the Respondent, the Defendant in the Civil Bill, was, and is, liable for the first gale of rent, but is not liable for the second; that the dismiss should be reversed, and that there should be a decree for the amount of the first gale. Of course, the Appellant must have the costs of the Appeal, of which I have no power to deprive him.

The case, however, being a novel one, and one on which I at first formed an opinion directly the reverse of that which I have here expressed, I consider that I ought, if either party shall so desire, to state a case, under the 27 & 28 Vict. c. 99, s. 35, for the opinion of one of the superior Courts of Common Law, for the purpose of obtaining the decision of such Court upon the point which I reserved at the Assizes.

The case may be framed in very brief terms. It would seem that the two first paragraphs of this judgment, ending with the words, 'and enjoyment of the lands,' would be sufficient for the purpose.

Note
See further *Irish Land Law*, para. 25.02 *et seq.*

HEAVEY V. HEAVEY
(1977) 111 I.L.T.R. 1 (High Court)

In 1967 Mr. Heavey purchased a house in Dublin in his wife's name and converted it into luxury flatlets, the total cost of purchase and renovation being in excess of £33,000, which was financed by a loan from the Bank of Ireland. The rents received from the premises were lodged in an account in the joint names of husband and wife.

In 1972 the wife began proceedings, inter alia, for a declaration under section 12 of the Married Women's Status Act, 1957, that she was the beneficial owner of the house. She subsequently applied for an account of the rents and profits of the house received by her husband and for a declaration that she was beneficially entitled to the sum of £23,000 lodged in their joint account under that heading.

Kenny J.:

The plaintiff married the defendant on 30th August, 1954. After their marriage they lived for some years in a house in Dublin which had been purchased by him in his name for £2,300. The plaintiff, who owned a business in Thurles where a grocery and confectionery trade was carried on, sold it in 1956 for £3,105 and this together with arrears of rent and £1,130 received on the sale of the fittings and stock were given by her to him and he lodged it in her name in the Educational Building Society. Between 1958 and 1961 three endownment policies, which she had taken out on her life, matured and she paid the £1,173 which she got from the insurance companies to him. She also had some savings certificates and when they became payable she gave the £402 which she got to him. She was also the owner of a one-seventh interest in a cinema in Thurles which yielded an annual income of £550 which she gave to him each year until 1968. From the time they were married until 1968, he gave her a generous housekeeping allowance, paid all the bills in connection with the household and the expenses of the education of the children. He opened a joint bank account in their names and lodged most of the money he got from her in it. Each could draw cheques on this account.

In 1957 the husband bought two houses in Haddington Road, Dublin, in his name and converted the two houses into flats. In 1959 he bought a house in Northumberland Road ('house A'), Dublin for £2,450 in his name and converted it in the same way. The family home in North Circular Road, which had been bought for £2,300, was sold in 1959 for £7,500 and with this he bought a fine house in Merrion Road, which was conveyed to him for £5,000 and he then spent about £12,000 in altering and decorating it. He and she and their children went to live in the house in Merrion Road where she still resides.

In 1967 another house in Northumberland Road ('house B') was purchased by him for £15,500 and on the 7th July, 1967, he had it conveyed into her name. Most of the purchase money came from the joint account. In an affidavit sworn on the 23rd April, 1974, the husband gave his reasons for having this property conveyed into the sole name of the wife: 'I purchased the premises. . . . in June 1967: I put the said premises in the plaintiff's (the wife's) name (a) to help avoid death duties after my death (b) to invest the plaintiff's money given to me over the previous years. When I purchased the said premises it was in three flats, unfurnished, undecorated, letting value about £20 per week. That is what I put in the plaintiff's name, a big empty house with no income from the same. When I put the said premises in the plaintiff's name it never occurred to me that the plaintiff would ever claim the said premises until after my death. I most definitely would not have put the said premises in the plaintiff's name if it ever entered my mind at that time that the plaintiff would claim the said premises or rents therefrom. The reason why I spent so much money converting the said premises into luxury flatlets was to give the plaintiff and our children a troublefree property after my death.'

The total cost of the purchase of that house including auctioneers' fees and solicitors' fees, was £16,904. The cost of converting the premises into luxury flats was £16,560 and this was financed by an overdraft given by the Bank of Ireland to the husband. He has a very prosperous business and the bank were prepared to advance this sum to him on the security of the title deeds of the two houses in Haddington Road and the other house he owned in Northumberland Road. The husband used this account for his business also and in April 1972, shortly after the banks in this country had decided to convert overdrafts into term loans, part of this overdraft became a term loan of £17,000 at interest of 16%. He received most of the rents from house B in Northumberland Road until the 19th May 1973, when the wife began to collect them. The conversion of the premises was done on such an elaborate scale that the annual gross income from them was £6,380 in 1969 and £6,747 in 1970.

In 1972 the wife began proceedings against him for a judicial separation, for custody of the children and for a declaration under the Married Women's (Status) Act, that she was the owner of the house in her name as from the date of purchase of it and of the other four houses. The three proceedings were heard together and I made an order for judicial separation because of his cruelty, awarded the custody of the children to her and fixed alimony at £75 per week. Subsequently, when I had heard further evidence, I found that she was beneficially entitled to the entire interest of the lessee in house B in Northumberland Road as from the date of purchase and that he was beneficially entitled to the other four houses and an order giving effect to this was made on 16th May, 1973. By it the husband was also restrained until further order from selling the house in Merrion Road until he provided such alternative suitable accommodation for the wife as might be sanctioned by the Court.

She subsequently applied for an account of the rents and profits of the house in Northumberland Road received by him from the 7th July, 1967, to the 19th May, 1973. On the 4th February, 1974, I directed the following accounts to be taken before the Examiner:

1. An account of the rents and profits of the premises in Northumberland Road in the City of Dublin received by the defendant (the husband) from the 7th July, 1967, to the 19th May, 1973.
2. An account of the amounts expended by the defendants in converting the said premises into flats between June, 1967, and May, 1973.
3. An account of the amount due by the defendant to the Bank of Ireland in connection with the purchase of the said premises by the defendant in the name of the plaintiff.

The Examiner made up his certificate on the 12th June, 1974. He found that the husband had received £30,514.11 of the rents and profits of the premises from the 7th July, 1967, to the 19th May, 1973, and that he had paid £7,472.89 on account thereof leaving a balance of £23,041.72 on that account. Bank interest paid by the husband on the amounts expended on the purchase and conversion of the premises was not included in this account. On the second account the Examiner found that the husband had expended £16,560 in converting the premises into flats between June, 1967, and May, 1973, and on the third account he found that on the 22nd October, 1973, £7,385 was due by the husband to the Bank of Ireland in connection with the purchase by him of the premises in the name of the wife. This was the proportionate part relative to the purchase price of the amount due by the husband to the bank.

Counsel for the wife have argued that she is entitled to be paid the £23,041.72 because the husband is not entitled to credit for the amounts expended by him in converting the premises into flats and so cannot claim that this should be paid out of the rents. It has also been submitted that he the husband is not entitled to credit for the sum which he owes the bank in respect of the purchase or conversion. The husband, who has appeared in person, did not direct his argument to any of the interesting legal questions which arise but abused his wife for her greed.

It is a presumption of law that when a husband makes a purchase of property or transfers money or securities into the name of his wife solely, it is intended as a gift to her absolutely at once and there is no resulting trust in his favour. (See: *In re Eykyn's Trusts* (1877) 6 Ch. D. 115; *In re Condrin, Colohan* v. *Condrin* [1914] 1 I.R. 89 and *McCabe* v. *The Ulster Bank Limited* [1939] I.R. 1, 14). The same principle applies when a husband expends his own money on the property of his wife even if that property has been transferred by him to her. It is, however, not an absolute rule of law that the wife gets the benefit of the expenditure, it is a presumption only which may be rebutted by evidence so that if the wife leads the husband to believe that money which he spends on improving her property will be repaid to him out of the rents of the property when improved, he has a valid claim to be reimbursed out of the rents. I agree with the statement of the law in the speech of Lord Upjohn in *Pettitt* v. *Pettitt* [1969] 2 All E.R. 385, at p. 409:

'It has been well settled in Your Lordship's house (*Ramsden* v. *Dyson* (1866) L.R. 1 H.L. 129) that if A expends money on the property of B, *prima facie* he has no claim on such property. And this, as Sir William Grant M.R, held as long ago as 1810 in *Campion* v. *Cotton* (1810) 17 Ves. 263, is equally applicable as between husband and wife. If by reason of estoppel or because the expenditure was incurred by the encouragement of the owner that such expenditure would be rewarded, the person expending the money may have some claim for monetary reimbursement in a purely monetary sense from the owner, or even, if explicitly promised to him by the owner, an interest in the land . . .'

It seems to me that it is unreal to approach the question of the ownership of or claims for shares in or reimbursement of expenditure on property as between husband and wife when each has made contributions to its purchase or improvement by trying to ascertain what the agreement between them was or what agreement can be implied from their behaviour. Husband and wife do not contemplate disputes or the break up of their marriage when they are getting married or when they are living happily together and the arrangements about domestic expenditure and their dealings in property are very informal and are not the result in legal agreements. I am fortified in this conclusion by the judgments of the Lord Chief Justice of Northern Ireland, Lord MacDermott, and of Mr. Justice Lowry (as he then was) in *McFarlane* v. *McFarlane* [1972] N.I. 59, from which I have got considerable assistance. When there is an express agreement, the Courts must give effect to it but, in the absence of a proved contract, I think that the question whether a husband has a claim for improvements carried out to his wife's property should be solved by the application of the flexible concept of a resulting or constructive trust (see the speech of Lord Pearson in *Gissing* v. *Gissing* [1970] 2 All E.R. 780). When this concept is adopted, the guiding principle is that stated by Lord Diplock in the same case:

'A resulting, implied or constructive trust – and it is unnecessary for present purposes to distinguish between these three classes of trust – is created by a transaction between the trustee and the cestui que trust in connection with the acquisition by the trustee of a legal estate in land, whenever the trustee has so conducted himself that it would be inequitable to allow him to deny to the cestui que trust a beneficial interest in the land acquired. And he will be held so to have conducted himself if by his words or conduct he had induced the cestui que trust to act to his own detriment in the reasonable belief that by so acting he was acquiring a beneficial interest in the land.'

This principle should, I think, be applied to a transfer of property by a husband to a wife and to expenditure on improvements carried out by him on her property. If he expended his money in improving his wife's property, particularly property which he has transferred to her, he has in my view, no claim to be repaid the amount which he spent even if he thought that the amount would be repaid out of the rents unless she led him to believe that it would be refunded.

This principle, however, does not apply when the husband has borrowed the money to purchase the property or to carry out the improvements. If the wife is aware that the husband is borrowing the money for either of these purposes, it would, in my view, be inequitable for her, when a dispute arises between them, to retain the rents for herself and to refuse to have the outstanding debt incurred by the husband paid out of them. In this case the wife was keeping the husband's books and knew that part of the cost of purchasing house B in Northumberland Road and the entire cost of converting them was being financed by a bank loan given to the husband.

The accounts, which were directed by the order of the 4th February, 1974, do not include an account of the amount due by the husband to the Bank of Ireland in connection with the conversion of the premises into flats between June, 1967, and May, 1973.

Subject to the result of this account, the financial position of the parties seems to me to be that the husband is entitled to credit against the rents which he collected for the amount which he owes the Bank of Ireland in connection with the purchase and conversion of the premises by him in the name of the wife together with the probable amount of interest which he will have to pay. The amount which he owes the bank in connection with the purchase is £7,385; the amount of interest which he will have to pay is not proved in evidence. At 16% the annual interest on £7,385 is £1,168 and the best estimate I can make of the interest which he will pay on the term loan is to allow five years at £1,168 and four years at £584 (which is half the original sum of interest) on the assumption that the husband will be repaying capital and interest each year. The total amount of interest is therefore £8,176 and when this is added to the principal, the total is £15,561. The husband is entitled to credit for this sum against the amount of the rents which he received. He will also be entitled to credit for the amount which may be found to be due by him to the Bank of Ireland for principal and interest in connection with the conversion of the premises into flats.

I regret the necessity of sending the case back to the Examiner for another account. If the husband had retained a legal adviser to conduct this case on his behalf, it would not have been necessary but the claim that part of the expenses of conversion had been financed out of a bank overdraft on which money is still due was not made until after the Examiner had made up his certificate.

There will accordingly be an account before the examiner of the amount due by the defendant to the Bank of Ireland for principal and interest in connection with the conversion of the premises house B in Northumberland Road by the defendant. When the result of this is known, it will be possible to dispose of the matter.

The wife is now receiving alimony of £75 a week, maintenance for the children and has a right to live in the house in Merrion Road without payment of rent. She is in receipt of an annual gross rental income from house B in Northumberland Road of about £7,000. Having regard to this income I think that the figure for alimony is too high and I propose to reduce it to £10 per week as from today. It may be that the wife at a subsequent hearing will be able to establish that the net income which she has from house B in Northumberland Road is not sufficient with the £10 per week and the children's maintenance to enable her to live in the house in Merrion Road. I have no evidence at the moment of the net income from house B in Northumberland Road which enables me to form a decision on this matter.

Notes

1. The princples stated by Kenny J. have been followed several times; see *Irish Land Law*, supp. (1975–80), p. 78. *Cf.* the statement of the principles involved by Finlay P. in *W.* v. *W.* [1981] I.L.R.M. 202 at 204–5:

   '1. Where a wife contributes by money to the purchase of a property by her husband in his sole name in the absence of evidence of some inconsistent agreement or arrangement the court will decide that the wife is entitled to an equitable interest in that property approximately proportionate to the extent of her contribution as against the total value of the property at the time the contribution was made.

   2. Where a husband makes a contribution to the purchase of property in his wife's sole name he will be presumed by a rebuttable presumption to have intended to advance his wife and will have no claim to an equitable estate in the property unless that presumption is rebutted. If it is, he would have a claim similar to that indicated in respect of the wife with which I have already dealt.

   3. Where a wife contributes either directly towards the repayment of mortgage instalments or contributes to a general family fund thus releasing her husband from an obligation which he otherwise would have to discharge liabilities out of that fund and permitting him to repay mortgage instalments she will in the absence of proof of an inconsistent agreement or arrangement be entitled to an equitable share in the property which had been mortgaged and in respect of which the mortgage was redeemed approximately proportionate to her contribution to the mortgage repayments: to the value of the mortgage thus redeemed and to the total value of the property at the relevant time. It is not expressly stated in the decisions to which I have referred but I assume that the fundamental principle underlying this rule of law is that the redemption of any form of charge or mortgage on property in truth consists of the acquisition by the owner or mortgagor of an estate in the property with which he had parted at the time of creating of the mortgage or charge and that there can be no distinction in principle between a contribution made to the acquisition of that interest and a contribution made to the acquisition of an interest in property by an original purchase.

   4. Where a husband contributes either directly or indirectly in the manner which I have already outlined to the repayment of mortgage charges on property which is in the legal ownership of his wife subject to the presumption of advancement and in the event of a rebuttal of that presumption he would have a like claim to an equitable estate in the property.

   5. Where a wife expends monies or carries out work in the improvement of a property which has been originally acquired by and the legal ownership in which is solely vested in her husband she will have no claim in respect of such contribution unless she established by evidence that from the circumstances surrounding the making of it she was lead to believe (or of course that it was specifically agreed) that she would be recompensed for it. Even where such a right to recompense is established either by an expressed agreement or by circumstance in which the wife making the contribution was lead to

such belief it is a right to recompense in monies only and cannot and does not constitute a right to claim equitable share in the estate of the property concerned.

6. A husband making contributions in like manner to property originally acquired by and solely owned as to the legal estate by his wife may again subject to a rebuttal of a presumption of advancement which would arise have a like claim to compensation in similar circumstances but would not have a claim to any equitable estate in the property.'

See also *F.G.* v. *F.G.* [1982] I.L.R.M. 155; *M.C.* v. *M.C.* Unreported (Supreme Court) (1982/52) (judgment delivered 24th March, 1984).

2. *Cf.* as regards an unmarried couple, *M'Gill* v. *S.* [1979] I.R. 283.

INDEX